Fundamentals of Criminal Justice

Steven E. Barkan
University of Maine

George J. Bryjak
University of San Diego

PEARSON
and

Boston • New York • San Francisco
Mexico City • Montreal • Toronto • London • Madrid • Munich • Paris
Hong Kong • Singapore • Tokyo • Cape Town • Sydney

Series Editor: Jennifer Jacobson
Editorial Assistant: Amy Holborow
Developmental Editor: Ohlinger Publishing Services
Senior Marketing Manager: Krista Groshong
Editorial-Production Administrator: Anna Socrates
Editorial-Production Service: Omegatype Typography, Inc.
Manufacturing Buyer: Megan Cochran
Composition and Prepress Buyer: Linda Cox
Cover Administrator: Linda Knowles
Interior Designer: Carol Somberg
Photo Researcher: Katharine S. Cook
Illustrations: Omegatype Typography, Inc.
Electronic Composition: Omegatype Typography, Inc.

For related titles and support materials, visit our online catalog at www.ablongman.com.

Between the time Website information is gathered and then published, it is not unusual
for some sites to have closed. Also, the transcription of URLs can result in unintended
typographical errors. The publisher would appreciate notification where these errors
occur so that they may be corrected in subsequent editions.

Library of Congress Cataloging-in-Publication Data

Barkan, Steven E.
    Fundamentals of criminal justice / Steven E. Barkan and George J. Bryjak.
      p. cm.
    Includes bibliographical references and index.
    ISBN 0-205-29518-5 (alk. paper)
    1. Criminal justice, Administration of. 2. Criminal justice, Administration of—United
States. I. Bryjak, George J. II. Title.

HV7419 .B37 2004
364—dc21

                                           2002038322

Printed in the United States of America

10 9 8 7 6 5 4 3 2 1   WEB   08 07 06 05 04 03

Brief Contents

Contents

chapter 2

Counting and Explaining Crime

To reduce crime, our society must first know how much crime we have and why it occurs. This chapter reviews the primary ways in which government officials and criminal justice researchers measure crime, and it outlines important explanations of crime from the fields of biology, psychology, and sociology.

p. 22

interchapter

UNDER Investigation:

Who Commits Crime?

Crime is socially patterned. This Under Investigation examines the kinds of people who are more likely to commit crime, and the kinds of places that are more likely to have crime. This section discusses how age, gender, race and ethnicity, social class, and urban residence all affect crime rates.

chapter 3

Crime in the United States

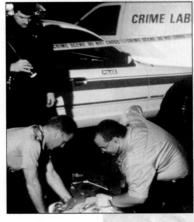

p. 60

This chapter is an up-to-date summary of the major forms of criminal activity in the United States, including stalking, prostitution, drunk driving, hate crimes, occupational crimes, and organized crime. A survey of illegal drug use is presented, including an examination of the drug distribution system beginning with the coca growing fields of South America.

part TWO
Crime and Victimization   104

chapter 4
Criminal Law

Criminal law governs what makes certain behaviors crimes and how the criminal justice system works. This chapter sketches the history of criminal law and discusses the elements of criminal acts, legal defenses to criminal prosecution, and the procedural rights afforded criminal suspects and defendants in the United States.

p. 104

chapter 5

Victims and Victimization

This chapter addresses the questions too often overlooked in criminal justice texts: Who is most likely to be a victim of street crime in the United States? Why are some people repeatedly victimized? What is the relation between victims and offenders? Is there a geography of victimization? What prompted the formation of the victims' movement, and what services do victims' organizations provide?

p. 130

interchapter

UNDER Investigation:

Terrorists and Victims—A World at Risk

This Under Investigation presents a typology of terrorist groups, explanations for terrorist behavior including target selection, and a look at the various strategies used by the United States and other nations to prevent terrorist attacks. This section concludes with a discussion of the impact of the attacks of September 11, 2001, on the criminal justice system, especially the police and the courts.

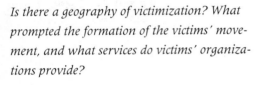

chapter 6

The Police: History, Organization, and Composition

An engaging social history of police in the United States, this chapter provides a context within which police issues and problems can be examined. It discusses the

p. 172

impact of technology on policing as well as the growth and function of police unions. Along with a survey of police at the local, state, and federal levels, this chapter examines the increasing participation of minority officers in American policing, especially African American, Latino, female, and gay officers.

interchapter
UNDER Investigation:
Community Policing and Militarizing the Police

This Under Investigation examines two simultaneous yet different developments in law enforcement in the United States over the past 30 years: community policing (working closely with members of the community in a joint effort to identify and solve local problems) and PPUs (police paramilitary units). The pros and cons of militarizing the police are discussed in this section.

chapter 7

Becoming a Cop and Doing Police Work

This chapter looks at the people who become police officers, why individuals choose this career, the strategies that police departments employ to attract young men and women to law enforcement, the difference between formal training in police academies and the informal socialization that occurs in on-the-job training on the streets, and the police subculture and its effect on police behavior. This chapter also provides a survey of police work, including patrol, traffic enforcement, criminal investigation, and undercover work.

p. 208

chapter 8

Police Misconduct

Why do some cops "go bad"? This chapter provides a typology of police misconduct as well as an examination of the evolution of a deviant career. Included is a thorough investigation of the most serious form of law enforcement deviance: police brutality. Topics discussed in this section include the use of force as a rite of passage, the "Dirty Harry" problem, and "contempt of cop." This chapter concludes with an overview of how various forms of police misconduct can be curtailed.

p. 240

chapter **9**

History, Organization, and Pretrial Procedures

p. 270

This chapter examines the organization of criminal courts in the United States as well as the principal players in the courts: judges, prosecutors, and defense attorneys. This chapter also presents pretrial procedures from arrest through discovery, with special emphasis on the pros and cons of the grand jury and bail (including bondsmen and skip-tracers) and pretrial detention.

chapter **10**

Bargaining and Jury Trials

p. 308

This chapter provides an in-depth look at the most misunderstood and controversial aspect of the criminal courts—plea bargaining. This chapter also presents the dynamics of the criminal trial from jury selection, composition, and voir dire through the appeals process. It examines an increasingly important phenomenon in the criminal trial—jury nullification. This chapter concludes with an overview of the numerous ways factually innocent people are falsely accused and convicted of crimes they did not commit.

chapter 11

Sentencing

Once someone is convicted of a crime, sentencing becomes the next phase of the criminal justice process—perhaps its most important. This chapter discusses the goals of sentencing, the types of sentences, and the various factors affecting judges' sentencing decisions.

p. 346

part FIVE
Punishment and Corrections   376

chapter 12

Prisons and Punishment: Yesterday and Today

This chapter discusses the history of prisons and examines the growing size and cost of the corrections system. It also examines several important and controversial correctional issues in the United States today, including the privatization of prisons and jails and the death penalty.

p. 376

interchapter

UNDER Investigation:

Health and Health Care in Prisons

p. 448

Convicted criminals bring with them many health problems when they enter prison, and prison conditions themselves can lead to further health problems. This Under Investigation discusses these problems and critically examines the quality of health care in U.S. prisons.

chapter 14

Community Corrections and Juvenile Justice

The U.S. correctional system includes community corrections for millions of adults and the juvenile justice system for youthful offenders. This final chapter examines both of these institutions. A major theme is the effectiveness and cost of community corrections for adults and juveniles compared to incarceration.

p. 452

Take a look
at the many exciting features inside the book . . .

questions *for* exploration

1. What are the four crimes of violence tabulated in the annual Uniform Crime Reports?
2. What are the four Index property crimes? How do burglary and robbery differ?
3. What is a hate crime? What constitutes stalking? Under what conditions does sex become the crime of prostitution?
4. How prevalent is drunk driving in the United States? Why do people abuse

drugs? What is the connection between drug use and criminal behavior?
5. What are the characteristics of organized crime groups? What are the models of organized crime in the United States?
6. What does occupational crime include?

The short life and tragic death of Jon-Benet Ramsey is one of the most unusual, widely reported, unsolved murders in U.S. criminal history.

According to police reports, the 6-year-old girl was put to bed at 10:00 P.M. on Christmas day 1996 in an upscale Boulder, Colorado, neighborhood by her parents, John and Patsy Ramsey. Just before 6:00 A.M. the next morning, Patsy Ramsey called the police after reportedly finding a ransom note on a back stairway demanding

$118,000 for the safe return of her dau... home a few hours later, John Ramsey disc... Benet in the wine cellar. Her hands were ... black duct tape covered her mouth; she ... molested, and strangled.

What propelled this murder into the ... above the brutality of the crime was the ... ily. John Ramsey was a millionaire busi... ished Jon-Benet with material comforts ... also managed his daughter's life in the ... pageants. In the days following the murd... replete with pictures of Jon-Benet ador... and tinted hair, looking more like a 16-y... pranced before contest judges; she even ... showgirl. This initial view of the toddle... struck many people as a vulgar exploita... dered on child pornography. Initial public... who could take pleasure in sexualizing a ... of killing that individual. By way of star...

In every chapter . . .

- Opening **Questions for Exploration** organize the student's study of the chapter content.

- Each chapter opens with a **real-life vignette** to bring the topics under discussion to life.

- **Clear topic headings** throughout the chapters reinforce this organized study. Charts, graphs, photographs, and interesting anecdotes within each chapter also reinforce learning. New terms are defined in the margins.

ish drug dealers. In February 1999, former New York City mayor Rudy Giuliani instituted a program in which individuals arrested for drunk driving had to surrender their vehicles to city officials. Even if drivers are acquitted of the drunk driving charge in a criminal court, they have to successfully sue the city in a civil court to get their cars back (Beals, 1999). City attorneys argue that just as drug dealers use their cars as instruments of crime, drunk drivers do the same. The constitutionality of this antidrunk driving strategy will certainly be challenged in the courts.

In 1997, a North Carolina man was sentenced to life in prison without parole for the death of two college students related to drunk driving. The prosecutor had sought the death penalty for the defendant who had two prior convictions of driving while alcohol impaired (Spaid, 1997).

Illegal Drugs

People use, abuse, and deal drugs for a variety of reasons: They do not have enough money or have too much; they are attempting to escape painful situations or seek adventure; they are depressed or overjoyed; they are bored or have too much to do. Regardless of whether people are pushed by emotional problems or pulled by the allure of money and excitement, drug use is learned and reinforced in a social context.

For whatever reason they initially use illegal drugs, the ingestion of these substances can lead to **drug dependence** (formerly called *drug addiction*), a condition that has three basic characteristics (Goode, 1991).

1. The user continues to ingest the drug over an extended period of time.
2. The user finds it difficult (if not impossible) to quit, taking drastic measures, such as stealing, dropping out of school or work, abandoning family and friends, to continue using the drug.
3. If the user stops ingesting the substance, he or she may experience painful physical symptoms as well as severe mental distress.

Drug dependence may well lead to criminal behavior. However, the association between drug use and crime is not a simple, straightforward cause-and-effect relationship. Drug use as a cause of criminal activity is only one of four feasible connections between these variables (Wilson and Herrnstein, 1985).

> drug dependence habitual use of a drug over an extended period of time

> Not all motorcycle riders are outlaws, but outlaw motorcycle gangs are involved in a significant amount of criminal activity including illegal drug distribution and prostitution.

"If utilized by students, these questions [for exploration] can be very effective tools. In essence, students have a study guide for each chapter without the additional purchase. The questions are specific enough to elicit a firm grasp of the material."

—Angela M. Nickoli, Ball State University

http://www.ablongman.com/barkan1e

xv

■ Focus On

Each chapter also features an international Focus On box that highlights an aspect of the criminal justice system from another society. These boxes familiarize students with the structure and workings of criminal justice around the world through a comparative perspective. For example, students see that dispensing justice in criminal courts in the United States is very different from determining guilt and innocence in other nations.

"The international focus clearly distinguishes this text from others on the market."

—Tod W. Burke,
Radford University

whether evidence [...] missible can be of utmost importance to the outcome of a trial.

Other pretrial motions submitted by defense attorneys include a request to dismiss the case because of the delay in bringing it to trial, and a motion for a change of venue (location) because an impartial jury cannot be found in a particular criminal court jurisdiction. An unsuccessful defense motion(s) may still benefit the defendant because it draws out the prosecution's case, educates the judge regarding the weakness of the district attorney's case, and sets the stage for a possible appeal (Reeves and Perez, 1994). Pretrial motions are filed in about 10 percent of felony cases and no more than 1 percent of misdemeanor offenses.

establish the individual's guilt

preventive detention
pretrial detention of defendants believed by the courts to be a threat to the community if released from custody

FOCUS on Islam

Islam and Criminal Justice

By the end of the tenth century, Islam had split into two distinct groups or sects, the Sunnis and Shiites. The

Sunni majority (with approximately 85 percent of the followers of the prophet Muhammed) can be further divided into four schools of jurisprudence (the science or philosophy of the law). These schools—the Hanifa, Shafi'i, Maliki, and Hanbal—are named for their founders and interpret aspects of the Shari'ah or holy law of Islam in various ways (Imber, 1997).

Recall from our discussion of criminal law in Islamic societies (Chapter 1) that the Koran is the Islamic holy book—"a code

302   chapter 9: Criminal Courts   http://www.ablongman.com/barkan1e

This 23-year-old Afghani woman in Kabul pleads with security officers to be released with fellow prisoners set free as a goodwill gesture during the holy month of Ramadan. She had no trial in any court of law and was imprisoned for adultery under harsh Shari'ah laws from the Taliban era.

which governs the religious and social life of mankind" (Sanad, 1991, p. 38). Whereas the Koran is thought to be the word of God as revealed to Muhammed, the Sunna is a compilation of the inspired sayings and deeds of the prophet (Sanad, 1991). Because Islamic law is derived from these sources, it is considered a "divinely inspired legal system" (Awad, 1982, p. 91). The Shari'ah is quite specific regarding substantive crimes and the punishment for these offenses, and there is little disagreement among Islamic jurists (legal scholars) regarding these issues. However, the apprehension of offenders and the overall administration of justice the responsibility of political authorities who make such decisions in accord with the best interests of their citizens. Because of this latitude, the four schools of jurisprudence have contrasting views on a wide variety of legal issues such as criminal responsibility, criminal investigation and prosecution, and the rights of defendants (Awad, 1982).

Children under the age of 7 are not considered rational human beings under Islamic law, and, as such, they lack the capacity to knowingly engage in criminal behavior under any circumstances. Individuals between the age of 7 and puberty (approximately age 11 or 12 or "by the signs of puberty") are not liable for *hudud* or *qisas* offenses (voluntary and involuntary murder and aggravated assault). In Egypt, juvenile law prohibits administering punishments for criminal code violations for persons under 15 years of age, although "security measures" can be applied to individuals in this category. After the onset of puberty in Islamic law, a person of sound mind is criminally liable

its is also inherent in the status of some authority figures. For example, a husband may physically discipline his wife as long he does so for the purpose of reforming her. However, "[i]f the husband exceeds his legal right so that his beating leaves marks, he is held responsible on both criminal and civil grounds, depending on the severity of the injury . . ." (Bahnassi, 1982, p. 182). Similarly, a father, grandfather, or instructor has the right to discipline a minor. Islamic jurists disagree as to the criminal responsibility of the individual administering the beating if the child dies. According to one school of jurisprudence "If the instructor beats the boy and the boy dies, then, if the father or guardian had not granted permission for the beating, the instructor is liable as an aggressor. If permission is granted for the beating, then he is not liable" (Bahnassi, 1982, p. 183). Disagreement exists regarding the culpability of mothers physically disciplining children. Some jurists support her right to do so, but others argue that she would be criminally liable for inflicting punishment on a child whom she has no authority.

As is the case in Western legal systems, under Islamic law, the accused is presumed innocent until proven otherwise. The burden of proof rests with the individual(s) making the complaint. False accusation is a serious offense that can result in punishment. According to a verse in the Koran, "And those who produce not four witnesses to support their allegations, flog them with eighty stripes" (Salama, 1982, p. 109). The Shari'ah also makes it clear that the accused has a right to legal counsel at all stages of criminal proceedings including the trial. While in custody defendants should not be subject to inhumane treatment (threats, beatings, torture, etc.). The prophet Mohammed said: "God shall torture, on the day of judgement, those who inflict torture on people in this life" (Sanad, 1991, p. 80).

Although the Shari'ah states that defendants are guaranteed freedom of movement until their cases are decided, most Islamic jurists advocate **preventive detention**, or "precautionary arrest," especially for persons accused of adultery, perhaps the most serious of the *hudud* crimes (adultery, theft, highway robbery, false accusations of unchastity, and for some jurists, forceful rebellion against Islamic leaders, drinking alcohol, and apostasy or rejecting Islam after having been a member of this religion). The justification for preventive detention is that the defendant may escape, attempt to destroy evidence, and/or influence witnesses. Incarcerating defendants using preventive detention is most likely to occur when the judge does not know the accused.

The role of the judge in Islamic courts concerning pretrial and extrajudicial knowledge of a case is a point of contention among the various schools of jurisprudence. From one perspective, any pretrial familiarity a judge has with the participants automatically disqualifies that judge from rendering a judgment [...]

cant obstacle to the development of free [...], free markets, and the legitimate institutions that support democratic capitalism (Coleman, 1997). Virtually all of the money produced

Davis Stalin (1998, p. 29) Stalin [...] away at the fabric of Russian society [...] prove impossible to overcome it."

summary

1. The four crimes of violence tabulated in the annual Uniform Crime Reports are murder, robbery, rape, and aggravated assault. First-degree murder is an unlawful killing that is willful, deliberate, and premeditated. In states with capital punishment, first-degree murder is punishable by death. Robbery involves taking something of value from an individual by force or the threat of force or placing an individual in a state of fear. Rape is the carnal knowledge of a female forcibly and against her will. Aggravated assault is the unlawful and intentional causing of serious bodily harm or the threat to do so.

2. The four Index property crimes are burglary, larceny–theft, motor vehicle theft, and arson. These crimes are committed without the threat or use of force. Burglary is the unlawful entry of a structure to commit a felony or theft. Larceny–theft is unlawfully taking property from the possession of another person. Shoplifting, pocket picking, and purse snatching are examples of this crime. Motor vehicle theft is the attempted or completed theft of automobiles, trucks, buses, or motorcycles. Arson is the willful or malicious burning or attempt to burn property with or without the attempt to defraud.

3. Hate crimes are committed against persons, property, or society and are motivated in part or whole by prejudice. These crimes are committed by individuals, groups, and mobs. Stalking is action directed at another person that would cause a reasonable individual to be fearful. California passed the first anti-stalking law in 1995. Often considered a "victimless" crime, prostitution is the sale of sex (oneself or another person) for money or something of value.

4. About 1.5 million people are arrested for drunk driving in the United States each year. One survey

found that 2.5 percent of [...] least one instance of alcohol-impaired driving [...] ing the past 30 days. People illegally use drugs for a wide variety of reasons. Rates of drug use are highest in the youngest age groups and decline as people age. Research consistently finds an association between drug use and criminal behavior.

5. Research suggests three primary interpretations of organized crime in the United States. According to the national conspiracy model, a nationwide alliance of 24 closely knit families operate in the country. All members of the Mafia or Cosa Nostra are of Italian or Sicilian descent. From the local, ethnic group perspective, crime families are highly organized at the local level but not at the national level. According to the enterprise model, organized criminals from a variety of racial and ethnic backgrounds meet the demands of millions of people for illegal products and services, such as drugs, gambling, and prostitution.

6. Street gangs have existed in the United States for more than 100 years. Gang membership and activity have increased significantly over the past 30 years. Estimates of the number of gang members nationwide range from 600,000 to 1.5 million. Gang members are often involved in a wide range of criminal activity including selling drugs, robbery, rape, and homicide.

7. Occupational crime is any act punishable by law that is committed from an opportunity created in a legal occupation. Organizational crime consist of price-fixing, bid-rigging, and any other illegal activity engaged in to increase corporate profits. State occupational crimes are offenses committed by individuals who are legally entitled to make and

Summary   95

■ Chapter Summary

All chapters end with a chapter summary and list of key terms to ensure that students understand the central concepts and facts of the chapter.

"The summaries at the end of each chapter are quite extensive and will be very helpful to students who are seeking to have main points synthesized in an orderly and comprehensive manner. This is much better than simple conclusions offered in other books."

—Tod W. Burke, Radford University

Questions for Investigation

These questions ask students to demonstrate their comprehension of the topics covered and to connect various related concepts.

"I especially like the Questions for Investigation as they give the student a chance to think critically about the subject and provide me with an excellent resource for essay-type or discussion topics."

–Robert Neville,
College of Siskiyous

It's Your Call

This feature invites students to assume a role in various hypothetical situations that people involved in the criminal justice system must face every day.

"These features are crucial in a shrinking world. The use of focus questions to each of these sidebars is great."

–L. Edward Day,
Pennsylvania State University, Altoona

---

enforce laws. Police corruption and the excessive use of force would fall under this category. Professional occupational crimes are committed by highly trained professionals, such as physicians and attorneys. Workers stealing from employees are engaging in individual occupational crime.

key terms

aggravated assault
arson
burglary
drug dependence
felony murder
first-degree murder
hate crimes
homicide
larceny-theft

manslaughter
motor vehicle theft
occupational crime
organized crime
prostitution
rape
robbery
stalking

questions for investigation

1. Research print and on-line sources of news information for your home or campus community, and answer these questions: How prevalent are crimes of violence and property crimes? How effective are the law enforcement agencies in arresting criminals? How effective is the criminal justice system in convicting criminals? Based on the answers to these questions, how would you rate the safety in your community?
2. What precautionary measures does your college or university take to prevent students from being victimized by rape? Motor vehicle theft? Hate crimes? Stalking? Drunk driving? Illegal drug distribution?
3. Some people believe that prostitutes should be considered a legal economic transaction between consenting adults rather than a crime. What do you believe? Why?
4. What is the difference between hate crimes and hate speech? Why is the latter protected by the First Amendment? Some people have argued that hate crime laws are unnecessary because existing statutes call for punishing convicted offenders regardless of the race, religion, or sexual orientation of their victims. Do you agree or disagree? Be prepared to de-

fend your position. Should the government prohibit organizations that espouse physically harming individuals and/or groups from having Internet sites? If someone is convicted of a hate crime and states that he or she was motivated in part or whole by material viewed on a specific Internet site, should the individuals or groups who posted that site be criminally prosecuted for the offense as well?
5. Suppose a sales representative, considered successful by his company and effective by his customers, is in the habit of padding his expense account so that, in effect, he can support himself reasonably on the expense account. The sales rep would consider padding the account to buy a golf membership or a vacation inappropriate; however, he believes he is justified in his current plan because he does spend most of his time traveling away from home. Explain your opinion of this sales rep's thinking and actions.
6. Consider the similarities and differences between Russian political and economic institutions and U.S. political and economic institutions. How do these similarities and differences impact criminal activity in each country?

IT'S YOUR CALL...

1. Choose one of these positions to defend in a debate: (a) You are a member of the National Rifle Association preparing for a debate on gun control. Your position is that, if more people owned and carried handguns, street

criminals would be deterred from committing a significant number of crimes. (b) As a member of Handgun Control, you are preparing to advocate the counterposition;

2. Choose one of these topics to defend in a debate: (a) As a member of the nonprofit group Crime Control in America—Alternative Strategies, you understand that the success and longevity of organized crime in this nation is a consequence of these groups providing illicit drugs, sex, and gambling to a public that has an insatiable demand for unlawful goods and services. Because there is little, if any, evidence that people can be dissuaded from pursu-

...believe it ...ly con... ...and ...page ...are ...ed by ...ly as ...'s Or... ...con... ...based pa-
...trary position. Prepare a two- or three... ...per arguing that the only way to diminish the wealth and power of organized crime is to substantially reduce the activity of these groups as well as zealously prosecute those individuals who use illegal drugs and engage the services of prostitutes and bookmakers.

UNDER Investigation

Terrorists and Victims— A World at Risk

On December 8, 1941, a somber Franklin D. Roosevelt addressed a joint session of Congress. "Yesterday," the president said, ". . . a date that will live in infamy—the United States of America was attacked by naval and air forces of the empire of Japan." Eighteen warships were sunk or severely damaged, and 2,403 people died as a consequence of the Pearl Harbor attack, an event that marked our entry into World War II. September 11, 2001, is a date that will also "live in infamy," to use Roosevelt's words, as terrorist attacks on New York City and Washington, D.C., took the lives of more than 4,000 individuals from the United States and 40 countries. Only 4 months after the execution of Timothy McVeigh, the former soldier convicted of planning and executing the Oklahoma City bombing that killed 168 people, Americans had to deal with the horror and magnitude of a terrorist strike that many believed could never happen in this country.

Complex in its nature and dimension, the first difficulty one confronts when examining this phenomenon is defining terrorism. According to Alex Schmid and Albert Jongman (1988) there are more than 100 definitions of this term, what Brian Jenkins (1992, p. 2168) refer to as the emotion-laden, "slippery-slope" of terrorism. The major reason for this large and disparate number of definitions centers on the question of what constitutes terrorist behavior? For example, were the reported 24 attempts on Cuban leader Fidel Castro's life (including the planting of poison cigars) by the Central Intelligence Agency (CIA) acts of terrorism? Were the U.S. Army Air Corps pilots terrorists when, in 1944, they dropped thousands of bombs on Tokyo that killed 180,000 individuals (mostly civilians)? Why is blowing

up people in a restaurant or government building a terrorist act, whereas burning to death men, women, and children with incendiary bombs an "unavoidable act of

"Why is blowing up people in a restaurant or government building a terrorist act . . . ?"

war" tolerated by the international community? One person's terrorist, as has been often noted, is another person's freedom fighter.

In spite of the difficulty of settling on a satisfactory definition of terrorism, this term must be operationalized if it is to prove useful. To that end we focus on the work of political scientist Ted Gurr (1989, p. 201), who views terrorism as "the use of unexpected violence to intimidate or coerce people in the pursuit of political objectives." The key words in this definition are *unexpected violence* and *political objectives*. Gurr notes that terrorism can occur at any place and at any time with the perpetrators of these acts rarely making a distinction between the innocent and the guilty, or between justifiable and unjustifiable victims: "The enemy is only incidentally particular individuals who cross the terrorist's path; more fundamentally it is civil order" (Lomasky, 1991, p. 107) and people's reaction to the temporary or long-lasting break in this order. Terrorists also have a political agenda (that may be quite specific or broad based), which can be loosely de-

164

---

or threatening to use violence to bring ...her some social, governmental, and/or ...tive.

...rists also have a ...itical agenda . . ."

...rist Typology

...on terrorism is so difficult to define is ...erous forms of this behavior. Just as ...icials and scholars have offered a ...s of terrorism, so too have they con... of these activities that consolidate ...errorism into a manageable num... ost typologies include at least two ...factors of terrorism: its purpose, its ...ers, and its location. We use the ...gy of Ted Gurr (1989) and add a ... contemporary terrorism. Gurr's ty... "political status and ...etrators" (p. 204).

...the United States it... is committed by pri... ther private citizens ...resist social change. ...victims of random ...ately after white ...e New World in the ...to be so far almost ...the only good In... "the phrase "the only good Indian" was a reality in many parts of the country as the indigenous people of the North American continent were attacked by settlers who coveted their land.

Formed in 1865 by ex-Confederate army officers, the Ku Klux Klan (KKK) is the most enduring and violent vigilante terrorist organization in U.S. history. What began as a fraternal association quickly turned into a brotherhood of racial bigots whose goal was to stop newly emancipated African Americans from realizing their recently gained social and political rights. Southern African Americans and white Reconstruction officials who sympathized with and aided former slaves were subject to beatings, torture, and murder. In subsequent years the Klan added Jews, Roman Catholics, and immigrants from non-Anglo Saxon groups to its list of victims. The KKK was especially active during the civil rights movement of the 1960s with Klan members charged in the deaths of four little girls who were killed when a bomb exploded in a Birmingham, Alabama, church (Cose, 2001).

issues-oriented groups (antiabortion, animal rights and environmental extremists) have used violence to promote their positions, or in the case of antiabortion and radical environmental groups, to obstruct behavior. For example, more than 60 abortion clinics were bombed in the 1980s and the trend continued in the 1990s. Based on their beliefs that, like humans, animals have certain inalienable rights, "ecoterrorist" groups, such as the Earth Liberation Front (ELF) and Animal Rights Militia, have attacked medical researchers (who conduct their experiments on animals), university agricultural stations doing research in biotechnology, meatpacking plants, and the fur industry. As of July 2001, the ELF claimed responsibility for 20 acts of violence (mostly arson) that resulted in $37 million in damages (Laurent, 2001). The individuals committing these acts would emphatically reject the terrorist label insisting that this violence is "justifiable," and that they are working for the greater good of the community, man, and/or planet earth (Barkan and Snowden, 2001).

Insurgent terrorism is committed "by private groups against public authorities and aims at bringing about

". . . the Ku Klux Klan is the most enduring and violent vigilante terrorist organization in U.S. history."

radical political change" (Gurr, 1989, p. 204). This form of terrorism has ebbed and flowed throughout our history and can be subdivided into the following three groups (Riley and Hoffman, 1995, pp. 13–17):

1. *Ethnic, separatist, and émigré groups.* Since 1898, when the United States obtained Puerto Rico via the Spanish America War, a number of Puerto Rican separatist groups have engaged in terrorist violence (on their island and in the United States) toward the goal of achieving an independent state.

2. *Left-wing radical organizations.* Left-wing radical groups have tended to engage in symbolic bombings (attacking uninhabited buildings in the middle of the night, for example), rather than attacks designed to result in a significant number of casualties. Their aim has been to call attention to themselves and the group's fundamental purpose or goals. Some antiwar groups during the Vietnam conflict were

165

■ A unique *format!*

Six "interchapters" located between chapters give the user the flexibility to branch out from the 14 chapters in several different directions. Topics of these interchapters include "Street Gangs and Motorcycle Gangs," "Health and Health Care in Prisons," and "Terrorists and Victims–A World At Risk."

There are countless ways to use these unique interchapters in your course: include them as assigned reading; use them for extra credit projects; assign one or two for in-depth study; ask your students to choose one to use as a launching point for a research project . . . it's up to you!

"It [the format] adds another dimension to the material in the text. This is a very good technique."

–Angela M. Nickoli, Ball State University

What your colleagues are saying about

Fundamentals *of* Criminal Justice

■ "Fundamentals of Criminal Justice *lucidly covers standard material for an introductory course, while maintaining a multicultural, comparative edge. This is the first introductory book I have seen that systematically includes issues pertinent to women and minorities, such as racial profiling in policing, stalking, jury nullification, hate crimes, female gang participation, habitual offender statutes, the family structure debate, and elaborate details about incarceration trends and what this means to the average citizen. I find it extremely enlightening and refreshing."*
— **Jana Bufkin, Drury University**

■ *"Students would respond favorably to this text. This is probably the one text that would pry me away from my current textbook. It is very well organized and the material is organized in an interesting and useful manner. Finally, an intro text that covers the essentials with exceptional analysis and practical examples. Nicely done!"*
— **Tod W. Burke, Radford University**

■ *"The overall approach of the text is simple, yet effective. Unlike other introductory texts, this text does not bog down the material with too much information; yet, it accents the material with* Focus On *boxes and the Under Investigation sections."*
— **Angela M. Nickoli, Ball State University**

■ *"I think this text will be a good addition to the options already available for introductory courses. I believe that the students will find the text stimulating yet comprehensive."*
— **Robert Neville, College of Siskiyous**

■ *"There is a certain set of topics that needs to be covered in all introductory criminal justice courses. This text hits the right spots. I was especially pleased to see jury nullification getting special attention. . . . Perhaps its best quality is that, as opposed to their competitors, the authors actually demonstrate a bit of courage. You can actually find critical evaluations of the system and our knowledge of it. When the textbooks we use provide few examples of critical thinking, it should be no surprise that our students don't either."*
— **L. Edward Day, Pennsylvania State University, Altoona**

Outstanding support materials
make it easy ...

... for instructors to teach!

Instructor's Manual and Test Bank

This Instructor's Manual/Test Bank includes unit objectives, unit outlines, a wealth of thought-provoking discussion questions, and activities. The Test Bank contains hundreds of challenging multiple-choice, true-false, short answer, and essay questions along with an answer key. The questions closely follow the text units and are cross-referenced with corresponding page numbers.

Online Text-Specific PowerPoint™ Lecture Presentations

A complete set of chapter-by-chapter PowerPoint™ lecture presentations, containing approximately 20 slides per chapter and specific to *Fundamentals of Criminal Justice*, is also available to adopters, giving instructors countless presentation options for their introductory course.

TestGen EQ: Computerized Test Bank

This computerized version of the Test Bank is available with Tamarack's easy-to-use TestGen software, which lets you prepare tests for printing as well as for network and online testing. It provides full editing capability for Windows and Macintosh. Fax-in testing is also available!

Videos

Qualified adopters receive one or more videos, including the Allyn and Bacon Interactive Videos for Criminal Justice, or "Prime Time Crime," and can also choose from a complete Video Library. Contact your publisher's representative for information on how you can access the latest news footage that relates directly to text content.

Digital Media Archive for Criminal Justice, Version 2.0

Newly updated for adopters of *Fundamentals of Criminal Justice*, this CD-ROM contains electronic images of charts, graphs, maps, tables, and figures; media elements such as video and audio clips and related weblinks; and introductory criminal justice PowerPoint™ lecture presentations. Instructors can customize pre-formatted PowerPoint™ lectures or import the media assets into their own presentations.

The Blockbuster Approach: Teaching Criminal Justice and Criminology with Video, 2/e

This supplement effectively guides the instructor on how to integrate feature films into the introductory course successfully and offers hundreds of film suggestions for the general topics covered in the course. Includes the latest Hollywood films!

CourseCompass for Introductory Criminal Justice

Instructors can focus on teaching the course—not on the technology—and create an online course with no headaches. CourseCompass combines the strength of Allyn and Bacon content with state-of-the-art technology that simplifies course management. This easy-to-use and customizable program enables instructors to tailor the content and functionality to meet their individual needs. Visit **www.coursecompass.com**

WebCT and Blackboard

A WebCT e-Pack or Blackboard Cartridge is available with published content that can be loaded into your course. See your Publisher's Representative or visit **www.ablongman.com/ techsolutions** for more information.

Custom Publishing Opportunities

Create your own customized reader with content and organization that matches your course syllabus. Select from hundreds of readings available through Boundaries, the Pearson Custom Publishing database in deviance, crime, and criminal justice. The anthology includes readings on the hottest topics such as terrorism and white collar crime, news articles from the latest headlines, and a wealth of state-specific information. You may also include your own writing, course-related information, or readings from outside sources. Contact your publisher's representative for more information on how easy and inexpensive it is to "go custom"!

... and for students to learn!

Practice Tests with Lecture Outlines

This workbook contains practice tests for every chapter and printouts of the PowerPoint™ lecture outlines with space for note taking.

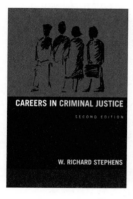

Careers in Criminal Justice, 2/e

Textbook + FREE *Careers in Criminal Justice,* Second Edition ValuePackage ISBN: 0-205-40672-6

This set of biographies of criminal justice professionals helps students and professors answer the often-asked question, "What can I do with a degree in criminal justice?" The text provides meaningful answers to a specific, targeted audience—typical students who are taking their first criminal justice course. The biographies are organized by various subfields and include discussions of what can be done with a B.A., M.A., Ph.D., or a combination of degrees.

Companion Website (www.ablongman.com/barkan1e)

This dedicated Website gives students the opportunity to quiz themselves on key chapter content online and to explore additional activities and resources.

State Supplements

Allyn & Bacon currently offers 11 state supplements with state-specific information on each state's criminal justice system. The following states are currently available and can be packaged FREE with *Fundamentals of Criminal Justice:* CA, FL, IL, KY, MI, NC, NY, OH, PA, TX, and WV.

eThemes of the Times for Introductory Criminal Justice

This online collection of about 30 contemporary articles from the award-winning *New York Times* brings currency and relevancy to the classroom. With additional pedagogy around eThemes articles, such as discussion and research questions, students practice their critical thinking and reading skills.

Research Navigator Guide: Criminal Justice

Textbook + FREE Research Navigator for Criminal Justice ValuePackage ISBN: 0-205-40673-4

This helpful booklet explains how to do high-quality online research and how to document it properly. It contains weblinks and activities specific to criminal justice. This booklet also contains an access code to Research Navigator.

Research Navigator™ (www.ablongman.com/researchnavigator)

Pearson's new Research Navigator™ is the easiest way for students to start a research assignment or research paper. Complete with extensive help on the research process and three exclusive databases of credible and reliable source material, including EBSCO's ContentSelect™ Academic Journal Database, *New York Times* Search by Subject Archive, and "Best of the Web" Link Library, Research Navigator™ helps students make the most of their research time.

Research Navigator™ requires a Pearson Access Code, which is included in Allyn & Bacon's Research Navigator for Criminal Justice.

A Message from the Authors

We finished writing this text after the tragic attacks of September 11, 2001, when commercial airliners hijacked by terrorists crashed into New York City's World Trade Center, the Pentagon, and farmland in western Pennsylvania. More than 3,000 people died that terrible day, including dozens of police officers who rushed into the World Trade Center before it collapsed.

In the aftermath of this tragedy, the nation struggled with many issues, including how best to balance the need for security with civil liberties guaranteed by the Constitution. Among other actions, the government detained hundreds of Middle Eastern immigrants, many of whom were neither informed of the charges against them nor allowed to consult attorneys; others who were allowed to consult lawyers were told that their conversations would be monitored. Critics charged that these actions violated constitutional safeguards, whereas defenders of these measures argued they were a necessary response to the continuing terrorist threat facing the nation.

This debate makes clear the fact that the criminal justice system—law enforcement, the criminal courts, and corrections—continues to play an important yet controversial role in life in the United States, both in ordinary times and during national crises. This book addresses several key topics and questions for understanding the role that criminal justice plays, the controversies it raises, and its potential for addressing the crime problem.

A first topic, and probably the most important for students to learn, is how the criminal justice system is structured and how it works in reality (as opposed to how it functions ideally). Because most students obtain their knowledge of this system from television programs and movies, their understanding of the practice of criminal justice is necessarily limited or even gravely mistaken. Our book provides them with an accurate and comprehensive view of the police, the criminal courts, and corrections in the United States.

A second and related topic is the role played by race, class, and gender in the operation of the criminal justice system. This role is both complex and significant, and most other texts do not treat it adequately. For a complete and accurate understanding of the criminal justice system, students must be aware of the impact of these essential components of contemporary U.S. society.

A third topic involves the tension between public safety and civil liberties that came to the forefront after the September 11 attacks. In a democracy, it is crucial to strike that delicate balance between these two goals, but this is extremely difficult to accomplish. We address this issue in the first chapter and return to it periodically throughout the book.

A final topic is the capacity of the criminal justice system (either as it currently exists or with appropriate reforms) to control criminal behavior and to reduce crime. This capacity is the very reason for having a criminal justice system, and our treatment will help students recognize both its potential and its limitations for protecting society.

In addressing these issues, the book casts a critical but balanced eye that draws on sociology and other disciplines and is grounded in the most recent empirical evidence. We recognize that students come from varied settings (like us, one a Californian and the other a Mainer), and that they have different views on, and experiences with, issues of crime and justice. Thus, we

Meet the Authors

Steven E. Barkan

Steven E. Barkan is the author of numerous books and articles on crime, criminal justice, and social movements. He is the author of *Criminology: A Sociological Understanding,* Second Edition (Prentice Hall, 2001), *Collective Violence* (with Lynne L. Snowden; Allyn & Bacon, 2001), *Discovering Sociology: An Introduction Using ExplorIt,* Second Edition (Wadsworth, 2003), and several articles on political justice and on racial prejudice and punitive attitudes toward criminals. He and his wife, Barbara Tennent, enjoy walking their dog, Sadie, whom they adopted from an animal shelter. Their older son, Dave, is a software engineer in the field of bioinformatics, while their younger son, Joe, is presently in college.

encourage students from both two-year and four-year institutions to draw their own conclusions on the many issues the text addresses, and we provide them with engaging yet comprehensive discussions of the latest research to help them do so.

We, the authors and publishers, would like to caution readers about the graphic subject matter and language within some of the chapters and interchapters in *Fundamentals of Criminal Justice*, especially within quoted materials. Changing such subject matter and language would have resulted in a lack of authenticity and jeopardized the integrity of such materials.

Acknowledgments

Writing a textbook requires a great deal of intellectual, and even physical, energy and has occupied much of our time. After completing such an endeavor, it is tempting to think in terms of "we did it," that is, the two authors. However, numerous people have given generously of their time and talent in the preparation of this book.

We are especially grateful to sociology editor Karen Hanson for having faith in our ability as sociologists and writers. Series editor Jennifer Jacobson prodded us (even pushed us a bit) down paths we did not always want to go. Monica Ohlinger and Joanne Vickers of Ohlinger Publishing Services did a terrific job in shaping the manuscript in the final months of the project. A special thanks to Joanne whose insightful comments and editorial skills contributed immeasurably to what we believe is a first-class textbook.

The University of San Diego provided two faculty research grants and a full-year sabbatical toward the completion of this project. The reference librarians at this institution never failed to provide needed information, in many cases long after hope had been lost of ever locating an obscure journal or foreign newspaper. Research assistant Kate Martin spent many summer afternoons in San Diego perusing library stacks and returning with an armload of books and journal articles. We would also like to thank the reviewers who carefully read early drafts of the manuscript, made innumerable comments (many of them incorporated in the final draft), and pointed out any mistakes or oversights. We sincerely appreciate your time and effort. These reviewers include: Roger C. Barnes, University of the Incarnate Word; Barbara Belbot, University of Houston, Downtown; Jana Bufkin, Drury University; Tod W. Burke, Radford University; Ligun Cao, Eastern Michigan University; Katherine A. Culotta, Indiana State University; L. Edward Day, Pennsylvania State University, Altoona; Thomas E. Fields, Cape Fear Community College, UNC–Wilmington; Ann-Victaire Lawrence-Robinson, Kean University; William J. Mathias, University of South Carolina; Nicholas Meier, Kalamazoo Valley Community College; Robert Neville, College of Siskiyous; Angela M. Nickoli, Ball State University; Jeannette M. Sereno, California State University, Stanislaus; and Brad Smith, Terra Community College.

Finally, we acknowledge our significant others, Diane Kulstad and Barbara Tennent. They endured an endless work schedule and our book-writing highs and lows during the preparation of this text. We are grateful for their understanding, support, and love.

George J. Bryjak

George J. Bryjak received his Ph.D. from the University of Oklahoma in 1980 and is a professor of sociology at the University of San Diego. His areas of interest include criminology, deviant behavior, the sociology of developing nations, and the sociology of sport. He is the co-author of three books (with Michael P. Soroka): *Sociology: Changing Societies in a Diverse World,* Fourth Edition (Allyn & Bacon, 2001), *Social Problems: A World at Risk,* Second Edition (Allyn & Bacon, 1999), *Sociology; The Biological Factor* (Peek Publications, 1985). He was the recipient of a summer Fulbright fellowship to India (1981), and was a visiting professor at a teacher's college in Zakopane, Poland (1993). His social commentary articles appear regularly in the *San Diego Union-Tribune.* He and his wife, Diane, have three passions in life: travelling, hiking in the mountains, and their granddaughter Elizabeth—not necessarily in that order.

chapter 1

Crime, Justice, and Law in American Society

questions *for* exploration

1. How real is the problem of crime in the United States?

2. What is public opinion about how criminals should be treated?

3. What are crime myths? How do they spread?

4. What is the "get tough" approach to crime?

5. What are the important events in the U.S. criminal justice system?

6. What are the models of the criminal justice system?

G ail Atwater, a respiratory therapist and former board member of the local parent–teacher association, was slowly driving her pickup truck on a road near her home in Lago Vista outside Austin, Texas. With her were her two young children, 4-year-old Mac and 6-year-old Anya. They were looking for Mac's rubber vampire bat that had fallen from the truck's window on the way home from soccer practice. She let her children unbuckle their seat belts so they could look out the window for the bat. "There was no one else on the road, and I was going so slowly," Atwater explained, "I thought it would be OK. But as soon as I saw the police car, I knew I was going to be stopped. I knew the law, and I deserved to be stopped." She expected to get a ticket for letting her children be unbuckled.

Atwater did get the ticket but was startled when she was also arrested and handcuffed while her children screamed in terror. The arrest startled her because seat-belt violations in Texas are punishable only by a fine, not by imprisonment. After being fingerprinted and put in jail until she made bail, she eventually paid a fine of $50 for each of her two children. Atwater sued the city for false arrest in violation of the Fourth Amendment's ban on unreasonable seizure. Four years later in April 2001, the U.S. Supreme Court rejected her suit in a close 5 to 4 vote and ruled that the police may arrest someone even for a minor violation punishable only by a small fine. A dissenting opinion by Justice Sandra Day O'Connor warned that handing the police "such unbounded discretion . . . carries with it grave potential for abuse" by giving the police a pretext for harassing. Atwater agreed, "If someone like me, a soccer mom, can be humiliated and handcuffed in front of her children, what happens to poor migrant workers or minorities when they're stopped?" Several legal observers agreed that the Court's ruling could increase the potential for such "racial profiling" and said it would also let police arrest people for minor violations, such as jaywalking, and then do full searches of their persons or vehicles. In contrast, police officials praised the ruling for allowing the police to do their job without fear of lawsuits (Denniston, 2001; Greenhouse, 2001, p. A1; Milloy, 2001).

Gail Atwater's arrest for not buckling up her children illustrates the difficulty in striking the correct balance between civil liberties and public safety in a democracy.

This case goes to the heart of some of the most important issues in criminal justice today. How much power should the police have to do their jobs? Where should we draw the delicate line between civil liberties and public safety? How punitive should the criminal justice system be? To what extent does the criminal justice system discriminate against poor people and people of color? How effective is it in preventing and reducing crime? All these questions became even more important after the terrorist attacks of September 11, 2001.

This book deals with all these issues and more. It presents a concise but comprehensive understanding of criminal justice in the United States. You will learn how the criminal justice system works, and you will also read about the issues just mentioned along with many others, such as the death penalty, the accuracy of crime statistics, police deviance, plea bargaining, prison rape and prison riots, and the legal response to juvenile violence. This first chapter discusses some basic features of crime, justice, and law in American society. Later chapters examine measurement and explanations of crime and victimization, types of crime, and the three major stages of the criminal justice system: police, courts, and corrections. An international Focus On box in each chapter provides a detailed look at criminal justice in other nations because learning about criminal justice elsewhere helps us better understand its operation and impact in our own society.

The Problem of Crime

As we move steadily into the twenty-first century, crime continues to be a major concern to many Americans. Crime, violence, and guns ranked third in a 2001 Gallup poll asking respondents to name "the most important problem facing this country today," just behind ethics and family decline, and the quality of education. Just 27 percent of Americans in a 2002 Gallup poll on social institutions professed much faith in the criminal justice system; only big business won less confidence. More Americans cite violence, gangs, or drugs than any other issue as the "biggest problem" facing the public schools in their communities. Almost half of the respondents in a 2000 Gallup poll thought there was more crime in the United States than a year earlier. About one-third report an area within one mile of their homes where they would be "afraid to walk alone at night"; this figure rises to about half of all women and all African Americans and other people of color and 60 percent of the residents of the largest cities (Maguire and Pastore, 2002).

These numbers reflect a gnawing concern over crime in our communities. Many of us hesitate to go out alone at night. We buy home security systems and lock our doors when we are away from our homes and our cars. Many keep handguns or other firearms in our houses for protection. Businesses and private citizens spend more than $90 billion annually on private security, such as alarm systems, guards, and special locks ("Welcome to the New World . . . ," 1997).

These concerns are real, and so is the problem of crime. The government estimates that more than 24 million violent and property crimes occur each year (2001 figures; Rennison, 2002). About 2.5 percent of the public are victims of violent crimes in any one year, and almost 17 percent are victims of property crimes. Because these risks accumulate over a lifetime, the government estimates high lifetime risks of being victimized by crime: 30 percent of Americans will be robbery victims at least once in their lives; 74 percent will be assault victims; and 72 percent will have their homes or apartments burglarized (Koppel, 1987). Certain types of crime affect women in particular; about one fourth of all women are victims of domestic violence or rape and sexual assault (Tjaden and Thoennes, 2000). "Street" crime costs Americans about $17 billion in direct costs—value of money or property stolen, medical expenses, and time missed from work—and much more than that, perhaps hundreds of billions of dollars, when intangibles, such as pain, suffering, and quality of life, are considered (Klaus, 1994; Miller, Cohen, and Wiersema, 1996). Homicide and robbery rates are higher in the United States than in other Western nations, and the U.S. rates of other serious street crimes generally rank among the highest in the Western world (van Dijk and Kangaspunta, 2000).

Public opinion reflects the reality of crime. About 60 percent of Americans think the United States is spending too little money to fight crime, and only one-fourth report much confidence in the criminal justice system (Maguire and Pastore, 2002). Moreover, the U.S. public is generally "punitive toward crime" (Cullen, Fisher, and Applegate, 2000, p. 57). Almost 70 percent favor the death penalty for people convicted of murder, although that support has declined since the late 1990s following revelations of innocent people being sent to death row (see Chapter 12). About three fourths of Americans think the courts in their communities do not deal harshly enough with criminals, and large majorities prefer imprisonment for most offenders and long prison terms for violent offenders. At the same time, Americans support alternatives to incarceration, such as supervision in the community, if they think public safety would not be at risk, and they continue to believe that the criminal justice system should try to rehabilitate offenders (Cullen et al., 2000). Thus, more than 80 percent of Americans think the U.S. prison system is doing only a fair or poor job in rehabilitating inmates, and another 60 percent think prisons are doing only a fair or poor job in keeping inmates safe while they are behind bars (Maguire and Pastore, 2002).

In sum, Americans think crime is a major problem and worry that efforts to deal with crime and criminals are not working. Crime rates are high in the United States, and so is the number of people in prison or jail or otherwise under correctional supervision. The criminal justice system costs taxpayers billions of dollars. The problem of crime is real for all of us whether we commit it or are victims of it.

The Problem in Understanding Crime

Although crime is a very real problem that needs to be addressed, much of what we think we know about crime may not be true or we may not fully appreciate its complexity. For example, Americans underestimate how many convicted offenders go to prison and the lengths of their prison terms (Cullen et al., 2000). As another example, although almost half of Americans thought in 2000 that the crime rate was rising (see the previous discussion), the U.S. crime rate in fact declined steadily from 1993 through 2000. And although Americans often have a sense that crime is a more serious problem than ever before, it turns out that crime has *always* been considered a serious problem. As a presidential commission reported in 1967, "There has always been too much crime. Virtually every generation since the founding of the Nation and before has felt itself threatened by the spectre of rising crime and violence" (quoted in Pepinsky and Jesilow, 1984, p. 21). Mob violence was common in major U.S. cities in the decades before the Civil War, for example, and teenage gangs were also a common threat. Concern over crime was a common theme in the development of criminal justice policy after the Civil War and in the early decades of the twentieth century (Friedman, 1993; Walker, 1998). In short, the United States has never been free from crime and has always been concerned about it. Recent concerns over crime have not abated, but they need to be considered in the larger historical context.

Current concerns about crime may both exaggerate the extent of violent crime and minimize the harm caused by other types of crime. Consider homicide, for example, which is a crime featured in countless movies, TV shows, books, and news crime stories. About 16,000 homicides occurred in 2001. This is no small number, but it does not even place homicide among the top ten causes of death (which are led by heart disease and include cancer, motor vehicle accidents, and suicide) (Census, 2000). Homicide thus receives much more media attention than its actual occurrence might warrant.

Homicide and other street crimes probably receive so much attention because they threaten us personally and violate our sense of security. Yet this fact leads us to neglect the gravity of white-collar crime, which in many ways is more harmful than street crime (see Chapter 3). Examples of white-collar crime include medical fraud, false advertising and price fixing, and "corporate violence" in the form of practices by corporations that threaten the health and safety of their workers or of the public. Estimates of the costs of white-collar crime dwarf those of street crime. For example, although the Federal Bureau of Investigation (FBI) estimates that property crime costs the public about $17 billion in direct costs, the monetary cost of white-collar crime probably exceeds $400 billion. And although, as just noted, about 16,000 people died from homicide in 2001, the annual number of deaths from white-collar crime (from such sources as pollution and unsafe workplaces and products) probably exceeds 100,000 (Barkan, 2001). Although white-collar crime is thus undoubtedly more costly than street crime, it receives far less media and public attention than street crime and much less attention from the criminal justice system.

Media Coverage and Myths about Crime

What accounts for this false or oversimplified understanding of crime? Many observers blame the news media (Kurtz, 1997). Because most people learn about crime from the media, the media should provide accurate details about the crime rate, the nature of crime, trends in crime rates, and the operation of the criminal justice system. Yet many studies confirm that the media, in fact, do not provide an accurate picture (Dorfman and Schiraldi, 2001; Surette, 1998; Warr, 2000).

The media overdramatize crime in at least two ways. First, they report many crime stories in order to capture viewer or reader attention. Local TV newscasts often report more stories about crime than about any other topic other than sports (Public Health Reports, 1998). If a particularly violent crime or series of crimes occurs, the media cover these heavily, contributing to false perceptions that crime is becoming more frequent. In this way, the media create "crime waves" by devoting so much attention to one crime or a small number of crimes that the public becomes excessively alarmed about the menace of crime (Fishman, 1978).

The media also overdramatize crime by giving disproportionate attention to violent crime, reflecting the belief that "if it bleeds, it leads." Studies have found that most crime stories on TV news or in the newspapers feature violent crime even though violent crime is much less common than other types of crime. For example, homicides comprise more than one-fourth of the crime stories on the evening news even though homicides comprise much less than 1 percent of all crimes (Dorfman and Schiraldi, 2001).

Such coverage yields the false impression that most crime is violent, which affects public perceptions of the amount of violent crime and subsequently their concern over it. One study asked several hundred college students in an introductory criminal justice class to estimate the annual number of U.S. homicides. Almost half the students thought this number to be at least 250,000; however, fewer than 24,000 homicides occurred in the year the study was done, 1994 (Vandiver and Giacopassi, 1997). Other studies of Baltimore and Philadelphia residents found that people who often watch TV news shows are more likely than those who watch them less often to worry about crime (Bunch, 1999; Farkas and Duffett, 1998).

In another problem, media coverage often highlights the involvement of minorities and teenagers in crime (Dorfman and Schiraldi, 2001; Entman, 1994). Some studies find that, in crime stories on the TV news and in newspapers, a greater proportion of the offenders are African American and Hispanic than is true in actual crime statistics. Conversely, a greater proportion of the victims are white than is true in actual statistics. Newspaper stories about white victims of homicide are longer than those of African American victims. Crime stories also disproportionately depict crimes in which African Americans are the offenders and whites are the victims even though most crime involves offenders and victims of the same race. A study of *Los Angeles Times* coverage of homicides illustrates these problems. Although 80 percent of Los Angeles homicide victims are African American or Hispanic, murders of white victims are much more likely than those of African American or Hispanic victims to be covered by that city's largest newspaper (Sorenson, Manz, and Berk, 1998).

In all these ways, media coverage exaggerates both the degree to which African Americans and Hispanics commit crime and the degree to which whites are victims of crime. Perhaps for this reason, one poll found that whites think they are more likely to be victimized by people of color than by whites even though about 75 percent of all crimes against whites are committed by other whites (Dorfman and Schiraldi, 2001). Another provocative study focused on subjects who watched news stories that did not depict the offender. Sixty percent of the subjects falsely remembered seeing an offender, and 70 percent of these subjects actually said the offender was African American (Gilliam and Iyengar, 2000)!

A similar bias exists in the coverage of youth crime (Dorfman and Schiraldi, 2001). A greater proportion of offenders in crime stories are teenagers, especially African American teenagers, than is true in actual crime statistics. For example, one study in California found that almost 70 percent of TV news stories on violence featured teenagers even though only 14 percent of all violent crime arrests in that state are of teenagers. In a related problem, newspaper and TV news stories about teenagers tend to show them committing violence rather than engaging in "prosocial" acts. Such coverage exaggerates the degree to which teenagers commit violence. Not surprisingly, therefore, 62 percent of respondents in a recent national poll said youth violence was increasing even though youth homicides actually had declined 68 percent from 1993 to 1999. Respondents in other polls say that teenagers commit most violent crime even though they actually only commit about 14 to 16 percent of it (Dorfman and Schiraldi, 2001).

These problems in media coverage help contribute to **crime myths,** or false beliefs about crime and criminal justice (Kappeler, Blumberg, and Potter, 2000). Like the *Emperor's New Clothes* fable, people may believe certain things are true when, in fact, they are not. Crime myths include the following: The public believes falsely that crime is rising when, in fact, it is not; people think that most crime is violent when, in fact, it is not; people overestimate the involvement of people of color and youths in crime and underestimate their victimization by crime; and people worry more about street crime than perhaps the facts warrant.

Statements by public officials contribute to crime myths. Politicians have regularly used harsh rhetoric, some of it racially "coded," about crime and criminals to win public support for harsher criminal sanctions and, not incidentally, for the politicians' campaign efforts (Beckett, 1997; Chambliss, 1999). A memorable example involved a

crime myth false belief about crime and criminal justice

1988 TV commercial aired on behalf of the presidential campaign of then–Vice President George Bush. The commercial featured convicts passing through a revolving door and showed a picture of an African American Massachusetts prisoner, Willie Horton, who had committed a vicious murder while on a prison furlough. The commercial was widely credited with hurting the campaign of Bush's Democratic Party opponent, Massachusetts governor Michael Dukakis, and was heavily criticized for its racial overtones (Mendelberg, 1997). After Bush became president, he gave a speech about drugs on Labor Day 1989 in which he held up a bag of crack cocaine that, he said, had been bought by undercover agents in Lafayette Park across the street from the White House. It was later revealed that the White House had asked federal agents to buy the crack in the park in order to provide a dramatic prop for the president's speech. When the agents were unable to find anyone selling crack in the park—because, they were told, it was too near all the police at the White House—they tricked a drug dealer into going to the park so that they could buy it there (Isikoff, 1989). Although both these examples involved a Republican president, Bush's successor, Democrat Bill Clinton, also engaged in harsh crime rhetoric when he sought congressional support for a major crime bill during his first term as president (Chambliss, 1999).

Whether promoted by the news media or by elected officials, crime myths help distort public understanding about crime. Crime itself is a real problem, but knowledge about crime and criminal justice gained from the media and from official statements may not be so real.

The Get Tough Approach

If the understanding of crime is confusing, the U.S. response to crime in the past few decades is quite certain. This response involves a concentrated, "get tough" approach of arrest and incarceration of many more offenders than previously, and it has prompted the extraordinarily high rates of incarceration noted earlier (Beckett and Sasson, 1999). It emphasizes the need to arrest and punish criminals rather than rehabilitating them and addressing the many social factors underlying criminal behavior. Other Western nations emphasize these latter needs much more. Their approach is more similar to the public health model used in the field of medicine (Moore, 1995). This model stresses the need to identify and address the causes of disease in order to reduce its incidence significantly. For example, unless the causes of cancer are identified and then eliminated, millions more people will get cancer no matter how many cancer patients are successfully treated. The public health model thus focuses on the prevention of disease and not only on its treatment. By neglecting the underlying causes of criminal behavior, the get tough approach to crime makes it likely that crime will continue no matter how many offenders are arrested and imprisoned.

This is a harsh charge, to be sure, and one with which get tough advocates would doubtless disagree (Robinson, 2001; Wilson, 1994). In their view, the get tough approach has reduced crime by imprisoning so many offenders. This view probably has some truth, and we examine it later in this book. Yet the bulk of the evidence indicates that the get tough approach has achieved only modest reductions in crime and that these reductions have come at a very heavy social and financial cost (Beckett and Sasson, 1999; Tonry, 1994).

What are some of these costs? The United States now imprisons about 2 million people and a greater proportion of its citizens than any other nation in the Western world; it also has almost 6.5 million citizens under correctional supervision of some form: incarceration, probation, or parole (Gainsborough and Mauer, 2000). The U.S. incarceration rate—about 700 jail or prison inmates per 100,000 residents—is more than five times greater that of any other Western nation and about five times greater than the U.S. rate only three decades ago. As one scholar notes, "Contemporary policies concerning crime and punishment are the harshest in American history and of any Western country" (Tonry, 1998a, p. 3). These policies have cost the nation tens of billions of tax dollars for more police and more prisons and jails, leaving higher education and various social programs to suffer in some states (Nolan, 1995).

This is a prison under construction, with workers pushing a prefab cell into place. The amount of money spent on the criminal justice system in the United States has increased tremendously during the last few decades, thanks in large part to the building of new prisons and the housing of many more inmates.

The get tough approach has fallen disproportionately on racial and ethnic minorities. Although the government estimates that more than 5 percent of all Americans will be put in prison at least once during their lifetime, this figure—in itself the highest by far in the Western world—rises to 16 percent for Hispanic men and almost 30 percent for African American men (Bonczar and Beck, 1997). About one-third of young African American men are currently under correctional supervision (Mauer, 1999).

In related problems, the get tough approach has destabilized urban neighborhoods because so many of their young males are in prison (Hagan and Dinovitzer, 1999). It has created a force of hundreds of thousands of inmates who are released from prison back into their communities every year with the same personal problems that helped put them into prison and with bleak chances of stable employment or social relationships (Gainsborough and Mauer, 2000). This fact leads one observer to warn, "We are creating a disaster that instead of dissipating over time will accumulate with the years" (Abramsky, 1999, p. 36).

We discuss these costs further in later chapters, but first examine the operation of the criminal justice system. The controversy over the get tough approach notwithstanding, the criminal justice system plays a fundamental role in U.S. society, and it is impossible to imagine our nation without it. It employs hundreds of thousands of people, costs billions of dollars, and processes millions of offenders annually. In one way or another, it touches all of our lives directly or indirectly. For all these reasons, it is important to understand the criminal justice system's operation, its strengths, its weaknesses, and its impact on the crime rate and other aspects of U.S. society. To begin this understanding, next we discuss several aspects of the criminal justice system.

The Criminal Justice System

The U.S. criminal justice system is only partly a "system" as usually defined. "System" implies a coordinated and unified plan of procedure. Criminal justice in the United States is only partly coordinated and unified. The basic stages of criminal justice—police or law enforcement, courts or judicial processing, and corrections—are the same throughout the nation, but the U.S. criminal justice system is really thousands of systems. The federal government has one system of criminal justice, each state has its own system, and each county and municipality has its own system. Although each system's components—police, prosecutors, judges, corrections officials—work together on occasion, they have separate budgets and work independently of one another for the most part. Inevitably, they also often work at cross-purposes. Thus, the police may crack down on drug trafficking in a particular neighborhood by making mass arrests, only to have this flood of cases overwhelm the prosecutor's office and judicial system. Or new legislation may require judges to put more people in prison, but the prisons have too few cells for them. This forces prison officials to release inmates early, overcrowd cells further, or request funds for new prison construction.

Events in the Criminal Justice System

Although U.S. criminal justice is composed of many systems, all involve a series of events, or stages, that are fairly similar from one jurisdiction to the next. These stages are outlined in Figure 1.1. Later chapters examine these stages extensively, but a brief discussion here is in order.

We start at the far left of the diagram with a crime being committed. Only if the police are aware of a crime can it enter the next stages of the criminal justice process. More than 60 percent of crime is *not* reported to the police and is not subject to the justice system. If the police learn about a crime, they investigate it. Although the chances of arrest vary from one crime to another, almost 80 percent of the crimes that come to the attention of the police do *not* end in arrest. Sometimes the police never find a suspect, and sometimes they find a suspect but decide not to make an arrest, often because the evidence is too weak to do so.

If an arrest does occur, then a series of stages, summarized in Figure 1.1 under the heading *prosecution and pretrial services*, ensues. The police provide information about the case to a prosecutor, who must decide whether to file formal charges with the court or

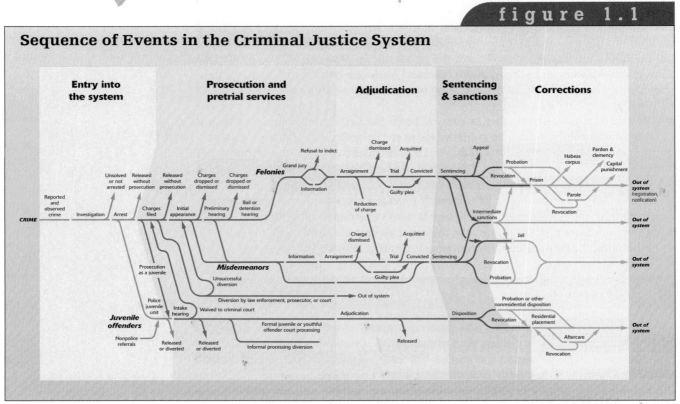

figure 1.1

Sequence of Events in the Criminal Justice System

Source: Bureau of Justice Statistics, U.S. Department of Justice. Available: http://www.ojp.usdoj.gov/bjs/flowchart.htm. Adapted from President's Commission on Law Enforcement and Administration of Justice. 1967. *The Challenge of Crime in a Free Society.*

In June 2000, rap singer Eminem (whose real name is Marshall Mathers) was arrested in Michigan and charged with carrying a concealed weapon. Here he faces a judge during a pretrial hearing. As this event reflects, decisions by judges and other criminal justice professionals characterize all stages of the criminal justice system.

to release the suspect. As Figure 1.1 indicates, the prosecutor may decide to release a suspect or drop the charges at several points in this part of the process even if formal charges are initially filed. Charges are sometimes dropped for any one of several reasons: The evidence may be too weak, a witness may be uncooperative, and so on. If the prosecutor chooses to proceed with a case after the initial arrest, defendants ordinarily appear before a judge to hear the charges against them and to determine whether the evidence is sufficient to allow the prosecution to proceed. Defense counsel is also often assigned at this appearance because most suspects cannot afford their own attorneys. At this or a later appearance, a judge decides whether to release defendants on their own recognizance or on bail, and, in the latter case, the amount of the bail.

Later a *preliminary hearing* determines whether there is "probable cause" to believe that a defendant committed a crime. If the judge makes this decision, the case is often sent to a grand jury. The grand jury hears evidence about the case and must decide whether the evidence is sufficient to justify a trial. If the grand jury decides in favor of a trial, it *indicts* the defendant. In some jurisdictions, grand juries are not used; instead, the prosecutor issues an "information" to the court, which is the equivalent to an indictment; such informations are also ordinarily used for minor offenses.

This series of decisions finally results in the *adjudication* stage (shown in Figure 1.1). After an indictment or information is filed, the defendant has an *arraignment* before a judge. Here the judge presents the defendant with the charges, advises the defendant of his or her legal rights, and asks for a plea to the charges. Defendants must decide whether they will plead guilty; those who plead not guilty must decide whether they will request their right to a jury trial or settle for a "bench trial" heard solely by the judge. Most defendants plead guilty in return for a reduction in the number or severity of the charges and the promise of a reduced sentence. If a defendant has a trial, the jury or judge must obviously decide whether the defendant is guilty or not guilty.

If the defendant is found guilty, the judge must decide on the appropriate sentence as the *sentencing and sanctions* stage shown in Figure 1.1 is reached. Often a sentencing hearing is held in which the judge considers all aspects of a case, including any aggravating or mitigating circumstances, and reviews a presentence report prepared by a probation officer or other legal official that presents the personal background of the defendant. The most important decision a judge makes at the sentencing stage is whether to incarcerate the defendant. Defendants convicted of minor offenses (misdemeanors) may be sent to jail for less than a year, whereas those convicted of serious offenses (felonies) may be sent to prison for one year or more. In lieu of incarceration, a judge may sentence a defendant to probation; in this case, the defendant remains in the community but must fulfill certain conditions and follow certain rules, such as drug testing under the supervision of a probation officer. Defendants may also be fined or sentenced to other types of *intermediate sanctions*, such as house arrest and electronic monitoring, that are stricter than routine probation but less harsh than incarceration.

Once defendants are sentenced, they enter the *corrections* stage. Many inmates serve their full prison terms less any time off for good behavior, but others are released early after a favorable decision by a parole board. Once inmates are released, they ordinarily are supervised by parole officers and must follow certain conditions similar to convicted offenders on probation. If they violate these conditions, they risk being sent back to prison. Once convicted offenders successfully complete the terms of their release (or, if not incarcerated in the first place, the conditions of their probation or intermediate sanctions), they leave the corrections system and are no longer under correctional supervision.

Note, as indicated in Figure 1.1, a separate process exists for juvenile offenders. The juvenile justice system is part of the broad U.S. legal system but separate from the adult criminal justice system. Its stages generally parallel those for the adult system but are more informal. In recent years, more juvenile offenders have been tried as adults in response to public perceptions of growing youth violence. We explore this recent trend and the entire juvenile justice system further in Chapter 14.

The Size and Cost of Criminal Justice

As noted previously, the U.S. criminal justice system costs billions of dollars. This expenditure breaks down as follows. In 1999, the latest year for which data are available, the entire nation spent $147 billion on criminal justice: about $22 billion at the federal level, $50 billion at the state level, and $75 billion at the local (county or municipality) level. These figures represent dramatic increases since 1982, when only about $36 billion was spent nationwide on criminal justice (Figure 1.2). The national cost of criminal justice quadrupled in only seventeen years. In 1982 the nation spent

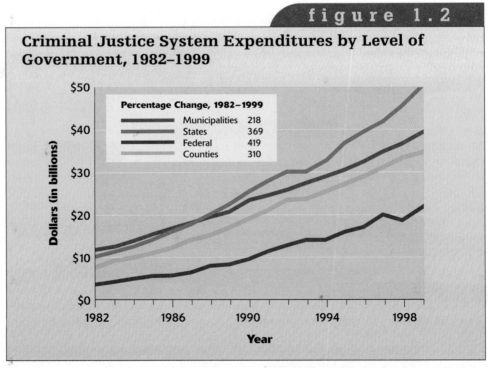

figure 1.2

Criminal Justice System Expenditures by Level of Government, 1982–1999

Percentage Change, 1982–1999
Municipalities	218
States	369
Federal	419
Counties	310

Source: Bureau of Justice Statistics, U.S. Department of Justice. Available: http://www.ojp.usdoj.gov/bjs/glance/expgov.htm.

about $155 for every American on criminal justice; in 1999 it spent more than $520 per capita (Maguire and Pastore, 2002).

Nationwide the single greatest expense is for police, followed by corrections, then judicial and legal expenses (Figure 1.3). Expenditures for each of these activities also soared from the early 1980s through the 1990s (Figure 1.4).

figure 1.3

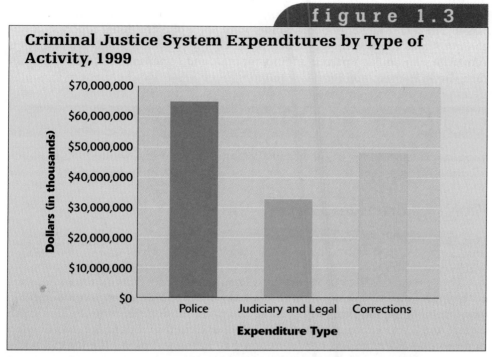

Criminal Justice System Expenditures by Type of Activity, 1999

Source: Data from Gifford, Sidra Lea. 2002. *Justice Expenditure and Employment in the United States, 1999*. Washington, DC: Bureau of Justice Statistics, U.S. Department of Justice.

figure 1.4

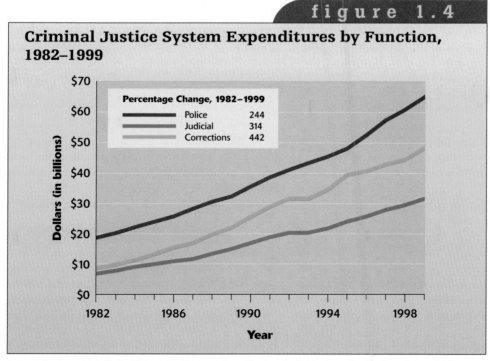

Criminal Justice System Expenditures by Function, 1982–1999

Percentage Change, 1982–1999

Police	244
Judicial	314
Corrections	442

Source: Bureau of Justice Statistics, U.S. Department of Justice. Available: http://www.ojp.usdoj.gov/bjs/glance/exptyp.htm.

A major reason for these costs is the fact that the criminal justice system employs hundreds of thousands of people (Gifford, 1999). In 1999, the latest period for which data are available, the system employed more than 2 million people. The single greatest number worked in policing, followed by corrections, then judicial and legal services. The more than 2 million employees in 1999 represents a 72 percent increase since 1982.

The criminal justice system also monitors millions of people. At midyear 2001, more than 3.8 million people were on probation; about 725,000 were on parole; more than 1.3 million were in prison, and another 700,000 were in jail or under jail supervision. The total number of people under some form of correctional supervision was about 6.5 million, representing about 3 percent of the U.S. adult population and 5 percent of all male adults, 7 percent of Hispanic men, and 16 percent of African American men (Beck, Karberg, and Harrison, 2002).

Understanding the Criminal Justice System

With the structure of the criminal justice system in mind, we now turn to its goals and models of operation to understand how and why it works the way it does.

Goals of Criminal Justice

Criminal justice in the United States serves several goals. How well it achieves these goals is, of course, a matter of debate. To understand the role played by criminal justice in American society, it is important to understand the goals it tries to accomplish.

The first goal, and arguably the most important for most Americans and the one with which you are probably most familiar, involves the *control and prevention of crime*. The criminal justice system tries to apprehend and punish people who commit crime and, through these and other measures, to prevent crime by deterring both offenders and potential offenders from committing crime in the first place. The larger goal, of course, is to keep the public as safe as possible from crime.

The police are the most visible branch of the criminal justice system as it tries to achieve this goal. Most people encounter the police only through traffic violations, but even here the police act, regardless of whether we like it, to maintain safe roads. As important and valuable as the police are in protecting the public from crimes, they are also highly controversial, as both the opening vignette to this chapter and the possibility of racial profiling suggest.

Another branch of the criminal justice system that gets much attention in its effort to control and prevent crime is the corrections system, which operates in several ways. (1) It "incapacitates" criminals by putting them behind bars where they do not pose a threat to the general public. (2) It tries to both scare and reform punished offenders with the hope that they will be less likely to break the law again. (3) It aims to deter potential offenders from committing crime by threatening incarceration. Whether the corrections system helps prevent crime in all these ways is a matter of some contention, which we explore in later chapters. Ironically, many observers now worry, as noted earlier, that the surge in incarceration in the past few decades is creating a dangerous flood of inmates whose sheer numbers as they are released from prison will exacerbate crime and other social problems.

The second goal of criminal justice is to *achieve justice* by protecting all citizens—those guilty of crimes as well as those not guilty—from governmental abuse of power. Jerome Skolnick (1994) refers to this as "the rule of law" and notes that, in the United States and other democratic societies, the police and other governmental agents must respect individual rights and freedoms as they pursue the goal of crime control. Otherwise, we would live in an authoritarian nation, not a democratic one. This goal of the U.S. criminal justice system is reflected in the U.S. Constitution and Bill of Rights, which guarantee several legal rights to people suspected or convicted of crimes. These provisions grew out of the colonial experience in which England abused the courts to harass the colonists. When the new nation began, this abuse was fresh in the minds of the framers of the Constitution and Bill of Rights, and they considered the legal rights of the criminally accused very important to protect.

These first two goals of the criminal justice system, to control crime and to achieve justice, sometimes clash. Skolnick (1994, p. 1) refers to this clash as a classic "dilemma of democracy." As the nation has adopted a get tough approach to the crime problem in recent decades, it has expanded the powers of police and increased the punishments for convicted offenders. As the opening vignette suggests, it is difficult to strike the correct delicate balance between the twin goals of controlling crime and achieving justice. As you read this book, keep this difficulty in mind.

The third goal of the criminal justice system is to *express the nation's morality and values* on important issues. For example, the laws nationwide against murder make very clear that we as a nation believe it is wrong to kill. Thus, criminal justice serves an important role in teaching moral lessons in addition to controlling crime and preserving justice. It is also true that this goal of criminal justice arouses much controversy regarding crimes that involve no unwilling victims, such as prostitution and drug use. Critics say the use of law to prevent these behaviors amounts to the state legislating morality by "coercing virtue" (Meier and Geis, 1997; Skolnick, 1968). In a free society, they say, people should be free to engage in such behaviors just as they are free to follow other potentially harmful actions, such as eating high-fat foods, parachuting, and gambling in the state lottery. The majority should not impose its sense of morality on the minority as concerns consensual behaviors, however objectionable these behaviors may be to some. On a more practical level, critics also say that the legal attempt to outlaw these behaviors may do more harm than good. Among other consequences, it may encourage police corruption, increase public disrespect for the law, and prompt the police to engage in unsavory practices such as wiretapping and using informants (Meier and Geis, 1997).

Models of Criminal Justice

In the social and natural sciences, a *model* is a simplified representation of a phenomenon or system that helps explain its operation and outcomes. Several models of criminal justice help us understand how it works and some of the dilemmas it faces.

System Model. The **system model** (refer to Figure 1.1) may be considered an "input–output" model in which crime is the input and entrance into corrections is the output. It involves a series of stages marked by limited cooperation among criminal justice officials. As was noted earlier, the criminal justice system is only partly a *system* as the term is usually understood; the branches of the criminal justice system are too independent for the tight coordination that the term *system* usually implies.

Discretionary Model. In the **discretionary model**, the criminal justice system involves a series of decisions at each stage of the process. Reread the earlier discussion of Figure 1.1, and note how often the words *decide, decides,* and *decision* are used. As these words suggest, **discretion** characterizes every event in the criminal justice system. Crime victims and witnesses decide whether to report a crime; police decide how intensively to investigate a crime and whether to arrest a suspect; prosecutors decide whether to prosecute a case and which charges to file; judges decide whether to dismiss a case and whether to release defendants on bail or on their own recognizance; defendants decide whether to plead guilty; and prosecutors and defendants decide on a plea bargain. If a trial occurs, juries or judges decide whether to convict a defendant; if a conviction occurs, judges decide on the appropriate sentence. And, finally, various corrections officials decide whether to release inmates early from prison or, for those in the community under supervision, whether to send them to prison for violating the conditions of their supervision.

The criminal justice system could not operate without all this discretion. No two cases are alike, and no two defendants are alike. Criminal justice officials recognize this, and they also recognize the need for a smooth and efficient process. Thus, discretion in the criminal justice system is necessary (Hawkins, 1993; Walker, 1993). Yet with so much

system model an "input–output" model of criminal justice in which crime is the input and entrance into corrections the output. It involves a series of stages marked by limited cooperation among criminal justice officials.

discretionary model a model of the criminal justice system that involves a series of decisions at each stage of the process

discretion in criminal justice, the power of officials to decide whether to take a particular course of action

discretion at every stage of the process, the opportunity for conscious or unconscious abuse of discretion arises. By this, we mean that criminal justice officials may make biased decisions, either consciously or unconsciously, based on such factors as a defendant's or victim's race, ethnicity, gender, or social class (Smith, Visher, and Davidson, 1984; Sorensen and Wallace, 1999; Steffensmeier, Ulmer, and Kramer, 1998). Attitudes toward the nature of certain criminal behaviors may also affect officials' decision making. For example, some officials in the past, and perhaps still currently, did not believe some crimes, such as rape and domestic violence, were serious and failed to arrest or prosecute to the fullest extent of their law (Schmidt and Steury, 1989). More generally, discretion may lead similar cases to have very different outcomes in different jurisdictions of the nation, raising important questions about the fairness of these outcomes. Discretion is thus a double-edged sword with profound implications for the operation of the criminal justice system. We explore these implications throughout the book.

Note also that in the earliest exercise of discretion victims decide not to report more than 60 percent of the crimes they suffer to the police. Also recall that most of the crimes known to the police do not end in an arrest. These two facts reveal serious obstacles the criminal justice system faces in addressing the crime problem in any significant way.

Wedding Cake Model. The system model depicted in Figure 1.1 distinguishes between felonies and misdemeanors but does not adequately present the vast differences in how the criminal justice system handles different types of crimes. In this regard, a *wedding-cake* model may be more useful (Walker, 2001).

As Figure 1.5 illustrates, a wedding cake has a small layer on the top and increasingly larger layers below. The criminal justice system may be understood using the **wedding cake model.** A very small number of *celebrated cases* is at the top of the model. These are cases that, because of the enormity of the crime and the fame of the offender and/or victim, receive heavy media attention and the utmost attention from criminal justice officials. The most celebrated case in recent years was probably the 1994 arrest and subsequent trial of football star and TV and movie celebrity O. J. Simpson for allegedly murdering his ex-wife and a friend of hers. A close second, perhaps, was the arrest and trial of Timothy McVeigh for bombing the Oklahoma City federal building in 1995. As Samuel Walker (2001, p. 29) notes, cases like these "usually involve the full criminal process, including that rare event, the criminal trial," which is filled with drama. Because they receive so much publicity, celebrated cases unduly influence

wedding cake model a model of the criminal justice system in which a very small number of celebrated cases is at the top of the model, and a greater number of serious felonies and greater numbers yet of less serious felonies and of misdemeanors are below

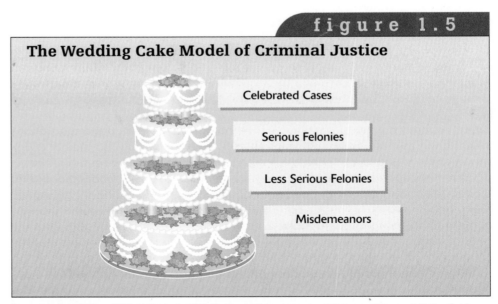

figure 1.5

The Wedding Cake Model of Criminal Justice

Celebrated Cases

Serious Felonies

Less Serious Felonies

Misdemeanors

Source: Adapted from Walker, Samuel. 2001. *Sense and Nonsense about Crime and Drugs: A Policy Guide,* 5th ed. Belmont, CA: Wadsworth.

When an offender is a celebrity, a criminal case is likely to receive heavy media attention and often a prolonged criminal trial, which otherwise is a relatively rare event. Here actress Winona Ryder listens with her defense attorney as the jury declares her guilty at the end of her 10-day trial for stealing more than $5,500 worth of designer clothes from Saks Fifth Avenue in Beverly Hills, California. The judge ordered her to undergo psychological and drug counseling and to do community service with babies with AIDS and other ill people.

public perceptions of how the criminal justice system works, but most criminal cases do not necessarily proceed as the celebrated ones do.

The second layer of the wedding cake model involves the most *serious felonies*. These cases are distinguished by the seriousness of the offense and the extent of the injuries involved, the extent of the defendant's prior record, whether the victim knew the offender, and other factors. Many homicides and robberies and some rapes fall into this category, although offenses in which the offender and victim are not strangers are apt to fall into the next layer. Although serious felonies represent only a small percentage of all crimes, they demand a disproportionate amount of the time, money, and energy in the criminal justice process. Because prosecutors believe that defendants in these cases should receive harsh punishments, they are reluctant to plea bargain, and a greater proportion of these cases than those in the remaining layers are likely to go to trial. In this second layer of the wedding cake model, the criminal justice system is very severe, as most people think it should be, because these cases involve serious crimes against strangers by offenders with long prior records.

The third layer of the wedding cake model involves *less serious felonies*. These are cases involving less serious charges, such as property crimes and violent crimes where little or no injury occurred and where the victim knew the offender. These are also cases where the defendant has little or no prior record. Compared to cases in the top two layers, cases in this third layer are more likely to be dismissed or to end in guilty pleas as a result of plea bargaining. Defendants convicted in these cases are more apt than those in the upper layers to avoid incarceration.

The fourth layer of the wedding cake model involves *misdemeanors*, which comprise the bulk of all criminal acts. The major violent and property crimes—homicide, aggravated assault, rape, robbery, burglary, larceny, motor vehicle theft, and arson (see Chapter 2)—comprise only about 16 to 17 percent of all arrests in any given year. About half of all arrests involve minor offenses, such as disorderly conduct, public drunkenness, prostitution, simple assault, and petty theft. Because so many cases are included in the fourth layer, they proceed very quickly. Public defenders or assigned counsel spend only a few minutes with their clients, if that, and the cases are resolved through plea bargaining and appearing before a judge one after another. Very few defendants in this layer are incarcerated.

In sum, the wedding cake model helps us understand that different kinds of cases in the criminal justice system are treated very differently. The heavy attention given to the celebrated cases at the top of the cake may lead to misperceptions of how the bulk of criminal cases in lower layers are handled.

Funnel Model. Another way of understanding the criminal justice system is to think of it as a funnel, with many cases entering the top of the system, and only a very few trickling out into prison at the bottom. Figure 1.6 illustrates the **funnel model,** which is partly the result of the discretion pervading the criminal justice process. Note that many crimes are investigated by police near the top of the funnel, but only relatively few lead to arrest. Fewer still are fully prosecuted, and fewer of those that are prosecuted end in convictions. For every 1,000 felonies that occur, only 11 result in a prison or jail sentence. Some of the remaining cases are dismissed by prosecutors or judges and others result in guilty pleas to misdemeanor charges that avoid incarceration. Although the figure does not show it, most arrests for serious crimes do result in some punishment for the offender and, as the wedding cake model reminds us, heavy punishment for those accused of the most serious crimes (Walker, 2001). But the funnel model also reminds us that most serious offenses do not lead to imprisonment. As we see in later chapters, this fact has important implications for the ability of the corrections system to influence the crime rate through increased incarceration rates.

Crime Control and Due Process Models. Herbert Packer (1964) long ago outlined two competing models of the criminal justice system: the crime control model and the due process model. These models help explain how the criminal justice system works and the dilemmas it faces.

As its name implies, the key objective of the **crime control model** is to prevent and punish crime and, by so doing, keep society safe. Because this model assumes that most criminal suspects are guilty, it emphasizes the need to process cases quickly and efficiently. According to Packer, the image of an assembly line conveyor belt best captures the operation of the criminal justice system under the crime control model. As with products on a conveyer belt, cases are passed quickly from one stage to another. The task of everyone on the criminal justice conveyor belt is clear and simple: to ensure that offenders are punished appropriately, quickly, and easily.

> **funnel model** a model of the criminal justice system in which many cases enter the top of the system and only a very few trickle out into prison at the bottom

> **crime control model** a model of the criminal justice system that emphasizes the need to prevent and punish crime and, by so doing, keep society safe

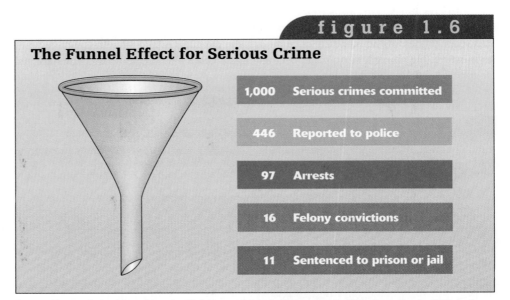

figure 1.6

The Funnel Effect for Serious Crime

1,000	Serious crimes committed
446	Reported to police
97	Arrests
16	Felony convictions
11	Sentenced to prison or jail

Source: Figures derived from Maguire, Kathleen and Ann L. Pastore (eds.). 1999. *Sourcebook of Criminal Justice Statistics* [Online]. Available: http://www.albany.edu/sourcebook; Ringel, Cheryl. 1997. *Criminal Victimization 1996: Changes 1995–96 with Trends 1993–96.* Washington, DC: Bureau of Justice Statistics, U.S. Department of Justice.

The **due process model** stands in sharp contrast. Its key goal is to prevent government abuse of the legal system against guilty and innocent people alike. This model assumes that some suspects are, indeed, innocent of the crimes with which they are charged. It also assumes that even guilty suspects deserve fair treatment in a democracy. Accordingly, it should be relatively difficult for the government to arrest, prosecute, and convict suspects. According to Packer, the image of an obstacle course best captures the operation of criminal justice under the due process model.

Packer (1964), Skolnick (1994), and other writers emphasize the tension between these two models of criminal justice. The get tough trend of the past few decades indicates that the crime control model has won out over the due process model. The reverse was true during the 1960s when the Supreme Court under the leadership of Chief Justice Earl Warren expanded the legal rights of suspects, defendants, and prisoners. Due process rights remain but have since been somewhat curtailed, and the crime control model is now more popular.

The clash between the two models became especially evident in the aftermath of the tragic attacks on September 11, 2001, when the hijacking of jet planes by Islamic extremists led to the deaths of more than 3,000 people at the World Trade Center, the Pentagon, and in western Pennsylvania. The U.S. Congress passed and President George W. Bush signed the U.S.A. Patriot Act, which authorized the detention and deportation of immigrants and the seizure of financial and medical records on grounds much weaker than had been acceptable in the past, and the designation of various domestic groups as terrorist organizations. The government quickly detained hundreds of Middle Eastern immigrants for intense secret questioning and denied many of them legal counsel or monitored attorney–client conversations of those who were allowed counsel. President Bush also announced that immigrants accused of terrorism could be tried by secret military tribunals where they would lack many of the rights of due process enjoyed by defendants in normal criminal proceedings, including the right to a jury trial and to the presumption of innocence. Officials also said that torture of suspected terrorists was under consideration. Critics charged that all these measures violated several amendments to the U.S. Constitution, whereas supporters claimed they were all necessary to ensure public safety against the threat of new terrorist acts (Purdy, 2001).

> **due process model** a model of the criminal justice system that emphasizes the need to prevent government abuse of the legal system against guilty and innocent people alike. This model assumes that some suspects are, indeed, innocent.

Richard C. Reid was arrested on December 22, 2001 for allegedly trying to blow up a trans-Atlantic flight by igniting explosive devices concealed in his shoes. The U.S. government's treatment of people of Middle Eastern descent in the aftermath of the attacks of September 11, 2001 reflects the tension between the crime control and due process models of criminal justice.

Adversarial versus Consensual Models. Closely aligned with these two models are the adversarial and consensual models of criminal justice, or, to be more accurate, of the criminal courts. The adversarial model is probably more familiar because the United States is often said to have an *adversary system* of criminal justice (Landsman, 1984). The **adversarial model** views court proceedings as a contest between the prosecution and the defense in which both parties do their best to win, often with fiery rhetoric. "Perry Mason" and other TV shows about lawyers feature this model, which theoretically gives defendants the opportunity to take advantage of their due process rights and thus to limit the arbitrary exercise of state power through the legal system.

The adversarial model is certainly highlighted in many law school courses and generally characterizes the celebrated cases at the top of the wedding cake model and some of the serious felony cases below them. But for most criminal cases, the adversarial model does not apply because prosecutors, defense counsel, and judges generally cooperate to push cases through as quickly and efficiently as possible. The **consensual model** characterizes this process, in which judges and attorneys share ideas of what "normal" crimes are and what appropriate punishments should be, and these shared ideas permit most cases to be resolved through plea bargaining (Nardulli, Eisenstein, and Flemming, 1988). Without such efficient case processing, the criminal court system would quickly break down. Ironically, then, U.S. criminal courts would be severely hampered if they actually did follow the adversary model for which the U.S. legal system is so renowned.

adversarial model a model of the criminal justice system that emphasizes fierce competition between prosecutors and defense attorneys to win their cases

consensual model a model of the criminal justice system that emphasizes cooperation among prosecutors, defense attorneys, and judges to expedite case processing

Focus on Islam

The Islamic Concept of Crime

By looking at crime and criminal justice in other cultures, we can better understand the problem of crime and the purpose and operation of the criminal justice system in our own nation. In this first Focus On box, we discuss the concept of crime in the Islamic world.

Islam is the second largest religion in the world today with more than 1 billion adherents called Muslims. Most Muslims live in the Middle East, northern Africa, and parts of Asia. Islam is the predominant or at least a major religion in several nations, including Afghanistan, Algeria, Egypt, Iran, Iraq, Jordan, Kuwait, Libya, Malaysia, Morocco, Pakistan, Saudi Arabia, Singapore, Sudan, Syria, and Tunisia.

Islam was founded by the prophet Muhammad in the seventh century A.D. The term *Islam* means "surrender" and connotes the idea that a devout Muslim is to surrender to the will of Allah, the Muslim term for God. The sacred book of Islam is the Koran (also spelled Quran), which is analogous to the Bible for Christians and Jews. It is considered to be the word of God as delivered to Muhammad by the angel Gabriel. Another important written source of Islamic principles is the Sunnah, which is a collection of the words and practices of Muhammad.

In the United States, the First Amendment to the Constitution guarantees the separation of church and state. This separation does not exist in Islamic nations, which are theocracies (nations in which the law of God is also the law of the land). Islamic law and the concept of crime that it involves are thus best understood as vehicles to enable Muslims to achieve the principles embodied in their faith.

Islamic law, or the *Shari'ah* (translated as "the path leading to the watering place"), derives from both the Koran and the Sunnah. The Shari'ah includes rules not only about an individual's relationship to the state and to other individuals—the scope of U.S. law—but also about religious practices, such as daily prayer and fasting, and about other practices, such as parenting, personal hygiene, diet, and giving charity to the poor. The Koran yields the principles that the Shari'ah embodies, whereas the Sunnah yields the practical application of these principles. These two sources complement each other nicely and together provide the basis for the Shari'ah: "The Sunnah provides essential and useful social and moral guidance and is viewed as indispensable in applying the principles of the Quran to daily life" (Holscher and Mahmood, 2000, p. 86). Accordingly, Islamic law reflects the religious beliefs and practices fundamental to the Islamic faith. Although many centuries have elapsed since Muhammad's time, the Koran "still wields tremendous influence in Muslim countries, since it largely determines what is sinful, and therefore illegal" (Holscher and Mahmood, 2000, p. 88).

The Shari'ah specifies three types of crimes: *hadd, qisas,* and *tazir. Hadd* offenses are considered the most serious because prohibitions against them exist in the Koran and Sunnah. They include theft, highway robbery, adultery, drinking alcohol, apostasy (abandonment) of Islam, and false accusation of adultery, all of which were considered serious misbehaviors in Muhammad's era. The Koran specifies that punishment of these offenses is the duty of the community, not the individual. In this way, the

Koran, which stresses compassion and forgiveness, attempts to prevent individuals from taking justice into their own hands. The Koran further specifies the exact punishment that each offense should receive. For example, the punishment for adultery is flogging (100 lashes with a whip) for someone who is unmarried or death by stoning for someone who is married; for theft, the amputation of a hand; for apostasy and highway robbery, death; for drinking, flogging (80 lashes).

Qisas offenses include homicide and assault. Traditionally, the victim or the victim's family may choose to forgive the offender, to be compensated by money or goods, or to request the death penalty. Yet so much proof of the crime, including eyewitnesses, is required under Islamic law that the death penalty in practice is difficult to carry out.

Unlike the previous two types of crimes, punishment for *tazir* offenses are not specified in either the Koran or the Sunnah; they are considered crimes against society, not against Allah. As such, they are deemed less serious than the other two types of crimes, and judges have great latitude in determining their appropriate punishment. Examples of *tazir* crimes include bribery, selling defective products or obscene materials, eating pork, and adultery not involving sexual intercourse. Common punishments for *tazir* crimes include home confinement, counseling, fines, confiscation of the offender's property, and flogging. In determining the appropriate punishment, judges consider the seriousness of the offense and the prior record and personality of the offender.

Many scholars of Islam and Islamic law rightly condemn prejudice against Muslims and common stereotypes about their religion. One such stereotype is that the principles of Islamic law and the practice of criminal justice are uniform from one Islamic nation to another. In fact, different nations practice Islamic law differently, and some have blended Islamic law with principles and practices from Western (Euro-American) law. Some nations, such as Iran, interpret Islamic law very strictly, whereas others, such as Egypt, use Islamic law for Muslims and other principles of law for other peoples.

A second, more common stereotype is that Islamic criminal justice is appallingly harsh. The fact that the Koran specifies harsh punishments, such as hand amputation for theft, suggests there might be some truth to this stereotype. However, scholars of Islamic law stress that "in practice, both in contemporary Muslim countries and historically, these traditional penalties have rarely been carried out" (Holscher and Mahmood, 2000, p. 88). When they do occur, according to these scholars, they often actually *violate* Islamic principles, so Islamic law should not be blamed for these harsh penalties. Instead these punishments are "distortions based upon pre-Islamic custom" (Griswold, 2001, p. 13).

Traditional penalties are rare because of the protections Islamic law allows criminal defendants. Islamic courts usually have such strict standards of evidence that it is difficult to prove defendants have committed the most serious crimes. For example, for a theft to be proven and hand amputation to be imposed, circumstantial evidence is not sufficient; instead, testimony from at least two male witnesses to the crime is required. Likewise, for adultery involving sexual intercourse to be proven, the law requires testimony by four males who actually witnessed the event. Because most sexual intercourse obviously does not occur in front of four witnesses, conviction of an adultery offense is rare. Thus, say Holscher and Mahmood (2000, p. 82), "By adopting a system of strict requirements of proof and testimony in criminal cases, Islamic law avoids despotic and arbitrary decisions and has limited the judges' discretion in the defendants' interest."

Although this is how Islamic law works in theory, and often in practice, in recent years harsh applications of Islamic law in certain nations have aroused international concern. In Nigeria, for example, several states adopted Shari'ah law beginning in 2000 as part of an Islamic revival in that part of the country. One such state was Zamfara, near the Sahara Desert. Groups of civilian police, termed *vigilantes* by some and carrying clubs, machetes, and whips, spread throughout the state, punishing people for alleged infractions, including drinking, gambling, and premarital sex. During the next year, many individuals were whipped for various violations, and a cattle thief's hand was amputated. The reported crime rate declined by more than 50 percent, a drop that most people attributed to the harsh punishments. One police officer claimed, "People here are afraid to commit crime. We don't have many thieves anymore" (Singer, 2001, p. 1). A Muslim citizen agreed, "Before there was no justice. The bad people were free. The police did nothing. Now with sharia, the bad people are afraid" (Singer, 2001, p. 1). The crime rate decline prompted other Nigerian states to adopt Shari'ah, but Western governments condemned the punishments as human rights violations, and Nigerian Christians said they were now being persecuted. Some Nigerian Muslims thought that "true" Shari'ah was not being practiced.

Iran is another nation in which a strict interpretation of Shari'ah was enacted. International controversy resulted when a German businessman, Helmut Hofer, 56, was arrested and sentenced to death in 1998 for having sex with a Muslim woman. The death sentence was declared even without the four witnesses that Shari'ah normally requires. After more than two years in Iranian jails, Hofer was finally allowed to leave Iran in January 2000 after paying a fine for the alleged assault of an Iranian police officer.

International concern also exists over the use of Shari'ah to restrict the freedom of Muslim women in many Islamic nations. Islam teaches that "all parts of the female body are sexual" and that femaleness is "an implicit moral weakness" (Truszkowska, 2001, p. 10). Islamic law thus requires women to cover their bodies fully and restricts their freedom of movement and their occupational choices. Although many Muslim women support these restrictions, human rights and women's rights organizations say they are discriminatory.

Sources: Abu-Hassan, 1997; Griswold, 2001; Holscher and Mahmood, 2000; Sanad, 1991; Singer, 2001; Souryal, Alobied, and Potts, 1994; Wiechman, Kendall, and Azarian, 1999.

1. Crime in the United States is a very real problem. Millions of serious crimes occur each year, and the public is very concerned about crime and about national efforts to deal with it.

2. Public beliefs about crime may neglect the complexity of crime. For example, the public underestimates the extent to which criminal offenders go to prison, and it is more concerned about street crime than white-collar crime, which is more costly in both financial and human terms.

3. The news media contribute to myths about crime in several ways. They overdramatize violent crime by airing or publishing so many stories about it, and they highlight the involvement of racial and ethnic minorities in crime. Such coverage reinforces the mistaken view that most crime is violent and exaggerates minority participation in crime. Politicians also contribute to crime myths with harsh rhetoric about crime, much of it racially tinged.

4. A get tough approach has characterized the nation's response to crime since the 1970s. This approach has dramatically increased the imprisonment rate and number of prisons. However, it has had only a modest effect on the crime rate and has proved costly in several ways. The United States has the highest incarceration rate by far in the Western world and spends tens of billions of dollars on corrections and other aspects of the criminal justice system. The war on crime has had a disproportionate impact on racial and ethnic minorities and created a wave of hundreds of thousands of prison inmates released back to their communities every year.

5. The U.S. criminal justice system is only partly a "system" and includes several stages from arrest through incarceration. Its goals include controlling and preventing crime, achieving justice, and expressing the nation's moral values. In a democracy such as the United States, the first two goals often clash.

6. Models of criminal justice help us understand how the criminal justice system is supposed to work and how it actually works. These models include the system, discretionary, wedding cake, funnel, crime control and due process, and adversarial and consensual models.

key terms

adversarial model
consensual model
crime control model
crime myth
discretion

discretionary model
due process model
funnel model
system model
wedding cake model

questions for investigation

1. What are the major sources of information about crime for most Americans? How reliable are these sources?

2. In a group, discuss the possible reasons why the public is more concerned about street crime than white-collar crime. Because the latter is so much more costly, what can be done to alert the public about it?

3. Discuss how various media treat crime—TV, news reports, in-depth TV news programs, daily newspapers, print news magazines, and Internet news sources. What differences do you see?

4. Discuss the pros and cons of the get tough approach to crime and the public health approach to crime.

5. Discuss the third goal of the criminal justice system: to express the nation's morality and values. How far-reaching should this goal be? What limitations, if any, do you think should be applied?

6. Discuss the use and abuse of the discretionary model of criminal justice. Do you think that abuse is an inherent part of the discretionary model? Explain your answer.

1. Suppose you are the producer of the 6:00 P.M. news show for a local television station in a small town, which traditionally has had a very low crime rate. One of your responsibilities is to determine the order in which the news stories your reporters have developed will be shown on the air and how much time will be devoted to each story. One day, a particularly grisly murder happens in your town. You realize that this is obviously a big story that should attract a lot of viewers, but you are reluctant to sensationalize what is, after all, a very unusual event in your town, needlessly worrying the public. What decisions will you make regarding how much attention to give to the murder and how graphic your coverage will be?

2. You are an assistant district attorney in a medium-sized city. A week ago, the police arrested a young man for killing a store clerk during an armed robbery. Having fit the general description of a witness, he was arrested three blocks from the store about fifteen minutes after the shooting occurred. The store's security video camera filmed the shooting, but its images are rather murky. No murder weapon has yet been found. This homicide was the lead story on the local TV news shows and was the lead article in your city's two major newspapers. The defendant's attorney comes to you to see if a deal can be struck before trial. Familiar with the wedding cake model, you realize that this case falls into the second tier of the model. Do you insist on a trial, or do you decide to strike a deal? Explain your decision.

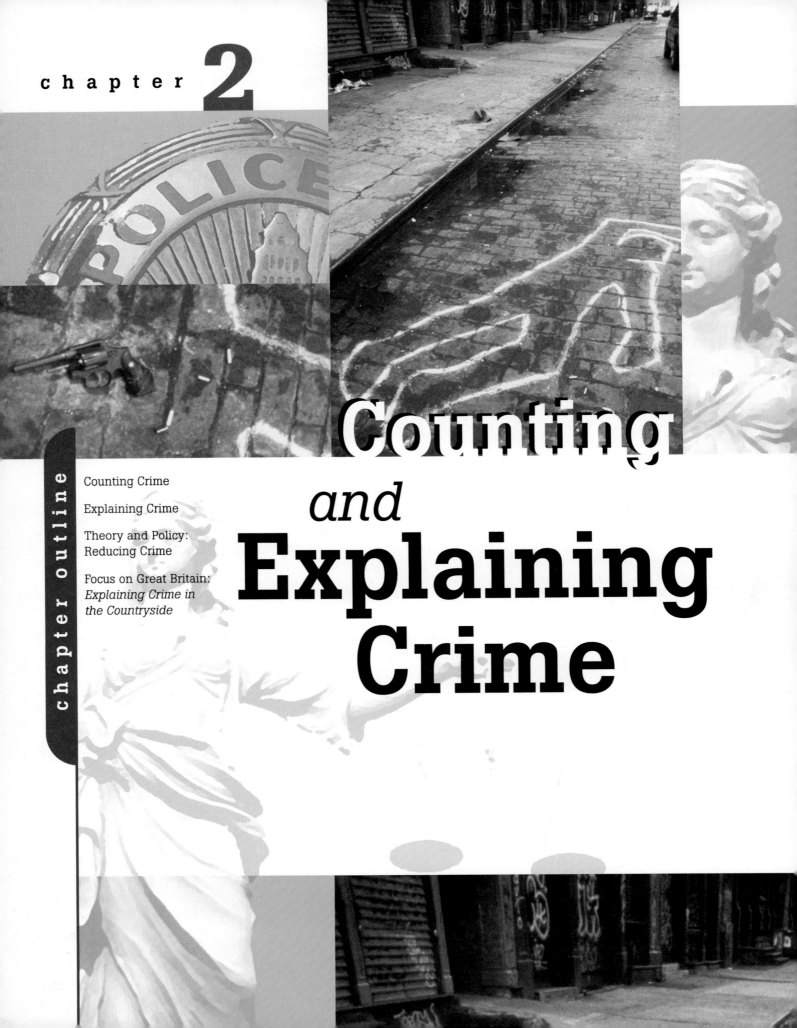

chapter **2**

Counting
and
Explaining
Crime

1. Why are accurate crime data essential? Why are accurate crime data difficult to obtain?

2. What are the Uniform Crime Reports (UCR)?

3. What is the National Crime Victimization Survey (NCVS)?

4. What is the importance of the self-report survey in crime data collection?

5. What information does field or ethnographic research on crime data provide?

6. On what factors does biological research on crime focus?

7. How does psychological research contribute to our understanding of crime?

8. What does sociological research contribute to our understanding of crime?

9. What do various sources of crime data reveal about the characteristics of offenders?

10. How does social environment influence an individual's chance of becoming an offender?

In December 2001, less than three months after the tragic events of September 11 that killed more than 3,000 people, U.S. troops in Afghanistan captured U.S. citizen John Walker Lindh, 20, who had been fighting for the Taliban regime in that nation. John Walker, as he came to be called, was returned to the United States for criminal prosecution and immediately branded a traitor by Americans filled with anger and grief.

Walker's case naturally attracted much media attention, and reporters tried to explain why a U.S. citizen was in Afghanistan fighting for the enemy. We soon learned that Walker was raised north of San Francisco in the liberal and wealthy Marin County, California. His parents, one of whom was an attorney, named him after Beatle John Lennon and Supreme Court Chief Justice John Marshall. By all accounts, Walker had a childhood typical of youngsters born into upper-middle-class affluence, although he was home-schooled for awhile and attended an alternative high school. By age 16, he had become fascinated with Islam and soon converted to that religion from his parents' Catholicism. He began wearing Islamic clothes and soon dropped out of school. When his parents separated in late 1998, Walker gave up his father's surname, Lindh, and adopted his mother's surname, Walker. More importantly, he moved to Yemen to further his Islamic education. There he began to adopt the anti-American beliefs of Islamic extremists and eventually made his way to Afghanistan (Thomas, 2001; Tyrangiel, Tumulty, Donnelly, Locke, and Perry, 2001).

After these details emerged, some observers blamed Walker's parents for being overly permissive and allowing him to undertake the spiritual journey that led him into Afghanistan and finally to a U.S. prison (Long, 2001). Other observers, however, dismissed Walker's story as an aberration not easily explained by parental upbringing because no other U.S. citizen with "permissive" parents ended up fighting for the Taliban. It might be fascinating to wonder why John Walker fought in Afghanistan, but we may never know the truth. Still, the question "why" remains fundamental to the study of crime and criminal justice, as scholars today offer many explanations of why some people are more likely than others to become involved in criminal behavior.

After John Walker Lindh was arrested, many people tried to understand why an American citizen would fight for the Taliban regime in Afghanistan. The effort to understand Lindh's behavior reminds us that the question "why" remains fundamental to the study of crime and criminal justice.

These explanations have advanced far beyond the more simplistic views of earlier decades. Take, for example, the fact that men commit more crime than women, a gender difference examined later in this chapter. Scholars have tried to explain this difference for at least a century, and their early answers now sound antiquated (Klein, 1995). One important figure in the rise of scientific criminology, Italian physician Cesare Lombroso, said a century ago that women committed less crime because they were naturally passive. His "evidence" for this was that sperm move around a lot more than does the egg. Sigmund Freud and his early followers thought that women were also naturally more passive but that, when they did commit crime, they did so out of penis envy: Because they were frustrated that they did not have penises, they committed crime to be more like men. In 1950, one sociologist even wrote that women committed more crimes than people thought but were especially good at hiding evidence of their crimes and thus more likely to evade arrest (Pollak, 1950). His "evidence" for this supposed skill at being deceitful was that girls and women learn at an early age to hide evidence of their menstrual flow and, when they are having sexual intercourse, to pretend that they are enjoying themselves!

Contemporary explanations of crime reject such wrongheaded ideas, and we explore these explanations later in this chapter. But first we discuss how crime is counted. As we shall see, accurate measurement of crime is essential for sound explanations of it, yet it is difficult to know exactly how much crime exists and which kinds of people are most likely to engage in it.

Counting Crime

Have you ever had anything stolen from you? Has anyone ever assaulted you? If either of these crimes has happened to you, did you tell the police (or, if it was at college, campus security) about it? If someone you know was ever victimized by crime, did that person tell the police about it? If the police never heard about a crime you or someone you know might have suffered, that crime never became part of the nation's official crime count. Even when the police do hear about a crime, they do not always, for reasons we shall see, count it as an official crime.

As these observations indicate, crime measurement is problematic. This is true even though the federal government, with the help of state and local agencies, devotes many resources to counting crime. Many criminal justice researchers gather information about crime on their own, often with the aid of federal funding. This huge effort reflects the importance of collecting accurate crime data, which are essential for several reasons.

First, they allow us to know whether crime is increasing, decreasing, or remaining at a stable level. If crime data are unreliable, we cannot be sure whether crime is rising or falling. And without this knowledge, we cannot know whether efforts to reduce crime are succeeding or whether economic and demographic changes in society are affecting the crime rate.

Second, accurate crime data enable us to determine where crime rates are high or low. Do urban areas have higher crime rates than rural areas? Do southern states have higher homicide rates than western states? Accurate determination of locations with different crime rates provides some clues about the characteristics that contribute to their crime rates. Knowledge of these characteristics helps criminal justice practitioners and researchers understand some of the reasons for crime and, in turn, to devise social and criminal justice policies for reducing crime.

It is difficult to know exactly how many crimes occur. This is particularly true for a crime like prostitution, as neither the prostitute nor her customer is likely to report the crime to the police.

Finally, accurate crime data allow us to know which people—in terms of age, gender, race and ethnicity, social class, family background, and other factors—are more or less likely to commit crime and to be victims of crime. Such knowledge again helps practitioners and researchers to better explain crime and to devise the best approaches to reducing it.

Accurate crime data are essential for all these reasons, but exactly how accurate are crime data? To answer this fundamental question, we turn to the major sources of information on crime, criminals, and victimization. We describe their various features, compare their strengths and weaknesses, and draw some conclusions about how accurately they portray the extent and distribution of crime and the characteristics of criminal offenders.

The Uniform Crime Reports (UCR)

Uniform Crime Reports (UCR) the U.S. government's official source of data on crime that relies on police reports of crimes that they hear about from citizens

The major source of official crime data is the **Uniform Crime Reports (UCR)** of the Federal Bureau of Investigation (FBI), U.S. Department of Justice. Based on police reports, the UCR was begun in 1930 and compiles several kinds of crime data. These include the numbers and rates of various types of crimes; the numbers of people arrested for these crimes; the percentage of all crimes that are cleared by arrest; and the rates of crime by geographical region and by social characteristics, such as age, race, and gender. Each year the FBI uses UCR data to produce its annual report, *Crime in the United States* (Federal Bureau of Investigation, 2002), which is published in the fall and summarizes crime statistics from the previous calendar year. Newspapers around the country usually devote at least one article to summarizing crime trends appearing in *Crime in the United States*. When you hear that crime is going up (or down), you will usually be hearing about UCR data.

Index offenses the term used by the Uniform Crime Reports for the eight felonies to which it devotes the most attention: murder and nonnegligent manslaughter, forcible rape, robbery, aggravated assault, burglary, larceny–theft, motor vehicle theft, and arson

The UCR provides data on two categories of crime: Part I crimes and Part II crimes. Part I crimes consist of eight so-called **Index offenses** that the FBI considers the most serious felonies. These are further broken down into two subcategories: *violent crime* and *property crime*. Violent Index crimes include murder and nonnegligent manslaughter, forcible rape, robbery, and aggravated assault; property Index crimes include burglary, larceny–theft, motor vehicle theft, and manslaughter. Part II includes such offenses as simple assault, forgery and counterfeiting, fraud, and gambling. A complete list of Part I and Part II offenses and their definitions appears in Table 2.1.

crime rate in the UCR, the number of crimes per 100,000 persons in some location or subgroup of the population; in the NCVS, the number of victimizations per 1,000 persons or 1,000 households

Crime Rates. The most important information the UCR provides concerns crime rates and arrest rates. A UCR **crime rate** is like a percentage: It compares the number of crimes to the size of the population (see Table 2.2). The UCR's crime rates reveal the number of crimes for every 100,000 people in the population; the size of this population depends on the geographical unit being examined. For example, consider City A of 300,000 people. A year ago 3,000 burglaries occurred in this city. To determine the crime rate, divide 3,000 by 300,000 (3,000 ÷ 300,000) to get a result of .01. Multiply this result by 100,000 to get a result of 1,000. This means that 3,000 burglaries in a city of 300,000 is equivalent to 1,000 burglaries for every 100,000 persons, so City A has a burglary rate of 1,000 per 100,000 persons.

The use of crime rates is important for two reasons. First, it allows us to determine whether one location has a greater crime problem than another location. Consider the burglary example. City A had 300,000 residents and 3,000 burglaries for a burglary rate of 1,000. Suppose City B has 500,000 residents and 4,000 burglaries. City B has more burglaries than City A, but does that mean that City B is less safe than City A when it comes to burglary? City B, after all, also has many more people than City A, so we would expect it to have more burglaries just as we would expect it to have more cars, TVs, and other elements. To compare the cities' burglary risks, we must compare their burglary rates. We have already seen that City A has a burglary rate of 1,000. To determine City B's burglary rate, simply divide its number of burglaries, 4,000, by its population size, 500,000, and multiply this result by 100,000. City B's burglary rate is 800,

table 2.1   The Uniform Crime Reports

Part I Offenses

Criminal homicide: (a) murder and nonnegligent manslaughter (the willful killing of one human being by another); deaths caused by negligence, attempts to kill, assaults to kill, suicides, accidental deaths, and justifiable homicides are excluded; (b) manslaughter by negligence (the killing of another person through gross negligence; traffic fatalities are excluded)

Forcible rape: the carnal knowledge of a female forcibly and against her will; includes rapes by force and attempts to rape, but excludes statutory offenses (no force used and victim under age of consent)

Robbery: the taking or attempting to take anything of value from the care, custody, or control of a person or persons by force or threat of force and/or by putting the victim in fear

Aggravated assault: unlawful attack by one person upon another to inflict severe bodily injury; usually involves use of a weapon or other means likely to produce death or great bodily harm; simple assaults are excluded

Burglary: unlawful entry, completed or attempted, of a structure to commit a felony or theft

Larceny–theft: unlawful taking, completed or attempted, of property from another's possession that does not involve force, threat of force, or fraud; examples include thefts of bicycles or car accessories, shoplifting, pocket-picking

Motor vehicle theft: theft or attempted theft of self-propelled motor vehicle that runs on the surface and not on rails; excluded are thefts of boats, construction equipment, airplanes, and farming equipment

Arson: willful burning or attempt to burn a dwelling, public building, personal property, etc.

Part II Offenses

Simple assault: assaults and attempted assaults involving no weapon and not resulting in serious injury

Forgery and counterfeiting: making, altering, uttering, or possessing, with intent to defraud, anything false in the semblance of that which is true

Fraud: fraudulent obtaining of money or property by false pretense; included are confidence games and bad checks

Embezzlement: misappropriation of money or property entrusted to one's care or control

Stolen property: buying, receiving, and possessing stolen property, including attempts

Vandalism: willful destruction or defacement of public or private property without consent of the owner

Weapons: carrying, possessing, etc.; all violations of regulations or statutes controlling the carrying, using, possessing, furnishing, and manufacturing of deadly weapons or silencers; attempts are included

Prostitution and commercialized vice: sex offenses such as prostitution and procuring

Sex offenses: statutory rape and offenses against common decency, morals, etc.; excludes forcible rape and prostitution and commercial vice

Drug abuse: unlawful possession, sale, use, growing, and manufacturing of drugs

Gambling: promoting, permitting, or engaging in illegal gambling

Offenses against the family and children: nonsupport, neglect, desertion, or abuse of family and children

Driving under the influence: driving or operating any vehicle while drunk or under the influence of liquor or narcotics

Liquor laws: state or local liquor law violations, except drunkenness and driving under the influence

Drunkenness: offenses relating to drunkenness or intoxication; driving under the influence is excluded

Disorderly conduct: breach of the peace

Vagrancy: vagabonding, begging, loitering, etc.

All other offenses: all violations of state or local laws, except as noted previously and traffic offenses

Suspicion: no specific offense; suspect released without formal charges being placed

Curfew and loitering laws: persons under age 18; offenses relating to violations of local curfew or loitering ordinances

Runaways: persons under age 18; limited to juveniles taken into protective custody under provisions of local statutes

Source: Federal Bureau of Investigation. 2001. *Crime in the United States: 2000.* Washington, DC: Federal Bureau of Investigation.

<table>
<tr><td>table 2.2</td><td>The Determination of a Crime Rate</td></tr>
</table>

$$\frac{\text{Crimes}}{\text{Population}} \times 100{,}000 = \text{Crime rate (number of crimes per 100,000 population)}$$

considerably lower than City A's rate of 1,000. Thus, although City B has more burglaries than City A, its burglary rate is actually lower, and we would say that City B is a safer city in terms of burglaries than City A.

The use of crime rates is important for a second reason: to determine whether crime is rising, staying the same, or declining. Because the population rises every year, a rise in the *number* of crimes does not necessarily mean that crime is getting worse. Consider the following hypothetical example. In 1993, City C had 1,500 robberies and 400,000 people. Ten years later, in 2003, City C had 2,400 robberies and 700,000 people. Did the robbery rate in City C increase or decrease during those ten years? The number of robberies rose from 1,500 to 2,400, an increase of 900. But (do the math on your own) its robbery rate actually fell from 375 (per 100,000 people) in 1993 to just under 343 in 2003. Criminal justice researchers would thus conclude that City C was a bit safer from robbery in 2003 than in 1993, even though the *number* of robberies rose.

crimes known to the police
the UCR's term for the "official" number of crimes that the police report to the UCR and that the UCR, in turn, reports to the public

The Production of UCR Data. UCR data are only as accurate as the information provided to the FBI. Unfortunately, the "production" of these data is imperfect for several reasons (O'Brien, 2000; Pease, 1995).

As noted earlier, UCR data are based on police reports. For this reason, the UCR calls the offenses on which it provides data **crimes known to the police.** How are

Accurate crime data allow us to determine which areas have more crime and which have less crime. Urban areas like the one depicted here tend to have much higher crime rates than rural areas.

table 2.3	The Production of UCR Crime Data

A crime is committed

↓

The victim or a witness decides to report the crime to the police

↓

The police decide to record the crime as an official crime
and to report it to the FBI

these data generated? Based on citizen complaints of crime, police agencies provide monthly reports to the FBI of the number and types of crimes in their jurisdictions (see Table 2.3). For each crime reported, the police tell the FBI whether someone was arrested for that crime or whether the crime was cleared for some other reason, including the death of the main suspect. For each arrest that occurs, the police tell the FBI the arrestee's age, gender, and race. UCR data are accurate only to the extent that the reporting process in each of these steps is accurate and complete. We examine these steps in detail.

Citizens' Complaints. The most important step in producing UCR data involves citizens reporting crime to the police. Police discover only about 3 percent of crimes on their own and thus must rely on citizens to tell them about crimes they experience as victims or, occasionally, see as witnesses (O'Brien, 2000). But victims of serious crime report less than 40 percent of all their victimizations to the police for reasons we examine later (Rennison, 2002b).

The low level of reporting has important implications for the production of UCR crime data. As Robert M. O'Brien (2000, p. 62) puts it, "Part I and Part II crimes usually come to the attention of the police through citizens' complaints; thus, the reporting behavior of citizens plays a major role in determining the number of crimes known to the police." The number of crimes the UCR lists must, therefore, always be lower, and usually much lower, than the number of crimes that *actually* occurs, with the large number of "hidden" crimes becoming what criminal justice researchers call the "dark figure of crime" (Biderman and Reiss, 1967). To illustrate this "dark figure," suppose 1,000 Index crimes occur in a town in a given year, but victims report only 38 percent of them, or 380, to the police. Let us assume (although this does not always happen; see below) the police record all these crimes and, in turn, report them to the FBI. Through the UCR, the FBI tells the public that 380 crimes occurred in the town in the past year when, in fact, 1,000 occurred. The number of actual crimes is thus almost three times higher than the public hears about, and the public may believe that the community is safer than it really is.

Police Underrecording of Crime. Victims' complaints of crime are problematic, but so are police recording and reporting procedures for the crimes victims do report to them. Once the police hear about an alleged crime, they must determine whether a crime actually occurred. This is called the *founding* stage. Sometimes citizens fabricate "victimizations" to get someone in trouble or to make themselves seem important. Sometimes citizens sincerely believe they have been victimized by a crime, but the circumstances do not lead police to conclude that any criminal law was violated. These two types of false or mistaken reports are thought to account for about 2 to 4 percent of all reports to the police. Even if police believe a crime has occurred, they do not always record it as a crime. If they are busy and think the crime was minor, they simply might not record it in order to save the time and energy of doing the paperwork.

Although the extent of such nonrecording is unknown, some evidence indicates the police fail to record up to one-third of all the crimes citizens report to them (Warner and Pierce, 1993).

Another problem at the police recording stage involves the fact that one criminal incident often includes many crimes (O'Brien, 2000). For example, suppose a burglar breaks into a house. The homeowner then comes home and surprises the burglar, who then hits the homeowner with a club before escaping. At least two felonies have occurred here, burglary and aggravated assault, but, following UCR procedures, the police record only the more serious of the two crimes, the assault. Thus, although a burglary also occurred, only the assault is recorded, and the burglary disappears from the official crime count.

Yet another problem stems from the fact that police agencies "exist in a sociopolitical environment in which their performance and needs are often evaluated on the basis of crime statistics" (O'Brien, 2000, p. 63). With a decrease in the crime rate, the police appear to be doing a good job of controlling crime. With an increase, the police appear less effective, but they could argue they need more resources to deal with the growing problem. Thus police agencies have a heavy investment in crime rate trends. At times, this investment has led individual police and entire agencies to "fudge" their crime reports by, for example, failing to record crimes they hear about or by downgrading serious crimes into misdemeanors: A burglary might be recorded as disturbing the peace. Either procedure makes it appear that fewer crimes were occurring.

Such fudging led to some serious scandals in the 1990s in cities such as Atlanta, Baltimore, Boca Raton (Florida), New York, and Philadelphia (Butterfield, 1998). One officer in Boca Raton downgraded almost 400 felonies to misdemeanors and thus artificially reduced the city's crime rate by more than 10 percent in 1997. In Philadelphia, the scandal was especially serious as police there regularly downgraded about 10 percent of all serious crimes into minor ones and counted crimes as occurring only when they were finally recorded, not when they actually took place. These problems forced the FBI to disregard the city's 1996 and 1997 crime statistics (Brown, J., 1997). In another problem, the city's police sex-crimes unit had, since the early 1980s, either failed to record or else downgraded thousands of reports of rape and sexual assault. The victims had no idea this was happening, and the police never followed up on their complaints by trying to catch the men who had assaulted them. In some cases, these men later raped and sexually assaulted other women (Fazlollah, Matza, McCoy, and Benson, 1999).

Fudging crime data also occurs at college and university campuses, where, it is charged, college administrators and campus security try to keep crimes hidden from the public. The campuses handle them internally in student disciplinary hearings rather than tell the police about them. Although the federal government requires colleges and universities to provide accurate data of the crimes occurring on and nearby their campuses, at some schools many crimes, especially those occurring just off campus, are not reported to the government (Chacon, 1998; Matza, 1997).

Other Problems in Police Recording. Several other problems also affect the accuracy of UCR crime data (O'Brien, 1985). First, despite UCR instructions, police agencies throughout the United States differ somewhat in their definitions of crime and, correspondingly, in their likelihood of recording an incident as a serious crime. For example, consider the difference between an aggravated assault and a simple assault. As Table 2.1 shows, an aggravated assault involves a serious injury and/or the use of a weapon, whereas a simple assault involves no weapon and only a minor injury. In many assaults, however, it is not clear whether an injury is serious or minor, and some police agencies are more likely than others to classify these assaults as aggravated rather than simple.

Second, different police forces have different "styles" of policing (see Chapter 6); some take a sterner approach than others to law enforcement and are more likely to record every crime about which they hear. Thus, the style of a police force can affect whether citizens' complaints are accounted for as official crimes in the UCR.

Third, police are more likely to record crimes involving certain kinds of victims. In the 1960s, several researchers accompanied police and observed their interactions with citizens who said a crime had been committed against them. The police were more likely to record these complaints as crimes when (1) the citizen complainant (victim) was polite; (2) the complainant and suspect were strangers or only acquaintances; and (3) the complainant preferred the police do something about the crime (Black, 1970). Once again, we see that citizen reports of crime are not automatically translated into official crimes.

Finally, the police sometimes stage *crackdowns* in which they flood a high-crime neighborhood to make arrests for illegal drug sales, prostitution, and other offenses (Sherman, 1990). The number of these crimes thus soars in police records and in the UCR even though the actual number of these crimes has not changed at all.

Arrest Statistics. If UCR crime data are inaccurate, what about UCR arrest data? Recall that police inform the FBI of every arrest they make and of the age, gender, and race of everyone they arrest. When someone is arrested for a crime, that crime is counted as being *cleared by arrest*. Overall, the police clear about 20 percent of all Index crimes, but the clearance rate varies greatly by the type of crime. It is highest for murder and lowest for burglary; more generally, it is higher for violent crime and lower for property crime (see Figure 2.1). If the police make arrests in only about 20 percent of all official crimes, can we assume that the characteristics of the persons arrested in terms of age, gender, and race accurately reflect the characteristics of *all* offenders, including the vast majority who are *not* arrested?

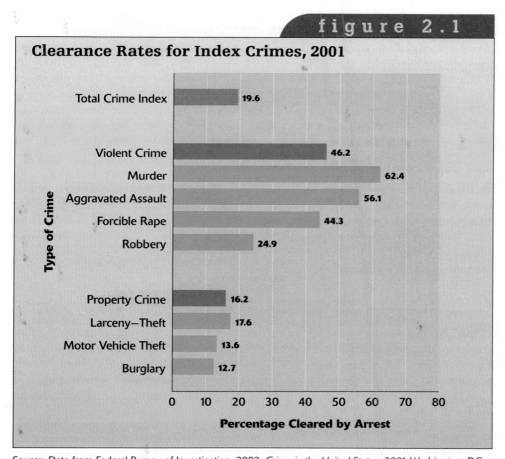

figure 2.1

Clearance Rates for Index Crimes, 2001

Source: Data from Federal Bureau of Investigation. 2002. *Crime in the United States: 2001*. Washington, DC: Federal Bureau of Investigation.

Many criminal justice researchers say no. They point to the low clearance rates just noted and say that, in numbers alone, it makes little sense to think the relatively few suspects who do get arrested represent the vast majority who escape arrest. These researchers further believe that the characteristics of arrestees may reflect police racial and other biases at least as much as they reflect the kinds of persons who commit crimes in the first place (Miller, 1996). Pointing to evidence that police focus their resources on poor minority communities (Smith, 1986), these critics add that it is no surprise that so many more arrests occur there than in wealthier white neighborhoods. Like UCR crime data, then, UCR arrest data might reflect police behavior more than crime reality. Arrest data might yield better ideas about police attitudes and behavior than about the kinds of people who commit crime.

Other researchers acknowledge that many more people commit crimes than get arrested and concede that police bias does exist. But they still maintain that the characteristics of arrestees do, in fact, fairly accurately represent those of suspects who do not get arrested (O'Brien, 2000; Tonry, 1994). They reach this conclusion by drawing on other sources of crime data as described later. If these researchers are correct, UCR arrest data provide a fairly good picture of who commits crime even if most crimes are not cleared by arrest.

The National Incident-Based Reporting System (NIBRS). The UCR provides very little information on the characteristics of crimes, the settings in which they occur, the relationships between offenders and their victims, and other such matters. In a major exception, detailed data on murders and nonnegligent homicides are supplied in the Supplementary Homicide Reports (SHR). These data include the victim–offender relationship in homicides; the race and ethnicity of offenders and victims in each homicide (so that we can tell, for example, what percentage of white homicide victims are killed by white offenders); and the use of weapons, alcohol, and other drugs. But this detailed information is lacking for other types of UCR offenses.

To remedy this problem, about a decade ago the UCR began the National Incident-Based Reporting System (NIBRS) to supply more complete data on criminal incidents (Chilton, Major, and Propheter, 1998). Under this system, the police gather and report a good deal of information on crimes they record; this information parallels the types of topics included in the SHR. About two dozen states now submit, or are preparing to submit, their crime information through NIBRS, and eventually NIBRS will replace the UCR. Although NIBRS will provide more complete information than the UCR, it will still be susceptible to the underreporting and underrecording problems that plague the UCR.

Strengths and Weaknesses of the UCR. The UCR has several strengths (Gove, Hughes, and Geerken, 1985). It is the nation's official compilation of statistics on crime and criminals, and its data have been used in numerous research studies. It also allows researchers to compare the crime rates of geographical areas (for example, urban versus rural crime rates) and to assess whether particular crime rates are associated with social and physical characteristics, such as poverty and unemployment rates.

Unfortunately, the UCR also has several weaknesses. The most important one, as we have seen, is that the UCR undercounts the true number of crimes. This makes it difficult to know whether changes in UCR crime rates reflect actual changes in the crime rate or, instead, changes in the likelihood of victims reporting crimes or of police recording the crimes they hear from victims. For example, although the UCR rates of rape rose steadily in the 1970s and 1980s, this increase probably did not mean that the actual rate of rape was increasing. Instead, it reflected both greater reporting by rape victims and the greater likelihood of police taking their reports seriously (Orcutt and Faison, 1988).

A related weakness is that UCR arrest data characteristics (age, gender, race) might not accurately reflect the characteristics of all criminal offenders. We return to this issue in the Under Investigation following this chapter.

Finally, the UCR does not include data on crime by corporations. This omission suggests that corporate crime is neither as important nor as serious as the street crime that the UCR covers (Simpson, Harris, and Mattson, 1995). Yet, as we discuss in Chapter 3, corporate crime can be more deadly and involve more financial loss than all street crime combined.

Despite the UCR's limitations, its strengths and widespread use in research show that it will remain an important source of crime data for many years to come. The UCR provides part of the picture of crime in the United States, but only one part. In an effort to improve our understanding of crime, other sources of crime information have been developed. We now turn to these.

The National Crime Victimization Survey (NCVS)

Concern over the UCR's limitations led the government to develop the **National Crime Victimization Survey** (NCVS; initially called the National Crime Survey) in 1973. Each year since then, the Census Bureau on behalf of the Bureau of Justice Statistics has surveyed tens of thousands of people age 12 or older from randomly selected households across the nation. In 2001, the NCVS sample consisted of about 44,000 households and 80,000 people age 12 or older. The NCVS's response rate is extremely high: in 2001, about 93 percent of eligible households and 89 percent of eligible individuals took part (Rennison, 2002).

In the survey, household residents are asked whether they have been a victim in the previous six months of several different kinds of personal crimes. These crimes include robbery, rape and sexual assault, aggravated and simple assault, and personal theft such as pickpocketing and purse snatching; the NCVS groups these offenses together and calls them *personal crimes*. One household member is also asked whether the family has been victim to a household burglary, other household theft, or motor vehicle theft; the NCVS calls these *property crimes*. To avoid influencing responses, interviewers do not use any of these crime terms in their questions; instead they read descriptions of the crimes.

If respondents have experienced personal crimes, they are then asked several questions about the offense, including whether and how they were threatened or hurt; the time and place of the victimization; whether a weapon was involved and, if so, what type of weapon; how well they knew the offender before the victimization; and whether they reported the offense to the police and, if not, why not. When respondents report a household victimization, they are asked further questions about it, including the value of the item(s) stolen and whether someone was at home at the time the theft occurred. (Chapter 5 further discusses the characteristics of crime victims and the process of victimization.)

Because the NCVS is a random sample of the entire nation, its results can be generalized to the rest of the population. For example, if 5 percent of NCVS respondents say their homes have been burglarized, we can be fairly sure that 5 percent of all U.S. homes have been burglarized. This fact allows NCVS researchers to make two important national estimates. The first is the actual number of victimizations in the United States. To use our burglary example, NCVS researchers would multiply the number of all U.S. households by 5 percent to estimate the number of household burglaries in the entire nation. The second estimate is the rate of victimization per 1,000 persons age 12 or older (for personal crime) or per 1,000 households (for property crime). To use our burglary example once again, a 5 percent finding in the NCVS translates to a rate of 50 per 1,000 households.

Although both the NCVS and the UCR measure street crimes, it is important to recognize differences in which crimes they measure (Biderman and Lynch, 1991). The NCVS does not include homicide (because homicide victims obviously cannot report their victimization); arson; or any commercial crime, such as shoplifting, robberies of store clerks, or after-hours burglaries of businesses. Another difference is that the NCVS includes simple assaults, but the UCR's data on Index crimes excludes them. Also, the NCVS includes sexual assault as well as rape, whereas the UCR's Index includes only rape. Finally, the NCVS measures personal victimizations only on people age 12 or older, whereas the UCR includes crimes that happen to children under age 12.

National Crime Victimization Survey (NCVS) an annual survey given by the government to people in thousands of randomly selected households around the nation that asks residents of these households a series of questions about crimes that they, other household members, and the household itself have experienced during the past six-month period

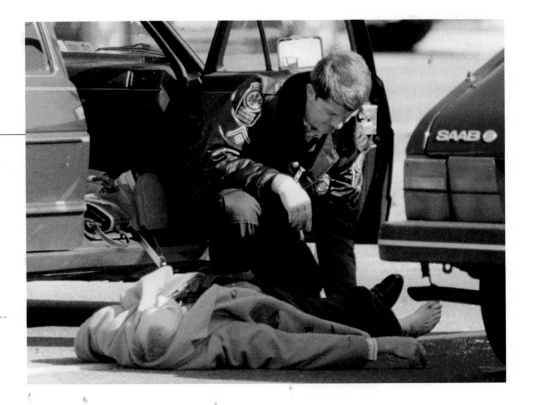

Although the National Crime Victimization survey yields very valuable information about crime victims and criminal victimization, it does not cover homicides, such as the one depicted here.

Therefore, to some extent, comparing crime data from the UCR and NCVS is like comparing apples and oranges (Biderman and Lynch, 1991). However, meaningful comparisons do exist. Table 2.4 lists the total UCR offenses known to the police and the totals estimated by the NCVS. Even allowing for the differences between the two data sources, it is obvious that the NCVS estimates that many more millions of crimes occur each year than become known to the police. As noted earlier, this huge disparity results because so many victims do not report their crimes to the police. About 19 percent of crime victims say they did not report their crime because it was a "private or personal matter"; 17 percent say the offender was unsuccessful; 17 percent say they reported the crime to "another official"; 6 percent say the crime was not important enough to report; 6 percent believed the police would not want to be bothered; 4 percent were afraid of reprisal by the offender; and 3 percent believed it would be too time consuming or inconvenient to report the crime (Bureau of Justice Statistics, 2002).

[handwritten margin note: Why don't report →]

Strengths and Weaknesses of the NCVS. The NCVS has several strengths and weaknesses. Its major strength is that it provides more accurate estimates than the UCR of the number of crimes. As Table 2.4 shows, many more crimes appear in the NCVS than in the UCR, and most researchers believe that the NCVS is the more reliable source of information on the number of crimes (O'Brien, 2000).

A second strength of the NCVS stems from its greater accuracy: It is probably a better barometer than the UCR of changes in crime rates. As we saw earlier, we cannot be sure whether changes in UCR crime rates reflect changes in actual crime rates or, instead, changes in police or citizen reporting practices. For this reason, many researchers use the NCVS rather than the UCR to measure crime rate trends for the years since the NCVS was implemented in 1973 (McDowall and Loftin, 1992).

A third strength is that the NCVS provides rich information on the context of criminal victimization and its effects on crime victims. Before the NCVS was established, the field of criminal justice knew much less about victims' experiences and the process of victimization than it does now.

Despite its considerable strengths, the NCVS also has several limitations (Biderman and Lynch, 1991). First, it does not include two very important types of crime, commercial crime and white-collar crime, and it does not cover crimes whose victims are

table 2.4	Number of Offenses, NCVS and UCR Data, 2001	
TYPE OF CRIME	**NCVS**	**UCR**
Violent crime	5,744,000	1,436,611
Homicide	—	15,980
Forcible rape	248,000[a]	90,491
Aggravated assault	1,222,000	907,219
Simple assault	3,643,000	—
Robbery	631,000	422,921
Property crime	18,472,000	10,412,395
Burglary	3,140,000	2,109,767
Larceny–theft	14,323,000[b]	7,076,171
Motor vehicle theft	1,009,000	1,226,457
Total crimes	24,216,000	11,849,006

[a]Includes sexual assaults
[b]Includes personal theft

Source: Data from Federal Bureau of Investigation. 2002. *Crime in the United States: 2001.* Washington, DC: Federal Bureau of Investigation; Rennison, Callie Marie. 2001. *Criminal Victimization 2001: Changes 2000–2001 with Trends 1993–2001.* Washington, DC: Bureau of Justice Statistics, U.S. Department of Justice.

under age 12. Because of these omissions, the NCVS itself underestimates the actual amount of crime in the United States even if it provides more accurate estimates than the UCR does.

Second, NCVS respondents can either forget about some of their victimizations or they can simply decide not to tell NCVS interviewers about them. This latter problem may be especially true for crimes such as rape, sexual assault, and domestic violence. Whether respondents forget about their victimizations or simply decide to remain silent, the NCVS fails to uncover these crimes and, as a result, underestimates the actual number of crimes.

If these problems lead to the NCVS underestimating the actual number of crimes, other problems might lead it to provide overestimates. Some respondents might believe they suffered a crime when, in fact, the circumstances would not fit the definition of a crime. Other respondents might mistakenly "telescope" crimes by telling NCVS interviewers about victimizations that happened before the survey's six-month reporting period. Despite these possibilities, most researchers think that underestimation is a more likely problem in the NCVS than overestimation (O'Brien, 1985).

Self-Report Surveys

Although both the UCR and NCVS provide useful information on crimes, they do not provide much information on offenders. **Self-report surveys** provide such information and help uncover the "dark figure of crime" noted earlier. These surveys are typically given to adolescents, usually students in high school classes, but a few notable surveys have been administered to random samples of all U.S. noninstitutionalized youths. Whatever their venue, self-report surveys ask whether respondents have committed various offenses within a particular time period (commonly called a *reference period*), usually

self-report surveys surveys in which respondents are asked to provide information on various offenses they may have committed

the past twelve months, and, if so, how often they committed the offense. They also ask several questions about respondents' personal backgrounds, including their relationships with their parents and friends and their involvement in school activities.

The first type of question allows researchers to determine both the prevalence and the incidence of offenses. **Prevalence** refers to the percentage of respondents who have committed an offense at least once within the reference period, whereas **incidence** refers to the average number of offenses committed per offender. For example, in a small survey of 200 respondents, 40 admit to having damaged school property in the past year and further report that they had done so 80 times altogether. The prevalence rate for this sample is .20 (40 ÷ 200), or 20 percent, and the incidence rate is 2 (80 ÷ 40) offenses per person.

Strengths and Weaknesses of Self-Report Surveys. Like the UCR and NCVS, self-report surveys have several strengths and weaknesses. Their strengths stem from the very nature of their research design, which "allows researchers to collect detailed information about individual offenders" (O'Brien, 2000, p. 70). Self-report surveys have been able to shed much light on the dark figure of crime by revealing both the prevalence and incidence of offending. This fact, along with their inclusion of items on many aspects of respondents' lives, has also enabled the surveys to shed much light on the causes of delinquency and, by extension, street crime in general.

Self-report surveys also have some weaknesses. Perhaps the most important problem is respondents' inability or unwillingness to respond truthfully when asked whether they have committed various offenses. Respondents may refuse to admit to an offense; they may admit to committing one when, in fact, they have not; or they may honestly forget whether they committed an offense (and how many of each offense) in the reference period. Thus, the *validity* of respondents' answers is a potential problem. Researchers have assessed this validity by comparing respondents' answers to police and court records, and they have found that respondents' answers are (perhaps surprisingly) accurate. Respondents only occasionally failed to report an offense they had committed, and they only occasionally claimed to have committed an offense they did not commit (Hindelang, Hirschi, and Weis, 1981).

A second problem is the research design of the self-reported survey. Recall that most self-report surveys have used samples of adolescents in high school or noninstitutionalized youths from around the nation. This research design omits certain groups of youths—those who have dropped out of high school, are homeless, or are in juvenile detention facilities—who might have especially high rates of juvenile offending (Cernkovich, Giordano, and Pugh, 1985). Thus, self-report surveys might themselves underestimate the prevalence and incidence of offending.

A third problem was truer in the early days of self-report surveys than it is today. The early surveys failed to include questions about serious offenses, such as rape and robbery, because the survey developers believed these offenses were so rare and so serious that too few respondents would admit to having committed them. Later surveys include serious offenses and have helped us to understand the extent and predictors of such behavior. Because some of these offenses are so rarely committed, however, they remain somewhat difficult to study even with self-report data (O'Brien, 2000).

Field Research

The UCR, NCVS, and self-report surveys are useful because they provide different kinds of numerical data on crime, offenders, and/or victims. A fourth source of information about crime, field research, does not provide numerical data but is important nonetheless. **Field research** (also called *ethnographic* research) involves intense interviewing and/or extended observations of criminal offenders and the settings in which they live. It can yield a much richer understanding than the other three sources of what makes criminals behave as they do, how they interact with other offenders, how they decide when to commit a particular crime, and other such issues.

prevalence in a self-report survey, the percentage of respondents who have committed an offense at least once within a certain time period

incidence in a self-report survey, the average number of offenses committed per offender

field research a research method involving extensive observation and/or intensive interviewing

Field research also has important limitations (Babbie, 1999). First, its results cannot be generalized beyond the subjects studied. However rich a portrait a field study yields of its criminal subjects, we cannot be sure whether this portrait can be generalized to any other group of offenders. Second, it is difficult to carry out. As might be expected, criminals do not like being interviewed, and field researchers may put themselves at some risk when they approach them. Finally, field researchers may unwittingly influence the behavior they observe. Their very presence may prompt their offender subjects to change how they normally act.

As a result of these problems, only a few field studies of criminals exist. In the 1990s, some researchers managed to interview and observe dozens of robbers and burglars in a few different cities, and the books and articles they later wrote yielded fascinating accounts of how their subjects became offenders, how they committed their crimes, and many other matters (Cromwell, Olson, and Avary, 1991; Tunnell, 1996; Wright and Decker, 1994; Wright and Decker, 1998). A field study by sociologist Elijah Anderson (1999) revealed eloquently the "code of the streets," which emphasizes toughness and the need for respect amid the despair of urban poverty. It provided a sensitive account of the urban poor that shed much light on why crime occurs in their neighborhoods.

Explaining Crime

As the story of John Walker reminds us, a critical question in the study of criminal justice is why crime occurs. Are parents too permissive? Do criminals have defective genes? Are poverty and overcrowding to blame? Unless we can determine the causes of crime and develop the best possible policies to reduce it, more people will continue to commit crime. Researchers in many disciplines have tried to understand why crime takes place, and we now turn to the explanations they have developed. Table 2.5 provides a summary of these explanations.

Rational Choice, Deterrence, and Routine Activities

Many scholars today favor a **rational choice theory** that criminals commit crime from their own **free will** by carefully weighing the potential rewards and risks before deciding to break the law (Clarke and Felson, 1993; Cochran, Chamlin, Wood, and Sellers, 1999). Much of the public shares this view (Gerber and Engelhardt-Greer, 1996).

An offshoot of rational choice theory is **deterrence theory,** which assumes that would-be criminals can be deterred from breaking the law by increasing the threat of arrest and punishment (Nagin, 1998b). Since the 1970s, this assumption has guided U.S. criminal justice policy, which has emphasized longer prison terms, the building of more prisons, and increases in the number and power of the police. Although the views of deterrence theory sound quite plausible, criminal justice researchers dispute whether the increased use of arrest and imprisonment has, in fact, deterred criminals and reduced the crime rate (Krohn, 2000; Walker, 2001). Chapter 11 discusses this issue in greater detail.

Another offshoot of rational choice theory is **routine activities theory,** which has stimulated much exciting research since its development about two decades ago (Cohen and Felson, 1979). According to this theory, crime is more likely when three factors converge in time and place: (1) motivated offenders, (2) attractive targets in the form of property or people, and (3) the absence of guardianship in the form of potential witnesses who can come to the aid of the victim (Felson, 2002). Thus, when someone who needs money sees a well-dressed person alone in a deserted neighborhood at night, a robbery is more likely to occur than in the daytime on a crowded street.

A routine activities perspective helps explain many crime rate trends. For example, the rise of ATMs and convenience stores probably led to more robberies because they were new attractive targets that often lack guardianship, and robbers responded accordingly. A routine activities view also suggests several steps to reduce crime. Called

rational choice theory the view that people act with free will and carefully weigh the potential benefits and costs of their behavior before acting

free will the view that human behavior is the result of personal, independent choices and not of internal or external forces beyond their control

deterrence theory closely related to rational choice theory, the belief that more certain and severe punishment reduces the crime rate

routine activities theory the belief that crime and victimization are more likely to occur with the simultaneous occurrence of motivated offenders, attractive targets, and low or no guardianship

table 2.5   **Explanations of Crime**

Rational Choice, Deterrence, and Routine Activities Theories

Rational choice: People commit crime after carefully weighing the potential rewards and risks of doing so.

Deterrence: Potential criminals can be deterred from committing crime by an increase in the likelihood of arrest and punishment.

Routine activities: Crime is more likely when three factors converge in time and place: (1) motivated offenders, (2) attractive targets in the form of property or people, and (3) the absence of guardianship in the form of potential witnesses who can come to the aid of the victim.

Biological and Psychological Theories

Biological

Genes and heredity: Criminal behavior is transmitted from parents to children through one or more genes that predispose individuals to criminality.

Hormones: High levels of testosterone produce criminal behavior in males, and premenstrual syndrome produces criminal behavior in females.

Pregnancy and child-birth complications: Problems during pregnancy and childbirth lead to developmental problems in newborns and young children and, in turn, to a greater likelihood of delinquency and crime when older.

Psychological

Psychoanalytic: Crime results from negative childhood experiences that cause an imbalance among the id, ego, and superego. More generally, crime is the result of mental illness.

Personalty problems: Impulsiveness, irritability, and other such problems underlie much antisocial behavior in children and their later criminality.

Sociological Theories

Social ecology: The physical and social characteristics of communities contribute to their crime rates.

Blocked opportunity and anomie: Crime results from the frustration stemming from lack of opportunity in a society that values economic success.

Peer influences and learning: Crime is the result of socialization by deviant peers who influence an individual to adopt their values and behavior.

Social controls: Crime results from weak social bonds to family, school, and other social institutions and from a lack of self-control.

Critical theories: Bias in the criminal justice system leads some individuals and behaviors to be more likely than others to be considered deviant. Crime is the result of class and gender inequality.

situational crime prevention, these suggestions include less attractive targets and increased guardianship (von Hirsch, Garland, and Wakefield, 2000). For example, lighting could be improved at outdoor ATMs and in other areas where people are vulnerable at night to criminals.

Biological and Psychological Explanations

Biological and psychological views obviously differ in many respects, but both assume that the root of crime lies within the individual rather than in the social environment, and both involve internal forces of which offenders might not be aware. According to these explanations, criminals are biologically or psychologically different from noncriminals. Certain biological and psychological problems make people more likely to commit crime, and criminals are more likely than noncriminals to have these problems.

Biological Views. Contemporary research addresses several biological factors. We do not have the space to discuss all of them here and will focus on genes, hormones, and pregnancy and childbirth complications.

Genes and Heredity. Although no specific gene for criminal behavior has been located, many scientists think crime has at least some genetic basis. They infer this from studies of identical twins. Because such twins have identical genes, we would expect them to behave similarly if genes affect behavior. Many twin studies indeed find that if one twin has a history of criminal behavior, so, often, does the other twin. Although not all twin studies find this pattern, they do lead many researchers to believe that some unknown gene or genes help produce criminal behavior (Fishbein, 1996; Jacobson and Rowe, 2000).

But other researchers point out that identical twins are similar in many respects other than their genes. They are socialized the same way by their parents, have the same friends, and spend much time with each other. Because all these similarities may lead twins to have similar behavior when it comes to crime, these researchers believe a strong genetic role in crime cannot be inferred (Walters, 1992). As a middle ground, some researchers believe that genes and the social environment interact in producing criminal behavior: Genes may predispose some individuals to crime, but this predisposition is not "activated" unless problems in the social environment exist (Jacobson and Rowe, 2000). Perhaps because no consensus yet exists, research on heredity and crime will continue to be a fascinating topic in the years ahead.

Hormones. The so-called male hormone, *testosterone,* is often mentioned as a reason for why some men are especially likely to commit serious crime. To test this hypothesis, researchers have assessed whether males with different testosterone levels also differ in their levels of criminal behavior and other forms of aggression. Several such studies find a link between higher testosterone levels and greater histories of crime and aggression (Booth and Osgood, 1993; Dabbs and Morris, 1990). Although this correlation might suggest that testosterone produces aggression, it is also possible that aggression (and the dominance it involves) increases testosterone. This possibility prompts some researchers to doubt that higher levels of testosterone in humans produce higher levels of aggression (Miczek, Mirsky, Carey, DeBold, and Raine, 1994).

In women, *premenstrual syndrome,* or PMS, has been linked in some research to greater aggression. The idea here is that some women in their premenstrual phase

Some scholars think that crime has a genetic basis. Studies of identical twins tend to support this view, but their similar behavior may also stem from their similar social environments.

become extremely irritable, tense, and/or depressed and that these changes increase their chances of becoming violent. Although an early study of women prisoners in Britain supposedly found this effect (Dalton, 1961), other researchers soon challenged the study's methodology, and a causal link between PMS and aggression cannot yet be assumed (Katz and Chambliss, 1995).

Pregnancy and Childbirth Complications. A promising line of research concerns the many problems that can occur during pregnancy and childbirth (Kandel and Mednick, 1991). If a fetus's neurological development does not proceed normally, a newborn can suffer long-lasting cognitive, emotional, and behavioral impairment. Several types of problems, including poor prenatal nutrition and the use of alcohol, tobacco, and other drugs, can affect this neurological development. If a birth is especially difficult, the baby can suffer a lack of oxygen and other problems that can also affect neurological development and, again, lead to various impairments. These impairments have, in turn, been implicated in aggressive behavior in children and later criminality (Loeber and Farrington, 1998). Thus, pregnancy and birth complications may contribute to criminal behavior many years later.

Psychological Views. Psychological views trace crime to various psychological problems that arise within the individual. In general, these internal problems are thought to stem from childhood experiences and difficulties.

Psychoanalytic Explanations. Drawing on the work of the great scholar Sigmund Freud (1856–1939), psychoanalytic views assume that criminal behavior stems from the failure of individuals to adjust their instinctive needs to the dictates of society (Bartol, 2002). In particular, Freud and his followers assume that the individual personality is composed of three components: the *id*, the instinctive part of the personality that selfishly seeks pleasure; the *ego*, the rational part of the personality that recognizes the negative aspects of pure selfishness; and the *superego*, the part of the personality that represents society's moral code and acts as the individual's conscience. These three components need to be in harmony for an individual to be mentally healthy. When this is not so—usually because of abnormal early childhood experiences—mental disorders, including criminal behavior, can result.

Although psychoanalytic explanations sound appealing, they are difficult to prove or disprove. For example, if a researcher studies someone with a history of crime, the researcher might conclude the person's superego is too weak, but if the person's criminality is used as evidence of a weak superego, the researcher is guilty of circular reasoning. Psychoanalytic views also imply that a person with a history of criminal behavior suffers from a mental disorder (Hodgins, 1993). Many criminal justice researchers dispute this point. While conceding that some criminals do have mental disorders, they argue that most criminals are not psychologically abnormal despite their history of crime (Vold, Bernard, and Snipes, 1998).

Despite these controversies, psychoanalytic explanations remain valuable because of their emphasis on early childhood experiences. Certain problems in early childhood can eventually lead to criminality and other behavioral problems. Regardless of the continuing value of psychoanalytic explanations, much research today focuses on negative childhood experiences and their consequences for later behavior (Wasserman, Miller, and Cothern, 2000).

Personality Problems. One consequence of negative childhood experiences might be various personality problems, including impulsiveness, irritability, and hyperactivity, that are thought to underlie aggression and other behavioral problems in children. These behavioral problems are, in turn, precursors for juvenile delinquency and adult criminality (Caspi, 2000).

To assess the role that personality problems play in criminality, it is important to determine first whether offenders do, in fact, have "worse" personalities than nonoffenders. To do so, many researchers use *personality inventories*—lists of true–false and other statements—to which subjects respond. These inventories have been administered to offenders in juvenile and adult institutions, and they often reveal personality problems (Eysenck, 1989). However, because personality problems may stem at least partly from the offender's institutionalization, this type of study leaves the nature of the personality–offending link unclear. A better research design would study children from infancy through at least young adulthood to determine whether personality differences at various ages predict later offending. A notable, ongoing research project in New Zealand has used this research design, and it finds that personality problems in childhood do predict later offending and other problems (Caspi, Wright, Moffitt, and Silva, 1998).

Despite this study's results, some criminologists remain skeptical of the importance of personality problems for criminal behavior because many studies fail to find clear personality differences between offenders and nonoffenders (Vold et al., 1998). Personality problems thus remain an appealing explanation for criminal behavior, but more research needs to be done before their importance can be adequately assessed. The New Zealand project just described suggests they do play an important role.

Sociological Explanations

Unlike their biological and psychological counterparts, sociological explanations suggest the causes of criminal behavior lie *outside* the individual in the *social environment*. The social environment does not totally determine who will commit crime, but it does have an important influence. Several sociological explanations exist, and we examine them in some detail.

Social Ecology Explanations. Social ecology approaches address the physical and social characteristics of communities that increase their rates of crime and victimization (Byrne and Sampson, 1986). Rodney Stark (1987) calls these approaches *kinds of places* explanations rather than *kinds of people* explanations. Different types of people, he notes, can move into and out of various neighborhoods, but certain types of neighborhoods will generally have higher crime rates no matter which kinds of people live there. The task of ecological approaches is thus to explain which place characteristics produce higher crime rates.

According to Stark (1987), several place characteristics matter, including residential density. In neighborhoods where residences are very close together, "good kids" are more apt to come into contact with "bad kids" and thus be more likely to break the law. Areas with another type of residential density, crowded households, will also have higher crime rates, in part because adolescents in these households often feel the need for "elbow room" and leave their homes to hang out with friends; once away from home, they have greater opportunity to get into trouble, and some do so.

Other ecological factors also affect neighborhood crime rates (Roncek and Maier, 1991; Sampson, 1997). Neighborhoods with higher rates of *collective efficacy*, in which neighbors watch out for each other's children, have lower crime rates. Neighborhoods with low rates of participation in voluntary organizations, such as churches and community groups, and higher numbers of bars and taverns have higher crime rates. Taken together, ecological explanations help us understand why some neighborhoods have higher crime rates than other neighborhoods. They suggest that criminality stems to a large extent from the social and physical characteristics of the places in which individuals live.

Blocked Opportunity and Anomie. Much sociological research emphasizes the importance of poverty for criminal behavior. Although several poverty-based explanations exist, most assume that poverty in a society like the United States that places such great value on economic success is especially frustrating for the poor, who feel *relative deprivation* as they compare themselves to other Americans who are wealthier (Blau and Blau, 1982). They face great difficulties in lifting themselves out of poverty: They have relatively little education, their children go to low-quality schools, and so

> **social ecology** in criminology, the view that certain social and physical characteristics of neighborhoods help explain their crime rates

forth. Their opportunity to move up the socioeconomic ladder, in short, is blocked by all sorts of factors, and such blocked opportunity is said to create "angry aggression" that translates into violence and other crime (Bernard, 1990).

Merton's Anomie Theory. This explanation echoes back to Robert K. Merton's (1938) classic **anomie theory** of deviance. Merton reasoned that the United States places much value on economic success and on working hard to achieve such success. The poor become frustrated as they realize that economic success for them is elusive: No matter how hard they work, they will have trouble achieving the "American dream" of economic success. Merton referred to their failure to become economically successful through hard work as *anomie*. Given this frustration, five adaptations to anomie are possible (see Table 2.6).

Despite their frustration, Merton noted, most poor people continue to accept the goal of economic success and continue to work hard. They are *conformists* and do not break the law. Other people continue to accept the goal of economic success and reject the means of working. Instead, they *innovate* with new means by engaging in forms of theft to obtain wealth and possessions. Others continue to work at jobs but have lost any ambition to become economically acceptable. Work has for them become a *ritual*. Next, some poor people give up on making money and give up on working. They turn to drugs or alcohol and/or live in the streets. Merton called their adaptation *retreatism*. Finally, some poor people reject both the goal of economic success and the means of working and engage in *rebellion* to achieve a new society with new goals and values.

Merton's theory, first presented in 1938, was for many years the most popular sociological theory of deviance and crime. It fell out of favor for several reasons, including its inability to explain most types of violence, which are not committed for economic reasons. Although the poor may commit violence out of "angry aggression," that reason was not part of Merton's explanation. However, anomie theory has been revived in recent years as researchers give new emphasis to the failures to reach the American dream and other important goals as significant reasons for higher crime rates among the poor (Agnew, 2000; Messner and Rosenfeld, 2001).

Differential Opportunity Theory. In 1960, Richard Cloward and Lloyd Ohlin (1960) presented an extension of Merton's anomie theory called **differential opportunity theory.** Extending Merton's notion of blocked opportunity for economic success, Cloward and Ohlin noted that the poor also have different levels of access to *illegitimate* means, leading to *differential opportunity* to achieve economic success through such means. Their degree of access depends on the types of neighborhoods in which they live. In some neighborhoods, a thriving criminal subculture with strong organized crime groups exists. In these neighborhoods, the poor who are so inclined can easily find opportunities to commit crime to get some money or possessions. Other neigh-

anomie theory Robert K. Merton's view that deviance among the poor results from their frustration over their failure to become economically successful through working

differential opportunity theory Richard Cloward and Lloyd Ohlin's view that poor people not only have blocked opportunities for success through legitimate means but also differential access to illegitimate means to achieve such success

table 2.6	Merton's Anomie Theory of Deviance	
	ECONOMIC SUCCESS	
WORKING AT A JOB	**Accept**	**Reject**
Accept	Conformity	Ritualism
Reject	Innovation	Retreatism

Note: A fifth category, *rebellion,* involves rejection of both the goal of economic success and the means of working and tries to achieve a new society with new goals and values.

Source: Adapted from Merton, Robert K. 1938. "Social Structure and Anomie." *American Sociological Review,* 3:672–682.

borhoods provide fewer such opportunities; in these, *random* violence or drug and alcohol use are much more common. Cloward and Ohlin's emphasis on differential opportunity to achieve economic success and to do so through illegitimate means helps explain why crime rates differ among the poor and between the poor and the nonpoor.

Peer Influences and Learning. An important part of the social environment, according to both psychologists and sociologists, is the various people with whom we interact. The greatest influence on young children is their parents, but, as they become preteens and then adolescents, their friends become increasingly important. Recognition of this fact led researchers long ago to consider the role played by peer influences in delinquent behavior. Although many types of learning theories formulated by both psychologists and sociologists exist, all of them emphasize that juveniles *learn* to break the law—or, more specifically, learn attitudes and values that help them decide to break the law—from their friends and acquaintances. They may also break the law simply because they want to conform to their friends' behaviors to "fit into the crowd" and avoid ridicule or even the loss of friendship (Akers, 2000).

Sutherland's Differential Association Theory. In sociology, the classic learning explanation is Edwin Sutherland's (1939) **differential association theory.** According to Sutherland, criminal behavior is learned from interacting with other people instead of being the result of biological factors. Such learning consists not only of certain values and attitudes that justify breaking the law but also of specific techniques for committing crime. When, said Sutherland, individuals acquire from their friends an "excess of definitions favorable to violation of law over definitions unfavorable to violation of law," they are more likely to break the law themselves.

Sutherland and other learning theorists suggest that crime stems from one of the most important, normal social processes: socialization. Just as most people are socialized to become law-abiding members of society, some people are socialized to become law-breaking members. Just as adolescents' friends influence them in all sorts of ways—for example, their taste in music and clothing—so do they influence them in many aspects of their behavior, including deviant behavior. Supporting this view, many studies find that adolescents with delinquent friends are more likely than those with fewer or no such friends to be delinquent themselves. Some scholars consider the effect of delinquent peers to be a more important cause of delinquency than any other factor (Akers, 2000).

Peers versus Mass Media. One interesting controversy concerns the impact of peer influences compared to that of the mass media. In saying that adolescents learn to be criminals from interacting with their friends, Sutherland implied that the mass media had little, if any, impact on crime. In formulating his explanation more than sixty years ago, Sutherland was writing, of course, long before the days of TV, modern music and movies, and the Internet. Today the public is concerned about the impact of mass media on youth violence, and many researchers have examined this issue.

In some studies, children and college students are shown violent videos and then watched as they play (children) or given questionnaires to complete (college students). When compared to control groups who watch a nonviolent video, the children play more violently, and the college students reflect more violent attitudes in their answers on the questionnaire. In other research, random samples of respondents are asked in self-report studies about the TV shows they watch, the movies they see, the music they listen to, and the video games they play. Those who report exposure to violent media in any of these forms also report being more violent in their behavior. These studies lead many researchers to conclude that violence in mass media has a strong influence on youth violence (Surette, 1998).

However, other researchers believe this conclusion is premature. The violence found among the studies involving children and college students who watched violent videos, they say, is only short term and does not necessarily mean that mass media violence has a strong influence in the "real world." They add that the correlations found

differential association theory Edwin Sutherland's view that deviance results from negative peer influences and, more specifically, from an excess of definitions favorable to violation of the law

in self-report studies between mass media exposure and violent behavior also do not suggest a cause-and-effect relationship (Surette, 1998). Perhaps individuals interested in violence are more likely to want to watch violent movies or play violent video games. No doubt the link between mass media violence and actual youth violence will arouse controversy for some years to come.

Social Controls. An important goal of any society is to control its members' behaviors. Émile Durkheim (1858–1917), one of the founders of sociology, recognized that a society is more stable if it has strong social bonds and can socialize its members to respect and conform to its moral codes of behavior. Reflecting Durkheim's insight, several sociological explanations highlight the factors that *keep* people from becoming deviant. In this sense, they represent the flip side of the explanations discussed so far that focus on the factors that *influence* people to be deviant. By understanding which factors help induce conformity, we better understand those that induce criminality.

Sociologists focus on two sorts of social controls: *internal* or *personal* ones, such as the ability to delay gratification, and *external* ones found in an individual's social environment (Krohn, 2000). Some of these external controls operate at the neighborhood level, as our earlier discussion of collective efficacy illustrates, whereas others operate at the family and school level.

Hirschi's Social Control Theory. Family and school bonds lie at the heart of Travis Hirschi's (1969) **social control theory,** which assumes that strong bonds to parents and schools help keep adolescents from becoming delinquent. These bonds have four dimensions: attachment, commitment, involvement, and belief. *Attachment* refers to how close we feel to our parents and teachers and how much we care about their opinions. The more we care about them, the more guilty we would feel if we violated their norms. *Commitment* refers to the importance we place on these activities. The more our commitment to these activities, the less likely we are to break the law. *Involvement* refers to the amount of time we devote to conventional activities; the more time we devote to them, the less time we have to get into trouble. Finally, *belief* refers to the extent to which individuals believe in society's norms. The more we believe in these norms, the less likely we are to break the law.

In support of Hirschi's theory, many studies find that adolescents with the strongest social bonds to their parents and schools are indeed less likely to be delinquent (Kempf, 1993). Citing a chicken-or-egg problem, some critics question whether this relationship shows that these social bonds reduce delinquency, as Hirschi assumes, or, instead, simply that delinquency weakens adolescents' bonds to their parents and schools (Krohn, 2000). Still, most sociologists would probably agree with Hirschi that social bonding reduces delinquency.

Hirschi's view has stimulated additional research on the roles played by the family and schools in delinquency. Many studies document the importance of *family interaction* for delinquency and other antisocial behavior. Harmonious families help produce well-behaved children, whereas conflict-ridden families are more apt to produce children with behavioral problems (Hirschi, 1995). Research is less clear on the importance of *family structure*. Some researchers find that children from single-parent households are at only slightly greater risk for delinquency, usually drinking and drug use and *status offenses* such as skipping school (Loeber and Stouthamer-Loeber 1986; Wells and Rankin, 1991). The major problem with single-parent arrangements, according to these researchers, is that they are more likely to be low-income ones, not that a single parent cannot be a good parent. Other researchers believe children of single parents are, indeed, at much greater risk for delinquency because the one parent is less able to supervise the children and to be a good parent in other respects (Popenoe, 1996). No doubt research on family structure and delinquency will continue to provoke debate.

Research also documents the importance of schooling for delinquency. Here the evidence is fairly clear: Students who get good grades, who like their schools and teachers, and who are involved in school activities are much less likely to be delinquent than those who get poor grades, who dislike their schools and teachers, and who are

social control theory Travis Hirschi's view that social bonds to family, school, and other conventional social institutions inhibit the development of criminal behavior

less involved in school activities (Cernkovich and Giordano, 1992). But the chicken-or-egg question remains a problem in interpreting this evidence: Are the good students less delinquent because they are good students, or are delinquents less likely to be good students because they are delinquents?

Hirschi and Gottfredson's Self-Control Theory.

Hirschi subsequently developed a **self-control theory** of delinquency with colleague Michael Gottfredson (Gottfredson and Hirschi, 1990). They said that a lack of self-control is responsible for all forms of crime. People who cannot restrain themselves, who are impulsive, and who can only live for the present are much more likely to commit crime than those who have more self-control in all these respects. Following up on Hirschi's original emphasis on family bonds, Gottfredson and Hirschi further said that low self-control stems from poor parenting starting in infancy and extending into adolescence.

Supporting self-control theory, much research finds that people who score low on various measures of self-control are more likely to have broken the law (LaGrange and Silverman, 1999; Schreck, 1999). Critics say that a chicken-or-egg problem again exists in some of these studies: Does low self-control promote criminality, or does criminality lead to low self-control (Krohn, 2000)? They also take issue with Gottfredson and Hirschi's assumptions that low self-control explains all crime and that low self-control is much more important than other factors, such as poverty and peer influences. Much white-collar crime, they say, involves *high* degrees of self-control; poverty, negative peer influences, and many other factors also are significant for street crime. As this brief summary should indicate, self-control theory has proven quite provocative in little more than a decade since its formulation and will continue to do so.

> **self-control theory** Michael Gottfredson and Travis Hirschi's view that all crime results from the inability to restrain one's own needs, aspirations, and impulses

Critical Views.

If a robber kills someone, the criminal justice system would ideally do its best to arrest and prosecute the robber for murder. If convicted, the robber would likely get a long prison term or even the death penalty. If a soldier kills several people on the battlefield, the soldier may well get a medal. In either case, killing has occurred, yet the circumstances affect how society thinks about the killing.

The sociological explanations discussed so far do not address society's reaction to crime and criminals. Other sociological views take a more critical look at crime and society. They say the definition of crime is *problematic* and question whether bias in the criminal justice system leads some people and behaviors to be more likely than others to be branded with a criminal label. They also say that much crime is rooted in the very way that our society is organized. Three general critical views exist: labeling theory, conflict views, and feminist perspectives. We look at each of these in turn.

Labeling Theory.

As the killing illustrates, whether a specific behavior is considered deviant may have more to do with the circumstances surrounding the behavior than with the behavior itself, which is the heart of **labeling theory**, a perspective on crime that emerged in the 1960s. According to this perspective, "deviance is not a quality of the act the person commits, but rather a consequence of the application by others of rules or sanctions to an 'offender'" (Becker, 1963, p. 9).

But if deviance results from decisions to label a person and that person's behavior as deviant, that raises the possibility that this labeling process may be inaccurate. Such inaccuracy may occur either from honest mistakes or, worse, from bias based on gender, race and ethnicity, social class, age, appearance, and other factors. Thus, not only is the definition of crime and deviance problematic but so is the process by which certain individuals come to be labeled criminals.

William Chambliss's (1973) famous study of the "Saints and the Roughnecks" illustrates labeling theory's view on bias. The Saints were a group of middle-class delinquents who skipped their high school classes without getting into trouble. They would drive to a nearby town and commit vandalism and other offenses with no one the wiser. Although some school officials and other townspeople suspected the Saints were up to no good, they considered the youths "good kids" from respectable, stable families and did not act on their suspicions. In contrast, the Roughnecks were a group of poor

> **labeling theory** the view that the definition of crime and deviance depend on the circumstances surrounding a behavior rather than on the qualities of the behavior itself, that labeling produces more deviance, and that the labeling process is biased and therefore problematic

delinquents who often got into trouble for fighting and other offenses. School officials and police tended to watch them carefully and to sanction them when they misbehaved. Overall, the Saints were more delinquent than the Roughnecks, wrote Chambliss, but got into trouble far less often. They entered professional careers after high school and college while the Roughnecks ended up in prison or with dead-end jobs.

Since labeling theory was developed in the 1960s, many studies have assessed the degree to which a suspect's gender, race and ethnicity, and social class affect the chances of being officially labeled a criminal. The evidence is mixed: Some research finds considerable bias on all these dimensions, whereas other research finds only a small amount of bias (Walker, Spohn, and DeLone, 2000). Some scholars say flatly that much bias exists in legal processing, whereas others say that any bias is fairly minimal and that legal factors matter more than nonlegal ones such as race and gender. We return to this issue in Chapter 11 on sentencing. For now suffice it to say that the absence of consistent support for labeling theory leads some critics to think it of little value. Labeling theory's supporters dispute this view and continue to believe the theory has much to offer (Wellford and Triplett, 1993).

Labeling theory makes one more provocative point: People who are labeled deviant become *more* likely to commit deviance because they were labeled. Labeled individuals develop a deviant self-image and find themselves shunned or suspected by law-abiding individuals. Faced with these problems, they become bitter and discover that it is easier to associate with other people who have also been labeled deviant. For all these reasons, they become more likely to commit deviance themselves *because* they were labeled. If this is true, labeling has the opposite effect from what is intended and from what deterrence theory would predict.

The labeling theory argument is appealing. Imagine you were just released from prison after spending five years there for armed robbery. Having paid your debt to society, you complete application forms for several jobs, and each form asks whether you have ever been convicted of any crimes. You write armed robbery on all the forms. How likely is it that you will get a job? Now suppose you are in a bar or at a party trying to meet people. You talk to someone who attracts you and who is evidently attracted by you. She or he asks you what you do for a living. You say you are looking for a job. You are then asked what you have been doing for the past few years. You respond that you were just released from prison for armed robbery. Would your companion respond enthusiastically, or would that person make an excuse to go to the restroom? As these scenarios suggest, once people are labeled criminals, they find it difficult to fit back into society. Sometimes they are even suspected of crimes they did not commit. Perhaps labeling theory, then, is correct in suggesting that labeling produces more deviance, not less.

Research on this issue is inconsistent. Some studies find that arrest and other labeling reduce future deviance, and some studies find that the opposite effect occurs (Wellford and Triplett, 1993). Nor do self-images often become more negative because of arrest. We return to this issue in Chapter 12 on prisons and punishment, but for now note that critics find fault with labeling theory. Still, its emphasis on the negative effects of labeling has led to efforts to keep juvenile and other offenders out of prison through what is called "alternative" or "community" corrections. We explore these alternatives in Chapter 14.

Conflict Views. The so-called "conflict tradition" in sociology began with the work of Karl Marx (1818–1883) and Friedrich Engels (1820–1895) in the nineteenth century. Marx and Engels thought that capitalist society is divided into two major social classes: the *bourgeoisie,* who owned the means of production such as factories and tools, and the *proletariat,* who worked for the bourgeoisie. Reflecting their class interests, the bourgeoisie aim to maintain their elite position by oppressing and exploiting the poor, whereas the proletariat aim to change society to make it more equal. This summary of Marx and Engels's philosophy is greatly simplified, but it reveals that they saw society as filled with class conflict. More to the point for our discussion, Marx and Engels thought that law played a key role in this conflict and wrote that the ruling class uses the law to maintain its power (Greenberg, 1993).

Various social scientists have developed Marx and Engels's ideas. Some call themselves Marxists and others call themselves conflict theorists, but all basically make at least one of two points. First, the structure of U.S. society leads to crime by the poor; second, the law reflects the interests of the ruling class and is used by the ruling class to reinforce its position at the top of society (Lynch, Michalowski, and Groves, 2000).

Reflecting the first argument, Dutch criminologist Willem Bonger (1876–1940) wrote long ago that capitalism produces crime by the poor because, as an economic system, it emphasizes competition, individualism, greed, and selfish behavior (Bonger, 1916). In such a system, people will be more likely to perform actions that help themselves even if they hurt others. Although all social classes commit various kinds of crime, the poor have an additional motivation, and that is economic need. Bonger thought that capitalism was a major cause of crime and predicted that crime would decline if capitalist nations became more socialistic.

Other scholars have focused on whether and how the law is used as a means to keep the poor in their place. Most research here focuses on the extent to which social class and race and ethnicity affect criminal justice outcomes. We commented on this research in the discussion of labeling theory and reiterate that its results are mixed. Some researchers believe that the strongest support for conflict theory is found in the way the legal system treats white-collar crime by corporations and wealthy individuals. Laws against such crime are weak, they say, and punishment is often minimal (Reiman, 2001). These scholars conclude that even if the law treats people who commit street crime fairly equally, it treats those accused of white-collar crime more leniently even though white-collar crime can be very harmful. We discuss conflict theory's assumptions again in Chapter 11 on sentencing.

Feminist Perspectives. Feminist work on crime and justice deals with several issues (Daly and Maher, 1998; Renzetti and Goodstein, 2000). One concerns the reasons why girls and women commit crime. Most of the sociological explanations previously discussed were developed with males in mind or tested only with data on males. Their neglect of girls and women leaves their relevance for female crime unclear. Researchers have begun to address this issue, and they generally find that the same factors that affect male criminality, including poverty and family problems, also affect female criminality (Baskin and Sommers, 1998). One interesting question is that even when these problems do exist, males are still more likely than females to commit serious crime. Researchers explain this fact by pointing to gender differences in socialization and opportunities to commit crime (Steffensmeier and Allan, 2000). According to some, male socialization patterns encourage male criminality and thus require significant changes in the ways boys are socialized (Messerschmidt, 1997).

A central concern of feminist work on women's criminality has been the ways in which the victimization of girls and women leads them to commit crime and to suffer other problems. Girls are much more likely than boys to be victims of sexual abuse. Such abuse has been implicated in various negative behaviors that girls and women later commit, including prostitution and drug and alcohol abuse (Chesney-Lind, 1997).

Other feminist-inspired work focuses on how females fare compared to males in the legal system. Are police more or less likely to arrest females than males? Once they are arrested, are females less or more likely to receive long prison terms? The evidence is inconsistent and depends to some extent on whether adolescents or adults are being considered (Daly, 1994). Some studies suggest that girls are more likely than boys to get into trouble for various delinquent offenses such as skipping school and sexual promiscuity, but a few studies find no such effect. Most studies find that adult women suspected of serious crimes are treated somewhat more leniently than their male counterparts, but they also find that this gender effect is only moderate. Gender thus seems to have some effect on legal processing, but overall the effect seems rather small (Steffensmeier, Kramer, and Streifel, 1993)

A final concern in feminist work has focused on the victimization of women. Before feminists began studying crime in the 1970s, rape, domestic violence, and other crimes in which girls and women are especially likely to be victims received little attention. In the 1970s, rape became a central concern of the women's movement as researchers emphasized that rape and sexual assault were widespread and stemmed from various cultural views and from gender inequality rather than from provocative behavior by women themselves (Griffin, 1971). The movement soon turned its attention to domestic violence and again emphasized the high incidence of such violence and its roots in cultural views and gender inequality. Researchers also documented how victims of rape and domestic assault were treated in the legal system where, it was said, a "second victimization" occurred as legal professionals doubted their word and often put them "on trial" (Spencer, 1987).

Since the 1970s, many scholars have studied rape, sexual assault, and domestic violence. They found that as many as one-third of U.S. women have been sexually or physically abused at some point in their lives (Tjaden and Thoennes, 2000). This body of research has led to major reforms in the criminal justice system. Victim advocate offices now exist in many communities, and various criminal justice procedures have been changed. For example, rape shield laws preventing rape victims from being asked in court about certain aspects of their sexual history now exist throughout the country (Samborn, 1994).

Theory and Policy: Reducing Crime

We noted earlier that sound explanations of crime are necessary for the development of social and criminal justice policies to reduce the crime problem. The discussions in this chapter have important implications for such policies.

The implications of biological explanations depend on which explanation we consider. Research on pregnancy and birth complications probably holds the most promise because it indicates that improvements in prenatal nutrition and other prenatal problems should help reduce crime rates at least to some degree. Other biological explanations might hold less promise, in part because their policy implications pose ethical and practical difficulties. For example, suppose scientists someday find specific genes that make people more likely to commit crime. How could this knowledge be used to reduce crime? Would genetic engineering be appropriate? Would children be tested to determine who has the "bad" genes? Once they were identified, what would their lives be like? As these questions suggest, crime reduction policies developed from genetic research will be fraught with ethical and practical dilemmas. The same problems affect hormonal research. Suppose high testosterone levels are eventually proven to increase criminality. A logical next step would then be to somehow identify males with high testosterone levels and to reduce these levels, perhaps by giving them a drug or even by castration. Any policy like this raises serious ethical and practical dilemmas even if we only reduced the testosterone levels of males who had already broken the law.

Important policy implications of psychological theories arise from their emphasis on negative childhood experiences and developmental impairments. The children at greatest risk for such problems are typically those born to young, poor, unwed mothers (Loeber and Farrington, 1998). Significant efforts are now underway to help these children. These efforts include home visitation programs in which nurses, social workers, and/or other trained professionals regularly visit these children's homes right after birth and for many weeks thereafter. During these visits, the professionals give the mothers valuable practical advice and moral support. Other efforts include *parent management training* programs in which parents of children with behavioral problems are instructed on discipline and other parenting skills. Although all these efforts are still fairly recent, a growing body of evidence indicates they are very effective at reducing later developmental and behavioral problems among high-risk children (Greenwood, 1998). For adolescent offenders, a multifaceted approach involving family therapy, parent management training, and conflict resolution counseling and programming in school and peer settings has also proven effective (Wasserman et al., 2000).

Sociological explanations also have important implications for crime reduction efforts, although the specific measures they suggest again depend on which explanation we have in mind. For example, ecological explanations suggest the need to focus on certain physical and social characteristics of communities. Although we cannot wave a magic wand and fix everything overnight, efforts that successfully reduce residential density, promote greater involvement in neighborhood voluntary associations, and address other criminogenic community characteristics should help reduce crime. A few such efforts have been attempted, but they have not been fully implemented and thus have not been proven very successful (Bennett, 1998). Ecological explanations suggest that full implementation of these programs should achieve greater success.

Explanations emphasizing blocked economic opportunities also suggest the need to reduce poverty. If poverty leads to feelings of angry aggression, relative deprivation, and other social psychological states that promote street crime, then efforts to reduce poverty should help greatly to reduce crime. The improved economy in the 1990s is widely cited as helping to reduce the crime rate in that decade (Butterfield, 2000a).

Hirschi's social control theory has several policy implications. It directs our attention to the family and school as critical sources of attitudes that either promote criminality or inhibit it. It suggests the need to help parents, especially those who are young, poor, and unwed, to improve their parenting skills; it also suggests the need to improve our schools with smaller class sizes and better school buildings because these measures could help improve students' attitudes toward their schools. Although little public policy has focused on school improvement, early childhood intervention programs show significant potential for crime reduction.

Finally, critical approaches to crime also have policy implications. Although support for labeling theory has been inconsistent, it does suggest caution in arresting and imprisoning at least some types of offenders lest they become worse as a result of their labeling. And it also suggests the need for careful attention to whether the labeling process itself is fair or biased. Conflict theory suggests a similar need, and it also highlights the possible criminogenic effects of values such as competition, individualism, and selfishness. Meanwhile, feminist research suggests the need to take all possible steps to reduce the victimization of women by rape, sexual assault, and domestic violence, and it reminds us of the need to change male socialization patterns in order to reduce male crime rates.

The policy implications of all the explanations discussed in this chapter suggest the need for a multifaceted approach in reducing crime (Lab, 2000; Sherman, Gottfredson, MacKenzie, Eck, Reuter, and Bushaway, 1998; Tonry and Farrington, 1995). Although the criminal justice system remains important in keeping us safe from offenders, efforts that *prevent* crime from arising in the first place are critical to ensure the safest society possible. Although all the explanations discussed in this chapter have different implications for how best to prevent crime, they hold more promise overall for crime reduction than a mere reliance on the criminal justice system.

Focus on Great Britain

Explaining Crime in the Countryside

In August 1999, Fred Barras, a 16-year-old teenager with twenty-nine convictions for assault, burglary, forgery, and theft broke into the British farmhouse of Tony Martin, 55, who kept an unregistered shotgun under his bed because his home had been burglarized many times before. Barras had driven to the farmhouse with two accomplices, both in their thirties, from his home in a housing development seventy miles away. All three burglars were unarmed. Martin confronted the intruders with his shotgun and shot at them as they fled. Barras was hit in the back, stumbled outside, and died. One of his accomplices was hit in the legs and seriously wounded, but survived the shotgun attack. In April 2000, a jury deliberated for about nine hours and convicted Martin of murder in the death of Barras. The defendant was sentenced to life in prison.

Martin's conviction and sentence unleashed a torrent of criticism throughout Britain. In one public opinion poll after another, more than 90 percent of Britons denounced his conviction.

Political leaders called for new laws to protect homeowners who use force to defend themselves or their homes. Some also urged that Britain's strict gun control laws be relaxed.

In the aftermath of the Martin case, attention also focused on rural crime in Britain. As noted, Martin himself had been a crime victim previously. Burglars had broken into his remote home repeatedly and stolen many items, including china, a dresser, and a grandfather clock. He stopped reporting the burglaries, he said at his trial, because the police did not seem concerned about them. Many other rural crime victims in Britain fail to report their burglaries and other crimes for the same reason.

Martin's case heightened concern about crime in the British countryside. As one of Martin's neighbors noted, "I know nobody who has not been a victim of crime. Whether it's burglary, mugging, theft—it's absolutely rampant" (Lyall, 2000, p. A1). A month after Martin was convicted, a couple who had planned to buy a home not too far from his changed their minds at the last moment. They and the owner had decided on a price of £160,000 (about $260,000), but the couple canceled the sale only a few weeks after Martin was convicted. The owner said they were afraid that the surrounding rural county, Norfolk, was rife with crime and that the police were too far away to help if a burglary occurred. Not surprisingly, the owner dismissed their fears. "I don't want to take away from the people who are afraid for their safety," he said, "and in certain parts of Norfolk people have had to take extreme measures against criminals. But every county has an area like that and I don't think if we take Norfolk as a whole that is the situation that exists" (Foss, 2000, p. 1).

In response to the alarm over rural crime in Britain after the Martin case, authorities took several steps. In May 2001, Kent County allocated more than £1 million for extra police and patrol cars. Kent authorities also hired several "crime wardens"—trained civilians wearing dark red jackets and black pants—to help patrol the county and perform other local governmental duties. One county official said, "We have been determined to tackle the problem of rural crime and have made this commitment from funds from our community safety programme." Another official said, "In Kent, we are very aware that for many people there is a very real and everyday fear of crime. Kent residents have told us that they want to feel more secure and see more police on the beat. Our demands for extra bobbies were getting nowhere, so we decided to [act] . . . ourselves" (Sapsted, 2001, p. 1).

Despite the heightened concern over crime in the British countryside, crime rates there remain lower than those in British cities. But certain aspects of life in the countryside lead rural residents to worry about crime. As one British official observed, "The problem in rural areas is that although the chances of being a victim are less than in urban areas, people nevertheless feel more vulnerable because they have fewer neighbors and police response times are likely to be longer than in urban areas" (Ford, 2000, p. 1).

Although it is clear that rural crime rates in Britain remain lower than urban crime rates, what remains less clear is whether the gap between the two areas is narrowing. Official crime statistics from police reports indicate that crime overall in Britain declined during most of the 1990s then showed an increase as the decade drew to a close, whereas victimization data from the British Crime Survey (similar to the U.S. NCVS discussed earlier) indicate that crime declined throughout the entire period in both urban and rural areas. Some police report data, however, suggest that crime was rising in rural areas even if it was declining overall. Other kinds of data support this finding. In 1998, British farmers reported more stolen farm equipment and other items than in 1994. More than half of 120 farmers surveyed a year later by the British Broadcasting Company (BBC) reported they had been victims of burglaries; farm machinery was most often stolen but also animals and crops. Almost half the farmers said their property had been vandalized, and one-fifth had been victims of arson.

Scholars have advanced several explanations for the possible rise in rural crime in Britain. Like the sociological theories discussed in the text, these explanations focus on factors in the social environment. Changes in the social environment may produce changes in crime rates. Several such changes in the British countryside have been noted.

First, rural areas in Britain have been losing farms and population. Since their homes were already far apart, making them easy targets for burglars, the decrease in farms and population makes the dwellings that remain even more isolated than before. This, in turn, makes them that much more tempting for burglars and other offenders.

Second, many rural residents have turned from farming to other occupations away from their homes. This means that their homes are more likely than before to be empty during the day, again making them more attractive targets for burglars.

A third reason involves a decrease in "citizen policing," which the Kent initiative described previously was designed to address. Many rural Britons who were not farmers worked in the shops in their small towns. There they "were able to walk about helping to police their own town" (Crime and Justice International, 2001, p. 11). But many village shops have closed, resulting in fewer people in town and thus less citizen policing. Another consequence of closing village shops is that towns reduced their regular policing because they had fewer stores to monitor. The reduced policing is thought to be yet another factor in the rise in rural crime.

Recall that Fred Barras drove seventy miles to Tony Martin's farmhouse to burglarize it. As this aspect of Martin's sad story might suggest, another reason for the rise in rural crime might be better transportation in the British countryside. The roads from London and other major cities to Britain's rural areas were greatly improved in the past decade or so. This fact has made it easier for criminals to drive longer distances to break into homes. Although most offenders continue to commit their crimes near their own homes and communities, the improvement of British roads may make crime in rural communities more likely. Yet another reason for the rise in rural crime results ironically from crime fighting efforts in British cities, many of which have installed closed-circuit TV cameras and other surveillance devices to try to reduce their own crime rates. These efforts have worked, but they have also displaced crime into more rural areas because criminals realize it is less risky to commit their crimes in the rural regions.

A final explanation focuses on tractor theft, which rose by 250 percent during the 1990s. With many tractors costing more than £30,000 each, even the theft of one tractor is very costly to a farming family and to their insurance company. Insurance officials believe the tractors are being stolen by organized gangs with ties to Northern Ireland terrorists. The tractors are shipped to Northern Ireland and sold, with the illegal profits helping to fund paramilitary activity.

These explanations obviously differ in many ways, but all illustrate that changes in crime rates occur from changes in the external environment and not from changes within individuals. As such, they reinforce the importance of explaining the causes of crime with a sociological lens.

Sources: Crime and Justice International, 2001; Ford, 2000; Ford and Tendler, 2001; Foss, 2000; Lyall, 2000; Naish, 2000; Sapsted, 2001.

summary

1. Accurate crime data are essential for several reasons. They allow us to determine crime rate trends, to know which kinds of places have higher and lower crime rates, and which kinds of people have higher and lower rates. However, much crime never comes to the attention of police, and this "dark figure of crime" makes it difficult to develop accurate crime data.

2. The Uniform Crime Reports (UCR) is the federal government's source of official crime data. It relies on police reports of crime they hear about from citizen victims and witnesses. Because the majority of victims do not tell the police about their crimes, the UCR undercounts the actual number of crimes. The production of crime rates in the UCR also may reflect the behavior of police. During the 1990s, the police in several cities downgraded crime reports from citizens in order to artificially lower the crime rates in their cities.

3. The National Crime Victimization Survey (NCVS) is the federal government's source of information on crime victims and their victimization. It probably provides a more accurate estimate than the UCR of U.S. crime and crime trends. At the same time, victims may sometimes forget or refuse to tell NCVS interviewers about the crimes they have experienced. So the NCVS itself may underestimate the actual amount of crime.

4. Self-report surveys help to reveal the dark figure of crime and have determined that people commit many more offenses than are found in the UCR. Although their respondents may fail to tell the truth about offenses they have committed, the best conclusion is that the reports are reliable. Early self-report surveys included only minor offenses, but more recent surveys have included items measuring more serious offenses.

5. Field, or ethnographic, research is another source of information on crime and offenders. Its major advantage is that it provides a rich portrait of offenders, their motivation for committing crime, and the ways in which they commit crime. One disadvantage is that field research is not necessarily generalizable beyond the subjects studied.

6. To reduce crime, it is important to understand why crime occurs. Today's biological research on crime involves such factors as heredity, hormones, and pregnancy and child-birth complications. Some evidence supports a strong criminogenic role of all these factors, but other evidence suggests only a weak role or none at all. From a policy standpoint, explanations involving pregnancy and child-birth problems most readily lend themselves to practical approaches to reducing crime.

7. Psychological explanations of crime involve psychoanalytic approaches and personality factors. Although evidence for both explanations is inconsistent, they nonetheless direct our attention to early childhood as a critical period for child development. Negative experiences during childhood may promote later criminality.

8. Several sociological explanations of crime exist. Ecological approaches focus on the social and physical characteristics of communities that raise or lower neighborhood crime rates. Blocked opportunity explanations emphasize the negative social psychological states induced by poverty in a society that values economic success. Learning theories emphasize the role played by negative peer influences, whereas social control explanations emphasize the various factors that keep individuals from deciding that crime is acceptable behavior. Critical approaches suggest that crime may result from inequality in society, from how offenders are treated by the

criminal justice system, and from male socialization; they alert us to possible biases in the application of the criminal label. Taken together, sociological explanations reinforce the need for a social policy that focuses on the causes of crime and not only on the apprehension and imprisonment of the criminal offenders we already have.

key terms

anomie theory
crime rate
crimes known to the police
deterrence theory
differential association theory
differential opportunity theory
field research
free will
incidence
Index offenses
labeling theory

National Crime Victimization Survey
  (NCVS)
prevalence
rational choice theory
routine activities theory
self-control theory
self-report surveys
social ecology
social control theory
Uniform Crime Reports (UCR)

questions *for* investigation

1. The FBI's annual *Crime in the United States* publication contains data from the Uniform Crime Reports and can be accessed through the FBI's Web site at www.fbi.gov. The Web site includes a link for Uniform Crime Reports, which takes you to pages from *Crime in the United States*. To access these pages, you will need the Adobe Acrobat program on your computer. If you do not have this program, go to http://www.adobe.com and download the Adobe Acrobat Reader appropriate for your operating system. Once you are ready to access *Crime in the United States,* go to http://www.fbi.gov/ucr/cius_01/01 crime2.pdf, which is one of the first sections of this publication and gives you some basic information on the crime Index (violent and property offenses combined) for 2001. Read this section to determine how many Index crimes occurred in 2001. What was this number?

2. Click on Murder on the left side of your screen to access this section from *Crime in the United States*. Scroll down until you find Table 2.3, which presents murder rates by month. For 2001, which month had the highest murder rate? Which month had the lowest murder rate? What conclusion, if any, can you draw from this comparison?

3. Discuss the value of the NCVS's distinction between sexual assault and rape. Do you think it is appropriate for the NCVS to include both sexual assault and rape in its measurement, or should it follow the UCR in including only rape?

4. Develop a self-report survey that focuses on interviewing people about Index II crimes they may have experienced. Remember to use language that does not prejudice respondents' answers. Survey five people. What do you discover about the survey writing and the interviewing process?

5. The U.S. Bureau of Justice Statistics (BJS) runs a useful Web site at http://www.ojp.usdoj.gov/bjs. Go to this site and click on Criminal victimization to read a summary of findings. According to findings from the NCVS, what percentage of all crimes in 2001 were crimes of violence?

6. Return to the main BJS page and click on Crime characteristics. Scroll down until you see material on the role of alcohol use in criminal victimization. About what percentage of all violent crimes involve an offender who had been drinking?

7. This chapter makes special note of the fact that victims of serious crimes report less than 40 percent of crimes they experience to the police for several reasons, such as fear of reprisal. Discuss ways that might encourage citizens in your community (hometown or college) to report their victimizations.

8. Suppose a woman shoots her husband and then at her trial claims diminished capacity because she was suffering from PMS (premenstrual syndrome). In small groups discuss the legitimacy of the PMS syndrome as a legal defense.

9. What social services or social programs does your community (hometown or college) have in various neighborhoods to prevent crime among young people (for example, block watch programs)? How effective are these services or programs?

IT'S YOUR CALL...

1. Suppose you are the police chief of a medium-sized city in a large state whose crime rate has been growing rapidly for the past two years. Police chiefs across the state are being criticized for allowing the crime rate to rise. You think this criticism is unfair, but you also know that your job may be at risk. One of your aides suggests that the police precincts in high-crime neighborhoods of the city be instructed to demand more "hard" evidence that the aggravated assaults and forcible rapes that come to their attention do, indeed, fit the definitions of those crimes. Because it is often difficult to determine exactly what type of crime occurred, your aide reasons, it would be appropriate to take this stricter approach to classifying crimes. Doing so, your aide speculates, would cause about half of the aggravated assaults and forcible rapes to be downgraded to simple assaults. If so, your city's crime rate would show at least a slight decrease, and your performance as its police chief would be widely applauded. Do you adopt your aide's suggestion? Why or why not?

2. The Under Investigation section following this chapter notes the higher street crime rates of African Americans and offers a structural explanation for racial differences in street crime. Suppose you are a police officer in a large northern city where about 60 percent of the population is African American, 30 person is white, and the remaining 10 percent are people of other races. You understand the racial differences in crime rates, but you also realize that the vast majority of African Americans do not commit crime. An armed robbery occurs in a mixed-race neighborhood of your city. Your partner, a white male officer with two years on the job, utters a racial slur and then says, "What do you expect from those people?" Do you say anything in response? If no, why not? If yes, what do you say?

UNDER
Investigation

Who Commits Crime?

Crime obviously is committed by individuals. But some kinds of individuals are more likely than others to commit crimes. By "kinds" of individuals, we mean individuals with certain social backgrounds or characteristics. Criminal justice researchers have examined several such characteristics: gender, age, social class, race and ethnicity, and geographical location. Our discussion of these characteristics relies heavily on the sources of crime data reviewed earlier in Chapter 2.

Gender

Criminal justice researchers may disagree on many issues, but one area on which they do agree is that men have much higher rates of serious crime than women. Evidence for this gender difference comes from both the UCR and the NCVS. The UCR reports the percentage of

> "... *men have much* *higher rates of serious crime than women.*"

all arrestees who are male and the percentage who are female; the NCVS asks its respondents who were victims of personal crime about their perceptions of the offender's gender, age, and race. Although sometimes victims might inaccurately perceive an offender's age and race, their perceptions of the offender's gender are probably accurate.

The UCR and the NCVS report almost identical results for the percentage of male offenders, lending confidence to their findings. For robbery, both data sources

find that almost 90 percent of all arrestees are male, and for aggravated assault both sources find that about 80 percent of offenders are male, even though males comprise just under one-half the population. Self-report data involving adolescents confirm that males are more involved in serious offenses but also find a much smaller or even no gender difference for minor offenses such as drinking and vandalism (Steffensmeier and Allan, 2000).

Why do males have much higher rates of serious crime? Scholars have tried to answer this question for at least a century, and, as we observed at the outset of Chapter 2, their early answers now sound antiquated. Contemporary explanations sound much more plausible (Steffensmeier and Allan, 2000). Girls and boys and women and men differ in many ways besides crime rates, and researchers specify many of these differences as reasons for the gender difference in criminality. Citing biological differences between the sexes, some researchers believe that males are naturally more aggressive than females and also have much higher levels of testosterone, which boosts their aggressiveness (Klein, 1995). According to other researchers, socialization and opportunity are more significant factors than biology (Steffensmeier and Allan, 2000).

It might sound like a cliché, but boys and girls continue to be socialized differently: Boys are raised to be more assertive and aggressive, whereas girls are raised to be more gentle and nurturing. Girls also become more attached to their parents and value their schooling more, and, as social control theory would predict (see Chapter 2), both these factors help keep them from offending. During adolescence, boys have more independence and hence have greater opportunity than girls to get into trouble. Boys' socialization thus helps them learn attitudes and behaviors that contribute to criminal behavior, whereas girls' socialization helps them learn attitudes and behaviors that contribute to a lack of criminal behavior (Kindlon and Thompson, 1999; Newburn and Stanko, 1994).

An interesting controversy on gender and crime developed during the mid-1970s when researchers noticed that women's arrests were rising faster than men's arrests. Some observers blamed this on the women's liberation movement, which was said to be turning women into men (Adler, 1975; Simon, 1975). But other researchers objected to the finding that a "new female criminal" was evolving (Steffensmeier, 1980). Women's arrests, they pointed out, began rising in the late 1950s, a full decade before the contemporary women's movement began. Thus, the women's movement could not have been responsible for the rise in women's arrests. These researchers instead attributed the increase in women's arrests to their greater poverty in the 1960s, which resulted from the rising divorce rate and other factors. The researchers also indicated that some of the increase stemmed from the fact that police were becoming more willing to arrest female suspects because of changing views on how women should be treated. This controversy over women's arrests notwithstanding, one conclusion seems clear: Although the percentage of female arrests is slightly higher than a few decades ago, data indicate that men still account for the vast majority of serious crimes (Steffensmeier and Allan, 2000).

Age

Age is another characteristic that heavily influences the likelihood of crime. Simply put, young people commit a disproportionately large amount of street crime, which, in general, peaks between ages 17 and 19, declines somewhat but still remains high in the early twenties, and declines further in the late twenties and beyond (Steffensmeier and Allan, 2000). UCR and NCVS data are illustrative. The figure on this page shows that, although less than 9 percent of the U.S. population is 15 to 20 years old, much higher percentages of offenders implicated by both data sources in robbery and aggravated assault are in this age group.

Why are crime rates higher for young people? Researchers cite several reasons primarily concerned with the nature of adolescence and young adulthood in our culture (Greenberg, 1977; LaGrange and White, 1985; Steffensmeier and Allan, 2000). First, adolescence and young adulthood are times of adventure, rebellion, and, sometimes, a lack of maturity. What seems to be fun

and daring to youths, including breaking the law, is often disapproved of by older age groups.

Second, during adolescence and young adulthood peer influences are especially important. As discussed in the text, peer influences play a strong role in decisions to commit crime: If your friends like getting into

> ## *"... young people commit a disproportionately large amount of street crime ..."*

trouble, you are that much more likely to do so yourself. If peer influences play such a role, it is no surprise that adolescents have high rates of offending.

Third, adolescents and, to a lesser extent, young adults want to own a lot of goods but often do not have the resources to buy them. The property crimes that young people commit partly stem from their need for money and possessions they otherwise would have trouble obtaining.

Finally, adolescence is a time when youths have few "stakes in conformity." Most are not yet married or parents, and most do not yet have full-time jobs. They do not have the sense of obligation arising from these responsibilities, and they are free of the time and

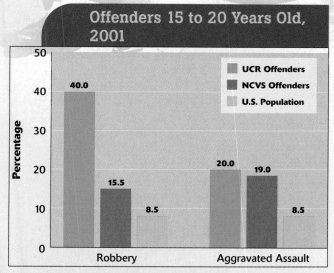

Offenders 15 to 20 Years Old, 2001

Legend: UCR Offenders, NCVS Offenders, U.S. Population

Robbery: UCR Offenders 40.0, NCVS Offenders 15.5, U.S. Population 8.5

Aggravated Assault: UCR Offenders 20.0, NCVS Offenders 19.0, U.S. Population 8.5

Source: Data from U.S. Bureau of the Census. 2001. *Current Population Survey, March 2001.* Washington, DC: U.S. Bureau of the Census; Federal Bureau of Investigation. 2002. *Crime in the United States: 2001.* Washington, DC: Federal Bureau of Investigation; Bureau of Justice Statistics. 2003. *Criminal Victimization in the United States, 2001: Statistical Tables.* Washington, DC: Bureau of Justice Statistics, U.S. Department of Justice. Available: http://www.ojp.usdoj.gov/bjs/pub/pdf/cvus0102.pdf.

energy constraints associated with them. Consequently, they are more likely to break the law.

Most youthful offenders "age out" of crime as they age chronologically (Steffensmeier and Allan, 2000). As we discuss in later chapters, an understanding of the age–crime relationship is important for criminal justice policy. It is also important for understanding crime rate trends. The crime rate declined during the 1990s, and this decline was likely caused in part by a decline in the number of young people during those years and the further aging of the baby boom generation beyond their high-crime years (Steffensmeier and Harer, 1999).

Social Class

Most prison and jail inmates are poor and lack even a high school degree. Many criminal justice researchers think this fact reflects large social class differences in se-

"Most prison and jail *inmates* are poor and *lack* even a high school *degree*."

rious offending (Harris and Shaw, 2000). However, other researchers believe it reflects a criminal justice system bias against the poor, and they call the presumed social class–crime rate relationship a "myth" (Dunaway, Cullen, Burton, and Evans, 2000; Tittle and Meier, 1990). They cite several self-report studies that find similar offending rates among poor and middle-class youths and adults.

Critics of the "myth" view challenge it on two counts (Hagan, 1992; Harris and Shaw, 2000). First, self-report studies that find no relationship often include only minor offenses and thus find only that no social class differences exist for these types of offenses. When serious offenses are examined, social class differences do emerge: Poor youths have higher rates of violence and other serious crime than nonpoor youths. Second, it is important to measure social class adequately by examining youths from the most deprived backgrounds. When very poor youths in self-report studies are compared to other youths, social class differences in serious offending are more apt to emerge than when such youths are not isolated for comparison (Farnworth, Thornberry, Krohn, and Lizotte, 1994).

To these critics, the social class–criminality relationship should be obvious. After discussing the views

of scholars who believe otherwise, one researcher wrote pointedly, "Yet, through it all, social scientists somehow still knew better than to stroll the streets at night in certain parts of town or even to park there . . . [and they] knew that the parts of town that scared them were not upper-income neighborhoods" (Stark, 1987, p. 894).

A recent self-report study of adults in a large midwestern city countered this general critique. The study included measures of serious offenses and of people with very deprived socioeconomic backgrounds. Despite the inclusion of these measures, the study concluded that "social class exerted little direct influence on adult criminality in the general population" (Dunaway et al., 2000, p. 589).

No doubt the debate among criminal justice researchers on the social class–crime relationship will continue for some years to come. Resolution of this debate is critical for an understanding of crime and for criminal justice policy. If social class does make a difference for serious street crime, this difference reflects the "fault lines" of a society with large pockets of poverty, unemployment, and other "structural" conditions that many researchers think contribute to crime (Currie, 1998). To the extent this is true, measures to improve these conditions should help reduce street crime. However, the lack of social class difference would mean these conditions do *not* matter for crime, and measures to improve them would do little to reduce crime. One point does seem clear: If we include white-collar crime, especially that committed by corporations, no social class–crime relationship exists. The people involved in such crime do not come from the ranks of the poor. Although poverty might explain street crime, it does not explain white-collar crime (Simon, 2002).

Race

When we ask who commits crime, perhaps the most controversial discussion centers on the issue of race and ethnicity. African Americans account for almost half of state prisoners, and about one-third of young African American men are under correctional supervision (in jail or prison or on probation or parole) at any one time. Clearly, African Americans are overrepresented as offenders in the criminal justice system. Latinos are also overrepresented (Walker et al., 2000). The fundamental question is this: Does this overrepresentation reflect actual racial and ethnic differences in offending, or does it reflect racial and ethnic bias in the criminal justice system?

Focusing mostly on African Americans, criminal justice researchers again disagree on answers to this question. Some believe that the African American overrepresentation mostly represents criminal justice system bias. According to these researchers, the United States has a system of unequal justice and is on a "search and destroy" mission to put African Americans, especially young male African Americans, behind bars (Mann, 1993; Miller, 1996). Other researchers concede some bias exists but believe that the African American overrepresentation reflects actual racial differences in offending much more than it reflects any bias. Even if no bias existed, they suggest, African Americans would still be overrepresented as offenders (Tonry, 1994; Walker et al., 2000).

Where does the truth lie? The evidence is complex, and we address it more extensively in later chapters. But for now, we agree with the researchers who concede some bias but still believe that African Americans have higher rates of offending. Evidence for this view is based on UCR arrest data and NCVS data victims' perceptions of offenders. For example, although African Americans represented 12.7 percent of the population in 1998, they accounted for much greater percentages of arrestees and NCVS offenders that year (see the figure below). Even allowing for the possibility that some NCVS victims misperceive the race of their offenders, African Americans do seem to have higher rates of offending for serious street crime.

Note that the African American percentage among UCR arrestees exceeds the percentage among NCVS offenders. Does this difference reflect racial bias in the

criminal justice system? Robert M. O'Brien (2000, p. 78) thinks not: "Whether these results indicate a bias in the criminal justice system is not clear because factors such as the differential reporting behavior of victims and the seriousness of the crimes have not been controlled." He concludes that both the UCR and NCVS do indicate that "African Americans constitute a much greater proportion of the offenders in street crimes than one would expect, given their percentages in the population" (O'Brien, 2000, p. 78). Other researchers concur. As Anthony R. Harris and James A. W. Shaw (2000, p. 134) comment, "Victims appear to be telling us that arrests are probably a reasonable indicator of real race-based differences in the commission of street crime."

What do self-report data indicate? The answer depends on which types of offenses are studied (Harris and Shaw, 2000). Self-report studies that examine only minor offenses find only small racial differences in offending, but those that examine serious violent offenses often, but not always, find substantial racial differences (Huizinga and Elliott, 1987).

Although the evidence on race and offending is inconsistent, most researchers would probably agree that African Americans do, in fact, have higher rates of serious street crime, notwithstanding any criminal justice system bias that might exist (Harris and Shaw, 2000; Sampson and Wilson, 1995; Walker et al., 2000). If such a racial difference does exist, it is important to explain it.

Researchers began to advance such explanations almost a century ago, and these early explanations were full of racial prejudice; they blamed high crime rates of African Americans on biological inferiority (Lewontin, Rose, and Kamin, 1984). More recent explanations center on several other factors: (1) a subculture of violence in African American communities; (2) the absence of fathers in African American families; and (3) structural problems facing African Americans, including extreme poverty and segregation (Harris and Shaw, 2000).

The term *subculture of violence* means a set of beliefs and values in which people are quite willing to use violence to resolve interpersonal disputes. Evidence on whether African Americans are more likely than whites to hold such values is mixed. Several surveys find that African Americans and whites give the same kinds of answers to questions asking about the use of violence in various situations. This suggests that a subculture of violence does not exist among African Americans and, further, that their higher rates of offending cannot derive from a subculture of violence (Cao, Adams, and Jensen, 1997). Other researchers, such as Elijah Anderson (1999), whose field study is discussed in Chapter 2, believe that African Americans in urban communities have values, such as the need for respect,

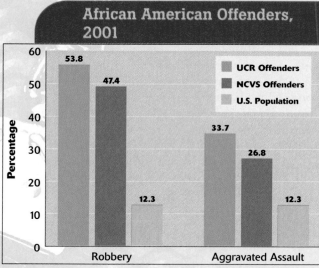

Source: Data from U.S. Bureau of the Census. 2002. *Current Population Survey, March 2002.* Washington, DC: U.S. Bureau of the Census; Federal Bureau of Investigation. 2002. *Crime in the United States: 2001.* Washington, DC: Federal Bureau of Investigation; Bureau of Justice Statistics. 2003. *Criminal Victimization in the United States, 2001: Statistical Tables.* Available: http://www.ojp.usdoj.gov/bjs/pub/pdf/cvus0102.pdf.

that promote the use of violence. However, Anderson is careful to add that if these values do exist, they arise from the structural deprivation in which many urban African Americans live.

Evidence on the African American family structure influence on criminality is also mixed. Although many more African American children than white children grow up without fathers (Census, 1999), evidence of the effects of living in single-parent households on juvenile offending is unclear. As Chapter 2 points out, some studies find that single-parent households greatly increase the likelihood of delinquency, but other studies find it has little, if any, effect.

Scholars are more confident about the importance of social structure problems for African American crime rates. Generally, African Americans are poorer than whites, have higher unemployment rates, and are worse off in other ways (Sampson and Wilson, 1995). According to many scholars, the higher African American crime rate results from the fact that they experience these problems (Harris and Shaw, 2000; Sampson and Wilson, 1995). Rodney Stark (1987, p. 906) says their higher crime rate also stems from where African Americans live: Outside the South, they are much more likely than whites to live in inner-city neighborhoods "where the probabilities of *anyone* committing a crime are high." This sort of structural explanation allows us to explain higher African American crime rates without resorting to a racist explanation that says African Americans are inferior or a blaming-the-victim (Ryan, 1976) approach that ignores the influence of the social environment on African American crime rates.

If African Americans do have higher rates of street crime, they have lower rates of white-collar crime. As Harris and Shaw (2000, p. 155) point out, if we focus on white-collar crime by corporate managers and executives, "we begin to see traces emerging of the photographic negative of the race–street crime relationship: an image in which whites are overrepresented by

> "**If African Americans do have higher rates of street crime, they have lower rates of white-collar crime.**"

a factor approximating African Americans' overrepresentation in street crime." If whites have higher rates of such white-collar crime because of their greater opportunities to be in white-collar positions in the first

place, then perhaps African Americans have higher rates of street crime because of their lack of opportunity to escape the kinds of structural conditions that promote such crime. We address white-collar crime further in Chapter 3.

The Geography and Climatology of Crime

So far we have considered who commits crime in terms of gender, age, social class, and race. But people are also more or less likely to commit crime depending on where they live. In the United States, the South and West have higher violent crime rates than the Northeast, and the Midwest has the lowest rate; the West also has the highest property crime rate. The reasons for these regional differences are not clear. Most scholarship on this issue tries to explain why the South's violent crime rate is so high. Some researchers believe the South has a regional subculture of violence in which slights and insults can easily escalate into violence. Other researchers, however, dispute this point, saying that southern violence instead stems from its high rate of poverty. Robert Nash Parker and Doreen Anderson-Facile (2000, p. 204) note that recent studies "do not find a great deal of evidence for the Southern subculture-of-violence thesis."

U.S. crime rates are also higher in urban areas than in rural areas; the violent crime rate is about three times greater in our largest cities than in rural areas. Why is the risk of crime greater in urban areas than in rural areas? Because crime rates take into account the number of people, it is not only that urban areas have more people than rural areas. Rather, there is probably something about urban living conditions that lead to higher crime rates. Although poverty is commonly cited as a reason for high urban crime rates, many rural areas are also poor and yet have lower crime rates than their urban counterparts. Thus, other features of urban life must contribute to criminality. As ecological approaches emphasize (see Chapter 2), these features include population density (many people living closely together), household overcrowding (crowded conditions within a household), and the presence of bars and other businesses where people "gather" and where violence and other crime can occur (Krivo and Peterson, 1996; Parker and McCall, 1999; Stark, 1987).

The evidence that geographical location affects crime rates is important for understanding why people commit crime because it reinforces the idea that the social environment influences the risk of crime.

Under Investigation: Who Commits Crime?

This idea is the basis of the sociological explanations of criminal behavior discussed in Chapter 2.

Climate also seems to affect crime rates. Generally, assaults, rapes, and burglary and larceny tend to increase in the summer and decrease in colder weather

"U.S. crime *rates* are also *higher* in *urban* areas than in *rural* areas . . ."

(Lab and Hirschel, 1988). Warm weather in the summer seems to explain the higher rates of violence at that time of year. In the summer, people become more irritable and lose their tempers more quickly. During the summer months, people spend more time outdoors, interacting with people. The more interaction, the greater opportunities for arguments, and the greater the opportunities for arguments, the more violence is likely to occur. People also spend more time away from home during the summer, leaving their homes vulnerable to burglars. If warm weather seems to promote several types of crime, that may explain why the South and West have such high crime rates: These regions are generally warmer than the Midwest and Northeast.

Chronic Offenders

Before we leave the subject of who commits crime, some discussion of chronic offenders is appropriate. *Chronic offenders* are people who commit serious crime at an early age, who continue to do so for many years, and who account for a very disproportionate amount of serious crime. Research finds that these offenders—about 5 to 6 percent of adolescents or adults—account for about 50 to 70 percent of all the serious offenses committed by their age group (Shannon, 1988; Tracey, Wolfgang, and Figlio, 1990).

What are the backgrounds of chronic offenders? Almost all are male. Most come from very poor families, many of which are headed by a single parent; most have little formal education; most live in poor, high-crime urban areas; and many have been victims of physical and sexual abuse during childhood. Although it is true that almost all people from these backgrounds do not become chronic offenders, it is also true that most chronic offenders come from these backgrounds (Loeber and Farrington, 1998).

Recognition of chronic offenders and knowledge of their backgrounds are important for criminal justice policy. If such a small number of offenders accounts for so much crime, any efforts that successfully improve the conditions that produce chronic offenders should also help reduce crime. Any efforts that can lead to the arrest and imprisonment of chronic offenders would likewise increase public safety. As we emphasize later in this book, however, efforts focusing on arrest and imprisonment are less promising for crime reduction than efforts focusing on the conditions that contribute to producing crime.

The idea of chronic offenders raises one additional issue. If we could determine which children are at risk for becoming chronic offenders, we could also help reduce the crime rate. Unfortunately, because most children with chronic offender backgrounds do not actually grow up to be chronic offenders, identification of such future offenders suffers from many "false positives." Accordingly, efforts to predict which children at risk for chronic offending actually become chronic offenders are notoriously inaccurate (Capaldi and Patterson, 1996). Despite this problem, the idea of chronic offenders reminds us that certain social conditions do contribute to criminality, and these conditions must be addressed for effective crime reduction to occur.

" . . . the idea of *chronic offenders* reminds us that certain *social conditions* do contribute to criminality. . ."

Crime
in the United
States

1. What are the four crimes of violence tabulated in the annual Uniform Crime Reports?

2. What are the four Index property crimes? How do burglary and robbery differ?

3. What is a hate crime? What constitutes stalking? Under what conditions does sex become the crime of prostitution?

4. How prevalent is drunk driving in the United States? Why do people abuse drugs? What is the connection between drug use and criminal behavior?

5. What are the characteristics of organized crime groups? What are the models of organized crime in the United States?

6. What does occupational crime include?

The short life and tragic death of Jon-Benet Ramsey is one of the most unusual, widely reported, unsolved murders in U.S. criminal history. According to police reports, the 6-year-old girl was put to bed at 10:00 P.M. on Christmas day 1996 in an upscale Boulder, Colorado, neighborhood by her parents, John and Patsy Ramsey. Just before 6:00 A.M. the next morning, Patsy Ramsey called the police after reportedly finding a ransom note on a back stairway demanding $118,000 for the safe return of her daughter. While searching the home a few hours later, John Ramsey discovered the tiny body of Jon-Benet in the wine cellar. Her hands were bound with a thin cord, and black duct tape covered her mouth; she had been beaten, sexually molested, and strangled.

What propelled this murder into the national spotlight over and above the brutality of the crime was the lifestyle of the Ramsey family. John Ramsey was a millionaire businessman who not only lavished Jon-Benet with material comforts but, along with wife Patsy, also managed his daughter's life in the world of children's beauty pageants. In the days following the murder, television coverage was replete with pictures of Jon-Benet adorned with lipstick, makeup, and tinted hair, looking more like a 16-year-old than a child as she pranced before contest judges; she even had the poise of a Las Vegas showgirl. This initial view of the toddler beauty queen subculture struck many people as a vulgar exploitation of little girls that bordered on child pornography. Initial public sentiment was that anyone who could take pleasure in sexualizing a 6-year-old was also capable of killing that individual. By way of standard procedure in virtually every case that a child is murdered at home, John and Patsy Ramsey became prime suspects in their daughter's murder.

Five years after her death, no one had been arrested for Jon-Benet's murder in spite of the staggering amount of time and effort expended to solve this crime. Police officers conducted 650 interviews, questioned 140 suspects, and followed up approximately 5,300 phone tips at a cost of $1.7 million to the city of Boulder and the state of Colorado. During the course of the investigation, 60 experts in various fields were consulted and more than 1,400 pieces of evidence collected. Police officers compiled some 43,000 pages of interviews and assorted information in a sweeping probe that reached into 18 states (Reid, 2001). Two documentaries about the murder were produced for British television, a miniseries aired in the United States, and a number of people associated with the case wrote "the truth about the Jon-Benet murder" type books.

The parents of Jon-Benet Ramsey hold a flyer offering a reward for information leading to the arrest and conviction of their daughter's killer.

These books were rife with allegations about who killed Jon-Benet, with the accusations triggering lawsuits. The Ramseys, an ex-Boulder police detective turned author, a housekeeper who worked for Jon-Benet's parents, a local journalist, the *New York Post,* and Time-Warner Company were involved in civil suits seeking just under $200 million in damages ("Five Years Later," 2001). The legal wrangling and nonstop verbal skirmishes provided material for radio and TV talk shows as well as numerous Internet sites devoted to Jon-Benet's murder, some of which received 2,000 hits a day.

Four major scenarios have been advanced to explain Jon-Benet Ramsey's death (Douglas, 2000, pp. 429–460):

1. Patsy accidentally killed her daughter in a fit of anger and rage. Jon-Benet wet her bed on a regular basis, and on this occasion her mother, angered, struck the child, not with the intent to kill but to punish. The little girl fell backward, hit her head on something, and died. Other scenarios with the same ending have Jon-Benet refusing to wear a dress her mother selected for her or telling her mother she wanted to quit the beauty pageant circuit. When she realized Jon-Benet was dead, Patsy wrote a ransom note and concocted a kidnapping crime. Unwilling to lose his wife as well as his daughter, John Ramsey went along with the hoax.

2. An intruder killed Jon-Benet, most likely a pedophile who had seen her at beauty pageants and broke into the house while the Ramseys and some friends were celebrating on Christmas day.

3. The culprit knew and hated John Ramsey, perhaps as a result of a business transaction gone bad or some other financial dealing. The killer decided to exact his revenge by destroying the most precious thing in Ramsey's life, his daughter.

4. The murder was the result of a planned kidnapping gone awry on the part of one or more teenagers. The language and syntax of the ransom note was similar to

ransom notes and expressions found in the movies *Speed, Ransom,* and *Dirty Harry* as well as television programs and video games popular with teenagers.

In October 1999, a grand jury announced that evidence was insufficient to indict (bring formal charges against) John and Patsy Ramsey or anyone else. However, the evidence the jurors heard and the reasoning they used in reaching their conclusion remains "the best-kept secret in Boulder County" (Douglas, 2000, p. 265; Sebastian, 2001). Under the penalty of fine and imprisonment, Colorado law prohibits grand jurors from discussing an investigation until an indictment has been handed down or a final report released. To date, neither has occurred in the Jon-Benet Ramsey case, and no juror has risked a jail sentence for revealing the grand jury proceedings (Sebastian, 2001).

As of December 2001, four detectives were still following leads and reviewing files. Some observers familiar with the investigation believe the chances of arresting and successfully prosecuting Jon-Benet's killer are all but nonexistent. However, Boulder Police Department chief Mark Beckner remains optimistic, stating that "we will never give up hope for finding justice in this case" (Reid, 2001, p. A1).

The great nineteenth-century French sociologist Émile Durkheim stated that crime is "normal" because it is impossible to imagine (or find) a society that does not have criminal behavior. Durkheim did not mean crime is normal in the sense that it is good. Rather, he used the term in the sense of statistical normalcy; crime is everywhere. Certainly, that is true in a modern industrial society such as the United States where millions of people commit crimes each year, and millions more are the victims of these unlawful acts. Moreover, the culture of crime and the criminal justice system is an integral part of our society as seen in the many movies, television series, novels, and short stories that have crime-related plots. For example, "Law and Order" has been a TV hit for almost 10 seasons, and novels such as *Silence of the Lambs, Presumed Innocent,* and *A Time to Kill* have been best-sellers.

Because of the overall impact crime has on society, most people know something about it. Unfortunately, much of this information is incomplete, inaccurate, or simply wrong. For example, most homicide victims are not killed by assailants who methodically plan their crimes down to the last detail. Also, crime victims lose significantly more money each year as a result of corporate crimes, such as price-fixing, than they do as victims of street crimes (robbery, burglary, motor vehicle theft, etc.).

In this chapter, we examine a wide variety of crimes and ask one or more of the following questions regarding these offenses. Is the crime rate increasing or decreasing? What is the profile of the typical offender? How are these crimes committed? What motivates offenders?

Crimes of Violence

The four crimes of violence (or crimes against persons) tabulated in the annual Uniform Crime Reports (UCR) are murder, robbery, rape, and aggravated assault. The overall rate of violent crime peaked in 1991 with 758.1 offenses per 100,000 population known to police, before declining to 610.8 in 1997. Figure 3.1 shows the overall drop in violent victimizations in the past decade, and Table 3.1 indicates the decline in crime-specific violent victimizations.

figure 3.1

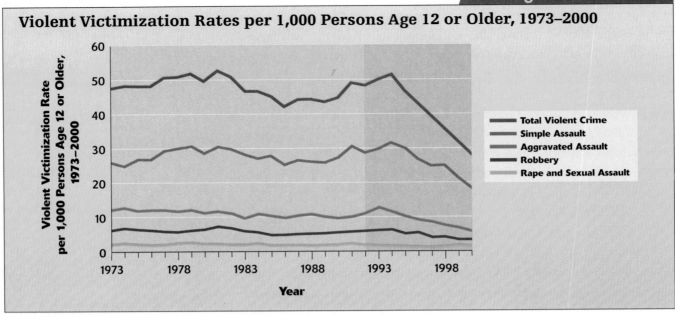

Violent Victimization Rates per 1,000 Persons Age 12 or Older, 1973–2000

Source: Rennison, Callie Marie. 2001. "Criminal Victimization 2000—Changes 1999–2000 with Trends 1993–2000." U.S. Department of Justice, Bureau of Justice Statistics.

Homicide

homicide the killing of one human being by another; not necessarily a crime

Homicide is the killing of one human being by another and is not necessarily a crime. The state-sanctioned death penalty and police officers taking a life in the line of duty are examples of noncriminal homicide. Most states make a distinction between five types of *unlawful* killings: (1) first-degree murder, (2) second-degree murder, (3) voluntary manslaughter, (4) involuntary manslaughter, and (5) felony murder (Gifis, 1996).

first-degree murder the willful, deliberate, and premeditated killing of one human being by another with "malice aforethought"; in states with capital punishment, this crime carries the death penalty

First-degree murder is a crime made famous by countless mystery novels and movies—the classic "whodunit?" theme. This unlawful killing is willful, deliberate, and premeditated. In other words, the offender makes a conscious decision to kill his or her victim that is formulated prior to committing the crime. This decision to take another life could be made months prior to the act or no more than a split second before the crime takes place. In states with capital punishment, first-degree murder carries the death penalty. In second-degree murder, although the offender may or may not have intended to take the life of the victim, the act occurs *without* deliberation and premeditation. In Boston, British born au pair Louise Woodward was convicted (1997) of second-degree murder in the death of an 8-month-old baby for whom she was caring. The prosecution argued that although the nineteen-year-old probably had not intended to kill the infant when she hit and shook Matthew Eapen in a fit of rage and frustration, she was responsible for his death ("U.S. Jury Finds Louise Guilty of Second Degree Murder," 1997).

manslaughter unlawful killings that are committed without "malice aforethought," and, as such, are considered less severe and more explainable

Manslaughter refers to those killings that, although unlawful, are committed without "malice aforethought." These homicides are considered less severe and more explainable. Voluntary manslaughter is an intentional killing under circumstances that make it less blameworthy, and, therefore, the offender's culpability is reduced. An example would be taking the life of another in the heat of intense emotion, such as anger or fear, that the behavior of the victim incites or brings about. Involuntary manslaughter is the death of an individual that results from the negligent or reckless behavior of the offender. The most common incident of this crime in modern industrial societies are deaths resulting from reckless and/or drunk driving.

table 3.1

National Crime Victimization Survey
Violent Crime Trends, 1973–1999

Adjusted violent victimization rates
Number of victimizations per 1,000 population age 12 and over

YEAR	TOTAL VIOLENT CRIME	MURDER	RAPE	ROBBERY	AGGRAVATED ASSAULT	SIMPLE ASSAULT
1973	47.7	0.1	2.5	6.7	12.5	25.9
1974	48.0	0.1	2.6	7.2	12.9	25.3
1975	48.4	0.1	2.4	6.8	11.9	27.2
1976	48.0	0.1	2.2	6.5	12.2	27.0
1977	50.4	0.1	2.3	6.2	12.4	29.4
1978	50.6	0.1	2.6	5.9	12.0	30.0
1979	51.7	0.1	2.8	6.3	12.3	30.3
1980	49.4	0.1	2.5	6.6	11.4	28.8
1981	52.3	0.1	2.5	7.4	12.0	30.3
1982	50.7	0.1	2.1	7.1	11.5	29.8
1983	46.5	0.1	2.1	6.0	9.9	28.3
1984	46.4	0.1	2.5	5.8	10.8	27.2
1985	45.2	0.1	1.9	5.1	10.3	27.9
1986	42.0	0.1	1.7	5.1	9.8	25.3
1987	44.0	0.1	2.0	5.3	10.0	26.7
1988	44.1	0.1	1.7	5.3	10.8	26.3
1989	43.3	0.1	1.8	5.4	10.3	25.8
1990	44.1	0.1	1.7	5.7	9.8	26.9
1991	48.8	0.1	2.2	5.9	9.9	30.6
1992	47.9	0.1	1.8	6.1	11.1	28.9
1993	49.1	0.1	1.6	6.0	12.0	29.4
1994	51.2	0.1	1.4	6.3	11.9	31.5
1995	46.1	0.1	1.2	5.4	9.5	29.9
1996	41.6	0.1	0.9	5.2	8.8	26.6
1997	38.8	0.1	0.9	4.3	8.6	24.9
1998	36.0	0.1	0.9	4.0	7.5	23.5
1999	32.1	0.1	0.9	3.6	6.7	20.8

Note: Estimates for 1993 and beyond are based on collection year, whereas earlier estimates are based on data year. Homicide rates for 1999 are estimated based on 1999 preliminary annual release data. 1973–1991 data adjusted to make data comparable to data after the redesign. (Homicide data were calculated from the FBI's Uniform Crime Reports.)

Source: "Criminal Victimization 2000 with Trends 1973–1999," U.S. Department of Justice, Bureau of Justice Statistics.

Felony murder is an unlawful homicide that occurs during the commission (or attempted commission) of a felony, most notably a robbery, rape, or arson. Two important aspects of this crime must be noted. First, in many states, the sentence for this unlawful act is the same as that for first-degree murder, which means that in death penalty states felony murder is a capital offense. Second, this crime does not require malice aforethought. If, during the commission of a convenience store robbery, a young offender panics and shoots and kills the clerk, the defendant can be charged with felony murder even though he or she had no intention of hurting, much less killing, anyone. "The evil mind or malice that is necessary to find someone guilty of murder is implied or imputed from the actor's intent to commit a felony" (Gifis, 1996, p. 199).

Keep in mind that murder and manslaughter categories are not always clear cut and require interpretation on the part of prosecutors regarding which charges to bring against a defendant. This "prosecutorial discretion" is discussed in Chapter 9.

Table 3.2 shows homicide trends in the United States between 1950 and 2000. Note, in particular, the decrease of the homicide rate since 1991. An examination of the Uniform Crime Reports data over the past 40 years reveals the following characteristics about murder in the United States.

1. Murder in the United States has traditionally been a crime wherein the killer and the victim know each other (family, friends, or acquaintances). However, in 1991, for the first time, more than half of the nation's murders were committed by strangers or under circumstances in which the relationship between the victim and offender was unknown. In 1965, one of every three murders was family related, a figure that has since decreased to one in eight.

2. This changing nature of the offender–victim relationship has had a significant impact on the number of murders solved by police. In 1965, police could (rightly) assume that the killer knew or was related to the victim and arrested someone in connection with the crime in 91 percent of the cases. By the mid-1990s, an arrest was made

table 3.2	Homicide Trends in the United States, 1950–2000	
YEAR	**HOMICIDE RATE PER 100,0000 POPULATION**	**ESTIMATED NUMBER OF HOMICIDES**
1950	4.6	7,020
1955	4.1	6,850
1960	5.1	9,110
1965	5.1	9,960
1970	7.9	16,000
1975	9.6	20,150
1980	10.2	23,040
1985	7.9	18,980
1990	9.4	23,440
1995	8.2	21,610
2000	5.5	15,517

Source: FBI, Uniform Crime Reports, 1950–2000. U.S. Department of Justice, Bureau of Justice Statistics.

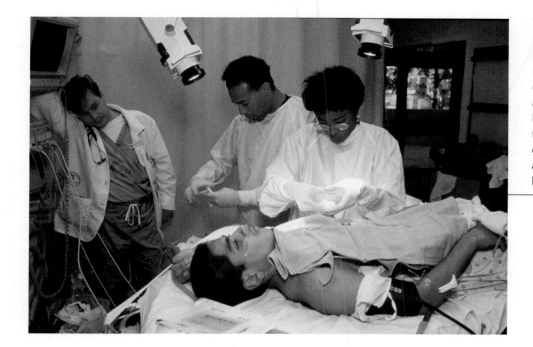

This man is undergoing surgery after being stabbed. If it were not for a faster response time on the part of emergency medical personnel, as well as more skilled and better equipped physicians, the number of criminal homicides in the United States annually would be significantly higher.

in only 65 percent of the murders, a number that decreased to 33 percent in some big-city neighborhoods.

3. In more than four of five murders both the offender and the victim are male. In 2001, 9 out of 10 female murder victims were murdered by males.

4. Murder is overwhelmingly an intraracial crime. In 2000, 90.7 percent of African American victims were slain by African American offenders, and 83.9 percent of white victims were killed by white assailants.

5. Although African Americans comprised only 13 percent of the population in 2000, one out of two murder victims was African American. The lifetime risk of being an unlawful homicide victim is 1 out of 26 for African American males, 1 out of 125 for African American females, 1 out of 170 for white males, and 1 out of 503 for white females (Dorbin, Wiersema, Loftin, and McDowell, 1996). If social class and residence were considered, the lifetime risk of being a homicide victim for poor, inner-city, young African American males could be as high as 1 out of 20. Using the 1 out of 26 figure, African American males in the United States are 19.3 times more likely to be murdered than white females.

6. The average age of people arrested for murder has declined from 32.5 years in 1965 to 27 in the mid-1990s, with many of these killings gang and drug related. Although the murder rate dropped by 10 percent for individuals 25 years of age and older in the early 1990s, it increased by 26 percent for teenagers. Juvenile homicides are overwhelmingly an inner-city phenomenon, with approximately one in three juvenile homicide arrests in 1995 occurring in only four cities: New York, Chicago, Detroit, and Los Angeles (Schiraldi, 1999). In fact, between 1984 and 1994, the number of teenage homicide offenders tripled (Snyder, Sickmund, and Poe-Yamagata, 1996). Criminologist Lawrence Sherman notes that "what we are seeing is the juvenilization of homicide in this nation" (Thomas, 1995, p. 26). Although it cannot be considered a crime trend, there have been more than 20 school shootings in recent years involving teenager offenders and multiple victims. The most infamous of these crimes was the 1999 mass murder at Colombine High School in Littleton, Colorado, where two students wearing long black trench coats opened fire on their classmates killing 13 and wounding 20.

7. Nearly three of every four children murdered in the 26 industrialized countries of the world are slain in the United States. Another way of looking at this relationship is that a child in the United States is five times more likely to be murdered than a child in the rest of the industrialized world (Havemann, 1997; "U.S. Called Capital of Gun Violence Deaths," 1997).

8. The geography of criminal homicide reveals that this behavior is disproportionately a big-city crime, with homicide rates in the nation's largest urban areas about twice as high as rates in suburban areas and rural districts. Although homicide rates are lowest in the Midwest, traditionally they have been the highest in the South, with the western United States a close second.

9. Peak periods for homicide are July, August, December, and the weekends when routine activities bring people together. As interaction increases, so, too, does the possibility that conflict will occur, which, in some cases, results in murder.

10. Firearms are the weapons of choice of murderers. Approximately 7 of 10 murders in 2001 involved a firearm, and in 77.9 percent of these cases the weapon was a handgun.

As noted previously, homicide rates have traditionally been the highest in cities and in the southern states. Sociologists David Luckenbill and Daniel Doyle (1989, p. 420) posed the following question: "What is there about residing in an urban or southern area that generates a high rate of violence?" They noted that a significant number of people in these areas (young, male, lower-income individuals) have a lifestyle characterized by "disputatiousness"; that is, these individuals share a culturally transmitted willingness to settle disputes (most of which are perceived as a threat to their masculinity or status) by using physical force. In an earlier and related work, Luckenbill (1977) stated that homicide is the product of a "character contest." During the course of an argument, insults and threats are traded until escalating tension brings the matter to a point of no return, with participants and bystanders agreeing that the "contest" can be resolved only by violence. Obviously, the more people settle disputes by physical force, the greater the likelihood that someone will be killed, even if the intent to take a life is absent. A significant number of homicides can be characterized as overly successful aggravated assaults.

Improvements in emergency services and care have dramatically reduced the deaths of assault victims according to a study headed by sociologist Anthony R. Harris of the University of Massachusetts. Harris noted that "People who would have ended up in morgues 20 years ago are now simply treated and released by a hospital, often in a matter of a few days" (Tynan, 2002, p. A2). In 1960, 1 out of every 18 aggravated assaults known to police ended with the death of the victim. By 1999, with almost six times as many attacks known to police, only 1 out of every 60 aggravated assaults resulted in death. In other words, modern medicine has dramatically reduced the number of assaults that become "overly successful," or criminal homicides. Using sophisticated statistical analysis, the researchers concluded that without these medical advancements as many as 45,000 to 70,000 homicides would have been recorded in recent years, the actual number is in the 15,000 to 25,000 range (Tynan, 2002).

The Horror of Serial Killers. While most Americans could name half a dozen serial killers, or at least are familiar with their media tags ("Son of Sam," the "Hillside Strangler," "Night Stalker," and the "Serial Sniper"), few individuals have more than superficial knowledge about the fundamental issues surrounding these criminals. How many serial killers are there in the United States? Over the course of their murderous careers how many lives do they take? How do these predators choose their victims? And, perhaps the most important question, why do they kill?

According to one estimate serial killers claim between 3,500 and 5,000 victims annually in this country. These figures are based on the fact that each year between 25 and 28 percent of "murder circumstances" are classified as "unknown." That is, these killing cannot be connected to factors such as arguments over property or money, a romantic triangle, or the commission of a felony (such as a drug deal or robbery). Twenty-five percent of the approximately 16,000 criminal homicides known to police in 2001 yields 4,000 unexplained murders—an overwhelming majority of which are believed to be serial killings.

The many critics of this line of reasoning contend that the fact that law enforcement personnel cannot provide an explanation for a killing does not necessarily mean that the crime in question was "motiveless." Also, murders solved months or, in some cases, years after they occurred may not be removed from the circumstances unknown category by overworked big-city homicide detectives.

The FBI estimates that there are approximately 35 but possibly as many as 100 serial killers active in the United States at any one time. (This does not mean that every year there are 35 to 100 new killers.) Collectively, these individuals are thought to murder about 200 to 300 people a year and account for between 1 and just over 2 percent of known murders annually. Almost all experts in homicide studies accept this much lower estimate of serial killings.

In their book *Overkill*, criminologists James Fox and Jack Levin (1994) offer a typology of serial killers based on motivation. *Thrill-oriented* killers murder for the fun of it, relishing the complete control they exercise over their victims. Fox and Levin note that these individuals rarely use a gun because a firearm results in a relatively rapid, painless death, a demise that would deprive them of their greatest pleasure—watching the victim die slowly and with as much suffering as they can inflict. Some thrill killers record their torture sessions on videotape so they can be viewed and enjoyed indefinitely. The overwhelming majority of serial killers fall in this category.

Mission-oriented killers are fanatics engaged in a campaign to rid the world of evil and filth. As opposed to experiencing some measure of psychological or physical ecstasy via their crimes, these individuals are attempting to further some social, political, and/or religious agenda. Mission killers target a particular group or category of individuals they deem reprehensible—usually prostitutes, homosexuals, homeless people, or drug users thought to be destroying the moral fiber of society. One mission killer specifically targeted young African American males who had white girlfriends. Rather than perpetrators of heinous crimes, these individuals see themselves as heroes, killing in the defense of some noble idea or eternal truth. A killer of prostitutes in Louisville, Kentucky, boasted to police that he was performing a valuable service for the community.

The *profit-driven* serial killer takes the lives of his victims in connection with another crime, typically a robbery. In a 1992 Midwest crime spree, thieves held up a number of small convenience stores, killing the proprietors and witnesses along the way. Unlike thrill-oriented killers, profit-motivated murderers favor a gun and dispatch their victims quickly. These individuals kill because they believe it is necessary lest they be identified, apprehended, and successfully prosecuted. For them, murder is not a form of pleasure but a requisite for survival.

The "sniper killers" in the Washington, D.C. area do not easily fit into this typology. Because the victims were murdered from a distance and the shooter and his accomplice had no intimate contact with them before or after the attacks, these killings cannot be considered thrill-oriented murders. A possible profit motive was noted in a demand for $10 million after the 13th shooting, but experts are not convinced that money was the prime motivation for the murderous rampage. Ranging in age from 13 to 72 and members of different racial and ethnic groups, the victims did not appear to be the target of a mission-oriented killer. However, John Allen Muhammad spoke on occasion of his hatred of the United States and support for the terrorists responsible for the September 11, 2001 attacks. The random shooting of 13 people, in a period of only three weeks, from a distance with a high-powered rifle is more akin to the philosophy of terrorists who embark on a deadly plan to psychologically and socially paralyze a population. The murderous spree of Muhammad and John Lee Malvo may represent a new form of serial killing/terrorism.

While serial killers have come from all racial and ethnic backgrounds and may be young or old, the "typical" offender is a white male in his late 20s and 30s. No more than 10 to 20 percent of known serial killers in this country have been females. Fox and Levin (1994, p. 18) argue that, with the exception of serial killers who murder because they hear voices or actually see their victims as devils, most of these individuals are "more cruel than crazy," with a "disorder of character rather than of the mind." They know right from wrong and can control their murderous desires. This latter point is of

Three weeks of terror ended on October 24, 2002, when two men were arrested for the random shooting deaths of 10 individuals in Maryland, Virginia, and Washington D.C. The FBI estimates that there are approximately 35, but as many as 100, serial killers active in the United States at any one time.

particular importance. If serial killers could not control their urges, they would make foolish mistakes and be apprehended rather quickly.

Often possessing above average intelligence, serial killers have posed as stranded motorists, utility company employees (to gain entrance to a residence), and even police officers. They can be charming, persuasive, and manipulative. In a prison interview Ted Bundy, who took the lives of at least 30 young females (between 16 and 26 years of age), stated that there was a rational, methodical element to his killings (Hickey, 1991). He noted that the serial killer learns to stalk, wait, and kill, and with each episode grows more proficient at his chosen crime. Because so many of these individuals (especially thrill-motivated serial killers) are rational and cunning, when they are caught it is often a matter of luck rather some mistake on their part (Fox and Levin, 1994).

To date, attempts at constructing profiles of serial killers have not proven to be very useful. For example, a number of psychiatrists are of the opinion that, as a consequence of repeated head trauma (from child abuse, for example), severe injury to the brain's limbic system predisposes an individual to violent behavior. A study of 15 inmates on Florida's death row revealed that all of these men exhibited signs of neurological damage. What is missing from this research (by way of comparison) is the prevalence of individuals in the non–criminally violent population who have also suffered severe head injuries. Fox and Levin note (p. 90) that "if head trauma were as strong a contributor to serial murder as some would suggest, we would have many times more serial killers than we actually do."

Understanding why some people choose to murder in a systematic and often horrific manner and ridding society of the factors that bring about this deadly motivation are not the same thing. Even if social and medical science advance to levels wherein an accurate profile of (for example) mission-oriented serial killers can be constructed, short of arresting everyone who conforms to that psychological portrait and incapacitating them in some kind of "preventative detention," serial killers will continue to walk among us. Unfortunately, the chances of significantly reducing, much less eliminating, serial killing are almost zero. In a society of 290 million people, it is inevitable that a very small number of individuals will be aberrant to the extent that they find killing pleasurable, profitable, or justified in the pursuit of some cause or twisted notion of religious purity. We can only be thankful that whatever ultimately causes this murderous behavior is present in so few people.

Robbery

Robbery involves taking something of value from an individual by force, by the threat of force, or by instilling fear in the victim. Unlike burglary, which involves an illegal entry but no contact with the victim, robbery is a crime of physical confrontation in which the perpetrator and target of the crime share the same physical space at the same time. Many robbery victims (especially those who resist) suffer severe personal injury. Robbery is predominantly a big-city crime, with rates of this offense in metropolitan centers of more than 1 million inhabitants (426.7) 25 times higher in 2001 than the rate (16.7) in rural areas of the country. Almost two-thirds of the robberies in cities with populations of more than 250,000 were street/highway crimes or muggings. In the rural United States, muggings accounted for just over one-third of total robberies.

> **robbery** taking something of value from an individual by the use or threat of force

In 2000, total losses from robberies were approximately $532 million. The average loss per robbery was about $1,258, just over 600 for convenience store crimes, and roughly $4,587 per bank robbery. Although they receive a good deal of media attention, only 2 percent of all robberies known to police were bank robberies.

Robbery is overwhelmingly a young man's crime: 62 percent of all those arrested in 2001 for robbery were under 25 years of age, and 89.9 percent were males. African Americans accounted for 53.8 percent of total robbery arrests and whites 44.5 percent.

In her study of 37 active street robbers (23 men and 14 women), sociologist Jody Miller (1998) discovered that the primary motivation for these crimes was economic, more specifically, to acquire "status-conferring goods" such as gold jewelry and spending money. Other motivating factors included the need for excitement, overcoming boredom, and revenge. Female street robbers commit this crime primarily in three ways: targeting other females in a physically confrontational manner, targeting men by appearing sexually available, and/or by working with males in the robbery of other males (Miller, 1998).

In his imaginative and insightful book, *Seductions of Crime*, sociologist Jack Katz (1988) argues convincingly that what motivates many street robbers is something quite different from the need or desire for money. Indeed, the amount of money gained from muggings is relatively small and hardly worth the risk of eventually being arrested. For Katz (1988), what drives many of these individuals is the need to establish and maintain a certain coveted identity—the "badass." Each robbery, therefore, is an affirmation of the badass identity to the victim who is terrorized and intimidated, and to the perpetrator who has thoroughly subjugated someone at his or her whim. Resistance to these individuals can be dangerous because they are likely to view self-defense as an affront to their identities that cannot be tolerated.

The robber as badass may partly explain why the males in Miller's (1998) sample of active street robbers are less likely to target females as victims. Inasmuch as women are defined as weak and passive, robbing these individuals is hardly a demonstration of masculinity much less the "super" masculine role coveted by the badass.

Although the overwhelming majority of robberies occur in the streets or places of business, about 10 percent of these crimes occur on private premises. This category of robbery involves breaking into homes or being admitted into a place of residence by an unsuspecting individual. Residential robberies are often committed by street gangs. In some cases, residents are intimidated by the threat of force and left unharmed, whereas in other crimes they are physically assaulted, and, on occasion, murdered.

Rape and Sexual Assault

rape carnal knowledge of a female forcibly and against her will

The Uniform Crime Reports define **rape** as the carnal knowledge of a female forcibly and against her will. UCR statistics include completed rapes and rape attempts, whereas statutory rape (sex involving a minor without the use of force) and other sexual offenses are omitted. Sexual assault includes a wide variety of behaviors in which some unwanted sexual contact (that does not include sexual penetration) occurs between the victim and the offender. In 1978, 31.0 rapes were known to police per 100,000 population, a figure that increased to 42.8 in 1992 and then declined to 31.8 in 2001.

Using a definition of rape that includes forced vaginal, oral, and/or anal sex, the National Violence against Women Survey concluded that 1 of 6 women in the United States as well as 1 of 33 men have experienced an attempted or completed rape as a child and/or as an adult ("Rape and Sexual Assault," 1999). According to one estimate, approximately 1.5 million women and 834,700 men are raped and/or physically assaulted by an intimate partner annually ("Rape and Sexual Assault," 1999).

In one of the most frequently cited studies of date or acquaintance rape, Koss and her colleagues (Koss, Gidycz, and Wisniewski, 1987) discovered that 15.4 percent of female college students surveyed reported that they had experienced at least one act in the previous year that met the legal definition of rape. In a similar study, Koss and Harvey (1991) found that 1 in 12 college males admitted to engaging in sexual acts that met the legal definition of rape or attempted rape. The policy director of the National Victims Center noted that "there is no question that acquaintance rape is more common than stranger rape. No one has the exact number, but the consensus is that in 80 to 85 percent of all rape cases, the victim knows the defendant" (*Crime—A Serious American Problem*, 1998, p. 23).

The fact that the offender and victim know each other is one of the major reasons why so few date rapes are reported to authorities. Because the offender was not a stranger who jumped from the bushes to attack them, some victims of date rape do not consider this crime a "real rape." Other victims may be too frightened and/or too embarrassed to call the police, or they may mistakenly believe that, if they did not physically resist their assailants, the sexual act was one of consent. The 1996 National Crime Victimization Survey reported that two-thirds of rape/sexual assaults were not reported ("Rape and Sexual Assault," 1999).

Another factor that rape victims take into consideration when deciding if they will inform authorities of the incident is the injury (if any) that they experienced. Females who suffered a physical injury as a result of the rape or sexual assault reported 37 percent of those attacks to authorities, whereas only 22 percent of rapes and sexual assaults that did not result in physical injuries were reported ("Rape and Sexual Assault," 1999).

The geography of rape reveals that of the rape/rape attempts known to police in 2000, 65 victimizations per 100,000 females occurred in metropolitan areas, 69 such crimes outside metropolitan areas, and 43 rapes/rape attempts per 100,000 females in rural regions of the country. Southern states had the highest rate of forcible rape, with 67 cases known to police per 100,000 females, whereas the northeastern states experienced the lowest incidence of this crime with a rate of 44 per 100,000 females. As is the case with other crimes of violence, a disproportionate number of offenders are young. Forty-six percent of individuals arrested for rape in 2000 were under 25 years of age, and 64 percent were white.

Criminologist William Sanders (1983, p. 266) has noted that rape is a unique crime in that forced sex (especially date rape) and sexual assaults "are very much subject to a double standard"; that is, there are a number of situations wherein individuals consider forced sex justifiable although illegal. Attitudes concerning what is acceptable sexual behavior are formed at an early age, as the following survey of Los Angeles high school students suggests (in Sanders, 1983, p. 266). Almost 50 percent of the respondents (54 percent of boys and 42 percent of girls) considered sexual assaults as possibly justifiable under the following circumstances:

1. The girl says "yes" to the boy and then changes her mind.
2. She has "led" him on.
3. The girl gets the boy "sexually aroused."
4. If they had sex before.
5. If he is "turned on."
6. If she has slept with other boys.
7. If she agrees to go to a party where she knows there will be drinking or drugs.

Although these justifications regarding forced sex are held by a significant number of people, consider how absurd they sound when given for virtually any other crime. Take robbery, for example. "Robbing a bank is acceptable under the following conditions:" (Sanders, 1983, p. 266).

1. The bank says "yes" to a loan and then changes its mind.
2. The bank has led the applicant to believe he/she will receive a loan.
3. Through advertisements, the bank has gotten the loan applicant "excited."
4. The bank has given the person a loan before.
5. The applicant "really needs" the money.
6. The bank has loaned other people money.
7. The loan officer goes to a party with the applicant where he knows drinking and drugs will be used.

Feminists argue that rape is an act of power and violence and not of sex (Brownmiller, 1975; Richardson, 1988). From this perspective, rape is an act of terrorism, a tangible and symbolic mechanism for keeping females in their supposed proper place. At the same time it is a symbolic act of violence of one male against another male, a husband, or boyfriend who has exclusive access to the girl or woman. From this perspective, rape is a form of property crime with the property in question being a woman.

In a six to one decision in January, 2003, the California Supreme Court ruled that a man can be convicted of rape if he continues to have intercourse with a woman who initially gave her consent but later changes her mind and asks him to stop. Writing for the majority, Justice Ming Chin stated "A withdrawal of consent nullifies any earlier consent and subjects the male to forcible rape charges if he persists in what has become nonconsensual intercourse" (Kravets, 2003, p. 1). This decision furthers a nationwide trend over the past 20 years that reduces the burden on females in bringing rape charges against males.

Although many psychological, sociological, and even economic theories attempt to explain or account for the "deviant motivation" of the rapist, the unique double standard surrounding this crime goes a long way toward understanding why so many females are the victims of forced sex and other forms of sexual assault.

This double standard may also explain in part why an estimated 180,000 to 500,000 "rape kits" across the country have not been processed by law enforcement agencies. Rape kits consist of the material—seminal fluid and pubic hair, for example—taken from victims after the attack. Obviously, this material is crucial in gaining a conviction. Speaking of unexamined rape kits, Delaware Senator Joseph Biden noted that "The cause of this backlog seems to be pretty straightforward—woefully inadequate funding and understaffing in forensic laboratories. And the result of this backlog is clear—justice delayed and sometimes denied" (Cantlupe, 2002, p. A16).

Aggravated Assault

Aggravated assault is the unlawful and intentional causing of serious bodily harm with or without a deadly weapon or the unlawful, intentional attempt or threat of serious bodily harm with or without a deadly weapon. This can be contrasted with simple

aggravated assault the unlawful and intentional causing of serious bodily harm with or without a deadly weapon or the unlawful, intentional attempt or threat of serious bodily harm with or without a weapon assault wherein the physical injury suffered by the victim is relatively minor. An example of the latter would be a fight in the stands of a football game where one or both of the participants suffer no more than a black eye or chipped tooth.

Of the four crimes of violence compiled in the UCR, aggravated assault is the most common and accounts for approximately 60 to 65 percent of these offenses annually. The rate of urban aggravated assault is typically two to three times higher than the rate of such assaults in rural areas; likewise the aggravated assault rate in the South is significantly higher than the rate in the Northeast and Midwest, the regions with the lowest rate of this crime.

Regarding weapons used in aggravated assaults in 2001: 36 percent of these attacks were committed with blunt objects, such as clubs or baseball bats; in 28 percent of cases known to police, attackers used their hands, fists, or feet; 18.3 percent of assailants used guns; and another 17.8 percent chose knives or other cutting instruments. The overwhelming number of offenders are males between 15 and 34 years of age. These defendants have been described as "spontaneous, heat of passion offenders" (Meithe and McCorkle, 1998, p. 25).

According to criminologist Marcus Felson (1998), fights typically occur among young males after they have consumed alcohol in bars or other locations. As noted in the section on murder, a significant number of aggravated assaults go beyond the intent of any of the combatants and culminate in criminal homicide.

Domestic Violence

Domestic violence, also called intimate violence, involves physical attacks by spouses, ex-spouses, boyfriends and girlfriends, or ex-boyfriends and ex-girlfriends. The physical abuse of children also falls into this category. These attacks range from the minor to the more serious and take the form of pushing, shoving, slapping, hitting with an object, beating, burning, sexual assault, and using or threatening to use a weapon. Domestic violence has received much attention in recent years, but many mistaken beliefs remain.

The National Crime Victimization Survey (NCVS) asks certain questions of its respondents to measure the amount of domestic violence throughout the nation. The NCVS estimates that just under 800,000 incidents of intimate violence (not including violence against children) occurred in 1999, the latest year for which data are available at the time of this writing. Of this number, women experienced about 671,000, incidents, or about 85 percent of the total; whereas men experienced approximately 120,000 incidents, or approximately 15 percent of the total. Risk also differs by age: Although 6 of every 1,000 women were victims of intimate violence in 1999, this figure rises to 16 per 1,000 for the 16 to 24 age group. Intimate violence rates do not differ by race (Rennison, 2001a).

How many women are assaulted at least once in their lifetime by a spouse or partner? One estimate comes from the National Violence against Women Survey, which asked respondents whether they had experienced one or more of several acts such as those listed previously. Slightly more than 22 percent of the women surveyed said they had been assaulted (Tjaden and Thoennes, 2000). A fair conclusion from this national survey is that more than one-fifth of all U.S. women will be assaulted at least once in their lifetime by a boyfriend or husband. About one in four violent offenders in local jails and 7 percent in state prisons committed their crimes against an intimate partner (*Violence by Intimates*, 1998).

Many scholars attribute the high rate of intimate violence against women to power differences and cultural beliefs in the larger society (Browne, 1995; Karmen, 1995). Men are not only usually bigger and stronger than women physically but they also traditionally have been considered the head of the family. Many men continue to accept this belief and further believe that their wives or girlfriends deserve to be hit for doing something that angers them.

In contemporary U.S. society a child is more likely to be killed by a parent than by a stranger. The U.S. Advisory Board on Child Abuse and Neglect states that each year an estimated 2,000 children die at the hands of their parents and primary caregivers ("Parents Who Kill Their Children," 1995; "Child Abuse and Neglect," 1997). A national survey of two-parent households concluded that an estimated 6.9 million children are physically abused each year by their parents (Rudo and Powell, 1998). Many children are abused repeatedly, even after their cases have been brought to the attention of local authorities (DePanfilis and Zuravin, 1998). Research indicates that mothers are somewhat more likely to physically abuse their children than are fathers because women usually spend considerably more time than men in the day-to-day socialization of their offspring and have to deal with children's misbehavior.

Property Crimes

The four Index property crimes are burglary, larceny–theft, motor vehicle theft, and arson. In the commission of these offenses, money and/or property is taken from the victim *without* the threat or use of force. Unlike crimes of violence, in the overwhelming majority of property offenses the victim is not present at the crime scene. Property crimes comprise the majority of Index crimes known to police, with approximately seven of eight offenses falling in this category. The total value of all property lost through these offenses was estimated at $16.6 billion in 2001 (excluding arson). Rates of property crime victimizations fell dramatically over the past quarter century, this drop being especially dramatic in the 1990s (see Table 3.3).

Burglary

Burglary is the unlawful entry of a structure to commit a felony or theft. The entry may or may not be forced (breaking a window, for example). Roughly two-thirds of burglaries known to police are residential crimes, with the remaining one-third involving commercial structures. Offenses for which the time of the crime was reported in 2000 reveal that 55 percent of burglaries occur in daylight hours with the remaining 45 percent happening at night. As is the case with robbery, burglary is overwhelmingly a youthful male activity. In 2000, 86.4 percent of suspects arrested for burglary were males, and 62 percent had not reached their twenty-fifth birthday. Almost 7 of 10 arrestees were white.

burglary unlawful entry of a structure to commit a felony or theft

In their study of 105 active burglars in St. Louis, Missouri, Richard Wright and Scott Decker (1994) discovered that these street criminals did not break into homes because of a need for money to realize some long-range goal. Rather, their crimes were motivated by more immediate financial problems. Money derived from criminal activity was spent in the following manner:

1. *To keep the party going.* Almost three of four subjects said they used money derived from burglary for good times, which typically involved purchasing drugs, most often cocaine.
2. *To keep up appearances.* Approximately half of the burglars motivated to steal for financial reasons stated they used the money to buy status items, especially clothing. One subject noted, "See, I go to steal money and go buy me some clothes. See, I likes to look good. I likes to dress" (p. 43).
3. *To keep things together.* About half of the burglars interviewed said they spent a portion of the money they made from breaking into homes for daily living expenses, such as food, shelter, and clothing for their children. A minority of the subjects spent all their illegally derived profits for this purpose.

Criminologists often make a distinction between novice or amateur burglars and professionals. Novices are typically young, lower-, or middle-class males who will engage in only a few burglaries and then abandon this criminal activity, or those who are beginning an extended criminal career. Miethe and McCorkle (1998, p. 140) note that "novices are not firmly entrenched in a burglar identity or criminal subcultures." Comprising the "elite" of the burglary world, professionals are relatively few in number. They differ from

table 3.3

National Crime Victimization Survey
Property Crime Trends, 1973–1999

Adjusted property victimization rates
Number of victimizations per 1,000 households

YEAR	TOTAL PROPERTY CRIME	BURGLARY	THEFT	MOTOR VEHICLE THEFT
1973	519.9	110.0	390.8	19.1
1974	551.5	111.8	421.0	18.8
1975	553.6	110.0	424.1	19.5
1976	544.2	106.7	421.0	16.5
1977	544.1	106.2	420.9	17.0
1978	532.6	103.1	412.0	17.5
1979	531.8	100.9	413.4	17.5
1980	496.1	101.4	378.0	16.7
1981	497.2	105.9	374.1	17.2
1982	468.3	94.1	358.0	16.2
1983	428.4	84.0	329.8	14.6
1984	399.2	76.9	307.1	15.2
1985	385.4	75.2	296.0	14.2
1986	372.7	73.8	284.0	15.0
1987	379.6	74.6	289.0	16.0
1988	378.4	74.3	286.7	17.5
1989	373.4	67.7	286.5	19.2
1990	348.9	64.5	263.8	20.6
1991	353.7	64.6	266.8	22.2
1992	325.3	58.6	248.2	18.5
1993	318.9	58.2	241.7	19.0
1994	310.2	56.3	235.1	18.8
1995	290.5	49.3	224.3	16.9
1996	266.3	47.2	205.7	13.5
1997	248.3	44.6	189.9	13.8
1998	217.4	38.5	168.1	10.8
1999	198.0	34.1	153.9	10.0

Note: Estimates for 1993 and beyond are based on collection year, whereas earlier estimates are based on data year. 1973–1991 data adjusted to make data comparable to data after the redesign.

Source: "Criminal Victimization 2000 with Trends 1973–1999," U.S. Department of Justice, Bureau of Justice Statistics.

amateurs in terms of technical skills, organizational abilities, and the status accorded them by other criminals and police. These individuals also have well-established contacts (professional "fences") for quickly selling stolen merchandise (Cromwell et al., 1991).

In many instances, skills learned in a noncriminal enterprise are effectively translated to illegal activities. Consider the following statement from a professional burglar (in Cromwell et al., 1991, p. 108):

> The military taught me what I needed to know as a burglar. Planning, that's what I learned in the Army. Laying out a map in your head, getting it all together and knowing who you're going to unload the stolen goods on before doing anything is also important. I guess my training in the Special Forces taught me to be sneaky and rehearse things in my mind ahead of time because, you know, you're scared. The military taught me to have confidence in myself.

Nationwide, people attempting to protect their homes from burglars via alarm systems have become a serious drain on law enforcement resources. According to the Justice Department, in 1998 police responded to 38 million burglar alarms at a cost of $1.5 billion—almost 98 percent of these calls for aid were false alarms. Annually, the time lost responding to false alarms by police in the United States is equivalent to the total work output of 35,000 officers. Burglar alarms are routinely triggered because homeowners do not understand their systems, the system was improperly installed, batteries are dead, or pets and insects move across motion detectors (Butterfield, 2003).

Larceny–Theft

Larceny–theft is the unlawful taking of property from the possession of another. This general category of crime includes shoplifting, pocket picking, purse snatching, theft of goods from inside motor vehicles, theft of motor vehicle parts and accessories, bicycle theft, and stealing money from coin-operated machines and telephones. Larceny–theft is the most common Index offense and accounts for more than 50 of these offenses. In a typical year, slightly more than one of three arrestees are female. This makes larceny–theft the Index crime with both the greatest number and percentage of female offenders.

Although overall theft of motor vehicle accessories dropped sharply in the mid-1990s, the number of air bags stolen increased dramatically, with estimates ranging from between 50,000 and 75,000 thefts annually. Air bags are easy to steal and sell, and air bag thefts cost the insurance industry an estimated $50 million a year. The thief (who is often recruited by dishonest auto body shops) gets between $100 and $600 per bag, whereas the shop defrauds the consumer or insurance company by selling the stolen air bag for up to $1,500 (Blake, 1995). With consumers becoming increasingly safety conscious and manufacturers outfitting more vehicles with sophisticated and expensive air bags, this crime is likely to grow in both volume and monetary loss.

The other high-incidence crime in this category is shoplifting, which results in billions of dollars of stolen merchandise each year. One study concluded that every U.S. consumer pays an extra $100 annually for purchases to partially compensate store owners for their losses ("More Than Sticky Fingers," 1988). Most studies of this offense identify three categories of offenders (Cleary, 1986). The *soft-core shoplifter* accounts for approximately 75 percent of individuals detained or arrested for shoplifting. These offenders who had no previous arrest for shoplifting, steal items for personal use and do not consider themselves criminals. A study of 1,700 shoplifters arrested for the first time over a 5-year period found that the average offender had committed this crime almost 100 times before being caught (Connor in Cleary, 1986). When offenders were asked why they stole merchandise from stores, typical responses included some version of the following: "Stores write off the losses on their taxes," and "I've spent plenty of money in that store and I'm entitled to get a little of it back." The lack of funds (at least at the time of the offense) does not appear to be a prominent factor for the average shoplifter. A study of 1,000 shoplifters in Texas discovered that 88 percent responded

larceny–theft unlawful taking of property from the possession of another; this category of crime includes shoplifting, pocket picking, purse snatching, and bicycle theft, as well as a number of other offenses

affirmatively when asked if they had the money to pay for the item they stole (Connor in Cleary, 1986). Most of the arrestees in this category are females, and about 20 percent are under 21 years of age.

One of every five arrestees is a *hard-core shoplifter*. These individuals steal goods for their personal use and have a criminal record either for shoplifting or for some other offense. The *professional shoplifter* (or booster) steals on a regular basis and sells the items, often to a fence (an individual who buys and then resells stolen merchandise). Professionals in this category make up no more than 5 percent of all shoplifters. Some observers think that the total number of boosters regularly "working" stores is quite small (Cleary, 1986). From what we know of these offenders, most work in pairs, regularly travel from one city to another, and can steal hundreds of thousands of dollars of merchandise in a year's time.

Professional shoplifters are clever and skillful and use specially designed implements to help them steal. Booster boxes look like wrapped packages, but have concealed openings or a false bottom to hide stolen goods. Booster jackets and coats have deep pockets sewn into the linings (Cameron, 1964). An adept professional can wrap a suit around a clothes hanger with a quick flick of the wrist and have the garment inside a booster box in 2 or 3 seconds. Unless someone, such as a security person, is looking right at the offender from the proper angle, this type of theft is almost impossible to detect.

Motor Vehicle Theft

motor vehicle theft
attempted or completed theft of automobiles, trucks, buses, and motorcycles

As defined by the UCR, **motor vehicle theft** is the attempted or completed theft of an automobile, truck, bus, or motorcycle. In the post–World War II era, this has been one of the fastest-growing crimes in the United States. In 2001, 1,226,457 cars, trucks, and buses were stolen, or approximately 1 of every 150 motor vehicles. Also, in a recent year, 1 of every 32 registered Miami motor vehicles was stolen, the highest auto theft rate in the nation. In 2001, automobiles accounted for just under three of every four vehicles stolen nationwide with autos comprising 70.1 percent of motor vehicle thefts in the western states and 87.9 percent of such thefts in northeastern states. Of the remaining vehicles stolen, the majority were trucks and buses. In 2001, the total value of all vehicles stolen was approximately $8.2 billion, with an average value per vehicle at the time of theft of $6,646.

Arrest data indicate that the typical car thief is a white male under 25 years of age with a prior arrest record. However, as Terrance Miethe and Richard McCorkle (1998) note, because this profile is based on such a small percentage of car thieves (approximately 85 percent of motor vehicle thefts are not cleared by arrest), it must be viewed with caution.

Arguably the most serious form of motor vehicle theft is carjacking—the attempted or completed theft of a vehicle by force or the threat of force. In more than 80 percent of cases a weapon is used, and, in completed carjackings, those weapons were typically firearms. Between 1992 and 1996, just less than 49,000 such crimes occurred annually in the United States (Klaus, 1999). One explanation for the relatively sudden rise of this form of auto theft is that many criminals have been forced to change their tactics. Car alarms and home security systems have made it much more difficult for amateur and opportunistic thieves to steal cars. It is easier for this type of auto thief to attack people while they are in a vehicle typically at a stop sign or traffic light or getting into or out of their cars.

The profit motive has been responsible for the overwhelming amount of motor vehicle theft in the United States over the past 35 years or about as long as organized crime has been involved in this offense. Although antitheft alarms and devices, such as the Club, have contributed to declining rates of auto theft of late, these mechanisms are no match for a skilled offender. A thief will gain entry to a locked vehicle by breaking the driver's side window. If an alarm goes off, the hood is popped open, and the alarm siren is disabled or smashed. When a Club is encountered, thieves cut through the steering wheel, and, if necessary, break the steering column. A New York City police detective (Brenner in Onishi, 1995, p. CY10) noted that it takes auto thieves "usually less than 20 seconds to start a car." A vehicle disabled during the course of a crime may be towed away by well-prepared offenders.

In some cities, 50 percent or more of stolen vehicles are taken to "chop shops" and disassembled. As of the mid-1990s in New York City, organized-crime–employed "steal men" received between $400 and $600 per stolen vehicle, and the chop shop crew of dismantlers was paid $1,800. Whereas an intact car may have a value of $5,000, the parts from that same vehicle can be worth between $15,000 and $20,000 when sold separately. Because the demand for parts for these vehicles is strong, reliable cars with a long road life are at the top of the stolen car list. This criminal enterprise also depends on illegal parts distributors and thousands of unscrupulous auto part store owners who knowingly (because of the heavily discounted price) buy stolen goods. Stolen parts are also sold in the black market and swap meets. Speaking of stolen Honda parts in his city, a Dallas police officer (Pierce in Coleman, 1999, p. 1A) asked, "Would you rather pay $500 in a store or $50 on the black market?" As of 1998, 5 of the 10 cars most likely to be stolen were Toyotas (especially the Camry), and the other 5 were Hondas, most notably the Accord EX model (McGoey, 1999).

Professional auto thieves working the lucrative "buy back" or "strip and run" scheme strip a car completely and discard the frame, which eventually is recovered by the police. Declared a total loss by the insurance company, the car frame (no longer considered stolen property) is eventually resold to a salvage company. At this point, organized crime thieves buy the frame, reassemble the car, and legally sell it.

Of the approximately 60 percent of stolen vehicles that are recovered, four of five have been vandalized or stripped. Forty percent of those never recovered (some 200,000 a year) are sent overseas. In light of this last statistic, it is hardly surprising that 20 of the 30 cities with the highest motor vehicle theft rates are near seaports or a national border (Canada or Mexico).

Arson

The UCR defines **arson** as any willful or malicious burning or attempt to burn, with or without the intent to defraud, a dwelling house, public building, motor vehicle, aircraft, or personal property of another. Only those fires that investigators determine are willfully set are classified as arson; fires of a suspicious or unknown origin are excluded. Arson statistics are not included with other Index crimes because the data are typically incomplete. Arson is primarily a big-city crime, with rates ranging from 19 in rural areas to 55.7 per 100,000 in urban areas with 1 million or more residents. Forty-four percent of arsons known to authorities in 2001 involve "structures" (homes, factories, public buildings, etc.), 32.5 percent were directed at "mobile property" (motor vehicles and trailers, for example), and 25.4 percent at other forms of property (crops, forests, etc.).

A government official who cochaired a task force on this offense noted that "Arsons are extremely difficult to solve. . . . Evidence burns" ("Panel Says Churches Are Still Targets," 1997). Arrest data from 2001 indicate that the typical arsonist is male (84.1 percent), white (76.9 percent), and under 18 years of age (49.4 percent), with this offense having an especially high rate of juvenile participation. A disproportionate number of child and juvenile arsonists come from the middle class.

Just as motor vehicle thieves steal cars for a variety of reasons, adult firestarters have different motives for their crimes. The following typology is a compilation of the work of Boudreau, Kwan, Faragher, and Denault, (1977); Inciardi (1970); and McCaghy (1980):

Revenge arsonists start fires to punish people they believe have wronged them in some capacity. Destroying the property of these individuals is a way of evening the score or deterring people from harming the arsonist in the future. Neighbors torching a crack house is an example of revenge arson, as is the burning of African American churches. From the arsonists' point of view, African Americans are being paid back for taking white jobs, being disrespectful toward whites, and/or not knowing their place (subordinate to whites) in society.

arson willful or malicious burning or attempt to burn, with or without the attempt to defraud, a dwelling house, public building, motor vehicle, aircraft, or personal property of another

Vandalism arson is a form of firestarting engaged in by both adults and teenagers. This crime has been especially problematic in deteriorating neighborhoods of industrial cities in the Northeast and Midwest. The migration of people to the suburbs in conjunction with closing factories has resulted in the abandonment of thousands of structures in these urban areas that are targeted by firestarters.

Crime concealment arson is a way for an offender to hide another crime. Examples include murder, burglary, and embezzlement. In the latter case, an accountant who had been embezzling from an employer for months (or years) may hear about an upcoming independent audit and set fire to the office in which ledgers he or she has altered are kept.

Sabotage arson is a fire deliberately set during labor disputes, race riots, prison riots, and other disturbances involving a large number of people. During prison riots, inmates often set fire to facilities in order to protest their living conditions, divert attention from an escape attempt, or gain access to prisoners they believe have been cooperating with corrections officials. During race riots, African Americans have set fires to those non-African American–owned local businesses they believe have been financially exploiting them.

Arson for profit refers to those fires typically set to defraud insurance companies. According to James Brady (1983), former director of the Boston Arson Strike Force, "escape fires" are set (or arranged) by landlords and small-business owners to collect insurance settlements on apartments and real estate holdings deemed unprofitable. Arson for profit also includes burning down the restaurant, store, or factory of one's economic rival(s).

Excitement arson are those fires started by people who not only like to watch things burn but also are excited by the chain of events their crimes trigger in terms of mobilizing firefighters, emergency rescue personnel, police officers, and the media. "Vanity arsonists" not only start fires but also notify fire departments and, in some cases (unbeknownst to authorities), help battle the conflagration (Impocco and Guttman, 1993).

Although arson is classified as a property crime, if a structure is inhabited at the time of the fire, the occupants may be seriously injured or killed. A person arrested for arson will be charged with first-degree arson if the premises were occupied and second-degree arson if the structure was vacant (Inciardi, 1987). If someone was killed in the blaze, the defendant may be charged with felony murder, a crime that carries the death penalty in many states.

Hate Crimes

hate crimes criminal acts against persons, property, or society that are motivated in part or whole by the offender's bias against the victim's race, religion, disability, sexual orientation, or ethnicity/nationality

Hate crimes, or bias crimes, are criminal acts committed against persons, property, or society that are motivated in part or whole by the offender's bias against the victim's race, religion, disability, sexual orientation, or ethnicity/nationality. Hate crimes include intimidating victims and destruction of property as well as the aforementioned Index crimes of murder, aggravated assault, burglary, and so on.

To be punished under a hate crimes statute, a person must have caused bodily injury or attempted to cause bodily injury. These laws do not apply to hate speech, name calling, or any manner of nonviolent expressive conduct. The underlying logic of hate crime laws is that bias crimes are more likely to provoke retaliatory offenses, inflict emotional injury on victims, traumatize other members of the victim's group, and instigate community unrest and problems ("Hate Crime Legislation and the First Amendment," 2001).

Of the 9,726 hate crimes reported to law enforcement authorities in 2001, just less than 45 percent were motivated by racial bias, 18.8 percent by religious bias, 14.3 percent by sexual orientation bias, and 21.6 percent by ethnicity/national origin bias. Crimes of violence accounted for 65 percent of these offenses, with property crimes making up the remaining 35 percent. The most frequently occurring hate crime was

John William King arrives at the Jasper, Texas, Courthouse for the second day of testimony during his capital murder trial. King was convicted of dragging an African American man, James Byrd Jr., to death behind a pickup truck in June 1998.

intimidation, which accounted for 39 percent of total offenses. Of known offenders, 65.5 percent were white and 20.3 percent African American.

Hate crimes can be committed by individuals, groups, or mobs. In 1999, a white supremacist walked into the North Valley Jewish Community Center near Los Angeles and fired more than 70 bullets, wounding three children, a teenage counselor, and one adult. He said he wanted to send a wake up call to America to kill Jews. A few hours later, he murdered a Filipino American postal worker because of the color of his skin (Stewart 2001; Borger, 2001). In Georgia, a carload of teenagers yelled racial slurs at an African American student telling her to "go back to Africa." Then the driver struck her with the car.

According to a report issued by the Southern Poverty Law Center, 537 hate groups existed in the United States as of 1998 ("Hate Group Count Tops 500," 1999). Of this number, 163 were Ku Klux Klan chapters, 151 neo-Nazi groups, 48 racist skinhead organizations, 29 black separatist groups, and 84 organizations that "followed a hodge-podge of hate-based doctrines." Although the total membership of these groups is relatively small, the potential for spreading racist propaganda has increased dramatically as a result of the Internet.

HateWatch.org has documented between 450 and 500 "hard-core" hate sites on the Internet and another 1,750 sites that are considered "problematic" regarding the circulation of inflammatory literature. Many of these sites have inoffensive sounding names, such as the Christian Bible Study, that are rife with hate material. For example, the aforementioned organization categorizes Jews as the children of Satan and implies that they should be killed (Bloom, 2000). However, the relation between these sites and hate crimes is unclear. Over the July 4 weekend in 1999, self-styled white supremacist Benjamin Nathaniel Smith went on a shooting rampage targeting Asians, African Americans, and Jews and later killed himself. Investigators speculated that Smith was inspired by material he found on the World Church of the Creator Web site, a charge the founder of that movement denied. HateWatch notes that many of these sites now "post disclaimers and warnings to protect them from liability and lawsuits if their patrons decide to attack one of the targets mentioned on their Web site" (Bloom, 2000, p. 2).

Stalking

A community college instructor was harassed by a former girlfriend shortly after ending their relationship. When he married and moved to another state the couple was barraged with unwanted and often obscene phone calls (up to 50 a day) and e-mails; his wife was routinely followed to and from work. The victims obtained a civil stalking protection order from local authorities but the abuse continued. Even after their tormentor was indicted by a grand jury, the harassment persisted.

With the exception of the occasional, highly publicized case that involves a celebrity or politician, stalking may be considered the nation's forgotten crime. **Stalking** is a "course of conduct directed at a specific person that involves repeated visual or physical proximity, nonconsensual communication, or verbal, written or implied threats, or a combination thereof, that would cause a reasonable person fear" (Tjaden and Thoennes, 1998, p. 2). California passed the first antistalking law in 1990, and by 1995 every state and the District of Columbia had enacted similar legislation. Although much has been written about this phenomenon over the past 15 years (especially celebrity stalking), a 1998 nationally representative telephone survey of 8,000 men and 8,000 women 18 years of age and older was the first comprehensive study of stalking (Tjaden and Thoennes, 1998).

Analysis of survey data indicated that stalking is considerably more prevalent than previously thought. Slightly more than 8 percent of women and 2.4 percent of men reported being stalked sometime in their lives. Seventy-eight percent of stalking victims are female, and 87 percent of stalking offenders are male. Women are most likely to be stalked (62 percent of female victims) by a spouse or ex-spouse, cohabiting partner or ex-partner, or a date or ex-date, whereas men are typically stalked (70 percent of male victims) by an acquaintance or stranger. Slightly more than four of five women stalked by current or former husbands, or cohabiting partners were also physically assaulted by that same individual at some point in their relationship. Thirty-one percent of females stalked by husbands or ex-husbands or cohabiting partners had been sexually assaulted by that same partner.

The overall pattern of victimization is different for men and women. Whereas an equal number of males and females report that they received letters or unwanted items and their property was vandalized, women were significantly more likely than men to say that stalkers followed them, spied on them, or appeared near their home, place of work, or place of recreation.

Women were also much more likely than men to report that they received unsolicited phone calls. When coupled with a history of battering and sexual abuse suffered at the hands of offenders, it is clear that stalking is a much more personal, physically threatening experience for female victims. Concerning male victimization, the authors speculate that some stalking occurs in the context of intragang rivalries (Tjaden and Thoennes, 1998).

About half of all stalking victims reported their problems to police, and about 50 percent of the individuals in this group stated that the suspect had been arrested. Overall, 12 percent of stalking cases resulted in criminal prosecution. Although antistalking laws have afforded victims a measure of protection, critics contend that many of these statutes will have to be refined if they are to be more than minimally effective.

> **stalking** behavior directed at a specific individual involving repeated verbal or nonverbal acts that cause a reasonable person fear

Prostitution

Prostitution is the sale of sex for money. Often thought of as a "victimless" crime because both individuals consent to a sex act, it is difficult to estimate both the number of acts of prostitution that occur annually and the number of people who make all or part of their living from prostitution. According to some estimates there are between 100,000 and 500,000 prostitutes in the United States (Clinard and Meier, 1992) and as many as 100,000 child prostitutes in the United States and Canada (Clayton, 1996). Data from

> **prostitution** the sale of sex of oneself or another person for money

recent Uniform Crime Reports indicate that approximately 100,000 people are arrested annually for engaging in prostitution; two of five individuals are male (Siegel, 1998).

The relationship between prostitution and drugs may not be as straightforward as most observers believe, that is, drug use causes prostitution. Criminologist Jocelyn M. Pollock (1999) notes that some prostitutes claim that they have to be in a drug-induced state in order to exchange sex for money. In these instances, the drug/prostitution relationship is circular—"women use drugs to help themselves perform as prostitutes, but they also engage in prostitution to help them buy drugs" (p. 56). Prostitution is associated with a significant amount of criminal activity. For example, in addition to acting as part-time drug dealers, prostitutes can rob their clients with the help of a pimp (a prostitute's agent, boss, protector, and, oftentimes, lover).

The majority of streetwalkers and bar girls live in a dangerous world. They are at risk of being physically abused by customers and pimps, arrested by police, and infected with sexually transmitted diseases including HIV. Streetwalkers are especially vulnerable when they get into a car with an unknown customer. *Mission-oriented* serial killers who believe it is their job to rid society of some undesirable category of people have often targeted prostitutes as their primary victims (Holmes and DeBurger, 1998).

Drunk Driving

Of the more that 120 million licensed drivers in the United States, almost 100 million drink alcohol to one degree or another (Clinard and Meier, 1992). It has been estimated that as many as 5 percent of drivers on the road at any time Monday through Friday may be legally drunk, with that figure approaching 12 percent (one of eight drivers) on the weekend (Jacobs, 1986; "Drunk Driving," 1999). A driver with a blood alcohol level of 0.15 percent is 18 times more likely to be involved in a traffic accident than a nondrinking driver and 200 times more likely to be involved in a *fatal* accident than a nondrinking motorist (Jacobs, 1986; Csere, 1998). Whereas 18,210 Americans were murdered in 1997, more than 16,000 individuals died as a result of alcohol-related traffic accidents. Another 327,000 people were injured in crashes where one or more individuals was drinking. According to one estimate, 3 of every 10 Americans will be involved in an alcohol-related motor vehicle accident at some point in their lives ("Drunk Driving," 1999).

Traffic accidents are the primary cause of death for people between 6 and 28 years of age, and almost 50 percent of these crashes are alcohol related. After drinking at a fraternity party, a student at a prestigious eastern university drove his sports utility vehicle into a tree at a high rate of speed. Four passengers were killed and two injured (all college students) in the crash. On waking in the hospital, the driver was read his rights, arrested, and incarcerated. He was charged with negligent homicide, four counts of vehicular manslaughter, and driving while intoxicated (Massey, 2000).

Even though approximately 1.5 million people are arrested annually for drunk driving, the probability of being apprehended by law enforcement officials for this offense has been variously estimated between 1 in 2,000 (Ross, 1984) and 1 in 82 (Liu et al., 1997). Only those individuals driving very erratically as a result of drinking or people that are unlucky are likely to be stopped by police. No doubt the slim chance of apprehension by law enforcement personnel is a major reason why so many people drink and drive on a regular basis. Among other facts, Table 3.4 shows that people arrested for driving under the influence of alcohol are disproportionately between the ages of 21 and 39.

In one of the most comprehensive studies of drinking and driving ever conducted in the United States, Simon Liu and his colleagues (1997) interviewed more than 100,000 noninstitutionalized adults 18 years of age and older from all 50 states and the District of Columbia and asked them the following question: "During the past month how many times have you driven when you've had perhaps too much to drink?" Overall, 2.5 percent of the respondents admitted to at least one instance of alcohol impaired driving in the past 30 days. Based on these findings, the researchers estimated that there

table 3.4 Licensed Drivers and Arrests for Driving under the Influence (DUI), by Age, 1986 and 1997

| | 1997 | | | 1986 | | | PERCENT CHANGE IN RATES, 1986–97 |
| | Percent of | | Arrests per 100,000 Drivers | Percent of | | Arrests per 100,000 Drivers | |
AGE	Drivers	Arrests		Drivers	Arrests		
Total[a]	100%	100%	809	100%	100%	1,124	–28.0%
16–18	3.7	3.2	696	4.3	3.8	990	–29.7
19–20	3.2	5.3	1,353	3.8	6.8	2,006	–32.6
21–24	6.7	14.1	1,695	9.3	19.7	2,384	–28.9
25–29	10.0	16.9	1,372	12.9	22.0	1,924	–28.7
30–34	10.8	16.3	1,227	12.3	15.8	1,445	–15.1
35–39	11.5	15.8	1,105	11.1	11.1	1,122	–1.5
40–44	11.0	11.5	849	8.8	7.2	921	–7.9
45–49	9.7	7.4	620	7.0	4.9	783	–20.8
50–54	8.0	4.3	438	6.2	3.4	613	–28.6
55–59	6.1	2.3	309	6.1	2.4	446	–30.7
60–64	5.0	1.3	213	5.8	1.5	299	–28.8
65 or older	14.3	1.4	78	12.3	1.2	114	–31.6

Note: Percents may not add to 100% because of rounding.

[a]Total includes a few licensed drivers and arrests for persons under age 16.

Source: *Sourcebook of Criminal Justice Statistics, 1997.* U.S. Department of Justice, Office of Justice Programs, Bureau of Justice Statistics.

were 123 million episodes of this behavior in the adult population in 1993–101 million among males and 22 million among females.

As of August 2000, 32 states had laws that make it illegal to drive a motor vehicle with a blood alcohol concentration (BAC) of .10, and 18 states plus the District of Columbia set the limit 20 percent lower, a .08 BAC (Plungis, 2000). The average 170-pound male reaches a BAC of .08 after consuming five 12 ounce beers (4.5 percent alcohol by volume) over a 2-hour period, whereas a 120-pound female reaches that same level on drinking three beers over that same time span. Even at low levels of alcohol consumption, reaction time, in applying the brakes, for example, increases, and tracking and steering become more difficult ("How Effective Are '.08' Driving Laws?" 1999).

In October 2000, President Clinton signed a law requiring states to lower their BAC levels from .10 to .08 by 2004. States that fail to comply will lose 2 percent of their federal highway money with the penalty increasing by an additional 2 percent per year with an 8 percent maximum until 2007 ("Clinton Signs Lower Drunk Driving Limit . . . ," 2000).

However, it is unclear if a simple cause-and-effect relation exists between lower BACs and a reduction in accidents and fatalities related to drunk driving. A study by the National Highway and Traffic Safety Administration (NHTSA) concluded that, in addition to lower BACs, public information, the enforcement of drunk driving laws, and penalties such as the revocation of drivers' licenses also have to be considered ("How Effective Are '.08' Driving Laws?" 1999).

Although the certainty of arrest for drunk driving is low, in some jurisdictions the severity of punishment for this crime is quite high. Using a city rule intended to punish drug dealers, in February 1999, former New York City mayor Rudy Giuliani instituted a program in which individuals arrested for drunk driving had to surrender their vehicles to city officials. Even if drivers are acquitted of the drunk driving charge in a criminal court, they have to successfully sue the city in a civil court to get their cars back (Beals, 1999). City attorneys argue that just as drug dealers use their cars as instruments of crime, drunk drivers do the same. The constitutionality of this antidrunk driving strategy will certainly be challenged in the courts.

In 1997, a North Carolina man was sentenced to life in prison without parole for the death of two college students related to drunk driving. The prosecutor had sought the death penalty for the defendant who had two prior convictions of driving while alcohol impaired (Spaid, 1997).

Illegal Drugs

People use, abuse, and deal drugs for a variety of reasons: They do not have enough money or have too much; they are attempting to escape painful situations or seek adventure; they are depressed or overjoyed; they are bored or have too much to do. Regardless of whether people are pushed by emotional problems or pulled by the allure of money and excitement, drug use is learned and reinforced in a social context.

For whatever reason they initially use illegal drugs, the ingestion of these substances can lead to **drug dependence** (formerly called *drug addiction*), a condition that has three basic characteristics (Goode, 1991).

> **drug dependence** habitual use of a drug over an extended period of time

1. The user continues to ingest the drug over an extended period of time.
2. The user finds it difficult (if not impossible) to quit, taking drastic measures, such as stealing, dropping out of school or work, abandoning family and friends, to continue using the drug.
3. If the user stops ingesting the substance, he or she may experience painful physical symptoms as well as severe mental distress.

Drug dependence may well lead to criminal behavior. However, the association between drug use and crime is not a simple, straightforward cause-and-effect relationship. Drug use as a cause of criminal activity is only one of four feasible connections between these variables (Wilson and Herrnstein, 1985).

Not all motorcycle riders are outlaws, but outlaw motorcycle gangs are involved in a significant amount of criminal activity including illegal drug distribution and prostitution.

To begin, the relation between drugs and crime may be spurious, meaning there is no causal connection. For example, one or more factors, such as an individual's personality or extreme poverty, is responsible for both occurrences—drug use and crime. Second, direct causality (drug use causes crime) has two sources. The pharmacological effects of drugs may produce behavioral changes, such as increased impulsivity and/or higher levels of aggression, that result in the commission of crime. Also, the prohibitive cost of illegal drugs may cause people to engage in criminal activity to support their drug taking (especially if they are physically and/or psychologically dependent on these substances). The drug–crime relationship may be conditionally causal; that is, drug use may cause criminal behavior provided some other condition(s) exist. Drug use may result in criminal behavior among adolescents when they are in the company of peers and experience the peer pressure of other young males. Although the final alternative is rarely considered, the ingestion of certain drugs may reduce crime, most notably crimes of violence. Narcotics such as heroin produce drowsiness and reduce both tension and sexual activity.

Numerous studies, such as those conducted by the National Institute of Justice/Drug Use Forecasting Program, have consistently found an association between drug use and criminal behavior. In 27 of 34 cities, more than 60 percent of adult male arrestees tested positive for the presence of at least one of five drugs, ranging from a low of 50 percent in San Antonio to 77 percent in Atlanta. For female adult arrestees the median figure for drug use was 67 percent, ranging from 22 percent in Laredo, Texas, to 81 percent in New York City (*1999 Annual Report on Drug Use*, 2000). Figure 3.2 illustrates the prevalence of drug use among detained arrestees in five English sites

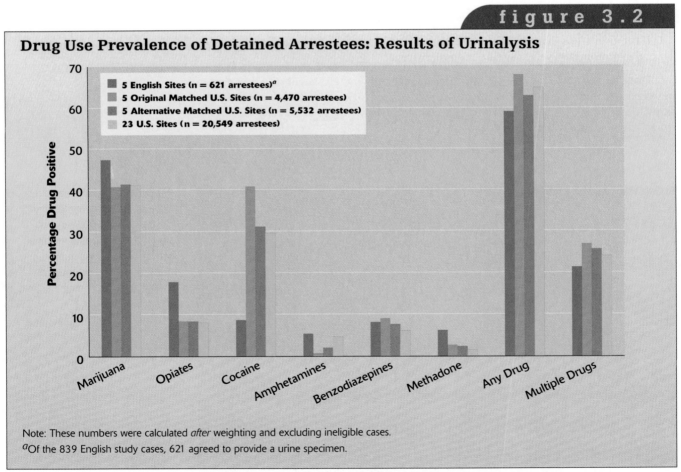

figure 3.2

Drug Use Prevalence of Detained Arrestees: Results of Urinalysis

Legend:
- 5 English Sites (n = 621 arrestees)[a]
- 5 Original Matched U.S. Sites (n = 4,470 arrestees)
- 5 Alternative Matched U.S. Sites (n = 5,532 arrestees)
- 23 U.S. Sites (n = 20,549 arrestees)

Categories: Marijuana, Opiates, Cocaine, Amphetamines, Benzodiazepines, Methadone, Any Drug, Multiple Drugs

Note: These numbers were calculated *after* weighting and excluding ineligible cases.
[a]Of the 839 English study cases, 621 agreed to provide a urine specimen.

Source: Taylor, Bruce and Trevor Bennet. 1999. "Comparing Drug Use Rates of Detained Arrestees in the United States and England." U.S. Department of Justice, Office of Justice Programs, National Institute of Justice.

(Cambridge, London, Manchester, Nottingham, and Sunderland) and 25 major U.S. cities. Note that the drugs of choice of these individuals are marijuana and cocaine and that between 20 and 30 percent of arrestees tested positive for multiple drugs. Keep in mind that some unknown portion of this observed association between drug use and persons arrested for committing a crime is, in fact, a cause-and-effect relationship, and that this percentage may be quite small.

We can be certain of at least one fact regarding the crime–illegal drugs association: Arresting, prosecuting, and imprisoning individuals for drug violations accounts for a significant amount of the total monetary expenditure of the criminal justice system. In recent years, approximately 10 percent of all arrests (about 1.5 million annually) have been for drug-related activities (possession and trafficking). In 1970, 16.3 percent of all inmates in federal prisons were convicted of drug offenses, a figure that increased to 59.5 percent in 1997. In 1996, more than $30 billion was spent imprisoning individuals who had a history of drug and/or alcohol abuse, were convicted of drug and/or alcohol violations, were high on one or more drugs and/or alcohol at the time of their crime, or committed an offense to obtain money to buy drugs ("Cost of Crime," 1999).

Figure 3.3 illustrates that drug offense arrests for juveniles and adults increased in the early to mid-1990s and then leveled off in the later years of that decade. This arrest increase could be a function of (1) more people using drugs, (2) police allocating more resources to drug crimes, or (3) some combination of the two.

Drug Use

The use of illicit drugs escalated in the United States in the post–World War II era. Marijuana, hashish, and LSD were especially popular during the "counterculture" and "antiwar" (the Vietnam conflict) years of the late 1960s and 1970s. Over the past 20 years, cocaine has been the drug of choice among middle-class and upper-middle-class users, whereas less expensive, and highly addictive crack-cocaine was pervasive among the nation's poor, inner-city residents.

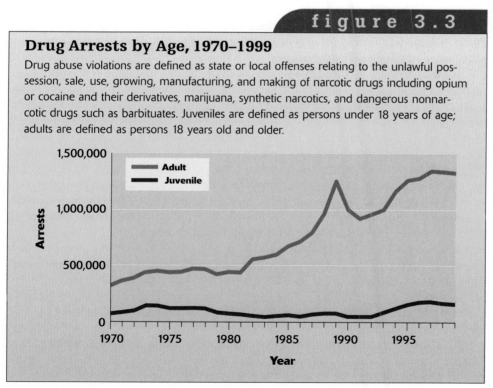

figure 3.3

Drug Arrests by Age, 1970–1999

Drug abuse violations are defined as state or local offenses relating to the unlawful possession, sale, use, growing, manufacturing, and making of narcotic drugs including opium or cocaine and their derivatives, marijuana, synthetic narcotics, and dangerous nonnarcotic drugs such as barbituates. Juveniles are defined as persons under 18 years of age; adults are defined as persons 18 years old and older.

Source: "FBI Uniform Crime Report—Crime in America 2000." U.S. Department of Justice, Bureau of Justice Statistics.

A 1993 nationwide survey of 50,000 junior and senior high school students revealed a marked increase in marijuana use (and smaller rises in the use of other drugs) among high school students. Data from the 1997 National High School Drug Abuse Society revealed that drug abuse among individuals 12 to 17 years of age was up as 11.4 percent of respondents admitted using an illicit drug within the past month. Although marijuana was the preferred drug in this age group, a total of 3.9 million teenagers used heroin for the first time in 1996; this latter number was a significant increase over the 2.2 million who used that narcotic for the first time in 1995.

High rates of drug use by young people coupled with a forthcoming "demographic explosion" of this age group does not bode well for the overall substance abuse problem in the United States. Speaking of the age–drug-use-rate relationship, Richard Clayton (in Kolata, 1996, p. B10) stated, "By 2010 we will have more teenagers than at any time in history. We are at the front end of what could be a disaster for the whole society."

The Drug Distribution System

The simple fact that citizens of the United States have a voracious appetite for mind-altering drugs and that most of these substances are illegal has led to a complex system of drug distribution that spans five continents and is unprecedented in terms of its economic might and ability to influence policy makers and the politicians of numerous countries. U.S. citizens spent almost $60 *billion* a year on drugs in the late 1990s, a figure greater than the gross national product of New Zealand (*World Almanac 2000,* 1999)

Just as organized crime in the United States met the demand for illegal alcohol during the Prohibition in the 1920s, today an assortment of criminals from different racial and ethnic groups in the United States and other countries is providing a similar service in the much more lucrative business of producing and distributing illegal drugs. Following is a classification and breakdown of the international drug distribution system as outlined by Michael Lyman (1987, pp. 62–63) and Joseph Albini (1992, pp. 92–103).

Growers plant, nurture, and harvest coca plants and opium poppies. By the early 1990s, well more than 520,000 acres were under coca cultivation in Bolivia, Peru, and Colombia, with growers employing between 500,000 and 1,500,000 people. Inasmuch as growing coca plants is labor intensive, requiring approximately 225 days of work from the beginning of the growth process until the plants reach maturity (Morales, 1989), hundreds of thousands of people earn much, if not all, of their income from this initial stage of the illegal drug business.

Manufacturers are involved in a process of changing raw materials, so to speak (coca plants and opium poppies), into finished products, the street-saleable drugs of cocaine and heroin. Regarding the production of cocaine, "mixers," "pit-laborers," and "pasters" are engaged in a chemical process that transforms coca leaves with a cocaine content of 0.5 percent into a paste that may have a cocaine content as high as 90 percent, although the drug that reaches the consumer is usually no more than 40 percent pure. This procedure takes place in rain forests and in villages on the outskirts of towns in the central Andes Mountains (Peru) (Morales, 1989). In some cases, a powerful individual will serve as both grower and manufacturer and possibly the importer as well.

According to sociologist Joseph Albini (1992), the next step in the distribution process requires the interaction and cooperation of three players: the importer, the smuggler, and the trafficker/primary distributor. The *importer* devises a plan by which the newly refined drug, now ready for shipment, will reach its final destination, most often the United States, Europe, and Japan. This may entail, in part, bribery and intimidation of officials ranging from rural police officers to officials at the highest level of government. Because importers often have a significant financial investment in these illegal substances, they frequently make enormous profits.

Inasmuch as an estimated 75 percent of all illegal drugs consumed in the United States come from other countries, the role of the *smuggler* is vital to the overall distribution system. Lyman (1987) notes that smuggling activities generally are distributed via one of the following methods: (1) private and commercial aircraft, (2) boat and ship, (3) ground vehicles (cars, trucks, trailers, etc.), and (4) body packing. Private planes with their cargos of cocaine and marijuana fly across the U.S.–Mexico border and land on lightly traveled highways, country roads, swamps, even fields. Once on the ground, they are met by trucks (which often illuminate the landing point with their headlights) that will transport the illicit cargo to distribution points throughout the country. A large oceangoing vessel (called a "mother ship") with a shipment of drugs will rest in international waters off the coast of the United States where it is met by numerous smaller boats. These latter vessels will carry reduced drug payloads to the mainland. Ground vehicles transport drugs into the United States as they cross into those states that border Mexico (California, Arizona, New Mexico, and Texas). Smugglers hide their illegal cargo in false-bottom gas tanks, hidden compartments, and other "inventive methods of concealment" (Lyman, 1987, p. 137).

"Body packers" attempt to conceal drugs (usually high-priced substances such as heroin and cocaine) on their persons as they enter the United States by plane or train. Female smugglers sometimes fill condoms with drugs and then insert them into their vaginas prior to going through customs. Other smugglers put drugs into balloons that are swallowed and later retrieved after vomiting or sifting through feces after defecation. Albini (1992, p. 98) notes that "One can safely conjecture that a substantial amount of cocaine has been brought into the United States from Colombia using this method. However, on occasion, digestive acids will eat through the balloon unleashing the contents and killing the smuggler in short order from a massive drug overdose."

The *trafficker/primary distributor* allocates the illegal drugs (often in significant quantities) once they have reached the port of entry by way of smugglers. Found in virtually every major city in the United States, *distributors* deal in multipound lots of cocaine, heroin, and/or marijuana. These individuals (some of whom have legitimate "front" occupations, such as bankers or attorneys) regularly resell the drugs they receive from traffickers. Distributors are usually well known to local law enforcement authorities (Lyman, 1987).

Dealers sell drugs to individual consumers. Because they are much more visible than those higher up on the drug distribution ladder, dealers are more likely to be observed, arrested, and convicted for their activities. Small-time *dealer-users* are often their own worst enemy. Frequently under the mind-altering influence of their own products, these individuals exercise poor judgement and often end up selling drugs to undercover officers. Fearful of arrest and incarceration, many of these individuals are turned into informers and used by police in their pursuit of distributors and traffickers.

Although drug *consumers* are not, by definition, part of the distribution chain, they are, as Albini (1992, pp. 93–94) correctly notes, "the most vital structural-functional component of syndication." Without the constant, heavy demand of consumers in the United States and other rich, industrially developed nations, all of the individuals involved in the illegal trade from field hands in Peru to a small army of urban dealer-users would be searching for other means of employment.

Organized Crime

Of the numerous definitions of **organized crime** (OC) offered by the FBI, law enforcement agencies, and criminologists, the most comprehensive and useful delineation of this phenomenon is the one presented by Howard Abadinsky (1997, pp. 7–8): For Abadinsky, OC has the following characteristics or attributes:

> *Nonideological.* OC groups are not motivated by political beliefs or ideological concerns. Their goals are simply money and power.
>
> *Hierarchical.* An OC group has a vertical or stratified power structure with three or more permanent ranks. A crucial point here is that authority is inherent in the position and not the person who occupies that position.
>
> *Self-perpetuating.* OC groups are designed to "persist through time" beyond the life of current members. The fact that authority resides in the position as opposed to the individual facilitates this goal.

organized crime self-perpetuating, hierarchical, nonideological group often with a specialized division of labor that exists for the purpose of committing crime for profit

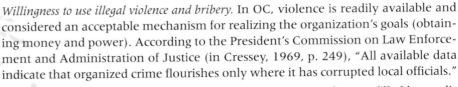

Willingness to use illegal violence and bribery. In OC, violence is readily available and considered an acceptable mechanism for realizing the organization's goals (obtaining money and power). According to the President's Commission on Law Enforcement and Administration of Justice (in Cressey, 1969, p. 249), "All available data indicate that organized crime flourishes only where it has corrupted local officials."

Specialization/division of labor. All OC groups have positions that are filled by qualified members. In addition to an *enforcer,* "if a group is sophisticated enough," it may have a *fixer,* the individual who bribes criminal justice officials and politicians, and a *money mover,* the individual who "launders" or cleans money obtained by criminal activity usually through banks and who also may invest some of these funds in legitimate businesses (Abadinsky, 1997, p. 7).

Monopolistic. OC groups do not like competition and will strive to dominate a particular area (city or section of that city), legitimate business (trucking, for example), or illegitimate enterprise (prostitution and drug distribution). An OC monopoly is established and maintained through corruption and intimidation.

Governed by rules and regulations. Like any other organization, OC has established rules and regulations that members must follow. Abadinsky (1997, p. 7) notes that individuals who violate these rules are more likely to be "fired upon" (shot) than fired.

Although the attributes of OC have been clearly spelled out by Abadinsky, researchers are divided on the question of just how organized is organized crime? In other words, do some or all OC groups resemble the highly structured organization implied in the definition of OC offered by Abadinsky and others? According to Jay S. Albanese (1989), three primary models of OC function in the United States: (1) the national conspiracy model; (2) the local, ethnic group model; and (3) the enterprise model.

The national conspiracy model is discussed by criminologist Donald Cressey in his book *Theft of a Nation* (1969), which is an extensive revision of a report he prepared for the President's 1967 Crime Commission. Cressey argued that a nationwide alliance of 24 "tightly knit" crime "families" operates in the United States. Controlled by a commission of the rulers of the most powerful families, members of the Mafia, or Cosa Nostra ("our thing"), are all Italians or Sicilians or of Italian or Sicilian descent. With approximately 900 members and 9,000 associates, five of these families operate in the New York City area, and they take in more than $1 billion in profits (Cook, 1991) from a variety of illegal activities especially gambling, loansharking, and drug dealing.

The local, ethnic group model of OC hypothesizes that "bonds of kinship—not crime or some network conspiracy—are what ties some Italian crime families together" (Ianni and Reuss-Ianni, 1972, p. 151). Anthropologist Francis Ianni lived with a crime family for 2 years and concluded that these groups "are structured by action rather than by a series of statutes" (p. 153). Leadership positions down to "middle management" are assigned on the basis of kinship, and the transfer of money does not take place through formal channels but is "part of the close kin-organization of the family" (p. 154). OC families, therefore, are closely organized at the local level, often comprised of individuals who share a common ethnic heritage (Albanese, 1991).

Some Italian crime families have been significantly weakened by a decade of aggressive police investigation, numerous arrests, and the successful prosecution of high-ranking members. In 1992, John Gotti, the reputed leader of the New York City's Gambino crime family, was convicted of numerous offenses and sentenced to life in prison without parole. With Gotti's incarceration, the size and importance of his crime family diminished prompting some observers to conclude that crime families in New York could be reduced to street gangs in the coming years. Other experts on OC believe that it is much too early to predict the demise of these organizations in the nation's largest cities.

According to the enterprise model, both OC and legitimate businesses exist for the same reason—to make money. However, the latter cannot legally meet the demands that millions of consumers have for drugs, gambling, prostitution, and the like, whereas "small, flexible organizations of criminals" attempt to meet these consumer cravings by moving into the illegal marketplace when opportunities present themselves

(Albanese, 1989, p. 98). Hardly limited to those of Italian and Sicilian extraction, these subterranean businesspeople come from a variety of racial and ethnic backgrounds.

Albanese (1989, p. 217) argues that "serious investigation" supports the enterprise model. These criminal associations are a local rather than a national phenomenon, and family ties are of little importance in the illegal marketplace. Robert Kelly (1997, p. 41) maintains that the highly structured Cosa Nostra that Cressey envisioned in his 1969 book has changed over the past 30 years because criminal opportunities are now available that "suggest that new roles and lines of activity, and therefore, organizations" have emerged.

Over the past 10 to 25 years, the nature of OC in the United States has changed significantly enough to warrant a fourth model. We are witnessing the proliferation of ethnic gangs (often first-generation immigrants) involved in illegal activities with strong ties to their homelands. Cuban, Colombian, Bolivian, Peruvian, Mexican, Chinese (from Hong Kong), Vietnamese, Israeli, Iraqi, Nigerian, Russian, YACS (Yugoslavians, Albanians, Croatians, and Serbs), and Jamaican gangs among others are engaged in a wide range of criminal activities including drug trafficking, smuggling, motor vehicle theft, prostitution, credit and identity theft, and supermarket and ATM robbery.

One of the most potent weapons the federal government has to combat organized crime activity is the Racketeer Influenced and Corrupt Organization Act (RICO) of 1970. Racketeering includes a long list of offenses including murder, gambling, robbery, extortion, loansharking (charging exorbitant and illegal interest rates for loaning money), prostitution, and drug violations. The main thrust of RICO is that it gives the federal government, by way of agencies such as the FBI and the Department of Alcohol, Tobacco and Firearms, jurisdiction to enforce laws that had been previously within the purview of state and local organizations (Abadinsky, 1997). For example, a 1997 FBI investigation led to the arrest of 16 men charged with running an extortion, loansharking, and gambling ring with ties to organized crime ("Loansharking Suspect Guilty on Two Counts," 1999).

Occupational Crime

Criminologist Gary S. Green (1990, pp. 12–13) defines **occupational crime** as "any act punishable by law which is committed through opportunity created in the course of an occupation that is legal." This form of criminal activity, also called white-collar crime, is by far the most commonplace in the United States as well as the most expensive in terms of money lost by victims. According to Green, four principal types of occupational crime exist in the United States: organizational, state authority, professional, and individual.

occupational crime criminal acts that are committed by way of legal employment

False and misleading advertising, price-fixing, bid-rigging, failing to provide safe working conditions for employees as well as selling unsafe products are examples of *organizational crime.* Many of these corporate law violations threaten the nation's health and safety. According to one estimate, each year corporate crime in the United States is responsible for approximately 1 million serious illnesses or injuries and 55,000 deaths (Barkan, 1997). This latter figure is about three times the number of homicides recorded annually by the UCR.

Organizational crimes against the environment, as aptly stated by Gilbert Geis (in Green, 1990, p. 135), result in the "compulsory consumption of violence" on the part of the public. Whereas people may be able to distance themselves from street predators through home and auto alarm systems, in most instances they can do little if anything to protect themselves from the harmful effects of environmental crimes. For example, the Rockwell International Corporation pleaded guilty to illegally disposing of radioactive waste near the Rocky Flats nuclear weapons site a short distance from Denver. Company employees dumped highly toxic and radioactive waste in streams that flowed through the industrial complex and then falsified records submitted to state and federal health officials (Abramson and Takahashi, 1992).

Enron employees remove their belongings from company headquarters in Houston, Texas, after Enron collapsed as the result of alleged massive fraud on the part of senior executives. Every year corporate crime costs consumers much more than the combined losses of street crimes such as robbery and burglary.

Billions of dollars are lost annually to telemarketing and direct personal marketing fraud operations. According to the National Fraud Information Center (Economic Crime, 1999), the top five telemarketing schemes are (1) phony prize/sweepstakes giveaways, (2) advance fees for loans that could have been acquired without fees or loans that are never forthcoming, (3) work-at-home plans (stuffing envelopes and stringing beads, for example) that never even result in recovering start-up fees much less a profit, (4) pay-per-call telephone services, and (5) "slamming" (consumers tricked into switching their phone service from one company to another, typically without their knowledge or consent).

Beginning in the fall of 2001, a number of corporate scandals rocked Wall Street and were, in part, responsible for declining investor confidence, which resulted in the stock market losing trillions of dollars in value. A top official of Enron Corporation, the giant energy trading company, was indicted on 78 counts of money laundering, obstruction of justice, and looting the company of so much money that it collapsed. Thousands of jobs were lost, as well as tens of billions of dollars of stock-capitalization owned by employees and shareholders all over the world. The value of Enron's stock plunged from $80 a share to ten cents a share in a short period of time (Smith, 2002).

Two executives of the telecommunications company WorldCom were charged with securities fraud, conspiracy to commit fraud, filing false documents with government agencies, and hiding billions of dollars in expenses to make the company appear profitable to investors and potential investors (Radelat, 2002).

Dennis Kozlowski, along with two other executives of the Tyco Corporation, were charged with stealing $600 million from their own company. Investigators alleged that among a long list of improprieties, Kozlowski spent $1 million in company funds on a lavish birthday party for his wife that included an ice sculpture of Michelangelo's David that sprayed vodka from its penis ("Three Former Tyco Executives Charged . . . ," 2002). Steven Cutler, director of the Security and Exchange Commission's enforcement division, stated that the defendants "treated Tyco as their private bank, taking out hundreds of millions of dollars of loans and compensation without ever telling investors" (p. A1).

U.S. Attorney General John Ashcroft noted, "Corrupt corporate executives are no better than common thieves" (Radelat, 2002, p. 1). They may be no better, but corporate criminals are certainly much richer, as their theft from the American public is many times greater than the combined annual monetary losses from all of the of the nation's robberies and burglaries combined. In addition, the few corporate criminals that are successfully prosecuted are much less likely to receive lengthy prison sentences than are street criminals.

State authority occupational crimes are those offenses committed by individuals legally entitled to make and enforce laws and command others. Examples of this criminal activity include police brutality and corruption (discussed in Chapter 8), various forms of corruption on the part of elected and appointed government officials, and torture administered by government employees and agencies. Posing as foreign Arab businesspeople, FBI agents conducted a "sting" operation and bribed a number of U.S. congressional leaders to invest money for them in violation of federal laws with some individuals accepting as much as $100,000 in illegal profits (Green, 1990). The so-called ABSCAM transactions were videotaped by FBI agents and later watched by the entire nation as well as the jurors who convicted the defendants.

Public officials may engage in this criminal activity to continue or enhance their political position or implement a specific goal-oriented policy. Regarding the former, in July 1972, President Nixon's reelection committee, or CREEP (Committee to Reelect the President), broke into the Democratic Party's national office located in the Watergate apartment-office building to tap telephone lines. In the months following the arrest of the Watergate burglars, federal prosecutors learned that CREEP had been involved in a variety of criminal activities including illegal wiretapping of citizens, improper campaign contributions to the Republican Party, obstruction of justice, and engineering smear campaigns against Democratic candidates.

In the early 1980s, Congress prohibited U.S. aid to right-wing military forces (the "contras") that were battling a communist government for the control of Nicaragua. High-ranking members of President Reagan's National Security Council planned and orchestrated the illegal sale of weapons to Iran with the proceeds of these transactions used to buy weapons and illegally supply the insurgent contra forces.

Professional occupational crimes are committed by highly trained individuals such as health care professionals (physicians, dentists, chiropractors, and veterinarians) and attorneys. Physicians have performed unnecessary surgery, filed fraudulent medical and insurance claims, and engaged in fee-splitting with other health care professionals. A government study estimated that 2.4 million unneeded operations costing more than $4 billion and killing almost 12,000 people occur every year in the United States (Coleman, 1995). Some psychiatrists, clinical psychologists, and therapists have sexual relations with their patients (a crime in many states) who are especially vulnerable as a consequence of their emotional problems.

Individual occupational crime is a "catch-all category" that includes occupational crimes other than those offenses committed by individuals *for* their organizations or in their role as government officials or professionals. For example, a bartender sells a $5 drink, rings up $3 on the cash register, and pockets the difference. This seemingly insignificant theft may be repeated dozens of times during the workweek.

Occupational crime is the most numerous, costly, and underreported crime in the United States. According to one estimate, more than 50 percent of U.S. workers steal from their employers. Whereas burglary victims lost almost $3 billion in 2000, employee theft ranging from extra-long lunch hours to stealing ("borrowing") company equipment or merchandise cost businesses, and eventually consumers who must absorb this loss, between $5 billion and $10 billion annually (Hagan, 1991). In many instances, people do not realize that they have been victims of occupational crime. Store owners who believe merchandise losses are the result of shoplifting may never know that the real problem is employee theft. A job applicant denied employment may attribute his or her failure to the existence of a more qualified applicant, although he or she was the victim of illegal racially discriminatory hiring practices. People in a certain locale may not link their high incidence of sickness and death to the dumping of hazardous waste that seeps into underground aquifers and poisons the area water supply (Miethe and McCorkle, 1998).

In 2001, arrests for embezzlement and fraud were slightly more than 20,000 and 323,000 respectively. Because the remainder of occupational offenders arrested fall under the category of "all other offenses" and so many people who engage in these illegal acts are never caught, our knowledge of occupational criminals is limited. Based on arrest data, Miethe and McCorkle (1998) constructed a profile of the "typical" occupational offender. This individual is most likely to be an educated and employed, white, home-owning, middle-class male between 20 and 29 years of age.

Focus on Russia

Organized Crime in a Changing Society

The collapse of communism in the former Soviet Union and Eastern European countries resulted in a tidal wave of organized crime activity, especially in Russia. Sociologist Joseph Albini and his colleagues (1997) argue that the roots of this latest period of lawlessness can be traced back almost 100 years when a series of political, economic, and social events traumatized Russian society. The Russian Revolution of 1917 that promised a workers' paradise quickly deteriorated into a dictatorship of an elite-driven Communist Party. In 1941, the USSR was invaded by Nazi Germany, and during the cold war, which lasted approximately 40 years, the nation was locked in a costly arms race with the West.

In each of these periods, everyday goods and services were in short supply. For example, because of the nation's commitment to gain military superiority over the United States and its allies, the Soviet government drastically cut back on the production of everything from food and clothing to automobiles and apartments. A black market emerged that traded in stolen (usually from the state) and illegally imported or smuggled goods. The situation was ripe for wide-scale corruption as well as organized criminal activity. "It seems then, that the period prior to the fall of communism and the breakup of the Soviet Union became the training and breeding ground for the development of syndicated crime in contemporary Russia" (Albini et al., 1997, p. 163).

The number of organized crime groups increased from 775 in 1990 the year prior to the collapse and fragmentation of the Soviet Union to 5,700 by the end of 1994 (Half, 1997) with hundreds of thousands of members. How can this tremendous increase in organized crime activity in such a short period of time be explained? Cameron Half (1997) offers a three-part answer. To begin, the almost overnight collapse of the Communist Party's monopoly across the executive, legislative, and judicial branches of government meant that the major forces in society that had previously managed to keep organized criminal groups in check ceased to exist. The collapse of the government created a power vacuum that organized crime was quick to exploit. Second, the privatization of the economy as Russia moved from a socialist to capitalist society opened up a wide range of previously nonexistent criminal opportunities. Finally, a lack of legal reform and often contradictory property laws meant that a businessperson facing extortion from an organized crime group was often reluctant to call the police for fear that he or she might be guilty of violating newly emerging property statutes. In addition, widespread police corruption could lead to a situation wherein extortion on the part of law enforcement was even worse (more costly) than extortion at the hand of organized crime.

With as much as 40 percent of the nation's economy controlled by organized crime (Nathan, 1998), President Boris Yeltsin noted his country was on its way to becoming a "superpower of crime" (in de Borchgrave, 1997). The Russian president stated, "Organized crime is destroying the economy, interfering in politics, undermining public morals, threatening individual citizens and the entire Russian nation . . . our country is already considered a great mafia power" (in Kelly, Schatzberg, and Ryan, 1997, p. 174).

The majority of Russian organized criminal activity may be grouped in the following categories (Handelman, 1994):

1. Organized crime controls banks, stock exchanges, and businesses across the country. According to one estimate, between 70 and 80 percent of private enterprises and banks make payoffs to organized crime groups. Much of this money comes via extortion, obtaining money from someone by way of threatening violence and/or the implementation of violence. Because of the "protection" racket (extortion) Russia has virtually no bank robberies although these institutions lose significantly more money by paying for protection than they would ever lose from robbery. Gang members who "guard" street corner kiosks in Moscow typically offer their services for 20 percent of the sales (Albini et al., 1997). More than 500 businesspeople were murdered in Russia in 1994 (Coleman, 1997), a fact that can convince the most stubborn businessperson not to resist the demands of organized criminals.

2. As is the case in virtually every country where organized crime flourishes, these groups satisfy the public's demands for illicit goods and services, such as prostitution, gambling, and drugs. Prostitutes (male and female) are found not only in urban areas but also are transported to various regions and other countries

(Albini et al., 1997). According to one estimate, 90 percent of prostitutes in Israel are Russian, many of whom were brought into that country by organized prostitution rings (Prusher, 1997).

3. Illegally exporting natural resources, nuclear and nonnuclear weapons as well as other military equipment is supported by organized crime. Between 1991 and 1994, German police recorded 440 cases of attempted smuggling of nuclear material from Russia into Germany. The illegal trade in military hardware supports armed conflict both within republics that were part of the Soviet Union and in other parts of the world (Albini et al., 1997). Organized crime as well as the corruption it generates is a significant obstacle to the development of free enterprise, free markets, and the legitimate institutions that support democratic capitalism (Coleman, 1997). Virtually all of the money produced by organized criminal activity is lost to Russia; that is, these funds are not reinvested in the economy. On the contrary, up to $2 billion a month leaves the country to be laundered in financial institutions around the world before they are invested in foreign legal enterprises (Half, 1997). In addition, a climate of fear and the political instability that Russian organized crime has helped generate make it exceedingly difficult to attract badly needed investment capital from abroad. The transition from a totalitarian, centrally planned economy to a democratic state with free market capitalism has been made much more difficult—if not imperiled—by the presence of organized crime. As Russian scholar David Slater (1998, p. 29) stated, "Organized crime has eaten away at the fabric of Russian society to such an extent that it may prove impossible to overcome it."

summary

1. The four crimes of violence tabulated in the annual Uniform Crime Reports are murder, robbery, rape, and aggravated assault. First-degree murder is an unlawful killing that is willful, deliberate, and premeditated. In states with capital punishment, first-degree murder is punishable by death. Robbery involves taking something of value from an individual by force or the threat of force or placing an individual in a state of fear. Rape is the carnal knowledge of a female forcibly and against her will. Aggravated assault is the unlawful and intentional causing of serious bodily harm or the threat to do so.

2. The four Index property crimes are burglary, larceny–theft, motor vehicle theft, and arson. These crimes are committed without the threat or use of force. Burglary is the unlawful entry of a structure to commit a felony or theft. Larceny–theft is unlawfully taking property from the possession of another person. Shoplifting, pocket picking, and purse snatching are examples of this crime. Motor vehicle theft is the attempted or completed theft of automobiles, trucks, buses, or motorcycles. Arson is the willful or malicious burning or attempt to burn property with or without the attempt to defraud.

3. Hate crimes are committed against persons, property, or society and are motivated in part or whole by prejudice. These crimes are committed by individuals, groups, and mobs. Stalking is action directed at another person that would cause a reasonable individual to be fearful. California passed the first anti-stalking law in 1995. Often considered a "victimless" crime, prostitution is the sale of sex (oneself or another person) for money or something of value.

4. About 1.5 million people are arrested for drunk driving in the United States each year. One survey found that 2.5 percent of respondents admitted to at least one instance of alcohol-impaired driving during the past 30 days. People illegally use drugs for a wide variety of reasons. Rates of drug use are highest in the youngest age groups and decline as people age. Research consistently finds an association between drug use and criminal behavior.

5. Research suggests three primary interpretations of organized crime in the United States. According to the national conspiracy model, a nationwide alliance of 24 closely knit families operates in the country. All members of the Mafia or Cosa Nostra are of Italian or Sicilian descent. From the local, ethnic group perspective, crime families are highly organized at the local level but not at the national level. According to the enterprise model, organized criminals from a variety of racial and ethnic backgrounds meet the demands of millions of people for illegal products and services, such as drugs, gambling, and prostitution.

6. Street gangs have existed in the United States for more than 100 years. Gang membership and activity have increased significantly over the past 30 years. Estimates of the number of gang members nationwide range from 600,000 to 1.5 million. Gang members are often involved in a wide range of criminal activity including selling drugs, robbery, rape, and homicide.

7. Occupational crime is any act punishable by law that is committed from an opportunity created in a legal occupation. Organizational crime consists of price-fixing, bid-rigging, and any other illegal activity engaged in to increase corporate profits. State occupational crimes are offenses committed by individuals who are legally entitled to make and

enforce laws. Police corruption and the excessive use of force would fall under this category. Professional occupational crimes are committed by highly trained professionals, such as physicians and attorneys. Workers stealing from employees are engaging in individual occupational crime.

key terms

aggravated assault
arson
burglary
drug dependence
felony murder
first-degree murder
hate crimes
homicide
larceny–theft

manslaughter
motor vehicle theft
occupational crime
organized crime
prostitution
rape
robbery
stalking

questions *for* investigation

1. Research print and on-line sources of news information for your home or campus community, and answer these questions: How prevalent are crimes of violence and property crimes? How effective are the law enforcement agencies in arresting criminals? How effective is the criminal justice system in convicting criminals? Based on the answers to these questions, how would you rate the safety in your community?

2. What precautionary measures does your college or university take to prevent students from being victimized by rape? Motor vehicle theft? Hate crimes? Stalking? Drunk driving? Illegal drug distribution?

3. Some people believe that prostitution should be considered a legal economic transaction between consenting adults rather than a crime. What do you believe? Why?

4. What is the difference between hate crimes and hate speech? Why is the latter protected by the First Amendment? Some people have argued that hate crime laws are unnecessary because existing statutes call for punishing convicted offenders regardless of the race, religion, or sexual orientation of their victims. Do you agree or disagree? Be prepared to de-

fend your position. Should the government prohibit organizations that espouse physically harming individuals and/or groups from having Internet sites? If someone is convicted of a hate crime and states that he or she was motivated in part or whole by material viewed on a specific Internet site, should the individuals or groups who posted that site be criminally prosecuted for the offense as well?

5. Suppose a sales representative, considered successful by his company and effective by his customers, is in the habit of padding his expense account so that, in effect, he can support himself reasonably on the expense account. The sales rep would consider padding the account to buy a golf membership or a vacation inappropriate; however, he believes he is justified in his current plan because he does spend most of his time traveling away from home. Explain your opinion of this sales rep's thinking and actions.

6. Consider the similarities and differences between Russian political and economic institutions and U.S. political and economic institutions. How do these similarities and differences impact criminal activity in each country?

IT'S YOUR CALL...

1. Choose one of these positions to defend in a debate: (a) You are a member of the National Rifle Association preparing for a debate on gun control. Your position is that, if more people owned and carried handguns, street

criminals would be deterred from committing a significant number of crimes. (b) As a member of Handgun Control, you are preparing to advocate the counterposition;

that is, a more heavily armed population will result in a dramatic increase in accidental shootings and suicides, and guns will end up in the hands of street criminals by way of home burglaries (theft of handguns) resulting in an increase in violent street crime. Keep in mind that your audience is interested in facts and not emotional arguments. Therefore, research this topic before presenting your case.

2. Choose one of these topics to defend in a debate: (a) As a member of the nonprofit group Crime Control in America—Alternative Strategies, you understand that the success and longevity of organized crime in this nation is a consequence of these groups providing illicit drugs, sex, and gambling to a public that has an insatiable demand for unlawful goods and services. Because there is little, if any, evidence that people can be dissuaded from pursu-ing prostitutes, illegal drugs, and gambling, you believe it is time for state and federal governments to seriously consider legalizing some, if not all, of these behaviors and mind-altering substances. Prepare a two- or three-page position paper for the governor and state legislature wherein you present your arguments (substantiated by data whenever possible) as clearly and convincingly as possible. (b) As the ranking member of your state's Organized Crime Task Force, outline and defend the contrary position. Prepare a two- or three-page data-based paper arguing that the only way to diminish the wealth and power of organized crime is to substantially reduce the activity of these groups as well as zealously prosecute those individuals who use illegal drugs and engage the services of prostitutes and bookmakers.

UNDER
Investigation

Street Gangs and Motorcycle Gangs

Street Gangs

Youth gangs have been part of the urban landscape in the United States for more than 100 years (Vigil and Long, 1990). As cities on the East Coast swelled with European immigrants between 1900 and 1930, teenagers who shared a common cultural heritage socialized with each other, some engaging in criminal activity. The combination of greater economic activity and more young people along the eastern seaboard explains why the growth of juvenile gangs has been more rapid in this region than in the Midwest and South (Taylor, 1990). However, gang activity and growth has increased significantly over the past 30 years in some midwestern cities, most notably Chicago and St. Louis.

The other area of the nation with a long history of gang activity is California, especially the cities of Los Angeles and San Francisco (Brantley and DiRosa, 1994). Chicano neighborhood ("barrios") gangs in southern California are among the longest lived gangs in America

> "...*gangs in southern California are among the longest lived gangs in America* ..."

ica with some maintaining a continuous presence in Los Angeles barrios since the 1930s (Vigil and Long, 1990). An especially heterogeneous area, Los Angeles and the surrounding region have gangs comprised of the following racial and ethnic categories: white, African American, Mexican, Chinese, Filipino, Vietnamese, Korean, Samoan, Jamaican, El Salvadoran, and Guatemalan (Vigil, 1988).

Prior to 1975, Asian street gangs were primarily limited to disgruntled Chinese youths living in "Chinatowns" of the nation's largest cities. However, beginning in the late 1970s and early 1980s, Asian gangs began to increase rapidly with the influx of immigrants from Vietnam (including ethnic Chinese-Vietnamese), Laos, Cambodia, and the Philippines. Some Asian gangs, most notably Vietnamese and Cambodian groups, are comprised in large measure of Amerasian children of U.S. military personnel who served in Vietnam during the war (Kodluboy, 1996; Le, 2002).

Active in major metropolitan areas on the West and East Coasts of the United States as well as in the largest cities in Canada, Asian gangs routinely victimize other Asians, especially recent immigrants to the United States. These newcomers often keep their money at home or place of business because they come from countries where the banking system is not well developed, or from rural areas where these institutions do not exist. Gang members know that Asians are much less likely than other individuals to notify the police when they are victimized. Many immigrants from South Korea, Indonesia, Burma, and other countries with less-than-democratic governments view the police as little more than repressive organizations controlled by those in power to crush political dissent. Rather than as a source of help and service, the police are viewed with suspicion and "extreme terror" (Le, 2002).

Ranging in size from 6 to 50 members, some Asian street gangs have close links to sophisticated criminal organizations in China such as the 14 K Triad. Founded in the seventeenth century to oppose the ruling dynasty, triads are criminal organizations that continue to flourish in Asian countries with ethnic Chinese populations. Triads are involved in money laundering, illegal gambling, counterfeiting, and the smuggling of illegal aliens into the United States. Asian gangs on the West Coast have been linked to the importation of drugs from the Golden Triangle region of Thailand, Burma, and Laos. Home invasion robberies are also a primary activity of Asian gangs, especially in the Chicago area ("Asian Street Gangs and Organized Crime in Focus," 2001).

Sporting names such as Black Dragons, Black Widows, and Street Killer Boys, many Asian gangs have adopted the hand signs, graffiti, manner of dress, and slang popular with African American and Hispanic street gangs. Some groups have named themselves after the infamous Bloods and Crips; Fresno, California, has the Asian Crips and Bloods, and Long Beach the Cambodian Crips.

The number of gangs and gang members in the United States is unknown, with available figures little more than wild "guesstimates." A March 1998 article in a National Institute of Justice publication noted that more than 16,000 gangs "with at least half a million members" existed (Huff, 1998a, p. 3). Seven months later, a research brief in the same publication stated there were an estimated 23,888 youth gangs with 664,906 members (Huff, 1998b). An *Office of Juvenile Justice and Delinquency Program* fact sheet concluded that the United States had 31,000 gangs and 816,000 gang members (Moore & Terrett, 1999). Other researchers have estimated that there may be as many as 1.5 million gang members active in the United States. The ten cities and counties with the most gang members (in descending order) are Los Angeles County, Los Angeles (city), Chicago, Santa Ana (California), Cleveland, Long Beach (California), San Antonio, and Gary (Indiana) (Gibeaut, 1998).

One reason for the vast discrepancy in gang members figures is the absence of a common definition of what constitutes a gang. According to one definition, gang members are between 10 and 22 years of age; however, other researchers include individuals well into their 30s (Huff, 1998b). Acknowledging the problem of gang definitions, a "Gang Manual" published by the National Law Enforcement Institute, Inc. (1999, p. 1) states, "Many of the definitions are so disparate, e.g., that the average, hard core street gang member

from California would not fit the definition established in Illinois."

Criminologists Robert Bursik and Harold Grasmick (1993) note that the money communities receive from federally funded law enforcement programs may be contingent on the volume of law-violating behavior in those communities. These "economic considerations," as the authors note (p. 105), "have been suggested as explanations of why police estimates of the number of gangs in Phoenix increased from 5 or 6 to over 100 in a very short period of time." However, fearing the loss of tourist and investment money, local officials may pressure police to publicly underestimate gang activity in a given community.

Three major questions regarding the relationship between street gangs and crime must be asked: (1) How much crime do gangs members commit, (2) what forms of law-violating behavior do they engage in, and (3) do gang members commit more crime than nongang members? Regarding the first two questions, researchers interviewed gang members in Denver and Aurora, Colorado; Broward County in southern Florida; and Cleveland, Ohio. Gang-described involvement in a wide range of criminal activity ranged from shoplifting, burglary, and selling drugs to robbery, rape,and homicide (see table on page 100) Note that across the four locations almost 75 percent of gang members carried concealed weapons and approximately one in six admitted involvement in a homicide. A study of 83 gang leaders and hard core members in Columbus, Ohio, concluded that between 1980 and 1994 these individuals had been collectively arrested 834 times. Thirty-seven percent of the arrests were for violent crimes (Huff, 1998a; Huff, 1998b). As of 1998 six of the 83 subjects had died, five were shot to death, and one was strangled. Data from the Cleveland sample indicated that gang members commit significantly more crime as well as more serious offenses than a group of at-risk but nongang youth. For example, the percentage of gang members who told interviewers they were involved in a homicide, robbery, or drive-by shooting were 15.2, 17.0, and 40.4 percent respectively. For nongang members, comparable figures were 2.0, 0.0, and 2.0 percent (Huff, 1998b).

Gang research in recent years has increasingly focused on the role of females in these organizations. Anne Campbell (1995) has identified three possible relations between female and male gang members: (1) gangs comprised exclusively of females that exist independent of male gangs, (2) "coed" gangs comprised of males and females with the former outnumbering the latter, and (3) females as subordinates in male-dominated organizations. In her study of the Vice Queens, a female gang associated with Chicago's Vice Kings, Laura Fishman (1995, p. 83) noted that

Type of Criminal Behavior in Which Gang Members Report Being Involved

	AURORA, CO N = 49	BROWARD COUNTY, FL N = 50	CLEVELAND, OH N = 47	DENVER, CO N = 41
Guns in school	53.1%	46.0%	40.4%	46.3%
Knives in school	50.0	58.3	38.3	37.5
Concealed weapons	87.8	84.0	78.7	88.1
Drug use	49.0	76.0	27.7	51.2
Drug sales (school)	26.5	34.0	19.1	38.1
Drug sales (other)	75.0	58.0	61.7	64.3
Drug theft	31.9	44.9	21.3	23.1
Drive-by shooting	51.0	68.0	40.4	50.0
Homicide	12.2	20.0	15.2	19.5
Auto theft	44.9	67.3	44.7	61.9
Theft (other)	59.2	80.0	51.1	52.4
Assault rivals	81.6	94.0	72.3	71.4
Assault own members	31.3	40.0	30.4	26.2
Assault police	28.6	22.0	10.6	31.0
Assault teachers	26.5	16.3	14.9	26.8
Assault students	58.3	66.0	51.1	53.7
Mug people	26.5	52.0	10.6	33.3
Assault in streets	42.9	56.0	29.8	52.4
Intimidate/assault victim or witness	39.6	46.0	34.0	47.6
Intimidate/assault shoppers	31.3.	42.0	23.4	40.5
Shoplifting	57.1	62.0	30.4	45.0
Check forgery	4.1	18.0	2.1	4.8
Credit card theft	12.2	46.0	6.4	9.5
Sell stolen goods	44.9	70.G	29.8	52.4
Bribe police	12.2	10.0	10.6	11.9
Burglary (unoccupied)	26.5	64.0	8.5	42.9
Burglary (occupied)	8.3	34.0	2.1,	14.6
Arson	12.2	12.0	8.5	14.3
Kidnapping	6.1	4.0	4.3	9.5
Sexual assault/molestation	4.1	4.0	2.1	0.0
Rape	2.0	4.0	2.1	0.0
Robbery	14.3	30.0	17.0	26.2

Source: Huff, R. 1998. "Comparing the Criminal Behavior of Youth Gangs and At-Risk Youths." *National Institute of Justice—Research in Brief* by C. Ronald Huff, October: 2. U.S. Department of Justice, Bureau of Justice Statistics.

Under Investigation: Street Gangs and Motorcycle Gangs

"Although female groups are still peripheral to the male gang," these organizations "have moved closer to becoming independent, violence-oriented groups." As is

"According to one estimate . . . 3.6 percent of all gangs are 'girl gangs'. . ."

the case with the Vice Queens, female gangs typically are offshoots of an established male organization and adopt a feminized version of the male group's name (Campbell, 1995). According to one estimate (Curry et al. in Pollock, 1999) based on law enforcement reports, 3.6 percent of all gangs are "girl gangs," with these groups accounting for 13.6 percent of all gang-related property crime, 12.7 percent of all drug crime, and 3.3 percent of all violent crime.

As members of predominantly male gangs, females are often initiated by being "sexed in," that is, the prospective members agrees to have sex with some or all of the male members. In other instances girls are raped. According to gang researcher John Walker (2001), one recent trend is for female initiates to have sex with someone known to be HIV positive. As they get older, have children, and want to leave the gang, females may have to undergo another rite of passage called "jumping out," a ritual which may include a severe physical beating that can lead to permanent injury or death (Walker, 2001).

Regardless of their relation to male gangs, many female gang members have no aversion to violence. On the contrary, some of these girls and women relish physical combat as much as their male counterparts. One female gang member described her sister's participation in a fight with rivals from another gang. "My sister had cracked a bottle and cracked her head open. She had her arm halfway sliced off. Just beat her up. Totally beat her up. They kicked her in the ribs a few times. She was all dazed down. Her face was all bruised up" (in Harris, 1997, p. 160).

In gangs comprised of both sexes, females often carry the group's weapons, act as lookouts for crimes such as burglary and drug deals, set up rival gang members for an attack by agreeing to date them, and procure nonmember girls for gang rapes (Campbell in

Pollock, 1999). As auxiliary members completely subordinate to males, females "hang out" in gangs where they drink, take drugs, and engage in sexual relations, often at the whim of male members. This latter form of female gang participation appears to be the most common.

A number of cities, including New York and Los Angeles, have introduced special antigang units to combat this form of street crime. Other locales have a coordinated antigang task force comprised of members of several agencies. For example, on Long Island, full-time members of the Hempstead Police, the Federal Drug Enforcement Agency, the federal Bureau of Alcohol, Tobacco and Firearms, the New York State Police, and other organizations make up one such unit (Celona, 1999; Domash, 2000).

In 1992, Chicago passed an antigang ordinance permitting police to disburse or arrest individuals at sidewalk gatherings ("people who remain in any one place with no apparent purpose" in the presence of a suspected gang member). The law was struck down by an Illinois appellate court in 1995 and the U.S. Supreme Court in 1999. The high Court stated that the law gave the police too much power to target innocent people (Epstein, 1999; "Gang Case Ruling Stings Chicago . . . " 1999).

To help federal, state, and local law enforcement organizations share and exchange information on gangs, the Clinton administration funded the National Gang Tracking Network. As a consequence of escalating gang-related crime, many big-city police departments have formed specialized antigang squads. For example,

". . . witness intimidation is a major problem in convicting street-gang defendants."

the New York City Police Department's CAGE unit (Citywide Antigang Enforcement) states that it attacks "gangs at all levels by any means legal to liberate neighborhoods from the scourge of gangsters" and has received numerous awards for its work ("Coming to a Hood Near You!" 2001, p. 3). However, arresting gang members does not always lead to a successful prosecution. A survey of 192 district attorneys discovered that 51 percent of prosecutors in large jurisdictions and 43 percent in smaller jurisdictions stated that witness intimidation is a major problem in convicting street-gang defendants ("Targeting Gangs and Violent Juveniles," 2001).

Motorcycle Gangs

Outlaw motorcycle gangs (OMGs) have their origin in the post–World War II and Korean War era, when many combat veterans returned home rife with feelings of hostility and alienation. Some vets joined motorcycle clubs and associations and continued their "quasi-military camaraderie" while using the motorcycle as a symbol of freedom from the responsibilities and restraints of a conventional lifestyle (Abadinsky, 1990, p. 215). One group of bike-riding southern California vets called themselves the Pissed Off Bastards of Bloomington (POBOBs), and engaged in various forms of deviant behavior. In 1947, a number of POBOBs in San Bernardino began calling themselves Hell's Angels, a name previously adopted by World War II fighter pilots (Abadinsky, 1997). In subsequent years, the ranks of motorcycle gangs have been partially replenished by military veterans of the Vietnam War.

According to Howard Abadinsky (1997), the Hell's Angels are one of the "big four" OMGs in the United States that can be described as "sophisticated criminal organizations." The remaining three national OMGs largely organized for criminal activity and the years they were founded are the Outlaws (1959), the Pagans (1959), and the Bandidos (1966) (see table below).

Together these organizations have 3 thousand to 4 thousand members, all of whom are white males. With the exception of the Pagans, all of these groups have international affiliations. Hell's Angels chapters outside the United States increased from 5 in 1965 to 108 in 1998 ("Hells Angels, Crime and Canada," 1998).

These gangs have been financially successful in the distribution of drugs, especially methamphetamimes (speed), phencyclidine (PCP or angel dust), cocaine, and LSD. Inasmuch as they are mobile, have connections throughout the country, and are prone to violence, OMGs "are excellent conduits for the distribution of illegal drugs" (Abadinsky, 1989, p. 227).

These criminal organizations also generate profits from running massage parlors, prostitution, gambling operations, trafficking in stolen motorcycle parts

> ## "Hell's Angels chapters outside the United States increased from 5 in 1965 to 108 in 1998."

as well as dealing in automatic weapons and explosives (Adler, Mueller, and Laufer, 1991). Money earned from these operations may be invested in legal profit-oriented enterprises. According to one estimate, the Hell's Angels' total worldwide revenue is in the *billions* of dollars, with most of this money coming from the drug trade ("Hells Angels, Crime and Canada," 1998).

With so much money to be made, rival motorcycle gangs routinely compete violently for exclusive access to distribution territories. Between 1994 and 1998, at least 60 people were killed in Quebec, Canada, as Hell's Angels and a local motorcycle gang (the Rock Ma-

Outlaw Motorcycle Gangs—Geographic Distribution

Hell's Angels	California and East Coast; mother club in Oakland, California.
Outlaws	Founded in Chicago; chapters in Michigan, Illinois, western New York, Ohio, western Pennsylvania, parts of Oklahoma, Arkansas, Kentucky, North Carolina, Georgia, and Florida; mother club moved to Detroit in 1984.
Pagans	Founded in Prince George County, Maryland; chapters in Pennsylvania, West Virginia, and New Orleans; mother club has no particular location.
Bandidos	Founded in Houston; chapters in Northwest and South, particularly Texas; mother club in Texas.

Source: Adapted from Abadinsky, Howard. *Organized Crime* 1997. 228. Chicago: Nelson-Hall.

chine) waged war on one another to determine which group would control the drug trade in that province. A Canadian investigator stated that the conflict had nothing to do with honor or gang pride; rather, "It's about business, market share, and greed" ("Hell's Angels, Crime and Canada," 1998).

The evolution of OMGs from bike-riding rebels looking for a good time to sophisticated crime networks took another turn in the 1980s. According to the President's Commission on Organized Crime, 1988 (in Abadinsky, 1997, p. 240), "there are growing reports that members are abandoning the outlaw image, wearing business suits and driving luxury cars, in essence, becoming an outlaw motorcycle gang without the motorcycles."

Women involved with OMGs are both victims and perpetrators of crime. They are expected to engage in economic activities (often prostitution) for individual members or the entire club. In his study of OMGs, James F. Quinn (1987) observed that female bikers have primarily three roles. "Ol' ladies" wear "property patches" on the back of their jackets designating they belong to a particular member and "through him, his club" (p. 53). "Mamas" are female companions or discarded ol' ladies who have been adopted by and belong to the entire chapter. Typically older than ol' ladies, they cannot compete successfully with younger prostitutes. A "sweetbutt" is a member's regular sex partner and/or source of income not protected by a property patch. As such, she is fair game for the sexual advances of any club member.

Often referred to as "sluts," "whores," "bitches," and "cunts," women are subordinate to biker males in every aspect of their lives. Women's inferior status is clearly spelled out in the following passage that has been incorporated into the marital ceremony of many OMGs

" . . . women are subordinate to biker males in every aspect of their lives."

(Hopper and Moore, 1997, p. 478): "You are an inferior woman being married to a superior man. Neither you nor any of your female children can ever hold membership in this club or own any of its property."

Although voluntary in some instances, group sex, or "pulling a train," is usually a female's punishment for some violation of the club's code of conduct or incurring the wrath of her partner. One woman told researchers that she had to pull a train because she failed to keep her man's motorcycle clean while another admitted to the same punishment for failing to notice that her mate was holding an empty beer bottle at a party (Hopper and Moore, 1997). One researcher stated that he had been offered females by bikers in the same manner that one might offer a neighbor the use of a tool (Watson, 1996).

Criminal Law

1. What is the history of criminal law?

2. How may law be classified? What are the elements of a crime?

3. What are the possible legal defenses that suspects and defendants may use?

4. As defined by the Constitution, what legal rights does a suspect or defendant have?

5. What is due process? How does it protect suspects and defendants?

6. How have recent Supreme Court rulings affected the legitimate powers of the police?

After only 8 years of marriage, Andrea Yates, 37, a former high school valedictorian and competitive swimmer, was already the mother of five young children: Noah, 7; John, 5; Paul, 3; Luke, 2; and Mary, 6 months. Yates had a history of severe postpartum depression and tried to kill herself on two different occasions after her fourth child was born in 1999. Although she and her husband were advised that any more children could trigger further depression and additional suicide attempts, she soon became pregnant again, and their fifth child was born the next year. Yates was again hospitalized for depression after her father died in March 2001. Three months later, on June 20 in her Houston, Texas, home, she methodically gathered her four youngest children, drowned them in a bathtub, and laid their bodies on her bed. Her oldest, Noah, tried to escape her grasp; she forced his head underwater while he tried desperately to get free. When she was done, she called 911 and her husband and told him to come home.

Yates later told a psychiatrist that Satan had taken over her body. She also said that her children were not growing properly and that characters on a TV cartoon had told her she was a bad mother. Adding that she had thought for at least 2 years about killing her children, Yates explained why she finally did so: "The way I was raising them, they could never be saved. They had to die to be saved." She concluded, "I need to be punished. I'm guilty. Destroy Satan." Yates also told the psychiatrist that she had heard Satan in her jail cell. The psychiatrist later appeared in court and testified, "Of all the patients I've treated for major depression with psychotic features, she was one of the sickest." A neuropsychologist also testified that Yates briefly considered stabbing Noah after he was born in 1994, when, according to Yates, she heard Satan's voice telling her to pick up a knife and stab her first child. A third doctor, who had treated Yates for her earlier suicide attempts and had seen thousands of patients in a 26-year career, testified that Yates "would rank up there with the five sickest patients I've ever seen" (Christian, 2002a; Gesalman, 2002, p. 32; Roche, 2002).

Andrea Yates was convicted of first-degree murder in the drownings of her five children, despite considerable evidence that she suffered from major depression and other psychosis. Her case highlights one of the elements that must be proven before someone is convicted of a crime—criminal intent.

After Yates was arrested, prosecutors charged her with first-degree murder and asked for the death penalty. In response, the defense pleaded not guilty by reason of insanity. When the case went to trial in January 2002, the prosecution conceded she was mentally ill but argued that she still knew right from wrong and should be found guilty of murder. The defense countered that her history of depression, coupled with her doctor's decision to take her off an effective antipsychotic drug 2 weeks before the tragic crime, made the killings happen and that she drowned her children as part of a psychotic episode.

The jury obviously had an important decision to make. The defendant had committed one of the most horrible crimes imaginable. If the jury found her guilty as charged, it further had to decide whether she deserved to be executed, which was favored by only 19 percent of respondents in a Houston poll (Hewitt, Stewart, and Cosgriff, 2002). If the jury instead found her not guilty by reason of insanity, she could be sentenced to a mental institution for life or until she was certified as no longer a threat to herself or to others. The verdict hinged on the jury's opinion about whether Yates understood that what she did was a crime and, ultimately, whether she should be held criminally responsible for her actions that tragic day in June. In the end the jury took somewhat of a middle ground: It found her guilty of first-degree murder, evidently deciding that she knew her actions were wrong, but determined she should not be executed. Instead, it sentenced her to life in prison (Christian, 2002b).

criminal law the body of law that prohibits acts that are seen as so harmful to the public welfare that they deserve to be punished by the state, and that governs how these acts are handled by official state procedures

This case highlights one of the elements, criminal intent, that must be proven before someone should be convicted of committing a crime. The study of criminal intent falls into the field of **criminal law,** the body of law that governs what makes certain behaviors crimes and how allegations of criminal behavior are handled by the criminal justice system. This chapter discusses the key aspects of criminal law in the United States. It first sketches the history of criminal law and then discusses the major types of crimes, the elements of criminal acts, legal defenses to criminal prosecutions, and the procedural rights afforded criminal suspects and defendants by the U.S. Constitution and Bill of Rights as interpreted by the Supreme Court.

History of Criminal Law

The earliest societies did not have criminal law as we know it today. Writing had not yet developed, and no formal criminal laws and criminal justice system existed. Still, these societies had several norms that guided their behavior, even if these norms did not take the form of written laws, and they also had standard ways of dealing with offenders. We see parallels to their informal, unwritten norms and means of social control in the societies that anthropologists have studied since the nineteenth century. Many of these societies also do not have written laws and a formal criminal justice system, but they do have informal norms and social control mechanisms that help to maintain social order and stability (Edgerton, 1976).

Ancient Societies

Key developments in written criminal law occurred in the great ancient societies in what is now the Middle East and parts of Europe (Watson, 1985). One of the first known bodies of criminal law originated in ancient Babylon while Hammurabi was king (2000 B.C.). Now called the Code of Hammurabi, this set of laws was written on stone tablets and stipulated property rights, banned behaviors, and the punishments for such behaviors. Although these punishments included death and *corporal punishment* (beatings and other types of physical violence), the Code of Hammurabi is regarded today as an advance over the vicious, vigilante-style justice that existed in Babylon before the code was written because it substituted state actions for those of vengeful individuals.

The ancient Hebrews also furthered the development of criminal law. As the Old Testament discusses, Moses received the Ten Commandments from God at Mount Sinai and then on behalf of God entered into a covenant with the people of Israel (about 1200 B.C.). In return for God's protection, they agreed to follow the rules of the Code (or Law) of Moses, as the ancient Hebrews' law is called today, contained in the Ten Commandments and in other pronouncements in *Deuteronomy*. The Code of Moses lies at the heart of much Judeo-Christian theology and, more important for our purposes, has served as the basis for criminal law in many Western societies since ancient times.

Early Roman law probably played an even more important role in the development of criminal law in these societies. Ancient Rome's laws were first written as the Twelve Tables around 450 B.C. and reflected Roman customs and beliefs. These laws identified property rights and rules for behavior, and their writing, or *codification*, was meant to ensure that all Romans would be governed by the same rules and restrictions. In the sixth century A.D., the Code of Justinian was developed during the reign of Emperor Justinian I. This code was a detailed collection of Roman criminal law and *civil law*, which is the body of rules governing interactions among individuals, such as the buying and selling of property. The Code of Justinian influenced the development of legal systems throughout Europe during the next several centuries (Lewis and Ibbetson, 1994).

English Common Law

Although ancient law was quite important, the most significant influence on the eventual development of U.S. criminal law was the system of **common law** that originated in England during the eleventh and twelfth centuries. The common law is essentially a system of *case law*, or laws derived from judges' rulings rather than from legislative statutes. During the eleventh and twelfth centuries and beyond, rulings by English judges reflected English customs and gradually established the laws of England. In so doing, they transformed several types of private harm into crimes against the state. Before this time, for example, if someone stabbed a victim, it would be the responsibility of the victim or the victim's family and friends to avenge this act of violence. Judicial rulings turned such acts into crimes against the crown and specified appropriate punishment for them. English common law also relied heavily on legal *precedence*, as later rulings by judges looked to earlier rulings for legal guidance.

A key event in the history of the common law was the writing of the **Magna Carta** in 1215. English nobles forced King John to sign this historic document, which recognized their rights and bound the king to the rule of law. In the early seventeenth century, British jurists considered the Magna Carta a document that guaranteed individual rights for all English citizens, and the Magna Carta is widely credited with helping to

common law system of laws derived from judges' rulings

Magna Carta historic document that asserts the rights of nobles and bound the king to the rule of law

establish the rights of citizens under the law and also the power of courts to overturn laws passed by legislatures that contradict these rights (Cantor, 1997).

American Colonial Law

When English colonists first came to the New World in the early seventeenth century, they brought with them their knowledge of English common law. It was quite natural for them to develop a new legal system based on the one with which they were already familiar. Thus, the colonial legal system closely resembled the English legal system in both substance and practice. In Massachusetts and other colonies, it was also influenced by the colonists' Puritan religious beliefs, which led them to ban many types of behavior on the Sabbath and to regard certain acts as morally depraved and sinful (Walker, 1998).

After the revolt against England succeeded, the new nation wrote the Constitution in 1787 and then the Bill of Rights, the first 10 amendments to the Constitution, in 1791. The influence of these documents on U.S. criminal law—and, indeed, on legal systems in several other nations—cannot be overstated. The colonial experience and, more specifically, the abuse by England of the legal system in its struggle with the colonists was fresh in the minds of the framers of the Constitution and the writers of the Bill of Rights. They saw the need to limit the ability of government to take away individual freedom and, more generally, to limit the ability of government to abuse its powers. Thus, the Bill of Rights specified not only the freedoms of speech, press, and religion but also the rights of individuals charged with criminal offenses and limits on government actions against such individuals. We return to the Bill of Rights later.

Types of Law and Crimes

Laws, crimes, and other illegal acts may be classified in several ways. We examine the most common classifications of law and types of crimes here (see Table 4.1).

Classifications of Law

Of the many types of cases that come before the courts, only some are criminal cases whereas many others are civil cases. Because these two types of cases are often confused, we begin by identifying the basic differences between them. The *criminal law* pro-

table 4.1 Classifications of Law

Administrative law: rules and regulations issued by governmental agencies, such as the Internal Revenue Service and the Food and Drug Administration

Case law: the body of laws derived from the decisions of judges and appellate courts

Civil law: laws that govern relationships between individuals, organizations, and governmental agencies; contracts, divorces, wills, and real estate transactions are examples of actions governed by civil law

Criminal law: laws that prohibit acts that are seen as so harmful to the public welfare that they deserve to be punished by the state, and specify how allegations of criminal behavior are officially handled

Procedural law: the body of law that governs how the courts handle criminal and civil cases

Substantive law: the body of law that specifies which behaviors are crimes and the appropriate punishments for these behaviors

hibits acts that are seen as so harmful to the public welfare that they deserve to be punished by the state, and it specifies how allegations of criminal behavior are officially handled. These prohibited acts are called **crimes,** and their official handling is performed through the criminal justice system, which is the subject of this book. (The criminal law is comprised of substantive law and procedural law, which are discussed later.) In contrast, the **civil law** governs relationships among individuals, organizations, and government agencies. Contracts, divorce, wills, and real estate transactions are examples of actions governed by civil law. Violations of the civil law are called **civil wrongs,** or **torts,** and it is the responsibility of the party that is harmed to take legal remedy in the form of a **civil suit.** Whereas the penalty for crimes is often imprisonment, the penalty for a suit is restitution, the payment of damages, or other actions that are meant to undo or compensate for the original civil wrong.

Other types of law include administrative law, case law, procedural law, and substantive law. **Administrative law** refers to the rules and regulations issued by governmental agencies, such as the Internal Revenue Service and the Food and Drug Administration. These agencies are authorized to impose fines or bring civil suits to end violation of their regulations. **Case law,** as noted earlier in our discussion of English common law, refers to the body of laws derived from the decisions of judges and appellate courts. In common law countries such as the United States, case law is very important because Supreme Court decisions become the law of the land, and decisions by lower courts become the law of the jurisdictions they cover. **Procedural law** refers to the body of law that governs how the courts handle criminal and civil cases. The legal rights enjoyed by criminal defendants fall under the rubric of procedural law, and we return to these rights later. Finally, **substantive law** refers to the body of law that specifies which behaviors are crimes and the appropriate punishments for these behaviors. A more familiar term for substantive law is the *penal code.*

As discussed previously, procedural law and substantive law combine to form the body of criminal law. As noted in Chapter 1, the United States actually has countless bodies of criminal law. The federal government has one body of law that defines the behaviors considered federal crimes and outlines how the federal system handles these offenses; each state has its own body of criminal law; and the many jurisdictions within each state also have their own bodies of criminal law. Fortunately, all these systems of law are much more alike than different, and serious offenses are both defined and handled fairly similarly from one jurisdiction to the next. For better or worse, however, some notable differences in criminal laws do exist. For example, nine states legally allow the medical use of marijuana by people who have certain serious illnesses, but the federal government and all other states ban such use (Gibeaut, 2001). Prostitution is legally permitted in certain rural areas of Nevada but prohibited in the major cities of Las Vegas and Reno and in the rest of the nation (Albert, 2001). These differences add to the richness of our criminal justice system but also to its complexity.

Serious Crimes versus Minor Crimes

The criminal law distinguishes between serious crime and minor crime (see Table 4.2). **Felonies** are serious crimes, such as homicide and rape, punishable by incarceration for at least 1 year, whereas **misdemeanors** are minor offenses, such as disturbing the peace, punishable by incarceration of less than 1 year. Someone incarcerated for a felony is ordinarily sent to a state prison for a state offense or a federal prison for a federal offense; someone incarcerated for a misdemeanor is ordinarily sent to a local or county jail. In many areas, misdemeanors are further divided into *gross* and *petty misdemeanors,* the former punishable by more than 30 days in jail and the latter punishable by fewer than 30 days in jail. The most minor offenses, such as many kinds of traffic offenses, are called **violations,** or **infractions,** and are punishable only by fines and do not yield a criminal record.

These distinctions apply to two other ways of categorizing crime, both with Latin roots. *Mala in se* crimes are those considered "evil in themselves," to paraphrase their Latin translation, and are offenses, such as homicide, that are so harmful or immoral that

crimes behaviors deemed so harmful to the public welfare that they should be banned by criminal law

civil law the body of law governing relationships among individuals, organizations, and government agencies

civil wrongs (torts) violations of the civil law

civil suit a legal action taken to remedy a civil wrong

administrative law rules and regulations issued by government agencies

case law laws derived from decisions by appellate courts, especially the Supreme Court

procedural law the body of law that governs how the criminal justice system handles criminal and civil cases

substantive law the body of law that specifies which behaviors are crimes and the appropriate punishments for these behaviors

felonies serious crimes punishable by a sentence of at least 1 year in prison

misdemeanors minor offenses punishable by a jail sentence of less than 1 year

violations (infractions) minor offenses punishable by only a fine

mala in se offenses that are inherently evil; serious crimes

table 4.2   Classifications of Crime

Felonies: serious crimes, such as homicide and rape, punishable by incarceration for at least 1 year

Infractions (or violations): the most minor offenses, such as many kinds of traffic offenses, punishable only by fines

Mala prohibita *crimes:* offenses, such as prostitution and the use of certain drugs, that are considered wrong only because the law forbids them; in general, these are crimes about which reasonable people disagree on the extent of their harm and/or on whether they should be prohibited by law

Mala in se *crimes:* offenses, such as homicide, that are considered so harmful or immoral that they would be wrong even if they did not violate the law

Misdemeanors: minor offenses, such as disturbing the peace, punishable by incarceration of less than 1 year

---

mala prohibita offenses that are crimes only because the law prohibits them; often applied to "victimless" crimes

they would be wrong even if they did not violate the law. In practice, of course, most such offenses are indeed punishable by law and roughly correspond to the felony crimes just described. ***Mala prohibita*** crimes are those that are wrong only because "the law forbids them," again to paraphrase their Latin translation; such offenses include prostitution and the use of certain drugs. In general, these are crimes about which reasonable people disagree on the extent of their harm and/or on whether they should be prohibited by law.

Elements of a Crime

Under the criminal law in a democracy such as the United States, a given behavior is generally a crime and punishable by the criminal law only if six distinct elements characterize it (see Table 4.3). As our discussion of the Andrea Yates trial mentioned, one of these is criminal intent. If this and the other elements of crime are not present, a defendant should not be found guilty of violating the criminal law by engaging in a specific behavior (Wallace and Roberson, 2001).

The first element is that the behavior must be *prohibited by criminal law,* and its punishment must also be specified by criminal law. This element seems so obvious that it

table 4.3   Elements of a Crime

A behavior is generally considered a crime and punishable by the criminal law only if the following elements apply to it:

1. The behavior must be *prohibited by a criminal law*

2. *Actus reus:* an actual act is required, not only the thought of doing the act

3. *Mens rea:* an act must be committed with criminal intent

4. *Concurrence:* a criminal act and criminal intent must occur at roughly the same time, with the intent preceding the act

5. *Causation:* the criminal act must actually cause the harm suffered by a victim

6. *Harm:* some injury or damage must actually occur to an individual, property, or society before a crime can be established

should go without saying. In fact, however, it is one of the most important cornerstones of criminal law in a democratic society. It would be patently unfair for someone to be arrested for committing a behavior that was not prohibited or for committing a behavior that was only later prohibited by a law enacted after the behavior occurred. Such arrests might be routine in some authoritarian regimes, but they clearly violate the fundamental standards of fairness expected in democratic societies. It is likewise essential that the possible punishment for a prohibited behavior also be provided. The lack of such a provision would allow authorities to be arbitrary in their use of punishment and, especially, to mete out overly punitive and hence unfair punishments for some offenders.

Two additional elements, and perhaps the most important ones, are *actus reus* and *mens rea*, Latin terms again. **Actus reus** means "guilty act" and refers to the idea that an actual act, not simply the thought of doing the act, is required before something can be considered a crime. Thus, you cannot be found guilty of merely thinking that you would like to shoplift or break some other law; instead you must actually commit some illegal act. This concept also implies that a law must actually prohibit an act before it can be considered a crime. **Mens rea** means "guilty mind" and refers to the idea that a criminal act must have been *intended* to happen before it can be considered a crime. Another way of saying this is that the offender must have had criminal intent. In practice, this means the offender wanted to do some harm and knew what he or she was doing—the key issue in the Andrea Yates trial—and that the act was not the result of a mere accident or of undue duress. Thus, a defendant should not be found guilty of a crime unless it is established that he or she committed the crime knowingly and willfully. The law also assumes that a criminal act has occurred even if it did so from extreme negligence or recklessness. Thus, if a parent accidentally leaves an infant inside a car on a hot, sunny day and the infant becomes very ill or even dies, the parent may be charged with a crime even though the parent did not intend to harm the child.

A fourth element of a crime is **concurrence.** This means that a criminal act and criminal intent must occur at roughly the same time, with the intent preceding the act. Of course, this is how most crimes occur. But suppose a man is planning to kill a business colleague by pushing him onto a subway platform. The day before he plans to carry out this act, he accidentally kills the colleague in a car crash. Even though the colleague is dead as the would-be offender was intending, no crime occurred because the actual act of murder that was intended did *not* occur.

A fifth element is **causation.** This means that the criminal act actually caused the harm suffered by the victim. Suppose a defendant tries to rob someone with a knife. During the robbery, the victim suffers a heart attack and dies. The prosecution might argue that the victim had the heart attack only because of the robbery and that the defendant is thus guilty of a homicide. For its part, the defense will probably look for any evidence that the defendant had a weak heart and, if such evidence exists, argue that the defendant should not be blamed for a death resulting from a weak heart, not from the robbery itself, especially if the defendant was not intending to harm the victim physically.

The idea of causation implies that the sixth and final element of a crime is **harm.** This means that some harm must actually occur to an individual or property before a crime can be established. This element raises the question of whether harm occurs in so-called "victimless" crimes, such as prostitution and illegal drug use, which involve willing participants and no actual victims as that term is usually understood. Even though participants in these behaviors participate willingly, the law assumes that they are harmed regardless of whether they agree with this assessment, and it also assumes that these behaviors harm society itself.

Criminal Responsibility and Legal Defenses

All the elements just discussed must be proven before a defendant should be found guilty of a crime. It is more difficult to prove these elements for some defendants and criminal acts than for others, and several legal defenses to criminal responsibility challenge the existence of one or more elements (see Table 4.4). Most of them challenge

actus reus as an element of crime, an actual act committed

mens rea as an element of crime, a guilty mind or criminal intent

concurrence as an element of crime, the correspondence of criminal intent and a criminal act

causation as an element of crime, the idea that an act actually caused some harm

harm as an element of crime, the requirement that some injury is done to an individual or property by a criminal act

table 4.4 — Legal Defenses to Criminal Responsibility

Accident, mistake, and ignorance: the defendant committed a harmful act by accident or mistake, or through either ignorance of the law or of the harm caused by one's action

Duress: the defendant was forced to commit a criminal act out of imminent threat to her or his safety or that of loved ones

Self-defense: the defendant's actions were necessary to prevent imminent harm to the defendant, a companion, or the defendant's property

Necessity: the defendant's behavior was necessary to prevent a greater harm from occurring

Entrapment: the defendant committed a crime only after strong inducements by law enforcement officials

Age, developmental disabilities, and insanity: the defendant was unable because of age, developmental disability, or mental illness to comprehend the criminal act the defendant committed

the existence of *mens rea,* or criminal intent. All these defenses involve many complexities in the law but can be summarized here briefly; we return to them in the discussion on the criminal courts in Chapter 9.

Accident, Mistake, and Ignorance

One set of legal defenses is that a defendant committed a harmful act by *accident* or *mistake,* or through either *ignorance* of the law or of the harm caused by one's action. For example, suppose someone gives you a package to mail that, unbeknownst to you, contains a bomb. If you had no reason to suspect a bomb was in the package, you should not be held criminally responsible. Of course, the question of whether you suspected there was a bomb in the package would be up to a jury if the case ever went to trial. The prosecution would probably try to prove that a reasonable person should have been suspicious, perhaps especially after the terrorist attacks of September 11, whereas the defense would try to establish that you had no knowledge of the package's contents and no reason to believe that it contained anything dangerous.

Duress

When under *duress,* a defendant is forced to commit a criminal act out of imminent danger to his or her safety or that of loved ones. If someone threatens to shoot you if you do not help with the commission of a robbery and if you have no realistic chance of escaping the robber's reach, you should not be found guilty if you then help commit the robbery. During the Vietnam War, some defendants arrested for civil disobedience in protest of the war tried to contend they were forced by their consciences to break the law as an act of moral witness against the situation in Vietnam. In this way, they tried to expand the concept of duress, which traditionally has comprised only the threat of bodily harm and not the pressure of conscience. Not surprisingly, judges routinely rejected this novel legal defense, and juries were not allowed to consider it (Barkan, 1985).

Self-Defense

Self-defense may be the legal defense with which you are most familiar. If someone is about to rob or attack you or a companion and you use a weapon in self-defense or otherwise harm the offender, you should not be found guilty of a crime as long as you can prove that the actions you took were necessary to prevent harm to yourself, your companion, or your property. A key issue is the degree of imminent peril the offender actually posed. If the offender was a big man holding a gun, your claim of self-defense might be more credible than if the offender was a small, slender youth with no weapon at all. Another key issue is the amount of force allowed to be used in self-defense. If you shoot an unarmed burglar, your force may exceed the amount that the legitimate use of self-defense permits. If you shoot an actual attacker, wound that person, and keep shooting, your force may again exceed the legitimate amount. It would be up to the criminal justice system to determine whether your claim of self-defense against criminal responsibility is legally valid.

Necessity

Sometimes defendants argue they commit their offense in order to prevent a greater harm from occurring. This is known as a *necessity* defense. Suppose a child is seriously injured and the child's parent, not wanting to wait for an ambulance, carries the child to the family car and then rushes to the hospital. Along the way, the car exceeds the speed limit and runs a red light or two. Technically, the parent has broken several traffic laws, but, if caught and cited by police, the parent could argue that this was necessary to help the injured child. If the parent is prosecuted, a judge and perhaps jury would have to decide whether the parent had a reasonable alternative and, more generally, whether the harm prevented was greater than the harm caused by the offense. During the Vietnam War, some defendants in civil disobedience cases tried to present a necessity defense by arguing that their illegal protests were necessary to call attention to their grievances against the war. As with the duress defense, judges routinely refused to allow defendants to present this defense and juries to consider it (Barkan, 1985).

Entrapment

The legal defense of *entrapment* is especially complex. If you commit a crime *only* because the police or other law enforcement agents induce you to do so, you may argue that you were entrapped and should not be found guilty. Such entrapment defenses are difficult to prove, but ordinarily they have the best chance of succeeding if the defendant is otherwise a law-abiding citizen who committed a crime only after repeated requests by law enforcement agents and/or after the use of particularly strong inducements by them.

Thus, if an undercover agent asks you to buy some illegal drugs for a small "reward" of $50 and you quickly agree, your entrapment defense might not succeed because you seemed too eager to oblige. But if you agree only after many requests to buy the drugs and the promise of a reward of several thousand dollars, your entrapment defense might seem more valid. If a man is cruising a "red-light" district filled with prostitutes and is arrested after agreeing to have sex with an undercover police officer posing as a prostitute, an entrapment defense probably will not work because it would be difficult to argue that the man would not have engaged the services of a prostitute if he had not been induced by the officer. A primary element in entrapment defenses is the *predisposition* of the defendant. In the prostitution case, the prosecutor will try to establish that the defendant was predisposed to pick up a prostitute and needed only some small inducement to break the law, whereas the defense will try to establish that the defendant had no such predisposition and broke the law only because of substantial inducements offered by the undercover officer. Entrapment defenses have their best chances of success if the defendant has no history of criminal behavior and especially no history of the offense with which he or she is charged.

Diminished Capacity: Age, Developmental Disabilities, and Insanity

Mens rea, or criminal intent, lies at the heart of a set of legal defenses that focuses on the capacity of defendants to comprehend their criminal acts because of a diminished capacity. Diminished capacity may derive from young age, developmental disabilities, or mental illness.

Age. Historically, the common law has recognized that some individuals, usually those under 17 or 18, are too young to be able to understand the consequences of their actions and to possess the required criminal intent. Thus, if a 5-year-old gets angry at a friend, finds and retrieves his parents' loaded and unlocked gun, points it at the friend saying "I'm going to shoot you," and pulls the trigger, our criminal law holds that the child was too young to understand what he was doing, however tragic the death that results.

An important issue in today's society concerns the exact age above which defendants are presumed old enough to understand their actions. Many states in recent years have begun to prosecute as adults offenders as young as 13 or 14 who commit serious crimes and to have the (adult) criminal justice system, rather than the juvenile justice system, handle their cases (Bishop, 2000). Proponents say this shift is necessary to reduce juvenile crime and to punish serious juvenile offenders severely. Opponents say children that young do not understand their actions sufficiently enough to justify being considered adults and that their criminal tendencies will simply be reinforced if the criminal justice system handles their cases. Chapter 14 discusses the age issue at greater length.

Developmental Disabilities. Some defendants have developmental disabilities that make it difficult, and perhaps impossible, for them to understand the nature and consequences of their actions. Whether such defendants should be held criminally responsible is also a matter of great dispute in the contemporary legal system. Some states allow developmentally disabled individuals who commit murder to be sentenced to death, whereas other states forbid their execution even if they permit executions more generally. Over the years, several such defendants have been executed. One such man was Ricky Ray Rector, who was executed by Arkansas in 1992; after eating part of his last meal, he said he would save the dessert for after he returned from his execution (Cohen, 2002). The U.S. Supreme Court last considered this issue in February 2002, when it heard the case of a Virginia death row inmate with an IQ of 59. The Court's deliberation hinged on the issue of whether a national consensus had developed in the United States against executions of the mentally disabled. Because about half the states with the death penalty allowed for such executions, it was not clear to some members of the Court that a national consensus against these executions yet existed (Greenhouse, 2002). In June 2002, however, the court banned them by a 6–3 vote.

Insanity. As the Yates case reminds us, a related issue is the *insanity defense,* which argues that certain defendants cannot by reason of mental defect appreciate the consequences of their actions and thus should not be held criminally responsible. The insanity defense is very complex but generally means that a defendant does not know right from wrong and/or was not able to control his or her behavior (Rogers, 2000).

American courts actually use several standards of insanity with the specific standard depending on the jurisdiction in which a case is heard. The oldest standard is the *McNaughtan Rule,* named after the case of Daniel McNaughtan, who assassinated Edward Drummond, the private secretary to the British prime minister, Edward Peel, in 1843. McNaughtan actually meant to kill Peel but shot Drummond by mistake after he mistook the secretary for his employer. During his trial, McNaughtan claimed he had been delusional, and he was found not guilty by reason of insanity. The case led to the development of the McNaughtan rule, which says that defendants cannot be held criminally responsible if they have a mental defect that prevents them from understanding the act of which they are accused or, if they did understand it, from understanding that their act was wrong (Moran, 1981). The McNaughtan rule, or the "knowing right from wrong rule," is still the standard in several U.S. states and governed the Yates trial.

Some individuals may have a serious mental illness that drives them to commit a criminal act even though they understand that the act is wrong. Recognizing this and believing the McNaughtan rule too limited in its application, many states have developed the *irresistible impulse test*. Under this standard, individuals are not held criminally responsible if it is proven that they had a serious mental condition that compelled them to commit a criminal act, even if they did understand that the act was wrong and violated the law.

A third standard, now used only in New Hampshire where it was developed, is the *Durham rule*, which holds that individuals may not be found guilty if their criminal act resulted from a mental disease or defect. Because this standard is both weaker and vaguer than either the McNaughtan rule or the irresistible impulse test, it has not proven popular elsewhere.

A fourth standard is the *substantial capacity test*, which is used by about half the states. This rule states that a defendant cannot be held responsible for a criminal act if, because of a mental disease or defect, he or she lacked "substantial capacity" to understand that the act was wrong or to obey the law. This standard integrates the McNaughtan rule and the irresistible impulse test; it is less stringent than the McNaughtan rule because it does not require that a defendant was completely unable to distinguish right from wrong, only that he or she lacked the "substantial capacity" to do so.

Current federal law is stricter than the substantial capacity test because it declares that defendants are not criminally responsible if they lacked the ability to understand that their actions were wrong. Because it demands that they lacked this understanding, it is more stringent than both the irresistible impulse test and the substantial capacity test; it allows for defendants to be criminally responsible as long as they understand their act was wrong, even if a mental condition compelled them to commit the act.

The insanity defense is quite controversial and often receives much media attention when it is used in cases involving serious crime. In addition to the Yates case, another celebrated case involving the insanity defense was the trial of John Hinckley, Jr., who was arrested in 1981 for shooting then-President Ronald Reagan. Hinckley said he shot Reagan in order to capture the interest of actress Jodie Foster. When the jury found him not guilty by reason of insanity, its verdict was condemned by many observers and much of the public. Despite this controversy, in practice very few defendants present insanity defenses, with Andrea Yates's sad story a notable exception to this general rule, and its use does not unduly impede the prosecution of criminal cases (S. Walker, 2001).

Constitutional and Procedural Rights

Recall that a body of procedural law defines how criminal cases should be conducted. This body of law, along with the Constitution, Bill of Rights, and judicial interpretations of these documents, provides several procedural rights to criminal suspects and defendants (see Table 4.5). These rights exist in theory but are not always provided in practice. For example, although criminal defendants enjoy the right to counsel, in practice poor defendants do not get effective counsel because their lawyers' caseloads are far too heavy to permit adequate legal representation (Fritsch and Rohde, 2001).

The Bill of Rights and Legal Protections

We noted earlier that many of the procedural rights enjoyed by suspects and defendants are provided for in the Constitution and Bill of Rights because England's abuse of the legal system was fresh in the minds of the citizens of the new nation. However, the Constitution specified only a few such rights. For example, Article 1, Section 2 guaranteed the right of *habeas corpus*, which requires that defendants be brought before judges to determine whether their arrest and detainment are lawful, whereas Article 3, Section 3 specified the right to trial by jury. The passage in 1791 of the Bill of Rights, the first 10 amendments to the Constitution, was intended in part to provide more legal rights to suspects and defendants. These rights were specified in the Fourth, Fifth, Sixth, and Eighth Amendments.

table 4.5   The Bill of Rights and Legal Protections for Individuals

The Fourth Amendment: The right of the people to be secure in their persons, houses, papers, and effects, against unreasonable searches and seizures, shall not be violated, and no Warrants shall issue, but upon probable cause, supported by Oath or affirmation, and particularly describing the places to be searched, and the persons or things to be seized.

    The police and other governmental agents may not search someone's person or property, seize that property, or arrest the person without adequate justification.

The Fifth Amendment: No person shall be held to answer for a capital, or otherwise infamous crime, unless on a presentment or indictment of a Grand Jury, except in cases arising in the land or naval forces, or in the Militia, when in actual service in time of War or public danger; nor shall any person be subject for the same offence to be twice put in jeopardy of life or limb; nor shall be compelled in any criminal case to be a witness against himself, nor be deprived of life, liberty, or property, without due process of law; nor shall private property be taken for public use, without just compensation.

    No one can be placed in double jeopardy by being prosecuted twice for the same crime; defendants may not be forced to testify against themselves; the processing of criminal cases must follow due process of law requirements.

The Sixth Amendment: In all criminal prosecutions, the accused shall enjoy the right to a speedy and public trial, by an impartial jury of the State and district wherein the crime shall have been committed, which district shall have been previously ascertained by law, and to be informed of the nature and cause of the accusation; to be confronted with the witnesses against him; to have compulsory process for obtaining witnesses in his favor, and to have the Assistance of Counsel for his defence.

    Defendants must have a speedy public trial; in addition, they enjoy the right to a trial by jury, they must be told the charges against them, and they have the right to question witnesses and to representation by legal counsel.

The Eighth Amendment: Excessive bail shall not be required, nor excessive fines imposed, nor cruel and unusual punishments inflicted.

    Excessive bail and fines, and cruel and unusual punishment are prohibited.

The Fourth Amendment. *The right of the people to be secure in their persons, houses, papers, and effects, against unreasonable searches and seizures, shall not be violated, and no Warrants shall issue, but upon probable cause, supported by Oath or affirmation, and particularly describing the places to be searched, and the persons or things to be seized.* Two phrases from the Fourth Amendment have entered the American lexicon: "unreasonable search and seizure" and "probable cause." Together, they mean that the police and other governmental agents may not search someone's person or property, seize that property, or arrest the person without adequate justification. In a democracy, such restrictions on the police are critical to protect personal privacy and to prevent abuse of police power.

The Fifth Amendment. *No person shall be held to answer for a capital, or otherwise infamous crime, unless on a presentment or indictment of a Grand Jury, except in cases arising in the land or naval forces, or in the Militia, when in actual service in time of War or public danger; nor shall any person be subject for the same offence to be twice put in jeopardy of life or limb; nor shall be compelled in any criminal case to be a witness against himself, nor be deprived of life, liberty,* *or property, without due process of law; nor shall private property be taken for public use, without just compensation.* The Fifth Amendment provides several important protections. First, it specifies that no one can be placed in "double jeopardy" (another familiar phrase) by being prosecuted twice for the same crime. This provision was meant to limit prosecutorial harassment. Second, it protects defendants from being forced to testify against themselves and, in so doing, to incriminate themselves. This provision was meant to limit police abuse and also to require prosecutors to prove a defendant's guilt without any help from the defendant. Third, it requires that the processing of criminal cases follow "due process of law" requirements. We return to the importance of this "due process" clause later.

The Sixth Amendment. *In all criminal prosecutions, the accused shall enjoy the right to a speedy and public trial, by an impartial jury of the State and district wherein the crime shall have been committed, which district shall have been previously ascertained by law, and to be informed of the nature and cause of the accusation; to be confronted with the witnesses against him; to have compulsory process for obtaining witnesses in his favor, and to have the Assistance of Counsel for his defence.* The Sixth Amendment also provides several rights. First, defendants must have a speedy, public trial. Both these features protect defendants from government abuse, particularly in the form of unjustifiably long detainment and secret legal proceedings. Second, defendants enjoy the right to a trial by jury. During the colonial period, juries often came to the aid of colonists unfairly prosecuted by England, and the inclusion of the right to jury trials in both this amendment and in Article 3, Section 3 (noted previously) reflects the importance that the new nation placed on the jury. Third, defendants must be told the charges against them and have the right to question witnesses. Again, these rights seem essential in any democracy's criminal justice system. Fourth, defendants must have the right to legal representation. Given the complexity of criminal proceedings, assistance of counsel is deemed necessary to protect defendants from governmental power.

The Eighth Amendment. *Excessive bail shall not be required, nor excessive fines imposed, nor cruel and unusual punishments inflicted.* The Eighth Amendment prohibits excessive bail and fines and, more importantly, "cruel and unusual punishment" (again a familiar phrase). During the 1960s and early 1970s, the U.S. Supreme Court interpreted the latter provision as requiring various reforms of prison and jail

The Sixth Amendment guarantees the right to a speedy, public trial by a jury of one's peers.

conditions (see Chapter 13). Critics of the death penalty assert that "cruel and unusual punishment" prohibits executions in today's society, but so far the Supreme Court has not supported this interpretation.

The Expansion of Due Process

For almost a century after the beginning of the United States, the provisions in all these amendments applied *only* to actions by the federal government. Defendants in most criminal cases thus did not enjoy these rights because most criminal cases involve state or local proceedings, not federal ones. The Fourteenth Amendment, passed in 1868 after the Civil War, began to present a change in this legal thinking. Designed to protect the rights of newly freed slaves, this amendment declared that no *state* could deprive anyone of "life, liberty, or property, without due process of law; nor deny to any person within its jurisdiction the equal protection of the laws." This amendment also theoretically prevented the states from denying citizens, including suspects and defendants, the rights and freedoms guaranteed by the Bill of Rights.

Despite this implication, it was left to the Supreme Court to determine the circumstances under which state actions were governed by the amendment. A series of Supreme Court rulings beginning in the first half of the twentieth century began expanding the rights that suspects and defendants in state cases enjoyed under the Fourteenth Amendment's due process clause. For example, the Court ruled in *Powell v. Alabama* (287 U.S. 45 [1932]) that poor defendants in capital (death penalty) cases must be provided counsel for their defense. During the 1960s, the Court greatly expanded legal rights in criminal proceedings. A hallmark case from this period was *Gideon v. Wainwright* (372 U.S. 335 [1963]), which required that counsel be provided to poor defendants in all criminal cases. Two other important rulings were *Mapp v. Ohio* (367 U.S. 643 [1961]), which extended the Fourth Amendment's protection from unreasonable searches and seizures to state actions; and *Miranda v. Arizona* (384 U.S. 436 [1966]), which established that criminal suspects have the right to remain silent and the right to have an attorney present during any questioning by the police. We discuss these and other important due process decisions later.

Suspects or defendants who believe they have been denied any legal right may challenge their prosecution. For example, they may believe they were arrested without probable cause and ask a judge to dismiss the charges. Or they may believe that their homes were searched without a proper warrant and ask a judge to exclude any evidence gathered during the search. They may also challenge their prosecution if they believe that either the police or the prosecutor engaged in various kinds of misconduct. In recent years, disclosures of police misconduct in cities such as Los Angeles and Philadelphia forced the dismissal of many charges and the reversal of convictions in cases already decided. In these cities, the police fabricated evidence against drug dealers and other suspects and lied on the witness stand (Fazlollah, 1997; Glover and Lait, 2000a).

The Supreme Court and the Police

As this discussion should illustrate, Supreme Court rulings governing police treatment of suspects have aroused much controversy, in part because they throw into sharp relief the fundamental conflict in democratic societies between public safety and protection from governmental abuse (Skolnick, 1994) (see Chapter 1). In totalitarian states, people have few (if any) individual rights, and the police can deal with the populace in virtually any manner the police deem appropriate. As we have indicated, however, police in democratic societies, such as the United States, must obey certain constitutional standards of behavior, as interpreted by the Supreme Court, in their effort to enforce criminal laws. As legal scholar J. Shane Creamer (1980, p. 1) has noted, "In Nazi Germany the Gestapo operated under a system of no limitations or legal constraints and literally could seize any citizen any time without cause. In our free society, the Constitution absolutely prevents this type of harrowing police tactic." Although Americans are protected from unlawful arrests, searches, and seizures, it is the Supreme Court that determines the limits of police power.

In the post–World War II era, a number of Supreme Court rulings have focused on the scope and dimension of police power (see Table 4.6). The most controversial of these decisions have involved the **exclusionary rule:** "Evidence obtained by violating the defendant's constitutional rights may not be introduced by the prosecution, at least for purposes of providing direct proof of the defendant's guilt" (Emanuel and Knowles, 1999–2000, p. 252). The Supreme Court developed this rule by extending several of the protections in the Bill of Rights that we have already examined: (1) The Fourth Amendment prohibits the introduction of physical evidence gathered through unreasonable searches and seizures; (2) the Fifth Amendment prohibits the use of confessions obtained in violation of the defendant's right against self-incrimination; and (3) the Sixth Amendment excludes the introduction of evidence obtained in violation of the defendant's right

exclusionary rule the principle that evidence obtained by the police in violation of a suspect's constitutional rights may not be used to prosecute the defendant

table 4.6

Selected U.S. Supreme Court Rulings and Restrictions on Police Behavior

Chimel v. California (1969): police must obtain a search warrant before searching a suspect's person and property

Escobedo v. Illinois (1964): suspects have the right to legal representation when being questioned by the police

Mapp v. Ohio (1961): evidence that the police gather without probable cause may not be used in court (the exclusionary rule)

Miranda v. Arizona (1966): the police must inform suspects that they have the right to remain silent, that any statement they make may be used against them, and that they have the right to consult with an attorney; any statements or evidence obtained in violation of the "Miranda" rule are not admissible in criminal court

Ohio v. Robinette (1996): the police are not required to inform a suspect that he or she is free to go before an officer conducts a consensual search

Tennessee v. Garner (1985): the police may not use deadly force to prevent a suspected felon from fleeing

Terry v. Ohio (1968): permits police to detain and search a suspect if the police have reasonable grounds to believe the suspect is about to commit a crime or is armed and dangerous

U.S. v. Leon (1984): the prosecution may introduce illegally obtained evidence if police officers obtained this evidence by relying on a search warrant that they reasonably, but erroneously, believed to be valid

Whren v. United States (1996): permits police to make "pretextual detentions" in which they stop a motor vehicle for a minor traffic violation when their real objective is to investigate the suspect for another offense for which there was not probable cause to detain the suspect

Wyoming v. Houghton (1999): after stopping a motor vehicle for an alleged traffic violation, the police may search the possessions of a passenger even though he or she had nothing to do with the alleged traffic violation and had done nothing to suggest that he or she was involved in criminal activity

to counsel. Following are some of the more salient decisions involving the exclusionary rule and other issues relating to police power (Samaha, 1990).

Mapp v. Ohio (decided 1961). In May 1957, three Cleveland police officers arrived at the home of Darlene Mapp and demanded admittance, stating that a person wanted in connection with a recent bombing was believed to be hiding at that location. Mrs. Mapp telephoned her attorney, who advised her not to let the police enter the home without a search warrant. A few hours later, four more officers arrived on the scene, and, when Mrs. Mapp did not come to the door, the police forcibly entered the home. Mrs. Mapp grabbed a piece of paper that one of the officers claimed was a warrant and "placed it in her bosom." After a struggle, the officers recovered the paper, handcuffed Mapp, and confined her in an upstairs room. The police then searched the premises and discovered obscene material. At a trial wherein Mrs. Mapp was convicted of possessing obscene material, no search warrant was produced by the prosecuting attorney, nor was the failure to exhibit such a document ever explained (Creamer, 1980).

On appeal, the Ohio Supreme Court upheld the conviction, although it noted that the evidence used to convict Mrs. Mapp (the obscene material) might have been seized illegally. The U.S. Supreme Court reversed the Mapp conviction, stating that the police lacked probable cause to arrest Mrs. Mapp. The information that the police "claimed to have that a fugitive was hiding in her home" could not justify the arrest of anyone (Creamer, 1980, p. 348). Because the police had no search warrant and no consent for the search, any evidence they found was obtained illegally and, as such, was not admissible in a court of law. The evidence should have been suppressed.

Before the *Mapp* decision, the exclusionary rule, originally created by federal judges in 1914, applied only to federal law enforcement officers. The *Mapp* decision extended the rule by creating "the first explicit, national, uniform standards in constitutional and criminal law" (Creamer, 1980). All police officers now operate under the same rules regarding a citizen's privacy and how that privacy relates to the introduction of evidence in criminal proceedings.

U.S. v. Leon (decided 1984). In *U.S. v. Leon,* the Court ruled that the prosecution may introduce illegally obtained evidence if police officers obtained this evidence by relying on a search warrant that they reasonably, but erroneously, believed to be valid (Emanuel and Knowles, 1999–2000). In their written opinion, the justices stated that "the exclusionary rule be more generally modified to permit the introduction of evidence obtained in the reasonable good-faith belief that a search or seizure was in accord with the Fourth Amendment . . ." (Samaha, 1990, p. 93). Simply stated, the Court permitted what is commonly referred to as a "good faith" exception to the exclusionary rule.

Escobedo v. Illinois (decided 1964). In January 1961, Danny Escobedo was arrested and interrogated for 15 hours regarding the fatal shooting of his brother-in-law. Eleven days later, he was arrested a second time and taken to a police station for further questioning. Escobedo's attorney arrived a short time later, and after repeated requests to see his client was told this was not possible. When Escobedo asked to see his lawyer, he was informed that the attorney did not want to see him. Police then told Escobedo that he could not make contact with legal counsel until they were finished with the interrogation. Escobedo then made self-incriminating comments that were later used against him in court, and he eventually was convicted for his involvement in his brother-in-law's murder. On appeal, the Supreme Court ruled that Escobedo had been denied the right to the assistance of legal counsel at a "critical stage" of a criminal proceeding. Refusal of the police to permit Escobedo access to his attorney constituted a denial of his Sixth Amendment rights (Creamer, 1980). J. Shane Creamer notes that this 5 to 4 decision was a "strong judicial attempt" to destroy prolonged police interrogations of suspects without the benefit of legal counsel. In the previous year (1963), George Whitmore, a New York City man, had confessed to the murders of two women following a grueling 26-hour interrogation session. After investigating some of the inconsistencies in the 60-page confession, a Manhattan district attorney was instrumental in gaining Whitmore's release. Shortly afterward, another man was indicted and convicted of the dual murders.

Miranda v. Arizona (decided 1966).

In 1963, Ernesto Miranda was arrested in connection with the forcible abduction and rape of an 18-year-old girl in Phoenix, Arizona. Two hours after being identified by the victim in a police lineup, Miranda signed a confession admitting his guilt. During the course of the trial, Miranda's attorney asked one of the police officers who had taken his client's statement if Miranda had been told that "he is entitled to the advice of an attorney" before he made it. The officer responded that he had not. The court admitted the confession into evidence and Miranda was convicted. On appeal, the Arizona Supreme Court affirmed the conviction and noted that, because Miranda had been arrested on two previous occasions (and convicted one time), he was familiar with criminal–legal proceedings and knowingly waived his rights. In 1966, the Supreme Court in a hotly contested 5 to 4 decision reversed the Arizona high court's judgment (Creamer, 1980).

In their majority statement, the justices wrote that "the prosecution may not use statements . . . stemming from custodial interrogation of the defendant unless it demonstrates the use of procedural safeguards effective to secure the privilege of self-incrimination" (in Gifis, 1980, p. 129). In other words, "custodial interrogation is inherently coercive" (Samaha, 1990). Detained in strange surroundings, devoid of the support of family and friends, and subject to skilled police officers who can and will use trickery and psychological pressure to obtain a confession, a suspect needs strong protection to counter the power of the state (Samaha, 1990). Before being questioned, suspects must be warned that: (1) They have the right to remain silent, (2) that any statement they make may be used against them, and (3) they have the right to consult with an attorney. Any statements or evidence obtained in violation of the *Miranda* rule are not admissible in criminal court (Gifis, 1980).

In July 2000, the Supreme Court reaffirmed *Miranda* by a 7 to 2 vote. Chief Justice Rehnquist stated that the 1966 ruling "has become embedded in routine police practice to the point the warnings have become part of our national heritage" (in Richey and Axtman, 2000, p. 1). At issue was a 1968 law passed by Congress that would have overturned *Miranda*, with the Court having to decide which rule has precedence. The Court ruled that *Miranda* was a "constitutional decision" that cannot

The *Miranda* warning, read here to a suspect, requires that the police tell people being arrested that they have the right to remain silent, that any statement they make may be used against them, and that they have the right to consult with an attorney. Any statements or evidence obtained in violation of the U.S. Supreme Court's *Miranda* rule are not admissible in court.

be overruled by Congress "and we decline to overrule Miranda ourselves" ("Miranda Survivor," 2000, p. 25).

***Chimel v. California* (decided 1969).** In 1965, police officers in Santa Ana, California, arrived at the home of Ted Chimel with a warrant for his arrest on a burglary charge. The suspect was placed under arrest, and the officers asked if they could look around. Chimel said no, but the officers conducted a search of the residence without a search warrant and found stolen property that was admitted into evidence over the objection of his attorney. Chimel was convicted of burglary. The Supreme Court reversed the conviction, stating that, if the arresting officers wanted to search Chimel's residence, they should have obtained a search warrant. The justices stated that, while making an arrest, the police are limited to searching the suspect and the area "within his immediate control" (which has subsequently been referred to as the "lunge area") so that he or she may not obtain a weapon or destroy evidence (*Chimel v. California,* 2001; Creamer, 1980).

***Terry v. Ohio* (decided 1968).** In 1963, a Cleveland plainclothes police officer observed two men walk back and forth along an identical route in front of a store. After each of these up-and-back strolls, the two men would stop and talk. At one point, the duo was joined by a third man. Thinking that the men were "casing a job, a stick up," the officer confronted the trio, asked a few questions, grabbed one of the suspects, and "patted him down." He found a revolver first on the person of Terry and another on a second suspect (Chilton). After the men were charged with carrying concealed weapons, the defense moved to suppress the evidence, arguing that the officer had no probable cause to arrest and then search the suspects. Terry's attorney contended that walking back and forth in front of the store could not be construed as a prelude to robbery. The court denied the motion to suppress and the defendants were convicted. An appellate court affirmed the convictions, and the Supreme Court dismissed Terry's final appeal (Creamer, 1980). Writing for the Court, Chief Justice Warren commented (Samaha, 1990, p. 166), "At the time he seized petitioner and searched him for weapons, Officer McFadden had reasonable grounds to believe that petitioner was armed and dangerous, and it was necessary for the protection of himself and others to take swift measures to discover the true facts and neutralize the threat of harm if it materialized."

***Ohio v. Robinette* (decided 1996).** A police officer pulled over Robert Robinette for speeding, issued him a warning, and returned his driver's license. The officer then asked Robinette if he was carrying any contraband, illegal drugs, or weapons. Robinette said "no" at which time the officer asked the defendant if he would consent to a search of his car. Robinette later testified that he "automatically" consented to the search. The officer found a small amount of marijuana and a methamphetamine pill. Robinettte was charged with the possession of a controlled substance. The Ohio Supreme Court ruled that the officer had extended the stop beyond its traffic enforcement purpose and used this "coercive setting" to gain consent for a search from Robinette. The court argued that both the state and federal constitutions require that people be secure in their property and possessions (Cole, 1999; "Traffic Detainee Need Not Be Advised," 1999). As such, police officers are required to inform individuals that they are free to go after a lawful detention but before the officer attempts to gain permission for a search. The Ohio Supreme Court stated that a "bright line rule" is necessary in such police–citizen encounters. In other words, before asking for consent to search, officers must inform the individual that "At this time you are free to go," or words to that effect. In an 8 to 1 decision, the U.S. Supreme Court reversed the Ohio ruling, arguing that the Fourth Amendment does not require that a legally detained individual be informed that he or she is free to go before an officer moves toward a consensual search. The Court stated that it would be "unrealistic" for police officers to routinely inform detainees that they are free to go before a consent to search may be considered voluntary (Cole, 1999; "Traffic Detainee Need Not Be Advised," 1999).

Whren v. United States (decided 1996).

In 1993, plainclothes Washington D.C. police officers riding in an unmarked car spotted two young males in a new sport utility vehicle (SUV) with temporary tags in a neighborhood known for drug activity. Under the pretext of making a traffic stop because the driver had waited more than 20 seconds at a stop sign (a violation in D.C.), the officers made a U-turn and headed back toward the vehicle, which then turned suddenly to the right and took off at an "unreasonable" rate of speed. The police pursued and quickly overtook the SUV. Michael Whren, the passenger, was holding a bag of cocaine in each hand. Whren's attorney moved that the cocaine be suppressed as evidence because the traffic stop was pretextual; the officers were primarily interested in finding drugs, not enforcing traffic laws. In court, the officers testified they had no intention of enforcing the traffic laws that they were not authorized to enforce under department regulations (in D.C., plainclothes officers can only enforce traffic laws if the violation in question presents an immediate safety threat). In a unanimous decision, the Supreme Court ruled that the traffic stop was constitutional. The court stated that "pretextual detentions" (stopping a vehicle for some minor traffic violation when the real objective was investigating something else for which there was no cause to detain) are lawful ("Administrative Notes," 1999; Cole, 1999; Urbonya, 1997).

Wyoming v. Houghton (decided 1999).

In July 1995, Wyoming police stopped a car occupied by David Young, his girlfriend, and Sandra Houghton for speeding and having a faulty brake light. After the stop, the officer, now joined by two other officers, noticed a syringe in Young's pocket and ordered him to step out of the car and put the syringe on the hood. On questioning, Young admitted that he used the device for taking drugs. The two passengers were ordered out of the vehicle and patted down for contraband and weapons. The officers then searched the car for drugs and found a closed "lady's purse" where the women, who had not given their consent for the search, were seated. The purse, which belonged to Houghton, contained drugs and drug paraphernalia. Young and his girlfriend were released, and Houghton was charged with possession of a controlled substance. Before the trial, Houghton's attorney moved to suppress the evidence, arguing that police had no probable cause to search her belongings. (During the trial the arresting officers testified that they did not believe any weapons were in the vehicle.) The presiding judge ruled that the officers had probable cause to search the car for contraband and that the drugs could be introduced as evidence. Houghton was sentenced to the Wyoming Women's Center for up to 3 years.

On appeal, the Wyoming Supreme Court ruled that the search violated Houghton's Fourth Amendment rights, and her conviction was reversed. In April 1999, the U.S. Supreme Court decided that the police can search the possessions of a passenger even though he or she had nothing to do with the alleged traffic violation and had done nothing to suggest that he or she was involved in criminal activity (Harris, 1999). The court reasoned that police officers with probable cause to search a vehicle may also inspect passengers' belongings that might conceal the object of that search (*Wyoming v. Houghton*, 1999).

Tennessee v. Garner (decided 1985).

All the cases just discussed concerned police powers of search and seizure. In *Tennessee v. Garner*, the Court addressed police use of deadly force. Searching for a prowler in 1974, Memphis police officers spotted a teenager in a residential backyard near a chain-link fence. The officers did not see a weapon and were "reasonably sure" that the youth was unarmed. One officer yelled, "Police, halt," and moved forward. When the suspect began to climb the fence, an officer fired. The bullet struck Edward Garner in the back of the head, and he died at a hospital a short time later. In 1980, Tennessee was one of 32 states that allowed police to use deadly force against fleeing felons (Creamer, 1980). The Supreme Court ruled that the officer in the Garner case could not have reasonably believed that the suspect posed any threat. The fact that an individual has burglarized a dwelling does not automatically mean that he or she is dangerous (*Tennessee v. Garner,* 2001). Justice Byron wrote, "The use of deadly force to prevent the escape of all felony suspects, whatever the circumstances, is constitutionally unreasonable. . . . It is no doubt unfortunate when a suspect who is in sight escapes, but the fact that the police arrive a little late or are slower afoot does not always justify killing a suspect. A police officer may not seize an unarmed, nondangerous suspect by shooting him dead" (*Tennessee v. Garner,* 2001, p. 1).

The Garner decision led law enforcement agencies to begin formulating a policy for use of deadly force. For example, in 1995, Attorney General Reno approved a procedure for all U.S. Department of Justice agencies that was later adopted by the Department of the Treasury (Hall, 1996, p. 26): "Law enforcement officers . . . may use deadly force only when necessary, that is, when the officer has a reasonable belief that the subject of such force poses an imminent danger of death or serious physical injury to the officer or to another person." In the post-*Garner* era, the number of individuals killed by law enforcement officers has been significantly reduced.

Have Supreme Court Decisions Helped or Hurt the Police?
The Supreme Court decisions of the 1960s (*Mapp v. Ohio, Miranda v. Arizona,* and *Escobedo v. Illinois*) were met with hostility by police officers across the country. Regarding the *Miranda* case, a police chief in Texas stated, "Damnedest thing I ever heard, we might as well close up shop" (in Brewster, 1991, p. 85). In 1968, President-elect Richard Nixon promised to appoint justices to the Supreme Court who were more receptive to the needs of the law enforcement community than they were to the arguments of criminal defendants (Biskupic and Witt, 1997). Nixon blamed the "liberal" Warren Court (Chief Justice Earl Warren was a member of the court from 1954 to 1969) for the nation's rising crime rates.

Peter Arenella (1997) argues that, over the years, *Miranda* has been embraced by an increasingly large number of police personnel. Police like this ruling because it provides them with clear guidelines for interrogating suspects and does not eliminate their power to manipulate suspects by deceiving them once they have been read their *Miranda* rights and waived them. Smith (1996, p. 823) suggests that *Miranda* has simultaneous and "roughly offsetting effects." Although *Miranda* rights may discourage people from making outright confessions of guilt, it also encourages suspects to talk to police and often incriminate themselves indirectly. "Understanding that they do not have to talk might sometimes make suspects more likely to talk because they feel more at ease or feel they are equal to the interrogators" (Smith and DeFrances, 1996, p. 831). The *Miranda* rights may also bring about a kind of "false consciousness" on the part of suspects inasmuch as police compliance with these rights deludes them into thinking they no longer have anything to fear from talking to authorities (Arenella, 1997).

A direct observation study of 118 interrogations conducted by the editors of the *Yale Law Journal* (1967) found no evidence that *Miranda* reduced the interrogation success rate (confessions). Some 30 years after this famous decision, another researcher concluded that studies indicated "no proof of a *Miranda* effect on the confession rate" (Thomas, 1996, p. 837). In addition, a number of studies find that, after being so informed by the police, a majority of suspects choose to waive their *Miranda* protections. In Salt Lake City, for example, researchers discovered that 83.7 percent of suspects chose this alternative (Cassell and Hayman, 1996). In other words, *Miranda* is a factor in only a small number of criminal interrogations.

In sum, the *Miranda* warning does not hamper the police because the majority of suspects waive their *Miranda* rights and answer police questions anyway, and many confess. They do so partly because they feel safe with the *Miranda* warning, partly because the police already have a lot of evidence against them, and partly because the police promise them a more lenient outcome or even lie about the strength of the evidence (Hoffman, 1998; Leo, 1996). If *Miranda* had retained its initial unpopularity with

the nation's police over the past 35 years, one would expect that law enforcement organizations and unions would have lobbied their state representatives to accept the Court's invitation to replace *Miranda* at the state level with alternative procedural safeguards (Arenella, 1997). However, rather than fight *Miranda,* the law enforcement community as a whole decided to live with the ruling and eventually discovered that *Miranda* was a positive step. A California sheriff stated, "When *Miranda* came down all of law enforcement thought the bad guys had won again. But after some reluctance and suspicion we began to work harder. We became more professional. Instead of relying on outwitting somebody in interrogation, we went and got good evidence" (in Brewster, 1991, p. 86). Another officer noted that the post-*Miranda* emphasis on gathering evidence resulted in an improvement in the quality of detective work as well as an acceleration of technological advancements to obtain this evidence.

What about the exclusionary rule resulting from the *Mapp v. Ohio* decision that suppresses illegally obtained evidence? Critics initially feared that the police would be unduly "shackled" in their crime-fighting ability. Strident opposition to the rule has since softened considerably. For example, all 26 Chicago Police Department narcotics officers that Myron Orfield (1987) interviewed asserted that the exclusionary rule should be retained along with a tightly worded "good faith" exception, meaning that, if an officer intended to comply with rules of gathering evidence but inadvertently made a mistake, the evidence would not be suppressed. One officer stated, "I would not do anything to the exclusionary rule . . . it is not a detriment to police work. In fact the opposite is true. It makes the police department more professional. . . . Throughout this department the majority of cases are not hurt by the exclusionary rule" (in Orfield, 1987, p. 1016). Another officer said, "In the old days if we knew something was in the house . . . we would just knock the door down. Now we use a search warrant" (p. 1052).

Studies of the exclusionary rule find it does not hamper police and prosecutors from carrying out their jobs (S. Walker, 2001). The exclusionary rule is only rarely applied, and conviction in most cases does not depend on evidence gathered from searches of a suspect's home or person. Motions to suppress evidence based on the exclusionary rule are made in only about 5 percent of all cases and only rarely granted. A study of more than 500,000 California cases found that prosecutors rejected less than 1 percent of the cases because of illegally gathered evidence (Fyfe, 1983).

As noted earlier, police powers expanded during the 1990s when several Supreme Court decisions (*Ohio v. Robinette, Whren v. United States,* and *Wyoming v. Houghton*) provided law enforcement with increased authority to stop and search individuals virtually anytime and for any reason. A number of people in the law enforcement community were overjoyed that the Supreme Court had made a shift to the ideological right regarding police powers. After the *Whren* decision one California highway patrol officer noted that the "the game was over. We won" (in Webb, 1999, p. 126). Critics charged that the Court had crossed the delicate line in a democracy between public safety and individual liberty. The proper extent of police power in U.S. democracy will undoubtedly remain an important debate for many years to come, with the attacks of September 11 only intensifying the controversy this debate represents between public safety and individual freedom.

Focus on International Law

The criminal law of the United States obviously governs the behavior of people who live within the nation's boundaries. If a U.S. citizen commits a crime in another nation, that nation's criminal law governs the definition of his or her conduct and the way the case will be officially handled. Regardless of the nation in which a crime is committed, the law is enforced by the police or other governmental agents who are authorized to use physical force, if necessary, to protect their society by enforcing the law.

In contrast, international law governs the conduct of individuals, organizations, and whole nations that involves the affairs or territory of more than one country. In one sense, the concept of international law is a bit of a paradox: It generally cannot be enforced because international police do not exist. Instead, international law relies for its enforcement and effectiveness on the cooperation and goodwill of the nations who subscribe to it. Although nations typically do feel pressured to follow international law, they certainly can refuse to do so with relative impunity beyond negative world opinion and, perhaps, the threat of international economic boycotts. In this respect, international law is perhaps least effective when it is needed most—when a nation feels so strongly about an issue that it refuses to obey international law. Despite this fundamental paradox of international law, over the years it has proven a very important vehicle for resolving international disputes and even maintaining world peace, even if its effectiveness may sometimes be less than ideal.

A major founder of international law was Hugo Grotius, a Dutch judge, legal scholar, and political leader, who believed strongly that international affairs needed to be conducted according to a body of international law. To this end, he published an influential book, *De Jure Belli ac Pacis* (*On the Laws of War and Peace*), in 1625. This book described his vision for international law and laid the groundwork for international conventions and treaties that were to be signed over the next two centuries.

Beginning in the nineteenth century, a series of international conferences began to establish international law as we now know it. An early and very influential conference was the 1815 Congress of Vienna, which was called to establish the territorial boundaries of Europe after the defeat of Napoleon. In addition, the conference also condemned the slave trade, passed resolutions concerning navigation on rivers that flowed into two or more nations, and established several rules for diplomacy. Some 40 years later, the Conference of Paris established several principles for maritime trade and maritime war.

Perhaps the most important early conference was held in Geneva, Switzerland, in 1864, when 12 European nations were invited by the Swiss government to discuss standards governing the treatment of wounded soldiers. The inspiration for the conference came from the efforts of Swiss philanthropist Jean Henri Dunant, who had been repulsed in 1859 when he visited a battlefield of the Austro-Sardinian War where 40,000 soldiers had been killed or wounded. His efforts led to an international meeting in Geneva in 1863 that initiated the establishment of the International Red Cross and the conference a year later that involved the 12 nations. Conference participants signed the first Geneva Convention, which was later ratified by the United States and several other nations. Geneva Conventions in 1906, 1929, 1949, and 1977 extended international wartime standards to the treatment of civilians and prisoners of war, the conduct of war, and other issues. Almost 200 nations have now signed onto the Geneva Conventions. Dunant's efforts won him a share of the first Nobel Peace Prize in 1901.

Today's international law derives not only from the Geneva Conventions but also from other international treaties and conventions. It governs not only the conduct of war and the treatment of people involved in war but also international commerce, diplomatic relations, and other international issues. In all these areas, the United Nations (UN) plays a fundamental role. Its charter emphasizes the importance of international law for world peace and nonviolent resolution of international conflict. Since its founding, the UN has convened many international conferences that have led to the adoption of treaties and conventions outlining human rights obligations and other matters of international significance.

The most important judicial body of the UN is the International Court of Justice, also known as the World Court, which is located in The Hague in the Netherlands. The court is composed of 15 judges selected by the General Assembly and the Security Council of the UN for a term of 9 years, and a majority vote of the judges constitutes the court's decision on any matter. When international disputes arise, they are often handled through the World Court but only with the consent of the nations involved. If a nation agrees to appear before the World Court, it usually also agrees to abide by the court's decision. More than 40 nations have generally agreed to accept the court's jurisdiction; the United States used to be one of these nations, but it withdrew its acceptance in 1985. Because other major nations, including France, Italy, and China, also do not accept the court's jurisdiction, its ability to resolve international disputes is hampered.

The Geneva Conventions became the subject of news stories in early 2002 after the United States captured several hundred members of the Al Qaeda and Taliban forces as part of its successful military effort to topple the Taliban government in Afghanistan after the terrorist attacks of September 11. After their capture, the Al Qaeda and Taliban forces were taken to the U.S. military base on Guantanamo Bay in Cuba. The United States said the captives were terrorists, not soldiers of a country, and declared they were "battlefield detainees" rather than "prisoners of war." U.S. officials acknowledged that this designation meant the detainees would not have to be treated in conformity with the Geneva Conventions but insisted the Geneva standards would be generally followed anyway. Several European governments criticized the United States for engaging in a verbal sleight of hand to justify its failure to conform to a strict interpretation of the Geneva Conventions. The United States responded that it was treating the detainees quite well and that the detainees had better food and medical treatment than they enjoyed in Afghanistan.

Sources: Bravin, 2002; Damrosch, 2001; Moorehead, 1999; Shaw, 1997.

summary

1. The written criminal law began in ancient times with the Code of Hammurabi, the Code of Moses, and early Roman law. English common law, based on judicial decisions, heavily influenced law in the U.S. colonies and today's U.S. criminal justice system.

2. Classifications of law include criminal law, civil law, administrative law, case law, and procedural law. Several elements of an act combine to make it a crime according to the law. One of the most important of these elements is *mens rea,* or criminal intent. Another important element is *actus rea,* or the commission of a criminal act.

3. Several legal defenses to criminal prosecution exist, including the claim that a defendant's behavior was the result of a mistake; accident; ignorance; duress; self-defense; entrapment; or diminished capacity owing to young age, developmental disability, or mental illness.

4. Suspects and defendants in the United States enjoy several legal rights guaranteed by the Constitution, and especially the Bill of Rights, as interpreted by the U.S. Supreme Court. These rights include protections from unreasonable search and seizure, double jeopardy, self-incrimination, excessive bail and fines, and cruel and unusual punishment. Suspects and defendants also have the rights to retain legal representation and to confront witnesses.

5. The Fourteenth Amendment expanded due process to the states. A series of decisions by the U.S. Supreme Court beginning in the first half of the twentieth century eventually extended the protections afforded by earlier amendments to suspects and defendants at the federal level to those at the state level.

6. Numerous Supreme Court rulings since the 1960s have concerned the legitimate powers of the police. Two of the most controversial rulings were *Miranda v. Arizona,* which required police to inform suspects of their rights to remain silent and to have an attorney at questioning, and *Mapp v. Ohio,* which established the exclusionary rule that prohibits evidence gathered as a result of an illegal search by police. Studies of these rights find that they do not unduly restrict police and prosecutors from doing their jobs.

- *actus reus*
  administrative law
  case law
  causation
  civil law
  civil suit
  civil wrongs (torts)
- common law
  concurrence
  crimes
- criminal law

- exclusionary rule
- felonies
  harm
- *Magna Carta*
- *mala in se*
- *mala prohibita*
- *mens rea*
- misdemeanors
  procedural law
  substantive law
- violations (infractions)

questions *for* investigation

1. This chapter notes that nine states (Alaska, Arizona, California, Colorado, Hawaii, Maine, Nevada, Oregon, and Washington) legally allow the use of marijuana by people who have certain serious illnesses. Research the process by which this use was made legal in one of these states. What evidence made it possible to legalize marijuana use?

2. Consider *mala prohibita* crimes such as prostitution and the use of certain drugs. Do you think the laws should govern such activities? Explain your answer.

3. Suppose someone wakes up to see a stranger entering her bedroom. She pulls out a gun, yells at the stranger to leave the room immediately, and then fatally shoots him when he continues to approach her. When the police arrive, they find no weapon on the intruder. If the woman is prosecuted for committing a homicide and claims self-defense at her trial, what do you think the jury's verdict should be?

4. Suppose that a Muslim living in the United States was attacked by two youths on September 12, 2001, the day after the terrorist attacks. The victim is beaten and subsequently hospitalized for 3 days. The youths are arrested and later claim in court that they were so enraged by the terrorism that they lost control when they saw the Muslim. Do you think they should be found guilty of aggravated assault?

5. What is your opinion of trying juveniles who commit serious crimes (e.g., murder) as adults? Where does the burden of proof for these offenses lie? How is such proof obtained? Is this proof, in your opinion, defensible?

6. Do you think that a national consensus against executions of juveniles is possible? If your answer is no, explain why not. If your answer is yes, explain how such a consensus could be reached and legally recognized?

7. Consider the recent Supreme Court decisions about police procedures and activities. Interview a few police officers in your community. Ask them if they believe these decisions hamper their jobs or boost professionalism in how they do their jobs.

IT'S YOUR CALL...

1. Suppose you are a judge in traffic court. Although people accused of speeding and other traffic offenses usually simply mail in their fines, some do come to court to plead their cases. The case before you is especially interesting. The defendant is a 42-year-old woman who was cited for driving at twice the speed limit, 50 miles per hour instead of 25 miles per hour in a residential area of your medium-sized city. She tells you that she was indeed driving that fast, but only to get her 10-year-old daughter to the hospital. The daughter, she says, had been playing softball and was hit in the head by a line drive while she was running the bases. Even though she was wearing a helmet, the blow knocked her over, and she was complaining of a severe headache and blurry vision. Not wanting to wait for an ambulance, the defendant decided to drive her daughter to the emergency room herself. That, she says, is why she was driving so fast. What do you decide?

2. In May 2002, the federal government announced that the FBI would have greater powers to monitor and infiltrate domestic political and religious groups to try to prevent terrorism. This action loosened restrictions that were imposed during the 1970s, after it was revealed that the FBI had infiltrated and harassed thousands of individuals and organizations suspected of criticizing the nation's domestic and foreign policies. After the May 2002 action, its supporters said it would enable the FBI to do a more effective job of countering terrorism, whereas critics said it would lead to government abuse of individual freedom and violate the Bill of Rights. Suppose you were a U.S. senator involved in hearings about the FBI's new powers. What would your position be? Why?

chapter 5

Victims and Victimization

1. What is victimology?
2. How do social science theories categorize crime victims?
3. How do age; gender; race and ethnicity; immigrant status; income; marital status; and region, urbanization, and home ownership correlate with a person becoming a crime victim?
4. What are the economic and medical costs of criminal victimization in the United States? What are the psychological consequences of victimization for individuals and their families and close friends?
5. What do victim typology theories teach us about victims?
6. How does one's residence and lifestyle affect his or her likelihood of becoming a crime victim?
7. How can a person precipitate the likelihood of becoming a crime victim? What factors contribute to a person's repeat victimization? What factors contribute to the interchangeability of victims and offenders?
8. What is restorative justice? What are the goals of victim offender reconciliation programs (VORPs) and victim–offender conferencing programs? How successful are such programs?
9. What is the purpose of a victim-impact statement? A victim statement of opinion?

With the exception of rape and sexual assault, the overwhelming number of street crime victims are male. In approximately 80 percent of criminal cases, both the killer and victim are males, and only one of three robberies and aggravated assaults outside the home involve female targets. Even more so than street crime, killing and dying on the battlefield are almost exclusively male endeavors. Of the 36,568 U.S. fatalities in the Korean War, only two were females, and, during our more than 10-year involvement in the Vietnam conflict, only eight of the 58,204 U.S. military deaths were women. Although the majority of victims in the September 11 attack on the World Trade Center were men, that terrorist strike claimed the lives of hundreds of women, the greatest number of female casualties as a consequence of a solitary crime or act of war in the nation's history.

When deaths resulting from an accident, natural disaster, or war go beyond a certain number, it is easy to lose sight of the fact that each victim was a unique individual, that family and friends who loved them were deeply, often permanently, affected by their demise. In June 1969, *Life Magazine* published a photo along with the military affiliation (Army, Navy, Air Force, Marine Corps) of the 242 Americans killed in action between May 28 and June 3 of that year. For the first time, the entire nation could see what a week's worth of dead service personnel looked like.

Shortly after the World Trade Center attack, the *New York Times* printed a daily "Portraits of Grief" page, some 10 to 20 photos and biographical sketches of those who died as result of the terrorist strike. Stories in other newspapers and numerous books published

131

about September 11 also gave us a glimpse of the people who died that day. However, unlike the Vietnam War pictures, this tragic assemblage of photos and stories was comprised of a significant number of women.

In *One Nation: America Remembers September 11, 2001* (2001, p. 120) we learned about Madeline Amy Sweeney, the senior flight attendant on the first plane to crash into the World Trade Center. She made two phone calls from the aircraft's galley on an in-flight pay phone, the first to her husband Matthew, and the second to the ground supervisor at Boston's Logan International Airport. In addition to describing the hijackers and providing their seat numbers so they could be identified, she noted how the attackers had killed one of the passengers and assaulted two flight attendants. Her brother-in-law stated that "The call made from the flight provided valuable information to the FBI and was instrumental in identifying the hijackers. In the most difficult circumstance she stayed calm. She did her job. Of course she tried to help. Helping was like breathing to her" (p. 120).

As the airliner crossed the Hudson River and the Twin Towers came into view she said the plane was flying low, too low. "She took a deep breath and very calmly spoke the words 'Oh, my God' one time. Not out of fear, but in her own amazement." (*One Nation: America Remembers September 11, 2001*, 2001, p. 120. Reprinted by permission of Little, Brown and Company.)

This woman fights back tears at a makeshift memorial to some of the victims of the September 11, 2001, terrorist attack on the World Trade Center in New York City.

In the colonial United States, the criminal justice system (to the extent that it existed) and the philosophy of that system were very different from what they are today. Victims or their agents were responsible for apprehending criminals and bringing them to justice. Crimes were thought of as injuries to the victim as opposed to injustices committed against the state. In other words, a crime was considered a conflict between two individuals, not an attack on society (Fattah, 1997). Convicted offenders were required to compensate the victims up to three times the amount of property and/or cash that was lost as a result of the crimes. Offenders who could not pay were legally given to victims as servants for a period of time equal to the amount owed. Victims also had the option of selling offenders so as to recoup their losses. Individuals who chose this latter option had 1 month to find a buyer; incarceration costs past 30 days were to be paid by the victim or the offender was released (McDonald, 1977).

In contemporary society, the status of crime victims is very different, having been reduced to little more than that of a witness for the prosecution or state. The criminal justice system no longer exists to redress the wrongs suffered by victims; rather, its primary focus is on the offender and his or her relation to the state. William McDonald (1977) notes that the primary purpose of the justice system is to deter crime as well as rehabilitate and punish criminals. Once a criminal has been punished, his or her debt to society is considered to have been paid regardless of the social, economic, and/or medical condition of the victim. This is what justice means not only in the United States but in most modern societies. Many social critics have noted that the victim has been "forgotten," if not completely disregarded, by the criminal justice system.

Criminologist Ezzat Fattah (1997, p. 264) no doubt echoes the sentiments of countless crime victims when he states: "It is difficult to understand how an act that hurts, injures, or harms a human being, an act that might thoroughly affect the person's life and

A candlelight vigil is held for Matthew Shepard, an openly gay student at the University of Wyoming who was killed because of his sexual orientation. The Uniform Crime Report now records the number of hate crimes known to police annually.

disrupt his or her existence, can be considered an offense not against that individual but against society." For Fattah, it makes no sense that, if the source of a physical injury or monetary loss is a criminal offense, the fine paid by the person who caused it goes to the state, whereas if the cause of the wrongdoing is defined as a civil matter (medical malpractice or negligence, for example), the damages go to the person who has suffered.

For most of its history, criminology focused almost exclusively on offenders. Leading textbooks in the field did not even have a listing for "victims" in the index, much less devote a chapter to this subject. Sociologist Andrew Karmen (1990, p. 8) notes that until the 1940s and 1950s "criminology could be characterized as 'offenderology.'" Researchers focused on offenders: "who they were, why they engaged in unlawful activities, how they were handled by the criminal justice system, why they were incarcerated, and how they might be rehabilitated" (p. 8). The central problem in an offender-driven criminology was the search for the origins of criminal motivation. Lombroso (1911) found the source of deviant motivation in the biological makeup of individuals. For Marx (1971), the economic structure of society and people's relation to the modes of production determined who violated the criminal law and what types of offenses they would commit. Robert Merton (1947) concluded that defects in the structure of society produced behavioral adaptations that led to crime. In his social learning theory of criminal behavior, Edwin Sutherland (1947) was interested in how individuals became exposed to definitions favorable to violating the criminal law and then internalized these definitions (Brantingham and Brantingham, 1981a; Sutherland and Cressey, 1970).

What these theorists and many others had in common was their lack of concern for the criminal event (including the role of the victim) as well as the victim's participation in the criminal justice system. Approximately 50 years ago, a number of academicians and researchers began considering the victim in the criminal event, and by 1970 victimology became a part of criminology. An interdisciplinary field comprised of social scientists, medical practitioners, and members of the criminal justice system, **victimology** explores a number of issues including how some individuals contribute to

victimology the study of the role of the victim in the criminal event and the relation between crime victims and the criminal justice system (the police, the criminal courts, and correction officials)

their victimization; the financial, physical, and psychological consequences of being a crime victim; and how the police, courts, and various social agencies deal with victims. In this chapter, we briefly examine each of these issues including the "victim's movement" and the successes and failures this movement has had in gaining additional legal and financial rights for crime victims.

Defining Crime Victims

Anyone who has suffered physically, emotionally, and/or economically as a result of a criminal offense is a crime victim. Although this may be correct in a literal sense, it is also true that not all crime victims are portrayed with the same degree of what might be called "victimness." In fact, Andrew Karmen (1990, pp. 10–11) maintains that social scientists and the larger society group victims into three categories—conservative, liberal, and radical-critical—depending on who is victimized and where the crime occurs.

Conservatives are concerned almost exclusively with victims of street crime, a view that has been perpetuated by the media, the primary source of information about crime and criminal justice for the majority of Americans. Robert Elias (1993) and his colleagues examined every crime story in *Time, Newsweek,* and *U.S. News & World Report* between 1956 and 1991 and found that crime was portrayed "primarily as lower-and-working class behavior." By comparison, both offenders and victims of corporate crime received significantly less news coverage. While not discounting street crimes, liberal victimologists focus on the victims of business, corporate, and government crime. An interesting aspect of this level of analysis is that many crime victims do not even know that they have been cheated. For example, tens of thousands if not millions of people can pay inflated prices for a variety of products because of corporate price-fixing and collusion.

Social scientists working from a radical-critical perspective believe that victimology should not limit itself to the study of casualties of strictly criminal behavior; that is, victimologists should consider how people are harmed, economically, physically, and emotionally, by "industrial polluters, owners and managers of hazardous workplaces, fraudulent advertisers, brutal police forces, discriminatory institutions, and other agents of power and privilege" (Karmen, 1990, p. 11). To the extent that victimologists focus primarily on street crime and exclude the suffering caused by the rich and powerful, they are turning a blind eye to some of the most blatant acts of criminal and noncriminal victimization that exist in this country. However, to date most researchers have focused on the victims of street criminals.

Paramedics assist an African American teenager after a shooting in the Washington D.C. area. Young, African American males are at greater risk of becoming criminal homicide victims than any other age, race, and gender group in the United States.

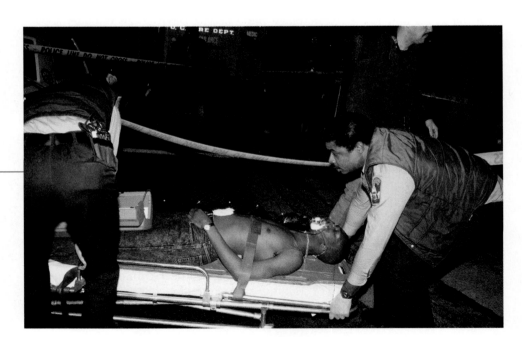

Not every resident of the United States has an equal chance of being a crime victim. Overall, some individuals are more likely to become targets of offenders than others, and the likelihood of being victimized for particular offenses, such as robbery and rape, is even more skewed. The National Crime Victimization Survey (NCVS) as well as other measures indicate that becoming a crime victim is correlated with age; gender; race and ethnicity; immigrant status; income; marital status; and region, urbanization, and homeownership.

Age

In general, the younger a person is the more likely it is that he or she will be the victim of a violent crime (see Figure 5.1). The victimization rate increases during the teenage years, peaks at about age 20, and then steadily declines through the remaining years of life. The rate of serious crime for 18 to 21 year olds is approximately 17 times higher than for persons age 65 and older. With a few exceptions, this pattern is found in all racial and ethnic groups and for both males and females. In a recent year, persons age 12 to 24 comprised 22 percent of the population and were 35 percent of murder victims as well as 49 percent of victims of all serious violent crimes (murder, robbery, rape, sexual assault, robbery, and aggravated assault). Persons age 50 and older made up 30 percent of the population and were 12 percent of the murder victims and 7 percent of overall serious crime victims (Perkins, 1997). The widely held perception that older persons are disproportionately victims of violent crime is false. However, there is one significant difference between older crime victims and other age categories: The elderly were more likely to be victimized in or near their home during the daytime (Klaus, 2000).

An examination of the entire spectrum of child victimization reveals that children are more likely to be victimized than are adults. The totality of crimes committed against children can be subdivided into three broad categories according to their seriousness and pervasiveness (see Figure 5.2). *Pandemic* victimizations are experienced by most children and include minimal assaults by siblings, physical punishment by parents, assault by other children, vandalism, and robbery. *Acute* victimizations are less

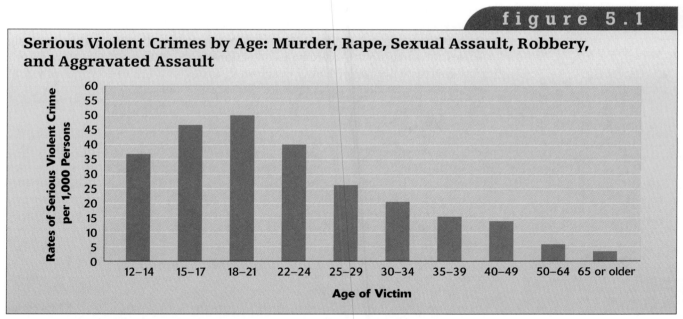

figure 5.1

Serious Violent Crimes by Age: Murder, Rape, Sexual Assault, Robbery, and Aggravated Assault

Source: Perkins, Craig A. 1998. *Age Patterns of Victims of Serious Violent Crime.* Washington, DC: U.S. Department of Justice, Office of Justice Programs.

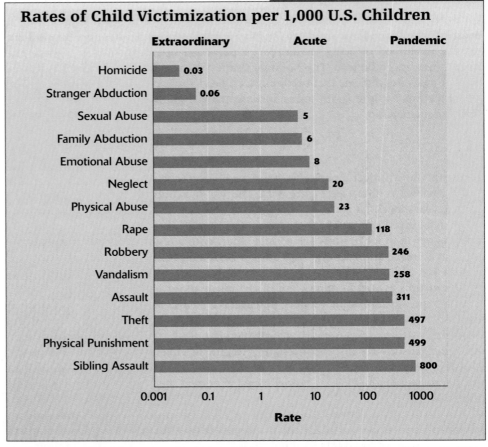

Rates of Child Victimization per 1,000 U.S. Children

	Extraordinary	Acute	Pandemic
Homicide	0.03		
Stranger Abduction	0.06		
Sexual Abuse		5	
Family Abduction		6	
Emotional Abuse		8	
Neglect		20	
Physical Abuse		23	
Rape		118	
Robbery		246	
Vandalism		258	
Assault		311	
Theft		497	
Physical Punishment		499	
Sibling Assault		800	

Source: Finkelhor, David. 1997. "The Victimization of Children: Developmental Victimology." Pages 86–107 in R. C. Davis, A. J. Lurigio, and W. G. Skogan, *Victims of Crime*. Thousand Oaks, CA: Sage. Copyright © 1997 by Sage Publications, Inc. Reprinted by permission of Sage Publications, Inc.

frequent and are experienced by a "sizeable minority" of children. These crimes include physical abuse, neglect, and physical abduction. Only a relatively small number of children experience the *extraordinary* crimes that attract a great deal of media attention. These offenses include child abuse, homicide, gang-related homicide, and nonfamily (successful) abductions. According to one estimate, more than 100,000 children primarily between the ages of 4 and 11 experience an attempted (unsuccessful) abduction by a nonfamily member each year (Finkelhor and Hotaling, 1995).

Gender

With the exception of rape and sexual assault, males had higher rates of victimization for violent crimes than females (see Figure 5.3). This gender gap exists at every age grouping and is pronounced for aggravated and simple assault with males experiencing rates for these crimes of 11 and 28 respectively per 1,000 persons and females being so victimized at rates of 5 (aggravated assault) and 19 (simple assault) per 1,000. In 1998, males had a slightly higher robbery victimization rate than females (Perkins, 1997; Rennison, 1999).

Estimates regarding the number of females victimized by their boyfriends and husbands each year range from slightly more than 1 million to as many as 18 million. This wide discrepancy is explained in part by the "type and purpose of the survey, the definition of violence used, and the political context" of the research ("Violent Relationships: Battering and Abuse among Adults," 2001, p. 12). Abused women are slapped, punched, kicked, burned, sexually assaulted, raped, and occasionally shot. A

figure 5.3

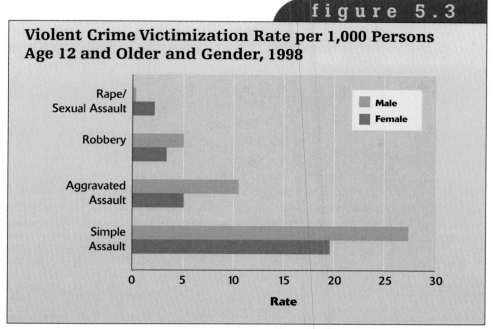

Violent Crime Victimization Rate per 1,000 Persons Age 12 and Older and Gender, 1998

Source: Rennison, Callie Marie. 1999. *Criminal Victimization 1998—Changes 1997–98 with Trends 1993–98.* Washington, DC: Department of Justice, Office of Justice Programs.

significant number of these victimizations do not come to the attention of the police, and, therefore, are not reflected in the Uniform Crime Reports. Abused women may be too embarrassed or frightened to inform crime victimization interviewers of their treatment or they may believe that only physical assault by a stranger is a "real" crime.

Race and Ethnicity

African Americans had somewhat higher rates of violent criminal victimizations than whites in 1998 and significantly higher rates than other races. Hispanics and non-Hispanics experienced comparable rates of victimization in 1998. Whereas non-Hispanics had higher rates of rape than Hispanics, the reverse was true for robbery. There was no difference between Hispanic and non-Hispanic rates of personal theft and aggravated assault (DeFrances and Smith, 1998). Native Americans are twice as likely to be victims of violent crime than other U.S. residents and four times more likely to be victims of rape, simple assaults, and aggravated assaults than Asian Americans—the least victimized racial/ethnic group across all categories. Approximately 7 of 10 violent victimizations of Native Americans involve an offender of a different race (Greenfield and Smith, 1999).

A significant amount of violent street crime involves victims and offenders of the same race. For example, in a typical year fewer than 15 percent of murders cross racial lines; that is, white victims are overwhelmingly killed by white offenders, whereas more than 90 percent of African American victims (in one victim and one offender homicides) had their lives ended by African American assailants. Similarly, about 75 percent of forcible rapes known to police are intraracial crimes.

Immigrants

Research indicates that immigrant populations are criminally victimized at rates similar to that of the larger population but that they are less likely to report these offenses to law enforcement personnel. A national survey of 92 police chiefs, prosecutors, and court administrators concluded that the crimes least likely to be reported to authorities by immigrants are domestic violence, sexual assault, and gang violence. Explanations these criminal justice officials offer for a low immigrant reporting rate are

- Fear of becoming involved with authorities
- Fear of embarrassing their families
- Difficulties speaking English
- Cultural differences in conceptions of justice
- Lack of knowledge of the U.S. criminal justice system

Income

For the most part violent victimizations decrease as household income increases (see Table 5.1). In 1998, households earning less than $7,500 annually experienced almost twice as many violent crimes as households earning $75,000 or more. This same relationship holds for burglary, with the nation's poorest households falling victim to this crime at approximately double the rate of that of the most affluent households in 1998 (Rennison, 1999).

Marital Status

In 1998, individuals who were never married, divorced, or separated had significantly higher rates of violent victimization than people who were married or widowed. People who were never married became crime victims at approximately 10 times the rate of widowed individuals and more than 3 times the rate of married persons (Rennison, 1999).

Region, Urbanization, and Home Ownership

Western households were the most vulnerable to property crimes in 1998, and northeastern households were the least likely to be victimized. City dwellers were more prone to burglary than suburban and rural households, and people who rent are more susceptible to property victimization (including motor vehicle theft) than homeowners.

table 5.1	Violent Crime Victimization and Household Income	
	VIOLENT CRIMES PER 1,000 PERSONS AGE 12 OR OLDER	
	1997	1998
Less than $7,500	71.0	63.8
$7,500–$14,999	51.2	49.3
$15,000–$24,999	40.1	39.4
$25,000–$34,999	40.2	42.0
$35,000–$49,999	38.7	31.7[a]
$50,000–$74,999	33.9	32.0
$75,000 plus	30.7	33.1

[a]1997–1998 difference is significant at the 95% confidence level

Source: Rennison, Callie Marie. 1999. *Criminal Victimization 1998—Changes 1997–98 with Trends 1993–98.* Washington, DC: U.S. Department of Justice, Office of Justice Programs.

The Costs and Consequences of Victimization

Economic and Medical Costs

It is hardly surprising to learn that criminal victimization results in the loss of significant amounts of money annually on the part of hundreds of thousands of individuals as well as the larger society. However, it is shocking to realize the magnitude of economic losses resulting from criminal activity and the financial impact this behavior has on both victims and nonvictims. A two-year multidisciplinary study conducted by Ted Miller and his colleagues (1996) for the National Institute of Justice concluded that personal crime (that is, street crime, child abuse, and drunk driving) cost the United States approximately $450 billion each year in the early 1990s (see Table 5.2). If this figure seems excessively high, consider that each attempted or completed rape costs the victim approximately $5,100 in out-of-pocket expenses. When the detrimental effects to one's quality of life are included, the monetary loss per rape victim escalates to $87,000 (Miller et al., 1996).

Note that the $450 billion figure only includes street victimizations. If the monetary losses resulting from employee theft and corporate offenses were factored in, the total cost of crime victimization would certainly exceed $1 trillion annually. Medical bills, lost earnings, and public programs related to street crime victim assistance cost $105 billion annually. Monetary losses for pain, suffering, and the reduced quality of life brought about by these law-violating acts add about $345 billion to the yearly crime tab. To put these numbers in perspective, the cost of operating the entire U.S. military in fiscal year 1999 was slightly more than $261 billion.

Violent crime accounts for about 3 percent of the nation's medical spending and 14 percent of injury-related medical spending. Based on a nationally representative survey of 168 mental health professionals, Mark Cohen and Ted Miller (1998) estimate that between 20 and 25 percent of the client populations of these practitioners are crime victims. More than half of this criminally victimized population are thought to be adults who suffered physical and/or sexual abuse as children. Inasmuch as the NCVS questions people about their physical injuries and medical expenses but not about mental heath counseling (and related costs), the direct psychological cost of victimization is one of the least well-known aspects of crime in the United States (Cohen and Miller, 1998).

Psychological Consequences

One of the major contributions of victimology has been an increasingly thorough examination of the psychological impact of being a crime victim. This is especially important in light of the fact that each year approximately one in four households is victimized by one or more acts of violence or theft. Numerous studies have indicated that the psychological consequences of victimization can be much more disruptive to people's lives than the loss of property and/or physical injury. In addition, although material losses can often be replaced quickly, the emotional pain resulting from criminal victimization can persist for years or, in some cases, a lifetime. Ongoing psychological problems are especially common among rape survivors. Victims of sexual assaults are often anxious, fearful, and depressed; and have low self-esteem, chronic physical ailments, sexual dysfunctions, and suicidal thoughts. Victims of robbery, burglary, and nonsexual assaults may suffer posttraumatic stress disorder (PTSD) that is, the persistent reexperiencing of the traumatic event by way of "intrusive memories" (flashbacks) and dreams. PTSD may be associated with a host of anxiety-related emotional and behavioral symptoms (Lurigio and Resick, 1990).

Arthur Lurigio and Patricia Resick (1990, pp. 52–59) examined a number of studies dealing with the psychological consequences of victimization. To date, much of this work has centered on rape survivors. Following is a brief summary of the major findings of this research:

- Younger people cope more effectively than older individuals with victimization.
- Women are generally more distressed than men by crime victimization.

table 5.2

Annual Losses (in millions) Due to Crime, 1993 Dollars

	MEDICAL	OTHER TANGIBLE	QUALITY OF LIFE	TOTAL
Fatal Crime (1990)	$ 700	$32,700	$ 60,000	$ 93,000
Rape/robbery/abuse/neglect/assault	510	24,200	46,000	71,000
Arson deaths	20	600	1,700	2,000
Drunk driving deaths (DWI)	140	7,100	12,300	20,000
Child Abuse	3,600	3,700	48,000	56,000
Rape	560	300	8,000	9,000
Sexual abuse	900	500	12,800	14,000
Physical abuse	1,240	2,000	20,400	24,000
Emotional abuse	910	1,000	7,100	9,000
Rape and Sexual Assault	4,000	3,500	119,000	127,000
Other Assault or Attempt	5,000	10,000	77,000	93,000
NCVS with injury	3,640	7,500	44,900	56,000
Age 0–1 with injury	220	400	3,900	5,000
Non-NCVS domestic	740	1,500	19,100	21,000
No injury	360	900	9,500	11,000
Robbery or Attempt	600	2,500	8,000	11,000
With injury	530	2,000	6,600	9,000
No injury	60	500	1,100	2,000
Drunk Driving	3,400	10,000	27,000	41,000
With nonfatal injury	3,300	8,000	24,600	36,000
No injury	150	2,200	2,500	5,000
Arson	160	2,500	2,400	5,000
With nonfatal injury	150	600	2,400	3,000
No injury	2	1,900	65	2,000
Larceny or Attempt	150	9,000	0	9,000
Burglary or Attempt	30	7,000	1,800	9,000
Motor Vehicle Theft or Attempt	9	6,300	500	7,000
Total	18,000	87,000	345,000	450,000

Note: Totals were computed before rounding. "No injury" cases involve no physical injury but may involve psychological injury. NCVS fatal crimes = all crime deaths except drunk driving and arson. Personal fraud/attempt is excluded to prevent possible double counting with larceny.

Source: Miller, Ted, Marc Cohen, and Brain Wiersema. 1996. *Victims Costs and Consequences: A New Look.* 1996. Washington, DC: National Institute of Justice, U.S. Department of Justice.

■ Victims with little formal education and low socioeconomic status are more traumatized than victims from higher socioeconomic classes and higher educational background.

■ Rape survivors with preexisting physical and/or emotional health problems are more likely to have difficulty coping with the experienced crime than women without these preexisting complications.

- A history of prior victimization is associated with more difficulty contending with the most recent crime.
- Some studies have concluded that the severity of a victim's symptoms is directly related to the degree of violence or injury that occurred in the criminal incident. Other researchers found that the amount of rape "trauma" experienced did not predict future reactions on the part of the victim. It is possible that the "actual violence of an attack is less crucial to victim reaction than the felt threat" (Seles et al., in Lurigio and Resick, 1990, p. 56).
- A number of studies have concluded that there were no differences in the psychological reactions of victims who were raped by their husband, a date, or a stranger.
- One study found that robbery and assault victims had more adjustment problems than burglary victims. Another researcher failed to discern any significant differences regarding the psychological difficulties experienced by these crime victims, although individuals whose homes were burglarized reported being more fearful and having more sleep disturbances than people who experienced robberies.

In the aftermath of a crime, victims typically strive to reorganize their world and make sense out of what has happened to them. Psychologists Morton Bard and Dawn Sangrey (1986, p. 54) stated that people want to be able to say, "I understand this thing, and I am no longer frightened by it." Only then can victims continue their lives with a minimal amount of emotional discomfort. To reach this psychological state of mind, victims usually start with the fundamental question of why the crime occurred. The obvious answer is that many people have few, if any, qualms about assaulting, robbing, raping, and killing their fellow citizens. Although this simple, straightforward cause-and-effect relationship between offender and victim is correct, in and of itself it is not very satisfactory; that is, this explanation does not answer the next question that invariably comes to mind, "Why me and not you?" Many individuals attribute their victimization to something they did or did not do; in other words, they blame themselves (Bard and Sangrey, 1986). Although these self-attributions may have some basis in reality, they are often exaggerated. For example, a burglary victim may blame herself for not locking the bathroom window. However, the unlocked window has nothing to do with why the offender chose this particular apartment building to burglarize as opposed to 10 other structures in the same complex. In addition, a secure window is hardly a guarantee that a crime will be prevented. Breaking and entering is all too common among residential burglars.

Family members and friends are not always supportive of crime victims; to the contrary, after the shock of hearing that someone they know and care about has been criminally attacked, they may become quite indignant. "Didn't you know better than to walk in that neighborhood after dark? Why didn't you make sure your door was locked? Why didn't you scream?" (Symonds, 1975, p. 92). This hostile reaction by people close to the victim has been called "secondary victimization." Similar to the thought processes of victims in their effort to make sense of crime, relatives and friends look for a rational explanation for the event. If these individuals can convince themselves that the victim did something or neglected to do something that brought about their own victimization, then they (the relatives and friends) can feel less helpless and vulnerable as they move about the social world.

Rape survivors may find that their friends are uncomfortable with them. A close friend of a woman who was raped noted how she struggled with her feelings (in Bard and Sangrey, 1986, p. 77):

> I remember feeling badly for a long time that I would look at her and I would think, you know that's the woman I know who was raped . . . and I was really feeling bad about this preying on my mind and I couldn't, you know, forget it. I felt that it was a real injustice to her that she had to carry this burden. . . . There is still that certain aura of being, ah, I think of it as tarnished. You're not quite whole and pure anymore and people remember that. And it's so unjust. . . . But I found those feelings myself.

Victims of robberies, physical assaults, and sexual assaults may also be stigmatized because they failed to forcefully resist their attackers. Bard and Sangrey (1986, p. 82)

A counselor talks with a client in a rape crisis center. The psychological trauma of a sexual attack can last for months or years, affecting the victim's emotional, social, and economic well-being.

argue, "Submission in our culture is viewed as cowardly and we tend to feel contemptuous of the victim who does not fight back." Some people may resist an assailant even against their better judgment (resistance may trigger an especially violent response on the part of the offender) simply because they fear being labeled a coward. This is probably more true of males than females in a culture that views physical courage as a component of manliness. It follows that some crime victims focus on the "hero fantasy" of self-defense (Bard and Sangrey, 1986). "This is what I should have done." "This is what I will do if I am ever attacked again."

Typology of Victims

In an oft repeated line from George Orwell's *Animal Farm,* one character notes that in the existing society, "Everyone is equal but some are more equal than others" (1949, p. 46). Similarly, victimologists have demonstrated that all crime victims are not equal regarding their blameworthiness for a crime. In fact, some individuals are not victims at all, but perpetrators of illegal acts. From the earliest days of the discipline, criminologists have divided crime and criminals into categories. Recall from Chapter 3 our discussion of street crime, violent crime, and organized crime. Most of these categories could be further subdivided into constituent offenses (for violent crime, murder, robbery, rape, and aggravated assault). Pioneer victimologists believed that the same could be done for crime victims, and they have constructed numerous typologies.

The German scholar Hans von Hentig (1948, p. 450) examined the "duet frame" or "interrelations between the doer and sufferer," that is, the offender and the victim. He was one of the first researchers to think of crime as an event comprised of two or more participants. According to von Hentig, crime could not be fully understood by focusing solely on the outcome of the criminal event. Rather, the dynamics of the situation had to be closely scrutinized. An examination of these events revealed that victims quite often contributed to their own victimization. Facilitating a criminal event was not always a function of what people did, but, rather, who they were. In other words, the personal attributes of individuals made them more or less vulnerable to crime in general and certain crimes in particular. Von Hentig (see Table 5.3) identified three categories of victims: biological, psychological, and social (or situational).

table 5.3 — Hans von Hentig's Victim Typology

GENERAL CLASSES OF VICTIMS	EXAMPLE
The young	Infants, children, and adolescents
The female	All women
The old	Elderly people
The mentally disabled and deranged	Individuals with mental problems and alcoholics
Immigrants	Foreigners unfamiliar with U.S. culture
Minorities	Individuals who, because of their race or ethnicity, do not receive equal protection under the law
Dull normals	Simpleminded, stupid people
The depressed	Individuals who, because of their psychological condition, are unsuspecting, careless, fearless, and/or have lost their sensibility to pain
The acquisitive	Greedy, often dishonest people looking to make a quick profit
The wanton	Sexually promiscuous men and women
The lonesome and heartbroken	Individuals whose "critical faculties" are reduced because they seek the companionship of other people
The tormentor	Physically abusive individuals who victimize a family member
The blocked, exempted, or fighting	Victims of blackmail, fraud, and extortion

Source: Adapted from von Hentig, Hans. 1948. *The Criminal and His Victim—Studies in the Sociobiology of Crime* (pp. 404–438). New York: Archon Books. Copyright © Yale University Press. Reprinted by permission.

Biological victims include both young and elderly individuals who are "feeble in body" as well as females, whom von Hentig considered the "weaker sex." These individuals are targeted by offenders because of their inability to physically fight off or deter predators. Individuals who are mentally disabled may inadvertently put themselves in situations where they are easily victimized. Chronically intoxicated people are all but defenseless against people who would shortchange them (give them incorrect change) and street muggers. Immigrants and minorities have an "artificial disadvantage" because of their social and legal status in society. Newly arrived immigrants are inexperienced in the customs of their adopted country and are easily victimized in a variety of circumstances including swindles or confidence games. The same can be said for dull normals whom von Hentig (p. 418) noted seem "born to be victimized in many ways."

Because racial minorities "do not receive the same protection of the law given to the dominating class," they make for easy targets (pp. 416–417). Note that some people may have two or more of these attributes that make them particularly susceptible to victimization, for example, a woman of color who has just arrived in the United

States from a poor, developing country. Her criminal vulnerability may be even higher if she has lived her entire life in a rural area and now resides in a big city.

According to von Hentig, people with psychological problems are typically apathetic, passive, and fatigued, characteristics that reduce their ability to discourage and/or fight off predators. Their mental and physical sluggishness may attract criminals who rightfully surmise that they can be victimized with relative impunity. Lonely and heartbroken individuals often prove to be naively trustworthy in their search for companionship and, therefore, leave themselves open to a variety of crimes. Greedy or acquisitive people are a fast-talking con man's dream because they can be easily duped in their effort to make a financial killing as quickly and effortlessly as possible. Tormentors are both victims and offenders. A middle-aged woman who was physically and/or sexually abused by her father as a child may torment and kill her then-elderly father. People of status and reputation are apt to be blackmailed if a motivated offender learns of a transgression from an earlier period in their lives. The aspiring politician may have to pay someone who learns that at one time the politician had a serious drug problem or cheated on a spouse.

As a consequence of situational factors, individuals are more likely to be criminally victimized at certain times and places than at others. Tourists, for example, are especially vulnerable. In south Florida in 1992 and 1993, ten travelers (four of them German) were murdered (Smith, 1993). Some of the victims were identified as tourists by their attackers because the cars they were driving had bumper stickers indicating the name of the rental company. Tourists are likely to have money, are usually preoccupied with local sights (and, therefore, less attentive to potential danger), and are less likely to return to the jurisdiction and testify against offenders if they are apprehended.

Unlike the classification scheme of Hans von Hentig, the typology of attorney and criminologist Benjamin Mendelsohn (in Schafer, 1968 p. 42) was an attempt to categorize the "correlation of culpability (imputability) between the victim and the delinquent." Mendelsohn had a five-step classification based on the victim's contribution to his or her victimization. "Completely innocent victims"—a category that includes all children—bear no responsibility for their misfortune. At Level 5, the "most guilty victim" enters the criminal event as the offender and actually becomes the victim, for example, the street mugger who is overpowered by a would-be victim and is stabbed to death with his or her own knife. Mendelsohn also had a sixth category: the "simulating" or "imaginary victim." This category is different from the previous five in that it is not a higher level of culpability on the part of the victim but, rather, a person who pretends to have been victimized for a variety of reasons. For example, a woman rejected by the man she believed would marry her informs the police that she has been sexually assaulted by this individual when, in fact, no such attack occurred. She is an imaginary victim.

Victimologist Andrew Karmen (1980) created a typology of victim culpability for the crime of auto theft (see Figure 5.4). Similar to Mendelsohn's work, this categorization classifies victims from "totally innocent"—individuals who employ antitheft devices and park their vehicles in garages and safe streets—to "largely responsible" and "fully responsible" owners who are not victims at all but active participants in crime. Karmen also examined the motivation of victims and the financial impact that vehicle theft had on them. Whereas the motivation of criminals has long been an important topic of criminology, victimologists have sensitized us to the motivation of victims and to what extent this mind-set bears on the crime in question.

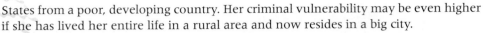

Victims and Offenders

The Geography of Crime

Crime is not randomly distributed in time and space; where people live affects victimization rates. Along with place of residence, the routine activities of individuals regarding the presence or absence of "capable guardians" of potential crime targets also influences the chances of becoming a victim. In the post–World War II era, people spend considerably more time away from home (both husbands and wives working, longer and more fre-

figure 5.4

Types of Victims of Auto Theft

TYPE OF VICTIM	TOTALLY INNOCENT	LARGELY INNOCENT	PARTLY INNOCENT	SUBSTANTIALLY RESPONSIBLE	LARGELY RESPONSIBLE	FULLY RESPONSIBLE
Actions of Victim	Conscientious —takes special precautions	Cautious— takes conventional measures	Careless— facilitates theft through negligence	Initiator— precipitates theft by leaving car exposed and vulnerable	Conspirator— provokes theft by arrangements with criminals	Simulator— fabricates theft of nonexistent car
Motivations of Victim	Seeks to minimize risks	Concerned about risks	Indifferent to risks	Wants car to be stolen	Determined to have car stolen	Seeks to make it look like car was stolen
Financial Outcome after Theft	Loses money	Loses money	Loses money	Gains money from victimization	Gains money from victimization	Makes large profit from alleged victimization
Approximate Proportion of All Victims	← 55% →		←20%→	← 25% →		
Legal Status	Actual victims →			Criminals posing as victims in order to commit insurance fraud →		

Source: Karmen, Andrew. 1980. "Auto Theft: Beyond Victim Blaming." *Victimology: An International Journal*, 5(2–4): 161–174.

quent vacations, for example) and interact with a larger network of people outside the home (Cohen and Felson, 1979). Time spent away from home means that one's residence is increasingly devoid of capable guardians, and interacting with nonhousehold members makes people viable targets for face-to-face physical and sexual assaults (Garofalo, 1987).

In a test of the residence and lifestyle hypothesis, Lawrence Sherman and colleagues (1989) analyzed all 115,000 addresses and intersections in Minneapolis over a 12-month period and discovered that 50 percent of calls to police for assistance came from only 3 percent of places. All of the calls regarding the predatory crimes of robbery, rape, and auto theft came from 2.2 percent, 1.2 percent, and 2.7 percent of locations, respectively. Every one of the almost 25,000 domestic disturbance calls were recorded at only 9 percent of addresses (although each address sometimes included many apartments). These intensely high crime areas are often referred to by law enforcement personnel as "hot spots." It is interesting to note that even in high-crime neighborhoods some addresses and locations had no calls to the police for assistance. High-crime areas, therefore, may contain "hot" and, one might say, "cold" spots. Obviously, living in and/or frequenting a high-crime area significantly increases one's chances of becoming a crime victim. Sherman and colleagues (1989) speculated that neighborhoods may not necessarily cause crime and produce victims. Rather, these locations host criminal activity that may well have occurred at another time and place.

What makes a neighborhood (or portion thereof) a hot spot, a zone of exceptionally high victimization? In their study of Cleveland, Ohio, Dennis Roncek and Pamela Maier (1991, p. 747) found that "the amount of crime of every type was significantly higher on residential blocks with taverns or lounges than on others." Locations with drinking establishments generate crime and victims for a number of reasons (p. 726): (1) Patrons of these establishments typically have cash on them and make for attractive targets, especially when they are intoxicated; (2) taverns and lounges are likely to have available cash, making them desirable robbery targets; (3) intoxicated individuals are likely to

engage in behavior that they would not exhibit when they are sober, such as fighting and sexual assault; (4) bars often attract a significant number of people (especially on weekends and "happy hour" periods) from other neighborhoods, and people may be more likely to engage in deviant and criminal behavior when they are in the presence of strangers and separated from local, informal agents of social control; and (5) businesses such as bars, lounges, and liquor stores may attract a clientele with a disproportionate number of offenders.

To the extent that individuals live in neighborhoods that have a significant number of offenders and potential offenders, their chances of becoming crime victims increase proportionately. Numerous studies have concluded that most perpetrators of street crimes commit a significant number of offenses close to home. Murders, rapes, and assaults often transpire within a few blocks of the offender's residence, whereas crimes such as burglary and larceny occur further from the transgressor's residence, sometimes requiring long "crime trips" (Brantingham and Brantingham, 1981a; Shover, 1973). The reduction of criminal activity as the distance from one's residence increases is called *distance decay*. Why this phenomenon occurs is relatively straightforward as Patricia and Paul Brantingham (1981b, p. 30) point out: "It takes money and effort to overcome distance." Offenders' lack of money for transportation to another neighborhood explains to some degree why poor people of color have such high rates of street crime victimization. They are victimized by the offenders among them (other poor people of color) who do not have the financial means to rob and burglarize individuals in more affluent neighborhoods. In addition, a racial or ethnic minority member is likely to arouse the suspicion of guardians in a locale primarily or exclusively comprised of members of a different racial or ethnic group.

Victim Precipitation

victim precipitation the chain of events started by the victim that culminates with his or her victimization

Criminologists have long known that some people contribute to their own victimization. The phenomenon wherein an individual starts or triggers a chain of events that culminates in his or her victimization is called **victim precipitation.** The esteemed criminologist Marvin Wolfgang (1958) was the first researcher to study victim-precipitated homicides. Wolfgang examined 588 homicides in Philadelphia between 1948 and 1952 and discovered that 26 percent of these crimes could be classified as victim precipitated. In these killings the victim was the first to exhibit deadly force, "the first to strike a blow or fire a shot" (p. 253). Following are examples of this category of homicide from Wolfgang's research (1958, pp. 253–254):

- A drunken husband beating his wife in the kitchen gave her a butcher knife and dared her to use it on him. She claimed that if he should strike her one more time she would use the knife whereupon he slapped her in the face, and she fatally stabbed him.
- A victim became concerned when his eventual slayer asked for money that the victim owed him. The victim grabbed a hatchet and started in the direction of his creditor who pulled out a knife and stabbed him.
- A drunken victim with a knife in hand approached his slayer during a quarrel. The slayer showed a gun, and the victim dared him to shoot. He did.

Wolfgang found that whereas homicide victims in general lose their lives by being stabbed in about a third of the cases, in victim-precipitated killings death came by way of a cutting or stabbing instrument in more than half of the crimes. Alcohol consumption was also more prevalent in victim-precipitated murders, with the victim most likely to have been drinking. Numerous investigators, including Wolfgang (1959), have speculated that some of these homicides were thinly masked suicides; that is, the victim wanted to die and used the killer to perform the act for him or her. Because the victims of these crimes cannot be interviewed, we will never know what percentage of them were consciously striving to end their lives at the moment of death.

Women who take their husbands' lives are more likely to be involved in victim-precipitated killings than incidents in which men kill their wives (Felson and Messner,

1998). Numerous investigators have concluded that women often kill their husbands in self-defense, a behavioral explanation commonly referred to as the *battered spouse syndrome*. As it addresses one element of the self-defense doctrine, the battered spouse syndrome has been used as a component in an overall defense strategy for the past 20 years. However, as Douglas Orr (2000) notes, this syndrome is not a complete defense strategy.

According to the battered spouse perspective, women are forced into the violent confrontations that result in the deaths of their spouses because they fear for their lives and, on many occasions, the safety of their children. In their study of 23 men and 18 women incarcerated for killing a domestic partner, Stout and Brown (1995) found that all of the women had high levels of fear before killing their partners, whereas 18 men (78 percent) said they had absolutely no fear of their wives or girlfriends. All of the respondents claimed that they were battered before the deadly incident. However, only the women reported receiving medical attention for their injuries.

Choosing a Victim and Repeat Victimization

Imagine that you desperately needed money as a result of some unexpected emergency. After selling your car and other possessions and borrowing money from family, friends, and lending institutions, you were still short. Financially trapped, you reluctantly decide that engaging in criminal behavior is the only solution. Upon deciding to commit residential burglary, you would be faced with the question of which home or homes to target. As a novice thief, you might decide to skip any home that advertises the presence of a burglar alarm. Like you, neither amateur nor professional criminals are likely to burglarize the first house they see. Victims (property or people) are rarely chosen haphazardly or randomly. Some amount of planning from a few minutes to a few months will produce a crime target.

So how do offenders decide whom or what they will victimize? Regarding street crimes such as physical and sexual assaults and muggings, David Finkelhor and Nancy Asdigian (1996, p. 6) argue that the physical characteristics of individuals may increase a person's chances of being victimized independent of his or her activities "because these characteristics have some congruence with the needs, motives, or reactivities of offenders." In other words, certain offenders are drawn to certain types of victims they perceive as being more vulnerable. This matching of offender's strengths and victim's weaknesses is called **target congruence.** This congruence helps explain the large amount of youth victimization in three ways (p. 6):

1. *Target vulnerability.* Characteristics of vulnerable targets include small stature, physical weakness, and/or psychological problems and indicate that the individual can be easily overpowered and will offer little, if any, resistance. Note the similarity to von Hentig's typology.
2. *Target gratifiability.* Some individuals have something that offenders want; a target may have possessions, for example, that are trendy, relatively expensive, and portable, or, in terms of female victims, are a sexual outlet. "Femaleness itself is a risk attribute" (p. 5).
3. *Target antagonism.* Some characteristics of victims arouse anger, resentment, jealousy, or destructive impulses in an offender. Victim characteristics in this category would include sexual orientation and one's racial/ethnic identification.

target congruence the matching of an offender's strength and victim's weakness

Target vulnerability is a common theme when offenders are questioned about victim selection. In their study of 65 arrested and/or incarcerated female robbers, Ira Sommers and Deborah Baskins (1993) recorded the following responses from these women (p. 145):

"Yeah, I would look for easy people. People who looked timid, who ain't gonna put up much of a fight."

"You know, I felt like if somebody looked soft, or you know young people they would have got stuck up."

"I would look for a certain type of person and I would plan what I was gonna say and when I was gonna make my move. I was looking for, uh, alcoholics, people who were coming out of bars drunk."

In what has been dubbed the law of "repeat victimization," Ken Pease (1992; 1997) states that the likelihood of being a crime victim is lower for individuals who have never been victimized and higher for those who have been victimized on one or more occasions. Individuals victimized three or more times have an even greater likelihood of falling prey to offenders in the future. A recent British Crime Survey found that 15 percent of all households suffered property crime victimization in a 12-month period with one-third of this group (or 5 percent of the total sample) experiencing multiple property offenses (Osborn, Ellingworth, Hope, and Trickett, 1996). Another survey in Great Britain discovered that 14 percent of adults suffered approximately 70 percent of all self-reported victimizations (Gottfredson, 1984).

Repeat victims of violent crimes in the United States are frequently admitted to urban trauma centers. Three studies concluded that between 33 and 44 percent of individuals who go to these facilities for medical care have been victims of violent crimes in the past, often in the past few weeks or months (Buss and Abdu, 1995; Morrissey, Byrd, and Deitch, 1991; Sims et al., 1989). All of these studies found that violent crime victims admitted to urban trauma centers are more likely to be young, male, African Americans, living in poverty, with low levels of education, and histories of alcohol and/or drug abuse. Many of these individuals had psychiatric problems, and few had medical coverage. The Buss and Abdu study (p. 188) found that victims of violent crime admitted to trauma centers "were more likely to carry a gun or a knife, and to put up a fight when attacked."

The reasons why some people become repeat targets of crime are similar to why they were victimized the first time; that is, they become known as vulnerable and/or attractive targets to one or more offenders. Certain people may be repeatedly victimized by the same individual, and it may become known to other offenders that this person can be robbed, burglarized, or physically assaulted with impunity. Individuals labeled as "easy" marks by local offenders will have difficulty losing this tag and can suffer a significant number of victimizations. As previously noted, some neighborhoods may be home to or attract a disproportionate number of offenders. People who live, work, or visit these neighborhoods, therefore, are at risk of becoming repeat victims (Lauritsen and Davis-Quintet, 1995).

A simple model examines repeat victimization within the context of decisions made by offenders (see Figure 5.5). The convergence of a suitable victim, a likely offender, and the absence of guardians produces a possible criminal event. If an offender decides to break the law, that event can result in a successful crime or an unsuccessful criminal attempt. If the attempt has been successful, a decision must be made whether to commit another crime. An affirmative decision triggers an additional question: Should another target be selected, or should the previous target be victimized again? If the offender defines the previous criminal event as one resulting in a relatively high reward with a minimal risk of apprehension, the forthcoming crime may be a repeat victimization (Bouloukos and Farrell, 1997). Note that the victim, in effect, has two strikes against her or him; the offender has some idea of the potential reward for committing the offense, and the perceived risk of apprehension is probably low because this individual has already been exploited without the offender being arrested.

Victims as Offenders and Offenders as Victims

We tend to think of criminals and victims as two distinct categories of individuals—the good guys and the bad guys. Victimologist Ezzat Fattah (1993, p. 239) states that his discipline rejects this false dichotomy and considers "the roles of 'victim' and 'victimizers' as neither fixed, assigned or predetermined." Rather, these roles are "interchangeable and may be assumed simultaneously or consecutively . . . with many individuals mov-

figure 5.5

Path Model of Repeat Victimization

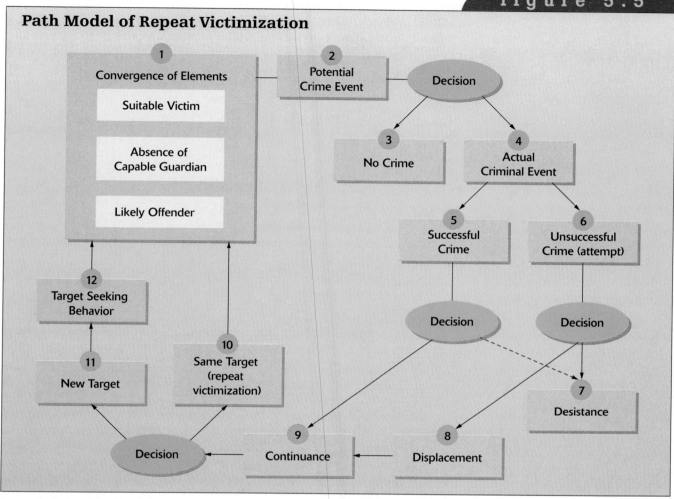

Source: Bouloukos, Adan C. and Graham Farrell. 1997. "On Displacement of Repeat Victimization." In *Rational Choice and Situational Crime Prevention,* edited by Ronald C. Clark and S. Giora Shoham. London: Athgate Aldershot. Reprinted by permission of Ashgate Publishing Limited.

ing alternatively between the two . . . as yesterday's victims become today's offenders and today's offenders becoming tomorrow's victims."

A number of studies have found that crime victims are much more likely than nonvictims to report a history of deviant behavior (Lauritsen, Sampson, and Laub, 1991). In their study of active armed robbers in St. Louis, Richard Wright and Scott Decker (1997) found that 6 of every 10 offenders specializing in street robbery stated that they usually targeted individuals who were involved in criminal pursuits, especially drug dealers. The comments of two of these robbers are telling (p. 63):

> "[I like robbing] them drug dealers [because] it satisfies two things for me: my thirst for drugs and the financial aspect. [I can] actually pay my rent, pay my car, [and things like that too.]"

> "[Dope men are perfect victims] 'cause they have money on them. . . . They carry all they money, jewelry, and all that on them, and all they drugs."

Janet Lauritsen and her colleagues (1991) argue that the delinquent lifestyles of adolescents place them at greater risk of criminal victimization. For example, gang members are often victimized by rival gang members in fights and drive-by shootings. Drinking and drug use at bars and parties increase the risk of physical and sexual assault on adolescents using mind-altering substances. If Lauritsen is correct, the victimization patterns of young people cannot be adequately understood apart from their criminal and deviant activities.

"Offender-victims" are especially vulnerable to other street criminals because they are viewed as less likely to call police than "nonoffender-victims." Offender-victims may believe that if they contact law enforcement officials their past or current criminal behavior will be discovered, thereby making an unfortunate situation even worse (Lauritsen et al., 1991). One might speculate that the more heavily involved an offender is in criminal activities the less likely he or she is to notify the authorities regarding a victimization. Offender-victims known to local officers may have less credibility and, therefore, are less likely to be believed by police and prosecutors.

Crime victims often become criminal offenders themselves. For example, victims of violent crimes may physically attack their victimizers (van Dijk and Steimitz, 1984). Property crime victims sometimes attempt to recoup their losses by stealing from others. Dutch criminologist Jan van Dijk (in Felson, 1998) notes that, in a country where bicycles are important and common vehicles of transportation, one bicycle theft may trigger a number of similar events as victims turn into offenders in a crime, victim, crime, victim sequence. "First A steals B's bike. Then B steals C's bike. Next C steals D's bike. Finally, D steals E's bike, but E is left out in the cold" (Felson, 1998, p. 128). Note that not only do victims shortly become offenders in this victim/offender chain, but the original victimization activates a chain of offenses that significantly contributes to both crime and victimization rates. Criminologist Marcus Felson (1998) speculates that **van Dijk chains** may contribute to the theft of certain items in this country, notably auto parts and car CD players.

Employees who rightly or wrongly believe that their employers are cheating them (for example, not paying them for the number of hours worked) may retaliate by stealing company property, embezzling, or sabotaging the workplace (Sykes and Matza, 1957). Children whose schoolbooks or other belongings are stolen may steal similar articles from their classmates. A multitude of research on family violence has made it painfully clear that abused children are more likely to be aggressive, delinquency-prone teenagers, and abusive adults than children not similarly victimized. It is not uncommon for rapists to have a history of childhood brutalization, and young victims can become lifelong offenders in a self-perpetuating cycle of violence (Fattah, 1993).

Crime Displacement and Victimization

Crime displacement is the transfer or movement of a crime from one place, time, or kind to another, place, time, or kind as a result of a change in the social and/or physical environment. When displacement occurs, the likelihood that one category of people will become crime victims decreases, whereas the probability that another category of individuals will be victimized increases. There are at least four types of crime displacement (Hakim and Rengert in Trasler, 1986, p. 18).

1. *Spatial displacement.* Offenders are deterred by increased police presence in one neighborhood and move to another neighborhood where the risk of being apprehended is lower.
2. *Temporal displacement.* Offenders change the time of day, the day, or the season to one in which it is considered safer to commit a crime(s).
3. *Target displacement.* Offenders search for new victims (people or property) when existing targets become difficult to penetrate ("target hardening"). Andrew Karmen (1990) refers to this type of displacement in terms of a "valve theory of crime-shift"; that is, when and where one area of illegal opportunity has been "shut off," offenders look for replacement targets. For example, if burglars discover that certain home alarms are difficult to disarm, they avoid households with these alarms and concentrate on dwellings with alarms they can readily disarm or homes without antitheft devices. If a bus company only accepts riders holding a prepurchased bus pass, offenders may shift their attention to cab drivers or pizza delivery employees.

> **van Dijk chain** the chain of events that is triggered with the first victimization. For example, if A has his bicycle stolen, he may steal B's bike who in turn may steal C's bike and so on.

> **crime displacement** the transfer or movement of a crime from one place, time, or kind to another place, time, or kind as a result of a change in the social and/or physical environment

4. *Type of crime displacement.* Offenders abandon what has become a high-risk crime and turn to offenses that are considered less risky. For example, bank robbers who realize that their chances of being apprehended have increased dramatically because of enhanced technological surveillance begin to rob supermarkets instead of financial institutions.

Because this type of "crime spillover" is difficult, if not impossible, to measure, the displacement of victims from one time, location, and type of crime to another is unknown and will never be more than conjecture.

The Victims' Movement

In December 1993, Mary Byron of Jeffersontown, Kentucky, was murdered by Donovan Harris, her estranged boyfriend. Harris, who raped Byron at gunpoint 3 weeks earlier, had been released from jail on bond. On the day of her death, Byron did not know that Harris was no longer in police custody because the Jeffersontown Police Department, which she had asked to notify her on Harris's release, failed to do so. Mary Byron's estate subsequently sued a detective and the police department. When the suit was dismissed, Byron's estate appealed the decision. The appellate court ruled that neither the city of Jeffersontown nor the detective had an obligation to notify Byron of Harris's release from custody ("Women in Criminal Justice," 1998).

The case of Mary Byron was an especially tragic example of what many people believe is the shameful way the criminal justice system treats crime victims. Although not as poignant as the Byron incident, there are numerous examples of how people who have suffered at the hands of criminals are, according to many observers, victimized a second time by the police, the courts, and/or the penal system. Whereas the Sixth Amendment to the Constitution guarantees the defendant's right to remain in the courtroom during a trial, crime victims have no such privilege. In most jurisdictions, victims appear in court only to give testimony (Kelly, 1990). When the defendants in the Oklahoma City bombing that killed 168 people were tried, the judge ruled that family members of 15 victims be excluded from the courtroom (Kyl and Feinstein, 1996). In 1983, Alabama became the first state to permit victims to sit at the prosecutor's table during the trial, and in the following years a number of other states permitted crime victims to remain in court at the judge's discretion (Kelly, 1990).

The plight of crime victims was rediscovered by some members of the media, "enlightened" criminal justice practitioners, social scientists, and advocacy groups beginning in the late 1950s and early 1960s (Karmen, 1990). Television, newspapers, and news magazines brought to the nation's attention stories focusing on the suffering of victims of crime. None of these cases was more chilling than that of a young New York woman named Kitty Genovese. Miss Genovese was attacked by a knife-wielding rapist as she was about to enter her apartment at 3:00 A.M. Her screams for help—"Oh my God, he stabbed me! Please help me! Please help me!"—aroused the attention of 38 of her neighbors, none of whom came to her aid. After struggling for 35 minutes, she finally escaped her attacker, and only then did someone call the police. Miss Genovese died a short time later (Darley and Latane, 1968).

Because of the media attention on such crimes, the get tough on criminals law and order movement of the 1970s advanced a campaign to convince the public that they had more to fear from becoming crime victims than of being falsely accused of violating the law. In addition to fighting for equality in the workplace and the political arena, the most recent phase of the women's movement zeroed in on females as victims of domestic abuse and rape. From the first crisis centers for female victims that began in Berkeley, California, and Washington D.C., in the early 1970s, shelters for abused women have spread across the country (Karmen, 1990). Groups such as Mothers Against Drunk Driving and Parents of Murdered Children also focused on victims of specific crimes. By the end of the twentieth century, a multifaceted victim's movement had helped bring about significant changes in the nation's perception of crime victims and, more importantly, how these individuals are treated by the criminal justice system. This section examines some of these changes.

Victims and Offenders—Restitution and Restoration

We noted at the beginning of this chapter that during the colonial era, offenders were required to compensate victims for up to three times the amount of property and/or cash that they had lost. The victims' movement resurrected this sentiment and had some measure of success in bringing about programs in which individuals convicted of property crimes make restitution to their victims even if so doing results in economic difficulties for the offenders. This philosophy was summed up in the 1982 President's Task Force on Victims of Crime (p. 79):

> It is simply unfair that victims should have to liquidate their assets, mortgage their homes, or sacrifice their health or education or that of their children while the offender escapes responsibility for the financial hardship he has imposed. It is unjust that a victim should have to sell his car to pay bills while the offender drives to his probation appointments. The victim may be placed in a financial crisis that will last a lifetime. If one of the two must go into debt, the offender should do so.

That criminals should make monetary restitution for their transgressions is part of a more comprehensive philosophy regarding offender/victim relations called *restorative justice*. From this perspective, the emphasis shifts from punishing offenders (retribution) to restoring the situation and well-being of victims prior to the crime. Table 5.4 summarizes the differences between these two perspectives along various dimensions.

table 5.4   Two Models of Justice

RETRIBUTION	RESTORATION
Crime defined as violation of or against the state	Crime defined as violation of one person by another
Emphasis is on establishing blame, on guilt, on the past (did he/she do it)	Focus is on problem solving, on liabilities and obligations, on the future (what should be done)
State imposes pain to deter or prevent future crime	Focus is on restitution as a means of restoring both parties; goal is reconciliation and restoration
One social injury is replaced by another	Emphasis is on repair of social injury
Action is directed from the state to offender; victims are ignored and the offender is passive	Victim's and offender's roles are recognized in problem/solution; victim's rights and needs are recognized, and offender is encouraged to be responsible for his/her actions
The offense is defined in purely legal terms devoid or moral, social, economic, or political dimensions	The offense is understood in whole context—moral, social, economic, and political
The offender's "debt" is owed to society in the abstract	Recognition that the debt or liability is owed to a specific victim(s)
Response of the state focuses on offender's past behavior	Response is shifted to the harmful consequences of the offender's behavior
The stigma of crime cannot be removed	Stigma of crime is removed via restorative action
No encouragement for repentance and forgiveness	Possibility of repentance and forgiveness

Source: Adapted from Zehr, Howard. 1985. *Retributive Justice, Restorative Justice*. Akron, PA: Mennonite Central Committee. Used by permission.

Note that, as in the colonial era, crime is viewed as a transgression against a person as opposed to an offense against the state. It follows from this position that offenders owe a debt not to society but to the individuals they have harmed. Restorative justice also emphasizes the possibility of reconciliation between offenders and victims.

The first **Victim–Offender Reconciliation Programs (VORPs)** in North America began in Ontario, Canada, in 1974 and Elkhart, Indiana, four years later. By 1998, there were almost 300 such programs in the United States, and 26 in Canada as well as a number of other countries, including Germany, Finland, France, and New Zealand. VORPs would never have succeeded in the United States if people did not embrace the philosophy of restorative justice. Although the punitive, get tough, "law 'n' order" perspective is part and parcel of many political campaigns, Mark Umbreit (1998, p. 11) argues there is a "growing body of evidence to suggest that the general public is far less vindictive than portrayed and far more supportive of the basic principles of restorative justice than many think, particularly when applied to property offenders." For example, in a survey of adults in Minnesota, nearly 75 percent of respondents said that having the offender compensate them for their losses was more important than a jail sentence for burglars. More than 80 percent of the respondents stated that they were interested in taking part in a face-to-face mediation with offenders (Pranis and Umbreit, 1992). These sentiments make VORPs possible.

VORPs are "dialogue driven" sessions that bring the offender and victim together in the presence of a trained mediator. The emphasis on these sessions or meetings is on victim healing, offender accountability, and the restoration of losses. Most VORPs are run by nonprofit community agencies and consist of a fourfold process, the centerpiece of which is the mediation session (Umbreit, 1998, p. 14). The mediator facilitates a dialogue between the victim and the offender focusing on how the crime has affected their lives. In most cases a written, mutually agreeable settlement is reached at this stage. The agreement may also take the form of monetary payments to the community or service to the victim and/or community (Zehr, 1990). The offender's behavior is monitored to ensure that all the terms of the agreement are being fulfilled. Additional sessions are scheduled if problems occur.

Both juveniles and adults are referred to VORPs by judges, probation officers, prosecutors, police, and, on occasion, defense attorneys and victim advocates. Referrals are usually made at the pre- or postadjudication level (see Chapter 10) although they can be made at any point in the criminal court proceedings. The settlement can become part of the sentence or some component of the court's overall decision in a case. Regarding court-referred cases, offenders are often on probation while fulfilling the stipulations of their contracts (Umbreit, 1998; Zehr, 1990).

Based on his evaluation of VORPs in four cities (Albuquerque, Austin, Minneapolis, and Oakland), Mark Umbreit (1994; 1998), who has studied these programs extensively, reached a number of conclusions:

- These mediation programs result in a high degree of satisfaction for victims (79 percent) and offenders (89 percent). More than 80 percent of respondents in both groups perceived the mediation process as fair. Offenders made the following comments: "I liked the fairness of it"; "To understand how the victim feels makes me different . . . I was able to understand a lot about what I did"; "I had a chance of doing something to correct what I did without having to pay bad consequences" (1998, p. 18). Victims were overwhelmingly positive about VORPs as indicated by their comments: "I was allowed to participate and I felt I was able to make decisions rather than the system making them for me"; "The mediation made me feel like I had something to do with what went on . . . that justice had been served."
- These mediation programs significantly reduce the fear and anxiety experienced by crime victims. Prior to their involvement in VORPs, 25 percent of victims feared they would be victimized again by the same offender. That figure dropped to 10 percent after the mediation.
- Juvenile offenders do not perceive their participation in VORPs as getting off easy or beating the system. Rather, they view the settlement as a demanding response

Victim–Offender Reconciliation Programs (VORPs) programs that bring the offender and victim together in the presence of a trained mediator for the purpose of reconciliation, which usually results in the offender making some form of the restitution to the victim or community

to their law-violating behavior, as severe as other options available to them via the courts.

- VORPs have been enthusiastically supported by judges and probation staff members and are increasingly becoming integrated into the juvenile court system.
- Significantly fewer and less serious additional crimes were committed by juveniles who participated in VORP-style programs during a 12-month period when compared to a group of offenders who committed similar crimes but did not participate in any form of mediation.

Similar to VORPs are *victim–offender conferencing programs* including family group counseling (FGC). This program usually includes a conference facilitator, the victim, the offender, members of their respective families, and support groups (Schweigert, 1999). Fundamental goals of FGCs are (1) to allow the victim to express the impact of the crime on him or her to the offender, (2) to help offenders recognize their criminal behavior by shaming them, and (3) to reach some agreement on a plan to compensate victims (Bazemore and Griffiths, 1997).

FGCs have been criticized for pressuring victims to forgive offenders to the point that some victims may fail to participate. As such, crime victims can be used as "props" to meet offender needs. Some observers have noted that these programs fail to protect victims against retaliation by offenders (Bazemore and Griffiths, 1997). To the extent that this criticism is true, individuals may be victimized a second time. Developed in New Zealand in 1989 (where all juvenile criminal matters are resolved with the exception of murder and rape), FGCs have been used in some cases in Montana, Minnesota, and Pennsylvania (Bazemore, 1999; Harris, Corbett, and Harris, 1998).

Despite the successes of victim–offender mediation and conferencing programs, the restitution/restoration strategy has significant drawbacks (Doerner and Lab, 1995). To begin, only about 20 percent of property crime offenses known to police via Uniform Crime Reports data result in arrests, meaning that no more than 1 in 5 such crimes lend themselves to VORPs. Simply stated, no offender, no restitution. Even when offenders are apprehended, there is no guarantee that a conviction will follow (Geis, 1990). Because most offenders come from the lower class or the poverty-stricken "underclass," their ability to make restitution in a reasonable amount of time is limited, if not impossible. For those offenders who can pay something, money diverted to victims may come at the expense of family members who eventually turn to the state for welfare benefits (Geis, 1990). Jobs created with public funds are not always available, and employers in the private sector may be reluctant to hire offenders. Also, when and where unemployment rates are relatively high, people may object to law-abiding citizens being denied work while offenders are given jobs. Although restitution is rather easy to quantify for property crimes, it is much more difficult to attach a dollar amount to crimes of violence. For example, how much money should a victim be awarded for pain and psychological suffering resulting from a debilitating physical assault or rape? VORPs do not readily lend themselves to crimes of violence. Finally, as previously noted, the philosophy of restitution is a dramatic shift from a criminal orientation that is offender based to a civil perspective that focuses on the victim (Doerner and Lab, 1995). As VORPs become more widespread, they may encounter resistance from conservative members of society with strong punitive orientations.

Victims of Crime Act

Deeply dissatisfied with the treatment of crime victims in her country, English magistrate and prison reformer Margaret Fry launched a campaign to have the state compensate crime victims in 1957. Although this initial attempt was unsuccessful, victim compensation programs were eventually introduced in New Zealand (1963), England (1964), and in California and New York (1965 and 1966, respectively). By the mid-1990s, all 50 states, the District of Columbia, and the Virgin Islands had established victimization programs. The 1996 Antiterrorism Act also provides compensation to U.S. residents who become victims of terrorist attacks within or outside this country ("State

Crime Victim," 2000). Established with the passage of the **Victims of Crime Act (VOCA) of 1984,** the **Crime Victims Fund** is a major source of revenue for state compensation programs (see Figure 5.6). Victims programs are subsidized by criminal fines, forfeited bail bonds, penalty fees, and special assessments collected by federal courts, the U.S. Attorney's Office, and the Bureau of Prisons. No funds come from federal tax dollars ("Victims of Crime Act Crime Victims Funds," 1999). Money deposited in state crime funds increased steadily from 1985 through 1996 before declining. The first $10 million placed in these funds each year is used to improve the investigation and prosecution of child abuse cases with the remaining money distributed in the following manner: 48.5 percent to state compensation programs, 48.5 percent to state assistance programs, and 3 percent to support training and improve the delivery of services to federal crime victims ("Victims of Crime Act Crime Victims Funds," 1999).

Victim compensation provides direct reimbursement to crime victims for medical costs, lost wages or loss of support, funeral and burial costs, and mental health counseling. Every state has a crime victims compensation program that it administers independently. The majority of states place a ceiling on awards distributed to victims in the $10,000 to $25,000 range. California caps awards at $46,000, whereas New York and Maryland have no specified limit. To be eligible for compensation, most states require the victim to notify law enforcement officials within 3 days of a crime and file a claim within a designated period of time, usually 2 years. These time limits can usually be extended for good cause. In addition, states have a number of program requirements that must be met before awards are granted. For example, most states closely examine the relationship between the offender and victim. Relatives, sexual partners, or residents of the same household as the offender are typically not eligible for compensation.

Victims of Crime Act (VOCA) of 1984 legislation that authorized federal funding for state-administered victim compensation programs; these funds are typically limited to victims of violent crimes with no other recourse to money or services

Crime Victims Fund established with the passage of VOCA in 1984, it is the major source of revenue for state compensation programs

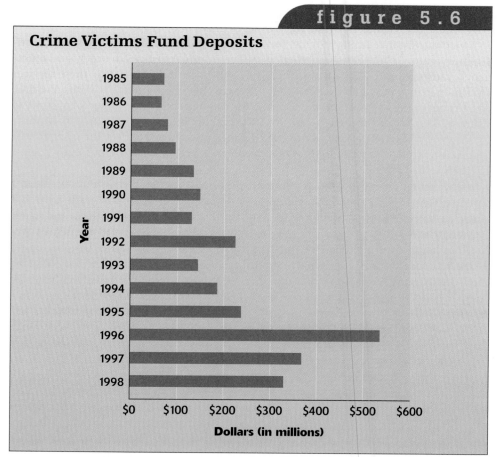

figure 5.6

Crime Victims Fund Deposits

Source: "Victims of Crime Act Crime Victims Fund." 1999. Washington, DC: Office of the Victims of Crime Fact Sheet, U.S. Department of Justice, Office of Justice Programs.

Fourteen-year-old Brandin Costin, seated next to a memorial to his deceased father, Michael Costin, becomes emotional as he delivers a victim impact statement at the sentencing hearing of Thomas Junta in Massachusetts in 2002. Junta was sentenced to six to ten years in prison for beating to death fellow hockey dad Michael Costin at their sons' hockey practice.

These individuals are disqualified for fear that the husband who has badly beaten his wife, for example, will be enriched by the money the woman receives from the victims' fund (Doerner and Lab, 1995). Figure 5.7 lists the major requirements of the California Crime Victims Program. Note that these programs only compensate crime victims to the extent that other forms of reimbursement, such as medical insurance, do not cover the loss ("Victims of Crime Act Crime Victims Fund," 1999).

Victim assistance funds provide, but are not limited to, the following services: crisis intervention, counseling, emergency shelter, criminal justice advocacy, and emergency transportation. Nationwide, roughly 10,000 organizations provide these services to crime victims, of which almost 3,300 receive some VOCA funds ("Victims of Crime Act Crime Victims Fund," 1999). From 1986 through 1998, the Office of Victims of Crime (OVC) has distributed more than $700 million in VOCA compensation funds—an impressive figure on one hand, but, on the other hand, almost inconsequential when compared to the hundreds of billions of dollars crime costs victims in this country each year.

Government compensation programs focus on victims of violent crimes for at least three reasons (Geis, 1990). First, victims of property crimes often have insurance that covers losses (or a portion of these losses) incurred from burglary, auto theft, and so on. Second, the loss of goods does not have as strong an emotional appeal as offenses that result in bodily injury or death. This being the case, using public funds to compensate property crime victims would not be enthusiastically supported by citizens. Finally, there are so many more property crimes than violent victimizations that an all-inclusive compensation program could not possibly help the vast number of individuals who suffer crime-related property losses annually without expending billions of dollars.

Government-sponsored compensation programs have generated controversy since their inception. Proponents argue that helping victims of violent crime is the latest step in a social welfare system that can be traced back to the Great Depression of the 1930s. Social Security, Medicaid, Medicare, workers' disability, and workers' compensation are all components of government-sponsored programs implemented to enhance the quality of life of citizens (Karmen, 1990). Besides, if public funds are used to help victims of natural disasters, such as hurricanes, floods, and tornadoes, why shouldn't federal and state money be used to help the victims of man-made disasters, such as violent crime? In both cases, people are the innocent victims of circumstances beyond their control. The final argument for compensation programs is that citizens in democratic states have entered into a "social contract" with the government. They have relin-

figure 5.7

California Board of Control: Crime Victim Compensation under the California Victims of Crime Program

Authority

Under California law (Government Code sections 13959–13969.4), qualifying victims of crime may receive financial assistance for losses resulting from a crime when these losses cannot be reimbursed by other sources. The State Board of Control (Board), Victims of Crime Program (Program), administers California's Crime Victim Compensation Program.

Losses That May Be Covered

- Medical/Dental
- Mental Health Counseling
- Wage/Income
- Financial Support
- Funeral/Burial
- Job Retraining

Losses That Are Not Covered

Personal property, losses, including cash, are not eligible for reimbursement under the Program. The Program also cannot reimburse applicants for expenses related to the prosecution of an alleged perpetrator or compensate applicants for "pain and suffering."

However, losses not covered by the Program may be recoverable either through court-ordered restitution as part of a convicted perpetrator's criminal sentence or through the enforcement of a judgment obtained in a civil lawsuit against the alleged perpetrator. For more information about these two methods of loss recovery, contact the Victim/Witness Assistance Center in your area (see the government listings of your local telephone directory).

Who Is Eligible?

- A victim who was injured, threatened with physical injury, or died as a result of a crime.
- A derivative victim who was not directly injured or killed as a result of a crime but who, at the time of the crime:
  - Was the parent, sibling, spouse, or child of the victim; or
  - Was living in the household of the victim; or
  - Had lived with the victim for at least two years in a relationship similar to a parent, sibling, spouse, or child of the victim; or
  - Was another family member of the victim, including the victim's fiancé(e), and witnessed the crime; or
  - Was not the primary caretaker of a minor victim but became the primary caretaker after the crime occurred; or
  - Pays for the medical and/or funeral/burial expenses of a deceased victim.

Who Is Not Eligible?

- Persons who commit the crime.
- Persons who contribute to or take part in the events leading to the crime.
- Persons who do not reasonably cooperate with law enforcement in the investigation and/or prosecution of known suspects.
- Persons who do not cooperate with the staff of the Board and/or the Victim/Witness Assistance Center in the verification of the claim.

Program Requirements That Must Be Met

- The crime must have occurred in California, or if the crime occurred outside of California, the victim must have been a California resident at the time of the crime.
- The crime must be reported to the police, sheriff, highway patrol, or other appropriate law enforcement agency.
- The victim must reasonably cooperate with law enforcement in the investigation and prosecution of any known suspect(s).
- The victim must cooperate with staff of the Board and/or the Victim/Witness Assistance Center in the verification of the claim.
- All other sources of reimbursement must ultimately be used to cover crime-related expenses.

Felony Convictions

The law places restrictions on Program-reimbursable expenses incurred by a victim or derivative victim who was also convicted of a felony on or after January 1, 1989. If you fall within this category, you may wish to seek further information or assistance from the Board or a local Victim/Witness Assistance Center.

Filing Deadlines

Applications for adult victims must be filed within one year of the date of the crime. The Board may, for "good cause," grant an extension for such applications filed up to three years after the date of the crime.

Applications resulting from crimes against a minor must be filed before the minor's 19th birthday. The Board may, for "good cause," grant an extension for such applications up to the minor's 21st birthday.

Source: State of California Victims of Crime Program, November 1999. Copyright © 2002 by California Victim Compensation and Governmental Claims Board. Used with permission of California Victim Compensation and Government Claims Board.

quished the right to engage in private vengeance (to "take the law into their own hands") in exchange for protection from the criminal justice system. If the police are too busy, too poorly trained, or too negligent to protect them from criminals, then the state has not lived up to its end of the bargain and is obligated to compensate crime victims (Karmen, 1990).

Opponents of state-sponsored compensation programs contend that they are basically government handouts that undermine the virtues of rugged individualism, self-reliance, and personal responsibility on which this country was built. These opponents maintain that government programs are but another example of "creeping socialism" that can only lead to economic and moral disaster. Detractors also point out that VOCA-type programs contribute to increased crime rates because people cognizant that the government will come to their financial aid in the event of a criminal victimization will become careless and foolish in their everyday behavior and, as such, are more likely to be victimized. Also, offenders can more easily rationalize their transgressions with the knowledge that crime victims will be compensated by the government (Karmen, 1990).

Victims and Sentencing

Advocating longer prison sentences, harsher treatment of convicted offenders, and speedy executions, one segment of the victim's movement has been called the "vengeance rights lobby." This faction of the movement scored a victory in 1974 when the criminal courts in Fresno, California, permitted victims to introduce a **victim-impact statement (VIS)** at the sentencing phase of the trial. These statements allow victims to tell the court in detail how they have been medically, financially, and emotionally affected by the crime *prior* to the offender's sentencing. In some jurisdictions, prosecutors send out VISs when charges are initially filed. Currently, all but two states have legislated VISs. In the federal justice system as well as many state systems, the VIS is prepared by a probation officer as part of the presentence investigation (which describes the offender's background and the criminal offense) that is forwarded to the judge (Wells, 1990). The judge gives the VIS as much or as little weight as he or she chooses in the sentencing determination. The **victim statement of opinion,** or VSO, is a much more subjective declaration allowing victims to tell the court what sentence they believe the offender should receive (Kelly, 1990). These written or oral statements are permitted in approximately 35 states.

Critics of VISs and VSOs argue that allowing victims to affect sentencing decisions makes for a dual track system of punishment. Tougher sentences are likely to be dealt to offenders whose victims submitted a VIS than to offenders who were fortunate enough to victimize more compassionate individuals (Elias, 1993). Several studies have concluded that VISs have had little impact on sentencing decisions primarily because victims do not exercise their right to use them. For example, only 3 percent of victims in California informed the court what impact a crime had on their lives (Villmoare and Neto, 1987). In many cases, victims are not aware that they have the right to participate at this stage of the proceedings. If a trial has had many continuances and/or has been particularly long, victims cannot always be located at the sentencing stage. Some people are aware of VISs but refrain from exercising their right to address the court because they are dissatisfied with the criminal justice system or fear their emotional well-being may be jeopardized at this stage of the healing process if they have to explain in detail yet one more time everything that happened to them as a result of the crime. Still other people may fear retaliation from friends and family members of the victim if they push for a more punitive sentence (Doerner and Lab, 1995).

A few years after Mary Byron was killed by her boyfriend on his release from jail (without her knowledge), the Victim Information Notification Everyday System was introduced. This technologically innovative system automatically dials jails and prisons every 10 minutes and informs individuals registered with it when a suspect or criminal (who had previously victimized them) has been released. This is but one of the many services that has come about since the victim's movement began more than 30 years ago. Figure 5.8 summarizes victims' rights and services circa 1970 and highlights those rights and services as of 1998. The overall welfare of crime victims was extended further in the latter part of the twentieth century than at any previous period in U.S. history.

victim-impact statement (VIS) a statement that allows victims to tell the court in detail how they have been medically, financially, and emotionally affected by a crime prior to the offender's sentencing

victim statement of opinion a subjective declaration by crime victims telling the court what sentence they believe offenders should receive

figure 5.8

Accomplishments for Crime Victims between 1970 and 1998

1970

No victim bills of rights or constitutional amendments.

Few victim-witness programs or crime victim compensation funds at the state or federal level.

No national organizations to assist crime victims and their survivors.

No organizations for people who survive homicide victims.

No discussion of domestic violence at the national level.

No discussion of sexual assault victims at the national level.

No organization working to change the laws on drunk driving or to assist the victims of these crashes.

No corrections-based victim services.

No programs to address staff as crime victims.

No programs for offenders to take responsibility for their crimes or the long-term impact of their crimes on their victims.

1998

Forty-eight state bills of rights introduced and 29 state constitutions amended.

Federal Victim/Witness Protection Act enacted. First victim compensation program started in 1965; others started in early 1970s. Victims of Crime Act enacted in 1984.

The National Organization for Victim Assistance formed in 1975 and the National Victim Center formed in 1982.

Parents of Murdered Children founded in 1978 now with thousands of members and many similar support groups, most started by women.

Thousands of programs established to serve domestic violence victims and the children who witness such violence. The 1994 Violence Against Women Act enacted and the Violence Against Women Grant Office established.

Hundreds of rape treatment programs established, and training has been improved for law enforcement, medical, and legal personnel to help these victims.

Mothers Against Drunk Driving, started by a woman, now has thousands of members, has been active in changing hundreds of laws, and claims to have saved thousands of lives.

Many departments of corrections implemented victim service programs based on the OVC-sponsored Victims and Corrections Grant in 1991.

Staff crime victims addressed as part of the Victims and Corrections Project.

The Impact of Crime on Victims classes started in 1985 and are now replicated in about 15 states.

Source: *Women in Criminal Justice—A Twenty-Year Update.* 1998. Washington, DC: U.S. Department of Justice.

Focus on Norway

Crime Victims in a Wealthy Society

As the world's second-largest producer of crude oil (Saudi Arabia is number one) with extensive reserves of this valuable commodity in the North Sea, Norway's only economic difficulties have been described as luxury problems. The Norwegian government has enough money to provide the majority of its citizens with funds or subsidies in the form of universal health care, inexpensive university education, and 10 months' maternity leave (at full pay) for all new mothers, to name but a few programs. The jobless rate is so low that guest workers have to be brought in from Sweden. If estimates of this Scandinavian nation's oil reserves are correct, all of this wealth is merely the beginning according to one Norwegian political consultant who noted that "we are going to be filthy rich." With a population of 4.5 million (only slightly less than the state of Arizona), Norway already is one of the wealthiest (per capita) nations in the world, with an amassed public fund of approximately $60 billion (Williams, 2001, p. A1).

In spite of this economic success, Norway is still plagued with the problem of law-violating behavior, with rates of criminality increasing fivefold between 1965 and 1995 even after adjusting for population growth (Rieber-Mohn, 1998). Although crime and victimization rates have risen dramatically in that 30-year period, Norway does have a lower rate of crime than most industrial nations. A victimization survey conducted in Norway in 1991 yielded a rate of 14 victimizations per 100 people for property crimes and 5 per 100 for crimes of violence including threats of violence (Bygrave, 1997).

As is the case in the United States, the role of crime victims in the prosecutorial stage of criminal court proceedings is limited to providing testimony and/or evidence. Currently, Norwegian courts do not provide for victim-impact statements, although changing the law to permit these reports is under consideration. In limited circumstances, victims have additional rights in the criminal courts where they can institute what might best be described as a "private prosecution." In these cases, victims have the prerogative to examine documents during the main court hearing as well as question witnesses (Bygrave, 1997).

Beginning in 1991, the prosecuting attorney had the authority to settle some criminal cases outside courts. For this to occur, the violation has to be relatively minor, meaning that a conviction would not result in imprisonment. In addition, the defendant has to be proven guilty of the offense with the victim agreeing to settle the case in this manner.

Conflict Resolution Boards deal primarily with young wrongdoers, preferably when both the victim and offender live in the same town. After a successful resolution, a contract is drawn up between the offender and victim stipulating the circumstances under which the guilty party will monetarily compensate the victim, repair damages, or do some other useful work in exchange for the state closing the case (Bygrave, 1997; "Victims of Crime in 22 European Criminal Justice Systems," 2001).

Crime victims in Norway have the right to demand monetary compensation from the state for physical and/or psychological injuries incurred as a consequence of a criminal offense. Maximum compensation payments total 200,000 krones (slightly more than U.S. $22,000) and can be awarded to foreign citizens living in or visiting Norway as well as Norwegian citizens victimized in a foreign country (Norway—Royal Ministry of Justice and the Police, 2001). Crime victims are also entitled to free legal advice during the prosecution phase of the proceedings regardless of their income. Victims have the right to sue offenders for monetary compensation in civil courts (Bygrave, 1997).

Although Norway does not have a national victim support movement, several organizations help individuals cope with their postcriminal encounter problems—especially victims of sexual and other violent offenses. For example, 19 Support Centers against Incest offer assistance to women who are sexually victimized by a family member(s) or are mothers of a child who is an incest victim. One of these centers deals exclusively with male victims. Also, 50 crisis centers throughout the country offer assistance to women survivors of rape and battering. These organizations offer victims and their children a variety of services including counseling, help contacting the police, legal aid, and medical help. About 25 medical emergency centers specialize in providing services to survivors of violent crimes, including rape ("Victims of Crime in 22 European Criminal Justice Systems," 2001).

Rates of crime and victimization that increased so dramatically in Norway from the mid-1960s to the mid-1990s have declined (Rieber-Mohn, 1998), and victimization rates for violent crimes in this Scandinavian country are significantly lower than in the United States. The victim's movement in both the criminal justice system and private sector (often funded in full or part by the government) have partially contributed to an overall living standard in Norway that some "quality of life" indexes rank as the highest in the world.

1. For most of the history of criminology, researchers focused almost exclusively on offenders and what motivated these individuals to commit crimes. About 50 years ago criminologists began examining the role of the victim in the criminal event, and by 1970 victimology became part of criminology.

2. Crime victims have been examined from three viewpoints, each roughly corresponding to a political philosophy. Conservatives are particularly concerned with victims of street crimes (robberies and burglaries, for example), whereas liberal victimologists focus on individuals who have been hurt by societal elites via corporate and government crimes. From a radical-critical perspective, the study of victims should not be limited to harm resulting solely from criminal acts. Rather, victimology must focus on the harm done by all forms of injurious behavior, including industrial pollution, discriminatory institutions, and abusive police forces.

3. Not every person in the United States has an equal chance of becoming a crime victim. Some individuals are more likely, and in the case of robbery and rape much more likely, to be victimized than others. Young people are more crime prone than older individuals. With the exception of rape and sexual assault, males have higher rates of victimization than females. African Americans have somewhat higher rates of violent victimization than whites and a significantly higher rate than people of other races. For the most part, violent victimizations decrease as household income increases.

4. Street crime, child abuse, and drunk driving cost Americans about $450 billion each year. When monetary losses resulting from employee theft and corporate offenses are included, the total cost of crime victimization exceeds $1 trillion a year. According to one estimate, between 20 and 25 percent of the client population of mental health professionals are crime victims. The emotional pain experienced by crime victims can last for months and in some cases a lifetime. Victims of robbery, burglary, and nonsexual assaults may suffer posttraumatic stress disorder, the ongoing reexperiencing of the criminal event in flashbacks and dreams. Crime victims often blame themselves, adding the pain of guilt to the pain of victimization. Family members and friends may blame crime victims in whole or part for their troubles, stating that they should have been more careful in their speech, behavior, attire, and so on.

5. Just as criminologists have divided crimes and criminals into categories, victimologists have constructed numerous typologies of victims. According to the German scholar Hans von Hentig, people often contribute to their own victimization. He examined the biological, psychological, and social characteristics of crime victims. The French attorney Benjamin Mendelsohn constructed a fivefold classification based on the victim's contribution to his or her victimization ranging from the completely innocent victim to the most guilty individual who enters the criminal event as the offender and becomes the victim.

6. Crime is not randomly distributed in time and space; that is, people are more or less likely to be victimized depending on where they live. One study of 115,000 addresses in a major U.S. city discovered that 50 percent of all calls to police for assistance came from only 3 percent of places. These high-intensity crime areas are called "hot spots"; these locations tend to have a significant number of businesses where liquor is bought and consumed. Most perpetrators of street crime commit their offenses close to home. People who live in neighborhoods with a disproportionate number of offenders have high rates of victimization. In his classic study of criminal homicide in Philadelphia, Marvin Wolfgang discovered that 26 percent of these crimes could be classified as victim precipitated; that is, the victim instigated the violence that led to his or her death.

7. Offenders often choose victims who are small in stature; physically weak; have something the offenders want; or arouse some negative emotion in them such as anger, resentment, or jealousy. Because some individuals become known as vulnerable and/or attractive targets, they are likely to be victimized on numerous occasions. The roles of offender and victim are not fixed; some victims become offenders and some offenders become victims. Regarding the latter, drug dealers are often favorite targets of robbers who realize that they (the drug dealers) have cash and drugs on them and are not likely to report their victimization to the police. The lifestyle of some delinquents, especially gang members, increases their chance of being victimized by rival gang members via fights and drive-by shootings. Victims of property crimes may attempt to recoup their losses by stealing from other people.

8. The first Victim–Offender Reconciliation Program (VORP) in the United States began in 1978. Run by nonprofit organizations, there are now more than 300 VORPs that mediate the terms of reconciliation

between offenders and victims, which usually takes the form of monetary payment or service to the victim or the community on the part of the offender. Analysis of these programs indicates a high degree of satisfaction on the part of victims as well as judges and probation officers. Established with the passage of the Victims of Crime Act (VOCA) of 1984, the Crime Victimization Fund is a major source of revenue for state-administered compensation programs. Subsidized by criminal fines, forfeited bail bonds, and assessments collected by the federal courts, VOCA compensates victims of violent crimes who have no other sources of money and services. Advocates of VOCA argue that, if the government cannot protect citizens from criminal victimization, it has the obligation to compensate them for their physical and mental suffering. Opponents believe that these programs are a form of socialism that undermines the individualistic ethos of capitalism.

9. Victim-impact statements permit victims to tell the court how they have been affected by the crime at the sentencing phase of the trial. Victim statements of opinion are declarations on the part of the victims allowing them to inform the judge what sentence they believe the offender should receive. Judges give these statements as little or as much weight as they choose in sentencing convicted offenders.

key terms

crime displacement
Crime Victims Fund
target congruence
van Dijk chain
victim-impact statement (VIS)
Victim–Offender Reconciliation
    Programs (VORPs)

victimology
victim precipitation
victim statement of opinion
Victims of Crime Act (VOCA)
    of 1984

questions *for* investigation

1. As a student of criminal justice, what are you most concerned about—the economic and medical costs of victimization or the psychological costs experienced by victims and their families and friends? Explain your answer.

2. After reading about the various characteristics of victims in this chapter, describe the precautions you might take to protect yourself from being victimized.

3. Explain the rights you think that victims should have in prosecuting and sentencing offenders. Why do you think the United States has moved from an offenderology approach back to a victimology approach in dealing with crime?

4. Consider the media coverage of violent crimes in your community. Explain how victims are perceived and treated by the local criminal justice system (note the source for your information on victims). How do the media treat and present victims to their audience? What is your opinion of this treatment? Are there any differences in treatment based on a victim's age, race, gender, neighborhood, and so on?

5. Are some crime victims more worthy of public sympathy than others? If so, list a few examples and defend your position. Do some crime victims "deserve what they get"? Explain.

6. Suppose you have been appointed by the governor of your state to lead a task force on crime victims and the criminal justice system. Prepare a list of recommendations that will both aid crime victims and facilitate the administration of justice, especially the crime courts. Be realistic in terms of the amount of time and money it will take to carry out these proposals.

7. Use the Internet or school library to gather information on victims programs in another country (preferably an African, Asian, or Latin American nation). Compare and contrast compensation programs in this country with those in the United States. What are the strengths and weaknesses of each program?

1. As an urban planner on the city payroll, you have been assigned to lead a task force designated to make the soon-to-be-renovated downtown area as free of street crime as possible. Research the geography of crime as background material for a one- or two-page report to be submitted to the mayor (by way of your instructor) that outlines an urban-center redevelopment strategy to keep visitors to your city from becoming crime victims. Consider any latent or unintended consequences of your plan.

2. Suppose you are running for governor of your state. Victims' rights groups are urging legislation that will significantly increase the scope of crime victims' benefits. Opponents of existing victims' rights provisions are calling for a dramatic reduction in these programs; they argue that government has no legal obligation to compensate these individuals. Develop a victims' rights package that will be minimally tolerable to both sides. Pay particular attention to the language in your report. Be as persuasive as possible.

UNDER
Investigation

Terrorists and Victims— A World at Risk

On December 8, 1941, a somber Franklin D. Roosevelt addressed a joint session of Congress. "Yesterday," the president said, ". . . a date that will live in infamy—the United States of America was attacked by naval and air forces of the empire of Japan." Eighteen warships were sunk or severely damaged and 2,403 people died as a consequence of the Pearl Harbor attack, an event that marked our entry into World War II. September 11, 2001, is a date that will also "live in infamy," to use Roosevelt's words, as terrorist attacks on New York City and Washington, D.C., took the lives of more than 3,000 individuals from the United States and 40 countries. Only 4 months after the execution of Timothy McVeigh, the former soldier convicted of planning and executing the Oklahoma City bombing that killed 168 people, Americans had to deal with the horror and magnitude of a terrorist strike that many believed could never happen in this country.

Complex in its nature and dimension, the first difficulty one confronts when examining this phenomenon is defining terrorism. According to Alex Schmid and Albert Jongman (1988) there are more than 100 definitions of this term, what Brian Jenkins (1992, p. 2168) refer to as the emotion-laden, "slippery-slope" of terrorism. The major reason for this large and disparate number of definitions centers on the question of what constitutes terrorist behavior. For example, were the reported 24 attempts on Cuban leader Fidel Castro's life (including the planting of poison cigars) by the Central Intelligence Agency (CIA) acts of terrorism? Were the U.S. Army Air Corps pilots terrorists when, in 1944, they dropped thousands of bombs on Tokyo that killed 180,000 individuals (mostly civilians)? Why is blowing

up people in a restaurant or government building a terrorist act, whereas burning to death men, women, and children with incendiary bombs an "unavoidable act of

"Why is blowing up people in a restaurant or government building a terrorist act . . . ?"

war" tolerated by the international community? One person's terrorist, as has been often noted, is another person's freedom fighter.

In spite of the difficulty of settling on a satisfactory definition of terrorism, this term must be operationalized if it is to prove useful. To that end we focus on the work of political scientist Ted Gurr (1989, p. 201), who views terrorism as "the use of unexpected violence to intimidate or coerce people in the pursuit of political objectives." The key words in this definition are *unexpected violence* and *political objectives*. Gurr notes that terrorism can occur at any place and at any time with the perpetrators of these acts rarely making a distinction between the innocent and the guilty, or between justifiable and unjustifiable victims. "The enemy is only incidentally particular individuals who cross the terrorist's path; more fundamentally it is civil order" (Lomasky, 1991, p. 107) and people's reaction to the temporary or long-lasting break in this order. Terrorists also have a political agenda (that may be quite specific or broad based), which can be loosely defined as using or threatening to use violence to bring about or hinder some social, governmental, and/or economic objective.

"Terrorists also have a political agenda . . ."

A Terrorist Typology

The principal reason terrorism is so difficult to define is that there are numerous forms of this behavior. Just as law enforcement officials and scholars have offered a variety of definitions of terrorism, so too have they constructed typologies of these activities that consolidate the many kinds of terrorism into a manageable number of categories. Most typologies include at least two of the three critical factors of terrorism: its purpose, its actions and supporters, and its location. We use the four-category typology of Ted Gurr (1989) and add a fifth dimension of contemporary terrorism. Gurr's typology focuses on the "political status and situation of the perpetrators" (p. 204).

Perhaps as old as the United States itself, *vigilante terrorism* is committed by private citizens against other private citizens to express hatred or to resist social change. Native Americans were victims of random violence almost immediately after white Europeans arrived in the New World in the 1600s and continued to be so for almost 300 years. The phrase "the only good Indian is a dead Indian" was a reality in many parts of the country as the indigenous people of the North American continent were attacked by settlers who coveted their land.

Formed in 1865 by ex-Confederate army officers, the Ku Klux Klan (KKK) is the most enduring and violent vigilante terrorist organization in U.S. history. What began as a fraternal association quickly turned into a brotherhood of racial bigots whose goal was to stop newly emancipated African Americans from realizing their recently gained social and political rights. Southern African Americans and white Reconstruction officials who sympathized with and aided former slaves were subject to beatings, torture, and murder. In subsequent years the Klan added Jews, Roman Catholics, and immigrants from non–Anglo Saxon groups to its list of victims. The KKK was especially active during the civil rights movement of the 1960s with Klan members charged in the deaths of four little girls who were killed when a bomb exploded in a Birmingham, Alabama, church (Cose, 2001).

Issues-oriented groups (antiabortion, animal rights, and environmental extremists) have used violence to promote their positions, or in the case of antiabortion and radical environmental groups, to obstruct behavior. For example, more than 60 abortion clinics were bombed in the 1980s and the trend continued in the 1990s. Based on their beliefs that, like humans, animals have certain inalienable rights, "ecoterrorist" groups, such as the Earth Liberation Front (ELF) and Animal Rights Militia, have attacked medical researchers (who conduct their experiments on animals), university agricultural stations doing research in biotechnology, meatpacking plants, and the fur industry. As of July 2001, the ELF claimed responsibility for 20 acts of violence (mostly arson) that resulted in $37 million in damages (Laurent, 2001). The individuals committing these acts would emphatically reject the terrorist label insisting that this violence is "justifiable," and that they are working for the greater good of the community, man, and/or planet earth (Barkan and Snowden, 2001).

Insurgent terrorism is committed "by private groups against public authorities and aims at bringing about

". . . the Ku Klux Klan is the most enduring and violent vigilante terrorist organization in U.S. history."

radical political change" (Gurr, 1989, p. 204). This form of terrorism has ebbed and flowed throughout our history and can be subdivided into the following three groups (Riley and Hoffman, 1995, pp. 13–17):

1. *Ethnic separatist and emigre groups.* Since 1898, when the United States obtained Puerto Rico via the Spanish American War, a number of Puerto Rican separatist groups have engaged in terrorist violence (on their island and in the United States) toward the goal of achieving an independent state.
2. *Left-wing radical organizations.* Left-wing radical groups have tended to engage in symbolic bombings (attacking uninhabited buildings in the middle of the night, for example), rather than attacks designed to result in a significant number of casualties. Their aim has been to call attention to themselves and the group's fundamental purpose or goals. Some antiwar groups during the Vietnam conflict were

organizations of this type. Unhappy with the failure of the antiwar movement to end the fighting in southeast Asia, some white radicals split off from the Students for a Democratic Society (commonly known as the SDS) and formed a revolutionary group called the Weather Underground. This group carried out a series of bombings in 1970 targeting police headquarters, and the Capitol and Pentagon in Washington D.C. (Barkan and Snowden, 2001).

3. *Right-wing, racist, antigovernment, and survivalist-type groups.* In the past 10 to 20 years, insurgent terrorism in this country has taken on a more right-wing bent, as members of militant militias and white supremacist groups have engaged in numerous acts of terrorism against the government and have been considerably more violent than their left-wing counterparts of the previous generation (Dees, 1996; Smith, 1994; White, 1991). Evidence indicates that many Klansmen traded in their white sheets for military garb and joined virulent antigovernment and typically anti-Jewish, -African American, -Hispanic, and -Asian groups. After the September 11 attack, a member of one militia hate group stated, "Anyone who is willing to drive a plane into a building to kill Jews is all right by me" (Sink, 2001, p. B1).

Leaders of these groups believe the federal government is hatching one conspiracy plot after another, all toward the ultimate goal of destroying the United States and enslaving its citizens. The United Nations is viewed as a front organization working to bring about a one-world government, and AIDS, they believe, was unleashed (by the federal government) on an unsuspecting public to divert people's time and energy away from what is really happening in this country—the erosion of individual freedoms. Espousing a Jewish conspiracy regarding the attacks of September 11, the leader of the Present Day Patriots (in Berlin, Wisconsin) stated that "4,500 Jewish workers didn't show up that day" (Sink, 2001, p. B1). Because of their contempt for the federal government, members of these organizations typically recognize no elected officials beyond the county level (Shafritz, Gibons, and Scott, 1991).

Timothy McVeigh had contact with members of various militant right-wing groups and was thoroughly familiar with their worldview. According to one terrorist expert, these organizations "have demonstrated that they are serious in their beliefs and dedicated to their causes—and that they are willing to use violence in the pursuit of their goals" (Hoffman, 1993 p. 224). Chip Berlet (in Knickerbocker, 2001, p. 3) of Political Research Associates would agree, noting that "Middle Eastern terrorists might have slipped some weapons-lab anthrax to a right-wing ally in the U.S." Since the early 1990s, a right-wing

terrorist philosophy called "leaderless resistance" has generated an unknown number of lone attackers who "act when they feel the time is right" as opposed to taking orders from an organization (Marlantes, 2001, p. 2).

Transnational terrorism begins in one country and takes place in another. There are two subcategories of this form of terrorism. First, individuals living in one nation strike at targets inside another nation(s). Second (as was the case in the September 11, 2001, attacks), individuals born and raised in one country move to the target nation, make preparations for an attack (which may take months or years), and strike that country from within. Regarding the first type of transnational terrorism (sometimes called *international terrorism*), in 1988, a Pan American airliner with 289 people on board (including 189 Americans) exploded in midair over Lockerbie, Scotland. A bomb had been hidden in a radio cassette player inside a suitcase. The United States and Great Britain accused two Libyan intelligence agents of the crime. The 19 suspected hijackers of the four planes that slammed into the World Trade Center, the Pentagon, and rural farmland in Pennsylvania entered this country legally on temporary visas issued in the Middle East and Europe. Fifteen of these young men were Saudis, two were citizens of the United Arab Emirates, one was Lebanese, and one Egyptian. State Department officials stated that the granting of their visas was in accordance with the law, that each applicant was checked against existing law enforcement databases, and that no criminal records emerged (McDonnell, 2001). Economically and politically advanced countries, such as the United States and European democracies, are especially prone to transnational terrorist violence because citizens of these nations have almost complete freedom of movement, and access to goods and services (such as flight lessons) is readily available to anyone who can pay for them.

In *state terrorism* governments use random violence to intimidate their own citizens for the purpose of crushing dissent and/or maintaining or increasing political power and control. This form of repression includes

"In state terrorism governments use random violence to intimidate their own citizens . . ."

beatings, torture, executions without due process, the assassination of dissident and opposition leaders, and mass murder. Because state terrorism is committed by

Under Investigation: Terrorists and Victims—A World at Risk the very government that makes the laws, these acts of violence are "legal" in the technical sense of the word (Barkan and Snowden, 2001).

Along with settlers hungry for land, U.S. Army troops killed tens of thousands of American Indians, with the federal government's complicity in these killings likened to genocide (the systematic extermination of a whole group of people because of their race, religion, ethnicity, or national origin) (Brown, 1971; Chalk and Jonassohn, 1993). During the French and Indian War (1754–1767), a British commander suggested using fomites (objects that carry and transmit disease agents) against American Indians hostile to his troops. After an outbreak of disease at Fort Pitt in Pennsylvania, contaminated blankets were distributed to enemy warriors. One British officer recorded in his diary, "I hope it will have the desired effect" (in Bryjak, 1998, p. B1).

During an 1897 coal miners strike in Pennsylvania, deputies fired their weapons into a group of peaceful miners, killing 18 and wounding 40; many of the victims were shot in the back. In Colorado in 1914, Colorado Fuel and Iron Company guards along with National Guard troops machine gunned families as they fled a tent city that the guards and troops had set afire. Among the dead were 13 children (McGovern and Guttridge, 1972).

The most barbaric example of state terrorism occurred during World War II when the Nazi Party orchestrated and carried out the mass murder of 6 million Jews as well as millions of Slavs, gypsies, and homosexuals (Gilbert, 1987). During the 1970s the Cambodian government (Khmer Rouge) slaughtered hundreds of thousands of people in order to solidify its rule. In the mid-1990s, the Rwandan government (comprised primarily of ethnic Hutus) indiscriminately killed up to 1 million Tutsis, the other major ethnic group in that central African nation. Chinese troops gunned down several thousand unarmed protestors in Tiananmen Square in Beijing in 1989. Hundreds of people were killed while others were arrested and imprisoned; an unknown number were executed (Black, 1993). In 2001, former Yugoslav president Slobodan Milosevic was indicted by the International Criminal Tribunal for his part in the slaughter of tens of thousands of Muslims and Croats by the Bosnian Serb military between 1992 and 1995. In the infamous Srebrenica massacre, more than 7,000 Bosnian Muslim men and boys were killed (Fletcher, 2001).

As this only partial list of gruesome incidents suggests, in the twentieth century significantly more people were killed, maimed, and imprisoned as a result of state terrorism than all other forms of terrorism combined. However, in spite of this staggering toll of death and suffering, state terrorism has received scant attention from scholars and other experts who have demonstrated a greater interest in other forms of terrorist activity. As John McCamant (1984, p. 11) has noted, the "bloody deeds of government," and "explanations of how and why these deeds are done" have been almost completely ignored by researchers.

To Gurr's typology we would add *narcoterrorism*, which involves crimes engaged in by members of drug cartels in order to prevent political officials and criminal justice practitioners from interfering with their (the drug dealers') trafficking in illegal substances. Over the past 20 years, hundreds of police officers, criminal court judges, and governmental officials in a number of South American countries have been beaten, tortured, and killed. In 1989, the Medellin (Colombia) Cartel blew up an Avianca Airlines passenger plane in midflight, killing 107 people. An anonymous caller told police the flight had been targeted to silence five informants on board (Shafritz et al., 1991).

Explaining Terrorism

To date, most explanations of terrorism have focused on insurgent, transnational, and, to a lesser extent, vigilante terrorism. As with other forms of collective violence, explanations of terrorism fall into two distinct categories: psychological perspectives and structural interpretations. In order to understand why people act as they do, Americans have traditionally favored an individualistic or psychological perspective rather than a broader, structural approach. Because terrorism involves wanton, random violence against innocent victims, many people assume that the perpetrators of these acts are mentally unbalanced, sadistic, "sick" individuals. In the aftermath of a terrorist attack, one often hears sentiments such as "those people are insane, how else could they do something so horrible?"

In spite of its popularity, there are at least three problems with the psychopathological, "terrorist personality" perspective. First, the available evidence suggests that most terrorists do not suffer from any severe mental disorder and that they are psychologically normal. As Richard Rubenstein (1987, p. 5) has noted,

"evidence suggests that most terrorists . . . are psychologically normal."

"Most terrorists are no more or less fanatical than the young men who charged into Union cannonfire at Gettysburg. . . . They are no more or less cruel and cold blooded than the Resistance fighters who executed Nazi officials and collaborators in Europe, or the American GI's ordered to 'pacify' [destroy] Vietnamese villages."

The second problem with the psychological viewpoint focuses on the manifestation of violent behavior: Even if terrorists are mentally disturbed in some manner that predisposes them to violence, why do they turn to terrorist violence as opposed to robbery, rape, or aggravated assault? To know that someone is prone to aggressive behavior is not the same as knowing why this predisposition is expressed in a specific way.

Finally, a strictly terrorist personality interpretation turns our attention away from the larger context within which this behavior occurs. This criticism is succinctly stated by Peter Sederberg (1998, p. 25): "While psychopathology offers some intriguing insights, it tends to discount the significance of the social and political environment. Indeed, under certain conditions, such as those of the [Nazi] death camps, terrorist acts may become the norm, and the deviant personality may be the one who resists committing acts of terrorism." As we learned in the aftermath of September 11, 2001, it would be both simplistic and naive to try to understand the motives of the men who turned passenger airplanes into guided missiles without understanding the social, political, and religious milieu from which they came.

It is this final psychological shortcoming that the structural interpretation of terrorism addresses. From this perspective terrorist violence is the ultimate form of protest—political action in its most extreme form. State terrorism within a structuralist framework can be seen as a violent response to dissenting (potentially revolutionary) citizens threatening the well-being (existence) of those in power. Vigilante terrorists target racial and ethnic minorities thought to be challenging the superiority and "way of life" of the dominant group(s) in society. The transnational terrorists who attacked New York City and Washington D.C. believe the United

> "... terrorist *violence* is the ultimate form of *protest*—political action in its most *extreme* form."

States is primarily responsible for the unrestricted spread of global capitalism that will eventually overwhelm Islam. International capitalism, therefore, is the evil empire that must be destroyed at any cost.

Countering Terrorism

Terrorist experts and military and law enforcement personnel continue to debate the most effective measures for countering terrorism, with the term *counterterrorism* now part of everyday language. Strategies for successfully combating attacks on innocent people and property are as controversial as other aspects of this phenomenon. The *soft-line* or passive approach advocates negotiating with terrorists in order to release hostages and/or to end a terrorist strike as quickly and bloodlessly as possible. Although governments hope that once they resolve a terrorist incident through negotiation or appeasement their tormentors will disappear never to return, typically just the opposite happens. Terrorists are likely to pounce on any evidence of governmental weakness and increase both the frequency of attacks and the boldness of their demands (Wilkinson, 1986). As Paul Wilkinson (p. 15) notes, "In terrorism, nothing succeeds like success."

> "*In terrorism, nothing succeeds like success.*"

For *hard-liners*, those individuals who promote an offensive, aggressive posture, any form of negotiation with, or concession to, terrorists is unacceptable. Offensive strategies include economic and diplomatic sanctions, military action, and, if terrorists are apprehended, long prison terms or the death penalty. Although this get tough, no-nonsense approach (especially executing terrorists) has a gut-level appeal to many people, there are some formidable arguments against it. Hard-core fanatical terrorists will hardly be deterred by the death penalty. In fact, they may relish the thought of becoming martyrs (after a highly publicized trial) and securing a niche, as Wilkinson (1986) notes, in "revolutionary history." Martyrdom can also be a powerful force in gaining converts to the terrorist cause and attracting new members to the organization. Finally, terrorists may engage in an escalated wave of attacks (assassinations, planting bombs in crowded locations, taking hostages) to secure the release of condemned colleagues, or they may extract a high measure of revenge if their comrades are executed.

Hard-liners, such as Paul Bremmer (1988), argue that after the United States bombed the headquarters of Libya's colonel Qaddafi in 1986, incidents of terrorism declined dramatically—as many as 35 attacks planned for the coming weeks were aborted. Opponents of this position counter by asserting that no nation has been more forceful in lashing out against terrorists than Israel. Yet terrorist attacks against Israel continue on a regular basis.

"*Hard-core fanatical terrorists will hardly be deterred by the death penalty.*"

Virtually everyone involved in counterterrorism agrees that target-hardening is a useful defensive strategy to be implemented whenever and wherever possible. *Target-hardening* involves making potential terrorist targets safe and secure, with airport metal detectors and random searches of luggage the most familiar examples of this tactic. Although target-hardening has been moderately successful, there are at least two drawbacks to this approach. First, implementing this strategy can be expensive as well as pose a significant inconvenience to the routine activities of a society. After Pan Am Flight 103 went down over Scotland, the U.S. government proposed more extensive baggage safety checks, but the airlines balked that the checks would take too long. The government backed down (Rohrlich, 2001).

Richard Ward (2001) of the College of Criminal Justice at Sam Houston State University noted that when he was part of an FBI-sponsored conference formed to assess terrorist threats, various target-hardening initiatives were recommended (including making the cockpits of commercial airliners more secure), but that they were eventually dismissed because of the expense involved. Airport security laws passed in the late 1990s were largely ignored because they fell victim to bureaucratic red tape and cost-conscious special interest lobbying (Cooper and Simon, 2001)

Even after September 11, 2001, there was resistance to installing about 2,000 baggage scanning machines at the nation's airports (at a cost of about $1 million each). Although this technology is effective, luggage scanners can only examine between 60 and 100 bags an hour. Nationwide, U.S. airports handle approximately 2 million pieces of baggage a *day*. Prior to the September 2001 attacks, federal government plans requiring 100 percent screening of checked bags at major, and eventually all, U.S. airports were not scheduled to go into effect until 2009 and 2017, respectively (Rohrlrich, 2001). In a fast-paced, modern, capitalist society such as ours, even something as seemingly basic as the safety and security of the populace must compete with profit making and convenience. Perhaps the most absurd reason for resisting baggage scanning machines was related to the U.S. Congress by Inspector General Kenneth Mead shortly after the World Trade Center was destroyed: "At one major airport, the airport operator would not approve a lobby installation because the machine did not fit the lobby's color scheme" (in Rohrlich, 2001, p. A1).

A second limitation to target-hardening is that not all possible targets can be adequately secured. Any location where people congregate for work, pleasure, or travel is a potential site for a terrorist strike. However, the fact that every school, hospital, or shopping center cannot be completely secured does not mean this strategy should be abandoned. Some aspiring terrorists with lesser resolve may be unwilling to risk capture or death (at the hands of sky marshals, for example). Target-hardening, therefore, is likely to deter some individuals from committing terrorist acts.

"*. . . not all possible targets can be adequately secured.*"

Terrorism, Criminal Justice, and the Future

The attacks on the World Trade Center and Pentagon were an aberration on at least two counts. First, the majority of terrorist incidents in the United States have been perpetrated by U.S. citizens (vigilante and insurgent terrorism). Second, the staggering number of casualties was higher than the relatively small number of people who are killed and wounded in most terrorist incidents. Because the September 11 strike was transnational in origin and more than 3,000 people were killed, the federal government considered it an act of war and responded with military force in Afghanistan.

The September 11 attacks resulted in tremendous burdens on police departments and other law enforcement agencies because these organizations were forced to respond to new demands. For example, the Los Angeles Police Department was overwhelmed by calls about suspected anthrax powder, receiving up to 44 reports a day (all unfounded) that took officers away from other duties. Between the September attacks and October 10, the nation's second-largest police department handled 375 bomb threats. Criminologist James Fox noted that while police officers are protecting buildings, bridges, and government facilities, some of the "highest crime neighborhoods are being relatively unprotected" (Wood, 2001, p. 2). The U.S. conference of mayors estimated that its 1,200 member cities would need at least $1.5 billion in the 12 months following the attacks to maintain current levels of security. The city of Baltimore paid $2 million in police and firefighter overtime in only the first 3 days after September 11, 2001 (Ritter, 2001; Sack, 2001). According to one estimate, the United States will spend as much as $370 billion by 2012 fighting terrorism and protecting citizens from terrorist attacks ("Cost of Fighting Terrorism . . . ," 2002).

Increased security demands mean that officers will be slower in responding to calls and less likely to devote the time and energy necessary in gathering evidence that results in successful prosecutions. And with thousands of FBI agents working on various aspects of terrorism, that agency may drop its traditional jurisdiction of drug trafficking and bank robbery cases, leaving the investigation of these crimes to overworked local and state police agencies. In the months following the terrorist attacks on New York City and Washington, DC, the FBI suspended all but the highest priority investigations (Sack, 2001).

The weeks following the September 11 attacks exposed the long-standing rift between state and local law enforcement departments on the one hand, and federal agencies on the other. Speaking of a simulated smallpox terrorist attack in his state in the summer of 2001, Oklahoma governor Frank Keating stated, "I was stunned and amazed at the patronizing, if not contemptuous, attitude of the federal government toward state officials" (Simon, 2001, p. A14). Police officials across the country complained that the FBI refused to inform them of suspicious persons (and federal investigations of these individuals) in their jurisdictions. Defending his agency's policies, an FBI spokesman stated, "We're not at war with state and local police. We're at war with terrorists and criminals" (Vance in Simon, 2001, p. A14). It is safe to assume that many local and state personnel were less than convinced with the sincerity of this statement.

Working under budget constraints and with a limited number of officers, law enforcement agencies will be forced to make decisions between local, short-term needs and long-term national security issues. One of the first casualties of deciding on the latter may be a drastic reduction in (if not elimination of) community policing (see Chapter 6) and crime prevention programs. This could be problematic; many individuals believe these operations contributed significantly to the 30 percent reduction in street crime between 1991 and 2001 (Sack, 2001).

State and federal officials have also clashed over the interpretation and implementation of state laws when those laws run counter to federal investigations. The police chief in Portland, Oregon, refused to help the FBI interview Middle Eastern immigrants, noting that state law prohibits questioning anyone not suspected of a crime. According to Chief Andrew Kirkland, "The law does not allow us to go out and arbitrarily interview people whose only offense is immigration or citizenship" ("Oregon City's Police Won't Aid FBI," 2001 p. A34). Police chiefs in several cities have much the same sentiment, arguing that interviewing Middle Eastern individuals simply because of their ethnic heritage is nothing more than racial profiling (see Chapter 7), and, therefore, is against departmental policy.

With few exceptions, terrorist defendants in the United States have been tried in civilian criminal courts. However, in November 2001, President Bush signed an executive order authorizing the use of military tribunals in terrorist cases with defendants placed under the control of the Secretary of Defense. In March 2002, that order was "refined" and the specifics of how the government intended to prosecute captured offenders was made public. Following are the most salient aspects of that ruling (Mintz, 2002; Saphire, 2002):

1. As in civilian criminal courts, defendants stand trial under the presumption of innocence.
2. Defendants have the right to an attorney of their choosing and to see the prosecution's evidence against them.
3. Trials will be public although classified information will be kept secret.
4. Defendants have the right to remain silent and no conclusions about their guilt or innocence are to be drawn as a result of this silence.
5. Prosecutors must prove guilt beyond a reasonable doubt, the same standard that is used in civilian criminal courts.
6. Guilt or innocence will be determined by military judges who can convict on a two-thirds majority vote. However, judges must vote unanimously to impose the death penalty.
7. Hearsay evidence inadmissable in civilian courts will be accepted by military tribunals. Hearsay is secondhand testimony. For example, John Smith saw the defendant running toward a building with a gun in his hand and later recounts this incident to Mary Jones. If Smith cannot or will not testify, the prosecution cannot substitute the secondhand testimony of Jones for what Smith saw (Steury and Frank, 1996). The admission of hearsay makes it easier for the prosecution to prove the state's case against the defendant(s).
8. If convicted, defendants do not have recourse to a civilian review of their case. Rather, an appeal is limited to judges appointed to or by the military.
9. If acquitted, captives will be sent back to their home country.
10. Captives that the U.S. government does not have sufficient evidence to prosecute, but are deemed too dangerous to release, will be detained indefinitely.

Under Investigation: Terrorists and Victims—A World at Risk

The September 11 attacks, as the president's move toward military tribunals indicates, forced people to make difficult choices in reaching that "delicate balance" between freedom and security in a democratic society. Speaking of the military tribunals, Secretary of Defense Donald Rumsfeld stated: "We have made every reasonable effort to establish a process that is just, one that protects both the rights of the defendant to a fair trial, but also protects the rights of the American people to live in freedom and without fear of terrorists" (Mintz, 2002, p. A1). However, not everyone shares this point of view. In their ruling against the government by way of declaring secret immigration hearings unconstitutional, a federal appeals panel in Cincinnati, Ohio, stated that "Democracies die behind closed doors. . . . When the government begins closing doors, it selectively controls information rightfully belonging to the people. Selective information is misinformation" (Kravets, 2002, p. A6).

In the weeks following the September 11 attacks, almost 1,200 people (most of Middle Eastern extraction) were collected and detained indefinitely without being charged. Two months after the strike about 600 were still in custody with some (if the Attorney General determined they were a threat to public safety) denied the right to private legal council (Chaddock, 2001; Serrano, 2001). With the exception of family members of those in custody and a few civil liberties organizations, the public was silent regarding these (in other circumstances) unconstitutional acts. On the contrary, many people seemed willing to suspend constitutional safeguards until the terrorist crisis had passed. A nationwide survey found that approximately one in three Americans favored state-sanctioned torture of terrorist suspects (McLaughlin, 2001). Even Alan Dershowitz, the well-known liberal Harvard University law professor, argued that the Constitution does not prohibit torture and that such practices can be kept within the legal system: "If we are to have torture, it should be authorized by the law. Judges should have to issue a 'torture warrant' in each case" (in Scheer, 2001, p. B13).

Writing in the *Journal of the American Medical Association*, Jeffrey Simon (1997, p. 429) stated that a biological warfare terrorist attack in this country could result in "hundreds of thousands, even millions of casualties." As tragic as the consequences of the September 11 attacks have been for the survivors, the families, and the nation as a whole, these strikes will pale in significance in the aftermath of a major biological warfare attack.

What measures should be implemented to prevent this from ever happening, and how will they impact civil liberties? Even before the attacks on New York City and Washington D.C., one poll found that 54 percent of respondents were willing to relinquish some civil liberties to combat terrorism (Gerstenzang, 1996). A June 2002 nationwide survey found that slightly more than 60 percent of respondents supported the loss of some individual freedoms (privacy rights, for example) for increased security from terrorism (Morin and Deane, 2002). However, the difficult questions remain unanswered: "Whose privacy, and how much, and will it actually do any good?" (Carney, Calabresin, and Dickerson, 2002, p. 27).

> "... The **September 11** attacks ... *forced people* to make **difficult** *choices* ... *between* **freedom** and *security* ..."

Many people believe fear of terrorism in the aftermath of September 11 will give already too intrusive law enforcement agencies more excuses to spy on citizens and groups. The American Civil Liberties Union (ACLU) noted that since 1999, police in Denver, Colorado, have maintained intelligence files on approximately 3,200 people in 208 organizations, including Amnesty International, the American Friends Service Committee, and the American Indian Movement (Dreyfuss, 2002). Mark Silverstein, legal director of the ACLU in Colorado sated, "Individuals who are not even suspected of a crime and organizations that don't have a criminal history are labeled criminal extremists" (in Dreyfuss, 2002, p. 15).

The balance between freedom and security is, arguably, the most fundamental issue both the citizens and government of a democratic society must address. However this issue is resolved, it is safe to assume that the criminal justice system will be affected for the foreseeable future. It remains to be seen whether these changes will be permanent.

> "... **biological** *warfare terrorist attack* ... *could* result in 'hundreds of **thousands**, *even* **millions** *of casualties.'*"

chapter **6**

The Police:
History,
Organization,
and
Composition

1. How did the police first become an organization in Europe? In the United States?

2. Which factors in society contributed to the formation of a permanent police department in the United States?

3. How has technology affected modern policing?

4. What is the organizational structure of police agencies in the United States?

5. What is the racial, ethnic, gender, and sexual orientation of police officers? What problems have individuals in these groups faced as police officers?

The 1960s and 1970s were years of political and social turmoil that affected virtually every major institution in the United States, including law enforcement. When an African American was promoted to police chief in Atlanta in 1974, many white officers were openly defiant of their new boss, with some individuals going so far as to physically block the entrance to his office. The police force in one of the South's largest cities was entangled in litigation as African Americans filed lawsuits charging discrimination in departmental patterns of hiring and promotion and white officers filed suits claiming they were the victims of "reverse" discrimination. Newly hired female officers were made to feel less than welcome by their male counterparts who considered law enforcement beyond the capabilities of women (Eddings, 1995).

It was during this volatile period that 21-year-old Beverly Harvard, a young African American woman from Macon, Georgia, with a bachelor's degree in sociology, joined the Atlanta Police Department (1973). After 2 years on the streets as a beat cop, Harvard's career path took her to a number of administrative positions (she also earned a master's degree in government administration). She was the first woman on the Atlanta Police Force to graduate from the Federal Bureau of Investigation Academy and also completed a course of study at the FBI's National Executive Institute (Atlanta Police Department, 2002).

In 1994, at age 43, Beverly Harvard became the first African American female chief of a major metropolitan police force in the

173

United States (Scruggs, 1994). Asked what it takes to be a good police officer Chief Harvard replied: "With the rise of women in the force in the past 20 years, we've learned that policing isn't all physical. You don't have to weigh 250 pounds to be a good cop. My whole philosophy has to do with service. It's not about power and authority. It's about wanting to help people" (Gregory, 1996, p. 56). Harvard was chief of the Atlanta Police Department until June 2002.

Prior to joining the Cleveland Police Department in 1980, Mary Bounds was a supermarket clerk. The rookie African American officer and single mother of three worked nights one month and days the next as she completed requirements for a bachelor's then master's degree. On her promotion from sergeant to commander of community policing in 1995, then–Chief of Police Patrick Oliver noted that Bounds was the hardest-working person he had ever met. She was instrumental in developing training programs on domestic violence and sexual assaults now used throughout Ohio. In August 2001, 54-year-old Mary Bounds was selected to lead the Cleveland Police Department (Fuetsch, 1995; Spencer, 2001).

Atlanta Police Chief Beverly Harvard makes comments on the results of a shooting investigation.

As of 2000, 190 women served as police chiefs nationwide, although nearly all of these individuals were in command of departments with fewer than 1,000 officers. According to the National Center for Women and Policing, among departments with 100 or fewer officers, only 7.3 percent of female officers held the rank of captain or higher, and only 1.7 percent of these "top command" positions were occupied by minority women ("Equality Denied—The Status of Women," 2001).

These numbers are indicative of the slow rate of female representation in law enforcement. In 2000, only 13 percent of police officers were female, an increase of only 4 percent since 1990. At this rate of growth—less than one-half of 1 percent a year—it will take about 70 years for women to achieve gender parity with men in law enforcement. Of the 10 big-city police departments with the greatest number of female officers, 8 were mandated to hire more women by federal court orders. In other words, "the glacial pace of gains for women" in the male stronghold of law enforcement would be even slower if it were not for judicial intervention. In small-town and rural police departments, females account for only 7.1 percent of police officers with women of color accounting for less than 1 percent of sworn personnel ("Equality Denied," 2001).

Police Chief Beverly Harvard realizes that many individuals are less than enthused about her rise to the position of Atlanta's top police official. "I'm sure that there are people who would like to see me fail. If it doesn't work, I will be singled out as proof that women are not cut out to be chief. And I know that's absolutely not true" (White, 1997, p. 116).

After serving as police chief for less than 6 months, Mary Bounds was removed as head of the Cleveland Police Department by newly elected mayor Jane Campbell and designated commander for minority recruitment and retention. Incoming Chief Edward Lohn stated that one of his priorities was to increase the number of female and minority officers in higher ranks. "I want to encourage diversity in the division of police by offering information and opportunities to excel" ("Campbell Picks a Cleveland Police Veteran to Be Chief," 2002, p. 1).

It is impossible to comprehend the role of the police in modern industrial societies without a thorough understanding of the social, political, and economic setting within which they exist. Consider that in totalitarian societies, such as China, police can do virtually anything they deem necessary to maintain order and apprehend suspects. However, in democratic nations, such as the United States, the police "are required to maintain order and do so under the rule of law" (Skolnick, 1994, p. 6). Whereas the concept of individual rights is all but nonexistent in one-party dictatorial states, in democratic societies these rights limit the behavior of police in their dealings with citizens. Whereas a police officer in China can simply arrest and detain someone as a matter of course, his or her counterpart in the United States must follow "procedural laws" of arrest, search, and seizure.

Criminologist Jerome Skolnick (1994) notes that police in democratic societies are faced with the difficult (if not impossible) task of maintaining order within the boundaries or limits of the law. Whereas the concepts of "law *and* order" are strongly associated in the United States (there is even a popular television drama by that name), they are often opposed to each other because law implies that the police will be restrained by (procedural) rules as they work to preserve order. Police can perform their duties with skill, discipline, and efficiency and crime rates may increase rather than decrease. This outcome is likely to trigger criticism on the part of conservative officials and citizens. However, if law enforcement personnel begin to bend or ignore procedural laws in their efforts to control crime and maintain order, they invite condemnation from more liberal members of society. In short, the police are in a very difficult situation as they attempt to keep the peace and pursue criminals under the rule of law.

In this, the first of three chapters on law enforcement, we examine the history, organization, and composition of police in the United States, considering the above-mentioned factors. Our discussion commences by investigating the interrelated questions of why, when, where, and under what circumstances modern policing began.

History

Origin and Development

The modern police force can be traced to medieval Europe (from 500 to 1500 A.D.) when cities were protected by paid "watchmen" who patrolled the streets looking for fires that could destroy wooden structures in a matter of minutes. These individuals were also charged with keeping travelers suspected of carrying the plague away from local inhabitants. In rural areas these citizen patrols were organized to protect crops and farm animals (Emsley, 1999; Rubenstein, 1973).

During the sixteenth and seventeenth centuries, London was a dangerous place, and the city's watchmen had a reputation for being incompetent cowards. Derisively referred to as "Charlies," these agents of social control were routinely taunted by young upper-class males who wrecked "watchhouses" and, in some instances, killed watchmen. Wealthy Londoners lived in well-guarded homes and traveled about the city armed (Rubinstein, 1973). Jonathan Rubinstein notes that "As for the poor, who were then as now the principal victims of crime, nobody cared" (p. 5).

Although crime was a serious problem in early eighteenth century England, the idea of a standing police force was resisted for fear that such an organization could easily abuse its power. Created as a result of the Metropolitan Police Act of 1829, the London police force was a compromise that limited police powers to the metropolitan London area ("Police," 2001). It was the first big-city law enforcement organization in the Western world. Under the direction of Sir Robert Peel (hence the nickname "Peelers" and, later, "Bobbies" given to officers), London was divided into 17 police districts

with 165 officers assigned to each of these sectors. Peel introduced military-type ranks and a hierarchical, authoritarian command structure that is characteristic of police departments around the world (Lundman, 1980; Walker, 1998). In addition to crime prevention, the new police force inherited many of the jobs previously done by watchmen including lighting lamplights (streetlights), announcing the time, and watching for fires. Even though the London Metropolitan Police Force was successful in the early years, it was not until 1856 that the English Parliament mandated that police departments be established in provinces throughout the country ("Police," 2001).

In North America, the colonists typically reproduced the institutions of social control that they had known in Europe, including the position of constable (Richardson, 1970). The "constableship" was a thankless duty that all able-bodied men of the community were expected to perform from time to time. In some locales, fines were levied against individuals who refused to serve (Parks, 1976). Constables were in part a kind of "morals" police charged with enforcing a series of oppressive laws against swearing, lying, not attending designated church services, and walking around at night. Historian Wilbur Miller (2000, p. 29) argues that at the heart of the formal system of social control in the colonial United States was reliance on public punishment designed to shame offenders, "the ducking stool for gossips, stocks for petty criminals, branding for thieves, hanging for murderers and other serious offenders. . . ."

Whereas constables served during daylight hours, watchmen patrolled the streets from dusk to dawn. Unlike modern police who focus on maintaining order, the duties of colonial watchmen were concerned with the general welfare of the township. For example, in addition to keeping a lookout for and reporting fires, these individuals would announce the time and weather conditions as they walked through city streets (Parks, 1976).

In lieu of regular salaries, New York City constables and marshals were compensated by fees for their services in line with a schedule determined by the state legislature. The problem was that these agents of social control were likely to devote their time and effort to those matters promising the greatest compensation as opposed to law enforcement issues of importance to the citizenry (Richardson, 1970). Regarding this practice of payment associated with specific services, a writer for the *Evening Post* noted "the abominable practices of the marshals, constables, law attorneys. . . . These are the worst bloodsuckers in that they prey upon the vitals of a great part of the community" (p. 19).

By 1800, some larger cities in the newly independent United States of America changed from the constabulary system to a voluntary, quasi-professional police force wherein individuals were appointed or elected and provided a regular salary (Parks, 1976). The first modern-style police forces appeared in the South primarily to control slaves. Washington, D.C. had a police department around 1820, whereas in the North, Boston (1838) and New York (1844) were the first cities to establish such agencies, and most other metropolitan areas followed suit in the years following the Civil War (1865).

Virtually all historians and police scholars believe that the transition from a part-time constabulary system to a larger, more complex, permanent police department is rooted in the increasing conflict, violence, and general civil disorder that engulfed most of the nation from the 1830s to the 1870s (Walker, 1977). Criminal justice historian Samuel Walker notes various aspects or dimensions of this conflict and disorder. Much of this tension was between ethnic groups, a consequence of a significant influx of immigrants most notably from Ireland and Germany. For example, on election day in St. Louis in 1844, Catholic Irish Americans fought with native-born Protestants. Five years later in that same city, Irish and native-born volunteer fire fighting companies battled each other in the streets.

Racial conflict was also common as mobs of white citizens attacked free African Americans and white abolitionists. Religious and other values figured prominently in the collective violence of this era as medical schools were attacked by people who objected to research done on cadavers. As routine fixtures in nineteenth-century urban America, brothels were targets of mobs determined to rid cities of evil and debauchery.

New York City police officers pose in front of their precinct house in the 1880s. Police officers of this era were poorly trained, earned low wages, and were often used by wealthy company owners to crack down on striking laborers agitating for higher pay and better working conditions.

A significant amount of violence in the mid to late 1800s that continued into the twentieth century was rooted in labor disputes. According to police historian Sidney Harring (1992, p. 315), the owners of corporate America fervently believed "they held the right to contract labor at the lowest price the market would bear as natural law." If that meant paying employees near starvation wages, then so be it. A Department of Labor study of six cities in the 1880s found that 74.3 percent of women working in factories and 66.2 percent of those working in stores earned less than a "living wage," defined as $8 a week. One manufacturer noted that "We try to employ girls who are members of families for we don't pay a living wage in this trade" (Montgomery, 1987, p. 137). Economists of that era considered $12 per week a subsistence wage for a family of five. Hundreds of thousands of workers across the country toiled for far less than that at a time when there was no minimum wage, no unemployment compensation, and no welfare benefits. Of the 25,000 Polish Americans living on Buffalo's East Side in 1893, a local newspaper reported that 5,000 were in "imminent danger of starvation" (Harring, 1983, p. 213).

Unable to secure higher wages by way of negotiations, workers resorted to strikes. In 1877, Chicago, Pittsburgh, St. Louis, and Buffalo were all but shut down by citywide work stoppages. The *Chicago Tribune* demanded that strikers, often referred to as "communards," "revolutionaries," and "anarchists" and considered as nothing more than common criminals by the paper, be massacred in the streets. Between 1881 and 1900 more than 8,500 strikes occurred in 10 major industrial cities—more than 5,000 alone in New York City (Harring, 1983). During the Great Strike of 1877, rioters in Pittsburgh destroyed 39 buildings, 104 locomotives, and 500 freight cars. More than 100 people were killed by the police and local militia (Wade, 1972). In 1904 in Chicago, there were 94 strikes in progress at one time, many of which were exceedingly violent and resulted in the deaths of well over 300 people.

From a conflict sociology perspective, modern police forces emerged in large measure as a result of the clash between wealthy corporate owners and impoverished workers. The capitalist class was able to accumulate enormous amounts of money by paying workers meager wages because it was backed by the physical power of local

police forces. From this perspective, urban law enforcement agencies of this period were the hired guns of the privileged minority. Harring (1983, p. 106) believes that the confrontations between the police and workers was so violent because "nothing less than the control of the labor process was at stake and, through that, the control of the entire national economy."

Passage of the Tramp Acts also involved police in class warfare. In the 1870s one state after another passed laws making it a crime for workers without any means of monetary support to travel freely (Harring, 1983). These laws effectively criminalized unemployment and prevented workers from moving from city to city to support each other in labor disputes. In 1894, the celebrated writer Jack London was arrested and jailed on tramp charges in Erie County, New York, and spent 30 days behind bars. London noted, "I was forced to toil hard on a diet of bread and water and to march the shameful lock-step with armed guards over me—and for what? What had I done?" (Kershaw, 1998, p. 265).

Samuel Walker (1977) argues that conflict criminologists have exaggerated the stridently probusiness and antilabor sentiments and behavior of the police in nineteenth-century America. Although he acknowledges that "Police history is indeed filled with incidents of police brutality against workingmen and strikers," in numerous cases, employers complained that they could not always depend on local police during strikes (p. 17). Walker makes the interesting observation that the primarily ethnic composition of the police and of the strikers was a factor in what action (if any) the former would take. "A police force dominated by Irish and Germans, for example, was far less likely to attack kindred [of the same ethnic background] skilled tradesmen than a strike by unskilled Eastern European immigrant laborers" (p. 18).

Because nineteenth-century capitalists could not rely on the police to intervene (on their behalf) in labor disputes, they established their own "special" police. In Pennsylvania, state officials granted railroads the right to mobilize private security forces. The coal and iron industries were extended the same authority 2 years later. In many communities the coal and iron police were little more than "legalized vigilantes" used to keep the labor movement in check.

It is hardly surprising that police officers were caught up in labor disputes because police departments of that era were intimately tied to local politics. In Philadelphia the mayor hired and fired command officers at his pleasure and determined which rules and regulations they would follow (Steinberg, 1989). Because local political bosses controlled law enforcement, a change in city hall often meant a dramatic overhaul of the police department. After the election of 1880 in Cincinnati, 219 members of the 295-strong police force were dismissed and another 20 resigned. In 1886, after another political transition an 80 percent turnover in personnel occurred (Walker, 1977). Chicago police were expected to contribute money to the incumbent political party on a regular basis. Partaking in activities that would be unthinkable today, police officers distributed campaign posters, sold tickets to party picnics, and, in some cases, worked the precincts to get out the vote (Haller, 1976). Late nineteenth-century New York City police officers learned from the first day on the job that their careers depended on satisfying the needs (legal or illegal) of district leaders (Richardson, 1970).

For approximately the first 50 to 75 years of their existence (depending on the city and the department), police officers in the United States were primarily untrained and unsupervised opportunists whose only qualification was loyalty to the political party in office. Before the advent of call boxes and two-way radios, officers were on their own once they left the station and spent a significant amount of time in saloons, pool halls, barbershops, and other neighborhood centers (Haller, 1976). In the 1850s, the Philadelphia marshall (chief of police) rebuked his men for spending too much time in "grog shops, taverns [and] houses of doubtful reputation" (Keyes in Steinberg, 1989, p. 152). Noting that many officers were "worthless, drunken, and totally unfit" to serve the community, he dismissed one-third of the force for intoxication and disorderly conduct (p. 152). Philadelphia police of this era routinely failed to appear in court and publicly fought with one another.

Police officers of this era did not hesitate to dispense "street justice" when they confronted wrongdoers or individuals who challenged their authority. Acting in an era before police cars and patrol wagons, officers had to physically escort (or drag in the case of drunks) people they arrested anywhere from a few blocks to a few miles to the nearest station house. Not only did this take time and effort but also the officers were subject to attacks by friends and relatives of the person in custody. Rather than go through all of this trouble, police physically punished individuals suspected of committing minor offenses without arresting them (Haller, 1976).

Early law enforcement personnel were also responsible for a variety of mundane tasks, including the care of street lights and sewers as well as the removal of dead animals from the streets. Police departments also served as social welfare agencies, maintaining soup kitchens and providing nightly lodging for homeless people (Lane, 1992).

Nineteenth-century police officers worked long hours and would have considered a 40-hour workweek a vacation. Prior to 1912, the Philadelphia Police Department was divided into two 12-hour shifts, with officers working 65 hours on "street duty" and another 42 hours on reserve or "house detail" for a total of 107 hours a week. When a three-platoon system came into effect, the workweek was reduced to 77 hours (Walker, 1977).

August Vollmer and O. W. Wilson

No history of police in the United States would be complete without noting the contributions of August Vollmer (1876–1955) who joined the Berkeley, California, police department in 1905 and directed that organization for many years. In 1914, Vollmer's entire 25-man staff patrolled the city in automobiles; this was the first totally mobile police force in the United States. At a time when most police personnel had a high school education at best, Vollmer began to actively recruit college students as part-time

August Vollmer was the chief of police in Berkeley, California, from 1909 to 1932. His department became a model for police organizations across the country. Vollmer was a lifelong advocate of professionalizing the police, in large measure by way of education. By 1930, his police recruits received 312 hours of formal training, including classes in psychology and criminal law.

officers. Shortly after World War I, he commissioned a psychiatrist to prepare a set of intelligence and neurological tests to screen applicants. During a brief period as police chief in Los Angeles, Vollmer promoted and reassigned personnel on the basis of army intelligence tests that all 3,000 officers were ordered to take (Douthit, 1992).

During the 1919 meetings of the International Association of Chiefs of Police (an organization he helped consolidate), Vollmer delivered an address entitled "The Policeman as Social Worker." He argued that rather than simply arresting youthful offenders, police should be actively involved in establishing programs that would attack teenage crime at it roots. The arrest and prosecution of juveniles should be a last resort. For Vollmer, only organized cooperation between the police and other social agencies would help solve the juvenile crime problem (Douthit, 1992; "Police," 2001). Although some police administrators supported the outspoken Californian, most chiefs were opposed to this restatement of the law enforcement role in society.

Vollmer was one of the first police administrators to see crime as a complex, multifaceted phenomenon that had to be studied from numerous perspectives, including psychiatry, neurology, medicine, psychology, and sociology. Armed with this philosophy, he sought to have police administrators educated at the college level in a course of study specifically designed for their profession. In 1931, Vollmer became the first professor of police administration at the University of California. Shortly thereafter, the first college-level training course of study for police officers was introduced at (then) San Jose State College where students took courses ranging from police science and typing to public health and foreign languages (Douthit, 1992). Vollmer wrote that "After spending nearly a quarter of a century instructing policemen I have come to the conclusion that the mechanics of the profession are of less importance than a knowledge of human beings" (p. 109).

Throughout his career, Vollmer was passionate about distancing police departments from the corrupting influence of local politics. Rather than having police chiefs appointed by mayors and city councils (as is still the case in many cities today), Vollmer urged that chiefs should be selected from a list of eligible candidates via a civil service commission. As such, chiefs would have the protection of civil service rules and could not be removed on the whim of local power brokers (Douthit, 1992).

Vollmer was a member of the 1929 National Commission on Law Observance and Enforcement, better known as the Wickersham Commission, chaired by U.S. Attorney General George W. Wickersham. According to Samuel Walker (1997, p. 1), that group's production of the Report on Lawlessness in Law Enforcement "is one of the most important events in the history of American policing." This report chronicled the widespread use of tactics employed by police to gain involuntary confessions, including physical brutality, illegal detention, and denying suspects access to legal counsel.

One of Vollmer's "college cops," O. W. Wilson (1900–1972) shared many of his mentor's professional views. Chief of the Wichita, Kansas, police from 1928 to 1939, Wilson fired or forced the resignation of 20 percent of a force reputed for corruption and brutality (Walker, 1998). Believing that a college educated officer was the "best hope" for making better police officers, Wilson became the dean of the School of Criminology at the University of California at Berkeley. According to Richard Lundman (1980), Vollmer and Wilson, as the leaders of the police professionalism movement, "championed" three causes: better educated police, a more efficient bureaucracy, and police independence from local political control. We add a fourth policing philosophy that both men shared: Police, no matter how well trained and organized, cannot successfully curtail crime on their own. The "co-production of order" also depends on citizen volunteers who work to solve social problems that generate criminal behavior (Thurman and Giacomazzi, 1993).

The Impact of Technology

Technological innovations during the past 100 years have left their mark on almost every aspect of society, and law enforcement is no exception. Although the advent of sophisticated weapons, fingerprinting, and crime laboratory techniques certainly has aided police officers, what radically transformed police work were patrol cars, two-way radios, and telephones. With the advent of patrol cars, officers in automobiles could cover much more territory than their counterparts on foot thereby affording citizens greater police protection. In conjunction with two-way radios, police supervisors could not only dispatch patrol officers quickly to calls for help but also command officers were only a radio call away from knowing the exact location of their personnel. Some people naively believed that these technological breakthroughs would dramatically reduce crime if not eliminate law-violating behavior entirely (Rubinstein, 1973). Although this utopian scenario never came to pass, the "conventional wisdom" of the massive shift from police walking beats to officers in patrol cars is that it isolated officers "from casual contacts with ordinary citizens" and damaged police–community relations (Walker, 1984, p. 80).

With the proliferation of telephones, almost every citizen had access to law enforcement on a moment's notice, and two-way radio communication made it possible for police to respond in a timely fashion. These technological advances also changed police–citizen relations in a dramatic way. Contacts with "ordinary" people while walking a beat decreased, but contacts with "problem" individuals, including not only criminals but also those with social problems (domestic violence and mental illness, for example), considerably increased.

The police, as Samuel Walker (1984, p. 82) notes, are both the "source and victims" of this technological revolution. As a result of emergency telephone numbers (911 in most cities), big-city police departments can receive tens of thousands of calls for assistance every day, which strains both human and physical resources. However, this burden is largely self-imposed because American police encourage the public to rely on professional law enforcement personnel to help solve their problems (Rubinstein, 1973; Walker, 1984). The long-term result of the "I'll just call the cops and they'll be right here" mentality is a "revolution of rising expectations" on the part of citizens regarding what the police can and *should* do. "Because it was now possible to call the police about even the smallest disturbance, the public gradually began to regard even the smallest disturbance as intolerable" (Walker, 1977, p. 137).

Police Unions

Police fraternal organizations, or **brotherhoods** date back to the late 1860s, approximately 30 years after the first metropolitan police departments were established. Because benefits for officers were relatively nonexistent at that time, these associations were formed to aid members who became ill or disabled in the line of duty as well as to help families of deceased officers. By the 1890s, these organizations began to focus on the overall economic well-being of their members. The major issues were increased pay, better working conditions, and greater job security (Vanagunas and Elliot, 1980). In 1892 the Police Benevolent Association of New York City was instrumental in obtaining a substantial pay increase for police officers. Seven years later the association also played a key role in bringing about an 8-hour workday.

Between 1898 and 1913, inflation in the United States increased 37 percent and jumped another 78 percent by 1918. However, a police recruit or "reserve man" in Boston in 1918 earned $2 a day, the same pay he would have received in 1854. In 1919, the salary of Boston police officers was approximately 50 percent of the wages of unskilled steelworkers, mechanics, carpenters, and streetcar conductors (Russell, 1975). Dissatisfied with their economic status, members of the Boston Social Club (the fraternal police organization) joined the powerful American Federation of Labor (AFL). A strident opponent of police unionization, the Boston police commissioner filed charges of insubordination against (and later dismissed) 19 officers, including the new union leaders. Failing to get their fellow members/officers reinstated through compromise with the commissioner, 1,117 of the department's 1,544 police officers went on strike (Vanagunas and Elliot, 1980). The governor of Massachusetts, Calvin Coolidge, lashed out at the striking officers declaring, "There is no right to strike against the public safety by anybody, anywhere, anytime" ("Boston Police Strike," 2000, p. 1).

police fraternal organizations or brotherhoods dating back to the 1860s, these associations were formed to aid members who became ill or disabled in the line of duty as well as to help families of deceased officers; by the 1890s, these organizations began to focus on the economic well-being of police officers

Following widespread looting, vandalism, and general disorder, Coolidge called on the National Guard to restore order to city streets. Approximately 300 Harvard undergraduates, including the 125-man football team, crossed the Charles River to protect Boston (Russell, 1975).

By this time, striking officers had voted to return to work, but it was too late. More than 1,000 officers had lost their jobs, and replacements were quickly hired. Perhaps to make their dismissals even more painful (and costly), the new officers received a substantial $300 pay increase, a $200 equipment allowance, and more days off. Governor Coolidge received favorable press on the national level; public sentiment was solidly against the striking officers. The importance of the Boston police strike cannot be overemphasized because it "killed police unionism for several decades" (Vanagunas and Elliot, 1980, p. 259).

With lingering memories of the Boston strike, followed by the Great Depression of the 1930s, and the United States entering World War II in 1941, police unionism would not be sought again until the 1960s. Stanley Vanagunas and James Elliot (1980) argue that police thinking and organization regarding their labor status changed from passivity to militancy in large measure because of the turbulence of this decade. Police battled anti–Vietnam War protesters, civil rights activists, and African Americans in riot torn cities. Demonstrations oftentimes culminating in violence were commonplace on college campuses across the country as police confronted militant students. Caught in the middle of these disturbances, the police were roundly criticized by conservatives for not being tough enough on demonstrators and by radicals who typically viewed them as fascists enforcing oppressive "establishment" laws. Believing that they were unfairly targeted by both sides, the police retreated into their own organizations and sought solidarity with fellow officers. This increased solidarity strengthened an emerging police labor movement.

At this time, when police were increasingly called on to maintain order in big cities and college towns, their wages were relatively low. For example, in the mid-1960s the average salary of a police officer in a large metropolitan area was approximately $5,300. Police officers were also concerned with other issues, including a lack of constitutional rights when they were investigated for misconduct (Vanagunas and Elliot, 1980). Fearing that they would be labeled "antipolice" during this raucous period, neither police chiefs nor local politicians aggressively opposed police unions.

By the early 1990s, officers in 73 percent of all urban police departments and 43 percent of sheriffs' departments were represented by unions. Police unionism was almost universal in large and medium-sized cities, but it was virtually nonexistent in departments with 10 or fewer officers (Walker, 1999). Today, most union objectives are realized using collective bargaining or political pressure on local governments by police allies (sympathetic politicians and community groups). However, should the implementation of their goals be thwarted, police do not hesitate to engage in behavior that will bring about desired changes. These tactics include work slowdowns or **"speedups,"** the latter often taking the form of an aggressive ticket writing campaign. A more drastic strategy is a partial immobilization of the entire department in the form of a **"sick in"** (a significant number of officers calling in sick when they are not ill), commonly referred to as the **"blue flu"** (Vanagunas and Elliot, 1980). Although strikes are relatively infrequent, police have used this tactic in several cities during the past 30 years, including Albuquerque, Baltimore, and Milwaukee.

Samuel Walker (1999, pp. 371–373) argues that police unions have had a significant impact on U.S. policing as follows: (1) They have been instrumental in achieving increased salaries and benefits for police officers. Higher salaries and more comprehensive benefits packages have resulted in an increase in highly qualified applicants, including some who are college educated. (2) Unions have decreased the power of police chiefs while concurrently strengthening the position of rank-and-file officers, producing a shared governance style of management. This form of administration has hindered police professionalism because, historically, department reforms were implemented by powerful chiefs whose ability to run agencies was now mitigated by unions. (3) Police organizations have introduced due process into discipline procedures, mean-

speedup usually manifested in the form of an aggressive ticket writing campaign, this tactic is used by police to bring public attention to some law enforcement goal, for example, a more comprehensive benefits package and/or a salary increase

sick in or **blue flu** a tactic wherein a significant number of police officers call in sick when they are not ill, resulting in a partial immobilization of the department; this strategy is used as a means for achieving a particular goal such as a pay increase or the hiring of additional officers

ing that police chiefs cannot arbitrarily punish officers. (4) Police unions have been divisive regarding police–community relations and, at times, intradepartmental relations. On the whole, police unions have represented white officers in their opposition to civil rights leaders and white officers against African American officers on issues such as affirmative action hiring and promotion.

The Organization of Law Enforcement

The defining characteristic of law enforcement in the United States since its inception has been decentralization. Whereas the police in many countries are organized at the national level and administered by the federal government, in the United States they are employed by local governments. There are two primary reasons for the historical emphasis on community control of police. First, since the colonial era, U.S. citizens have been afraid to allow the federal government too much control over their daily lives. This was especially true regarding the police, an agency with the power to arrest and detain people. Second, Americans have long believed that local problems are best solved at the community level by people intimately familiar with the issues. An extension of this perspective holds that what may be an effective law enforcement strategy in Los Angeles will be a complete failure in rural Mississippi (and vice versa).

There are a number of disadvantages to organizing police primarily at the community level: (1) No overarching agency ensures uniform standards across departments. For example, police recruits in big cities are apt to receive extensive training in modern police techniques, but recruits in smaller towns usually receive much less comprehensive instruction. (2) A significant amount of law enforcement duplication exists in this country because jurisdictions of two or more agencies overlap. This is a waste of time, money, and effort. (3) Whereas communication in a national police force is apt to be direct and expedient, communication (and coordination when necessary) among multiple agencies is likely to be slow and cumbersome. It is not unusual to find less than full cooperation between law enforcement agencies that view each other as rivals. Although communities are entitled to administer their own police departments, they cannot exclude state and federal agencies from investigating crimes over which the state and federal agencies have jurisdiction ("Police," 2000).

Municipal Police and Sheriffs' Departments

Of the almost 19,000 publicly funded law enforcement agencies in the United States, almost 90 percent are local, **municipal police** and sheriffs' departments. The largest of these organizations, the New York [City] Police Department (NYPD), has almost 45,000 full-time employees including slightly less than 37,000 sworn officers. Four cities have 5,000 or more sworn officers: Chicago (13,237), Los Angeles (11,998), Philadelphia (6,398), and Houston (5,298). To put these numbers in perspective, consider that 1 in 12 full-time police officers works for the NYPD, and approximately 1 in 6 is employed by one of the five largest forces. Big-city police forces such as the San Diego Police Department are highly structured, complex organizations subdivided into numerous divisions (see Figure 6.1).

These large departments are atypical in that 61.5 percent of local agencies employed fewer than 10 full-time officers, and almost 20 percent had only one full-time or one part-time officer (Reaves, 1998a). In departments with 100 or more officers, slightly less than three in four officers were uniformed police whose duties included responding to calls for service. In addition to their law enforcement duties, local police (especially in small departments) often provide other services. For example, 49 percent of these agencies were involved in animal control and 20 percent offered emergency medical services (Reaves, 1996).

Organized primarily at the county level, **sheriffs' departments** provide countywide police services outside cities and towns. These law enforcement agencies may be staffed by only a few officers or they may have thousands of members as does the Los

municipal police law enforcement officers in the employ of a town or city; these departments range in size from a few officers to the NYPD with almost 37,000 sworn officers

sheriff's departments organized primarily at the county level, these law enforcement agencies provide police services to people who do not reside in cities or towns; these departments range in size from a few officers to thousands of members; for example, the Los Angeles County Sheriff's Department has more than 8,000 full-time sworn officers

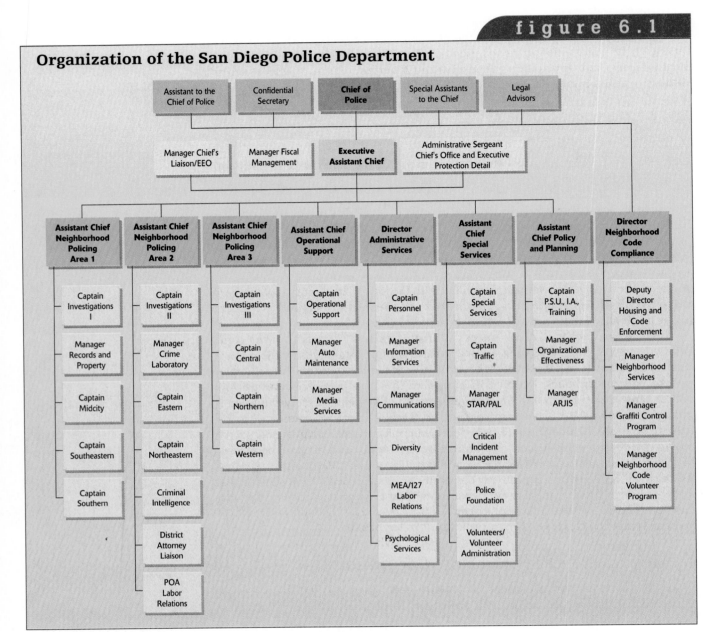

Organization of the San Diego Police Department

figure 6.1

Source: Reprinted by permission of the San Diego Police Department, San Diego, California.

Angeles County Sheriff's Department with almost 12,000 employees and slightly more than 8,000 full-time sworn officers. Whereas 22 percent of employees in local police departments are nonsworn civilian workers, 40 percent of employees in the nation's sheriffs' departments have the same status (Reaves, 1992).

With few exceptions, all sheriffs' departments perform work related to the courts, and almost 9 out of 10 have duties pertaining to jails. For example, in the Los Angeles Sheriff's Department 28 percent of officers were assigned to jails, and 19 percent had court related duty. Sheriffs may also be involved in tax assessment and collection; various inspection services; and overseeing public buildings, roads, bridges, and parks (Adler et al., 1991).

Both municipal police and sheriffs' departments are becoming increasingly racially and ethnically diverse. In 1987, minorities comprised 14.6 percent of municipal police departments, and that number increased to 21.5 percent in 1997 ("Local Police Departments, 1997," 1999). Corresponding figures for sheriffs' departments are 13.4 and 19 percent ("Sheriffs' Departments, 1997," 1999).

State Police

There are 66 state law enforcement agencies, which can be classified under one of three categories: **state police,** highway patrol, and state investigative departments. Many of these agencies exist within the context of a larger organization (a Department of Public Safety, for example) and are under the authority of the governor or state attorney general. Although most states have one state-level law enforcement agency, 13 have two such organizations, and Oklahoma has three (Torres, 1987). Hawaii is the only state without a law enforcement agency at this level. Collectively these organizations employ about 84,000 personnel, approximately two-thirds of which are full-time sworn officers. The number of officers at the state level ranges from 120 in North Dakota to 6,219 in California (Reaves, 1998a).

Established as a paramilitary unit in 1835 to fight American Indians and bandits from Mexico, the **Texas Rangers** were the nation's first state-level law enforcement agency, although Texas was not annexed by the United States until 1845. Almost all of the remaining state police agencies were established between 1900 and 1930. Donald Torres (1987, pp. 6–7) argues that "the state police were created in some situations because governors did not have anyone to enforce the will of the state in municipal and county areas; they were seen as a power symbol and as a security force of the governor's office."

As was the case with municipal police, some state law enforcement agencies were established in the midst of class conflict. This is evident in both the New York State Police (NYSP) and Pennsylvania State Police (PSP). Created as a result of the Great Anthracite Coal Strike (1902–1905), the PSP were despised by workers and union leaders who viewed them as nothing more than strikebreakers. In their early years of existence, the NYSP and the PSP were thoroughly racist, sexist, and anti-immigrant. Workers often referred to the state police of this period as Cossacks (peasant soldiers in the Russian Empire of the seventeenth and eighteenth centuries) (Miller, 2000).

In her book, *Justice for All: The Story of the Pennsylvania State Police,* a work that was favorably reviewed by the state's leading newspapers and carried an introduction by (then) former President Theodore Roosevelt, Katherine Mayo writes that the state police had not been needed "when the mass of people came from generations of law-revering people" (Gerda, 1995, p. 572). However, this was not the case with newly arrived immigrants. Italians and Slavs had to be ruled with an iron hand, and Poles and

A tribal police officer takes notes. Because they are separate nations existing within the confines of the United States, Native American tribes have their own police departments. On the vast Navajo reservation in the Southwest, a small number of officers provides police services for thousands of square miles of territory.

Hungarians, described as only slightly better than animals, had to be controlled in much the same manner. Similarly, *Grey Riders: The Story of the New York State Troopers*, written by Frederic Van de Water and endorsed by Governor Alfred Smith, was a diatribe against minorities. American Indians were described as "native born aliens" who had returned to "savagery" (Gerda, 1995, p. 580). A 1918 annual report of the NYSP contained a photo of an elderly African American man holding a sack full of chickens. The accompanying caption read, "I ain't never stole no chickens in my life" (Gerda, 1995, p. 382). Not surprisingly, state police organizations excluded African Americans, members of numerous ethnic groups, and women.

Today, state police have statewide powers regarding traffic regulation and criminal investigation and are comprised of both uniformed and plainclothes officers. Highway patrol agencies have statewide traffic regulation powers and also have the authority to arrest nontraffic violators. Most of these organizations do not employ plainclothes investigators (or very few) and are engaged in criminal investigation only to a limited extent. State investigative agencies assist other law enforcement on request (Torres, 1987).

Federal Agencies

The federal government employs almost 89,000 full-time personnel authorized to carry firearms and make arrests. Approximately 60 percent of these individuals work for the Immigration and Naturalization Service (INS), the Federal Bureau of Prisons (BOP), the Federal Bureau of Investigation (FBI), and U.S. Customs Service (see Table 6.1).

Perhaps the most well-known law enforcement agency in the United States is the **Federal Bureau of Investigation (FBI),** which has been surrounded by controversy since it was established nearly 100 years ago. Frustrated and angry by Congress's failure to pass legislation that would regulate corrupt politicians and businesses as well as a belief that crime would have to be dealt with at the national level, President Theodore Roosevelt created the Bureau of Investigation in an executive order in 1908. The bureau was stridently opposed by many individuals who feared that it could easily become a politically motivated secret police (Adler et al., 1991; Walker, 1998). Appointed by President Coolidge in 1924, J. Edgar Hoover served as director of the bureau until his death in 1972. Hoover was a master at manipulating the media and politicians to his agency's advantage. Congress expanded the bureau's jurisdiction in 1934, and a year later its name was changed to the Federal Bureau of Investigation. The FBI became a household word in the 1930s and 1940s because of its investigation and capture of a number of high-profile criminals including Baby Face Nelson, Pretty Boy Floyd, John Dillinger, Bonnie Parker, and Clyde Barrow (Adler et al., 1991).

However, a sinister side of the bureau emerged that would prove the earliest critics of that organization correct—political spying. Shortly after its inception in 1908, members of the (then) Bureau of Investigation were caught opening the mail of individuals who had opposed its creation (Walker, 1998). With the outbreak of World War II in Europe in 1939, the FBI began gathering information to discredit groups opposed to the United States' involvement in the hostilities. The "isolationist" America First Committee, which boasted members such as famed aviators Charles Lindbergh and Eddie Rickenbacker as well as Alice Roosevelt (daughter of President Theodore Roosevelt), was a major target of FBI surveillance. The agency attempted to impugn Lindbergh's character and to discover any information that would question his loyalty to the United States (Charles, 1999).

The FBI was especially suspicious of African American leaders and conducted surveillance on prominent African Americans from Marcus Garvey (leader of the Back to Africa Movement) in the 1920s to Malcolm X and Martin Luther King, Jr., during the civil rights struggle in the 1960s. Hoover had gathered so much information on so many prominent people during his tenure as FBI director that in the final year of his life he was beyond the control of anyone in the country including the president. The systematic abuses of power (spying on political groups out of favor with Hoover and/or the current administration and compiling secret files) did not become public knowledge until Hoover's death. While searching for communists and bank robbers, the FBI under

Federal Bureau of Investigation (FBI) established in an executive order in 1908, this agency investigates corporate crime, political corruption, and more than 250 federal offenses

table 6.1

Federal Agencies Employing 500 or More Full-Time Officers with Authority to Carry Firearms and Make Arrests, June 2000

AGENCIES	FEDERAL OFFICERS
Immigration and Naturalization Service	17,654
Federal Bureau of Prisons	13,557
Federal Bureau of Investigation	11,523
U.S. Customs Service	10,522
Internal Revenue Service	2,726
U.S. Postal Inspection Service	3,412
U.S. Secret Service	4,039
Drug Enforcement Administration	4,161
Administrative Office of the U.S. Courts	3,599
U.S. Marshals Service	2,735
National Park Service	2,188
Bureau of Alcohol, Tobacco and Firearms	1,967
U.S. Capitol Police	1,199
U.S. Fish and Wildlife Service	888
GSA—Federal Protective Service	803
Bureau of Diplomatic Security	617
U.S. Forest Service	586

Source: Reaves, B., and T. C. Hart. 2001. *Federal Law Enforcement Officers, 2000*. Washington, DC: U.S. Department of Justice, Office of Justice Programs.

Hoover all but ignored street crime, white-collar crime, organized crime, and violations of civil rights laws (Walker, 1998).

The FBI has wide-ranging investigative powers, and in the post-Hoover era the agency became involved in discovering corporate and organized crime as well as political corruption and more than 250 other federal offenses. Numerous crime family figures were convicted and sent to prison as a result of investigations by bureau agents, local police departments, and state agencies. During this period, the FBI continued to grow, and by the late 1990s the agency had approximately 10,400 agents in field offices across the country. Of the almost 7,000 agents who perform investigative work, the majority have backgrounds in law or accounting.

In 1996, FBI investigations resulted in 11,855 convictions, a number hailed by supporters of the agency as proof that it is doing a good job. However, detractors note that more than half of these convictions were for drug violations, credit card offenses against financial institutions, and bank robbery, whereas in that same year FBI investigators won only two convictions for antitrust violations and 35 for environmental crimes. As it was during the Hoover era, critics contend that today's FBI is much more concerned with crime in the streets than it is with crime in the suites.

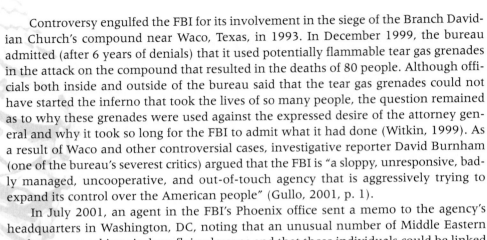

Controversy engulfed the FBI for its involvement in the siege of the Branch Davidian Church's compound near Waco, Texas, in 1993. In December 1999, the bureau admitted (after 6 years of denials) that it used potentially flammable tear gas grenades in the attack on the compound that resulted in the deaths of 80 people. Although officials both inside and outside of the bureau said that the tear gas grenades could not have started the inferno that took the lives of so many people, the question remained as to why these grenades were used against the expressed desire of the attorney general and why it took so long for the FBI to admit what it had done (Witkin, 1999). As a result of Waco and other controversial cases, investigative reporter David Burnham (one of the bureau's severest critics) argued that the FBI is "a sloppy, unresponsive, badly managed, uncooperative, and out-of-touch agency that is aggressively trying to expand its control over the American people" (Gullo, 2001, p. 1).

In July 2001, an agent in the FBI's Phoenix office sent a memo to the agency's headquarters in Washington, DC, noting that an unusual number of Middle Eastern students were taking airplane flying lessons and that these individuals could be linked to Osama Bin Laden's terrorist network. The memo urging that all flight schools in the United States be investigated for possible student–terrorist associations never reached senior-level officials (Lichtblau and Meyer, 2002). Senator Bob Graham of Florida, head of the Senate Intelligence Committee stated, "How in the world could somebody have read this [FBI] document and not had lights, firecrackers, rockets go off in their head that this is really important?" (in Lichtblau and Meyer, 2002, p. A19).

A former federal law enforcement official believes FBI field managers are interested in high-profile crimes, such as bank robberies and multimillion dollar illegal drug transactions, that play well on television when arrests are made. He noted, "They [the FBI] looked down on people who worked for counterintelligence because they couldn't show results. They were not arresting people" (in Karkorian and Connell, 2002, p. A20). According to Johnston and Van Natta, Jr. (2002, Sec. 1, p. 1), in the macho culture of the FBI, intelligence analysts and linguists were disdained as "desk-bound pencil-pushers."

In announcing the reorganization of the FBI in May 2002, Director Robert Mueller, III, said that the bureau would hire 400 new analysts. On September 10, 2001, a day before the terrorist attacks, Attorney General John Aschcroft declined to endorse an FBI request for 149 new counterterrorism field agents, 200 intelligence analysts, and 54 additional translators (Johnston and Van Natta, Jr., 2002).

A former senior agency official stated that "The FBI is the greatest in the world at investigating a crime after it happened, but it is not equipped to prevent crimes. It wasn't in the 90's, it wasn't on 9/11" (in Johnston and Van Natta, Jr., Sec. 1, p. 1). Few if any law enforcement agencies have the human, monetary, and/or technological resources to thoroughly investigate each tip, lead, and shred of evidence that becomes available. Therefore, to condemn the FBI for every breach of security and act of terrorism is unfair and unrealistic. In spite of substantial criticism, the FBI is still regarded by many people as one of the world's preeminent crime-fighting organizations (Burnham, 2001).

Almost half of the INS personnel are Border Patrol agents charged with interdicting undocumented aliens and stopping the flow of contraband (including illegal drugs) to the United States. Approximately 25 percent of INS employees are immigration inspectors assigned to ports of entry. Other INS personnel work in criminal investigation, detention, and deportation (Reaves, 1998b). In addition to interdicting contraband entering this country U.S. Customs Service officers are responsible for enforcing more than 400 laws relating to drugs, customs, export control, and revenue fraud.

During the past 25 years federal law enforcement agencies have become more diverse regarding race, ethnicity, and gender. Data covering about 90 percent of federal officers (approximately 67,000 individuals) indicate that 14 percent are women and 28 percent are racial/ethnic minorities. More than 40 percent of INS and Federal Protective Service agents are minorities. Other agencies with at least 25 percent minority composition include the BOP (35.6 percent), the U.S. Postal Inspection Service (33.4 percent), the U.S. Capitol Police (30.9 percent), and the U.S. Customs Service (28.9 percent) (Reaves, 1998b).

Special Police Forces

In addition to municipal police and sheriffs' departments, there are slightly more than 1,300 special police agencies employing more than 43,000 full-time sworn officers. The largest category of these special geographic jurisdiction or special function law enforcement personnel are college/university campus police with more than 10,000 officers employed by public institutions of higher learning across the country. Departments charged with enforcing natural resources and conservation laws (the California Department of Fish and Game, for example) comprise the second-largest category of special police with approximately 8,400 officers. With almost 3,000 special officers, the New York City Public School Police employs more than half of the country's public school district personnel in the largest category of special function police. Other agencies with 1,000 or more sworn officers work in the following areas: transportation systems/facilities, parks/recreation facilities, airports, waterways/harbors/ports, public housing, and alcohol control (Reaves, 1998a).

Composition of Police Departments

African American Police

African Americans served as police officers as early as 1861 in Washington, D.C. In the years following the Civil War (1861–1865), newly emancipated African Americans demanded the rights of free men—including the right to become police officers in southern cities then increasingly populated by former slaves. The thought of African American police officers arresting white citizens was almost too outrageous to think about for many people. A July 1863 headline in a Raleigh, North Carolina, newspaper boldly stated: "The Mongrel Regime!! Negro Police." The story detailing the hiring of four African American police officers concluded that "this is the beginning of the end" (Rabinowitz, 1991, p. 595). To make the presence of African American police less offensive to their white constituents, local southern governments prohibited "Negro" officers from arresting white citizens. In the mid-1870s the mayor of Greenville, North Carolina, stated, "I have expressly ordered Negro policemen not to arrest any white person, but to report any disturbance and the white policemen would make the arrest" (Rabinowitz, 1991, p. 598). By 1910 no African Americans were on southern police forces, and the entire country had fewer than 600 African American officers (Dulaney, 1996).

The policy of largely segregating African American police officers from white citizens lasted for more than 100 years in the South. A 1959 survey of 130 cities in that region revealed that in 69 of these municipalities (43.3 percent) African American officers were required to call white officers to arrest white suspects. In 107 cities (67.2 percent), African American officers patrolled only in African American neighborhoods, and some southern towns had squad cars marked "Colored Police" (Rudwick in Peak, 1997). An African American officer (Dixon in Dulaney, 1996, p. 52) noted that when he and seven other African Americans were appointed to the Atlanta police force in 1948 they had to stand up and say, "I do solemnly swear as a nigger policeman that I will uphold the segregation laws of the city of Atlanta."

Blatant discrimination against African Americans in law enforcement was also prevalent in other regions of the country. The first African American hired in New York City (1911) received the silent treatment by fellow officers for almost a year (Walker, 1998). As late as the 1940s, St. Paul, Minnesota, had an unwritten law against African American police officers riding in patrol cars, and some of these officers were not allowed to wear uniforms lest they offend local white citizens (Peak, 1997). Patrol cars were racially segregated in Los Angeles and Cleveland until 1961 and 1968, respectively, and an African American officer was not promoted to the rank of sergeant in the latter city until 1949 (Walker, 1998). Until the 1950s, the St. Louis Police Department had two annual picnics, one for white and the other for African American officers (Walsh, 1995).

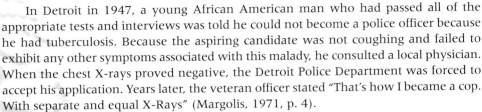

In Detroit in 1947, a young African American man who had passed all of the appropriate tests and interviews was told he could not become a police officer because he had tuberculosis. Because the aspiring candidate was not coughing and failed to exhibit any other symptoms associated with this malady, he consulted a local physician. When the chest X-rays proved negative, the Detroit Police Department was forced to accept his application. Years later, the veteran officer stated "That's how I became a cop. With separate and equal X-Rays" (Margolis, 1971, p. 4).

The relationship between African American police officers and many white citizens reflects the racial prejudice and hatred that has long existed in this country. Intolerance of African Americans on the part of some individuals can even be self-destructive. Consider the following incident as related by an African American New York City police officer during the civil rights era of the late 1960s (Alex, 1969, p. 178):

> My partner and I are on radio motor patrol duty. It's an ambulance call. When you arrive you find a low income [white] family . . . and the grandmother is hurt with a broken arm. We respond, my white partner and I, and the ambulance which has a white driver and a Negro attendant. . . . And the patrolmen are attempting to help her. She turns to the Negro policeman and says to him, "Don't put your hands on me!" I can't touch her. Can you imagine that. I come to her aid, and she tells me to get my hands off her.

In 1910, no more than 1 percent of police officers in this country were African American, with that figure declining to .9 percent by 1940. In a more racially tolerant post–World War II America, African Americans have gained entrance to many professions from which they had been mostly barred, including law enforcement. By the late 1990s, about one out of eight police officers was African American. Although the number of African Americans in law enforcement has increased significantly, the same cannot be said for African American officers in supervisory positions. For example, whereas slightly less than 14 percent of the NYPD is African American, only 3.8 percent of the command-level jobs (from captain on up) are filled by members of that racial group. In Baltimore, 33 percent of the police force is African American as are 18 percent of command-level officers (Moss, 1996). A number of cities with significant African American populations have police forces in which the majority of officers are African American. Fifty-three percent of police officers in Detroit and almost 7 out of 10 officers in Washington, DC, are African American (Walker et al., 1996). During the past 20 years, African Americans have become police chiefs in some of the nation's largest cities including New York, Los Angeles, Philadelphia, and Chicago (Walker, 1998).

Kenneth Peak (1997) argues that, historically, there have been two general reasons for the small number of African Americans in police work. *Institutional barriers* are those formal and informal obstacles erected by police administrators and governmental officials to dissuade minority men and women from seeking jobs in law enforcement. Little if any time, energy, and/or money is expended recruiting African American candidates, and job applications are often complicated and confusing. *Personal preferences* refers to African Americans choosing jobs in professions other than law enforcement. Many African Americans continue to believe the police are the enemy, an occupying army of mostly white males that represent a racist and highly discriminatory government.

During the civil rights movement of the 1960s and 1970s, virtually all white police departments enforced segregation laws, arrested peaceful demonstrators (African American and white), and, in some cases, assisted extremist groups carrying out vigilante-style justice (Glover, 1992). Becoming a police officer, therefore, became the equivalent of selling out and joining one's hated foe. The argument that African American police officers would be more understanding of and sympathetic toward the African American community often fell on deaf ears. As one individual noted, "It doesn't matter what color the officer is, it's the police mindset of dehumanizing whoever is black or brown or of color" (Rodriguez in Zuniga, 1999, p. 33).

The verdict in the O. J. Simpson murder trial revealed just how deep the chasm between African American and white police officers is in many police departments. One veteran St. Louis officer stated that when the "not guilty" verdict was read by the jury

http://www.ablongman.com/barkan1e

foreperson "The white coppers sulked, some of them looked down and shook their heads. The blacks high-fived, cheered, and applauded" (Johnston in Walsh, 1995, p. 8).

Much of the animosity between African American and white officers in large, urban departments is embedded in hiring and promotion issues. Many white officers believe African American and women gained admittance to the force (and were later promoted ahead of whites) because of a governmental mandated quota system. "Affirmative action" programs that gave preferential treatment to qualified minorities are increasingly being referred to as "reverse discrimination," programs that penalize or discriminate against whites. Referring to the economic tension between African American and white police officers, Samuel Walker states, "There's a sense of limited job opportunities and a fight over the good ones that exist" (Walsh, 1995, p. 8).

Big-city police administrators often find themselves in difficult positions. On his appointment as police chief in New York City, Raymond W. Kelly came under pressure from some African American community leaders to hire more African American officers. The new chief embarked on a recruiting strategy that included an "all out" marketing campaign in African American neighborhoods as well as sending recruiting teams to African American churches (Wolff, 1992). However, success in bringing African Americans into the department in New York as well as other cities may trigger not only resentment but also legal action on the part of white officers.

In addition to the Houston Police Officers Union, which has existed for decades, other groups, such as African Americans and the Organization of Spanish Speaking Officers, have been formed to address the concerns of a specific constituency. Founded in 1993, the White Officers Association (WOA) has a membership of 700 officers "of all races" and is strongly opposed to any preferential treatment in the workplace on the basis of race or ethnicity.

> Our organization is founded on the democratic values that people, regardless of race, religions, or sex should have an equal opportunity. . . . While a more descriptive name for our organization would be the Association for Equal Opportunity for Everyone, the name lacks the impact of denoting the race currently experiencing discrimination. We firmly feel that discrimination against anyone is wrong—ethically, morally, and legally. ("White Officers Association," 1999, p. 1)

Ten white police officers in Hartford, Connecticut, filed a federal lawsuit alleging that they were not promoted to the rank of sergeant because of their race ("Police Claim Reverse Discrimination," 1996). In 1999, white police officers won a lawsuit when a federal judge ruled that the racial quota hiring system used by the Memphis Police Department for more than 20 years was unconstitutional. More than 100 white officers filed discrimination suits after they had been passed over for promotion ("An Equal Force," 1999). In Houston, the WOA strongly opposes the more than 100 promotions ("welfare promotions") it alleges were given to African Americans and Hispanics rather than more qualified white officers in the name of affirmative action and consent decrees ("White Officers Association," 1999). Minority group officers state that they deserve the promotions they receive and that a hiring quota system is necessary to make up for well over 100 years of systematic discrimination in law enforcement.

In the 1920s sociologists introduced the term *social marginality*—the state of being both an insider and an outsider to a social group (Jary and Jary, 1991). In other words, although some individuals (such as ethnic and racial minorities) are formal members of a group, they are shunned by other members who resent their inclusion in that organization. Nicholas Alex (1969) argued that African American police officers are in a position of "double marginality." Not only are they members of an organization (the police department) in which they are treated as outsiders by many whites (the first form of marginality) but they also find themselves in a state of conflict because of the expectations of contradictory roles—police officer and member of a racial minority group. This latter conflict represents the second form of marginality. In an effort to test the double-marginality thesis, Valencia Campbell (1980) surveyed 576 African American male officers employed in a metropolitan area to determine whether occupational status and race explained the attitudes and behavior of these individuals across a number of issues. The data did not support the double-marginality perspective, and the author concluded that African American police are comfortable with both their race and profession.

Some individuals have argued that the law enforcement needs of African Americans would be best served by the presence of primarily (if not exclusively) African American police officers. Samuel Walker and his colleagues (1996, p. 109) reject this policing strategy for three reasons: (1) No evidence suggests that African American, white, and Hispanic officers behave differently to any significant degree. Departmental policies and situational factors, rather than race or gender, are the strongest determinants of police conduct. (2) To assign only African American officers to African American neighborhoods would "ghettoize" these individuals by denying them the experience of working in a variety of assignments and perpetuating the stereotype that these officers can best handle problems in the African American community. We would add that this policy would be a step backward to the days when "colored" officers were limited to patrolling "colored" neighborhoods. (3) Although many urban neighborhoods are almost exclusively African American, white, or Hispanic, many more are not. What officers would be assigned to these multiracial/ethnic neighborhoods? Finally, communities are not static; their racial/ethnic composition is continually changing. "Any attempt to draw precinct boundaries based on race and ethnicity would be quickly outdated" (Walker et al., 1996, p. 109).

Hispanic and Asian Police Officers

Little if any systematic research has been done on Hispanic Americans in law enforcement. According to the U.S. Bureau of the Census, in 1983, 4 percent of all police and detectives in this country were Hispanic. By 1997, 7.6 percent of a much larger population of police and detectives were Hispanic. Cities with large Spanish-speaking populations are likely to have a significant number of officers with Latin American roots. For example, by 1992, 47.5 percent of police officers in Miami were Hispanic. In 2001, that figure was more than 33 percent in the Los Angeles Police Department (personal correspondence, LAPD, 2001). Like their African American colleagues, Hispanic officers have had to deal with significant individual as well as institutional discrimination.

Samuel Walker and colleagues (1996) noted that some Hispanic officers were not raised in Spanish-speaking households, and, therefore, do not speak Spanish well or cannot speak the language at all. Their ethnic background may be of little or no value in dealing with primarily Spanish-speaking people. On the contrary, police officers who "look" Hispanic but cannot speak Spanish may alienate some native speakers who mistakenly believe these individuals choose not to communicate in Spanish because they are ashamed of their heritage.

Information regarding Asian American police officers is sparse. However, it is reasonable to assume that in cities with a significant Asian American population (New York, San Francisco, and Los Angeles among others), the number of officers from this racial background has increased in the past 10 to 15 years just as the number and percentage of Hispanic officers has gone up. In 2001, 6.8 percent of Los Angeles police officers (including Filipino officers) were Asian (personal correspondence, LAPD, 2001).

During one entry examination period, the NYPD had almost 1,100 Asian applicants although it is not known how many of these individuals eventually graduated from the police academy. During that same year, Thomas M. Chan became the first Asian American captain in that city's history. The Supreme Council of Asians in Law Enforcement is an umbrella organization that includes Asian officers at city, state, and federal levels (English, 1995).

Female Police Officers

Women have served as police officers in the Untied States for almost 100 years. However, because of widespread gender discrimination, both the scope of their activities and the number of females serving in law enforcement have been limited compared to male officers. Sociologist Susan E. Martin (1980, pp. 21–34) outlined four periods regarding the social history of police women in this country.

The Prepolicewomen Phase. The prepolicewomen period extended from before the Civil War (1861–1865) through the first decade of the twentieth century. Social reformers sought to have women and girls who were held in custody in governmental institutions supervised by women. Samuel Walker (1977) argued that the policewomen's movement can be traced to the latter years of this period when Mrs. Lola Baldwin of Portland, Oregon, became the first female known to have full police powers in the United States in 1905.

The Specialist Phase: 1910–1930. With the appointment of Alice Stebbins Wells to the Los Angeles Police Department in 1910, the policewomen's movement gained considerable momentum. A highly sought after speaker, Mrs. Wells traveled extensively as she addressed women's groups and national organizations (including the International Association of Chiefs of Police) about the virtues of women in law enforcement (Walker, 1977).

By 1916, between 16 and 40 towns and cities had at least one policewoman, and that number rapidly increased to 220 municipalities by 1918. In this phase the emerging policewoman's movement was involved in a struggle on two fronts (Walker, 1977). First, it had to fight and overcome strong opposition to creating new roles for women. In some cases, this resistance came from other, more conservative women's groups. The policewoman's movement was also part of a larger campaign on the part of the police to redefine (or at least significantly modify) their role in society. In this latter pursuit, women were helped by the emerging philosophy that crime prevention should be a fundamental responsibility of the police. One strategy toward this end was to prevent juveniles from starting down the slippery slopes of criminal careers. Samuel Walker (1977, p. 89) noted that the new emphasis on crime prevention "provided the entry wedge for the policewomen's movement; that is, because of their attributed natural nurturing qualities, females were perfectly suited for this line of police work." Policewomen dressed in street clothes could patrol those areas (dance halls, skating rinks, and movie theaters, for example) where children were likely to engage in illegal behavior as well as come in contact with criminals.

Speaking of their "child saving" role, Mary Hamilton (1924/1971, p. 4), the first female police officer in New York City, stated that "In many ways the position of a woman in a police department is not unlike that of a mother in a home. Just as a mother smooths out the rough places, looks after children and gives a timely word of warning, advice or encouragement so the policewoman fulfills her duty." Hamilton noted

A line of newly recruited policewomen report for work at a munitions factory during World War I. African American, Hispanic, Asian, and Native American women were almost entirely excluded from law enforcement at this time.

that a policewoman's role was different from that of her male counterparts, and she did not believe that women should attempt to move into the policemen's domain.

> When policewomen put on uniforms, carried guns and clubs they became little men, but when they did their work as women, they rendered a great service. And it is certainly a fact that no woman can really be a good policewoman unless she works as a woman and carries with her into a police department a woman's ideals. (p. 5)

Female officers of this period faced a number of obstacles including higher entrance standards than males, admission quotas, and a separate promotion track. Opponents of women in law enforcement questioned their (female officers') physical and emotional capacity to do police work as well as their ability to function in a disciplined, military-style environment (Martin, 1980). A final point of interest and importance is that, much unlike contemporary feminists, the policewomen's movement of this period did not seek equality with men regarding their role and duties in law enforcement. Rather, they accepted the prevailing gender-based division of labor and were willing to work in "areas of policing believed to be less dangerous and less demanding of physical strength, in which they could utilize their 'feminine' skills" (Martin, 1980, p. 24).

The Latency Phase: 1930–1970. The Great Depression of the 1930s halted the policewomen's movement because women's bureaus within urban police departments were considered "expensive frills" that could be eliminated. Martin (1980) notes that for most of this 40-year period female officers worked with "juveniles, prisoners, and typewriters" with few changes in their overall status or duties. The number of policewomen and detectives in both public and private agencies increased only slightly in the depression years from 1,534 in 1930 to 1,775 in 1940. By 1970, departments employed approximately 11,000 female officers, comprising only 2 percent of all police personnel in the United States.

The slow growth of the policewomen's movement in this phase can be explained in large measure by another redefinition of police work. Under the influence of August Vollmer and O. W. Wilson, "professional" departments moved away from a "crime prevention" model and "concentrated on the law enforcement and crime fighting aspects of police work . . . " (Walker, 1977, p. 93). Policewomen's social work/crime-prevention activities were no longer considered "real" policing. *Police Administration,* the highly regarded textbook by O. W. Wilson, had a strident antifemale point of view. According to Wilson, men were "less likely to become irritable and overcritical under emotional stress" and as such, were better suited to administrative positions (Walker, 1977, p. 94).

The Contemporary Period. With the passage of the Equal Rights Employment Opportunity Act of 1972, which outlawed discrimination by government agencies on the basis of race, color, religion, sex, or national origin, women obtained an equal opportunity to pursue a law enforcement career (Martin, 1994; Martin, 1997). In 1971, the percentage of female officers in cities with populations of more than 400,000 people was 2.3 percent, ranging from a low of 0.1 percent (Boston) to 6.9 percent (Indianapolis). By 1998, 9.8 percent of all sworn officers in this country were women with almost 15 percent of big-city departments comprised of female officers (see Figure 6.2). In some cities both the number and proportion of women officers increased as a result of legal pressures, that is, fear of lawsuits and/or court orders mandating that a specified number of females be hired (Martin, 1980). The number and percentage of female officers employed by big-city departments may be a factor of the racial composition of those municipalities. Martin (1980, p. 27) argues that in cities with significant African American populations (Washington, Atlanta, and Detroit, for example) "the sexual and racial integration of police departments have proceeded furthest." By way of comparison, in "ethnic group dominated" cities, such as Buffalo, Boston, Philadelphia, and Minneapolis (Irish, Polish, Italian, German), the forces of "traditionalism" have tended to resist change including the integration of women and African Americans in law enforcement.

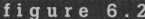figure 6.2

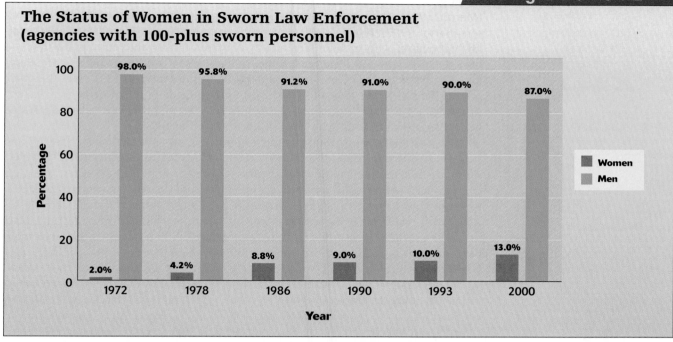

The Status of Women in Sworn Law Enforcement (agencies with 100-plus sworn personnel)

Source: Harrington, P. E. 2001. "Equality Denied—The Status of Women in Policing: 2000." National Center for Women and Policing. Reprinted by permission of National Center for Women and Policing, a division of the Feminist Majority Foundation.

In a 1978 civil case (*Brace v. O'Neill*), Penelope Brace, a member of the Philadelphia Police Department instituted a suit "on behalf of herself and all others similarly situated" against Police Commissioner Joseph O'Neill and a number of city officials alleging sex discrimination in department hiring practices. The following exchange occurred between Commissioner O'Neill (in Sass and Troyer, 1999, p. 573) and an attorney. When asked why women were not allowed on patrol duty, the commissioner responded:

O'Neill: Because God, in his wisdom made them different.

Attorney: From what respect?

O'Neill: Physically and psychologically.

Attorney: Physically, what differences . . . render females incapable of performing street work?

O'Neill: In general, they are physically weaker than males . . . I believe they would be inclined to let their emotions all too frequently overrule their good judgement . . . I don't mean to embarrass either of the ladies, but there are periods in their life they are psychologically unbalanced because of the physical problems that are occurring within them.

Susan Martin (1994) argued that the resistance to assigning women to patrol work was strong and organized. The first generation of women officers in this latest era faced insufficient instruction, co-worker hostility, the "silent treatment," and close, punitive supervision. They also had to deal with both the extremes of exposure to danger (with insufficient backup) and "paternalistic overprotection." One officer related the following incident (p. 390):

My first day of on the North side, the assignment officer looked up and said, "oh shit, another fucking female." That's the way you were treated by a lot of the men. The sergeant called me in and said the training officer doesn't want to ride with you but I've given him a direct order to work with you.

Female officers have encountered sexual harassment for the past 100 years, and although this form of discrimination is not as systematic as in years past, it still exists (Martin, 1994). The primary culprits of this sexist behavior appear to be male supervisors (Bartol, 1997). A female officer reporting to a new district was greeted with the following remark: "Officer, I don't mean any harm but I just want you to know that you have the biggest breasts I've ever seen on a policewoman" (Martin, 1980, p. 145). Serving as a reserve police officer in the mid-1970s, Susan Martin (1980) notes that male officers did not relate to her "comfortably" until they determined if she was "taken" (married) or "available" (unmarried). Male patrol officers she had never met addressed her as "sweetheart" and "dear."

Language is very revealing regarding how one group of individuals perceives and treats another group. Male officers often keep female colleagues "in their place" by referring to them in terms of cultural stereotypes—"ladies" or "girls"—that suggest weakness and passivity, people who need protection. Female officers who challenge this gender typecasting by being more aggressive (that is, behaving in a manner traditionally associated with males) risk being labeled a "butch," "bitch," or "lesbian" (Martin, 1994; Martin, 1997). Women police officers may find themselves in a no-win situation, caught between stereotypical extremes in an organization where they have little authority. (See Box 6.1, in which Nancy L. Herrington reflects on her 13 years of police experience.)

In her study of 106 African American and white (male and female) officers in five municipal police departments, Susan E. Martin (1994) observed that when a male officer failed to provide expedient and reliable backup in a dangerous situation, he was shunned and labeled a coward. However, when a female officer exhibited the same behavior, rather than being viewed as an individual shortcoming "the stigmatizing label is generalized to all women" (p. 391).

Although African American males have been the victims of systematic discrimination and stereotyping in law enforcement, some of the most common behavioral

In their struggle for equality within the world of law enforcement, minority group officers such as this African American policewoman have faced prejudicial attitudes and discriminatory behavior on the basis of both race and gender.

box 6.1   **On Being a Female Police Officer**   197

Joseph Wambaugh has accurately described the police code of silence—that inbred culture that can lead to personal and professional success or suicide. I believe that for women, being accepted within that culture is difficult at best. Women must accept and endure constant sexual harassment and the continual challenge to personal values. Acceptance generally requires becoming one of the boys and sacrificing femininity to play the police role. A woman can maintain her stance, but she will suffer the slings and arrows of disapproval from her peers and supervisors. The only option other than endurance is quitting. Fighting back is not an option unless she is willing to live the rest of her professional life being ostracized. While an organization can legislate behavior, it can do nothing with attitudes that have chilling effects. I have constantly juggled between wanting to be accepted as just one of the guys to being obstinate and stalwart in my opinions and actions. Only now do I feel confident and truly comfortable with myself in my job.

As a rookie officer, I remember one night at shift change asking for a portable radio from a male rookie officer. Exchanging equipment at shift change was our typical procedure. The best equipment generally went to the buddies who shared it with their buddies. On this particular night, I asked this officer for his portable radio. His response was, "I wouldn't let you lick the sweat off my balls if you were the last woman on earth." He then heartily laughed all the way into the station. I was devastated. It had been drilled into my head at the academy and with my field-training officers,

you don't rat on another officer. Ironically, a few of the younger officers on my shift overheard the comment. Later in the shift, a couple of them approached me individually to encourage me to report the incident to my sergeant. Facing the fear of retaliation from my peers was not something I wanted to do. I did finally muster the courage to talk with my sergeant. Needless to say, I was scared to death. The offending officer was "talked to" and the incident was never brought up again—to my face. Today he's a high-ranking officer in the department.

It took me two tries to make lieutenant. There were supposedly two budgeted positions for lieutenant open. The first time I took the test, I missed second place by seven-tenths of a point. The second time, I placed first on the promotional list and left my closest competitor 100 points behind. (Oh how sweet the taste of revenge.) On the first test, I was left hanging on the list even though it was known that two lieutenants would be retiring within the year. On the second promotional list, they promoted the last guy hanging on the list even though there was no budgeted position and no one was known to be leaving. They literally "created" a new position miraculously on the day the promotional list was to expire. Something just doesn't seem fair about all of that. Unfortunately, my options have never changed. If I wanted to continue my career in policing, my most viable option was to overlook the discrimination and try to make a difference by example rather than by accusation—which would only isolate me further.

Source: Adapted from Herrington, N. L. 1997. "Female Cops—1992." Pages 385–390 in *Critical Issues in Policing*, edited by Roger C. Dunham and Geoffrey P. Alpert. Prospect Heights, IL: Waveland Press. Reprinted by permission of Waveland Press, Inc. All rights reserved.

characteristics attributed to this racial–gender group (physically strong, aggressive, and streetwise) are valued in the police culture. In addition, whereas integrating African American men into law enforcement does not require any organizational changes, bringing women into this traditionally (white) male dominated profession requires altering facilities, uniforms, and physical training programs (Martin, 1994). An argument could be made that females have faced more strident opposition in their struggle to move into law enforcement than have African American males. African American female officers have encountered resistance on the part of both African American and white male officers. Subject to discrimination on the basis of both their race and gender, these women have been referred to as the "outsider within" (Collins in Martin, 1994).

On a more optimistic note, the overall situation for females in law enforcement may well change for the better because women could account for more than 25 percent of the nation's police officers in the next 2 decades (Bartol, 1997). Both the number and percentage of women supervisors and chiefs of police will also increase although that number is not likely to correspond to the 25 percent figure.

Gay and Lesbian Police Officers

Because the majority of gay and lesbian police officers choose to conceal their sexual orientation, the number of homosexual men and women in law enforcement is unknown (Leinen in Blair, 1999). In the mid- to late 1990s, some metropolitan police forces attempted to recruit homosexuals, ending decades-long systematic exclusion of these individuals. For example, the NYPD sent 55,000 fliers and applications to gay residents via mailing lists obtained from local gay and lesbian groups. A similar campaign was launched by the Los Angles Police Department (LAPD), an organization with "dozens" of officers who identify themselves as homosexual. Bernard Parks, former chief of the LAPD, stated, "I am pleased with the work of these officers. As chief of police, I set the tone for the LAPD. In that capacity I have made it quite clear that gay and lesbian officers will not be treated as second class citizens by anybody under my command" (Meers, 1998, p. 27).

Treatment as second-class citizens was precisely the point of a lawsuit filed by The Gay Officers' Action League (GOAL) against the NYPD in 1996. With 500 sworn officers, the New York City chapter of GOAL contends that it was not given the same consideration as other fraternal police organizations (Sudetic, 1996).

Anecdotal incidents indicate that homosexual male officers face more prejudicial attitudes and discriminatory behavior from other police personnel than do lesbian officers. In a profession dominated by heterosexual males, a homosexual male officer is a threat to the "macho mystique." An openly lesbian officer may be treated as "one of the guys." One woman noted that "My [male police] partners love the fact that I'm gay. They can talk about their girlfriends with me. They think women are women and gay women are cops" (Meers, 1998, p. 30).

Focus on France

The French Police—Two Forces Are Better Than One

When Napoleon Bonaparte (1769–1821) had himself crowned emperor of France in 1804, the country was still reeling from the civil disorder brought about by the revolution of 1789. The diminutive ruler inherited two very different police forces from the revolutionary government that he overhauled to suit his own purposes as well as to restore order and stability to the nation. Both of these law enforcement agencies still exist albeit in an altered state of organization.

Much as it is today, the Gendarmerie (now the Gendarmerie Nationale) was a paramilitary force established to police the countryside. Napoleon wanted an elite police organization comprised of honest, impartial, and reliable men who could instill confidence and gain the trust and respect of the public. The ideal gendarme was a noncommissioned officer in the regular army with an honorable service record who could read and write and was about 6 feet tall (Broers, 1999). Dressed in elegant uniforms and armed with the latest breach-loading rifles (carbines), as opposed to cumbersome and often wildly inaccurate muskets, gendarmes projected an image of "reliability, professionalism, even glamour" (Broers, 1999, p. 28).

By way of ensuring loyalty to the regime and exercising impartiality in the administration of their duties, Napoleon mandated that gendarmes should be detached from the communities they served. This was accomplished in the following manner: First, all gendarmes and their families (the government preferred unmarried men whenever possible) lived in barracks apart from local residents. Second, gendarmes could not be local men. Rather, they worked in regions in France other than where they lived. Lastly, the Gendarmerie was not accountable to local authorities but to the minister of war. Although they policed local citizens, gendarmes were soldiers in the service of the state (Broers, 1999).

Some 200 years later the Gendarmerie Nationale, with approximately 95,000 officers and men, continues to police the French countryside (approximately 95 percent of the nation's territory). Nationwide the Gendarmerie is divided into some 3,700 *brigades* consisting of between 5 and 55 men depending on the size of the *commune* (France has more than 36,000 communes or administrative districts).

There are two additional components of this quasi-military organization. The Mobile Gendarmerie are a fast-moving, heavily armed (with machine guns, tanks, armored personnel carriers, helicopters, and light aircraft) riot police who can be deployed anywhere in the country. Divided into 130 squadrons of about 134 men each, the more than 17,000 personnel in this organization represent 18 percent of total Gendarmerie manpower (Horton, 1995; Stead, 1983). Consisting of a cavalry regiment and two infantry regiments (about 3,000 men), the prestigious Republican Guard is permanently stationed in Paris. Its primary duties are ceremonial and stately; these gendarmes guard the president and high-ranking government officials (Horton, 1995; Stead, 1983).

The second major branch of law enforcement in France is the Police Nationale, an organization that operates predominantly in metropolitan areas with populations of 10,000 or more. With more than 125,000 personnel, this police force is under the direction of the Ministry of the Interior. The Directorate of Criminal Investigation (Police Judiciare) works serious crimes as well as those cases beyond the scope and resources of the city police or Gendarmerie (Stead, 1983). The Compagnies Republicaines Securite (the Republican Security Companies) are the civil version of the Mobile Gendarmerie. This force consists of 61 companies each staffed with between 210 and 255 personnel (Horton, 1995; Stead, 1983).

Although this organization is not part of the French army, it has a military structure with men living in barracks and officers holding the ranks of lieutenant, captain, major, and colonel. Like their counterparts in the Mobile Gendarmerie, the Republican Security Companies are a rapid deployment force (61 companies of about 250 men each) chiefly concerned with maintaining and restoring order in and around urban centers (Horton, 1995). These two police organizations provide the federal government with a well-trained, well-armed force of 32,000 men that can deal with a variety of emergency situations. This is an impressive number of personnel in a nation of 54 million people (roughly equivalent to the combined populations of California and New York).

One of the more interesting components of the Police Nationale is the Renseignements Generaux (Directorate of Intelligence). Unlike any police organization in the United States, the sphere of interest of this department is public opinion "which it seeks to measure by the collection, collation, and interpretation of data from a wide variety of sources including the mass media, periodicals, books, statistics, opinion polls, neighborhood gossip . . ." (Stead, 1983, p. 7). The Directorate of Intelligence has been referred to as France's "political police," the "eyes and ears" of the government. The roughly 3,000 officers in this department also infiltrate extremist groups, militant unions, and any other groups considered a threat to the state. When deemed necessary, individual or organizational phones are tapped, and mail is intercepted. The Directorate of Intelligence also keeps detailed files on an unknown number of people (Horton, 1995; Stead, 1983).

The Directorate of Counter Espionage (Surveillance du Territoire) is a 1,600-member strong plainclothes organization with the mission of protecting the republic from foreign agents and terrorists working in France (Horton, 1995). Because Paris is the center of government, business, and banking, as well as an international tourist destination and the venue of foreign embassies and consulates, the French capital city has its own prefect of police. John Stead (1983) notes that this department is a "microcosm" of the Police Nationale with its own administration, patrol force, and criminal investigation and intelligence units. A "force within a force," the Paris Prefecture of Police comprises slightly more than 16 percent of the entire Police Nationale.

The major problems associated with a dual national police system include the duplication of resources and confusion resulting from a "complex territorial division" of responsibility throughout the nation (Horton, 1995). For example, if the suspect of a crime committed in the countryside lives in a city, which organization should investigate the case? Some tension exists among members of the two forces because personnel in the Police Nationale often resent the higher esteem in which their colleagues in the Gendarmerie are held by the public (as measured by opinion polls). The latter organization has traditionally been favored by a more generous budget and superior resources (Horton, 1995). One plainclothes inspector of the Police Nationale stated, "We don't get on well. The gendarmes are favored by the powers that be. They have more sophisticated telecommunication systems . . . computer terminals in their cars. . . . We're lucky if we have working radios" (p. 77).

Interagency problems and rivalries notwithstanding, two national police forces appear to satisfy the government, the judiciary, and the French public (Horton, 1995). The government feels secure with a "divide and rule" police system wherein one force serves to check the other and neither poses a threat to the state. The judiciary favors two law enforcement agencies because any malpractice or corruption in one department can be kept in check by the other. "If one police force seems likely to be compromised by a case, then the case can be passed on to the other force" (p. 76). The public favors a dual police system because it is more likely that justice will be served if two criminal investigation departments check each other. And for those people who reside near a Gendarmerie and Police Nationale borderline they have an element of "consumer choice"; they can call either agency regarding a police matter.

Until the early 1970s, no female officers were in the Police Nationale, and recruiting posters declared that policing was "a man's job." However, much as they were in the United States, female "police assistants" had long been employed by law enforcement in France to work with children. Since 1972, females have been admitted to all departments in the Police Nationale although a quota was established to cap their number. This quota was later declared illegal by the European Court and withdrawn. To circumvent this ruling, a height requirement ("selection by measuring scale") was imposed that effectively eliminates the majority of French women from applying to the Police Nationale. In 1992, females accounted for slightly less than 6 percent of the personnel in this organization (Horton, 1995).

1. Although the organization of police forces can be traced to medieval Europe, the first modern police department in a major metropolitan area was established in London in 1829. In North America, the colonists usually reproduced the institutions of social control that they were familiar with in Europe. A system of constables and watchmen performed community service on a regular basis, which gave way to quasi-professional police forces wherein individuals were elected or appointed and received regular pay. Police forces in the southern states were primarily oriented to catch runaway slaves. Boston and New York were among the first cities to establish what would evolve into big-city police departments.

2. The creation of police departments is rooted in the increasing levels of conflict, violence, and general civil disorder the country experienced between the 1830s and 1870s. Much of this conflict, which continued into the twentieth century, was rooted in violent labor disputes. The owners of corporate America believed that they had the right to pay workers the lowest wages the market would bear. Unable to get salary increases, laborers often resorted to work slowdowns and strikes. From a conflict perspective, police forces emerged as a consequence of the clash between factory owners and impoverished workers. Other scholars believe that the upper class could not always count on the police to intervene on their behalf, especially when the police were from the same ethnic background as the workers. Early police departments were often intimately intertwined with local politics and, as such, were thoroughly corrupt. Police officers of the latter half of the nineteenth century often administered physical beatings or street justice when they encountered offenders or anyone who challenged their authority.

3. Technology has significantly affected policing; the introduction of patrol cars, two-way radios, and telephones completely changed the way officers interact with each other and the public. Patrol cars removed officers from face-to-face contact with citizens in the streets, and the telephone has made the police accessible to almost everyone in a moment's notice. August Vollmer (1876–1955) was arguably the most influential police administrator of the twentieth century. His Berkeley, California, department was to patrol a city entirely by automobile. Vollmer believed that police officers should be college educated if possible and believed crime was a multifaceted phenomenon that should be studied by many disciplines including sociology, psychology, and medicine. O. W. Wilson, one of Vollmer's disci-

ples and chief of police in Wichita, Kansas, became dean of the School of Criminology at the University of California at Berkeley. Police unions emerged from police benevolent associations, which began in the 1860s. By the 1990s, 73 percent of police departments and 43 percent of sheriffs' departments were unionized.

4. Whereas police in many countries are organized at the national level, the defining characteristic of law enforcement in the United States is decentralization and administration at the local level. Almost 90 percent of the nearly 19,000 law enforcement agencies are local police and sheriffs' departments. Although five cities had 5,000 or more sworn officers (including New York City with slightly less than 37,000), three of five local police agencies were comprised of fewer than 10 full-time officers. Sheriffs' departments are typically organized at the county level and provide police services outside cities and towns. State law enforcement agencies (state police, highway patrol, and state investigative departments) are under the authority of the governor or state attorney general. Approximately 60 percent of the 75,000 full-time law enforcement personnel at the federal level authorized to carry guns and make arrests work for the Immigration and Naturalization Service, the Federal Bureau of Prisons, The Federal Bureau of Investigation, and the U.S. Customs Service. The 43,000 officers employed by special police forces work in transportation systems/facilities, airports, public housing, among other types of employment.

5. African Americans first served as police officers in Washington D.C. in 1861. Racial discrimination was widespread on integrated police forces, and, as late as 1959, in 43 percent of the 130 cities surveyed, African American officers were required to call white officers to arrest white suspects. In 1940, just under 1 percent of police officers were African American, a figure that increased to 12 percent in the late 1990s. African Americans are underrepresented in command-level positions although in recent years African Americans have been appointed police chiefs in some of the nation's largest cities. Nationwide just under 8 percent of police officers are of Hispanic heritage although that figure approaches 50 percent in cities with a significant Latin population, such as Miami. The number and/or percentage of Asian American law enforcement personnel nationally is unknown. It is highly likely that their numbers have also been increasing in metropolitan areas with significant Asian populations.

Some police departments have actively recruited in the gay and lesbian community in recent years. With the passage of the Equal Rights Opportunity Act of 1972, the number of women police officers rose dramatically from 2.3 percent of the force in cities with populations more than 400,000 in 1971 to about 15 percent of big-city departments in 1998. The resistance to women doing patrol work has been strong. Female officers continue to be victims of job-related sexual harassment.

key terms

Federal Bureau of Investigation (FBI)
municipal police
police fraternal organizations or
  brotherhoods
sheriffs' departments

sick in or blue flu
speedup
state police
Texas Rangers

questions *for* investigation

1. Find out what made London so dangerous in the sixteenth and seventeenth centuries and how Sir Robert Peel created the London police force in 1829. Describe the jobs of officers in this early force.
2. Research the formation of the police in the United States between the 1830s and 1870s. Find specific examples of how the force was developed by politics and capitalist interests in cities such as New York, Boston, Buffalo, Washington, DC, Pittsburgh, Chicago, and St. Louis.
3. Consider the issue of police unionization as discussed in this chapter. Do you believe unions are appropriate for police? Defend your answer.
4. In a group, discuss the effectiveness of the FBI today.

5. From reading this chapter's coverage of the emergence of women in police work, identify the various physical and psychological biases about women that have led to discrimination against them as police officers.
6. Compare and contrast the structure and organization of police departments in the United States and France. Go to the library and find material on the structure and organization of police in a developing nation such as Peru, India, or Egypt. What can law enforcement agencies in this country learn from the organization of police in other nations that might prove beneficial to their (police in the U.S.) overall effectiveness?

IT'S YOUR CALL . . .

1. You are a rookie police officer fresh from the academy. Your partner, an officer with 19 years of experience, thinks that "community policing" is a ridiculous philosophy as well as an unworkable strategy for maintaining "law 'n order." As tactfully as possible, try to convince her of the merits of community policing. If necessary, do some research to find additional material on community policing.

2. You are the chief of one of the nation's largest police forces—a department that has rejected community policing in favor of a military strategy, especially in dealing with street gangs and highly organized drug dealers. Last week, a 5-year-old child was accidentally shot and killed by a SWAT team officer during a successful drug bust. Outraged by the child's death and the department's "Rambo police philosophy," thousands of people in the community (by way of protest rallies and demonstrations) are calling for an end to military-style drug busts as well as your ouster as chief. The mayor has ordered you to make a televised address to the city. What will you say?

UNDER
Investigation

Community Policing and Militarizing the Police

Community Policing

Beginning in the 1970s, the philosophy, and, to a lesser extent, the organization of numerous police departments began to change in the direction of community policing (CP). Steven Mastroski, Worden, and Snipes (1995) note that CP is the kind of catch-all label for an outlook on policing that rejects law enforcement as the single most important function of police and that officers must be more cooperative with "those who are not police." CP has been described as a plastic concept that has different meanings to different people (Eck and Rosenbaum, 1994). David Bayley (1988, p. 225) notes that variations of CP have encompassed one or more of the following: "public relations campaigns, shopfronts and mini-stations, rescaled patrol beats, liaison with ethnic groups, permission for rank-and-file to speak to the press, Neighborhood Watch, foot patrols, patrol–detective teams, and door-to-door visits by police officers."

CP is based on the fundamental premise that police officers cannot do their jobs alone. If law enforcement is to be effective, it must work closely with members of the community in a joint effort to solve mutually defined problems (Roberg, 1994). For the director of the

National Institute of Justice, CP recognizes that "the police and the community are co-producers in safety," and that the police are open to "public involvement and scrutiny" (Travis, 1996, p. 112). Ultimately, CP is a re-

> " ... community policing ... is based on the fundamental premise that police officers cannot do their jobs alone."

jection of the long-established premise that the police and only the police are capable of handling societal problems of crime and disorderly behavior. CP is a radical innovation in U.S. policing because it redefines the overall philosophy of law enforcement and the relation between the police and society. By 1997, more than 60 percent of police departments serving populations of 100,000 or more residents had formal community policing plans, and, overall, about 9 in 10 local police officers worked for a department with some form of community policing policy (Reaves and Goldberg, 2000).

In an effort to more fully answer the question "What is community policing?" Gary Cordner (1997, pp. 452–464) has neatly summarized the four major dimensions of this concept as follows:

The Philosophical Dimension. In a democratic society the public should have access to police organizations, including departmental policies and decision making. This can be achieved by police officials meeting on a regular basis with local citizen advisory boards, members of the business community, and minority group representatives. Whereas police activity has traditionally focused on fighting crime, under CP, non–law enforcement tasks take on greater importance. Their tasks include order maintenance, dispensing some social services, and general assistance to the public. The police assume a greater role in protecting and improving the quality of life of some of society's most vulnerable members, including the poor, juveniles, the disabled, and the homeless. A major benefit of this expanded role is increased police status and legitimacy in the local community. This is hardly inconsequential in neighborhoods where the police are viewed as the enemy. Currently, officers make a decision to arrest someone based on a combination of legal (the penal code), bureaucratic (what laws police administrators determine should be enforced), and personal (the individual officer's interpretation of what transgressions should result in an arrest) criteria. Under CP, police officers consider the "will of the community" when deciding if the behavior in question warrants arrest. This strategy of personalized policing means that behavior leading to an arrest in one community (for example, a fight that does not lead to serious injury) would not lead to legal intervention in another neighborhood.

The Strategic Dimension. One component of CP that most advocates of this form of policing agree on is taking officers out of squad cars and assigning them to foot patrol beats, thereby generating more face-to-face interaction with the public. Police administrators have been increasingly critical of officers randomly cruising neighborhoods in patrol cars. A former police chief in San Diego referred to this activity as "little more than sleeping on duty" (Burgreen in Eggers and O'Leary, 1995, p. 9). It is widely assumed that officers on foot patrol are more likely to get a "feel" for the community

than their motorized counterparts. In addition, police on foot have an opportunity to interact with citizens in a routine, friendly manner (as opposed to only when a problem arises) thereby gaining the trust of local citizens.

In addition to foot patrols, in some departments police ride on bicycles and horses. As one NYPD police captain noted, "the patrol car is the barrier, the bike is a bond" ("On Your Bike," 1993, p. 28). In 1895, when Teddy Roosevelt was police commissioner in New York City, officers routinely controlled traffic riding bicycles. This trend continued until the mid-1930s when bicycles were discarded in favor of motorcycles and squad cars (Petracca, 1996). Besides the NYPD, which now has more than 2,000 officers deployed on bicycles, Seattle, San Jose, and San Francisco, to name only a few cities use bicycle patrols (Flynn, 2000a; "On Your Bike," 1993). Similarly, the use of officers on horseback has increased in cities across the country. Officers report that the number of contacts with civilians increases dramatically as people pet the animals and talk to the riders. Anecdotal evidence suggests that crime rates in some horse patrolled areas have declined (Clayton, 1996).

For most of their history, police in this country have taken a *reactive* or "incident-driven" posture; that is, they

> " . . . officers on *foot* patrol are more *likely* to get a '*feel*' for the community than their *motorized* counterparts."

wait until they are called and then respond. CP advocates a *proactive*, preventive approach. Instead of waiting for the next call and/or randomly patrolling in police cars, officers spend time between calls engaged in designated crime prevention efforts, problem solving, interacting with community members, and other specified activities. If the police can discover (and begin to rectify) the conditions that generate crime in a particular neighborhood, they can reduce the number of future incidents of this behavior and improve the quality of life of all concerned.

The effectiveness of preventive policing is evident in the following example. A trucking company in a large city had 32 of its trailers broken into during an 18-month period. These burglaries became predictable as the crimes were reported and the police arrived and recorded the pertinent information. Tiring of financial losses and the inconvenience of these thefts, the owner of the trucking company informed local political leaders that, unless something was done to rectify the situation, he was taking his multimillion dollar business (and a significant number of jobs) to another city. The police convinced the owner to improve the lighting in the truck yard as well as increase the height of the fence. Police officials also worked with other city agencies, and a barricade was erected between the truck yard and an adjacent lot that served as a getaway for thieves. The burglary problem was solved via a proactive, prevention-oriented approach. When a detective in Newport News, Rhode Island, wanted to reduce domestic homicides he established a task force consisting of local hospitals, military bases, women's groups, the local newspaper, and other organizations (Eck and Rosenbaum, 1994).

The Tactical Dimension. The emphasis on crime prevention leads to partnerships with citizens either individually or in groups. Herman Goldstein, who has written extensively on CP, notes, "We must restore a balance between citizen and police responsibilities [for] effective social control cannot possibly be achieved by hired hands alone" (Eggers and O'Leary, 1995, p. 74). Individuals can donate their time to a police department as volunteers, reserves, or auxiliaries. Collectively, people can form local revitalization groups, neighborhood watch organizations, and youth-oriented educational programs and recreational programs. As a disproportionate number of street crimes are committed by young offenders, youth-centered organizations are especially important. Cordner (1997) notes that police should refrain from claiming that they alone can solve society's crime and drug problems while simultaneously encouraging citizens and community groups that they are also responsible for dealing with these issues. As one police officer noted, "The community has to recognize it has a responsibility for governing its own value standards. . . . People choose the way they want to live, and police can't remove that responsibility" (Coleman in Eggers and O'Leary, 1995, p. 78).

The Organizational Dimension. Although the organization of a police department is not part of CP per se, the command structure of a law enforcement agency may well determine whether the implementation of this strategy is successful. According to Cordner (1997) the following types of "restructuring" are associated with CP: Departments can *decentralize* so commanders, supervisors, and officers are independent, make decisions quickly, and, therefore, are more responsive to citizens' needs. *Flattening* reduces the layers of bureaucracy within a department whenever possible in order to remove communication barriers and increase flexibility. *Despecialization* reduces the number of specialized units and frees up resources that then can be delivered directly to the public. People working in *teams* are often much more effective than individuals in solving problems and/or improving the quality of work. The *civilianization* of some positions means that work currently done by sworn officers can be done by civilian personnel. Besides saving departments money in many instances, this latter strategy typically results in effective use of police officers. In a move that was challenged by the local police union, the mayor of Jersey City, New Jersey, reassigned two officers who had been delivering interoffice mail to street patrols. Mayor Bret Schundler stated, "Our crime problem is not the result of our spending too little on policing, but rather, of our getting too little policing for our money . . . " (Eggers and O'Leary, 1995 p. 76).

A very different philosophy and style of policing logically requires an alternative way of evaluating police performance at both the individual and departmental level. Cordner (1997) suggests that instead of evaluating officers on traditional performance indicators such as tickets, arrests, and calls handled, police personnel should be graded "on the quality of their community policing and problem solving activities and perhaps the results achieved" (p. 463). Departments could be assessed on the basis of citizen satisfaction of their performance and the level of fear in the community as opposed to crime rates and response time to calls.

To date, the overall effectiveness of CP is anything but certain. Summarizing the available data in this area, Mark Moore (1994) notes that citizens appear to respond favorably to this type of policing. The evidence is "slightly less strong" that CP can reduce citizens' fear of crime, and weaker still that this form of policing can successfully mobilize a community to deal with its problems of crime and disorder. Finally, there is almost no evidence to prove that CP can reduce rates of crime and criminal victimization (Moore, 1994).

Although the effectiveness of CP remains to be seen, it appears that the majority of police officers in a number of departments believe this organizational philosophy will remain popular. In their survey of 866 officers in one Canadian (Edmonton) and five U.S. cities

"... there is almost **no** evidence *to prove that* **CP** *can* reduce *rates of* crime *and criminal* victimization."

(Savannah, Philadelphia, Las Vegas, Newport News, and Santa Barbara), Deborah Weisel and John Eck (1994) found that between 64 and 80 percent of respondents in each agency noted that CP as it was currently practiced or in some other form was "here to stay." One supervisor with more than 20 years' service noted that police officers come in three "flavors" or personality types. Vanilla officers are willing to obey orders and when trained properly will follow departmental directives to the best of their ability. Chocolate officers may be critical and outspoken against any organizational change unless they can be convinced of the value, logic, and merits of that change. Stubborn and resistant, strawberries resist any form of change and no amount of training or inducements are likely to change their minds. If Weisel and Eck's (1994) survey results reflect police personnel in departments around the country regarding CP, most officers are in the vanilla and chocolate categories.

A study of the Houston Police Department concluded that officers hostile to CP often felt overwhelmed by their new assignments, believed they were not adequately prepared for the tasks they were required to perform, and questioned the program's overall goals. Some officers regarded CP as little more than a gimmick and resented doing work "more like social workers than police officers" ("Study Criticizes Community Policing," 1991). Officers working in CP are sometimes referred to as "the smile and wave squad."

Militarizing the Police. Criminologists Peter Kraska and Victor Kappeler (1997) note that, although

the well-publicized community policing movement has taken center stage in U.S. law enforcement, a less frequently reported backstage development has been occurring simultaneously—the militarization of the U.S. police. This militarization is in the form of police paramilitary units (PPUs). Kraska and Kappeler (1997) surveyed all 690 state and local law enforcement agencies in the United States serving jurisdictions of 50,000 or more residents and employing at least 100 officers. Of the 548 departments that responded, 89.4 percent (490) had PPUs and more than 20 percent of agencies without such units were "planning on establishing one in the next few years" (p. 6).

PPU members often refer to themselves in military jargon ("heavy weapons units") and have a variety of weapons and high-technology devices unavailable to other units. These weapons include Heckler & Koch MP5 submachine guns, 12 round shotguns ("street sweepers"), M16 rifles, sniper rifles, C4 explosives, and flash grenades. According to one estimate, between 1995 and 1997, the Department of Defense gave police departments 1.2 million pieces of military hardware ("Policing: The Sultans of Swat," 1999). Mission-ready PPU members look more like combat soldiers than po-

"... PPU members ... **see** themselves *as members of an* elite *unit* ..."

lice officers. Their attire typically consists of battle dress uniforms (BDUs), combat boots, full body armor, Kevlar battle helmets, and in some instances, ninja-style hoods. These officers see themselves as members of an elite unit, a view that is promoted by police administrators (Kraska and Kappeler, 1997).

This elite self-perception and elevated status in the law enforcement community is a consequence in no small measure of the training PPU members receive. When asked about the sources of training that were influential during the start-up period of their PPUs, 46 percent of departments reported that they gained expertise from "police officers with special operations experience in the military," whereas 43 percent of the agencies with such units reported that they trained with "active-duty military experts in special operations" (Kraska and Kappeler, 1997, p. 11). Twenty-three percent of departments noted that they were instructed by Navy Seals or Army Rangers. Speaking of these organizations, one respondent stated:

> We've had special forces folks who have come right out of the jungles of Central and South America. These guys are into real shit. All branches of the military are involved in providing training to law enforcement. . . . We've had teams of Navy Seals and Army Rangers come here and teach us everything. We just have to use our judgment and exclude information like: at this point we bring in the mortars and blow the place up. (p. 12)

Not only have the number of PPUs increased significantly over the past 20 years but their use of "call-outs" has risen markedly as well both in scope and quantity. Between 1980 and 1983, PPUs averaged about 13 call-outs per year, or slightly more than one a month. By 1995 that number had quadrupled to four or five calls for service per month. Just over 75 percent of the deployments were for drug related "high risk warrant work" while other call-outs were dispatched to barricaded persons (13.4 percent), hostage situations (3.6 percent), civil disturbances (1.3 percent), and terrorist incidents (0.9) percent. A significant number of paramilitary units conduct between 200 and 700 warrants/drug raids annually (Kraska and Kappeler, 1997). As these statistics clearly indicate, PPUs are predominantly proactive units in the war on drugs.

The notion that PPUs are a "domestic army engaged in a 'war' on crime" is grounded in three themes (Klockars, 1999, p. 431). First, by associating the police with military heroes and victories as opposed to the often-sordid side of local politics, militarization confers

" . . . PPUs are predominantly proactive units in the war on drugs."

honor and respect on the police profession. Second, the notion of a "war" on crime creates a sense of urgency

and heightened importance. Denying police the necessary resources to battle criminals is like "siding with the enemy and metaphorically tantamount to treason" (p. 431). Third, just as generals make battlefield decisions in combat, militarizing the police is a way for police administrators to gain more control of their departments (at the expense of local politicians) in terms of hiring, firing, assignments, and disciplinary matters that are necessary to manage these quasi-military organizations.

Although many police administrators and officers are enthusiastic about PPUs, arguing that they are necessary to preserve order and control law-violating behavior in a society characterized by high crime rates (especially violent crime), other members of the law enforcement community are adamantly opposed to these

"Some officers think that PPUs pose a danger to team members and civilians."

units. Some officers think that PPUs pose a danger to team members and civilians. One police captain who had a negative view of paramilitary drug raids recounted the following incident:

> We did a crack-raid and got in a massive shoot-out in an apartment building. Shots were fired and we riddled a wall with bullets. An MP5 round will go through walls. When we went into the next apartment where bullets were penetrating, we found a baby crib full of holes; thank god those people weren't home. (in Kraska and Kappeler, 1997, p. 9)

Joseph McNamara, former chief of police in Kansas City and San Jose, California, considers PPUs a "disaster," resulting in now routine levels of force that would have been unacceptable in the past ("Policing: The Sultans of Swat," 1999). Ron Hampton, executive director of the National Black Police Association believes that the militarization of the police is dangerous and that departments so organized will begin attracting applicants who

Under Investigation: Community Policing and Militarizing the Police

are not oriented toward community service but motivated by the "thrill of chasing criminals and the excitement of the weapons" (Lindorff, 1999, p. 20). Although opponents of PPUs are often dismissed as little more than misguided liberals, some conservatives have also been highly critical of these paramilitary groups. Diane Weber of the conservative Cato Institute stated that the mind-set of a soldier is not appropriate for civilian law enforcement personnel. "Police officers confront not an 'enemy' but individuals who are protected by the Bill of Rights. These units are going into public housing projects, into black neighborhoods, as if they're in hostile territory" ("Policing: The Sultans of Swat," 1999, p. 29).

Although PPUs are almost universally considered necessary in certain hostage-related tasks and antiterrorist situations, this activity comprises only a small fraction of their work. Research indicates no correlation between overall paramilitary policing and crime rates. According to Peter Kraska, the number of PPUs is increasing not as a result of rising crime or any evidence that these units can reduce law-violating behavior, but simply because police departments want them ("Policing: The Sultans of Swat," 1999).

Becoming *a* Cop *and* Doing Police Work

1. Why does a person choose to become a police officer? What are the minimum requirements? What formal and on-the-job training do officer candidates receive?

2. How effective are police at preventing crime?

3. What are the principal functions of uniformed police in a community?

4. Which situational factors are necessary for officers to decide that a criminal investigation is necessary?

5. What are the most frequent points of contact between police and the general public?

6. Why is discretion necessary in police work?

7. What is profiling and why is it an issue in policing?

8. What is the police subculture?

Although women have made substantial gains politically, economically, and socially in the post–World War II era, their advances in law enforcement have been less noteworthy. The "cult of masculinity," as Smith and Gray (1985) have noted, is alive and firmly entrenched in the police culture, and it continues to be a formidable obstacle to gender parity. During the approximately 300 hours he spent in the field with Los Angeles police officers, Steve Herbert (1997; 2001) discovered that the "manly" characteristics of courage, aggressiveness, and physical toughness were an integral part of their normative order or occupational worldview. The emphasis on masculinity served as a framework for how male officers interacted with each other as well as how they viewed and interacted with female officers.

For example, the LAPD personnel Herbert observed made a sharp distinction between two ideal types of officers: "hard-chargers" and "station-queens." The former are "real men," "real cops" who relish danger, whereas the latter are believed to prefer the safety and sanctuary of precinct house duty. These less than full-fledged officers are labeled as effeminate with the designation "queen," a term that also has a homosexual connotation. Even detectives are routinely denigrated by patrol officers "because they [detectives] avoid the test of masculinity that the danger of the street presents" (Herbert, 2001, p. 57).

Will female officers ever be fully accepted as equals in the "macho" world of law enforcement?

This masculine/feminine dichotomy contributes to a kind of social geography with some neighborhoods designated "antipolice" (where many residents are openly hostile to officers) and others labeled "propolice," areas that are officer friendly. Officers who request assignment to a quiet beat find that they are downwardly mobile in the status hierarchy of the police subculture, while those working "antipolice" neighborhoods (often locales with a significant amount of gang activity) have a "chance to demonstrate the courage and strength so central to the adventure/machismo normative order" (Herbert, 1997, pp. 88–89).

Sociologists Susan Martin and Nancy Jurik (1996) comment on how this adventure/machismo conceptualization of policing compels female officers to make difficult decisions. *Police*women who identify with the male-centered and male-dominated world of law enforcement attempt to gain acceptance by acting like "real cops," that is, by being as aggressive, loyal, courageous, and street smart as their male counterparts. However, women who choose this alternative risk the indignity of being labeled a bitch, lesbian, or dyke. As much as these officers crave the acceptance of their comrades, they will never be accepted as "one of the boys" (p. 97).

Conversely, police*women* are unable or unwilling to become street cops. They may be uncomfortable on patrol, fearful of physical injury, and/or reluctant to take control of street situations patrol officers routinely encounter. Uncomfortable around men's locker-room language, they try to remain "ladies" by accepting the "paternalistic bargain." These women accept or tolerate the protection of male officers and may conform to gender stereotypes, such as seductress, helpless maiden, or mother, in their interaction with them. Although most female officers contend with work-related sexism by adopting one of these strategies, many women respond with elements of both as situations dictate (Martin and Jurik, 1996).

Susan Martin (1980, p. 79) argues convincingly that integrating women into "police patrol work as coworkers threatens to compromise the work, the way of life, the social status, and the self-image of the men." As long as male law enforcement personnel adhere to an occupational worldview that denigrates the feminine and females, they will continue to demonstrate the perceived differences between male and female officers by way of "doing gender" during the course of their work.

In its final report concerning the LAPD, the Christopher Commission commented on computer messages sent between patrol cars. Female officers were referred to as "sweet cakes . . . babes . . . Barbie dolls . . . Sgt. Tits . . . " Another message asked: "Hey slut, when do you want to take a code 7 (a break)?" (Segrave, 1995, p. 147). When a

Soviet policeman visiting Los Angeles stated that female officers in his country were limited to desk jobs and juvenile duties, male officers in the back of the room cheered.

Becoming a Cop

Why would anyone want to be a police officer? Although the job certainly offers more excitement than most occupations (teaching at a university, for example), routine police work is a far cry from the nonstop, action-packed, crime-fighting activity it is portrayed as on television and in movies. While shoot-outs and vehicle pursuits do occur, most police work is less adventuresome and dangerous. Many officers describe answering service calls, writing traffic citations, and dealing with "fender benders" as downright boring. Coupled with this everyday tedium, law enforcement personnel routinely complain about the lack of respect and appreciation they receive from the public. Society has also "dumped on the police" the job of implementing laws that are more or less unenforceable—laws regarding alcoholism, gambling, sexual activity, and drug use.

In the post–World War II era, the primary motivating factors for choosing police work have remained fairly consistent: job security and working with others or "helping people" (Lefkowitz, 1975; Walker, 1999). One survey of two midwestern departments found that the top five reasons for choosing a law enforcement career were (1) to "help people," (2) "job security," (3) to "fight crime," (4) "excitement of job," and (5) "prestige of job." Little difference in ranking occurred between male and female officers (Meagher and Yentes, 1986).

Table 7.1 shows the starting and maximum salaries for police departments around the country in three categories: population group, geographic location, and metro status (central, suburban, and independent). Notice that, in general, as the population a department serves increases in size, police salaries rise. Whereas southern police departments pay the least, law-enforcement agencies in the North and (especially) the Pacific Coast pay the most. One southern city of approximately 150,000 starts academy trainees at $9.62 an hour, a figure less than twice the minimum wage. In 2001, New York City Police Department rookies earned $31,305, a sum considerably less than the $45,331 salary graduates of the Downey, California, Police Academy were paid ("City of Downey," 2001; Flynn, 2000a). Police officers have complained that the maximum wage they can earn is not significantly higher than the starting salary of rookie officers. For example, the average maximum salary of a New England police officer ($38,223) is slightly less than 24 percent higher than the average compensation of first-year officers ($30,721). By comparison, full professors may earn more than twice as much as an assistant professor fresh from graduate school.

If police departments across the country are to attract some of society's best and brightest members, municipal governments will have to compensate them accordingly, and many have moved in that direction. In a competitive society where wages have increased dramatically in hundreds of occupations, individuals who must develop the skills necessary to deal with people from diverse backgrounds in stressful situations (and, on occasion, make life or death decisions), should be paid at least as much as automobile assembly line workers. This is especially important because tens of thousands of officers born in the baby boom era (1946–1964) are beginning to retire, and their numbers will have to be replenished.

Requirements and Selection

Virtually all police departments have minimum requirements an individual must meet in order to be accepted as a candidate in a police academy. Eighty-eight percent of departments require a high school diploma or GED, and 12 percent of police agencies require new officer recruits to have some college background. For example, as of 1999,

table 7.1 Police Salaries

Entrance and maximum salaries, and mean number of years to reach maximum salary, for police officers in cities of 10,000 persons and over

By population group, geographic division, and metro status, United States, as of Jan. 1, 1998

	ENTRANCE SALARY		MAXIMUM SALARY		NUMBER OF YEARS TO REACH MAXIMUM	
	Number of Cities Reporting	Mean	Number of Cities Reporting	Mean	Number of Cities Reporting	Mean
Total, all cities	1,274	$29,192	1,250	$39,907	1,011	7
POPULATION GROUP						
Over 1,000,000	3	33,381	3	49,966	3	9
500,000 to 1,000,000	6	34,032	6	47,534	6	8
250,000 to 499,999	14	30,087	14	43,204	13	10
100,000 to 249,999	66	31,392	65	42,904	54	8
50,000 to 99,999	154	32,211	154	43,314	125	7
25,000 to 49,999	325	30,522	319	41,667	265	7
10,000 to 24,999	706	27,639	689	37,870	545	6
GEOGRAPHIC DIVISION						
New England	91	30,721	89	38,233	80	5
Mid-Atlantic	150	30,745	147	48,850	137	5
East North Central	267	30,588	267	40,690	242	6
West North Central	129	27,293	128	36,994	102	7
South Atlantic	169	24,475	163	35,655	87	10
East South Central	68	22,256	68	30,128	48	10
West South Central	148	24,400	138	32,612	99	7
Mountain	76	27,870	76	39,301	55	9
Pacific Coast	176	38,163	174	48,002	161	5
METRO STATUS						
Central	242	28,890	237	39,347	200	8
Suburban	727	31,121	718	43,164	595	6
Independent	305	24,835	295	32,428	216	7

Source: Evelina R. Moulder, "Police and Fire Personnel, Salaries, and Expenditures for 1998," in *The Municipal Year Book 1999*. Washington, DC: International City/County Management Association, 1999, p. 124, Table 3/6.

the Metro Nashville Police Department required applicants to have earned at least 60 units of college credit. One percent of local departments demand four-year college degrees of their officers (Reaves, 1996). Although specific height and weight requirements have been eliminated (in part because of more female recruits), departments typically stipulate that weight must be proportionate to height. Apart from being a U.S. citizen, some departments have a residency requirement as a condition of employment. To become a Philadelphia police officer, an individual must be a resident of that city for one year "immediately prior to appointment" ("Philadelphia Police Recruitment," 1999). Residency requirements in other departments are less stringent, stipulating that an officer reside in the county of employment or one of several adjoining counties.

The application and selection process in big-city departments is similar to that of the San Diego Police Department ("Testing and Selection Process," 1999). The following sections describe the requirements.

Written Examination. Applicants must pass a general aptitude test based on the skills considered necessary to be a competent police officer. This test may measure observation and decision-making skills, map reading and directional orientation, reading comprehension, as well as report writing and written communication. Many departments now use videos as part of their observation and memory testing procedures. Individuals who fail these tests can usually take them again after a designated waiting period (often 6 months).

Personal History Statement. On successful completion of the written examination, applicants must provide a lengthy personal history statement for the Background Investigation Unit.

Physical Ability Test. Physical ability tests are designed to measure general physical fitness and/or the bodily attributes thought to be essential for patrol work. Some departments have structured these tests so that they are both age and gender specific. For example, the Phoenix Police Department requires male applicants between 20 and 29 years of age to minimally bench press .99 percent of their body weight, whereas 30- to 39-year-old recruits must bench press .88 percent of their body weight. Comparable numbers for female applicants are .59 and .53 percent ("Police Officer Recruitment," 2001). The San Diego Police Department has a 500-yard obstacle course that measures a number of physical abilities that might be needed when pursuing a fleeing suspect. These include climbing ladders and stairs, jumping, dodging low-hanging objects, and climbing over 3-, 4-, and 6-foot fences. The Denver Police Department also has a pursuit simulation physical abilities test, as shown in Figure 7.1.

Investigation. Applicants are asked to authorize individuals and organizations to release pertinent information to police investigators. In addition to positive attributes, such as good work records and the ability to get along with others, investigating officers are looking for factors that may be problematic, including past criminal involvement and behavioral difficulties. In some departments, the use and/or possession of any illegal drugs in the previous 6 months will lead to disqualification, whereas other departments extend this period to 1 year. Drug use prior to a department's designated time period is likely to be evaluated on a case-by-case basis. About one-third of departments test applicants for drug use (Walker, 1999). Excessive past or current alcohol use is typically subject to a case-by-case review. A felony conviction or a pattern of misdemeanor convictions or traffic violations will lead to disqualification in almost all departments. At this stage in the application process, potential recruits may have an in-depth interview with an investigator.

Polygraph Examination. The truthfulness of an applicant's responses may be tested using a polygraph (lie detector). Examiners ask questions regarding prior employment, alcohol and drug use, gambling habits, driving record, and possible criminal activities.

figure 7.1

Denver Civil Service Physical Ability Test

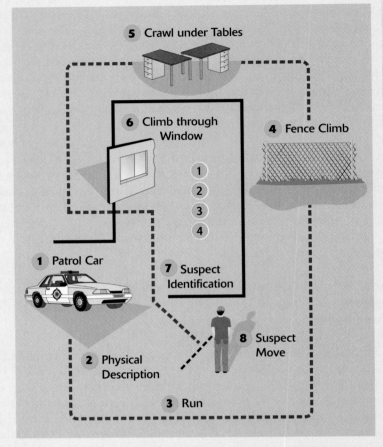

1 To begin the test, the candidate will sit in the driver's seat of a patrol car with the doors closed and await further instructions.

2 A test monitor will give the candidate verbal instructions to pursue a fleeing felony suspect (fictitious) by providing a description of what the suspect is wearing (for example, a baseball hat and a red T-shirt). The test monitor will provide two pieces of descriptive information. Finally, the test monitor will tell the candidate to "GO." The applicant must then complete the following physical tasks.

3 The candidate must get out of the car and run a distance of about 130 yards. Timing begins when the candidate opens the car door.

4 At some point approximately midway through the course, the candidate will encounter and **climb over an approximately 6 foot chain link fence.**

5 On the other side of the fence, the candidate will **crawl under two standard-size office tables.**

6 After crawling under the tables, the applicant must run to and **climb through an approximately 30 inch by 30 inch opening** with the bottom of the opening located approximately 50 inches from the ground.

7 After climbing through the opening, the applicant must identify the proper suspect from four targets, each numbered and dressed differently.

8 The candidate will then **move a dummy weighing approximately 150 pounds** to a designated line 5 feet away. Timing of the events stops when the entire dummy passes over the line.

A candidate who is able to complete the entire series of events successfully, in proper sequence, within 63 seconds passes the test. Note the sample map illustrating the entire test sequence.

Source: Reprinted by permission of the City of Denver, Denver, Colorado.

Hiring Interview. The hiring interview is conducted by one or more (typically the latter) officers to determine whether the individual is ready to enter the academy and begin a career as a police officer.

Psychological Examination. A clinical psychologist interviews candidates to determine their overall psychological fitness for police work. Individuals are likely to be asked a wide variety of questions such as "Why do you want to be a police officer?" "What are your greatest strengths?" "Weaknesses?" "What could make you lose your temper?" "How do you deal with panic?" "Your own?" "That of others?" "Are you afraid of dying?" "What would you do with the rest of your life if your legs were crippled in an injury?" (O'Neill et al., 1999, pp. 49–50). Many departments also use pencil-and-paper standardized personality inventories that contain 100 or more questions.

Medical Examination. A major component of the medical exam is to determine whether an applicant has vision problems that are not correctable that would impair him or her from doing police work.

Samuel Walker (1999) notes that, although departmental selection procedures are adequate for screening *out* individuals "clearly unqualified" for police work, they are not very good at screening *in* those men and women most likely to make good police officers. People who score well on written examinations may have limited social skills and be unable to work effectively with others. Whereas psychological tests and interviews may eliminate candidates with severe emotional problems, they do not necessarily identify people who can exercise sound judgement under pressure (Walker, 1999).

A strong economy coupled with a growing number of police officers (a 9 percent increase from 1992 to 1996) has made recruitment difficult in many parts of the country. A spokesperson for the King County Sheriff's Department in Washington noted that, whereas his department typically received 1,200 to 1,600 applicants for every test, in recent years that number has dropped to 400 (Salkever, 1998). Even a large pool of applicants is no guarantee that a department will meet its need for new personnel. In May 1999, the city of Detroit had 1,200 applicants for the police academy ("Cop Out: The Thinning Blue Line," 1999). Of that number

- 4 were not U.S. citizens
- 13 had outstanding arrest warrants for offenses ranging from traffic violations to felonies
- 211 had been convicted of felonies or misdemeanors that disqualified them from police work
- 126 were ineligible for a variety of reasons
- 66 were disqualified because of poor work records or admitted drug use
- 126 failed the written exam or the physical agility test
- 326 did not show up for examinations
- 287 or 24 percent of the original 1,200 were qualified

The recruiting situation is much the same in Los Angeles where between 1,200 and 1,500 applicants are needed to fill a class of 80 at the police academy. Applications for

This police officer is standing next to a bus adorned with a recruiting message. Some police departments in large cities are finding it increasingly difficult to attract and retain qualified individuals for careers in law enforcement.

the New York City Police Department declined from more than 20,000 annually in the mid-1990s to just more than 10,000 in 1999, and the department was unable to fill a 2000 police academy class for the first time in recent history (Flynn, 1999; Flynn, 2000b). In an effort to hire new officers, some departments seem to have informally lowered their standards and/or become sloppy conducting background investigations. The Chicago police force discovered it had gang members on the force, and the Miami Police Department found that some academy graduates had felony drug convictions (Greengard, 1996).

From the Academy to the Street

For at least the first 75 years of policing in this country, officers rarely received any pre-service training. New patrol officers were given badges and batons and sent out to do police work (Walker, 1999). Today, virtually all police officers receive some formal training, typically at a police academy. The length of training is highly correlated with the size of the population the department serves (see Figure 7.2). Whereas departments in small towns average about 375 hours of training (or slightly more than ten 40-hour weeks), recruits in cities of more than 250,000 can expect to receive approximately 1,200 hours of formal instruction (or thirty 40-hour weeks). A significant majority of cities with a quarter of a million inhabitants or more operate training academies, but only 10 percent of cities with 50,000 or fewer residents have such facilities (Reaves, 1996).

Victor Kappeler and his colleagues (1998) have criticized the content of this training. They note that relatively little time is spent on subjects such as constitutional law, civil rights, and ethical considerations regarding the enforcement of laws, whereas "differential importance" is given to weapons training, patrol procedures, and the use of force in restraining and arresting people (see Table 7.2). The latter three areas of instruction are also given greater emphasis in scoring the performance of police recruits. These researchers concluded that "much of the material provided to new police officers serves to reinforce the existing police view of the world rather than to educate police recruits . . . " (p. 82). Police scholar Samuel Walker (1999) notes that many academy curriculums still ignore important subjects such as **discretion** and the use of informants.

Police Lieutenant Michael Birzer (1999) argues that, as the community-oriented policing philosophy gains momentum, the academy curriculum will have to change.

discretion having the ability or power to decide on a course of action without having one's decision questioned or overruled by others

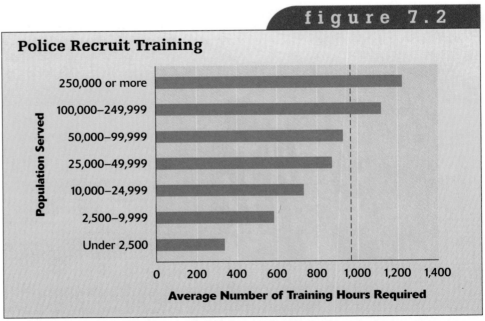

figure 7.2

Police Recruit Training

Source: Reaves, Brian A. April 1996. *Local Police Departments 1993*. Washington, DC: U.S. Department of Justice, Office of Justice Statistics.

table 7.2	Typical Law Enforcement Basic Training Program	
TOPIC	**PERCENTAGE OF TIME**	**WEIGHT**
Administration	6.13	(—)
Introduction to law enforcement	5.00	1.00
Firearms (skills development)	14.10	2.00
Vehicle operation (pursuit driving)	6.40	1.00
First aid/CPR	4.00	.50
Accident investigation	3.80	.50
Criminal law (statutes)	13.80	1.00
Patrol procedures (crime detection)	12.50	2.00
Criminal investigation	4.80	.50
Specific investigations (street crime)	7.80	1.00
Arrest and restraint/physical fitness	16.90	2.00
Practical performance exercises	4.75	1.00

Source: Adapted from Kappeler, V. E., R. D. Sluder, and G. P. Alpert. 1998. *Forces of Deviance—Understanding the Dark Side of Policing* (p. 93). Prospect Heights, IL: Waveland Press. Reprinted by permission of Waveland Press, Inc. All rights reserved.

For example, as officers increasingly become "proactive problem solvers" more time will have to be spent teaching them conflict resolution skills and less attention will be focused on the mechanical and technical aspects of the job. Birzer (1999) believes that this new training should also continue after recruits leave the academy. Just as most departments mandate that officers regularly qualify with firearms, they should also schedule training for communication skills on a systematic basis. The way officers interact with citizens often determines how a situation is resolved (with or without the use of force, for example).

To better understand how individuals become police officers (including socialization into the police culture), sociologist John Van Maanen (1973) spent 3 months as a "fully participating member" of a training academy in a big-city department. Afterward, as a civilian, he rode in a patrol car with officers 8 to 10 hours a day, 6 days a week for 4 months. Van Maanen concluded that the academy was characterized by absolute obedience to departmental rules, dull lectures devoted to various technical aspects of police work, rigorous physical training, and "ritualistic concern" for detail.

Along with formal training that may be considered rites of passage, recruits were exposed to many hours of "war stories" by veteran officers who served as instructors. These stories dealt with past events (especially the shooting of police officers), places, and local personalities as well as an informal history of the department. As opposed to regular lectures that were presented in a highly structured environment, war stories unfolded in a relaxed atmosphere of comraderie. Van Maanen (1973) notes that relating these experiences in an informal manner serves the important function of establishing both "congeniality and solidarity" with veteran officers in what is typically a "harsh and uncomfortable environment." Outside the classroom, recruits spent considerable time discussing various aspects and nuances of war stories. These stories help recruits to begin to fully understand and internalize the emotional reality of police work.

Police recruits also learn that when the department (at this point in their careers, academy instructors) notices their behavior it is usually to punish and not to praise them. Recruits learn to avoid punishment by staying low and keeping out of trouble, a strategy that many officers will carry with them throughout their careers. Another consequence of being punished much more than being praised is that officers learn to identify with each other rather than with the larger department. As we will see in Chapter 8, this loyalty first and foremost to one's comrades influences police deviance.

On graduating from the academy, the new officer is assigned (in the majority of departments) to a field training officer (FTO) for a designated period of time. As a form of apprenticeship, the time spent with an FTO can be considered the second phase of training. It is not uncommon for FTOs to have little regard for academy training, referring to this instruction as nothing more than an ordeal that all police officers must endure. An FTO told Van Maanen (p. 412) on his first day of patrol:

> I hope the academy didn't get to you. It's something we all have to go through. A bunch of bullshit as far as I can tell. . . . Since you got through it all right, you get to find out what it's like out here. You'll find out mighty fast that it ain't nothing like they told you at the academy.

The first few weeks on patrol are difficult for a rookie officer, and he or she is unlikely to do anything without clearing a proposed course of action with an FTO. While the newcomer is learning to be a cop, the FTO is evaluating the rookie officer's behavior. FTOs may withhold final judgment on a new officer until they see how he or she responds (in the jargon of the department Van Maanen observed) to a "heavy" call or a "hot one"—calls of a crime in progress or to an officer that needs assistance. A police sergeant told Van Maanen (p. 413), "You've got to be tough on this job and situations like these separate the men from the boys. I know I'd never trust my partner until I'd seen him on a hot one." Because these calls are relatively rare, training officers may deliberately place rookies in difficult situations. One FTO had his junior partner check identifications, make cursory body searches, and even eject customers from bars in one of the tougher sections of town. New officers were also evaluated regarding how fast they got out of the patrol car, their hesitation (if any) when approaching a suspicious person, and their willingness to lead the way while pursuing a suspect up a darkened stairwell (Van Maanen, 1973).

Depending on department policy, new officers are on probationary status after they leave the academy for 6 months to 2 years. During this period, an officer may be dismissed without cause at any time.

Doing Police Work

The Police and Crime

In a chapter entitled "The Myth of the Police," David H. Bayley (1994, p. 3), one of the foremost authorities on the police in the United States, notes that "The police do not prevent crime. This is one of the best kept secrets of modern life. Experts know it, the police know it, but the public does not know it." Although such an assertion may seem brash and unfounded to many, Bayley presents a good deal of evidence to bolster his claim. First, numerous studies have failed to show any relation between the number of police officers in a given locale and the crime rate in that venue. For example, in 1995, there were 3.1 full-time law enforcement officers per 1,000 population in cities of more than 250,000 and 1.9 officers per 1,000 residents in cities between 10,000 and 24,999 population. However, the larger urban centers had a significantly higher crime rate (especially violent crime) than did the smaller cities (Uniform Crime Report, 1995). Bayley notes that, at some point, increasing the number of police in a given area would result in a reduced crime rate. A police officer "on every corner and on every doorstep" would probably make a difference; that is, there is some threshold beyond which an additional number of law enforcement personnel would deter a significant amount of criminal behavior. However, this "magic number" is unknown, and, even if it could be discerned, the cost of training and employing so many additional officers would probably be prohibitive.

Second, a good deal of research indicates that the number of officers in a given area at a particular time has virtually no impact on crime rates, victimization rates, or the public's satisfaction with local police. In numerous experiments, the number of patrol officers in neighborhoods has been doubled, reduced by 50 percent, or officers have been removed completely without changing crime rates. While "saturation patrolling" or inundating a precinct with uniformed officers does depress the crime rate, "it is too expensive to be more than a short term expedient" (Bayley, 1994, p. 5).

Finally, no evidence proves that decreasing the time it takes police to report to a crime scene will increase the chances of apprehending an offender. Unless police arrive at the locale within 1 minute (which is both highly unlikely and an impossible standard to hold police to) they will usually not make an arrest. Otherwise their chances of taking a suspect into custody are probably less than 1 in 10 (Bayley, 1994). Although the preceding information may appear to be a sharp indictment of police and police practices, it is not Bayley's intent (nor ours) to chastise the law enforcement community for failing to effectively control (much less solve) the crime problem in this country. Blaming the police for a society's penchant for criminal behavior makes about as much sense as holding physicians responsible for escalating rates of lung cancer. As Bayley (1994, p. 10) notes, "Police shouldn't be expected to prevent crime. They are outgunned by circumstances." In other words, crime is a product of conditions well beyond the scope of police resources and authority. As we saw in Chapter 3, crime is primarily a consequence of the distribution of income and wealth, and poverty and unemployment; the racial and ethnic composition of an area; family structure, age, and gender; and a host of more subtle psychological, sociocultural, and economic variables.

For Bayley (1994), police in modern industrial states perform two major functions: *authoritative intervention* and *symbolic justice*. The responsibility of patrol and traffic officers, authoritative intervention is an almost completely reactive attempt to restore order resulting from disruptive behavior such as public drunkenness, automobile crashes, barroom brawls, and full-scale riots. An important point here is that virtually no attempt is made to rectify the conditions that resulted in a breakdown of order and the need for police intervention. Also a primarily reactive mode, symbolic justice is the job of detectives and traffic officers. Through their work, these officers demonstrate to offenders and

These mounted police officers wait for a traffic light to change on a busy city street in Atlanta, Georgia. Some evidence indicates that police on horseback create an increased number of positive encounters with citizens; people approach mounted officers to pet the animal, which often leads to conversations with the officers.

the general public that "a regime of law exists." As we see in our review of detectives and criminal investigation, the success police have in rendering symbolic justice depends almost completely on the information they receive from the public.

One last point worth noting is that police spend little time and few monetary resources on anticipating and, therefore, trying to prevent the crimes that people are most fearful of—murder, robbery, rape, and assault. These transgressions are ignored by law enforcement until they occur (Bayley, 1994) primarily because they are difficult to predict, and, therefore, prevent.

On Patrol

On virtually every police force, patrol officers comprise the majority of departmental personnel (see Table 7.3). Officers on patrol are sometimes referred to as "peacekeepers," an accurate description, especially in big-city departments. No more than 30 percent of all calls for service are about crime, and even that figure may be much too high. Responding officers often find that the reported law-violating incident was not a crime. For example, lonely senior citizens report nonexistent burglaries simply so they can talk to someone for a few minutes (Bayley, 1994; Mastrofski, 1983; Walker, 1999). David Bayley (1994) estimates that the real proportion of crime-related calls for police assistance is no more than 7 to 10 percent, with the vast majority of these requests related to property offenses.

Patrol officers are the first public servants to be summoned when the relative harmony and order of everyday life has been disrupted and must be restored. As peacekeepers, patrol officers routinely deal with rowdy teenagers who may be harassing people at a shopping center, neighbors arguing loudly over a petty dispute, a dog barking nonstop in the middle of the night, homeless people panhandling too aggressively, a drunk pedestrian wandering mindlessly across a busy street, an apartment dweller playing a stereo at an earsplitting level, and an individual who is mentally impaired threatening passersby with a knife (Bayley, 1994). The most common as well as the most difficult situations patrol officers must deal with on a regular basis are those involving family disputes. On arriving at a domestic dispute, police must determine whether a crime has been committed, who is the offender, and who is the victim. The answers to these questions are not always apparent and may not be readily determined by questioning individuals who will relate an incident to officers that puts them in the best light. A major difficulty police have in their role as peacekeepers is that people regularly and brashly lie to them. This is a major reason why officers "become cynical and hard to convince" (Bayley, 1994 p. 20).

table 7.3	Division of Labor in Select Number of U.S. Police Departments
ASSIGNMENT	**PERCENTAGE OF OFFICERS**
Patrol	65
Criminal investigation	15
Traffic	7
Administration	7
Operational support and crime prevention	7

Source: Adapted from Bayley, David H. 1994. "What Do the Police Do?" Chapter 2, pages 15–35, in *Police for the Future*. New York: Oxford University Press.

John Van Maanen (1999a, p. 348) suggests that police view their "occupational world" (those people they come into contact with on a regular basis) as comprised of three types of citizens: (1) "Suspicious Persons" are people whom police believe may have committed a serious offense. Because of their possible criminal involvement, these individuals are treated in a "brisk" yet "thoroughly professional manner." (2) "Assholes" are people whom police treat harshly because these suspects fail to accept (and meet) officers' expectations based on the "interaction situation itself" as opposed to anything they might have done in the past. In other words, these individuals are (or are perceived to be) disrespectful, difficult, and/or confrontational. Assholes are prime candidates for "street justice" (this topic is discussed in detail in Chapter 8), physical attacks aimed at teaching an individual a lesson, at rectifying an insulting behavior. Because they engage in stupid, senseless behavior, assholes "are not granted status as worthy human beings" (p. 349). (3) "Know Nothings" are average citizens whose only encounters with police are as requests for assistance. They are so labeled because as civilians they cannot know (according to officers) what the police and police work is all about. Van Maanen is careful to point out that he is not suggesting that a "general moral order is shared by all policemen" (p. 349). Rather, certain situational conditions "predispose policemen toward certain perceptions of people" (pp. 349–350), resulting in three categories.

Using Van Maanen's typology, one important aspect of a patrol officer's peacekeeping/order maintenance role is to make sure persons in category 2 (assholes) are held in check. As one veteran officer stated (p. 346):

> I guess what our job really boils down to is not letting the assholes take over the city. Now I'm not talking about your regular crooks . . . they're bound to wind up in the joint anyway. What I'm talking about are those shitheads out to prove they can push everybody around. Those are the assholes we gotta deal with and take care of on patrol. . . . They're the ones that make it tough on the decent people out there. You take the majority of what we do and it's nothing more than asshole control.

Patrol officers are society's frontline troops when it comes to maintaining and restoring order and are summoned when people believe no one else can help them. These calls for help, as Bayley's (1994) examples demonstrate, range from the silly and absurd to the poignant and tragic. A man stops a patrol car and asks officers if they have needle-nosed pliers to fix the zipper on his pants. A woman brings her parakeet to the

These heavily armed police officers are preparing to enter a home suspected of being a drug distribution center. The militarization of the police has been one of the more controversial developments in contemporary law enforcement.

station house to be weighed because she thinks it is ill. An invalid falls out of bed and calls for assistance. A man wants the police to notify his sister (who does not have a phone) that their brother has died.

Many police officers think that it is impossible for the average citizen to understand and appreciate what they do. Although this perception may well be exaggerated, it is certainly true that very few nonpolice individuals are called on to perform what patrol officers routinely experience during their careers on the street. As one young patrol officer stated (in Van Maanen, 1999b, p. 221):

> I'll tell ya, as long as we're the only sonofabitches that have to handle ripe bodies that have been dead for nine days in a ninety degree room or handle skid row drunks who've been crapping in their pants for 24 hours or try to stop some prick from jump'en off the Liberty Bridge or have to grease some societal misfit who's trying to blow your goddam head off, then we'll never be like anyone else . . . as far as I can see, no one is ever gonna want to do that shit. But somebody's got to do it and I guess it'll always be the police. But hell, this is the only profession where ya gotta wash your hands before you take a piss!

A significant amount of a big-city patrol officer's time and energy is spent dealing with individuals who are typically seen by middle-class America only on the evening news: the chronically poor, the unemployed, the homeless, impoverished mentally ill people, teenage runaways, and hardcore substance users. Both "victims and victimizers," these are "life's refugees" (Bayley, 1994), those expendable people in a modern society who have fallen through the organizational cracks and are now little more than "police property." Urban patrol officers deal with these individuals for the simple reason that in many instances no other agency will.

Patrol officers spend approximately 40 percent of their time "in-service" handling calls and 60 percent of their shift "out-of-service" available for the next call. Walker (1999) notes that tremendous variation occurs among cities, precincts, and shifts regarding in- and out-of-service time. Within the same city some patrol assignments are very busy, whereas other officers spend much of their shift cruising in the squad car.

The boredom that is occasionally part of every patrol officer's workday may be punctuated at any moment by one of the approximately 100,000 high-speed pursuits that occur annually in the United States (Greenhouse, 1998; Sharkey, 1997). Although this figure is based on official records, the actual number may be much higher because an unknown number of chases of short duration are not recorded by police (Walker, 1999). About 300 people a year are killed in high-speed pursuits, thousands more are injured, up to a third of whom are innocent bystanders (Milner, 1999).

Approximately 75 percent of pursuits are triggered by traffic offenses, and according to one informed estimate, less than 5 percent of high-speed chases involve suspects wanted for violent crimes (Manak in Sharkey, 1997). Research indicates that younger male officers are more likely to take part in high-speed chases than older and female colleagues, and women are less likely than males to engage in this behavior. Law professor and former police officer James Ginger (Sharkey, 1997) argues that pursuing fleeing cars is embedded in the police culture. Officers are likely to think in terms of "Here's a bad guy and it's my job to catch him" (p. B3). Whereas police may or may not have adequate training in high-speed driving techniques, depending on departmental priorities and resources, they typically have little if any instruction on whether to begin or intensify a high-speed pursuit (Sharkey, 1997).

In a 9 to 0 decision (*County of Sacramento v. Lewis*) the Supreme Court ruled that high-speed chases resulting in injury or death do not violate the Constitution unless an officer deliberately acted with a "purpose to cause harm" (Greenhouse, 1998, p. A1). One of the justices noted, "The Constitution does not guarantee due care on the part of state officials" (p. A1). This ruling established that it is all but impossible to successfully sue an officer or police department for damages resulting from a high-speed pursuit–related accident. Commenting on this decision, criminologist Geoffrey Alpert (in Yi, 1998, p. B3), who has studied this form of police behavior extensively, noted, "You will see a lot more pursuits, injuries, and deaths." One such death occurred when a San

Diego squad car rammed into an oncoming vehicle and killed a 32-year-old woman and mother of a 4-year-old girl. The officer was described as being very distraught as he replayed the incident over and over in his mind (Thornton, 1999).

The number of high-speed chases officers are involved in is directly related to departmental policies regarding this action. For example, as a result of revamped guidelines, both the Los Angeles and Orange County (California) sheriffs' departments have witnessed declines in high-speed pursuits and chase-related deaths and injuries. Between 1996 and 1998, Alpert (in Yi, 1998) found that almost half of the police departments surveyed had modified their pursuit policies, with 9 of 10 of these organizations restricting conditions under which police could chase a vehicle. Many of these reforms include engaging in hot pursuit only if the occupants of the pursued vehicle are thought to be felony suspects.

High speed chases that turn into accidents can also result in high monetary losses for cities and counties. San Diego officials approved a $1.95 million settlement with the family of the victims of the squad car crash (Chacon, 2002). In the last six months of 2001, the city of Los Angeles paid out $1.32 million in liability claims from police pursuits that resulted in injury and death (Blankstein, 2002).

Criminal Investigation and Undercover Work

On determination that a crime has occurred, plainclothes detectives may be called in to analyze the situation. These officers talk to victims, witnesses, and suspects to determine what happened and to decide whether an investigation should be pursued. The decision on whether to extend their inquiry depends on two factors: (1) Has a "credible perpetrator" been "fairly clearly" identified? and (2) is the crime serious enough to attract public attention?

The key factor in solving crimes is whether information passed on to police by victims and witnesses will help identify a suspect. Because they are significantly outnumbered, detectives are not inclined to investigate an offense if a suspect has not been identified. This means that very few burglaries and only a limited number of robberies will be seriously pursued by detectives (Bayley, 1994). A citizen's request (or demand) that police "dust" a crime scene for a burglar's fingerprints is likely to be met with controlled anger or muted laughter depending on how busy officers are at the time. Generally speaking, if a case is not solved quickly, it is dropped. "Cold cases" are not likely to be reopened because the chances of identifying a suspect—the major factor in solving a crime—diminish as time passes (Bayley, 1994).

The gap between what detectives actually do and how citizens and politicians expect these officers to act is often significant. In 1999, San Diego police chief Dave Bejarano stated publicly that officers would investigate burglaries only when there is a known suspect, a compelling lead, or extensive evidence. (Many people believe that this had been the department's policy all along.) The mayor responded to the chief's proclamation, "As a citizen of this community I want to know if I'm burglarized, somebody's going to investigate" (Golding in Thornton and Huard, 1999, p. AI). The mayor's comments notwithstanding, the reality of criminal investigation given departmental time and resource constraints was accurately conveyed by San Diego detective Greg Myers (in Rowe, 1999, p. E1): "People get the idea from watching TV or whatever that officers and detectives are sitting around, waiting for the phone to ring and then they and the lab spring into action. But you are constantly in a juggling act, prioritizing." Criminal investigation could well be characterized as "paperwork intensive." For every hour detectives spend talking to people and looking for evidence, they spend 30 minutes on paperwork (Bayley, 1994).

Another inaccurate perception the public has about detective work involves the role of physical evidence in solving crimes. Mystery stories are replete with examples of criminal investigators painstakingly searching a crime scene and eventually finding clues that lead to the perpetrator's identity and eventual arrest. However, physical evidence gathered at a real-life crime scene is seldom used in the apprehension of a suspect. Rather, this evidence is used as confirmation or supporting testimony once an

offender has been identified. As Bayley (1994, p. 27) notes, detectives "begin with an identification, then collect evidence; they rarely collect evidence and then make an identification." Although television programs such as *CSI* (Crime Scene Investigation) and *CSI Miami* make for interesting television drama, a significant number of cases (some would argue a majority of cases) are solved by nothing more than chance. In the aftermath of the Washington, D.C. area serial sniper killings in October, 2002—one of the most intensive criminal manhunts in U.S. history—Montgomery County Maryland Police Chief Charles A. Moose stated, "As a police chief I know you need a lot of luck. I'd like to say it's all skill, moxie, and brains. But it's mostly luck" ("Quote of the Day," 2002, p. A1).

Criminal investigation can be viewed as an ongoing search for information—information that will lead to the identification of a suspect and/or evidence to convict that individual. No matter how dedicated, skillful, and hard working detectives may be, they often depend on knowledge about crimes that can only be provided by informants. This is especially true in policing drug offenses and drug-related crimes. The police–informant relationship is best understood in terms of a bargain with both parties having something to gain. The price for gaining the cooperation of informants involved in illegal activities (which is often the case) may well be turning a blind eye toward this behavior (Marx, 1985). In his study of a big-city police department, Jerome Skolnick (1994) found that it was "not uncommon" for bartenders to be fences (individuals who buy and sell stolen merchandise). Police would overlook this criminal activity in exchange for information that led to the arrest of addicts.

Skolnick (1994) notes, however, that it would be foolish to believe that criminal informants have a license to break the law as long as they are providing useful information. He observed that narcotics detectives did not hesitate to arrest a prostitute or addict informer if they had good evidence against that person.

> This arrest then becomes an added value to the officer's bargaining position. The officer might offer to recommend a fine in return for that prostitute's cooperation in making a narcotics purchase. The good arrest, however, provides the police officer with a commodity to exchange for this type of service. To assert that police ignore the infractions of persons who have acted as informers in order to maintain their "good will" is to overlook that informers have no specific affection for police and are themselves often coercively persuaded to play their roles by threat of legal sanction. (p. 121)

Although money can and does buy information from law violators, this incentive is limited to available funds. Skolnick (1994) argues that the reduction of a jail or prison sentence is usually superior in the purchase of "more and better information" than cash payments. This is accomplished by way of the number of charges brought against an individual. He suggests that charge reduction is the "primary coin" in the world of informers (p. 122).

Being a police informer can be dangerous. After his arrest for possession of half an ounce of methamphetamines in 1998, a 17-year-old California youth agreed to cooperate with local authorities in their ongoing drug investigations (the boy's mother signed a waiver authorizing this role). The young informant made a drug buy while wearing a "wire" (recording device) but was soon kicked out of the informant program after his second arrest for drug violations. Less than two weeks later the youth was robbed and killed in a local drug house. His girlfriend was raped, shot in the head, and abandoned. The three men convicted of these crimes stated that they knew one of their victims was an informant and killed him in retaliation for working with the police (Pfeifer, 2002).

One of the more interesting and controversial aspects of criminal investigation concerns the use of deception by police. Criminologist and attorney Jerome Skolnick (1985, p. 75) asks the question: "To what extent, if at all, is it proper for law enforcement officials to employ trickery and deceit as part of their law enforcement practices?" In some situations, the answer is rather straightforward because deception or outright lying to offenders may be the only way to resolve a situation. Deceiving kidnappers, terrorists, and known rapists to save the lives of innocent people presents few, if any, moral dilemmas. However, other instances of police deception are not as clear-cut, either morally or legally. Consider the following cases presented by Gary Marx (1985, pp. 103, 105):

Rommie Loudd, the first black executive with a professional sports team, organized the Orlando, Florida, franchise in the World Football League. With the failure of the WFL, Loudd went broke. A man whom he did not know called and offered him one million dollars to reorganize his team. The caller promised to bring wealthy colleagues into the deal, and instructed Loudd initially to loosen up the financiers with cocaine. Loudd resisted the offer but eventually introduced the caller (an undercover agent) to two people who sold him cocaine. Loudd, with no previous criminal record, was sentenced to a long prison term. On tape, the agent involved said to his partner, "I've tricked him worse than I've tricked anybody before."

Former Assistant U.S. Attorney Donald Robinson was accused of taking money for information from persons he thought were organized crime figures, but who were actually police. Robinson at first ignored their approaches, but became involved only after persistent phone calls, a threatening call to his wife, and a warning that he might turn up missing.

Marx (among others) has been critical of the type of police undercover work that fails to make a distinction between trying to determine whether a suspect *is* breaking the law and those undercover operations undertaken to see if a person *can be induced* to engage in criminal behavior (1985). In other words, Marx is critical of police "entrapping" citizens. The entrapment defense has been successfully used by defendants as it was in the case of the U.S. attorney in the preceding example. This defense strategy requires the accused to demonstrate that, if it were not for objectionable and contrived police conduct, he or she would not have committed the crime (Gifis, 1996).

In recent years, undercover police activity has increased not only in the areas of white-collar and political corruption but also in combating street crime as well. Examples of the latter include policewomen posing as prostitutes and undercover officers offering to buy and sell drugs and stolen goods (Marx, 1985).

Undercover work (especially for prolonged periods) can be hazardous to an officer's mental and physical well-being. For an undercover cop to pass for and be accepted as a criminal, he or she has to think and act like a habitual offender. The work is stressful because the individual is always on stage and must perform accordingly. As the officer develops relationships with those he or she is investigating, feelings of ambivalence and guilt may ensue at the thought of eventually betraying their trust. Undercover officers may even become consumers and/or suppliers of the illegality they are attempting to control (Marx, 1985).

Marx (1985) relates the story of a "deep cover" operation wherein an officer rode with the Hell's Angels for 18 months. The officer was responsible for the arrest of numerous people, including previously high-level untouchable drug dealers, and was highly praised for doing a "magnificent job." The cost, however, of doing outstanding police work was heavy drug use, alcoholism, the breakup of his family, and the inability to readjust to everyday police work. The officer eventually resigned, committed several bank robberies, and ended up in prison.

Deception may also occur when a suspect is questioned. Most interrogations are simple, straightforward procedures; detectives confront the suspect with the evidence they have marshaled and the individual confesses. However, in those cases in which a suspect does not confess, detectives may resort to deception or, more accurately, outright lying. For example, investigators may tell a suspect that her or his fingerprints were found at a crime scene, that a witness has positively identified her or him, and/or that she or he has failed a lie detector test (Wilkens and Sauer, 1999). Police typically defend the practice of deceiving suspects in several ways: (1) In the end justifies the means argument, if detectives cannot bend the truth on occasion, many guilty people will never confess; (2) because of liberal court rulings, such as the *Miranda* decision, police already have one hand tied behind their backs—lying to suspects during an interrogation is one way of evening the score; it gives the police a fighting chance of bringing the guilty to justice; and (3) using the "It's all part of the game" interpretation, as one detective put it; "Yes, you can lie to a person in an interrogation—they lie to you."

One problem with police deceiving suspects is that this practice can result in false confessions—innocent people may confess to crimes they have not committed. As ACLU attorney Jordan Budd (in Dolbee, 1999) noted, some people "become disoriented, they lose their sense of what happened and what didn't happen. And more than anything else, there is just this incredible desire to get this over with." Innocent people who are in awe of the police may well come to doubt their own minds, eventually coming to believe that "If the police said I committed this crime, then I probably did." Social psychologist Richard Ofshe, an expert on false confessions, notes that these admissions of guilt rank third behind perjury and eyewitness error as the cause of wrongful homicide convictions in the United States (Jerome, 1995). Note that police officers do not knowingly and willfully try to gain confessions from people they believe are innocent. Rather, detectives in their zeal to solve a crime along with a sincere belief that the suspect is factually guilty may unwittingly coerce innocent suspects into making false confessions (Jerome, 1995).

In southern California, a 12-year-old girl was brutally stabbed in her bedroom during the night. Because her 14-year-old brother appeared to detectives to be unaffected by the tragedy, and, according to the boy's story, because he walked by his sister's room 2 hours before the body was found without noticing anything, the youth became a primary suspect. Following are excerpts from the interrogation (Wilkens and Sauer, 1999, p. A1):

> **Detective:** We found blood in your room already.
>
> **Suspect:** God, where did you find it?
>
> **Detective:** I'm sure you know. It's easy to make mistakes in the dark. [No blood was found in the suspect's room. The detective would say later that he thought he saw blood.]

At another point in the interrogation:

> **Detective:** We can prove that nobody came into the house. So we know that the person who did this was inside the house.

The detective told the suspect that all the doors and windows were locked, and that the house showed no signs of entry. This was a lie. The sliding glass door from the master bedroom to the backyard was unlocked.

In a portion of the interrogation that was not videotaped, the suspect stated that a detective told him that his parents believed that he was the killer and they never wanted to see him again. Later, under oath, the detective stated that he "may have" said this to the suspect, but that he doubted he would ever tell an individual that his or her parents never wanted to see him or her again. The victim's blood was eventually found on the shirt of a local transient (evidence that was missed when this individual was questioned and his clothing examined shortly after the murder), and the case against the boy was dismissed.

Although deception can be an effective strategy for obtaining confessions, this policy may well come at the expense of some public trust and support of the police. After details of the murder case just discussed were published in the newspaper, one woman stated: "Yes, find the murderer and bring him/her to justice—but not like this. Reading those articles has shaken my faith in both justice and the police, and I for one, will never believe anything they say again" (in Dolbee, 1999, p. E1).

Traffic Enforcement

Departments with 200 or more officers typically assign about 7 percent of their personnel to traffic units. These individuals enforce traffic laws, control the flow of traffic on major thoroughfares, and conduct investigations of motor vehicle accidents (Bayley, 1994). They are also responsible for maintaining order at traffic accidents and anywhere large numbers of people congregate in a confined area, such as sporting events, rock concerts, and political rallies (Skolnick, 1994). Bayley (1994) reports mixed findings regarding how police view traffic enforcement duty. Although they often feel "beleaguered" and "unappreciated," many traffic officers believe that what they are doing is important. Other officers believe traffic regulation is "chicken shit work," insignificant labor that is resented by the public. Many police officers dislike traffic duty for at least two reasons (Skolnick, 1994, p. 142): (1) Stopping a vehicle for a traffic violation is one of the most dangerous components of police work; of those officers wounded and killed annually, a significant number are victimized after stopping armed and dangerous offenders; and (2) traffic stops represent the most frequent point of contact between the police and the public and are the source of low-level but significant discord between these two groups. Many people resent being stopped, detained, and sometimes lectured to by police officers. Regarding the second point, police are in a no-win situation as they issue traffic tickets to the very group ("mainstream America," so to speak) that they count on for political and economic support. The public especially resents receiving tickets they believe are primarily (if not exclusively) driven by a quota system. Although many police chiefs deny that their officers must issue a specific number of tickets within a specified time period, the evidence clearly indicates that ticket quotas are part and parcel of departments across the country. According to criminologist Lawrence Sherman (Reid, 1998, p. 1), "Quotas have been widely used in regulatory work. . . . But they are rarely admitted." New York City police officers picketed traffic courts in their protest of ticket-writing quotas. A police union secretary and 30-year department veteran stated, "These cops are hustled and harangued to give out more and more tickets. Time off and holidays are rewarded by the number of tickets you write" (Cooper, 1997, p. B3). The police commissioner denied the existence of a quota system.

Partly as a result of a quota system, Metro Transit Police in Washington, DC, issued more than twice the number of tickets and citations in the first 10 months of 1998 than they did in the same time frame the previous year (Reid, 1998). In a police department in Ohio, the number of tickets issued dropped sharply after a new policy was adopted that no longer evaluated police performance (partially) on the basis of the number of tickets written and arrests made (Ott, 1998). Two officers from a small-town New Jersey department went to court arguing that the quota of writing 20 tickets a month in a rural environment with little traffic was unattainable. The judge disagreed, stating that this performance standard was "reasonable and attainable" and did not violate any public policy or constitutional principles (Riley, 1999, p. 1). Ticket quotas are routinely opposed by police unions.

This officer confronts a potentially dangerous suspect in an automobile. Although policing is not as life threatening as some other occupations, an average of 155 officers were killed each year in the 1990s, a figure down from 185 annually in the 1980s.

If the public dislikes being stopped by traffic cops, these officers object to their treatment by drivers, although some citizen responses can be quite humorous, as noted in Table 7.4. Bayley and Bittner (1997) note that officers especially disdain wealthy people driving expensive cars who threaten to complain to the "the chief" or the mayor about their treatment.

Traffic enforcement is a component of police work that has an especially high degree of discretion. At the point of "contact," the initial phase of the police–citizen encounter, Bayley and Bittner (1997, pp. 125–126) note officers can engage in 1 of 10 courses of action, including ordering the driver out and leaving the passengers in the vehicle or ordering the passengers out while asking the driver for documents. Concerning the outcome of the stop, traffic officers usually choose one of the following courses of action (Skogan in Bayley, 1994): (1) a citation is written 43 percent of the time; (2) the driver is released with a warning 20.7 percent of the time; (3) the driver is arrested for being intoxicated or for another crime (14 percent); (4) the driver is simply let go (13.4 percent); and (5) 12 percent of the time the driver is given a stern lecture along with a citation.

Police Discretion

Discretion can be defined as the "liberty or power of deciding or acting without other control than one's own judgement" (Webster, 1983, p. 522). The criminal justice system can be considered as an unfolding series of "situations and decisions" (Daudistel, Sanders, and Luckenbill, 1979), with police officers making one of the first decisions (for example, whether to arrest someone) in a chain of events. The police not only decide which laws will be enforced but also when, where, and under what circumstances legal statutes are implemented (Delattre, 1994). Samuel Walker (1999) considers police officers the "gatekeepers" of the system in that their decisions regarding arrest determine in large measure the workload of prosecutors, probation officers, judges, and parole officers as well as prison guards and administrators.

Discretion is an inescapable part of a police officer's job because laws are written in generalized language that may be difficult to interpret (some much more than others), and they must be interpreted. No law, statute, or departmental regulation can possibly cover each and every situation to which it might be applied. Consider patrol officers responding to a call for assistance at a local nightclub, arriving just as a barroom brawl has ended. The officers must decide which (if any) of the patrons will be arrested and on what charges: Should some or all of the combatants be taken into custody for simple assault (a misdemeanor) or aggravated assault (a felony)? Summoned to a convenience store, police find the clerk physically restraining a shabbily dressed old man. The clerk states the man shoplifted about $10 worth of food. Learning that the individual is homeless and possibly mentally impaired, the officers must decide if the petty thief should be arrested, escorted to a homeless shelter, taken to the county mental hospital for observation, or simply released.

Discretion is also built into police work because officers are, to a certain extent, future-oriented in their work (Bayley and Bittner, 1997). Regarding the elderly shoplifter, officers must decide whether arrest or referral to a social service agency is the most appropriate response (Walker, 1999). In other words, what is the best course of action to pursue for all concerned, including the police. The likelihood that they will be called on again to deal with the same people in a similar situation may be a factor in the decision-making process. James Q. Wilson (1968) argues that police practice a kind of "distributive justice," making decisions (exercising discretion) about situations and individuals based in part on their evaluation of the moral character of victims and suspects. Police perceptions, therefore, of "good guys" and "bad guys" will determine in part how they deal with people.

Police discretion exists at the departmental or administrative level as well as at the individual level. Departmental discretion involves such decisions as the allocation of personnel and resources and regulations regarding the use of deadly force and high-speed pursuits (Brooks, 1997). Because there is "an almost inexhaustible supply of offenses" and a finite number of officers, police administrators must prioritize their objectives and decide how to allocate available personnel (Bayley, 1994, p. 47). Should they concentrate their efforts on vice (gambling, prostitution, and drug dealing), gang-related crime, or routine street offenses? The local political structure may directly or indirectly influence departmental decisions. For example, the city council may receive an inordinate number of complaints from store owners regarding gang activity in their area. Council members, in turn, pressure the police chief to rectify the situation.

Joseph Goldstein (1960) conceptualizes police discretion in terms of full enforcement and actual enforcement of the law. *Full enforcement* means investigating every event that is reported to or observed by police that might be a violation of the law. However, *actual enforcement* is the reality of policing after pressure from local politicians, the media, and influential citizens on departments is considered in addition to budgetary and personnel constraints. Because full enforcement of the law is impossible, police must use discretion.

Although police discretion is inevitable and, to a certain extent, desirable, *uncontrolled* discretion is problematic (Walker, 1999). This behavior can result in the unequal treatment of citizens because the power to exercise discretion is also the power to engage in discriminatory behavior. Racial profiling (see the next section) is a perfect example of the undesirable application of discretion. When and where discretion-based discrimination becomes systematic and widespread, police–community relations are almost sure to deteriorate. To the extent that police accuse (and harass) suspected offenders of engaging in prostitution, dealing drugs, and/or gambling illegally without arresting them, they are denying these individuals due process. If discretion on the part of police personnel is completely unregulated by departmental policy, it becomes impossible to evaluate officers' performance via any uniform criteria because each officer is basically engaged in his or her own brand of police work (Brooks, 1997; Walker, 1999).

The Police and Profiling

In 1998, a young man from the West African nation of Liberia attending college in the United States was pulled over by police in Maryland for not wearing a seat belt. The man, Nelson Walker, and two passengers were detained for 2 hours while officers searched the car for illegal drugs, weapons, or other contraband. After their initial search turned up nothing out of the ordinary, the officers began dismantling the car by removing part of the door panel, the seat panel, and a portion of the sunroof. When this more comprehensive search also failed to yield any illegal material, one of the officers handed Walker a screwdriver and said, "You're going to need this." The police then drove away (Harris, 1999).

In 1997, Aaron Campbell, while driving on the turnpike, was stopped by Orange County (Florida) sheriff's deputies for allegedly making an illegal lane change and having an obscure license tag. During the course of the encounter, Campbell was wrestled to the ground and blasted with pepper spray. Campbell, an African American, is a major and decorated officer of the Metro–Dade Police Department. That same year, then–San Diego Charger football player Shawn Lee and his girlfriend were pulled over by local police, handcuffed, and detained for 30 minutes. The police stated that the vehicle Lee was driving matched the description of one that was stolen earlier that day. Lee was driving a Jeep Cherokee (a sport utility vehicle) and the stolen car was a Honda sedan. Shawn Lee is an African American (Harris, 1999).

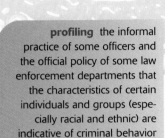

profiling the informal practice of some officers and the official policy of some law enforcement departments that the characteristics of certain individuals and groups (especially racial and ethnic) are indicative of criminal behavior

Profiling is the long-held, widespread police practice of viewing certain characteristics of individuals and situations as indicative of criminal behavior. For example, U.S. customs agents are alert for people who appear particularly nervous when they enter the United States, and these people are subject to routine questions and possibly searches. Their anxiety is likely to be interpreted as a sign that the individual is attempting to smuggle illegal drugs or other contraband into the country. *Racial profiling* is the police practice of stopping, questioning, and searching a disproportionate number of racial and ethnic minorities (especially African Americans and Hispanics). This practice is predicated on the belief that these individuals are involved in a significant amount of crime, especially the use and distribution of drugs. The three police/driver accounts at the beginning of this section would be considered by many routine examples of racial profiling or, as this practice has been dubbed by opponents, DWB—driving while black (or brown).

No doubt, some people would argue that if minorities are heavily involved (disproportionate to their numbers) in the drug trade, racial profiling is not only justified but also a useful strategy in combating the drug trade. However, the government's own statistics undermine this perspective. Approximately 80 percent of cocaine users are white, and the "typical user is a middle-class, white suburbanite" (Harris, 1999, p. 6).

Although police departments across the country have been accused of racial profiling by individuals and civil rights groups for decades, law enforcement officials have steadfastly denied engaging in this practice. However, in the past few years, both anecdotal and social science research has supported the belief that racial profiling is a fundamental component of policing in much of the nation. For example, after denying that New Jersey troopers engaged in racial profiling for more than 5 years, the state attorney general admitted that troopers routinely use this strategy (Marks, 1999; Peterson, 1999). None of the troopers was convicted of any wrongdoing. In a sworn statement, one trooper admitted that he was trained to target African Americans and Hispanics for traffic stops. An Alabama state trooper testified that traffic stop indicators included "Texas plates" and "Mexicans." Testifying in a drug interdiction case, a police officer in Lexington, Kentucky, reported that race and out-of-state plates were indicators used in his department (Webb, 1999). A training film used by the Louisiana State Police Department encourages officers to use traffic stops to conduct drug searches when they encounter "males of certain nationalities, mainly Cubans, Columbians, Puerto Ricans, or other swarthy outsiders" (Cole, 1999, p. 41). The Florida Department of Highway Safety and Motor Vehicles issued a guideline for police officers entitled *The Common Characteristics of Drug Couriers*. Indicators that officers were to be aware of included drivers wearing "lots of gold" or those who did not "fit the vehicle" and "ethnic groups associated with the drug trade" (Harris, 1999, p. 6).

In 1992, Robert L. Wilkins and his family were returning home from a funeral in Chicago when they were stopped on Interstate 95 for allegedly speeding by Maryland State Police (MSP). When the trooper asked if he could search the car, Wilkins refused. The Harvard trained, African American public defender and his family were ordered out of the vehicle and forced to stand in the rain while drug-sniffing dogs searched their car. The American Civil Liberties Union (ACLU) successfully sued the MSP on behalf of Wilkins. As part of the settlement, the MSP agreed to keep detailed records of individuals detained during traffic stops (including their race and ethnicity) for 3 years (Webb, 1999).

The ACLU conducted a "rolling survey" to identify both the race and ethnicity of drivers, and the number of individuals violating the law (mostly speeding) on a stretch of Interstate 95 in Maryland over a 42-hour period. Of the 5,741 drivers observed, 5,354 (93.3 percent) were violators and, therefore, eligible to be stopped by the police (see Tables 7.5 and 7.6). Slightly less than 75 percent of the violators were white, and 21.8 percent were minorities. MSP records mandated by the courts because of the Wilkins/ACLU lawsuit revealed that, between January 1995 and September 1996, 823 motorists on Interstate 95 north of Baltimore were stopped. Of those drivers pulled over

table 7.5 — Maryland State Police Searches on Interstate 95 North of Baltimore, January 1995 to September 1996

	NUMBER	PERCENTAGE
White	162	19.7
Black, Hispanic, and other minority	661	80.3
Total stopped and searched	823	100.0

Source: "Driving While Black: Racial Profiling On Our Nation's Highways." An American Civil Liberties Union Special Report, June 1999, p. 24. Available: http://www.aclu.org/profiling/report/index.htm. Reprinted by permission of the American Civil Liberties Union.

table 7.6 — Drivers and Traffic Law Violators by Race from I-95 Corridor Study

	WHITE	BLACK	OTHER	UNKNOWN	TOTAL
Number of drivers observed	4,314	973	241	186	5,741
Number of violators observed	4,000	938	232	184	5,354
Percentage of drivers (by race)	75.6%	16.9%	4.3%	3.2%	100%
Percentage of violators (by race)	74.7%	17.5%	4.4%	3.4%	100%

Source: "Driving While Black: Racial Profiling On Our Nation's Highways." An American Civil Liberties Union Special Report, June 1999, p. 24. Available: http://www.aclu.org/profiling/report/index.htm. Reprinted by permission of the American Civil Liberties Union.

661, or 80.3 percent, were African Americans, Hispanics, or other minorities. Slightly less that 20 percent were white (Harris, 1999). Regarding these findings, psychologist and statistician John Lambert (in Harris 1999, p. 26) stated:

> The evidence examined in this study reveals dramatic and highly statistically significant disparities between the percentage of black Interstate 95 motorists legitimately subject to stop by MSP troopers on this roadway. While no one can know the motivations of each individual trooper in conducting a traffic stop, the statistics presented herein, representing a broad and detailed sample of highly appropriate data, show without question a racially discriminatory impact on blacks and other minority motorists from state police behavior along I-95.

Along with the belief that racial and ethnic minorities are the chief culprits in the nation's drug problem, the increase in racial profiling during the past few years has been attributed to the stepped up war on drugs on the part of law enforcement, specifically "Operation Pipeline." This highway drug interdiction program has trained approximately 27,000 officers in more than 300 departments in 48 states (Harris, 1999; Webb, 1999). John Harris argues that the instructions officers have received via Operation Pipeline have "been instrumental in spreading the use of pretext stops, which are at the heart of [the] racial profiling debate" (p. 8). He notes that training materials have implicitly—if not explicitly—encouraged targeting African American and Hispanic drivers.

In a move lauded by opponents of racial profiling, police departments in San Jose and San Diego, California, indicated that they would begin collecting data on the race of drivers in routine traffic stops. Although information on the gender and race of the driver is recorded when a traffic citation is written, these data are *not* collected when officers pull over motorists and release them without taking official action. Law enforcement personnel have generally opposed collecting racial data on traffic encounters, arguing that this policy will increase rather than decrease race consciousness. As of 1999, 12 states were considering legislation that would require collecting data on race during vehicle stops (Stetz and Thornton, 1999; Van Slambrouck, 1999).

Profiling as it pertains to drug offenders is not limited to minorities, as Gary Webb (1999), an investigator for the California legislature, learned when he attended Operation Pipeline training. One instructor provided a list of physical "indicators" of drug involvement (especially transporting these substances) that police officers could use as they patrolled the nation's streets and highways (in Webb, 1999, pp. 122–123).

> *Air fresheners,* most notably the ones shaped like little pine trees, are referred to by Pipeline officers as "the felony forest." These devices along with fabric softener, laundry detergent, and coffee grounds can be used to mask the scent of drugs.
>
> *Fast-food wrappers on the floor* are indicative of "hard travel"; someone does not want to leave a drug payload unattended. Pillows and blankets in the vehicle also fall in this category.
>
> *Maps with cities circled on them* may be a "drug source" or a "drug destination."
>
> *Tools on the floor* may have been used to open and close compartments in the vehicle where drugs have been stashed. Tinted windows, new tires on an old car, and vehicles with especially high mileage are also signs that the driver is transporting something other than vacation luggage.
>
> *A single key in the ignition* suggests that the driver was given a vehicle for transporting drugs and handed a key.
>
> *Not enough luggage for a long trip or too much for a short journey* suggests that something is out of the ordinary. Officers are also taught to be wary of rental cars.

Although any one of these indicators does not necessarily demonstrate drug-related wrongdoing, some combination of these signs may well point to criminal activity. Drivers' characteristics that may indicate drug involvement according to some Pipeline instructors include long hair, beards, earrings, nose rings, eyelid rings, and tattoos (especially tattoos of marijuana leaves) (Cannon, 1999; Webb, 1999). One instructor noted that "Deadhead stickers . . . are almost always associated with drugs" (in Webb, 1999, p. 5).

The Police Subculture

A **subculture** is a group that holds values, norms, and patterns of behavior in common with the dominant society but also has its own worldview and design for living. Occupations and professions are subcultures; members of these groups typically do the same work in the same manner (often in close proximity to one another) and have the same job-related advantages and disadvantages. Much has been written about the police subculture, especially the high degree of solidarity and intragroup loyalty of these groups. Other characteristics associated with the police subculture are secrecy, suspicion of outsiders, an emphasis on masculinity, and a focus on risk or danger (Herbert, 1998).

Perhaps the defining feature of the police subculture is the "us–them" perspective that many officers internalize. Officers learn that, although the public may be highly supportive of police and police work via opinion polls, they resent being reprimanded or told what to do by law enforcement officials. In other words, citizens often react negatively when they receive traffic citations or are ordered about at accidents, crime scenes, sporting events, and political rallies (Skolnick, 1994). In turn, this challenge to (if not outright contempt for) their authority can lead to antagonistic feelings toward the public on the part of police officers. The belief that the general public does not understand, appreciate, and respect them is not uncommon among police in this country. In the extreme, officers can become alienated from the very people they are hired to serve and embrace the conviction that other cops are the only ones who understand them, the only people they can relate to and trust.

In a matter of months after leaving the academy, officers learn that various aspects of the criminal justice system are even more troublesome and inefficient than they had realized. As "insiders" they regularly observe incompetent prosecutors, attorneys, and judges. They realize that the hard work that led to an arrest typically does not result in a jury trial but is adjudicated by way of plea bargaining and a "negotiated" sentence. Officers also come to learn that some of their own supervisors are inefficient and that the police department is not exempt from everyday management and overall leadership problems. To add insult to injury, officers often realize that they receive little, if any, respect from judges, lawyers, and other members of the criminal justice system (Walker, 1999). All of these findings can result in greater or lesser degrees of cynicism and reinforce the "us–them" worldview.

Sociologist Steve Herbert (1998, p. 347) has a somewhat different interpretation of a subculture, viewing it as a collection of *normative orders:* a "set of generalized rules and common practices oriented around a common value." In this view, the common value is doing police work and being a good cop. We briefly examine three of the six normative orders that police officers construct (pp. 351–361): morality, safety, and competence.

Morality. Police officers tend to see themselves not only as upholders of the law but also as participants in the "wider struggle between good and evil" (p. 361). Herbert notes that the labels *bad guy* and *predator* are used frequently by police, the latter word conveying a sense of "evil devouring good; like some unwanted carnivore," vile individuals who "prey upon the unsuspecting and vulnerable" (p. 31). These terms not only denigrate offenders but they also serve to glorify police work and cast law enforcement officers as "defenders of the good." This sharp distinction between good and evil no doubt contributes to police cynicism; that is, although the police define their work largely in terms of protecting the public from criminals, they perceive the public as ungrateful if not outwardly hostile to law enforcement (Prenzler, 1997).

Safety. Although many officers welcome the chance to demonstrate their courage and bravery, they also value personal safety and the physical well-being of their comrades. Roll calls typically end with the admonition "stay safe out there." The Los Angeles police officers Herbert observed made a distinction between propolice areas (locales where residents were believed to support law enforcement) and antipolice areas (neighborhoods hostile to the police). When entering the latter, officers' concerns with safety was evident as they unbuckled seat belts enabling them to exit squad cars quickly, unlatched their shotguns, and informed dispatchers of their location should they need assistance.

> **subculture** a group that holds values, norms, and patterns of behavior in common with the dominant society but also has its own worldview and design for living

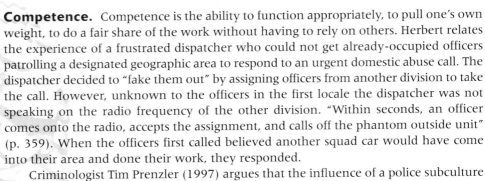

Competence. Competence is the ability to function appropriately, to pull one's own weight, to do a fair share of the work without having to rely on others. Herbert relates the experience of a frustrated dispatcher who could not get already-occupied officers patrolling a designated geographic area to respond to an urgent domestic abuse call. The dispatcher decided to "fake them out" by assigning officers from another division to take the call. However, unknown to the officers in the first locale the dispatcher was not speaking on the radio frequency of the other division. "Within seconds, an officer comes onto the radio, accepts the assignment, and calls off the phantom outside unit" (p. 359). When the officers first called believed another squad car would have come into their area and done their work, they responded.

Criminologist Tim Prenzler (1997) argues that the influence of a police subculture on the attitudes and behaviors of law enforcement officers (especially as it relates to police misconduct) has been exaggerated. To begin, the characteristics of this subculture (secrecy, resistance to outside scrutiny, stereotyping, and the protection of colleagues) are hardly unique to police; they are found in numerous other occupations and professions, including medicine and law. To the extent that a predominantly white male police culture exists, it is being eroded by increasing numbers of female officers who tend to be less authoritarian and ethnocentric than their male counterparts. Racial and ethnic minority officers are also less ethnocentric, and increasingly better educated recruits are more likely to resist informal, occupational socialization.

The Police and Suicide

Police officers are more likely to take their own lives than they are to be killed by others, and the suicide rate for law enforcement personnel is more than three times that of the general population (Slovenko in Violanti, 1996). However, the validity of police suicide statistics is suspect because investigators may want to protect a comrade and his or her family (the overwhelming majority of police suicide victims are males) from the stigma associated with a self-inflicted wound. As Violanti (1995, p. 19) notes, "The police represent a highly cohesive subculture whose members tend to 'take care of their own.'" For example, a 1982 study discovered that 15 possible suicides in the Chicago Police Department were officially listed as "accidental gunshot wounds." The following is a likely (deliberate) misclassification of a police suicide (Cronin in Violanti, 1996, p. 27):

> A police officer was found dead in bed in a rear bedroom. The officer was to report to work at 5 P.M. but failed to appear. Police arrived at the scene and received no response at the door. They forcibly entered the apartment and found the officer lying on his bed. There was a bullet wound to the left side of the head, and the gun was in the officer's hand. The officer was lying on his back in bed. The apartment was locked, there was no sign of forcible entry, and the officer's own gun was in his hand. Cause of death: Undetermined.

John M. Violanti (1995; 1996), the foremost researcher of police suicides in this country, offers the following explanations for why law enforcement officers take their lives:

Frustration, helplessness, and stress. Some of the major stressors associated with police work are danger, shift work, public apathy and hostility, boredom, a sense of uselessness, and dealing with trauma and the misery of death. Commenting on the death of a New York City police officer, Violanti (in Zeilbrauer, 1999, p. B5) stated: "We have a lot of people out there who think they have to be perfect cops. If, in some way, they feel they've failed that image of themselves, it's devastating." The initial enthusiasm of officers to help people, to make a difference in society "may transform into hard core cynicism" (Violante, 1995, p. 123). In addition, troubled officers trained to be physically and mentally strong and in control of situations may have difficulty confiding in comrades and family members, leaving the officers to cope with problems on their own.

Access to firearms. Whereas firearms are involved in slightly less than 50 percent of suicides in the general population, approximately 95 percent of self-inflicted deaths of police officers involve the use of the officer's service weapon. Violanti (1995;

1996) makes some interesting observations regarding the police suicide–firearm relationship. First, many police departments encourage officers to carry firearms when they are off duty in case some emergency arises. This means that an officer can shoot himself or herself when an impulse to commit suicide arises with little if any time to reconsider the action. "Accessibility to firearms may also limit any pre-attempt opportunity for intervention by others" (1996, p. 45). Violanti (1995) argues that firearms have a special significance for police officers; firearms are weapons issued to protect people from harm and misery. Despondent officers may view self-inflicted gunshot wounds with service weapons as appropriate and legitimate ways of ending their own misery.

Alcohol abuse. Stress can lead to alcohol abuse, which in turn can lead to more problems (high absenteeism, traffic accidents, and/or intoxication on duty) and even greater stress. One study found alcohol abuse in 60 percent of suicides in the Chicago Police Department (Wagner and Brzeczek in Violanti, 1996).

Retirement and fear of separation from the police subculture. Violanti (1996, p. 48) notes that police officers have a love–hate relationship with their profession: "[T]hey find it difficult to stay beyond 20 years and even more difficult to leave." Upcoming retirement has two meanings for many officers: (1) moving into a (nonpolice) society that they have long viewed as different, alien, and hostile; and (2) leaving a job and subculture that has been an integral part of their lives, that is, leaving the only group of individuals who really understand them. One officer noted (in Violanti, 1996, p. 48):

> It's like I belonged to a big club. I made my mark, I was one of the guys. I did my job. . . . Suddenly all of that is gone and you are on the outside looking in. I felt so different . . . I played golf with the guys, went to all the parties. Somehow it wasn't the same. I wasn't one of them anymore. It's hard to explain. I retired, but I couldn't let go of this strong attachment.

In a study of police suicides in the Buffalo, New York, police department between 1950 and 1990, Violanti (1996) found that retired officers had similar rates of suicide to other occupations, but the rate was significantly higher for officers just prior to retirement.

In the wake of a sharp increase in suicides among New York City police officers in 1994, the Police Organization Providing Peer Assistance (POPPA) was formed in 1996. After undergoing training, 50 police officers began manning telephones at a 24-hour hot line to assist colleagues experiencing difficulties. The first year POPPA received 250 calls; this number increased to approximately 1,500 in 2001 (prior to the September 11 terrorist strike on the World Trade Center). According to one clinical "guesstimate," about eight lives a year have been saved as a result of the counseling this organization provides. In the days after the terrorist attack in 2001, about 20 to 265 officers with POPPA inscribed on their jackets began handing out brochures to police officers (Scherer, 2002).

Focus on Japan

Police in the Land of the Rising Sun

Being a police officer is a relatively well paid, high-status occupation in Japan. As such, it attracts a significant number of applicants each year of which no more than 12 percent are accepted. Almost 50 percent of successful candidates are university graduates. One reason entrance requirements are so stringent is because the police training system is "long, extensive, and systematic" (Ueno, 1994). Beginning in 1959, preservice (the police academy in U.S. parlance) lasted for a year, and that time period was extended to almost 2 years by the 1990s. Police recruits follow a challenging schedule that begins with a 6 A.M. wake-up call (all recruits live in dormitories at the police school) and ends with the completion of a mandatory evening study hall at 9:30 P.M. Instruction is conducted 6 days a week (Ueno, 1994).

Whereas police recruits in this country are thought to be in "training," future Japanese police officers receive an "education." This distinction reflects very different views of the role of the police. Former Japanese detective Huaro Ueno (1994, p. 254) notes that, in his country, "An officer should have a bit of knowledge of a lawyer, a doctor, an engineer. He or she must possess the tough-mindedness of an athlete, the insight of a scientist, and the compassion of a priest." The more than 3,000 hours of education include the following topics (Ueno, 1994, p. 255):

SUBJECT	HOURS
General culture	256
Civics	25
Ethics	25
Health care	24
Japanese language	40
Current topics	30
Natural sciences	16
Law	248
Criminal law	80
Criminal procedure	80
Civil law	28
Police activities	692
Patrol duties	384
Criminal investigation	86
Communication	110
Role playing	112
Physical training	548
Etiquette and drill	112
Firearms	72
First aid	40
Judo and kendo	136
Athletics	50
Driving	34
Miscellaneous	324

On completion of their education, new officers are sent to the field for approximately 1 year where they are under the tutelage of carefully selected veteran police officers. Then they return to the academy for a 4-month refresher course and additional training that completes the initial phase of educating a police officer. At this stage in their careers, young officers can expect to be assigned to patrol duty for a few years. Individuals who demonstrate ability and desire after they have sufficient patrol experience can take a career advancement test to become detectives, for example. Successful candidates receive additional training and once again are assigned to an experienced officer in their area of specialization (Ueno, 1994).

Of Japan's 230,000 police officers, approximately 4,300 are women. Females receive less training than their male counterparts and are not issued firearms (Ueno, 1994). About 50 percent of women officers have traffic-related duty (ticketing and impound-

ing illegally parked cars), and 20 percent counsel juveniles. Some women work undercover in stores where they apprehend shoplifters. Bayley (1994, p. 71) notes that women officers "invariably serve tea to male officers and visitors," and one city has a drum majorette corp of female officers adorned in miniskirts.

Almost all police officers in Japan have had duty (for some, a significant portion of their careers) in a *koban* or *chuzaisho;* these uniquely Japanese aspects of policing have been translated into English as police boxes, substations, or ministations. The approximately 6,600 *kobans* (as of 1997) are found throughout urban Japan, with Tokyo alone having more than 1,000 police boxes. They are, in fact, the fundamental component of big-city policing in Japan with four of five Osaka (the nation's second-largest city) patrol officers working out of *kobans.* Depending on the area of the city and the size of the *koban,* anywhere from 2 to 12 officers are assigned to these substations. David Bayley (1991, p. 17), who has studied policing in Japan extensively, notes that officers in *kobans* "are the foot soldiers of Japanese police work—jacks-of-all-trades but masters of none."

Japanese people regard a *koban* as "an all purpose source of help" (Bayley, 1991, p. 17). Of the 62 percent of the public (more than 50 million visits) that came to *kobans* in 1988, 31.5 percent reported a lost item or turned one in and 19 percent asked directions (a common police service in a country where few streets are named and many homes are not numbered). Police routinely counsel people with a variety of troubles, lend them

A Japanese police officer gives directions in front of a *koban* or "police box." *Kobans* are small neighborhood police stations staffed by four to twelve officers. A *chuzaisho* is a small residential post with one or two officers on duty around the clock. Japan has over 16,000 *kobans* and *chuzaishos,* and people are encouraged to seek out officers for assistance in both criminal and non–crime-related matters.

bus fare home, and even make hotel reservations for tourists unfamiliar with a neighborhood. People who are drunk and unruly or have committed some minor transgression may be gently reprimanded or scolded by *koban* officers. Some *kobans* equipped with loudspeakers even make announcements of general interest (Bayley, 1991).

Chuzaishos are essentially rural substations manned by one and sometimes two officers and their families. Currently, there are 8,300 *chuzaishos* throughout the country, although this number has been declining as Japan becomes an increasingly urban society. The underlying premise of these ever-present rural and urban substations is that if family and neighborhood problems can be nipped in the bud they are less likely to erupt into criminal behavior.

The majority of patrol officers in Japan work a three-shift system that entails a 56-hour workweek. The first begins at 8:30 A.M. and ends at 5:15 P.M.; the second starts at 8:30 A.M. and ends the following day at the same time (a 24-hour shift). The third day is for rest and then the cycle begins again. Tokyo prefecture has a four-shift system. On their 24-hour shift, officers are allowed to rest for up to 8 hours, circumstances permitting. However, on a busy day, officers may get only a few minutes of sleep whenever they can and eat on the run. Bayley (1994, p. 22) notes that patrol work is not easy, and tiredness resulting from the twice-a-week day-long shift "becomes a way of life."

> Patrol officers spend much of their time on their feet, standing in front of a *koban* answering questions. By nighttime the urge to sit is overwhelming; an officer's feet seem to grow hot and expand in size. But it is precisely at night, when fatigue is the greatest that police officers are busiest. They particularly dread getting a call at 2:30 A.M. just before most of them are due to get their first break in eighteen hours of duty. (p. 22)

The physical demands of the job notwithstanding, David Bayley (1991, p. 1) argues that Japan "is heaven for a cop," and he adds "with respect for law enforcement [comes] a different world." To begin, the rate of crime (particularly violent crime) is very low in Japan when compared to other modern industrial states, especially the United States. One reason for low rates of violent crime in Japan is the almost total absence of firearms among the general public. Even criminals rarely use guns. Bayley (1991, p. 6) notes that robbery rates are negligible in Japan because thieves "are less able, perhaps less willing to injure people." The ban on firearms also protects Japanese police officers who are significantly less likely to be shot in the line of duty than are their U.S. counterparts.

In a typical year, U.S. homicide and robbery rates are five to nine times and well over 100 times, respectively, greater than the corresponding rates of those crimes in Japan. As a result of low crime rates, Japanese police can spend more time and assign more officers to each case, which translates into a higher clearance rate (that is, crimes that are "cleared" by the arrest of suspects in connection with those offenses). Although about two of every three homicides in the United States are cleared by ar-

rest, in Japan no more than four or five of every hundred homicides known to police are *not* cleared by arrest.

Arguably, the most important reason for high clearance rates is the presence of a legal system that favors the state as opposed to individuals suspected of committing a crime. For example, although someone arrested in Japan has the constitutional right to remain silent and retain an attorney, the country has relatively few lawyers and their services are expensive (Miyazawa, 1992). In addition, Japan has no criminal defense specialists, public defenders, or legal aid attorneys. Even if a suspect hires an attorney, the police and prosecutor have the legal right to determine when, where, and for how long the accused can meet with his or her legal counsel.

Once arrested, a suspect can be held for 3 days before a prosecutor has to gain the permission of a judge for further detention. Suspects can be interrogated for up to 15 hours a day, and their statements are neither transcribed verbatim nor tape recorded. A detective rewrites what the suspect says and the suspect is expected to sign these papers. People arrested in Japan are presumed guilty, and detectives work under the assumption that suspects will eventually confess. Referring to the Japanese criminal justice system, Setsuo Miyazawa (1992, p. 25) of Kobe University states, "The whole system is designed and implemented in such a way that the suspect will offer apparently voluntary confessions to his captors."

If confessions are not forthcoming, Japanese police have allegedly resorted to extralegal methods of persuading suspects to admit their guilt. Grueling interrogation sessions have reportedly lasted from morning till night for 23 straight days (Jameson, 1984). There are also reports of physical abuse during these sessions. Suspects are handcuffed and tied to chairs where they are shouted at by police all day long. They are often kept under surveillance, "deprived of sleep, fed meager rations of food and denied the toilet for long periods" (Schoenberger, 1989, p. A1). The Japanese Bar Association notes that these practices have resulted in a "hotbed of wrong verdicts" (Watanabe, 1992, p. A1), and in recent years many convictions based on forced confessions have been overturned.

Why would people in a democratic nation such as Japan tolerate the heavy-handed, if not outright abusive, behavior of the police? The usual answer is that the Japanese are well socialized to follow the cultural imperatives of duty, conformity, obedience, and deference to individuals and institutions in positions of authority. However, Patricia Steinhoff (1993, p. 847) rejects this explanation favoring an interpretation that focuses on power relations:

> [The] institutional arrangements of modern Japanese life tend to make people economically and emotionally dependent on their employers, co-workers, and family to a greater degree than is generally true in the United States. Consequently, people in Japan simply have more at risk if they violate social expectations, resist authority, or strain their reputations. Under these circumstances they may choose to acquiesce, to conform, to avoid, or to put up with conditions over which they have little control.

1. All police departments have minimum requirements that prospective officers must meet. These typically include height in proportion to weight, a minimum level of education, and, in some cases, residency requirements. The application process in big-city departments typically includes a written examination; a personal history statement; a physical ability test; a background investigation; polygraph, psychological, and medical examinations; and a hiring interview. A robust economy beginning in the early 1990s made recruitment difficult in some parts of the country. The length of training an officer recruit receives is highly correlated with the size of the population the department serves; recruits in large cities receive significantly more training than prospective officers in small cities and towns. Veteran officers often view the training academy as a rite of passage that must be endured, and they believe the real training necessary to become an efficient law enforcement agent can only be learned on the streets.

2. Numerous studies have concluded that no relationship exists between the number of police officers in a given locale and the crime rate in that area or the public's satisfaction with local police. The police perform two major functions in modern industrial societies. Authoritative intervention is an almost completely reactive attempt to restore order in situations ranging from public drunkenness to full-scale riots. Through their work, police officers demonstrate to both offenders and the general public that laws exist that must be obeyed. This is symbolic justice.

3. In almost all police departments, the majority of uniformed personnel are engaged in patrol activities. Less than a third of all calls for police assistance are concerned with criminal behavior. Patrol officers are peacekeepers routinely summoned when some disruption of the social order occurs that citizens cannot or will not deal with by themselves. One study noted that police see the social world as comprised of three distinct groups of people: (a) Suspicious persons are individuals thought to have committed a serious offense; (b) "assholes" are disrespectful to officers, difficult to deal with and/or confrontational; (c) "know nothings" are average citizens whose only contact with police is when they request assistance.

4. If a crime has occurred, nonuniform detectives may be called in to analyze the situation. The decision on the part of detectives to conduct an investigation is contingent on two factors: (a) Has a perpetrator been clearly identified? and (b) Is the crime serious enough to attract public attention? Because there are so many more crimes than detectives, the police are not likely to fully investigate an offense unless a suspect has been identified. No matter how skillful detectives may be, they often depend on knowledge about crimes that can only be provided by informants; this is especially true in drug offenses and drug-related crimes. Detectives may deceive or lie to suspects during questioning, telling these individuals that they have been identified by a witness or that they have failed a polygraph test.

5. Officers working traffic enforcement control the flow of traffic on major roads and investigate motor vehicle accidents. They also maintain order at events where large numbers of people congregate, such as sporting events and rock concerts. Many officers resent traffic duty because a significant number of the police personnel wounded or killed annually are victimized after stopping dangerous offenders for traffic violations. Traffic stops are also a point of friction between the public and the police because the former believe that the police are stopping them to fulfill department-mandated ticket quotas.

6. Police officers have a great deal of discretion in their daily activities. They decide not only which laws will be enforced but also when, where, and under what circumstances legal statutes will be implemented. Discretion is an unescapable part of police work because many laws are vague and can only be interpreted within the context of a given situation.

7. Profiling is the police practice of viewing certain characteristics of individuals and situations as being indicative of criminal behavior. Racial profiling is the police practice of stopping, questioning, and searching a disproportionate number of racial and ethnic minorities, notably African Americans and Hispanics. Proponents of racial profiling argue that this strategy is justified because minorities are heavily involved in certain crimes, especially drug use. Critics contend that governmental statistics contradict this assertion. Anecdotal evidence over the past few years indicates that racial profiling is a fundamental component of police departments across the country. Much of the increase in racial profiling over the past few years has been attributed to the nation's war on drugs. Some departments are now collecting data on the races of drivers in routine traffic stops to determine if racial profiling is occurring.

8. The most prominent aspect of the police subculture is the "us–them" perspective that many officers internalize. Only street cops understand what police work is all about; therefore, they are the only individuals who can be trusted. All others are outsiders to be regarded with skepticism. Within a few months after leaving the police academy, young officers may learn via the police subculture to view prosecutors, attorneys, judges, and their own supervisors with misgivings. One sociologist sees the po-

lice subculture as a set of a generalized rules and common practices including an emphasis on morality, safety, and competence.

9. The law enforcement rate of suicide is three times that of the general population. However, the actual rate may be even higher inasmuch as police departments, in their effort to protect the reputation of an officer and spare his or her family the stigma associated with a self-inflicted wound, may list possible suicides as accidental gunshot wounds. Explanations for police suicides include job stress, access to firearms, alcohol abuse, and separation from the police subculture via retirement.

key terms

discretion   profiling   subculture

questions *for* investigation

1. This chapter notes that departmental selection procedures are adequate for screening *out* individuals unqualified for police work; it also notes that the selection process is not very good for screening *in* individuals who are likely to be good police officers. Suggest some policies or training that would identify potentially effective police officers.

2. What formal and on-the-job training do police candidates receive in your community (hometown or college location)? Discuss its effectiveness. What works? What needs to be changed? Compare this training with that given recruits in a large metropolitan area (or, if you are using a metropolitan area as a base, compare it with a nearby small town).

3. Describe the functions of authoritative intervention and symbolic justice. Provide examples of these functions.

4. Many police officers think the average citizen does not understand and appreciate their work. This includes both uniformed officers and plainclothes detectives. In a group, discuss this assertion. Do you agree or disagree? Explain your reasoning drawing from personal experience as well as this chapter's discussion.

5. What is your opinion of the policy of ticket quotas?

6. How does a police officer develop discretionary skills?

7. Do instances of racial or ethnic profiling exist in your community's police operations? Check Internet news sources available to you, and summarize your findings.

8. What are the pros and cons of a police subculture?

9. Compare and contrast the police academy training of Japanese and U.S. police officers. Suppose you have just been appointed chief of a police department in this country, and your first order of business is to examine, and possibly change, police academy training. Search the Internet for the police academy curriculum of a large or medium-sized city and prepare a list of possible changes to this course of study and training. Be prepared to defend your plan.

IT'S YOUR CALL . . .

1. Imagine you work for a large advertising agency and your firm has been hired to develop a campaign that will attract young men and women (including racial, ethnic, and sexual orientation minorities) to police work. Create Internet and newspaper ads as well as 30-second television and radio commercials that will persuade members of your target audience to seriously consider careers in law enforcement.

2. You are the chief training officer of a metropolitan police force. Always looking for ways to improve officer effectiveness, the police commissioner assigns you the task of examining the course content of police academies in four or five countries. You are to determine which aspects of training in those nations will work in the United States. Remember, the commissioner is a stickler for details and will want to know why some aspect of training that works in the Czech Republic, for example, will be equally effective in big-city America. Write a report of your recommendations with appropriate details.

Police Misconduct

1. What constitutes police deviance? How frequent is it?

2. How does police corruption impact a community?

3. How does an officer become a crooked cop?

4. What is the typology of corrupt police departments?

5. What is legitimate use of force in police work?

6. When does an officer's legitimate use of force become police brutality?

7. Why does police violence occur?

Bonnie Hanssen had reason to be suspicious when she walked in on her husband who was awkwardly concealing a letter. Twelve years earlier, she learned that Bob had sex with a former girlfriend within days of their marriage. But Bob wasn't having an extramarital affair. FBI agent Robert Hanssen was drafting a letter to a Russian military intelligence agency in which he was selling government secrets to the Russians for $20,000 (Vise, 2002).

When Bonnie discovered the truth, she convinced her husband—a recent convert to Roman Catholicism—to talk to a local priest, confess his transgression, and seek counsel for a resolution. The priest advised Bob to sever his contact with the Russians and donate the ill-gotten money to charity. Robert Hanssen told his wife how much he loved her and promised he would never repeat his treasonable behavior. He was lying (Vise, 2002).

The son of a police officer, Hanssen followed in his father's footsteps joining the Chicago Police Department where he worked in the internal affairs unit. His job was to find and gather evidence against corrupt cops. Five years later, he was at the FBI Academy in Quantico, Virginia, training to become a member of one of the nation's elite law enforcement agencies. After graduation he embarked on a career in counterintelligence—"the art of preventing other people from stealing your secrets" (Mangold, 2002, p. A15).

From that day in 1980 when Bonnie stumbled on her husband's first transaction with the Russians, Robert Hanssen sold more than

6,000 pages and some 24 computer disks of valuable, often top-secret, material to the Russians. Leaving the information at prearranged drop sites for pick-up by Russian agents, Hanssen used his considerable skill to avoid detection by the agency that trained him in counterintelligence tactics. In an intermittent spying career that lasted almost 21 years, even the Russians did not know the identity of the man with whom they were dealing ("Robert Philip Hanssen Espionage Case," 2001; Vise, 2002).

FBI agents make sketches in the front yard of the home of fellow agent Robert Hanssen. Hanssen was convicted of espionage and sentenced to life in prison without parole.

For $1.4 million in cash and jewelry, Hanssen sold information to the Russians in what some observers believe was the most damaging security breach in U.S. history. The *Washington Post* investigative reporter David Vise stated that the disgraced FBI agent "gave away the store of national security secrets" ("The Spy in the FBI," 2001, p. 1).

- He gave the Russians detailed intelligence about U.S. nuclear weapons capabilities, including information about the early warning system that would be deployed in the event of a large-scale nuclear attack.
- He told the Russians how the president, the vice president, and Congress were to be kept safe and continue to function during a nuclear war.
- He revealed the identities of nine Russian officials who were spying for the United States (double agents). Three of these individuals were called back to their homeland under false pretenses, tried for espionage, and executed.
- He told the Russians about a secret spy tunnel under the Russian Embassy in Washington, DC.

The master spy could have been stopped in 1990 with damage to the nation's military and security secrets far less severe. Hanssen's brother-in-law, also an FBI agent, noticed that Bob had a significant amount of cash at home and was spending more money than he was making at the bureau. Agent Mark Wauck informed his superiors that Hanssen might be selling secret information. But for reasons that are still unclear, the FBI failed to launch an investigation (Vise, 2002). In retrospect, a 38-year veteran of the bureau stated that the FBI's performance (or lack thereof) regarding the Hanssen case was abysmal. "We just dropped the ball so many times, you are embarrassed by it" (Curran in Pound and Duffy, 2001, p. 32).

When asked why he sold out his country's military secrets Hanssen replied, "Fear and rage."

"Fear of what?"

"Fear of being a failure and fear of not being able to provide for my family" Hanssen responded (Vise, 2002, p. W22).

David Vise, author of *The Bureau and the Mole* (2001), believes that although financial pressures may have had something to do with Hanssen's initial transaction with the Russians, what drove the counterintelligence agent to continue selling his country's secrets was the rage that resulted from a "fractured ego seeking recognition." According to Vise (2001, p. 2), Hanssen "felt that the FBI didn't recognize his brilliance, and so he went to prove to the bureau, to the world, that he was a player. That he was an important guy, that the mole inside the FBI couldn't be caught. . . ."

On July 6, 2001, Robert Hanssen pled guilty to 13 charges of espionage. America's most infamous double agent will spend the rest of his life in prison without the possibility of parole. In return for his plea, prosecutors agreed not to seek the death penalty.

Most Americans have a positive image of the police, an image that goes back to childhood when they were taught that police officers were their friends. Although the vision of the hard-working, scrupulously honest, courageous cop on the beat is certainly true in most cases, the police in this country have another dimension. As Kappeler, Sluder, and Alpert (1998, p. 28) note, "To study the history of police is to study police deviance, corruption, and misconduct."

In 1895, the Lexow Commission, one of the first formal organizations to study police deviance in the United States, concluded that in New York City "almost every conceivable crime against the elective franchise [citizens] was either committed or permitted by the police . . . " (Chevigny, 1995, p. 119). Captain Timothy Creeden told the commission that he paid $15,000 (a significant amount of money in the 1890s) for his promotion to captain, a position that paid approximately $3,000 a year (Richardson, 1974). Like others who paid for their promotions, Creeden knew that he could get the money he borrowed to acquire his job and much more via corruption in precincts that were rife with gambling and prostitution. As long as alcohol, illicit sex, and gambling were illegal or controlled, and the populace wanted to partake of these goods and services, the police had a steady source of corruption money. During Prohibition (1919–1929), a New York City police commissioner stated, it was understood that police would be paid for every half barrel of beer sold. The city had more than 32,000 "speakeasies" at that time (Skolnick and Fyfe, 1993).

In a series of magazine articles, muckraking journalist Lincoln Steffens chronicled a century ago how criminals with the full cooperation of local officials and the police force virtually took control of Minneapolis in the early 1900s (Worsnop, 1995). During the 1940s, police officers in Los Angeles protected hundreds of local prostitutes at the rate of $100 per week per woman. Approximately 30 Denver officers were involved in a burglary ring in the 1960s, and in Chicago the police served as lookouts and planners for local burglars. When the thefts were completed, the two groups split the profit (Kappeler et al., 1998).

Another aspect of police deviance is the use of excessive force. The National Commission on Law Enforcement and Observance appointed by President Herbert Hoover found widespread use of the "third degree" by the police. The 1931 report commonly known as the Wickersham Commission (named after the chairperson, George Wickersham) stated that "the inflicting of pain, physical or mental, to extract confessions or statements" was accomplished through the application of beatings with fists, blackjacks, and rubber hoses (the latter preferred because they left no marks). Suspects were battered over the head with phone books and hung out windows from a high floor until they confessed (Skolnick and Fyfe, 1993, p. 45). People accused of crimes were also subject to illegal detention and denied access to attorneys.

In this chapter, we examine various aspects of police deviance. Much of our attention will focus on the excessive use of force and the causes of this misconduct.

A Typology of Police Deviance

Although police deviance is not as pervasive in the post–World War II era as it was in the past, this behavior continues to be a serious problem. Former FBI director Louis J. Freeh noted that one form of police wrongdoing—corruption—exists in every region of the country in departments large and small, rural and urban from inner-city precincts to small-town sheriffs' offices (U.S. Department of Justice, 1999). Between 1994 and 1997, FBI investigations resulted in the arrest and conviction of 508 law enforcement personnel. In New Orleans during that same period, 79 officers were arrested for various crimes, 64 resigned under investigation, and another 272 were disciplined (Pederson, 1997). During the late 1980s, approximately 100 of the 1,060 Miami police officers had been or were currently under investigation for corruption-related matters (Dombrink, 1994).

Broadly speaking, two categories of police deviance can be identified. Occupational deviance is the violation of regulations or the "commission of crime while on the job or by using some aspect of the occupational position to carry out illegality" (Kappeler et al., 1998, p. 1). Non–work-related wrongdoing or nonoccupational deviance are those activities that have little if anything to do with police work. Following are examples of non–work-related police deviance. A San Diego police officer and his wife presented themselves to social workers as single individuals so the woman could pose as an unwed mother and receive welfare benefits. Both were charged with fraud in the illegal acquisition of more than $30,000. Seventeen off-duty policemen engaged in a drunken melee in downtown Indianapolis. The officers pointed their guns at people, taunted minority group members with racial slurs, and gestured lewdly at women. Two officers were fired, five were demoted or suspended without pay, and the police chief resigned (Tyson, 1996). Some police officers in Staten Island, New York, planned a Fourth of July party with local drug dealers. The party was advertised as "BYOD," slang for "bring your own drugs" (DeRienzo, 1999). After a police academy graduation dinner in San Francisco in 1985, a recruit was handcuffed to a chair and a prostitute was brought in to perform oral sex on him (Dombrink, 1994). In arguably the most egregious incident of off-duty police deviance in recent history, New Orleans police officer Antoinette Frank and a civilian accomplice robbed a Vietnamese restaurant. During the course of the crime, three people were murdered, including an off-duty officer who was moonlighting as a security guard. The slain officer had been Frank's patrol partner on at least one occasion. Frank and the individual she committed this crime with were convicted of first-degree murder and sentenced to death (Sanz and Hermes, 1995).

One area of work-related police deviance that has received relatively little attention from researchers is *sexual misconduct*. In an effort to better understand this phenomenon, Allen Sapp (1994) conducted in-depth interviews (some lasting up to 5 hours) with police officers for more than 10 years. Of the six types of sexual misconduct engaged in by police officers, we examine three. *Nonsexual misconduct* is a form of harassment that while sexually motivated does not involve direct physical contact or inferences. In many instances, the subject of an officer's attention does not realize that an impropriety is occurring. The most common example of this behavior is the unwarranted or invalid traffic stop. One officer recounted inappropriate behavior as follows (Sapp, 1994, p. 189):

> Sure? I see a good-looking chick driving around by herself or even a couple of foxes together, I pull them over and check them out. You can always claim a stoplight isn't working or something like that. . . . Lots of times it sure doesn't lead anywhere but you'd be surprised how much action I get from stopping chicks.

Many of the contacts police officers have with offenders are also opportunities for *sexual harassment*. Officers realize that if a female suspect complains about inappropriate sexual advances she may not be taken seriously. No doubt many women share this same definition of the situation and remain silent. A detective in a big-city department stated (Sapp, 1974, p. 192):

> You bet I get (sex) once in a while by some broad who I arrest. Lots of times you can just hint that if you are taken care of, you could forget about what they did. One of the department stores here doesn't like to prosecute, but they always call us when they catch a shoplifter. Usually we just talk to them and let them go. If it's a decent looking woman, sometimes I'll offer to take her home and make my pitch.

Sexual shakedowns target individuals who are habitually engaged in some form of illegal behavior. Prostitutes are especially vulnerable to this form of police misconduct. Following is one report (Sapp, 1994, p. 195):

> I know several dozen guys who have worked vice in the ten years I've been assigned to the vice squad. I believe everyone of them has gone beyond the rules on sex with prostitutes. Sometimes the officer goes ahead and has sex and then makes the arrest and files a report saying he followed procedures. If the whore claims otherwise, no one believes her anyway since they think she is just trying to get her case tossed out. . . . Guys that would never even consider taking money will take (oral sex or intercourse) from a good looking woman. I don't know if the guys who are oversexed get assigned to vice or if being exposed to so much of it makes the vice squad oversexed, but it seems more is going on in vice than anywhere else.

In January 2003, a Los Angeles police officer was convicted of 14 felony offenses including sodomy and three counts of rape. The officer threatened his victims with arrest or deportation (if they were in the United States illegally) ("L.A. Cop Convicted of 3 Rapes on Duty," 2003)

In addition to sexual misconduct, a significant amount of occupational police deviance is related to *corruption,* which McMullen (in Kappeler et al., 1998, p. 23) defines as accepting "money or money's worth for doing something that [police are] under a duty to do anyway . . . under duty not to do, or to exercise a legitimate discretion for improper reasons." In New York City, police discovered some 300 stolen televisions stashed in a store. Approximately half of these items were "vouchered" (duly noted and accounted for), whereas the remaining 150 were taken by officers for their own use (Daley, 1978). The 1972 Knapp Commission that investigated **police corruption** in New York City (see Table 8.1) made a distinction between "grass eaters," officers who accepted bribes for not making an arrest when they should have, and "meat eaters," law enforcement personnel who aggressively demanded some manner of payment for not doing their duty (Walker, 1999).

> **sexual shakedown** a form of sexual misconduct on the part of police wherein an officer will forgo arresting a female suspect (often a prostitute) in exchange for sexual favors

> **police corruption** a catchall term that covers a wide variety of police misconduct including accepting money, illegal drugs, or articles of value for not arresting law violators, committing burglaries or robberies, selling illegal drugs confiscated in drug busts, and so on

table 8.1	**Major Investigations of the New York City Police Department**	
YEAR	**NAME OF INVESTIGATION**	**FOCUS OF INVESTIGATION**
1894	Lexow Committee	Corruption from gambling and prostitution operations. Extortion of money from legitimate businesspersons. Collusion with criminals. Intimidation, harassment of citizens.
1913	Curran Committee	Corruption from gambling and prostitution operations.
1932	Seabury Committee	Corruption from the manufacture, distribution, sale and consumption of illegal alcohol. Extortion of money from prostitutes.
1949	Brooklyn Grand Jury	Corruption from gambling payoffs.
1972	Knapp Commission	Corruption from gambling and drugs. Payoffs from citizens and the operators of legal and illegal businesses.
1994	Mollen Commission	Drug corruption. Robberies and thefts committed by officers. On-duty substance abuse. Excessive use of force. Effectiveness of internal affairs in detecting and investigating police wrongdoing.

Source: Kappeler, V. E., Richard D. Sluder, and Geoffrey P. Alpert. 1998. *Forces of Deviance—Understanding the Dark Side of Policing* (p. 175). Prospect Heights, IL: Waveland Press. Reprinted by permission of Waveland Press, Inc. All rights reserved.

In Philadelphia in the late 1970s, bars and taverns began purchasing video poker machines for their establishments; owners and machine vendors split the profits in this lucrative but illegal form of entertainment. Police officers used the threat of arrest and seizure of the machines to extort money on a regular basis from vendors (Dombrink, 1994). This police extortion racket was cracked by the FBI, and 31 officers were eventually convicted, including four lieutenants, a captain, an inspector, a chief inspector, and the deputy commissioner. One inspector was receiving approximately $10,000 a month in gambling-related extortion from vice lieutenants. The FBI investigation revealed plans to eventually operate a citywide police-run extortion ring (Dombrink, 1994).

In recent years, a significant amount of both individual and systematic police corruption has been drug related. Of the 508 police convictions for criminal activity between 1994 and 1997 noted earlier, almost 45 percent were drug related. Forty-two police and corrections officers from five Cleveland area agencies were arrested in an FBI sting operation and charged with conspiracy to distribute cocaine. Police cars were used to transport the cocaine, and one officer routinely arrived late for narcotics transactions because he was giving antidrug lectures at local schools (Cohen, 1998).

Drug-related corruption reached new highs (or lows) in New York City in the 1980s. The Christopher Commission found that police officers provided assistance and protection to narcotics organizations for payoffs. Officers sold confidential information (for example, who was being investigated and forthcoming drug busts) to drug dealers, provided protection for the transportation of illegal substances and drug money, became active drug entrepreneurs, and harassed competing traffickers. Some officers also robbed drug dealers and burglarized known drug locations. The stolen drugs were sold to other dealers, other police officers, and back to the dealers from whom they were stolen ("Corruption in the New York City Police Department," 1995). On one occasion in the 1980s, two officers (members of the self-named "Buddy Boys," a group of corrupt officers) from the NYPD's notorious Seventy-Seventh Precinct raided a drug house with guns drawn. As the dealers fled and the officers located a large stash of marijuana, customers unaware of what was happening inside lined up at the door to buy some "smoke." Rather than confiscating the drugs and taking them to the station house, the two officers sold packages of marijuana until they ran out of customers (McAlary, 1987).

There is an important question concerning drug corruption: How could people sworn to uphold the law violate these statutes so flagrantly and habitually? A related issue involves how these officers manage to keep a positive self-image. In other words, if drug dealers were the bad guys, in what sense were police officers now engaged in the same activity any different from narcotics traffickers? Consider the following interpretation of police drug trafficking by one of the Buddy Boys (in McAlary, 1987, pp. 170–171):

> Even though I was a bad guy, I had the feeling, "Hey I'm bad on one side, but on this side I'm making up for it." If people really needed us, we were there. We weren't taking anything from honest workers. I know it doesn't matter whether it's an honest worker or a skell (criminal or low life), it's still wrong. I know that. But we were taking money that was illegal to begin with. Drug money. It's weird but I never thought I was robbing people. I was robbing lowlife. A drug dealer. Someone who shouldn't be there to begin with. The law couldn't touch these guys. If we caught them they just went down and paid the fine. They could afford the fines. Hell, they were making money hand over foot. I know it sounds like a rationalization. But what we did worked. We ripped these guys off and they moved out. They should legalize that. Go in and rip all these guys off and they'll all disappear.

This officer, who eventually became a police informer, rationalized his criminal behavior in three ways: (1) He cited the analogy of a ledger used to keep financial transactions. On one side is a list of money coming in (profits) and on the other side is a record of funds used to pay expenses (debits). The corrupt officers emphasized that they were not all bad ("on this side I'm making up for it") and that their good work more than compensated for ongoing criminal behavior. Implicit in this line of reasoning is the idea that if one does enough good deeds he or she is entitled to do some illegal behavior (Klockars, 1974). (2) As a second rationalization, if an officer was stealing from a criminal ("I was robbing lowlife"), a person who by definition is evil and deserves to be punished, then the action was neither immoral or illegal. (3) This leads to the final interpretation, an extension of number two. Stealing drugs from drug dealers is not only acceptable but it is also desirable because these individuals are rarely punished by a too-lenient criminal justice system.

Officers who rejected bribes from drug dealers on the strength of their belief that narcotics money was "dirty money" had no compunctions about stealing from drug dealers headed for prison (in Sherman, 1974a, p. 139).

> The general feeling was that the man was going to jail, was going to get what was coming to him, so why should you give him back his money and let him bail himself out. In a way we felt that he was a narcotics pusher, we knew he was a narcotics pusher, we kind of felt he didn't deserve no rights since he was selling narcotics.

Once again, the "self-talk"/rationalization is that, by taking the drug dealer's profits, the officers are doing what is right because they are assisting the criminal justice system. Police officers also used drugs in another manner that undermined the criminal justice system, perhaps in an even more insidious manner than dealing illegal substances. On many occasions police officers are convinced that, although someone is "legally innocent," he or she is "factually guilty"; in other words, because of a lack of evidence and/or witnesses, legal guilt cannot be proven in a court of law. To help bring about a conviction, police may engage in what New York City officers referred to as "flaking" and "padding" (Sherman, 1974a). Planting illegally obtained drugs on a person for the purpose of making a narcotics arrest is called flaking. Drugs obtained from a previous arrest (or stolen from drug dealers) which are added to the quantity of narcotics found on a person to upgrade a charge from a misdemeanor to a felony (or multiple felonies) is padding. This practice effectively turns police officers into judge, jury, and executioner. By planting drugs on people, they make the determination of guilt, and, to a certain extent, decide what punishment the individual will receive.

As researchers, David Carter and Darrel W. Stephens (1994, p. 105) have noted, "The extent of on-duty drug use by officers is simply not known." A study of a small 50-person department found that 10 individuals (20 percent) used marijuana while on duty two or more times a month (Kraska and Kappeler, 1988). Anecdotal evidence suggests marijuana is the on-duty drug of choice because it is easy to obtain, relatively inexpensive, and does not carry the stigma associated with other mind-altering substances such as cocaine and heroin (Carter and Stephens, 1994).

It is hardly surprising that police officers actively dealing drugs sometimes also ingest these substances. One of the Buddy Boys told the Mollen Commission that officers routinely drank and used drugs on duty, sometimes snorting lines of cocaine off the dashboard of their patrol cars (Kappeler et al., 1998). Another New York City police officer explained his on-duty drug use in the following manner (in McAlary, 1987, p. 108):

> I wasn't an addict or anything. It's like—say you're doing an eight-to-four tour, you wind up going through the four-to-twelve to the midnight-to-eight, then come back, you work and do another eight-to-four. You're tired. You do some coke. It was a nice feeling. Kept you up, kept you aware, kept you awake.
>
> Much later, if we hit a place and got drugs, I might have dipped into a package. I can look back and say I was stupid because you don't know what the hell you're getting from these people. But if we got a lot of coke, I'd open up one package in the car, taste it, snort maybe a little and say, "Yeah, this is good stuff, we'll get good money for this." Then I'd be ripped for the whole rest of the night. I'd say, "Yeah, let's go do this job. Let's go do that job."

Not only are on-duty drug-taking officers committing crimes, but they are also less effective workers if for no other reason than the use (especially the habitual use) of mind-altering substances, does just that—alters the way people perceive their surroundings. An inaccurate perception of the social world will result in faulty decisions that can be dangerous to all concerned. A police officer whose mind has been clouded by some substance is in no position to engage in a high-speed chase or use a weapon safely and effectively.

Carter and Stephens (1994) reject the argument that recreational drug use on the part of police officers is a function of job stress and job assignment. Rather than high stress leading to drug use as a coping mechanism, they submit that officers using drugs are more likely to experience stress because discovery of their deviant behavior could lead to disciplinary measures including termination. Concerning the second argument, that officers (especially undercover drug personnel) because of extended exposure to the "drug culture" could eventually be socialized into that culture, to date no evidence supports this claim.

The Impact of Corruption

Samuel Walker (1999) argues that corruption has a significant impact on the police and courts and also the larger society. Besides being illegal, this behavior undermines the integrity of law enforcement not only in the department where it occurs but also, to some extent, in all police agencies. When a community loses respect for police and distrusts them because of corruption, it becomes more difficult for officers to do their job. As we discuss later in the chapter, the use of excessive force on the part of law enforcement is more likely to occur in those communities where the police and local citizens have an antagonistic relationship.

Because a significant amount of corruption protects illegal gambling, prostitution, and drug trafficking, much of which is linked to organized crime, corruption contributes to the nation's overall crime problem by allowing individuals and organizations that pay off police to violate the law with impunity. Walker (1999) notes that police corruption undermines the effectiveness of the criminal courts when officers on the take perjure themselves while testifying. Bribed officers will "lose" damaging evidence as well as interpret criminal events (if not lie outright) in a manner that is favorable to the defendant. Another form of perjury occurs when police officers lie in an attempt to convict someone who is legally innocent. In one of the most celebrated cases regarding this form of police deviance, 116 convictions in Philadelphia were overturned in the mid-1990s because officers planted false evidence and lied under oath. In addition, 1,400 other convictions in that criminal court jurisdiction had to be reconsidered ("Policing the Cops," 1996).

Finally, police professionalism is undermined as crooked cops lie to protect one another. Internal discipline is also thwarted as corrupt supervisors (often known to patrol officers and detectives) are always at risk of being exposed by disgruntled subordinates (Walker, 1999).

Becoming a Crooked Cop

As we have seen, some police officers engage in a variety of criminal behavior over an extended period of time. Although police deviance has been documented in departments across the country, it is less clear how an officer becomes capable of providing armed protection for drug traffickers and/or offering to obtain "hit men" to kill potential witnesses against these individuals (Sherman, 1974a). It is highly unlikely that a rookie officer fresh from the police academy would immediately begin shaking down crack-cocaine dealers.

In an article entitled "Becoming Bent—Moral Careers of a Police Officer," Lawrence Sherman (1974b) hypothesizes that the deviant career of an officer is a gradual process of refining one's self-concept to accept increasingly more serious forms of law-violating behavior from the original frame of reference a new officer has on leaving the police academy. For Sherman (1974b) the transition from honest officer to thoroughly corrupt cop occurs in six stages.

Stage 1. Shortly after the rookie cop has completed training and is working the streets with a veteran officer, he or she may accept free coffee and meals at local restaurants. These initial acts of deviance are usually the result of peer pressure as the officer's self-image begins to change slightly.

Stage 2. With a somewhat modified sense of self and duty (concerning appropriate and inappropriate behavior), the new officer is ready to engage in more serious wrongdoing. For example, the officer may accept free drinks in exchange for permitting bars to stay open after hours.

Stage 3. Next an officer may accept a $20 bill tucked in behind a driver's license in lieu of writing a traffic ticket. Individuals paying for favors and special treatment are viewed matter-of-factly, as the officer internalizes a "that's the way the world works" mentality.

Stage 4. Stage 4 is a transition stage from relatively minor wrongdoing to more serious violations of the law. Officers may be offered and regularly accept money from bookmakers and illegal card parlor owners in exchange for turning a blind eye to what is happening on their watch. Sherman notes that this level of illegality is qualitatively significant as the now-increasingly corrupt officer is extended "an offer of solidarity" with his new "significant others" (fellow corrupt officers), "an invitation that he is loathe to reject" (p. 199).

Stage 5. Stage 5 marks the regular taking of bribes from pimps, streetwalkers, and the operators of houses of prostitution. Because the illegal sex industry is closely associated with drugs, this escalation in corruption is often a prelude to the sixth and final stage.

Stage 6. Sherman argues that getting involved with illegal drugs is the most difficult moral decision an officer has to make "since the initial frame of reference of most policemen would abhor the thought of helping drug pushers" (p. 200). After accepting money from drug traffickers it is a small step to selling drugs and doing whatever is necessary to make sure that one is not caught.

Police corruption depends on more than the strength or weakness of individual personalities. Situational factors include opportunities for engaging in corruption and the informal police culture that may support or discourage police deviance. Officers may never embark on a deviant career; if they do, these individuals may well remain at a level short of becoming thoroughly corrupt. However, one or more experiences of police deviance may be so severe that an officer may internalize the label of corrupt cop and accelerate the process. "What the hell, I'm a crook, so I'll make the most of it" (Sherman, 1974b, p. 201).

By way of conclusion, Lawrence Sherman (1974b) makes the thought-provoking observation that, if becoming a police officer capable of drug trafficking is a *gradual* process of redefining one's self-concept to accept ever more serious criminal behavior, corruption might be reduced by making the process less gradual; that is, if gambling and prostitution were legal, it would be a tremendous moral leap from accepting money to ignore a speeding violation to selling drugs, a jump requiring a radical redefinition of self that is very difficult to make. "Thus, a society concerned with police *narcotics* graft is well advised to legalize gambling and prostitution" (p. 205).

Corrupt Police Departments

Just as every organization has some members who at least occasionally act in an inappropriate manner, all police departments experience some corruption. However, the level of corruption across law enforcement agencies varies tremendously. In some departments, police deviance is limited to a few officers who violate regulations and (possibly) criminal laws infrequently, whereas other departments (or subsections of these departments, such as much of New York City's Seventy-Seventh Precinct in the 1980s) are thoroughly corrupt. Lawrence Sherman (1974c) offers a typology of corrupt police departments (grounded in data from actual departments) based on "the *pervasiveness* of corruption, its *organization,* and the *sources* of bribes" (pp. 7–12, emphasis added).

Type I: Rotten Apples and Rotten Pockets. Type I is the most common and least serious form of wrongdoing. A small number of uniformed patrol officers—the "rotten apples"—acting independently engage in low-level corrupt acts such as taking bribes from motorists for not issuing tickets. Regardless of the seriousness of the corruption problem, police administrators and local political officials are likely to invoke the **rotten apples explanation** should this behavior become public. The rotten apples interpretation is a face-saving rendering for police administrators in at least two ways. First, it minimizes the size and scope of the problem. Rather than being seen as widespread, police deviance is viewed as a minor problem confined to no more than a handful of ("rogue") officers. Second, because the corrupt individuals are "morally weak," the police chief and other high-ranking officers bear no responsibility for their (the corrupt officers') actions. Comments about rotten apples are invariably followed by a statement(s) regarding the honesty, integrity, and effectiveness of the department as a whole regardless of whether these statements are true.

"Rotten pockets" (or small work groups) is a form of police deviance that exists in departments where corruption is a more frequently occurring and accepted practice. Whereas rotten apples are apt to be patrol officers, rotten pockets are plainclothes detectives and vice officers. These latter individuals are typically corrupted by people with whom they come in contact, such as prostitutes, pimps, and individuals involved in the illegal gambling industry. This level of deviance entails "very little organization" because the corrupters are paying off individual police officers and possibly a "rotten pocket" rather than a significant portion of the department.

Type II: Pervasive Unorganized Corruption. The defining characteristic of Type II police deviance is that, even though a *majority* of personnel are corrupt, they have little if any relationship with one another. Each officer on "the take" accepts his or her bribery money when the opportunity presents itself. No formal organization for receiving bribes exists.

Type III: Pervasive Organized Corruption. Type III departments are thoroughly corrupt with illegal behavior organized from the top down in an authoritarian hierarchy. These departments are embedded in a network of wrongdoing that includes corrupt judges and officials at the highest levels of local government. In addition, there is a close association among police officers at all levels and the illegal businesses of gambling, prostitution, and drug trafficking controlled by organized crime.

According to Sherman (1974c), the difference between Type II and Type III corruption can be clearly seen from the vantage point of a young police recruit. In a Type II department, the new officer learns from colleagues that opportunities for making money via corruption exist and are not only welcome but also should be "actively sought out" (p. 11). In Type III organizations, the rookie cop is told by superiors when and where payoffs from gambling houses and other illegal activities are to be made, how much goes to those higher up the chain of command, and how much the rookie can keep. Remaining an honest cop in a Type III department is much more difficult than in Types I and II departments.

Police and the Use of Force

Few people question the need for police to use necessary force in the performance of their duty because many individuals they encounter will resist arrest, run away from officers, attack them, and on occasion, attempt to kill them. The issue, therefore, is not whether force should be used, but how much force and under what circumstances. More specifically, there are two fundamental issues regarding use of force by police.

First, was the use of force justified? Was it necessary, or could the situation have been resolved in a nonphysical manner? Was the force administered within the confines of the law and/or departmental policy? Second, if the use of force was needed, was it administered at the appropriate level, or was more force used when a lesser application of force would have achieved the desired result?

Police Brutality—Definition and Frequency of Occurrence

If legitimate force is a necessary and inescapable part of police work, then police brutality is "the use of excessive physical force or any force that is more than reasonably necessary to accomplish a lawful police purpose" (Walker, Spohn, and DeLane, 1996, p. 96). The difficulty with this and similar definitions is determining what constitutes reasonable force. This point was duly noted by Sergeant Anthony Miranda of the New York City Police Department: ". . . but what's reasonable force in a moment of real danger to a cop who thinks he's in trouble, and what's reasonable in a courtroom can often be open to interpretation" (Marks, 1999, p. 1). That well-meaning, intelligent people can disagree on what constitutes excessive force was demonstrated more than 30 years ago when investigators working for the President's Commission on Law Enforcement and the Administration of Justice documented 37 cases of what they believed involved the improper use of force. When a panel of "experts" reviewed these incidents, they concluded that only 20 of 37 situations fit the definition of unreasonable force (Adams, 1996, p. 53). In other words, one group of observers determined that the cases included almost twice as many examples of excessive force as the second group agreed on. Whose interpretations were correct? Kenneth Adams (1996, p. 5) noted that this question may be impossible to answer because "applications of definitions to incidents will always be open to challenge."

Determining the number of incidents of excessive force in police departments across the country is problematic for other reasons as well. For example, what specifically should be counted? Consider the following example provided by Adams. Two police officers pull over a car occupied by five drunken teenagers, then hit three of the adolescents with their batons even though the youths offered no resistance. Should this situation be counted as one incident of excessive force, or as two police officers using unreasonable force, or as three citizens victimized by the officers? Another problem concerns comparing rates of excessive force. Although City A may have twice the rate of excessive force incidents as City B, a closer look at these urban areas reveals that the former has twice the number of violent offenders in the population (individuals at high risk for being on the receiving end of unreasonable force) as the latter.

In addition to violent offenders, there are other factors that affect the use of excessive force. After examining a number of studies in this area, Kenneth Adams (1996) offers the following list of attributes that increase the likelihood that excessive force will be used:

1. Low social class of the suspect
2. The presence of two or more officers
3. Alcohol use by the suspect or the officer
4. A relatively young suspect and officer
5. An inexperienced officer(s)
6. Although Adams does not mention it, other investigators include minority group status as an attribute.

A final method for determining the amount of excessive force on a police force is to ask the officers themselves. Although individual officers are reluctant to implicate themselves, police personnel are much less hesitant to answer questions regarding the use of excessive force on the department as a whole. For example, the Christopher Commission found that 30 percent of officers surveyed agreed that "the use of excessive force is a serious problem facing the Department" (in Adams, 1996, p. 75). Slightly less than 5 percent of the officers agreed that "an officer is justified in administering physical punishment to a suspect who has committed a serious crime" (p. 75).

In recent years, officers in departments across the country have been formally charged (and some have been convicted) with the unlawful use of force or what is commonly referred to as "police brutality." Following are some of the most well known instances of police and the use of extralegal force.

■ In 1991, Rodney King and two passengers were in a vehicle speeding on a Los Angeles area freeway. When California Highway Patrol officers attempted to signal King to pull over, he ignored them, triggering a pursuit. (King would later testify that he feared that if he received a moving violation ticket his probationary status following a robbery conviction would be revoked.) By the time King's vehicle stopped, between 24 and 27 police officers from several agencies were on the scene. When King failed to get out of the car (his two companions did so without incident) he was shocked with a 50,000 volt Taser (stun gun) by one of the officers. Once on the ground, King was hit at least 56 times by nightstick-wielding police (Kappeler et al., 1998). Nurses at Pacific Hospital where King was taken for treatment noted that officers joked and bragged about the number of times they hit the suspect, often using baseball analogies. "We played a little ball tonight, didn't we Rodney. . . . You know, we played a little hardball tonight, we hit quite a few home runs. . . . Yes, we played a little ball and you lost and we won" (Christopher Commission, in Kappeler et al., 1998, p. 142).

■ In August 1997, Abner Louima, a Haitian immigrant, was arrested in New York City and taken to a Brooklyn precinct house where he was handcuffed, beaten, and dragged into the restroom. A police officer jammed a broom handle up his rectum then waved the feces-covered stick under Louima's nose and threatened to kill him if he ever told anyone what happened. Louima suffered extensive internal injuries (Morganthau, 1999). The officer who perpetrated the attacked eventually confessed and was convicted of crimes carrying a minimum 30-year prison sentence. In February 2002, a Federal Appeals Court overturned the convictions of three other officers sentenced in the brutalization of Abner Louima. This decision prevented two of the officers from being retried for their involvement in this incident (Getlin, 2002).

■ In February 1999, Amadou Diallo, a 20-year-old immigrant from Guinea, Africa, was returning to his Bronx residence when he was stopped by four plainclothes New York City police officers for questioning. Within a few seconds of the encounter, Diallo was

Perhaps the most well known example of the use of excessive force by law enforcement personnel in the United States occurred in Los Angeles in 1991. More than 20 officers from numerous agencies watched or took part in the beating of Rodney King, who was struck with police batons approximately 56 times.

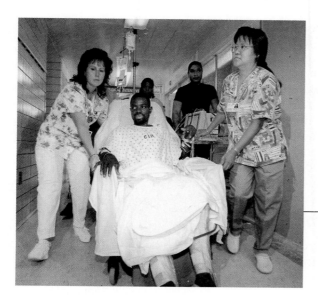

Haitian immigrant Abner Louima, a victim of police brutality at Brooklyn, New York's 70th precinct, is wheeled from his room at Coney Island Hospital. How many incidents of excessive force on the part of police officers never come to the attention of their superiors because victims are intimidated by the threat of future attacks?

dead, struck 19 times by the 41 bullets officers fired at him. Police maintain that Diallo did not respond to their questions and appeared to be reaching for a gun. The young African had no criminal history. When one officer realized the victim was unarmed, he administered CPR. Two other officers reportedly began weeping at the realization of what they had done. The four police officers involved in the shooting were charged with second-degree murder but later acquitted by a jury (Gleick and Epperson, 1999; Rogers and Campbell, 1999). The U.S. Department of Justice declined to file federal civil rights charges against the officers (Milton, 2001).

Police Violence—Why Does It Occur?

There are a number of explanations why some police officers engage in excessive force. While reading the following interpretations for this behavior, recall the discussion on police subcultures in Chapter 7. The values, norms, and patterns of conduct learned via this subculture may encourage, condone, and/or even demand that officers engage in the use of excessive force in some circumstances.

Excessive Force Is Tolerated

The Christopher Commission, the investigatory body that critically examined the Los Angeles Police Department in the wake of the Rodney King incident, concluded that excessive force was treated leniently at the command level because this behavior did not violate the department's "internal moral code." One officer told the commission that "some thumping" was permissible as a matter of course (Chevigny, 1995, p. 41). Anthony Bouza (1991), a 24-year New York City Police Department veteran and commander of a Bronx precinct, stated that "Cops develop the sense that they can exercise power without too great a risk of being called . . . strictly into account for its use" (p. 77).

Excessive Force as a Rite of Passage

The Commission to Investigate Allegations of Police Corruption and the Anti-Corruption Procedures of the New York City Police Department chaired by Milton Mollen (hereafter referred to as the Mollen Report) found that a willingness to abuse people who challenge police authority on the street or in the station house is a mechanism for officers to show that they are tough cops who can be trusted by fellow officers. "Brutality, like other forms of misconduct, thus sometimes serves as a rite of initiation into aspects of police culture . . . " ("Corruption in the New York City Police Department," 1995, p. 35).

Jennifer Hunt (1999) argues that it is a much graver error for a street cop to use too little force and begin developing a reputation among fellow officers as a "shaky" officer than to engage in excessive force and be told by colleagues to calm down. This is especially true of female officers who are often viewed by their male counterparts as "physically weak, naturally passive, and emotionally weak" (p. 309). Hunt relates an incident in which a female officer learned that she was the target of a police brutality suit while watching the evening news. She was fearful of going to work the next day and encountering angry colleagues, but the woman was instead greeted with a standing ovation. One male officer commented, "You can use our urinal now" (p. 309). Using excessive force may establish an officer's status as a "street cop" who does "real police work" rather than an "inside man" (Hunt, 1999, p. 309).

The "Dirty Harry" Problem

In the Dirty Harry films popularized by leading man Clint Eastwood, Inspector (Dirty) Harry Callahan of the San Francisco Police Department has no compunction about using excessive force to obtain information he deems necessary to solve crimes and save lives. In the first movie, Harry stomps on the bullet-mangled leg of a kidnapper in order to find the location of a kidnapped girl who will suffocate if she is not quickly located (Klockars, 1999). Some officers regard procedural laws (laws of search and seizure, for example) as little more than legal obstacles in the apprehension and conviction of criminals. Hence these laws are disregarded as officers resort to "dirty means" such as intimidation and torture in their roles as professional crime fighters. Criminologist James Fyfe (1997), a former New York City police officer, notes that these officers work on the presumption of a suspect's guilt. Regarding police violence in New York City, the Mollen Commission stated (in Chevigny, 1995, p. 78):

> Officers also told us that it was not uncommon to see unnecessary force used to administer an officer's own brand of street justice: a nightstick to the ribs, a fist to the head, to demonstrate who was in charge of the crime ridden streets they patrolled and to impose sanctions on those who "deserved it" as officers, not juries, determined. As was true in other forms of wrongdoing, some cops believe that what they are doing is morally correct—though technically unlawful—when they beat someone who they believe is guilty and who they believe the criminal justice system will never punish.

One Bronx, New York, police officer told commission members that he was called "the Mechanic" because he routinely "tuned people up," a "police word for beatin' people up" (in Cole, 1999, p. 23). This officer testified that tuning people up was widespread in his precinct.

Question: Did you beat people up who you arrested?

Answer: No. We just beat people up in general. If they're on the street, hanging around drug locations. Just—it was a show of force.

Question: Why were these beatings done?

Answer: To show who was in charge. We were in charge, the police.

Dirty Harry strategy the disregard of procedural laws (law of search and seizure, for example) and the use of "dirty means" such as intimidation and torture by police officers in their roles as professional crime fighters; named for the Dirty Harry movies starring Clint Eastwood

Officers adopting the **Dirty Harry strategy** may engage in violence to gain information about crimes and criminals, punish people they believe will escape successful prosecution, and/or establish a climate of fear in their jurisdictions. This latter strategy is based on the assumption that fearful individuals are more compliant and, therefore, a more easily controlled populace.

Police Mistakes

Whereas *extralegal violence* is the willful and wrongful use of force by officers who knowingly exceed the limits of their authority, *unnecessary violence* occurs when well-meaning officers prove incapable of dealing with a situation without resorting to force too hastily or to a greater extent than is actually needed (Fyfe, 1997). This latter type of violence occurs when officers "lack—or fail to apply—the expertise required to resolve as bloodlessly as possible the problem their work requires them to conduct" (Fyfe, 1997, p. 534). The 1992 Kolts Commission that investigated the Los Angeles County Sheriff's Department stated that "Our staff reviewed many cases in which officers unnecessarily walked into or created situations which ultimately required the use of deadly force" (Chevigny, 1995, p. 53).

In December 1998, police officers in Riverside, California, found a young woman passed out in the driver's seat of a locked car with a pistol in her lap. The four officers testified that they spent approximately 7 minutes trying to wake Tyisha Miller by shouting at her and banging on the car (Gorman, 1999). When this course of action failed, the officers decided to break a window and take the weapon so that forthcoming medical personnel could render aid if necessary. According to police testimony, when the window was smashed, Miller woke up and reached for the gun. At this point, the four officers opened fire with 12 of the 24 shots striking the young woman and killing her instantly. The officers and their defenders argued that, although Miller's death was a tragic occurrence, they acted properly. Other "experts" stated the four policemen erred in breaking the window. They also should have anticipated Miller reaching for the weapon on being suddenly awakened by the sound of breaking glass (Gorman, 1999). In December 2002, the civil rights division of the Justice Department concluded that there was insufficient evidence to prosecute the four officers. Any negligence, poor judgment, or mistakes on the part of the police did not warrant criminal charges. The report stated that although Ms. Miller's death was a tragedy, the officers fired "out of fear for their safety" (Rosenzweig, 2002, p. B1).

Some decisions police officers are required to make occur in the context of what has been called the "split-second syndrome"; that is, a decision about whether to fire has to be made instantly lest a police officer(s) or bystander(s) risk injury or death at the hands of an assailant. According to James Fyfe, several aspects of the split-second syndrome must be understood and examined. Because no two police problems or encounters are exactly the same, no specific rules or regulations can be applied to the diagnosis of individual situations as they arise. Therefore, police officers will always have to make spur-of-the-moment decisions. Because of the stress police experience in potentially life-threatening situations (in addition to the time constraints they face), a significant number of inappropriate decisions are to be expected. Therefore, any subsequent criticism of police behavior is unwarranted. "Thus, if we are to maintain a police service whose members are decisive in the crisis to which we summon them, we had best learn to live with the consequences of the decisions we ask them to make. If we do not, we risk damaging police morale and generating a police service whose members are reluctant to intervene on our behalf" (Fyfe, 1997, p. 541).

Although former police officer Fyfe concedes that street cops often have to make almost instantaneous decisions, he also notes that the split-second syndrome can serve as an after-the-fact justification for unnecessary police violence. He notes that, even in the few minutes that it takes to respond to a robbery in progress or a man brandishing a gun, officers may be able to avoid making spur-of-the-moment decisions by analyzing the available evidence and planning their response(s). According to sociologist Carl Klockars (1996, p. 8), "Excessive force should be defined as the use of more force than a highly skilled police officer would find necessary to use in that particular situation." The problem here is that we can no more expect every weapon-carrying police officer to be "highly skilled" than one might realistically expect from any other occupation or profession.

Police Violence and Race

The relationship between the police, racial minorities, and police violence is complex and exists on several levels. In the United States, most police officers are white, and the people suspected of committing the crimes that they deal with on a regular basis (street crimes as opposed to white-collar crimes) are disproportionately African American

and Hispanic. Of the 59 cities with populations of more than 50,000 where racial/ethnic minorities are the numerical majority, only three had police departments in which minority group officers were equal to or exceeded the percentage of racial/ethnic minorities in that city (Kappeler et al., 1998). Whereas poor African Americans, Hispanics, and Native Americans collectively represent a significant portion of the police clientele (both as perpetrators and victims of street crime), for most of the history of this country, police officers have had little training in dealing with people from different backgrounds whose first language is often not English.

Speaking of policing minority neighborhoods, sociologist James Marquart (in Dudley, 1991, p. 13) argues that "white officers don't understand a lot of things that go on in these areas. One way to deal with that is to use force. It goes across all cultural boundaries." One Los Angeles police officer told the Christopher Commission that the prone-out technique (in which suspects are made to lie face down on the pavement) was "pretty routine" in minority communities because officers had been taught that "aggression and force are the only things these people understand" (Chevigny, 1995, p. 45). Stereotyping in a police–citizen encounter works in both directions (Geller and Toch, 1996). An officer who stops a "typical black gang member," who he believes is probably involved in the drug trade, is seen by the youth as the "typical ugly white cop" out to hassle African Americans. The youth's hostile reaction reinforces the officer's stereotype and leads to an arrest. The move to arrest confirms the young man's worst expectations of the officer, leading him to resist being taken into custody and thereby inviting the use of force or excessive force. As Geller and Toch (1996, p. 307) note, this experience not only reinforces stereotypes for all concerned, it also "increases the chance that the next prophecies on both sides also will be self-fulfilling."

If officers are taught to act more aggressively with certain groups of people, excessive force can be viewed in part as a consequence of institutionalized racism. After monitoring thousands of police radio transmissions over a 6-month period, the Christopher Commission found that racist messages were routinely transmitted by both officers and supervisors. Some of these messages are as follows (in Kappeler et al., 1998, p. 140):

- "Well . . . I'm back over here in the projects, pissing off the natives."
- "Sounds like monkey slapping time."
- "Lt. says learn Spanish bone head . . . Sgt. (A) says tell them to go back to Mexico."

Former Los Angeles police officer Mark Fuhrman (who testified in the O. J. Simpson murder case) told a screenwriter about his life as a big-city cop. He recounted his handling of African Americans (using the word *nigger* repeatedly) suspected of killing two police officers. "We basically tortured them. We broke 'em. Their faces were just mush. They had pictures of the walls with blood all the way to the ceiling and finger marks from trying to crawl out [of] the room" (in Witkin, 1995, p. 20). (Fuhrman later stated that this and other aspects of his conversation with the screenwriter were purely fiction; he was just giving the interviewer enticing material for her story.)

Much has been written about the police worldview of an "us" versus "them" society. The police are the "us," and everybody else falls into the "them" category. This polarization of the world is not uncommon in professions characterized by highly specialized training and a stressful, often dangerous working environment. Jerome Skolnick (1994) has written of the "working personality" that police develop along two significant aspects of the law enforcement occupation: danger and authority. "Police officers . . . develop a perceptual shorthand to identify certain kinds of people as symbolic assailants, that is, as persons who use gestures, language, and attire that the police have come to recognize as a prelude to violence" (p. 44).

Although this typology is useful, perhaps a more accurate way to conceptualize this polarized worldview is in terms of "insiders" and "outsiders." Even family, friends, fellow officers, and police administrators who do not "work the streets" (and do not experience and understand the world as street cops do) are often considered outsiders. However, some outsiders are much more distant than others. This latter group is likely to include people from different racial and ethnic groups as well as individuals suspected of being or known to be troublemakers and criminals. These extreme outsiders are most likely to be recipients of excessive force. Poor people of color file the majority of brutality complaints leveled against police in virtually every big city in the nation.

To categorize all police officers as racial bigots would be both flat out wrong and grossly unfair to the hundreds of thousands of officers who are not prejudiced. However, to dismiss discrimination as a contributing factor in attempting to explain police and excessive force would be equally naive.

Fear and Fun

Fear is a normal reaction to finding oneself in a threatening situation. Recruits in military boot camp are taught that although fear cannot always be overcome, it can be managed to the extent that individuals are capable of performing their duty while still being frightened. Hans Toch (1996) found that police officers in fearful situations who could not admit to themselves that they were afraid tended to get angry beyond the point of control. These officers were most likely to use excessive force. One police chief stated that he believed some of his officers were fearful of African American suspects. The manifestation of this fear (in the form of nervousness, for example) might provoke resistance on the part of some African Americans who would in turn provoke a forceful response by officers. In addition, fearful officers may use force unnecessarily to mask their anxiety, which in turn might trigger resistance on the part of suspects. In order to control this defiance, officers may well engage in additional force. The Mollen Commission concluded that "some police officers use violence gratuitously . . . for power and thrills" ("Corruption in the New York City Police Department," 1995).

The War on Crime

Over the past 30 years, we have heard much about the **war on crime** and the war on drugs. These clichés are routinely used by politicians, police officials, police officers, and the media as well as the general public. In 1988, after an innocent bystander was killed in a shoot-out near the UCLA campus, the Los Angeles Police Department launched "Operation Hammer." Over the next 2 years, thousands of African American and Hispanic youth who made their way into the mostly white Westwood area were arrested. Many were forced to "kiss the concrete," then searched, and later released for lack of evidence (Chevigny, 1995). In a combat situation, soldiers attempt to overwhelm and destroy enemy forces. To the extent that patrol officers have internalized the war on crime mentality, they are more likely to brutalize the distant outsiders they encounter. When the police perceive themselves as an occupying army and local residents perceive them in much the same manner, they lose their connection to the local community. This bond is a fundamental requirement for doing police work both effectively and peacefully (Chevigny, 1995). The more unpopular police become, the more likely they are to resort to force, which leads to even greater local resentment, thereby escalating the cycle of violence.

The war analogy is often nourished by ranking police administrators. Referring to Operation Hammer, one LAPD official said, "This is Vietnam," and then–Police Chief Daryl Gates stated, "We're in a war . . . and even casual drug use is treason" (Chevigny, 1995, p. 40). Speaking of the war on drugs mentality that was prevalent during the crack-cocaine epidemic of the mid-1980s to mid-1990s, criminologist Samuel Walker noted, "It sent a message to police officers that you can go out and kick some butt, do whatever you need to do" (Harrison, 1991, p. 18). Patrick Murphy, who headed police commissions in three cities (Detroit, New York City, and Washington, D.C.) stated, "There is no doubt that this war-on-drugs rhetoric is part of the problem . . . raiding all these crack houses, more guns on the street, cops getting automatics . . . It has cops so psyched up they think they're in combat" (Dudley, 1991, p. 12).

Although police work can be dangerous especially in high-crime neighborhoods, the police are not soldiers and their risk of becoming fatalities in the line of duty is significantly less than that of combat troops and people in a number of civilian occupations.

war on crime a phrase often used by politicians, police officials, police officers, the media, and the general public to denote an all-out effort on the part of the city, state, or larger society to eradicate street crime

In 1996, the number of on-the-job fatalities per 100,000 police officers and detectives was 10.8. For select other occupations, work-related fatality rates per 100,000 in that same year were heavy equipment operators at 24.4; mining machine operators, 71.8; airplane pilots and navigators, 87.7; civilian sailors and dockhands, 132; and lumberjacks, 157.3.

"Contempt of Cop"

The two most prominent components of police work are authority and the ever-present threat of danger (Bittner, 1970). The Kolts Commission concluded that police brutality (especially against racial and ethnic minorities) was often directed against individuals who defied or criticized them (Chevigny, 1995). "This is the worst aspect of police culture, where the worst crime of all is 'contempt of cop.' The deputy cannot let pass the slightest challenge or failure immediately to comply" (Chevigny, 1995, p. 43). **Contempt of cop** reflects defiant attitudes of individuals for the authority of a police officer. Some officers consider a verbal affront no different from a physical assault inasmuch as verbal defiance can lead to a loss of control, which in turn increases the risk of danger. To maintain (or regain) control of a situation, some officers may resort to force.

Police are very likely to interpret flight from them as an act of defiance that cannot be tolerated. Individuals who attempt to escape a police–citizen encounter by way of a motor vehicle and trigger a high-speed chase undoubtedly place officers and the public in a precarious position. An individual who attempts to evade officers in this manner is likely to generate an "enraged reaction by the police" (Chevigny, 1995, p. 140). Skolnick and Fyfe (1993, p. 11) argue that motorists fleeing even minor traffic violations are "prime candidates for painful lessons at the end of police nightsticks." This contempt of an officer's authority and increase in the risk of danger by attempting to outrun police partially explains the beating administered to Rodney King in 1991. The fact that a pursuit can trigger strong emotions and violent behavior appears to be common knowledge for some officers. One veteran officer advised a rookie, "The only reason to go in on a pursuit is not to get the perpetrator but to pull the cop who gets there first off the guy before he kills him" (Hunt, 1999, p. 319).

In communities where police have reputations (as perceived correctly or incorrectly by residents) for using excessive force, a "spiraling effect" of police brutality may occur as suspects resist or flee arrest because they are fearful of what will happen to them in police custody (Harrison, 1991). This action both increases the chances that force will be used against a suspect and reinforces the belief of some officers that residents of this neighborhood must be dealt with aggressively.

Contempt of cop behavior that triggers excessive force often leads to additional incidents of police deviance. In categorizing Rodney King as a highly dangerous individual who required a savage beating to be subdued, officers stated that they reached speeds of 115 miles per hour in pursuing King. However, the manufacturer of the car King was driving reported it was impossible for that model vehicle (even a new one) to travel at such a high rate of speed (Kappeler et al., 1998). A subsequent investigation by the California Highway Patrol concluded that King was never going more than 65 miles per hour. The arresting officers also portrayed King as a drug-crazed madman who was impervious to pain. However, a blood test taken of King at the hospital revealed only a moderate amount of alcohol (0.075) and a small measure of marijuana. No PCP or other mind-altering substances were discovered in King who behaved in a quiet, cooperative manner according to medical personnel (Kappeler et al., 1998).

The Code of Silence

Officers who witnesses the use of excessive force by a colleague often have a difficult decision to make, which involves the **code of silence.** If the action is ignored, the use of force has been tacitly condoned, increasing the likelihood that it will happen again.

contempt of cop defiant attitudes of individuals (often those suspected of crimes) for the authority of a police officer; examples include direct profanity at an officer and fleeing after being stopped for questioning

code of silence the unwritten norm adhered to by officers not to inform on a colleague even if that individual has violated police procedures, for example, by engaging in excessive force

In addition, officers who remain silent are trampling the rights of individuals they are duty bound to protect and serve. However, if they are forthcoming to superiors regarding this police deviance, officers may face a variety of informal sanctions at the hands of their colleagues. According to one Los Angeles police officer, "What do you do if you see your partner do something wrong? If you can't stop him from doing it you're supposed to tell the watch commander. But if you squeal, no one will want to work with you" (in Dudley, 1991, pp. 12–13). Former New York police officer Frank Serpico, who was forced to leave the department in the early 1970s after he helped expose internal corruption, noted: "Why does the blue wall exist? Because there's a code that says, 'Keep your mouth shut and you will be taken care of' " (Serpico in Marks, 1999b, p. 1). According to Serpico, little has changed in the NYPD since he was a police officer.

Both the Christopher and Mollen Commissions found that officers who break the code of silence are not only ostracized but they also become the object of complaints and physical threats from colleagues. Perhaps the greatest fear an officer contemplating breaking the code has is that he or she will be left alone in a dangerous situation (Collins, 1999). The Mollen Commission discovered that, in the New York City Police Department, the code of silence also extended to supervisors who protected subordinates from charges of brutality and other irregularities and, in so doing, shielded their own careers from the taint of scandal ("Corruption in the New York City Police Department," 1995). With few exceptions, the code of silence would be more aptly named the iron law of silence. Regarding approximately 8,000 civilian complaints against police that were investigated in New York City in 1987 and 1988, not one case of an officer coming forward with incriminating information about a colleague arose (Harrison, 1991).

Some observers believe that the "blue wall of reluctance" is eroding and that "Good officers are anxious to weed out the bad ones when they crop up" (Pasco in Marks, 1997, p. 1). The officer who provided key evidence in the prosecution of New York City Police Officer Justin Volpe in the brutal assault of Abner Louima was motivated by the seriousness of the crime. However, he and his family were placed in protective custody as a result of threats against them. Other officers who testified against Volpe waited days and in some cases weeks to come forward, and they did so only out of fear of getting caught up in a widening federal investigation. One of those officers also requested police protection (Marks, 1997; White, 1997).

It would not be an exaggeration to say that overcoming the wall of silence is the most critical factor in significantly reducing police misconduct. Criminologist James

Alan Fox (in White, 1997, p. 63) stated that "Whistleblowers who come forward need to feel admired, not detested. It is the only way the system can be freed of corruption, misconduct, and brutality."

Department Philosophy and Accountability

A police department's objectives and overall philosophy appear to be related to officers' use of excessive force. For example, the Christopher Commission (1994, p. 299) concluded that "LAPD officers were trained to command and to confront, not to communicate." Officers were evaluated and rewarded on the basis of "high citation and arrest statistics and low response times" (Toch, 1996, p. 98). Although this philosophy may generate favorable arrest statistics, it does so at the expense of building the goodwill, trust, and respect of the community. The Christopher Commission noted that when officers made a mistake they had no time to explain their actions or apologize to people. They had to write up a citation or make an arrest as quickly as possible and rush off to the next call. An 8-hour shift of short, sometimes tense, interactions with officers continually watching the clock and hurrying to the next call can result in a great deal of stress. This stress, in turn, can produce short-tempered police likely to engage in excessive force.

We began this section by noting that the informal moral code of the department can foster the use of excessive force. We conclude by noting that arguably the major reason for the use of excessive force in many police departments is the lack of accountability for such actions. Officers who engage in this behavior believe that they can get away with it. Officer John Volpe, who pleaded guilty in the torture case of Abner Louima, boasted "I broke a man down" with impunity. Likewise, prior to the Rodney King affair, Los Angeles police officers transmitted hundreds of improper messages including dozens in which they referred to beating suspects ("Capture him, beat him, treat him like dirt") with little if any fear of being disciplined. The Christopher Commission found that 44 Los Angeles police officers were cited for six or more allegations of brutality over a 4-year period, and all received favorable fitness reviews from the department (Dudley, 1991). A former LAPD assistant chief told the commission that management's inattention to the problem along with a lack of accountability were the "essence of the force problem. . . . We know who the bad guys are. Reputations become well known, especially to the sergeants and of course to lieutenants and captains in the area. . . . But I don't see anyone bringing these people up" (Brewer in "Brutality in the Los Angeles Police Department," 1995, p. 19).

In a 440-page report based on research of 14 big-city police departments over a 2-year period, Human Rights Watch stated: "Police Departments like to claim that each high-profile case of abuse is an aberration, committed by a 'rogue' officer. But these human rights violations persist because accountability systems are so defective" (Human Rights Watch, 1998, p. 1). According to Samuel Walker this is precisely the situation that exists in the Los Angeles Police Department 11 years after the Rodney King incident. Walker (in Wood, 2002, p. 2) stated that "the LA police leadership simply continues to operate with an in-your-face attitude . . . that they know all the problems and no one else can possibly understand. Therein lies their problem."

James Fyfe (in Gleick and Epperson, 1995, p. 39) argues that ranking police officers in the chain of command with the most power to correct brutality and racism "are products of the system." As such, their loyalties are more in line with the department than with the public. Rather than punish individuals for lying when they got caught, the Mollen Commission discovered that NYPD supervisors instructed patrol officers how to prepare convincing false testimony. At the academy, police recruits learned what was considered a fundamental survival tactic: "cover your ass" (in Chevigny, 1995, p. 80). Until police officers come to realize that they will be held accountable for their actions by a department that refuses to tolerate the implementation of excessive force, this type of police deviance will not only persist, but in some departments it will be relatively routine behavior.

Devil Cops in the City of Angels

It has been called the worst scandal ever to hit Los Angeles and possibly the most shameful episode in the history of U.S. law enforcement. What started out as a routine internal investigation of a single cop quickly spread to a probe of an entire police station. Officer Rafael Perez was caught removing 8 pounds of cocaine from an evidence room, drugs he intended to sell on the streets. Convicted of the cocaine theft and hoping to reduce his sentence, Perez told investigators about widespread corruption at the Rampart Division, a police station in a neighborhood notorious for gang activity. The investigation uncovered evidence of false arrests, beatings, unjustified shootings, evidence planting, witness intimidation, and perjury (Glover and Lait, 2000a). Twenty officers were relieved of their duties, two others fired, and dozens more investigated for either committing crimes or knowing about these offenses and covering them up (Glover and Lait, 2000b).

Undoubtedly, the most shocking details to emerge from the corruption probe were the unjustified shootings and how these incidents were covered up. In one episode, Perez and his partner shot an unarmed 19-year-old gang member, Javier Francisco Ovando, and then planted a rifle next to him to make it look as if he attacked the officers. During the course of the trial, the presiding judge severely chastised Ovando for endangering the lives of two heroic police officers. Paralyzed from the waist down as a result of the shooting, Ovando was sentenced to 23 years in prison (Cohen, 2000). Released after being incarcerated for almost 3 years, he is suing the city of Los Angeles.

In another incident, Perez and a partner shot a gang member they were chasing through the halls of an apartment building. On reaching the fallen suspect, the officers discovered that he was not armed. Although 21-year-old Juan Saldana was bleeding profusely, police delayed calling an ambulance while they planted a gun where he fell and concocted stories that would justify the shooting. Saldana died shortly after arriving at a trauma center. An autopsy revealed that he was shot once in the chest and once in the back (Lait and Glover, 2000a).

On a third occasion, police kicked down the door of an apartment and found a suspect fast asleep. Two officers jumped on the man and began beating him with their fists and flashlights. Perez told investigators that "This guy didn't run. This guy was asleep—legitimately asleep" (Lait and Glover, 2000b, p. A1). Realizing that a police brutality complaint was a virtual certainty, the officers discussed how they were going to explain their behavior. When a sergeant arrived, Perez and the other officers told him two stories. "At first we told him how it actually happened and how this guy was beat down. And then, uh, we told him how we were going to explain it" (Lait and Glover, 2000b, p. A1). The sergeant instructed the officers to pour beer on the fire escape to bolster their story that the suspect received some of his injuries when he fell down the stairs during the chase.

The officers involved in these crimes were members of the Rampart Division anti-gang unit known as CRASH—Community Resources Against Street Hoodlums. Ironically, this organization took on numerous characteristics of the street gangs they were attempting to control. To become a member of CRASH, an individual had be sponsored by other officers. When an individual joined the unit, CRASH members allegedly beat him in an initiation ceremony similar to what street gangs call "jumping in." According to Perez, for an officer to be considered a "stand-up" guy, he had to do whatever was deemed necessary (legal or illegal) to fight gang activity. Allegedly, some Rampart officers wore "colors," had special handshakes, hand signs, and tattoos, all trappings of gang behavior. After a civilian was pummeled by a CRASH member, an officer leaving the scene allegedly turned and yelled "Puro Rampart!" (totally Rampart) imitating a gang slogan (Cohen, 2000). A sign above Rampart offices proclaimed: "We intimidate those who intimidate others" (Glover and Lait, 2000a, p. A1).

Perez stated that the standard practice among Rampart officers after a shooting was to "celebrate." The night Juan Saldana was shot and killed, Perez and two other officers drank in a local bar until 6 or 7 A.M., the bartender letting them stay long after closing

time. Rampart officers also had shooting parties where they drank beer, barbecued steaks, and awarded their comrades plaques for wounding or killing someone. One officer stated, "It might seem kind of barbaric . . . they're glorifying it in a way. But it's good for morale. They talk about the shooting, how they're heroes or whatever" (Glover and Lait, 2000c, p. A1). Officer Perez received an award for shooting and paralyzing Javier Ovando. Speaking of the plaques that consist of a playing card with two bullet holes in it, Perez told investigators that "Uh, if the guy dies, the card is a black number two. If he stays alive, it's a red number two." Asked if it is more prestigious to get a card that is black than red, Perez responded, "Yeah, I mean, you know, the black one signifies that a guy died" (Glover and Lait, 2000c, p. A1). Hardly secret events, shooting parties were sometimes held at the Police Academy, and on at least one occasion a captain was present.

As egregious as the unjustified beatings and shootings were, the heart of the LAPD scandal is the widespread perjury on the part of the many Rampart officers who joined the "liars club." Perez told investigators that "90 percent of officers who work CRASH, and not just Rampart CRASH, falsify a lot of information. They put cases on people . . . it hurts me to say this but there's a lot of crooked stuff going on in the LAPD" (Lait and Glover, 2000b, p. A1). Perez identified 57 cases involving 99 defendants wherein he and his partner perjured themselves and fabricated evidence, mostly false drug and weapons charges. Some Rampart officers specialized in particular kinds of misconduct; one planted guns on people, whereas another, dubbed the "Candyman," concealed crack-cocaine on unsuspecting individuals (Lait and Glover, 2000c, p. A1).

As of March 2000, more than 40 criminal convictions had been overturned, and as many as 17,000 cases involving the testimony of 71 officers would have to be reviewed. Los Angeles district attorney Gil Garcetti said this reevaluation process could take months, possibly years. The number of civil suits brought against the city as the Rampart scandal unfolds could run into the thousands. One attorney had already filed 10 suits and was in the process of filing 190 more. According to initial estimates, the city of Los Angeles might have to pay as much as $125 million in damages. That figure has been revised upward to hundreds of millions of dollars, and some observers believe Los Angeles could wind up bankrupt.

The impact of the scandal will affect the criminal courts to some unknown degree. One judge noted that in the future both he and juries will be less likely to believe the testimony of law enforcement personnel. This means that the honest and forthright testimony of police officers may well be discounted by many jury members resulting in fewer convictions of guilty defendants.

The LAPD released a 362-page inquiry report of the Rampart scandal, a document that was greeted with limited praise and much criticism. To begin, the department's hiring process is insufficient. Four of the 14 Rampart officers at the heart of the scandal were hired despite some combination of the following: a criminal record, narcotics involvement, and histories of violent behavior and financial problems including bankruptcy. Seven of the officers were hired from outside California without the benefit of face-to-face interviews ("LAPD's Unlearned Lessons," 2000). This lax recruiting and hiring system dovetails with the "few bad apples" and "no more than a handful of rogue cops" explanation favored by police administrators.

The report failed to state how many officers were directly or indirectly involved and how high up the administrative ladder misconduct occurred. It is hard to fathom that criminal behavior on the part of so many officers for an extended period of time was not noticed by supervisors. For example, on many occasions, arrest reports of different individuals were almost identical with suspects supposedly having said and done the same thing. How did these "one size fits all" reports escape the attention of commanding officers? The code of silence must have been operative for much if not all of the time this illegal behavior was occurring, an issue the report does not address. The report also failed to recommend any new oversight boards or special prosecutors to deal with police corruption. Former LAPD Police Chief Leonard Parks was adamantly opposed to any external review process (Chemerinsky, 2000).

In the aftermath of individual officers being punished and the absence of any new external mechanisms to oversee the behavior of LAPD officers, no reason exists to believe that widespread police corruption will not happen again, possibly in the near future. Warren Christopher, chair of the 1991 Christopher Commission that investigated the wrongdoing of the Los Angeles police officers, stated, "It's troubling to find that there are matters of real importance that were discussed in our report of nine years ago that remain unaddressed or not fully resolved today" ("LAPD's Unlearned Lessons," 2000, p. B4).

Policing the Police

Accountability, as Samuel Walker (1999, p. 268) has noted, is a complex issue that raises two basic questions: "*What* should the police be held accountable for?" and "What *procedures* are necessary for holding police accountable?" Regarding the first question, even the staunchest defenders of law enforcement admit that the use of excessive force on the part of police officers cannot be tolerated. As was noted previously, reasonable people can disagree on what constitutes excessive force. The second question is just as difficult. Who shall decide that an officer acted improperly, and what procedures shall be followed in arriving at this decision? To date there have been three types of **police accountability** or oversight: internal control, government control, and community control.

> **police accountability** the philosophy that individual officers and the department as a whole should be accountable for police behavior

Internal Control

For most of their history, police *departments* in the United States were not accountable to anyone (Walker, 1999), although *individual* patrol officers and detectives answered to superiors within the department. In other words, the police were policing themselves. David Bayley (1985) argues that internal mechanisms of accountability can be effective for three reasons: (1) Because determined command officers can hide just about anything from outside investigators, an internal control and accountability process is much more likely to discover what is really happening within a department. (2) Because internal affairs officers are intimately familiar with their departments, in-house investigations can be much more thorough than external inquiries, and as such, are likely to focus on a whole range of police activities and not only the visible incidents in question. (3) Because the investigators are police officers knowledgeable about police culture, they are capable of making subtle inquiries that can be quite revealing, inquiries that an outsider could never make.

Like members of other highly trained, specialized professions, the police have long held that only they are capable of understanding police work and problems, and, therefore, of disciplining fellow officers. A policy of internal review can be effective if it is carried out in a conscientious manner that is fair to all concerned. This, as the many critics of internal police control have pointed out, is the heart of the problem. Police officers who know the system well enough to uncover wrongdoing also know the wrong-doers well enough to protect them and the entire department.

Individuals and various groups across the country have complained bitterly over the years about what they believe are the systematic injustices perpetrated by internal reviews of police misconduct, especially police brutality. For example, it is often very difficult for a citizen to have his or her complaint accepted and acted on by the police. When Rodney King's brother went to the station to file a grievance, the designated officer refused to fill out the form (Chevigny, 1995). In multiethnic neighborhoods where many residents speak a language other than English, complainants may find that no officers at the desk can help them. In addition, investigations are often "lax and incomplete," and the person making the complaint may never be informed how the case was resolved (Chevigny, 1995).

John Crew, head of the Police Practices Project of the ACLU, believes that internal mechanisms for dealing with misconduct will never be effective. He argues that politicians, and police administrators in particular, lack "the will to take steps necessary to institute real [police] oversight, real accountability, real scrutiny. It is a pattern that stretches from the president to the Department of Justice, to statehouses, down to the local city council and police chief" (in Wood, 1999, p. 1).

Government Control

The U.S. Department of Justice (DOJ) plays a significant role in dealing with police misconduct at the local, state, and federal levels. In 1997, the Civil Rights Division of the DOJ reviewed approximately 8,000 complaints filed against police officers primarily at the local (city and county) level. FBI agents conduct an investigation and submit their reports to the Civil Rights Division and the U.S. attorney's office. After reviewing these reports, prosecutors decide whether to (1) decline prosecution based on their interpretation of the evidence, (2) request a more comprehensive investigation before making a decision, or (3) determine that there is sufficient evidence to present to a federal grand jury (Perez, 2000).

The DOJ can investigate police misconduct where other mechanisms of accountability are ineffective or simply do not exist. For example, in 1990, the FBI received complaints of excessive force on the part of local police from two residents of a small Ohio town. During the course of their investigation, the agents learned that the chief of the approximately 20-person department sent a memo to his officers stating that they were not required to cooperate with the FBI. Most of the officers interpreted this to mean that they were not permitted to talk to federal agents, and one officer was told that if he testified in court he would be fired. Because of the difficulty in gaining the cooperation of witnesses and police officers, a federal grand jury investigation (which allows individuals to give testimony in secret) was launched. One officer (the chief's son-in-law) was eventually charged with five violations of federal law stemming from excessive force incidents, and the chief was charged with two counts of obstruction of justice. The chief and his son-in-law were sentenced to 46 and 63 months in prison, respectively (Perez, 2000).

Community Control

During the past 15 to 20 years, communities have been moving toward independent citizen review boards to investigate police misconduct, especially the use of excessive force. Currently, about 100 such fact-finding bodies exist in this country. In her research, Sandra Bass (2000) found that cities with significant African American political participation and leadership were most likely to establish civilian review boards and confront difficult police policy issues. Police unions and associations have been highly critical of civilian oversight, arguing that only law enforcement personnel understand the pressures and demands of police work, and they have vigorously opposed such groups. Mary Powers of the National Coalition on Police Accountability believes that civilian review boards are a necessity if police misconduct is to be curtailed. "Without watchdog organizations that have teeth, police know they can hide behind civil-service protections until the latest scandal passes by. Then they come out again when the coast is clear" (in Wood, 1999, p. 3). This does not mean mutual trust and respect cannot exist between the police and civilian oversight groups. San Francisco and Pittsburgh are two cities where this relationship has been reported to work. Elizabeth Pittinger of the Pittsburgh Citizen's Police Review Board stated, "If you are going on a witch hunt or cop chase just for the chase, it won't work. The key is being fair and balanced" (in Wood, 1999, p. 3).

An often-overlooked problem regarding the use of excessive force on the part of police and the community are the mixed messages citizens may be sending law enforcement personnel. Bass (2000, p. 162) discovered that communities experiencing serious

problems with violence and drug use "condone and even encourage aggressive action against 'known' offenders while deploring these same police practices against 'innocent' members of the community." In some instances, citizens encouraged police to behave in a manner that was not only questionable but also quite possibly illegal.

All review boards, be they internal or external, substantiate no more than 20 percent of the complaints they receive. Many of the accusations against officers are without merit. Some people are simply mistaken about what constitutes excessive force, whereas others are attempting to shift the focus of attention from their own criminal behavior to the contrived misconduct of the police. Most complaints are impossible to authenticate because of lack of witnesses. Finally, because of the code of silence, many cases end up a matter of the complainant's word against the interpretation of the police (Chevigny, 1995).

A final point by Paul Chevigny (1995) about police review boards is worth noting. Regardless of whether they are internal (police) or external (civilian), these investigatory bodies cannot discipline anyone. On reaching the findings from the review board, the police chief alone has the authority to determine who shall be disciplined and in what manner. No serious movement to alter this system of control has emerged and state legislators are not likely to grant review boards the authority to punish public officials.

Based on their 1998 report of the use of excessive force by police, Human Rights Watch offered the following recommendations for reform (Human Rights Watch, 1998):

- Make federal aid to police departments contingent on regular reporting about the use of excessive force.
- Create among police and political leaders a policy of zero tolerance for abuse.
- Establish early warning systems at the departmental level to identify officers at risk for engaging in abusive behavior and remove those individuals who engage in this manner of misconduct.
- Hire special prosecutors in each state to handle criminal prosecutions of police.

In the years since the report was published, to our knowledge, none of these recommendations has been implemented in a systematic "official policy" manner.

FOCUS on Mexico

Police Deviance in a Developing Nation

In most societies, people view the police with a combination of respect, fear, and anger, depending on the local crime rate and whether they have received a speeding ticket in the past few months. This is not the case in Mexico where citizens have strong feelings about the police. "To say that Mexicans hate their police doesn't quite capture the feeling. Abhor? Loathe? Revile? Well, yes, those are closer but still not quite it. Abominate? Yes, that's the feeling I encountered when talking to Mexicans about their police. Mexicans abominate their police" (Oster, 1989, p. 166). In addition, the people are fearful of extortion, robbery, torture, even murder. "That's what happens after the police arrive" (Oster, 1989, p. 166). A national joke in Mexico is that a kid can play cops and robbers—by himself. Since journalist Peter Oster wrote those words almost 15 years ago, overall police deviance in this Latin American country has become an even greater problem.

Between 1995 and 1997, crimes increased at a rate of 30 percent in Mexico City. One reason an estimated 96 percent of these offenses remains unsolved is that no more than one in five people report criminal victimizations to police for fear of being preyed on a second time (Padgett, 1998). Another reason for the low clearance rate is that police themselves commit a significant number of these offenses ("Policing the Capital," 1998). When Mexico City police opened a substation in a middle-class neighborhood, the residents protested until the office was closed (Holmstrom, 1997). Police deviance is so pervasive in Mexico that even former president Ernesto Zedillo was forced to acknowledge its existence. He stated that "we have no police forces to trust in Mexico and I must be very frank with you, very blunt about it" (Winner, 1995, p. G5).

Police officers engage in at least three types of criminal behavior at local, state, and federal levels in Mexico.

1. Police often victimize citizens in much the same manner as street criminals, that is, via robbery, burglary, sexual assault, rape, and kidnapping. In the aftermath of the 1985 Mexico City earthquake that killed 30,000 people and left hundreds of thousands homeless, reports of police looting the homes and apartments of victims appeared (Riding, 1989). Between late May and early June 1997, 14 street children were arbitrarily arrested and then beaten by Mexico City police. Two of the youths were raped while in custody (Amnesty International Report, 1998: Mexico, 1998). In July 1998, three girls were kidnapped by a group of police officers and repeatedly raped over a 4-day period. None of the 15 officers charged with the latter crime was brought to trial ("Policing the Capital," 1998). High-ranking Mexican police are thought to be heavily involved in the nation's billion dollar kidnap/ransom industry (Padgett, 1998).

2. Many observers think that Mexican police are routinely used by the Partido Revolucionario Institucional (Institutional Revolutionary Party) to curtail political opposition. In June 1995, police in the southern state of Guerrero set up roadblocks, ostensibly to capture local kidnappers. When truckloads of peasants were stopped and a shot was fired (by the peasants according to Mexican authorities), police opened fire. Seventeen people were killed, and 20 more were wounded. Critics of the "massacre" contend the police—under the direction of state officials—deliberately murdered these impoverished people who were on their way to an antigovernment political rally. In 1997, several Jesuit priests along with leaders of Mexico's indigenous community and human rights organizations were arrested, beaten, burned, and subjected to mock executions by police before being released (Amnesty International Report 1998: Mexico, 1998). Journalists and television reporters investigating police corruption and other issues that would prove embarrassing to the government have been subject to arbitrary arrests, beatings, and death threats.

3. The most visible and ubiquitous form of police corruption is *la mordida*—the "bite" of the traffic cop (Riding, 1989). Police in Mexico may stop any moving vehicle and take a bribe in lieu of writing a ticket. This procedure is simple and straightforward because most drivers would rather pay off the police than take the time and trouble of paying a more expensive fine. In some areas of the country, *la mordida* is so common and institutionalized that truck drivers simply stop when they see a parked Federal Highway Patrol car and hand over money as if they had encountered a toll booth.

This form of police corruption can be explained in part by the fact that Mexican police are paid so poorly. One government official noted that if police had to exist only on their salaries, "they would live in cardboard boxes in the slums" (Scott, 1992, p. 3). Not only are wages low but also the typical officer has to buy his or her uniform, pistol, and even bullets. Also, many police in Mexico do not "have" jobs as much as they "rent" them. This rent, so to speak, must be paid off on daily basis to supervisors who in turn pay off their superiors. This system of tribute "can add up to hundreds of dollars a week, and that kind of money can only come from extortion or other illegal sources" (Garcia in La Franchi, 1994, p. 9). To get a good assignment, that is, duty at a location where it is easy to extort motorists, a Mexico City officer has to pay an immediate superior about $125 a shift. To recoup this outlay and turn a profit, the officer charges people $6 to overlook a parking violation and $12.50 to ignore running a stop sign. One Mexican police officer stated that "the best assignments are in sections where working-class people live. They don't want problems and they don't have any influence. They pay up on the spot" (Sanchez in Golden, 1997a, p. A14).

Low salaries (a watch commander earns about $900 a month and a patrol officer approximately $200 to $300) are also a major reason why so many Mexican police have been corrupted by drug smugglers. So much money is being made on cocaine passing through Mexico from Colombia on its way to the United States that drug barons spend an estimated $500 million on bribes. When the leader of one of the nation's largest drug cartels was arrested in the state of Jalisco, 33 police officers moonlighting as his bodyguards were also taken into custody (Holmstrom, 1997). In 1997, the director of the National Institute to Combat Drugs was arrested for corruption. In April 2002, 41 officers were arrested for their alleged involvement with the Arellano Felix Drug Cartel. Among those caught in the sting operation was the city of Tijuana's police chief and several high-ranking state police commanders (Dibble, 2002). Richard Cohen (1997, p. 29) is correct when he notes that "It's utterly naive to believe that non-Americans will turn down great riches, or even, moderate bribes, so that American drug users will have to pay a bit more—maybe even go without drugs."

In an effort to rid the 27,000-member Mexico City police force of corruption, the police chief was removed and replaced with a high-ranking officer from the Mexican Army. General Enrique Salgado's first action was to dismiss 900 police officers for taking bribes and other offenses and to assign approximately 150 military officers to key positions in the department. Although this action may well be a step in the right direction, many observers remain skeptical. A member of the Mexico City Representative Assembly stated that "Police corruption here is a monstrous problem . . . embedded in the very bone and marrow of the department." Everything that new rookie police officers "learn in the academy about honesty and values vanishes the moment they arrive at the station house" (Penaloza in Golden, 1997b, p. A1).

summary

1. Although most Americans have a positive image of the police, the history of law enforcement in this country has been replete with corruption and scandal. A former FBI director noted that police corruption exists in every region of the United States in departments that are large and small, in inner cities, and in affluent suburbs. Two categories of police corruption exist: (a) Non–work-related wrongdoing or nonoccupational deviance consists of those activities that have little if anything to do with police work. An officer writing bad checks would be an example of this form of police deviance. (b) Work-related police misconduct occurs in the course of performing one's duties. Accepting money in exchange for not arresting someone or shaking down drug dealers falls into this category. In recent years, a significant amount of police misconduct has been drug related. Police officers may rationalize their deviant behavior by telling themselves ("self-talk") that, although they are doing something illegal, they are doing much more good for society as a whole, their wrongdoing is inconsequential, and either no one or only criminals are hurt by their transgressions.

2. Police corruption has a significant impact on the police, the courts, and the larger society. When corruption is uncovered, citizens are likely to lose respect for the police, making their job more difficult. The public may generalize the wrongdoing in one precinct or department to all law enforcement officials. The effectiveness of the criminal courts is un-dermined when officers perjure themselves. Innocent people may be falsely convicted, and if the perjury is later discovered, juries may be less inclined to believe the testimony of officers when they are telling the truth. Internal discipline may be compromised when corrupt supervisors effectively lose control of their command for fear of being exposed by subordinates who are aware of (the supervisors') wrongdoing. An officer does not become a "crooked cop" overnight. Rather, the deviant career of an officer is a gradual process of redefining one's self-concept to accept increasingly more serious forms of law-violating behavior.

3. The level of corruption across law enforcement agencies varies considerably from a few officers violating rules and laws to entire precincts or even departments that are thoroughly corrupt. In some agencies, a few rotten apples acting independently engage in various forms of corruption. Rotten pockets (or small work groups) are those departments where corrupt behavior on the part of officers is a more frequently occurring and widely accepted practice. In departments characterized by pervasive unorganized corruption, although the majority of officers are corrupt, they have little if any relationship with one another because each person engages in work-related deviant behavior on his or her own. Pervasive organized corruption characterizes those law enforcement agencies that are thoroughly corrupt with illegal behavior being highly organized from the top (police administrators) on down.

4. The administration of legitimate force is an inescapable part of police work. Police brutality can be defined as the use of excessive physical force or any force that is more than reasonably necessary to accomplish a lawful police purpose. The difficulty with this and similar definitions is what constitutes excessive force, with even experts disagreeing on what physical action in a given situation should be condoned and what actions should be condemned. A number of factors increase the likelihood that an individual will become a victim of excessive force including: (a) low social class of the suspect, (b) the presence of two or more officers, and (c) a relatively young suspect and officer. The rate of excessive force complaints varies considerably across departments.

5. Police officers engage in excessive force for a number of reasons. The Christopher Commission, which investigated the use of excessive force in Los Angeles, concluded that this behavior was treated leniently at the command level because it did not violate the department's internal moral code. Excessive force may be considered a rite of passage, a mechanism to show officers that one is a tough cop who can be trusted by colleagues. According to the Dirty Harry explanation, officers may deliver street justice in the form of beatings because lenient judges and juries fail to give offenders the punishment they deserve. Police may resort to excessive physical violence because they are not properly trained or lack the personal skills to handle a situation in a less confrontational manner. Officers may physically abuse offenders because of outright racial prejudice or the mistaken belief that force is the only thing certain individuals understand. Excessive force may be the result of fear; that is, officers who were anxious might strike out first in anticipation of a situation escalating into a physical conflict. The war on crime has generated an us–them mentality with some officers viewing suspects in much the same way military personnel view enemy soldiers—individuals to be destroyed. Police officers may use excessive force against people who openly defy them according to the contempt of cop interpretation. Officers who witness colleagues using unreasonable force may fail to inform superiors because of the code of silence that is typically an integral component of the police subculture.

6. Arguably the worst scandal in U.S. law enforcement history recently occurred in the LAPD. Officers shot unarmed suspects, then planted weapons next to them. At shooting parties, officers awarded their comrades plaques for wounded or killing alleged offenders. Some officers perjured themselves in court and fabricated evidence. Over 40 criminal convictions had to be overturned; thousands more had to be reviewed.

7. According to police scholar Samuel Walker, the two most critical questions regarding the use of excessive force involve what police should be accountable for and what procedures are necessary for holding them accountable. For most of their history, police departments in the United States have not been accountable to anyone regarding the issue of excessive force. At best, individuals officers were accountable to their superiors, which resulted in the situation of police policing themselves. Police departments have long resisted being held accountable to external, independent review boards investigating any form of police misconduct including the use of excessive force.

key terms

code of silence
contempt of cop
Dirty Harry strategy
police accountability

police corruption
rotten apples explanation
sexual shakedown
war on crime

questions for investigation

1. How do you respond to police officers' rationalization about planting drugs on a person to secure a narcotics arrest?

2. There are few accounts of female officers sexually harassing citizens. Explain.

3. If a community knows that its police department is corrupt, what action can its members take to remedy this problem?

4. This chapter outlines six stages by which a rookie cop becomes corrupt. Is every rookie cop susceptible to this process? Explain your answer.

5. If a rookie cop discovers that he or she has become part of a Type II or Type III corrupt police department, what options does he or she have besides joining in the corruption?

6. List police behaviors that describe legitimate uses of force in various situations. Are there any circumstances when police brutality is excusable? Explain and be prepared to defend your answer.

7. What factors make identifying and defining police brutality so difficult?

8. What types of officer training might reduce the incidence of police violence? Consider this chapter's explanation for police violence as you answer this question.

9. Suppose you are appointed police chief of a department that has been described as "thoroughly corrupt" (officers on the take, numerous incidents of sexual harassment and police brutality). How would you go about solving these problems (a) without alienating your officers and (b) to gain the respect, support, and trust of community leaders?

IT'S YOUR CALL...

1. Your brother-in-law confides in you that he is being pressured by fellow police officers to accept bribes in the form of cash and jewelry from drug dealers in exchange for not arresting them as well as informing these individuals of the department's drug enforcement strategy. During the past year, he has learned that dozens of local police are on the take. He does not want to get involved but fears that he will be ostracized by these officers who may not come to his aid if and when he requires their assistance. He has considered quitting the force, talking to the precinct commander directly, and sending an anonymous letter regarding the situation to the police commissioner and the local media. He says that the tension and anxiety are affecting his health and his marriage. What advice do you give him? Be specific.

2. Gotham City has just experienced a second day of rioting following the shooting death of a teenage convenience-store robber at the hands of the police. This is the fourth questionable shooting death in the past 3 years, and, while the circumstances surrounding the current incident remain unclear, the rioters are especially angry at what they believe is a complete lack of police accountability. As one of the nation's foremost experts on police and police behavior, you have been hired by Gotham City to devise a procedure of police accountability that will satisfy the community but will not alienate on-the-street patrol officers. Submit a one- or two-page outline of your accountability plan to the mayor by way of your instructor. Remember, your plan should be as precise and straightforward as possible, including the place (if any) of civilians and nonpolice city officials in the accountability process.

Criminal
Courts:
History,
Organization,
and Pretrial
Procedures

1. What is jurisdiction? What are the important distinctions of jurisdiction in the U.S. court system?

2. Who are members of the courtroom workshop, and what is their goal?

3. Describe the function of criminal court judges.

4. What is the function of the prosecutor?

5. What is the function of the defense attorney? What are the systems for representing indigent defendants?

6. Identify the major steps in pretrial procedures.

7. What is the function of the grand jury?

8. Name the factors that decide whether a defendant should be detained before trial or released on bail.

For most of our history as a nation, the criminal justice system ignored domestic violence. Police were apt to view spousal abuse as a family matter and made arrests in only the most egregious cases. Likewise, prosecutors were typically loathe to file charges against an abusive husband and bring the defendant to trial. Feminists have argued that the failure of the police and courts to intervene on behalf of battered women was rooted in a male-dominated criminal justice system. Men did not arrest and prosecute other men for "disciplining" their wives.

As a result of mandatory arrest laws and the courts taking a much more aggressive stance against domestic violence defendants, the situation has changed dramatically in recent years. Women who are abused by boyfriends and husbands routinely petition domestic violence courts for protective or restraining orders to keep their attackers away.

Although protective orders may literally save the lives of abuse victims, judges exhibit a growing concern that these judicial shields are being undermined by the very individuals they are designed to protect—the women who requested them. Within days of their issuance, it is not uncommon for domestic violence victims to return to court "arm in arm" with the men they said they feared. Many judges find this rapid turnaround in attitude and behavior reprehensible and are taking steps to discourage it. In rural Kentucky, judges are sending women to jail for contacting their husbands after restraining orders have been issued. North Carolina judges fine women $65 for applying for a protective order and then deciding to drop the matter. In Illinois, some judges hold females in contempt of court for dropping their initial complaints and reconciling with boyfriends and husbands (Simon, 2002).

In Fayette County, Kentucky, a judge issued a temporary restraining order barring the husband "from any contact or communication" with his wife or baby and ordered the couple to return in 2 weeks to decide on a more permanent solution. By the time of their scheduled appearance before the court, the couple had reconciled. Judge Megan Thornton Lake was furious. "I have [no-contact] orders in place, [and then] folks walk into the courtroom . . . and everything's all hunky-dory. When these orders are entered, you don't do whatever you damn please and ignore them" (in Clines, 2002, p. A12).

The Clothesline Project is a collection of shirts created with stories from survivors, family, and friends of women who have been victims of violence.

In another instance, Thornton fined a woman $200 for returning to an abusive boyfriend. "Somebody with a fourth-grade education ought to be able to read this [no-contact order] and understand what it says" (Simon, 2002, p. A14).

Advocates for battered women argue that punishing victims of domestic violence for reconciling with their husbands demonstrates a complete lack of understanding of the difficult situations in which these women find themselves. For example, abused women—especially women who are poor and have little education—depend on their husbands for financial support both for themselves and their children. Some victims may be coerced into reconciliation by husbands who threaten escalated violence and tell them that the courts and police will not always be able to protect them. When she applies for a protective order, a woman wants the court's assistance in putting an end to the violence, but she does not necessarily want the judge to terminate the relationship (Simon, 2002).

Women's advocates acknowledge that some victims misuse the system, but they believe that punishing females for reconciling with their mates will discourage an unknown number of individuals trapped in violent relationships from seeking protective orders. Carol Jordan, director of Kentucky's Office of Child Abuse and Domestic Violence, stated that these rulings will "absolutely increase abused women's level of risk" and establish a barrier that prevents them from "seeking protection of the courts" (Clines, 2002, p. A14).

Supporters of disciplining women who return to abusive partners in the aftermath of a protective order counter these assertions by maintaining that, if restraining orders are routinely circumvented, judges will be less likely to issue them. This will keep women imprisoned in a cycle of violence with little hope of escape.

Informal judicial policy to punish women for reconciling may become law in some states as legislation is introduced to make the provisions of restraining orders binding on both parties. This will force the more than 30,000 women annually in Kentucky alone to make an important decision at a time when they are under tremendous emotional pressure and fear for their safety.

As one abuse victim told reporter Stephanie Simon (2002, p. A12) "Maybe they did explain to me [the restrictions a protective order would entail], but it's not the time you can look clearly at the pros and cons. . . . When I went to court [to get the order], I was thinking, 'Please stop him from hurting me. Please protect my children. . . .' I didn't think through whether I ever wanted to see him again."

Celebrated as the cornerstone of democracy in the United States, the Bill of Rights comprises the first 10 amendments of the Constitution, with four of these amendments delineating individual rights as they relate to criminal procedure. The Sixth Amendment states that "In all criminal prosecutions, the accused shall enjoy the right to a speedy trial . . . and have the assistance of counsel for his defense." However, for most of our history many states only recognized the right of poor people to have qualified legal representation in capital cases, that is, offenses punishable by death (Steury and Frank, 1996).

In the late 1930s, Smith Betts was indicted by a Maryland state court for robbery. During the **arraignment** (the first step in criminal proceedings when the defendant is formally charged with a crime), Betts told the trial judge that he did not have money to hire an attorney and asked the court to appoint one for him. The judge informed Mr. Betts that in this criminal court jurisdiction legal counsel was only provided for murder and rape cases. Betts proceeded to conduct his own defense and was convicted at a bench trial (a trial before a judge but without a jury); he was sentenced to 8 years in prison. After considering Mr. Betts's appeal in 1942, the Supreme Court ruled (in *Betts v. Brady*) that due process (in this instance the right to an attorney in a criminal case) did not mean defense attorneys had to be provided by the courts in all felony cases, but that due process required the state to appoint legal counsel to poor people only in special circumstances, such as capital cases, when a defendant is mentally impaired, and/or when the case involved complex legal issues (Findlaw, 2000; Israel and LaFave, 2001; Steury and Frank, 1996).

In 1961, Clarence Earl Gideon was arrested and charged with a felony for breaking and entering into a poolroom in Florida. As in the Betts case, Gideon stated that he did not have enough money to retain an attorney and asked the state to provide him with legal counsel. The following exchange took place in the courtroom (Findlaw, 2000, p. 2):

> **The Court:** Mr. Gideon, I am sorry, but I cannot appoint Counsel to represent you in this case. Under the laws of the State of Florida, the only time the Court can appoint Counsel to represent a Defendant is when the person is charged with a capital offense. I am sorry, but I will have to deny your request to appoint Counsel to defend you in this case.

> **Defendant:** The United States Supreme Court says I am entitled to be represented by Counsel.

Like Betts, Gideon was forced to argue his own case. He made an opening statement to the jury, cross-examined the prosecution's witnesses, called individuals to testify on his behalf, and presented a brief closing argument, performing "about as well as could be expected from a layman" (in Sexton and Brandt, 1986, p. 235). He was convicted and sentenced to 5 years in prison. After the Florida Supreme Court failed to overturn his conviction, Gideon submitted a handwritten petition to the U.S. Supreme Court asking the justices to review his case. The court responded affirmatively.

Reversing the Betts decision, the justices in a 9 to 0 vote agreed with the petitioner (*Gideon v. Wainright,* 1963). In the written opinion drafted by Justice Black, the court stated that "reason and reflection require us to recognize that in our adversary system of criminal justice, any person haled into court, who is too poor to hire a lawyer, cannot be assured a fair trial unless counsel is provided for him. . . . The right of one charged with crime to counsel may not be deemed fundamental and essential in some countries, but it is in ours . . . " (in Bartholomew and Menez, 1990, p. 284). The guiltless poor man who cannot afford a lawyer like the layman with no legal training "faces the danger of conviction because he does not know how to establish his innocence" (in Sexton and Brandt, 1986, p. 236). At a subsequent trial where he was provided legal counsel by the state, Gideon was acquitted.

In the years following the *Gideon* decision, many states provided legal counsel to all poor defendants regardless of whether they were charged with felonies or misdemeanors. However, other states limited state-appointed attorneys to those indigents accused of felonies and serious misdemeanors. A 1972 Supreme Court decision (*Argersinger v. Hamlin*) stated that the *Gideon* ruling applied to all misdemeanor defendants who are sentenced to jail time. In yet a further clarification of *Gideon* in 1979, the

arraignment the proceedings by which an individual is formally charged and required to enter a plea of guilty, not guilty, or nolo contendere; if the individual refuses to plea, the judge will enter a plea of not guilty on his or her behalf

Supreme Court ruled (*Scott v. Illinois*) that a defendant convicted of shoplifting—a crime punishable by imprisonment of up to 1 year in Illinois—but who was sentenced to a fine of $50 was not entitled to a court-appointed attorney. This ruling gave judges the discretion to deny appointing counsel in misdemeanor cases if they chose to punish offenders with something other than confinement on conviction. In other words, it is not the threat of incarceration but actual imprisonment that guarantees the right to counsel (Steury and Frank, 1996). However, in 2002, the Supreme Court ruled that an indigent defendant charged with a misdemeanor must have a court-appointed lawyer even if incarceration is only a remote possibility (Greenwood, 2002).

The history of the Sixth Amendment illustrates that laws have no single, inherent meaning clearly and unequivocally known to all. Rather, laws are reinterpreted at the macrolevel as well as on the specific occasions of their application (by police officers and judges, for example) in societies that are continually changing.

In this chapter we present an overview of the history and structure of criminal courts in the United States; consider the roles of judges, prosecutors, and defense attorneys; and examine the daily dynamics of criminal courts. Finally, we look at pretrial procedures that commence with a defendant's arrest. Plea bargaining and the criminal trial are analyzed in the next chapter.

History

The esteemed American legal historian Lawrence Friedman (1985) states that despite a fair amount of diversity and experimentation, the courts in the colonial United States were patterned after the judicial system in Great Britain. "English models, English terms, and English customs were more or less influential everywhere" (Friedman, 1985, p. 46). The colonial court system was a triangle-shaped hierarchy with justices of the peace courts at the base. Established in 1327 in England and 1634 in the Pennsylvania colony, these courts were the "workhorses of the legal system" (Walker, 1998, p. 28), and the **justice of the peace** had jurisdiction over civil and criminal matters at the local level. Often men (never women) of property and status, justices were appointed by the governor and had numerous duties that extended beyond the courtroom. These duties often included, but were not limited to, issuing licenses, keeping streams and rivers free of obstacles, collecting taxes, and supervising the construction of roads (Surrency, 1967).

justice of the peace a judge or magistrate of limited jurisdiction who presides over minor civil and criminal cases, including preliminary stages in the latter

This courthouse and jail in Marrieta, Ohio, was built in 1798, 10 years after the settlement was founded. During this period, judges often traveled from one settlement to another in a mostly rural, agricultural society. By the American Revolution, an official similar to the contemporary prosecutor, or district attorney, existed in many colonies.

Justices considered it part of their duty to maintain not only order but also standards of decency based on prevailing morals and values. For example, in the Massachusetts Bay Colony in 1636, a woman and two men convicted of adultery were whipped and banished. In one Virginia county between 1632 and 1645, the most common criminal court entries were for slander (making false and injurious statements about another person) and defamation, blasphemy (disparaging God or sacred things), adultery, and public drunkenness. Punishments for misdemeanor offenses typically involved amputating a body part, whipping, or sitting in a pillory for a designated period of time. One man was convicted of having sex with a calf (a capital offense) (Chapin, 1983; Surrency, 1967). Decisions reached by justices of the peace were often influenced by friendships, family ties, and economic relationships (Walker, 1998).

In the mid-Atlantic and southern states, justices of the peace also presided over slave courts that tried captive African Americans accused of crimes. Because they were valued for their labor, convicted slaves were rarely imprisoned. Rather, African Americans in these states received various forms of corporal punishment, usually a bare-backed whipping. Friedman (1985, p. 227) notes that slaves found guilty of some criminal transgression were whipped "throughly, soundly, and often." In the years after independence in 1776, the punishment of slaves in southern courts became even more severe. One of 12 slaves convicted in South Carolina received more than 100 lashes. Mississippi law stated that any "Negro or mulatto" giving false testimony in court would be nailed by the ear to the pillory for one hour at which time the ear was to be cut off. Then the other ear was to be likewise nailed and later removed (Friedman, 1985). In an informal system of *injustice* that has been called "plantation justice," slave owners were judge, jury, and executioner regarding infractions of personal plantation laws as they applied to slaves (Hindus in Friedman, 1985).

Immediately superior to the justices of the peace courts in the colonial United States were various trial courts, including the especially unpopular admiralty courts. These judicial bodies enforced trade acts thought to favor British navigation laws and seamen's wages; they also were used to conduct trials without juries (Friedman, 1985). With the exception of Virginia, the governor and his council comprised the **appellate court,** the highest tribunal in the state. Later, the appellate function was turned over to a chief justice and a number of associate judges (Surrency, 1967).

> **appellate court** a court of review that determines whether the rulings of a lower court—usually a trial court—were correct

In the years following the Civil War (1861–1865) urbanization, industrialization, and population increased dramatically as the United States was making the transition from an agricultural to a factory-based economy. The structure of the judicial system remained intact, and the number of courts grew rapidly. This proliferation was especially evident in cities expanding with immigrants from Europe and the South. By 1931, Chicago had 556 courts, mostly at the justice of the peace level (Friedman, 1985; Glick and Vines, 1973; Neubauer, 1999).

In the period between 1870 and 1900, state supreme courts reflected the nation's economic growth: One-third of the cases these judicial bodies decided were issues of debt and contracts, and another 21 percent dealt with property law. Only 10 percent of the state high-court decisions at this time involved criminal cases. U.S. proclivity for local control has resulted in 50 different state court systems distinct enough to make generalization about these judicial networks "difficult" (Stump, 1988). Friedman (1985) notes that for of all of its growing pains the judicial system worked and has provided "stability and certainty" to the nation's legal affairs. However, this stability came at a price as the courts developed a standardized set of procedures that has resulted in "assembly-line justice" for routine civil and criminal cases.

Formal Organizations

An understanding of the court system in this country begins with an understanding of **jurisdiction**—the power or authority to hear and decide a case. The court system involves three major categories or dimensions of jurisdiction starting with the distinction between courts with civil jurisdiction (bankruptcy courts, small claims courts,

> **jurisdiction** the power to hear and decide a case, for example, some courts have jurisdiction over civil matters, whereas others decide criminal cases

Formal Organizations **275**

family courts, etc.) and those with criminal jurisdiction. Inferior or lower courts have jurisdiction over matters of relatively lesser consequence, whereas superior or general trial courts have jurisdiction over the most significant of human affairs. Courts of original jurisdiction (or "courts of the first instance") have the authority to try cases, and appellate courts have the authority and responsibility to correct any errors that were made in trial courts. Appellate courts may alter or reverse decisions made in trial courts (Holten and Lamar, 1991).

The United States has a diverse and complex dual court system comprised of independent state courts and federal judiciaries that coexist in the same geographical areas. State courts have jurisdiction over matters that occur within their borders and concern the residents of that political entity; federal courts have jurisdiction over all states and territories of the United States (Smith, 1997).

State Courts

Both the state and federal courts systems are hierarchical, with the lower courts or courts of limited jurisdiction handling the vast majority of cases (see Figures 9.1 and 9.2). Comprising about 90 percent of all courts, they have diverse names, including dis-

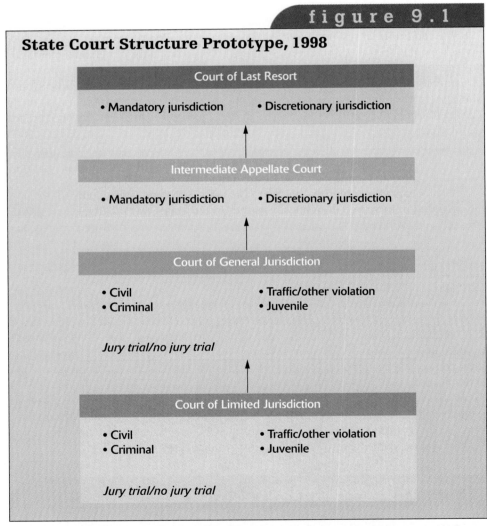

figure 9.1

State Court Structure Prototype, 1998

Court of Last Resort
- Mandatory jurisdiction
- Discretionary jurisdiction

Intermediate Appellate Court
- Mandatory jurisdiction
- Discretionary jurisdiction

Court of General Jurisdiction
- Civil
- Criminal
- Traffic/other violation
- Juvenile

Jury trial/no jury trial

Court of Limited Jurisdiction
- Civil
- Criminal
- Traffic/other violation
- Juvenile

Jury trial/no jury trial

Source: Adapted from Rottman, David B., Carol R. Flango, Melissa T. Cantrell, Randall Hansen, and Neil LaFountain. 2000. *State Court Organization, 1998.* Washington, DC: U.S. Department of Justice, Office of the Justice Bureau, Bureau of Justice Statistics, U.S. Government Printing Office.

figure 9.2

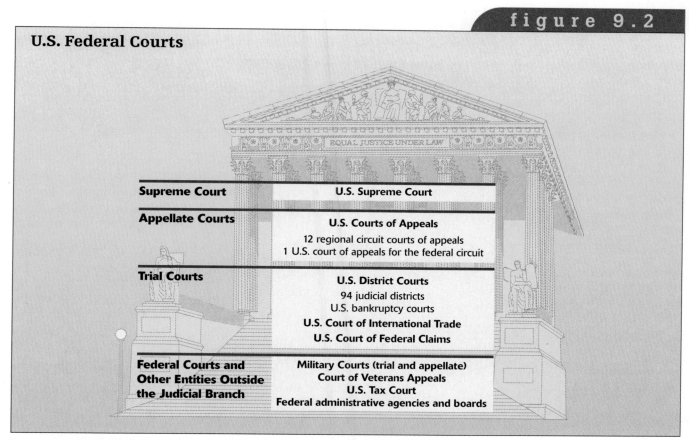

U.S. Federal Courts

Supreme Court	**U.S. Supreme Court**
Appellate Courts	**U.S. Courts of Appeals** 12 regional circuit courts of appeals 1 U.S. court of appeals for the federal circuit
Trial Courts	**U.S. District Courts** 94 judicial districts U.S. bankruptcy courts **U.S. Court of International Trade** **U.S. Court of Federal Claims**
Federal Courts and Other Entities Outside the Judicial Branch	**Military Courts (trial and appellate)** **Court of Veterans Appeals** **U.S. Tax Court** **Federal administrative agencies and boards**

Source: *Understanding the Federal Courts.* 1999. Federal Judiciary Home Page. Available: http://www. uscourts.gov/about/html.

trict court, municipal court, magistrate court, city court, county court, juvenile court, domestic relations court, police court, and justice of the peace court (Carp and Stidham, 1996; Rottman, Flango, Cantrell, Hansen, and LaFountain, 2000). These courts may have jurisdiction over an entire county or have authority that is limited to a city or even a village. As noted by their names, many of these courts are limited to specific matters such as juvenile offenses or family matters. They deal with minor infractions (e.g., parking tickets) and misdemeanors wherein fines and jail sentences are usually no more than $1,000 or 1 year in jail. The judicial officers of these courts are called judges, magistrates, referees, or justices of the peace. In some states lay judges (some of whom are part-time government employees) with little if any legal training preside over these courts. Juries are not common at this level of jurisdiction, with judges making the determination of guilt or innocence at criminal proceedings. In poor, rural areas lacking funds and other resources, these courts may convene in grocery stores, restaurants, or private homes. Five states and the District of Columbia do not have courts at this level (Carp and Stidham, 1996; Rottman et al., 2000; Smith, 1997).

There are more than 3,500 courts of general jurisdiction, with the least populous states having only four such courts each and Texas having more than 250. Called circuit, district, or superior courts (and in New York state "supreme courts"), these are the highest trial courts in the state; they hear felony criminal cases and civil cases involving substantial amounts of money. Table 9.1 indicates the types of felony cases heard by nine state criminal courts from various parts of the country. These courts are divided into or encompass one or more counties and are usually case specific (for example, criminal

table 9.1

Composition of Cases in Nine State Criminal Trial Courts

TYPE OF FELONY CASE (AS A PERCENTAGE OF TOTAL CASELOAD)	OVERALL	CINCINNATI	GRAND RAPIDS, MI	PORTLAND, OR	OAKLAND	SACRAMENTO	ALBUQUERQUE	AUSTIN	BIRMINGHAM	HACKENSACK, NJ
Most violent crimes[a]	6	4	5	5	8	12	5	7	7	5
Other violent crimes[b]	17	13	15	13	23	27	26	17	11	15
Burglary, theft	32	28	45	24	14	18	40	36	36	35
Drug sale, possession	34	49	19	53	45	32	18	28	39	30
Other felonies[c]	11	15	17	6	9	12	11	12	7	15
Total[d]	100	100	101	101	99	101	100	100	100	100
Number of cases	3,779	485	463	455	417	200	375	499	478	407

[a]Most violent crimes include capital murder, homicide, and rape.

[b]Other violent crimes include robbery, assault, kidnapping, manslaughter, and child abuse.

[c]Other felonies include weapons possession, DWI, destruction of property, and escape from confinement.

[d]Totals may not equal 100 due to rounding.

Source: Ostrom, Brian J., and Roger A. Hanson. 2000. *Efficiency, Timeliness, and Quality: A New Perspective from Nine State Criminal Trial Courts*. Washington, DC: U.S. Department of Justice, Office of Justice Programs, National Institute of Justice.

courts, probate courts, and family courts). It is not unusual for general jurisdiction courts to have an appellate function; that is, to rule on appeals originating in trial courts of limited jurisdiction.

Intermediate appellate courts occupy an organizational position between general jurisdiction courts and a state's **court of last resort** (COLR). Whereas only 13 states had appellate courts in 1911, the vast majority of states now have courts at this level of decision making. The reason for this proliferation is a significant increase in the number of cases tried at the general jurisdiction level that are subsequently appealed. In other words, these courts were created to take some of the burden off COLRs. Keep in mind that appellate courts do not conduct trials or hear the testimony of witnesses. Rather, they make decisions on an appeal. For example, the attorney of a defendant found guilty at a jury trial may argue that a judicial mistake during the proceedings resulted in his or her client's conviction. An attorney's argument is presented to the appellate court via a detailed written brief, and in some courts lawyers may address the judges for limited periods of time. Decisions are made by a majority vote of three or more judges (Smith, 1997).

COLRs exist in every state with Texas and Oklahoma sharing the appellate process at this level between one court that has jurisdiction over civil cases and another that rules on criminal trial appeals. To eliminate deadlocks or ties, CORLs have an odd number of judges (sometimes called justices at this level). Eighteen states have five justices, 27 have seven, and seven states have decided that nine justices is the optimum number. Similar to the intermediate appellate courts, appeals are presented to COLRs by way of written briefs and oral arguments. In all but three states (Tennessee, Ohio, and Alabama), appeals in death penalty cases bypass intermediate appellate courts and go straight to COLRs (Rottman et al., 2000).

court of last resort the highest appellate court in a geographical jurisdiction. In the United States, that would be a state or the entire nation

http://www.ablongman.com/barkan1e

Federal Courts

Because of their responsibility to protect the rights and liberties guaranteed U.S. citizens in the Constitution, the federal courts have been called the "guardians of the Constitution" ("Understanding the Federal Courts," 1999). As is the case with state courts, the federal court system is a hierarchical network of tribunals whose judges are appointed by the president and confirmed by Congress. Although the Supreme Court—the nation's COLR—was the only judicial body created by the U.S. Constitution, as a result of the Judiciary Act of 1789, Congress established federal trial and appellate courts.

District courts, the trial courts of the federal system are divided into 94 judicial districts with at least one district in each state as well as the District of Columbia, Puerto Rico, the Virgin Islands, Guam, and the Northern Mariana Islands. Twenty-three states each comprise one district; numerous states are divided into two or three districts; and New York, California, and Texas have four district court regions. District courts are courts of general jurisdiction in both civil and criminal cases, the latter dealing with violations of the federal criminal code such as bank robbery, kidnapping, transporting stolen goods across state lines, and some drug offenses. In 1998, U.S. attorneys initiated 115,692 investigations. Almost one-third of these inquiries involved drug crimes, and slightly more than 77,000 people were prosecuted in federal courts resulting in almost 61,000 convictions ("Federal Criminal Case Processing, 1998," 1999). These are relatively small numbers when compared to the millions of criminal cases that are processed by courts of limited and general jurisdiction within the state court systems.

Collectively, the more than 500 federal district judges have appointed hundreds of U.S. magistrate judges who serve 8-year terms in limited or inferior court systems within the framework of the district courts. These judges perform some of the same functions as limited court judges in the state system, including determining probable cause at **preliminary hearings** and setting **bail** (Holten and Lamar, 1991). (These and other pretrial procedures are discussed later in the chapter.)

The 94 judicial districts are assembled into 12 regional circuits with each region having a U.S. Court of Appeals that serves as an intermediate appellate court in the federal system. Appeals courts have between 3 and 15 judges who have three primary responsibilities. The first is correcting judicial mistakes by way of monitoring the performance and decisions of district court judges. Second, appeals courts supervise federal agencies regarding how these agencies apply and interpret national and state laws. Finally, federal appellate courts screen out, begin to develop, and pass forward the small number of cases that merit the attention of the Supreme Court (Carp and Stidham, 1996).

First assembled in February 1790, the Supreme Court of the United States handed down its first decision two years later. This COLR accepts cases from federal appellate courts and directly from state courts if the latter raise issues that concern or challenge federal laws or the U.S. Constitution. The often-heard sentiment "I'll take this case all the way to the Supreme Court" is hardly likely because the Court typically hears oral arguments and provides complete written opinions for only a small number of the many petitions it receives annually. For example, of the 6,996 petitions filed between October 1994 and July 1995, only 82 cases (1.2 percent) were disposed of by a full opinion. If the Supreme Court declines to hear a case, the decision of the lower court stands.

Because of their authority to interpret federal laws and the U.S. Constitution, the nine members of the Supreme Court can be viewed as policy makers. For example, we saw that, as a result of the *Gideon v. Wainright* decision, indigent defendants accused of felony offenses were entitled to an attorney provided by the state. Whereas the *Plessy v. Ferguson* decision of 1896 established segregation via the "separate but equal" policy, 58 years later the court struck down this policy in the nation's classrooms with *Brown v. Board of Education* (Carp and Stidham, 1996). These three decisions (and many others) profoundly affected the lives of tens of millions of people and changed the social course of the entire nation. The Supreme Court does not necessarily have the final say in all legal and constitutional matters because the Court's decisions may be altered by a constitutional amendment or an act of Congress. However, instances of changing or negating the Court's decisions in this manner are infrequent.

preliminary hearings proceedings to determine if there is cause to subject someone legally to a criminal trial; states without a grand jury use preliminary hearings

bail money or other security given to the court to ensure that a defendant will appear at every stage of the legal proceedings

Companies, associations, and government agencies of any appreciable size typically have a *table of organization* that illustrates the positions in the group and how individuals who occupy these positions relate to one another in terms of authority and status. For example, the table of organization for a private university would probably list the board of trustees at the top. Subordinate to the trustees would be the president, followed by the vice president or provost; deans of the various colleges and professionals schools would be next. Although these tables are useful in understanding the formal structure of an organization, only a knowledge of the informal makeup and everyday working relations will reveal how that group actually functions.

The major players in the courtroom workgroup include judges; members of the state's attorneys office, which provides **prosecutors** and district attorneys; and members of the public defender's office, which furnishes defense counsel for indigent (poor) persons accused of committing crimes (Eisenstein and Jacob, 1991; Neubauer, 1999). Judges, prosecutors, and defense attorneys share one goal: to move cases through the criminal courts at a rapid pace. They work together in interrelated and interdependent informal workgroups, although they often disagree on how the goal is to be achieved. In one way or another, these courthouse players are rewarded for expediting cases and penalized for letting a backlog of cases build up. For example, **public defenders** are evaluated on the number of cases they handle, not on the number of not-guilty verdicts they obtain. "As long as the office represents most indigents without disrupting the flow of cases, it will be considered successful" (Eisenstein and Jacob, 1991, p. 49). Conversely, if public defenders push for too many time-consuming and resource-consuming jury trials, rather than plea bargaining the vast majority of cases, they may experience a cutback in funds and suffer reprimands from superiors. (*Plea bargaining*, the procedure wherein the defendant pleads guilty to a crime with the expectation of receiving some benefit from the state—typically a reduction in the number of charges and/or the severity of these charges—is discussed in the next chapter.) Prosecutors who do not engage in delaying tactics (from the perspective of judges) may be rewarded accordingly. As one district attorney noted (in Clynch and Neubauer, 1981, pp. 81–82):

> You might have 10 or 15 preliminary hearings any given morning and you need a little time to talk to a witness you didn't have a chance to talk to or you need

prosecutors public officials either elected or appointed who represent the government in all phases of criminal proceedings

public defenders attorneys employed by the state who represent indigent defendants during criminal proceedings

A young public defender talks to a juvenile incarcerated in a Los Angeles detention center. Will this young man receive the same legal expertise as a youth from an affluent family whose parents can hire an experienced private attorney?

time, a break say, to talk to defense counsel. If you have a good rapport with that judge, you get that time. You, in fact run that calendar, not the judge. That's only possible if you have rapport.

In their book *Felony Justice—An Organizational Analysis of Criminal Courts,* James Eisenstein and Herbert Jacob (1991) ask and answer the following question: How do courtrooms dispose of or process criminal cases? Their answer is the performance of the courtroom workgroup. More specifically, workgroup characteristics determine in large measure how successful the group is in moving cases through the system. One important component for success is familiarity. When workgroup members know one another, uncertainty is reduced and they can predict each other's reaction to proposals with a high degree of accuracy. "It is hard to negotiate with strangers . . . the process is full of nasty surprises" (p. 61).

The distribution of influence and power in a workgroup affects the stability of the group, which in turn impacts the disposition of cases. If either judges or prosecutors dominate (defense lawyers are rarely in a superordinate position), cases will be disposed of rapidly because one faction of the workgroup determines and implements the rules of the negotiating game. However, if power and influence are more evenly distributed, disposition time is likely to increase as each faction attempts to push forward aspects of its own agenda. In his study of a rural Pennsylvania courtroom workgroup, Jeffery Ulmer (1994) discovered a rather serious conflict between judges and district attorneys. Because neither side was strong enough to dominate the working environment, they were locked in an ongoing conflict (the public defenders were aligned with the judges) that negatively affected the processing of a heavy caseload. Ulmer's work is a good example of the strains that may develop in a courtroom workgroup even when all members of that group share a common goal.

Courtrooms are also affected by the number and type of offenses they process. During the course of a year, judges, prosecutors, and defense attorneys in big cities will deal with thousands of burglaries, street robberies (muggings), and assaults. These offenses become "normal crimes" (Sudnow, 1965) in that the circumstances of these events (offender and victim backgrounds, degree of injury suffered by the victim) are similar. The similarity of these crimes provides a common frame of reference for the members of the workgroup. Because the burglary case being negotiated today falls in the normal crime category, it can be routinely disposed of in the same manner as those disposed of countless times in the past and those processed in the foreseeable future will also be disposed of in the same manner. A high volume of similar cases, therefore, greatly facilitates the speed in which they can be disposed of, that is, moved through the criminal court system.

In a classic article entitled "The Practice of Law as a Confidence Game," sociologist Abraham Blumberg (1967) views the defense lawyer as a "double agent" whose goals are more aligned with the courtroom workgroup than with the welfare of his or her client. Blumberg found that, of 724 individuals convicted by way of a negotiated plea (plea bargaining), in 411 cases (56.7 percent) the defendant's attorney had the greatest influence on the final decision to plead. In the 16.5 percent of the cases wherein the wife of the defendant influenced the plea bargaining decision, this suggestion on her part was usually "sparked and initiated by defense counsel" (p. 36).

The working relation between prosecutors and defense attorneys is clearly evident in one southern California locale. The Orange County Attorney's Association is a union comprised of prosecuting attorneys *and* public defenders. When the county board of supervisors recommended cutting the salaries of public defenders (which is the same as that of prosecutors), the district attorneys threatened to strike if the pay cuts were implemented. The county backed off, and no pay reductions were made. Joint prosecutor/public defender unions also exist in two Minnesota counties ("Improving State and Local Criminal Justice Systems," 1998).

Courtroom workgroups are also influenced by external forces, such as the police, the prisons, and the media (Eisenstein and Jacob, 1991). Prosecutors cannot obtain convictions without the investigative work of police who provide the necessary evidence and witnesses to build a case. Therefore, district attorneys are likely to give high priority to cases that are important to law enforcement personnel and will often check with officers before plea bargaining with some defendants. "Physical assaults on police officers are prosecuted vigorously" (Eisenstein and Jacob, p. 55), and defense attorneys know that the rules of the game are different in these situations.

Members of the workgroup also consider the prison situation and parole practices in their states in the negotiation process. For example, a 5-year sentence may really mean parole after 3 years, and in some instances only the most violent offender can be sent to overcrowded correctional institutions.

Judges, prosecutors, and defense attorneys are also considerate of the media. All seek favorable publicity, especially those workgroup members who have elected positions or aspire to a higher political office. In small towns and predominantly rural jurisdictions, most felony cases are covered in the newspapers (and, possibly, by television stations), whereas in big cities only those especially egregious or unusual cases draw media attention. Depending on the local political climate, some newspaper editors and television station managers will push for a hard-line punitive criminal court system, whereas others will advocate a more defendant-oriented due process approach to crime (Eisenstein and Jacob, 1991). Workgroup members who buck the prevailing media orientation are likely to trigger negative publicity. Any conflict within the workgroup that affects the disposition of cases (charging decisions and/or sentence recommendations, for example) are likely to draw media attention.

The Major Players

Regular courtroom personnel include judges, prosecutors, defense attorneys, bailiffs, court stenographers, probation officers, and bail bondsmen. In this section we present a brief overview of the principal actors involved in criminal court proceedings: judges, prosecutors, and defense attorneys.

Judges

The primary responsibility of criminal court judges is to *adjudicate*, that is, to reach a formal legal decision based on evidence presented (Gifis, 1996). Decisions as to whether evidence was obtained illegally and should be suppressed (not allowed to be introduced during the trial) are reached "backstage," so to speak, in the judge's chambers after careful examination of the material and the conditions under which it was obtained. Decisions to overrule or sustain (to permit or approve) an attorney's objection to some aspect of the proceedings are made in open court with little time for thoughtful reflection. In some instances, judges also decide on the guilt or innocence of a defendant at a bench trial—a trial heard by a magistrate alone (without a jury). Sentencing determinations are reached by judges in conjunction with other members of the criminal justice system, most often probation officers. Because judicial decisions are supposed to be grounded in existing constitutional and statutory laws, judges are expected to keep abreast of current legal rulings (Steury and Frank, 1996).

Historically, criminal court judges in the United States have been white males in their mid-forties to late fifties, from upper-middle-class families who have had successful law practices prior to being selected for the "bench" (Baum, 1994). Paul Wice (1985) found that about 25 percent of judges were former prosecutors or defense attorneys. Table 9.2 indicates the racial and ethnic composition of U.S. Court of Appeals judges appointed by presidents Johnson through Clinton.

Judges at the U.S. district courts and appellate levels as well as justices of the U.S. Supreme Court are nominated by the president and confirmed by the Senate. Traditionally, the president nominated a federal district judge according to the desires of a senator from the state in which the judge was to serve, a practice known as *senatorial courtesy*. This procedure began to change during the Carter administration (1977–1980) when senators from various states formed a commission to recommend nominees to fill vacant judicial district court positions in their states (Steury and Frank, 1996).

table 9.2

Characteristics of Presidential Appointees to U.S. Court of Appeals Judgeships by Presidential Administration, 1963–1998

	JOHNSON APPOINTEES, 1963–68 (N = 40)	NIXON APPOINTEES, 1969–74 (N = 45)	FORD APPOINTEES, 1974–76 (N = 12)	CARTER APPOINTEES, 1977–80 (N = 56)	REAGAN APPOINTEES, 1981–88 (N = 78)	BUSH APPOINTEES, 1989–92 (N = 37)	CLINTON APPOINTEES, 1993–98 (N = 48)
SEX							
Male	97.5%	100%	100%	80.4%	94.9%	81.1%	63.7%
Female	2.5	0	0	19.6	5.1	18.9	33.3
RACE, ETHNICITY							
White	95.0	97.8	100	78.6	97.4	89.2	77.1
African American	5.0	0	0	16.1	1.3	5.4	10.4
Hispanic	0	0	0	3.6	1.3	5.4	10.4
Asian	0	2.2	0	1.8	0	0	2.1

Source: *Sourcebook of Criminal Justice Statistics, 1998*, adapted from "Characteristics of Presidential Appointments to U.S. Courts of Appeals Judgeships" (p. 58). Washington, DC: U.S. Department of Justice, Office of Justice Programs, Bureau of Justice Statistics, U.S. Government Printing Office.

President Carter was the first chief executive to begin appointing women and minority racial/ethnic members to the appellate courts in any significant number. This policy was reversed under Presidents Reagan and Bush but renewed in the Clinton administration. Lower-court judges are a more racially and ethnically diverse group, with one study finding that about a third of trial judges in two large cities had working-class backgrounds (in Baum, 1998).

At the state level, judges are either appointed or elected; most states use some form of appointment process. For example, slightly more than over 30 states have commissions that help governors select or appoint judges. This selection process is quite different from the appointment of judges in many other countries that have a kind of judicial civil service wherein individuals decide early in their legal careers to become judges and move through the ranks to increasingly more important and prestigious positions (Baum, 1994). For example, in France aspiring judges receive a 28-month intensive training course and enter judicial service only after passing rigorous examinations (Carp and Stidham, 1998). The major shortcoming of the U.S. system is that newly appointed or elected judges have little if any preparation for a difficult job. One judge noted, "when I was appointed to the court, I was left to stumble, bumble, and do injustice to other people. I was given no manual, no orientation . . . I was abandoned" (in Baum, 1994, p. 151).

The lack of judicial know-how is alleviated by a combination of on-the-job training and socialization by other judges, members of the court staff, prosecutors, and defense attorneys (Baum, 1994; Wice, 1985). Judicial socialization is especially important because it relates to sentencing decisions. According to Steffensmeier and Hebert (1999), the sentencing determination learning process "emphasizes the interplay" of the following: (1) the offender's blameworthiness and the amount of harm he or she caused the victim; (2) the defendant's prior record, facts of the crime including the use of a weapon, and concern for the protection of the community; and (3) the practical implications of sending someone to prison including the impact on the corrections system. Does the system have enough space for first-time property offenders, or should the limited prison resources be used exclusively for violent offenders?

In addition to how judges reach sentencing determinations, scholars have examined the impact of gender and race on these decisions. For example, some people believe that more compassionate female judges pass lighter sentences on convicted felons than their male counterparts, except in the cases of rapists and other sex offenders who receive harsher sentences from female judges who identify with same-sex victims (Steffensmeier and Hebert, 1999). Research in this area finds few if any differences in sentencing decisions on the basis of gender, but where these differences do exist women judges are more punitive. In their study of 39 white female judges and 231 white male judges in 18 Pennsylvania counties, Steffensmeier and Hebert (1999, p. 1177) concluded that "women judges are somewhat more likely to incarcerate defendants and impose somewhat longer prison terms than men judges." In addition, "women judges are particularly harsh toward repeat black offenders."

With few exceptions, researchers have found no substantial differences in the sentencing determinations or other legal decisions of African American and white criminal court and appellate judges (Gottschall, 1983; Spohn, 1990a; Spohn, 1990b; Walker and Barrow, 1985). Samuel Walker and his colleagues (1996) identify three reasons for the insignificance of the race of judges in sentencing decisions: (1) The judicial recruitment process selects conventional, politically moderate members of the legal community regardless of race; (2) these similarities are reinforced via the judicial socialization process that encourages judges to go along with existing norms and courtroom practices; and (3) the norms are supported by the day-to-day activities of the courthouse workgroup.

Although African American and white judges as a whole make comparable sentencing determinations, the judicial profession is not free of racist individuals. Judges have been censured, suspended, and occasionally removed from the bench because of prejudicial statements. Prior to the trial of the African American militant H. Rap Brown, the presiding judge informed an attorney "that he was going to get the nigger" (Kennedy, 1997, p. 282). Between the guilty verdict and penalty phase of a capital trial, a judge, referring to attendant parents of the defendant, said (according to the defense attorney), "Since the niggers are here maybe we can go ahead with the sentencing phase" (p. 283).

Because of their decision-making power at all phases of criminal proceedings, judges command a great deal of respect. Anyone who has spent time in a courthouse knows that judges are routinely addressed as "your honor" by virtually everyone. One observer noted that attorneys routinely "compliment the judge's appearance, lavish him with honorifics, pore over his decisions, praise his erudition, [and] double over with laughter at even his lamest jokes" (in Baum, 1994, p. 153).

As powerful individuals often with substantial egos, judges may occasionally use their authority in an inappropriate or illegal manner. Consider the following three examples:

> A Washington D.C. judge discovered that a defendant awaiting trial had fallen asleep in court. For this lapse, he not only sentenced the defendant to thirty days in jail but also gave the same sentence to a nonsleeping codefendant. When the codefendant protested, the judge declared, "You are guilty by association." (Baum, 1994, p. 159)

> A Michigan woman went to court wearing a campaign button for the local mayor who happened to be a political enemy of the judge. The judge ordered the woman to remove the button, and when she refused she was found in contempt and sent to jail. When the police chief released her three hours later, the judge ordered the chief jailed as well. (Baum, 1990, p. 157)

> A superior court judge in California had sex with a woman whose husband was a defendant in his courtroom. According to investigators he told her she would have to "pay the price" by having sexual intercourse with him unless she wanted her husband to spend the rest of his life in prison. The judge was criminally prosecuted and the defendant given a new trial. (Meyer and Weinstein, 2000)

Prosecutors

Prosecutors or district attorneys "represent the state at every stage of a criminal proceeding" (Holten and Lamar, 1991, p. 122). Their primary responsibility is to ensure that a significant number of individuals arrested by law enforcement authorities are prosecuted and convicted (Eisenstein and Jacobs, 1991). Former Supreme Court justice Robert Jackson stated that "the prosecutor has more control over life, liberty, and reputation than any person in America" (in Miller, McDonald, and Cramer, 1978, p. 47). This bold pronouncement is no exaggeration. Although the police have the authority to arrest, detention will be short-lived if a prosecutor decides a suspect should not be charged. The prosecutor decides what charges to bring, at what level, at what number, whether to plea bargain, and whether to *nolle prosequi* (not to charge) a case. Former assistant U.S. attorney and now law professor Kenneth Mellili (1992) notes that even if a criminal charge is later dismissed or does not result in a conviction at a jury trial, the mere filing of a charge can significantly impact an individual's life by potential pretrial incarceration, possible loss of employment and reputation, embarrassment, the financial cost of providing a defense, and having to cope with stress and anxiety while waiting for a final disposition.

Prosecutorial power has additional dimensions. Because they are typically determined in secrecy behind closed doors, charging decisions are not subject to review by other branches of government and are often influenced by local politics and other non-legal factors (Davis in Miller et al., 1978, p. 48). Because prosecutorial decisions are not open to external review or reversal, a district attorney may decide to prosecute someone based on little if any available evidence or may decide not to file charges against an individual who is obviously guilty of a crime (Schmidt and Steury, 1989).

Clearly, district attorneys are *the* pivotal actors in the criminal justice system. They not only determine what percentage of those individuals arrested will proceed through the criminal court system (and what percentage of arrests will be dismissed) but also, by their charging and plea bargaining decisions, how many people will eventually go to prison and for what length of time. In this latter capacity, prosecutors serve as gatekeepers to the jailhouse door. Other titles for prosecutors at the state level include district attorney, county attorney, prosecuting attorney, commonwealth attorney, and state's attorney (DeFrances and Steadman, 1998).

In 2001, 79,000 employees were in state prosecutor's offices across the country. About 34 percent of these individuals (slightly less than 27,000 people) were prosecutors, and the remaining 66 percent were employed as investigators and other support personnel. Table 9.3 presents basic information about prosecutorial staffs serving populations of various sizes. Note that in big cities these staffs include hundreds of people and have budgets in the tens of millions of dollars. More than 95 percent of chief prosecutors in big cities are elected officials; all others are appointed. At the federal level, prosecution is the responsibility of the 93 U.S. attorneys appointed by the president and subject to Senate confirmation and their staffs ("Report to the Nation on Crime and Justice," 1988). Because they help send people to prison (872,217 felony convictions in state courts in 1994), prosecutors are subject to threats and physical assaults. Almost 73 percent of prosecutor's offices in big cities reported that one or more assistant district attorneys had been threatened or assaulted in 1996 (DeFrances and Steadman, 1998).

Returning to prosecutorial discretion, social scientists have long been interested in how district attorneys decide what to do when they are presented with an arrest report. After a comprehensive study of prosecutors, George Cole (1992, pp. 362–364) concluded that three types of considerations affect charging decisions: evidential considerations, pragmatic considerations, and organizational considerations. *Evidential considerations* refer to the presence or absence of proof about required legal elements necessary in a criminal case. Did the suspect commit the crime, and did he or she do so with criminal intent? Is evidence available (a confession, witness statements, and/or physical evidence) that connects the suspect to the criminal event?

Pragmatic considerations result from the prosecutor's duty to both society and the accused. In cases involving possible mental illness or youthful offenders, district attorneys may decide that all parties would be best served if the accused was channeled into

table 9.3

Budget for Prosecutorial Functions in Prosecutors' Offices, 2001 (in thousands)

	ALL OFFICES	FULL-TIME OFFICES (POPULATION SERVED)			PART-TIME OFFICES
		1,000,000 or More	250,000– 999,999	Under 250,000	
Total	$4,680,000	$1,910,000	$1,580,000	$1,120,000	$78,788
Median	$318	$32,115	$6,100	$379	$95
Mean	$2,000	$56,223	$8,119	$706	$148
Minimum	$6	$7,200	$200	$6	$7
Maximum	$373,000	$373,000	$53,351	$13,113	$2,268
Number of offices	2,341	34	194	1,581	532

Source: DeFrances, Carol J. 2002. *Prosecutors in State Courts, 2001.* Washington, DC: U.S. Department of Justice, Office of Justice Programs, U.S. Government Printing Office.

a *pretrial diversion* program. Using these alternatives to formal charging, a prosecutor can allow those he or she considers good-risk defendants to be removed (at least temporarily) from the criminal justice system. For example, the accused could be diverted to a victim–offender reconciliation program, a drug rehabilitation center, anger-management counseling, or a vocational training program. *Unconditional diversion* means that no monitoring or follow-up of the accused will occur while he or she is in a diversion program. With *conditional diversion,* the accused's activities are monitored (Cole, 1992). If the conditions of diversion are met and the individual refrains from criminal activity, charges are dropped and court records destroyed. If prescribed conditions are not satisfied, the prosecutor refiles criminal charges (Wice, 1985).

Organizational considerations refer to an array of internal and external pressures that district attorneys deal with on a continual basis. Regarding internal factors, prosecutors are cognizant of the volumes of their caseloads; the availability of resources, such as staff investigative support; and the number of cases on criminal court dockets (court congestion). Externally, prosecutors are acutely aware of public opinion, particularly as it relates to cases involving significant levels of violence (the rape of a child), famous offenders and/or victims, and large sums of money.

The number of cases that are ultimately rejected and diverted by prosecutors varies—often significantly—from one jurisdiction to another. For example, one study found that in Manhattan (New York) only 3 of 100 cases were rejected at screening and no one was channeled into diversion programs. In Salt Lake City, 21 percent of cases were rejected by prosecutors and 5 percent were diverted to noncriminal court programs. Although some prosecutorial screening units reject cases at the earliest point in the process (shortly after arrest), others (such as Manhattan) accept most arrest cases, many of which are later dismissed by judges further up the adjudication ladder ("Report to the Nation on Crime and Justice," 1988). Table 9.4 is a compilation of the most common reasons prosecutors reject or later dismiss cases.

District attorney's offices that screen out a relatively high number of cases are likely to have strained relations with the police, at least with some officers. The police are likely to believe that much of their hard work is wasted inasmuch as prosecutors routinely fail to charge individuals they have arrested. However, prosecutors may believe that some officers are poorly trained, sloppy in their work, or simply incompetent when they arrest people and present the district attorneys' office with insufficient evidence to gain a conviction.

table 9.4   The Main Reasons Cases Are Rejected or Dismissed

Many criminal cases are rejected or dismissed because of—

- *Insufficient evidence* that results from a failure to find sufficient physical evidence that links the defendant to the offense

- *Witness problems* that arise, for example, when a witness fails to appear, gives unclear or inconsistent statements, is reluctant to testify, is unsure of the identity of the offender or where a prior relationship may exist between the victim/witness and offender

- *The interests of justice,* wherein the prosecutor decides not to prosecute certain types of offenses, particularly those that violate the letter but not the spirit of the law (for example, offenses involving insignificant amounts of property damage)

- *Due process problems* that involve violations of the constitutional requirements for seizing evidence and for questioning the accused

- *A plea on another case,* for example, when the accused is charged in several cases and the prosecutor agrees to drop one or more of the cases in exchange for a plea of guilty on another case

- *Pretrial diversion* that occurs when the prosecutor and the court agree to drop charges when the accused successfully meets the conditions for diversion, such as completion of a treatment program

- *Referral for other prosecution,* such as when there are other offenses, perhaps of a more serious nature, in a different jurisdiction, or deferral to federal prosecution

Source: *Report to the Nation on Crime and Justice.* 1988. Washington, DC: U.S. Department of Justice, Bureau of Justice Statistics, U.S. Government Printing Office.

Defense Attorneys

Defense lawyers represent defendants at all critical stages of criminal proceedings and ostensibly strive for the most favorable dispositions of their clients' cases. With the *Gideon v. Wainright* decision of 1963, stating that indigent defendants must be provided legal counsel in noncapital cases, a number of questions were raised that had to be addressed immediately. Who would defend poor people? How would a program to provide legal aid to indigents be coordinated and administered? And finally, who would pay for attorney services? These were no small matters; between 60 and 90 percent of all criminal cases involve indigent defendants ("Contracting for Indigent Defense Services," 2000). If these numbers seem high, remember that crime has been defined by legislatures and the public in large measure and reacted to by police as wrongdoings engaged in primarily by young, poor, African American and Hispanic males. Offenses committed by more affluent, middle-age, white males (white-collar and corporate crimes) who can afford to hire private attorneys receive a much lower priority by criminal justice officials.

In the United States there are three primary systems for representing indigent defendants. The first and most prevalent is the *defender* system (see Table 9.5). Existing at both the county and state levels in 32 states, public defender programs are especially numerous in big cities with heavy criminal caseloads. In 1992, these full- or part-time government employees provided legal counsel for 59 percent of indigent defendants in the nation's 75 largest counties (Smith and DeFrances, 1996). On notifying a judge of the indigent status of his or her client, a public defender is appointed at the individual's first court appearance (Wice, 1985). Defendants assigned to public defenders and critics of this form of representation in the criminal justice system repeatedly cite three problems with it. First, because these attorneys are usually appointed on a "who gets the next case" basis, defendants have no choice of who will be their legal advocate. Second, the typical public defender's office works on an assembly line basis wherein the indigent accused is likely to be assigned a different attorney at each stage of the pretrial proceedings (see the following section) until the arraignment. Not only does this

table 9.5   **Who Defends Indigents?**

Public defender: A salaried staff of full-time or part-time attorneys that renders indigent criminal defense services through a public or private nonprofit organization, or as direct government paid employees.

Assigned counsel: The appointment from a list of private bar members who accept cases on a judge-by-judge, court-by-court, or case-by-case basis. This may include an administrative component and a set of rules and guidelines governing the appointment and processing of cases handled by the private bar members.

Contract: Nonsalaried private attorneys, bar associations, law firms, consortiums or groups of attorneys, or nonprofit corporations that contract with a funding source to provide court-appointed representation in a jurisdiction.

- In 1999, 21 state governments funded virtually all indigent criminal defense services; 20 states had a combination of state and county funds; and 9 states relied solely on county funds.

- The 21 states, accounting for 27% of the U.S. population, spent $662 million on indigent criminal defense services in 1999, more than double the total amount in 1982 in constant dollars.

- *Public defender programs:* 19 of the 21 states funded public defender programs. Over 726,000 criminal cases were received by the public defender programs in the 17 states reporting criminal caseload data.

- *Assigned counsel programs:* 19 states provided indigent defense services through assigned counsel programs. Ten states maintained a roster of private attorneys who could be appointed to represent indigent criminal defendants. Five of the ten states had formal procedures for removing attorneys from the roster.

- *Contract attorney programs:* 11 states funded contract attorney programs. Contracts were administered to public defender offices, law firms, individual solo practitioners, nonprofit organizations, or groups of private attorneys or law firms. Five states reported competitively bidding for indigent criminal defense services.

Source: DeFrances, Carol J. September 2001. *State-Funded Indigent Defense Services, 1999.* Washington, DC: U.S. Department of Justice, Office of Justice Statistics.

---

undermine the confidence of the defendant in his or her legal representation but also every time a file is passed from one attorney to another there is the risk that some information will be misinterpreted or lost (Anderson, 1997; Wice, 1985).

The final area of concern is that caseloads can vary significantly across jurisdictions. However, the typical big-city public defender is involved with hundreds of cases annually (Steury and Frank, 1996). Each attorney in the Louisville, Kentucky, Public Defenders Office handles about 750 cases a year ("Too Poor to Be Defended," 1998). A public defender in Minnesota stated: "We are operating with twice the caseload recommended. . . . The reality of our work is like M*A*S*H—the public defenders are operating, and they hear the helicopters bringing in new clients" (in Rovella, 2000, p. 9).

With so many impoverished defendants to represent, public defenders can do little more than "meet 'em and plead 'em," that is, plea bargain as many cases as possible and move on to the next group of indigents accused of committing crimes. Numerous commentators have observed that justice is not being served if defendants have lawyers whose primary work is plea bargaining as opposed to being staunch advocates marshaling a strong defense on their behalf.

Regarding the competency of public defenders based on extensive observations, Paul Wice (1985, p. 64) concluded that the middle 50 percent of public defenders and private attorneys "were operating at similar levels of efficiency and achieving nearly identical results." However, the top 25 percent of private attorneys were "clearly superior" to the best public defenders, whereas the bottom 25 percent of public defenders were much better at their jobs than the bottom 25 percent of private lawyers. Beginning public defenders earn between $25,000 and $35,000 annually and veteran attorneys typically make between $71,000 (Cheyenne, Wyoming) and $152,000 (San Diego, California) a year ("Public Defenders," 1999).

Assigned counsel or court-appointed counsel systems are most numerous in jurisdictions with small populations (especially rural counties of less than 50,000 population) with approximately 22 percent of poor defendants represented in this manner. A judge or the court assigns private attorneys to indigent defendants as the need arises either from a list of volunteers or from a file of all practicing lawyers in that jurisdiction. In the nation's 75 largest counties, just over two of five prosecutors offices report using both the public offender and assigned counsel program (Smith and DeFrances, 1996).

The major criticism of assigned counsel is represented by the old adage "you get what you pay for." Attorneys receive little monetary compensation for their work with indigent defendants, and, on occasion, some jurisdictions that have run out of money require lawyers to defend people without being paid. Assigned attorneys in Virginia receive a maximum of $265 for a felony case carrying a sentence of up to 20 years and $575 if the offense is punishable by more than 20 years. In Alabama assigned counsel earns $20 an hour with a maximum payment of $1,000 for death penalty cases. At these rates of compensation, attorneys cannot even pay for routine expenses (office space, investigators, secretarial help), much less make a profit ("Too Poor to Be Defended," 1998). Prior to 1992, attorneys in South Carolina were paid $10 an hour for out-of-court work and $15 an hour for court work before this rate of payment was struck down by that state's supreme court. This pay rate was only two to three times more than the minimum wage at that time.

Judges motivated to process as many cases as possible can assign attorneys whom they know will routinely plead one case after another of indigent defendants. In Houston, judges have continually appointed an attorney with a "greased lightning" record of rushing defendants through the system; 10 of this attorney's clients have been sentenced to death ("Too Poor to Be Defended," 1998). A court-appointed attorney in Texas fell asleep numerous times during the proceedings at which his client received the death sentence. Although the defendants's appeal was rejected, a U.S. district judge ordered a stay of execution 13 hours before Calvin Jerold Burdine was scheduled to die. Five years later he was released from prison because the state attorney general's office missed a court-ordered deadline to retry him (Ballard, 1995). A study of the 461 death row inmates in Texas as of May 2000 discovered that one in four of these individuals were represented by court-appointed lawyers with records of professional misconduct ("Death Row Lawyers Not Cream of Crop," 2000). In 1995 Texas began allowing new claims of innocence to be raised in capital offenses because of trial misconduct or ineffective counsel. A 2002 study by the *Texas Defender Service* examined hundreds of capital cases and found that a "high number of death row inmates are being propelled through the state habeas corpus proceedings . . . with unqualified, irresponsible, or overburdened attorneys" (Vertuno, 2002, p. 1). Habeas corpus is a judicial procedure for determining the legality of an individual's confinement (Gifis, 1996).

Since the mid-1980s, the use of the **contract system** for defending indigents has increased dramatically. Under this system, a local governmental agency engages in a contractual relationship with a law firm or individual attorneys to provide the necessary services. Table 9.6 outlines the various forms these contracts can take. As of late, some jurisdictions have replaced assigned counsel programs with contract systems ("Contracting for Indigent Defense Services," 2000). The major criticism of contract programs is that they emphasize "cost over quality" as local governments accept the lowest bid from a law firm regardless of the caliber of representation it will provide. (See Box 9.1, "Cheap Justice.") As is the case with poorly paid, assigned counsel, it is much more cost effective for low-bid contract attorneys to plea bargain cases as early as possible rather than to take a case to trial.

A contract lawyer in Georgia who had represented about 300 indigent defendants never took a case to trial. Rather, he encouraged all of his clients to plead guilty. In one

assigned counsel a system wherein a judge or court assigns attorneys to represent indigent defendants either from a list of volunteers or a file of all practicing lawyers in that jurisdiction

contract system a system of defending indigents accused of committing crimes by which a governmental agency enters into a contractual agreement with a law firm or individual attorneys to provide the necessary services

table 9.6 — Contracting for Indigent Defense Services

TYPES OF CONTRACTS

Across the nation, jurisdictions are using a variety of contracts to provide indigent defense services. The following is a brief description of each type.

Fixed-fee, all cases: Specifies the total amount of compensation the lawyer will receive for work on all cases he or she is assigned during a specified contract period. The number of cases assigned to the attorney is not capped; he or she is expected to accept all appointments that arise in the jurisdiction except those in which there is a conflict of interest.

Fixed-fee, specific type of case: Establishes the total amount of compensation the lawyer will receive, but it specifies a particular type of case as well (e.g., all misdemeanors). There is no limit to the number of cases an attorney will be assigned during the contract period.

Flat fee, specific number of cases: Pays a flat fee for all work completed based on a specific number of cases the attorney agrees to accept during the contract period.

Flat fee per case: Establishes a fee by case type (e.g., $150 per misdemeanor), and the attorney agrees to take all cases of that type that arise in the jurisdiction during the contract period.

Hourly fee with caps: Pays the attorney an hourly fee established in the contract but includes a cap on the total amount of compensation he or she can receive. Once the ceiling is reached, the attorney may be required to perform additional work without compensation.

Hourly fee without caps: Pays the attorney an hourly fee established in the contract, but also covers the actual expenses of each case.

In jurisdictions using fixed-fee and flat fee, specific number of cases contracts, the funding agency knows in advance the total costs associated with representation, regardless of fluctuations or peculiarities in charging practices, caseloads, or case type during the course of the contract. As a result, these types of contracts appeal to funding agencies. The regularity of payment appeals to some attorneys, too. These systems have been criticized by many observers, however, because of the pressure they create to resolve cases as early as possible.

Under flat fee per case and hourly fee contracts, total costs to funding agencies can vary over the course of the contract, depending on variables outside the control of the contracting attorney and the funding agencies. As a result, some funding agencies have concluded that these types of contracts do not adequately guarantee the contract's maximum cost.

Source: Spangenberg Group. April 2000. *Contracting for Indigent Defense Services—A Special Report.* Washington, DC: U.S. Department of Justice, Office of Justice Programs.

case, a client pleaded guilty to injuring someone while driving drunk and received a 15-year sentence. During the 13 months this individual spent in jail before entering a plea, he never conferred with his lawyer, nor had his attorney interviewed a single witness (Weinstein, 2002). Another Georgia contract lawyer stated that it was "a grave error for a defense attorney to assume" his clients were innocent (Weinstein, 2002, p. A38). This attorney's contract with the state was later revoked.

In addition to high-caseload limits or no limits at all, contracts typically provide little if any money for investigators or other support staff. In Jones County, Mississippi,

box 9.1   Cheap Justice

In 1997 and 1998, a rural county in California agreed to pay a low-bid contractor slightly more than $400,000 a year to represent half of the county's indigent defendants. The contractor was a private practitioner who employed two associates and two secretaries, but no paralegal or investigator. The contract required the contractor to handle more than 5,000 cases each year. All of the contractor's expenses came out of the contract. To make a profit, the contractor had to spend as little time as possible on each case. In 1998, the contractor took fewer than 20 cases—less than 0.5 percent of the combined felony and misdemeanor caseload—to trial.

One of the contractor's associates was assigned only cases involving misdemeanors. She carried a caseload of between 250 and 300 cases per month. The associate had never tried a case before a jury. She was expected to plead cases at the defendant's first appearance in court so she could move on to the next case. One afternoon, however, the associate was given a felony case scheduled for trial the

following week. The case involved multiple felony and misdemeanor charges. When she looked at the case file, the associate discovered that no pretrial motions had been filed, no witness list had been compiled, no expert witnesses had been endorsed, and no one had been subpoenaed. In short, there had been no investigation of any kind into the case, and she had no one to help her with the basics of her first jury trial.

The only material in the case file was five pages of police reports. In these reports she found evidence of a warrantless search, which indicated strong grounds for suppression. She told the judge she was not ready to proceed and that a continuance was necessary to preserve the defendant's Sixth Amendment right to counsel. The continuance was denied. The associate refused to move forward with the case. The contractor's other associate took over the case and pled the client guilty to all charges. The associate who had asked for a continuance was fired.

Source: Spangenberg Group. April 2000. *Contracting for Indigent Defense Services—A Special Report.* Washington, DC: U.S. Department of Justice, Office of Justice Programs.

in 1992, two attorneys were hired for $13,000 each and awarded a combined $6,000 for their annual expenses ("Contracting for Indigent Defense Services," 2000).

In the 1980s, the Reagan administration and a Republican-dominated Congress shifted responsibility for many domestic programs from the federal government to the states and sharply cut back funds for many of these agencies (Wice, 1985). As spending for police, prosecutors, and prisons has increased steadily during the past 10 to 15 years, funds for representing indigent defendants have not kept pace ("Too Poor to Be Defended," 1998). The consequences of shortchanging poor defendants (both literally and figuratively) are, according to Stephen Bright, director of the Southern Center for Human Rights, the creation of a "wealth-based system of justice." "For the wealthy, it's gold-plated. For the average person, it's like being herded to the slaughterhouse. In many places the adversary system barely exists for the poor" ("Too Poor to Be Defended," 1998, p. 27). For Bright and others, the promise of *Gideon v. Wainright* has yet to be realized.

If at all possible, criminal defendants hire private attorneys. The major advantages for doing so are (1) personalized attention, (2) with much smaller caseloads, private attorneys are more accessible to their clients, and (3) because they are not members of the courtroom "working group," private attorneys are more likely to take an aggressive posture in their dealings with prosecutors and judges (Wice, 1985). Many defense attorneys are former prosecutors and note this in their "yellow page" advertisements. This suggests that they have special knowledge about the workings of the local criminal courts and/or useful contacts in the prosecutor's office.

Eisenstein and Jacob (1991, p. 50) note that private attorneys "must maintain a reasonable balance between the amount of money they receive from clients and the amount of time they spend on their cases," which is a difficult task because the majority of criminal defendants are not rich. Blumberg (1967) argues that a major problem of the many private criminal attorneys who are defending people only slightly more prosperous than those being served by court-appointed counsel is how they are going

to be paid. This is especially true if the case goes to trial and the prosecution gains a conviction, which is what usually occurs. (See the discussion of criminal trials in Chapter 10.) A client behind bars has no incentive to pay for an unsuccessful defense and is in no position to find employment in the near future. A partial solution to this difficulty is for attorneys to collect fees in stages prior to necessary court appearances such as the preliminary hearing. Blumberg (1967, p. 35) notes that attorneys may also "enlist the aid of relatives" for payment if necessary. Because of the complexity of criminal cases, attorneys' fees vary considerably. Although a small percentage of lawyers charge a specific amount of money for a misdemeanor or felony charge, most private criminal attorneys bill their clients contingent on the time and effort needed to properly defend them. A felony defendant who hires a lawyer for a flat fee of $1,000 or $2,000 dollars may not realize that (1) this relatively minor cost is a function of an inexperienced attorney trying to build a practice, and/or (2) unbeknownst to the client, the attorney has no intention of taking the case to trial and will attempt to persuade the defendant that the best course of action is to plea bargain the case (Smith, 1997).

Highly experienced and well known defense attorneys may charge $100,000 or more to defend clients facing homicide, rape, or major drug charges (Smith, 1997). O. J. Simpson's attorneys' fees for his "Dream Team" were estimated at about $1.8 million.

Regardless of how much money they earn or whether their practices are in the private or public sector, defense attorneys are often faced with the prospect of making difficult decisions and/or taking uncomfortable positions. Suppose, as Alex Roth (2002) postulates, a man charged with murder confides to his attorney that he committed the crime. In the course of his investigation the defense attorney discovers a witness who firmly believes she saw a different person kill the victim and is willing to testify for the defense. Should the attorney call this witness to the stand? Many experts are of the opinion that not only would it be ethical for the defense attorney to call such a witness, but it is his professional duty to do so (Roth, 2002). Alameda County (California) prosecutor Jim Anderson argues that "If a defense attorney can find a guy who believes the sun rises in the west and sets in the east, and that testimony will somehow help his client out, he has a duty to put that guy on the stand" (p. A1).

In 2002 in San Diego, David Westerfield was charged with the murder of seven-year-old Danielle van Dam although the girl's body had not been found. Just before the case came to trial, Westerfield informed prosecutors that he would tell them the location of Danielle's body in exchange for a sentence of life in prison without parole instead of the death penalty. However, the deal collapsed when the body was discovered by volunteer searchers. Even though they knew their client was guilty, Westerfield's highly competent attorneys launched a vigorous courtroom defense on his behalf. Neither of the attorneys lied to the jury via the presentation of evidence that the presiding judge ruled was admissible (Roth, 2002). Rather, they "offered the jury interpretations of that evidence" and "It was up to the jurors to decide whether those interpretations were reasonable" (p. A1). The defense attorneys came under a barrage of criticism for their actions.

Getting Busted: Pretrial Procedures

Arrest

For a person to move through the criminal court system, he or she must be arrested. Recall from our discussions in previous chapters what has to transpire for this to happen. First, someone has to become aware that something that might be considered a crime has occurred and then must decide to call the police. In a very real sense, citizens are the gatekeepers of the criminal justice system because police discover only about 3 or 4 percent of criminal activity themselves. In other words, law enforcement agencies (not only in this country but also throughout the world) are reactive agents of social control who respond to calls for assistance. Second, the police must answer the call for help. If they are occupied with other matters that have higher priorities, officers may arrive after a caller has left the scene or, in some cases, they may not respond to that particular request for assistance at all. On arrival, the police must determine whether what has been described to them and the visible evidence they see constitutes a criminal event. The caller may be known among local officers as someone with a vivid imagination who embellishes events or simply makes them up. Third, if the officers decide that the event was, in fact, a crime, the culprit must be identified and located. Regarding property crimes such as larceny–theft and burglary, if the victim cannot tell police who the perpetrator was, he or she is not likely to be apprehended. Fourth, arrests are also a function of departmental priorities. Because police agencies have limited resources, if an emphasis is on arresting street-level drug dealers, burglary arrests are likely to go down and vice versa. The full enforcement of all laws is not even a remote possibility because such a policy would be prohibitively expensive and require the services of significantly more police officers than are now employed at all levels of government.

The two basic types of arrests in the United States are those with and those without a warrant. A warrant is issued after a *complaint* is filed by one person (the *complainant*) against another individual, and, on reviewing this document, a judge decides that "probable cause" for arrest exists. Arrests without warrants occur when police officers witness criminal events or when law enforcement personnel have probable cause to believe that someone has committed (or is about to commit) a crime. About 95 of every 100 arrests are made without a warrant. After a suspect has been arrested and brought to a police station, the facts regarding the arrest are recorded, and the individual may be fingerprinted and photographed (Carp and Stidham, 1996).

Initial Appearance

Typically occurring within a few hours of arrest, defendants make their **initial appearance** before a magistrate where they are informed of the charges against them as well as their right to remain silent, have a lawyer assigned to them, and, in felony cases, to have a preliminary hearing. In crowded, big-city courts, defendants may be advised of their rights in groups (Neubauer, 1997). Because the initial appearance occurs in a court of limited jurisdiction, magistrates have no authority to accept a plea in felony cases. Judges may also set bail at this time (see Bail and Preventive Detention later in this section). Regarding misdemeanor offenses, most defendants enter a guilty plea and are sentenced. The Supreme Court has determined that the initial appearance constitutes a "critical stage" in criminal proceedings, and, as such, defendants are entitled to the assistance of legal counsel. Toward this end, many jurisdictions have public defender's office attorneys on duty to provide assistance to indigent offenders (Emanuel and Knowles, 1999–2000; Israel and LaFave, 1988; Neubauer, 1999). In a 1991 Supreme Court decision (*County of Riverside v. McLaughlin*), the justices ruled that an individual arrested without a warrant can be detained for up to 48 hours without a court appearance to determine whether the arrest was justified (Carp and Stidham, 1996).

initial appearance the first appearance before a judicial officer of a person who has been arrested; at this appearance (1) the individual is informed of his or her constitutional rights; (2) the terms of bail or other forms of pretrial release are set; and (3) if the defendant is indigent, counsel is appointed

Charging

The defendant is informed of the charges against him or her at the initial appearance. Legal scholar David Neubauer (1999, pp. 239–240) notes that there are four types of *charging documents* (documents that describe the date and time of the offense): complaint, information, arrest warrant, and indictment. A *complaint* must be supported by an oath on the part of a witness or arresting officer. An *information* is the same as a complaint except that it is a document filed by a prosecutor stating that sufficient evidence against an individual exists to justify an arrest, and he or she directs the police to do so. As previously noted, an **arrest warrant** is issued by a magistrate, typically a lower-court judge. Indictments are discussed in the section on grand juries.

arrest warrant a document issued by a judge or court having the authority to do so that directs or sanctions the arrest of one or more persons

Preliminary Hearing

States that do not have a grand jury system (about 50 percent) use a preliminary hearing or preliminary examination to determine whether the accused is to be subjected to a criminal trial. The preliminary hearing, therefore, is a screening device in which some cases will proceed to the next level and others will be dismissed. The fact that these proceedings are not circumscribed by a uniform set of definitive rules means that some judges adhere to a probable-cause criterion in making their decisions, whereas other magistrates do not. This latter category of judges "raises the bar," so to speak, and will only subject defendants to criminal trials if they believe there is sufficient evidence to demonstrate proof beyond a reasonable doubt. Also, some jurisdictions compel magistrates to follow the usual rules of evidence at preliminary hearings, whereas other jurisdictions have no such requirements (Saltzburg and Capra, 1992). Hearsay or secondhand evidence is usually permitted and defense counsel may or may not have the right to cross-examine witnesses (Carp and Stidham, 1996; Neubauer, 1997). Defense attorneys use preliminary hearings to gauge the strength of the government's case against their clients. District attorneys often play the information game at this stage of the proceedings by presenting enough evidence to warrant continued prosecution without revealing all of the evidence they will present at a trial (Smith, 1997). If defense attorneys come to believe (correctly or incorrectly) that prosecutors have an especially strong case, the defense attorneys may be more willing to plea bargain (see Chapter 10 for a full discussion of plea bargaining).

Grand Jury

grand jury a jury of between 12 and 23 individuals who determine whether an individual should be indicted; grand juries also have the power to investigate crimes in specified jurisdictions

The **grand jury** can be traced back to twelfth-century England when King Henry II declared that 12 "good and lawful men" of every 104 law-abiding village males would divulge (under oath) the names of those community members believed to have committed crimes. *Grand* and *petit* are the French words for *large* and *small*, respectively, with the grand jury so named because it consists of between 12 and 23 members (16 and 23 for federal grand juries), and petit juries are usually comprised of 12 individuals. The term *grand* does not imply that this jury is more important than the smaller petit jury; both are integral components of the legal system (Saltzburg and Capra, 1992).

Similar to that of the preliminary hearing, the purpose of the grand jury is to determine whether a crime was committed, if the person accused of this offense is the likely culprit, and, therefore, if he or she should face criminal prosecution. If the grand jury determines by a majority vote that the state's charge(s) has a basis against the accused, then an **indictment** or *true bill* is presented. When jury members are not satisfied with the weight of the evidence against the defendant, a decision of *no bill* is rendered. The petit or common jury is the trier of facts and determines the guilt or innocence of a defendant through a criminal trial.

indictment a formal, written accusation written by the prosecuting attorney and submitted to a grand jury charging individuals with a crime. If jury members agree by a majority vote that the charges as outlined in the indictment are valid, they return a true bill

The grand jury is supposed to be an institutional safeguard that prevents prosecutors and the government from using the criminal courts to harass citizens for personal and political reasons. In addition, this system is supposed to be a mechanism for ensuring that, before the state spends the time, money, and energy on a jury trial, there is sufficient evidence against the accused to warrant such action (Carp and Stidham, 1996). However, the workings of the grand jury have been sharply criticized by those who argue that the prosecutor—whose power that body is supposed to check—is the jury's legal advisor and coordinator of its proceedings. The district attorney calls witnesses and determines which individuals should be issued subpoenas and compelled to testify. The defendant and his or her legal counsel are excluded from grand jury proceedings (Carp and Stidham, 1996). In a 1978 decision, the California Supreme Court presented a scathing criticism of the grand jury system (Saltzburg and Capra, 1992, p. 681):

> The prosecuting attorney is typically in complete control of the total process in the grand jury room: he calls the witnesses, interprets the evidence, states and applies the law, and advises the grand jury on whether a crime has been committed. The grand jury is independent only in the sense that it is not formally attached to the

prosecutor's office; though legally free to vote as they please, grand jurors virtually always assent to the recommendations of the prosecuting attorney.

Critics who contend that grand juries do little more than "rubber stamp" the district attorney's agenda note that, in a recent year, federal grand juries returned more than 23,000 indictments and only 123 no bills. In other words, federal grand juries agreed with district attorneys almost 99.5 percent of the time. According to law professors Stephen Saltzburg and Daniel Capra (1992), this almost perfect prosecutorial batting average does not necessarily mean that grand juries are the lackeys of district attorneys. What critics do not understand is that prosecutors rarely seek indictments against defendants if they do not have the evidence to substantiate their assertions. The overwhelming number of indictments as opposed to no bills is a result of district attorneys screening out weak cases before they reach the grand jury.

Grand juries also have far-reaching investigative powers and can summon anyone to testify before them based "upon a hint of suspicion" of being involved in criminal activity as determined by a prosecutor. Any aspect of a person's life that may have relevance for a criminal investigation falls under the scope of a grand jury inquiry. Grand jury service usually lasts from 1 month to 1 year, and jurors can hear up to 1,000 cases during this period (Carp and Stidham, 1996; Saltzburg and Capra, 1992).

Arraignment

After the information or indictment has been presented to the court, the defendant is arraigned. During this formal proceeding, the accused stands before a judge in open court and hears the charges against him or her read by a clerk or district attorney. Once again, the individual is informed of his or her constitutional rights including the right to legal counsel provided at state expense. At this juncture of the criminal proceedings, the defendant is asked to enter a plea of guilty, not guilty, or, in many jurisdictions, nolo contendere (no contest). Strictly speaking, not a plea, **nolo contendere** means that the defendant will not formally contest or refute the charges against him or her. By way of a nolo contendere plea, the defendant can later claim that technically no guilty verdict was reached (even though he or she was punished for an offense); therefore, the defendant may be spared the civil penalties that result from a guilty plea or conviction (Carp and Stidham, 1996). In other words, the nolo contendere plea is an implied confession only to the offense charged and cannot be used against the defendant in another criminal or civil case. These pleas are often entered in tax fraud cases where a civil suit is likely to follow (Marcus and Whitebread, 1996; Gifis, 1996). Most defendants plead not guilty, and the proceedings move toward a criminal trial.

David Neubauer (1999) keenly observes that the significance of the arraignment is the signal it sends to the courtroom workgroup that the defendant is probably guilty and will most likely be convicted via a trial or a negotiated plea of guilt. However, between the arraignment and the trial or guilty plea, one of two possible scenarios can lead to the termination of the case in the defendant's favor. Changing circumstances, such as the uncovering of new evidence that bolsters the defendant's case or the refusal or inability of prosecutorial witnesses to testify, may lead the district attorney to dismiss all charges. This happens in about 5 to 15 percent of all cases. In no more than 5 percent of all cases, pretrial motions are granted by defense counsel (such as a request to suppress evidence that was illegally obtained) that undermine the prosecution's case to such an extent that charges against the defendant are dropped (Kamisar, LaFave, and Israel, 1999).

If a defendant pleads guilty, the judge may impose a sentence immediately or postpone sentencing until some future date. On occasion, individuals refuse to plea, and the court enters a plea of not guilty on their behalf.

Bail and Pretrial Detention

In medieval England defendants were typically confined to squalid, disease-infested prisons where they awaited trial by traveling judges whose visits were few and far between. Local sheriffs whose duty it was to ensure that prisoners did not escape welcomed the

> **nolo contendere** strictly speaking, not a plea, it is a statement in which the defendant does not admit guilt but submits to the charges and punishment against him or her

intervention of friends, relatives, or a property owner who accepted defendants into custody or "bailment" under the condition that they turn themselves over to authorities if the defendant failed to appear in court. The English Parliament passed two acts in the late 1600s outlining procedures by which prisoners became eligible for bail and prohibiting judges from demanding excessive amounts of money or property for pretrial release. The U.S. Constitution guarantees an individual in police custody the right to seek a writ of habeas corpus (a document that challenges the lawfulness of detention or imprisonment) and, via the Eighth Amendment, the right to be free of excessive bail, although it does not grant access to bail in all cases. The right to bail for most offenses was established by state and federal statutes early in U.S. history ("Report to the Nation on Crime and Justice," 1988; Saltzburg and Capra, 1992).

Pretrial Release and Detention

When an individual is taken into custody and probable cause is demonstrated to the satisfaction of the court, that person is legally presumed to be innocent because he or she has not been convicted of any criminal wrongdoing. However, inasmuch as the person is detained against his or her will, this incarceration can be viewed as a form of punishment. This preconviction detention is costly for both the individual and the criminal justice system. A person's demeanor or "presentation of self" may impact how a jury ultimately votes in a criminal trial. As Saltzburg and Capra (1992, p. 702) note, an individual who has spent any time in an overcrowded big-city jail is likely to appear "unshaven, unwashed, unkempt, and unhappy" as he or she is brought into the courtroom under guard. The hopelessness and lowered self-esteem projected by pretrial detainees is unlikely to positively influence jurors and may result in detainees pleading guilty to crimes they did not commit simply to get out of jail, even if this means going to prison, which is often considered a less dehumanizing experience than incarceration in "central lockups."

Pretrial detention can also result in a prolonged absence from employment, loss of a job, and the inability to meet financial obligations, the latter possibly being one of the reasons an individual committed a criminal act (most notably property or drug offense). In addition, a defendant behind bars is less able to help an attorney prepare his or her legal defense (Broderick, 1993). Incarcerating pretrial defendants is also a potential double financial burden on the state. Not only must the government pay for that individual's detention but also taxpayers may have to subsidize his or her family (especially single-parent families headed by women) through welfare payments (Saltzburg and Capra, 1992).

The primary justification for detaining defendants prior to a trial is to ensure they appear in court and accept the lawful disposition of their cases. The U.S. Justice Department's periodic survey of the nation's 75 largest counties reports that 64 percent of felony defendants were released prior to their trial (see Table 9.7). Regarding minor infractions, the police issue the defendant a summons or ticket, informing the individual when he or she is to appear in court. This saves law enforcement personnel much time and energy because they do not have to take defendants to the station house for booking and to the courthouse for arraignment (Cole, 1992). About 25 percent of all felony defendants are "released on recognizance" (ROR), that is, they promise to appear in court on a specified date (see Table 9.8). Primarily a function of nonfinancial releases, slightly more than 50 percent of all pretrial discharges occur within 48 hours of arrest, and approximately 90 percent take place prior to 30 days of confinement (Reaves and Perez, 1994).

However, judges may disallow pretrial release if they believe a defendant is a threat to the community. For example, if, in the judge's opinion, the individual is likely to commit additional crimes, attempt to intimidate witnesses or the victim, and/or destroy evidence on discharge from custody, pretrial release will be denied. About 60 percent of states have *preventive detention laws,* and the Bail Reform Act of 1984 authorizes the pretrial confinement of defendants charged with felony offenses by the federal courts. Of the almost 57,000 defendants arraigned on federal charges in

table 9.7

Felony Defendants Released before or Detained until Case Disposition, by Most Serious Arrest Charge, 1998

MOST SERIOUS ARREST CHARGE	NUMBER OF DEFENDANTS	PERCENTAGE OF DEFENDANTS IN THE 75 LARGEST COUNTIES		
		Total	Released before Case Disposition	Detained until Case Disposition
All offenses	54,458	100%	64%	36%
Violent offenses	13,241	100	55	46
Murder	409	100	13	87
Rape	723	100	47	53
Robbery	3,386	100	38	62
Assault	6,705	100	62	38
Other violent	2,017	100	63	37
Property offenses	15,860	100	66	34
Burglary	4,116	100	50	50
Larceny/theft	5,316	100	73	27
Motor vehicle theft	1,551	100	50	50
Forgery	1,556	100	78	22
Fraud	1,312	100	84	16
Other property	2,010	100	70	30
Drug offenses	20,346	100	68	32
Trafficking	9,751	100	63	37
Other drug	10,595	100	72	28
Public-order offenses	5,011	100	69	31
Weapons	1,567	100	64	36
Driving-related	1,819	100	78	22
Other public-order	1,625	100	63	37

Note: Data on detention/release outcome were available for 94% of all cases. Detail may not add to total because of rounding.

Source: Reeves, Brian A. 2001. *Felony Defendants in Large Urban Counties, 1998.* Washington, DC: U.S. Department of Justice, Office of Justice Programs, U.S. Government Printing Office.

1996, a detention hearing was ordered in 46 percent of the cases (see Figure 9.3). In more than 73 percent of these hearings, pretrial release was denied for one or more of the following reasons (Sciala, 1999, p. 9):

1. The defendant was charged with a drug offense carrying a penalty of 10 or more years in prison.
2. The defendant was charged with specific firearms violations.
3. The defendant was convicted of any offense with a statutory maximum sentence of life imprisonment or death, a crime of violence, or a drug-related offense carrying a statutory maximum of 10 years or more.
4. The crime was committed while the defendant was free but pending the trial for another offense.
5. The crime was committed within 5 years of a previous conviction or release from prison.

table 9.8   Pretrial Release Options

Both financial bonds and alternative release options are used today.

FINANCIAL BOND

Fully secured bail: The defendant posts the full amount of bail with the court.

Privately secured bail: A bondsman signs a promissory note to the court for the bail amount and charges the defendant a fee for the service (usually 10% of the bail amount). If the defendant fails to appear, the bondsman must pay the court the full amount. Frequently, the bondsman requires the defendant to post collateral in addition to the fee.

Deposit bail: The courts allow the defendant to deposit a percentage (usually 10%) of the full bail with the court. The full amount of the bail is required if the defendant fails to appear. The percentage of bail is returned after disposition of the case, but the court often retains 1% for administrative costs.

Unsecured bail: The defendant pays no money to the court but is liable for the full amount of bail should he or she fail to appear.

ALTERNATIVE RELEASE OPTIONS

Release on recognizance (ROR): The court releases the defendant on the promise that he or she will appear in court as required.

Conditional release: The court releases the defendant subject to his or her following specific conditions set by the court, such as attendance at drug treatment therapy or staying away from the complaining witness.

Third-party custody: The defendant is released into the custody of an individual or agency that promises to assure his or her appearance in court. No monetary transactions are involved in this type of release.

Citation release: Arrestees are released pending their first court appearance on a written order issued by law enforcement personnel.

Source: U.S. Department of Justice, Bureau of Justice Statistics. 1999. *Report to the Nation on Crime and Justice, 1998* (p. 76). Washington, DC: U.S. Department of Justice.

Federal defendants charged with violent or drug-related crimes were significantly more likely to have detention hearings than individuals charged with other offenses (Sciala, 1999). Critics contend that the ability of social scientists and criminal justice practitioners to predict who is prone to dangerous behavior is negligible at best and nonexistent at worst. This means that thousands of people are unnecessarily subject to preventive detention annually.

Bail

A judge may decide that releasing a defendant on his or her recognizance is too risky and opt for a financial bond that is forfeited if the individual fails to appear in court. The next issue is the monetary amount at which bail should be set. Almost all felony court judges use three primary criteria in determining the amount of bail a defendant will have to post (Saltzburg and Capra, 1992, pp. 711–712): (1) the seriousness of the offense (despite a lack of evidence linking the gravity of the crime to the defendant's likelihood of appearing for trial); (2) the strength of the case against the accused, information that is usually passed on to judges by prosecutors (a positive relation exists between the strength of the government's case and the likelihood of the accused not appearing in court and, therefore, the greater the bail amount; (3) the defendant's prior criminal record because individuals with numerous criminal convictions are more likely to have a higher bail set than people with no or limited criminal backgrounds. Judges also consider character references and an individual's ties to the community. For example, people employed full time or full-time students are considered less likely to flee; therefore lower bail amounts are set for these individuals (Saltzburg and Capra, 1992).

Judges are influenced in their bail determinations by prosecutors who typically push for high amounts in a number of ways (Wice, 1985). The prosecutor determines

figure 9.3

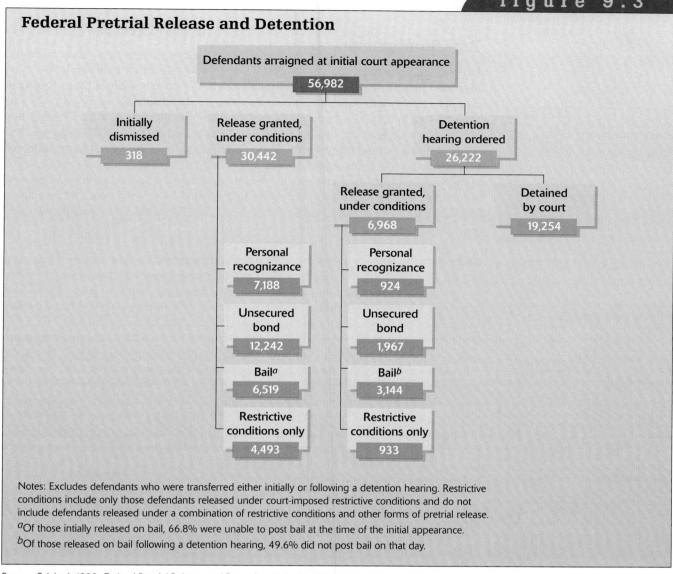

Federal Pretrial Release and Detention

Defendants arraigned at initial court appearance
56,982

Initially dismissed
318

Release granted, under conditions
30,442

Detention hearing ordered
26,222

Release granted, under conditions
6,968

Detained by court
19,254

Personal recognizance
7,188

Personal recognizance
924

Unsecured bond
12,242

Unsecured bond
1,967

Bail^a
6,519

Bail^b
3,144

Restrictive conditions only
4,493

Restrictive conditions only
933

Notes: Excludes defendants who were transferred either initially or following a detention hearing. Restrictive conditions include only those defendants released under court-imposed restrictive conditions and do not include defendants released under a combination of restrictive conditions and other forms of pretrial release.
^{a}Of those intially released on bail, 66.8% were unable to post bail at the time of the initial appearance.
^{b}Of those released on bail following a detention hearing, 49.6% did not post bail on that day.

Source: Sciala, J. 1999. *Federal Pretrial Release and Detention, 1996* (p. 3). Washington, DC: U.S. Department of Justice, Office of Justice Programs, U.S. Government Printing Office.

the level of charges (felony or misdemeanor) and the number of counts brought against the defendant. The more serious the charge, the higher bail is likely to be. District attorneys also control data regarding a defendant's background that is made available to the judge. Finally, judges learn of the strength of the state's case via the prosecutor's office. As the likelihood of conviction increases so, too, does the risk of a defendant fleeing, which, in turn, drives up the amount of bail the accused will have to post. Defense attorneys showcase the positive attributes of their clients and argue that their clients present little if any risk of fleeing the jurisdiction prior to the trial.

Judges are also sensitive to public opinion and the media in making their bail decisions. A man charged with spousal abuse in a city where local citizens' groups have received significant media coverage for harsher penalties for wife batterers is likely to have his bail set at a relatively high amount. Fearing negative public reaction in controversial cases, judges may set bail at an amount they know a defendant cannot meet, a practice called *sub rosa* preventive detention (Steury and Frank, 1996). Of the slightly more than one-third of felony defendants detained until their cases were disposed of in state courts in the nation's largest 75 counties, 83 percent had bail set but were unable to obtain the funds necessary for release.

Bail Bondsmen

Almost one in five defendants secures their freedom through bail bondsmen who advertise their 24-hour, 365-day-a-year service in the yellow pages of phone books in every city in the nation. Bondsmen can be thought of as insurance agents whose companies guarantee the courts that on a specified date the defendant will appear or they will be responsible for the full amount of the bond. It works like this: If a judge sets bail at $10,000 the defendant or family and friends pays the bondsmen a nonrefundable sum equal to 10 percent of bail, in this case $1,000. If the defendant appears in court at the required time and date, the bond company has profited by $1,000. To prevent themselves from being stuck paying the courts $9,000 if the defendant fails to appear, bondsmen may purchase a "surety bond" from a large insurance company for 30 percent (in this example, $300) of the bondsmen's fee (Neubauer, 1999).

Once a contact has been made with a potential client (often by way of defense attorneys), the bondsmen must decide if the company will do business with this individual. Keep in mind that bondsmen are not part of the criminal justice system. They are private businesspeople and as such they can choose who they accept as clients and who they reject. Professional criminals and individuals with extensive crime histories are good risks because they know the ins and outs of the system; they have been this route before and can be expected to appear in court when required. Narcotics users are acceptable risks because they have to stay close to their supply of drugs. First-time offenders charged with serious crimes are considered poor risks because they may panic and flee. Violent offenders pose a threat to the bondsmen and are less likely to secure financial backing (Saltzburg and Capra, 1992). Profit-oriented bail bondsmen have long been associated with corruption; some individuals in this highly competitive business pay off police officers, jailers, and attorneys to steer clients in their direction (Smith, 1997). Bondsmen may also work covertly with prosecutors and judges to deny bail money to defendants these criminal justice officials believe should be punished before going to trial (Dill, 1975).

The overwhelming majority of people who secure their freedom via a bail bondsman appear in court as required, meaning that forfeitures (the money bondsmen must pay the courts when an individual does not appear) are low. Most states have a grace period (30

Bail bond offices spouting ads such as "Quick Release," "Fastest 'Out' in Town," and "Ask About Our Freedom Guarantee" are located in neighborhoods adjacent to criminal courts all over the country.

days in New York, 185 in California) to locate a truant defendant before the bondsman must make good on the money now owed the state (Black, 1996). A bail or bond jumper can be certain that one of the estimated 2,500 to 5,000 "skip tracers" (bounty hunters) will be looking for him or her intently in a matter of days (Drimmer, 1997). Depending on their experience and state laws, bounty hunters receive between 5 and 20 percent of the bail bond amount when they apprehend a fugitive (Colloff, 1997). The bounty hunting profession has become increasing controversial in recent years. On the positive side, these individuals are credited with making approximately 30,000 arrests annually (many of dangerous criminals), saving taxpayers money and police time.

However, because the failure to live up to the terms of a bail agreement is considered a civil as opposed to criminal matter, bounty hunters are not limited by the rules of due process and extradition (if the defendant flees to another state or country) that law enforcement personnel must follow (Neubauer, 1999). For example, (1) bounty hunters may enter the residence of a suspect or third party believed to be sheltering the suspect without an arrest warrant; (2) they may enter or burst into a dwelling without the "knock-and-announce" requirement that law enforcement personnel must abide by; and, (3) bounty hunters may imprison a suspect until he or she can be returned to the state where the bond was secured ("Bounty Hunters: Legal Loose Cannons on Prowl," 1998; Drimmer, 1997). Bounty hunters have these sweeping powers because defendants, by entering into a bail contract, have consented to broad search and arrest rights.

The negative consequences of these far-reaching legal rights become apparent when bounty hunters target the wrong individual, which is not an uncommon occurrence. In Kansas City, bounty hunters broke into the house of an innocent man and shot him three times. The victim was African American; the defendant they were looking for was Hispanic. In Colorado, four armed bounty hunters crashed into a motel room, threw two innocent people to the floor, and handcuffed them. Because bounty hunters are hired as independent contractors by bond agents, these agents have little if any liability if they are sued for the actions of skip tracers. Few bounty hunters have the financial assets to make civil suits worthwhile ("Bounty Hunters: Legal Loose Cannons on Prowl," 1998). This leaves the innocent victims of bounty hunter mistakes with no meaningful civil or criminal court recourse.

Discovery and Pretrial Motions

Discovery is the pretrial procedure by which the prosecution and defense gain information regarding each other's case. It is the disclosure of deeds, facts, documents, and other material that may be necessary to present an adequate defense or aggressive prosecution. Perhaps the primary rationale for discovery is to remove the surprise witness or piece of evidence presented by one side during the course of a trial that catches the opposition completely off guard and renders it unable to make on a moment's notice an effective response. The Constitution mandates that the prosecution disclose to defense counsel any exculpatory evidence within its possession. **Exculpatory evidence** "refers to evidence and/or statements which tend to clear, justify, or excuse a defendant from alleged fault or guilt" (Gifis, 1996, p. 75). The federal government and most states now have statutory pretrial discovery stipulations. Following is an overview of disclosure requirements that the prosecution must satisfy (Emanuel and Knowles, 1999–2000, pp. 347–348):

discovery the pretrial procedure by which the prosecution and defense gain information about each other's case

exculpatory evidence evidence that tends to clear, justify, or excuse a defendant from alleged fault or guilt

1. On request, the prosecution must provide the defense with copies of previously recorded statements by the defendant. Many states also require any statements made by codefendants.
2. The defense is entitled to copies of medical and physical examinations and scientific tests made for the prosecution.
3. Most states give the defense counsel access to documents and tangible objects that will be presented by the district attorney during the trial.
4. Many states require the prosecution to present the opposing attorney(s) with a list of witnesses who will be called to testify as well as any prior written or recorded statements made by these individuals.

Although the prosecution has no constitutional right to defense disclosure, the federal government and most states provide the prosecution with some discovery rights, which tend to be less broad in their scope than the rights given to the defendant's counsel (Emanuel and Knowles, 1999–2000, p. 348):

1. Defense counsel must inform the district attorney if he or she (the defendant's attorney) intends to present an alibi defense. (Alibi defenses, which provide an excuse or justification for committing a crime, are discussed in Chapter 10).
2. Defense counsel must inform the prosecution if an insanity defense will be introduced or if expert witnesses will be called to testify that the defendant lacked the mental capacity necessary to commit the offense.
3. Some states require defense counsel to provide the prosecution with the names and addresses of witnesses it plans to call as well as any previously recorded statements made by these individuals.
4. In some states, prosecutorial discovery is contingent on defense disclosure; that is, if the defense counsel does not seek discovery, then the prosecution has no right to information in the possession of the defendant's attorney.

Discovery does not provide access to the opposition's *work product*—the opinions, thoughts, strategies, and theories of an attorney that are a part of his or her trial strategy (Gifis, 1996). Work product also includes reports of private investigators as well as a list of witnesses in the order they will be called. Because the work product is not evidence, it is not subject to discovery as outlined in state and federal statutes (Steury and Frank, 1996).

In the period between the arraignment and beginning of a trial, the prosecutor and/or defense counsel can file **pretrial motions**—petitions to the court requesting orders or rulings favorable to the applicant's case (Gifis, 1996). Submitted to the court by way of a written brief, judges make their rulings on these motions after reading the briefs, after hearing the oral arguments of the competing attorneys, and/or after an extensive fact-finding hearing (Steury and Frank, 1996). Arguably the most important pretrial motions filed by defense attorneys are motions to exclude a confession or suppress evidence they contend was illegally obtained. For example, a pretrial motion may ask the court to deny the admission of a confession as evidence because the declaration of guilt was involuntary or obtained prior to the defendant being informed of his or her *Miranda* rights. According to the **exclusionary rule,** evidence obtained in violation of a defendant's rights may not be used by the prosecution for the purpose of establishing that individual's guilt (Emanuel and Knowles, 1999–2000). Obviously, the judge's ruling on whether evidence is admissible can be of utmost importance to the outcome of a trial.

Other pretrial motions submitted by defense attorneys include a request to dismiss the case because of the delay in bringing it to trial and a motion for a change of venue (location) because an impartial jury cannot be found in a particular criminal court jurisdiction. An unsuccessful defense motion(s) may still benefit the defendant because it draws out the prosecution's case, educates the judge regarding the weakness of the district attorney's case, and sets the stage for a possible appeal (Reeves and Perez, 1994). Pretrial motions are filed in about 10 percent of felony cases and no more than 1 percent of misdemeanor offenses.

pretrial motions petitions to the court requesting orders or rulings favorable to the applicant's case; for example, the defense may submit a motion requesting that some or all of the prosecution's evidence be suppressed because it was illegally obtained

exclusionary rule evidence obtained in violation of a defendant's rights may not be used by the prosecution to establish the individual's guilt

Focus *on* Islam

Islam and Criminal Justice

By the end of the tenth century, Islam had split into two distinct groups or sects, the Sunnis and Shiites. The Sunni majority (with approximately 85 percent of the followers of the prophet Muhammed) can be further divided into four schools of jurisprudence (the science or philosophy of the law). These schools—the Hanifa, Shafi'i, Maliki, and Hanbal—are named for their founders and interpret aspects of the Shari'ah or holy law of Islam in various ways (Imber, 1997).

Recall from our discussion of criminal law in Islamic societies (Chapter 1) that the Koran is the Islamic holy book—"a code

This 23-year-old Afghani woman in Kabul pleads with security officers to be released with fellow prisoners set free as a goodwill gesture during the holy month of Ramadan. She had no trial in any court of law and was imprisoned for adultery under harsh Shari'ah laws from the Taliban era.

which governs the religious and social life of mankind" (Sanad, 1991, p. 38). Whereas the Koran is thought to be the word of God as revealed to Muhammed, the Sunna is a compilation of the inspired sayings and deeds of the prophet (Sanad, 1991). Because Islamic law is derived from these sources, it is considered a "divinely inspired legal system" (Awad, 1982, p. 91). The Shari'ah is quite specific regarding substantive crimes and the punishment for these offenses, and there is little disagreement among Islamic jurists (legal scholars) regarding these issues. However, the apprehension of offenders and overall administration of justice is left to political authorities who make such decisions in accord with the best interests of their citizens. Because of this latitude, the four schools of jurisprudence have contrasting views on a wide variety of legal issues such as criminal responsibility, criminal investigation and prosecution, and the rights of defendants (Awad, 1982).

Children under the age of 7 are not considered rational human beings under Islamic law, and, as such, they lack the capacity to knowingly engage in criminal behavior under any circumstances. Individuals between the age of 7 and puberty (approximately age 11 or 12 or "by the signs of puberty") are not liable for *hudad* or *qisas* offenses (voluntary and involuntary murder and aggravated assault). In Egypt, juvenile law prohibits administering punishments for criminal code violations for persons under 15 years of age, although "security measures" can be applied to individuals in this category. After the onset of puberty in Islamic law, a person of sound mind is criminally liable for his or her conduct (Sanad, 1991).

The law in Islamic societies permits the use of force (including deadly force) in cases of self-defense and in the defense of others. The right to discipline individuals physically within lim-

its is also inherent in the status of some authority figures. For example, a husband may physically discipline his wife as long he does so for the purpose of reforming her. However, "if the husband exceeds his legal right so that his beating leaves marks, he is held responsible on both criminal and civil grounds, depending on the severity of the injury . . ." (Bahnassi, 1982, p. 182). Similarly, a father, grandfather, or instructor has the right to discipline a minor. Islamic jurists disagree as to the criminal responsibility of the individual administering the beating if the child dies. According to one school of jurisprudence, "If the instructor beats the boy and the boy dies, then, if the father or guardian had not granted permission for the beating, the instructor is liable as an aggressor. If permission is granted for the beating, then he is not liable" (Bahnassi, 1982, p. 183). Disagreement exists regarding the culpability of mothers physically disciplining children. Some jurists support her right to do so, but others argue that she would be criminally liable for inflicting punishment on a child over whom she has no authority.

As is the case in Western legal systems, under Islamic law, the accused is presumed innocent until proven otherwise. The burden of proof rests with the individual(s) making the complaint. False accusation is a serious offense that can result in punishment. According to a verse in the Koran, "And those who produce not four witnesses to support their allegations, flog them with eighty stripes" (Salama, 1982, p. 109). The Shari'ah also makes it clear that the accused has a right to legal counsel at all stages of criminal proceedings including the trial. While in custody defendants should not be subject to inhumane treatment (threats, beatings, torture, etc.). The prophet Mohammed said: "God shall torture, on the day of judgement, those who inflict torture on people in this life" (Sanad, 1991, p. 80).

Although the Shari'ah states that defendants are guaranteed freedom of movement until their cases are decided, most Islamic jurists advocate *preventive detention,* or "precautionary arrest," especially for persons accused of adultery, perhaps the most serious of the *hudad* crimes (adultery, theft, highway robbery, false accusations of unchastity, and for some jurists, forceful rebellion against Islamic leaders, drinking alcohol, and apostasy or rejecting Islam after having been a member of this religion). The justification for preventive detention is that the defendant may escape, attempt to destroy evidence, and/or influence witnesses. Incarcerating defendants using preventive detention is most likely to occur when the judge does not know the accused.

The role of the judge in Islamic courts concerning pretrial and extrajudicial knowledge of a case is a point of contention among the various schools of jurisprudence. From one perspective, any pretrial familiarity a judge has with the participants automatically disqualifies that judge from rendering a judgment in that case. The danger is that familiarity may influence a verdict without evidence to support that decision. An alternative view holds that it would be unjust for a judge knowing a particular defendant is guilty not to punish this individual; that is, justice would be better served if a judge reached a decision on the basis of personal knowledge than if he accepted the testimony of witnesses he knows to be unreliable. A third interpretation holds that judges should refrain from making decisions influenced by pretrial knowledge only in cases involving *hudad* crimes (Salama, 1982). The majority of Islamic jurists favor prohibiting judges from rendering decisions on the basis of personal knowledge because this procedure undermines public trust in the judicial system.

A related issue involves what constitutes evidence in Islamic criminal courts. Three of the four major schools of jurisprudence argue that verses in the Koran stipulate that evidence is primarily the testimony of witnesses. Other jurists believe that what constitutes proof in criminal proceedings should not be limited to witnesses; "evidence is a name for whatever manifests the truth" (Salama, 1982, p. 110). According to this latter perspective, a just determination of guilt or innocence can only be reached (in many instances) when evidence from any source can be presented to the court.

Whereas the proof of a defendant's guilt in Western legal systems must be established beyond a reasonable doubt, in Islamic law that burden is more accurately construed as *well* beyond a reasonable doubt. Evidence to convict someone must be unambiguous and explicit: It should have no need for explanation or interpretation. For example, in the case of adultery "the testimony of *every* witness must clearly and explicitly prove the act of adultery" (Salama, 1982, p. 112). At any time during the criminal proceedings prior to the execution of punishment, if the evidence "loses its conclusiveness" (for example, a witness changes testimony), the verdict that it was based on is no longer valid. Some Islamic jurists believe that, for *hudad* crimes, evidence that is not presented in a specified period of time is doubtful evidence, and, therefore, loses its credibility. For less serious crimes, evidence can be presented to the courts without time constraints.

Most Muslim legal scholars believe that for *hudad* and *qisas* crimes two witnesses must provide consistent testimony for the defendant to be convicted. However, in cases of adultery, the requirement is four witnesses (Salama, 1982; Sanad, 1991). With few exceptions Islamic jurists agree that for *hudad* and *qisas* offenses prosecution witnesses must be males. The Zahiri sect considers the testimony of two females equivalent to the testimony of one man. In adultery cases, this 2-for-1 rule leads to the following combinations: four males, three males and two females, two males and four females, one male and six females, or eight females (Sanad, 1991). A woman's testimony is acceptable on behalf of the defendant, and in some adultery cases only the testimony of females will be considered for the defense.

Some jurists posit that only the testimony of Muslims can be accepted. Legal scholars in the Hanafi tradition will accept the testimony of one non-Muslim against a Muslim, whereas other jurists accept this arrangement only when no Muslim witnesses exist. All witnesses are to be of good character. For some jurists, a person is considered to be of satisfactory reputation unless proven otherwise to the satisfaction of the court, whereas other

Islamic courts dealing with domestic issues are comprised exclusively of men. Is this an example of blatant gender discrimination, or a manifestation of religious precepts that rightfully delineate the roles of men and women?

legal traditions require the judge to verify the trustworthiness of witnesses even if their competence has not been challenged by the prosecution or defense (Salama, 1982).

Along with the testimony of witnesses, confession takes one of the two forms of evidence accepted by most Islamic schools of jurisprudence in determining guilt. The individual making the confession must be mature (having reached the age of puberty) and sane. Confessions must occur during the course of a legal hearing and the defendant must repeat this declaration as many times as the number of legal witnesses that are required. In adultery cases, the confession must be repeated four times. Confessions do not implicate other individuals who may be involved in an offense. A man admitting an adulterous liaison will not automatically render his partner guilty if no independent evidence corroborates the confession. If the judge is not convinced that the confession can be confirmed by additional circumstances, it will be rejected. The defendant may withdraw his admission of guilt at any time prior to the administration of punishment, and, if self-incrimination is the only evidence against him or her, a verdict of not guilty is rendered.

Although Islamic criminal law may seem fragmented in light of the four major schools of jurisprudence, it is more harmonious than Western law when one considers the variation among legal systems in the United States, France, Germany, and the Scandinavian countries, to name only a few. The major difference between Islamic and Western legal systems is that the former is charged with upholding laws outlined in the Shari'ah as proclaimed by God. The separation of church and state, which most people in the West hold as fundamental to the rights of citizens, is unacceptable in the Muslim world. The word of God is and always will be the law. On this, there can be no disagreement. The only question to be resolved by mortals is how these laws will be administered.

summary

1. The colonial court system was patterned after the judicial system of Great Britain. Justice of the peace courts were the workhorses of the early legal system, performing duties such as tax collecting that extended beyond the courtroom. Slave courts in the mid-Atlantic states and the South dispensed severe physical punishment to slaves convicted of any wrongdoing. Both the state and federal courts are hierarchical systems with the lower courts of limited jurisdiction handling most of the cases. Intermediate appellate courts occupy an organizational position between general jurisdiction courts and a state's or the federal government's court of last resort (COLR). These high courts exist in every state, with Texas and Oklahoma having two COLRs, one for civil cases and a second that rules on criminal trial appeals. Because it has authority to interpret federal laws and the U.S. Constitution, the nation's Supreme Court can also be viewed as a policy-making body.

2. The courtroom workgroup is a convergence of three criminal court practitioners: judges, prosecutors, and defense attorneys. Although these individuals have different tasks and responsibilities, they share a common goal as members of an interrelated and informal courthouse workgroup. This goal is the processing or disposing of criminal cases at a pace fast enough that it does not create a significant backlog. In one way or another, judges, prosecutors, and defense attorneys are rewarded for expediting cases through the system and penalized for allowing the disposition of cases to slow to unacceptable levels. The distribution of power within the group, the level of familiarity, and the number and type of cases handled affect workgroup performance levels.

3. The fundamental responsibility of criminal court judges is to adjudicate or make a formal decision based on available evidence. For most of our history judges have been middle-age, white males from affluent families who have had successful law practices. Judges are either appointed or elected, with most states using an appointment process. New judges have little if any formal preparation for their work and receive on-the-job training through an informal socialization process by more experienced judges, members of the courtroom staff, and the attorneys who appear before them. Some studies indicate that female judges are more punitive in sentencing decisions than their male counterparts. With few exceptions, researchers have found no substantial differences in the sentencing determinations or other legal decisions made by African American and white criminal court or appellate judges.

4. Prosecutors represent the state at all phases of criminal proceedings. Because of the charging decisions they make, prosecutors have significant amounts of power over citizens. Prosecutors decide what charges to bring, at what level, at what number, whether to plea bargain or take a case to trial, or to dismiss a case. Their decision-making power is typically exercised behind closed doors and is not subject to review by other branches of government. Because prosecutors determine what percentage of individuals arrested will proceed through the courts, they are the pivotal actors in the criminal justice system. One study found that prosecutors consider various factors in reaching a charging decision. *Evidential considerations* refer to the presence or absence of proof needed to prosecute a defendant. *Pragmatic considerations* are a function of a prosecutor's perceived duty to the accused, victim, and society as a whole. For example, would all parties be better served if the defendant was prosecuted or channeled into a diversion program? *Organizational considerations* refer to internal and external pressures in the district attorney's office such as current caseload volume and public opinion regarding a specific case.

5. The *Gideon v. Wainright* decision raised questions about who should defend indigents accused of committing crimes and how these services would be organized and compensated. Three primary systems are available for representing indigent defendants. Existing at both the county and state level in 32 states, public defenders are prevalent in big cities with heavy caseloads. Assigned counsel or court-appointed counsel systems are most numerous in jurisdictions with small populations. Under this system, a judge or a court assigns private attorneys to poor defendants from a list of volunteers or a file of all practicing lawyers in that jurisdiction. With the contract system of defending indigents, local government agencies engage in a contractual relation with a law firm or individual attorneys to provide the necessary legal services. All three of these indigent defense systems have been criticized for providing inadequate representation for their clients primarily as a consequence of heavy caseloads and/or meager financial compensation. The majority of criminal defendants who can afford to do so hire private attorneys. These lawyers may be more interested in financial rewards than in providing vigorous defenses for their clients.

6. Individuals may be arrested with or without a warrant. A warrant is issued after a complaint is filed by one person against another if a judge determines

that probable cause for the arrest exists. About 95 percent of arrests occur without a warrant when police officers witness a crime or believe that someone has committed or is about to commit a criminal act. Usually within a few hours of being arrested, defendants make an initial appearance before a magistrate where they are informed of the charges against them and their constitutional rights. The Supreme Court has ruled that the initial appearance is the first critical stage in criminal proceedings, and, as such, defendants are entitled to legal counsel. States that do not have a grand jury system use a preliminary hearing or preliminary examination to determine whether the accused should stand trial. In making their decision, some judges adhere to a probable cause standard, whereas others believe that prosecutors must demonstrate that the evidence is sufficient to prove guilt beyond a reasonable doubt.

7. Composed of 12 to 23 members, grand juries determine whether a crime was committed and whether the accused is the likely culprit and should face criminal prosecution. If the grand jury determines that there is a basis for the state charge, it returns an indictment, or true bill. Grand juries have been criticized for being controlled by prosecutors who advise jurors as to who they want indicted. Defendants and their attorneys are excluded from the grand jury process. During an arraignment, the accused is formally charged and once again informed of his or her constitutional rights. The defendant is required to enter a plea of guilty, not guilty, or nolo contendere (no contest). Most defendants plead not guilty and the proceedings move toward a criminal trial.

8. Defendants can be released from jail prior to trial through several of mechanisms, including bail. In reaching a bail determination, that is, whether to grant bail and at what amount, judges must decide whether the defendant is likely to flee the jurisdiction prior to appearing in court and if he or she is likely to engage in criminal behavior while free. Discovery is the pretrial procedure by which the prosecutor and defense attorney gain information about each other's case. The Constitution mandates that the prosecutor disclose any exculpatory evidence, that is, evidence excusing the defendant from criminal prosecution. Between the arraignment and trial the prosecutor and/or the defense attorney can file pretrial motions—petitions to the court requesting favorable rulings on matters considered important to the applicant's case. Defense motions often ask the court to suppress prosecutorial evidence they believe was illegally obtained.

key terms

appellate court
arraignment
arrest warrant
assigned counsel
bail
contract system
court of last resort
discovery
exclusionary rule
exculpatory evidence

grand jury
indictment
initial appearance
jurisdiction
justice of the peace
nolo contendere
preliminary hearings
pretrial motions
prosecutor
public defender

questions for investigation

1. This chapter explains several influences on the operation of the courtroom workshop as well as the consequences of these influences. Discuss both. What conclusions can you reach about the efficiency and ethics of courtroom workshop operations?

2. U.S. judges have little or no formal training as they begin their careers on the bench. Should they have such training? If your answer is no, explain your reasons. If your answer is yes, identify the formal training you think would be useful.

3. Discuss the legal and ethical dimensions of prosecutorial discretion.

4. This chapter describes the shortcomings of the three systems for representing indigent defendants. As a group, discuss possible remedies for these shortcomings.

5. Discuss the importance of the preliminary hearing for judges, prosecutors, and defense attorneys.
6. Should the defendant and his or her legal counsel be included in grand jury proceedings? Explain your answer.
7. Are the disclosure requirements for the prosecution and the defense fair? Defend your answer.

8. What are the primary similarities and differences between the Islamic criminal court system and the criminal court system in the United States? Are there any aspects of the Islamic court system that should be incorporated into our system? What are they? Be prepared to defend your position.

IT'S YOUR CALL . . .

1. A successful revolution in Libreland has resulted in independence for that country after 137 years of colonial rule. The commanding general of the revolutionary forces was educated in the United States and has requested assistance from the U.S. Department of Justice in establishing a criminal court system in his country. As a Justice Department official, you have been selected to lead the task force and prepare a final report for the general (now interim president). This is an opportunity to establish an organization using the best elements of the U.S. criminal courts while eliminating the worst elements of this system. Design a criminal court system at the state and national level paying particular attention to the following: How will judges be trained and selected? Will there be a jury system, or will guilt and innocence be determined by one or more judges? If you decide on a jury system, must the jury reach a unanimous verdict of guilty for all crimes under all circumstances, or will three-quarters of the jury or a simple majority be sufficient for some offenses? Will defendants be presumed innocent until proven guilty, or guilty until proven innocent? Will pretrial procedures be similar to those in the United States, or will you make significant changes?

2. Newly retired reverend Billy Lee Scruggs has been arrested and charged with sexually molesting teenage girls and boys at Sunday school services 6 years ago. Church members are outraged at what they consider ridiculous charges and demand that the reverend be released on his own recognizance; they maintain that he poses no threat to the community and, because he has lived in the community his entire life, is not likely to flee. The parents of the allegedly molested children see the situation differently. Their attorney argues that the reverend may still be a pedophile and, with the lucrative retirement package he received from the church, could leave the country on a moment's notice. As the judge, you must determine the reverend's pretrial fate. Do you release him on his own recognizance, deny him bail, or set bail at a figure you believe he could or could not make? The news media are outside the courtroom door and will be asking questions about your decision.

Plea Bargaining *and* Jury Trials

1. What is plea bargaining? Why are many people opposed to plea bargaining?

2. What are the roles and responsibilities of prosecutors, judges, and public defenders in plea bargaining?

3. How are juries formed, and how many people are required for a jury? What is voir dire? What are possible challenges to potential jurors in the voir dire process?

4. What is involved in an opening statement? What is involved in the examination of witnesses? What four types of evidence are presented during a trial? How can closing arguments be made effective?

5. In instructing jurors about their deliberation, what factors must the judge consider? How do jurors arrive at a determination of guilt or innocence? How does the appeals process work?

6. What is jury nullification? What are the pro and con arguments about jury nullification?

7. What factors contribute to erroneous convictions of innocent individuals? What remedies have been proposed to correct this problem?

I n March 1999, the life of soft-spoken, 59-year-old Wen Ho Lee took a dramatic turn when he was accused of mishandling classified information and funneling this data to Communist China. A Taiwanese-born, naturalized U.S. citizen, Lee was a scientist at New Mexico's Los Alamos National Laboratory where he worked in the top secret "X Division" as part of a team designing nuclear weapons. He was eventually charged with 59 counts of breaching national security, almost 40 of which could have put him in prison for life. The prosecution contended that without proper authorization Lee had downloaded the "crown jewels" of U.S. science onto his personal computer (Benke, 2001a, 2001b). In December 1999, Dr. Lee was arrested and, allegedly, because of the seriousness of the charges against him and the highly sensitive nature of the knowledge he possessed, denied bail.

The conditions of his detention were particularly harsh: He was locked in solitary confinement for 23 hours each day; the light in his cell was never turned off; he was allowed to exercise only once or twice a week; and, while exercising, he was restrained by shackles on his wrists, waist, and ankles ("Amnesty International Protests Solitary Confinement, Shackling of Dr. Wen Ho Lee," 2000). Lee was denied phone calls, and visits were restricted to members of his family and defense counsel.

Members of the Asian American community and others argued that, because he was Chinese, Lee was singled out for investigation, arrest, and prosecution ("racial profiling"). FBI and Justice Department officials vehemently denied these accusations and repeatedly asserted that Lee was arrested because of what he did, not because of his Chinese heritage. However, when an investigation into the mishandling of classified information by John Deutch was undertaken, the former CIA director was treated so leniently that it prompted Republican senator Charles Grassley of Iowa to state, "Mr. Deutch is being investigated for not just downloading CIA information but also Defense Department Information while he was at [the Pentagon]. . . . Yet, I don't see him in solitary confinement with no bail, even though he acknowledged he downloaded information that Wen Ho Lee could never get access to" (in "Wen Ho Lee Freed in Plea Bargain," 2000, p. 1).

A jubilant Wen Ho Lee is shown immediately following his release after 9 months of confinement.

The government's case began to unravel when the lead FBI investigator admitted that he might have misled the court with false information regarding Dr. Lee's action. The FBI had been watching Lee for more than 2 years after the Central Intelligence Agency had assured them that Lee was not a spy. It also became evident that the documents in question were not classified as secret until sometime after they were downloaded by the defendant. In addition, lawyers for Dr. Lee offered statements from three Los Alamos scientists asserting that the contention the accused had downloaded the "crown jewels" of our national defense system was an "unbridled exaggeration" (Benke, 2001; "Wen Ho Lee Released," 1999).

At his sentencing, Lee, who spent the 9 months in solitary confinement, received something from the presiding judge that angered many and was thought to be long overdue by others: an unqualified apology for how he had been treated. U.S. District Court judge James Parker stated: "What I believe remains unanswered is the question: what was the Government's motive in insisting on your being jailed pretrial under extraordinarily onerous conditions of confinement until today, when the Executive Branch agrees that you may be set free essentially unrestricted? This makes no sense to me. . . . I sincerely apologize to you, Dr. Lee, for the unfair manner [in which] you were held in custody by the Executive Branch" ("Wen Ho Lee Freed in Plea Bargain," 2000, p. 2).

Alan Dershowitz, professor of law at Harvard University, noted, "This case stinks, and the resolution doesn't make it smell any better. It only makes the contestant [Wen Ho Lee] happy, but it shouldn't make the public happy. If he pleaded innocent, he had to remain in jail, but if he pleads guilty, he gets out of jail, it's so Soviet, it is un-American" ("Wen Ho Lee Freed in Plea Bargain," 2000, p. 3).

The case of Wen Ho Lee illustrates the decision making that occurs at every stage of the criminal court process following arrest. For example, prosecutors determine how many charges will be brought against a defendant and at what level (felony or misdemeanor). Judges decide whether the accused shall be released on bail (and how high bail shall be set), released on his or her own recognizance, or held in jail. District attorneys determine whether a case will be adjudicated by way of a jury trial or a negotiated plea (plea bargaining), and, along with defense counsel, what the terms of that agreement will be. Judge Parker's stinging rebuke of the government demonstrates that actions of the major players in the criminal courts (judges, prosecutors, and defense attorneys) are highly controversial and subject to the often harsh criticism of observers both inside and outside the courtroom.

We tend to think of a jury trial as a form of verbal combat, with the attorney having the strongest case, quickest mind, and sharpest tongue winning the battle. In medieval Europe, criminal cases that could not be decided by the presentation of evidence and/or the testimony of witnesses were often settled by "judicial combat" or, as it is more commonly referred to, "trial by battle" wherein opposing parties engaged in armed conflict, often to the death.

This form of judicial resolution began among the Germanic people and spread to other parts of Europe by the end of the eleventh century. In some locales, it was viewed as a logical alternative to widespread perjury by those "who do not fear God." An Italian law book of the era listed 23 "actions" that could result in a judicial duel, including adultery, fornication, arson, some forms of murder, and property crimes above a certain limit. "Another legal text stipulated the size and location of the place of battle, weapons to be used, oaths to be sworn by the combatants, and the regulation of crowd behavior" (Bartlett, 1990).

Although females were sometimes active participants in trials by combat, women, the young, the old, and the sickly were almost always excused from fighting. These noncombatants typically offered a proxy, or substitute, known as a "champion," who, for a fee, fought their battles for them. Some affluent individuals retained champions who, for agreed-on sums of money, were on call should the affluent individuals become involved in a matter that could only be settled by physical combat.

"At first glance, the obvious problem with determining guilt and innocence by combat is that the guilty but physically powerful offender could defeat a righteous but physically weaker victim, a perfect example of might makes right." Defenders of trial by ordeal believed that, by divine intervention, God would ensure that the just party would always prevail regardless of his (and occasionally her) physical condition and fighting prowess. However, this system of justice was often harshly criticized by the Catholic Church, which was one reason for its demise in the thirteenth century and its almost complete disappearance from Europe by the end of the fifteenth century (Bartlett, 1990). As one observer noted, "the duel was opposed to Christian charity, to reason, to experience . . . the duel was opposed to the nature of judgement, which consists of wise investigation not brutal power" (in Bartlett, 1990, pp. 117–118). By the year 1250, trial by battle was giving way to jury trials.

Plea Bargaining

In this chapter, we examine the manner in which the overwhelming majority of convictions are obtained by plea bargaining. We also consider the contemporary criminal trial in the United States from the selection of jurors to the final verdict. Table 10.1 provides definitions of relevant terms.

Definition and Criticism of Plea Bargaining

A **plea bargain** is an agreement between the state (represented by the prosecutor) and the defendant (typically represented by an attorney) wherein each side gives up something and receives something in return. For example, the accused may plead guilty to a less serious charge (or to a reduced number of charges) than the state would have brought had the case gone to trial. Pleading to a lesser offense results in a lighter sentence. However, the state gains a measure of control over the now-convicted defendant (a jail or prison sentence or probation). If the case had gone to trial and the jury had voted to acquit, the state would have achieved nothing. Plea bargaining allows the state to win a conviction while expending little time and effort compared to a trial and, in the case of a capital offense, potentially a lengthy trial.

plea bargain an agreement between the state and the defendant wherein each side gives up something and receives something in return

table 10.1 **Criminal Justice Legal Terms**

Acquittal: judgment that a criminal defendant has not been proved guilty beyond a reasonable doubt; a verdict of not guilty

Affidavit: written statement of facts confirmed by the oath of the party making it, before a notary or officer having authority to administer oaths

Appeal: request made after a trial by a party that has lost on one or more issues that a higher court (appellate court) review the trial court's decision to determine if it was correct; to make such a request is "to appeal" or "to take an appeal"; one who appeals is called the *appellant,* the other party is the *appellee*

Arraignment: proceeding in which an individual who is accused of committing a crime is brought into court, told of the charges, and asked to plead guilty or not guilty

Bail: security given for the release of a criminal defendant or witness from legal custody (usually money) to ensure appearance on the day and time set by the court

Bench trial: trial without a jury in which a judge decides which party prevails

Brief: written statement submitted by each party in a case that explains why the court should decide the case, or particular issues in a case, in that party's favor

Chambers: judge's office, typically including workspace for the judge's law clerks and secretary

Conviction: judgment of guilt against a criminal defendant

Counsel: legal advice; also refers to lawyers in a case

Cross-examination: questioning of a witness by opposing counsel, for example, a defense attorney's questioning of a prosecution witness

Defendant: in a civil case, the person or organization against whom the plaintiff brings suit; in a criminal case, the person accused of a crime

Direct examination: questioning of a witness by the party on whose behalf he or she has been called

Discovery: process by which lawyers learn about their opponent's case in preparation for a trial; typical tools of discovery include depositions, interrogatories, requests for admissions, and requests for documents; these devices help lawyers learn the relevant facts, and collect and examine relevant documents or other materials

Evidence: information presented in testimony or in documents that is used to persuade the fact finder (judge or jury) to decide in favor of one side or the other

Felony: serious crime carrying a penalty of more than a year in prison

Grand jury: body of 16 to 23 citizens who listen to evidence of criminal allegations, which is presented by the prosecutors, and determine whether there is probable cause to believe an individual has committed an offense; see also *indictment*

Hearsay: statements by a witness who did not see or hear the incident in question but heard about it from someone else; usually inadmissible as evidence in court

Indictment: formal charge issued by a grand jury stating that there is enough evidence that the defendant committed the crime to justify a trial; used primarily for felonies

Information: formal accusation by a government attorney that a defendant committed a misdemeanor

Jurisdiction: legal authority of a court to hear and decide a case; also, the geographic area in which a court has authority to decide cases

Jury instructions: judge's directions to the jury before it begins deliberations regarding the factual questions it must answer and the legal rules that it must apply

Misdemeanor: offense punishable by 1 year of imprisonment or less

The Supreme Court both affirmed and advocated plea bargaining in a 1971 decision (*Sontobello v. New York*). According to Chief Justice Warren Burger (http://www. caselaw.lp.findlaw.org, 2002), "plea bargaining is an essential component of the administration of justice. Properly administered, it is to be encouraged. If every charge were subjected to a full-scale trial, the States and the Federal Government would need to multiply by many times the number of judges and court facilities."

Plea bargaining has been much maligned by the general public in large measure because people do not fully understand the concept. Many individuals are confused about the term *bargain,* which is supposed to convey a sense of compromise, but which often has another connotation as in "I got a real bargain on a sweater I bought yester-

Mistrial: invalid trial caused by a fundamental error; when a mistrial is declared, the trial must begin again with the selection of a new jury

Motion: request by a litigant to the judge for a decision on an issue relating to the case

Nolo contendere: no contest; a plea of nolo contendere has the same effect as a plea of guilty, as far as the criminal sentence is concerned, but may not be considered as an admission of guilt for other purposes

Petit jury (or trial jury): group of citizens who hear the evidence presented by both sides at a trial and determine the facts in dispute; federal criminal juries consist of 12 persons; state criminal juries may have as few as six jurors

Plea: in a criminal case, the defendant's response of guilty or not guilty to the charges

Presentence report: report prepared by a court's probation officer, after a person has been convicted of an offense, summarizing for the court the background information needed to determine the appropriate sentence

Probation: (1) sentencing alternative to imprisonment in which the court releases convicted defendants under the supervision of a probation officer, who ensures defendants follow certain rules (e.g., get a job, get drug counseling, etc.); (2) a department of the court that prepares a presentence report

Prosecute: to charge someone with a crime; a prosecutor tries a criminal case on behalf of the government

Rebuttal: the introduction of refuting evidence indicating that the statements of a previous witness are not true or accurate; the stage of the trial at which this evidence may be introduced

Sentence: the punishment ordered by a court for a defendant of a convicted crime

Sequester: to separate; sometimes juries are sequestered from outside influences during their deliberations

Subpoena: a command issued under the authority of a court or other authorized governmental entity to a witness to appear and give testimony

Testimony: evidence presented orally by witnesses during trials or before grand juries

U.S. attorney: lawyer appointed by the president in each judicial district to prosecute and defend cases for the federal government; the U.S. attorney employs a staff of assistant U.S. attorneys who appear as the government's attorneys in individual cases

Venue: geographical location in which a case is tried

Verdict: decision of a trial jury or a judge that determines the guilt or innocence of a criminal defendant, or that determines the final outcome of a civil case

Voir dire: process by which judges and lawyers select members of a trial jury from among those eligible to serve by requesting them to ascertain that they would fairly decide the case; *voir dire* means "to speak the truth"

Warrant: written order authorizing official action by law enforcement officials, usually directing the arrest of the individual named in the warrant; a search warrant orders that a specific location be searched for items, which, if found, can be used as evidence

Witness: person called on by either the prosecution or defense to give testimony before the court or jury

Source: Adapted from "Understanding the Federal Courts," 1999. Available: http://www.uscourts.gov/UFC99.pdf2000.

day." People have a sense that criminals are getting a "good deal" at the expense of the victim and the criminal justice system.

There are two main types of bargains: explicit and implicit. In some situations, defendants negotiate for **explicit bargains** from the state through their lawyers:

> **explicit bargains** specific considerations, such as charge or sentence reductions from the state, that defendants negotiate for through their attorneys

1. Defendants may negotiate for charge reductions. This can include both the number and/or type of charges, for example, a reduction from five to two counts of felony burglary, from armed robbery to unarmed robbery, or from rape to sexual assault. In the latter two examples, although all of the crimes are felonies, unarmed robbery and sexual assault are not as serious (or punitive) as armed robbery and rape.

A prosecutor and defense attorney involved in a plea negotiation confer with a judge. In the United States, a large number of criminal prosecutions never go to trial and are adjudicated through plea bargaining.

2. They may negotiate for a specific sentence recommendation (typically, a reduced sentence) in terms of months or years of incarceration. For example, in exchange for a guilty plea, the district attorney may recommend the defendant serve 2 years of a possible 7-year sentence.

3. Defendants may request a promise by the district attorney not to oppose the defense attorney's request for probation.

4. Other specific considerations may be requested, for example, that the offender be incarcerated at a local prison.

implicit bargaining defendants, through their attorneys, learn that if they do not plead guilty and are convicted of a crime(s) at a jury trial they will be punished more severely than if they would have pled to an agreed-on offense(s)

Implicit bargaining occurs when a defendant, through his or her attorney, comes to believe that if he or she does not plead guilty and is convicted at trial, the sentence will be harsher than if he or she would have pled guilty to the charges offered by the district attorney (i.e., accepted the deal). This form of bargaining more difficult to detect. Researchers have discovered that in many jurisdictions defendants who pled guilty consistently received lighter sentences than those individuals who took their cases to trial when "relevant variables," such as age, gender, race/ethnicity, and previous criminal record, were held constant (Jost, 1999).

Since its inception, the primary criticism of plea bargaining is that offenders are not punished severely enough and, as a result, are prematurely released from prison and often continue their criminal careers. A vocal opponent of plea bargaining, law professor and legal historian John Langbein (1992) argues that at least three "evils" are associated with this nontrial procedure. First, because plea bargaining negates both the jury and the trial, it concentrates the ominous power to punish completely in the hands of the state. Inasmuch as governmental officials become the "judge, jury, and executioner," citizens are removed from the everyday allocation of justice. In addition, high visibility trials are replaced with behind-the-scenes decision making, and the central figure in these negotiations (the prosecutor) is not directly accountable to the public for her or his actions.

Second, plea bargaining is wrong because it is based on coercion; the defendant is pressured to bear witness against herself or himself. For Langbein, "A legal system that comes to depend upon coercing people to waive their supposed rights is by definition a failed system" (p. 214). Because the disparity grows between the sentence offered a defendant via plea bargaining and the punishment threatened as a result of a jury trial, the pressure to confess intensifies. Because prosecutors routinely "overcharge," (that is, charge offenders with crimes prosecutors know they could not prove at a trial), defendants often end up pleading guilty to crimes they may have been acquitted of had the case gone to trial. Langbein would agree with those who believe the term *plea bargaining* is a misnomer that should be changed to reflect what it really is, "plea pressure" (Stitt and Chaires, 1993).

Finally, negotiated justice makes a mockery of criminal statistics. A person arrested and charged with multiple rapes may plead to one or more counts of sexual assault. Because approximately 90 percent of all criminal convictions in both state and federal courts (see Figure 10.1) are the result of plea bargaining, there is virtually no correspondence between what individuals are arrested for and the offenses for which they have been convicted (Langbein, 1992).

A staunch defender of negotiated pleas, New York state supreme court justice Carolyn Demarest (in Palermo, White, Wasserman, and Hanrahan, 1996) argues that plea bargaining offers significant benefits to the community, including many crime victims. She notes that testifying and undergoing rigorous cross-examination can be very difficult for the young, the old, and the infirm, as well as sexual abuse and rape survivors who may be reluctant to take the witness stand because of shame and/or the fear of public humiliation. Plea bargaining may also be the best prosecutorial strategy when witnesses are truthful but not credible, for example, when a known prostitute informs authorities that she has been raped. Figure 10.1 shows that most federal cases are settled by guilty pleas negotiated in bargaining.

Prosecutors and Plea Bargaining

In Chapter 7 on doing police work, we saw that officers have significant discretionary power and continually make decisions regarding the specific course of action they will follow. Similarly, after a decision has been made to prosecute, district attorneys must

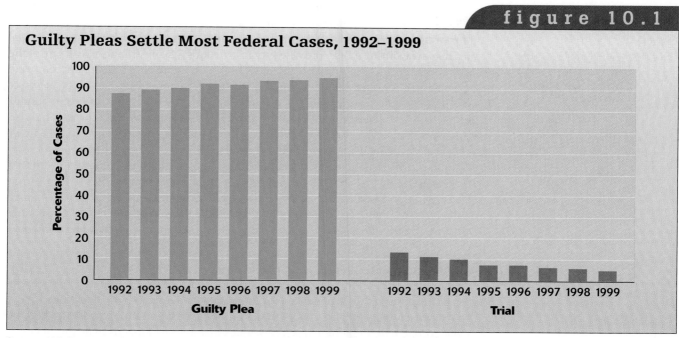

figure 10.1

Guilty Pleas Settle Most Federal Cases, 1992–1999

Sources: U.S. Sentencing Commission. 1996. *Sourcebook of Federal Sentencing Statistics.* Washington, DC: Bureau of Justice Statistics, U.S. Government Printing Office; U.S. Sentencing Commission. 1999. *Sourcebook of Federal Sentencing Statistics.* Washington, DC: Bureau of Justice Statistics, U.S. Government Printing Office.

determine whether they take a case to trial or plea bargain. The following questions may help influence a prosecutor's decision (Baker in Miller et al., 1978, p. 61):

1. If I go to trial, will I have credible witnesses? Do my witnesses have criminal records? Are they believable? Will they crumble under rigorous cross-examination?
2. If I go to trial, what are my chances of gaining a conviction?
3. Is the opposing attorney an efficient and capable advocate who will provide his or her client with a first-rate defense?
4. Will he or she get continuances and prolong the proceedings until my case is worn out?
5. Is the defense attorney capable of swaying the jury to his or her point of view?
6. Will this trial be so long and arduous that it will take time and energy away from other cases?
7. Would the judge and police chief want the case concluded without a trial?
8. What would the public want me to do?
9. Should I accept a plea of guilty (the sure thing) and a lesser term than this case may deserve, or should I take a chance and gamble for a longer sentence by going to trial, risking a not guilty verdict and no punishment?

Of these considerations, the most important appears to be the prosecutor's perception of the strengths and weaknesses of the state's case. Other major factors include the seriousness of the offense; the suspect's past record, and the reputation of the defense attorney.

Judges and Plea Bargaining

In their national survey of more than 2,800 criminal court judges, John Ryan and James Alfini (1979) learned that almost 70 percent of these officials at both felony and misdemeanor court level did not actively participate in or attend plea negotiation sessions (see Table 10.2). Nevertheless, judges are important in the plea bargaining process if for no other reason than they "ratify" the agreements that prosecutors and defense attorneys have reached. In other words, plea bargaining cannot exist where judges are unwilling to give their approval of negotiated settlements (Worden, 1995). If judges do not accept deals that are presented to them by district attorneys, prosecutors lose credibility with defense attorneys, and the process of negotiating guilty pleas comes to a standstill.

In his landmark study of plea bargaining, Milton Heumann (1981) noted that judges are typically forceful advocates of plea bargaining for at least four reasons: (1) Bargaining makes their jobs easier because they do not have to prepare for a trial, rule on legal issues that arise during a case, or write jury instructions; (2) on striking a deal, one of the most difficult decisions criminal court judges face—sentencing offenders—is removed; (3) plea bargaining expedites "moving the business," a euphemism for processing cases through the system (judges state that they are pressured by colleagues and court administrators to dispose of cases as readily as possible); (4) plea bargaining significantly reduces the chances that judicial decisions will be reduced by an appellate court. Judges abhor having their legal determinations publicly reversed.

Similar to district attorneys, criminal court judges work under the assumption that the overwhelming number of defendants are guilty. Heumann (1981) found that judges are not opposed to these guilty individuals taking their case to trial if they have a realistic, contestable issue "justifying" this course of action. What judges readily object to is the frivolous legal maneuvering in an unnecessary trial that serves no purpose. As one judge noted (Heumann, 1981, pp. 142–43),

> The circumstances are these: If a fellow tries a case where he is obviously guilty, where it is sheer folly to try the case, and yet the accused is insisting on trying the case, he deserves to be penalized for the trial because he takes up court time, there is expense involved, and so on. On the other hand, if a situation [arises] where he had a good defense, where it is a close question, and he happens to be found guilty, I would not penalize him for trying a case like that. He's got a right to try a case where he has [a] reasonable position, and it happens not to prevail.

table 10.2 — Trial Judges' Level of Participation in Plea Bargaining: Felony and Misdemeanor Judges

FELONY

Q. Which one of the following roles do you *most typically* assume with respect to plea negotiations?

"Attend plea negotiation discussions, and recommend dispositions to the D.A. and/or defense counsel"
(RECOMMEND)   7%

"Attend plea negotiation discussions, and review recommendations of the D.A. and/or defense counsel"
(REVIEW)   20

"Attend plea negotiation discussions but do not participate"
(ATTEND)   4

"Do not attend plea negotiation discussions, only ratify in open court dispositions agreed to outside your presence"
(RATIFY)   69%
    100%

N^a (2187)

MISDEMEANOR

Q. To the extent that plea negotiation takes place, which statement best characterizes your role generally?[b]

"I participate in plea discussions"
(PARTICIPATE)   21%

"I am present during plea discussions but do not participate in the discussions"
(ATTEND)   12

"I only ratify agreements reached outside my presence"
(RATIFY)   67%
    100%
    (616)

[a]Responses include only those judges whose *current* assignment involves the hearing of criminal cases.

[b]This question was preceded by a question asking the judge about the frequency of plea bargaining (as to charge or sentence) in misdemeanor cases in his court. Eight percent (N = 57) reported that plea negotiations "never" take place.

Source: Ryan, John Paul, and James J. Alfini. 1979. "Trial Judges' Participation in Plea Bargaining: An Empirical Perspective." *Law & Society Review*, 13(2): 479–507. Reprinted by permission of the Law and Society Association.

Judges are also responsible for ensuring that the rights of the defendant are protected and that factually innocent people are not pleading guilty to crimes they did not commit. This is ostensibly accomplished in a public ritual (sometimes referred to as the "litany") where the judge formally accepts the guilty plea (McConville and Mirsky, 1995, pp. 217–218):

Judge: Have you had an opportunity to consult with your lawyer, Mr. _____, and to discuss the matter with him/her before choosing to plead guilty?

Defendant: Yes.

Judge: Do you understand that by pleading guilty you have given up your right to confront and cross-examine witnesses against you, to testify, and to call witnesses on your own behalf?

Defendant: Yes.

Judge: Do you understand that you have given up your right to remain silent and your privilege against self-incrimination?

Defendant: Yes.

Judge: Do you understand that at a trial you are presumed innocent and that the prosecution has to prove you're guilty beyond a reasonable doubt?

Defendant: Yes.

Judge: Has anybody threatened or coerced you?

Defendant: No.

Judge: Is your plea voluntary and of your own free will?

Defendant: Yes.

Judge: Do you understand that in pleading guilty you have given up all these rights and that the conviction entered is the same as a conviction after a trial?

Defendant: Yes.

Critics contend that this procedure is nothing more than a sham to mask the "assembly line justice" (or injustice) that our criminal court system has become. The guilty plea is hardly given voluntarily because the defendant has learned (either explicitly or implicitly) that if he or she requests a jury trial and is convicted, the punishment will be more severe. In some cases, the judge is a player in this coercive process.

Public Defenders and Plea Bargaining

Plea bargaining can be stressful for public defenders in criminal court jurisdictions that have a judicially created "no trial option," that is, where going to trial is an infrequent occurrence. Sociologist David Lynch (1999) sent 375 questionnaires to all chief and assistant public defenders in New York state exclusive of New York City. Data from the 217 respondents (58 percent) indicated that not having the option of taking a case to trial was the third (of 17) most stressful aspects of public defenders' working environments. Only interacting with a judge whom they perceived as partial to the prosecution and actually going to trial were more taxing.

A qualitative aspect of the study using in-depth interviews with 20 public defenders in New York, North Carolina, and South Carolina revealed stress-producing conflicts that public defenders have with judges, prosecutors, clients, and their families. Almost all of the attorneys interviewed said that judges routinely mete stiffer punishments (often the maximum sentence) to defendants who go to trial and lose. An attorney in New York commented that judges often say: "How could you be trying this stupid case, how dare you" (Lynch, 1999, p. 226). A public defender in the Carolinas noted what happens when attorneys fail to convince their clients to accept a deal. "We go back and say, I've done everything I can, judge. He screams at you" (Lynch, 1999, p. 226).

Respondents in the Lynch study believed that most prosecutors did not take advantage of the fact that many judges excessively punished defendants who insisted on going to trial. However, they were hostile to those who did capitalize on this situation. A Carolina public defender stated that "some [prosecutors] are not merely unreasonable. They are astronomically unreasonable" (Lynch, 1999, p. 227). Lynch (p. 227) notes that the comment from a New York defender summed up the feelings of many defense attorneys who are forced to deal with prosecutors in jurisdictions where a jury trial is not a viable option: "You want to go to the district attorney's office and say, You self-righteous son-of-a-bitch, who the hell do you think you are?"

Public defenders routinely have conflicts with defendants and their families regarding their (the attorney's) competency. One respondent stated that "your clients will say to you after you talked to them initially [about an offer] in the jail, This doesn't look very good. I think I need to hire a real lawyer" (Lynch, 1999, p. 226). Defendants also accuse public defenders of not really caring about them and of working hand in hand with the district attorney.

Let's Make a Deal

Rather than a single decision, plea bargaining is best understood as a *process* involving a number of decisions (Walker, 1993) occurring over a period of a few days to a few weeks. Debra Emmelman's (1996) observational study of plea bargaining in southern California is a rich account of this dynamic component of the criminal justice system. Emmelman observed 15 attorneys employed by a private nonprofit organization that had a contract with "Smith County" (a fictitious name) to defend indigent persons. The organization had a reputation for providing "high-quality defense service." In Smith County, plea negotiations include the judge, the prosecuting attorney, the defense attorney (defender), the defendant, and, on rare occasions, the victim. Judges in this locale are encouraged to promote plea bargaining and to minimize jury trials. Emmelman found that pleas could be negotiated almost anywhere (in the judge's chambers, in hallways outside the courtroom, and in "holding tanks" where defendants awaited their court appearances) and at almost any time or juncture of an ongoing criminal case.

In some cases, pleas may be successfully bargained in one session, whereas in other instances negotiators will meet several times. A decision on the part of the defender to reach a settlement immediately or to continue the process involves the following three activities: (1) assessing the prosecutor's offer for pleading guilty, (2) negotiating the terms of the deal, and (3) conferring with the defendant and deciding what should be done. These steps do not necessarily occur in this order, for example, a defender may discuss possible terms offered by the prosecutor before meeting with that individual (see Table 10.3) (Emmelman, 1996).

Assessing a prosecutor's offer as acceptable or unacceptable is in large measure a function of the defense attorney's understanding of the value of the case. This value is determined by several factors beginning with the seriousness of the charge and the circumstances of the case. Although both crimes are technically the same offense (aggravated assault), prosecutors are likely to consider beating a helpless senior citizen a more serious offense than beating a rival gang member. Case value is also contingent on the strength of the state's evidence as interpreted by the defender and his or her perception of how successfully this evidence can be refuted. Finally, the defendant's background is assessed including prior criminal convictions (Emmelman, 1996).

After estimating the value of a case, defenders reach "tentative conclusions" on how they should proceed; some cases will be bargained immediately, and in others the

table 10.3	Hypothetical Plea Negotiation

The procedure for plea bargaining is not standard. It can take place formally or informally, with a plea negotiated in one session or in numerous meetings that transpire over several weeks. In most instances, the district attorney and defense counsel are the only active participants in the process, and they eventually reach a settlement on approval of the defendant. Following is a typical chronology of a negotiated plea for a defendant charged with armed robbery.

The defense attorney considers the prosecutor's offer in exchange for a guilty plea, for example, a charge reduction from armed robbery to simple robbery.

The prosecutor offers 2 years in prison in exchange for a guilty plea. The defense attorney counters with 1 year of incarceration contingent on acceptance of the plea by the client. (At this point, the prosecutor may accept or reject the counteroffer).

The defense attorney confers with the defendant. If the prosecutor rejects the 1-year offer, the defense attorney may (1) advise the client that 2 years is still a "good deal" to consider or accept, (2) suggest countering with 18 months (for example), (3) suggest making the 1-year offer again, or (4) suggest another strategy.

During this initial stage, both prosecution and defense attorneys calculate the current "value" of the case in that particular jurisdiction. For example, the defense attorney may stress that, although a weapon was used during the crime, no one was hurt, and similar offenses have had a value of 1 year in prison in exchange for a guilty plea. If the defendant has a prior armed robbery conviction, the prosecutor is likely to counter that such cases have a value of 2 years in prison in return for a plea of guilty.

negotiations will continue while the remaining defendants move toward a jury trial. One defender explained this decision-making process as follows (in Emmelman, 1996, p. 341):

> There are cases that you know [in the beginning] are gonna settle. . . . You know that there's simply no defense to the case . . . not a defense that's gonna be worthwhile in terms of having, exposing the person to a state prison sentence and drawing out the procedures for three to six months. . . . There's [another] category of case where it's not a triable case. You see it's not a triable case. However, the [first] offer is bad. Something may shake out at the [preliminary hearing] that is useful. Or the offer may be better in Superior Court than in Municipal Court. Or there's a motion that needs to be run . . . you do whatever needs to be done and you settle the case in Superior Court. But all along you know this isn't going to trial. . . . The third case is the case you know is going to go to trial. You know from the day that you get the case that it's going to be tried. That's because your client has no record and it's clear from talking to the client and reading discovery that a jury could acquit.

Even when district attorneys make a reasonable offer in exchange for a guilty plea, defenders may hold out for a better deal, believing that subsequent offers will not be more punitive. This is usually the case because over time the prosecutor loses witnesses, or evidence may appear that is favorable to the defense (Emmelman, 1996). However, in some instances, prolonging the culmination of a plea bargain may work against the accused. One defender noted (in Emmelman, 1996, p. 342), "I have a case now, I think the client was offered local time [in municipal court]. They just came up with two prison priors on this guy. He swears they aren't his. I don't believe him. I think they're his. . . . In which case the deal's gonna get worse." An often-overlooked aspect of plea bargaining is that both the prosecutor and defender are playing an information game. Who knows (or believe they know) what at a given stage of the proceedings will, in part, determine if a case is negotiated and what the settlement is likely to be.

Most of the defenders Emmelman observed and interviewed said that they negotiated pleas because judges and prosecutors were under a great deal of pressure to adjudicate cases in this manner. Others noted that the primary rationale for bargaining is that this process is almost always in their client's best interest. When asked why not take every case to trial, one defender stated (in Emmelman, 1996, p. 344):

> Because it's not in the client's best interests. [Interviewer: Why not?] Because if the defendant has no good case he's gonna be found guilty, and—say he's charged with a whole bunch of forgery counts, and he's gonna get ten counts, and he's gonna be found guilty on all of them, and the DA says instead of taking this case to trial, I'll give you one count. Obviously it's better to have him plead guilty to one count and have the others dismissed than go down on all counts. . . . [In addition] not that many are going to trial because the District Attorney can't try everything. And they have an incentive to offer you something because they can't try everything."

Is Plea Bargaining Here to Stay?

During the past 30 years, a number of criminal court jurisdictions and a few states have attempted to limit or eliminate plea bargaining with various degrees of success (Blum, 1996; Carns and Kruse, 1992; Holmes, Daudistel, and Taggart, 1992; McDonald, 1985). Typically, these efforts have done little more than shift negotiations from a visible process to a more covert or hidden stage (Fisher in Jost, 1999). If legislators or a district attorney bars plea bargaining, prosecutors simply consult with defense counsel *before* charges are officially filed and make a deal at that time. As Stanford law professor George Fisher notes: "The form of the plea becomes, I will seek only these charges if you will promise that your client will plead guilty" (in Jost, 1999, p. 121).

The most frequently given explanation for the existence and persistence of plea bargaining is the sheer number of criminal defendants that the courts have to process. However, Milton Heumann (1981, p. 287) has presented compelling evidence that "guilty pleas characterize high and low volume courts" and have done so since the late 1800s. If plea bargaining is not driven by necessity, then why is it the most frequently used method of case disposition across the country? Based on his research, Heumann argues that, through the course of their work, judges, prosecutors, and defense attorneys are taught and learn that, because most defendants are both legally and factually guilty, plea bargaining is the most "realistic" and beneficial method of dispensing justice. Judges learn that any case not worthy of a trial because of legal issues that may be contested should be bargained. Prosecutors learn that adequate punishments relative to the seriousness of the crime can be achieved via bargaining. Defense attorneys believe that, because their guilty clients will get a better deal if they bargain than if they go to trial and are convicted (as almost all of them will), plea bargaining works on their (the defendants') behalf. "As the actors spend more time in the system, these assumptions become so ingrained that they no longer think in terms of a trial" (Heumann, 1981, p. 157).

The Trial

The single most distinguishing feature of the U.S. system of justice (both civil and criminal) is the jury trial. The right to a jury trial in the case of criminal defendants is guaranteed by the Sixth Amendment: "In all criminal prosecutions, the accused shall enjoy the right to a speedy and public trial, by an impartial jury of the State and district wherein the crime shall have been committed." The Sixth Amendment also states that the defendant has the right to be informed of the charges prior to the trial so that a proper defense can be mounted and the accused can confront those individuals (witnesses) who are making accusations against him or her. However, as we learned in the discussion on plea bargaining, the overwhelming majority of criminal defendants waive their right to a jury trial.

Of the estimated 120,000 trials conducted in the world annually, more than 90 percent take place in the United States ("Jury," 1999–2000). When the Virginia Company was granted a charter in 1606, the colonists as English citizens were guaranteed the right to trial. Juries were composed of 12 (in some cases 13 or 14) *men*, all of whom were property owners with assets of at least £100. Felony cases were usually settled in 1 day because jurors were confined without food or water until they reached a decision. In addition to convicting or acquitting defendants of the crimes for which they were being tried, under certain circumstances, jurors could return a guilty verdict to a lesser offense. By the 1760s, the independence of North American juries from British control became one of an increasing list of demands (Simon, 1975) as the colonists and England moved ever closer to war.

Legal scholars Harry Kaven and Hans Zeisel (1966, p. 4) have characterized the jury as "an exciting experiment in the conduct of serious human affairs," one that has been "the subject of deep controversy, attracting at once the most extravagant praise and the most harsh criticism." We examine a number of issues in the chronological context of how a criminal jury trial unfolds:

- Jury selection, composition, and voir dire
- Prosecution's opening statement
- Defense's opening statement
- Presentation of prosecution's evidence
- Presentation of defense's evidence
- Rebuttal by prosecution
- Defense's closing arguments
- Prosecutor's closing arguments
- Instructing the jury and jury deliberation
- Returning a verdict
- Appeals

Jury Selection, Composition, and Voir Dire

The first step in selecting a jury is compiling a roll from which individuals can be selected. In an effort to remove discretion from local authorities who could include and/or exclude people (or categories of people) from serving at trials as they so pleased, voters' lists are used to draw the names of prospective jurors. These lists typically contain the names of 60 to 80 percent of the 18-and-older population. To generate a more inclusive jury list, a number of states have supplemented voter registration with an index of people with driver's licenses. In addition, some states have gathered names from city directories, motor vehicle registration, and telephone books as well as lists of taxpayers, welfare recipients, recent high school graduates, naturalized citizens, hunting licenses, utility customers, and, in some jurisdictions, dog licenses (Munsterman and Munsterman, 1986). Multiple lists are used to select names from a representative cross-section of the population by race, gender, religion, and socioeconomic status. The final list from which names are selected is called a *master jury list* or a *jury wheel*. The use of some highly inclusive lists, such as from the Census Bureau, Internal Revenue Service, and Social Security Administration, is prohibited by law. The federal court system develops a plan for the random selection of jurors on a district-by-district basis.

Jury Composition. In a 1970 Supreme Court decision (*Williams v. Florida*) affirming the constitutionality of 6-person juries (if so desired by the states), the justices ruled that the difference between a 12- and 6-person deliberating body regarding the representation of a cross-section of the community "seems likely to be negligible." Examining this decision from a mathematical perspective, law professor Michael J. Saks (1996, p. 264) argued that the high court was dead wrong in their ruling: "If we draw juries at random from a population consisting of 90 percent one kind of a person and 10 percent another kind of person (categorized by politics, race, religion, social class, wealth, or whatever), 72 percent of juries of size 12 will contain at least one member of a minority group, compared to only 47 percent of juries of size six."

People between the ages of 18 and 64 are usually employed or attending school, which makes jury service of more than a few days burdensome if not impossible. Some surveys indicate that juries serving on trials that exceed 20 days tend to have fewer college graduates and more unemployed and retired individuals as well as a disproportionate number of females and single people. Trials of this duration often involve murder charges, meaning that defendants in capital punishment cases may have their fates decided by a less-educated segment of the population (Dolan, 1994a).

Almost all states have a literacy and language requirement stating that jurors must speak and understand the English language. Twenty-six states stipulate that exemptions from jury duty are not possible. The remaining states excuse a variety of state officials and employees, with Nevada adding to that list physicians, dentists, optometrists, attorneys, state legislators (when in session), and locomotive engineers (*State Court Organization*, 1998).

Voir Dire. Voir dire (literally "to see, to tell," also translated as "to speak the truth") is the procedure by which opposing attorneys gain information about prospective jurors. As such, it is a crucial part of the trial process. There are three types of challenges that, if successful, will prevent an individual from being selected as a juror (Fried, Kaplan, and Klein, 1975): (1) In the *to the array* challenge, the master list is thought to be less than representative of the community or the names included improperly selected. Challenges to the array regarding the representativeness of the jury pool are rare. A challenge to the array of a seated jury can occur if either the prosecution or defense believes that the jury has been "stacked" on the basis of gender, race, or some other characteristic. In the trial of professional football player Rae Carruth charged with the murder of Cherica Adams, the defense argued that jury selection had been biased against African Americans, especially African American males. The judge asked the prosecutor to give reasons other than race or gender for dismissing 8 of 11 potential African American jurors (including four African American males). The prosecution provided answers (juror's age being too close to that of defendant, which might illicit sympathy for the defendant, for example) to the judge's satisfaction (Cronin, 2000). (2) When a challenge is *for Cause,* a juror is believed to be unfit for service because of his or her past experiences, occupation, bias, or relationship with the defendant or victim. Challenges for cause (which are unlimited in number) may be overruled by the judge, and the prospective juror would remain. (3) In a *peremptory* challenge, one of the attorneys may deem for any reason a prospective juror unacceptable. Traditionally, attorneys did not have to justify or explain challenges in this latter category, which were often based on "hunch, insight, whim, prejudice, or pseudoscience" (Neubauer, 1999, p. 341). However, in *Batson v. Kentucky* (1986), the Supreme Court ruled that the equal protection clause forbids prosecutors to peremptorily challenge potential jurors solely on the basis of their race or to make such challenges on the assumption that African Americans as a whole are unable to impartially consider the state's case against an African American defendant.

The number of peremptory challenges allowed per jury selection event varies by seriousness of the offense and state. For example, in misdemeanor cases, municipal courts in Connecticut permit only two challenges each for the prosecution and the defense, whereas New Jersey allows 10. In death penalty cases, Virginia law stipulates four challenges; at the other extreme, Connecticut permits 25 for each side. A few states give the defense more challenges than the prosecution, especially in capital cases. In these trials, Georgia, for example, grants the prosecution 12 challenges and the defense 20 (*State Court Organization,* 1998).

In Connecticut and North Carolina, questions at the voir dire are posed by attorneys, whereas in Arizona, California, Illinois, Massachusetts, New Hampshire, and New Jersey, questioning is restricted to judges (but usually with input from the prosecution and defense). In the remaining states, both the judge and opposing attorneys participate in the voir dire process. In most federal courts, questions are asked exclusively by judges (Small, 1999; *State Court Organization,* 1998).

During the course of the voir dire, attorneys attempt to educate jurors so that the jurors understand (1) certain aspects of the law as they apply to the case, (2) the burden of proof by which they will be evaluating evidence, and (3) the general theories or overarching arguments to be used during the course of the trial.

Regarding the standard of evidentiary proof, although there has been no systematic investigation of this subject, it appears that the popular television programs *CSI* (Crime Scene Investigation) and *CSI: Miami* may be altering the way some jurors interpret physical evidence. Because the investigators in these programs solve crimes with state-of-the-art technology such as DNA analysis and chemical tests that are sensitive to minuscule amounts of blood, some jurors may set impossibly high standards of physical evidence before they will vote to convict. During the voir dire, some prosecutors are asking potential jurors about their television viewing habits and if they can "distinguish between real-life forensics that take time, luck, and money, and make-believe" television cases that are irrefutably solved in less than an hour (Franzen, 2002, p. D6).

Attorneys may also try to elicit information from prospective jurors about certain relevant factors in the case. Attorneys may try to discover whether the prospective jurors have had similar experiences in their own lives. For example, "This is a simple case involving greed and guilt, so I'd like you to tell me whether you yourself have experienced being a victim of either greed or guilt" (Starr, 1994, p. xiv). Voir dire is also the occasion when opposing attorneys attempt to develop a relationship with prospective jurors, an ease of communication they hope will carry over into the trial. In his book *Going to Trial,* Daniel Small states (1999, p. 165): "This is an extraordinary chance to develop a rapport with the jury in a way not available once the jury has been empaneled. At no other time during the trial will counsel enjoy the opportunity to essentially engage in a conversation with members of the jury."

However, the overriding purpose of voir dire as viewed by the prosecution and defense is to select jurors who are sympathetic to their particular arguments. In other words, neither side wants completely open-minded, objective jurors (Steury and Frank, 1996). Rather, they are seeking individuals who are predisposed to a greater or lesser degree to their positions and hostile to the arguments that will be presented by their counterpart. James Gould (2000, p. 103) states that opposing attorneys "use challenges (peremptory and for cause) to exclude jurors they don't like. What is left is the jury that hears the case." Toward this end, the prosecution is looking for jurors said to have an *authoritarian personality,* a worldview characterized by submission to legitimate authority figures and conformity to a value system that clearly designates what is appropriate and inappropriate behavior. Authoritarian jurors are thought to be more susceptible to the arguments of the prosecutor because he or she is a legitimate government authority (Fried et al., 1975). However, defense attorneys are seeking egalitarians who are more likely to examine the evidence objectively or individuals hostile to authority figures. Table 10.4 delineates the aims of the prosecution and defense in the selection of jurors, and Table 10.5 notes the lighter side of the voir dire process.

During the past 30 to 35 years, social scientists and others who believe that they can identify salient personality characteristics in prospective jurors (and determine whether they are more likely to convict or acquit) have become increasingly more influential in U.S. courts, both civil and criminal. The practical application of social science to the justice system has resulted in the neolegal profession of "jury consultants." In 1982, there were 35 jury consultants in the United States and in 1994 there were 250 (Gollner, 1994). As of 2000, the American Society of Trial Consultants claimed 340 members.

Although some of the reasoning employed by these consultants (especially in the late 1960s and 1970s) is grounded in research, other strategies for choosing prospective jurors are little more than pop psychology. Consider the following examples:

> The young lady who lets her foot slip out of her shoe may be outwardly well balanced, but inwardly feel threatened by men. Life to her is a tight-fitting shoe from which she desires to escape. Like a dog straining at the leash, such a woman will be sympathetic with a defendant who has been fenced in, subjugated and squashed until finally the defendant broke out from the hated pattern of living by committing some unlawful act. She is not willing to punish this kind of defendant because she longs to do the same thing herself. (Bryan, 1971, p. 161)

> A nice suit with dirty shoes usually indicates an uncoordinated mind. . . . A female juror who is fearful of adult sexuality might compensate with seductive clothes and makeup. A short juror may dress flamboyantly, denoting an inner inferiority complex." (Mitcham, 1980, pp. 53–54)

table 10.4	Differential Aims of Attorneys in the Selection and Influence of Jurors
PROSECUTION	**DEFENSE**
Select authoritarian jurors	Select egalitarian jurors
Select jurors with a closed or rigid mind-set	Select jurors willing to consider conflicting information
Convince jurors of high probability of guilt	Convince jurors of low probability of guilt
Establish in jurors a low criterion for conviction	Establish in jurors a high criterion for conviction

Source: Adapted from Fried, Michael, Kalman J. Kaplan, and Katherine W. Klein. 1975. "Jury Selection: An Analysis of Voir Dire." Pages 47–66 in *The Jury System in America,* edited by Rita James Simon. Beverly Hills, CA: Sage. Copyright © 1975 by Sage Publications, Inc. Reprinted by permission of Sage Publications, Inc.

table 10.5   Voir Dire—Humor in the Court

Attorneys questioning prospective jurors during voir dire often elicit unexpected responses.

Question: What do you do in your spare time?
Answer: (from a 64-year old, gray-haired, conservative-looking farmer) I smoke marijuana.

Question: Can you tell me about your job?
Answer: Very boring.
Question: Even more boring than this voir dire procedure?
Answer: No, not this boring.

Question: I see that you have a large family. Have you and your husband been able to spend time alone together?
Answer: That is apparent, isn't it?

Question: Can you hear me all right?
Answer: Pardon?

Question: Did you enjoy your previous experience on the jury?
Answer: To this day I wonder what really happened.

Question: Would you like to serve on a jury?
Answer: I wish you paid more.

During a moment of silence in the courtroom a prospective juror said,
Juror: Can I ask a question?
Attorney: Yes?
Juror: Why can't those Cubs ever win a pennant?

Source: Walsh, Michael S. 1994. "Voir Dire Follies—Humor in the Court." *Trial,* February: 52–54. Copyright © 1994 by the Association of Trial Lawyers of America. Reprinted by permission.

Body language such as folding and unfolding arms and legs and rapid changes in facial expression may be indicative of people's feelings and underlying personality characteristics, but it does not necessarily follow that these gestures can be accurately interpreted. Social psychologist James Weyant (1986, p. 176) noted that individuals "can detect deception from non-verbal cues at only slightly better than at chance level, and there is no evidence that psychologists can do any better."

Jury consultants may be quite effective when advising attorneys on what questions to ask and how to pose their queries during voir dire. At a murder trial where the defendant was charged with murdering a 16-year-old girl, the first question the defense attorney asked potential jurors was, "Can you look Kevin in the eyes and say, 'Kevin, I can give you a fair trial'?" Individuals who hesitated or looked away from the attorney (although they responded affirmatively) were excluded by the defense (in Gollner, 1994). Table 10.6 is a sample of the more than 200 voir dire questions attorneys asked prospective jurors at a murder trial. (No one juror was asked all of the questions).

The problem with selecting the right jurors is that both attorneys are using the same strategy and may use peremptory challenges to exclude individuals they believe their opponents have designated as highly desirable. Because the ability to mold a jury to one's liking is limited, consultants are most effective in advising lawyers how they should proceed with a case once jurors have been chosen. In other words, instead of

table 10.6 Voir Dire Examination

In a high-profile murder trial in South Dakota, the defense attorney prepared a list of 201 questions to be asked during the voir dire. The first 25 items elicited demographic information such as age, gender, marital status, number of children, residence, education, employment, religious affiliation, and military experience. Following is a sample of some of the other questions that were asked of prospective jurors.

Do you believe that police officers are human just like you and me? By that I mean, do you believe they are subject to the same human weaknesses as you and I?

Do you believe that under certain circumstances, a police officer could make a mistake, maybe even a serious mistake?

Do you think it is the obligation of police officers to investigate all the evidence or just to find evidence until they feel that they can prove someone is guilty?

Do you think a police officer should be working for the prosecution, or do you think a police officer is the objective gatherer of facts?

Would you say that you have a fixed opinion in your mind about this case?

You know, don't you, that the state and the prosecutor have the burden of proof?

The burden of proof means that the state must prove its case against _____ to your satisfaction beyond a reasonable doubt to a moral certainty. Do you think that is placing too much of a burden on the state?

Would the fact that _____ has been arrested and charged with this crime create an inference in your own mind that there must be some truth or they wouldn't be holding this man all these months for trial?

And then the fact that the state's attorney general has filed an information against him, does that create within you a state of mind that _____ must have done it or he wouldn't have been charged?

Would you generally take the position that where there is smoke, there must be fire? Is that the way your mind works?

Would you believe that you had not heard "both sides of the story" if you had not heard _____ testify on his own behalf?

If _____ is advised by his lawyers that it is best for him not to take the stand, would you feel that there must be some negative reason for his electing not to testify?

If the defendant in this case were to testify, would you give him the same credence that you would give to any other witness; specifically, would you feel that he were any less likely to tell the truth than, let us say, a police officer?

If you are chosen for this case, do you know of any reason why you could not sit as a fair and impartial juror?

Is there anything that you have felt, seen, or heard since you came here for jury duty that would lead you to believe that you might have a propensity or a tendency to accept one view, either that of the prosecutor or the defendant more than you would accept the other view?

Source: Adapted from Starr, V. Hale (ed.). 1994. *Jury Selection—Sample Voir Dire Questions*. Boston: Little, Brown. 1994. Reprinted by permission of V. Hale Starr.

trying to match jurors to the facts of the case, the presentation of the case is shaped to the composition of the jury ("Shrinking Courtrooms," 1995). For example, consultants can tell lawyers which evidence should be stressed and the most effective way to make a point. This is accomplished in part by using a "shadow jury," that is, individuals hired by consultants who follow the trial closely and inform the consultants what they are feeling and thinking as the case unfolds (Dolan, 1994b).

How effective are jury consultants in helping to bring about a verdict that is favorable to their clients? Jo-Ellan Dimitrius (in Gollner, 1994) claims a 90 percent success rate in the more than 100 cases on which she has worked. The unanswerable question is in how many of these cases would the jury have returned the same verdict had she not provided her services? Most social scientists believe that jury selection techniques may well make a difference in those close cases where evidence is ambiguous (Weyant, 1986). However, in trials where one side or the other has a demonstrably stronger case, jury selection is most likely irrelevant.

Opening Statements

When the voir dire process has been completed and the jury is sworn in, the trial begins. Each side has the opportunity (although it is not required) to make an opening statement beginning with the prosecution. The opening statement is the first opportunity for the state, and then the defense, to present to the jury the thrust of the case from their respective positions. Although some judges will permit the attorneys to speak at length, others place specific time constraints on opening statements. Attorneys consider this initial contact with the jury an important part of their overall trial strategy because "repeated studies and experience have demonstrated that the lawyer who wins the opening statement, in the great majority of cases, will ultimately receive a favorable verdict" (Small, 1999, p. 181). Attorneys will present some or all of the following information in the opening statement (Small, 1999, p. 18):

1. *A case summary.* The jurors will be told what the case is about, what happened, and why they should care about successfully prosecuting or acquitting a defendant.
2. *Cast of characters.* The jury is informed of the major players in the drama.
3. *The chronology.* The jury is given an overview of the time sequence of the significant facts and events.

At this juncture of the trial, the attorneys are not permitted to argue the facts of the case (as they perceive them), and they cannot try to convince the jury to return a verdict of guilt or innocence.

Presenting the Evidence

The presentation of evidence by the opposing attorneys constitutes the bulk of the trial. In its attempt to demonstrate that a defendant is guilty beyond a reasonable doubt, the state/prosecutor presents its case (evidence) first. It is imperative to understand exactly what "reasonable doubt" entails in a legal sense. It means that the evidence "must be so conclusive and complete that all reasonable doubts of the fact are removed from the mind" (Gifis, 1996, p. 170). However, "It does not require that the proof should be so clear that no possibility of error can exist" (p. 170). If this latter—and much more stringent—criterion of reasonable doubt was used, far fewer guilty verdicts would be reached. Four types of evidence are presented during a trial (Neubauer, 1999, p. 347):

Testimony. Testimony includes any statement made by a witness under oath.

Direct evidence. Direct evidence is derived by way of the physical senses (sight, hearing, taste, touch, and smell); for example, testimony that the defendant was seen pulling a knife from a jacket pocket is direct evidence.

Real evidence. Real evidence involves tangible objects, for example, the knife with the defendant's fingerprints on it and the receipt for the purchase of this object.

Circumstantial or *presumptive evidence.* Circumstantial or presumptive evidence is inconclusive because it is not based on a witness's direct experience. Testimony that a defendant was seen walking out of the park sweating profusely with a tennis racket under his arm is circumstantial evidence that he or she had been playing tennis. This form of evidence is treated as true until it is refuted by other evidence.

When a district attorney calls witnesses who will testify on the state's behalf, he or she is engaging in *direct examination.* The purpose of this form of questioning is for witnesses to tell their stories and, in so doing, to make emotional connections with the jury. Small (1999, p. 197) notes that direct examination has at least three primary objectives: First, it serves to introduce and validate the witness, that is, to convince the jury by way of the individual's testimony that he or she is a credible (believable) person; second, it serves to present a dramatic and persuasive picture of the principal facts in the case; and finally, by way of testimony, it introduces real, tangible evidence. In planning their trial strategy, attorneys must determine which witnesses have what information and in what order they should testify. Because attorneys want "their" witnesses to speak to jurors in a persuasive, unrestrained manner, they ask the witnesses open-ended or general response questions. For example, "Mr. Jones, on the Saturday night in question, what did you see as you approached in your car?"; "Mr. Smith, what did you and the defendant talk about on that occasion?" This type of questioning is predicated on the assumption that, although attorneys shape and direct a case, it is ultimately the testimony of the witnesses (and through them the introduction of real evidence) that will determine the outcome of a trial.

When a defense attorney questions a prosecution witness (and vice versa), he or she is conducting a *cross-examination.* One of the goals of cross-examination is to undermine the credibility of a witness. If an attorney can show that the witness has a prior criminal record or has engaged in previous acts of dishonesty, jurors may conclude that, if this individual has lied in the past, he or she may be lying now. Cross-examination is also used for directly attacking the testimony of a witness by demonstrating that he or she has had a long-standing hatred of the defendant, that there are inconsistencies in his or her testimony, and/or that the ability of the witness to hear or see things accurately is impaired for some reason (Small, 1999). Simply stated, the overall purpose of cross-examination is to undermine the witnesses, the evidence, and, therefore, the case of opposing counsel.

According to John Wigmore (in Black, 1999) of Northwestern University School of Law, "cross-examination is the greatest engine for determining the truth." Defense lawyer Roy Black maintains that more defendants end up in prison because of inept "cross" than any other legal mistake. During this type of questioning, lawyers attempt to get witnesses to say only what they (the attorneys) believe will support their case. To this end, attorneys want to control the testimony of the witness as much as possible. This is accomplished by asking short questions that can only be answered by a "yes" or "no" response.

"The formula for successful cross-examination is simply stated: Use plain declarative sentences, add only one new fact per question. . . . Think of cross-examination as a series of statements by the lawyer only occasionally interrupted by a yes from the witness" (Black, 1999, p. 43). In the following example, a skillful attorney cross-examines a police detective (p. 43–44):

Attorney: And your interview with Officer Alvarez took place at 6:35?

Detective: Yes, sir.

Attorney: By then the crowd was even larger?

Detective: Yes, sir.

Attorney: Still a steady stream of rocks and bottles?

Detective: Yes.

Attorney: Did people begin pounding on the windows of the arcade?

Detective: Yes.

Attorney: Were the officers handling the crowd outside forced back inside the arcade?

Detective: Yes, sir.

Attorney: Things were too hot for them standing outside the front doors?

Detective: Yes, sir.

Famed defense counsel F. Lee Bailey and his colleague Henry Rothblatt (1978) suggest that during cross-examination attorneys stand close to the witness without blocking the view of jurors. This nearness can create a tension between attorney and witness that can help break down the latter's testimony. However, this tactic would not work in states where attorneys must gain the judge's permission to approach the witness. Granted only when it is thought to be absolutely necessary, this rule is intended to keep witnesses from being harassed.

After the prosecution has presented its case, the defense will likely enter a motion for a *directed verdict* (sometimes called "judgment of acquittal") stating that the prosecution has not presented a case strong enough to warrant a continuation of the trial and that the defendant should be acquitted of all charges. These motions are rarely granted, and defense counsel then proceeds with its case using a predetermined strategy. One such strategy is the *alibi defense* wherein the contention is made that the defendant was someplace else when the crime was committed. Witnesses are then called to testify that the defendant was with them or was seen at a location other than the crime scene when the criminal event occurred. During cross-examination, prosecutors may attack the credibility of these witnesses and/or search for inconsistencies in their stories. In an *affirmative defense,* the defendant's attorney does not deny the charge but rather introduces new evidence that will avoid a judgment (guilty verdict) against his or her client. Entrapment and self-defense are affirmative defenses. Note that in all affirmative defenses the burden of proof rests with the defendant (see Table 10.7); that is, the defendant must demonstrate why he or she should be legally excused from conviction and punishment.

One of the most difficult decisions a defense attorney must make is whether to put a defendant on the witness stand. The Fifth Amendment provides legal protection against self-incrimination, and judges instruct the jury that they can make no inferences from the fact that a defendant does not testify. However, this does not prevent jurors from wondering why an innocent individual (as the defendant claims to be) would not testify on his or her own behalf (Neubauer, 1999). Some jury members may take this line of reasoning a step further and conclude that only a guilty person would choose not to testify. Defendants who testify are subject to cross-examination, questioning that will be observed very closely by the jury as they evaluate not only what is being said but also the defendant's emotional state as he or she answers questions. The prosecuting attorney is likely to attack the defendant's credibility, by revealing any prior convictions (Neubauer, 1999).

When the defense rests, the prosecution may choose to call rebuttal witnesses. The purpose of rebuttal evidence is (1) to undermine or directly attack the defense case, and (2) to buttress any weaknesses in its own case that have been exposed by the defense counsel. For example, if the defendant's attorney has presented a highly credible witness whose testimony was not damaged in cross-examination, this testimony can be contested by rebuttal witnesses. The "expert" testimony of a defense witness is likely to be called into question by the introduction of another expert witness who contradicts that testimony (Small, 1999). Rebuttal witnesses are subject to cross-examination. Table 10.8 summarizes the types of questioning of witnesses.

Closing Arguments

After the prosecution and defense have presented their cases, each side has the opportunity to address the jury in closing arguments: first, the prosecution, then the defense, with the prosecution having a final opportunity (because it has the burden of proof) to refute the assertions of defense counsel (Neubauer, 1999). Typically the most dramatic part of the trial process, Steven Goldberg (1997, p. 391) refers to the closing argument as "pure persuasion" in which each side ties elements of the case together and attempts to convince the jury of the righteousness of its position. This is the last chance for opposing attorneys to refute each other's position as well as to shore up weaknesses in their own cases. The prosecution will argue that the state has met its obligation because the evidence clearly demonstrates that the defendant is guilty beyond a reasonable doubt. Conversely, the defense counsel will state emphatically that the state clearly failed to overcome the reasonable doubt criteria.

In their closing arguments, Daniel Small (1999, p. 276) advises attorneys to "use powerful, descriptive, catchwords, and phrases . . . use all the tools at your disposal . . . use silence, and contrast, use movement and body language." Jurors are often reminded that they are part of an honorable judicial position and that the outcome of the trial now rests with them and them alone. Finally, opposing attorneys virtually always tell jurors that the only fair and just verdict is a vote for their side.

table 10.7   Affirmative Defenses

Several defenses are recognized by the courts that allow defendants to escape conviction even though the prosecution may be able to prove all the elements of a crime. However, the burden of proof in these defenses falls on the defendant. Affirmative defenses can be thought of as excuses for why an individual should be acquitted of the crime(s) that he or she is accused of committing. Law professor Steven L. Emanuel has outlined eight affirmative defenses.

Duress: A defendant can be said to have committed a crime under duress if he or she performed a criminal act because of the threat of, or use of, force by a third person sufficiently strong that the defendant's will was overcome. The term applies to force on the defendant's mind, not the body. For example, suppose that X forces D to rob Y by threatening D with immediate death if D refuses. This is duress because the force from X operates on D's mind.

Necessity: The defense of necessity can be raised when the defendant has been compelled to commit a criminal act by nonhuman events rather than by coercion by another person. For instance, a husband who must get his seriously sick or injured wife to a hospital could claim the necessity defense if he was ticketed for speeding. The essence of this defense is that the offender has committed the lesser of two evils. In this instance it is a lesser evil to violate traffic laws than to jeopardize someone's health by not providing medical care as soon as possible.

Self-defense: There is a general right to defend oneself against the use of unlawful force. Depending on the circumstances, this use of force may or may not be deadly. A number of requirements must be met for the successful use of this defense. For example, the use of force must not be more than reasonably necessary to defend oneself against the threat. If A slaps B in the face, A is not justified in pulling out a gun and killing A. In other words, the force used by the defendant may not be deadly unless the danger being resisted was also deadly.

Defense of others: An individual has the right to use force in the defense of others under approximately the same circumstances that he or she would be justified in his or her own defense.

Defense of property: Individuals have a limited right to protect their property against wrongful taking. However, the degree of force may not be more than

appears reasonably necessary to prevent the taking. Because the law regards human life as more valuable than property, generally speaking, an individual may not use deadly force in the defense of property. A few courts have allowed the use of deadly force on the forcible entry to one's dwelling provided the intruder has not desisted when warned to do so.

Law enforcement: A law enforcement agent has the general privilege of violating the law when it is reasonable in the commission of his or her duties. A police officer who strikes and kills a pedestrian while chasing a known felon is typically acquitted of manslaughter charges if it can be shown that he or she was appropriately performing his or her duties even though the speed limit was being exceeded during the chase.

Maintaining authority: Parents of minor children, school teachers, and other persons with supervisory duties have a limited right to use force in the course of their duties. A person who spanks a child will not be guilty of battery provided the use of force is reasonable under the circumstances, which include, but are not limited to, the child's age, gender, and the severity of misbehavior.

Entrapment: The defense of entrapment exists when a law enforcement official, or someone cooperating with him or her, has induced the defendant to commit a crime. A number of courts and the U.S. Supreme Court have ruled that entrapment exists "when the criminal design originates with the officials of the Government, and they implant in the mind of an innocent person the disposition to commit the alleged offense and induce its commission in order that they may prosecute." The entrapment defense is usually raised by defendants who argue that undercover officers have induced them to engage in illicit sexual behavior or become involved in the manufacture, distribution, or use of drugs.

Source: Adapted from Emanuel, Steven L. 1988. *Criminal Law.* Larchmont, NY: Emanuel. Reprinted from Emanuel Law Outline Series with the permission of Aspen Law & Business.

table 10.8	**Questioning Witnesses**
TYPE OF EXAMINATION	**MAJOR OBJECTIVES**
Direct examination	Introduce and legitimate witness with convincing testimony
	Present jury with dramatic and persuasive exposition of principal facts
	Introduce real evidence
Cross-examination	Undermine credibility of witness
	Attack testimony of witness by demonstrating it is inaccurate, inconsistent, and/or inconclusive
	Undermine opposing attorney's case by exposing deficiencies of his or her witness

Instructing the Jury and Jury Deliberation

After the attorneys have addressed the jury in their closing arguments, the judge "charges" (or instructs) the jurors as to the issues of the case and the applicable points of law that must be observed during their deliberation (Starr and McCormick, 1993). Educating jurors at the conclusion of the proceedings is based on the assumption that people are more likely to remember and use what they have just heard. However, instructing the jury after, as opposed to before, the trial begins has been harshly criticized by many practitioners in both criminal and civil courts. One judge noted that this practice is comparable to "telling jurors to watch a baseball game and decide who won without telling them what the rules are until the end of the game" (in S. J. Adler, 1994, p. 129). A team of researchers concluded that when jurors received instructions both before *and* after the trial they were better able to ascertain the relevant evidence as well as remember more accurately what they heard (Elwork, Sales, and Alfini, 1982). Yet another alternative is to present the jurors with instructions during the course of the proceedings as the need arises (Starr and McCormick, 1994). Whenever the jury is addressed by the judge, the instructions are not likely to provide any guidance if they are presented in "legalese" or "lawyerspeak." Consider the following paragraph excerpted from 81 pages of jury instructions in a civil case (in S. J. Adler, 1994, p. 131):

> The outer boundaries of a product are determined by the reasonable interchangeability of use or the cross-elasticity of supply and demand between the product itself and substitutes for it. . . . The average variable cost test is a double inference test because if you find that Brown & Williamson priced below its reasonably anticipated average variable cost. . . ."

Attorney Stephen Adler (1994) notes that this was not a case of jurors being unable to understand some of the instructions; rather, they did not comprehend anything they were told. It is little wonder that many jurors are incapable of making informed decisions. Although some attempt has been made to render instructions in "plain English," what is straightforward and understandable to lawyers may remain unclear to jurors.

The Florida Standard Jury Instructions video stresses that a defendant is presumed to be innocent until he or she is proven guilty by the presentation of the evidence beyond a reasonable defense. In a startling and worrisome discovery, researchers found that after viewing this film only 50 percent of the jurors fully understood the reasonable doubt concept (Strawn and Buchanan, 1976). Ten percent of the viewers were

These jurors are voting on the guilt or innocence of a defendant whose trial they have just witnessed. Currently there is a debate about the placement of cameras in jury rooms to record the deliberation and voting procedure. Will some jurors "grandstand" or show off in front of the cameras while others (perhaps less articulate and educated) remain silent and follow the majority so as not to have the lens focus on them? In short, will the presence of a recording device impact the outcome of trials by way of altering the jury's decision-making process?

confused as to what the presumption of innocence meant, and 2 percent believed that the burden of proof of innocence rested with the defendant.

In *Williams v. Florida* (the 1970 decision permitting six-person juries), the Supreme Court essentially said that a jury divided 10 to 2 is the social psychological equivalent of a jury split 5 to 1. However, the juror who is the lone holdout on a six-member panel is in a much different (and weaker) position than are the two contrary individuals on a 12-person jury. In the latter instance, each dissenter has an ally and is in a much stronger psychological position to hold out against the majority (Saks, 1996). The argument has also been made that a larger group will make better decisions because more resources are available to solve the problem. If six heads are better than one, then 12 minds are superior to six (Saks, 1996).

In a 1978 decision (*Ballew v. Georgia*), the Supreme Court ruled that five-person criminal juries were too small and cited a number of social scientific studies that evaluated the performance of six-person juries. This was a radical departure from *Williams v. Florida* 8 years earlier. Some of the major findings of these studies were as follows (Gobert and Jordan, 1990): (1) Smaller juries were less likely to promote effective group deliberation; (2) smaller juries were not as likely to overcome the biases of individual members; (3) the risk of convicting innocent people increases as the size of the jury decreases; and (4) smaller juries are less likely to result in a hung jury to the detriment of defendants who benefit from mistrials. Although the court did not overturn *Williams v. Florida*, it stated that "the purpose and functioning of the jury in a criminal court is seriously impaired, and to a constitutional degree, by a reduction in size to below six members" (Gobert and Jordan, 1990, p. 59).

The very important question of how individuals arrive at a determination of guilt or innocence has been investigated by social scientists. A juror's vote can be viewed as the result of a twofold decision-making process. The first step is the individual juror's evaluation of the defendant's guilt or innocence at the end of the trial but *before* deliberations commence. The second part of this process is an examination of group dynamics, that is, the deliberation process of the jury as a whole and how this process affects the vote of constituent members.

In their investigation of jurors' initial opinions, Barbara Reskin and Christy Visher (1986) interviewed 331 of 456 jurors who served in 38 sexual assault trials. They also observed the ongoing trial proceedings. Reskin and Visher (1986) concluded that jurors' "predeliberation verdict" was a consequence of at least three factors: (1) The jurors used trial evidence in determining a defendant's guilt or innocence; (2) evidence was selectively interpreted because jurors tended to ignore available eyewitness testimony and focused on evidence of the force and seriousness of the assault; and (3) when the prosecution presented substantial "hard evidence" (a recovered weapon, other physical evidence, eyewitness testimony, and physical injury to the victim), jurors were more likely to believe the defendant was guilty without considering "extralegal evidence." This latter evidence consisted of the jurors' perceptions of the defendant's physical and social attractiveness and any reference to employment. Other extralegal factors were negative comments about the victim's moral character and the jurors' perceptions of the victim's carefulness or carelessness when assaulted. When the prosecution presented a weak case and the guilt of the defendant was in doubt, jurors reached a pre-deliberation decision by incorporating their personal values (attitudes about crime) and the extralegal values concerning the defendant and victim. The weaker the state's case against the defendant, the more likely a juror's sentiments were to impact his or her decision to acquit or convict. In a similar vein, Kalven and Zeisel (1966) noted that the "closeness of the evidence" to jurors' beliefs, values, and experiences allows them to avoid considering the case solely in terms of how it is presented by the prosecution and defense. Under these circumstances, jurors may interject their personal sentiments into the decision-making process, a phenomenon known as the *liberation hypothesis*.

Because a person's life experiences are likely to affect the way he or she interprets evidence and because one's experiences are in large measure a function of gender, race, age, social class, occupation, and personality traits, these factors have been examined as they relate to jurors' decisions in criminal trials. However, after reviewing dozens of studies, Marilyn Chandler Ford (1986, p. 19) found that "the influence of social and demographic factors on juror behavior is unclear." In other words, we cannot say with any certainty that African Americans, women, or college-educated jurors are likely to vote one way or another in certain cases.

Numerous studies have concluded that authoritarian personalities are more likely to convict (Ford, 1986). Recall from our previous discussion that authoritarian individuals tend to follow rules uncritically, obey people in positions of authority, and typically adhere to conventional values that have been endorsed by political and religious leaders (Gergen and Gergen, 1986). People who score high on authoritarianism are especially punitive to low-status defendants, a group that includes minority members who are often perceived as leading unconventional lifestyles.

Authoritarianism is also correlated with attitudes favorable to the death penalty. This is very important in light of two Supreme Court decisions (*Witherspoon v. Illinois,* and *Wainwright v. Witt*) stating that individuals opposed to the death penalty or who had reservations about this form of punishment could be excluded from jury panels in capital cases. The jury composition in death penalty cases, therefore, may be qualitatively different from the makeup of juries in noncapital cases (Ford, 1986).

Apart from personality characteristics, a juror's mood at the time of the trial may be relevant to the decision-making process. A person who has recently received a speeding ticket (thought to be undeserved) or had an unpleasant experience with a governmental official may not believe the testimony of police officers and generally may be hostile to the prosecution's case (Gobert and Jordan, 1990). The overall "psychological baggage that human beings bring to the jury room may render illusory any talk of a truly representative jury" (p. 57).

The Verdict

After the jury has reached a verdict, it returns to the courtroom and announces the decision. Although it is uncommon, either attorney may request that the court *poll the jury,* with the judge asking each juror if the verdict reflects his or her decision. Approximately two-thirds of all criminal trial juries find for the state; that is, the defendant is convicted. There is significant variation among states ranging from 59 percent of defendants being declared guilty by juries in Florida to 83 percent in California (Vidmar, Beale, Rose, and Donnelly, 1997). This number is not particularly high considering that district attorneys are loathe to invest time and human resources in a trial that they do not believe with a high degree of certainty will result in a guilty verdict. An unknown but significant percentage of criminal trials are "slam dunk" cases. Just as a slam dunk is rarely missed on the basketball court, the state's case is so strong because of eyewitness testimony and physical evidence that the chances of a not guilty verdict are the proverbial "slim and none."

In about 5 percent of cases, even after prolonged deliberation, the jury cannot reach a unanimous verdict or the designated majority vote for a conviction or acquittal in that state. This is a *hung jury* with the judge declaring the proceedings a mistrial; it is a scenario likened to a draw in a prize fight—nobody wins and nobody loses. Defense attorneys routinely ask the judge to order the acquittal of the defendant in the aftermath of a hung jury. Should this request be denied, the prosecutor must decide whether the case warrants a second trial or if the charges against the accused should be dismissed (Steury and Frank, 1996). A high-profile case in which the district attorney believes that the reputation of the department is at stake and/or believes that the public wants the case tried again is likely to result in a retrial.

In a nonjury or *bench trial,* the judge is both the trier of the law and the fact finder. As such, in addition to reaching a decision to convict or acquit, the judge must write *findings of fact* and a *conclusion of law* to support that decision (Steury and Frank, 1996).

Appeals

After a guilty verdict, a defendant can appeal points of law that resulted in his or her conviction. Although there is no constitutional right to appeal, the prerogative to do so is granted by state and federal statutes. All criminal court jurisdictions provide defendants with at least one direct appeal of a conviction. The appeal is sent to an appellate court in a written brief summarizing the legal error that was allegedly made during the trial. If the court finds that a brief has merit, the attorneys in the contested case (that is, the prosecutor and defense counsel) argue the issue raised in that document. (At the federal level, overburdened appellate courts are deciding cases without oral arguments in about one in three appeals [Cecil and Stienstra, 1987].) On listening to both presentations and discussing the disputed point of law, the appellate judges have several options. They can vote to *affirm* (uphold) the conviction, *reverse* the conviction with no further action needed, or *reverse and remand,* meaning that the decision has been overturned and the case is sent back to a lower court for further proceedings. These additional proceedings include holding a new trial or changing the original judgment. Appellate judges may also *remand* a case to a lower court with specific instructions for additional proceedings (Neubauer, 1999).

If the conviction is upheld, the defendant may appeal to the court of last resort overseeing that jurisdiction, which is usually the state supreme court. However, this judicial body decides which appeals it will hear and which it will reject. In other words, this second appeal is not a right and far from automatic. The final court of appeal, should the defendant be unsuccessful at the state level, is the U.S. Supreme Court. The chances of the nation's highest judicial body hearing an appeal to reverse a criminal conviction are remote.

An appellate court may conclude that a procedural blunder did occur during a trial but that it was a *harmless error* that did not affect the outcome or the fairness of the hearing, and, therefore, it will not negate the guilty verdict. Convictions are overturned only when a violation of a fundamental right of the defendant transpired or some error affected the outcome of the case (Steury and Frank, 1996). Appeals are much more the exception than the rule as only 6 percent of criminal appeals produces "a tangible victory for the defendant" (Neubauer, 1999, p. 442).

Jury Nullification

There are two primary types or facets of jury nullification. In its original form, the jury decides that, even though an act has been prohibited by law, it is not a crime and, therefore, should not be punished (Simon, 1992). This form of nullification dates back to the colonial era when juries refused to convict defendants charged with crimes against the "crown" (England). In the nineteenth century, juries in northern states often acquitted defendants charged with harboring runaway slaves, an act that was explicitly prohibited by the Fugitive Slave Law of 1850 (Barkan, 1983; Brown, 1997; Holden, Cohen, and deLisser, 1995). During Prohibition, some juries failed to return guilty verdicts in cases where individuals were charged with making and distributing whiskey. Vietnam War protestors, motorcycle helmet law opponents, and individuals who use marijuana for medical purposes have benefited from juries who believed the laws that they violated were unjust ("The Jury, 1999–2000," 2000). More recently, juries are returning not guilty verdicts in some drug possession cases that would result in a "three strikes and you're out" sentence, that is, life in prison for conviction of a third felony. Another instance where jurors' values have clashed with the law are "assisted suicide" prosecutions. Jurors sympathetic to medical practitioners or family members who help terminally ill people in severe pain end their lives have voted to acquit (Biskupic, 1999). In San Diego, just as Operation Rescue defendants accused of trespassing and other offenses near a medical clinic were about to be tried, a three-quarter-page ad appeared in a local newspaper (Scheflin and Van Dyke, 1995, p. 1165), which stated:

ATTENTION JURORS & FUTURE JURORS

You Can Legally Acquit Anti-Abortion

"Trespassers" Even If They're "Guilty"

The second form of nullification involves a jury's decision based on how a law is being applied to a specific category of defendants. In the aftermath of the Civil War, all-white juries (especially in the South) routinely convicted African Americans accused of crimes against whites regardless of the strength or weakness of the evidence. Conversely, whites on trial for physically assaulting, raping, and killing African Americans were exonerated (Barkan, 1983; Holden et al., 1995).

This latter form of nullification has increased dramatically in recent years. In Albany, New York, 11 white jurors concluded that an African American man tried for distributing cocaine was guilty. The twelfth juror, an African American man, refused to convict arguing that he was sympathetic with African Americans struggling to make a living. He chastised his fellow jurors for their lack of understanding of the economic difficulties that racial and ethnic minorities face on a daily basis (Biskupic, 1999).

In another case, after an all–African American jury acquitted an African American man accused of murder, an anonymous juror sent a letter to the court stating that, even though the majority of individuals deciding the defendant's fate believed he was guilty, they changed their verdicts to accommodate the holdouts who "didn't want to send anymore Young Black Men to Jail" (Holden et al., 1995, p. A1). Paul Butler, an African American criminal law professor at George Washington University, believes "African American jurors are doing a cost benefit analysis" and concludes that "defendants are better off out of jail, even though they're clearly guilty." Butler argues that jury nullification is not simply a matter of race per se: "It's life experiences. Blacks are more likely to have been jacked by the police, and less likely to view police testimony with quite the same pristine validity as a white male from the suburbs" (Holden et al., 1995, p. A1). Butler is most likely correct in this latter assertion; the late 1990s police scandal in Los Angeles in which officers perjured themselves and planted evidence on primarily minority suspects will only lead to an increase in racially motivated jury nullifications in the future.

The number of juries failing to reach a consensus in criminal trials (hung juries) remained relatively constant for decades at about 5 percent. However, in some parts of the country in recent years, that figure has doubled and even quadrupled (Biskupic, 1999). Much, if not most, of this increase has been attributed to race-based decisions. Race also seems to be a factor in the dramatic rise in acquittals of criminal cases. In the New York City borough of the Bronx in the mid-1990s where more than 80 percent of juries are comprised of African Americans and Hispanics, African American defendants are acquitted in 47.6 percent of felony cases, a figure almost three times the national average of 17 percent for all races. Hispanic defendants are acquitted 37.6 percent of the time. An interesting side note to these Bronx statistics is that, in a majority of instances, the victims of these crimes are also African Americans and Hispanics (Holden et al., 1995).

A survey conducted by Decision Quest and the *National Law Journal* concluded that 75 percent of Americans would vote to convict or acquit based on their own values even when instructed by a judge that they were bound to follow the law in making their decision (Biskupic, 1999). Jury nullification activists across the country are working to change the jury system. Consider the following excerpt from the the "Fully Informed Jury and the Jury Nullification" Web site (2000):

> If you find yourself on a trial jury in a criminal case, especially in a federal court, you need to research the Constitution and the laws applicable to the case. You will be instructed not to do that, but do it anyway. Your duty to the Constitution overrides any promise you make to the judge. If the judge and the prosecutors are lying to you, that may make it necessary to deceive them and to violate the instructions of the court in the cause of justice and constitutional compliance. It is sad that it has come to that, but it has.

Advocates of jury nullification also contend that it is one way that the imperfections of the law can be corrected (D. K. Brown, 1997). In other words, this process serves as a check by citizens on the power of legislatures to create laws that may be contrary to the will of the people. This is a philosophical position that was clearly articulated by some of the founding fathers of the United States. Speaking of a juror in 1771, John Adams, who would become the nation's second president 26 years later, stated that "it is not only his right, but his duty . . . to find the verdict according to his best understanding, judgment, and conscience, though it be in direct opposition of the court" (quoted in Barkan, 1983, p. 32). Alexander Hamilton, secretary of the treasury under George Washington, said that jurors should disobey a judge's instructions and find for the defendant "if exercising their judgment with discretion and honesty they have a clear conviction that the charge of the court is wrong" (quoted in Barkan, 1983, p. 32).

Currently, only Maryland and Indiana instruct jurors that they are triers of the law as well as the facts of the case although they are cautioned against making arbitrary decisions.

> Members of the jury, under the Constitution of Maryland the jury in a criminal case is the Judge of the law as well as the facts. Therefore, anything which I may say about the law, including any instructions which I may give you, is merely advisory and you are not bound by it. You may feel free to reject any advice on the law and to arrive at your own independent conclusions. . . ." (quoted in Barkan, 1983, p. 30)

Opponents of jury nullification note that this process is completely contrary to and undermines the notion of the "law of the land." Jurors voting to convict or acquit based on their own values of right and wrong or the race of the defendant reduce the law to what a particular group of people believes at a given time as it applies to a specific individual. From this perspective, justice would have little if anything to do with the strength of the evidence against the accused or the skill of lawyers presenting or refuting that evidence. Rather, guilt or innocence would be primarily a matter of chance; that is, are any jurors in this particular case proponents of jury nullification? Former federal judge Simon Rifkind (quoted in Barkan, 1983, p. 37) noted that informing juries of their power to nullify would lead to "a lawless society, a society without laws, without regulations. That is a monstrosity."

A 1997 ruling by the U.S. Court of Appeals for the Second District stated that, by definition, nullification is a "violation of a juror's oath to apply the law as instructed by the courts" (Biskupic, 1999, p. 8). Prosecutors have brought charges against jury nullification activists distributing literature at courthouses.

Convicting the Innocent

How many factually innocent people are wrongfully convicted in the United States each year? In an effort to answer this question, sociologists C. Ronald Huff, Arye Rattner, and Edward Sagarin (1997) surveyed 353 criminal judges, prosecutors, and public defenders around the country. Based on this research, the investigators concluded that during a 10-year period almost 100,000 individuals were punished for crimes they did not commit. Keep in mind that this figure does not include the wrongful conviction of people for dozens of non-Index offenses. The obvious question arising from these findings is, "How can so many people be convicted of crimes they did not commit?" (See Table 10.9.) As a result of interviewing attorneys, convicted innocents, and others as well as analyzing hundreds of cases, the researchers concluded that erroneous conviction is primarily the result of eyewitness errors, prosecutorial and police misconduct and errors, plea bargaining, community pressure for conviction, inadequacy of counsel, accusations against the innocent by the guilty, criminal records, the race factor, or DNA testing (Huff et al., 1997, pp. 260–274).

Eyewitness Errors. Four of five respondents to Huff and colleagues' (1997) false conviction questionnaire stated that the "good faith" misidentification of suspects by witnesses was the major factor responsible for this problem. "Aside from the prejudices of police, prosecutors and jurors, [person's] being of a race different from that of witnesses may increase the possibility of misidentification" (p. 272). A significant amount of research supports the *cross-race effect*. In general, African Americans and whites recognize faces of individuals of their own group more accurately than they do the faces of the other race (Ng and Lindsay, 1994). In Tennessee, Eddie L. Coley, a convicted robber serving a 20-year sentence, was given an additional 12 years for a robbery he says he did not commit. Coley, who is African American, was convicted solely on the testimony of two white clerks. No material evidence, no weapon, and no fingerprints linked him to the crime (Gibeaut, 1999).

table 10.9 Legally Guilty—Factually Innocent

MARK DIAL BRAVO (LOS ANGELES COUNTY, CALIFORNIA)

Factual background: On February 20, 1990, a patient at the psychiatric hospital where Bravo worked claimed she had been raped in an alcove earlier that afternoon. During the course of police interviews, she named several different people as her assailant. One of those she named was Bravo. She later stated she was sure Bravo was the attacker.

A Los Angeles County jury found Mark Diaz Bravo guilty of rape in 1990. He was sentenced by the court to a prison term of 8 years.

Prosecutor's evidence at trial: The prosecution based its case on several points:

- The victim named Bravo as the assailant and made an in-court identification.

- Bravo had misrepresented himself in the past on applications and on his business card.

- Blood tests done on a blanket near the crime scene showed a blood type consistent with Bravo's blood type, which is found in only 3 percent of the population.

- Bravo's alibi defense was not aggressively pursued.

Postconviction challenges: Bravo's appeal to the intermediate court of appeals was denied. Before his appeal was decided in 1992, he filed a postconviction motion in the superior court of Los Angeles County. In 1993 a superior court judge granted Bravo's motion to release a blanket, a sheet, and a pair of panties to the defense for DNA testing.

DNA results: Prosecutors received a report from Cellmark Diagnostics on December 24, 1993, stating that none of the tested semen had DNA that matched Bravo's.

Conclusion: On January 4, 1994, Bravo's lawyer filed a writ of habeas corpus. A Los Angeles County superior court judge ordered Bravo to be released on January 6, 1994. The judge stated that Bravo had not received a fair trial, that the victim had recanted her testimony, that Bravo's alibi was unimpeachable, and that the DNA tests were irrefutable. On January 7, 1994, Bravo was released from prison after serving 3 years of his sentence.

Source: Connors, Edward, Thomas Lundregan, Neal Miller, and Tom McEwen. 1996. *Convicted by Juries, Exonerated by Science: Case Studies in the Use of DNA to Establish Innocence after the Trial.* Washington, DC: U.S. Department of Justice.

It is reasonable to assume that a significant number of innocent people have been imprisoned on the basis of eyewitness identification error because juries give so much credibility to eyewitness testimony. Compounding the problem is the fact that courts have traditionally prohibited expert testimony (from psychologists) on the cross-race effect regarding eyewitness identification. In the Coley case, the trial judge referred to such evidence as "hooey" and would not allow the jury to hear the expert testify on the issue (Gibeaut, 1999).

Prosecutorial and Police Misconduct and Errors. Overzealous district attorneys may be procedurally sloppy in their desire to rid the streets of as many criminals as possible. However, this zeal may also be a result of the desire to enhance one's reputation as being tough on crime, especially during election years. More convictions suggests greater success to the public. Political candidates may boast having successfully prosecuted 85 percent of the criminal cases that have come through their offices. Wrongful convictions can also result from the "inability, unwillingness, or lack of funds and personnel available to make true and proper investigations" (Huff et al., 1997, p. 264). Both prosecutors and the police may be pressured to close as many cases as possible. In Chapter 8 on police misconduct, we noted that some officers routinely plant false evidence on suspects and perjure themselves in court.

False Confessions. Innocent defendants can make false confessions during the course of a police interrogation for a number of reasons including duress, coercion, alcohol intoxication or drug-induced diminished capacity, mental impairment, and ignorance of the law (Innocence Project, 2002). In Alabama three "poor, black, and retarded" defendants confessed to killing a newborn infant and were sentenced to prison. However, there was no evidence that the baby ever existed, and a fertility expert testified that because one of the defendants had undergone a sterilization procedure (a tubal ligation) years prior to the alleged birth, she could not have become pregnant. When asked what evidence he had that a baby had been born and killed, the prosecuting attorney stated, "Well, they all told us that" (Keahey in Herbert, 2002, p. D10). The defendants' lawyer believes that police interrogators "planted that idea [the killings] in the minds of these mentally retarded people" (Hutchinson in Herbert, 2002, p. D10). The Alabama Court of Appeals ruled that "a manifest injustice" occurred in this case (Herbert, 2002).

In April, 1989, a young white female jogging in New York's Central Park was savagely beaten, raped, and left for dead. Within days, five African American and Hispanic youths between 14 and 16 years of age were arrested and charged with the crime. The youths confessed to the crimes, were eventually convicted, and all served time in prison. In 2002, Matias Reyes, serving a 33-years-to-life sentence for murder and rape stated that he alone attacked the Central Park victim. DNA evidence corroborated his jailhouse confession. An examination of the boys' confession disclosed that their statements were replete with errors. For example, several boys said that they stabbed the victim repeatedly, yet the victim did not suffer any knife wounds. Eyewitness accounts on the night of the assault suggest that at the time the jogger was being attacked, the boys were in another part of the park harassing, intimidating, and robbing other people. With numerous evidentiary problems, why were these youths singled out for prosecution? Roger Wareham, the attorney for three of the boys, stated that the police "had made up their minds" regarding the guilt of the suspects, and "They weren't going to let anything spoil their neatly tied package of convictions . . . " (in Stodghill, 2002, p. 65). A Manhattan district attorney successfully moved to have the boys' convictions reversed (Stodghill, 2002; McFadden and Saulny, 2002).

In his book, *Troubling Confessions: Speaking of Guilt in Law and Literature,* Yale Humanities Professor Peter Brooks states: "I have read a number of police interrogation manuals and it's clear that they've become sophisticated in playing on psychological weaknesses. That's their business, trying to get a confession" (in Sealey, 2002, p. 1). Psychologist Saul Kassin of Williams College, an expert on false confessions, notes that after hours of interrogation, exhausted suspects are often looking for a way out of their predicament. At this point in the questioning, police may suggest that although the suspect committed the crime, he or she did not intend to do so, or hint that the punishment may not be so harsh if the individual confesses. In addition, because the police are not obliged to tell suspects the truth, they may falsely represent the evidence by informing a suspect that his fingerprints were found at the scene of the crime when they were not, or that he failed a lie detector test (Sealey, 2002).

One possible solution to the problem of false confessions is to have the entire interrogation videotaped from the beginning to the end, a procedure that is currently mandated in Alaska, Minnesota, and a few jurisdictions around the country. While many law enforcement agencies record confessions, these admissions are typically given at the end of an interrogation session. Saul Kassin notes that this procedure is all but useless. "Asking a jury to judge the credibility of a confession without seeing the interrogation is like a medical examiner conducting an autopsy without the body" (in Sealey, 2002, p. 4).

Plea Bargaining. An unknown number of innocent defendants are convicted after pleading guilty to one or more offenses. Through the influence of prosecutors and/or defense attorneys, individuals may come to believe that the state has an airtight, "can't lose" case against them, and that if they go to trial, they will surely be convicted and punished more harshly than if they engage in plea bargaining. Because most plea bargains result in immediate freedom, a suspended sentence, or probation, innocent defendants may decide to reduce their losses rather than sitting in jail until they are tried and possibly convicted. Some people may plead guilty to crimes they did not commit in order to save themselves and their families legal fees that can be very high, especially if the case goes to trial.

Community Pressure for Conviction. When crime rates are high, the public may pressure criminal justice officials to increase their efforts and put more offenders behind bars. Special interest groups, such as women's organizations (regarding domestic violence and rapes), racial/ethnic groups, and homosexual advocates, may demand that authorities be especially strident in their prosecution of hate crimes. Public pressure can be intensified when these groups receive media coverage.

Inadequacy of Counsel. Individuals can be convicted of crimes they did not commit when their lawyers are inexperienced, have heavy caseloads, and lack the resources to carry out in-depth investigations. In some instances, defense attorneys are incompetent and/or have little interest in their clients. Law professor and attorney Barry Sheck (a member of O. J. Simpson's defense team) stated that "nothing guarantees the conviction of an innocent person faster than a lawyer who is incompetent or lacks resources. It's terribly risky to be poor, or even middle-class, and unable to afford a good attorney" (in Longley and Sheck, 2000, p. 12). Supreme Court Justice Ruth Bader Ginsburg stated that she has "yet to see a death case, among the dozens coming to the Supreme Court on the eve of execution petitions, in which the defendant was well-represented at trial" (in Lane, 2002, p. A7).

While watching court-appointed attorneys enter guilty pleas on behalf of their clients in Texas, one of the authors of this text observed that many of the lawyers, who had met with their clients perhaps no more than once weeks or months prior to that moment, did not recognize these individuals or remember their names when they were ushered into the courtroom from the county jail. When the judge was trying to determine if there was a factual basis for the plea by asking the defendant questions about the offense, it became clear that these poorly paid attorneys had little, if any, knowledge of the crimes their clients supposedly committed.

Accusations against the Innocent by the Guilty. Trading their cooperation with the district attorney for sentencing considerations or immunity from prosecution, criminals have testified against and helped convict other wrongdoers as well as innocent people. Individuals have also been convicted of crimes that were never committed. After spending the night with a woman in a coed dormitory, a young man was arrested the following evening and charged with rape based on her accusation. The man had a past criminal record while the young woman "appeared to be the epitome of everything righteous and proper" (Huff et al., 1997, p. 271). He was convicted and sent to prison. Later, the woman was arrested for arson and claimed her behavior was related to rape trauma. A curious prosecutor learned she had a history of mental illness and was being treated by a therapist. The therapist said that he knew the woman had not been raped but could not inform the police because of doctor–patient confidentiality.

Criminal Records. Having a criminal record significantly increases one's chances of being wrongfully convicted. Prior arrests and convictions means that a person's photo will be in police files where it is likely to be mistakenly singled out by crime victims. Because they open their previous criminal history to scrutiny during cross-examination, innocent defendants are less likely to take the stand and testify on their own behalf. If they do not take the stand, these individuals are depriving themselves of testimony that could refute the prosecution's case. As noted in our discussion of criminal trials, even though judges inform jurors that a defendant's failure to testify cannot be construed as an admission of guilt, this directive may be ignored. Jurors may also believe that, even if a defendant with a criminal history is not guilty of this particular crime, the defendant is still bad, and it is a good idea to put these individuals behind bars when one has a chance to do so.

The Race Factor. Although many people found guilty of crimes they did not commit are white, a disproportionate number are African American and Hispanic, with some of these latter individuals convicted by all-white juries. An unknown number of these convictions were the result of racial prejudice.

DNA Testing. Since the death penalty was reinstated in 1976, more than 600 people have been executed and 87 exonerated because the introduction of new evidence eventually proved their innocence. Of those individuals who escaped execution, eight were cleared by DNA testing. **DNA** is deoxyribonucleic acid, a substance containing genetic material that is unique to the individual except in cases of identical twins. In February 2001, Earl Washington, Jr., was released from a Virginia prison after serving almost 18 years, 9½ on death row. Postconviction DNA testing proved that he was wrongly convicted of the rape and murder of a woman in 1982 (in Masters, 2001). In one form or another, DNA evidence is admissible in every state and federal circuit court (Levy, 1996).

Between 1992 and January 2002, the Innocence Project, a nonprofit legal clinic housed in the Benjamin N. Cardozo School of Law in New York City, helped secure the release of 100 people who were incarcerated although factually innocent of the crime for which they were convicted ("Innocence Project Honors 100th Freed Inmate," 2002). The organization "only handles cases where postconviction DNA testing of evidence can yield conclusive proof of innocence" (Innocence Project, 2002). Since the FBI began DNA analysis in murder and sexual assault cases in 1989, approximately 25 percent of primary suspects have been cleared (see Table 10.9). This figure raises the disturbing question of how many innocent people have been imprisoned and executed prior to sophisticated biological testing. Currently, 33 states have statutes of limitations of 6 months on introducing new evidence (Longley and Sheck, 2000). If these laws are not changed, more innocent people will be convicted regardless of the sophistication of DNA testing.

Reforming the Criminal Courts

Many criminal court practitioners and social scientists have been highly critical of the administration of justice in this country. Former Washington D.C. prosecutor Craig M. Bradley (1995) has commented on how needlessly inefficient and cumbersome jury trials have become and offers a number of solutions to remedy these difficulties (pp. 418–422).

Bradley suggests that we examine (and learn from) the administration of criminal justice in Germany, which has a system wherein serious cases are tried before a panel of three judges and two laymen, and a 4-to-1 vote is needed for conviction. There is no voir dire, and, therefore, no selection of juries by the opposing attorneys. Because jurors have read a dossier on the case before the trial begins, protracted arguments by the attorneys are unnecessary, and the typical felony trial is concluded in 2 or 3 hours.

In Germany, no more than 30 percent of criminal convictions are obtained by plea bargaining, with negotiated settlements rarely occurring in cases of violence or other serious offenses. When a bargain has been reached and the defendant makes a formal confession at a preliminary hearing, the prosecution must be prepared to present witnesses if the court determines they are needed to support the guilty plea. In the German criminal justice system, "a confession does not replace a trial but rather causes a shorter trial" (Hermann in Bradley, 1995, p. 419). Bradley suggests that in "run-of-the-mill-cases" the voir dire process could be dramatically curtailed if judges ask prospective jurors only two questions: "Do any of you have personal knowledge of the participants and events of this case?" and "Is there any reason why any of you cannot render a fair and impartial verdict in this case?" (p. 420). If the circumstances necessitate, as they would in death penalty cases, additional questions could be asked. The preliminary screening of jurors by a jury commissioner could further expedite the process.

As we have seen, peremptory challenges designed to shape a jury are often little more than guesswork grounded in pop psychology. And "[t]o the extent that they are not wild guesses, they are worse: an exercise in cooking the jury to be more favorable to the view of the attorney exercising the challenge" (Bradley, 1995, p. 420). Bradley agrees with late Supreme Court justice Thurgood Marshall who steadfastly believed that peremptory challenges should be banned.

Trials often drag on for days or weeks because attorneys (especially prosecutors) call numerous witnesses who testify to the same thing. Bradley believes that attorneys should have to justify (to the satisfaction of the judge) the need for hearing the testimony of witnesses. Another strategy that would be particularly helpful in relatively simple cases is to limit each side in its presentation of evidence and witnesses to a specified time, 2 hours, for example.

Jury deliberations that can also take significant time can be facilitated by permitting nonunanimous verdicts and juries with fewer than 12 members. Whereas the Supreme Court has upheld verdicts of 11 to 1 and 10 to 2 (*Apodaca v. Oregon*, 1972), and 9 to 3 (*Johnson v. Louisiana*, 1972), Bradley suggests that 8-person juries returning verdicts of 6 to 2 would be minimally acceptable.

Craig Bradley is not the first person to recommend sweeping changes to the nation's criminal courts, and he certainly will not be the last. Although some modifications have occurred, the courts of today operate in much the same manner they did 100 years ago. Most convictions are the result of plea negotiations, and the entire trial process has remained relatively constant. For whatever reason—a reverence for tradition, lack of resources, and/or a fear of change—the likelihood that we will witness any significant alterations in the administration of criminal justice in the foreseeable future is remote.

Focus on China

Crime and Justice in a Marxist Society

From a Marxist–Leninist perspective, the law represents the will of the dominant class in society. As such, it is primarily a tool of the ruling party. In a "bourgeoisie" or capital-

ist state, the law (especially the criminal law) is used to oppress and exploit the proletariat or working class. In a society characterized by the "dictatorship of the proletariat," such as China, the law functions to suppress capitalist "counterrevolutionaries" as the nation transforms itself into a workers' paradise, that is, a socialist state (Gregor, 1988; Michael, 1988). Whereas legal systems in democratic societies are designed to protect individuals from the power of the state, in Marxist–Leninist regimes, the law is fashioned to serve the ideological and practical interests of the ruling Communist Party (Gregor, 1986).

Criminal trials and the role of defense attorneys in these proceedings illustrate the pronounced differences between the rights of individuals accused of crimes in a democratic nation, such as the United States, and China, a totalitarian state. In the years following the formation of the People's Republic of China (1949), denial of guilt was a crime that further complicated the already dire situation of defendants (Michael, 1988). Although defense attorneys are currently permitted to "assist" the accused, the legal well-being of those charged with criminal offenses in China has only marginally improved. Defendants are entitled to legal counsel only *after* they have been indicted. This means that defense attorneys enter the criminal court process on completion of the police and prosecutors' investigation, after these agencies have gathered all of the information they believe will result in a conviction. As stipulated in the Law on Criminal Procedure, the court is directed to decide before the trial "whether the facts are clear and the evidence sufficient" to bring the case before a judge. In other words, the trial is relatively meaningless; it is little more than a formality because a conviction is "probably inevitable" (Lubman and Wajnowski, 1986). Acknowledged by Chinese officials, this system of justice is referred to as "verdict first, trial second" (Asia Watch Committee, 1990, p. 2).

Inasmuch as all of the evidence has been gathered by the police and prosecution, defense attorneys have no right to introduce additional evidence that would suggest alternative theories to the one presented by the state. As opposed to having an adversarial relationship, as they do in democratic societies, prosecution and defense attorneys are considered teammates working toward the same goal—justice from a Marxist perspective. As one Chinese defense attorney stated, "I represent the facts and the law, not the client. In our society the lawyer works for the state. In yours he works for the client" (Baker, 1986, p. 232). The primary duties of defense attorneys as uniformed state officials are to "help the court to understand the true substance of the case," to "help the prosecutor and the court to influence the defendant to admit his guilt," and "help the court to match the punishment to the crime" (Michael, 1988, p. 51).

Given the role of defense attorneys in the Chinese justice system, it is hardly surprising to learn that they play such an insignificant role in criminal trials (Leng and Chiu, 1985). Reluctant to challenge the prosecution or cross-examine witnesses, they confine their activity to pleading for leniency on behalf of defendants. In a robbery trial open to foreign observers, the defense counsel spoke only one time in a 3-hour session when he petitioned the court for a reduced sentence based on his client's confession and previous contributions to society. This same inactivity on the part of defense lawyers has been witnessed by outside observers at other trials (Leng and Chiu, 1985). Chinese criminal courts do not have a jury system; rather, guilt or innocence is determined by a judge and two lay jurors called assessors. In important cases, the deciding panel may consist of three judges (Lubman and Wajnowski, 1986).

The revised criminal law statutes of 1979 specify eight categories of crimes and their corresponding penalties. The first and most important group of crimes are counterrevolutionary offenses defined as "acts done for the purpose of overthrowing the political power of the dictatorship of the proletariat and the socialist system and endangering the People's Republic of China" (Leng and Chiu, 1985, p. 125). A number of offenses are clearly specified in this group, such as conspiring with foreign agents to jeopardize the autonomy and security of China, plotting to overthrow the government, instigating armed rebellion, and committing sabotage with a counterrevolutionary motive. However, using a very broad interpretation and application of these laws, individuals engaging in virtually any behavior deemed counterrevolutionary by authorities are subject to arrest and prosecution.

Chinese authorities charged thousands of people with this category of offenses in the aftermath of the "prodemocracy" movement that was centered in Beijing's Tiananmen Square during the summer of 1989. Participants in the movement were routinely arrested for "disrupting traffic, damaging vehicles, and sabotage" (Wing-hung Lo, 1995, p. 305). Other people were apprehended, prosecuted, and sentenced for what are typically considered political crimes, that is, acts such as public demonstrations against the government and writing and/or distributing articles critical of the ruling party. One man who spoke to a U.S. television crew about the brutal treatment of student demonstrators by soldiers that he witnessed was sentenced to 10 years in prison for "carrying out counterrevolutionary incitement" (p. 306). A young man accused of telling the Voice of America that students in Zhejiang Province had persuaded local officials to fly their flag at half mast in honor of people killed in Beijing was punished by 9 years imprisonment for "counterrevolutionary propaganda and incitement" (Wing-hung Lo, 1995, p. 306).

As arrests and prosecutions continued into the 1990s, secret trials were common and punishments were harsh, including at least 50 executions. Although "procedural niceties were observed," criminal proceedings occurred at a speed most observers in the West would argue completely undermined justice (Wing-hung Lo, 1995, p. 310). For example, in some instances, individuals were arrested one day, tried on the second and/or third day, and executed on the fourth (Wing-hung Lo, 1995). "I think there are very, very few cases of innocent people who are executed, and, anyway, that's better than letting some criminals get away to harm other people," said Li Boyu, a 19-year-old female college student sipping a cup of tea at a fashionable café in the university district of Shanghai. "In China, the interests of the nation or the community are always more important than the interests of the individual" (Smith, 2001a, p. A1).

Political prisoners in China are often held in "administrative detention" outside the criminal justice system. Amnesty International estimates that hundreds of thousands of people are held incommunicado for months and in many cases years without being charged or tried. Torture is not uncommon for many of these individuals who live in atrocious prison conditions ("Seven Years after Tiananmen Repression Continues Unabated," 1996).

In the mid-1990s, the Chinese government embarked on a campaign called *yanda* ("strike hard" or "severe crackdown") aimed at reducing serious street crime. One consequence of this strategy was a significant increase in the number of people executed, often after unfair and summary trials. In 1996, Amnesty International was aware of 6,100 death sentences and 4,367 confirmed executions in China. This latter figure represents an average of almost 12 government-sanctioned killings a day, and even these extraordinarily high numbers are believed "to fall far short of reality" ("The Death Penalty in China" 1997). "According to a report by the Supreme People's Procuracy (Chinese government department), torture cases surged to their highest level in six years during the 1996 Strike Hard campaign" (Smith, 2001a, p. A12). Throughout the 1990s, China executed more people than the rest of the world combined ("People's Republic of China: The Death Penalty Log in 1998," 1998).

More than 60 crimes carry the death penalty in China, including approximately 20 "economic" crimes such as tax fraud. In most instances the condemned prisoner is taken to an open field, forced into a kneeling position, and shot in the back of the head. A few provinces are experimenting with lethal injections to terminate the lives of individuals convicted of capital crimes (Smith, 2001a).

In recent years, the Chinese criminal justice system has focused on another group of "dissidents." In July 1999, the gov-

A line of uniformed police officers in China's capital city of Beijing forcefully hold down the heads of prisoners at an arrest ceremony. In the 6 weeks prior to this display of public humiliation in 1996, Chinese authorities executed 500 individuals in a nationwide crackdown on violent crime.

ernment formally denounced and banned the Falun Gong as an "illegal organization." Falun Gong is a worldwide association with as many as 100 million adherents in China committed to improving the physical and psychological well-being of individuals through a program of exercise and meditation. Outlawing both the public and private practice of Falun Gong, the Chinese Ministry of Civil Affairs stated that this quasi-religious group advocates "superstition and spreading fallacies" that jeopardize "social stability" ("U.S. Asked to Intervene to Protest Falun Gong's Rights," 1999, p. 1).

In the first 8 months after Falun Gong was outlawed, tens of thousands of people were arbitrarily detained by police for short periods of time, some on multiple occasions. Detainees reported being ill treated and tortured, and some were sent to psychiatric hospitals. Others were held in "re-education through labor camps" (without being tried) or sentenced to prison after unfair trials ("Falun Gong Practitioners, 2000, p. 2). According to Amnesty International, "All the information available indicates that the crackdown is politically motivated with legislation being used retroactively to convict people on politically driven charges, and new regulations introduced to further restrict fundamental freedom" ("China: Falun Gong Deaths," 2000, p. 2). In February 2001, 37 people were sentenced to between 3 and 10 years in prison for distributing information about their group. Most were convicted of "using a cult to obstruct the law" ("37 from Falun Gong Sentenced to Prison," 2001, p. A19). According to Amnesty International (China, 2001; China, 2002), tens of thousands of Falun Gong members are in prison and approximately 200 of these detainees have died from mistreatment or torture. Many devotees are placed in detention camps and forced to attend "study classes" until they recant their religious beliefs. Evangelical Protestants and Roman Catholics are routinely subject to arrest, fine, and imprisonment. In 2000, 24 nuns were arrested and 22 are still unaccounted for; a priest was beaten until he vomited blood.

During the past 20 years, the Chinese economy has grown on average between 6 and 10 per year, one of the healthiest rates of increase in the world. However, although China's industrial and financial sectors modernize, the criminal justice system continues to be repressive; it routinely engages in human rights violations. Referring to imprisoned supporters of the democracy movement awaiting trial in 1990, the Asia Watch Committee stated, "There is simply no rule of law in China worth mentioning, and no justice can be expected." The recent crackdown on Falun Gong members indicates that little has changed in the ensuing years.

summary

1. A plea bargain is an agreement between the accused and the state. The accused agrees to plead guilty to a charge in return for consideration from the prosecution typically in the form of a reduction in the number of charges and/or the seriousness of the charges brought against her or him. Plea bargaining has been opposed by many people who perceive this process as the state submitting to criminals and permitting wrongdoers to escape the punishment they justly deserve. Explicit bargaining occurs when

defendants, through their lawyers, negotiate for specific concessions from the state. Implicit bargaining takes place when the defendant, also through an attorney, comes to believe that, if he or she does not plead guilty and is convicted at a trial, the punishment will be harsher than if he or she would have pled to an agreed-on offense(s).

2. In deciding whether they will take a case to trial or plea bargain, prosecutors must make a number of decisions, including the following: (a) Will my witnesses stand up in court to rigorous cross-examination? (b) Is the defense attorney a capable advocate? and (c) How serious is the offense (that is, the more serious the crime, the more likely prosecutors are to take the case to trial and seek the maximum penalty)? Judges typically favor plea bargaining because they are under pressure to adjudicate or settle as many cases as possible. Plea bargaining also makes judges' lives easier because they do not have to prepare for trial, write jury instructions, or worry that their decisions will be reversed by appeal. Defense attorneys usually welcome deals knowing that the vast majority of their clients are guilty of the crimes they are accused of and could face harsh sentences if convicted at a jury trial. On the basis of his research, Milton Huemann states that judges, prosecutors, and defense attorneys are taught and learn that plea bargaining is the most realistic and beneficial method of administering justice.

3. More than 90 percent of the civil and criminal trials that are conducted annually in the world occur in the United States. Jurors are selected from a master jury list or a jury wheel. In 1970, the Supreme Court affirmed the constitutionality of six-person juries if so desired by the states. Small juries have been criticized for reducing the chances of minority group members being selected. The voir dire ("to see and tell the truth") is the procedure by which attorneys obtain information about prospective jurors. There are three type of challenges to potential jurors in the voir dire process: (a) a challenge to the array, (b) challenges for cause, and (c) peremptory challenges. Depending on the state, voir dire questioning may be conducted by the attorneys, the judge, or the attorneys and the judge. Over the past 35 years, jury consultants who believe that they can determine which prospective jurors are more likely to acquit and which individuals are more inclined to convict have become influential in U.S. courts. Jury consultants can make a difference in close cases where evidence is ambiguous but not in trials where one side has a much stronger case.

4. In the opening statement of a criminal trial, attorneys present the jury with a case summary, a cast of characters, and/or an overview of the significant facts and events. The presentation of the evidence constitutes the bulk of a trial. The prosecution at-

tempts to introduce evidence that proves the defendant is guilty beyond a reasonable doubt. When a district attorney calls witnesses who will testify on the state's behalf, he or she is engaging in direct examination. When defense attorneys question a prosecution witness (and vice versa), they are conducting a cross-examination. The purpose of cross-examination is to attack the testimony of a witness and/or undermine his or her credibility. A defense attorney may introduce an affirmative defense wherein the charge is not denied, per se, but new evidence is introduced that will prevent a guilty verdict. Self-defense and entrapment are examples of affirmative defenses. The last phase of the trial are the closing arguments, first the prosecution, then the defense, and finally the prosecution again because the state has the burden of proof in these proceedings.

5. On conclusion of the trial, the judge "charges" or instructs the jury about the issues of the case and the points of law they must observe during their deliberation. Some observers have noted that jurors should be instructed by the judge before the trial begins and/or during the trial as needed. The size of the jury may be a crucial factor in the decision to convict or acquit. The lone holdout on a six-member jury is in a much weaker psychological position than are two dissenters on a 12-person jury. In the latter case, each holdout has an ally in their disagreement with the majority. A juror's vote results from a two-part decision-making process: (a) the individual's evaluation of guilt or innocence at the end of the trial but before deliberations begin, and (b) the deliberation process of the jury as a whole. A number of studies have concluded that people with authoritarian personalities are more likely to vote for conviction and are especially punitive to lower-class offenders. A juror's mood at the time of trial may also be a factor in how he or she votes. Approximately 75 percent of criminal juries convict the defendant. Although there is no constitutional right to appeal a conviction, the prerogative to do so is granted by federal and state statutes.

6. There are two types of jury nullifications: (a) a jury's decision that, even though an act is prohibited by law, it is not a crime, and, therefore, the defendant should not be punished, and (b) a jury's decision to acquit based on jury members' beliefs that, even though the defendant is guilty of the crime, the law is being unfairly applied to a specific category of defendants. This second form of nullification has increased significantly in recent years because juries refuse to convict African Americans and Hispanics who are "factually" guilty *or* who they have determined are factually guilty. Advocates of jury nullification argue that it is a mechanism that can be used to correct imperfections in the law. Opponents contend that nullification is morally wrong and illegal

and can only undermine the law and, ultimately, the entire criminal justice system.

7. Some research indicates that about 10,000 people are wrongfully convicted of Index crimes in the United States each year. These erroneous convictions are the result of eyewitness errors, prosecutorial and police misconduct and errors, plea bargaining, community pressure for conviction, ill-prepared and incompetent defense attorneys, false accusations by the guilty, criminal records, racial prejudice, and inadequate DNA testing. Many criminal justice practitioners and social scientists have been highly critical of the administration of criminal justice and offered a number of remedies. Among these are abolishing or revising the voir dire process, having attorneys justify the need to hear the testimony of witnesses, limiting both the prosecution and defense to a specified time limit in the presentation of their cases, and allowing nonunanimous verdicts with fewer than 12-person juries.

key terms

DNA
explicit bargains

implicit bargaining
plea bargain

questions for investigation

1. Do you favor plea bargaining for serious felony cases? Why or why not?
2. This chapter identifies the potential abuses of plea bargaining by prosecutors, defense attorneys, and judges. How can such abuses be prevented or minimized?
3. After reading this chapter's coverage on peremptory challenges to jurors, discuss your opinion of these challenges. Should any factors, such as race, gender, occupation, age, income, education, be allowable as the basis of a challenge?
4. Think about how you and your peers learn, for example, in a classroom. Given your academic experiences, when and how do you think a judge should provide instructions to a jury?
5. Do you agree with the proposition that jury nullification is a legitimate way to correct the imperfections of the law? Why or why not?
6. This chapter describes nine possible factors that can contribute to wrongful conviction. Has the court system in your community wrongfully convicted a defendant? If so, which factor(s) led to the conviction, and what action has the court system taken to ensure this won't happen again?
7. Should defendants in a court trial testify on their own behalf? Why or why not?

IT'S YOUR CALL . . .

1. Suppose you are the defense attorney of a woman charged with the drunk-driving death of a nine-year-old boy. Prepare a list of 10 questions you would ask prospective jurors at the voir dire. Also, on what type of prospective jurors (what age, gender, race, occupation, education, religion, hobbies, etc.) would you use the 10 peremptory challenges allotted each attorney? Be prepared to defend your choices.

2. As the district attorney of a medium-sized city you give final approval on all the negotiated pleas of assistant district attorneys. You have just approved a plea to one count of aggravated assault and one count of sexual assault of a defendant charged with raping a 19-year-old woman. According to the prosecutor handling this case, although she is convinced of the "factual guilt" of the defendant, there is less than a 40 percent chance that "legal guilt" can be proved beyond a reasonable doubt in a rape trial. The phone rings, and your secretary informs you that the victim's father is on the phone. In a previous conversation, this man has referred to you as an incompetent coward for even suggesting plea bargaining—a concept you believe he doesn't fully understand. What do you tell him?

chapter **11**

Sentencing

1. What is judicial discretion? How much discretion do judges have today?

2. What are the goals of sentencing?

3. What are the major types of sentences for offenders?

4. What are the major sentencing reforms since the 1970s?

5. What are presentence reports? What information do they include?

6. What is the significance of sentencing guidelines and victim impact statements?

7. Why does sentencing disparity occur?

S uppose you are a judge who must hand down sentences for the following convicted offenders:

■ **Person A was convicted of armed robbery at a convenience store. He threatened the cashier with a gun and stole $150. This is his fourth conviction for armed robbery. He is 22 years old, not married, and has never held a steady** job. The maximum prison sentence the law allows for armed robbery is 10 years.

■ Person B was convicted of shoplifting blouses at a department store. This is her first conviction for shoplifting. She is 18 years old, unmarried, and works as a waitress. The maximum sentence for shoplifting is 2 years.

■ Person C was convicted of simple assault after a fight at a bar. He and another bar patron began arguing after one of them bumped the other and then began hitting each other. This is his first conviction for any crime. He is 28 years old, married, and works in construction. The maximum sentence for simple assault is 3 years.

■ Person D was convicted of burglary. He broke into a house and stole about $400 worth of CDs and jewelry. This is his second conviction for burglary. He is 19 years old, not married, and works occasionally at a fast-food restaurant. The maximum sentence for burglary is 10 years.

As the judge, you have to decide what the *appropriate* sentence is for each of these offenders. To simplify matters, suppose that each of these offenders is allowed by law to receive a sentence of a fine only, probation only, fine and probation, or a prison term. If you decide on a prison term, you also have to decide how long that term should be; suppose it can be anywhere from 1 month in prison up to the maximum the law allows. On the accompanying worksheet, indicate the sentence you would give to each offender:

Because a judge has the power to take away a defendant's freedom for many years, sentencing is perhaps the most important phase of the criminal justice process.

	FINE ONLY	PROBATION ONLY	FINE AND PROBATION	PRISON TERM (HOW MANY MONTHS OR YEARS?)
Person A				
Person B				
Person C				
Person D				

Consider your sentences. Who got the most severe sentence? Who got the least severe? As you think about your decisions, what factors affected the sentence you gave each offender? The seriousness of the offense? Whether the offender had prior convictions? Whether the offender was married or employed? The gender of the offender? What if one offender had been white and another had been African American? Would that have affected your sentence? If your answer is "no," can you be sure that race would *not* have unconsciously affected your decision? If you have a chance, compare your sentences to those handed down by your classmates who are also reading this book. Does everyone give about the same sentence for each of the offenders, or are there large differences in the sentences for at least one or two of the offenders?

Once police arrest somebody and the prosecutor obtains a conviction through a guilty plea or jury trial, sentencing becomes the next phase of the criminal justice process and perhaps its most important. A judge has the power to take away a defendant's freedom for many years. As we hope our sentencing exercise indicated, many factors affect sentencing, and it is often difficult for judges to decide what sentence is the most appropriate.

The public and other members of the criminal justice system trust judges to make the best sentencing decisions possible. But what does "best" mean here? Is "best" whatever keeps the public the safest? Is it whatever satisfies a victim's desire for justice? Is it whatever gives the offender a chance to be reintegrated into society as a law-abiding citizen? As these questions suggest, sentencing has many goals. For better or worse, judges, other criminal justice professionals and researchers, and members of the public often disagree on these goals.

Such disagreement is hardly a new phenomenon. During the days of the "Wild West," for example, a few so-called "hanging judges" were the law of the land. They ruled with an iron fist and sentenced scores of defendants to death. One of the most notorious of these judges was Isaac C. Parker, who presided from 1875 to 1896 in the Western Judicial District of Arkansas. Before he was done, Parker sentenced 79 defendants to be hanged (Tuller, 2001). Critics back then criticized the harsh punishment these judges meted out, but their supporters and the judges themselves said their draconian sentences were necessary to bring law and order to the territories. Parker defended his actions by observing

> Cruel they have said I am, but they forget the utterly hardened character of the men I dealt with. They forget that in my jurisdiction alone 65 deputy marshals were murdered in the discharge of their duty. The good ladies who carry flowers and jellies to criminals mean well. There is no doubt of that. But what mistaken goodness. Back of the sentimentality are the motives of sincere pity and charity, sadly misdirected. They see the convict alone, perhaps chained in his cell. They forget the crime he perpetrated and the family he made husbandless and fatherless by his assassin work. (Haines, 2002)

Sentencing has changed considerably in many ways since the days of the hanging judges, but the issues their practices raised still remain. This chapter discusses the goals of sentencing and the types of sentences, and it critically examines whether today's sentences are achieving their goals. It also discusses the sentencing process and the various factors affecting judges' sentencing decisions. By focusing on sentencing, this chapter serves as a bridge between the previous few chapters on the court system and the next few on corrections.

Judicial Discretion and Sentencing Policy: An Overview

Just as police have discretion in deciding whether to arrest someone who has allegedly committed a crime, so do judges have discretion in deciding how severe a convicted offender's sentence should be. State legislatures determine the minimum and maximum sentences for any given crime, and judges then decide how severe a sentence should be within these limits. As we shall see, judges generally have less discretion now than a few decades ago.

Whether judicial discretion is good or bad is a matter of some dispute (Hawkins, 1993). Should judges consider only the severity of the crime and the offender's prior record in determining a sentence? Or should they also consider the circumstances surrounding the crime, the offender's general attitude, and various aspects of the offender's personal background? For example, suppose two offenders have committed the same crime, but one sounds genuinely remorseful whereas the other seems proud of the behavior. Supporters of judicial discretion believe judges should be allowed to take these offenders' attitudes into account before deciding on their sentences. More generally, they believe judicial discretion allows judges to decide on the best sentence possible after considering all relevant factors and that the "best" sentence is one that balances the needs of society and the needs of the individual offender.

Critics of judicial discretion cite at least two reasons for opposing it (Walker, 1993). First, discretion allows judges to impose sentences that are too lenient and that, therefore, endanger public safety. Second, discretion leads to inconsistency in sentencing: Some judges may impose a harsh sentence for certain crimes, whereas other judges may impose a more lenient sentence. This makes the law too much of a "crapshoot," the critics say, and sentencing thus needs to be more uniform.

Partly because of these criticisms, judicial discretion began to be narrowed during the 1970s, and sentences became more severe. This change led to what critics call a "race to incarcerate" (Mauer, 1999) and an "imprisonment binge" (Austin and Irwin, 2001). In 1970, the number of U.S. prison and jail inmates was about 326,000. Today, only three decades later, it is more than 2 million. In 1970, the incarceration rate was about 160 inmates for every 100,000 Americans; today the rate has more than quadrupled to 690 per 100,000 residents (see Figure 11.1; Reitz, 1998; The Sentencing Project, 2003). Because of such sentences, almost 6.6 million American adults, or about 3.1 percent of the adult population, were under some form of correctional supervision as of 2001, up from 1.84 million in 1980 (see Figure 11.2). The correctional population thus more than tripled in only 21 years.

Goals of Sentencing

The increase in incarceration reflects an important shift in sentencing goals since the 1970s. Over the years sentencing has had several objectives: rehabilitation, retribution, incapacitation, and deterrence. Rehabilitation was the most popular goal before the 1970s but has since been supplanted by the other goals. In this section, we examine each of the goals of sentencing and review the research on the extent to which criminal justice policy can achieve these goals.

Rehabilitation

rehabilitation the reform of offenders through various kinds of programs in prisons and in the community

For many decades before the 1970s, the primary goal of sentencing in the United States was **rehabilitation,** or the reform of offenders through various programs in prisons and in the community (Reitz, 1998). It was thought that these programs rehabilitated inmates in at least two ways. First, they could change prisoners' attitudes and help them see the error of their ways. Second, they could help inmates learn useful skills and receive help for psychological problems, drug and alcohol abuse, and other

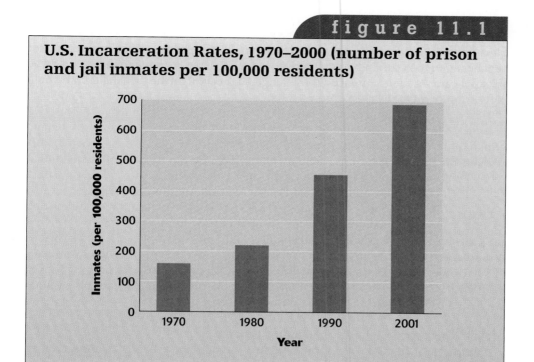

Source: Data from Reitz, Kevin R. 1998. "Sentencing." Pages 542–562 in *The Handbook of Crime and Punishment*, edited by Michael Tonry. New York: Oxford University Press; The Sentencing Project. 2003. *Facts about Prisons and Prisoners*. Washington, DC: The Sentencing Project.

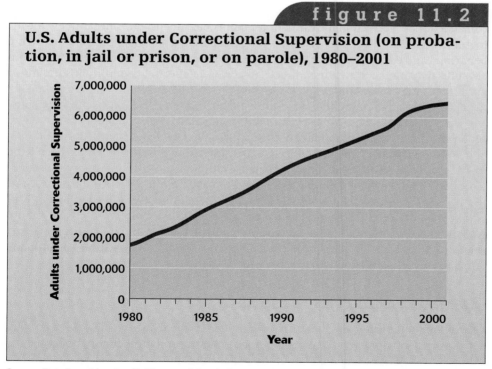

Source: Data from Maguire, Kathleen, and Ann L. Pastore (eds.). 2002. *Sourcebook of Criminal Justice Statistics 2000* [Online]. Available: http://www.albany.edu/sourcebook.

difficulties. Most prisons had some mixture of rehabilitation efforts, including vocational training; classes in reading, math, and other subjects; and drug and alcohol counseling. To make rehabilitation more likely, judges typically assigned *indeterminate* sentences (discussed later in the chapter) involving a range of years in prison, such as

a minimum of 2 years and a maximum of 10 years. These types of sentences were thought to encourage inmates to behave well in order to be released as early as possible, and they also allowed prison officials to retain inmates as long as was needed for rehabilitation to occur. Inmates who were judged to have been rehabilitated would be released early in their sentences; those judged in need of further rehabilitation would serve most or all of their maximum sentences.

By the mid-1970s, the goal of rehabilitation was largely abandoned for at least two reasons (Reitz, 1998). First, rising crime rates in the 1960s and 1970s convinced many criminal justice professionals and researchers that a more punitive approach in corrections was needed. Second, a number of studies questioned whether traditional rehabilitation programs were doing much good, and the view that "nothing works" soon developed (Lipton, Martinson, and Wilks, 1975; Martinson, 1974). These concerns prompted calls to abandon rehabilitation as a sentencing goal in favor of retribution and especially incapacitation and deterrence (Wilson, 1985). In the years since, these latter goals have guided criminal justice policy, and a huge increase in criminal justice resources and the use of imprisonment has been the result. At the same time, fewer dollars have been spent for individual treatment and training programs in prisons. The era of rehabilitation popular before the mid-1970s is no longer popular, and there is little likelihood of its renewal. According to Kevin R. Reitz (1998, p. 545), "the public, and public officials, are now less likely to view criminals as disadvantaged, ill-treated members of society who can be changed for the better."

Many criminal justice researchers continue to question whether offenders can be rehabilitated, and they think rehabilitation simply does not work, or at least does not work very well (von Hirsch, 1998; Walker, 2001). But others think rehabilitation can work well for at least some offenders, and they say that one problem with past rehabilitation efforts is that they were not funded appropriately and not used often enough. After reviewing the latest research on rehabilitation, Federal Bureau of Prisons official Gerald G. Gaes and colleagues (Gaes, Flanagan, Motiuk, and Stewart, 1999, p. 414) concluded that "correctional treatment for adults has modest but substantively meaningful effects." The most effective adult programs, they reported, were those involving behavioral and cognitive skills training. Drug treatment programs for prison inmates are also effective, but such treatment needs to continue after release from prison. Prison vocational and educational programs help improve the behavior of inmates who participate in them and modestly help improve their behavior after release from prison.

Gaes and colleagues make several other points. First, most offenders have several problems, including procriminal attitudes, weak self-control, and a lack of educational and vocational skills. To be most effective, treatment and training programs need to be *multimodal* by addressing all these problems rather than only one or two. Second, although treatment and training programs in prison can be effective, those in community settings are usually more effective. Third, "treatments initiated in institutions will be more successful if there is continued care in the community. Aftercare is more effective if it is a continuation of the type of treatment delivered in the institutional setting" (p. 365). Overall, then, some rehabilitation seems to be possible, even if the emphasis on rehabilitation ended three decades ago.

Retribution and Just Deserts

retribution a society's punishment of criminal offenders to avenge a wrong done to a member of the society and thus to the society as a whole

One of the sentencing goals that drove the shift in criminal justice policy three decades ago was **retribution,** which refers to a society's punishment of criminal offenders to avenge a wrong done to a member of the society and thus to the society as a whole. A retributive philosophy, thus, holds that a society has the right and even the need to punish an offender for violating the society's moral code. Retribution is currently popular in the United States. In a recent national survey, more than half of Americans named retribution as the most important goal of sentencing; in contrast, only 21 percent named rehabilitation, and only 13 percent named either incapacitation or deterrence (Gerber and Engelhardt-Greer, 1996).

An extreme statement of the retributive philosophy is found in the familiar phrase from the Old Testament: "an eye for an eye" (Leviticus 25:17–22). Some people and some societies interpret this literally: Whatever harm a criminal inflicts on a victim should be inflicted on the criminal. Most biblical scholars today interpret the "eye for an eye" adage less literally; they say it simply meant that an offender *deserves* to be punished, but not necessarily with the same exact harm inflicted. Still, a literal application of the "eye for an eye" philosophy remains in the use of the death penalty because many people believe that someone who wantonly takes a human life forfeits his or her own right to live.

The goal of retribution is the basis for various theories of punishment. According to several eighteenth-century philosophers, the chief goal of sentencing and punishment should be retribution (Jones, 1986). Accepting the more literal interpretation of the Bible, they believed that criminals should be punished with the same behavior they themselves had committed. The nineteenth-century sociologist Émile Durkheim (1901/1983), a founder of sociology whose views were introduced in Chapter 2, did not take this position but still thought that punishment of offenders served the important function of allowing a society to express its moral outrage.

The most notable proponent today of a retributive, or *just deserts,* philosophy is probably Andrew von Hirsch, whose writings on the subject have been very influential (von Hirsch, 1976; 1985). Von Hirsch believes that the primary function of the criminal law and the criminal justice system should be to *blame* and *censure* criminal offenders. Thus, the foremost goal of sentencing should be retribution. Von Hirsch specifically indicates that punishment should not try to serve any other goals and that it probably cannot achieve these other goals in any event. When judges decide on sentences, the only factor they should consider is what punishment the offender *deserves,* based on the gravity of the offense and, perhaps, the history of criminal behavior.

Von Hirsch and other sentencing scholars stress that the severity of a sentence, and thus the degree of punishment, should be *proportional* to the seriousness of the offense (von Hirsch, 1998). This is the principle of **just deserts.** The key question, of course, is what degree of punishment is appropriate and what degree is too harsh or too mild. Von Hirsch and others who stress retribution (and also incapacitation and deterrence) above all else would likely favor longer prison terms for many types of crimes, whereas scholars who stress rehabilitation would favor shorter terms or, for some offenders and some crimes, probation or intermediate sanctions (discussed later).

just deserts the idea that the degree of punishment should be proportional to the seriousness of the offense

In an extreme position by today's U.S. standards, Graeme Newman argues the equivalent of an "eye for an eye" position. In his book, *Just and Painful: A Case for the Corporal Punishment of Criminals,* Newman (1983) asserts that most convicted offenders should be *physically* punished through electric shock and sometimes whipping instead of being imprisoned: The more serious the offense, the more severe the shock or the more prolonged the whipping. Newman's policy was obviously never adopted, but it is worth noting the positive reaction among many Americans in 1994 when a U.S. teenager living in Singapore was caned after being accused of vandalism. Almost 40 percent of U.S. residents approved of his punishment, and several state legislatures considered legislation that would allow the flogging of criminals, a practice still used in many nations but one that had long ago been abandoned in the United States and other Western democracies (Wilkie, 1995; Witt, 1994).

Sentencing: Harsh or Lenient? Many people who favor retribution (and also incapacitation and deterrence) as key goals of sentencing probably believe that the average sentence in U.S. courts is not severe enough. In the 2000 General Social Survey, a national sample of U.S. residents similar to the Gallup poll, respondents were asked, "In general, do you think the courts in this area deal too harshly or not harshly enough with criminals?" About 75 percent responded "not harshly enough."

Clearly, most of the public thinks the courts are too lenient. Some criminal justice researchers agree with them, but other researchers disagree. Several kinds of evidence suggest the courts are not nearly as lenient as the public thinks. When U.S. courts are compared to those in other democracies, they do not seem at all lenient because the sentencing of criminals is harsher in the United States than in Canada, England, France, and other nations (Kappeler et al., 2000). In 1995, the U.S. imprisonment rate was about 600 persons for every 100,000 residents; this rate was 4 times greater than Canada's and 6 to 10 times greater than that of western European nations (see Figure 11.3). Although some of this difference stems from higher U.S. crime rates (Lynch, 1993), the terms of

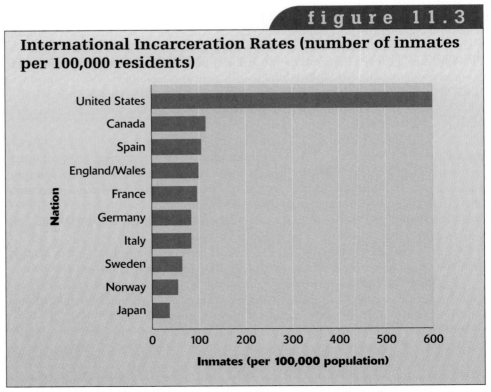

figure 11.3

International Incarceration Rates (number of inmates per 100,000 residents)

Source: Data from The Sentencing Project. 1997. *Americans behind Bars: U.S. and International Use of Incarceration, 1995.* Washington, DC: The Sentencing Project. Copyright © The Sentencing Project.

U.S. offenders sentenced to prison are also generally longer than those given to other offenders. For example, James P. Lynch and William J. Sabol (1997, p. 3) note that in the mid-1980s "the average time served for theft in the U.S. was 1.5 times that served in England and 3.5 times that served in Canada." In another comparison, U.S. offenders convicted of violent crime and serious theft are much more likely than their German counterparts to be sentenced to at least 1 year in prison (Feeney, 1998).

Within the United States, more than 90 percent of adults prosecuted for felonies are convicted of a crime, and 80 percent of them are sentenced to prison or jail with the remainder put on probation. More than 90 percent of offenders who are convicted of violent felonies and who have more than one prior felony conviction are sentenced to prison or jail. The average prison term for all those convicted of felonies is almost 8 years; this term rises to 11 years for those convicted of rape and 36 years for those convicted of murder (Hart and Reaves, 1999).

Figures such as these lead criminologist Samuel Walker (2001, p. 37) to conclude that "our criminal justice system is already fairly tough on serious crime." Victor E. Kappeler and colleagues (2000, p. 270) agree and say that the belief that U.S. sentencing is too lenient is merely a "myth" fueled by the attention the news media give to the relatively few cases where serious offenders receive lenient treatment: "Unfortunately, citizens often do not appreciate that such accounts receive so much press attention precisely because they are atypical. Thus, events that are relatively rare . . . are viewed as everyday occurrences. The reality of the situation is that most serious offenders are not treated leniently by the courts."

Incapacitation

Another goal of sentencing is **incapacitation:** depriving offenders of the ability to commit new offenses and thereby improving public safety (Zimring and Hawkins, 1995). In the United States and other democracies, incapacitation occurs through incarceration because offenders confined behind bars cannot endanger the public. In authoritarian regimes, incapacitation can occur in other ways. For example, amputating a pickpocketer's hands effectively prevents an offender's repeat pickpocketing. The ultimate incapacitation, of course, is the death penalty: Someone who has been executed cannot murder or commit any other crime again. Critics of the death penalty say the same goal could be accomplished by life imprisonment with no chance of parole. We return to the death penalty in Chapter 12.

incapacitation depriving offenders of the ability to commit new offenses and thereby improving public safety

The sentencing goal of incapacitation stresses the need to promote public safety by keeping offenders in prison and away from the public.

Because incapacitation as a sentencing goal has guided criminal justice policy since the 1970s, it is appropriate to ask two related questions. First, does incarceration help reduce crime because of its incapacitation effect? Second, is the size of this effect large or small? On the face of it, these are silly questions because America's 2 million prison and jail inmates obviously cannot hurt the public while they remain behind bars. As Daniel S. Nagin (1998b, p. 365) notes, "To be sure, there would be a sizable increase in the crime rate from the wholesale release of the incarcerated population." Thus incarceration has a strong incapacitation effect in *absolute* terms.

As a practical matter, however, the question of incapacitation and crime prevention is not one of the "wholesale release" of everyone in prison or jail. Instead, it is a question of the "incapacitation impact of *incremental* changes in prison population" (Nagin, 1998b, p. 365, emphasis added). In the real world, we can add (or subtract) only a certain number of people to prisons and jails in any one year, although these numbers obviously add up over time. If we put *more* people behind bars, how much more incapacitation occurs? How many crimes are prevented because these additional prisoners are *not* out in the public? Answers to these questions are critical for crime policy. If incapacitation is large, that might yield a strong argument for putting more people behind bars. If incapacitation is small, or even nonexistent, such an argument becomes weaker.

The evidence on incremental incapacitation is very complex, but overall it suggests that increased incarceration has only a weak incapacitation effect on the crime rate that must be weighed against the huge economic costs of the incarceration. Several considerations support this pessimistic appraisal. A major problem is that in any one year the vast majority of crimes do *not* result in anyone behind bars. Figures from 1998, the latest year for which relevant data are available, illustrate this problem. Although the National Crime Victimization Survey estimated that about 26,100,000 felonies (homicide, rape and sexual assault, aggravated assault, robbery, burglary, larceny, and auto theft) occurred in 1998, only about 312,000 persons were incarcerated that year for one of these felonies (Durose, Levin, and Langan, 2001; Maguire and Pastore, 2002). Thus, only about 1.2 percent of the total number of felonies resulted in anyone being convicted and incarcerated as a felon. Although these 312,000 inmates could no longer endanger the public, the incapacitation effect of incarcerating them was still only 1.2 percent. If we somehow doubled the number of people going to prison (at the cost of billions of dollars), the incremental incapacitation effect of incarcerating the additional 312,000 inmates would once again only be 1.2 percent.

This example is admittedly a bit simplistic because it assumes that each incarcerated offender commits only one felony per year. If each one committed many felonies per year, the incapacitation effect would obviously be much higher, and perhaps its expense could be justified. Thus, a central task of incapacitation research has been to determine how many felonies per year the average offender commits (Nagin, 1998b). Some studies examine the arrest histories of offenders who are arrested for any one crime, whereas other studies involve self-reports of prison inmates on the numbers of burglaries and robberies they committed in the year before incarceration. A small percentage of inmates committed dozens of these crimes before they were put behind bars, but the vast majority committed only a handful. For example, in one study 5 percent of California inmates said they had committed an average of 180 robberies per year, but about half said they had committed fewer than four (Visher, 1986). Thus, a small percentage of offenders commit the vast majority of crimes committed by all offenders.

If we could determine which individuals are such high-rate, or *chronic*, offenders (see Chapter 2) at the time of their arrest, then incarcerating them for many years would help greatly to lower the crime rate and thus have a large incapacitation effect at much lower cost than incarcerating many more low-rate offenders. This strategy is called **selective incapacitation**. Although this idea sounds good in theory, it has proven virtually impossible in practice (Nagin, 1998b). One problem is that it is very difficult to identify high-rate offenders. Prior arrest and conviction records, which judges typically consider as they decide on a sentence, are unreliable indicators of future criminality. The reasons for this are simple: Most crimes do not end in arrest and conviction, and offenders obviously cannot be relied on to tell judges how many crimes

selective incapacitation reduction of crime through the incarceration of chronic offenders

they have committed without being arrested or how many crimes they plan to commit after they are released from prison.

A lengthy record may also simply indicate that an offender has aged beyond early adulthood because he or she has had more years to commit crime. Because criminal behavior declines after early adulthood (see Chapter 2), a long criminal record may simply indicate that an offender is nearing the end of a criminal career anyway. Such offenders, says Daniel Nagin (1998b, p. 364), are "poor candidates for incarceration from an incapacitation perspective." Christy Visher (2000, p. 611) adds that because many offenders with long histories of crime would be near the end of their criminal careers, "part of the time incarcerated would not prevent any crimes."

To overcome the unreliability of prior records, various *prediction instruments* have been developed to help judges determine who is most likely to commit crime again. These instruments include not only the offender's prior record but also such factors as history of drug use, unemployment, and commission of crime before age 16. Unfortunately, these instruments are no more accurate in predicting offending patterns than simply flipping a coin and, thus, do not help to identify high-rate offenders (Walker, 2001). As a major study of these instruments concluded, "There are no reliable methods for either measuring or predicting future offense rates" (Greenwood and Turner, 1987).

A second problem with selective incapacitation is that many, and perhaps most, high-rate offenders are probably already behind bars. Although their chances of getting arrested for any one crime are extremely low, their chances of *eventually* getting arrested increase with each offense and become fairly high after dozens of offenses. Nagin (1998b, p. 364) provides a hypothetical example: If the chances of arrest are 1 percent for any one crime, an offender who commits 100 crimes a year has a 64 percent chance of eventually being arrested.

A third problem is that much crime is committed by groups of offenders. Nagin (1998b, p. 365) points out the obvious implication: "Thus, it is unclear whether the incarceration of one member of a group will avert any crimes at all. Perhaps the group will continue on with one fewer member; alternatively, a new team member may be recruited." As this comment implies, *replacement* can also occur; a new offender may simply fill in the gap created by the incarceration of any one offender.

Because selective incapacitation is virtually impossible to achieve, the United States has in effect been following a policy of **gross incapacitation** (also called *collective incapacitation*), which involves imprisoning large numbers of offenders without much regard to their criminal histories or propensities for future offending. The major problem with this approach should be obvious from our discussion of selective incapacitation: If the worst offenders are probably already behind bars, most of the additional people incarcerated under an incapacitation policy commit relatively few crimes per year. Thus, the incapacitation effect of such a policy must be small. Samuel Walker (2001, p. 133) points out, "As we lock up more people, we quickly skim off the really high-rate offenders and begin incarcerating more of the less serious offenders. Because they average far fewer crimes per year . . . , we get progressively lower returns in crime reduction."

Research on imprisonment and crime rate trends yields little evidence for a strong gross incapacitation effect. As Visher (2000, p. 609) observes, "The greater use of incarceration in general during the 1970s and 1980s led to dramatic increases in prison populations, but it did not bring about any significant reduction in serious crime." For example, although incarceration rose throughout the 1980s, violent crime increased in the latter part of the decade after an initial decline in the early part. Although virtually all the states had higher incarceration rates, some states actually experienced higher crime rates (Zimring and Hawkins, 1995). Even when crime rates did lower in many states during the 1980s, it was not clear whether the reason was incarceration or, instead, demographic changes and other social factors. The same uncertainty over the meaning of incarceration and crime rates held true for the 1990s. Although imprisonment increased and crime declined throughout the nation in that decade, an improved economy and other factors may have been much more responsible than increased imprisonment for the crime rate decline (Lynch and Sabol, 1997). We return to this issue in Chapter 12.

gross incapacitation the imprisonment of large numbers of offenders without much regard to their criminal histories or propensities for future offending

All these considerations lead to a conclusion shared by many researchers: Incapacitation through imprisonment is *not* a promising crime control strategy. Reflecting this view, Daniel Nagin (1998b, p. 365) observed that "the crime prevention effects of incapacitation are highly uncertain." Samuel Walker (2001, p. 134) agrees: "Because no clear link between incarceration and crime rates is apparent, and because incapacitation locks up many low-rate offenders at a great cost to society, . . . incapacitation is not an effective policy for reducing serious crime."

Deterrence

A final goal of sentencing is **deterrence.** As Chapter 2 pointed out in discussing deterrence theory, the idea is that would-be criminals will refrain from committing crime because they are deterred by the prospect of being arrested and punished. A logical extension of this theory is that increasing both the *certainty* and *severity* of punishment should reduce the crime rate by increasing the *deterrent effect* of the criminal justice system. A belief in this effect is yet another reason for the increased use of imprisonment during the past three decades. As noted in Chapter 2, this belief rests on the assumption that would-be criminals consider the potential threat to their freedom as they decide whether to commit crimes.

Criminal punishment may have several kinds of deterrent effects (see Table 11.1). First, people in general may decide not to break the law because they do not want to risk being arrested and punished. This effect is called **general deterrence.** Second, criminals who have already been punished may decide not to break the law again because they do not want to pay another fine or go back to jail. This effect is called **specific deterrence** (also *individual deterrence*).

How significant is either deterrent effect of criminal punishment? Let's first discuss general deterrence. Before doing so, we should distinguish between absolute and marginal deterrence. **Absolute deterrence** refers to the effect of criminal punishment (either the threat or the actual use) compared to *no* punishment at all. Most scholars think that the criminal justice system has a strong absolute deterrent effect: If all the police quit their jobs or all the prisons shut down, the crime rate would probably rise dramatically (Nagin, 1998b). No doubt many people would remain law abiding, obeying the law not because of deterrence but because of their own moral code, but no doubt many other people would commit at least some crimes if they knew they would not be criminally punished. As evidence, when U.S. and Canadian police have gone on strike in a few cities, looting and other crimes soared (Sherman et al., 1998). No massive shutdown of prisons has occurred, but it makes sense to think that, if incarceration were no longer possible, crime rates would also rise.

In the real world, absolute deterrence is not an issue because our society is not about to eliminate the criminal justice system. The question of general deterrence

table 11.1	**Types of Deterrence**

Absolute deterrence: the deterrent effect of criminal punishment, either its threat or actual use, compared to *no* punishment at all

General deterrence: the effect that occurs when people in general decide not to violate the law because they do not want to risk being arrested and punished

Marginal deterrence: the deterrent effect of a relatively small increase or decrease in the threat or use of punishment, for example, raising the maximum sentence for aggravated assault from 6 to 8 years in prison

Specific deterrence: the effect that occurs when criminals who have already been punished decide not to violate the law again because they do not want to be punished again by the legal system; also called *individual deterrence*

then becomes a question of **marginal deterrence,** which refers to the deterrent effect of a relatively small increase or decrease in the threat or use of punishment. For example, if the maximum sentence for aggravated assault were raised from 6 years in prison to 8 years, deterrence theory would predict that the rate of such assaults should decline. The research on general deterrence, then, is really research on marginal deterrence, just as the research discussed on incapacitation is really research on marginal incapacitation.

marginal deterrence the deterrent effect of an incremental increase or decrease in the threat or use of punishment

Evidence from the research on general deterrence is inconsistent (Nagin, 1998a; Walker, 2001). Recall from Chapter 2 that rational choice and deterrence theories predict that the greater use of imprisonment, the hiring of more police, and other increments in the criminal justice system should reduce the crime rate. Supporting these theories, some studies find that such measures do have a strong general (marginal) deterrent effect. Specifically, they find that increases in the rate of incarceration and in the number of police help greatly to reduce crime rates by deterring criminals, and they conclude that the more punitive criminal justice policy of the past three decades has helped lower crime (Marvell and Moody, 1994, 1996).

However, other studies conclude that harsher and more certain punishment has only a limited effect on crime rates and perhaps no effect at all (Walker, 2001). They reach this conclusion for several reasons. First, imprisonment rates are not consistently related to crime rates. We addressed this issue in our earlier discussion of incapacitation. To reiterate, in the past two decades the imprisonment rate has risen steadily, and four times as many people are in prison now than in 1980. If deterrence theory is correct, we would have expected the crime rate to have declined steadily during this time. The crime rate did decline during the early 1980s, but then it rose from the mid-1980s through the early 1990s before falling once again for the rest of the decade. As just noted, although some researchers believe the 1990s decline stemmed from increasing imprisonment, others cite the improved economy and other factors.

Second, deterrence theory assumes that criminals carefully calculate the potential benefits and costs of their planned criminality. Yet two important types of violent crimes, homicide and assault, are not the types of crimes in which people pause to assess the consequences of their actions before trying to injure and even kill someone. Instead, they are emotional, spontaneous, *expressive* crimes where offenders often act without thinking (Chambliss, 1967) (see Chapter 3). Thus, even if criminal punishment can deter some types of crimes, it cannot deter these types of violent crimes. As these remarks imply, some types of crimes might be inherently more "deterrable" because of the evident planning they involve. Such *instrumental* crimes include robbery, burglary, and other property crimes (Chambliss, 1967). Yet studies of active robbers and burglars generally find that even though they plan their crimes to some extent, they still do not give much thought to their risk of getting caught or, when they do give it some thought, simply decide they will not be caught or else fatalistically resign themselves to being caught (Tunnell, 1996; Wilson and Abrahamse, 1992). Once they make sure that no police or bystanders are nearby, they proceed with their crimes. Assessing this evidence, Samuel Walker (2001, p. 117) concludes, "Actual offenders do not appear to make their decisions about criminal activity on the basis of a rational and carefully calculated assessment of the costs and benefits." If studies of criminals find they do not make such assessments, then it is no surprise that many studies fail to find a general deterrent effect.

Third, deterrence theory assumes that criminals are aware of their chances of being arrested, prosecuted, and imprisoned. If they are *not* aware of these chances, then incremental changes in the certainty and severity of punishment can have no effect on their behavior. If, for example, the chances of arrest rise by 5 percent from one year to the next or sentences for violent crime become 1 year longer, criminal justice professionals and researchers might know this, but most criminal offenders will not, so they will not be deterred from committing their crimes. Unfortunately, we have little reason to believe that criminals have the required awareness to be deterred by incremental changes in the certainty and severity of punishment.

What about *specific* deterrence? Does punishing criminals deter them from committing new offenses because they will not want to risk returning to jail or prison? Again, research on this issue fails to find a deterrent effect. If anything, it finds an opposite effect: More severe punishment makes individuals more likely to commit new offenses, perhaps because they become more embittered and have more time in jail or prison to be influenced by other inmates.

Several kinds of evidence support this pessimistic conclusion. In the past few decades, increasing imprisonment rates have forced criminal justice officials to release offenders prematurely. Researchers have compared the **recidivism** (repeat offending) rates of these offenders to those of similar offenders who stay behind bars, serving out their sentences. If a specific deterrent effect exists, the recidivism rate of the latter offenders should be lower than that of the ones who get out early. However, research on this issue does not find this difference: The offenders who stay behind bars do *not* have lower recidivism rates, and sometimes they even have higher ones (Austin, 1986; Petersilia, Greenwood, and Levin, 1978).

In another line of research, several states got tough on juvenile offenders during the 1980s and 1990s by transferring many of their cases to the adult criminal courts where, it was believed, their punishment would be more severe. If a specific deterrent effect exists, the recidivism rate of juvenile offenders transferred to adult criminal courts should be lower than that of similar offenders in the juvenile justice system. In a major study of this hypothesis, Donna M. Bishop and colleagues (Bishop, Frazier, Lanza-Kaduce, and Winner, 1996) compared the recidivism rates of Florida juveniles transferred to adult criminal courts and a matched group of juveniles who stayed in the juvenile justice system. They found that the ones transferred to adult criminal courts had a *higher* recidivism rate when they finally got back to their communities than the ones who remained in the juvenile justice system. Once again, then, no specific deterrent effect was found: Harsher treatment of juvenile offenders in their study increased recidivism, the opposite of what deterrence theory would predict.

Overall, research on deterrence does *not* suggest that more certain and severe punishment can lead to significant crime reduction through marginal deterrence. By drawing this conclusion, we do not mean to imply that the criminal justice system is ineffective. As noted earlier, it probably has a strong absolute deterrent effect because its very existence helps keep the crime rate lower than it would otherwise be. But the relevant issue is marginal deterrence: whether relatively small changes in the certainty and severity of criminal punishment affect crime rates to a substantial degree. Despite many studies, the size of this type of deterrent effect remains unclear.

Types of Sentences

The major types of sentences today are *probation; intermediate sanctions* such as fines, boot camps, and community service; and *incarceration* in prison or jail (see Table 11.2). Both probation and intermediate sanctions place the offender in the community, and we treat them in more detail in Chapter 14. We introduce them briefly in the following sections and then turn our attention to the various sentences involving incarceration.

table 11.2	Types of Sentences

Incarceration: confinement in prison or jail

Intermediate sanctions: a miscellaneous category of sentences that are somewhat more severe than probation but less severe than incarceration; examples include community service, boot camps that place offenders in quasi-military settings, electronic monitoring, and house arrest

Probation: a substitute for incarceration that involves placing a convicted offender in the community under the supervision of a probation officer as long as the offender meets certain standards of behavior

Probation

Probation is a substitute for incarceration and involves placing a convicted offender in the community under the supervision of a probation officer as long as the offender meets certain standards of behavior. Typically, the offender must be in regular contact with the probation officer, be at home by a certain time in the evening, and abstain from illegal drug use and excessive alcohol use. Many offenders on probation are also required to seek regular employment, to take part in drug and alcohol counseling, and other such efforts.

Of the almost 6.6 million adults under correctional supervision in 2001, more than half, or 3.9 million, were on probation. Of this number, 53 percent had been convicted of a felony, 45 percent of a misdemeanor, and 1 percent of other infractions. About one-fourth were on probation for violating drug laws, and 18 percent for driving under the influence of alcohol (Glaze, 2002).

In 1980, about 1.1 million adults were on probation. The number on probation thus more than tripled during the 21-year period from 1980 to 2001. Despite this huge increase, probation budgets have lagged far behind, and probation officers have much larger caseloads than in the past. Because of this, many offenders receive less supervision than they should or no supervision at all, increasing their chances of recidivism. Partly for this reason, says Joan Petersilia (1997, p. 150), probation has a negative, "soft on crime" image among many people who view it as "permissive, uncaring about crime victims, and committed to a rehabilitative ideal that ignores the reality of violent, predatory criminals." Yet Petersilia adds that probation actually has much potential that is not realized because it is so underfunded and because probation officers have such huge caseloads. In a review of probation research, Petersilia (1997, p. 149) concluded that "probation programs, if properly designed and implemented, can reduce recidivism and drug use," and she called for greater funding for probation and for more research on its effectiveness. Chapter 14 discusses various issues surrounding probation and the research on its potential for reducing crime.

Intermediate Sanctions

Intermediate sanctions comprise a miscellaneous category for sentencing that is somewhat more severe than probation but less so than incarceration. As their name implies, they fall somewhere in between probation and incarceration and are meant to be "more intrusive and burdensome than standard probation" (Tonry, 1998a, p. 202). Offenders facing intermediate sanctions typically have to do something more than their counterparts on probation but obviously are not confined behind bars. Although many types of intermediate sanctions exist, community supervision, boot camps that place offenders in quasi-military settings, electronic monitoring, and house arrest are common examples of these sanctions. They are used as both "front-end" and "back-end" programs. Offenders enter the former after being sentenced by judges in lieu of incarceration; they enter the latter after being released from prison or jail on parole.

This technical issue aside, intermediate sanctions are a recent development. Before the 1980s, these sanctions hardly existed because most offenders were sentenced to either probation or incarceration. Ironically, one reason for their growing popularity was the massive increase in incarceration beginning in the 1970s. As more and more people went to prison, legislators worried about the financial costs of incarcerating so many offenders. They reasoned that punishment for nonviolent offenders that fell short of incarceration would save money and keep prison cells free for violent offenders. They also thought that intermediate sanctions would be more effective than imprisonment in reducing recidivism (Tonry, 1998a). By and large, however, these hopes have not been fulfilled because intermediate sanctions appear to produce the same recidivism rates as imprisonment. Moreover, many offenders in front-end programs violate the terms of their sanctions and end up in jail or prison anyway, nullifying any savings in prison costs that these programs might have had. Back-end programs are

probation a substitute for incarceration that involves placing a convicted offender in the community under the supervision of a probation officer as long as the offender meets certain standards of behavior

intermediate sanctions sentences that fall in between probation and incarceration

more effective in this regard because offenders enter them after being released from prison; although some do violate the terms of their sanctions, the ones who do not still represent a net decrease in prison inmates and thus incarceration costs (Tonry, 1998a).

Intermediate sanctions remain popular because they are perceived as more punitive than probation and because some research suggests that intermediate sanctions combined with effective treatment programs can produce lower recidivism rates than incarceration (Petersilia, 1997). Back-end programs, at least, also appear to reduce prison crowding and costs when properly administered. These considerations lead Michael Tonry (1998a, p. 203) to conclude that "intermediate sanctions can be used to save money and prison use, without significant sacrifices in public safety." We discuss intermediate sanctions further in Chapter 14.

Incarceration

incarceration confinement in prison or jail

Incarceration involves confinement in prison or jail and is the most severe sentence a judge can impose. *Prisons* are run by states or the federal government and house offenders serving long sentences, usually a year or more; *jails* are run by local governments and house offenders serving short sentences or awaiting pretrial hearings or trials themselves. At midyear 2001, about 1.3 million Americans were in prison, and more than 630,000 were in jail (Beck, Karberg, and Harrison, 2002). Both these numbers represent huge increases from two decades earlier (see Figure 11.4). Close to 70 percent of all convicted felons in any one year are incarcerated, with almost all the remainder receiving probation. Of those incarcerated, roughly equal numbers are sentenced to prison or to jail. However, this ratio varies by offense: Among offenders convicted of violent crime, 51 percent are sentenced to prison (including all those convicted of murder and 71 percent of those convicted of robbery) and 29 percent to jail; among those convicted of property crime, 30 percent are sentenced to prison and 32 percent to jail (Hart and Reaves, 1999).

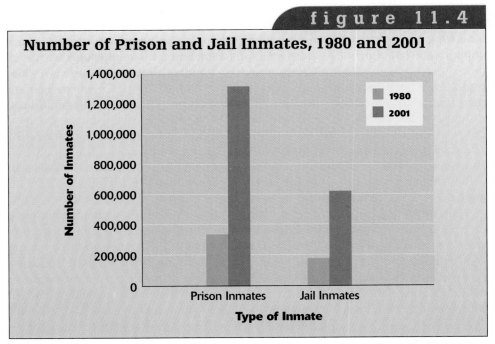

figure 11.4

Number of Prison and Jail Inmates, 1980 and 2001

Sources: Maguire, Kathleen, and Ann L. Pastore (eds.). 2002. *Sourcebook of Criminal Justice Statistics 2000.* Available: http://www.albany.edu/sourcebook; Beck, Allen J., Jennifer C. Karberg, and Paige M. Harrison. 2002. *Prison and Jail Inmates at Midyear 2001.* Washington, DC: Bureau of Justice Statistics, U.S. Department of Justice.

table 11.3	Two Types of Sentencing Reforms

Determinate sentences: sentences that require offenders to receive fixed terms of imprisonment and also require judges to impose such sentences; these replaced indeterminate sentences that sent offenders to prison for a minimum of years ranging up to a maximum of many years more

Mandatory minimum sentences: sentences that require judges to sentence offenders to some minimum prison term; a recent example includes "three strikes" laws that require long prison terms, including life terms for offenders convicted of a second or third felony, depending on the jurisdiction

Sentencing Reforms and Incarceration

Much of the increase in incarceration since the 1970s stemmed from sentencing reforms that made it much more likely that offenders would be incarcerated at all and incarcerated for longer terms than previously (see Table 11.3). These reforms were mandated by legislatures across the country that wanted to reduce judges' discretion, which, they thought, produced too much sentencing disparity (discussed later) and sentences that were too lenient. Supporters of these reforms applaud them for producing longer, more uniform sentences. Critics attack them for the same reasons: They say sentences for some offenders and some crimes are far more severe than they should be, and they lament the fact that judges increasingly are being prevented from taking the complex circumstances of many cases into account before deciding on sentencing. They also believe that the increased incarceration stemming from sentencing reforms has cost the nation billions of dollars with little or no benefit in crime reduction.

One of the most significant reforms was a shift from *indeterminate* to determinate sentencing. As noted earlier, **indeterminate sentences** send offenders to prison for a minimum of years ranging up to a maximum of many years more. Their aim was to encourage good behavior by inmates and to allow them to be rehabilitated. Because of the concerns just cited, legislatures began to favor **determinate sentences** that require offenders to receive fixed terms of imprisonment and also require judges to impose such sentences. For example, an offender who under indeterminate sentencing might have received 1 to 6 years in prison would now receive a flat sentence of 5 years. Almost two dozen states now use determinate sentencing; they have coupled this use with the abolition of parole because offenders now are expected to serve their full sentence. Judges still retain some discretion in deciding to sentence an offender to prison at all, but once incarceration is the decision, the offender receives a fixed sentence as mandated by the legislature (Reitz, 1998).

Another, related reform was the establishment of **mandatory minimum sentences.** As their name implies, these require judges to sentence offenders to some minimum prison term. Mandatory minimum sentencing is used throughout the country in every state and in the federal judicial system. The offenders targeted vary from one state to another, but they generally include offenders who have committed violent crimes (especially those involving guns or other deadly weapons) or drug offenses or who are repeat offenders.

Mandatory sentencing was established in reaction to rising crime rates and the perception that judges were too lenient. It was meant to achieve lower crime rates through both incapacitation and deterrence. However, many trial judges criticize mandatory sentencing laws for being too harsh on individual offenders. Reitz (1998, p. 551) notes that judges "encounter offenders across a spectrum of blameworthiness and apparent dangerousness. Over a period of time, many judges have accumulated experiences in which the mandatory penalty was far removed from their sense of justice in a given

indeterminate sentences sentences involving a range from a minimum of years to a maximum of many years more

determinate sentences fixed terms of imprisonment

mandatory minimum sentences as required by legislatures, sentences involving a minimum prison term

case." Judges also say that mandatory sentencing can lead to problems that actually make the public less safe. As one New York judge declared, "A terrible idea. Facing a surefire stiff penalty, the defendant, with nothing to lose, asks for a trial. The court can't lock people up indefinitely, so he's back on the streets on a pretrial release. What does a robber do when he's back on the street? He robs" (Machan, 2000, p. 133).

Another problem is that many criminal justice researchers think mandatory sentences have not achieved their goals of incapacitation and deterrence; Reitz (1998, p. 551) says "overwhelming evidence" exists that they have failed to do so. Our earlier discussion of these goals suggests several reasons for this failure, including the facts that many serious offenders are already in prison and that offenders in general pay little attention to the possibility they will be caught and punished.

A related problem is that mandatory sentences lead members of the courtroom "workgroup" to devise ways of avoiding them. As Walker (2001, p. 137) notes, "An increase in the severity of the potential punishment creates pressure to avoid its actual application." Walker illustrates this problem in a discussion of a 1973 New York state law that imposed long mandatory prison terms on drug traffickers and users and abolished plea bargaining in their cases. In the aftermath of the law, fewer drug arrests than before led to prosecution, perhaps because prosecutors and judges worried about the effects on prison crowding or even thought the sentences were too severe. They may have also feared that defense attorneys and their clients would insist on time-consuming and costly jury trials, which is precisely what happened. Although drug offenders who were convicted under the law received much longer prison terms than before, the percentage of people arrested for drug offenses who went to prison was the same after the law as before the law. Walker also reports that the law probably did not reduce crime or drug use in New York. Even with new prison construction, the New York law and other mandatory sentencing laws have forced prison officials to release inmates earlier than usual. The intent of mandatory sentencing is thus ironically undermined by the very increased incarceration it creates.

For all these reasons, mandatory sentencing does not appear to reduce crime to any significant degree. A U.S. Justice Department report, says Walker (2001, p. 139), noted that "it is difficult, perhaps fundamentally impossible, to substantiate the popular claim that mandatory sentencing is an effective tool for reducing crime."

"Three Strikes" Legislation. "Three strikes and you're out" laws, a popular form of mandatory sentencing, emerged in the mid-1990s. These laws required prison terms of at least 25 years, and sometimes life, for offenders convicted of their third felony (or in some locations, only a second felony). Used most extensively in California, three strikes legislation was passed in about two dozen states altogether. As with other forms of mandatory sentencing, legislators hoped that three strikes laws would help keep dangerous criminals off the streets and deter other offenders from committing crime (Shichor and Sechrest, 1996; Turner, Sundt, Applegate, and Cullen, 1995).

Three strikes rules have not achieved these goals. The reasons for their failure are the same as those already discussed for mandatory sentencing in general (Walker, 2001). Because most repeat offenders already receive long prison terms, three strikes laws were in effect reinventing the wheel. Also, because many offenders also give little thought to their chances of being imprisoned, three strikes laws were not capable of deterring them. Another problem is that many three strikes offenders were sentenced to long prison terms that would keep them behind bars long after they would have stopped offending anyway because of their advanced age. Finally, because courtroom "workgroups" believed that three strikes laws were too punitive and also believed that their implementation would slow case processing and worsen prison crowding, they found ways of avoiding the laws. Prosecutors, for example, have charged three strikes offenders with misdemeanors to avoid jury trials and other problems three strikes prosecutions would create (Austin, Clark, Hardyman, and Henry, 1999).

Three strikes laws also created other problems (Butterfield, 1995; Dickey and Stiebs, 1998; Harris and Jesilow, 2000). Many offenders were sentenced to long terms, including life, for third felonies that turned out to be fairly minor. In California, for example, several offenders received sentences of 25 years to life for stealing objects such as pizza and video tapes. Many three strikes defendants demanded jury trials and brought some California courts almost to a standstill. Finally, three strikes laws in California have increased jail and prison crowding as more than 50,000 offenders have received longer sentences under three strikes provisions. This influx has cost California tens of millions of dollars in increased incarceration costs and forced the release of other offenders. Because three strikes laws do not seem to reduce crime, or do so only at a great economic cost, and because they create so many other problems, Walker (2001) calls them "a terrible crime policy."

How Sentencing Happens

The sentencing of criminal offenders follows certain procedures. Ideally, these procedures result in appropriate sentences for all offenders. In practice, this does not always happen. Next we examine the sentencing process, and then we discuss the various factors that affect sentencing severity.

Presentence Reports and Sentencing Hearings

The exact nature of the sentencing process depends partly on the seriousness of the crime for which an individual offender is being sentenced. When a defendant pleads guilty to (or much less often, after a trial is convicted of) a misdemeanor, judges usually announce the sentence immediately. In these cases, the sentence is usually a fine or fairly short jail time; because so little is at stake, there is no need for sentencing to be delayed pending further information.

When a defendant is found guilty of a felony, however, the process is usually much different. Typically, the judge will request that a **presentence report** be prepared by a presentence investigator, normally a probation officer or sometimes a social worker. The preparation of this report can take several weeks. Presentence reports consist of various kinds of information, including a defendant's family and work history, a list of any prior arrests and/or convictions, and insights gathered from interviews with police officers and other people with helpful knowledge of the defendant. Often the report includes the presentence investigator's recommendation about the sentence, either probation or incarceration (Storm, 1997).

The judge uses the information in the report to help decide what kind of individual the defendant is, whether the defendant shows potential for future offending, and other such factors. All this information helps the judge decide what an appropriate sentence for the defendant will be. For this reason, the presentence report is "a critically important document," says Joan Petersilia (1998, p. 571), especially because judges adopt recommendations for probation in 65 to 95 percent of all cases.

One problem with presentence reports is that they sometimes include mistakes or show bias on the part of the presentence investigator. Although few studies of the extent of this problem exist, the available research suggests that the accuracy of presentence reports could stand improvement (Gelsthorpe and Raynor, 1995). Some critics also say that the sentencing recommendations that presentence investigators often include in their reports are too lenient because they are apt to be more likely than judges to favor probation or other sanctions that avoid incarceration. Because the recommendations included in presentence reports do often influence judges' decisions, these recommendations may make judges more lenient in their sentencing than otherwise. Whether this is a valid criticism, of course, depends on whether sentencing is indeed too lenient, a belief we addressed earlier.

Once the judge is ready to announce the sentence, a **sentencing hearing** takes place. At this hearing, the prosecutor and the defense attorney both give sentencing recommendations and discuss the reasons for the recommendations. The judge then asks the defendant whether he or she has anything to say. After hearing from all these parties, the judge then announces the sentence and often adds some comments that

presentence report a report prepared by a probation officer or social worker that includes information on a defendant's background and, usually, a recommendation for his or her sentence

sentencing hearing a courtroom meeting at which a judge pronounces the sentence of a convicted offender

explain its severity. If sentencing guidelines exist, the judge's sentence should conform to these guidelines. Because these guidelines are becoming increasingly important, we now discuss them in further detail.

Sentencing Guidelines

Recall that sentencing reforms begun in the 1970s aimed to reduce judicial discretion and judicial leniency. An important component of these reforms was the creation in several states of **sentencing commissions** and the development of **sentencing guidelines** by these commissions (Frase, 1995). The first four states to establish commissions were Florida, Minnesota, Pennsylvania, and Washington. By the late 1990s, almost two dozen states and the federal judicial system had created commissions. They have become so important that Reitz (1998, p. 547) called them "the most popular vehicle of sentencing reform in the last decade of the twentieth century."

Sentencing commissions were first conceived in the 1970s out of concern over the wide disparity in sentences given to similar kinds of offenders, creating what one critic called "law without order" (Frankel, 1973). It was believed that sentencing decisions by judges "followed no rhyme or reason beyond their own personal instincts" (Reitz, 1998, p. 548) and that guidelines developed by sentencing commissions would lead sentencing to become more uniform and thus more fair. As sentencing commissions developed, they had various goals for developing sentencing guidelines. Some commissions wanted to make sentencing more uniform, whereas others wanted to make sentencing more harsh or, alternatively, somewhat more lenient in order to reduce prison crowding (Reitz, 1998). Most sentencing guidelines have focused on whether offenders should be put in prison and, if so, for how long. They have paid less attention to probation and intermediate sanctions. According to Reitz (1998, p. 557), it is easier to determine which offenders should be incarcerated and which should not be incarcerated than it is to "prescribe the type and intensity" of the many types of intermediate sanctions that may exist in any one jurisdiction. Some sentencing commissions have tried to do just that. In Pennsylvania, guidelines passed in 1994 required incarceration for the most serious cases but recommended intermediate sanctions, including victim restitution and community service, for less serious offenses (Reitz, 1998).

Sentencing guidelines are sometimes called *presumptive* sentencing guidelines because they establish sentences that are *presumed* to be appropriate for offenders based on two considerations: their prior record and the seriousness of the offense for which they are convicted. Sentencing commissions have developed sentencing matrices or grids that judges consult before handing down a sentence. The grid typically includes three variables: the offender's prior record at the top, the seriousness of the offense for which the offender was convicted at the left side, and the sentence guideline in the middle. Judges are supposed simply to impose the sentence indicated on the grid by intersecting the offender's prior record and offense seriousness. If a judge departs from the required sentence, he or she must provide a written statement explaining the reasons for the departure. Table 11.4 provides a simplified, hypothetical example of a sentencing grid. In this grid, if an offender with two prior felony convictions is convicted of an armed robbery, the judge is expected to hand down a sentence of a prison term between 108 and 119 months.

What impact have sentencing guidelines had? Research on the issue is mixed because they have made sentencing more uniform in several states but not in all states (D'Alessio and Stolzenberg, 1995; Kramer and Ulmer, 1996; Stolzenberg and D'Alessio, 1994; Ulmer and Kramer, 1996). Even where greater uniformity has been achieved, criminal justice researchers and professionals disagree on whether this effect is good or bad. Although many applaud the fairness they see in more uniform sentencing, others, and especially judges, think they are too inflexible and prevent judges from giving enough attention to differences among individual offenders. In some states, sentencing guidelines have also made sentencing more harsh. This is especially true for drug offenses because various federal and state laws enacted since the 1970s have established long mandatory prison terms for drug offenders (Tonry, 1996). Although harsher sen-

sentencing commissions commissions that were established beginning in the 1970s to develop sentencing guidelines and to consider other aspects of sentencing

sentencing guidelines recommendations that judges are expected to follow in determining an offender's sentence

table 11.4 — Hypothetical Sentencing Guidelines Grid

SERIOUSNESS OF CONVICTION OFFENSE	NUMBER OF PRIOR FELONY CONVICTIONS			
	0	**1**	**2**	**3 or more**
Level I: Minor theft; marijuana possession	12	14	15	12–13
Level II: Burglary	15	16	15–16	20–22
Level III: Simple assault; unarmed robbery, no injury	18	15	17–19	24–28
Level IV: Aggravated assault	24–26	32–36	33–38	36–40
Level V: Armed robbery; rape	84–90	96–106	108–119	120–130
Level VI: Attempted murder	180–190	200–220	240–280	300–380

Note: The cells above the heavy lines represent a sentence of probation; the cells below or to the right of the heavy lines represent a sentence of incarceration. The numbers in each cell represent the number of months of probation or incarceration that the offender is expected to receive. In some cases, a range of months is listed; the sentence is expected to fall within this range. Mitigating circumstances would normally yield a sentence on the lower end of the range, whereas aggravating circumstances would normally yield a sentence on the higher end of the range.

tencing like this has been in accord with public and political sentiments, it is questionable, as we noted earlier, whether it has also helped increase public safety.

Victim–Impact Statements

Another influence on sentencing is the **victim-impact statement.** Used in more than half the states across the country, victim-impact statements allow crime victims to discuss how their victimization has affected their physical and mental health, their social relationships, their economic situation, and other aspects of their lives. Arising from the victim rights movement (see Chapter 5), they are meant to give victims (mostly those of violent crime) a role in the criminal justice system and to help increase their satisfaction with the system. After an offender has been convicted, a judge asks the victim to complete an impact statement before sentencing is pronounced. The judge considers all the information contained in the statement, and the victim is often in court when the defendant is sentenced.

When they were first proposed in the 1980s, victim-impact statements aroused some controversy. Critics feared that victim statements could sway judges to give unduly harsh sentences to defendants, especially when victims were perceived as virtuous and clean-cut. Those concerns still remain (Phillips, 1997). But in 1991, the U.S. Supreme Court said victim-impact statements were constitutional. After that decision, victim-impact statements grew quickly in popularity.

The influence of these statements on sentencing remains an open question. A study of 500 felony prosecutions in Ohio found that impact statements made imprisonment more likely, but a study of New York City cases found no such effect (Davis and Smith, 1994; Erez and Tontodonato, 1990). In the Ohio study, completing the impact statements did *not* increase victims' satisfaction with the criminal justice system. Ironically,

victim-impact statements information provided by victims that is meant to aid in sentencing

some even became more dissatisfied because they felt the sentencing of their offenders was too lenient (Erez and Tontodonato, 1992).

Determinants of Sentencing

Because sentencing is so important, much research has focused on the various factors that affect the type and severity of the sentences that judges pronounce. These factors include at least two that are legally permissible, the defendant's prior criminal record and the seriousness of the offense for which he or she was convicted, as well as several "extralegal" factors that should not influence sentencing. These latter factors include the race, ethnicity, age, and gender of the defendant. To the extent these extralegal factors influence sentencing, they contribute to sentencing disparity, the different sentencing of offenders who have similar criminal histories and who have committed similar kinds of crimes. As noted previously, a major aim of sentencing guidelines and other sentencing reforms has been to limit and even eliminate sentencing disparity. In this section, we examine the determinants of sentencing and review the research on sentencing disparity.

Prior Record and Seriousness of Offense

As our discussion of sentencing guidelines indicated, the two most important factors affecting sentence severity are the offender's prior criminal record and the seriousness of the offense for which he or she is being sentenced. Martha A. Myers (2000, p. 458) summarizes the evidence on this issue: "The most striking and consistent finding of empirical research is that the offense and the offender's prior criminal record are pivotal considerations during sentencing." Although survey evidence indicates that the public thinks it makes sense to give so much weight to these two variables (Roberts, 1997), scholars raise several questions about them.

Let's start with the seriousness of the offense. As noted earlier, a modern sentencing principle (just deserts) is that the severity of the sentence should be *proportional* to the seriousness of the offense for which someone is being sentenced. This implies that we must first have some idea of, and consensus on, how serious various offenses are (von Hirsch, 1998). Surveys given to national samples of U.S. residents do just that: They ask people to rank the seriousness of many kinds of offenses. These surveys find that violent crimes are considered more serious than property crimes, and they also find consensus among various demographic subgroups in their rankings of crime seriousness (Wolfgang, Figlio, Tracy, and Singer, 1985). This consensus is, in turn, reflected in sentencing policy because violent crimes are usually given harsher sentences than property crimes (Warr, 2000). However, some critics point out that crimes by corporations can be very serious but still receive only mild sentences that are not proportional to the severity of the offense (Reiman, 2001). Others say that if too much weight is given to offense seriousness, circumstances such as a defendant's level of remorse that should influence sentencing receive too little weight or none at all.

The influence of prior criminal record on sentencing raises even more questions. As von Hirsch (1998, p. 670) points out, "It has been a matter of controversy how much weight the criminal record should have, and why." According to the just deserts principle, the major goal of sentencing should be retribution, and the seriousness of the current offense should thus have the most weight by far. Although prior record might predict future offending, that is irrelevant from a just deserts standpoint, and it should play little or no role in sentencing decisions.

Another philosophical issue is one of ethics. Julian V. Roberts (1997) questions the morality of punishing a defendant more severely for offenses that have already been punished. Once offenders have been punished, they are supposed to have paid their debt to their society. As Roberts (1997, p. 316) asks, "If a defendant has already discharged the previous sentence of the court, is he not being sentenced a second time for the same criminal conduct?" He notes that some legal scholars say that giving a defendant a more severe sentence because of past criminal conduct violates the constitutional ban on double jeopardy, which prohibits someone from being punished twice for the same crime.

Beyond these philosophical issues, several practical concerns can also be raised about basing sentencing on prior record (Roberts, 1997). First, how should prior criminal record be defined? Should previous arrests be used, or only previous convictions? Should only felony convictions count, or should misdemeanor convictions also count? How much weight should misdemeanors receive compared to felonies? Even if only felony convictions are used, should all felonies count the same? Should an armed robbery count more than a burglary? As these questions indicate, it is surprisingly difficult to "operationalize" prior criminal record in any logical way.

Second, should juvenile offenses be included in the prior record? As Chapter 14 discusses, juvenile offenses are usually treated differently from adult offenses because adolescents are not yet legal adults and thus not thought to be as responsible for their behavior. If someone commits an offense at age 14 and then is being sentenced at age 30 for a new offense, should his juvenile record be held against him?

This consideration raises a third question of *time factor*. As Julian V. Roberts (1997, p. 307) puts it, "Should the weight of a previous conviction decline if the offender lives a crime-free life? At that point should previous convictions cease to count against a defendant? Should they ever cease to count?" How would *you* answer these questions?

Fourth, as our discussion of incapacitation indicated, prior record may not be a very accurate record of someone's actual history of offending. Someone with few or no prior convictions may actually have committed many more offenses than someone with more prior convictions. Sentencing based on prior record may thus be based on flawed information.

A final concern relates to the one just stated. To the extent that race and other extralegal factors influence arrest and sentencing (see the following discussion), some innocent people may be arrested and even convicted because of their race and other factors. Even if they actually commit a future offense and are convicted for it, basing their sentencing on their mistaken prior record in effect doubles the wrong already done to them.

Sentencing Disparity

We have noted more than once that a major aim of sentencing reforms, including the establishment of sentencing guidelines, was to reduce **sentencing disparity,** which is the use of very different sentences for offenders who have been convicted of similar crimes and who have similar prior records. Despite the reforms and guidelines, sentencing disparity still remains.

Some of the reasons for the disparity lies in inevitable differences in the attitudes and backgrounds of judges. Some judges favor harsher sentences, whereas others favor more lenient sentences. When judges are asked what sentence they would impose in hypothetical cases, their responses vary widely precisely because they are different people with different views of punishment and sentencing (Austin and Williams, 1977).

Sometimes laws themselves lead to sentencing disparity. A key example here is federal law enacted in the mid-1980s to curtail the use and sale of cocaine and its derivative, crack (Duster, 1995; Tonry, 1996). Although pharmacologically the two drugs are very similar, the law punished the possession and sale of crack more severely than that of powder cocaine, with the penalty for possessing 1 gram of crack as severe as that for possessing 100 grams of powder cocaine. Because crack is used more in urban African American neighborhoods and powder cocaine is used more in white, middle-class neighborhoods, the federal law has had a much more severe impact on African Americans than on whites, a consequence we explore further in Chapter 12.

Since at least the 1970s, many studies have assessed the degree to which race and ethnicity, social class, gender, and other extralegal factors affect sentence severity. The evidence is complex, and researchers differ on how to interpret it. Many share the view of Martha A. Myers (2000, p. 457) that the seriousness of the offense and prior record

sentencing disparity unequal legal treatment of offenders convicted of similar crimes and with similar prior records

play the major roles in sentencing and that extralegal factors play only "smaller and intermittent roles." In this view, then, discrimination in sentencing does exist, but it is fairly small and unsystematic and even subtle.

Let's look first at *race and ethnicity*. Criminal justice researchers have heatedly debated the role that race and ethnicity play in sentencing (Mann, 1993; Wilbanks, 1987), and a large body of research exists on this issue (Walker et al., 2000). Most of this research has concerned how African Americans are treated. Although, as noted in Chapter 2, African Americans are disproportionately incarcerated, many researchers attribute this fact to their higher rates of criminal offending and not to sentencing discrimination (Tonry, 1996). Racial discrimination in sentencing does exist, but its extent is fairly small, and some studies uncover no discrimination at all once relevant variables such as offense seriousness and prior record are taken into account (Walker et al., 2000). A notable exception to this general conclusion is sentencing under federal cocaine laws, which, as we just noted, serve to imprison African Americans much more than whites.

This general conclusion also masks subtle differences in how whites and African Americans are treated (Myers, 2000; Walker et al., 2000). For example, prior record plays a more important role in the sentencing of African Americans than in that of whites. Also, some studies of murder and rape cases find that sentencing is harsher if the victim is white than if the victim is African American, implying that judges place more importance on the lives of white victims than on those of African American victims. Race also affects sentencing more in cases involving less serious crimes than those involving more serious crimes. Apparently, the greater discretion that judges have in less serious cases provides more of a possibility for race to affect their sentencing decisions. To the extent that race does matter, it also appears to matter more for the decision to incarcerate (the "in–out" decision) than for the length of the prison term for those who are incarcerated.

Sentencing guidelines have reduced the importance that race plays in sentencing, but it still plays some role nonetheless. Myers (2000, p. 460) offers this conclusion about race and sentencing: "In sum, the significance attached to race varies, and African Americans are often but not always punished more severely than whites."

Much research on sentencing disparity examines the degree to which African Americans receive harsher sentences because of racial bias.

Less research has been conducted on ethnicity and sentencing, with studies focusing on Hispanic Americans. This evidence is again inconsistent (Myers, 2000). In some locations, Hispanics receive harsher sentences than non-Hispanic whites, but in other locations they receive the same sentences. Whether disparate treatment emerges depends on the type of offense: Hispanics receive harsher sentences for drug offenses but more lenient sentences for violent crimes. In general, prior records have a larger effect on the sentencing of Hispanics than on the sentencing of whites.

The evidence for *gender* and sentencing is fairly clear: Taking everything into account, women are treated somewhat more leniently than men (Daly and Bordt, 1995; Steffensmeier et al., 1998). This is especially so for the in–out incarceration decision; women are 10 to 30 percent less likely than men to be incarcerated for similar crimes. Leniency for women is also more likely when they have children, and scholars have debated whether this type of leniency makes sense.

Research on *social class* and sentencing is fairly meager, and it suggests that social class makes little difference in sentence severity (Chiricos and Waldo, 1975; D'Alessio and Stolzenberg, 1993; Myers, 2000). To the extent it has any effect, this effect probably stems from the influence of social class on bail decisions and type of defense counsel: Poorer defendants are less likely to be released on bail before trial and less likely to hire a private attorney.

Randall G. Shelden (1982) thinks the research on social class and sentencing misses the mark. Because most defendants accused of street crimes are fairly poor, he says, researchers do not have enough social class differences for a link between social class and sentencing to emerge. Too few middle-class and upper-class people are arrested for street crimes, Shelden says, for meaningful social class comparisons to be possible. Picking up on this perspective, critics say that considerable social class differences in sentencing do emerge when the fate of street crime offenders is compared to that of white-collar crime offenders, especially those involved in crime by corporations. These offenders are treated much more leniently, according to these critics, even though their offenses cause more public injury than street crimes (Rosoff, Pontell, and Tillman, 1998; Tillman and Pontell, 1992). This difference leads political scientist Herbert Jacob (1978, p. 185) to observe that criminal courts are "fundamentally courts against the poor." White-collar crimes, he points out, receive less legal scrutiny and less severe punishment when they do attract such scrutiny.

A Final Word on Sentencing

Our discussion has questioned whether the massive incarceration since the 1970s has had the incapacitation and deterrence effects that its proponents proclaim. Even if these effects did exist, that does not necessarily mean it would be wise to build more prisons and to put more offenders in them. First, it is quite expensive to do so, and any crime reduction from more imprisonment must be balanced against the huge costs—in the tens of billions of dollars—of such efforts (Tonry and Farrington, 1995). Second, a reliance on harsher and more certain punishment may also endanger civil liberties, and, once again, the goal of crime reduction must be weighed against this possible danger (Krohn, 2000).

Third, and perhaps most ominously, as we put more and more people behind bars, we have more and more inmates who eventually are released back to their communities after they serve their sentences. In any one year, more than 40 percent of prison inmates are released. In 2001, about 600,000 inmates were released, and this number is projected to grow to 1 million or more per year by 2010. As writer Sasha Abramsky (1999, p. 33) observes, "That is an awful lot of potential rage coming out of prison to haunt our future." Abramsky points out that the released inmates will have few job skills and will thus have trouble getting stable jobs. Because of this, they may easily end up committing more crime. Their presence will also lower wages (through simple processes of supply and demand of labor) and increase unemployment and worsen other problems in their communities. All these reasons may further drive up the crime rate and prompt the communities' law-abiding people to move elsewhere. Thus, even if the current policy of massive arrest and imprisonment does have strong incapacitation and general deterrent effects (which we doubt), in the long run it may well cause much more harm than good. Abramsky (1999, p. 36) thinks that "we are creating a disaster that instead of dissipating over time will accumulate with the years."

In view of these concerns, debate over sentencing and crime policy is important and sure to continue. In the next few chapters, we turn our attention to the final stage of the criminal justice system, corrections, to which offenders move once they are sentenced. These chapters complete our examination of the criminal justice system in the United States.

Focus on Australia

Mandatory Sentencing Down Under

Australia's origins as a British colony began in the late 1700s when Britain decided to relieve jail overcrowding by transporting convicts to what was then called New South Wales. Britain had previously used America for this purpose, but its defeat in the American Revolution forced Britain to send convicts to this new location. Despite its origins as a penal colony, Australia has long been acclaimed for its criminal justice system's focus on rehabilitative programs. However, Australia changed its sentencing practices a few years ago in ways that have proven at least as controversial as the U.S. sentencing reforms discussed in the text.

In 1996 and 1997, two Australian regions, the Northern Territory and Western Australia, established mandatory minimum sentences for adult and juvenile offenders convicted of property crimes. For adults in the Northern Territory, the minimum sentences are 14 days in jail for first-time offenders; 90 days for second-time offenders; and 1 year for third-time offenders. For juveniles ages 15 or 16, the minimum sentences are 28 days for those convicted of at least their second property offense and 1 year for those convicted of additional offenses. The property crimes receiving these sentences include minor offenses such as smashing a street lamp bulb and stealing objects such as cigarette lighters, biscuits, and paint. Western Australia's mandatory sentencing legislation was less sweeping: Adults or juveniles convicted of at least their third burglary receive a minimum term of 1 year behind bars.

Australian critics say these mandatory sentences pose several problems similar to those cited by critics of U.S. mandatory sentencing. First, many of the property crimes receiving automatic jail terms are very minor, and the penalties are thus disproportionately harsh. In one case, a 22-year-old man received a 1-year prison term for stealing a box of biscuits. Second, these offenses tend to be committed by young people and by persons from poor socioeconomic circumstances, particularly Aborigines, Australia's indigenous population that historically has lived in poverty

and been the victim of prejudice and discrimination. Mandatory sentencing thus falls most heavily on young Aborigines.

Third, mandatory sentences eliminate judicial discretion. As noted in the text, this means that judges no longer have the ability to consider an offender's individual circumstances when they assign a sentence. Fourth, mandatory sentencing has reduced the number of guilty pleas and prolonged the length of cases. This consequence means that courts are more congested than before and legal costs are greater. To avoid a mandatory sentence, some defendants are also pleading guilty to nonmandatory offenses when perhaps they might not be guilty of any crime.

A fifth criticism is that mandatory sentencing does not, in fact, lower the crime rate. As U.S. critics have noted, low-level property crime is fairly impulsive and spontaneous, and offenders do not take time to consider their risk of receiving a mandatory term.

Next, mandatory sentencing has increased prison costs in Australia because it has increased the number of people going to prison. Critics say that these increased costs make it more difficult to fund social services and other kinds of support for crime victims. They also say that, because prisons can be "breeding grounds" for criminal behavior, mandatory sentencing may be making offenders more likely to commit crime. Nonprison alternatives would save money and also reduce their chances of reoffending.

Begun in controversy, mandatory sentencing in Australia became even more controversial after a 15-year-old Aboriginal boy who received a mandatory sentence died in custody in February 2000. His name was Johnno Wurramarrba, and his crime was stealing some pens and pencils. Because this was his second offense, Johnno received a mandatory 28-day term in a juvenile detention center. Depressed at being separated from his family, he hanged himself with a bed sheet shortly thereafter. His suicide provoked an even more heated debate in Australia over mandatory sentencing.

Not surprisingly, much of this debate focused on the impact of mandatory sentencing for petty offenses on the Aboriginal population. Two years after mandatory sentencing began in the Northern Territory, the number of Aborigines imprisoned there had increased by 22 percent. Although Aborigines comprise only about 28 percent of the Northern Territory's population, they comprise 72 percent of its prison population. In

Western Australia, the incarceration rate for the indigenous population is 2,272 per 100,000 people, a rate much higher than that for the general population (212 per 100,000 people). One Aboriginal leader charged, "The fundamental nature of something like mandatory sentencing within the legal framework is totally wrong. It is fundamentally directed at the indigenous youth. That's only going to compound the situation" (Donnan, 2000, p. 8). A Northern Territory official denied that mandatory sentencing was directed at young Aborigines. Instead, he said, the mandatory sentencing law is intended to deter "grubs who break into homes, steal cars and anything else that is not nailed down" ("An Apology Delayed," 2000, p. 42).

The controversy over Australia's mandatory sentencing policy soon extended beyond its borders when international organizations took notice. The United Nations High Commissioner for Human Rights investigated the new legislation to determine whether its provisions for juveniles violated the 1989 United Nations Convention on the Rights of the Child. This convention condemned mandatory sentencing that would imprison a high proportion of any racial group that is economically marginalized, a description that fit the Aborigines. The UN body reportedly bowed to pressure from the Australian government and failed to conclude that the mandatory sentencing legislation did violate the convention. Another UN body, the United Nations Committee on the Elimination of Racial Discrimination, issued a statement that expressed its "grave concern" over the mandatory sentencing legislation and criticized it for targeting offenses "that were committed disproportionately by indigenous Australians, leading to a racially divisive impact on their rate of incarceration" (Duffy and Warby, 2000, p. 6). Noting that Australia had done much to promote human rights around the world, an Amnesty International official commented, "But it recently seems to be undoing all its good work," and he worried that other nations could follow Australia's example and adopt mandatory sentencing practices of their own (Donnan, 2000, p. 8).

In return, Australia's federal government attacked the international criticism of its mandatory sentencing legislation and accused its critics of interfering with Australia's domestic policies. Despite the government's response, the international criticism apparently proved effective. In July 2000, the Northern Territory decided that the mandatory sentencing provisions would not apply to first-time juvenile offenders convicted of a minor property crime. Instead, they would be diverted into counseling and community programs. In return, the Australian government gave the Northern Territory several million dollars to support rehabilitation programs for juvenile offenders (Colman, 2000). Although this change eased some of the impact of mandatory sentencing in the Northern Territory, critics say such sentencing continues to pose the problems previously discussed and, in particular, has a discriminatory impact on the young Aboriginal population.

Sources: "An Apology Delayed," 2000, Bessant, 2000; Colman, 2000; Donnan, 2000; White, 2000; Wilson, 2000.

summary

1. Judges have some discretion in sentencing convicted offenders. Proponents of judicial discretion say it allows judges to take the individual circumstances of a case into account and to fit a sentence to the needs of the offender. Critics say it leads to sentencing disparity and to sentences that are too lenient. Concern about judicial discretion led to sentencing reforms beginning in the 1970s that have greatly increased the rate of incarceration and the number of people under correctional supervision.

2. Sentencing goals include rehabilitation, retribution, incapacitation, and deterrence. Rehabilitation was the primary goal in the United States before the 1970s, but concern at growing crime rates led to less emphasis on this goal. Although incapacitation and deterrence are now the major goals guiding U.S. criminal justice policy, research questions whether these goals are being achieved.

3. The major types of sentences today are probation, intermediate sanctions, and incarceration. Probation involves supervision by a probation officer in lieu of imprisonment, whereas intermediate sanctions fall in between probation and incarceration and impose more severe conditions on offenders than those imposed by probation.

4. The sentencing reforms that began in the mid-1970s included a shift to determinate sentencing and mandatory minimum sentences. These reduced judges' discretion but led to a rise in incarceration and to other problems. Research does not appear to indicate that mandatory sentences have helped to lower the crime rate.

5. Presentence reports play an important role in judges' sentencing decisions. They are usually prepared by probation officers and include various kinds of information about the defendant and usually a sentencing recommendation by the probation officers. Most judges rely heavily on these reports in their sentencing decisions.

6. Sentencing guidelines and victim impact statements also affect contemporary sentencing. Passed by sentencing commissions, sentencing guidelines often take the form of sentencing grids based on the seriousness of the convicted offense and the prior criminal record

of the offender. Victim-impact statements are becoming increasingly popular, although their actual effect on sentence severity remains unclear.

7. Sentencing disparity results from differences in judges' beliefs and attitudes and, sometimes, from

certain laws that end up treating different kinds of offenders differently. Overall, offense seriousness and prior record play the major roles in sentencing; the effect of extralegal factors such as race and ethnicity, gender, and social class is weaker and inconsistent.

key terms

absolute deterrence
determinate sentences
deterrence
general deterrence
gross incapacitation
incapacitation
incarceration
indeterminate sentences
intermediate sanctions
just deserts
mandatory minimum sentences
marginal deterrence

presentence report
probation
recidivism
rehabilitation
retribution
selective incapacitation
sentencing commissions
sentencing disparity
sentencing guidelines
sentencing hearing
specific deterrence
victim-impact statements

questions *for* investigation

1. This chapter notes that judges' sentencing discretion has been considerably narrowed and that legislatures determine minimum and maximum terms of incarceration for any given crime. What is your opinion of this change in sentencing policy?

2. This chapter asserts that treatment and training rehabilitation programs are more effective in communities than in prisons and jails. Discuss possible reasons for this.

3. Do some research on intermediate sanction programs in your state. Identify the features of such programs. Also, find out whether your state has information on the recidivism rates of offenders taking part in such

programs. If such information is available, use it to assess the effectiveness of these programs in preventing recidivism.

4. Discuss the pros and cons of mandatory sentencing policies.

5. Can you suggest ways in which to reduce or eliminate bias in presentence reports?

6. In your opinion, should an individual's prior criminal record have any significance on his or her sentencing for a current crime?

7. This chapter notes that sentencing for women is somewhat more lenient than for men. Identify possible reasons for this leniency.

IT'S YOUR CALL...

1. Suppose you are a criminal court judge who had just presided over a case in which the defendant was found guilty. The defendant is a 21-year-old man who was accused of armed robbery; he had brandished a kitchen knife and asked his victim, a 50-year-old male, for his wal-

let. The older man handed over his wallet and the defendant fled, only to be caught two blocks away by the police. This is the defendant's first conviction for a serious crime. His only other involvement with the criminal justice system occurred when he was arrested at age 18 for shoplifting a baseball glove; the charges were dropped because the prosecutor decided it would be difficult to prove criminal intent. You think the defendant is basically a decent person who has been going through some tough times lately, but you also recognize that his crime was very serious. What sentence do you give the defendant? Why?

2. Your house is burglarized and you lose all your jewelry, your two computers, and your home theater equipment.

The total loss runs into the thousands of dollars. Although your homeowners insurance covers your losses, you have many sleepless nights and finally go to your doctor to have a sedative prescribed. You are doing better 1 month later but still feeling very vulnerable. The police tell you that two young men, both in their early 20s, have been arrested for burglarizing your house and a dozen others. You soon hear from the prosecutor that the men are pleading guilty, and you are invited to render a victim-impact statement before sentencing. Would you make such a statement? If so, what would you say? If not, why not?

Prisons *and* Punishment: Yesterday *and* Today

1. Before the eighteenth century, what were the common forms of punishment for a crime?

2. What is the history of incarceration as a punishment?

3. In the history of incarceration in the United States, how have women been treated?

4. What are the major types of prisons? What is the difference between a prison and a jail?

5. What is the incarceration rate in the United States? What are the annual costs of incarceration?

6. What is privatization?

7. What do proponents and critics say about the death penalty?

Ernie Preate, Jr., was once a "tough on crime" advocate without peer. After graduating law school, he served as an assistant prosecutor for several years in the Scranton, Pennsylvania, area before winning election as district attorney in 1977. He won one guilty verdict after another and 19 murder cases in a row. He put five murder defendants on death row and was a passionate advocate of capital punishment. He also urged mandatory sentences for drug offenses and recalls, "I was the prosecutor's prosecutor" (Bleyer, 2001, p. 28). When he became the attorney general of Pennsylvania in 1988, Preate continued to press his tough approach to fighting crime and drugs.

Several years later, Preate found himself on the other end of the law when he was accused of hiding $20,000 in campaign contributions from operators of illegal video-poker machines. In 1995, he pleaded guilty to mail fraud, resigned as attorney general, and was sentenced to a federal prison in Duluth, Minnesota (Reske, 1995). There he saw that many of the inmates were African Americans serving long terms for minor drug offenses. He recalls, "I'll never forget it. In January of 1996, I walked into the mess hall the first night

I was up in Duluth, and I turned around and I said, 'Oh, my God, what have we created?' It was a sea of black and brown faces" (Bleyer, 2001, p. 28). Preate was also shocked by the conditions he found in his prison. When he was released after spending 14 months in the prison, Preate emerged as a prison reformer and has since urged an end to capital punishment, a reconsideration of the nation's harsh sentencing policy for drug offenders, and a renewal of rehabilitation efforts for inmates. He says, "Hey, look, this is common sense. We can't keep building prisons, or pretty soon we're going to wind up with more people in prisons than we have kids in school" (Bleyer, 2001, p. 30).

Ernie Preate entered prison as a disgraced state attorney general and emerged as a prison reformer because of the conditions he observed while incarcerated.

Preate's story reminds us that many divergent views exist on how best to punish criminals. Like the United States, all societies have ways of dealing with people who violate their norms. Historically, these ways have varied from one society to another. Some societies have relied on informal means, such as ridicule and shunning, whereas others have used more formal means, such as banishment, corporal punishment, confinement, and even death. Although the United States and other nations today rely primarily on imprisonment and other legal sanctions, these forms of punishment are actually a fairly recent development in the course of human history.

Their relative "newness" makes them no less important and no less fascinating. As Francis T. Cullen and Jody L. Sundt (2000, p. 473) point out, "Prisons are a continuing source of curiosity and controversy. For most Americans, prisons remain much like a distant foreign land—exotic enough to excite our voyeuristic impulses but sufficiently unfamiliar to inspire trepidation, if not fear." In fact, prisons and legal punishment have long been a staple of Western literature and popular culture. Great novels, such as Fyodor Dostoyevsky's *Crime and Punishment,* Alexandre Dumas's *The Count of Monte Cristo,* and Victor Hugo's *Les Misérables,* concern incarceration or the threat of punishment. They are far more than that, of course, but their plots involve a legal system intent on punishing an offender and the offender's response to this threat. If your tastes run more to theatrical films, prisons can be found there as well. In the past decade, many popular U.S. films have featured prisons and prison life: *Dead Man Walking,* with Susan Sarandon and Sean Penn; *Double Jeopardy,* with Ashley Judd and Tommy Lee Jones; *The Green Mile,* with Tom Hanks; *Out of Sight,* with George Clooney and Jennifer Lopez; and *The Rock,* with Sean Connery and Nicolas Cage, to name only a few.

Legal punishment fascinates us because it represents the loss of freedom and, perhaps, because it tells us something about what kind of society we have. As noted in

Chapter 11, Émile Durkheim thought that punishment served an important function for society because it expresses society's moral outrage over violation of important social norms. Durkheim and other social theorists believe that fundamental links exist between a society's values and its mode of punishment. Reflecting this view, Dostoyevsky (1957, p. 76), the great nineteenth-century Russian author, once wrote that "the level of civilization in a society can be judged by entering its prisons." His statement reminds us that prisons can reflect well or poorly on the society that builds and runs them.

If social theorists and authors such as Dostoyevsky are right in believing that a society's choice of punishment reflects its values and beliefs, then by studying this choice we can learn something about the society itself. By studying punishment, we also can learn about a fundamental aspect of society and its potential for controlling crime and deviance. Accordingly, this and the next two chapters introduce punishment and corrections in the United States. This chapter discusses the history of prisons and examines the growing size and cost of the corrections system. It also discusses several important and controversial correctional issues in the United States today: (1) the surge in incarceration since the 1970s (the subject of an Under Investigation feature), (2) the privatization of prisons and jails, and (3) the death penalty. Chapter 13 examines life in prison and jail, and Chapter 14 considers community corrections and the juvenile justice system, both of which involve alternatives to traditional incarceration.

Punishment in Historical Perspective

Ancient societies did not have prisons; instead, they used other forms of punishment. Some favored public humiliation and ridicule, especially for minor offenses, to teach offenders a lesson and to deter other individuals from violating social norms. In some societies, punishment often took the form of restitution; offenders would be expected to compensate their victims for the wrongs they had committed. In other societies, punishment was more retributive and involved fines, banishment from the society, corporal punishment, or execution (Farrington, 1996).

Ancient societies and their medieval counterparts developed many types of corporal punishment, including beating, whipping or flogging, branding, mutilation, and the use of devices such as the rack and pillory. Torture in medieval Europe was common, both as a punishment and as a means of making individuals confess to alleged offenses. Corporal punishment in the Western world lasted well into the nineteenth century when, thanks to efforts begun a century earlier by criminal justice reformers in Britain, Italy, and elsewhere, it finally fell out of favor. It did not disappear altogether, however; flogging remained a possible form of legal punishment in Great Britain for at least some offenses until 1967. In the United States, floggings occurred in Delaware as late as 1952, and Delaware did not ban them until 1972 (Walker, 1998). Flogging and other corporal punishment are prohibited by various international human rights treaties but continue to be practiced in many nations in the Middle East and elsewhere.

As a form of punishment, confinement (or **incarceration**) did not really exist anywhere in the world before the eighteenth century. Some offenders *were* confined even in ancient times, but not as a form of punishment. Instead, they were confined until they could be tried or until they could be given some other form of punishment, such as flogging or banishment. In one exception to this general rule, debtors in medieval Europe were confined until they could pay the money they owed.

Several institutions resembling prisons were established during the sixteenth century in Britain and other parts of Europe. The first was the *workhouse,* in which poor people lived and had to work hard under the supervision of guards. Workhouses were developed to help the poor by providing them with food and lodging and helping them to learn good work habits, but, in effect, they were a way of confining them and controlling their behavior. A second quasi-prison that developed during this time was the *house of correction,* in which people charged with minor offenses lived and, like their workhouse counterparts, had to work hard under the supervision of guards. Finally, the

incarceration confinement in prison or jail following conviction of a crime

gaol (jail) also developed and was used to detain suspects until they could be tried. But until well into the eighteenth century, incarceration in prison or jail as a form of punishment was not used (Foucault, 1977).

That changed by the end of the eighteenth century, in large part due to the efforts of the European criminal justice reformers noted earlier. These reformers were appalled by the massive use of torture and executions in Europe and argued that punishment should be proportional to the offense. They were also appalled by the conditions in the European prisons that were used to hold people for the reasons just cited. Their efforts helped improve prison and jail conditions but also gave rise to the idea that imprisonment should replace corporal punishment as the dominant mode of punishment. Thus, as the 1700s passed, more and more people were punished by being put behind bars. Although that was a reform over corporal punishment, the prisons in which they were put continued to suffer from terrible conditions. They were filthy and overcrowded; men, women, and children were confined together as were violent and minor offenders. Rape and other abuses were common. The crowded and dirty conditions made communicable diseases rampant, and these diseases routinely killed inmates, guards, and even, sometimes, lawyers and judges. At the same time, many British prisoners who were awaiting *transportation,* or banishment, to Australia lived in the hulls of ships docked in England and often never left for Australia. The conditions in the hulls were often even worse than those in the prisons.

Criminal justice reformers continued to call attention to all these decrepit conditions. One British reformer, John Howard, wrote a 1777 book in which he said that prisons should become places in which offenders could learn the error of their ways and repent the offenses they had committed. His work helped motivate Britain to build prisons, which came to be called **penitentiaries,** designed to accomplish this goal. The age of the modern prison had finally begun (Foucault, 1977).

penitentiaries early prisons that were built to hold inmates so they could repent for their offenses

The U.S. Colonial Experience

The development of corrections in the United States largely mirrored the European experience. During the colonial period, jails were used mainly to hold debtors until they paid their debts or defendants for trial or other kinds of punishment. Like their British counterparts, colonial jails were filthy and overcrowded and the repositories of communicable disease (Walker, 1998).

Many kinds of behaviors that are not criminal today were considered serious crimes during the colonial period, including adultery, blasphemy, gossip, and swearing. Public drunkenness and disorderly conduct were also severely punished. Because most of the colonies were essentially religious societies with strong views on morality, this list of "serious" offenses is perhaps not that surprising. Because the colonists believed that affronts to morality were sins and that people with sin were not capable of being reformed, they thought these behaviors deserved strong and swift punishment to teach offenders and would-be offenders alike a clear lesson.

Punishment in the colonies took four primary forms: fines, shaming, flogging, and execution. Fines were used for minor offenses, whereas shaming was used both for minor and more serious offenses. A famous literary example of shaming is Nathaniel Hawthorne's *The Scarlet Letter,* where young Hester Prynne was forced to wear a red "A" on her chest for committing adultery. More common forms of shaming involved the use of the *pillory* or *stocks,* which were wooden frameworks with holes in them for the offender's arms, legs, and head. The offender would be placed in these devices for several days at a time in the town center, subjected to taunting and ridicule by passersby. Sometimes these offenders would also be whipped or the target of launched stones, eggs, or other objects. *Ducking stools* were also used; an offender would be tied to a chair at the end of a long plank which would then be dunked into a pond or river.

People accused of serious crimes would typically be flogged or occasionally executed, usually by hanging, although wealthy offenders sometimes would only be fined. Instead of being executed, some offenders were banished, but banishment was generally uncommon because the colonies could not afford to lose people, even offenders, who were needed to perform the many tasks of colonial life (Walker, 1998). One of the most famous hanging victims in the colonial period was Mary Dyer, a Quaker, who was hanged by Boston Puritans in 1660 for sedition in practicing her faith. Despite this example, executions in the colonies were relatively infrequent. To prevent executions, juries often found defendants guilty of manslaughter, and many defendants who were sentenced to death were later pardoned.

An important exception to the widespread colonial use of corporal punishment and public shaming was developed in Pennsylvania, founded by William Penn, a Quaker who believed in the possibility of redemption. As a result of his Quaker beliefs, Pennsylvania abolished corporal punishment except in the case of murder. Penn enacted the *Great Law of 1692*, which, in effect, mandated that prisons would be built to take the place of corporal punishment. Penn thus established prisons as the major form of punishment a century earlier than Britain and other U.S. colonies. The intent of the Great Law was not always followed, however, because many offenders continued to be flogged and publicly shamed, and it was repealed one day after Penn's death in 1718.

After the Revolution with Britain, the new United States ushered in an era of criminal justice reform. Many of the grievances outlined in the Declaration of Independence had centered on British abuses of the criminal justice system, and the Constitution and Bill of Rights included many protections for people suspected of crimes. Inspired by the European criminal justice reformers and by William Penn's vision a century earlier, U.S. reformers determined to devise a system of punishment that would limit executions and avoid public humiliation, flogging, and other corporal measures (Rothman, 1995).

In the post-Revolutionary period, the first key event in the development of the modern prison was the opening in 1790 of the Walnut Street Jail in Philadelphia. Devised by that city's Quakers, the Walnut Street Jail was meant to be a penitentiary in which inmates lived in solitary confinement and had no contact with other inmates, even during the day. This solitude, it was thought, would allow inmates time for reflection, Bible

A key event in the development of the modern prison was the 1790 opening of the Walnut Street Jail, seen in this early engraving. Devised by Philadelphia's Quakers, the Walnut Street Jail was meant to be a penitentiary in which inmates lived in solitary confinement and had no contact with other inmates. Their solitude would allow them time for Bible reading and prayer that would help reform them.

reading, prayer, and other activities that would help reform them. Male and female inmates were kept apart as were minor and serious offenders, and guards were prohibited from abusing inmates. However, overcrowding and other problems plagued the Walnut Street Jail and prevented inmates from being isolated from each other. Although, like the earlier houses of correction, inmates were supposed to work steadily and thereby develop good work habits, not enough work was available to keep everyone busy (Walker, 1998). Also, to the extent it occurred, solitary confinement, however well intended, did not prove an effective instrument of rehabilitation; it impaired prisoners' mental health and led to several other problems.

Prisons in the Nineteenth Century

Despite the Walnut Street Jail's problems, it continued to serve as a model for building new prisons in Pennsylvania and other states. During the 1820s, Pennsylvania built two additional large prisons in Philadelphia and Pittsburgh, and other states also followed suit. These prisons used solitary confinement, allowed little or no contact among prisoners, and urged reflection and prayer. At the Philadelphia prison, called the Eastern Penitentiary or Cherry Hill (because its site had once been a cherry orchard), prisoners did craft work in their cells, were not allowed to talk to each other, and even wore blindfolds when they were taken outside their cells. They spent 23 hours a day in their cells and exercised solitarily for 1 hour in a nearby yard (Walker, 1998).

The Pennsylvania model, as it was called, involving solitary confinement soon gave way to the Auburn or New York model, named after a prison opened in 1817 in Auburn, New York. The key difference in the two models was that the Auburn prison did not practice continuous solitary confinement. Inmates were housed separately at night but worked and ate together during the day, although they still were not allowed to talk with each other. Because of this limited physical contact, the Auburn model is often called a *congregate* model, whereas the Pennsylvania model is often called a *solitary* model.

At least three reasons prompted the decision to discontinue complete solitary confinement in the Auburn prison and those that followed it. First, absolute solitary confinement was impractical because of prison overcrowding. Second, it was causing many behavioral and psychological problems in the Pennsylvania prisons. Third, the Auburn cells were too small for inmates to use certain craft equipment, such as spinning wheels (Walker, 1998).

Despite the differences between the Auburn and Pennsylvania models, both assumed that crime was the result of problems in the external social environment rather than of personal moral problems and even sin. As a result, both also assumed that prisoners could be rehabilitated through reflection and hard work, both of which would help them overcome the negative influences of their social environments. At the same time, the substitution of confinement for the public shaming and flogging that were so popular during the colonial period meant that the criminal was now perceived "not as a fallen member of the community who could be reintegrated into it by a public shaming ritual but as a threat to the social order who needed to be set apart" (Walker, 1998, pp. 82–83).

As the nineteenth century proceeded, prison conditions began to alarm many observers. As Walker (1998, p. 88) notes, "No one fully anticipated the problems involved in confining hundreds of men, all of whom had displayed some form of antisocial behavior, against their will in close quarters for long periods of time." Prison conditions, including overcrowding, filth and lack of sanitation, and abuse by guards, caused prisoners to die "at an extraordinarily high rate" (Walker, 1998, p. 90), with 15 to 20 percent of many states' prisoners dying each year. These problems stimulated a large prison reform movement that began after the Civil War, spread throughout the nation during the 1870s, and lasted well into the next century. This movement stressed the need to improve prison conditions not only as a humane gesture but also as a way to help rehabilitate prisoners. It also advocated the use of *indeterminate sentences* (see Chapter 11) to permit prison officials to determine how long inmates needed to stay behind bars in order to be rehabilitated.

Beginning in the late 1870s, these principles were instituted at a prison in Elmira, New York, which became known as the Elmira Reformatory. This prison coupled indeterminate sentencing with awarding inmates points for good behavior and for achievement in work and educational programs. When they earned enough points, inmates would receive certain privileges, including more comfortable clothing and a better mattress, and they could eventually achieve early release from prison on parole. It was thought that these incentives would motivate inmates to behave well and to become fully rehabilitated. Inmates earned 56 cents a day working in various industries, took classes every evening, and attended religious services every Sunday. Despite the many innovations in the Elmira Reformatory, living conditions there were no better than those at other prisons. Guards routinely whipped or beat prisoners for almost any misbehavior, and homosexual rape was common (Shelden, 2001; Walker, 1998).

Twentieth-Century Developments

The Elmira model quickly became popular, and by the 1920s nearly every state had adopted it. The goal of rehabilitation, aided by indeterminate sentencing and parole, guided corrections throughout the nation. As the field of criminology developed during the 1920s and 1930s, so did knowledge of the causes of crime and optimism that effective correctional treatment could rehabilitate offenders and reduce recidivism. Still, most treatment programs in prisons "existed in name only" (Walker, 1998, p. 165) because prisons devoted most of their attention to maintaining inmate discipline. Prison conditions continued to be horrid.

After World War II, criminal justice scholars and professionals devoted new attention to correctional treatment programs. The leading state in this effort was California, which established new treatment programs and a comprehensive system of parole. At the same time, the post–World War II years saw increasing numbers of prisoners in many states and a wave of prison riots in the early 1950s, including more than 40 in 1952 and 1953, that contemporary scholars attribute to squalid prison conditions.

During the 1960s and 1970s, the U.S. Supreme Court and other federal courts rendered several important decisions about prison conditions and prisoners' rights. In one of the first decisions, a federal court in 1970 declared the entire Arkansas prison system unconstitutional because of its appalling conditions; 6 years later, another court reached the same conclusion for an Alabama prison. Inspired by the southern civil rights movement, prisoners and lawyers became active in seeking legal redress for prisoners, and the federal courts were sympathetic to their claims. Prisoners won the right to engage in certain religious practices, to communicate with family and friends, and to receive reading material that had previously been banned. They also won certain due process rights when confronted with disciplinary procedures. All these court rulings ended many of the worst abuses in the nation's prisons but not all of them. As Walker (1998, p. 188) notes, "Prisons remained dreadful and very dangerous places."

Even as these court reforms were being instituted, the Elmira model's focus on rehabilitation, indeterminate sentencing, and parole, which had been popular for most of the century, was becoming less popular. As discussed in Chapter 11, during the 1970s the goal of rehabilitation and the use of indeterminate sentencing began to give way to the goals of incapacitation and deterrence and the use of determinate sentencing. An oft-cited quote from a 1975 book by criminologist James Q. Wilson (1975, p. 209) reflects this new philosophy: "Wicked people exist. Nothing avails except to set them apart from innocent people." As Chapter 11 also noted, this new philosophy ushered in a "get tough" era of crime policy that led to an unprecedented surge in imprisonment and prison construction. We discuss this trend later in the Under Investigation feature.

Women's Prisons

During the colonial period, women offenders were often considered worse than their male counterparts: Because women were much less likely than men to commit offenses, those who did break the law had to be especially bad. The colonists also assumed that women tempted men to violate norms themselves, and they feared that women offenders would bear children with criminal tendencies. For all these reasons, women's behavior was closely watched, and penalties for deviance were harsh (Freedman, 1981).

After incarceration became the dominant mode of punishment, female offenders faced special problems. Early prisons and prisonlike structures, both in Europe and in the United States, housed men, women, and children in the same cells and buildings. Not surprisingly, rape and other abuses were common. Because women were only a small proportion of all prisoners, officials did not consider it cost effective to build separate buildings for them. Women also had other needs and problems that men did not have. One set of concerns was medical: Few, if any, prisons had gynecologists on staff. Also, women were far more likely than men to be the primary caretaker of one or more children, and their imprisonment raised serious issues of child welfare that were largely irrelevant to men's imprisonment. We return to some of these issues in the next chapter on prison life.

These problems led some criminal justice reformers and women's rights activists to focus on improving the conditions facing women prisoners. An early activist on this count was Elizabeth Fry, a British Quaker, who was shocked by the conditions she observed at Newgate Prison in 1813. She worked for the establishment of vocational training—involving a traditional female task, sewing—for women prisoners and for schooling for child prisoners. After the Civil War, U.S. women's rights activists and criminal justice reformers urged that separate units in men's prisons be built for women. Their efforts succeeded and helped reduce rape and other abuses of women prisoners. However, the segregation of the sexes meant that women now had less or no access to treatment programs, exercise yards and equipment, and other services and programs that were available to men (Rafter, 1985).

A few states began building separate prisons for women. The first such prison was the Indiana Women's Prison, which admitted its first inmate in 1873; both Massachusetts and New York opened women's prisons within the next decade. Women's prisons took two forms: *custodial* and *reformatory* (Rafter, 1985). Reformatories housed younger women who had committed minor offenses; custodial prisons housed older women who had committed more serious offenses. Although either type of prison theoretically should have provided women with more access to exercise, treatment programs, and the like than was possible in men's prisons, that did not happen for the most part because these prisons were underfunded. To the extent that women prisoners received vocational training in the nineteenth and early twentieth centuries, it centered on teaching them to be good housewives and mothers. As at Newgate Prison, they were taught sewing, domestic chores, and other traditional women's tasks. Conditions in women's prisons were little better than those in men's prisons; abuse both by guards and by other prisoners was common. During the Great Depression of the 1930s, financial problems forced many women's custodial and reformatory prisons to merge and other women's prisons to close. Some prisons were converted into men's prisons, and the women in those prisons once again encountered the various problems already noted facing women in men's institutions.

Today about 167,000 women are confined in the nation's prisons and jails (midyear 2001). They represent about 6.7 percent of the total prison population and 11.6 percent of the total jail population (Beck, Karberg, and Harrison 2002). About 75 percent of all female prisoners are housed in women's institutions, and the remainder live in institutions that house both women and men, often because their state lacks a separate women's prison (Greenfeld and Snell, 1999). Women inmates face problems both similar to and different from those facing male inmates, and we discuss these problems further in the next chapter.

Prisons and Jails Today

The next chapter discusses prison and jail life in detail and explores several issues facing inmates, guards, and other prison personnel. In this section, we sketch the structure of the U.S. correctional system.

http://www.ablongman.com/barkan1e

The United States actually has many correctional systems. The federal government administers the federal prison system, and each state has its own prison system. At the local level, counties and cities around the country run their own jails. This multitude of systems can cause confusion at times and makes it difficult to gather systematic data about the number of inmates, their backgrounds, and the costs of corrections. Fortunately, various federal agencies publish regular reports on all levels of the correctional system, and we include some of the information they provide in the following pages. We first discuss several aspects of prisons and jails and then examine the size and cost of the correctional enterprise.

Prisons

Prisons house offenders who have been found guilty of felonies and are sentenced to at least 1 year of incarceration. They are run by the 50 states, by the federal government, and by private companies contracting out to the states. Each state has at least a few prisons, and some big states, such as California and Texas, have many prisons. In 2000, when the most recent census of adult correctional facilities was conducted, 1,320 state prisons, 84 federal prisons, and 264 privately operated facilities (238 housing state inmates and 26 housing federal inmates) existed, for a total of 1,668 overall. The number of all state facilities, public and private, has risen by 351, or 29 percent, since 1990. Both state and federal prisons are filled beyond capacity. State prisons overall operate at capacity or up to 15 percent more inmates than they have room for, whereas federal prisons house 31 percent more inmates than capacity (Beck and Harrison, 2001).

The word *prison* probably brings to mind a massive structure with high towers, heavily armed guards and searchlights, and long, bleak hallways of cells. This is one kind of prison, but other kinds of prisons exist. The one just described fits the portrait of a **maximum-security prison,** more commonly called the "big house" (Shelden, 2001). These grim places hold inmates who are thought to be the most violent and dangerous to the outside community. Although maximum-security prisons have vocational and educational programs, their main function is strict monitoring of inmates' behaviors. Several maximum-security prisons in use today were built a century or more ago and include San Quentin in California (just north of San Francisco) and Leavenworth in Kansas. San Quentin opened in 1852 in response to high crime rates following the discovery of gold in California in 1848 and the resulting influx of thousands of men

> **prisons** penal institutions that house offenders who have been found guilty of felonies and are sentenced to at least 1 year of incarceration

> **maximum-security prison** large, forbidding prison that holds inmates who are thought to be the most violent and dangerous to the outside community

Maximum-security prisons hold inmates who are thought to be the most violent and dangerous to the outside community. They feature one cell after another on long, bleak hallways.

seeking their fortunes. Inmates built the prison during the day and slept on a prison ship at night. It held both male and female inmates until 1933 when a separate women's prison was built. Today, San Quentin serves as death row for all California men who have been sentenced to death, and, 150 years after it was built, contains some 6,000 inmates behind its ominous walls. Several other big houses built years ago have closed, but some, such as Alcatraz, remain notorious in popular lore.

Medium-security prisons hold property offenders and other inmates who are considered less dangerous than those in maximum-security institutions. Instead of high towers and walls with armed guards and searchlights, they typically are enclosed with barbed-wire fences. In many of these prisons, inmates live in large rooms, similar to a military barracks or summer camp cabin, rather than in small cells. They are less expensive to build and maintain than maximum-security prisons and usually have more educational and vocational programs and drug and alcohol counseling.

Minimum-security prisons hold inmates, typically property and drug offenders, who are considered the least dangerous and who are serving the shortest sentences. They typically lack even fences and instead rely on locked doors and various electronic equipment to detect escape attempts. Inmates are allowed much more freedom of movement than their counterparts in the other types of prisons and are offered a greater number of programs and services. Some offenders from more secure prisons who are ready to be released back into the community are put in minimum-security institutions for a short period of time to begin the transition process.

The number of state and federal correctional facilities at different levels of security is listed in Table 12.1. As you can see, just under half of all state facilities are minimum security, compared to almost three-fourths of federal facilities. Similarly, only 14 percent of state inmates are in minimum-security facilities, compared to 57 percent of federal inmates. As these numbers suggest, federal facilities house inmates who overall are considered less dangerous than those in state facilities. The major reason for this is that federal prisons hold inmates convicted of federal crimes. These crimes tend to be property crimes, white-collar crimes, and drug offenses. Most violent crimes fall under state jurisdiction, and people convicted of such crimes end up in state prisons.

Jails

Jails are important for many reasons, not the least of which is that so many people enter them in any given year. Despite their significance, jails have received much less attention than prisons (Klofas, 1998). Accordingly, this section outlines some important facts and issues about jails.

---

medium-security prisons prisons that hold property offenders and other inmates who are considered less dangerous than those in maximum-security institutions

minimum-security prisons prisons that hold inmates, typically property and drug offenders, who are considered the least dangerous and who are serving the shortest sentences

---

table 12.1 | U.S. Correctional Facilities and Security Levels, 1995

	STATE				FEDERAL			
	Facilities	%	Inmates	%	Facilities	%	Inmates	%
Maximum security	289	21	354,500	38	9	7	9,272	11
Medium security	438	32	454,057	48	25	20	26,156	32
Minimum security[a]	648	47	133,085	14	91	73	46,502	57
Total	1,375		941,642		125		81,930	

[a]Minimum-security facilities include 291 state and 13 federal facilities that are *community-based* facilities, such as halfway houses and work-release centers. The remaining facilities in the table are *confinement* facilities (prisons).

Source: Data from Stephan, James J. 1997. *Census of State and Federal Correctional Facilities, 1995.* Washington, DC: Bureau Justice Statistics, U.S. Department of Justice.

Jails are run by towns, cities, and counties and hold several kinds of offenders and other individuals: (1) people who have been arrested and are awaiting arraignments, trials, or other procedures (about half of all jail inmates); (2) people convicted of misdemeanors and sentenced to less than 1 year behind bars; (3) people convicted of felonies who are waiting to be sentenced; (4) people convicted of felonies and sentenced to more than 1 year behind bars but for whom no room in a state prison is available; (5) inmates who have completed their sentences and are awaiting release to the community; (6) individuals held for contempt of court, for military legal action, or for protective custody; (7) mentally ill persons awaiting movement to a health facility; and (8) inmates awaiting transfer to other correctional facilities (Stephan, 2001). About 3,365 jails exist throughout the United States, and as many as 16 million Americans (including repeat admissions) enter a jail each year for at least one of these reasons. As a result, "the jail touches more people's lives than does any other form of correctional service" (Klofas, 1998, p. 245).

Conditions in jails are worse than those in prisons in many ways. They generally are more overcrowded and dilapidated. Because jails are intended for short-term confinement, they also lack the vocational, educational, and drug treatment programs found in state and federal prisons. A special problem of jails is that they confine people awaiting arraignments or trials (and thus in *pretrial detention*) with those already convicted of crimes, some of which are quite serious. Although the pretrial detention inmates have not yet been convicted of any crime and some may well be innocent of any wrongdoing, their confinement with convicted criminals subjects them to the possibility of violent assaults and negative peer influences, to use some sociological jargon. Even if they emerge from jail unharmed physically, they may emerge very much harmed emotionally and perhaps more apt to commit crime than before they were placed in jail. As sociologist John Irwin (1998, p. 228), a former prison inmate himself, observes, "The experiences prisoners endure while passing through the jail often drastically influence their lives."

An interesting controversy about jails concerns the kinds of people they confine. Irwin (1998, p. 228) disputes the common view that jails hold "a collection of dangerous criminals." Instead, he says, most jail inmates have committed only minor offenses. More tellingly, he says, they come overwhelmingly from the ranks of the poor and unemployed and share two characteristics: detachment and disrepute. By *detachment,* Irwin means that they have few or no ties to conventional social networks or institutions, and, by *disrepute,* he means that they are perceived as offensive and threatening. These characteristics led Irwin to call the kinds of people in jail the *rabble*. As such, Irwin argues, the police monitor the activities of the rabble very closely and are especially apt to arrest them for petty crimes, such as public drinking and rowdy behavior. These observations led Irwin to conclude that the major goal of the jail is to "manage society's rabble," more because they are perceived as offensive than because they are actually dangerous. This leads to a double standard in law enforcement, adds Irwin: "The police are always on the lookout for purse-snatching, theft from cars, and shoplifting, but they almost never patrol used-car lots or automobile repair shops to catch salesmen or repairmen breaking the law, and they never raid corporate board rooms to catch executives fixing prices" (p. 229).

John A. Backstrand and colleagues (Backstrand, Gibbons, and Jones, 1998) dispute Irwin's contention that most jail inmates are only petty offenders. In a study of jail inmates in Oregon and Washington, Backstrand and colleagues found that more than 82 percent of the inmates in the jails they studied had been charged with or convicted of felonies. Because so few had been accused of only petty offenses, Backstrand and colleagues (1998, p. 241) concluded that their findings cast "a good deal of doubt on Irwin's claims." At the same time, they agreed with Irwin that members of the rabble sometimes are arrested and placed in jail even in the absence of serious lawbreaking.

The Size and Cost of Corrections

As noted in Chapter 11, the United States has by far the highest incarceration rate of any Western democracy. At midyear 2001, the nation's prisons housed 1,328,063 inmates: 1,187,322 in state prisons and 140,741 in federal prisons. The total number

Construction of new jails and prisons, such as the $43 million prison in Wisconsin shown in this photo, has added considerably to the cost of the U.S. criminal justice system.

of prisoners was up by more than 550,000 inmates, or more than 71 percent, from the total of 773,905 prisoners in 1990 (Figure 12.1). Not surprisingly, the rate of incarceration had also risen: at midyear 2001, it was 472 prisoners for every 100,000 U.S. residents, compared to the 1990 rate of only 292 per 100,000 (Beck et al., 2002).

Turning to jail inmates, at midyear 2001 the nation's jails housed 631,240 inmates, representing an increase of about 53 percent from the 1990 figure of slightly more than 400,000 inmates (Figure 12.2) (Beck et al., 2002). More than 70,000 offenders were also supervised by jail authorities outside jail facilities (for example, in home detention or work programs). As high as they are, these figures mask the fact, noted previously, that up to 16 million people enter jails in any given year for at least one of the many reasons that jails hold offenders. Adding the number of jail inmates to the number of prison inmates brings the total number of U.S. inmates to almost 2 million and the U.S. incarceration rate up to 690 per 100,000 residents, by far the highest in the Western world.

figure 12.1

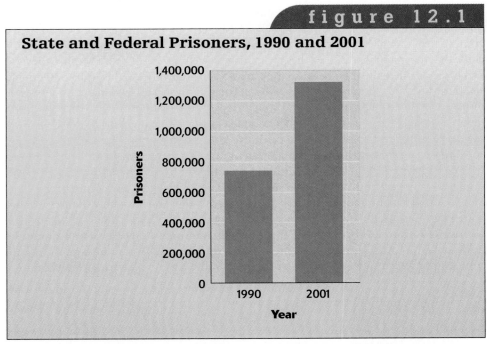

State and Federal Prisoners, 1990 and 2001

Source: Data from Beck, Allen J., Jennifer C. Karberg, and Paige M. Harrison. 2002. *Prison and Jail Inmates at Midyear 2001.* Washington, DC: Bureau of Justice Statistics, U.S. Department of Justice.

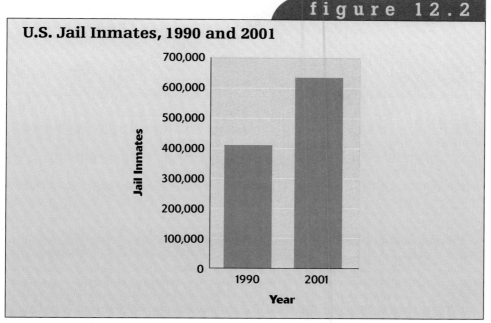

U.S. Jail Inmates, 1990 and 2001

figure 12.2

Source: Data from Beck, Allen J., Jennifer C. Karberg, and Paige M. Harrison. 2002. *Prison and Jail Inmates at Midyear 2001*. Washington, DC: Bureau of Justice Statistics, U.S. Department of Justice.

With so many prison and jail inmates, it is not surprising that the correctional enterprise employs many people and costs billions of dollars. In 1999, the latest year for which data are available, the U.S. corrections system employed about 716,000 people, almost two-thirds at the state level (Table 12.2), and expended more than $49 billion (Table 12.3). This expenditure amounted to about $175 for every person in the United States and represented about an 80 percent increase since 1990 (Gifford, 2002).

As these figures suggest, the corrections system in the United States is a huge enterprise that increased every year during the past three decades. As with any expensive effort, it is important to determine whether dollars are being wisely spent. This determination is no less important for corrections. What is our society "getting" for the billions of dollars it spends each year on corrections? Is the expenditure worthwhile? We return to this issue later in the Under Investigation feature on the surge in incarceration, but first we discuss two other important correctional issues: (1) the privatization of prisons and jails and (2) the death penalty. Although there are no easy answers to the questions they raise, we hope this discussion will help you better understand the issues and begin arriving at your own conclusions.

table 12.2

U.S. Corrections Employees, 1999

Federal	30,974
State	456,753
Local	228,846
Total	716,573

Source: Data from Gifford, Sidra Lea. 2002. *Justice Expenditure and Employment in the United States, 1999*. Washington, DC: Bureau of Justice Statistics, U.S. Department of Justice.

table 12.3	Direct Expenditures for U.S. Corrections, 1999
Federal	$ 4,080,000,000
State	34,680,000,000
Local	15,096,000,000
Total	$49,007,000,000

Source: Data from Gifford, Sidra Lea. 2002. *Justice Expenditure and Employment in the United States, 1999.* Washington, DC: Bureau of Justice Statistics, U.S. Department of Justice.

Privatization

privatization in corrections policy, the involvement of private corporations in the building and operation of prisons and jails

The building and operation of prisons and jails are ordinarily public enterprises performed by employees of the local, state, and federal governments. In recent decades, however, prisons have undergone increasing **privatization.** This process involves two aspects: (1) outsourcing corrections functions such as food service to private companies (similar to what many colleges and universities now do); and, more importantly, (2) private companies building and operating prisons and jails. For better or worse, privatization has aroused much controversy.

History of Privatization

The roots of modern privatization go back to the earliest days of the U.S. colonies in the early 1600s (Austin and Irwin, 2001). Back then, private merchants transported convicted felons from England to Virginia and the other colonies in exchange for the right to sell them as indentured servants. During the next two centuries, privately operated jails were common, and private facilities continued to operate well past the Civil War. In the postbellum South, this system of privatization took an ugly turn when the southern states leased out many of their prisons and inmates to private companies. These companies charged the inmates (or their families) for housing them and also required them to work as laborers, with any profits returning to the company.

Although this system enabled the southern states to handle the surge in prisoners resulting from economic problems in the South after the Civil War, it was also, according to one scholar, "corrupt and brutal. Prisoners' rights were nonexistent, conditions inhumane, and any notion of rehabilitation or improvement inconsequential" (Harding, 1998, p. 626).

By the 1920s, privatization of corrections had faded in the South and elsewhere. There were three reasons for its demise (Harding, 1998; Tipp, 1991). First, acceptance of privately run prisons gave way to the view that the government should handle offenders' custodial care because the offenders violated governmental laws. Second, the living conditions in many private facilities were horrid: "Prisoners were little more than slave laborers, subject to the brutality and greed of the jailer and the turnkeys, and were housed and maintained in cramped and filthy conditions" (Tipp, 1991, p. 159). Third, the growing interest in rehabilitation (noted previously) in the early 1900s led public officials to conclude that rehabilitation was not possible amid the conditions in private prisons.

Privatization Today

Although privatization essentially disappeared for several decades after the 1920s, it regained popularity in the early 1980s when the increasing number of prisoners led states to worry about the costs of prison construction and operation. Sensing a potential source of profits, private corporations began to build prisons and jails and to offer to operate ones that already existed. At midyear 2001, more than 90 private facilities (all built since 1980) in 31 states, Washington, DC, and the federal system held almost 95,000 inmates, or 6.8 percent of all state and federal inmates (Austin and Irwin, 2001).

Although the U.S. proportion of privately held inmates is relatively low, they do involve tens of thousands of inmates and, perhaps more significantly, vary around the country. For example, although private facilities hold 8.8 percent of all inmates in the southern states, they hold only 1.8 percent of all inmates in the northeastern states. Moreover, they hold more than 30 percent of the inmates in four states: Alaska, Montana, New Mexico, and Oklahoma (Beck et al., 2002).

For some companies, new prison construction has meant big business during the past two decades. With names such as the Corrections Corporation of America, they have paid for building new prisons and run them once they were built. As private enterprises, they claim to have lower construction and operation costs than are possible when states pay for prison construction and operation. As a result, many states have been very happy to let these companies build and run at least a few of the prisons within their borders.

Concerns about Privatization

On the surface, privatization seems like a mutually beneficial arrangement for both the corporations and the states. But critics worry about such a system of "punishment for profit" (Austin and Irwin, 2001; Bates, 1998; Lilly and Deflem, 1996; Shichor, 1995, p. 1). Perhaps their most important concern centers on inmate safety and welfare. Because the corporations that build and run private prisons naturally have profit as their most important motive, they may feel constrained to cut corners on operation costs and on screening and training guards and thus put their inmates at risk for abuse and neglect.

Although private prisons are not necessarily worse than public ones in this respect (Harding, 1998), examples of such abuse abound in private facilities. A study of Oklahoma prisons found that twice as many "serious" incidents occurred in private prisons as in public institutions over a 3-year period (Slevin, 2001). In 1997, guards at a private facility in Texas were videotaped as they fired stun guns at inmates. They had been hired even though they had abused inmates in previous jobs as guards (Welch, 1999). More recently, in March 2000, a state judge in New Orleans removed six adolescent boys from a juvenile prison run by the Wackenhut Corrections Corporation after determining that they had been "brutalized by guards, kept in solitary confinement for months and deprived of shoes, blankets, education and medical care," according to a news report (Butterfield, 2000, p. A14). In one incident, a youth who was wearing a colostomy bag after having an operation for gunshot wounds was forced to lie on his stomach with a guard's knee in his back. Investigators also found that one-fourth of the inmates had been injured in a 2-month period by untrained guards who threw them into walls or onto the ground. They often lacked clean underwear for days and would even fight for their share of newly washed clothes. Investigators found that the company had tried to save money by neglecting to provide sufficient food, clothing, educational programs, and medical treatment for the prison's inmates and had also failed to provide sufficient training for its guards. It had even hired guards with arrest records because background checks would have cost too much money. As one inmate put it, "Wackenhut was using us kids to make money." The news report said that "this situation raises a fundamental question about privately run prisons: Can corporations operate them more efficiently than state governments without skimping on essential services and proper training" (p. A14)?

Critics of privatization also question whether private prisons are more cost efficient to build and operate. In a capitalist economy, the free-enterprise system theoretically ensures that competition between companies to provide goods and services will help keep prices as low as possible. Yet if only a few companies are competing, such competition is minimized, keeping prices higher. That is the situation today in the private corrections industry because only two companies controlled three-fourths of the market at the end of the 1990s (Welch, 1999). Beyond this problem, factors such as the size and age of prisons may affect their operating costs at least as much as whether the prison is publicly or privately run. Investigating this issue, a recent study concluded that "private prisons were no more cost-effective than public prisons" (Pratt and Maahs, 1999, p. 358). Another study by the Oklahoma Corrections Department found that private cells were actually slightly more expensive than public ones (Slevin, 2001).

A third concern is that the private corrections industry naturally does its best to encourage the increased use of imprisonment and to discourage alternatives to incarceration. The industry's emphasis on imprisonment stems from its desire for increased profit and not from what may be best in the long run for offenders, taxpayers, and public safety. Guards and wardens at private prisons end up with a terrible conflict of interest. Because they receive stock options in the companies that run their prisons, they ultimately profit if they discipline prisoners and thus revoke the "good time" that lowers the number of days inmates stay in prison. Not surprisingly, such loss of good time is precisely what happens. In one New Mexico private prison, for example, prisoners lost "good time" eight times more often than their counterparts at a public state prison (Welch, 1999).

By the end of 2000, the private prison industry was experiencing financial and public relations problems (Haddad, 2000; Slevin, 2001). The stock value of several prison companies had declined, and public officials' faith in private prisons had been shaken by the escape of several dozen inmates from these prisons since their inception. The industry had built several prisons "on speculation," hoping that they would then win contracts from state agencies. When they did not win as many contracts as they anticipated, thousands of their prison cells remained empty. One example was in Georgia: The Corrections Corporation of America (CCA) had built a $45 million private prison that remained empty. CCA's stock, which traded at $44 per share in 1998, was only 18 cents per share at the end of 2000. Despite these problems, financial analysts predicted that the private prison industry would continue to grow, if more slowly than before, and remain profitable, and that it was likely to branch out into institutions for the elderly and for people with drug problems and mental disorders.

The Death Penalty

Although this chapter discusses incarceration, the ultimate punishment is death. The United States is the only Western democracy that executes offenders; other democracies decided decades ago that the death penalty violates modern standards of punishment. Partly because the United States stands alone and partly because executions raise so many issues for any system of punishment, the death penalty continues to be one of the most hotly debated topics in criminal justice today. We examine the issues it raises next.

History of Executions

Executions go back at least to the days of the Old Testament. Many passages there support the idea that people who commit various offenses, not only murder but many others, should themselves be put to death. According to Genesis 9:5–6, "Who so sheddeth a man's blood, by man shall his blood be shed: for in the image of God made he man," and Deuteronomy (19:21) gives us the familiar phrase: "Life for life, eye for eye, tooth for tooth, hand for hand, foot for foot." Exodus and other books of the Old Testament call for the death of someone who commits any one of at least 21 offenses, including adultery, bestiality and sodomy, blasphemy, cursing or hitting parents, defiling sacred objects or places, homosexuality, incest, kidnapping, murder, premarital sex, prostitution, witchcraft, and working on the Sabbath (Costanzo, 1997).

Although the Bible apparently supports executions, "there is much even in the Old Testament to suggest that killing may not be the appropriate penalty for murder" (Costanzo, 1997, p. 130). For example, the Old Testament also says that vengeance belongs to the Lord (Psalms 94:1) and that we should love our neighbors as ourselves (Leviticus 19:18). In practice so many procedural restrictions were imposed on the use of the death penalty that it was almost impossible to execute anyone (Costanzo, 1997). Further, as the list of capital offenses in the Old Testament suggests, the Bible contains many beliefs and practices that even very devout people today no longer accept: Few Americans today would say that someone who commits adultery, engages in premarital sex, or works on the Sabbath should be executed. Thus, although the Bible continues to inspire many people, according to many theologians it provides no clear guidance on the morality of executions (Megivern, 1997).

This theological issue notwithstanding, it remains true that executions in ancient times were quite common (Costanzo, 1997; Johnson, 1998). The usual method was stoning. The ancient Greeks and Hebrews required that two witnesses make an accusation before execution by stoning could take place. With no trial, the "offender" would be stripped naked, tied, and pushed from a tall platform by one witness; then the second witness would stone the victim. If the offender managed to survive this initial stoning, the crowd watching the execution would join in the stoning. The ancient Chinese sometimes executed people by cutting away small bits of the victim's flesh for several days.

During the Middle Ages, burning at the stake was a popular method of execution, especially for women. About 300,000 women thought to be witches were burned at the stake or otherwise executed in Europe from the 1400s to the early 1700s (Hoyt, 1981). From the Middle Ages until the early nineteenth century, hanging was a common mode of execution, and capital offenses in England included vagrancy, heresy, rape, witchcraft, murder, and some 45 others. Those hanged in England would often be disemboweled and decapitated, and the rest of their bodies would then be cut into quarters. This yielded five body parts that would be placed around the region to deter criminal behavior. During the eighteenth century, Germany and France executed offenders via the "breaking on the wheel" method. An executioner would tie the offender to a large cart wheel, slowly use an iron bar or similar object to break many bones in the arms and legs, and then strike the heart or throat to kill the offender. It sometimes took up to 2 hours to perform such an execution. England and other nations also executed people by "pressing" them. In this method, a naked prisoner would be tied face up to a floor while heavy weights were put on him or her over a period of several days. The goal was to get the prisoner to confess even if he or she was innocent, but those who refused to confess would finally die from their maltreatment.

Executions in the United States. When English and other settlers came to the New World, they brought the practice of execution with them (Bohm, 1999). Hanging was the preferred method in the colonies. Capital offenses in Puritan Massachusetts included adultery, bestiality, blasphemy, rebellion, and witchcraft, whereas those in North Carolina included slave stealing and helping to free slaves. Virginia had five capital offenses for whites, but 70 for African Americans. One colony, Pennsylvania, founded by William Penn, a Quaker, prohibited capital punishment because it violated Quaker beliefs in the sanctity of life.

During the mid-1800s, a few states, including Rhode Island and Wisconsin, abolished capital punishment, but the death penalty remained on the books throughout most of the country. The number of U.S. executions peaked in the late 1930s but then dwindled through the late 1960s until finally ending altogether by 1967. Public support for executions had waned, and some observers thought that the United States would follow the example of other Western democracies that were beginning to abolish capital punishment during this time: Every democracy that still allowed capital punishment by the 1960s eventually abolished it by the end of the 1990s.

Indeed, a notable U.S. Supreme Court decision in 1972, *Furman v. Georgia* (408 U.S. 238), seemed to put an end to capital punishment. In this decision, the Court ruled that the arbitrary way the death penalty was carried out violated the Eighth Amendment's prohibition of "cruel and unusual punishment" and the Fourteenth Amendment's guarantee of "equal protection." The death penalty, the Court ruled, was thus unconstitutional as it was currently being administered. The Court was particularly concerned that jurors had too much discretion in deciding whether to impose the death penalty.

The Court's ruling left open the possibility that changes in the way the death penalty was administered could allow it to pass constitutional muster. Over the next few years, state legislatures made several such changes in the hope of appeasing the Court. In perhaps the most important change, capital punishment would be allowed only for certain types of murder, and capital defendants would be tried by a jury in two stages. In the first stage, the jury would determine the defendant's guilt or innocence. If the defendant were found guilty, the jury in the second stage would decide whether the death penalty was deserved. In making this decision, the jury would take into account *special circumstances,* such as the way in which the murder was committed, and also *mitigating circumstances,* such as the background of the defendant, that would argue against capital punishment. Accepting these and other changes, the Court ruled in a series of decisions in 1976 that the death penalty was constitutional as long as its administration followed these new guidelines (Bohm, 1999).

This decision allowed executions in the United States to resume. At the same time, public support for the death penalty was rising because the violent crime rate was increasing. The result of the Court's decision and this increase in public support was that both the number of people sentenced to death (and on "death row" in prisons) and the number of executions began to increase rapidly (see Figures 12.3 and 12.4). This increase enabled the total number of executions from 1930 to 2001 to reach 4,608.

The Death Penalty in the United States Today

As Figures 12.3 and 12.4 indicate, more than 3,500 Americans now sit on death row, and the annual number of executions in recent years has exceeded 60. Thirty-eight states and the federal government authorize the use of the death penalty; 12 states and the District of Columbia do not (Figure 12.5). Although three-fourths of the states permit capital punishment, in practice not all these states use it, and a small number of states account for the bulk of executions. In 2000, for example, southern states accounted for 80 of the 85 executions that occurred that year; Texas alone accounted for 40, and Oklahoma for another 11 (Snell, 2001).

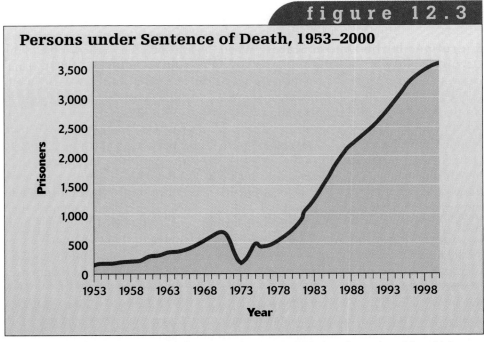

figure 12.3

Persons under Sentence of Death, 1953–2000

Source: Bureau of Justice Statistics, U.S. Department of Justice. Available: http://www.ojp.usdoj.gov/bjs/glance/dr.htm.

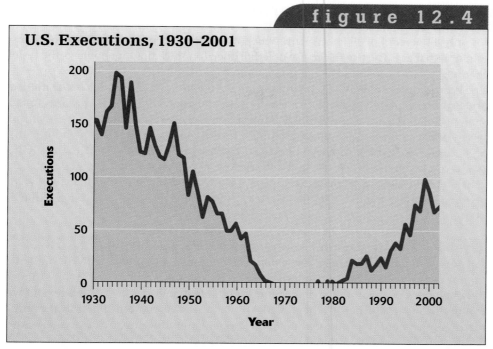

figure 12.4

U.S. Executions, 1930–2001

Source: Bureau of Justice Statistics, U.S. Department of Justice. Available: http://www.ojp.usdoj.gov/bjs/
glance/exe.htm.

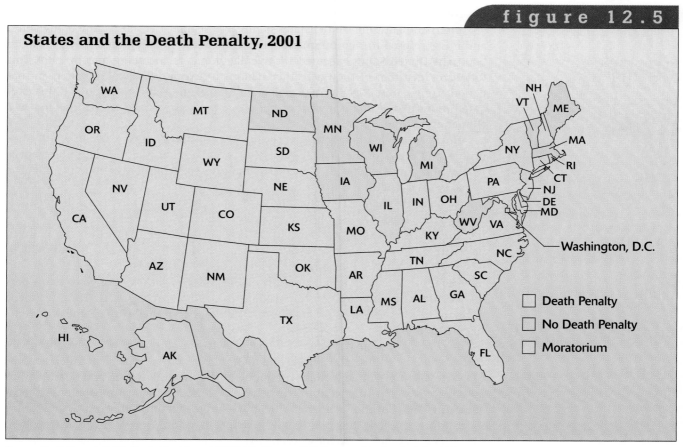

figure 12.5

States and the Death Penalty, 2001

Washington, D.C.

☐ Death Penalty
☐ No Death Penalty
☐ Moratorium

Source: Snell, Tracy L. 2001. *Capital Punishment 2000.* Washington, DC: Bureau of Justice Statistics, U.S.
Department of Justice.

Most executions are now carried out by lethal injection, which accounted for 100 percent (66 out of 66) of the executions in 2001. In 1989, lethal injections accounted for only 44 percent of all executions, which were more often carried out by electrocution or lethal gas. The rise in the use of lethal injection since that time reflects the belief that it is a more humane way of ending a life (Bohm, 1999).

Who is on death row? Compared to the U.S. population, prisoners on death row are disproportionately male, African American, and poor. Of the 3,593 persons under sentence of death at the end of 2000, almost 99 percent were men. About 43 percent were African American (compared to only 13 percent of the general population), and 55 percent were white. Almost 11 percent were Hispanic. Slightly more than half did not have a high school diploma, and only 10 percent had gone to college. About 40 percent of all the people on death row were 24 years old or younger when they were arrested for their capital offense, whereas 2.4 percent were 17 or younger (Snell, 2001).

Juveniles and the Death Penalty. This preceding statistic raises the controversial question of whether executions should be permitted for anyone who committed a capital offense as a juvenile (under age 18). This question reflects the larger issue of how juveniles who commit serious crimes should be treated in the first place, and we explore this issue further in Chapter 14. But because capital punishment is the "ultimate" punishment, this question takes on special importance in any discussion of the death penalty. The U.S. Supreme Court prohibits executions for youths under age 16 at the time of their capital offense (*Thompson v. Oklahoma*, 487 U.S. 815 [1988]), but it allows the individual states to determine whether youths who are 16 or 17 years old at the time of their offenses may be executed. Currently, 13 states permit the death penalty for youths who are age 16, and 4 more permit it for youths who are age 17. Fourteen states stipulate age 18 as the minimum age, whereas seven states do not specify any minimum age (Snell, 2001).

Internationally, the United States stands almost alone in its execution of juveniles, and it has refused to sign international agreements prohibiting them. From 1990 to 2000, the United States executed 14 juvenile offenders, including four in 2000. This total exceeded that of the only other nations to execute juvenile offenders in that period: Congo, Iran, Nigeria, Pakistan, Saudi Arabia, and Yemen. Although China executed more people than any other nation, it banned juvenile executions in 1997 (Rimer and Bonner, 2000).

How old should capital offenders be before it is appropriate to execute them? Supporters and critics of the death penalty for juveniles continue to debate the answer (Rimer and Bonner, 2000; Streib, 2001). Supporters say that some crimes by juveniles are so heinous that the death penalty is a just punishment. The juveniles who commit them, they add, are so brutal and heartless that they have no hope for rehabilitation. Executing them sends a message that their monstrous violence will not be tolerated. As one district attorney put it, "If you do an adult crime, the jury ought to have the option to come back with the death penalty" (Rimer and Bonner, 2000, p. A1). The mother of a teenage girl who was raped and murdered by a 17-year-old male echos this view: "I don't care how old he was. He was old enough to know better. I could pull the switch on him and never have any remorse. He shot her three times in the forehead. He shot her eye out. He shot her in the heart" (Rimer and Bonner, 2000, p. A1).

According to some critics, most teenagers who murder have themselves been victims of childhood abuse and neglect and thus are not fully responsible for their actions. They are also too young to fully comprehend the meaning of life and death and to appreciate the consequences of their behavior. Although the death penalty may be a "quick fix" for youthful violence, it does not address the underlying causes of this violence. More generally, these critics say, juveniles are simply too young to be executed, even if they commit a heinous crime. A district attorney who supports the death penalty for adults shares this view: "It offends my conscience to execute someone who was under 18 at the time of the crime" (Rimer and Bonner, 2000, p. A1).

Executions of the Mentally Retarded. The debate over executions of juvenile offenders hinges partly on the crucial question of whether these offenders are fully responsible for their actions. A similar question arises in executions of the mentally retarded, a diagnosis that applies to about 10 percent of all U.S. death row inmates. Before 2002, 20 of the 38 states that have the death penalty permitted executions of people who are mentally retarded. According to the human rights organization Amnesty International, the United States had executed 35 mentally retarded defendants since 1976, and only the United States, Japan, and Kyrgyzstan (a Central Asian nation that was part of the Soviet Union until 1991) had executed such defendants since 1995.

Although a U.S. Supreme Court ruling in 1989 allowed these executions to continue, the Court reversed itself by a 6 to 3 vote in June 2002 when it declared in *Atkins v. Virginia* (No. 00-8452) that they now were banned by the Eighth Amendment's prohibition against cruel and unusual punishment. The Court's majority ruled that a national consensus had developed in the United States against executions of the retarded and that these defendants do not sufficiently comprehend their actions.

In response, the Court's minority questioned whether the consensus claimed by the majority actually existed (Greenhouse, 2002). In the wake of the Court's ruling, observers noted several legal and practical difficulties in determining which defendants already on death row are, in fact, mentally retarded, and thus should not be executed. For example, because the Court's ruling did explicitly say it applied retroactively to these defendants, it is possible that those who did not raise the issue of retardation during their appeals may thus not be allowed to raise the issue even after the Court's ruling (Duggan, 2002).

The Death Penalty Debate

The controversy over the executions of juveniles is only part of a larger and very heated debate over the death penalty itself. Proponents say, as we noted previously with juveniles, that some crimes are so heinous that the people who commit them deserve to die. In effect, they have forfeited their right to live. Proponents also say that the death penalty saves lives by deterring homicides by would-be murderers and that it saves money because otherwise capital offenders would need to stay in prison for life. Opponents of the death penalty reply that it is wrong in a civilized society for the state to take anyone's life. They add that the death penalty has no general deterrent effect and that executions are actually more expensive than life imprisonment because of increased judicial costs. Opponents also assert that the death penalty is racially discriminatory and that it ensures a great chance of innocent people being convicted of capital crimes and later executed (Smith, 2000).

What does the literature in the field of criminal justice say about all these issues? It has little to say about the moral argument on whether some vicious criminals deserve to die because capital punishment raises moral and religious questions more suited for the fields of philosophy and theology than for a social science such as criminal justice. Certainly, these questions are not easy to answer. As the biblical passages cited earlier suggest, both proponents and opponents of the death penalty may find grounds in the Bible to support their views, and, at best, the Bible is ambiguous on the justness of capital punishment. Despite this ambiguity, most organized religious bodies in the United States have made official statements opposing the death penalty on the grounds that it violates the sanctity of human life and emphasizes revenge over redemption. And despite these statements, most people who consider themselves religious, and most Americans generally, support the death penalty (Bohm, 1999).

Criminal justice researchers have more to say about the other issues in the death penalty debate because these are social science issues on which much empirical evidence exists. What is this evidence?

Does the Death Penalty Deter Homicides? Many studies have tried to answer the question as to whether the death penalty deters homicides, and almost all fail to find a deterrent effect (Bailey and Peterson, 1999). As Robert Bohm (1999, p. 85) summarizes,

> There is no scientific evidence showing conclusively that the death penalty has any marginal deterrent effect. There is no evidence showing that capital punishment deters more than an alternative noncapital punishment, such as life imprisonment without opportunity for parole. Instead, statistics indicate that capital punishment makes no discernible difference on homicide or murder rates.

What is the nature of this evidence? For one, states with the death penalty do not have lower homicide rates than states without it. Relatedly, states that eliminated the death penalty at one time or another in the past century did not see their homicide rates increase, and states that adopted it, including some in the past 30 years, did not see their homicide rates decline.

There is other evidence from studies that examine the effect of well-publicized executions on homicide rates. Although the results are inconsistent, these studies generally fail to find that such executions lower subsequent homicide rates. In fact, some studies find a "brutalization" effect, with the homicide rate *increasing* after publicized executions (Bailey, 1998). Other studies find that whether publicized executions have a deterrent or brutalization effect might depend on what types of homicides are considered. For example, a recent study found that a highly publicized execution in California increased murders between strangers based on arguments but decreased murders of strangers committed in the course of felonies such as armed robberies. These two effects canceled each other out, with the result that these executions had no net effect on the number of California homicides (Cochran and Chamlin, 2000).

If, as seems likely, the death penalty does not deter homicide, the reason may well lie in the type of crime homicide is. For the death penalty to deter a homicide, a would-be murderer has to have the penalty in mind while planning a crime and have time to carefully weigh the possible risk of getting caught and eventually being executed. This, in turn, implies that homicide would have to be the type of crime that is carefully planned by someone who is acting rationally and unemotionally. Yet homicide is *not* such a crime. As discussed in Chapter 3, homicide is best considered a relatively spontaneous crime in which someone becomes angry or vengeful and lashes out without really thinking through the possible consequences for his or her future. If homicide is indeed such a crime, then capital punishment probably cannot deter it. As Bohm (1999, p. 93) points out, "Most murderers, especially capital murderers, probably do not rationally calculate the consequences of their actions before they engage in them."

Does the Death Penalty Save Money? Many people, up to 70 percent of respondents in national surveys in the 1990s, believe the death penalty is cheaper than life imprisonment, and a small number, 13 percent, cite the lower cost of the death penalty as a reason for their support of it (Bohm, 1999). How much does the death penalty cost compared to life imprisonment?

It turns out that the death penalty is actually two to three times *more* expensive than life imprisonment. Capital cases are extraordinarily time consuming and, therefore, costly. Various procedures followed closely at the pretrial and trial stages (for example, a prolonged voir dire, or selection of potential jurors) are not followed in noncapital cases. Appeals following conviction are mandatory, time consuming, and again costly. At all these stages, the state incurs its own costs for prosecution and appeals, and it must almost always also pay these costs for capital defendants, who are typically too poor to afford their own attorneys. As a result, the average capital case costs $2 million to $3 million. In contrast, life imprisonment costs about $1 million in current dollars, assuming 40 years in prison and $25,000 in annual incarceration costs per capital defendant. Thus, the average capital case costs $1 million to $2 million *more* than life imprisonment (Costanzo, 1997).

If we apply these figures to capital cases nationwide, the death penalty becomes very expensive. In 2000, 214 people were sentenced to death. Multiplying this number by the $1 million to $2 million *extra* cost of capital punishment means that these 214 cases will eventually cost their states an extra $214 million to $428 million as compared to life imprisonment. If we apply the extra cost of capital punishment to all 3,593 people on death row at the end of 2000, then this extra cost is between about $3.6 billion and $7.2 billion in current dollars. Capital punishment turns out to be quite costly indeed.

Is the Death Penalty Racially Discriminatory? We saw earlier that the people on death row are disproportionately African American. Does that mean the death penalty is racially discriminatory? Not necessarily. Recall from Chapter 2 that African Americans have higher rates of homicide and other serious street crime. They account for about 49 percent of all arrests for homicide but only about 13 percent of the national population (Federal Bureau of Investigation, 2001). Perhaps their overrepresentation on death row compared to their representation in the population simply reflects their greater arrests rates for homicide.

Many studies have addressed this possibility, and they do find racial discrimination in the application of the death penalty. But the discrimination they find is both subtle and complex. Several, but by no means all, studies find that, when the defendant is African American, prosecutors are more likely to lodge capital charges (without which there could be no death penalty), and jurors are more likely to find the defendant guilty and to sentence him or her to death. But other studies do not find these differences, and thus the evidence of discrimination based on the race of the offender is inconsistent.

However, evidence of discrimination is clearer and more consistent when the race of the *victim* is considered. Simply put, when whites are victims, death penalty charges and sentences are much more likely than when African Americans are victims (Sorensen and Wallace, 1999). In effect, the judicial system places more value on the lives of white victims than on the lives of African American victims.

Research suggests that the death penalty is a more likely outcome when a white person is murdered than when an African American is murdered.

We see evidence of this in at least two ways. The first kind of evidence compares the percentage of white victims of people who are executed to the percentage of all murder victims who are white. For example, about 80 percent of the victims of people executed since the *Furman* decision in 1972 have been white, even though only about 50 percent of all murder victims are white (Bohm, 1999). In Texas, 34 percent of the victims of executed offenders are white women, even though only 1 percent of all murder victims in Texas are white women (Jackson, 2000). In North and South Carolina, 70 percent of the victims of death row inmates are white, compared to only 40 percent of all murder victims in these states (Rimer, 2000).

The second kind of evidence comes from studies of whether death penalty charges and sentences are forthcoming in actual murder cases. In a widely cited investigation, David C. Baldus and colleagues (Baldus, Woodworth, and Pulaski, 1990) found that Georgia prosecutors were about five times more likely to seek the death penalty, and jurors seven times more likely to impose it, when the victim was white than when the victim was African American. A similar study in South Carolina found that, in murder cases with African American defendants, prosecutors were about four times more likely to seek the death penalty when whites were victims than when African Americans were victims (Paternoster, 1984). This body of evidence strongly suggests that the application of the death penalty is racially discriminatory.

How Possible Are Wrongful Executions? In January 2000, the governor of Illinois, conservative Republican George Ryan, suspended executions in his state after newspaper investigations revealed that 13 innocent men had been sentenced to death in Illinois during the past dozen years. Although these men were subsequently released from prison, the governor did not want to risk the possibility of a **wrongful execution** (one where an innocent person is executed).

wrongful execution the execution of an innocent person

His unprecedented action occurred in the wake of reports in several other states of innocent people on death row. Of the more than 6,000 people sentenced to death since *Furman* in 1972, more than 90 have been released from prison after their innocence was established (Rimer, 2001). Two of these men were Michael Ray Graham, Jr., and Albert Ronnie Burrell, who were released in December 2000 and January 2001, respectively, after spending 14 years on death row in Louisiana for the 1986 murders of an elderly couple. They were convicted mainly on the testimony of a "jailhouse snitch" who said the two men had told him they had committed the murders. This witness had spent time in mental hospitals for manic depression and had a history of writing bad checks. No other witnesses saw them at the home of the murdered couple, and ballistics tests of their guns proved negative. An appellate judge later found that the prosecutor had failed to reveal that the jailhouse witness was mentally incompetent (Rimer, 2001).

Another wrongfully convicted death row inmate was Rolando Cruz, who was convicted of murder in 1985 of a young girl in a Chicago suburb despite the lack of any physical evidence linking him to her death. DNA evidence later cleared him, and a police officer later revealed that he had lied under oath when he implicated Cruz in the murder. Cruz spent 10 years on death row. Another man released from death row—after 21 years—was James Richardson, who had been convicted of murdering his seven children. He was released after it was discovered that the prosecutor had hidden evidence of his innocence and that witnesses against him had committed perjury (Berlow, 1999).

Death penalty supporters say these cases prove that the "system works" because these men never were executed and it has never been proven that an innocent person has been executed since *Furman*. Opponents reply that some of these men nonetheless came dangerously close to being executed. They concede that no wrongful execution has been "proven," but they cite several cases in which the guilt of an executed person was at least highly questionable and subject to much more than reasonable doubt (Bedau and Radelet, 1987; Bohm, 1999).

One example was the case of Gary Graham, who was executed in Texas in June 2000 for the 1981 murder of a drug dealer. The only evidence against him was one witness's testimony that was contradicted by two other witnesses whom the defense attorney never called to the stand or even interviewed. The gun used in the murder was never found, and no physical evidence implicated Graham (Miller, 2000). Another such case was that of Roy Roberts, who was executed in Missouri in 1999 for a murder conviction even though "there was no physical evidence, witnesses changed their stories and Roberts passed three lie-detector tests" (Alter, 2000b, p. 31). A third possible wrongful execution was that of James Adams, an African American, who was executed in Florida in 1984 for the 1974 murder of a white man. A witness who said he saw Adams driving his car from the victim's home turned out to have a grudge against Adams because Adams had dated his wife. Hair found inside the victim's hand did not match Adams's hair. These facts were not known during the trial and were uncovered only a month before Adams's execution, too late to save him. Death penalty scholars think that at least 12 innocent people, and probably more, have been wrongly executed since the mid-1970s; this figure represents almost 3 percent of all executions through the late 1990s (Bohm, 1999).

Why are innocent people sentenced to death, and why are some of them executed? As some of the preceding examples suggest, police, prosecutors, and witnesses may lie or conceal evidence. As in noncapital cases, honest mistakes by police or witnesses can also occur. But perhaps the most important reason is that capital defendants are routinely represented by attorneys who are unqualified to handle capital cases. Although such cases, as just noted, require careful preparation and investigation, most of the attorneys for capital defendants are public defenders or assigned counsel with no experience in these cases. Even if they are skilled, they do not have the estimated $250,000 that it takes to defend a capital defendant adequately because states typically provide them no more than about $2,000 to $3,000 in legal expenses.

Worse yet, some of these attorneys have been notoriously inept. They fail to call important witnesses to the stand or to present important evidence, and some even fall asleep during the trial. In one capital trial in Houston, the defense attorney slept throughout an afternoon's testimony. "Every time he opened his eyes," a report later said, "a different prosecution witness was on the stand" (cited in Bohm, 1999, p. 135). The trial judge said the attorney's slumber did not violate his client's right to counsel because "the Constitution doesn't say the lawyer has to be awake" (cited in Bohm, 1999, p. 135). In another case where the lawyer slept throughout the trial, he also did not object when the prosecutor urged the jury to sentence the defendant, who was gay, to death because "sending a homosexual to the penitentiary certainly isn't a very bad punishment for a homosexual" (Herbert, 2000, p. A27). At a hearing after the trial, the defense attorney used derogatory terms in talking about his client and other gay men (Herbert, 2000).

Various reports confirm the inadequate representation of capital defendants. One found that about one-fourth of death row prisoners in Kentucky were defended by attorneys who were later disbarred or resigned to avoid disbarment, and another noted that at least 33 death row inmates in Illinois had attorneys who were later suspended or disbarred (Johnson, 2000; Perez-Pena, 2000). An investigation by the *Chicago Tribune* of 131 executions in Texas while George W. Bush was governor found 43 cases where the defense attorney was later disbarred or disciplined. More generally, it concluded that "Texas has executed dozens of Death Row inmates whose cases were compromised by unreliable evidence, disbarred or suspended defense attorneys, meager defense efforts during sentencing and dubious psychiatric testimony" (Mills, Armstrong, and Holt, 2000, p. A1).

As this brief discussion indicates, wrongful convictions for murder and wrongful executions are indeed possible. A news analysis of this possibility observed that "it's impossible to know just how many other prisoners are living the ultimate nightmare," and, citing the moratorium on executions imposed by the governor of Illinois, asked, "How can the 37 other states that allow the death penalty be so sure that their systems don't resemble the one in Illinois?" (Alter, 2000a, p. 27). Citing continuing concern over the possibility of wrongful executions, Governor Ryan of Illinois commuted the death sentences of the 167 people on death row in his state in January 2003. In a statement accompanying this decision, the governor said, "Our capital system is haunted by the demon of error: error in determining guilt and error in determining who among the guilty deserves to die" (Wilgoren, 2003, p. A1).

FOCUS on Scandinavia and the Netherlands

Prisons and Punishment

As discussed in this and the previous chapter, the United States since the 1970s has reacted to crime with longer prison terms and more prisons. Criminal justice scholars and officials continue to debate the effects of this surge in incarceration, and this chapter reviews the debate.

To help understand this debate further, it is instructive to examine the very different reaction to crime in Scandinavia (Norway, Sweden, Denmark, Finland, and Iceland) and the Netherlands. Consider first some illuminating differences between Americans and the residents of some of these nations in popular support for imprisonment in the 2000 International Crime Victimization Survey (ICVS). The ICVS is a survey given regularly to random samples of the residents of several nations and includes many questions about their experiences as victims of crime and about their views on crime and punishment. The 2000 ICVS included a question asking respondents to name their preferred sentence for a hypothetical 21-year-old male convicted of his second burglary offense (stealing a color TV). Respondents could choose between imprisonment as their preferred sentence, a fine, community service, a suspended sentence, or some other sentence. U.S. residents led the 16 nations in the survey in their preference for imprisonment, with 56 percent of Americans favoring a prison sentence for this recidivist burglar. Much lower public support for a prison sentence for the burglar was found in the Netherlands (37 percent), Sweden (31 percent), Denmark (20 percent), and Finland (19 percent). Americans were thus two to three times more likely than their Scandinavian counterparts to favor a prison sentence for this type of offender.

The ICVS also asked respondents in each nation who favored a prison term how long that term should be. It then calculated the average length of imprisonment preferred by each nation's respondents who preferred a prison term at all. In the United States, the average length was 31 months. This figure was much higher than that for the Netherlands (19 months) or the Scandinavian nations (Sweden, 11 months; Finland, 8 months; and Denmark, 7 months). The average sentence length preferred by Americans was thus three to four times longer than that preferred by their Scandinavian counterparts.

Conversely, residents of the Scandinavian nations and the Netherlands were much more likely than Americans to favor community service for the hypothetical recidivist burglar. About half of the residents of the Scandinavian nations favored this type of punishment (Denmark, 50 percent; Sweden, 47 percent; Fin-

land, 46 percent; and the Netherlands, 30 percent), compared to only 20 percent of Americans. Scandinavians were thus more than twice as likely as Americans to prefer community service.

These international survey data find more popular support for imprisonment in the United States than in the Netherlands and Scandinavia. This difference reflects differences in incarceration rates between these nations. In the Northern European nations, the imprisonment rate per 100,000 population is up to 10 times lower than the U.S. rate. Part of this difference stems from the Northern European nations' lower crime rates, but part also stems from their criminal justice policy, which places much more emphasis on alternatives to prison for most offenders. In these nations, imprisonment is used primarily for violent offenders only, whereas in the United States it is also used for drug and property offenders. Their sentence length for violent offenders is also generally lower than the typical sentence length in the United States for these offenders.

Even as the United States reacted to crime in the past three decades with longer prison terms and more prisons, the Scandinavian nations and the Netherlands made a conscious effort to deal with their own rising crime rates with nonprison alternatives. For example, after its crime rate rose in the 1960s and 1970s, Denmark decided that lengthening prison terms and building more prisons would do much more harm than good. These measures, Danes thought, would be far too expensive and would lead to many more prisoners who would be likely to become more crime prone from their imprisonment than less crime prone. Instead, Denmark shortened prison terms and reduced the number of crimes punishable by imprisonment. These measures made it possible for the country to reduce the costs of incarceration and to spend the saved funds on various community-based corrections, such as counseling.

Finland had a similar experience. In the 1960s, Finland had a higher incarceration rate than other Scandinavian nations even though its crime rate was lower than some of these nations' rates. Its prison sentences were also longer than those in its Scandinavian counterparts. This situation led criminal justice experts in Finland to conclude that its "high prison rate was a disgrace and that the number and length of prison sentences should be reduced" (Shinkai and Zvekic, 1999, p. 100). The Finnish government adopted their view and instituted a series of reforms similar to Denmark's that lowered the imprisonment rate. One of these reforms involved the greater use of fines in lieu of incarceration for theft crimes. Another reform required the time spent in pretrial detention to be subtracted from whatever sentence was imposed after conviction. A third change involved the use of parole. Previously, prisoners were eligible for parole and released from prison only after serving at least 6 months behind bars. In 1976, this minimum term was reduced to 4 months, and, in 1988, it was reduced to only 2 weeks.

In another reform, Finland also abolished the crime of public drunkenness. Before this abolition, people could be fined for being drunk in public. Many could not pay their fines and went to prison. By decriminalizing public drunkenness, Finland helped reduce its number of prisoners. In a related area, Finland also reduced the use of imprisonment for driving under the influence, limiting it to offenders who had high blood alcohol levels and/or had been in accidents.

Like its Scandinavian counterparts, the Netherlands has a "humane prison system" (van Dijk and Waard, 2000, p. 12) that reserves incarceration only for the most serious offenders. Several figures present a striking contrast to the United States. The Netherlands imprisons only 4.2 persons for every 1,000 serious crimes, compared to 22.5 per 1,000 serious crimes in the United States. Because the Netherlands has many more educational, vocational, and other rehabilitative programs for prison inmates than does the United States, its cost per inmate is about 2.6 times greater than the U.S. cost. Even so, its lower imprisonment rate saves it much money overall: The amount it spends on prisons for each crime is only about one-fourth that spent in the United States, and its per capita spending on incarceration is only one-third that of the United States. Prison overcrowding is also not a serious problem in the Netherlands because its prisons operate at about 100 percent of capacity, whereas U.S. prisons operate at 125 percent of capacity.

Another difference between the Netherlands and the United States lies in the legal response to drug users. The Dutch criminal justice system distinguishes between drug users and drug traffickers and views the former as people needing help rather than punishment. Drug users in the Netherlands are arrested only if they are engaging in disorderly conduct or committing other crimes. When they are arrested, they are typically sentenced to treatment programs, not to prison. The Netherlands also distinguishes between "soft drugs," mainly cannabis (marijuana) products, and "hard drugs." Possession of minor quantities of cannabis products for one's own use is generally allowed, and "coffee shops" may sell cannabis products under certain conditions, including no sales to anyone under age 18 and no sales of more than 5 grams to any customer. In contrast, the United States makes about 600,000 arrests per year for marijuana possession, and about one-fourth of all U.S. prisoners are incarcerated for drug offenses, most of them possession rather than trafficking.

Sources: Brydensholt, 1992; Downes, 1996; Ministry of Justice, 2001; Moran, 2000; Shinkai and Zvekic, 1999; van Dijk and Waard, 2000.

summary

1. Incarceration as a form of punishment is a relatively modern phenomenon; it did not really exist before the eighteenth century. Before this time, corporal punishment such as flogging was the norm. Although prisons developed as a reform in the criminal justice system, in practice, they were decrepit institutions that did little or nothing to rehabilitate their inmates.

2. In the United States, prisons were first established in the late eighteenth and early nineteenth centuries. The Pennsylvania model involved constant solitary confinement, whereas the Auburn model allowed prisoners to work and eat together during the day. Nineteenth-century U.S. prisons suffered from overcrowding, filth and lack of sanitation, and abuse by guards. A prison reform movement after the Civil War helped improve prison conditions and prison life, although poor conditions continued to exist. Reform efforts and a renewed focus on rehabilitation continued past the middle of the twentieth century, when a growing crime rate led to a decreased emphasis on rehabilitation and a greater focus on harsher punishment.

3. When prisons first began to be used, women and girls were initially housed with male inmates. There they were subject to sexual abuse by the male inmates and also by prison guards. The women's and prison reform movements after the Civil War em-

phasized the need to build separate institutions for female inmates. Although these institutions helped reduce sexual abuse, they were less funded than male institutions and had fewer training, treatment, and other programs. That problem continues to exist today.

4. Prisons house offenders who have been found guilty of felonies and sentenced to at least 1 year of incarceration. They are run by the 50 states, by the federal government, and by private companies; almost 1,700 prisons exist at all levels. The three major types of prisons are maximum-security, medium-security, and minimum-security institutions. Jails are run by towns, cities, and counties. They house several kinds of offenders, including people awaiting arraignment, trial, or some other procedure; people sentenced for misdemeanors to less than 1 year behind bars; people convicted of felonies and waiting to be sentenced; people convicted of felonies and sentenced to more than 1 year behind bars but for whom there is no room in a state prison; and others. About 3,360 jails exist throughout the United States, and as many as 16 million Americans (including repeat admissions) enter a jail each year for at least one of these reasons.

5. The United States has the highest incarceration rate of any Western democracy and an incarceration rate that has risen dramatically during the past three

decades. The corrections system employs more than 700,000 people and costs almost $50 billion annually.

6. Privatization involves building and operating prisons by private companies. Although privatization was meant to save the states money, the available evidence indicates that they are not cost-effective for the states. Concerns about privatization include inmate safety and welfare and the involvement of private prison companies in promoting increased incarceration.

7. The death penalty goes back to ancient times and has been used in the United States since colonial times. The United States is now the only Western democracy to retain and use the death penalty, and both the number of people on death row and the number of executions have risen since a series of U.S. Supreme Court decisions in the 1970s affirmed the constitutionality of capital punishment as long as certain procedures were followed. Critics of the death penalty assert that it does not deter homicide, that it costs more than life imprisonment, that it is racially discriminatory, and that wrongful convictions and executions are very possible.

key terms

incarceration
jail
maximum-security prison
medium-security prisons
minimum-security prisons

penitentiaries
prisons
privatization
wrongful execution

questions for investigation

1. Consider flogging as a punishment. Do you think it is less humane than incarceration?

2. Discuss the various possible reasons for inmate abuse in the early prison models discussed in this chapter.

3. Discuss reasons why female penal institutions are less funded for various programs than men's institutions. What is necessary to correct this problem?

4. Look up a maximum-security prison (e.g., Leavenworth or San Quentin) on the Internet. Describe the features it uses to monitor inmates' behavior. What educational or treatment programs are available to inmates?

5. This chapter notes that the U.S. corrections system employs more than 700,000 people. Do some research on the Internet to find out what jobs these people perform, what training they receive for their jobs, how their job performance is monitored and evaluated, and how much they are paid. What conclusions can you draw from your research? One site to start your investigation is http://www.drc.state.oh.us/web/ocac.htm.

6. What is your opinion of the "punishment for profit" venture? For further information on perhaps the most notable company in prison privatization, go to the Web site of the largest corrections company, the Corrections Corporation of America. Its URL is http://www.correctionscorp.com.

7. Do you think that the death penalty should be retained or abolished? Explain your answer.

IT'S YOUR CALL...

1. Suppose you are a state legislator who is running for reelection. The crime rate in your state has been rising for the past 3 years even though your state has built three new prisons during the past decade at a cost of more than $250 million. You think that other methods of reducing crime must be pursued, but, at the same time, your opponent in the election is calling you soft on crime for not yet

declaring your support for the construction of yet another prison. Will you decide to support this prison's construction? Why or why not?

2. Although you generally favor the death penalty, you have never really given it that much thought. You are called to jury duty and serve on the jury for a case in which the defendant was accused of fatally shooting a gas station attendant during an armed robbery. The jury finds him guilty of first-degree murder and then must decide whether he will be executed or, instead, spend the rest of his life in prison. What are your thoughts as the jury prepares to hear arguments during this sentencing phase of the case?

UNDER
Investigation

The Surge in Incarceration

We have noted in Chapters 11 and 12 the great surge in incarceration that has highlighted U.S. corrections policy since the 1970s. To reiterate briefly, in 1970 the number of U.S. prison and jail inmates was about 326,000. At midyear 2001, only 3 decades later, it was almost 2 million, an increase of about 800,000 since 1990 alone. In 1970 the incarceration rate was about 160 inmates for every 100,000 Americans; today the rate has more than quadrupled to almost 700 per 100,000 residents. About 6.5 million American adults, or 3.1 percent of the adult population, are now under some form of correctional supervision; this proportion rises to about one-third of African American males in their 20s. Corrections now cost us almost $50 billion per year. In this section, we outline the reasons for this surge in incarceration and then examine some of its effects.

Reasons for Rising Incarceration

Why has incarceration risen during the past few decades? It would make sense to think that a rise in the crime rate is an important reason, but that does *not* seem to be true. During the 1990s, for example, the crime rate fell by about 22 percent overall, but the number of prison and jail inmates still increased by about 67 percent. Examining the tripling of the prison inmate population from 1980 to 1996, a recent study concluded that crime rate increases explained only 12 percent of the growth in the prison population during that time. Policy changes in the sentencing of offenders instead accounted for the remainder of this growth (Blumstein and Beck, 1999).

Three policy changes seem especially important (Blumstein and Beck, 1999; Gainsborough and Mauer, 2000). The most important is the implementation, dis-cussed in Chapter 11, of mandatory sentences and other sentencing reforms that make it much more likely that offenders will be incarcerated at all, and incarcerated for longer terms, than was true before the 1970s. These reforms have had their intended effect, and the longer sentences they produce have swelled the nation's prisons and jails. These longer sentences mean that, in any one year, a smaller proportion of inmates is released from prison than was true in the past. As new inmates continue to be admitted to prison, the number of inmates inevitably increases (Beck, 2000).

A second reason is an increase in the number of people on parole who are being returned to prison, either for being arrested or convicted of new offenses or for violating the conditions of their parole. The number of such *parole violators,* for example, rose more than 54 percent from about 134,000 in 1990 to 207,000 in 1998 (Beck, 2000). Surprisingly, the number of *new* court commitments to prison *cannot* be said to account for the sharp rise in the total number of prisoners during the 1990s. The number of new commitments was only 7.5 percent higher in 1998 than 1990, and during the years in between it fluctuated with no clear pattern.

A third reason for the rise in incarceration is the war against drugs that has highlighted U.S. drug policy since the 1980s. We noted previously that about 20 to 25 percent of all prison and jail inmates are behind bars for drug offenses; this figure translates to about 500,000 inmates altogether. These figures were much lower two decades

"A third **reason** *for the* **rise** *in incarceration is the* **war** *against drugs . . ."*

ago. In 1980, for example, just under 24,000 drug offenders were in state and federal prisons, but, by 1999, this number had risen to more than 300,000. Arrests for drug offenses also soared during this same period from about 580,000 in 1980 to almost 1,600,000 by the late 1990s. The nation's war against drugs, then, has helped fuel the rise in incarceration (Blumstein and Beck, 1999; Gainsborough and Mauer, 2000).

The Prison-Industrial Complex. If policy changes account for most of the growth in incarceration, a growing prison-industrial complex, as it is labeled by its critics, has facilitated this growth. Also called the "corrections-commercial complex," this phenomenon is a set of political and economic interests that has encouraged increased spending on imprisonment (Lilly and Deflem, 1996; Schlosser, 1998). The name is adapted from the term *military-industrial complex*, coined by President Dwight D. Eisenhower 40 years ago to describe the combined efforts of military, political, and corporate officials to maximize military spending even when such spending was excessive and dangerous to the welfare of the planet (Eisenhower, 1960).

Critics say a similar situation now exists in the world of incarceration (Christie, 2000; Schlosser, 1998). Many companies provide goods and services for prison construction and operation, and these companies lobby political officials to build more facilities so that they can increase their profits. Meanwhile, these officials are already receptive to such lobbying: They favor more prisons and jails so that they can appear "tough" on crime, and they also realize that these new facilities will bring many jobs to the regions—usually poor, rural areas—where they are built. Just as retired military officers join defense contractors, so do corrections officials now join the companies that build and supply the nation's prisons. According to writer Eric Schlosser (1998, p. 54), this "confluence of special interests . . . has given prison construction in the United States a seemingly unstoppable momentum." This momentum, he notes, has its own "inexorable logic": If crime is rising, we need to build more prisons; if crime is falling, we need to build more prisons to ensure that it keeps falling.

Whether this reasoning makes sense, of course, depends on how much imprisonment does, in fact, lower crime rates and at what cost. We now consider these issues.

Effects of Rising Incarceration

The surge in incarceration has placed millions of Americans under correctional supervision and cost the nation tens of billions of dollars. These consequences are easy

> "The surge in incarceration has . . . cost the nation tens of billions of dollars."

to document. Are they worth it? Part of the answer to this question depends on your view of the proper goals of sentencing discussed in Chapter 11. But part of the answer must also depend on an understanding of how successful the incarceration boom has been in keeping society safe and also on an understanding of its other "collateral effects." To aid your understanding of all these effects, we examine here the impact of the surge in incarceration on the crime rate and on its most important side consequences, including its disproportionate impact on African Americans.

Impact on the Crime Rate. In Chapter 11, we presented a theoretical argument on why increasing incarceration cannot have large deterrent or incapacitation effects on the nation's crime rate. However, the experience of the 1990s suggests that such effects may be possible: Incarceration *increased* (by 67 percent), and the crime rate *decreased* (by 22 percent). This correlation has led several observers to claim that rising incarceration played a dominant role in the crime rate decrease during the 1990s by having large incapacitation effects (Witkin, 1998). If they are right, then incarceration may be worth the money it costs, and the nation would be wise to continue to build more prisons and to put more inmates in them.

However, according to other observers, the conclusion of large incapacitation effects during the 1990s is too simple, and they present several kinds of evidence to support their skepticism. For example, the states with the largest increases in incarceration in the 1990s actually had *smaller* crime rate declines than the states with the lowest increases in incarceration (Gainsborough and Mauer, 2000). Further, although the U.S. incarceration rate has increased steadily since the 1970s, its crime rate has fluctuated. It declined and then rose during the 1980s, for example, even though incarceration soared steadily during that time. Although the crime rate finally fell during the 1990s as incarceration continued to rise, other factors were probably at work, including a robust economy, stabilizing crack cocaine trafficking in our major cities, and the aging of the large baby boom generation, whose sheer size had helped fuel the crime rate increase during the 1960s (Butterfield, 2000a; Fletcher, 2000). Such evidence leads The Sentencing Project, a national nonprofit criminal justice research and advocacy organization, to find "little support for the contention that massive prison construction is the most effective way to reduce crime" (Gainsborough and Mauer, 2000, p. 3). If this conclusion is correct, then incarceration may *not* be worth the money it costs, and the nation would be wise to develop nonprison alternatives to prevent and address the crime problem.

Where does the truth lie? How effective has our surge in incarceration been in reducing crime, especially during the 1990s? On this as on so many other issues in criminal justice, we may never know the exact answer, but a recent series of studies sponsored by the National Consortium on Violence Research and the Harry Frank Guggenheim Foundation began to shed some light on the question. Published in an edited collection called *The Crime Drop in America* (Blumstein and Wallman, 2000), these studies examine the many possible causes of the crime drop during the 1990s. In general, they support the view that the thriving economy during that decade, the stabilizing of crack cocaine trafficking, and changing demographics were the most important reasons for the crime drop in that decade.

Two of these studies focused specifically on the extent to which increasing imprisonment during the 1990s also helped lower the crime rate. One concluded that "the prison buildup was responsible for about one-fourth of the crime drop. Other factors are responsible

"... *imprisonment* is *still* 'an incredibly inefficient means of reducing crime'"

for the vast majority of the crime drop" (Spelman, 2000, p. 123). Although this study did find some incapacitation effects, its author concluded that imprisonment is still "an incredibly inefficient means of reducing crime" (Spelman, 2000, p. 124).

The second study found that rising incarceration accounted for slightly more than 25 percent (or 100 homicides per year) of the drop in homicides during the first half of the 1990s. This study's author, Richard Rosenfeld, calls his finding "good news," but notes its "huge price tag," as the $40 billion now spent on corrections reduces the money that could be spent on education, health, employment, child welfare, and other areas that could have large crime preventive effects. He adds that each homicide averted during the early 1990s by incarceration cost more than $13 million per year in prison costs. Thus, the 100 homicides averted annually during this period cost

more than $1 billion per year. This expenditure leads Rosenfeld to ask, "Would we better off if the $1 billion were spent on preschool programs, parent training, vocational training, drug treatment, and other promising prevention programs" (Rosenfeld, 2000, p. 151)?

The body of research on the incapacitation effects of the surge in incarceration thus yields several conclusions. First, rising incarceration has probably had small but still significant effects on the crime rate, especially during the 1990s when incarceration had reached such high levels that it was bound to have some effect. Second, any effect that incarceration had in reducing crime during the 1990s was much smaller than that of the other factors previously cited, including a thriving economy and changing demographics. Third, incarceration is extremely expensive and thus a very cost-inefficient way of lowering the crime rate. Most criminal justice scholars believe that the billions of dollars spent on incarceration now and during the past few decades would be much more effective in lowering the crime rate were they spent instead on crime prevention programs such as early childhood intervention programs and on drug treatment and other programs for convicted offenders (Greenwood, 1998; Sherman et al., 1998).

Some Collateral Consequences. Sometimes a well-intended policy has untended collateral effects that indicate the policy is doing more harm than good when these effects are considered. Many observers fear that the surge in incarceration is one such policy because they worry about the effects of increasing incarceration on *future* crime and violence and on other problems in urban communities (May, 2000).

A major reason for this fear is that prisons can be "factories for crime" (Schlosser, 1998, p. 77). While an inmate is in prison or jail, he or she is exposed to many other offenders and squalid living conditions (see Chapter 13). When they leave prison, inmates may often be worse than when they entered.

As noted in Chapter 12, hundreds of thousands of inmates are now being released back to their communities, most of them inner-city neighborhoods, every year, with this number projected to rise to 1 million by the end of this decade. This fact contributes to many problems in these communities (Gainsborough and Mauer, 2000; Hagan and Dinovitzer, 1999; Petersilia, 2000b; Rose and Clear, 1998). Once back home, the ex-inmates have few job prospects because they have few job skills, and up to 60 percent remain unemployed 1 year after their release. These problems drive up unemployment rates in their communities and, as a result, crime rates. The surge in incarceration and massive increase in "prisoner reentry" have led to other problems as well. For example, many inner-city communities have seen large numbers of their young males go to prison or

Under Investigation: The Surge in Incarceration

jail. The absence of so many young adults weakens these communities' social cohesion and thus indirectly raises their crime rates. Other problems from the great increase in prisoner reentry include increased child abuse and family violence, the spread of AIDS and other infectious diseases, and an increase in homelessness.

Many observers especially worry about the collateral effects of the surge in imprisonment on the children of inmates. About 1.5 million children now have a parent in prison, and many others also have a sibling behind bars. The Sentencing Project notes the conse-

> ## "About 1.5 million children now have a parent in prison, and many others also have a sibling behind bars."

quence: "As more young people grow up with parents and siblings incarcerated and a view of time in jail as a normal aspect of one's life experience, the deterrent effect of prison is diminished" (Gainsborough and Mauer, 2000, p. 25). Parental imprisonment also leads to less effective socialization of children and a disruption in their family stability and financial well-being. For all these reasons, children's crime and delinquency rates probably rise when one of their parents is imprisoned. The surge in imprisonment is thus creating a group that has been called the "children of the prison generation," whose increased criminality may soon be coming back to haunt us (Hagan and Dinovitzer, 1999, p. 153).

All these problems indicate that the U.S. incarceration policy of the past few decades may well be exacerbating some of our most serious social problems and ironically contributing to the crime rates our nation has now and will have in the future (May, 2000). These possibilities led Rosenfeld (2000, p. 152) to conclude that "it would be unwise" to use his findings on the incapacitation effects on homicide rates during the early 1990s "to justify the cost of current policy or future increases in incarceration."

Disparate Impact on African Americans.
One of the most serious collateral effects of the surge in incarceration has been its disparate impact on the African American community. This impact has been well documented (Beckett and Sasson, 1999; Mauer, 1999; Miller, 1996; Tonry, 1994). In the past two decades, the number of African Americans under such control increased by a much greater rate than that for any other racial or ethnic group in the United States.

One-third of all African American males in the 20 to 29 age group are now under correctional control: They are in prison or jail, or on probation or parole. If current trends continue, newborn African American males have more than a 25 percent chance of going to prison during their lifetimes, whereas newborn white males have only a 4 percent chance (Bonczar and Beck, 1997).

Because African Americans appear to have higher rates of street crime (see Chapter 2), the rise in incarceration was bound to have a larger impact on this racial group than on others. But this impact has been much greater than what might have been expected because of the nation's "war against drugs" that has relied on arrest and imprisonment as the primary means of combatting drug trafficking, possession, and use. Much of this war has focused on crack cocaine, with much higher mandatory penalties imposed for possession of this drug than for its close cousin, powder cocaine. Whites tend to use powder cocaine, whereas African Americans tend to use crack cocaine. This difference means that the war on drugs with its focus on crack has disproportionately affected African Americans. This fact, in turn, has led to large racial disparities in imprisonment for drug offenses, as African Americans represent 74 percent of those sentenced to prison for drug possession (The Sentencing Project, 2001). From 1986 to 1991 alone, the number of African Americans in state prisons for drug offenses increased by almost 466 percent. During the 1990s, drug offenses accounted for 25 percent of the total growth among African American prisoners versus 18 percent of the total growth among Hispanic inmates and only 12 percent of the growth among white inmates (Beck, 2000). Many critics decry these racial disparities; a former president of the American Society of Criminology called the war on drugs "a major assault on the black community" (Blumstein, 1993, p. 5) and another scholar called it a "search and destroy" mission against African American males (Miller, 1996).

The sheer number of African Americans under correctional supervision has important implications for the African American community. For example, because felons in most states lose their right to vote, about 1.4 million African American men, or 13 percent of all African American men, are currently or permanently disenfranchised. This fact reduces the political clout of African Americans in many states and communities. Further, because so many African Americans are under correctional control, the collateral effects noted in the previous section are apt to be especially severe in African American neighborhoods. The surge in imprisonment, then, has had a serious collateral effect on African Americans, an impact that is likely to have serious repercussions for many years to come.

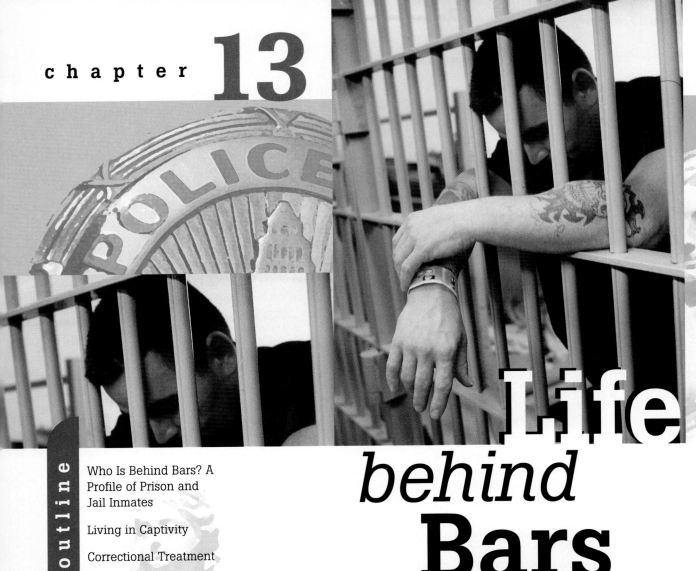

chapter 13

Life behind Bars

1. Describe the profile of a male state prison inmate. Does the profile of a jail inmate differ significantly?

2. What features characterize the prison as a total institution?

3. What is an inmate subculture? What is prisonization?

4. What is it like to live on death row? What is it like to live in a supermax prison?

5. What correctional treatment programs may exist in prisons? How effective are these programs in preventing recidivism?

6. What types of violence occur in prisons, and why do they occur?

7. What is the profile of a female inmate? What special problems do women inmates face in prison? What special needs do women prisoners have?

8. What rights should inmates have in prison?

9. What problems do offenders face when they leave prison?

10. What roles do correctional officers play in prison life?

As noted in Chapter 12, eighteenth-century jails and prisons in Europe and the U.S. colonies were filthy, decrepit, and overcrowded. These living conditions led to epidemics of communicable diseases that killed inmates and guards alike. Rape and other violence and abuse were also quite common. Reformers maintained that these conditions were inhumane and would only harden inmates' criminal tendencies, leading them to be even more of a threat to society when they finally left prison. Eventually, prison reform movements arose on both continents, and over time living conditions in correctional facilities improved.

How far have we come today? Consider Washington D.C.'s Central Detention Facility, more commonly known as the D.C. jail, which holds almost 1,700 inmates and employs about 450 corrections officers. About two-thirds of the inmates are awaiting trial, and the rest are serving misdemeanor sentences or awaiting sentencing. In fall 2000, a troubling report cited substandard conditions at the jail that threatened both inmates and guards. The ventilation system was so dirty that summertime room temperatures would sometimes become dangerously high; the lack of adequate ventilation was also implicated in a case of Legionnaires' disease that almost killed a corrections officer. Many sinks and showers simply did not work.

Laundry machines did not work either, forcing the inmates to wash their clothes and sheets in their toilets. A lack of jumpsuits meant that some inmates would wear only their underwear for days on end. Mice and rats scurried everywhere, and roaches and other insects bred in puddles of water caused by leaky plumbing. One inmate said, "I see rats and mice running from cell to cell, and roaches are everywhere, big ones that crawl in your ears and all over you" (Kovaleski, 2000, p. A1). Since the jail opened in 1976, the report said, "it has been plagued by chronic sanitary and maintenance deficiencies despite protracted litigation on behalf of inmates and extensive intervention by the federal courts" (Kovaleski, 2000, p. A1).

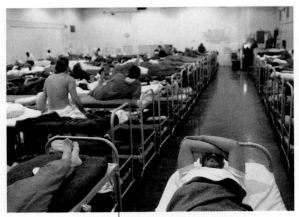

Overcrowding is a serious problem in jails and prisons throughout the United States.

The conditions in the D.C. jail sound eerily similar to those afflicting its eighteenth-century counterparts. Just how typical are these conditions today? And what is their significance for society at large? Perhaps the most important answer to the latter question is this: Virtually all inmates return to society. This unavoidable fact means that what happens to them behind bars is crucial not only for their own welfare but also for public safety when they are released. Understanding what happens behind bars helps us appreciate whether the incarceration experience is more likely to rehabilitate inmates or, instead, to reinforce and even increase their criminality.

Accordingly, this chapter presents a picture of life in prison and jail. First we sketch the characteristics of prison and jail inmates, including their demographic backgrounds and the health and other problems they bring into their facilities. Then we examine what it is like to live in captivity and critically address several issues of the prison and jail experience, including living conditions and problems in health and health care. A separate section focuses on women prisoners, whose numbers are rising rapidly, and who face problems both similar to and different from those of their male counterparts. Separate sections also focus on treatment programs, prison violence, prisoners' rights, and correctional officers.

Criminal justice scholars and officials, politicians, and the public routinely debate many of the issues discussed in this chapter, and our discussion will help you understand the nature of these issues. We begin our exploration of life behind bars with a profile of *who* these inmates are.

Who Is Behind Bars? A Profile of Prison and Jail Inmates

The federal government regularly gathers information on prison and jail inmates. Some of this information comes from correctional authorities, whereas other information is based on surveys of inmates themselves. This body of information includes demographic data, such as the age, sex, and race and ethnicity of inmates, and other personal data, such as their history of drug use and of physical abuse during childhood.

From all these sources, we gain a profile of prison and jail inmates that helps us understand whether their needs are being met as they live behind bars.

Prison Inmates

The U.S. government publishes annual reports on prison inmates (Beck et al., 2002; Beck and Harrison, 2001). At midyear 2001, the nation's prisons housed about 1.4 million inmates, with almost 25 percent of all state prisoners found in only two states: California and Texas.

Gender, Race, Ethnicity. The 1.4 million figure includes vast differences by gender, race, and ethnicity. More than 93 percent of all prisoners are men; slightly less than 7 percent are women. Across the nation, 1 of every 111 men is in prison and 1 of every 1,695 women. These rates vary dramatically by race and ethnicity. For example, about 3,457 of every 100,000 (or almost 3.5 percent) African American males are in prison compared to only 449 of every 100,000 (or 0.45 percent) white males. The incarceration rate of African Americans is thus 7.7 times greater than that for whites. Figure 13.1 depicts these disparities. As this figure shows, African Americans and Hispanics are disproportionately likely to be in prison. There is further evidence of this in Figure 13.2, which depicts the racial and ethnic breakdown of U.S. prisoners.

More than 46 percent of all prisoners are African American compared to just less than 13 percent of the U.S. population; likewise, more than 17 percent of prisoners are Hispanic compared to only about 13 percent of the population. This racial and ethnic disparity in imprisonment is reflected in the high incarceration rates of African American men in their late 20s (ages 25 to 29): Almost 10 percent of African American males in this age group were in prison in 2000 compared to 3 percent of Hispanics in their late 20s and less than 1 percent of whites.

Socioeconomic Backgrounds. Prisoners tend to be undereducated, unemployed, and poor. About 43 percent of state prisoners never graduated high school; this figure

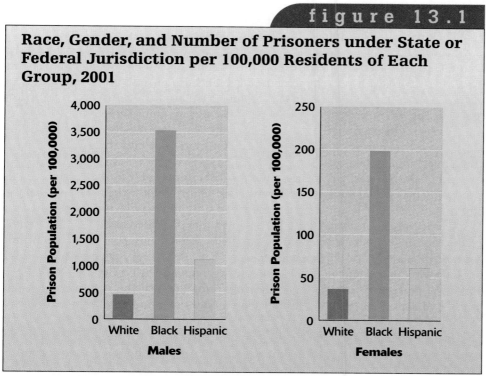

figure 13.1

Race, Gender, and Number of Prisoners under State or Federal Jurisdiction per 100,000 Residents of Each Group, 2001

Source: Data from Harrison, Paige M., and Allen M. Beck. 2002. *Prisoners in 2001.* Washington, DC: Bureau of Justice Statistics, U.S. Department of Justice.

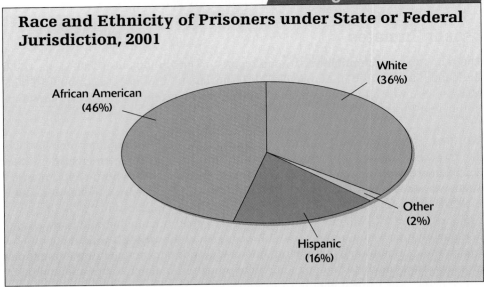

figure 13.2

Race and Ethnicity of Prisoners under State or Federal Jurisdiction, 2001

White
(36%)

African American
(46%)

Other
(2%)

Hispanic
(16%)

Source: Data from Harrison, Paige M., and Allen M. Beck. 2002. *Prisoners in 2001*. Washington, DC: Bureau of Justice Statistics, U.S. Department of Justice.

includes 14 percent who never reached the ninth grade. Another 44 percent have a high school diploma (including those with a GED). Only 3 percent are college graduates (Beck et al., 2000). During the month before their arrest, one-third of state prisoners were unemployed, and only 55 percent were employed full time. More than half of state prisoners in 1991, the latest year for which data were available at the time of this writing, earned less than $10,000 in the year before their incarceration (Beck et al., 1993). Because the poverty level in 1991 for an individual was only about $6,900 (U.S. Census Bureau, 1991), it is apparent that large numbers of prison inmates were living in poverty or near poverty at the time of their arrest. Reflecting this fact, 13 percent of male inmates and 38 percent of female inmates were receiving welfare or other aid before their incarceration (Beck et al., 1993).

Drug Use and Other Problems. The prison population also generally suffers from a series of health-related problems, including alcohol and drug use, a history of victimization (sexual and physical abuse), and various mental disorders and physical illnesses. The federal government has gathered extensive information on the extent of these problems through surveys of prison inmates. The following discussion focuses primarily on inmates in state prisons, who exhibit more problems than their far fewer counterparts in federal prisons.

Although the exact role that alcohol and other drugs play in the commission of crime remains unclear (Dorsey and Zawitz, 1999; Roth, 1994), what *is* clear is that the vast majority of state prisoners had a history of drug use before entering prison. In a 1997 survey of prison inmates, 83 percent said they had tried an illegal drug (marijuana, cocaine or crack, heroin and other opiates, depressants, stimulants, hallucinogens, or inhalants), and 70 percent said they had used drugs regularly. Figure 13.3 breaks down the percentage who had used drugs regularly by type of drug. Moreover, almost 57 percent of inmates said they were using drugs in the month before their arrest, and almost 53 percent said they were under the influence of alcohol or drugs or both at the time of their offense (Beck et al., 2000).

Smaller but still large numbers of state prisoners report having been physically or sexually abused *before* they were put in prison. Almost one-fifth (18.7 percent) reported ever being physically or sexually abused. This figure includes a sizeable gender difference: Whereas "only" 16.1 percent of male inmates reported being abused either physically or sexually, 57.2 percent of female inmates reported being abused (see Figure 13.4). More

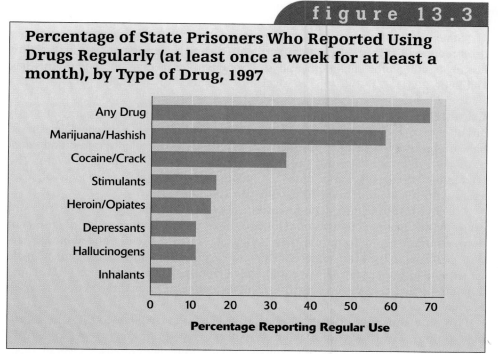

figure 13.3

Percentage of State Prisoners Who Reported Using Drugs Regularly (at least once a week for at least a month), by Type of Drug, 1997

Source: Data from Beck, Allen J., Thomas P. Bonczar, Paula M. Ditton, Darrell K. Gilliard, Lauren E. Glaze, Caroline Wolf Harlow, Christopher J. Mumola, Tracy L. Snell, James J. Stephan, and Doris James Wilson. 2000. *Correctional Populations in the United States, 1997.* Washington, DC: Bureau of Justice Statistics, U.S. Department of Justice.

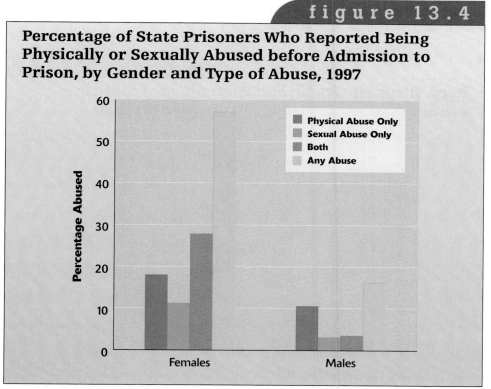

figure 13.4

Percentage of State Prisoners Who Reported Being Physically or Sexually Abused before Admission to Prison, by Gender and Type of Abuse, 1997

Source: Data from Beck, Allen J., Thomas P. Bonczar, Paula M. Ditton, Darrell K. Gilliard, Lauren E. Glaze, Caroline Wolf Harlow, Christopher J. Mumola, Tracy L. Snell, James J. Stephan, and Doris James Wilson. 2000. *Correctional Populations in the United States, 1997.* Washington, DC: Bureau of Justice Statistics, U.S. Department of Justice.

Who Is Behind Bars? A Profile of Prison and Jail Inmates   **415**

than one-third (37.3 percent) of the female inmates reported being raped before their incarceration (Beck et al., 2000).

State prisoners also report significant mental or physical problems: Almost one-third reported having a physical impairment (such as a learning or speech disability, hearing or vision problem, or other physical condition) or mental condition (Maruschak and Beck, 2001).

Criminality. Although all prisoners have been, by definition, found guilty of a serious offense, the type of offense for which they are incarcerated varies widely. Almost half (48 percent) of all state prisoners are behind bars for violent crimes, and equal numbers are incarcerated for property and drug offenses (21 percent each). The remaining 10 percent are imprisoned for public order crimes, such as weapons offenses and driving while intoxicated (Beck and Harrison, 2001).

These figures include some important racial, ethnic, and gender differences in drug offenses. Such offenses account for only 13 percent of white inmates' offenses, but they account for 26 percent of African American inmates' offenses and about 24 percent of Hispanic inmates' offenses. They also account for only 20 percent of male inmates' offenses, but for 32 percent of female inmates' offenses (Figure 13.5). These disparities reflect the uneven racial impact of the nation's war on drugs, a point stressed in Chapter 12.

Not surprisingly, most state prisoners have been convicted previously. One-fourth have no previous convictions, about 29 percent have prior convictions for violent offenses, and 47 percent have prior convictions for nonviolent offenses. Overall, then, about three-fourths of state prisoners have prior convictions for at least one violent or nonviolent offense (Beck et al., 2000). As Figure 13.6 shows, many offenders have several prior convictions, with 6 percent having at least 11 prior convictions.

Jail Inmates

In most respects, the profile of jail inmates is strikingly similar to that of their prison counterparts. Our profile again comes from government reports.

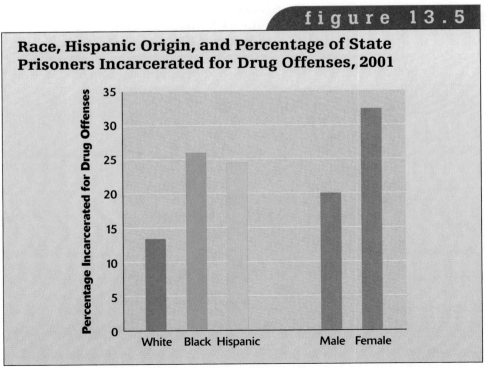

figure 13.5

Race, Hispanic Origin, and Percentage of State Prisoners Incarcerated for Drug Offenses, 2001

Source: Data from Beck, Allen J. 2002. *Prisoners in 2001.* Washington, DC: Bureau of Justice Statistics, U.S. Department of Justice.

figure 13.6

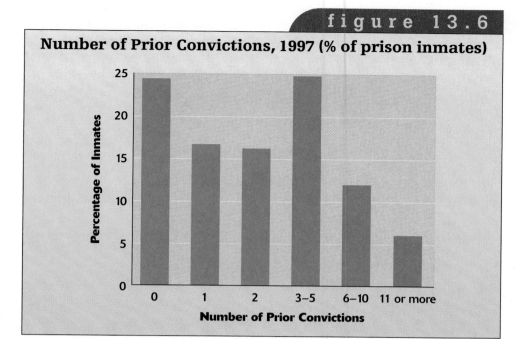

Number of Prior Convictions, 1997 (% of prison inmates)

Source: Data from Beck, Allen J., Thomas P. Bonczar, Paula M. Ditton, Darrell K. Gilliard, Lauren E. Glaze, Caroline Wolf Harlow, Christopher J. Mumola, Tracy L. Snell, James J. Stephan, and Doris James Wilson. 2000. *Correctional Populations in the United States, 1997.* Washington, DC: Bureau of Justice Statistics, U.S. Department of Justice.

Gender, Race, Ethnicity. About 88 percent of the more than 600,000 jail inmates (midyear 2001 figures) are men: 40.6 percent are African American; 43 percent are white, non-Hispanic; and 14.7 percent are Hispanic. Like their prison counterparts, then, jail inmates are disproportionately likely to be male and to be African American or Hispanic (Beck et al., 2002). Figure 13.7 depicts racial and ethnic differences in jail incarceration.

Socioeconomic Backgrounds. In other respects, the profile of jail inmates also mirrors that of prison inmates, as they, too, tend to be poor and uneducated and to have a variety of personal problems. The most recent survey of jail inmates conducted by the U.S. government found that almost 47 percent never graduated high school, and another 40 percent had only a high school diploma. More than one-third (36 percent) of jail inmates were unemployed at the time of their most recent arrest. Almost half (45.6 percent) were earning less than $600 per month (or $7,200 per year) in the month before their arrest, and slightly more than 20 percent were receiving government public assistance such as welfare or food stamps. While they were growing up, 60 percent of jail inmates did not live with both of their parents, and slightly less than 14 percent had lived in foster homes or institutions. Almost 40 percent grew up in families that received public assistance from the government. About 46 percent had an immediate family member (parent, sibling, spouse, or child) who had been incarcerated. Almost one-third had a parent or guardian who abused alcohol and/or drugs while the inmate was growing up (Harlow, 1998).

Personal Problems. Jail inmates also report a history of victimization by physical and sexual abuse and their own abuse of drugs and alcohol that again parallels the profile of prison inmates. Slightly more than 16 percent of jail inmates reported having been physically or sexually abused at some time in their lives before entering jail. As with prison inmates, this figure includes an important gender difference: Almost half of female inmates reported being physically or sexually abused, and about one-third reported being the victims of completed or attempted rapes. More than 80 percent of jail inmates had used an illegal drug before entering jail; 64 percent had used drugs

figure 13.7

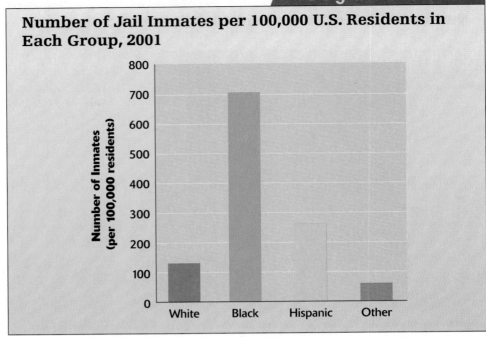

Number of Jail Inmates per 100,000 U.S. Residents in Each Group, 2001

Source: Data from Beck, Allen J., Jennifer C. Karberg, and Paige M. Harrison. 2002. *Prison and Jail Inmates at Midyear 2001*. Washington, DC: Bureau of Justice Statistics, U.S. Department of Justice.

regularly; and 55 percent of convicted inmates had used drugs during the month before committing the offense that led to their jailing. Additionally, 60 percent of convicted inmates were using drugs or alcohol or both at the time of their offense.

Like prison inmates, jail inmates report a high rate of physical and mental impairment, with almost 37 percent reporting a physical, mental, or emotional condition or difficulty in seeing, hearing, speaking, or learning. About 13 percent said they had been injured in an accident or a fight since entering jail.

Criminality. Although in many respects the profile of jail inmates is very similar to that of prison inmates, they do differ somewhat in one important area: the nature of the crime that led to their incarceration. Befitting their jail status, jail inmates were accused of fewer violent crimes and of more public order crimes than their prison counterparts: About 26 percent of inmates were being held for violent offenses, 27 percent for property crimes, 22 percent for drug offenses, and 24 percent for public order offenses. Like prison inmates, however, the offense patterns of jail inmates exhibit racial disparities in drug offenses: Whereas these offenses account for only 14 percent of white inmates' offenses, they account for 28 percent of African American inmates' offenses and also 28 percent of Hispanic inmates' offenses. Finally, only about 29 percent of jail inmates had no previous convictions for criminal offenses, a figure that is only slightly higher than that for prison inmates (Harlow, 1998).

Inmate Characteristics and Prison Life

This statistical portrait of prison and jail inmates is disheartening because it depicts an inmate population that is generally poor, undereducated, and rife with personal problems, such as drug and alcohol abuse, mental and physical illness, and physical and sexual victimization. This picture may not be surprising, but it nonetheless reinforces the discussion in Chapter 2 of the factors *underlying* criminal behavior. It also has an important implication for life behind bars: If inmates' personal problems are not addressed before they reenter society, these problems are apt to get worse, not improve. Inmates themselves and society at large, thus, will ultimately be at greater risk. We return to this point later.

Next we examine life behind bars in detail. Most of the discussion in the following sections focuses on prisons and prisoners, not on jails and jail inmates. The reason for this is based on a point made in the previous chapter: Prisons have been studied more than jails. Thus, most of what we know about life behind bars is about prison life, not jail life. Because prison and jail life have much in common, we believe we are presenting a picture of life behind bars in general.

Living in Captivity

What is it like to live in captivity? Perhaps only people who have this experience will ever know for sure, but for the past half-century social scientists have been interviewing inmates from prisons, jails, and other captive settings such as Nazi concentration camps to find out. Inmates themselves have also written about their lives in captivity. From these sources emerges a fairly clear picture of what it is like to live in captivity in general, and in prison in particular.

The Prison as a Total Institution

One of the first and still best discussions of life in captivity was Erving Goffman's (1961) classic book, *Asylums: Essays on the Social Situation of Mental Patients and Other Inmates*. According to Goffman, the mental asylum is an example of a **total institution** because it has complete control over the lives of its inmates. Other examples of total institutions include Nazi concentration camps, military boot camps, and prisons. These institutions obviously differ in many ways, and we may view some of them positively and others negatively. For better or for worse, though, all strongly control the lives of the people who live in them. The people who live there (Goffman called them inmates) are not free to leave and have little or no autonomy; they are told what to do, when to do it, and how to do it. Violation of the many rules for their behavior can lead to severe punishment.

In the total institution inmates lose their individual identity. They usually wear uniforms and, in some total institutions, have their heads shaved and are assigned a number or a new name. These measures are intended to weaken self-identity and increase conformity.

Goffman also asserted that inmates often suffer physical and mental abuse by those in charge. The torture and extermination of Nazi concentration camp inmates are, of course, infamous (Gilbert, 1987), but abuse also takes place in other total institutions. The prison is no exception. One form of such abuse, according to Goffman, is the **degradation ceremony** in which an individual is humiliated in front of the total institution's officials and/or other inmates. In a mental asylum or prison, inmates may be stripped naked in front of several people and their private parts checked for lice and other insects.

All these features of total institutions can have considerable influence on inmates. At a minimum, their beliefs and values may change drastically. Whether such *resocialization* is good or bad depends on whether a particular institution is perceived positively or negatively. Life in some total institutions may decrease the will to live or, alternatively, increase alienation and bitterness. Perhaps worse, it may also cause various mental disorders to develop or intensify. In short, after living in a total institution, people may emerge as very different and, depending on the type of institution, much worse in a social and psychological sense from who and what they used to be.

There is striking evidence of this influence in a famous mock prison experiment conducted by Stanford University psychologist Philip Zimbardo (1972). Zimbardo

total institution Erving Goffman's term for an institution that has complete control over the lives of its inmates

degradation ceremony any public activity that humiliates an individual

converted the basement of a Stanford psychology building into a mock prison and recruited male Stanford students to take part in the experiment. After screening his subjects for mental disorders and other problems, he randomly assigned them to play either prisoners or guards in the experiment. The "prisoners" were taken into custody by real police, booked, and fingerprinted, and then transported to the mock prison. They were stripped naked, deloused, and given gowns to wear in lieu of uniforms. In addition, they wore stockings on their heads in lieu of having their heads shaved. Each prisoner was assigned a number and then referred to by that number instead of his name. The goal was to remove the prisoners' identities and, perhaps, their will to resist.

The guards wore khaki uniforms and dark sunglasses and were simply told they should keep order. Although the guards initially did not take their roles very seriously, by the end of the first day they had already begun treating the prisoners harshly by insulting them, humiliating them in front of their fellow prisoners, and forcing them to stand at attention for hours at a time. The next day some prisoners refused to come out of their cells. In response, the guards rushed in and pulled the prisoners out, sprayed them with a fire extinguisher, and put some of them in solitary confinement. This harsh treatment began to destroy the will of the prisoners, and by the third day they had become passive in the face of continued verbal abuse by the guards. Unexpectedly, one prisoner then manifested symptoms of a nervous breakdown. When the researchers told him he should leave the mock prison, he had to be convinced that he was not really a prisoner. Within the next day or two, other prisoners began to suffer symptoms of nervous breakdowns, and Zimbardo and his associates decided to end the experiment at least 2 weeks before they had intended to. What had started out as a fake prison had become all too real.

Because Zimbardo had randomly assigned the students to be either prisoners or guards, the extreme behaviors they later exhibited could not have stemmed from preexisting personality problems. Instead, they arose from the social structure of the prison experience, as captured by Goffman's concept of the total institution, and from the roles the prisoners and guards were playing. If this short-lived mock prison had such a dramatic impact on the thinking and behavior of its participants, then real prisons may have the same or an even more severe impact. Although prison conditions have improved in the past 40 years, they continue to exhibit features supporting the insights of Goffman and Zimbardo.

The Pains of Imprisonment

In his classic book, *The Society of Captives*, Gresham M. Sykes (1958, p. 64) discussed several "deprivations or frustrations of prison life" that reflect the prison's status as a total institution. He referred to these deprivations as the **pains of imprisonment.** He said they undermine the inmate's sense of self-worth, and for this reason, he asserted, they can be just as painful in their own way as the physical punishment used against offenders in the past.

The first deprivation is the *loss of liberty*. Prison inmates are obviously not free to leave the prison, and they are deprived of contact with family, friends, and relatives. In this sense, the loss of liberty represents society's moral condemnation of the offender and its rejection of him or her as a contributing member of society. For these reasons, writes Sykes, the deprivation of liberty impairs inmates' self-esteem.

The second deprivation is the *loss of goods and services*. Sykes writes that inmates live a meager existence in a Spartan setting. Although their basic needs—food, clothing, shelter—are met, and some may actually be better off inside prison because of this, most inmates think they could have more possessions and be leading a better life outside prison. As a result, they consider the loss of goods and services a painful deprivation. They want not only the necessities of life but also the amenities that most of us take for granted: their own clothing rather than prison uniforms; a variety of good food rather than monotonous prison fare; privacy rather than a shared, overcrowded cell.

pains of imprisonment
Gresham Sykes's term for the deprivations of prison life

http://www.ablongman.com/barkan1e

In a society that values an individual's worth in terms of the material possessions he or she enjoys, the loss of goods and services is a painful deprivation for inmates. As Sykes (1958, p. 69) puts it, "[M]aterial possessions are so large a part of the individual's conception of himself that to be stripped of them is to be attacked at the deepest layers of personality."

The third deprivation is the *loss of heterosexual relationships*. Although home furloughs and conjugal visits have become more common since Sykes wrote his book, the lack of heterosexual outlets for prison inmates remains a serious problem. Their involuntary celibacy is obviously frustrating sexually and emotionally, but it can also further impair their self-worth and, even worse, prompt some prisoners to sexually assault or threaten others.

The fourth deprivation is the *loss of autonomy*. This loss, of course, is a key feature of the prison as a total institution. According to Sykes (1958, p. 73), inmates are "subjected to a vast body of rules and commands which are designed to control [their] behavior in minute detail." Inmates believe many of the rules governing their behavior are arbitrary, pointless, and designed simply to harass them. The loss of autonomy, Sykes writes, again impairs inmates' self-worth by treating them as helpless, dependent children and, in this way, humiliating them.

The final deprivation is the *loss of security*. Inmates' physical safety is always at risk, most often by other inmates, but also by corrections officers. Recall that many inmates had previously been convicted of violent offenses; others may have no violent convictions yet have violent tendencies. Life behind bars aggravates these tendencies (see the following discussion). As a result, new inmates quickly realize they are potential targets of violence. Sykes (p. 77) quotes one New Jersey inmate as saying, "The worst thing about prison is you have to live with other prisoners." Inmates are aware that they will be tested physically and that they must be prepared to fight to defend both themselves and their possessions. Their loss of security makes them anxious because they realize they can never be safe.

Sykes believes that these deprivations are psychologically harmful to inmates. Although they agree with Sykes's general point, scholars disagree on the extent of this harm (Adams, 1992; Goodstein and Wright, 1989). Some believe it can be quite severe and that inmates leave prison much worse off than when they entered it (Toch, 1993). Others believe this harm is less severe, perhaps because inmate subcultures (discussed later) help them cope with the pains of imprisonment and thus minimize whatever harm does occur (Zamble, 1992). A conservative and admittedly indecisive conclusion is that imprisonment is more psychologically harmful for some inmates than for others. As Francis T. Cullen and Jody L. Sundt (2000, pp. 495–496) observed, "In general, it has been found that the effect of prison is not uniform; rather, prisons seem to make some people worse, have no effect on others, and make some better."

Two other conclusions also seem justified. First, incarceration "magnifies problems people bring to jail and prison" and can thus exacerbate preexisting psychological problems (Tewksbury, 1997, p. 147). Second, some prisons are worse than others for inmates' psychological health. The more overcrowded a prison is, for example, the worse the psychological effects on inmates; and the better its treatment programs are, the better the psychological effects.

Adapting to Prison Life: Inmate Subcultures

As noted previously, inmates typically develop **inmate subcultures** that include a set of beliefs, values, roles, and norms for behavior. These behaviors and attitudes are often referred to simply as the **inmate code**. Inmate subcultures may also have a specialized language, commonly called the **prison argot**. When inmates enter prison, they learn the inmate subculture, a process called **prisonization**. The term *prisonization* was coined by Donald Clemmer (1940) many years ago in what was perhaps the first systematic study of prison life. Prisonization enables new inmates to learn how to behave in prison and how to function as members of the inmate community.

inmate subculture the norms, values, beliefs, behavior, and language of inmates

inmate code set of rules that governs how inmates should behave

prison argot a special language that is part of the inmate subculture

prisonization the learning of the inmate subculture

Many authors have examined inmate subcultures, and Sykes's (1958) discussion remains valuable. Sykes said the inmate code consists of several rules and beliefs, including the following:

- *Mind your own business.* Let other inmates do their activities, legitimate or illegitimate, and, above all, do not squeal on them.
- *Be strong and tough.* Complaining about your imprisonment or showing signs of physical or emotional weakness reduces your status in the prison community and can even increase your risk of becoming a target of violence.
- *Do not trust or toady up to the prison staff.* If you seem too friendly with corrections officers and other prison staff, you risk being seen as a traitor by the other inmates. This in turn can again make you a target of violence.

Cullen and Sundt (2000, p. 492) noted that this sort of inmate code is "decidedly pro-criminal and antisocial." They add that these "rules" are less prevalent today than they were in Sykes's day, in part because inmate populations are now more racially and ethnically diverse than they were then. Other scholars agree that these social influences "have contributed to the demise of a singular prison subculture (Greer, 2000, p. 465). Still, the values Sykes identified remain common in prison populations. Note that Sykes and most other observers of prison communities have studied male prisoners. Women prisoners have distinctive subcultures, and we discuss these later in the chapter.

As part of the inmate subculture, inmates adopt various roles. According to Cullen and Sundt (2000), the early works by Clemmer (1940) and Sykes (1958) identified several roles: (1) the *right guy* or *real man* who follows the inmate code; (2) the *square john* who, as the name implies, holds noncriminal values; (3) the *punk* who allows himself to be bullied by aggressive homosexuals; and (4) the *rat* who squeals on fellow inmates. Later, John Irwin (1980), a sociologist and former convict, identified several lifestyles: (1) *doing time,* in which inmates try to avoid trouble and get out of prison as soon as they can; (2) *gleaning,* in which inmates try to rehabilitate themselves with the help of prison treatment and educational programs; (3) *jailing,* in which inmates strictly follow the inmate code; and (4) the *disorganized criminal lifestyle,* involving inmates who cannot adapt to prison, often because they have mental disorders or other problems.

Why Inmate Subcultures Develop. An interesting debate concerns why inmate subcultures develop. Sykes (1958) stressed that inmates adopt the inmate code and other aspects of the inmate subculture to help cope with the "pains of imprisonment." This view is known as the **deprivation model.** As Cullen and Sundt (2000, p. 494) note, "Inmate behavior can be understood as a response to the deprivations that inmates experience in prison."

John Irwin and Donald Cressey (1962) presented another view called the **importation model.** They argued that inmates import, or bring, certain norms and values with them when they enter the prison. These norms and values reflect their race, ethnicity, and other aspects of their personal backgrounds. In this model, then, inmate subcultures reflect the inmates' backgrounds more than they reflect their attempt to cope with the pains of imprisonment. Thus, chronic violent offenders from urban areas might adopt an inmate subculture that emphasizes toughness and competition for personal gain, whereas first-time offenders might place more emphasis on improving themselves during their time behind bars.

Although both the deprivation and importation models have their advocates, it seems apparent that both can help us understand why inmate subcultures develop (Adams, 1992; Goodstein and Wright, 1989). More generally, they tell us that inmates' personal backgrounds and the pains of their imprisonment influence both how and why inmate subcultures develop.

Conditions behind Bars

The report on the D.C. jail at the beginning of this chapter reminds us that squalid prison and jail conditions are not new. Few people want to coddle prisoners or jail

deprivation model the view that inmate subcultures result from the need of inmates to cope with the pains of imprisonment

importation model the view that inmate subcultures reflect the values prisoners bring into their institutions and other aspects of their backgrounds

inmates, but most would presumably want them to be treated humanely. Some might prefer humane treatment out of a basic sense of decency, whereas others might prefer it simply to reduce the risk that inmates will be any more threatening to society when they are released back to it. Are the conditions in the D.C. jail typical, or are they rare exceptions to a pattern of generally decent living conditions?

In trying to answer this question, we implicitly address a widespread belief about prisons—labeled the "country club myth" by Victor E. Kappeler and colleagues (Kappeler et al., 2000)—that inmates live a pampered life behind bars with color TVs, VCRs, DVD players, and exercise gyms. Although equipment such as this is sometimes available, inmates are hardly pampered. They still suffer the "pains of imprisonment" that Sykes (1958) and others have documented. As Kappeler and colleagues (2000, pp. 239–240) note, quoting another scholar, "The idea of a country club correctional center is about as viable a notion as the existence of the Loch Ness monster—many people believe in it but nobody has ever seen one." They add, "In reality, prison is [a] harsh and painful experience . . . that provides inmates with few amenities" (p. 240).

What makes prison, and also jail, a "harsh and painful experience" beyond the pains of imprisonment previously described? One common problem is *overcrowding;* many prisons and jails contain many more inmates than they were intended to facilitate. In 1999, 22 states had prison systems that were operating at or above capacity (Beck, 2000), and a recent report concluded that "three out of four inmates are housed in facilities where the living space for two people is the size of a walk-in closet" (King, 1998, p. 616). This situation has led Human Rights Watch (2001b), an international human rights organization, to charge that U.S. prisons are "dangerously overcrowded."

As an example, a federal judge recently ordered Alabama to remove state prisoners who were being housed in a county jail because of overcrowding in the state's prisons. He issued the ruling after first touring the jail, which was holding 256 inmates despite being built for only 96. The jail's inmates were sleeping on the floor next to toilets and on top of shower drains because there was no room for beds. The judge wrote in his ruling, "The sardine-can appearance of its cell units more nearly resemble the holding units of slave ships during the Middle Passage of the 18th century than anything in the 21st century" (Firestone, 2001, p. A1).

Unfortunately, overcrowding can be expected to continue. As James Austin and John Irwin (2001, p. 94) note, "The bottom line is that crowding is now an accepted way of operating a prison system." Overcrowding can have psychological consequences and is thought to be a prime contributor to prison violence.

A second problem involves the *substandard living conditions* in many of today's facilities, which resemble the D.C. jail in this regard. As one correctional officer in Chicago described his facility, "You ever had a dream where there is a huge ball of fire and you're entering hell? Well, this is it. This is worse than hell" (in Kappeler et al., 2000, p. 239). In 1998, 35 states and the District of Columbia were under court order to improve their prison systems (Austin and Irwin, 2001). Litigation and reports by human rights and prison reform organizations continue to allege inhumane and unconstitutional conditions in the nation's prisons and jails. According to Human Rights Watch (2001b), "barely tolerable physical conditions" exist in many U.S. prisons and jails. Many facilities, it finds, are "dirty, unsafe, vermin-infested, and lacked areas in which inmates could exercise or get fresh air." Reflecting some of these problems, in January 2001, 22 years after New York City agreed to improve its jails, a federal judge ruled that certain jail conditions in the city continued to be inadequate. The substandard conditions he criticized included poor ventilation systems, which help transmit airborne disease and aggravate asthma and other respiratory illnesses; broken windows and lack of adequate heat; decrepit bathrooms and showers; and dirty cells and other areas (Lipton, 2001).

Other problems contributing to the "harsh and painful experience" behind bars include inadequate physical and mental health care, prison violence, and mistreatment by guards. These problems are examined later in greater detail. When problems such as severe overcrowding, decrepit living conditions, inadequate health care, and mistreatment and violence are common in correctional facilities, it is a fair conclusion that life behind bars is anything but a country club.

Living on Death Row

As noted in Chapter 12, more than 3,500 inmates live on death row, awaiting execution by legal injection or, more rarely, electrocution. What is it like to live on death row? The literature on death row depicts a bleak, harsh reality (Christianson, 1999; Johnson, 1998; Von Drehl, 1995). As one writer observed of a prison's death row, "The place was a dungeon, full of men who were as good as dead" (in Johnson, 1998, p. 33). Condemned prisoners usually spend many years on death row as their appeals continue. They live in virtual solitary confinement in a separate part of the prison. The result, according to Robert Johnson (1998, p. 35), perhaps the most perceptive observer of death row life, is this:

> The psychological impact of death row confinement is such that most condemned prisoners gradually waste away as human beings. By the time they reach the deathwatch, the condemned lead lives not much richer than that of a maggot. . . . Death row is indeed a living death, a place where the body is preserved while the person languishes and ultimately dies awaiting execution.

To reach this conclusion, Johnson interviewed death row inmates and their guards in a southern state. Johnson noted that death row inmates are treated differently from regular inmates. The latter spend about 8 to 12 hours in their cells each day; death row inmates spend 20 to 22 hours in theirs. They receive fewer visitors and cannot participate in prison recreation or treatment programs. In many prisons, the cells in which condemned prisoners spend virtually all their time are usually no larger than 6 × 9 feet and include a cot, toilet, and sink. The goal of death rows across the nation is simple, he says: "that condemned prisoners be treated essentially as bodies kept alive to be killed" (p. 48).

Living on death row magnifies the psychological consequences that regular inmates often face from the pains of imprisonment. Condemned prisoners feel especially powerless, lonely, hopeless, depressed, and vulnerable to harm by guards. As a result, says Johnson (1998, p. 57), they "give up on life as we normally know it. They exist rather than live."

In the last day or so before a scheduled execution, a condemned prisoner actually receives better treatment because prison officers want to keep the condemned calm for the execution. Coffee, cigarettes, and good food are given to the inmate, and he is attended to virtually around the clock by officers who try to establish friendships with him in order to "manipulate the prisoner's behavior so that he will comply with the etiquette of a dignified execution" (Johnson, 1998, p. 87).

Despite this treatment, condemned prisoners often break down emotionally as the execution hour arrives. After changing their clothes, eating their last meal, and talking with a chaplain, they walk to the death chamber. By this time, they have become completely numb, "more like an object without sensation than like a flesh-and-blood person on the threshold of death" (Johnson, 1998, p. 94). Their will to live is gone, and they are already spiritually dead.

Life in the Supermax

Although many maximum-security prisons exist throughout the country, a few are specifically designed to accommodate serial killers and others considered especially violent and dangerous. They are popularly known as **supermax** prisons (National Institute of Corrections, 1997). At the time of this writing, 57 supermax prisons, 16 of them in Texas alone, were in operation; other supermax units exist within regular prisons. About 20,000 prisoners live in supermax facilities (Human Rights Watch, 2000).

Security at these prisons and units includes the latest electronic surveillance and high guard-to-inmate ratios in order to prevent escapes and inmate uprisings. Accordingly, these supermax prisons are very expensive to run. Inmates in supermax prisons live little better than those on death row. Although they do not face death sentences, they, like their death row counterparts, live in virtual isolation. Inmates in an Ohio supermax prison spend 23 hours a day in 8- × 10-foot cells. They watch TV, eat in their

supermax a supermaximum-security prison or wing within a prison specifically designed to accommodate serial killers and others considered especially violent and dangerous

cells, and are permitted out for only 1 hour each day under heavy guard to shower and exercise. Beatings and other abuse by guards are thought to be especially common (Cullen and Sundt, 2000).

Human rights organizations, such as Amnesty International and Human Rights Watch, denounce these harsh conditions. According to Human Rights Watch (2000), the worst aspect of life in supermax facilities may be the extreme social isolation in which inmates live, which is "emotionally, physically, and psychologically destructive." One federal judge has observed that life in supermax facilities may thus "press the outer bounds of what most humans can psychologically tolerate" (Human Rights Watch, 2000).

Psychologist Craig Haney (1997, p. 429) visited one of the most notorious supermax prisons, Pelican Bay in California. He found a grim facility with no windows or natural light. The "yard" to which prisoners are taken for exercise is a "barren concrete encasement" with no exercise equipment. In their 8- × 10-foot cells almost every hour of the day, the prisoners, two to a cell, have nothing to do except watch TV or listen to the radio. Like their counterparts in the Ohio supermax, Pelican Bay prisoners eat in their cells and receive no vocational or educational training. When prisoners leave their cells to shower or go to the yard, they are first strip-searched in front of several guards and other prisoners. The humiliation of this degradation ceremony discourages many inmates from going to the yard. The prisoners who do leave their cells always wear chains around their waists and ankles.

According to Haney (1997, p. 430), Pelican Bay inmates "are deprived of human contact, touch and affection for years on end." They have virtually no contact with anyone on the outside. "The psychological significance of this level of long-term social deprivation," he adds, "cannot be overstated." He found evidence of serious mental disorders, with many inmates telling him they were suicidal or self-mutilating.

Human Rights Watch (2000) recommends that the use of supermax facilities be strictly limited. Many inmates in them, it says, are not violent or dangerous enough to justify this punishment. People confined in supermax units should spend as little time there as legitimate safety and security grounds dictate. Human Rights Watch also calls for better living conditions in supermax facilities, including adequate ventilation and heating and cooling systems, the addition of windows to allow natural light, larger cells, and adequate outdoor recreation areas and equipment. More frequent contact with family members is also encouraged, and abuse by prison staff should be strictly prohibited.

Correctional Treatment

We have noted that many offenders enter prison with a history of problems. In addition to the health problems previously discussed, many inmates suffer from poverty, lack of formal education, unemployment, prior drug and alcohol abuse, and physical and sexual victimization. Many prison-based programs have been developed to deal with these problems and to encourage inmates to become noncriminal, functioning members of society when they are released back into their communities. These programs include *educational and vocational programs* in which inmates take classes to receive high school equivalency degrees or to learn trades such as auto repairs, and *drug and alcohol treatment programs* in which inmates receive counseling and therapy to reduce their drug and alcohol dependence. How effective are such programs in preventing recidivism and other problems when inmates are released from prison? How adequate are these these programs in prisons?

Effectiveness

The responses of criminal justice researchers to the question of treatment program effectiveness have varied over the years. As was noted in the previous chapter, rehabilitation was a key goal of corrections before the 1970s. To encourage rehabilitation, prisons developed a number of treatment and vocational programs for inmates. The rising crime rate of the 1960s and 1970s and the corresponding movement from rehabilitation

Vocational, education, and substance abuse programming in prisons can be very helpful, but these programs are often unfunded and poorly designed. Here an instructor is assisting several inmates in the use of computers.

to retribution, deterrence, and incapacitation as the key goals of the criminal justice system reduced the enthusiasm for these programs. Studies suggested these strategies were largely ineffective anyway in reducing recidivism. The most influential study was that of Robert Martinson (1974), who concluded that almost all rehabilitation programs, including individual and group counseling and educational and vocational training, had virtually no effect on recidivism.

Martinson's study led to the belief that "nothing works," but his study was challenged by other researchers who said that Martinson had ignored evidence of effective programs (Lipton et al., 1975). Since the 1970s, researchers, adopting a "what works" perspective, have considered which programs might work best for certain offenders. A major problem in gauging the effectiveness of correctional programs is that relatively few studies use an adequate research design involving appropriate control groups and sample sizes that are high enough to permit statistical analysis. These problems aside, recent reviews of correctional treatment indicate that researchers are now more optimistic than Martinson was some 30 years ago.

One review concluded that correctional treatments "probably have modest positive effects" (Gaes et al., 1999, p. 361). Another reported that, "an impressive body of research has shown that, in fact, many interventions with offenders are effective in lowering future criminal participation" (Cullen and Sundt, 2000, p. 481). Less enthusiastically, a third review concluded that "some rehabilitation programs are successful with some offenders in some settings when applied by some staff" (Antonowicz and Ross, 1994, p. 97). The successful programs identified by the first review are those that involve (a) a cognitive–behavioral model that includes, among other factors, training in interpersonal skills; (b) multifaceted programming that focuses on the many problems that inmates have; and (c) role playing positive behaviors such as empathy and problem solving.

Considering specific programs, drug treatment in prison seems to work, but its positive effects tend to end when offenders are released from prison unless treatment continues when they are back in the community. Vocational and educational programs reduce recidivism by at least a small amount and also help to produce better inmate behavior in prison. At least some evidence suggests that treatments for sex offenders can reduce their recidivism, but well-designed studies of these programs are too sparse to know for sure (Gaes et al., 1999).

Adequacy in Prisons

Correctional treatment is not a panacea, but if it can work, as now seems true, then it is important for prisons to provide their inmates with adequate programs and services. A group of criminal justice officials and researchers recently noted, "The best intervention will fail if there are insufficient funds or if there is a lack of commitment from treatment staff, administrators, or support staff" (Gaes et al., 1999, pp. 364–365). This, in fact, is a public safety issue. As Cullen and Sundt (2000, p. 481) note, "The public's stake in reforming offenders is clear, for the average prison inmate will be returning to the community thirty months after being placed behind bars." If treatment in prisons is inadequate, the various problems inmates have will not go away, and society as a whole will be at greater risk when they are released.

Unfortunately, many correctional treatment programs remain poorly designed and inadequately funded. The move in the 1970s away from rehabilitation reduced the emphasis on such programs. Despite court orders to provide adequate programming and despite the presence of vocational, educational, and drug treatment programs in the nation's prisons, correctional treatment overall remains inadequately funded, designed, and implemented. To help pay for the building and operating costs of new prisons, some states have even cut back on their correctional treatment programs.

By 2001, there were signs of a renewed emphasis on inmate rehabilitation because some states had begun to worry about the high recidivism rates of ex-inmates and the cost of reincarcerating them. This concern led these states to improve their correctional programs. For example, Oregon established comprehensive training programs for inmates in telemarketing and computer operations to enhance their employment prospects after release from prison. The state also increased its literacy classes, drug treatment programs, and other rehabilitative efforts. This strategy seems to have succeeded in reducing recidivism by ex-inmates because the percentage of returning parolees among new admissions to Oregon's prisons declined from 47 in 1995 to 25 in 2000 (Butterfield, 2001).

An interesting controversy concerns the impact of funding and implementing adequate rehabilitation efforts in prison. Two critics of the "imprisonment binge," James Austin and John Irwin (2001, p. 180), worry that faith in correctional treatment may ironically contribute to support for even more imprisonment. "[I]n a strange and twisted way," they say, "the need for treatment has served to justify the use of incarceration. No matter how well intentioned, imprisonment in the name of treatment should be strongly resisted." Although Austin and Irwin recognize that effective correctional treatment can help prisoners and humanize the prison experience, they do not want evidence of correctional treatment success to justify the use of imprisonment in dealing with the nation's crime problem.

Prison Violence

One of the facts of life behind bars is violence: inmates against inmates, inmates against guards and other correctional staff, and guards against inmates. In this section, we discuss violence by inmates, whether violence against other inmates or against correctional staff, and focus on both interpersonal and collective violence. *Interpersonal violence* involves one or more inmates physically attacking one or more other inmates. Although psychological and economic victimization among inmates also occur, they are, strictly speaking, not examples of interpersonal violence (Bowker, 1980). Meanwhile, *collective violence* involves prison uprisings or riots. Its goal is to express group grievances and to bring about changes in prison conditions. The key difference, then, between interpersonal violence and collective violence by prison inmates is that the former "poses no decisive challenge to the continued smooth functioning of the prison as an organization" (Bottoms, 1999, p. 206).

Interpersonal Violence

Interpersonal violence in prisons is relatively common. Prisoners have been stereotyped as monsters, but the harsh reality is that many are violent. Many prisoners have violent pasts. When they enter prison, their violent tendencies are not likely to stop. They are being retained against their will, and for many the pains of imprisonment create even more hostility. Then, too, aspects of prison life, such as overcrowding and substandard living conditions, foster interpersonal violence. If a correctional facility were designed that would be guaranteed to produce violence, it would look very much like the prisons and jails that exist today. Interpersonal violence in prisons, then, results not only from inmates' personal backgrounds and attitudes but also from the uglier aspects of prison life (Bottoms, 1999).

Although many scholars have written about prison violence, it is surprisingly difficult to know how much violence actually occurs. The problem is similar to that discussed in Chapter 2 on crime statistics: Violence that occurs in prisons is not always reported to correctional staff and, if reported to staff, it does not always get reported to the outside world. Also, many types of violence exist, ranging from pushing or shoving to biting, beating, stabbing, or worse. Should all these types be included in the measurement of prison violence, or only the more serious forms? We also need to distinguish violence used in self-defense from more culpable violence, and it is not always easy to do so. By the same token, we must distinguish threats of physical force from the actual use of physical force.

As with crime statistics in the outside world (Chapter 2), the best gauge of prison violence is probably the victimization survey. Inmates can fill out anonymous surveys. Although this is not a perfect gauge, it does provide valuable information.

Although the amount of prison violence varies from one prison to another, a few U.S. surveys have suggested the depth of the problem (Cullen and Sundt, 2000). For example, a survey of inmates in three Ohio prisons found that 10 percent had been assaulted in the previous 6 months (Wooldredge, 1998). A similar survey of New Mexico inmates found that 14 percent had been assaulted in the previous 3 months (Wooldredge, 1994). The character of inmates most apt to commit violence should not be surprising: They tend to be young, to have prior records of violent crime, to be emotionally unstable, to be from urban areas, and to be in crowded facilities (Cullen and Sundt, 2000).

There are fairly reliable data on prison homicides. As Figure 13.8 indicates, there were 56 such homicides in 1999. This compares to 124 in 1973 when the number of prisoners was much lower. The 1999 rate of homicides was 5 per 10,000 inmates, compared to 61 per 10,000 back in 1973. Thanks to court orders, the much lower recent rate probably reflects improvements in prison conditions over the past 3 decades (Bottoms, 1999).

Prison Gangs

Prison gangs are a relatively recent development and have become a prime contributor to prison violence. Before the 1960s, a few individual white inmates dominated the social system in major prisons and used their influence to maintain order. As crime rates and prison admissions grew in the 1960s and 1970s, this social system began to change as new, more violent inmates challenged the authority of traditional inmate leaders. As African American and Hispanic urban inmates were incarcerated in greater numbers, they imported gang structures which soon dominated many prisons; they also changed inmate subcultures by no longer giving as much respect to older inmates, leaving prison life more unpredictable than before (Cox, 1986; Hunt, Riegel, Morales, and Waldorf, 1993). In particular, prison gangs now account for much of the violence that occurs. As a recent study notes, "The behavior of gangs has resulted in an increased

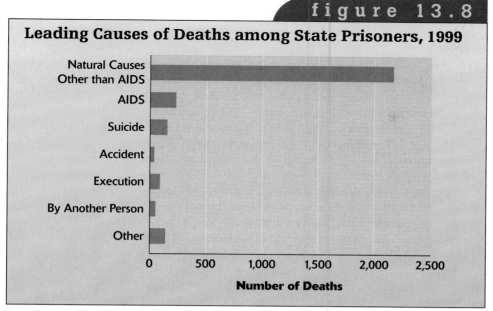

figure 13.8

Leading Causes of Deaths among State Prisoners, 1999

Source: Data from Maruschak, Laura M. 2001. *HIV in Prisons and Jails, 1999.* Washington, DC: Bureau of Justice Statistics, U.S. Department of Justice.

acceptance of predatory violence [and] interracial victimization" (Ralph, 1997, p. 183). Although gang members comprise less than 3 percent of California's prison population, they are thought to be involved in more than half of all prison violence (Ralph, 1997).

Much of this violence helps prison gangs secure economic profits illegally, for example, through drug trafficking and extortion. In this regard, prison gangs closely resemble organized crime gangs in the outside world (Ralph, 1997). Like their organized crime counterparts, prison gangs sell protection, drugs, and other contraband. Some have contacts with youth gangs and other illegal enterprises in the outside world, and, when inmates from the gangs are released, they work for these groups.

In terms of membership, three types of prison gangs predominate: white supremacist gangs, African American gangs, and Hispanic gangs. Although gang procedures vary, many take great care in their selection of new recruits. Usually, a recruit must be sponsored by a current member, and the gang must vote to admit a new member. As part of their initiation, the new recruits sometimes must assault rival gang members (Ralph, 1997). White supremacist prison gangs became notorious in Texas in the late 1990s after three white men tied an African American man to a pickup truck and dragged him to his death in Jasper, Texas. Two of the defendants, who were later convicted of the murder, had previously spent 2 years together in a Texas prison for burglary and drugs. While incarcerated, one of them came under the influence of a white supremacist gang and emerged 2 years later with white supremacist views that, according to his friends, he had not held before entering prison (Galloway and Selcraig, 1999).

Prison authorities have responded to prison gangs in several ways. For example, Arizona officials have transferred gang leaders to prisons across the country. To help ensure that the transferred gang leaders are ineffective in their new facilities, the state tries to send white supremacist leaders to prisons where most inmates are African American or Hispanic, and African American or Hispanic leaders to prisons where inmates from those racial and ethnic backgrounds are fewer in number. Whether this transfer procedure has helped reduce the gang problem in Arizona's prisons is questionable. As with juvenile gangs in the outside world, it is common for a regular member to ascend to gang leadership. As one prison reform advocate notes, "Gangs will only regenerate if they lose a leader. There's always someone waiting in the wings." Arizona authorities defend the practice, pointing to reduced gang activity in their prisons (Martinez, 1999, p. 2).

Sexual Violence

Prison rape and other sexual assaults, either completed, attempted, or threatened, are specific types of interpersonal violence in prisons that continue to be serious problems. Prison rape has been called "the plague that persists" (Dumond, 2000, p. 407) and "the most terrifying of all prison punishments" (Weiss and Friar, 1974, p. x), and it is "tacitly accepted by much of the criminal justice system" (Sennott, 1994, p. 1). It has been likened to an "unwritten code that warns 'one strike and you're raped' " (Goodman, 1994, p. 79). Such remarks may sound extreme, but sexual assault in prisons and jails seems to be a common fact of life behind bars, especially in prisons that are large and more overcrowded (Lewin, 2001). (We discuss sexual assault here and return to it in a later section on women in prison.)

As with physical, nonsexual violence in prison, it is difficult to derive accurate estimates of sexual assault, which has been called "one of the most illusive statistics in the criminal justice field" (Struckman-Johnson and Struckman-Johnson, 2000, p. 379). A survey of male inmates in several midwestern prisons found that 21 percent of them had been sexually assaulted since entering prison, including 7 percent who had been raped in their current facility (Struckman-Johnson and Struckman-Johnson, 2000). Another survey of male prisoners in Nebraska found that 22 percent of inmates in medium- or maximum-security institutions had been sexually assaulted, including 12 percent who had been raped (Struckman-Johnson, Struckman-Johnson, Bumby, and Donaldson, 1996).

Given such surveys, it seems fair to say that at least one-fifth of prison inmates are sexually assaulted and that at least 10 percent are raped. These proportions amount to a significant number of rapes and sexual assaults. A recent estimate by Stop Prisoner Rape (2001), a California nonprofit organization, assessed the annual number of sexual assaults at about 600,000 and the number of rapes at more than 250,000. Most inmates who commit prison rape are not gay themselves but use rape to exert dominance. The fear of being raped helps maintain the inmate social system hierarchy (Sennott, 1994). Inmates who seem to be at high risk for sexual victimization include those who are young, small, suffering from mental disorders, not gang affiliated, thought to be gay or effeminate, or convicted of sexual crimes themselves. Inmates who have squealed on other inmates are also at great risk for sexual victimization. Another risk factor is race because racial tension within prisons contributes to interracial sexual assaults (Dumond, 2000).

Although most observers attribute prison sexual assault to inmates' violent tendencies and to negative aspects of prison life such as overcrowding, it is also true that "a pattern of indifference on the part of the prison system" bears some responsibility for the problem (Sennott, 1994, p. 1). There are too few correctional officers in overcrowded facilities, and officers receive little or no training on rape and other sexual assault. Mental health counseling for rape victims is rare. Many guards believe that rape victims are gay and consent to the sex that victimizes them. Even when guards do believe a sexual assault has occurred, they ignore it, believing that prison rape is to be expected. As one correctional official put it, "Well, that's prison. Boys will be boys, prisoners will be prisoners" (Goodman, 1994, p. 79).

Some critics paint an even more ominous picture of the complicity of prison staff in prison rape. According to these critics, staff allows, and sometimes even encourages, prison rape because it helps them maintain order in the prison. There are at least two explanations for this. First, prison rape channels prisoners' aggression from guards to other prisoners. As one guard noted, "They could take this place anytime they want. The only thing that matters here is me and my staff going home at night safe" (Marano, 2001). Second, inmates know that, if they do not obey guards, they may be assigned to cells with known sexual aggressors. Guards may also coerce inmates into becoming informers by threatening them with a known aggressor if they refuse to squeal. Some guards have taken bribes from inmates to put young, new prisoners into their cells (Lehrer, 2001; Marano, 2001).

As with sexual assault outside prison, sexual victimization in prison can be "pervasive and devastating, with profound physical, social, and psychological components"

(Dumond, 2000, p. 409). These effects include posttraumatic stress disorder, helplessness, fear, depression, and suicidal thoughts. Inmates are also at increased risk of contracting HIV and other sexually transmitted diseases. Rape in prison that infects the victim with HIV can be the equivalent of a death sentence. As a Massachusetts inmate convicted of assaulting a teenager and subsequently raped in prison recalls, "What I did was stupid. We hurt that kid bad. It was wrong. But nowhere in the book of rules was it written that I got to be here to get raped, that I have to have them destroy my mind, that I am supposed to get AIDS. That wasn't supposed to be the deal." Another inmate recounted, "I was coming out of the shower. Him and another inmate came and pegged the door shut. One sat on my arms and the other one did it. I reported it to the guards. If I got AIDS, I'd probably kill myself. You walk around thinking about that every day" (Sennott, 1994, p. 1).

Recognizing the effects of prison rape, the U.S. Supreme Court ruled in *Farmer v. Brennan* (511 U.S. 825 [1994]) that prison officials must take measures to prevent it. An opinion by one of the Court's justices declared

> The horrors experienced by many young inmates, particularly those who are convicted of nonviolent offenses, border on the unimaginable. Prison rape not only threatens the lives of those who fall prey to their aggressors, but it is potentially devastating to the human spirit. Shame, depression, and a shattering loss of self-esteem accompany the perpetual terror the victim thereafter must endure. (511 U.S. 854 [1994])

Despite this ruling, prison rape continues to be "the plague that persists."

Prison Riots

Inmate collective violence takes the form of riots against prison authorities. The first reported prison riot in the United States occurred in 1774, and since then more than 300 riots have rocked prisons throughout the nation. Most of these have occurred since the early 1950s (Martin and Zimmerman, 1990). In several instances, prisoners have taken hostages for one of two reasons. First, they hoped to gain concessions from the prison warden and state officials on improving the prison conditions that contributed to instigating the riot in the first place. Second, they hoped that holding hostages would prevent or at least reduce the likelihood of a violent response by police, state troopers, and other law enforcement officials.

Explaining Prison Riots. It is tempting to try to explain prison riots by blaming inmates' violent tendencies and the poor conditions of prisons themselves, including overcrowding, lacking food quality, and harsh treatment by guards, which may anger inmates and spur them to riot. Violent inmates and poor conditions exist in virtually all of the prisons where riots have occurred. However, most prisons have these same underlying factors and have never experienced riots. Although prison riots might not occur without these factors, these factors in and of themselves only rarely lead to riots. Indeed, a recent study found little relationship between variation in prison conditions and the likelihood of prison riots (McCorkle, Miethe, and Drass, 1995). When riots do erupt, then, other processes must be at work (Useem and Resig, 1999).

One of these processes is a weakening of the formal and informal social control mechanisms that characterize prisons. Here **formal social control** means the rule of prison officials and guards over inmates, and **informal social control** means the understandings that inmates have among themselves and with prison staff about how prisons should operate. When these mechanisms are disrupted, social control in the prison breaks down, and the potential for a riot increases (Martin and Zimmerman, 1990). Another process underlying some prison riots comes from **rising expectations theory,** which assumes that unfulfilled expectations can lead to frustration and thus to collective violence. If inmates expect improved prison conditions and the improvements are not forthcoming, their increased discontent may lead to rioting.

formal social control in prisons, the rule of prison officials and guards over inmates

informal social control in prisons, the understandings that inmates have among themselves and with prison staff about how prisons should operate

rising expectations theory regarding prison riots, the view that riots occur when inmates' expectations for improved conditions have been raised and then frustrated

A fire set by inmates smolders in the aftermath of a prison riot in Atlanta, Georgia. Prison riots result in part from a weakening of the formal and informal social control mechanisms that characterize prisons.

Both weakened social controls and rising expectations seem to explain two major prison riots from the 1980s. The first is the West Virginia State Penitentiary (WVSP) riot that broke out on January 1, 1986. In the years before the riot, the conditions at WVSP were widely viewed as substandard, and in 1983 the West Virginia Supreme Court ordered massive changes that were not implemented because of inadequate funds. Then, in September 1985, a new warden restricted visitation rights and limited inmates' rights to private possessions. These and other incidents made it clear that the promised reforms would not occur. On January 1, 1986, several guards on the evening shift called in sick, and some critical guard posts were left empty. Although this situation usually would require a lockdown, none occurred, reducing the formal control the inmates would face if they rebelled. Taking advantage of the opportunity, the inmates took control of the dining hall during dinner and then captured the prison's north wing along with 16 hostages. After 3 days of negotiations with the governor, leading to a promise to improve prison conditions, the inmates surrendered (Martin and Zimmerman, 1990; Useem and Kimball, 1989).

Although conditions at the WVSP had been substandard, other prisons at the time had similar conditions and did not experience riots. Thus, the conditions by themselves cannot explain the WVSP uprising. Instead, the harsh measures of the new warden were responsible because they antagonized inmates, who believed their rising expectations of improved prison conditions were being crushed, and thus their interest in helping to maintain order in the prison was weakened. By January 1, then, the prison's "informal control system was in disarray" (Martin and Zimmerman, 1990, p. 729), and on that day the reduced staff numbers gave the inmates the opportunity for which they evidently had been waiting.

A second riot that stemmed from weakened controls and rising expectations occurred on February 2, 1980, in the Santa Fe, New Mexico, state prison. This riot was arguably the worst in U.S. history, costing $200 million and resulting in the deaths of 33 inmates and the injury of some 400 others (Colvin, 1992; Useem and Kimball, 1989). It began when some inmates attacked and beat four prison guards in the south wing, after which the other guards in this wing were captured. Inmates began to attack, beat, torture, and kill other inmates; several guards were also beaten and raped. Interviewed later, most inmates blamed the riot on the substandard living conditions of the prison. One inmate said, "It's been too crowded, the food is bad, the goddamned guards talk to you like you're a dog. We're not dogs." Another recalled, "There was one dormitory designed for 45 men, and they had 120 in there. It is a jungle after lights out.

You couldn't go to the restroom at night without stepping on someone, and that was all it took for a fight to break out" (Useem, 1985, p. 672).

Although, as noted previously, prison conditions typically are substandard, by themselves, they cannot explain why a riot begins. The New Mexico inmates, similar to their West Virginia counterparts, believed that the conditions in the prison had worsened. In the New Mexico situation, a popular prison warden had left his position some 5 years earlier. In addition, a reduction in the educational and vocational programs during this period angered inmates, weakened their informal social control networks, and reduced their incentive to be obedient and to behave. The establishment of a system of prison snitches during this time led inmates to distrust each other further. As with the West Virginia prison riot, an increased sense of deprivation combined with weakened social controls set the stage for the New Mexico uprising.

The Consequences of Prison Riots. The immediate consequences of prison riots are obvious: property destruction, injury, and death. Inmates sometimes kill each other and also prison guards, and guards and other law enforcement agents sometimes kill the rioters. Perhaps the most notable example of this latter dynamic occurred after inmates in the Attica, New York, state prison rioted in 1971. The inmates, most of them African American, had been angered by their alleged mistreatment at the hands of white prison guards at the Attica facility. They rioted, held prison guards hostage, and took control of the prison for 4 days while negotiating with state officials for the release of the hostages and for improvement in prison conditions. Then, acting on the orders of the New York governor, state troopers stormed the prison. In the process they killed 32 prisoners and 11 guards whom the prisoners had been holding hostage. Critics denounced the governor's decision to storm the prison, saying he should have allowed more time for the negotiations to progress (Mahan, 1985; Wicker, 1975).

The longer-term consequences of prison riots are less obvious but just as important. Often, but not always, they lead to improved living conditions in the prison experiencing the riot because prison officials want to keep their inmates peaceful (Useem, Camp, and Camp, 1996). Yet any such improvements in living conditions are fairly limited.

Another longer-term consequence of prison riots concerns how these institutions are administered (Useem et al., 1996). In response to riots, some prison administrators strengthen their control over inmates with stricter rules on behavior. The administrators believe such a "crackdown" is needed to ensure and maintain order. Other administrators have instead loosened their control while still maintaining proper security measures, as these administrators believe inmates' satisfaction with life behind bars should be improved. The dilemma for prison administrators is to strike the right balance between these two responses. Prison discipline must be maintained but not at the expense of inhumane treatment that increases the risk of future prison violence.

Women in Prison

Most studies of prisons and prisoners have focused on male inmates. Because women inmates are much fewer in number and perceived as less dangerous, they are often considered "forgotten offenders" (Greer, 2000, p. 444). In this section we present a profile of female prisoners and discuss important aspects of their life experiences behind bars.

At midyear 2001, women comprised 94,336, or 6.7 percent, of the nation's 1,405,531 state and federal prisoners. The total number of female prisoners increased 106 percent during the 1990s compared to a 75 percent increase for male prisoners (Beck, 2000). Although men are still 15 times more likely than women to be in prison, the growing number of women represents a significant change in prison admissions.

Despite their growing numbers, women inmates exhibit a different pattern of convictions than do male inmates. In particular, they are more likely to be incarcerated for drug offenses and less likely for violent offenses. For example, only 29 percent of women inmates in state prisons were convicted of violent offenses (often against male intimates who had abused them) compared to 49 percent for male inmates. Also, 34

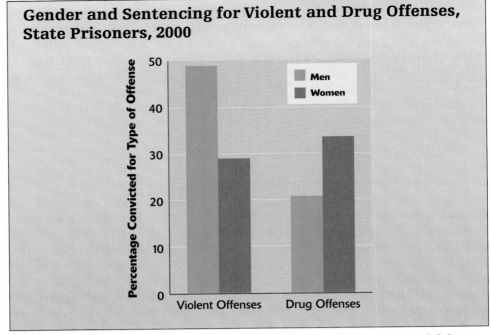

figure 13.9

Gender and Sentencing for Violent and Drug Offenses, State Prisoners, 2000

Source: Data from Beck, Allen M. and Paige M. Harrison. 2001. *Prisoners in 2000.* Washington, DC: Bureau of Justice Statistics, U.S. Department of Justice.

percent of women inmates were convicted of drug offenses compared to only 20 percent for male inmates (see Figure 13.9) (Beck, 2000). In some states, the percentage of women inmates convicted of drug offenses is especially high. In New York, for example, 60 percent of female prisoners are behind bars for drug offenses. In this regard, the war on drug's reliance on arrests and the courts has had a disproportionate impact on women, and has accounted for about half of the overall increase in female prisoners (Asseo, 1999).

Female inmates differ from male inmates in other ways as well. As we noted earlier, they are much more likely to have been physically or sexually abused before their incarceration. Almost 60 percent of women inmates and only 16 percent of male inmates report such abuse, and more than one-third of women inmates report having been raped before entering prison. Female inmates are also poorer on average than their male counterparts. Only 40 percent of women inmates were employed full time before their incarceration compared to 60 percent of male inmates; almost 30 percent of women inmates were receiving welfare aid compared to slightly less than 8 percent of male inmates. Women inmates also report higher rates of drug use, but lower rates of alcohol use, than male inmates (Greenfeld and Snell, 1999).

In other differences, 65 percent of women prisoners have children under age 18 compared to only 55 percent of male inmates, and, more importantly, 64 percent of these mothers were living with their children at the time of their incarceration compared to only 44 percent of the fathers. Breaking that down further, 31 percent of mothers in prison had been living alone with their children compared to only 4 percent of fathers (Mumola, 2000). We return to these differences in parenthood later.

On average, then, women prisoners are—compared to male prisoners—poorer, less violent, more likely to have used drugs, much more likely to have been sexually or physically abused, and more likely to be living with their young children before incarceration. Because of these differences, imprisonment creates special problems for women. We saw evidence of this in Chapter 12 in the discussion of the rise of women's prisons. These institutions developed in response to the sexual and other abuse that women and girls faced from male inmates in what were essentially men's institutions. The rise of separate prisons for women helped to reduce these abuses, but women still face a variety

This inmate is in her ninth month of pregnancy. Although women prisoners have medical needs that differ from those of male prisoners, the medical services they receive are often inadequate.

of problems in their own institutions, which receive less funding than men's prisons and have fewer educational, vocational, and treatment programs. Some of the problems women inmates face are similar to those of male inmates, but some are quite distinctive because of the nature of women's institutions and because of women's particular medical and other needs. Although both sexes suffer the pains of imprisonment, women face additional problems because of their gender and different life experiences.

Inmate Subcultures

We have already seen that the inmate code in prisons emphasizes toughness, minding one's own business, and not being too friendly with prison staff. Most of the early studies about inmate subcultures were actually studies of men's prisons and thus of *male* inmates' subcultures. Given this fact, these studies did not necessarily reveal anything about the subcultures women prisoners develop.

As women began to enter prison in greater numbers, studies found gender differences in inmate subcultures that partly reflect differences in gender socialization (Bowker, 1981; Wilson, 1986). One difference is that women seem less committed than men to the inmate code. Another is that women's prisons have less racial conflict and interpersonal violence and more cooperation with prison staff. They also generally lack the prison gang problem found in men's prisons and are much less violent than men's prisons. Early studies of women's prisons found a social structure characterized by close friendships, many of them homosexual, and "pseudofamilies" where inmates play the roles of parents, children, grandparents, and other relatives in order to make up for the loss of these roles in their lives before incarceration (Giallombardo, 1966; Ward and Kassebaum, 1965). More recent studies have questioned the extent and importance of this pseudofamily structure among current women prisoners. Some find it continues to be important, whereas others find some female inmates very involved in pseudofamilies and other inmates very opposed to them (Girshick, 1999; Owen, 1998; Pollock, 1998).

A recent study by Kimberly R. Greer of 35 women in a midwestern state prison found a complex situation. The friendship structure there was "based on manipulation and mistrust" (Greer, 2000, p. 447). Despite their forced interaction in a crowded environment, the inmates viewed themselves as "loners," suspicious of their fellow inmates. They considered prison friendships risky because they could not predict how any inmate might behave one day or another. They also worried that any friendships they did develop would end once one of the friends left the prison. Given this fear, it was easier for them not to become friends in the first place. Despite these concerns, most of the prisoners did have at least one strong friendship, but the pseudofamilies highlighted in earlier studies were largely absent in this midwestern prison (Greer, 2000).

Although earlier studies found homosexuality in women's prisons very common, less than 30 percent of these midwestern inmates had been involved in a sexual relationship in prison. When asked why they thought other inmates became so involved, the sample of respondents cited reasons including loneliness and a desire to improve one's financial situation by having a relationship with an inmate who had more money. One similarity between this and earlier studies of women inmates was the relative absence of racial tension and prison gangs. As we saw earlier, these are pervasive features of men's prisons, but they apparently are rarer in women's institutions.

Sexual Victimization

As in men's institutions, sexual victimization in women's prisons is a common problem, but, unlike men's institutions, the offenders are often prison guards, not other inmates. Studies of male prisons find that up to 20 percent of sexual victimization is committed by prison staff (Struckman-Johnson and Struckman-Johnson, 2000). In women's prisons, most sexual violence and other types of sexual victimization are committed by prison staff. Although women's institutions developed in part to reduce sexual abuse by male inmates and guards, most of the guards in women's prisons are men. Given their authority and control over inmates, the potential for sexual abuse is high and translates into actual abuse. As a recent study noted, "[W]omen in confinement face substantial risk of sexual assault by a small number of ruthless male correctional staff members, who use terror, retaliation, and repeated victimization to coerce and intimidate confined women" (Dumond, 2000, p. 410).

Although the exact prevalence of sexual victimization is difficult to estimate, a report by Amnesty International (2001) found more than 1,000 cases of sexual abuse in prisons in 49 of the 50 states from 1997 to 1999. Because of fear of retaliation, most of the victims did not report their abuse. The report called such abuse a "major systemic problem" not limited to only a "few bad apples" (Fleming, 2001, p. A7). As late as 1999, 14 states had no laws prohibiting sexual relations between prison staff and inmates; by early 2001, this number dropped to five, although in 19 states the laws prohibiting sexual relations do not cover all forms of sexual abuse, such as threats and oral sex. Only 10 states prohibit sexual relations by all prison staff, including medical personnel and kitchen staff as opposed to only guards. In some states the laws prohibiting sexual misconduct by correctional staff apply only to prisons and not to jails, even though much of the sexual abuse occurs in jails. In another problem, four states allow an inmate to be charged with a criminal offense for having sex with a prison official despite the obvious power difference between the two (Amnesty International, 2001).

Much of the sexual abuse Amnesty International (2001) found was in the form of rape and other types of sexual assault, where physical force or threats of force were used. But some also involved sexual encounters achieved through bribery and other inducements. For example, a guard at a Boston correctional facility was fired after allegedly having sex with two women inmates to whom he had given extra food, jewelry, and recreation time (Kim, 2001).

Amnesty International also found that all but three states permit male guards to do "pat down" searches of female inmates, which the report called "inherently abusive." Susan McDougal, who went to prison for almost 2 years as part of the White-water scandal several years ago, reported, "I had pat down searches the entire time I was in prison" (Fleming, 2001, p. A7). Between 1995 and 1999, the sheriff's department in one Massachusetts county strip-searched every one of the 5,500 women arrested by Boston police no matter what the charge; female guards would also search the women's vaginas and rectums for drugs and other contraband. The sheriffs did not strip-search male suspects (Ellement, 2001).

Prison staff commit other forms of sexual misconduct. McDougal said male guards in her prison watched women inmates undress and use toilet facilities. She also recounted one incident in which a mentally ill girl walked around nude in a recreation area while the male guards simply watched (Fleming, 2001).

Medical Needs and Services

The medical needs of women prisoners differ from those of male prisoners. As noted previously, women inmates are more likely to have prior histories of drug abuse and sexual victimization. In another, perhaps more obvious difference, women need adequate gynecological care. As we shall see in the Under Investigation feature following this chapter, prisons lack adequate medical and mental health care and services. Given that female inmates have more medical and mental health needs than their male counterparts, this lack of adequate medical care in prison affects women severely (Acoca, 1998; Morash, Bynum, and Koons, 1998). For example, although women inmates have a greater need for drug treatment, they are less likely than male inmates to receive it (Cullen and Sundt, 2000). A study of services for women prisoners nationwide concluded that "the availability of treatment for women offenders falls far short of what is needed, and the treatment that is available does not necessarily offer the types of services that women need," for example, counseling for the sexual victimization that is so often a cause of their drug abuse (Prendergast, Wellisch, and Falkin, 1997, p. 324).

Women prisoners also receive inadequate gynecological care. For example, only half of state prison systems offer mammograms and Pap smears (Amnesty International, 1999). Such care can also lead to exploitation. In a 1999 ABC *Nightline* show, Ted Koppel interviewed inmates at a California women's prison. Koppel asked the prison's head physician about reports by the inmates that they had to submit to unwanted and unneeded pelvic exams in order to get medical treatment. The physician replied that the women liked the exams: "It's the only male contact they get." He was later reassigned from patient care to research (Chevigny, 2000).

All these problems led journalist Cynthia Cooper (2002, p. 30) to charge that "medical treatment in women's prisons ranges from brutal to nonexistent." One female prisoner she interviewed recounted her treatment by prison guards following mastectomy of her right breast for breast cancer. The guards signed her out of the hospital before the doctors believed she was ready to leave and refused to let her take her pain medication. Although she was scheduled for chemotherapy at regular intervals, the guards did not take her to her appointments. Within 2 years, her cancer had spread, and she had to have her remaining breast removed.

Women Prisoners as Mothers

Recall that women inmates are much more likely than male inmates not only to be parents but also, before incarceration, to be the primary caretakers for their children. As a result, incarceration poses a more serious emotional and practical problem for women inmates than it does for male inmates (Enos, 2001). As Cullen and Sundt (2000, p. 502) observe, "One of the most painful and distressing aspects of incarceration for women is being separated from their families." The children of incarcerated women must be cared for by other people, usually relatives but sometimes the state, and some of the women even face losing custody of their children permanently. Prisons vary in their rules on visitation rights and in their facilities for young children, and the majority do not permit extended visits. The majority of incarcerated mothers (and also fathers) report never having been visited by their children since entering prison, in part because their institutions are usually more than 100 miles from their last place of residence (Mumola, 2000).

About 5 percent of women offenders are pregnant when they enter prison (Greenfeld and Snell, 1999). These women face special problems. Like nonpregnant women inmates, they already come from backgrounds of poverty, drug and alcohol abuse, smoking, poor nutrition, and other problems that render their pregnancies high risk. Once they enter prison, conditions may further increase the chance of pregnancy complications. As with other health services in prison, obstetrical care can be inadequate. When the baby is born, inmates in most prisons must give up the baby within a few weeks although a few institutions have nurseries where the children live up to age 1 or so.

These problems led some scholars to question whether pregnant offenders, most of whom are not violent, should be incarcerated or whether they should be sentenced to community-based corrections. These scholars stress the inadequacy of prenatal and obstetrical care in prisons and worry about the lack of mother–child bonding and thus the child's later development when the newborn is so quickly removed from the mother's life. Defenders of the incarceration of pregnant women reply that prenatal care in prison may be better than the care pregnant offenders would receive outside prisons, and that newborns can bond well with any adult who cares for them (Ayers and Moriarty, 1999).

A final problem facing some pregnant inmates is shackling during childbirth. Amnesty International (2001) reports that 18 states allow pregnant inmates to be shackled while they give birth even though there is obviously no chance the woman will try to escape. The organization considers such shackling a form of abuse of women in custody. According to one Amnesty International official, "There is simply no reason to shackle a woman who is in labor or giving birth. These laws were clearly written by largely male legislators" (Fleming, 2001, p. A7).

Treatment and Vocational Programs

We have previously examined the extent, quality, and effectiveness of treatment and vocational programs in the nation's prisons. In this regard, once again women seem to be at a disadvantage. Although the situation is improving, women's prisons typically have fewer treatment and vocational programs than men's prisons. Because most prisoners are men and because men are thought to be more dangerous to society, the attention and funding of the corrections system has traditionally focused on male prisoners. This, in turn, has led to a neglect of the needs of female prisoners (Tewksbury, 1997).

A more subtle bias also exists in the nature of vocational programming in women's prisons. Although the situation is improving, vocational programing has typically focused on preparing women inmates for traditionally "female" jobs, such as secretarial work, sewing, and food service, and not for traditionally "male" jobs, such as carpentry, plumbing, and auto repair. Training for the latter jobs remains much less available in women's prisons than in men's prisons, even though these jobs pay much more than traditional women's jobs (Morash, Haarr, and Rucker, 1994).

To the extent that treatment and vocational programs in prisons can be effective (see previous discussion), it is important that they be as available in women's prisons as in men's prisons. The fact that they continue to be less available in women's prisons adds to the pains of imprisonment that women inmates face because of their gender.

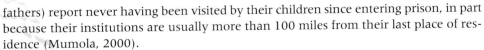

Litigation and Prisoners' Rights

In 1871, the U.S. Supreme Court ruled in *Ruffin v. Commonwealth* (62 Va. 790 [1871]) that prisoners were "slaves of the state" and, as such, could be treated as harshly as prison officials deemed appropriate. The ruling reflected a view in the English common law, from which U.S. law is derived, that convicted felons suffer "civil death" and have no rights. In turn, it reinforced a "hands-off" policy toward U.S. prison conditions that prevailed despite some court rulings in favor of prisoners' rights for almost a century (Wallace, 1997). As a result, the U.S. courts before the 1960s considered prison conditions and the treatment of prisoners largely beyond their scope.

This view began to change in the early 1960s with U.S. Supreme Court decisions that applied the Civil Rights Act of 1871, passed after the Civil War to help the newly freed slaves, to prisoners (*Monroe v. Pape*, 365 U.S. 167 [1961]) and that allowed African American Muslim inmates to read the Koran and to worship in their faith (*Cooper v. Pate*, 376 U.S. 546 [1964]). These cases signaled that the courts would now be willing to hear litigation by and on behalf of prisoners, and many cases have since focused on freedom of religion and speech in prisons, and also on the poor living conditions discussed previously (Cullen and Sundt, 2000). State and local officials fought back vigorously in the courts but lost many of these legal battles. The entire prison systems in several states were judged unconstitutional. As noted earlier, 35 states and the District of Columbia were under court order in the late 1990s to improve their prison conditions.

The prisoners' rights litigation movement that began during the 1960s emerged in the wake of the civil rights movement in which the federal courts played an important role in giving African Americans equal protection under the law. The new political consciousness that marked that decade found its way into the nation's prisons and jails where some prominent African American activists had been incarcerated. Lawyers who had worked for the civil rights movement later became prisoners' rights lawyers. Some inmates studied the law, and these "jailhouse lawyers" became involved in prison litigation.

This wave of litigation is widely credited with achieving significant improvements in prison conditions, but it has also caused problems (Cullen and Sundt, 2000). Court rulings have forced states to spend more money on corrections, money that might have been put to better use in noncorrectional areas such as improving schools. As litigation forced prisons to loosen their control over inmates, the opportunity for prison violence may have increased although scholars dispute this point (Crouch and Marquart, 1990). Overall, though, prisoner litigation has done much more good than harm. As Cullen and Sundt (2000, p. 483) note, "the prison environment has been unalterably affected by the prisoners' rights movement, giving inmates redress against the truly inhumane and brutal treatment that once existed unnoticed behind the high walls of the prison." Despite this redress, prison conditions continue, as we have seen, to magnify the pains of imprisonment that inmates experience even in the best of prisons.

The major U.S. Supreme Court decisions advancing prisoners' rights came under the so-called Warren Court named after its chief justice, Earl Warren. By the late 1970s and continuing into this decade, the Court has taken a decidedly conservative turn under the leadership of William Rehnquist. As such, it has been less amenable to the idea of prisoners' rights than its predecessor, and it has reversed several of the rights that prisoners had previously won in the lower federal courts. It has also made it more difficult for inmates to prove in court that their rights have been violated. In particular, the Court has restricted the degree to which the Eighth Amendment's prohibition on "cruel and usual punishment" and the Fourteenth Amendment's "due process" clause apply to deprivations that prisoners suffer beyond their sentences (Wallace, 1997).

In 1996, the U.S. Congress passed, and President Bill Clinton signed, the Prison Litigation Reform Act. This act limited the ability of inmates to file suit in federal court and, therefore, the ability of federal courts to reinforce and expand their rights. A few of its provisions illustrate these effects. First, the act requires that inmates must exhaust the grievance process within their facilities before they file suit; this process may take a long time, and inmates may be intimidated from filing grievances at all. Second, the act requires that inmates pay their own court filing fees, which many cannot afford to do. The act also states that inmates cannot file suits for mental or emotional harm unless they can also show evidence of physical harm (American Civil Liberties Union, 1999). The American Civil Liberties Union and other groups have lobbied Congress to overturn the act or repeal some of its provisions.

What Rights Do Inmates Have?

Inmates now have rights in theory although, as we have seen, not always in practice. Here, briefly, are some of the rights they legally enjoy (Branham, 1998):

- *Disciplinary sanctions.* Prisons and jails have wide latitude in disciplining inmates but may not impose abnormal hardships on them.
- *Medical care.* Prisoners must receive adequate medical care under the Eighth Amendment. Those who believe their care is inadequate must prove that prison officials deliberately ignored their medical needs.
- *Protection from inmate violence.* Prisons may be held liable under the Eighth Amendment for inmates' interpersonal violence only if officials recklessly disregarded the safety of inmates. In practice, this means that it is difficult for inmates to bring suits when they are victimized because court rulings allow for the everyday risk of inmate violence. Victimized inmates must prove that officials knew of imminent violence and failed to prevent it.
- *Reading materials.* Prisoners must have reasonable access to mail and reading materials, although prisons may limit this access if it poses a threat to security.
- *Religious rights.* Inmates may worship in their chosen faith but may not have religious symbols or engage in religious practices that threaten prison security.
- *Use of force by prison staff.* Staff may use reasonable force to subdue and discipline inmates but may not use force that is malicious and sadistic.

Leaving Prison

How prepared are inmates for life outside when they finally leave prison? This chapter has stressed that many inmates are, in fact, ill prepared for jobs, social relationships, and other aspects of the outside world. Even as the number of inmates has increased in the past few decades, correctional services for them have been cut, making it even more difficult for them to succeed in the outside world. As one news report noted, "Because states sharply curtailed education, job training and other rehabilitation programs inside prisons, the newly released inmates are far less likely than their counterparts two decades ago to find jobs, maintain stable family lives or stay out of the kind of trouble that leads to more prison" (Butterfield, 2000b, p. A1). These problems have important implications for the effectiveness of parole, which we discuss in Chapter 14. Here we outline some of the difficulties inmates immediately face when they leave prison.

To recall a mental exercise from Chapter 2, imagine you have just been released from prison for armed robbery. You apply for a job, and write "yes, armed robbery" on the application form when it asks whether you have ever been convicted of a felony. How likely are you to get this position? You apply for more jobs and write the same information on the application forms. How likely are you to get these positions?

Now imagine you are in a bar and meet someone to whom you are attracted. You strike up a conversation. When your potential friend asks, "What do you do?" you reply, "Well, I just got out of prison for armed robbery." The person makes an excuse to go to the restroom, never to be seen again.

As these vignettes suggest, ex-prisoners face harsh realities in the outside world. As we have seen, many have emotional and physical problems that the prison experience may have exacerbated. Many also have drug and alcohol problems and are functionally illiterate or at least undereducated. A Massachusetts study estimated that 70 percent of ex-inmates in the state are unable to complete job applications, write letters, or read bus schedules, and 80 percent have substance abuse problems (Larivee and Davis, 2001). A California study found that 85 percent of ex-inmates abuse drugs or alcohol, 50 percent are illiterate, and 10 percent are homeless (Butterfield, 2000b). Ex-prisoners also have trouble getting jobs because of their criminal records. As one ex-convict who had served 34 months for selling cocaine commented, "I need a steady job. I've been all over New Orleans filling out applications. But they don't call. All the applications ask if you have ever been convicted of a crime, and that kills the whole thing right there" (Kilborn, 2001, p. A16).

With hundreds of thousands of inmates being released every year (see Chapter 12), services for them cannot meet the demand. In Boston, for example, one job training program for inmates with drug problems can handle only 70 offenders annually, even though Boston receives close to 4,000 released inmates with drug problems each year (Larivee and Davis, 2001).

The story of Mitzi Ann Shepard, a licensed practical nurse, illustrates the problems ex-inmates face even when they are capable of working. Shepard was convicted of manslaughter for killing her boyfriend after, she says, he violated a restraining order, came to her home, and raped her. Released after 15 months in prison, she listed her conviction on 13 job applications and never received a call from any of the prospective employers. She finally secured a job almost 3 years after her release with a doctor who was a family friend. When she was interviewed by a reporter, she said she wanted to get more schooling in order to become a nurse practitioner and triple her salary, but was worried no college would accept her. "Maybe I don't deserve this, but I do know I can do more than I'm doing now. I know I can better myself and I can better the lives of others by pursuing my dream" (Larivee and Davis, 2001, p. H2).

Guarding Inmates

This chapter has focused on the lives of inmates, but correctional officers also spend much of their time in prison. What do we know about prison guards and their work?

In prison movies and other transmitters of popular lore, the prison guard is often portrayed as a sadistic brute who takes pleasure in mistreating inmates. The Zimbardo experiment discussed earlier suggests that the prison experience affects guards' personalities and behavior at least as much as those of inmates. Although guards do sometimes mistreat prisoners, prison litigation and other prison reforms, including better selection and training of new officers, have from all reports greatly reduced the amount of abuse that occurs.

Although correctional officers in the past were primarily white males living in rural areas, these days they come from diverse racial and ethnic backgrounds (Britton, 1997). About two-thirds are white, one-fourth African American, and 7 percent Hispanic. This greater diversity is thought to have eased relations between correctional staff and inmates, the majority of whom are not white, but to have complicated relations among the officers themselves. About one-fifth of correctional officers are women.

Scholars dispute whether correctional officers have their own subculture. Some say that guards do not communicate much with each other and do not agree on ideas about how punitively they should treat inmates (Hepburn, 1984; Philliber, 1987). Others say that a guard subculture does exist, and that, like the police subculture (see Chapter 6), it includes a code of behavior that emphasizes the need for officers to "stick together." At a minimum, this means that they must immediately help an officer who is being threatened by one or more inmates, that they never "rat" on a fellow officer, that they always take an officer's side in a dispute with an inmate, and that they do nothing to make an officer look bad in front of inmates (Kauffman, 1988). As this code implies, correctional officers see inmates as an opposing force and, like police officers with the public, exhibit an "us against them" mentality. If this mentality does exist, it reflects correctional officers' perception (which they share with police officers) that their safety and lives are constantly at risk.

Although the popular image of the prison guard is that of an individual who is authoritarian, prejudiced, and brutal, this presumption may well be a myth. As Robert Johnson (1996, p. 201) notes, "there is no evidence that guards as a group are distinctively prejudiced or authoritarian, or indeed share any personalty type at all. . . . Guards are neither congenital sadists, rabid racists, nor ex-military officers looking for another uniform and more men to boss around."

Prisonization of Correctional Officers

Earlier we discussed inmates' "prisonization" whereby they learn the inmate subculture and the prison routine. Correctional officers undergo a similar process. One thing they learn is that reality does not always conform with perception. To the outside world, correctional officers control the prison, which is, of course, the main purpose of their job. However, control in the prison is actually accomplished somewhat differently. Although officers are obviously in charge, they nonetheless make deals with inmates to maintain order (Philliber, 1987). In return for inmates' good behavior and attempts to make other inmates behave, guards often grant prisoners small privileges; they also reward prison "snitches" who inform on other inmates. This general process, however, subjects officers to the risk of becoming too dependent on inmates for their own safety.

Other differences between outside perception and inside reality also exist. Correctional officers in some prisons play important roles in maintaining the inmates' contraband economy. They profit financially from their involvement but also help maintain order among inmates. In yet another difference, some try secretly to help inmates with personal problems. They do this in secret to avoid being perceived as too inmate friendly by other guards and inmates (Johnson, 1996).

Correctional officers must also learn about the roles they are expected to play (Johnson, 1996; Lombardo, 1997). One is *human services*. They view themselves as human service workers at least as much as prison guards. In this role, guards provide inmates with various goods and services, including food, clothing, and medication. They also help inmates handle "institutional" problems, such as lack of money and visitation rights, and they help inmates deal with the personal pains of imprisonment. Finally, they learn that if they say they will help an inmate, they have to follow through, lest the inmate lose trust in them and become resentful and hostile.

A second key role is *order maintenance*. Although officers are concerned for their own safety, they also recognize the need to keep inmates in line so that they do not harm each other. In this respect, they see themselves "as police officers who intervene in family quarrels to maintain social order" (Lombardo, 1997, p. 197). As one officer put it, "It's like a city within a city and we're the policemen" (Lombardo, 1997, p. 197).

A third role is maintaining prison *security* by preventing escapes. Officers realize they are in the prison to prevent escapes, but do not believe this role is as important as the previous two.

A final role is *rule enforcement*. Officers realize they need to enforce numerous rules, especially those designed to prevent drug use and other illegal inmate activity. To help control such behavior, they often rely on information supplied by inmate informants.

As the number of prisoners has increased dramatically over the past few decades and as prison gangs have come to dominate prison life, some evidence suggests that correctional officers' perceptions of their roles have changed as well. In particular, officers now seem to emphasize personal security and rule enforcement roles. As prison systems have themselves provided more rules to govern officers' behaviors and duties, officers now have less discretion over their own behavior than in years past (Lombardo, 1997, p. 197).

Alienation and Stress

According to some research on correctional officers, their work can lead to several personal problems (Johnson, 1996). Job satisfaction is low and work conditions are stressful. These factors affect officers' well-being. The longer guards serve as officers, the more stress they feel and the more negative their attitudes toward inmates become (Philliber, 1987). This stress contributes to high divorce rates and health problems such as high blood pressure, ulcers, and heart disease.

Correctional work can also be alienating. Like inmates, correctional officers are cut off from the outside world and have little freedom of movement or excitement in their lives. They work amid the same prison conditions as inmates and often find prison rules contradictory or difficult to follow. Despite this alienation, many correctional officers continue to believe that the work they do is important and worthwhile (Johnson, 1996). That they continue to be optimistic and idealistic underscores their commitment to a human services orientation. Although many do find their work alienating and stressful, others find it rewarding.

In assessing the influence of correctional work on prison guards, it is important to distinguish among the kinds of institutions in which they work and the kinds of work they do (Cullen and Sundt, 2000). For example, officers in maximum-security prisons experience more stress than those in other types of prisons. Regardless of where they work, officers who believe their work is dangerous experience more stress, whereas those who can do more human service work find their jobs more rewarding.

The overall alienation and stress of prison work has made it difficult to recruit and retain enough guards for the nation's prisons, and several states lose more guards every year than they hire. This problem increased during the past decade for two reasons. First, more prisons were built and more guards needed to be hired. Second, and as noted earlier, inmates have become more violent than before, in part because their mandatory sentences gave them no incentive for good behavior. As one observer noted (in Belluck, 2001, p. A1), "If prisons were to honestly advertise the job, they might say, 'Come to work with us. Have feces thrown at you. Be verbally abused every day.' People don't advertise the job that way, but that often is what they have to deal with." Some states have responded to this staffing problem by reducing the minimum age for corrections work to 19 or even 18, and some have had to delay the opening of new prisons that were already built (Belluck, 2001, p. A1).

Women as Correctional Officers

As noted previously, about one-fifth of correctional officers are women. Because they work in a male-dominated occupation, they experience problems similar to those of women in other such occupations, including lower salaries, reduced chances for promotion, and hostility and sexual harassment from fellow officers and supervisors (Belknap, 2000). As with their police counterparts, doubts persist whether women correctional officers can perform their jobs as well as men. Also as with police, the evidence suggests that women are at least as capable as men, and that, in fact, their presence in a prison may help to calm inmates (Zimmer, 1986). Female guards are no more likely than male guards to be attacked or injured by inmates, and they respond at least as aggressively as male guards to signs of inmate trouble (Jenne and Kersting, 1996). Although male guards continue to believe that the presence of women guards undermines prison security, the evidence does not support this view.

Female and male guards have similar attitudes toward crime and punishment and the treatment of inmates (Jurik, 1985). Given this similarity, one interesting question concerns whether women correctional officers perform their jobs in the same way as male officers. To answer this question, Lynn Zimmer (1987) interviewed 70 women guards in New York and Rhode Island male prisons. These women were more likely than male guards to develop friendships with the prisoners, and some even play a nurturing role in contrast to the more "macho" role that male guards often play. The female guards spent much time talking with the prisoners and helping them with personal and institutional problems. Zimmer believes that the women guards' different approach reflects their own gender socialization, including the skills of "communication and persuasion and the ability to generate voluntary cooperation from others" (p. 423).

In sum, the entrance of women into the field of correctional work has been a positive development, not only for the women themselves but also for the inmates they guard and the prisons in which they work. Barriers to female participation as guards still exist despite a lack of evidence that they pose any special problems.

Focus on Brazil

Hell on Earth in a Prison Cell

The director of Human Rights Watch/Americas stated: "The Brazilian prisons system is a time bomb" (Cavallaro in Epstein, 1998, p. 7), with the bomb exploding on a regular—often monthly—basis in the form of prison riots. Some of these uprisings have been particularly tragic. After a riot erupted in the state of Sao Paulo's Casa de Detencao (located in the Carandiru prison complex) in 1992, police invaded the compound and eventually gained control of the situation. Police ordered the inmates to strip and began shooting them. One hundred and eleven prisoners were killed. None of the officers were injured by gunfire, undermining the official version of the massacre that prisoners opened fire on the police ("Behind Bars in Brazil," 1998).

In February 2001, a coordinated series of riots ripped through 21 prisons in the state of Sao Paulo where 40 percent of the nation's inmates are housed. Armed with knives, guns, and clubs, the prisoners took more than 1,000 hostages, including a significant number of women and children. By the time the police commandos squelched the uprising, at least 12 people had been killed (Rotella and Gobbi, 2001).

Almost every problem a penal system can experience is found in Brazil, and experts agree the crux of this disastrous situation is rooted in overcrowding. Brazil has more than 170,000 inmates in 512 prisons and municipal jails, and thousands of local police lockups (Brazil, Annual Report, 2000). However, the system is designed to hold approximately 65,000 individuals.

Many prison facilities have two to five times the number of inmates they were designed to hold. A Human Rights Watch inspection team visiting Sao Paulo's Casa de Detencao discovered that single-person cells contained eight to ten prisoners, with some inmates tied to windows to reduce demand for floor space. While some slept in hammocks suspended from the ceiling, others were forced to lie on top of hole-in-the floor toilets. In some overcrowded institutions, prisoners sleep in shifts ("Behind Bars in Brazil," 1998). It is hardly surprising that human beings living in such miserable conditions would engage in rebellious behavior on a regular basis.

Overcrowding contributes to the spread of contagious diseases such as tuberculosis and HIV/AIDS, which have reached epidemic levels in the Brazilian penal system. Severely ill and dying prisoners receive little if any medical care and are typically incarcerated with other inmates. One study concluded that approximately 20 percent of Brazil's prison population was HIV-positive. The lack of proper medical treatment not only places inmates at increased risk but it also facilitates the spread of these

maladies in the general public through conjugal visits and when prisoners are released ("Behind Bars in Brazil," 1998).

Violent repeat offenders routinely share the same cells with first-time petty thieves, a situation that leads to a significant amount of prisoner-on-prisoner abuse. In the more dangerous institutions, the strongest, most violent inmates brutalize and often kill weaker prisoners with impunity. Even in relatively tranquil prisons, lesser forms of physical violence and extortion are common occurrences. A recent prison census recorded 131 prisoner-on-prisoner homicides and 45 suicides over a 12-month period, with some of these latter deaths thought to have been coerced ("Behind Bars in Brazil," 1998).

Inmate gangs are responsible for much of the violence; rival groups fight to control the lucrative prison drug trade. After the Carandiru riot in 2001, prison officials transferred 10 gang leaders to other facilities and confiscated cell phones, guns, and hand grenades from their quarters. Although prison gangs such as the First Command of the Capital (known by the initials PCC in Portuguese) are dangerous, they have spearheaded protests for better conditions for all inmates (Rotella and Gobbi, 2001).

A major contributing factor to prisoner-on-prisoner violence is the lack of funds necessary to maintain Brazil's penal system. In many prisons, inmates must supply their own mattresses, bedding, clothing, and toiletries. In some facilities prisoners rely on family and friends to provide them with food or give them money to buy nourishment. The struggle for basic necessities means that physically strong prisoners lacking a support system will exploit weaker inmates who receive money, goods, and food from the outside ("Behind Bars in Brazil," 1998).

Individuals accused of crimes may spend extended periods of time in local jails housed in police precincts. Many of these jails have a torture room. This facility is commonly referred to as the sala de pau (perch room) because the pau de arara, or parrot's perch, is a favorite torture technique of the Brazilian police ("Behind Bars in Brazil," 1998).

> The parrot's perch is a bar on which the victim is suspended from the back of the knees, with his hands tied to his ankles. Once on the perch, the victim, usually stripped naked, is subjected to beatings, electric shocks, and near-drowning. Near-drowning, in turn, is a torture technique in which the victim's head is submerged in a tank of water, or water is forced into the mouth and nostrils. According to those who have undergone this form of torture, the experience produces a terrifying sensation of impending death" (p. 39).

Guards can be particularly brutal in the aftermath of an escape attempt or riot. Individual and group beatings occur with inmates stripped naked and flogged with police batons, wooden sticks, and/or iron bars. Prisoners have been forced to run a gauntlet with guards striking them as they pass, and inmates who run too quickly are forced to pass through a second time. Guards are rarely charged with brutality, and convictions for torturing prisoners are relatively nonexistent ("Behind Bars in Brazil," 1998).

Prison guards in Brazil are underpaid, poorly trained, and often corrupt ("Brazil: Prison Uprisings Reflect Deep-Seated Crisis," 2000). Guards often take money from prisoners in return for letting them smuggle contraband into their cells from visiting areas. The head of a Sao Paulo police lockup stated, "I have only a few jailers, and most of them are corrupt. . . . These guys, they make 300 to 400 reais [approximately U.S.$265–$355] a month. Prisoners offer them huge amounts of money to bring in electric drills. . . . I'm trying to implement a new policy requiring that jailers be searched when they enter" ("Behind Bars in Brazil," p. 72). One prisoner stated that for 30 reais [U.S.$26] a guard will give you the key to another inmate's cell.

Prison conditions have become so unbearable that inmates occasionally conduct a "death lottery," a form of protest wherein the name of a prisoner is drawn and the "winner" is strangled. The lottery continues until some or all of the prison reform demands are met (Epstein, 1998).

The plight of Brazil's almost 9,000 female prisoners (slightly more than 4 percent of the prison population) is not as desperate as that of their male counterparts. Managed by Catholic nuns until 1980, women's detention facilities are not as crowded as male prisons, and riots are infrequent occurrences. However, Human Rights Watch investigators observed a holding cell approximately 16 feet long and 3 feet wide that held 10 women. A significant number of female prisoners are incarcerated for drug offenses, which partially explains the high rate of HIV/AIDS among female detainees. The majority of these women contracted HIV via shared contaminated needles ("Behind Bars in Brazil," 1998).

Most women's prisons allow conjugal visits to inmates who comply with a set of requirements including a history of good behavior, a stable relationship with a male, and the passing of a medical examination that screens for HIV and venereal diseases. Both the woman and her male partner must be interviewed by a prison social worker. Brazilian law states that women prisoners be allowed to keep their babies for the duration of the lactation period. However, this regulation is not always followed. In some cases babies are taken away from their inmate mothers almost immediately after birth, and the women rarely see their newborn children ("Behind Bars in Brazil," 1998).

Brazil's deplorable prison conditions have generated scant attention from a public much more concerned with high rates of crime than the welfare of inmates ("Reforming Sao Paulo's Prison System," 2001). Prisoners come almost exclusively from the poverty-stricken, undereducated, and powerless groups in society and, as such, have few political allies. Data indicate that 95 percent of prisoners are poor, 44 percent are African American or mulatto, 87 percent have less than an eighth-grade education, and 85 percent could not afford a lawyer ("Behind Bars in Brazil," 1998; Epstein, 1998).

In 2000, money was allocated for facilities to house 25,000 additional prisoners and 3,500 top-security places. If these measures come to pass, perhaps authorities can act on some of the 250,000 arrest warrants that were "on hold" because of lack of prison space ("Brazil Grapples with Crime, Punishment, and Policing," 2000; Epstein, 1998).

summary

1. Prison and jail inmates share certain characteristics. In particular, they tend to be poor, undereducated, and African American or Hispanic. They also tend to enter prison with histories of drug and alcohol abuse, mental and physical problems, and sexual and physical victimization. If their prison experience does not alleviate these problems, inmates are likely to emerge from prison worse off than when they entered.

2. The prison is a total institution that controls its inmates' lives. As such, the prison experience includes several pains of imprisonment, including the loss of liberty, goods and services, heterosexual relationships, autonomy, and security.

3. Early prison literature discussed the existence of inmate subcultures that help inmates cope with the pains of imprisonment. More recent literature finds that such subcultures are now more varied than in the past because of the entrance of many new offenders from urban backgrounds who import their own values into the prison. This shift has disrupted the traditional prison social system in which older, white prisoners commanded respect.

4. Despite popular myths, prison and jail conditions are often harsh and grim. This is especially true for inmates living on death row or in supermax facilities. These inmates live mostly in solitary confinement and often lack the amenities that their counterparts in other types of prisons sometimes enjoy.

5. Correctional treatment takes the form of educational and vocational programs and drug and alcohol treatment. It has been shown to be somewhat effective in reducing recidivism and in helping inmates gain employment after they leave prison. Despite this evidence, treatment programs in prisons continue to be poorly designed and inadequately funded.

6. Interpersonal violence is a fact of prison life because of inmates' violent tendencies and prison conditions, such as overcrowding. Sexual violence is common and can have devastating psychological and practical consequences. Prison riots represent a form of collective violence and arise from a weakening of social control in the prison and from rising expectations that are then frustrated.

7. Women prisoners face problems both similar to and different from those encountered by male prisoners. These include sexual victimization by guards and various medical needs and services. They also have important parental needs as mothers. Their inmate subcultures differ from men's in several ways, including the importance placed on close friendships.

8. Three decades of prison litigation have greatly increased prisoners' rights. However, in recent years the U.S. Supreme Court and the Congress have passed various rulings and legislation that have curtailed the ability of prisoners to bring lawsuits and to extend their rights.

9. Release from prison can be frustrating. Inmates reenter society with a prison record, little education, drug and alcohol abuse histories, and other problems that prevent them from finding jobs and otherwise becoming fully functional members of society.

10. Correctional officers play an important role in prison life. They have several complementary views of their role in the prison, with most favoring a human services or order maintenance orientation. Theirs is often a stressful, alienating job, although the degree of stress and alienation depends on the type of prison in which they work and on other aspects of their jobs. Women have proven themselves fully capable as correctional officers despite continuing doubts about their ability to do their job.

key terms

degradation ceremony
deprivation model
formal social control
importation model
informal social control
inmate code
inmate subculture

pains of imprisonment
prison argot
prisonization
rising expectations theory
supermax
total institution

questions *for* investigation

1. As discussed in this chapter, incarceration "magnifies problems people bring to jail and prison." From your reading about the structure and resources of a prison as well as the profile of inmates, elaborate on some possible examples of how prison affects certain inmates.

2. According to this chapter, "few people want to coddle prison and jail inmates, but most would presumably want them to be treated humanely." Discuss "coddling" and "humane treatment."

3. Describe how the conditions behind bars, as discussed in this chapter, affect the pains of imprisonment.

4. Should prisons treat death row prisoners as described in this chapter? Explain your answer.

5. How would you design and manage an educational program for prisoners who want a high school or college degree?

6. Discuss steps or precautions that might be helpful in preventing sexual assault and rape in prisons.

7. Compare the prison subcultures of male and female inmates. Suggest reasons for the differences between them.

8. Consider the problems, needs, and treatment programs for women inmates identified in this chapter. Based on this information, how would you design an appropriate incarceration program for women offenders?

9. If you were the manager of a retail business, such as a restaurant or department store, would you hire a nonviolent ex-convict? Why or why not?

10. Would you consider a career as a prison correctional officer? Why or why not?

1. Suppose you are a guard in a medium-security prison. Several of the guards take petty bribes from inmates to look the other way when trouble occurs, but you believe in enforcing prison rules about behavior and safety to the best of your ability. Your fellow guards sometimes mock your position, but generally treat you well enough. One day three inmates rape another inmate. Two other guards and you discover the incident seconds after the rape has ended, and the situation is relatively clear. The three offenders have been among the most active in paying the other guards to look the other way; they offer to do so again, and the other two guards accept their offer. Now you have to decide whether to take a bribe and remain silent, or, instead, to report the occurrence. What do you do?

2. Suppose you are a woman serving 3 years in a state prison for drug possession. You notice a suspicious lump on your breast and ask to see the prison doctor, who only visits the prison once per week. Your request is noted, but no medical appointment is scheduled for the next 3 weeks. You ask for an appointment again, but this time the guard simply laughs at you and calls you a malingerer. What do you do now?

UNDER Investigation

Health and Health Care in Prisons

Many inmates suffer from a host of mental and physical problems and have histories of drug and alcohol abuse. These problems make it especially important that inmates receive adequate care while incarcerated. How adequate is this care?

Before the 1970s, it was, according to a recent review, "substandard at best, relative to the quality of care available in the larger society, and appallingly negligent and even brutal at worst. . . . Health care was often delivered, if at all, by persons having little or no medical training—sometimes, even other prisoners—or by small numbers of qualified physicians overwhelmed by huge caseloads" (McDonald, 1999, pp. 427–428). As late as the early 1970s, inmates in Alabama's prisons would extract teeth, perform minor surgery, prescribe drugs, and use X-ray machines. Only three nurses were available for the 4,000 inmates in the state's prisons. In Pennsylvania prisons, guards would block entry to "sick call," special diets for diabetics were unknown, psychiatric services were rare, and one large prison had no registered nurses. Studies in other states found similar conditions (McDonald, 1999).

Beginning in the late 1960s, however, a series of federal court decisions established several health care standards for correctional facilities to follow. Health care spending in these institutions rose dramatically, and correctional health care improved greatly. Despite these rulings, however, several serious problems in such care remain. Human Rights Watch (2001b) charges that health care in many of the nation's correctional institutions remains "inadequate."

One reason for this inadequacy is that prison guards and medical personnel often doubt the claims of prisoners that they are ill. Instead, they believe these claims are pretenses for malingering (Dabney and Vaughn, 2000). Second, and more important, it is dif-

> "*. . . it is **difficult** to **recruit qualified physicians** to work in prisons and jails.*"

ficult to recruit qualified physicians to work in prisons and jails (McDonald, 1999). Not surprisingly, most physicians do not view these settings as desirable places to practice, and their compensation is generally lower than in the outside world. As a result, prisons and jails typically attract and employ physicians who are less qualified than their noncorrections counterparts and those who are apt to have faced disciplinary charges by medical review boards. As a recent review noted, "There is a widespread belief in the medical community that correctional physicians are inept and cannot find free-world (non-prison) employment, necessitating their appointment in prisons and/or jails" (Dabney and Vaughn, 2000, p. 184). Supporting this view, several studies have found that at least 25 percent of correctional physicians in some states have been disciplined by medical boards compared to less than 3 percent of noncorrectional physicians, and many courts have con-cluded that correctional physicians and other medical staff are unqualified or inept (Dabney and Vaughn, 2000).

A recent report by the Correctional Association of New York, a prison reform group, supports this con-clusion. For 18 months in 1998 and 1999, the group interviewed 1,300 inmates and 100 medical profes-sionals in 22 prisons in that state. Although it found that the prisons had improved their medical treatment, it also found that several health care problems remained. One of the most important was a shortage of board cer-tified physicians, meaning that many physicians in the prisons were unqualified. The executive director of the Correctional Association said, "We got the impression that the prison system was the employer of last resort for that doctor, and as a result health care in those fa-cilities is compromised." In response, the state defended the qualifications of its prison physicians ("Group Finds Health Care . . . ," 2000, p. B4).

A third reason for inadequate correctional medical care is the lack of adequate health facilities and diag-nostic equipment (McDonald, 1999). Many prisons

"Many prisons have no way to isolate prisoners with infectious diseases . . ."

have no way to isolate prisoners with infectious dis-eases, and their infirmaries lack 24-hour nursing. Pris-oners with chronic illnesses are not separated from other inmates. This means that prisons often have to rely on nearby hospitals to care for some of their in-mates. But because at least one guard must take an in-mate to the hospital and stay with the inmate until he or she is released, such hospital visits are "exceedingly limited" (McDonald, 1999, p. 443).

Special Health Problems in Prison: HIV/AIDS and Tuberculosis

Inmates have many physical and mental health prob-lems; one of the most serious is HIV/AIDS. In 1999, 2.3 percent of all state and federal prisoners were known to have the human immunodeficiency virus, or HIV

(Maruschak, 2001). The actual number of HIV-positive inmates was 25,757, of whom about one-third were confined in New York state and another 10 percent in Florida. Of the total number of HIV inmates nationally, 6,642 were confirmed AIDS cases; 242 prison inmates died from AIDS complications in 1999, down from 1,010 in 1995. The 1999 figure represented about 8 per-cent of all deaths among state prisoners that year, and AIDS complications were the second leading cause of death after natural causes other than AIDS (see Figure 13.8). A small gender difference exists for HIV: 3.4 per-cent of female state prison inmates were HIV-positive at year end 1999 compared to 2.1 percent of male in-mates (Maruschak, 2001).

The rate of confirmed AIDS cases among prison in-mates is about twice as high as that for the entire U.S. population. A major reason for this disparity is the high number of intravenous drug users among prison in-mates. Many inmates, as we have seen, used drugs be-fore entering prison; moreover, many are also in prison for drug possession. These two facts contribute to the concentration of HIV and AIDS in the nation's prisons (McDonald, 1999). The type of drug used also makes a difference: Of inmates who ever shared a needle as part of drug use, 7.7 percent tested positive compared to only 2.3 percent of those who had used drugs but had never shared a needle and 1.7 percent of those who had never used drugs (Maruschak, 1999).

Human Rights Watch (2001a) points out that "[n]ot only do people entering prison tend to have a relatively high incidence of HIV, pris-ons provide a perfect breeding ground for trans-mission of the virus." Unprotected homosexual sex and prison rape are certainly not unknown, and when they involve a partner or rapist with HIV, the risk of infection for a non-HIV inmate is great. Another high-risk behavior, injection drug use, also occurs in prisons, as do fighting, stabbings, and other actions that can shed blood. Prisons could reduce the risk of HIV transmission by providing condoms and bleach for ster-ilizing needles and syringes, but this is rarely done; in-stead, condoms are considered contraband. In contrast, Canada distributes condoms in all its federal prisons, placing them in shower areas, the canteen, and en-trances to prison infirmaries. Most other Western na-tions also distribute condoms in their prisons. U.S. prison officials reply that condoms could be used to strangle other inmates and to hide drugs (MacKeen, 1999).

Critics say that prison and jail inmates with HIV or AIDS do not receive adequate treatment (Cusac, 2000). Guards and medical staff, they say, have prevented in-mates from taking their daily, three-drug regimen. An

Amnesty International official notes, "We routinely get letters from people who are not getting their medica-

"Critics say that prison and jail *inmates* with *HIV* or *AIDS* do *not* receive adequate treatment."

tions" (in Cusac, 2000, p. 22). A prison in Mississippi required HIV or AIDS inmates to prove that they could handle a two-drug regimen for 6 months before allowing them to take the third drug. Inmates from the prison filed suit in 1999, and a physician who testified for them later said, "What they were doing [in the prison] was barbaric" (Cusac, 2000, pp. 22–23). A study in South Carolina in 2000 found the same problem occurring in that state's prisons. Prisons in other states force their inmates to take their medication at mealtime even though having food in the stomach can reduce the effectiveness of the drugs they take.

One reason prisons deny HIV and AIDS inmates their required medication is because the medication is very expensive, with an annual cost of about $12,000 per inmate. The lack of doctors and other medical personnel is another reason inmates with HIV or AIDS fail to get their proper medication. The lack of proper treatment endangers not only the inmates' health but also that of the larger society because it can prompt drug-resistant strains of HIV to develop. When inmates with these strains are released back into society, these strains can then be transmitted to people outside prison (Cusac, 2000).

"The *TB* prison rate is *six* times higher than that of the U.S. population . . ."

Tuberculosis (TB) is another special health problem in prison; like HIV and AIDS, it is much more common in prisons than in the outside world. The TB prison rate is six times higher than that of the U.S. population, and

at least 15,000 prisoners are thought to have TB nationwide. The prison rate is so high because prisoners come from backgrounds—poverty and poor health care, crowded housing, prior intravenous drug use—that put them at high risk for TB. Moreover, prisons and jails are "nearly ideal places for transmitting the disease" (McDonald, 1999, p. 451) given their frequent overcrowding and poor ventilation. This again poses a danger to the larger society: When prisoners with TB are released, they return to their communities, many of which have living conditions conducive to TB infection. Recognizing this threat, the corrections system established better TB testing and treatment procedures during the 1990s, but TB remains a significant health problem in U.S. prisons and jails (McDonald, 1999).

Health Care for Older Prisoners

About 50,000 state and federal prisoners—or more than 3 percent of all prisoners—are age 55 or older; this number is seven times higher than it was at the beginning of the 1980s. This increase stems from the greater number of prisoners in general since that time, but also from such factors as "three strikes laws" (see Chapter 11) and the lowered use or abolition of parole. According to a recent estimate, it costs almost $70,000 per year to incarcerate an elderly inmate, or more than $2 billion annually, compared to about $25,000 per year for younger inmates (Drummond, 1999).

The major reason for the high cost of elderly inmates is medical care. As prisoners age, their medical problems multiply (Stolberg, 2001). For example, almost half of prisoners age 45 or older report physical impairment or a mental condition compared to less than one-fourth of those 24 or younger (Maruschak and Beck, 2001). Inmates 65 and older spend twice as much time in medical facilities and incur medical costs that are three times higher than those for younger inmates.

As the Coalition for Federal Sentencing Reform (2001) notes, "Many medical problems of the elderly ultimately require constant bed care and intensive medical supervision. These problems stretch the resources and capabilities of correctional institutions while providing no additional safety to the community." An example of such intensive treatment is a prison near Pittsburgh that provides extensive nursing home facilities. It includes an 85-bed, long-term care unit that employs 48 nurses. Many of the prisoners watch TV all day; several are confined to wheelchairs; and many take med-

Under Investigation: Health and Health Care in Prisons

ication for heart disease, diabetes, and other problems (Drummond, 1999).

Ironically, elderly prisoners might actually receive better care in prison than they would outside prison

> **"Ironically, elderly prisoners might actually receive better care in prison than they would outside prison . . ."**

where, Medicare notwithstanding, elderly medical care can be prohibitively expensive. Moreover, inmates who have spent their whole lives in prison often have no family or friends left to care for them on the outside (Drummond, 1999). These problems underscore the difficulty of deciding what to do about health care for elderly prisoners. But many observers think that keep-

ing them in prison is unnecessarily expensive, especially because they are thought to pose only minimal threats to public safety. As a news report on elderly prisoners asked, "just how much sense does it make for society to keep these mostly nonviolent, broken old men incarcerated?" (Drummond, 1999, p. 60). The executive director of the Pennsylvania Prison Society also observed, "To keep some of these folks in prison for the length of time we do is purely punitive and serves no purpose to society" (Drummond, 1999, p. 60).

Prison reform groups call for nonprison alternatives for elderly inmates who need nursing home care and, further, for the release of elderly inmates convicted of nonviolent offenses. The Coalition for Federal Sentencing Reform (2001) recommends "structured supervised release" for nonviolent offenders 55 or older who have served more than one-third of their sentence and who are not considered a threat to public safety. It estimates this proposal would save nearly $1 billion in prison costs in the first year after its implementation. Such a program would help keep society safe while saving a considerable sum of money.

Community
Corrections
and Juvenile
Justice

1. What does community corrections involve? What is the difference between probation and parole?

2. What problems are associated with probation?

3. Is probation effective?

4. What are intermediate sanctions?

5. What problems are associated with parole?

6. What changes have occurred in the history of the juvenile justice system?

7. Which intermediate sanctions have been effective for serious and violent juvenile offenders? How have early childhood and adolescent programs combated juvenile problems?

In May 2001, Judge Manuel Banales of Corpus Christi, Texas, ordered 14 sex offenders who were on probation to post warning signs in their yards and bumper stickers on their cars. The signs in the yards proclaimed, "DANGER. Registered Sex Offender Lives Here," and the bumper stickers gave similar warnings. The judge's action was in keeping with a 1999 Texas law that gave judges the authority to require public punishment for crimes such as drunk driving and sex offenses. He selected the 14 probationers after consulting with probation officers to determine which sex offenders on probation showed the greatest risk for committing new sex crimes.

The effects of his order on the sex offenders were quite apparent. One of the offenders said, "I made my mistake, and I'm paying for it. I can't even go out and cut my yard. I just stay in the house. . . . I was doing good in therapy. How is this helping me?" (Thomas and Hylton, 2001, p. 82). Another offender tried to commit suicide, and members of the offenders' families worried about possible violence from people incensed by the presence of a sex offender in their midst. Critics charged that Judge Banales's action violated the rights of the probationers and punished their families as well. But probation officers applauded his move. One officer said, "It's definitely a deterrent now. Other offenders are saying to us, 'We'll do whatever it takes not to have signs' " (Thomas and Hylton, 2001, p. 82).

Attorneys for the probationers filed suits in the Thirteenth Court of Appeals in Corpus Christi to overturn the judge's order on the grounds that it was cruel and unusual punishment, and that it violated the probationers' rights to privacy. In a February 2002 ruling on one of the cases, the Thirteenth Court said that Judge Banales had exceeded his discretion, and it reversed his order for one of the probationers, who had plead guilty to indecency with a child. A month later, the Texas Office of the Attorney General filed a motion on behalf of Judge Banales to the Texas Court of Criminal Appeals to overturn the Thirteenth Court's ruling (*Texas Lawyer,* 2002).

This is one of the signs that Judge Manuel Banales ordered fourteen sex offenders to place in their yards. This example reminds us that corrections take place in the community as well as in a jail or prison.

As this Texan tale reminds us, corrections do not take place only in a prison or jail cell. Many convicted offenders are sentenced to probation or intermediate sanctions such as electronic monitoring and serve their sentences in the community. Many prisoners leave prison on parole, and they, too, serve the remainder of their sentences in the community. In fact, slightly more than two-thirds of the 6.5 million Americans under correctional supervision are actually in the community and not behind bars.

These figures apply only to adults. About 2.5 million arrests of juveniles (persons under age 18) occur each year, but only about 170,000 youths are then placed in juvenile correctional institutions or other residential facilities. In between these two stages of the juvenile justice system is a series of stages that determine the fate of youthful offenders, most of whom are given probation or other sanctions. They, too, serve their sentence in the community.

To understand the U.S. correctional system fully, we must appreciate the types of community corrections that millions of adults experience and also the system of justice used for juvenile offenders. This final chapter thus examines community corrections and juvenile justice in the United States. A major theme is the effectiveness and cost of community corrections for adults and juveniles compared to incarceration.

Community Corrections

An Overview

correctional supervision
incarceration, probation, intermediate sanctions, and parole

Incarceration in prison or jail is obviously one major way in which people come under **correctional supervision** and undoubtedly the form of supervision with which most people are familiar from films, books, TV, and the news media. Two other forms of correctional supervision include probation and parole. Although offenders on probation or parole are out in the community and not behind bars, they are not totally free; their movements are at least partly under correctional control. Intermediate sanctions are also used to control offenders.

Probation refers to the sentence of a convicted offender to supervision in the community by an agent of the court called a **probation officer;** this sentence is in lieu of incarceration as long as the offender obeys all terms of the probation. These conditions vary from one case to another but typically include reporting to the probation officer regularly, abstaining from alcohol and drug use, not engaging in criminal behavior, observing a curfew, looking for work, and working once a job is obtained. If an offender violates any of these conditions, he or she risks incarceration.

Parole is often confused with probation because it also occurs in the community, but it refers to the supervision of an offender who is released from prison after serving a term of incarceration. The person who supervises an offender on parole is the **parole officer.** The conditions of parole are similar to those for probation, and an offender who violates any condition also risks being returned to prison.

As their name implies, **intermediate sanctions** occur "in between" probation and incarceration. They are meant to be more punitive than probation but less punitive than incarceration. They are really a special form of probation and include several types as discussed shortly.

Having reviewed the terminology, we now examine some of the statistics and trends in probation and parole. Figure 14.1 shows the trend in all forms of correctional supervision since 1980. Note two things: First, the number of people in all forms of correctional supervision has increased greatly since 1980. Second, the number of people on probation dwarfs the number in any other form of supervision and, in fact, exceeds the three other forms combined.

About 6.6 million people, or 3.1 percent, of the adult U.S. population are under correctional supervision (year end 2001). This number includes more than 4.6 million under *community* supervision (3.93 million on probation and 731,000 on parole), representing about 2.2 percent of the adult population and about a 45 percent increase during the 1990s. More than 1 million of all probationers and parolees live in Texas or California. Several states, led by Georgia with about 5.5 percent, have more than

probation supervision in the community of a convicted offender in lieu of imprisonment

probation officer a legal official who handles the cases of people on probation

parole supervision of an offender released from prison after serving a term of incarceration

parole officer a legal official who handles the cases of people on parole

intermediate sanctions social controls that are supposedly more punitive than routine probation but less punitive than incarceration

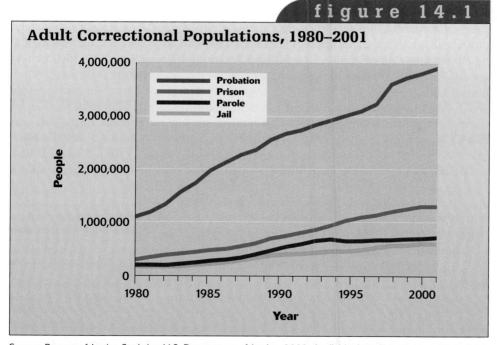

figure 14.1

Adult Correctional Populations, 1980–2001

Source: Bureau of Justice Statistics, U.S. Department of Justice. 2003. Available: http://www.ojp.usdoj.gov/bjs/glance/corr2.htm.

3 percent of their populations under community supervision (Bureau of Justice Statistics, 2001).

In any given year, many people are terminated from probation or parole and thus leave community corrections for one of two opposite reasons: either they successfully complete the terms of their supervision or they violate at least one such term. Almost 2 million probationers and 460,000 parolees left community supervision for either reason in 2000 (Bureau of Justice Statistics, 2001). They were, of course, replaced by even more people because the number of people on probation and parole continues to rise each year. Next, we examine discharge from probation and parole.

Probation

As noted previously, more than 3.8 million people, or 59 percent of the correctional population, are on probation in lieu of incarceration. With such a massive number of convicted offenders in the community, it is important to understand how probation works and how effective it is. To begin understanding these issues, we sketch the history of probation since its origins and development and present its current problems and prospects.

History of Probation. The roots of probation in the United States are based in the colonial era. Recall from Chapter 12 that colonial jails held debtors or people awaiting trial. Instead of incarceration, the primary punishments were fines, shaming, flogging, and, occasionally, execution. But in addition to these forms, courts sometimes allowed offenders to post a cash "peace bond" in lieu of another punishment. Under the terms of the bond, offenders reported to the court regularly. Sometimes courts required peace bonds even for people who had not been convicted of crimes but who were considered potential offenders. The goal was to supervise them and prevent misbehavior. Under the concept of "judicial reprieve," judges could postpone a flogging sentence as long as the offender obeyed the law. Somewhat later, prosecutors would lay the cases of some offenders "on file" and not prosecute as long as the offender behaved. Similar to modern-day probation, these actions kept offenders from being punished provided they obeyed the law (Walker, 1998).

The formal system of probation, however, did not develop until just before the Civil War when incarceration had become the standard punishment. The key impetus was the work of a wealthy Boston shoemaker named John Augustus, a religious man who posted bail for almost 2,000 offenders between 1841 and 1858. Most of them were first-time offenders charged with vice or drinking violations. He then supervised their behavior and helped some find jobs, get educations, or find living accommodations. When defendants came before a judge for sentencing a few weeks later, Augustus would vouch for the offenders' behavior, who were then assessed a small fine instead of incarceration. The amount of bail Augustus paid for all the defendants he helped was $243,234, a figure equal to about $5 million in today's dollars. Augustus's efforts initially met with resistance because judges and police thought offenders should be punished, rather than helped, but his persistence was rewarded because it persuaded some officials that alternatives to incarceration could make sense (Petersilia, 1997; Walker, 1998).

More importantly, Augustus's strategy helped lead to the nation's first formal system of probation some years later. A Boston police captain named Edward H. Savage had performed the equivalent of presentence investigations of prostitutes in 1858 after a mass arrest. He recommended that the judge give the arrestees suspended sentences and that they be allowed to continue living in the community. Savage later became the Boston police chief, then resigned in 1878 to become the first probation officer for Suffolk County, where Boston is located, after Massachusetts passed the nation's first state statute authorizing probation officers. The Massachusetts statute initially authorized probation officers only in Suffolk County, but it created a statewide system by 1891. Missouri followed suit in 1897 and, in turn, was followed by Rhode Island in 1899, and New Jersey and Vermont in 1900. By the early twentieth century the system of probation had spread throughout the country as the nation began to emphasize, as was discussed in Chapter 12, the goal of rehabilitation and the need for individual treatment (Walker, 1998).

As probation developed, it drew heavily on Augustus's work with Massachusetts offenders. As Joan Petersilia (1997, p. 156) notes, "Virtually every basic practice of probation was conceived by him. He was the first person to use the term 'probation'—which comes from the Latin term *probatio,* meaning a 'period of proving or trial.' He developed the ideas of the presentence investigation, supervision conditions, social casework, reports to the court, and revocation of probation."

Although probation was a notable reform in the early twentieth century, it faced several problems. One was the lack of qualified probation officers: It was difficult to hire competent people who would take the job seriously. Another problem was the inability of even competent probation officers to provide the supervision and treatment offenders needed. As Samuel Walker (1998, pp. 124–125) noted, "Because of enormous caseloads, supervision amounted to little more than an occasional contact." Caseloads averaged 150 to 300 offenders per probation officer, far more than the maximum of 50 that was recommended back then. During the early 1900s, probation officers in New York spent only 10 minutes per year with each probationer, and some Chicago probation officers could not find their clients' files and did not even know where they lived (Walker, 1998).

How Probation Works. Although probation is one type of community corrections, probation officers actually are involved in all stages of the criminal justice system. They first gather information to help judges determine whether defendants should be released on their own recognizance or on bail. If a defendant is convicted, a probation officer gathers more information and files a presentence report with the court (see Chapter 11). As such, probation officers serve an *investigation* function in addition to the *supervisory* function usually associated with them (Storm, 1997).

The judge's sentence usually follows the sentence recommendation contained in the probation officer's report. For every 100 defendants convicted of felonies, 31 percent are sentenced to straight probation (with no jail or prison time to serve), either with or without a suspended term of incarceration, and another 27 percent receive "split sentences," meaning they receive a combination of probation and incarceration in prison or jail. Adding these figures together, 58 percent of convicted felons receive probation sentences, which average almost 3.5 years each (Levin et al., 2000).

What determines whether someone is sentenced to probation rather than incarceration? As noted in Chapter 11, the seriousness of the offense and the defendant's prior record have the greatest influence in general sentencing decisions, and personal factors, such as race, play more subtle, complex roles (Myers, 2000). The probation literature reports similar findings. One of the best probation studies analyzed the cases of 16,500 California males convicted of various felonies. The researchers found that defendants were more likely to receive probation rather than imprisonment if, among other factors, they had fewer than two prior convictions, were not using drugs, did not use a weapon to commit the crime, and did not seriously injure the victim. They were also more likely to receive probation if they had private attorneys rather than public defenders and if they had been out on bail before their trials. All these factors accounted for 75 percent of the cases in the study; this means that no identifiable factors could explain why 25 percent of the defendants got either probation or imprisonment. This finding led the authors to conclude that many offenders who get probation are no different from those who are incarcerated (Petersilia and Turner, 1986).

When judges sentence defendants to probation, they list the conditions the probationers must follow; these conditions form a contract between the court and the offender. Usually, the conditions have been recommended by a probation officer in the presentence report, but judges also sometimes develop their own. Three types of conditions exist. *Standard conditions,* as their name implies, are given to virtually all probationers and involve such requirements as looking for work, reporting changes of address, and not associating with known criminals. *Punitive conditions* are given to more serious offenders and include intermediate sanctions discussed later. *Treatment conditions* are sometimes required for offenders with various personal problems such as drug or alcohol abuse. Various court rulings have established that all these conditions must be reasonable and constitutional; for example, they cannot take away a probationer's freedom of speech (Reichel, 2001).

Several outcomes are possible if a probationer violates the terms of probation. First, the judge may simply continue the probationary sentence without any changes in the conditions. Second, the judge may extend the length of the sentence and/or impose new, more restrictive conditions. Third, the judge may revoke probation and order the probationer to prison or jail.

As previously noted, almost 2 million people left probation in 2000. About 60 percent of these were "successful completions": They simply completed their probationary term. About 15 percent were incarcerated after having their probation revoked for violating at least one condition. The remainder left probation for other reasons, including 3 percent who absconded and 1 percent who died (Bureau of Justice Statistics, 2001). It is estimated that on any one day about 10 to 20 percent of adult probationers officially abscond with no known address. Warrants are usually issued for their arrests but no one really tries to find and arrest them (Taxman and Byrne, 1994).

Certain personal characteristics predict who is most likely to complete probation successfully. In general, successful completers include those who are married and who have children, who are employed, who are educated, and who have few prior arrests and convictions. Probationers with fewer or no substance abuse problems also are more likely to complete probation successfully (Morgan, 1994).

Who Is on Probation? Of the more than 3.8 million people on probation, 52 percent were convicted of felonies and 46 percent of misdemeanors. Seventy-eight percent of all probationers are men, and 22 percent are women; 64 percent of all probationers are white and 34 percent are African Americans. Hispanics, who can be of any race, comprise 16 percent of all probationers. Southerners comprise about 41 percent of all probationers (Bureau of Justice Statistics, 2001).

Is Probation Effective? The effectiveness of probation depends on the criteria that are used to asses it. The two most common criteria in measuring correctional effectiveness (and two used in assessing the impact of incarceration discussed in Chapter 12) are cost and recidivism. When it comes to dollars, probation is very effective even if it is difficult to accurately determine how much probation costs. Some estimates simply total the salaries of probation officers, whereas others add in other costs, such as the salaries of office staff, office overhead, and the costs of services and programs provided to probationers. Because of these different standards, estimates of the cost of probation range widely from about $200 to $2,000 per probationer per year (Petersilia, 1998). Yet even the higher figure in this range is much lower than the more than $20,000 per year it costs to imprison one person. If we venture to say that probation saves at least $18,000 per year, and then assume for the sake of argument that half of all probationers, or about 1.9 million people, would need to be added to our nation's prisons if probation did not exist, prison costs would rise by $34 billion annually. This figure does not even include the extra 1,900 prisons that would have to be built (assuming 1,000 persons per prison) at a cost of close to $200 billion. Probation obviously saves a lot of money.

But does probation keep society safe? When it comes to recidivism, the effectiveness of probation depends on how we view the data. On the one hand, 60 percent of probationers end their terms successfully. The majority, then, do well, especially given their backgrounds and lack of help and supervision while on probation (discussed later). On the other hand, 15 percent, or almost 300,000 people, were incarcerated in 2000 after failing probation. The majority of these revocations are for new offenses, amounting to many thousands of serious crimes, and not only for the violation of a probation condition.

Felons and misdemeanants each comprise about half the probationary population, and the failure rate, including recidivism, is much higher if we examine only felons.

Almost three-fourths of misdemeanants complete probation successfully, but about 60 percent of felons do *not* complete probation successfully. Most of the latter are rearrested for new crimes; one study found that 43 percent of felons on probation were rearrested for serious crimes (Langan and Cunniff, 1992). Recidivism rates for felons on probation are thus high nationwide but vary greatly by location: Depending on the area studied, rearrest rates vary from 12 to 65 percent (Geerken and Hayes, 1993). By the same token, recidivism rates for misdemeanants are low, and for financial reasons it might not be cost effective to put them on probation in the first place (Petersilia, 1997).

Close to 30 percent of prisoners overall were on probation at the time they committed the crime that put them behind bars. This amounts to several hundred thousand crimes. If all the felons who fail probation had been put in prison originally instead of on probation, their many crimes would not have occurred. However, it would have been impossible to predict these failed probationers at the time of sentencing. Although we know the factors that predict probationary success and failure (see prior discussion), using this information at the time of sentencing to predict failure would lead to many "false positives" and "false negatives" (Petersilia, 1997). Thus the only way to prevent new crimes during probation would be to end probation altogether. As we have seen, however, that would be prohibitively expensive.

Todd Clear and Karen Terry (2000) argue that assessing the effectiveness of probation by looking *only* at the recidivism of people on probation misses the point. A more relevant question, they say, is this: How does the effectiveness of putting offenders on probation compare to the effectiveness of putting them in prison? Unfortunately, only a few studies have tried to answer this question. They find that the recidivism rates of felons sentenced to probation are very similar to those of matched groups of felons sentenced to prison. Put another way, the high recidivism of offenders put on probation is *not* higher than that of similar offenders put in prison, but neither is it lower. This is a bad news/good news situation. The bad news is that probation is not more effective than imprisonment, but the good news is that probation is also not *less* effective.

The Problems with Probation. Two problems with probation explain why recidivism of felon probationers is as high as it is, even if it is not higher than that of people put in prison. These problems are similar to those besetting probation in the early twentieth century. The first problem is that probation officers have caseloads that are far too heavy (Petersilia, 1997). The recommended caseload for optimal supervision is about 30 to 50 adult probationers for every probation officer, but, according to recent estimates, the average caseload nationwide is about 260 persons for every officer; this figure varies by location and is as high as 400 in California and 1,000 in Los Angeles. Caseloads are thus more than five to eight times larger than they should be. The typical probationer sees a probation officer no more than once a month and often less than that; the typical probationer in Los Angeles spends less than 2 hours per year with a probation officer. About 20 percent of probationers nationwide never see their probation officer at all.

With slightly fewer than 4 million people on probation, the nation thus needs many more probation officers than it now has. Despite this need, the emphasis in recent decades on incarceration has led probation to be underfunded. In Los Angeles, for example, where the caseloads are so high, the city's probation budget has been cut repeatedly since the 1970s even though the number of people on probation and the number of defendants needing presentence investigations have risen dramatically (Petersilia, 1997).

The second problem is the lack of programs and services for probationers. As discussed in Chapter 13, many offenders have low levels of education and high levels of drug and alcohol abuse, mental and physical problems, and sexual and physical victimization; these problems are much more common than in past generations. Yet less than 30 percent of all probationers receive drug or alcohol abuse treatment or vocational training (S. Walker, 2001). Petersilia (1998, p. 579) says that in many jurisdictions "the services are woefully inadequate to meet the needs of today's community corrections clients."

The low supervision stemming from heavy caseloads and lack of programs and services in turn help produce the high recidivism rates by felon probationers. As Petersilia (1998, pp. 581–582) puts it, "It is no wonder that recidivism rates are so high. In a sense, we get what we pay for, and, as yet, we have never chosen to invest sufficiently in [probation]."

Improving Probation. This last point suggests that more money should be invested in probation. The needed dollars could come from a decreased emphasis on imprisonment, say for the many offenders now in prison for property and drug offenses not involving violence who could instead be put on probation.

This increased funding for probation would have two important benefits. First, it would save money because the increased cost of probation would still be less than the cost savings achieved by lower imprisonment rates. Second, it would make society safer because it would facilitate hiring many more probation officers, reduce caseloads and thus increase supervision, and pay for more numerous and effective treatment programs and other services. Where it has been tried, the combination of increased supervision and greater treatment and programming achieves significant reductions in recidivism (Petersilia, 1997). We return to this point later in our discussion of intensive supervision as one of the intermediate sanctions.

Intermediate Sanctions

Because felons on probation have high recidivism rates, probation came under attack in the early 1980s as the nation abandoned rehabilitation as a goal of punishment in favor of retribution, deterrence, and incapacitation. This attack coincided with increased overcrowding in the nation's prisons from the surge in imprisonment that began in the 1970s (see Chapter 12). Interest heightened in developing different forms of probation for property offenders and some violent offenders involving more supervision and greater restrictions. These new forms would be harsher than routine probation but not as harsh as imprisonment. The goal was to make probation and also parole work better while still avoiding the extra cost of incarceration and associated overcrowding (Tonry, 1998b).

These new forms of punishment came to be known as *subincarceration* or, more commonly, intermediate sanctions, because they come "in between" routine probation and incarceration (Clear and Terry, 2000). Conservatives favored them because they seemed harsher than routine probation and promised lower recidivism rates at a lower cost than incarceration. Liberals also favored them because they stopped short of imprisonment and allowed offenders to remain in the community. With so much support from opposite sides of the political spectrum, intermediate sanctions quickly became popular. Today about 10 percent of adult probationers and parolees, or about 450,000 people, participate in them.

In this section, we discuss the most popular types of intermediate sanctions; the focus is on their effectiveness, using recidivism as our main criterion but also considering other criteria. In general, we note that, with one or two exceptions, intermediate sanctions have largely failed to achieve lower recidivism rates than routine probation. At the same time, the success of some intermediate sanctions suggests that their promise can be achieved with suitable funding and adequate program design. We discuss several types of intermediate sanctions separately, but note that two or more sanctions are often combined in practice (see Table 14.1).

house arrest an intermediate sanction involving confinement in one's home

electronic monitoring an intermediate sanction that uses an electronic device to pinpoint the location of an offender

House Arrest and Electronic Monitoring. Two intermediate sanctions have been **house arrest** and **electronic monitoring**. Although in theory they are different sanctions—an offender could be restricted to home without electronic monitoring or be monitored without being restricted to home—in reality, they often occur together, and we treat them here as one sanction.

The problem with requiring house arrest without electronic monitoring is that it is very difficult to determine whether the offender really stays at home. When tech-

table 14.1

Types of Intermediate Sanctions

Community service: work in the community under close supervision; imprisonment is a possible penalty if offenders fail to complete their service

Day-reporting centers: locations where offenders attend required treatment and vocational programs during the daytime and then leave to go home for the night

Fines, restitution, and forfeiture: financial sanctions. Fines are payments of money to a court; restitution is the payment of money or provision of services to the offender's victim(s); forfeiture involves taking personal property from an offender.

House arrest and electronic monitoring: confinement to one's home with electronic devices to ensure compliance to such confinement

Intensive supervision: surveillance of offenders that is more intense than routine probation in frequency and behavioral restrictions

Shock probation (boot camp): confinement in a paramilitary setting intended to instill respect for authority, a sense of responsibility, and a reluctance to reoffend

nological advances by the 1980s made electronic monitoring possible, the combination of house arrest and electronic monitoring became a popular option. It was first used for minor property offenders and for those convicted of driving while intoxicated. Later it was used for other types of offenders. Used separately or in combination, house arrest and electronic monitoring are now used in all 50 states. About 1 percent of probationers

Electronic monitoring, such as the ankle device shown here, is a type of intermediate sanction that is intended to save prison costs while still maintaining public safety.

and parolees, some 40,000 in number, are monitored (Petersilia, 2000a). Typically, the offender wears a device on his or her wrist or ankle that sends a signal through a device placed in the home to a computer that can tell whether the signal is coming from the offender's home. The offender cannot remove the wrist or ankle device without alerting authorities.

Despite many hopes, house arrest and electronic monitoring have not proven very workable (Baumer, Maxfield, and Mendelsohn, 1993; Bonta and Wallace-Capretta, 2000; Clear and Terry, 2000). Two problems concern the monitoring equipment: It is very expensive and often produces both "false positives" (false reports that the offender *is* at home) and "false negatives" (false reports that the offender is *not* at home). It is also difficult to determine what the penalty should be if the offender leaves home. Imprisonment seems too harsh for this sort of violation, but what other penalty would be appropriate? Yet if no penalty occurs, the offender has no incentive to stay at home. Another problem is that, when offenders are imprisoned for violating house arrest, more prison beds are filled than would occur if the offenders were simply on routine probation, "widening the net" of incarcerated offenders and thus defeating one of the prime goals of intermediate sanctions. House arrest and electronic monitoring also do not prevent the offender from committing crimes such as domestic violence and drug use and trafficking at home. Finally, this form of probation has been used primarily for low-risk offenders who probably would not commit new crimes even if they were not being monitored. Perhaps for this reason, house arrest and electronic monitoring do not appear from the few studies that have evaluated them to produce lower recidivism rates than those achieved by similar, low-risk offenders on routine probation.

Shock Probation: Boot Camps. Another intermediate sanction for which there was initial enthusiasm that has since waned is **shock probation** in the form of the **boot camp.** Offenders, typically young males convicted of property crimes and other less serious offenses, are sent to a paramilitary setting for several months where they receive similar treatment to that greeting new recruits in military boot camps. The harsh treatment offenders receive is meant to instill in them respect for authority, teach them responsibility, and "shock" them into not wanting to reoffend. The goal is not only to reduce their recidivism but also to reduce prison crowding by placing them in boot camp instead of prison. Depending on the boot camp, offenders usually stay from 3 to 6 months. All boot camps emphasize discipline achieved through military drill, hard labor, and intense exercise, but some also use drug treatment and other programs. Georgia and Oklahoma created the first two boot camps in 1983. A decade later they

shock probation an intermediate sanction, usually in the form of a boot camp, meant to "shock" offenders into obeying the law

boot camp an intermediate sanction involving a paramilitary environment

The "boot camp" is a form of shock probation in which offenders, typically young males convicted of property crimes and other less serious offenses, are sent to a paramilitary setting for several months where they receive similar treatment to that greeting new recruits in military boot camps.

were found in 30 states, and now exist in 35 states. About 10,000 adult probationers and parolees participate in boot camps, and about half that number are juvenile offenders (later discussion) (Petersilia, 2000a; Selcraig, 2000).

As Tonry (1998b) notes, boot camps have inherent appeal. Many U.S. men and some women have experienced the "original" boot camp after joining the military and recall learning discipline and teamwork. Public opinion polls indicate that the public supports boot camps because they are believed to be justifiably harsh punishment for certain offenders.

Despite this enthusiasm, boot camps have largely failed to achieve their goals (Mackenzie, Brame, McDowall, and Souryal, 1995; Tonry, 1998b). They do not reduce recidivism beyond that achieved by routine probation (which is also less expensive), perhaps because, as Walker (1998, p. 224) points out, they encourage "the most aggressive definition of masculinity" through their emphasis on military drill. Walker (1998, p. 224) observes, "Yelling at inmates, treating them with disrespect, and forcing them to undergo painful physical exercises may be counterproductive, teaching inmates that disrespect and verbal abuse are the keys to success in life." Another problem is that boot camps, like electronic monitoring, have also increased the number of offenders sent to prison (the "widening the net" problem). This occurs for two reasons. First, up to one-half of boot camp offenders are sent to prison after failing to complete boot camp. Second, those who do complete boot camp receive close surveillance afterward; such surveillance yields technical violations of probation conditions and thus revocation to prison.

Tonry (1998b, p. 688) summarizes the literature:

> The emerging consensus from assessments of boot camps must be discouraging to their founders and supporters. Although promoted as a means to reduce recidivism rates, corrections costs, and prison crowding, most boot camps have no discernible effect on subsequent offending and tend to increase costs and crowding.

Tonry adds, however, that the "news is not all bad" (p. 688). Some programs involve imprisoned offenders who are placed there by corrections officials. Because these offenders serve their time in boot camp and not in prison, these programs do save money. However, these programs also have high failure rates and high rates of revocations after release. In another "good news" finding, boot camp participation seems to increase the self-esteem of offenders who complete boot camp. The bad news is that the increased self-esteem vanishes soon after the offenders leave boot camp.

Overall, then, boot camps have not lived up to their promise, but they do offer some glimmer of hope: Boot camps that place much emphasis on drug treatment and other rehabilitative programs appear to reduce recidivism beyond routine probation (MacKenzie, 1997). This is an important point, and we return to it in the next section on intensive supervision.

Intensive Supervision. **Intensive supervision,** also called *intensive probation* or *strict probation,* involves surveillance of offenders that is more careful than routine probation in frequency and behavioral restrictions. It comprises about 6 percent of adult probationers and parolees, or probably more than 240,000 overall. It is the oldest intermediate sanction and the most widely studied. Evaluations of its effectiveness thus tell us much not only about the problems of intermediate sanctions but also about their potential.

intensive supervision an intermediate sanction involving more careful supervision and control than routine probation

As its name implies, the supervision is intensive. The first major intensive supervision program occurred in Georgia in the 1980s. Two probation officers were given a combined caseload of 25 offenders. One officer monitored the offenders' behaviors, while the other provided counseling and arranged various kinds of treatment and training programs. Each offender was seen five times weekly, did community service, and either had a job or was enrolled in vocational training or other educational programs (Petersilia, 2000a). The offenders had very low recidivism rates and good employment histories. The apparent success of the program led to much national publicity, and many other states soon established intensive supervision programs of their own. Today, the average caseload in intensive supervision programs remains about 25 offenders per probation officer. Each offender typically sees an officer several times weekly, has regular urine tests for drug and alcohol use, and participates in various treatment programs when they are available.

Although intensive supervision imposes many burdens on offenders, criminal justice and elected officials disagree over which types of offenders should go into intensive supervision instead of prison. Many prosecutors and state legislators think that intensive supervision should be restricted to first-time property offenders and not drug offenders or repeat offenders who, they say, would endanger public safety. In contrast, many probation officials think that intensive supervision could be used for these other types of offenders as well.

A recent controversy in Massachusetts reflected this debate. Offenders in the state's intensive supervision programs are required to wear electronic bracelets, to take daily drug or breath-analysis tests, to do community service, to attend drug treatment or anger management classes, and to learn job and life skills. When the state decided to expand the number of programs, prosecutors and legislators said drug offenders should go to prison under the state's mandatory drug sentencing laws rather than into the programs. One defense attorney noted, "A lot of prosecutors won't touch [the programs] with a 10-foot pole" (Ranalli, 2000, p. B1). He had a client who was a bank teller with no prior criminal record who was arrested for selling $50 worth of crack cocaine. Although he argued that his client would be a good candidate for intensive supervision, the prosecutor was able to have him sentenced to prison under the state's drug sentencing laws. Another attorney said that it is wrong to think that intensive probation is only a mild sanction, noting that "a lot of offenders view this as tougher and more onerous" than prison (Ranalli, 2000, p. B1). Studies of offenders' views on intensive probation support his claim (Petersilia, 1997).

Despite the evident success of the 1980s Georgia program noted previously, intensive supervision has, overall, not fulfilled its initial promise (Clear and Terry, 2000; Tonry, 1998). Perhaps somewhat surprisingly, recidivism rates of offenders on intensive supervision are no lower than the rates of those on regular probation. Worse yet, because offenders on intensive supervision are monitored so closely, they have higher revocation rates from technical violations and other misbehavior. These offenders are sent to prison, again widening the net and reducing cost savings compared to routine probation. These problems now lead many observers to doubt the ability of intensive supervision to enhance public safety.

Amid this pessimism, however, lies some hope. Recall that the relatively few boot camps that emphasize drug treatment and other rehabilitation programs do appear to lower recidivism. The same is true for intensive supervision: A growing body of evidence indicates that surveillance *combined with* drug treatment (and, although the evidence is less strong, perhaps with other rehabilitation services) can be very effective in reducing recidivism. Intensive supervision that requires drug treatment increases offenders' participation in such treatment, and such participation, in turn, helps lower their recidivism rates (Tonry, 1998).

Thus, programs that combine surveillance and drug tests with mandatory participation in drug treatment and other services have been shown to reduce recidivism by 20 to 30 percent (Petersilia, 1997). A 3-year study of 1,500 Connecticut offenders on intensive supervision with life-skills training found they were 35 percent less likely than those sent to prison or jail to be rearrested (Ranalli, 2000). This type of evidence leads Joan Petersilia (1997, p. 187) to conclude that "the first order of business must be to allocate sufficient resources" to implement programs combining surveillance and treatment. Echoing the Massachusetts attorney just cited, she adds that offenders often view such programs as harsher than imprisonment because of their many restrictions and the lowered stigma that a prison record offers because incarceration is now so common. Thus, they can enhance public safety while also satisfying the public's desire for harsh sanctions. Petersilia (1997, p. 191) notes that these combined programs can be expensive, but adds, "in terms of crime and health costs averted, it is an investment that pays for itself immediately." She cites a California study that found that every dollar spent on drug and alcohol treatment for offenders saved the state $7 in crime and health care expenses.

Day-Reporting Centers. **Day-reporting centers** are facilities where offenders attend required treatment and other programs during the daytime and then leave to go home or elsewhere for the night; the maximum amount of time one can attend a day center varies by facility but can be up to 9 months. These centers combine and even intensify the surveillance of intensive supervision with the treatment and other services that intensive supervision often fails to provide. They were first used in England in the early 1970s and quickly became popular there, with dozens of centers now in operation. Recidivism rates by offenders involved in the English centers are similar to those for offenders sentenced to prison (Mair, 1995).

The first U.S. centers were established in Connecticut and Massachusetts in the mid-1980s. By 1990, only 13 centers were operating in the United States, but this number grew quickly over the next few years, with almost 120 operating by 1995 (Parent and Corbett, 1996). They vary widely by size; some serve as few as 14 offenders, whereas others serve more than 300. The average number of clients is about 50. Almost all U.S. centers provide drug treatment, group and individual counseling, educational programs, advice on job seeking, and other services. Their advantage is that they combine these services with surveillance, including random drug testing, at a lower cost than incarceration. But they also accept offenders who would not have been sentenced to prison. About half these offenders reoffend or commit technical violations by, say, not reporting to the center as required. Many are then sentenced to prison as punishment. As is true of other intermediate sanctions, this process widens the net of imprisoned offenders and ironically increases prison costs (Marciniak, 2000).

Few U.S. studies exist of the impact of involvement in day-reporting centers on offenders' criminal behavior and other problems, and the little evidence that exists is mixed. A study of drug offenders who were assigned to a day-reporting center in Cook County, Illinois, reported very positive results. The offenders significantly reduced their drug use, had a very low rearrest rate, and became more willing to take part in other treatment programs and services (McBride and VanderWaal, 1997). Another study compared recidivism rates of North Carolina offenders sentenced to intensive probation plus a day-reporting center to those of offenders sentenced to intensive probation alone. Recidivism of the two groups was the same, perhaps because the increased surveillance of the offenders in the center increased the likelihood that any offenses they committed would be discovered. This consequence countered any positive effect on reoffending that center involvement may have had (Marciniak, 2000).

Community Service. In several European countries, **community service** is a common penalty for even moderately severe offenses in lieu of imprisonment. Offenders typically work 40 to 240 hours under close supervision, with imprisonment the penalty if they fail to complete their service. In contrast, community service "is the most underused intermediate sanction in the United States" (Tonry, 1998, p. 695). Many U.S. officials and much of the public think it too mild a punishment and one that may put the public at risk because the offender remains in the community doing his or her service (Nasser, 1995). It is thus used mainly for very minor offenses such as moving vehicle violations or disorderly conduct.

The first known community service for U.S. offenders in modern times occurred in the 1960s when judges in Alameda County, California, decided they did not want to fine low-income women for traffic violations. They feared the women would be unable to pay their fines and would thus have to go to jail. Instead, they ordered them to do community service. This allowed them to stay out of jail while still paying their debt back to society (Morris and Tonry, 1990).

This program attracted much attention and led officials to develop other community service programs in the United States and other nations. Community service was perhaps most fully implemented in England, Wales, Scotland, and the Netherlands, but, after an initial burst of enthusiasm, it never really caught on in the United States. What little we know about the nature and effectiveness of community service comes from studies of the programs in these other nations (McIvor, 1995; Pease 1985; Spaans, 1998; Tak, 1995).

day-reporting centers buildings to which persons on probation report daily for monitoring and various programs and services

community service an intermediate sanction in which an offender performs service for the community, often in the form of menial labor

Michael Tonry (1998b) notes several findings from these studies. In both England and Scotland, about half the offenders given community service would otherwise have gone to prison, and half would have received more minor punishments. Recidivism rates are about the same as those for similar offenders sent to prison, indicating that community service keeps the British public as safe as imprisonment while costing much less. In the Netherlands, at least 10 percent of convicted offenders receive community service, and they, too, have recidivism rates similar to those for offenders sent to prison for similar crimes.

To date, only one major study of community service has been performed. Douglas McDonald (1992) evaluated a New York City program for repeat property offenders. Like the European programs, offenders who failed to complete their service could be sent to prison. Again, like the European programs, the New York effort had recidivism rates no higher than incarceration while costing much less.

Tonry (1998b, p. 697) concludes from these studies that community service "can serve as a meaningful, cost-effective sanction for offenders who would otherwise have been imprisoned." He deems community service a viable sanction for nondangerous offenders because it has recidivism rates no higher than imprisonment and costs much less. These benefits prompted Tonry to term its underuse in the United States a "pity" (p. 695).

Fines, Restitution, and Forfeiture. A final category of intermediate sanctions involves financial sanctions. **Fines** were used widely in medieval times for a variety of crimes and then again in colonial America for relatively minor offenses (Walker, 1998). Today they are widely used in the United States for traffic offenses and many other minor crimes, and large fines have been imposed on corporate and other white-collar offenders. But they are rarely used for serious "street crimes" in lieu of more serious sanctions. In contrast, fines for serious offenses are very common in many European nations. In the Netherlands, fines are considered the preferred sanction for every crime. In fact, judges there are required to explain in writing any decision *not* to use a fine. In other European nations, fines are imposed in at least half of all convictions for serious offenses in lieu of imprisonment. Some of these fines take into account the seriousness of the crime and the defendant's financial status (Tonry, 1998).

This latter criterion has not been widely used in the United States, where the amount of a fine has been based more on the seriousness of the offense than on the offender's ability to pay. It is thus easier for wealthier offenders to pay a given fine than poorer offenders who commit the same crime. This problem, along with the success of means-based fines in Europe, has prompted many judges to begin considering the offender's ability to pay, and means-based fines have become more popular in recent years.

Restitution, the payment of money or provision of services by offenders to their victims, is another monetary sanction that has deep historical roots and was widely used in colonial America for minor offenses (Walker, 1998). Community service, previously discussed, is thus a form of restitution. In the United States, restitution, whether in the form of money or services, is usually used as a sanction in addition to probation or imprisonment, not instead of them. Studies of restitution programs find that offenders usually pay the money and/or perform the services required of them, but it is unlikely that restitution will be used as an exclusive penalty for anyone but a minor offender.

Forfeiture, also known as asset forfeiture, is a third type of monetary intermediate sanction. This penalty involves taking personal property from a suspect. It has deep historical roots; it was a common penalty in medieval times when the state would seize offenders' property. In the contemporary United States, forfeiture has often been used in recent years in drug cases, with cars, boats, or large sums of money confiscated by police from persons suspected of drug possession or trafficking. The police, the U.S. Drug Enforcement Agency, and the U.S. Customs Service confiscate assets—money and property such as cars or boats—worth several hundreds of millions of dollars per year. Because local police and other law enforcement agencies often are allowed to keep the cars, money, and other assets they confiscate, forfeiture has been a key source of income for them.

fines the payment of money to the state or community, often in lieu of incarceration

restitution the payment of goods and services by offenders to their victims

forfeiture the seizing of assets such as cars and money by police and other law enforcement agents from suspected offenders

This fact—sometimes termed "policing for profit"—troubles many criminal justice observers. They worry that police and other law enforcement personnel may focus on offenders more because they have many assets to confiscate than because they pose serious threats to society. The police may thus target people and perhaps even "invent" crimes because they have financial incentive to do so. Another problem is the fact that many of the assets that are forfeited are taken from people who have been suspected of drug offenses and other crimes but not convicted. They are thus being punished without first being found guilty. A related problem is that sometimes the property of family members or friends of offenders is confiscated even though they were not involved in any crime (Jensen and Gerber, 1996; Kaplan, 2000).

The Future of Intermediate Sanctions. Many types of intermediate sanctions exist. They have some problems but also offer some hope. Two related problems are "net widening" of offenders committed to prison for technical violations and the associated increased prison costs. Another problem is that recidivism rates are often about as high as those for routine probation and for imprisonment. Thus, intermediate sanctions generally cost more than routine probation but do not have lower recidivism rates.

Despite these problems, intermediate sanctions have potential. Although they do not have lower recidivism rates than imprisonment, they also do not have higher recidivism rates even though they cost much less. Net widening exists but could be reduced if imprisonment were used less often for technical violations. Perhaps more important, intermediate sanctions that combine surveillance with effective drug and other treatments produce recidivism rates lower than those for routine probation and imprisonment. It thus seems that a model for successful intermediate sanctions exists. As Tonry (1998b, p. 704) observes, "for offenders who do not present unacceptable risks of violence, well-managed intermediate sanctions offer a cost-effective way to keep them in the community at less cost than imprisonment and with no worse later prospect for criminality." Whether national policy will begin to recognize the potential of this model remains a key issue. Until the "modern American preoccupation with absolute severity of punishment and the related widespread view that only imprisonment counts" (Tonry, 1998, p. 701) begins to change, intermediate sanctions will not be able to fulfill the promise they ultimately could have.

A Massachusetts legislator's comment reflects the obstacles that well-designed and well-funded intermediate sanctions face. Referring to a bill in his state House of Representatives that would let more offenders receive intensive supervision rather than a prison sentence, he commented, "I understand that it's not a slap on the wrist. But does the public believe that? No. The public's perception for criminal justice is strong. How do I know that the headline the next day isn't going to be 'House Frees Drug Offenders?' " (Ranalli, 2000, p. B1).

Parole

As noted earlier, parole involves supervising offenders released to the community after serving a prison sentence. Two types of parole exist. *Discretionary parole* occurs because parole boards decide to grant early release to inmates serving indeterminate sentences. *Mandatory parole* occurs without a parole board decision and takes place because of good-time provisions under determinate sentencing statutes. Inmates receiving either type of parole typically leave prison *before* their full sentences expire. Regardless of the reasons for their release, they report to a parole officer and must heed various restrictions on their behavior. They also take part in many of the intermediate sanctions we have already discussed.

In many respects, probation and parole are very similar. As noted earlier, the key difference is this: Probation is used in lieu of imprisonment, where parole is used *after* imprisonment. Like probationers, parolees can be sent (back) to prison if they commit either new crimes or technical violations of the conditions of their supervision. In general, parolees pose more potential danger than probationers to the community because they have usually committed more serious offenses and may have developed more criminal inclinations during their time behind bars. They are thus generally supervised much more closely than probationers and, as a result, are more likely to be caught in technical violations. These violations and the new offenses parolees may commit lead to high rates of readmission to prison (discussed later).

History of Parole. Parole began in the nineteenth century when prison over-crowding forced prison wardens to release inmates and governors to pardon other inmates. The promise of early release from prison for either reason was also thought to promote good behavior by inmates. With so many inmates leaving prison before their terms had expired, it became necessary to supervise them in the community. At the same time, granting pardons was "inevitably arbitrary and capricious" because wealthy people or those with connections were better able to secure pardons (Walker, 1998, p. 101). States thus established "boards of pardons" to bring some order to the process, and these gradually evolved by the early twentieth century into parole boards.

The first actual parole system was established at the Elmira Reformatory in New York in the 1870s under the leadership of Zebulon Brockway. As noted in Chapter 12, this prison innovated in coupling indeterminate sentencing with awards for good behavior. These awards included early release from prison on parole. Inmates would stay on parole for up to 6 months and had to report on the first day of every month to a volunteer guardian. This prison's policies and procedures soon became very popular, and by 1927 only three states—Florida, Mississippi, and Virginia—had no parole system. By 1942, these three states had followed suit. The proportion of all prisoners released on parole grew rapidly over the decades and reached a high of 72 percent in 1977 (Petersilia, 1998).

At that time, most inmates were serving open-ended, indeterminate sentences (see Chapter 12). They would come before parole boards that would determine whether they should be released early from prison or serve their maximum sentence. This process of discretionary parole came under attack by the end of the 1970s (Petersilia, 2000b). Conservatives believed it was returning dangerous criminals to the community too soon, whereas liberals thought the process was arbitrary and racially discriminatory. In response to this criticism from both sides of the political spectrum, several states, led by Maine in 1976, abolished discretionary parole; the number of such states is now 14 and includes California, Illinois, Virginia, and Washington. These states use determinate sentencing and automatic release from prison. Thus, as Petersilia (2000b, p. 2) notes, "there is no parole board to ask whether the inmate is ready for release, since he or she *must* be released once his or her term has been served." Most such inmates remain under parole supervision for at least 1 year after their release. More than 20 other states have restricted the use of discretionary parole (Petersilia, 1999). Today the number of mandatory releases to parole exceeds the number of discretionary releases, whereas in 1990 the opposite was true (Bonczar and Glaze, 1999).

Ironically, the abolition of discretionary parole for good behavior has made it even more difficult for inmates to succeed in the outside world after release from prison because they have less incentive to take part in rehabilitation programs while still behind bars (Butterfield, 2000a). Some observers also think it has increased misbehavior in prison because inmates no longer have incentive to behave well. Another problem is that parole officers are now more apt than in the past to send a parolee back to prison for technical violations of parole conditions. In California, for example, 68 percent of the people admitted to prison in 1999 were on parole at the time of their admission, compared to only 21 percent in 1980. Moreover, four out of every five parolees returned to prison in 1999 were sent back for technical violations and not for new crimes. This process not only increases prison costs and overcrowding but also helps create a "self-perpetuating prison class" (Butterfield, 2000a, p. A1). In fact, California's prison population would have declined in the 1990s as crime dropped there and nationwide if so many parolees had not been returned to prison; instead it grew dramatically (Butterfield, 2000a).

The abolition of discretionary parole in several states has led to one further problem. Although it was abolished in part based on concern that it allowed dangerous

criminals to be released too early, this abolition has, in fact, had the opposite effect. Inmates released in states that have abolished discretionary parole serve terms 7 months *shorter* than those released in states that still have it (Petersilia, 2000b). The reason for this surprising outcome stems from the discretion of parole boards. Although they have been criticized for letting dangerous inmates out early, they, in fact, can identify these inmates and have them stay behind bars longer. States that have moved away from indeterminate sentences and discretionary parole to determinate sentences and automatic release, in effect, "replace a rational, controlled system of 'earned' release for *selected* inmates with 'automatic' release for nearly *all* inmates," including ones that are still dangerous (Petersilia, 2000b, p. 5). The abolition of discretionary parole has thus had the opposite effect from what its conservative critics intended.

The Effectiveness of Parole. In October 1993, a parolee named Richard Allen Davis kidnapped 12-year-old Polly Klaas from a slumber party in her bedroom in Petaluma, California, and then murdered her. A nationwide manhunt resulted in his capture weeks later. The fact that he was on parole when he committed this vicious crime outraged the public and led to new calls for the restriction or abolition of parole.

When parolees do commit new, serious crimes, the public is justifiably outraged. Because many parolees are serious offenders who have been released from prison, their recidivism rates are of special importance in judging the effectiveness of parole. These rates are apt to be high for two reasons. First, as noted in Chapter 13, ex-inmates have many of the same personal problems, and, in some cases, even worse problems as when they entered prison. These include drug and alcohol abuse, functional illiteracy and a lack of employable skills, and mental and emotional disorders. They also have prison records that may limit their opportunities for gainful employment and for friendships with law-abiding citizens. As Petersilia (1999, p. 501) notes,

> Persons released from prison face a multitude of difficulties in trying to reenter the outside community successfully. They remain largely uneducated, unskilled, and usually without solid family support systems—and now they bear the added burdens of a prison record and the distrust and fear that inevitably result.

A labor economics professor adds, "Many of these guys come out with almost every characteristic that makes employers reluctant to hire. They're not just ex-offenders. They're high school dropouts. They have poor skills and substance-abuse problems" (Kilborn, 2001, p. A16). Many studies find that prison records significantly increase the likelihood of unemployment and of low earnings even by those ex-inmates who do find jobs. These employment problems, in turn, increase the likelihood that ex-convicts will commit new crimes (Western and Pettit, 2000).

Parolees' personal histories and difficulties explain much of their high recidivism rates. But some of the blame also must be attributed to the lack of services for them. As Petersilia (1999, pp. 501–502) asks, "But what assistance are parolees given as they reenter our communities? Sadly, while inmates' need for services and assistance has increased, parole in some (if not most) states has retreated from its historical mission to provide counseling, job training, and housing assistance." As states have spent more of their money to build new prisons, she notes, they have cut back on services for parolees. California, for example, has only 200 shelter beds for more than 10,000 homeless parolees, only four mental health clinics for 18,000 parolees with mental disorders, and only 750 places in residential treatment programs for 85,000 parolees with drug and alcohol problems. In that state's prisons, only about 3,000 of the 130,000 inmates who have drug problems receive any drug treatment. Nationally, although up to 85 percent of state prison inmates need drug treatment, only 13 percent receive it (Petersilia, 1999).

For all these reasons, it would be surprising if parolees did *not* have high recidivism rates. Unfortunately, such high rates do exist. About 60 percent of parolees are rearrested for a felony or serious misdemeanor within 3 years of their release from prison, and slightly more than 40 percent are sent back to prison for these offenses (Beck and Shipley, 1989). About one-third of all new prison admissions are these parolees (Petersilia, 2000b). The factors predicting their recidivism are similar to those for probationers (see previous discussion) and include greater prior criminal records, unemployment, criminal friends, and drug use (Gendreau, Little, and Guggin, 1996). Similar factors also predict the approximately 11 percent of parolees who simply abscond by fleeing parole supervision (Williams, McShane, and Dolny, 2000).

The Future of Parole. Like probation and intermediate sanctions, parole has been criticized by observers from both sides of the political spectrum. Conservatives continue to criticize it for allowing dangerous offenders to leave prison early and thus endanger public safety, whereas liberals criticize it for still being an arbitrary process and for lacking adequate rehabilitation services. As noted previously, discretionary parole became less popular in the 1970s, continued to decline through the 1900s, and shows no signs of making a comeback.

Our discussion of intermediate sanctions, however, suggests it is possible to have ex-prisoners in the community on parole without endangering public safety unduly as long as they are in programs combining adequate supervision with adequate treatment. A lack of interest in providing appropriate funding has hampered the establishment and development of such programs. Yet a decreased reliance on imprisonment for many types of offenders would free up the funds needed for the types of community corrections for parolees that, like those for probationers, show strong promise of satisfying public concerns for both punishment and safety. As Petersilia (1999, p. 479) observes, "Such reforms are more promising than parole abolition, in that they reduce the public safety risks posed by parolees and increase the chances that offenders will succeed."

Many observers also think that discretionary parole should be restored in the states that abolished it. It could be made less arbitrary and discriminatory with appropriate standards and due process procedures. The restoration of discretionary parole could also help ensure that dangerous offenders stay longer in prison (Petersilia, 2000b).

Juvenile Justice

In March 2001, a 15-year-old boy named Charles Andrew Williams, tired of being teased for being scrawny and having big ears, took a handgun to his Santana High School in suburban Santee, California, near San Diego. He began firing it in a bathroom

Andy Williams, 15, was accused of going on a sho[ot]ing spree at his high school [in] California in 2001. Here he appears with his public defenders at his arraignment as they try to prevent him from being tried as an adult. Since the 1980s, the "get tough" movement in criminal justice has led prosecutors in many states to attempt to try the cases of juveniles accused of serious offenses in criminal (adult) court.

and within 6 minutes killed two students and wounded 13 other people, including two adults (Reno and Smalley, 2001). This tragic act followed a string of well-publicized school shootings beginning in the late 1990s and marked by the infamous April 1999 massacre by two students of more than a dozen other students and adults at Columbine High School in Littleton, Colorado.

These and other violent acts by juvenile offenders keep juvenile crime in the headlines and highlight the need to address the role of the juvenile justice system in reducing such crime. This section first offers a brief explanation of juvenile delinquency and examines trends in juvenile crime to help put the juvenile justice system in context. It next sketches the history of the juvenile justice system and describes how it operates today. We finish by examining the impact of the current emphasis on treating serious juvenile offenders more harshly than was done in the past and, in particular, on transferring their cases into the adult legal system.

Understanding Juvenile Delinquency

Whole books exist on juvenile delinquency and its causes. Here we simply sketch some of the most important facts and issues in understanding juvenile delinquency in order to provide a context for the discussion of juvenile justice.

Juveniles age 10 to 17 comprise nearly 12 percent of the U.S. population but account for about 17 percent of all arrests, including 16 percent of all violent crime arrests and 32 percent of all property crime arrests. As Figure 14.2 shows, these percentages vary greatly by the type of crime and are as high as 53 percent of all arson arrests and as low as 1 percent of all arrests for driving under the influence. Although almost 620,000 arrests of juveniles for UCR Index offenses (including about 98,000 for violent crimes and 519,000 for property crimes) occur every year (2000 figures), these arrests actually comprise only a very small percentage of the more than 31 million youths in the 10 to 17 age group. In 2000, about one-third of 1 percent of all such juveniles were arrested for violent crimes, and about 1.7 percent of all juveniles were arrested for property crimes (Snyder, 2002). Put another way, more than 99 of every 100 juveniles age 10 to 17 were *not* arrested for violent crimes, and more than 98 of every 100 juveniles were *not* arrested for property crimes. Even allowing for the possibility of "hidden" crime that does not end in arrest (see Chapter 2), the vast majority of juveniles do *not* commit serious offenses.

The *serious and violent juvenile (SVJ) offenders* who do commit these offenses have concerned public officials and captured scholarly attention. The roots of their actions are generally identified in the explanations of criminal behavior discussed in Chapter

figure 14.2

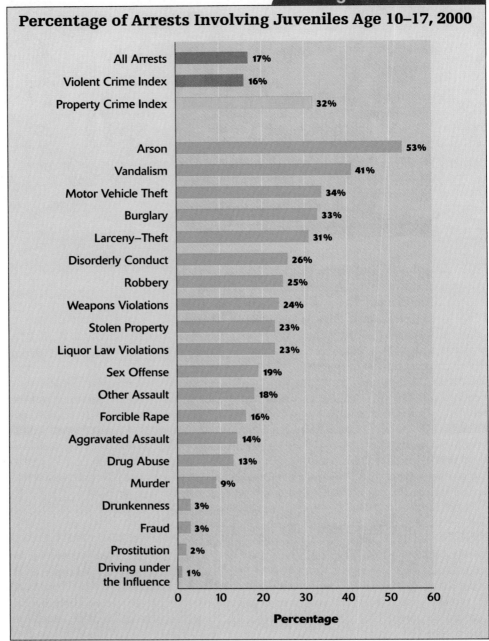

Percentage of Arrests Involving Juveniles Age 10–17, 2000

Category	Percentage
All Arrests	17%
Violent Crime Index	16%
Property Crime Index	32%
Arson	53%
Vandalism	41%
Motor Vehicle Theft	34%
Burglary	33%
Larceny–Theft	31%
Disorderly Conduct	26%
Robbery	25%
Weapons Violations	24%
Stolen Property	23%
Liquor Law Violations	23%
Sex Offense	19%
Other Assault	18%
Forcible Rape	16%
Aggravated Assault	14%
Drug Abuse	13%
Murder	9%
Drunkenness	3%
Fraud	3%
Prostitution	2%
Driving under the Influence	1%

Source: Snyder, Howard. 2002. *Juvenile Arrrests 2000.* Washington, DC: Office of Juvenile Justice and Delinquency Prevention.

2, but scholarly research has pinpointed more specific factors underlying their behavior (Hawkins et al., 1998). In general, the youths who become SVJ offenders exhibited relatively high levels of aggression and impulsiveness during early childhood and tend to begin committing their serious offenses early in their teenage years rather than later. They are overwhelmingly male and generally grew up in poverty and in dilapidated urban neighborhoods. They are also disproportionately likely to have been abused or neglected by their parents during their childhoods and to have grown up in families beset by marital conflict. They are also more likely to have seriously delinquent friends and to use illegal drugs.

In general, then, the backgrounds of SVJ offenders resemble those of the average prisoner discussed in Chapter 13. Without trying to defend or excuse their actions, it is fair to say they typically come from very troubled backgrounds. This fact forces us to ask whether these offenders are fully responsible for their crimes. It also suggests that, to reduce SVJ offending, our society must adequately treat the problems these backgrounds cause for SVJ offenders and also alleviate the problems that lead to such backgrounds in the first place. We return to this issue later when we discuss ways of reducing delinquency.

Trends in Juvenile Crime

The school shootings and other youth violence of the 1990s helped fuel an important misconception, also called a "myth" by some observers, regarding youth crime (Glassner, 1999; Kappeler et al., 2000; Males, 1999; Zimring, 2000). This myth is that youth crime rose dramatically throughout the 1990s and into the 2000s and that adolescents are becoming more violent all the time. Alarmist declarations by some social scientists in the mid-1990s that a new generation of "superpredators" was threatening America reinforced this myth (Bennett, Dilulio, and Walters, 1996). As one criminologist warned ominously, "So long as we fool ourselves in thinking that we're winning the war against crime, we may be blindsided by this bloodbath of teenage violence that is lurking in the future" (Zoglin, 1996, p. 52). Media coverage of teenage violence also fuels the myth of unprecedented teenage violence. One study found that 40 percent of newspaper stories featuring children and 48 percent of the stories on the TV network news shows featuring children focus on violence and other illegal behavior. Another study of local TV news stories found that 68 percent of the stories about violence concern youth violence, and 55 percent of the stories of youths concern their violence (Dorfman and Schiraldi, 2001).

Despite the impression these warnings and media coverage create, the reality is quite different. Although youth violence in the United States did rise in the late 1980s and early 1990s, it has actually been *declining* since 1994; arrests for youth violence reached a peak that year and declined steadily through the end of the decade before reaching a level almost as low as in 1980. And although 40 to 55 percent, depending on the source, of news stories of youths focus on their violence, teenagers commit, as we have seen, only about 16 percent of all violent crime, and less than one-half of 1 percent of all adolescents are arrested each year for violent crimes (Snyder, 2002). The news stories apparently affect public views: Although youth homicides declined 68 percent from 1993 to 1999, 62 percent of the public think youth crime increased during those years (Dorfman and Schiraldi, 2001).

The myth of rising juvenile violence spills over into school shootings. Many of these shootings gained nationwide publicity, fueling concern over school safety and fear that schools were becoming more dangerous. Once again, however, the reality is quite different. The number of school homicides and other acts of serious violence actually *declined* steadily after the early 1990s as did the amount of violence reported in surveys of secondary school students and high school principals. Given that about 50 million children attend school and that about 50 homicides of children occur each year at school, the odds of a child being killed at school are about one in a million. Less than 1 percent of all murdered children are killed at school. When it comes to serious violence, children are actually much safer at school than elsewhere (Kappeler et al., 2000; Snyder and Sickmund, 1999). Despite this fact, 71 percent of respondents in a recent national poll thought a school shooting was likely in their town. Although fatal school shootings declined from 1998 to 1999, respondents in another poll were much more likely to be concerned about violence in their schools in 1999 than in 1998 (Dorfman and Schiraldi, 2001).

An old sociological adage says that if things are perceived as real, then they are real in their consequences (Thomas and Thomas, 1928). One consequence of the myth of rising youth violence is that it has prompted more and more youth crimes to be removed from the juvenile justice system to the adult criminal justice system (discussed later). As one observer notes, "Exaggerated depictions of America's youth as budding criminals lead to bad public policy that condemns 14-year-olds to life without the possibility of parole" ("Building Blocks for Youth," 2001). Has this shift in the treatment of youth crime helped or hurt public safety? What does it mean for the future of the juvenile justice system? We try to answer these questions after looking at the origins of the juvenile justice system to see what lessons the past might hold for the present and the future.

History of Juvenile Justice

As a separate institution for dealing with youthful offenders, the juvenile justice system is actually a relatively recent invention, having begun only in the late nineteenth century. Its origin illustrates a fundamental relationship: The way a society deals with youthful offenders is intimately related to its ideas of the nature of children and childhood and the reasons for children's misbehavior.

From Ancient Times to the Renaissance. Children have probably misbehaved, and sometimes very seriously, since ancient times. But for most of human history, their misbehavior was not regarded as very different from adult misbehavior, and they were punished in the same way that adults were punished. The reason for this is simple but might also be difficult to comprehend: Childhood as a separate stage of the life cycle is a relatively recent development, and, for most of human history, children were viewed as miniature adults. We can see this in the paintings and sculptures created before the thirteenth century that depicted children as "shrunken" adults, their bodies out of proportion to what children's bodies really look like.

Why were children not viewed as *children?* The reason seems to be that the majority of children in ancient and medieval times died from disease and malnutrition. With so many children dying, parents did not allow themselves to become emotionally attached to their children. Given this lack of emotional attachment, it is not surprising that children were not seen as different from adults, with special needs, and no separate concept of childhood existed.

Such a concept finally began to develop with the advent of the Renaissance that began in Italy in the fourteenth century and eventually spread to the rest of Europe. Whereas medieval thinkers believed that society made people wicked, Renaissance thinkers believed society could civilize them. This led Renaissance thinkers to look to education and moral training as a way of improving children's behavior. This emphasis intensified with the arrival of the Protestant Reformation in the early sixteenth century. Because Protestantism emphasized the importance of hard work and success in life for winning God's favor, education became a key tool for children's success as they grew older. Education became even more significant as Europe gradually changed from an agricultural to a mercantile (trade) economy and then to an industrial economy by the nineteen century. Because it was more important to be literate in either a mercantile or industrial economy than it was in an agricultural society, the importance of education grew as well.

Thus, the Renaissance, the Protestant Reformation, and the Industrial Revolution combined to produce a greater interest in the need for children to be educated and, more generally, a greater interest in children themselves. This recognition included the idea that children were not simply miniature adults and that they had different needs from adults, including adequate education and supervision, if they were to succeed in life. By the fifteenth century, paintings no longer depicted children as shrunken adults, and children's clothing was "invented" during the seventeenth century. This period also included the writing of the first fairy tales. The idea began to develop that children were innocent and needed protection and guidance by adults. No separate juvenile justice system yet existed, but the groundwork for one had been laid.

Colonial and Nineteenth-Century America. In colonial America, preventing and handling children's misbehavior was the responsibility of their parents because no juvenile justice system yet existed. Because most American colonists accepted the concept of original sin, they thought that children were quite capable of misbehaving. This belief led the colonists to advocate strict discipline involving many rules for children's behavior and whipping and other corporal punishment, usually administered by their parents, for any misbehavior. Laws in many communities prohibited children from such activities as sledding on the Sabbath, playing ball in the streets, idleness, rudeness, lying, and rebelliousness. If parents were thought incapable of controlling their children's behavior, authorities would intervene by administering corporal punishment themselves, by taking children away and assigning the responsibility of raising them to someone else, or, in extreme cases, by expelling an adolescent from the community (Walker, 1998).

Views of children's misbehavior and the ways of dealing with their misbehavior gradually changed during the nineteenth century thanks to two related social trends: industrialization and urbanization. As society became more and more industrialized, cities began to grow by leaps and bounds. As children began working in factories, many people began to worry about what the long, grueling hours and harsh working conditions would do to them. This concern led to the development of the more general view that children were weak and needed protection.

At the same time, urbanization was causing increased poverty and crime and, more to the point, increased juvenile crime. In many U.S. cities, mobs of teenagers would roam the streets and attack and rob people. Many were arrested and imprisoned with adult criminals, who taught them even more criminal ways and sometimes sexually abused them. Social reformers began to say that juvenile offenders should be kept apart from adult offenders and, more generally, from the adult criminal justice system because youthful offenders needed help and not simply punishment.

All these changes—industrialization, urbanization, increasing poverty, juvenile crime, and the growing concern for children's well-being—led to the development of a child welfare movement. This movement's main goal was to protect children from the corrupting influences of urban life. Child welfare agencies were established to help children who were living in the streets or who were unable to be controlled by their parents. The focus of the child welfare movement was children from poor families and immigrant families because these children were thought to be at the greatest risk for parental neglect and thus for crime and other problems. Modern critics say the movement was thus biased against children who were not from white and middle-class backgrounds and born in the United States (Platt, 1969; Walker, 1998).

In the early 1800s, a notable achievement of the child welfare movement was the development of "houses of refuge" for children who had broken the law, children who were orphans, children whose parents had abandoned them, and children whose parents were abusing or neglecting them. These houses of refuge were the first separate facilities for juvenile offenders and other children in trouble and were the forerunners of a separate juvenile justice system. The first house of refuge opened in New York City in 1824; within the next few years others opened in Boston and Philadelphia. Most major cities had them by 1850. Most of these houses were run with strict order and discipline and provided educational lessons and religious instruction. Unfortunately, houses of refuge never achieved their proponents' hopes and became less popular by the beginning of the Civil War. Many were very large and filthy, and their administrators were overly strict in their discipline. In these and other ways they resembled prisons more than "houses."

The first reform schools for serious juvenile offenders were opened in the late 1840s in Massachusetts and New York, and 51 reform schools had appeared throughout the nation by 1876. Their development was prompted by concern over what would happen to juveniles who were put in prisons with adult criminals. Like the houses of refuge, reform schools intended to rehabilitate their residents and not punish them. Because authorities worried that treating juvenile offenders like criminals would only make them more likely to become criminals, they called these new institutions "schools" rather than prisons and built some of the reform schools in the form of a series of cottages to better resemble a home environment. In several states, offenders could be sent to reform schools without an actual trial. This informal procedure was again meant to "decriminalize" the treatment of juvenile offenders lest they become more hardened lawbreakers as a result, but it also meant that the state had considerable powers to remove youths from their parents' homes without legal recourse, raising important constitutional questions (Walker, 1998).

The Development of the Juvenile Court. In their emphasis on separate facilities for children, on rehabilitation, and on informal proceedings, the houses of refuge and reform schools marked the beginnings of a separate juvenile justice system for youthful offenders. All these developments reflected a new philosophy of children and their misbehavior that, as noted previously, had been gradually developing since the early nineteenth century. According to this philosophy, children in trouble should not be punished because they were not responsible for their misbehavior. Instead, they were victims of problems in their social environment such as poverty, neglectful or abusive parents, and substandard living conditions in their neighborhoods. The new philosophy also asserted that these children were capable of being reformed and needed help, not punishment. They thus needed to be kept out of jails, prisons, and adult courts whenever possible because these institutions would not help children but, instead, would subject them to sexual abuse and lessons in crime from adult offenders. Juvenile offenders, in short, were no longer regarded as criminals. Instead, they were regarded as children in need of moral guidance, discipline, and other kinds of help.

This new philosophy guided the development of the houses of refuge and reform schools and also began to affect the legal handling of juvenile offenders more generally. By the 1870s, a few states had begun to keep juvenile offenders separate from adult criminals at arraignments, trials, and other legal proceedings. The nation's first juvenile court was finally established in Chicago in 1899. In the legislation that enacted this court, the word *delinquency* was used for the first time to describe juvenile misbehavior. Ten states had juvenile courts by 1904, and almost all states had them by the early 1920s.

The goal of these courts was to help and rehabilitate youthful offenders, not punish them. They would provide children the equivalent of parental care and treat their problems individually. The procedures they followed were more personalized and informal than those in adult courts in order to project a "caring" atmosphere and to keep juveniles from being stigmatized as criminals. Written transcripts were not kept, lawyers were often not allowed, and witnesses could not be confronted. Juveniles were also kept out of jail and prison whenever possible, and they were especially kept from contact with adult offenders. Instead of being punished, most juveniles were put on probation and ordered to take part in various kinds of treatment programs. In all these ways, the creation of these juvenile courts "completed the development of a separate juvenile justice system" (Walker, 1998, p. 115).

Changes during the Twentieth Century. The procedures of the juvenile courts and the philosophy guiding them continued until the second half of the twentieth century. Until then, the juvenile justice system continued to act very informally because it was believed that more formal rules and procedures would have impeded the quest for individualized justice catered to the needs of individual juveniles. But this informality also meant that juvenile offenders did not have the same legal rights, such as the right to counsel and to a jury trial, that the U.S. Constitution and, beginning in the 1960s, U.S. Supreme Court rulings gave to adult offenders. By the 1960s many legal observers had decided that the informality of the juvenile court led to arbitrary procedures that were not in the best interests of juvenile offenders. Several Supreme Court decisions in this period expanded the rights of juvenile offenders, who, for example, won the right to have counsel and to cross-examine witnesses.

The key case involved a 15-year-old boy named Gerald Gault who was sent to a reform school for up to 6 years for making an obscene phone call. He did not have a lawyer, was not allowed to question any witnesses, and was not allowed to appeal his sentence. The Supreme Court overturned his conviction in 1967 because he had been denied these rights (*In re Gault*, 387 U.S. 1 [1967]). In ringing terms, the Court's decision said that "under our Constitution, the condition of being a boy does not justify a kangaroo court." Despite this ruling, Walker (1998) notes that years later many juvenile offenders still did not have lawyers when they appeared in juvenile court and that the ones who did have lawyers were more likely to be placed in a juvenile institution.

At about the same time, there was growing acceptance of labeling theory's view (see Chapter 2) that treating people as criminals increased their likelihood of a criminal self-concept and of criminal behavior. This belief led reformers to argue that involvement in juvenile court and placement in juvenile detention centers only led youthful offenders to be more likely to reoffend when they were eventually released. This view led to growing efforts to divert juveniles who had committed minor offenses from the juvenile justice system. In 1974, the U.S. Congress passed the Juvenile Justice and Delinquency Prevention Act, which required that status offenders (juveniles who violate curfew, run away from home, and commit other behaviors that would be legal for adults) not be placed in detention. The act and later congressional legislation also required that juvenile offenders and adult offenders be separated at all times. As part of this "deinstitutionalization" movement, diversion of juvenile offenders from the juvenile courts and community-based programs for them multiplied during the 1970s and early 1980s.

These efforts continue today, but have begun to lose ground. As crime increased during the 1970s and 1980s, concern about juvenile delinquency also grew. As with adults (see Chapter 11), this concern led to a new "get tough" movement that required harsher treatment of juvenile offenders. States passed laws requiring the cases of juveniles accused of certain serious offenses to be handled in criminal (adult) court. Other laws gave prosecutors the discretion to transfer these cases to criminal court without first needing (as was true in the past) the permission of a juvenile court judge. Still other laws provided mandatory penalties for serious juvenile offenses. This movement accelerated during the 1990s; 45 states between 1992 and 1997 made it easier to transfer juvenile cases into criminal court, and the penalties for juveniles convicted of various offenses became harsher (Snyder and Sickmund, 1999), even though, as we have seen, youth violence actually declined during most of the 1990s.

All these changes reflect a new philosophy that blames juveniles for their offenses instead of the social environment in which they had been raised; it maintains that they need to be punished, not rehabilitated. This new philosophy represents a dramatic turn from the philosophy that led the development of the juvenile court system slightly more than a century ago and that continued to guide its operation well into the twentieth century. We examine the impact of this fundamental change next.

The Juvenile Justice Process

The stages of the juvenile justice system generally parallel those in the adult criminal justice system that previous chapters examined. However, juvenile justice procedures are generally more informal, even after the Supreme Court rulings discussed earlier, than the corresponding procedures in the adult system, and they include slightly different terminology. Figure 14.3 depicts the several stages of the juvenile justice system. Because processing juvenile offenders varies from state to state, and even from city to city within a state, the diagram in Figure 14.3 and the following discussion provide a general explanation of the juvenile justice system across the nation but not a specific explanation of any one system.

Arrest and the Police. When a juvenile allegedly breaks the law, the police exercise their discretion in deciding whether to arrest the offender or to take some other action, such as talking with his or her parents. If an arrest does occur, the police then decide, often in consultation with juvenile justice officials and the offender's parents, whether to divert the case from juvenile court or to refer it to the court. The police divert about one-fourth of all arrests and refer about 70 percent to juvenile court. Juveniles awaiting court disposition must not be held with adult offenders. Instead, they simply live at home or, occasionally, are sent to juvenile detention facilities.

Intake and Adjudication. When a case is referred to juvenile court, the *intake* process begins. Similar to the prosecution stage for adult offenders, the intake process is generally handled by the juvenile probation department or the prosecutor's office. Its main purpose is to determine whether to dismiss the case, to divert it from the court by handling it informally (perhaps also requiring certain conditions such as restitution,

figure 14.3

Stages of the Juvenile Justice System

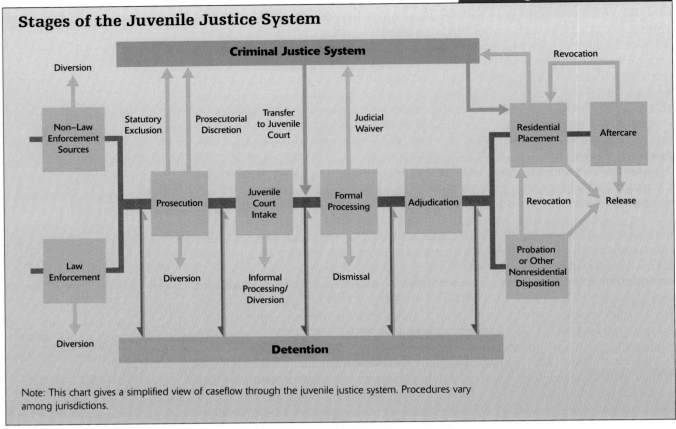

Note: This chart gives a simplified view of caseflow through the juvenile justice system. Procedures vary among jurisdictions.

Source: Snyder, Howard, and Melissa Sickmund. 1999. *Juvenile Offenders and Victims: 1999 National Report.* Washington, DC: Office of Juvenile Justice and Delinquency Prevention.

curfews, and treatment programs), or to *petition* it to juvenile court. About half of all cases reaching the intake stage are handled informally. When this is the outcome, juveniles and their parents typically sign a "consent decree" in which the juvenile admits to having committed the act. A juvenile probation officer usually monitors the youth's compliance with any conditions of this *informal probation.* As with an adult offender, a juvenile who violates his or her probation conditions risks having the case return to juvenile court with possible incarceration in a juvenile detention facility the result.

If, instead, a case is petitioned into juvenile court, the juvenile court judge's task then becomes whether to transfer the case to adult court, if so requested by intake officers, or to *adjudicate* the youth as delinquent if no transfer request is made. Almost all petitioned cases result in adjudicatory hearings, the equivalent of a trial in the adult criminal justice system. At these hearings, the juvenile court judge hears testimony from various witnesses and decides whether the youth was delinquent. About 58 percent of all cases petitioned to juvenile court result in adjudications of delinquency, the equivalent of a guilty verdict in criminal court.

Disposition. If a youth is adjudicated as delinquent, the judge's next decision is the *disposition,* or sentencing, of the case. Before the disposition hearing, juvenile probation officers prepare a set of recommendations for the judge after interviewing the youth, speaking with his or her parents, and, perhaps, having psychological evaluations performed. The judge's disposition can include *formal probation,* with conditions such as restitution and drug treatment attached, or placement in a juvenile detention facility. Slightly more than half of all dispositions result in formal probation, and slightly less than 30 percent result in residential placement. The juvenile's offense and prior record help determine whether placement is in a secure facility resembling a prison or in an "open" facility resembling cottages or homes.

In any one year, the juvenile courts handle about 1.7 million to 1.8 million cases. Figure 14.4 represents the outcomes for a hypothetical 1,000 cases. As the diagram depicts, processing juvenile cases is complex, with many different results possible. Residential placement is the most serious outcome, but it occurs for less than 10 percent of all cases. Thus, only about 160,000 of the 1.7 million cases end with residential placement.

Factors Affecting Juvenile Processing Decisions. We have just seen that a series of decisions accompanies every stage of the juvenile justice process: Should a police officer arrest a juvenile? If an arrest does occur, should the case be diverted or referred to juvenile court? If referred, should the case be handled informally or petitioned to juvenile court? If petitioned, should it be transferred to criminal court? If it stays in juvenile court, should the juvenile be adjudicated as a delinquent? If such adjudication occurs, what should the disposition be?

What factors affect all these decisions? The most important factors are the seriousness of the alleged offense and the prior arrest record of the juvenile (Bynum and Thompson, 2002; Vito, Tewksbury, and Wilson, 1998). Youths accused of serious offenses and those with previous arrests are more likely at all decision points of the juvenile justice process to receive the more punitive outcome—to be arrested, to be

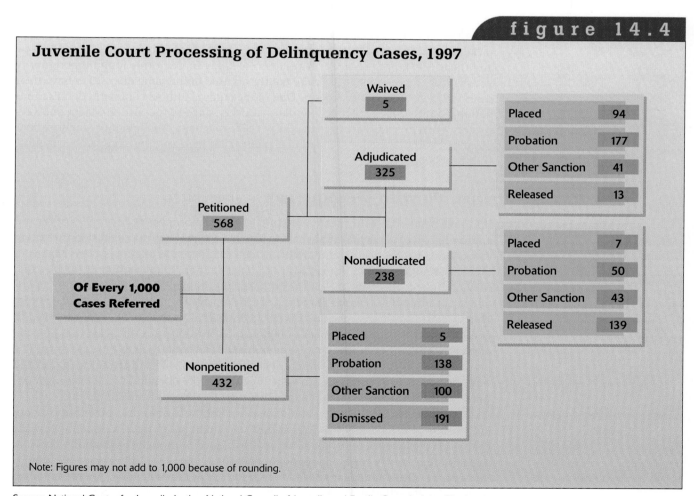

figure 14.4

Juvenile Court Processing of Delinquency Cases, 1997

Waived	5

Adjudicated	325

Placed	94
Probation	177
Other Sanction	41
Released	13

Petitioned	568

Nonadjudicated	238

Placed	7
Probation	50
Other Sanction	43
Released	139

Of Every 1,000 Cases Referred

Placed	5
Probation	138
Other Sanction	100
Dismissed	191

Nonpetitioned	432

Note: Figures may not add to 1,000 because of rounding.

Source: National Center for Juvenile Justice, National Council of Juvenile and Family Court Judges, Charles Puzzanchera, Anne L. Stahl, Terrence A. Finnegan, Howard N. Snyder, Rowen S. Poole, and Nancy Tierney. 2000. *Juvenile Court Statistics 1997.* Washington, DC: National Center for Juvenile Justice, National Council of Juvenile and Family Court Judges.

petitioned to juvenile court, and so forth. Some evidence also suggests that girls receive more lenient treatment than boys for criminal offenses but harsher treatment for status offenses (Chesney-Lind, 1995; Johnson and Scheuble, 1991).

Scholars have also considered the effects of race and ethnicity on juvenile case processing. African American youths and other minorities are greatly overrepresented in the juvenile justice system (Butterfield, 2000b). For example, although African Americans comprise 15 percent of all youths, they represent 26 percent of all the youths who are arrested, 31 percent of those referred to juvenile court, 46 percent of those whose cases are waived to adult criminal court, 40 percent of those placed in juvenile detention centers, and 58 percent of those placed in adult prisons. Among those charged with violent crimes who have never been in juvenile prison, African Americans are more than nine times more likely than whites to be sentenced to such prisons. African American youths charged with drug offenses are 48 times more likely than their white counterparts to be sentenced to juvenile prison. Among youths accused of violent crime, African Americans spend an average of 254 days in prison after trial and Hispanics, 305 days, compared to only 193 days for whites.

Do these disparities reflect racial discrimination, or do they simply reflect the greater likelihood of African American youths being involved in serious crime? Many studies have addressed this issue, and they generally find that race, ethnicity, and also poverty do affect juvenile case processing even after differences in criminal involvement are considered (Bynum and Thompson, 2002; Joseph, 1995; Leonard, Pope, and Feyerherm, 1995). As a review of the evidence on class and racial/ethnic discrimination in juvenile case processing noted, "The preponderance of evidence within the juvenile justice system suggests that race does make a difference and that underclass poverty and racial inequality have a major impact on the administration of juvenile justice" (Pope and Clear, 1994, pp. 132–133). Thus, a recent study in California found that minority youths were twice as likely as white youths accused of the same offenses to have their cases transferred to criminal court. One of the study's authors commented, "Discrimination against kids of color accumulates at every stage of the justice system and skyrockets when juveniles are tried as adults. California has a double standard: Throw kids of color behind bars, but rehabilitate white kids who commit comparable crimes" (Lewin, 2000, p. A14).

Dealing with Delinquency

We have seen that a fundamental shift in our philosophy of juvenile justice and approach to juvenile delinquency has occurred in the past two decades. At its inception, the juvenile justice system embraced the idea that juvenile offenders were victims of their environment and in need of help and rehabilitation. It now embraces the idea that they are hardened criminals who need harsh punishment to deter even more delinquency. A philosophy of punishment has thus replaced a philosophy of rehabilitation. This shift involves a greater emphasis on the transfer or waiver of SVJ offenses to adult criminal court. Underlying this get-tough transfer movement is the belief that juvenile offenders will receive harsher punishment in criminal court than in juvenile court. The juvenile justice system also hopes that such punishment will have greater "general" and "specific" deterrent effects (see Chapter 11) on juvenile offenders by decreasing delinquency in general and by reducing recidivism by the juveniles tried in adult court.

Has the transfer movement accomplished these twin goals of harsher punishment and greater deterrence? The answer seems to be no in both cases. Considering first the goal of harsher punishment, there is mixed evidence. Although some studies find that adult criminal courts impose longer sentences than juvenile courts on juvenile offenders, several others find that criminal courts actually impose more lenient sentences (Feld, 1998; Fritsch, Hemmens, and Caeti, 1996; Podkopacz, 1996; Vito et al., 1998). The latter evidence leads researcher Dean Champion (1989, p. 584) to wonder, "If waivers are not resulting in more severe penalties for juveniles, what are they accomplishing?"

They do not seem to be accomplishing either general or specific deterrence because the evidence on both kinds of deterrence is also negative. First, in terms of general deterrence, a few studies examine the impact in several states of new legislation that required or eased the transfer of serious juvenile offenses to criminal court (Jensen and Metsger, 1994; Singer and McDowwall, 1988). These studies fail to find a general deterrent effect of waivers to adult court. As one review summarized these studies, "There is no evidence to indicate that treating young people as adult criminal offenders has any impact on serious juvenile crime" (Kappeler et al., 2000, p. 190). The evidence on specific deterrence is no more encouraging. At least two studies compare the recidivism of juvenile offenders tried in adult criminal court with matched samples of offenders processed in juvenile court (Bishop et al., 1996; Fagan, 1995). Both of these studies found that the youths tried as adults were often more likely than their juvenile court counterparts to commit more new offenses and more serious offenses and to do so more quickly. Sending juvenile cases to adult court thus seems to endanger public safety in the long run, not protect it.

The evidence on general and specific deterrence thus suggests that transferring SVJ cases to adult court does much more harm than good. As Kappeler and colleagues (2000, p. 191) note, "There appear to be few benefits from treating juvenile offenders as adults. No general deterrent impact on juvenile crime has been observed. . . . In addition, the research suggests that young persons tried and sentenced as adults are more likely, not less, to commit future crimes." They add that transfers to criminal court have other negative effects. Juveniles convicted in adult court will face decreased job opportunities after release from prison. They are also less likely than their counterparts held in juvenile institutions to receive various kinds of counseling and other programming and are much more likely to be sexually and physically abused while behind bars.

New Approaches to Delinquency. If transferring juvenile offenders to adult criminal court does more harm than good, how else could the United States deal with SVJ offenders? Some observers suggest that all offenders, juveniles and adults, be tried in an "integrated" criminal justice system, with "youth discounts" given at sentencing to adolescents in recognition of their diminished responsibility (Feld, 1998). Under this plan, a 14-year-old may receive, say, 25 percent of the adult penalty, and a 16-year-old, 50 percent. An integrated system of this kind would permit better recordkeeping, avoid the need for transfer hearings and for proceedings that treat adolescents like adults, and acknowledge that youths are less responsible than adults for their misbehavior. Youthful offenders would still be kept separate from adults at all stages of the proceedings and would fully enjoy the same legal rights that adults have. As one advocate puts it, an integrated criminal court "permits a nuanced response to youth crime" (Feld, 1998, p. 250). It recognizes that adolescents do bear some responsibility for their crimes but not full responsibility. Its "discounted" sentencing would thus serve both their needs and the needs of public safety.

Other observers object to this plan, which would essentially abolish the juvenile court (Lindsay, 1998; Rosenberg, 1993). They fear that the more formal legal proceedings that juveniles would face would stigmatize them and produce harsher punishments than they now receive. They also say that abolitionist proposals romanticize adult courts because adult courts often fail to provide due process and in this and other ways are no better than juvenile courts. For example, the right to counsel exists in adult courts, but in practice it is the right to *inadequate* counsel because public defenders have heavy caseloads, and "assembly line" justice is the norm in many urban areas.

According to a different strategy, some scholars suggest that new or better funded and designed forms of intermediate sanctions be used for SVJ offenders (Altschuler, 1998). We saw earlier that intermediate sanctions that combine surveillance *with* drug counseling, vocational training, and other programs offer some hope in reducing recidivism among adults. The same seems true for juvenile offenders (Altschuler, 1998). For these sanctions to work, they must be better funded so that important kinds of treatment, counseling, and training are readily available. Unfortunately, as with adults, most intermediate sanctions programs for juveniles remain focused on surveillance and control, not on counseling and rehabilitation. For these programs to reduce recidivism, a different approach is needed.

The most promising strategy, however, is one aimed at *preventing* SVJ offending before it starts (Howell and Hawkins, 1998; Wasserman and Miller, 1998). This strategy recognizes the risk factors for SVJ offending described earlier and involves early childhood and adolescent intervention programs aimed at the children and youths most at risk for such offending. Some programs involve prenatal and postnatal visits by nurses, social workers, and other professionals to the homes of poor, teenage pregnant women. Their offspring are more likely than those born to more advantaged circumstances to grow up to be delinquent. These visits help improve the physical health of the mothers and their infants and the latter's cognitive development. Studies show they more than pay for themselves by helping to prevent childhood cognitive and behavioral problems, child abuse and neglect, and later delinquency. School-based programs focusing on conflict resolution and after-school recreation also have been shown to reduce SVJ offending. Again, greater funding of these programs is necessary if they are to succeed in preventing SVJ offending to any great degree, but any dollars spent on these programs save many more dollars in reduced crime, prison costs, and other problems (Greenwood, 1998).

Focus on Canada

Juvenile Justice in Transition

The juvenile justice system in Canada illustrates some of today's possibilities and problems in dealing with delinquency. In 1984, the Canadian Parliament passed the Young Offenders Act (YOA), which replaced earlier legislation that had treated young offenders as wayward children in need of protection, guidance, and support ("Youth and the Criminal Justice System," 1998). The emphasis under this earlier legislation was on timely intervention and individualized sentencing—that is, let the punishment fit the individual, not necessarily the crime.

The YOA raised the lower age of criminal responsibility from 7 to 12 with the upper limit established at 17 years. It placed more emphasis on the offense than on the needs or individual characteristics of the offender. Since its full implementation in 1986, the YOA has been severely criticized by mostly conservative detractors who believe the range of penalties that can be imposed on young offenders is far too lenient. For example, the maximum punishment for individuals convicted of first-degree murder is 10 years (raised from the original 2 years). Yielding to public criticism that the YOA is soft on teenage criminals and to the erroneous perception that youth crime is on the rise, Parliament increased some penalties by amending the act in 1986, 1992, and 1995. Although youth crime declined 21 percent during the 1990s, many observers believe that the stiffer penalties had little if anything to do with this decrease (Cunningham, 1998; "Youth and the Criminal Justice System," 1998).

The cases of older youths—those 16 and 17 years of age—charged with murder or other serious crimes are commonly transferred to adult courts, where conviction yields an adult sentence. Youthful defendants 14 and 15 years old and who are charged with a serious offense or who have a prior criminal record *may*

be tried in adult court. However, all youthful offenders are eligible for parole (including those convicted of murder) after serving fewer years than adults found guilty of the same crime. Youths convicted as adults serve their time in juvenile detention facilities until they reach their eighteenth birthday, at which time they are transferred to adult prisons (Cunningham, 1998; McNaught, 2000; "Youth and the Criminal Justice System," 1998).

Compared to other nations, the Canadian system of juvenile justice is quite punitive. The rate of youth incarceration in Canada is approximately twice that of the United States and 10 to 15 time as great as that of numerous European countries, Australia, and New Zealand. The Canadian criminal justice system also treats youths more harshly than adults. In 1992, the incarceration rate for individuals 18 years of age and older was 151 per 100,000 adults, compared to a higher 219 per 100,000 youths between the ages of 10 and 17 (Rubec, 2000; "Youth and the Criminal Justice System," 1998).

About two-thirds of juvenile offenders appearing in youth courts are convicted. Of these, slightly more than one-third are sentenced to "secure custody" (a youth prison), or "open custody" (a group home or wilderness camp). Secure custody sentences vary significantly across Canada: Ontario incarcerates youthful offenders at twice the rate of the provinces of Quebec and British Columbia. Most of these custodial dispositions are for a period of 3 months or less and are sometimes referred to as "short shock" sentences. In the 1998 to 1999 period, only 2 percent of offenders sentenced to custody received a punishment of more than 1 year in prison (Doob, 1999; Rubec, 2000).

The youth justice system has no form of early release such as time off for good behavior or parole; convicted offenders must serve their sentences (McNaught, 2000). The individual deterrent impact of this form of punishment has been questioned. In 1993 and 1994, 40 percent of those serving time were second offenders and 25 percent were persistent offenders (three or more prior convictions) ("Youth and the Criminal Justice System," 1998).

Over the past 20 years, the youth justice system in Canada has become increasingly punitive toward adolescent girls, who comprise about one-fifth of all juvenile arrests. In 1982, slightly less than 33 percent of youth court outcomes involving girls were minimal including suspended sentences. By 1995 and 1996, minimal sanction dispositions had plunged to 4.2 percent. Historically, a disproportionate number of First Nation (the Canadian equivalent of Native American) and females of color have been caught up in the Canadian juvenile justice system (Reitsma-Street, 1999).

A significant number of youths guilty of minor infractions are processed outside the criminal justice system. They may be directed to apologize, make restitution to the victim(s), and/or engage in volunteer work. In a recent year in Newfoundland, 880 cases were referred by crown attorneys to 27 volunteer work programs involving more than 500 volunteers ("Youth and the Criminal Justice System," 1998).

In its 1998 Report on Youth Crime, the Ontario Crime Commission called for additional amendments to the YOA including ("Youth and the Criminal Justice System," 1998)

- Lowering the maximum age for a young offender from 17 to 15 so that those 16 years of age and over can be prosecuted as adults.
- Lowering the minimum age for prosecution from 12 to 10.
- Eliminating the prohibition against publishing the names of youths charged with serious crimes or repeat offenders.

In an attempt to create a juvenile justice system that will satisfy the majority of Canadians, the Youth Criminal Justice Act (YCJA) has been proposed as a replacement for the YOA. Introduced in February 2001, this legislation provides for tougher penalties for violent offenders and more community-based diversion alternatives for nonviolent lawbreakers. Conservatives and liberals immediately criticized this proposal. Conservatives said it was unmanageable and too expensive as well as a continuation of "the molly-coddling of dangerous young offenders ..." (in Ford, 2000, p. A18). They added that the list of "serious" crimes does not include aggravated assault, sexual assault, or armed robbery and that judges have too much discretion when passing sentence (Williamson, 2001). Speaking from the other side of the political spectrum, a liberal group in Quebec said that penalties outlined in the bill were too harsh (MacCharles, 2001).

Many schools in Canada have a zero tolerance policy regarding disruptive student behavior. For example, students who bully classmates and swear at teachers are removed from the traditional academic environment and sent to a youth court. According to a youth court judge, this strategy is a way of transferring misbehaving students from "the school system into young offenders facilities. And it's paying off" (in Landon, 2000, p. A10).

Teachers in Ontario have recently been granted the authority to temporarily send disruptive pupils to boot-camp style programs modeled on youth correction centers. Children suspended from school must attend alternative classes, including sessions on anger management. To enhance their respect for authority, disruptive students start the day by reciting an oath of allegiance to the queen of England. The power to expel students for infractions such as weapons possessions and sexual assault has been transferred from local boards of education to school principals. These students will also be sent to boot-camp style programs (Greenfield, 2000).

Although many teachers welcome the opportunity to remove misbehaving students from their classes, they are wary of infringing on individuals' constitutional rights. The president of a teacher's union noted, "Teachers want the right to remove [problem pupils] from their class. But they do not want to be judge and jury at the same time as teachers" (in Greenfield, 2000, p. 14).

Trampling individual rights is just what many people believe happened to a 16-year-old boy from a small town near Ottawa in early 2001. As part of a drama class assignment, he was instructed to write a story and read it aloud. Entitled "Twisted," the story was about a student who, tormented for years by local bullies, gained revenge by blowing up the school. The author of the story was arrested on a charge of uttering death threats and held in custody for 34 days. He told authorities that horror-story author Stephen King was one of his heroes and that he had no plans or desire to hurt anyone. A thorough search of his home failed to yield any incriminating evidence. The boy's parents told officials that their son had been verbally and physically abused by school bullies for years. A week before the incident the boy had been thrown to the ground by a group of 11 students and repeatedly kicked in the head (Sands, 2001a; Sands, 2001b).

summary

1. Community corrections involve probation, intensive supervision, and parole. These efforts aim at keeping society safe while saving money that incarceration would otherwise cost.

2. Probation began in the nineteenth century as a way of reducing prison overcrowding and costs, and helping offenders to rehabilitate. But it soon led to heavy caseloads, a lack of qualified probation officers, and a lack of meaningful treatment and educational programs.

3. Many people on probation today fail to follow the conditions of their release into the community. They commit technical violations of these conditions and also commit new offenses. The recidivism rate of probationers is high but not higher than that for comparable offenders who are sent to prison. Probation thus saves a good deal of money while keeping society as safe as imprisonment. Recidivism by probationers could be lower if more programs and services for probationers were available.

4. Intermediate sanctions include house arrest and electronic monitoring, boot camps, intensive supervision, day-reporting centers, community service, and fines and other monetary penalties. In general, intermediate sanctions do not produce lower recidivism rates than incarceration, but neither do they produce higher recidivism rates. Like probation, they thus keep society as safe as incarceration while costing much less. Evidence suggests that intermediate sanctions combining surveillance with adequate programs and services would produce lower recidivism rates than now exist.

5. Parole began in the nineteenth century as a way of reducing prison crowding. Because parolees have high recidivism rates, parole has come under attack in recent decades, and some states have abolished discretionary parole involving parole boards. This abolition has arguably reduced participation in various programs during incarceration; it has also led to more behavioral problems because inmates no longer have incentives to take part in these programs and to engage in good behavior. Recidivism rates among parolees could be reduced if adequate drug treatment and other programs and services for them were available.

6. The juvenile justice system has its roots in the nineteenth century, when a new understanding of childhood and a new philosophy of juvenile misbehavior developed. This philosophy began to change during the 1970s and especially the 1980s and 1990s when perceptions of rising juvenile crime fueled a get tough movement involving the transfer of serious juvenile offenders to adult court. However, these transfers have done more harm than good because they seem to increase recidivism by the juvenile offenders, who end up in adult court and, if incarcerated, become subject to sexual and physical victimization by adult offenders.

7. Promising new approaches to serious and violent juvenile offending include well-funded intermediate sanctions combining surveillance with adequate programs and services and, especially, early childhood and adolescent programs and services. The latter have been shown to be very effective in preventing delinquency and other childhood and adolescent problems while saving society money in the long run.

key terms

boot camp	intensive supervision
community service	intermediate sanctions
correctional supervision	parole officer
day-reporting centers	parole
electronic monitoring	probation
fines	probation officer
forfeiture	restitution
house arrest	shock probation

questions *for* investigation

1. Would you feel safe working with a person on probation or parole? Explain your answer.
2. Using the information given in this chapter on probation, design, in chart form, a set of guidelines that identifies various factors a judge might consider when deciding whether to put an individual on probation. Then elaborate on this chart to include all the relevant factors, such as the various conditions, you would incorporate into the probation term.
3. Further extend the guideline chart from Question 2 to identify the factors a judge might consider if an individual violates his or her terms of parole.
4. In a group, design an intensive supervision program that you think would be effective for first-time drug offenders. Provide a rationale for each feature of the program.
5. Do some research on parole in your community (college or hometown). Find out which programs—drug treatment, anger management, job skills, others—are usually incorporated into parole terms.
6. Do you think that community service programs would be effective for nonviolent juvenile offenders? For violent juvenile offenders? Explain your answer.
7. This chapter introduces the concept of an "integrated" criminal justice system that handles both adults and juveniles. Do you favor such a system? Explain your answer.

1. Suppose you have just been released from prison after serving a 5-year term for armed robbery. You spend the next 3 weeks applying for menial labor jobs, only to be told repeatedly that you're not wanted because of your criminal past. You finally get a job doing some light construction work but are accused of theft when some power tools are discovered to be missing, and you lose your job. What do you do now?

2. Suppose you are the juvenile intake officer for a 15-year-old girl who has been arrested for prostitution and drug use. You talk with her family members and teachers and discover that she has probably been sexually abused by her father for several years and that her parents have a very argumentative relationship with each other and with her. You have to decide how the juvenile justice system should treat this girl in view of her alleged offenses. What do you decide and what actions do you take?

Criminal Justice Information on the Internet

Hundreds of Web sites on crime and justice populate the Internet. We obviously do not have space to list them all, but following is an annotated list of a dozen of the most important and informative Web sites. They link to many more sites that provide information on virtually any crime and justice topic imaginable.

1. Bureau of Justice Statistics, U.S. Department of Justice   **http://www.ojp.usdoj.gov/bjs**

   This is the Web site for the branch of the U.S. Department of Justice that gathers, analyzes, and presents statistics on crime and criminal justice in the United States. It covers topics including crime and victims, law enforcement, prosecution, criminal offenders, courts and sentencing, corrections, drugs and firearms, and the federal justice system. The site includes spreadsheets and graphics on crime statistics and links to many reports about crime and criminal justice.

2. The Uniform Crime Reports, Federal Bureau of Investigation   **http://www.fbi.gov/ucr/ucr.htm**

   The FBI's Uniform Crime Reports is the nation's leading source of "official" crime statistics. This site has links for *Crime in the United States,* the FBI's chief publication on UCR data for the past several years, and it also has links for hate crime statistics and for data on the number of law enforcement officers killed and assaulted in the line of duty.

3. Office of Juvenile Justice and Delinquency Prevention   **http://ojjdp.ncjrs.org/facts/facts.html**

   This site of the branch of the U.S. Department of Justice focuses on juvenile delinquency and juvenile justice. It has links to numerous publications and to statistics, charts, and tables that provide a comprehensive look at delinquency and juvenile justice in the United States.

4. Sourcebook of Criminal Justice Statistics   **http://www.albany.edu/sourcebook**

   The *Sourcebook of Criminal Justice Statistics* is an annual compilation of data on crime and criminal justice in the United States. It contains hundreds of statistical tables that are organized into six sections: (a) characteristics of the criminal justice systems, (b) public attitudes toward crime and criminal justice–related topics, (c) the nature and distribution of known offenses, (d) characteristics and distribution of persons arrested, (e) judicial processing of defendants, and (f) persons under correctional supervision. The *Sourcebook* is published in hard copy but is easy to use on-line.

5. Office for Victims of Crime   **http://www.ojp.usdoj.gov/ovc**

   The Office for Victims of Crime is the branch of the U.S. Department of Justice that focuses exclusively on crime victims. It sponsors and oversees several programs designed to help such victims. Its site contains links to sources of grants and findings on victim-related matters, to sources of help for crime victims, and to publications about criminal victimization.

6. National Institute of Justice   **http://www.ojp.usdoj.gov/nij**

   The National Institute of Justice (NIJ) is the branch of the U.S. Department of Justice that conducts research on criminal behavior and criminal justice. It is a major source of grant funding for scholars in the field of crime and criminal justice and sponsors many workshops and conferences designed to further scholarly and professional understanding of crime and justice issues. Its Web site includes links to the NIJ's programs, funding sources, and publications.

7. Violence against Women and Family Violence Program
   http://www.ojp.usdoj.gov/nij/vawprog/welcome.html

   The Violence against Women and Family Violence Program is a special initiative of the National Institute of Justice that focuses on rape and domestic violence. It aims to understand the nature and extent of violence against women and family members, to identify the causes and consequences of this violence, and to evaluate the effectiveness of prevention and intervention programs designed to reduce such violence and to help its victims and survivors. Its Web site contains links to projects, funding sources, and publications in all these areas.

8. National Center for State Courts
   http://www.ncsconline.org

   The National Center for State Courts is an independent, nonprofit organization that provides leadership and service to the nation's state courts. Its Web site contains links to court statistics, publications, and programs provided by the center.

9. Justice Research and Statistics Association
   http://www.jrsainfo.org

   The Justice Research and Statistics Association (JRSA) is a national, nonprofit organization of criminal justice researchers and practitioners from every state. It sponsors statistical analysis centers in the states that gather and analyze crime and justice data for policy purposes. Its Web site includes links to JRSA publications, programs, and conferences.

10. Death Penalty Information Center
    http://www.deathpenaltyinfo.org

    The Death Penalty Information Center is a private, nonprofit organization that advocates for the abolition of capital punishment. Its site contains links to other sites related to the death penalty, including those that provide data on the use of the death penalty and analyses of its cost and effectiveness.

11. Academy of Criminal Justice Sciences
    http://www.acjs.org

    The Academy of Criminal Justice Sciences (ACJS) is an international professional society established in 1963 to promote the understanding of criminal justice and to foster interaction among criminal justice practitioners and researchers. It sponsors an annual conference where hundreds of papers on crime and justice are presented, and it also includes several regional associations that sponsor their own conferences. This site provides important information about the ACJS and includes links to other criminal justice resources.

12. American Society of Criminology
    http://www.asc41.com

    The American Society of Criminology (ASC) is the leading international professional society of criminologists. Its members include scholars from many academic disciplines, as well as criminal justice professionals. Like the ACJS, it sponsors an annual conference where research on crime and justice issues is presented. Its site contains links to the ASC's activities and to various topics on criminal behavior and criminal justice.

Glossary

absolute deterrence   the effect of criminal punishment (either the threat or the actual use) compared to *no* punishment at all

actus reus   as an element of crime, an actual act committed

administrative law   rules and regulations issued by government agencies

adversarial model   a model of the criminal justice system that emphasizes fierce competition between prosecutors and defense attorneys to win their cases

aggravated assault   the unlawful and intentional causing of serious bodily harm with or without a deadly weapon or the unlawful, intentional attempt or threat of serious bodily harm with or without a weapon

anomie theory   Robert K. Merton's view that deviance among the poor results from their frustration over their failure to become economically successful through working

appellate court   a court of review that determines whether the rulings of a lower court—usually a trial court—were correct

arraignment   the proceedings by which an individual is formally charged and required to enter a plea of guilty, not guilty, or nolo contendere; if the individual refuses to plea, the judge will enter a plea of not guilty on his or her behalf

arrest warrant   a document issued by a judge or court having the authority to do so that directs or sanctions the arrest of one or more persons

arson   willful or malicious burning or attempt to burn, with or without the attempt to defraud, a dwelling house, public building, motor vehicle, aircraft, or personal property of another

assigned counsel   a system wherein a judge or court assigns attorneys to represent indigent defendants either from a list of volunteers or a file of all practicing lawyers in that jurisdiction

bail   money or other security given to the court to ensure that a defendant will appear at every stage of the legal proceedings

boot camp   an intermediate sanction involving a paramilitary environment

burglary   unlawful entry of a structure to commit a felony or theft

case law   laws derived from decisions by appellate courts, especially the Supreme Court

causation   as an element of crime, the idea that an act actually caused some harm

civil law   the body of law governing relationships among individuals, organizations, and government agencies

civil suit   a legal action taken to remedy a civil wrong

civil wrongs (torts)   violations of the civil law

code of silence   the unwritten norm adhered to by officers not to inform on a colleague even if that individual has violated police procedures, for example, by engaging in excessive force

common law   system of laws derived from judges' rulings

community service   an intermediate sanction in which an offender performs service for the community, often in the form of menial labor

concurrence   as an element of crime, the correspondence of criminal intent and a criminal act

consensual model   a model of the criminal justice system that emphasizes cooperation among prosecutors, defense attorneys, and judges to expedite case processing

contempt of cop   defiant attitudes of individuals (often those suspected of crimes) for the authority of a police officer; examples include direct profanity at an officer and fleeing after being stopped for questioning

contract system   a system of defending indigents accused of committing crimes by which a governmental agency enters into a contractual agreement with a law firm or individual attorneys to provide the necessary services

correctional supervision   incarceration, probation, intermediate sanctions, and parole

court of last resort   the highest appellate court in a geographical jurisdiction. In the United States, that would be a state or the entire nation

crime control model   a model of the criminal justice system that emphasizes the need to prevent and punish crime and, by so doing, keep society safe

crime displacement   the transfer or movement of a crime from one place, time, or kind to another place, time, or kind as a result of a change in the social and/or physical environment

crime myth   false belief about crime and criminal justice

crime rate   in the UCR, the number of crimes per 100,000 persons in some location or subgroup of the population; in the NCVS, the number of victimizations per 1,000 persons or 1,000 households

Crime Victims Fund   established with the passage of VOCA in 1984, it is the major source of revenue for state compensation programs

crimes   behaviors deemed so harmful to the public welfare that they should be banned by criminal law

crimes known to the police the UCR's term for the "official" number of crimes that the police report to the UCR and that the UCR, in turn, reports to the public

criminal law the body of law that prohibits acts that are seen as so harmful to the public welfare that they deserve to be punished by the state, and that governs how these acts are handled by official state procedures

day-reporting centers buildings to which persons on probation report daily for monitoring and various programs and services

degradation ceremony any public activity that humiliates an individual

deprivation model the view that inmate subcultures result from the need of inmates to cope with the pains of imprisonment

determinate sentences fixed terms of imprisonment

deterrence the prevention of crime through the threat or actual use of legal punishment

deterrence theory closely related to rational choice theory, the belief that more certain and severe punishment reduces the crime rate

differential association theory Edwin Sutherland's view that deviance results from negative peer influences and, more specifically, from an excess of definitions favorable to violation of the law

differential opportunity theory Richard Cloward and Lloyd Ohlin's view that poor people not only have blocked opportunities for success through legitimate means but also differential access to illegitimate means to achieve such success

Dirty Harry strategy the disregard of procedural laws (law of search and seizure, for example) and the use of "dirty means" such as intimidation and torture by police officers in their roles as professional crime fighters; named for the Dirty Harry movies starring Clint Eastwood

discovery the pretrial procedure by which the prosecution and defense gain information about each other's case

discretion in criminal justice, the power of officials to decide whether to take a particular course of action

discretionary model a model of the criminal justice system that involves a series of decisions at each stage of the process

DNA deoxyribonucleic acid, a substance containing genetic material that is unique to an individual except in the cases of identical twins

drug dependence habitual use of a drug over an extended period of time

due process model a model of the criminal justice system that emphasizes the need to prevent government abuse of the legal system against guilty and innocent people alike. This model assumes that some suspects are, indeed, innocent.

electronic monitoring an intermediate sanction that uses an electronic device to pinpoint the location of an offender

exclusionary rule the principle that evidence obtained by the police in violation of a suspect's constitutional rights may not be used to prosecute the defendant

exculpatory evidence evidence that tends to clear, justify, or excuse a defendant from alleged fault or guilt

explicit bargains specific considerations, such as charge or sentence reductions from the state, that defendants negotiate for through their attorneys

Federal Bureau of Investigation (FBI) established in an executive order in 1908, this agency investigates corporate crime, political corruption, and more than 250 federal offenses

felonies serious crimes punishable by a sentence of at least 1 year in prison

felony murder unlawful homicide that occurs during the commission of a felony, usually robbery, rape, or arson

field research a research method involving extensive observation and/or intensive interviewing

fines the payment of money to the state or community, often in lieu of incarceration

first-degree murder the willful, deliberate, and premeditated killing of one human being by another with "malice aforethought"; in states with capital punishment, this crime carries the death penalty

forfeiture the seizing of assets such as cars and money by police and other law enforcement agents from suspected offenders

formal social control in prisons, the rule of prison officials and guards over inmates

free will the view that human behavior is the result of personal, independent choices and not of internal or external forces beyond their control

funnel model a model of the criminal justice system in which many cases enter the top of the system and only a very few trickle out into prison at the bottom

general deterrence the effect that occurs when would-be criminals decide not to commit crime because of their concern about being apprehended and punished

grand jury a jury of between 12 and 23 individuals who determine whether an individual should be indicted; grand juries also have the power to investigate crimes in specified jurisdictions

gross incapacitation the imprisonment of large numbers of offenders without much regard to their criminal histories or propensities for future offending

harm as an element of crime, the requirement that some injury is done to an individual or property by a criminal act

hate crimes criminal acts against persons, property, or society that are motivated in part or whole by the offender's bias against the victim's race, religion, disability, sexual orientation, or ethnicity/nationality

homicide the killing of one human being by another; not necessarily a crime

house arrest an intermediate sanction involving confinement in one's home

implicit bargaining defendants, through their attorneys, learn that if they do not plead guilty and are convicted of a crime(s) at a jury trial they will be punished more severely than if they would have pled to an agreed-on offense(s)

importation model the view that inmate subcultures reflect the values prisoners bring into their institutions and other aspects of their backgrounds

incapacitation depriving offenders of the ability to commit new offenses and thereby improving public safety

incarceration confinement in prison or jail

incidence in a self-report survey, the average number of offenses committed per offender

indeterminate sentences sentences involving a range from a minimum of years to a maximum of many years more

Index offenses the term used by the Uniform Crime Reports for the eight felonies to which it devotes the most attention: murder and nonnegligent manslaughter, forcible rape, robbery, aggravated assault, burglary, larceny–theft, motor vehicle theft, and arson

indictment a formal, written accusation written by the prosecuting attorney and submitted to a grand jury charging individuals with a crime. If jury members agree by a majority vote that the charges as outlined in the indictment are valid, they return a true bill

informal social control in prisons, the understandings that inmates have among themselves and with prison staff about how prisons should operate

initial appearance the first appearance before a judicial officer of a person who has been arrested; at this appearance (1) the individual is informed of his or her constitutional rights; (2) the terms of bail or other forms of pretrial release are set; and (3) if the defendant is indigent, counsel is appointed

inmate code set of rules that governs how inmates should behave

inmate subculture the norms, values, beliefs, behavior, and language of inmates

intensive supervision an intermediate sanction involving more careful supervision and control than routine probation

intermediate sanctions social controls that are supposedly more punitive than routine probation but less punitive than incarceration

jail penal institutions run by towns, cities, and counties that house several kinds of offenders

jurisdiction the power to hear and decide a case, for example, some courts have jurisdiction over civil matters, whereas others decide criminal cases

just deserts the idea that the degree of punishment should be proportional to the seriousness of the offense

justice of the peace a judge or magistrate of limited jurisdiction who presides over minor civil and criminal cases, including preliminary stages in the latter

labeling theory the view that the definition of crime and deviance depend on the circumstances surrounding a behavior rather than on the qualities of the behavior itself, that labeling produces more deviance, and that the labeling process is biased and therefore problematic

larceny–theft unlawful taking of property from the possession of another; this category of crime includes shoplifting, pocket picking, purse snatching, and bicycle theft, as well as a number of other offenses

Magna Carta historic document that asserts the rights of nobles and bound the king to the rule of law

mala in se offenses that are inherently evil; serious crimes

mala prohibita offenses that are crimes only because the law prohibits them; often applied to "victimless" crimes

mandatory minimum sentences as required by legislatures, sentences involving a minimum prison term

manslaughter unlawful killings that are committed without "malice aforethought," and, as such, are considered less severe and more explainable

marginal deterrence the deterrent effect of an incremental increase or decrease in the threat or use of punishment

maximum-security prisons large, forbidding prisons that holds inmates who are thought to be the most violent and dangerous to the outside community

medium-security prisons prisons that hold property offenders and other inmates who are considered less dangerous than those in maximum-security institutions

mens rea as an element of crime, a guilty mind or criminal intent

minimum-security prisons prisons that hold inmates, typically property and drug offenders, who are considered the least dangerous and who are serving the shortest sentences

misdemeanors minor offenses punishable by a jail sentence of less than 1 year

motor vehicle theft attempted or completed theft of automobiles, trucks, buses, and motorcycles

municipal police law enforcement officers in the employ of a town or city; these departments range in size from a few officers to the NYPD with almost 37,000 sworn officers

National Crime Victimization Survey (NCVS) an annual survey given by the government to people in thousands of randomly selected households around the nation that asks residents of these households a series of questions about crimes that they, other household members, and the household itself have experienced during the past six-month period

nolo contendere strictly speaking, not a plea, it is a statement in which the defendant does not admit guilt but submits to the charges and punishment against him or her

occupational crime criminal acts that are committed by way of legal employment

organized crime self-perpetuating, hierarchical, nonideological group often with a specialized division of labor that exists for the purpose of committing crime for profit

pains of imprisonment Gresham Sykes's term for the deprivations of prison life

parole supervision of an offender released from prison after serving a term of incarceration

parole officer a legal official who handles the cases of people on parole

penitentiaries early prisons that were built to hold inmates so they could repent for their offenses

plea bargain an agreement between the state and the defendant wherein each side gives up something and receives something in return

police accountability the philosophy that individual officers and the department as a whole should be accountable for police behavior

police corruption   a catchall term that covers a wide variety of police misconduct including accepting money, illegal drugs, or articles of value for not arresting law violators, committing burglaries or robberies, selling illegal drugs confiscated in drug busts, and so on

police fraternal organizations or brotherhoods   dating back to the 1860s, these associations were formed to aid members who became ill or disabled in the line of duty as well as to help families of deceased officers; by the 1890s, these organizations began to focus on the economic well-being of police officers

preliminary hearings   proceedings to determine if there is cause to subject someone legally to a criminal trial; states without a grand jury use preliminary hearings

presentence report   a report prepared by a probation officer or social worker that includes information on a defendant's background and, usually, a recommendation for his or her sentence

pretrial motions   petitions to the court requesting orders or rulings favorable to the applicant's case; for example, the defense may submit a motion requesting that some or all of the prosecution's evidence be suppressed because it was illegally obtained

prevalence   in a self-report survey, the percentage of respondents who have committed an offense at least once within a certain time period

prison argot   a special language that is part of the inmate subculture

prisonization   the learning of the inmate subculture

prisons   penal institutions that house offenders who have been found guilty of felonies and are sentenced to at least 1 year of incarceration

privatization   in corrections policy, the involvement of private corporations in the building and operation of prisons and jails

probation   a substitute for incarceration that involves placing a convicted offender in the community under the supervision of a probation officer as long as the offender meets certain standards of behavior

probation officer   a legal official who handles the cases of people on probation

procedural law   the body of law that governs how the criminal justice system handles criminal and civil cases

profiling   the informal practice of some officers and the official policy of some law enforcement departments that the characteristics of certain individuals and groups (especially racial and ethnic) are indicative of criminal behavior

prosecutors   public officials either elected or appointed who represent the government in all phases of criminal proceedings

prostitution   the sale of sex of oneself or another person for money

public defenders   attorneys employed by the state who represent indigent defendants during criminal proceedings

rape   carnal knowledge of a female forcibly and against her will

rational choice theory   the view that people act with free will and carefully weigh the potential benefits and costs of their behavior before acting

recidivism   repeat offending

rehabilitation   the reform of offenders through various kinds of programs in prisons and in the community

restitution   the payment of goods and services by offenders to their victims

retribution   a society's punishment of criminal offenders to avenge a wrong done to a member of the society and thus to the society as a whole

rising expectations theory   regarding prison riots, the view that riots occur when inmates' expectations for improved conditions have been raised and then frustrated

robbery   taking something of value from an individual by the use or threat of force

rotten apples explanation   a common interpretation of police deviance stating that unbeknownst to senior police officials and administrators, a small number of officers are engaging in corrupt behavior; this explanation minimizes the scope of the problem and insulates police officials from any blame regarding the deviant behavior of subordinates

routine activities theory   the belief that crime and victimization are more likely to occur with the simultaneous occurrence of motivated offenders, attractive targets, and low or no guardianship

selective incapacitation   reduction of crime through the incarceration of chronic offenders

self-control theory   Michael Gottfredson and Travis Hirschi's view that all crime results from the inability to restrain one's own needs, aspirations, and impulses

self-report surveys   surveys in which respondents are asked to provide information on various offenses they may have committed

sentencing commissions   commissions that were established beginning in the 1970s to develop sentencing guidelines and to consider other aspects of sentencing

sentencing disparity   unequal legal treatment of offenders convicted of similar crimes and with similar prior records

sentencing guidelines   recommendations that judges are expected to follow in determining an offender's sentence

sentencing hearing   a courtroom meeting at which a judge pronounces the sentence of a convicted offender

sexual shakedown   a form of sexual misconduct on the part of police wherein an officer will forgo arresting a female suspect (often a prostitute) in exchange for sexual favors

sheriff's departments   organized primarily at the county level, these law enforcement agencies provide police services to people who do not reside in cities or towns; these departments range in size from a few officers to thousands of members; for example, the Los Angeles County Sheriff's Department has more than 8,000 full-time sworn officers

shock probation   an intermediate sanction, usually in the form of a boot camp, meant to "shock" offenders into obeying the law

sick in or blue flu   a tactic wherein a significant number of police officers call in sick when they are not ill, resulting in a partial immobilization of the department; this strategy is used as a means for achieving a particular goal such as a pay increase or the hiring of additional officers

social control theory Travis Hirschi's view that social bonds to family, school, and other conventional social institutions inhibit the development of criminal behavior

social ecology in criminology, the view that certain social and physical characteristics of neighborhoods help explain their crime rates

specific deterrence the effect that occurs when criminals who have been sanctioned by the criminal justice system decide not to commit crime again because of their concern about facing additional such sanctions

speedup usually manifested in the form of an aggressive ticket writing campaign, this tactic is used by police to bring public attention to some law enforcement goal, for example, a more comprehensive benefits package and/or a salary increase

stalking behavior directed at a specific individual involving repeated verbal or nonverbal acts that cause a reasonable person fear

state police established between 1900 and 1930, these agencies enforce state laws and are especially active in the area of traffic law and motor vehicle accidents; with the exception of Hawaii, every state has a state police force

subculture a group that holds values, norms, and patterns of behavior in common with the dominant society but also has its own worldview and design for living

substantive law the body of law that specifies which behaviors are crimes and the appropriate punishments for these behaviors

supermax a supermaximum-security prison or wing within a prison specifically designed to accommodate serial killers and others considered especially violent and dangerous

system model an "input–output" model of criminal justice in which crime is the input and entrance into corrections the output. It involves a series of stages marked by limited cooperation among criminal justice officials.

target congruence the matching of an offender's strength and victim's weakness

Texas Rangers established as a paramilitary unit in 1835, this agency is the nation's oldest state-level law enforcement organization

total institution Erving Goffman's term for an institution that has complete control over the lives of its inmates

Uniform Crime Reports (UCR) the U.S. government's official source of data on crime that relies on police reports of crimes that they hear about from citizens

van Dijk chain the chain of events that is triggered with the first victimization. For example, if A has his bicycle stolen, he may steal B's bike who in turn may steal C's bike and so on.

victim-impact statement (VIS) a statement that allows victims to tell the court in detail how they have been medically, financially, and emotionally affected by a crime prior to the offender's sentencing

Victim–Offender Reconciliation Programs (VORPs) programs that bring the offender and victim together in the presence of a trained mediator for the purpose of reconciliation, which usually results in the offender making some form of the restitution to the victim or community

victimology the study of the role of the victim in the criminal event and the relation between crime victims and the criminal justice system (the police, the criminal courts, and correction officials)

victim precipitation the chain of events started by the victim that culminates with his or her victimization

victim statement of opinion a subjective declaration by crime victims telling the court what sentence they believe offenders should receive

Victims of Crime Act (VOCA) of 1984 legislation that authorized federal funding for state-administered victim compensation programs; these funds are typically limited to victims of violent crimes with no other recourse to money or services

violations (infractions) minor offenses punishable by only a fine

war on crime a phrase often used by politicians, police officials, police officers, the media, and the general public to denote an all-out effort on the part of the city, state, or larger society to eradicate street crime

wedding cake model a model of the criminal justice system in which a very small number of celebrated cases is at the top of the model, and a greater number of serious felonies and greater numbers yet of less serious felonies and of misdemeanors are below

wrongful execution the execution of an innocent person

References

Abadinsky, H. 1989. *Drug Abuse—An Introduction.* Chicago: Nelson-Hall.

Abadinsky, H. 1990. *Organized Crime,* 3 ed. Chicago: Nelson-Hall.

Abadinsky, H. 1997. *Organized Crime,* 5 ed. Chicago: Nelson-Hall.

Abramsky, Sasha. 1999. "When They Get Out." *The Atlantic Monthly,* June:30–36.

Abramson, R., and Takahasi, D. 1992. "Rockwell Agrees to $18.5 Million Fine." *Los Angeles Times,* March 26:A14.

Abu-Hassan, Muhammad. 1997. "Islamic Criminal Law." Pages 79–89 in *Justice and Human Rights in Islamic Law,* edited by Gerald E. Lampe. Washington, DC: International Law Institute.

"Abusive Behavior." 1998. *The Economist,* November 10:32.

Acoca, Leslie. 1998. "Defusing the Time Bomb: Understanding and Meeting the Growing Health Care Needs of Incarcerated Women in America." *Crime and Delinquency,* 44:49–69.

Adams, K. 1996. "Measuring the Prevalence of Police Abuse of Force." Pages 52–93 in *Police Violence: Understanding and Controlling Police Abuse and Force,* edited by W. A. Geller and H. Toch. New Haven: Yale University Press.

Adams, Kenneth. 1992. "Adjusting to Life in Prison." *Crime and Justice: A Review of Research,* 16:275–359.

Adler, F., G. O. W. Mueller, and W. S. Laufer. 1991. *Criminology.* New York: McGraw-Hill.

Adler, Freda. 1975. *Sisters in Crime: The Rise of the New Female Criminal.* New York: McGraw-Hill.

Adler, Jeffrey S. 1994. "The Dynamite, Wreckage, and Scum in Our Cities: The Social Construction of Deviance in Industrial America." *Justice Quarterly,* 11(1):33–49.

Adler, S. J. 1994. *The Jury—Trial and Error in the American Courtroom.* New York: Random House.

Administrative Notes. 1999. *San Diego Legal Update Bulletin,* 3:3. Available: http://www.clew.org/CLEW/LEGAL/V3N3.htm.

Agnew, Robert. 2000. "Sources of Criminality: Strain and Subcultural Theories." Pages 349–371 in *Criminology: A Contemporary Handbook,* edited by Joseph F. Sheley. Belmont, CA: Wadsworth.

Akers, Ronald L. 2000. *Criminological Theories: Introduction and Evaluation,* 3 ed. Los Angeles: Roxbury.

Albanese, J. 1989. *Organized Crime in America.* Cincinnati: Anderson.

Albanese, J. S. 1991. "Organized Crime—The Mafia Mystique." Pages 201–208 in *Criminology,* edited by J. F. Sheley. Belmont, CA: Wadsworth.

Albanese, J. 1995. "Organized Crime: The Mafia Mystique." Pages 231–248 in *Criminology: A Contemporary Handbook,* edited by J. F. Sheley. Belmont, CA: Wadsworth.

Albert, Alexa. 2001. *Brothel: Mustang Ranch and Its Women.* New York: Random House.

Albini, J. 1992. "The Distribution of Drugs: Models of Criminal Organization and Their Integration." Pages 79–108 in *Drugs, Crime, and Social Policy: Research Issues and Concerns,* edited by T. Meiczkowski. Boston: Allyn & Bacon.

Albini, J. L., R. E. Rogers, V. Shabalin, V. Kutushev, V. Moiseev, and J. Anderson. 1997. "Russian Organized Crime: Its History, Structure and Foundation." Pages 153–173 in *Understanding Crime in Global Perspective,* edited by P. Ryan and G. Rush. Thousand Oaks, CA: Sage.

Alex, N. 1969. *Black in Blue: A Study of the Negro Policeman.* New York: Appleton-Century Crofts.

Alter, Jonathan. 2000a. "The Death Penalty on Trial." *Newsweek,* June 12:24–34.

Alter, Jonathan. 2000b. "A Reckoning on Death Row." *Newsweek,* July 3:31.

Altschuler, David M. 1998. "Intermediate Sanctions and Community Treatment for Serious and Violent Juvenile Offenders." Pages 367–385 in *Serious and Violent Juvenile Offenders: Risk Factors and Successful Interventions,* edited by Rolf Loeber and David P. Farrington. Thousand Oaks, CA: Sage.

American Civil Liberties Union. 1999. *Prisoners' Rights.* New York: American Civil Liberties Union.

Amnesty International. 1999. *'Not Part of My Sentence': Violations of the Human Rights of Women in Custody.* New York: Amnesty International USA.

Amnesty International. 2001. *Abuse of Women in Custody: Sexual Misconduct and Shackling of Pregnant Women.* New York: Amnesty International USA.

"Amnesty International Protests Solitary Confinement, Shackling of Dr. Wen Ho Lee." Amnesty International. Available: http://www.amnestyusa.org/news/2000/usa08162000.html.

Amnesty International Report 1998: Mexico. 1998. Available: http://www.amnesty/org/ailib/aireport/ar98/amr41.htm.

"An Apology Delayed." 2000. *The Economist,* March 4:42–43.

Anderson, D. C. 1997. *Public Defenders and Neighborhoods.* Washington, DC: National Institute of Justice, Bureau of Justice, U.S. Government Printing Office.

Anderson, Elijah. 1999. *Code of the Street: Decency, Violence, and the Moral Life of the Inner City.* New York: W. W. Norton.

"An Equal Force." 1999. *The Economist,* May 29:26–27.

Antonowicz, Daniel, and Robert Ross. 1994. "Essential Components of Successful Rehabilitation Programs for Offenders." *International Journal of Offender Therapy and Comparative Criminology,* 38:97–104.

Arenella, P. 1997. "Miranda Stories." *Harvard Journal of Law and Ethics,* 20(2):375–387.

Armstrong, S., and D. B. Wood. 1991. "Curbing Police Brutality: An Overview." Pages 103–105 in *Police Brutality,* edited by W. Dudley. San Diego: Greenhaven Press.

"Asian Gangs." 2002. Koch Learning Systems. Available: http://www.kic.org/seminars/modules/po015.htm.

"Asian Street Gangs and Organized Crime in Focus." 2001. Available: http://www.ispn.org/asg08107.html.

Asia Watch Committee. 1990. "Punishment Season—Human Rights in China after Martial Law." New York: Asia Watch Committee.

Asseo, Laurie. 1999. "Study Ties Drug War, Rise in Jailed Women." *The Boston Globe,* November 18:A18.

Atlanta Police Department. 2002. Available: http://www.atlantapd.org/staff/chief.html.

Austin, James. 1986. "Using Early Release to Relieve Prison Crowding: A Dilemma in Public Policy." *Crime and Delinquency,* 32:391–403.

Austin, James, John Clark, Patricia Hardyman, and D. Alan Henry. 1999. *Three Strikes and You're Out: The Implementation and Impact of Strike Laws.* Washington, DC: National Institute of Justice, U.S. Department of Justice.

Austin, James, and John Irwin. 2001. *It's about Time: America's Imprisonment Binge,* 3 ed. Belmont, CA: Wadsworth.

Austin, William, and Thomas A. Williams, III. 1977. "A Survey of Judges' Response to Legal Cases: Research Notes on Sentencing Disparity." *Journal of Criminal Law and Criminology,* 68:306–310.

Awad, A. M. 1982. "The Rights of the Accused under Islamic Criminal Procedure." Pages 91–108 in *The Islamic Criminal Justice System,* edited by M. C. Bassiouni. London: Oceana.

Ayers, Ken, and Laura J. Moriarty. 1999. "Should Incarceration of Pregnant Women Be Avoided?" Pages 90–104 in *Controversial Issues in Corrections,* edited by Charles B. Fields. Boston: Allyn & Bacon.

Babbie, Earl. 1999. *The Basics of Social Research,* 7 ed. Belmont, CA: Wadsworth.

Backstrand, John A., Don C. Gibbons, and Joseph F. Jones. 1998. "Who Is in Jail? An Examination of the Rabble Hypothesis." Pages 236–244 in *Incarcerating Criminals: Prisons and Jails in Social and Organizational Context,* edited by Timothy J. Flanagan, James W. Marquart, and Kenneth G. Adams. New York: Oxford University Press.

Bahnassi, A. F. 1982. "Criminal Responsibility in Islamic Law." Pages 171–194 in *The Islamic Criminal Justice System,* edited by M. C. Bassiouni. London: Oceana.

Bailey, F. L., and H. B. Rothblatt. 1978. *Cross-Examination in Criminal Trials.* Rochester, NY: Lawyers Co-Operative.

Bailey, William C. 1998. "Deterrence, Brutalization, and the Death Penalty: Another Examination of Oklahoma's Return to Capital Punishment." *Criminology,* 36:711–733.

Bailey, William C., and Ruth Peterson. 1999. "Capital Punishment, Homicide, and Deterrence: An Assessment of the Evidence and Extension to Female Offenders." Pages 257–276 in *Homicide: A Sourcebook of Social Research,* edited by M. Dwayne Smith and Margaret Zahn. Thousand Oaks, CA: Sage.

Baker, B. G. 1986. "Chinese Law in the Eighties: The Lawyer and the Criminal Process." Pages 230–233 in *Law in the People's Republic of China,* edited by R. H. Folsom and J. H. Minan. New York: Professional Seminar Consultants.

Baldus, David C., George Woodworth, and Charles A. Pulaski. 1990. *Equal Justice and the Death Penalty: A Legal and Empirical Analysis.* Boston: Northeastern University Press.

Ballard, M. 1995. "Sleeping Lawyer Claim Brings Stay of Execution." *Texas Lawyer,* April 17:6.

Bard, M., and D. Sangrey. 1986. *The Crime Victims Handbook.* New York: Bruner/Mazer.

Barkan, Steve. 1983. "Jury Nullification in Political Trials." *Social Problems,* 31(1):28–45.

Barkan, Steven E. 1985. *Protesters on Trial: Criminal Prosecutions in the Southern Civil Rights and Vietnam Antiwar Movements.* New Brunswick, NJ: Rutgers University Press.

Barkan, Steven E. 1997. *Criminology.* New York: Prentice Hall, College Division.

Barkan, Steven E. 2001. *Criminology: A Sociological Understanding,* 2 ed. Upper Saddle River, NJ: Prentice-Hall.

Barkan, Steven E., and Lynne L. Snowden. 2001. *Collective Violence.* Boston: Allyn & Bacon.

Bartholomew, P. C., and J. F. Menez. 1990. *Summaries of Leading Cases on the Constitution.* Savage, MD: Littlefield Adams Quality Paperbacks.

Bartlett, R. 1990. *Trial by Fire and Water—The Medieval Judicial Order.* Oxford: Clarendon Press.

Bartol, Curt R. 1997. "Police Psychology: A Profession with a Promising Future." Pages 98–113 in *Critical Issues in Policing: Contemporary Readings,* edited by R. G. Dunham and G. A. Alpert. Prospect Heights, IL: Waveland Press.

Bartol, Curt R. 2002. *Criminal Behavior: A Psychological Approach,* 6 ed. Upper Saddle River, NJ: Prentice-Hall.

Baskin, Deborah R., and Ira B. Sommers. 1998. *Casualties of Community Disorder: Women's Careers in Violent Crime.* Boulder, CO: Westview Press.

Bass, S. 2000. "Negotiating Change: Community Organizations and the Politics of Policing," *Urban Affairs Review,* 36(2):148–177.

Bates, Eric. 1998. "Private Prisons." *The Nation,* January 5:11–16.

Batson v. Kentucky. 2001. Available: http://web.lexis-nexis.com/universe/docu.

Baum, L. 1990. *American Courts—Process and Policy.* Boston: Houghton Mifflin.

Baum, L. 1994. *American Courts—Process and Policy.* Boston: Houghton Mifflin.

Baumer, Terry L., M. G. Maxfield, and R. I. Mendelsohn. 1993. "A Comparative Analysis of Three Electronically Monitored Home Detention Programs." *Justice Quarterly,* 10:121–142.

Bayley, D. 1985. *Patterns of Policing.* New Brunswick, NJ: Rutgers University Press.

Bayley, D. H. 1988. "Community Policing—A Report from the Devil's Advocate." Pages 225–238 in *Community Policing: Rhetoric or Reality?* edited by J. R. Green and S. D. Mastrofski. New York: Praeger.

Bayley, D. H. 1991. *Forces of Order—Policing in Modern Japan.* Berkeley: The University of California Press.

Bayley, D. H. 1994. *Police for the Future.* New York: Oxford University Press.

Bayley, D., and E. Bittner, 1997. "Learning the Skill of Good Policing." Pages 114–138 in *Critical Issues in Policing,* edited by R. C. Dunham and G. A. Alpert. Prospect Heights, IL: Waveland Press.

Bazemore, G. 1999. "The Fork in the Road to Juvenile Court Reform." *Annals of the American Academy of Political and Social Science,* 564:81–116.

Bazemore, G., and C. T. Griffiths. 1997. "Conferences, Circles, Boards, and Mediations: The 'New Wave' of Community Decisionmaking." *Federal Probation,* 61(2):25–37.

Beals, G. 1999. "Rudy Takes the Keys." *Newsweek,* March 8:28.

Beck, Allen J. 2000. *Prisoners in 1999.* Washington, DC: Bureau of Justice Statistics, U.S. Department of Justice.

Beck, Allen J., Thomas P. Bonczar, Paula M. Ditton, Darrell K. Gilliard, Lauren E. Glaze, Caroline Wolf Harlow, Christopher J. Mumola, Tracy L. Snell, James J. Stephan, and Doris James Wilson. 2000. *Correctional Populations in the United States, 1997.* Washington, DC: Bureau of Justice Statistics, U.S. Department of Justice.

Beck, Allen, Darrell Gilliard, Lawrence Greenfeld, Caroline Harlow, Thomas Hester, Louis Jankowski, Tracy Snell, James Stephan, and Danielle Morton. 1993. *Survey of State Prison Inmates, 1991.* Washington, DC: Bureau of Justice Statistics, U.S. Department of Justice.

Beck, Allen J., and Paige M. Harrison. 2001. *Prisoners in 2000.* Washington, DC: Bureau of Justice Statistics, U.S. Department of Justice.

Beck, Allen J., and Jennifer C. Karberg. 2001. *Prison and Jail Inmates at Midyear 2000.* Washington, DC: Bureau of Justice Statistics, U.S. Department of Justice.

Beck, Allen J., Jennifer C. Karberg, and Paige M. Harrison. 2002. *Prison and Jail Inmates at Midyear 2001*. Washington, DC: Bureau of Justice Statistics, U.S. Department of Justice.

Beck, Allen, and Bernard Shipley. 1989. *Recidivism of Prisoners Released in 1983*. Washington, DC: Bureau of Justice Statistics, U.S. Department of Justice.

Becker, Howard S. 1963. *Outsiders: Studies in the Sociology of Deviance*. New York: Free Press.

Beckett, Katherine. 1997. *Making Crime Pay: Law and Order in Contemporary American Politics*. New York: Oxford University Press.

Beckett, Katherine, and Theodore Sasson. 1999. *The Politics of Injustice: Crime and Punishment in America*. Thousand Oaks, CA: Pine Forge Press.

"Becoming a Member of FDNY." 2001. Available: http://www.ci.nyc.ny/fdny/html.

Bedau, Hugo Adam, and Michael L. Radelet. 1987. "Miscarriages of Justice in Potentially Capital Cases." *Stanford Law Review*, 40:21–179.

"Behind Bars in Brazil." 1998. New York: Human Rights Watch.

Belknap, Joanne. 2000. *The Invisible Woman: Gender, Crime, and Justice*, 2 ed. Belmont, CA: Wadsworth.

Belluck, Pam. 2001. "Desperate for Prison Guards, Some States Rob Cradles." *The New York Times*, April 21:A1.

Benke, R. 2001a. "Judge Unseals Documents in Lee Case." Associated Press Wire Service. Available: http://associatedpresswireservice.

Benke, R. 2001b. "Wen Ho Lee's Agreement About to Expire." Associated Press Wire Service. Available: http://associatedpresswireservice.

Bennett, Trevor. 1998. "Crime Prevention." Pages 369–402 in *The Handbook of Crime and Punishment*, edited by Michael Tonry. New York: Oxford University Press.

Bennett, William J., John J. Dilulio, Jr., and John P. Walters. 1996. *Body Count: Moral Poverty—and How to Win America's War against Crime and Drugs*. New York: Simon & Schuster.

Berlow, Alan. 1999. "The Wrong Man." *The Atlantic Monthly*, November:66–91.

Bernard, Thomas J. 1990. "Angry Aggression among the Truly Disadvantaged." *Criminology*, 28:73–96.

Bessant, Judith. 2000. "International Obligations and Mandatory Sentencing." *Social Alternatives*, 19(2):53–56.

Biderman, Albert D., and James P. Lynch. 1991. *Understanding Crime Incidence Statistics: Why the UCR Diverges from the NCS*. New York: Springer-Verlag.

Biderman, Albert D., and Albert J. Reiss, Jr. 1967. "On Exploring the 'Dark Figure' of Crime." *Annals of the American Academy of Political and Social Science*, 374:1–15.

Birzer, M. 1999. "Police Training in the Twenty-First Century." *FBI Law Enforcement Bulletin*, 68(7):16–19.

Bishop, Donna. 2000. "Juvenile Offenders in the Adult Criminal Justice System." *Crime and Justice: A Review of Research*, 27:81–167.

Bishop, Donna M., Charles E. Frazier, Lonn Lanza-Kaduce, and Lawrence Winner. 1996. "The Transfer of Juveniles to Criminal Court: Does It Make a Difference?" *Crime and Delinquency*, 42:171–191.

Biskupic, J. 1999. "Veto by Jury." *The Washington Post National Weekly Edition*, March 29:6–8.

Biskupic, J., and E. Witt. 1997. *The Supreme Court and Individual Rights*, Washington, DC: Congressional Quarterly Inc.

Bittner, E. 1970. *The Functions of the Police in Modern Society*. Rockville, MD: The National Institute of Mental Health.

Bittner, E. 1999. "The Capacity to Use Force as the Core of the Police Role." Pages 123–133 in *The Police and Society*, edited by V. E. Kappeler. Prospect Heights, IL: Waveland Press.

Black, Donald. 1970. "Production of Crime Rates." *American Sociological Review*, 35:733–748.

Black, G. 1993. *Black Hands of Beijing: Lives of Deviance in China's Democracy Movement*. New York: John Wiley.

Black, K. 1996. "Hot Job." *Rolling Stone*, August 22:60–66.

Black, R. 1999. *Black's Law*. New York: Simon & Schuster.

Blair, J. 1999. "Quietly, Police Are Making Largest Efforts in U.S. to Add Gay Officers." *New York Times*, September 7:B1.

Blake, K. 1995. "What You Should Know about Car Theft." *Consumer's Research Magazine*, October:26–28.

Blankstein, A. 2002. "L.A. Police Chief Proposes Ban on Majority of Police Pursuits." *Los Angeles Times*, December 17:A1.

Blau, Peter M., and Judith R. Blau. 1982. "The Cost of Inequality: Metropolitan Structure and Violent Crime." *American Sociological Review*, 47:114–129.

Bleyer, Jennifer. 2001. "Prison Converts." *The Progressive*, June:28–30.

Bloom, L. 2000. "As Internet Grows, So Does the Number of Hate Sites." United Methodist News Service. Available: http://www.unms.org.

Blum, A. 1996. " 'No Plea' Policies Sprout across U.S." *The National Law Review*, 19(2):A1–A2.

Blumberg, A. S. 1967. "The Practice of Law as a Confidence Game—Organizational Cooptation of a Profession." *Law and Society Review*, June:15–39.

Blumstein, Alfred. 1993. "Making Rationality Relevant—The American Society of Criminology 1992 Presidential Address." *Criminology*, 31(1):1–16.

Blumstein, Alfred, and Allen J. Beck. 1999. "Population Growth in U.S. Prisons, 1980–1996." *Crime and Justice: A Review of Research*, 26:17–61.

Blumstein, Alfred, and Joel Wallman (eds.). 2000. *The Crime Drop in America*. New York: Cambridge University Press.

Bohm, Robert M. 1999. *Deathquest: An Introduction to the Theory and Practice of Capital Punishment in the United States*. Cincinnati: Anderson.

Boland, B., and B. Forst. 1985. "Prosecutors Don't Always Aim to Pleas." *Federal Probation*, 49(2):10–15.

Bonczar, Thomas P., and Allen J. Beck. 1997. *Lifetime Likelihood of Going to State or Federal Prison*. Washington, DC: Bureau of Justice Statistics, U.S. Department of Justice.

Bonczar, Thomas P., and Lauren E. Glaze. 1999. *Probation and Parole in the United States, 1998*. Washington, DC: Bureau of Justice Statistics, U.S. Department of Justice.

Bonger, Willem. 1916. *Criminality and Economic Conditions*. Boston: Little, Brown.

Bonta, James, and Suzanne Wallace-Capretta. 2000. "Can Electronic Monitoring Make a Difference? An Evaluation of Three Canadian Programs." *Crime and Delinquency*, 46:61–75.

Booth, Alan, and D. Wayne Osgood. 1993. "The Influence of Testosterone on Deviance in Adulthood: Assessing and Explaining the Relationship." *Criminology*, 31(1):93–117.

Borger, J. 2001. "Racist Killer Jailed for Life." *The Guardian*, January 25:15.

"Boston Police Strike." 2000. Available: http://www.britannica.com.

Bottoms, Anthony E. 1999. "Interpersonal Violence and Social Order in Prisons." *Crime and Justice: A Review of Research*, 26:205–281.

Boudreau, J. F., Q. Y. Kwan, W. F. Faragher, and G. C. Denault. 1997. *Arson and Arson Investigation*. Washington, DC: U.S. Government Printing Office.

Bouloukos, A. C., and G. Farrell. 1997. "On the Displacement of Repeat Victimization." Pages 219–231 in *Rational Choice and Situational Crime Prevention*, edited by G. Newman, R. C. Clarke, and S. Giora Shoham. London: Athgate Aldershot.

"Bounty Hunters: Legal Loose Cannons on Prowl." 1998. *Fulton County Daily Report*, January 13:17–20.

Bouza. A. V. 1991. "Police Officers' Attitudes toward Civilians Causes Police Brutality." Pages 77–79 in *Police Brutality*, edited by W. Dudley, San Diego, CA: Greenhaven.

Bowker, Lee. 1980. *Prison Victimization*. New York: Elsevier.

Bowker, Lee H. 1981. "Gender Differences in Prisoner Subcultures." Pages 409–419 in *Women and Crime in America*, edited by Lee H. Bowker. New York: Macmillan.

Bradley, C. 1995. "Reforming the Criminal Trial." Pages 418–424 in *Courts and the Justice System*, edited by G. L. Mays and P. R. Gregware. Prospect Heights, IL: Waveland Press.

Brady, J. 1983. "Arson, Urban Economy, and Organized Crime: The Case of Boston." *Social Problems*, 31(1):21.

Branham, Lynn S. 1998. *The Law of Sentencing, Corrections, and Prisoners' Rights in a Nutshell*, 5 ed. St. Paul, MN: West Group.

Brantingham, P. J., and P. L. Brantingham. 1981a. "Introduction: The Dimensions of Crime." Pages 7–26 in *Environmental Criminology*, edited by P. J. Brantingham and P. L. Brantingham. Beverly Hills, CA, Sage.

Brantingham, P. L., and Brantingham P. J. 1981b. "Notes on the Geometry of Crime." Pages 27–57 in *Environmental Criminology*, edited by P. J. Brantingham and P. L. Brantingham. Beverly Hills, CA: Sage.

Brantley, C. A., and A. DiRosa. 1994. "Gangs—A National Perspective." *FBI Law Enforcement Bulletin*, May:1–6.

Bravin, Jess. 2002. "Bush Says Taliban, Al Qaeda Fighters Aren't POWs under Geneva Conventions." *The Wall Street Journal*, February 8:A20.

Brazil: Annual Report 2000. 2000. Amnesty International. Available: http//www.web.amnesty.org/web/ar2000web.

"Brazil Grapples with Crime, Punishment, and Policing." 2000. *The Economist*, June 24:39–40.

"Brazil: Prison Uprisings Reflect Deep-Rooted Crisis." 2001. Available: http://amnesty.org.

Bremmer, B. 1996. "Terrorism: Myth and Realities." *Department of State Bulletin*, Vol. 88, May:61–64.

Brewster, T. 1991. "Law and Order." *Life*, 14(13):85–87.

Britton, Dana M. 1997. "Perceptions of the Work Environment among Correctional Officers: Do Race and Sex Matter?" *Criminology*, 35:505–524.

Broderick, V. L. 1993. "Pretrial Detention in the Criminal Justice Process." *Federal Probation*, 57(1):4–8.

Broers, M. 1999. "The Napoleon Police and Their Legacy." *History Today*, May 49(5):27–34.

Brooks, L. W. 1997. "Police Discretionary Behavior: A Study of Style." Pages 149–166 in *Critical Issues in Policing*, edited by R. C. Dunham and G. A. Alpert. Prospect Heights, IL: Waveland Press.

Brown, D. 1971. *Bury My Heart at Wounded Knee: An Indian History of the American West*. New York: Holt, Rinehart, and Winston.

Brown, D. K. 1997. "Jury Nullification within the Rule of Law." *Minnesota Law Review*, 81(5):1149–1200.

Brown, Julie Knipe. 1997. "FBI Dumping City's 96–97 Crime Stats." *The Philadelphia Daily News*, October 20:1.

Browne, A. 1995. "Fear and Perception of Alternatives: Asking 'Why Battered Women Don't Leave' Is the Wrong Question." Pages 228–245 in *The Criminal Justice System and Women: Offenders, Victims, and Workers*, edited by B. R. Price and N. J. Sokoloff. New York: McGraw-Hill.

Brownmiller, S. 1975. *Against Our Will: Men, Women and Rape*. New York: Simon & Schuster.

"Brutality in the Los Angeles Police Department." 1995. Independent Commission on the Los Angeles Police Department. Pages 17–29 in *Policing the Police*, edited by P. A. Winters. San Diego, CA: Greenhaven Press.

Bryan, W. J. 1971. *The Chosen Ones*. New York: Vantage Press.

Brydensholt, H. H. 1992. "Crime Policy in Denmark: How We Managed to Reduce the Prison Population." Pages 185–191 in *Prisons around the World: Studies in International Penology*, edited by Michael K. Carlie and Kevin I. Minor. Dubuque, IA: William C. Brown.

Bryjak, G. 1998. "The Specter of Biological Terrorism." *San Diego Union-Tribune*, January 13:B1.

"Building Blocks for Youth." 2001. *Press Release: News Coverage Skews Picture of Youth Crime*. Washington, DC: Building Blocks for Youth.

Bunch, William. 1999. "Survey: Crime Fear Is Linked to TV News." *The Philadelphia Daily News*, March 16:A1.

Bureau of Justice Statistics. 2001. "National Correctional Population Reaches New High." Washington, DC: Bureau of Justice Statistics, U.S. Department of Justice. Available: http://www.ojp.usdoj.gov/bjs/pub/pdf/ppus00.pdf.

Bureau of Justice Statistics. 2002. *Criminal Victimization in the United States, 2000: Statistical Tables*. Washington, DC: Bureau of Justice Statistics, U.S. Department of Justice. Available: http://www.ojp.usdoj.gov/bjs/pub/pdf/cvus9902.pdf.

Bureau, U.S. Census. 1991. "Current Population Survey." Washington, DC: U.S. Census Bureau.

Burnham, D. 1997. "The F.B.I.: A Special Report." *The Nation*, August 8–11:9–15.

Bursik, R. J., and H. G. Grasmick. 1993. *Neighborhoods and Crime: The Dimensions of Effective Community Control*. San Francisco: Jossey-Bass.

Buss, T. F., and R. Abdu. 1995. "Repeat Victims of Violence in an Urban Trauma Center." *Violence and Victims*, 10(3):183–194.

Butterfield, Fox. 1995. "California's Courts Clogging under Its 'Three Strikes' Law." *New York Times*, March 23:A1.

Butterfield, Fox. 1998. "As Crime Falls, Pressure Rises to Alter Data." *New York Times*, August 3:A1.

Butterfield, Fox. 2000a. "Cities Reduce Crime and Conflict without New York-Style Hardball." *New York Times*, March 4:A1.

Butterfield, Fox. 2000b. "Often, Parole Is But One Step on the Way Back to Prison." *New York Times*, November 29:A1.

Butterfield, Fox. 2000c. "Privately Run Juvenile Prison in Louisiana Is Attacked for Abuse of Six Inmates." *New York Times*, March 16:A14.

Butterfield, Fox. 2000d. "Racial Disparities Seen as Pervasive in Juvenile Justice." *New York Times*, April 26:A1.

Butterfield, Fox. 2001. "Inmate Rehabilitation Returns as Prison Goal." *New York Times*, May 20:A1.

Butterfield, Fox. 2003. "Alarms without Burglars Put Strain on Police Budgets." *New York Times*, January 17:A1.

Bygrave, L. 1997. "World Factbook of Criminal Justice." Available: http://www.ojp.usdoj.gov/bjs/pub/ascii/wfbcjnor.txt.

Bynum, Jack E., and William E. Thompson. 2002. *Juvenile Delinquency: A Sociological Approach*, 5 ed. Boston: Allyn & Bacon.

Byrne, James M., and Robert J. Sampson (eds.). 1986. *The Social Ecology of Crime*. New York: Springer-Verlag.

Cameron, M. O. 1964. *The Booster and the Snitch*. New York: Free Press.

Campbell, A. 1995. "Female Participation in Gangs." Pages 70–77 in *The Modern Gang Reader*, edited by M. W. Klein, C. L. Maxxon, and J. Miller. Los Angeles: Roxbury.

"Campbell Picks a Cleveland Police Veteran to Be Chief." 2002. Associated Press State and Local Wire Service. Available: http://web.lexis-nexis.com/universe/docu.

Campbell, V. 1980. "Double Marginality of Black Policemen." *Criminology*, February 17(4):470–484.

Cannon, A. 1999. "DWB: Driving While Black." *U.S. News & World Report*, March 15:72.

Cantlupe, J. 2003. "Rape Evidence Sits Unprocessed." *San Diego Union Tribune*, January 23:A1.

Cantor, Norman F. 1997. *Imagining the Law: Common Law and the Foundations of the American Legal System.* New York: HarperCollins.

Cao, Liqun, Anthony Adams, and Vickie J. Jensen. 1997. "A Test of the Black Subculture of Violence Thesis: A Research Note." *Criminology,* 35:367–379.

Capaldi, Deborah M., and Gerald R. Patterson. 1996. "Can Violent Offenders Be Distinguished from Frequent Offenders: Prediction from Childhood to Adolescence." *Journal of Research in Crime and Delinquency,* 33:206–231.

Carney, J., M. Calabresi, and J. F. Dickerson. 2002. "How Far Do We Want Them to Go?" *Time,* June 10:24–28.

Carns, T. W., and J. A. Kruse. 1992. "Alaska's Ban on Plea Bargaining Reevaluated." *Judicature,* 75(6):310–317.

Carp, R. A., and R. Stidham. 1996. *Judicial Process in America.* Washington, DC: CQ Press, A Division of Congressional Quarterly Inc.

Carter, D. L., and D. W. Stephens. 1994. "An Overview of Issues Concerning Police Officer Drug Use. '' Pages 101–122 in *Police Deviance,* edited by T. Barker and D. L. Carter. Cincinnati: Anderson.

Caspi, Avshalom. 2000. "The Child Is Father of the Man: Personalities Continuities from Childhood to Adulthood." *Journal of Personality and Social Psychology,* 78:158–172.

Caspi, Avshalom, Bradley R. Entner Wright, Terrie E. Moffitt, and Phil A. Silva. 1998. "Early Failure in the Labor Market: Childhood and Adolescent Predictors of Unemployment in the Transition to Adulthood." *American Sociological Review,* 63:424–451.

Cassell, P. G., and B. S. Hayman. 1996. "Police Interrogations in the 1990s: An Empirical Study of the Effects of Miranda." *UCLA Law Review,* 43(February):839–898.

Cecil, J. S., and D. Stienstra. 1987. *Deciding Cases without Appeals: An Examination of Four Courts of Appeals.* Washington, DC: Federal Judicial Center.

Celona, L. 1999. "NYPD Gathers Its Troops for All-Out War on Gangs." *The New York Post,* May 29:A4.

Census, U.S. Bureau of the. 1999. *Statistical Abstract of the United States: 1999.* Washington, DC: U.S. Government Printing Office.

Census, U.S. Bureau of the. 2000. *Statistical Abstract of the United States: 2000.* Washington, DC: U.S. Government Printing Office.

Cernkovich, Stephen A., and Peggy C. Giordano. 1992. "School Bonding, Race, and Delinquency." *Criminology,* 30(2):261–291.

Cernkovich, Stephen A., Peggy C. Giordano, and Meredith D. Pugh. 1985. "Chronic Offenders: The Missing Cases in Self-Report Delinquency Research." *Journal of Criminal Law and Criminology,* 76(Fall):705–732.

Chacon, D. J. 2002. "Law Enforcement Blamed in 6 of 10 of Its Wrecks." *San Diego Union-Tribune,* January 27:A1.

Chacon, Richard. 1998. "Questions Raised on Campus Crime." *The Boston Globe,* February 8:A1.

Chaddock, G. R. 2001. "Why Congress Is Quiet on Liberties." *Christian Science Monitor,* November 16:2.

Chalk, F., and K. Jonassohn. 1993. "Genocide: An Historical Review." Pages 72–76 in *Violence and Terrorism,* edited by B. Schechterman and M. Slann. Guilford, CT: Dushkin.

Chambliss, William J. 1967. "Types of Deviance and the Effectiveness of Legal Sanctions." *Wisconsin Law Review,* Summer:703–719.

Chambliss, William J. 1973. "The Saints and the Roughnecks." *Society,* 11:24–31.

Chambliss, William J. 1999. *Power, Politics, and Crime.* Boulder, CO: Westview Press.

Champion, Dean J. 1989. "Teenage Felons and Waiver Hearings: Some Recent Trends, 1980–1988." *Crime and Delinquency,* 35:577–585.

Chapin, B. 1983. *Criminal Justice in Colonial America, 1606–1660.* Athens: University of Georgia Press.

Charles, D. 1999. "Franklin D. Roosevelt, J. Edgar Hoover, and FBI Political Surveillance." *USA Today Magazine,* 128(2652):74–76.

Chemerinsky, E. 2000. "Report on Rampart Scandal Has a Hollow, Disturbing Ring." *The Los Angeles Times,* March 3:B7.

Chesney-Lind, Meda. 1995. "Girls, Delinquency, and Juvenile Justice: Toward a Feminist Theory of Young Women's Crime." Pages 71–88 in *The Criminal Justice System and Women: Offenders, Victims, and Workers,* edited by Barbara Raffel Price and Natalie J. Sokoloff. New York: McGraw-Hill.

Chesney-Lind, Meda. 1997. *The Female Offender: Girls, Women, and Crime.* Thousand Oaks, CA: Sage.

Chevigny, Bell Gale. 2000. "Prison Activists Come of Age." *The Nation,* July 24/31:27–29.

Chevigny, P. 1995. *Edge of the Knife: Police Violence in the Americas.* New York: New Press.

"Child Abuse and Neglect Still a Widespread Problem in America Today." 1997. *Nation's Health,* May/June:9–10.

Chilton, Roland, Victoria Major, and Sharon Propheter. 1998, November. *Victims and Offenders: A New UCR Supplement to Present Incident-Based Data from Participating Agencies.* Paper presented at the annual meeting of American Society of Criminology, Washington, DC.

Chimel v. California. 2001. Available: http://www.jus.state.nc.us/NCJA/legaug94.htm.

"China." 2001. *Annual Report.* Amnesty International. Available: http://www.amnesty.org/ar2001.

"China." 2002. *Annual Report.* Amnesty International. Available: http://www.amnesty.org/ar2002.

"China: Falun Gong Deaths in Custody Continue to Rise as Crackdown Worsens." 2000. Amnesty International Library. Available: http://web.amnesty.org/ai.nsf/index/ASA.

Chiricos, Theodore G., and Gordon P. Waldo. 1975. "Socioeconomic Status and Criminal Sentencing: An Empirical Assessment of a Conflict Proposition." *American Sociological Review,* 40:753–772.

Christian, Carol. 2002a. "Doctor: Yates' Illness Severe." *Houston Chronicle,* February 27:A1.

Christian, Carol. 2002b. "Jury Gives Yates Life Term with No Parole for 40 Years." *The Houston Chronicle,* March 16:A1.

Christianson, Scott. 1999. *Condemned: Inside the Sing Sing Death House.* New York: New York University Press.

Christie, Nils. 2000. *Crime Control as Industry: Towards GULAGS, Western Style,* 3 ed. New York: Routledge.

Christopher, W. 1994. "Report of the Independent Commission of the Los Angeles Police Department." Pages 291–304 in *Police Deviance,* edited by T. Barker and D. L. Carter. Cincinnati, OH: Anderson.

"City of Downey." 2001. Available: http://downeypd.org/recpolic.htm.

City of Los Angeles—Personnel Department. 2001. Available: http://www.lacity.org/PER/lafd.htm.

Clarke, Ronald V., and Marcus Felson (eds.). 1993. *Routine Activity and Rational Choice.* New Brunswick, NJ: Transaction Books.

Clayton, M. 1996. "Prostitution Circuit Takes Girls across North America." *Christian Science Monitor,* August 23:10.

Clear, Todd, and Karen Terry. 2000. "Correction beyond Prison Walls." Pages 517–537 in *Criminology: A Contemporary Handbook,* edited by Joseph F. Sheley. Belmont, CA: Wadsworth.

Cleary, J. 1986. *Prosecuting the Shoplifter—A Loss Prevention Strategy.* Boston: Butterworths Press.

Clemmer, Donald. 1940. *The Prison Community.* Boston: Christopher.

Clinard, M. B., and R. F. Meier. 1992. *Sociology of Deviant Behavior.* Fort Worth, TX: Harcourt Brace Jovanovich.

Clines, F. X. 2002. "Judge's Domestic Violence Ruling Creates an Outcry in Kentucky." *New York Times*, January 8:A14.

"Clinton Signs Lower Drunk Driving Limit." 2000. *Pittsburgh Post-Gazette*, October 24:A1.

Cloward, Richard A., and Lloyd E. Ohlin. 1960. *Delinquency and Opportunity: A Theory of Delinquent Gangs*. New York: Free Press.

Clynch, E. J., and D. W. Neubauer. 1981. "Trial Courts as Organizations." *Law and Public Policy*, 3(1):69–94.

Coalition for Federal Sentencing Reform. 2001. *Executive Summary on Elderly Prisoners*. Available: http://www.sentencing. org/exec.pdf. Alexandria, VA: Coalition for Federal Sentencing Reform.

Cochran, John K., and Mitchell B. Chamlin. 2000. "Deterrence and Brutalization: The Dual Effects of Executions." *Justice Quarterly*, 17:685–706.

Cochran, John K., Mitchell B. Chamlin, Peter B. Wood, and Christine S. Sellers. 1999. "Shame, Embarrassment, and Formal Sanction Threats: Extending the Deterrence/ Rational Choice Model to Academic Dishonesty." *Sociological Inquiry*, 69:91–105.

Cohen, A. 2000. "Gangsta Cops." *Time*, March 6:30–34.

Cohen, Lawrence, and Marcus Felson. 1979. "Social Change and Crime Rate Trends: A Routine Activity Approach." *American Sociological Review*, 44:588–607.

Cohen, M. A., and T. R. Miller. 1998. "The Cost of Mental Health Care for the Victims of Crime." *Journal of Interpersonal Violence*, 13(1):93–110.

Cohen, R. 1997. "A Crusade That Spreads Corruption." *The National Post National Weekly Edition*, March 10:29.

Cohen, Richard. 2002. "Why Kill Andrea Yates?" *The Washington Post*, February 21:A21.

Cohen, W. 1998. "The Feds Make a Cop Drug Bust." *U.S. News & World Report*, February 2:36.

Cole, D. 1999. *No Equal Justice*. New York: New Press.

Cole, G. W. 1992. *The American System of Criminal Justice*. Pacific Grove, CA: Brooks/Cole.

Coleman, J. W. 1995. "Respectable Crime." Pages 249–269 in *Criminology*, edited by J. F. Sheley. Belmont, CA: Wadsworth.

Coleman, R. 1999. "Doing Their Civic Duty: Thieves Taking a Liking to Late-Model Hondas." *Dallas Morning News*, March 22:1A.

Coleman, S. 1997. "Crime in Russia: Implications for the Development of Training Programs for Russian Entrepreneurs." *Journal of Business Management*, 35(1):78–82.

Collins, A. 1999. "No Joy in Louima Verdict, the Blue Wall Still Stands." *The Record* (Bergen County, NJ), July 10:L9.

Colloff, P. 1997. "Outlaw Blues." *Texas Monthly*, 25(11):82–86.

Colman, Adrian. 2000. "Crime and Justice." *Youth Studies Australia*, 19(3):4–5.

Colvin, Mark. 1992. *The Penitentiary in Crisis: From Accommodation to Riot in New Mexico*. Albany: State University of New York Press.

"Coming to a Hood Near You!" 2001. Available: http:// members.aol.com/_ht_a/NYPD CAGE/yearbook.

Connors, Edward, Thomas Lundregan, Neil Miller, and Tom McEwen. 1996. *Convicted by Juries, Exonerated by Science: Case Studies in the Use of DNA to Establish Innocence after the Trial*. Washington, DC: U.S. Department of Justice.

"Contracting for Indigent Defense Services." 2000. Washington, DC: U.S. Department of Justice, Office of Justice Programs. U.S. Government Printing Office.

Cook, J. 1991. "But Where Are the Don's Yachts?" *Forbes*, October 21:121–126.

Cooper, Cynthia. 2002. "A Cancer Grows: Medical Treatment in Women's Prisons Ranges from Brutal to Nonexistent." *The Nation*, May 6:30–34.

Cooper M. 1997. "Police Picket Traffic, as Pact Protests Go On." *New York Times*, January 29:B3.

Cooper, M. 1999. "Citing Recruitment Lag, Police Union Leader Says Pay Is Too Low." *New York Times*, August 12:6.

Cooper, R. T., and R. Simon. 2001. "Doubts Linger on Airport Safety." *Los Angeles Times*, November 17:A1.

"Cop Out: The Thinning Blue Line." 1999. *Newsweek*, May 3:8.

Cordner, G. W. 1997. "Community Policing—Elements and Effects." Pages 452–467 in *Critical Issues in Policing— Contemporary Readings*, edited by R. G. Dunhan and G. P. Alpert. Prospect Heights, IL: Waveland Press.

"Corruption in the New York City Police Department." 1995. Pages 28–44 in *Policing the Police*, edited by W. Dudley. San Diego: Greenhaven Press.

Cose, E. 2001. "The Lessons of Birmingham." *Newsweek*, May 14:27.

Costanzo, Mark. 1997. *Just Revenge: Costs and Consequences of the Death Penalty*. New York: St. Martin's Press.

"Cost of Crime." 1999. *Victims' Voices: Silent No More*. Washington, DC: U.S. Department of Justice. Available: http://www.ojp.usdoj.gov/ovc/ncvrw/1999/cost.htm.

"Cost of Fighting Terrorism Since Last Fall Closes in on $37 Billion." 2002. *San Diego Union-Tribune*, September 6:A13.

Cox, V. 1986. "Prison Gangs: Inmates Battle for Control." *Corrections Compendium*, 10:6–9.

Creamer, J. S. 1980. *The Law of Arrest, Search and Seizure*. New York: Holt, Rinehart & Winston.

Cressey, D. 1969. *Theft of a Nation*. New York: Harper & Row.

Crime & Justice International. 2001. "Rural Crime on the Rise." *Crime & Justice International*, April:11–12.

Crime—A Serious American Problem. 1998. Wylie, TX: Information Plus.

Criminal Case Processing, 1998. 1999. Washington, DC: Bureau of Justice Statistics, Office of the Justice Program, U.S. Government Printing Office.

Cromwell, Paul F., James N. Olson, and D'Unn Avary. 1991. *Breaking and Entering: An Ethnographic Analysis of Burglary*. Newbury Park, CA: Sage.

Cronin, D. 2000. "Agassi Rallies, Wins Opener in Lyon." *USA Today*, November 8:19C.

Crouch, Ben M., and James W. Marquart. 1990. "Resolving the Paradox of Reform Litigation, Prisoner Violence, and Perceptions of Risk." *Justice Quarterly*, 7:103–122.

Csere, C. 1998. "The More You Drink, The Worse You Drive." *Car and Driver*, 44(3):116.

Cullen, Francis T., Bonnie S. Fisher, and Brandon K. Applegate. 2000. "Public Opinion about Punishment and Corrections." *Crime and Justice: A Review of Research*, 27:1–79.

Cullen, Francis T., and Jody L. Sundt. 2000. "Imprisonment in the United States." Pages 473–515 in *Criminology: A Contemporary Handbook*, edited by Joseph F. Sheley. Belmont, CA: Wadsworth.

Cunningham, A. 1998. Overview of the Criminal Justice System of Canada. Available: http:www.cjprimer.com/ canada.htm.

Currie, Elliott. 1998. *Crime and Punishment in America*. New York: Henry Holt.

Curtis, L. A. 1974. "Victim Precipitation and Violent Crime." *Social Problems*, 21:594–605.

Cusac, Anne-Marie. 2000. "'The Judge Gave Me Ten Years. He Didn't Sentence Me to Death.'" *The Progressive*, July:22–26.

Dabbs, James, and Robin Morris. 1990. "Testosterone and Antisocial Behavior in a Sample of 4,462 Men." *Psychological Science*, 1:209–211.

Dabney, Dean A., and Michael S. Vaughn. 2000. "Incompetent Jail and Prison Doctors." *The Prison Journal*, 80:184–209.

D'Alessio, Stewart J., and Lisa Stolzenberg. 1993. "Socioeconomic Status and the Sentencing of the Traditional Offender." *Journal of Criminal Justice*, 21:61–77.

D'Alessio, Stewart J., and Lisa Stolzenberg. 1995. "The Impact of Sentencing Guidelines on Jail Incarceration in Minnesota." *Criminology*, 33:283–302.

Daley, R. 1978. *Prince of the City: The True Story of a Cop Who Knew Too Much.* Boston: Houghton Mifflin.

Dalton, Katharina. 1961. "Menstruation and Crime." *British Medical Journal*, 2:1752–1753.

Daly, Kathleen. 1994. *Gender, Crime, and Punishment.* New Haven: Yale University Press.

Daly, Kathleen, and Rebecca L. Bordt. 1995. "Sex Effects and Sentencing: An Analysis of the Statistical Literature." *Justice Quarterly*, 12:141–175.

Daly, Kathleen, and Lisa Maher (eds.). 1998. *Criminology at the Crossroads: Feminist Readings in Crime and Justice.* New York: Oxford University Press.

Damrosch, Lori. 2001. *International Law: Cases and Materials*, 4 ed. St. Paul, MN: West Group.

Darley, J. M., and B. Latane. 1968. "Bystander Intervention in Emergencies: Diffusion of Responsibility." *Journal of Personality and Social Psychology*, 8:377–383.

Daudistel, H. C., W. B. Sanders, and D. F. Luckenbill. 1979. *Criminal Justice—Situations and Decisions.* New York: Holt, Rinehart & Winston.

Davis, R. C., and E. Erez. 1998. *Immigrant Populations as Victims: Toward a Multicultural Criminal Justice System.* Washington, DC: U.S. Department of Justice, Office of Justice Programs.

Davis, Robert C., and Barbara E. Smith. 1994. "The Effects of Victim Impact Statements on Sentencing Decisions: A Test in an Urban Setting." *Justice Quarterly*, 11:453–469.

"The Death Penalty in China: Breaking Records, Breaking Rules." 1997. Available: http://www.amnesty/org/ailib/aipub/1997/SUM/31703897.htm.

"Death Row Lawyers Not Cream of Crop." 2000. *San Diego Union-Tribune*, September 11:A6.

de Borchgrave, A. 1997. "Ignoring Russia's Crisis of Crime." *The Washington Times*, July 25:A19.

Decker, S. H., and R. T. Wright. 1997. *Armed Robbers in Action: Stickups and Street Culture.* Boston: Northeastern University Press.

Dees, M. 1996. *Gathering Storm: America's Militia Threat.* New York: Harper Collins.

DeFrances, C. J., and S. K. Smith. 1998. *Perception of Neighborhood Crime, 1995.* Washington, DC: U.S. Department of Justice, Office of Justice Programs.

DeFrances, C. J., and G. W. Steadman. 1998. *Prosecutors in State Courts, 1996.* Washington, DC: U.S. Department of Justice, Office of Justice Programs, U.S. Government Printing Office.

Delattre, E. J. 1994. *Character and Cops—Ethics in Policing.* Washington, DC: AEI Press, Publisher for the American Enterprise Institute.

Denniston, Lyle. 2001. "Police Gain in Powers of Arrest." *The Boston Globe*, April 25:A1.

DePanfilis, D., and S. J. Zuravin. 1998. "Rates, Patterns, and Frequencies of Child Maltreatment Recurrences among Families Known to CPS." *Child Maltreatment*, February:27–43.

DeRienzo, P. 1999. "Mollen Commission Says Cops Can't Police Themselves." Available: http:/:www.mediafilter.org/MFF/Mollen.htm.

Dickey, Walter J., and Pam Stiebs. 1998. *"Three Strikes": Five Years Later.* Washington, DC: Campaign for an Effective Crime Policy.

Dill, F. 1975. "Discretion, Exchange and Social Control: Bail Bondsmen in Criminal Courts." *Law & Society Review*, 9:639–674.

Doerner, W. G., and S. P. Lab. 1995. *Victimology.* Cincinnati: Anderson.

Dolan, M. 1994a. "Why Jurors Err: They're Human." *Los Angeles Times*, September 25:A1.

Dolan, M. 1994b. "Role of Jury Consultants Controversial and Extensive." *Los Angeles Times*, September 26:A1.

Dolbee, S. 1999. "The Lying Game—Coaxing Confessions with Lies May Be Legal, But Is It Ethical?" *San Diego Union-Tribune*, May 21:E1.

Domash, S. F. 2000. "War against Gangs Ratchets Up." *New York Times*, Long Island edition, December 31:3.

Dombrink, J. 1994. "The Touchables: Vice and Police Corruption." Pages 61–100 in *Police Deviance*, edited by T. Barker and D. L. Carter. Cincinnati: Anderson.

Donnan, Shawn. 2000. "Mandatory Sentencing Gets Closer Look in Australia." *Christian Science Monitor*, April 10:8.

Doob, A. N. 1999. "Youth Justice Research in Canada: An Assessment," *Canadian Journal of Criminology*, 41(2):217–224.

Dorbin, A., B. Wiersema, C. Loftin, and D. McDowall. 1996. *Statistical Handbook on Violence in America.* Phoenix: The Oryx Press.

Dorfman, Lori, and Vincent Schiraldi. 2001. *Off Balance: Youth, Race and Crime in the News.* Washington, DC: Building Blocks for Youth.

Dorsey, Tina L., and Marianne W. Zawitz. 1999. *Drugs and Crime Facts.* Washington, DC: Bureau of Justice Statistics, U.S. Department of Justice.

Dostoyevsky, Fyodor. 1957. *The House of the Dead.* New York: Grove Press.

Douglas, J. 2000. *The Cases That Haunt Us.* New York: Simon & Schuster.

Douthit, N. 1992. "August Vollmer, Berkeley's First Chief of Police, and Emergence of Police Professionalism." Pages 92–119 in *Policing and Crime Control, Part 2*, edited by E. H. Monkkonen. Westport, CT: Meckler.

Downes, David. 1996. "The Case for Going Dutch: The Lessons of Post-War Penal Policy." Pages 243–253 in *Criminology: A Cross-Cultural Perspective*, edited by Robert Heiner. St. Paul, MN: West Group.

Dreyfuss, R. 2002. "The Cops Are Watching You." *The Nation*, 274(21):12–15.

Drimmer, J. 1997. "Frontier Justice; Open Bounty Hunting Is Out of Date." *Texas Lawyer*, September 27:37–39.

Drummond, Tammerlin. 1999. "Cellblock Seniors." *Time*, June 21:60.

"Drunk Driving." 1999. Available: http://www.ojp.usdoj.gov/ovc/ncvrw/1999/drunk.htm.

Dudley, W. 1991. *Police Brutality.* San Diego, CA: Greenhaven Press.

Duffy, Michael, and Michael Warby. 2000. "The Stolen Generations." *IPA Review*, 52(2):6–9.

Duggan, Paul. 2002. "New Rulings Don't Fling Open Death Row Doors." *The Washington Post*, June 27:A02.

Dulaney, W. M. 1996. *Black Police in America.* Bloomington: Indiana University Press.

Dumond, Robert W. 2000. "Inmate Sexual Assault: The Plague That Persists." *The Prison Journal*, 80:407–414.

Dunaway, R. Gregory, Francis T. Cullen, Velmer S. Burton, Jr., and T. David Evans. 2000. "The Myth of Social Class and Crime Revisited: An Examination of Class and Adult Criminality." *Criminology*, 38:589–632.

Durkheim, Émile. 1983. "Two Laws of Penal Evolution." Pages 102–132 in *Durkheim and the Law*, edited by Steven Lukes and Andrew Scull. New York: St. Martin's Press. (Original work published 1901.)

Durose, Matthew R., David J. Levin, and Patrick A. Langan. 2001. *Felony Sentences in State Courts.* Washington, DC: Bureau of Justice Statistics, U.S. Department of Justice.

Duster, Troy. 1995. "The New Crisis of Legitimacy in Controls, Prisons, and Legal Structures." *The American Sociologist*, 26:20–29.

Eck, J. E., and D. P. Rosenbaum. 1994. "The New Police Order—Effectiveness, Equity, and Efficiency in Community Policing."

Pages 3–23 in *The Challenge of Community Policing,* edited by D. P. Rosebaum. Thousand Oaks, CA: Sage.

"Economic Crime." 1999. Available: http://www.ojp.usdoj.gov/ovc/ncvrw/1999/econ.htm.

Eddings, J. 1995. "Atlanta's New Top Cop Makes Her Mark." *U.S. News & World Report,* December 26:82.

Edgerton, Robert. 1976. *Deviance: A Cross-Cultural Perspective.* Menlo Park, CA: Cummings.

Eggers, W. D., and J. O'Leary. 1995. "The Beat Generation." *Policy Review,* 74(Fall):4–10.

Eisenhower, Dwight David. 1960. "Farewell Speech." *New York Times,* November 15:A1.

Eisenstein, J., and H. Jacob. 1991. *Felony Justice—An Organizational Analysis of Criminal Courts.* Lanham, MD: University Press of America.

Elias, R. 1993. *Victims Still—The Political Manipulation of Crime Victims.* Newbury Park, CA: Sage.

Ellement, John. 2001. "Judge's Removal Sought in Rights Suit." *The Boston Globe,* March 15:B5.

Elwork, A., B. D. Sales, and J. Alfini. 1972. "Juridic Decisions in Ignorance of the Law or in Light of It?" *Law and Human Behavior,* 1:169–190.

Elwork, A., B. Sales, and J. Alfini. 1982. *Making Jury Instructions Understandable.* Charlottsville, VA: The Michie Company.

Emanuel, S. L., and S. Knowles. 1999–2000. *Criminal Procedure.* Larchmont, NY: Emanuel.

Emanuel, Steven L. 1988. *Criminal Law.* Larchmont, NY: Emanuel.

Emmleman, D. S. 1996. "Trial by Plea Bargain: Case Settlement as a Product of Recursive Decisionmaking." *Law & Society Review,* 30(2):335–361.

Emsley, C. 1999. "The Origins of the Modern Police." *History Today,* 49(4):8–14.

English, T. J. 1995. "Forget Jake, It's Chinatown." *Village Voice,* February 28:4.

Enos, Sandra. 2001. *Mothering from the Inside: Parenting in a Women's Prison.* Albany: State University of New York Press.

Entman, Robert M. 1994. "African Americans According to TV News." *Media Studies Journal,* 8:29–38.

Epstein, A. 1999. "Supreme Court Rules Out Chicago's Anti-Gang Law." *Pittsburgh Post Gazette,* June 11:A1.

Epstein, J. 1998. "No Vacancy in Brazil's Big House." *Christian Science Monitor,* January 5:7–8.

"Equality Denied—The Status of Women in Policing in 1998." 1999. Washington, DC: The National Center for Women and Policing, a division of the Feminist Majority Foundation.

"Equality Denied—The Status of Women in Policing: 2000." 2001. Washington, DC: The National Center for Women and Policing, a division of the Feminist Majority Foundation.

"Equality Denied—The Status of Women in Small and Rural Police Agencies: 2000." 2001. Washington, DC: National Center for Women and Policing, a division of the Feminist Majority.

Erez, Edna, and Pamela Tontodonato. 1990. "The Effect of Victim Participation in Sentencing on Sentence Outcome." *Criminology,* 28:451–474.

Erez, Edna, and Pamela Tontodonato. 1992. "Victim Participation in Sentencing and Satisfaction with Justice." *Justice Quarterly,* 9(2):393–417.

Eysenck, Hans J. 1989. "Personality and Criminality: A Dispositional Analysis." Pages 89–110 in *Advances in Criminological Theory,* edited by William S. Laufer, and Freda Adler. New Brunswick, NJ: Transaction.

Fagan, Jeffrey. 1995. "Separating the Men from the Boys: The Comparative Advantage of Juvenile versus Criminal Court Sanctions on Recidivism among Adolescent Felony Offenders." Pages 238–260 in *Serious, Violent, and Chronic Juvenile Offenders: A Sourcebook,* edited by James C. Howell, Barry

Krisberg, J. David Hawkins, and John J. Wilson. Thousand Oaks, CA: Sage Publications.

"Falun Gong Practitioners: List of Sentences, Administrative Sentences, and Those Detained." 2000. Available: http://www.amnesty.org/ailib/aipub/2000/SUM/31701200/htm.

Farkas, S., and A. Duffett. 1998. *Crime, Fears and Videotape: A Public Opinion Study of Baltimore-Area Residents.* Washington, DC: Public Agenda.

Farnworth, Margaret, Terence P. Thornberry, Marvin D. Krohn, and Alan J. Lizotte. 1994. "Measurement in the Study of Class and Delinquency: Integrating Theory and Research." *Journal of Research in Crime and Delinquency,* 31(1):33–61.

Farrington, Karen. 1996. *Dark Justice: A History of Punishment and Torture.* New York: Smithmark.

Fattah, E. A. 1993. "The Rational Choice/Opportunity Perspectives as a Vehicle for Integrating Criminological and Victimological Theories." Pages 225–258 in *Routine Activity and Rational Choice,* edited by R. V. Clarke and M. Felson. New Brunswick, NJ: Transaction Books.

Fattah, E. A. 1997. "Toward a Victim Policy Aimed at Healing, Not Suffering." Pages 257–272 in *Victims of Crime* by R. C. Davis, A. J. Lurigio, and W. B. Skogan. Thousand Oaks, CA: Sage.

Fazlollah, Mark. 1997. "Eleven More Cleared Due to Scandal." *The Philadelphia Inquirer,* March 25:A1.

Fazlollah, Mark, Michael Matza, Craig R. McCoy, and Clea Benson. 1999. "Women Victimized Twice in Police Game of Numbers." *The Philadelphia Inquirer,* October 17:A1.

Federal Bureau of Investigation. 2001a. *Crime in the United States: 2000.* Washington, DC: Federal Bureau of Investigation.

Federal Bureau of Investigation. 2001b. Available: http://www.britannica.com.

Federal Bureau of Investigation. 2002. *Crime in the United States: 2001.* Washington, DC: Federal Bureau of Investigation.

"Federal Criminal Case Processing, 1998." 1999. Washington, DC: Bureau of Justice Statistics, U.S. Department of Justice, Office of Justice Programs.

Feeney, Floyd. 1998. *German and American Prosecutions: An Approach to Statistical Comparison.* Washington, DC: Bureau of Justice Statistics, U.S. Department of Justice.

Feld, Barry C. 1998. "Juvenile and Criminal Justice Systems' Responses to Youth Violence." *Crime and Justice: A Review of Research,* 24:189–261.

Felson, M. 1998. *Crime and Everyday Life.* Thousand Oaks, CA: Pine Forge.

Felson, Marcus. 2002. *Crime and Everyday Life: Insights and Implications for Society,* 3 ed. Thousand Oaks, CA: Pine Forge Press.

Felson, R. B., and S. F. Messner. 1998. "Disentangling the Effects of Gender Intimacy on Victim Precipitation in Homicide." *Criminology,* 36(2):405–423.

Findlaw. 2000. *Gideon v. Wainright.* U.S. Supreme Court Cases. Available: http://caselaw.findlaw.com.

Finkelhor, D. 1997. "The Victimization of Children: Developmental Victimology." Pages 86–107 in *Victims of Crime,* edited by R. C. Davis, A. J. Lurigio, and W. G. Skogan. Thousand Oaks, CA: Sage.

Finkelhor, D., and N. L. Asdigian. 1996. "Risk Factors for Youth Victimization: Beyond a Theory of Lifestyles/Routine Activities Theory Approach." *Violence and Victims,* 11(1):3–19.

Finkelhor, D., and G. Hotaling. 1995. "Attempted Non-Family Abductions." *Child Welfare,* 74(5):941–955.

Firestone, David. 2001. "Crowded Jails Create Crisis for Prisons in Alabama." *New York Times,* May 1:A1.

Fishbein, Diana H. 1996. "The Biology of Antisocial Behavior." Pages 26–38 in *New Perspectives in Criminology,* edited by John E. Conklin. Boston: Allyn & Bacon.

Fishman, L. T. 1995. "The Vice Queens: An Ethnographic Study of Black Female Gang Behavior." Pages 83–92 in *The*

Modern Gang Reader, edited by M. W. Klein, C. L. Maxxon, and J. Miller. Los Angeles: Roxbury.

Fishman, Mark. 1978. "Crime Waves as Ideology." *Social Problems,* 25:531–543.

"Five Years Later." 2001. *The Daily Camera,* December 16:A1.

Fleming, Sue. 2001. "Abuse of Women Inmates Seen Rampant." *The Boston Globe,* March 7:A7.

Fletcher, M. 2001. "Milosevic Is Charged with Genocide." *The Times* (London), October 20:A1.

Fletcher, Michael A. 2000. "We Seem to Be Winning the War on Crime. But How?" *The Washington Post,* January 16:F1.

Flynn, K. 1999. "Applicants for Police Test Are Down Despite Big Drive." *New York Times,* August 28:2.

Flynn, K. 2000a. "No Day in the Park for Police Officers on Bike Paths." *New York Times,* May 29:B4.

Flynn, K. 2000b. "Police Feel Scorn on Beat and Pressure from Above." *New York Times,* December 26:A1.

Ford, C. 2000. "We Have to Use Reason, Not Rage, to Help Young Offenders." *The Calgary Herald,* March 23:A18.

Ford, Marilyn C. 1986. "The Role of Extralegal Factors in Jury Verdicts." *The Justice System Journal,* 11(1):16–39.

Ford, Richard. 2000. "Country Is Safer Than Towns, Says Crime Survey." *The Times* (London), October 17:1.

Ford, Richard, and Stewart Tendler. 2001. "Straw Blames Gangs for Rise in Violence." *The Times* (London), January 17:1.

Foss, Edward. 2000. "Couple Pull Out of West Norfolk House Deal: 'We're Afraid.' " *Eastern Daily Press,* May 3:1.

Foucault, Michel. 1977. *Discipline and Punish: The Birth of the Prison,* trans. Alan Sheridan. New York: Pantheon Books.

Fox, J. A., and Levin, J. 1994. *Overkill—Mass Murder and Serial Killing Exposed,* New York: Plenum Press.

Frankel, Marvin E. 1973. *Criminal Sentences: Law without Order.* New York: Hill and Wang.

Franzen, R. 2002. "'CSI' Effect on Potential Jurors Has Some Prosecutors Worried." *San Diego Union-Tribune,* December 16:D6.

Frase, Richard S. 1995. "State Sentencing Guidelines: Still Going Strong." *Judicature,* 78:173–179.

Freedman, Estelle B. 1981. *Their Sisters' Keepers: Women's Prison Reform in America, 1830–1930.* Ann Arbor: University of Michigan Press.

Fried, M., K. J. Kaplan, and K. W. Klein. 1975. "Jury Selection: An Analysis of Voir Dire." Pages 47–66 in *The Jury System in America,* edited by R. J. Simon. Beverly Hills, CA: Sage.

Friedman, L. M. 1985. *A History of American Law.* New York: Simon & Schuster.

Friedman, Lawrence M. 1993. *Crime and Punishment in American History.* New York: Basic Books.

Fritsch, Eric, Craig Hemmens, and Tory J. Caeti. 1996. "Violent Youth in Juvenile and Adult Court: An Assessment of Sentencing Strategies in Texas." *Law and Policy,* 18: 115–136.

Fritsch, Jane, and David Rohde. 2001. "Lawyers often Fail New York's Poor." *New York Times,* April 8:A1.

Fuetsch, M. 1995. "Challenge No Novelty for Commander Bounds." *The Cleveland Plain Dealer,* February 13:1B.

"The Fully Informed Jury and Jury Nullification." 2000. Available: http://www.freeandrea.org/jurynull.htm.

Fyfe, J. J. 1997. "The Split Second Syndrome and Other Determinants of Police Violence." Pages 531–547 in *Critical Issues in Policing,* edited by R. G. Dunham and G. P. Alpert. Prospect Heights, IL: Waveland Press.

Fyfe, James J. 1983. "The NIJ Study of the Exclusionary Rule." *Criminal Law Bulletin,* 19:253–260.

Gaes, Gerald G., Timothy J. Flanagan, Laurence L. Motiuk, and Lynn Stewart. 1999. "Adult Correctional Treatment." *Crime and Justice: A Review of Research,* 26:361–426.

Gainsborough, Jenni, and Marc Mauer. 2000. *Diminishing Returns: Crime and Incarceration in the 1990s.* Washington, DC: The Sentencing Project.

Galloway, Joseph L., and Bruce Selcraig. 1999. "Into the Heart of Darkness." *U.S. News & World Report,* March 8:18–20.

"Gang Case Ruling Stings Chicago; Supreme Court Overturns Tough Anti-Loitering Law." 1999. *The Patriot Ledger,* June 11:20.

Gang Manual. 1999. Washington, DC: National Law Enforcement Institute, Inc.

Garofalo, M. 1987. "Reassessing the Lifestyle Modes of Criminal Victimization." Pages 23–42 in *Positive Criminology,* edited by M. R. Gottfredson and T. Hirshi. Beverly Hills, CA: Sage.

Geerken, Michael, and Hennessey D. Hayes. 1993. "Probation and Parole: Public Risk and the Future of Incarceration Alternatives." *Criminology,* 31(4):549–564.

Geis, G. 1990. "Crime Victims—Practices and Prospects." Pages 251–267 in *Victims of Crime—Problems, Policies, and Programs,* edited by A. J. Lurigio, W. G. Skogan, and R. C. Davis. Newbury Park, CA: Sage.

Geller, W. A., and H. Toch. 1996. "Understanding and Controlling Police Abuse of Force." Pages 292–328 in *Police Violence,* edited by W. A. Geller and H. Toch. New Haven: Yale University Press.

Gelsthorpe, Loraine, and Peter Raynor. 1995. "Quality and Effectiveness in Probation Officers' Reports to Sentencers." *British Journal of Criminology,* 35:188–200.

Gendreau, Paul, Tracy Little, and Claire Goggin. 1996. "A Meta-Analysis of the Predictors of Adult Offender Recidivism: What Works?" *Criminology,* 34:575–607.

Gerber, Jurg, and Simone Engelhardt-Greer. 1996. "Just and Painful: Attitudes toward Sentencing Criminals." Pages 62–74 in *Americans View Crime and Justice: A National Public Opinion Survey,* edited by Timothy J. Flanagan and Dennis R. Longmire. Thousand Oaks, CA: Sage.

Gerda, R. W. 1995. "From Cossack to Trooper: Manliness, Police Reform, and the State." *Journal of Social History,* 28(3):565–586.

Gergen, K. J., and M. J. Gergen. 1986. *Social Psychology.* New York: Springer-Verlag.

Gerstenzang, J. 1996. "Poll: Safety Key Concern." *The Las Vegas Review Journal,* August 8:A1.

Gerstenzang, J. 2001. "Bush Defends Trying Terror Suspects in Secret Military Tribunals." *Los Angeles Times,* November 20:A3.

Gesalman, Anne Belli. 2002. "A Dark State of Mind." *Newsweek,* March 4:32.

Getlin, J. 2002. "N.Y. Cops Freed in Brutality Case." *Los Angeles Times,* March 1:A16.

Giacopassi, D. J., and J. R. Sparger. 1992. "The Effects of Emergency Medical Care on the Homicide Rate: Some Additional Evidence." *Journal of Criminal Justice,* 20:249–259.

Giallombardo, Rose. 1966. *Society of Women: A Study of a Women's Prison.* New York: Wiley.

Gibeaut, J. 1998. "Gang Busters." *American Bar Association Journal,* 84(1):64–68.

Gibeaut, J. 1999. " 'Yes, I'm Sure That's Him.' " *ABA Journal,* 85:26–27.

Gibeaut, John. 2001. "The Grass May Still Be Greener." *ABA Journal,* 87(10):90.

Gideon v. Wainright, 1963. 2000. Civnet. Available: http://org/resources/.

Gifford, Lea S. 1999. *Justice Expenditure and Employment in the United States, 1995.* Washington, DC: Bureau of Justice Statistics, U.S. Department of Justice.

Gifford, Sidra Lea. 2002. *Justice Expenditure and Employment in the United States, 1999.* Washington, DC: Bureau of Justice Statistics, U.S. Department of Justice.

Gifis, S. H. 1980. *Law Dictionary.* Woodbury, NY: Barron's Educational Series, Inc.

Gifis, S. H. 1996. *Law Dictionary.* Woodbury, NY: Barron's Educational Series.

Gilbert, Martin. 1987. *The Holocaust: A History of the Jews of Europe during the Second World War.* New York: Henry Holt.

Gilliam, F. D., and S. Iyengar. 2000. "Prime Suspects: The Influence of Local Television News on the Viewing Public." *American Journal of Political Science,* 44:560–573.

Girshick, Lori B. 1999. *No Safe Haven: Stories of Women in Prison.* Boston: Northeastern University Press.

Glassner, Barry. 1999. *The Culture of Fear: Why Americans Are Afraid of the Wrong Things.* New York: Basic Books.

Glaze, Lauren E. 2002. *Probation and Parole in the United States, 2001.* Washington, DC: Bureau of Justice Statistics, U.S. Department of Justice.

Gleick, E., and S. E. Epperson. 1999. "The Crooked Blue Line." *Time,* September 11:38–42.

Glick, H., and K. Vines. 1973. *State Court Systems.* Englewood Cliffs, NJ: Prentice-Hall.

Glover, Scott, and Matt Lait. 2000a. "Police in Secret Group Broke Law Routinely, Transcripts Say." *Los Angeles Times,* February 10:A1.

Glover, Scott, and Matt Lait. 2000b. "A Tearful Perez Gets 5 Years." *Los Angeles Times,* February 26:A1.

Glover, Scott, and Matt Lait. 2000d. "4 Officers Back Tales of Parties after Shooting." *Los Angeles Times,* February 12:A1.

Glover, T. L. 1992. "Careers in Law Enforcement." *Black Collegian,* January/February 22(3):102–105.

Gobert, J. J., and W. E. Jordan. 1990. *Jury Selection—The Law, Art, and Science of Selecting a Jury.* New York: Sheppard's/McGraw-Hill.

Goffman, Erving. 1961. *Asylums: Essays on the Social Situation of Mental Patients and Other Inmates.* Garden City, NY: Anchor Books.

Goldberg, S. H. 1997 *The First Trial—Where Do I Sit? Where Do I Stand?* St. Paul, MN: West Group.

Golden, A. 1997a. "Honest Cops Group Fight Rogues." *San Diego Union-Tribune,* February 10:A14.

Golden, A. 1997b. "General Targets Crooked Cops." *San Diego Union-Tribune,* February 10:A1.

Goldstein, J. 1960. "Police Discretion Not to Invoke the Criminal Process: Low Visibility Decisions in the Administration of Justice." *Yale Law Review,* 69(4):543–588.

Gollner, P. M. 1994. "Consulting by Peering into the Minds of Jurors." *New York Times,* January 7:A23.

Goode, E. 1991. *Deviant Behavior.* Englewood Cliffs, NJ: Prentice-Hall.

Goodman, Ellen. 1994. "The Double Punishment in American Prisons." *The Boston Globe,* June 12:79.

Goodstein, Lynne, and Kevin N. Wright. 1989. "Inmate Adjustment to Prison." Pages 229–251 in *The American Prisons: Issues in Research and Policy,* edited by Lynne Goodstein and Doris L. MacKenzie. New York: Plenum.

Gorman, T. 1999. "Riverside to Fire Four Officers Who Killed Woman." *Los Angeles Times,* June 12:A1.

Gottfredson, M. 1981. "On the Etiology of Criminal Victimization." *Journal of Criminal Law and Criminology,* 72(2):714–734.

Gottfredson, M. 1984. *Victims of Risk: The Dimensions of Crime.* London: Home Office Research and Planning Unit No. 87, Her Majesty's Stationery Office.

Gottfredson, Michael, and Travis Hirschi. 1990. *A General Theory of Crime.* Stanford: Stanford University Press.

Gottschall, J. 1983. "Judicial Appointments: The Influence of Affirmative Action and Merit Selection on Voting on the U.S. Courts of Appeals." *Judicature,* 67:165–173.

Gould, J. 2000. "Twelve Good Men and True." *Managing Intellectual Property,* September:102–113.

Gove, Walter R., Michael Hughes, and Michael Geerken. 1985. "Are Uniform Crime Reports a Valid Indicator of the Index Crimes? An Affirmative Answer with Minor Qualifications." *Criminology,* 23:451–501.

Green, G. 1990. *Occupational Crime.* Chicago: Nelson-Hall.

Greenberg, David F. 1977. "Delinquency and the Age Structure of Society." *Contemporary Crises,* 1:66–86.

Greenberg, David F. 1993. "Introduction." Pages 1–35 in *Crime and Capitalism: Readings in Marxist Criminology,* edited by David F. Greenberg. Philadelphia: Temple University Press.

Greenfeld, Lawrence A., and Tracy L. Snell. 1999. *Women Offenders.* Washington, DC: Bureau of Justice Statistics, U.S. Department of Justice.

Greenfield, L. A., and S. K. Smith. 1999. *American Indians and Crime.* Washington, DC: U.S. Department of Justice, Office of Justice Statistics.

Greenfield, N. 2000. "Respect Hinges on Oath to Queen." *The Times Educational Supplement,* May 19:14.

Greengard, S. 1996. "Under Fire at the LAPD." *Personnel Journal,* April 75(4):98–103.

Greenhouse, L. 1998. "Supreme Court Eases Liability on Police in Chases." *San Diego Union-Tribune,* May 27:A1.

Greenhouse, Linda. 2001. "Divided Justices Back Full Arrests on Minor Charges." *New York Times,* April 25:A1.

Greenhouse, Linda. 2002. "Top Court Hears Argument on Execution of Retarded." *New York Times,* February 21:A1.

Greenwood, L. 2002. "Right to Counsel Expanded by a Divided Court." *New York Times,* May 22:A1.

Greenwood, Peter W. 1998. "Investing in Prisons or Prevention: The State Policy Makers' Dilemma." *Crime and Delinquency,* 44:136–142.

Greenwood, Peter W., and Susan Turner. 1987. *Selective Incapacitation Revisited: Why the High-Rate Offenders Are Hard to Predict.* Santa Monica, CA: Rand Corporation.

Greer, Kimberly R. 2000. "The Changing Nature of Interpersonal Relationships in a Women's Prison." *The Prison Journal,* 80:442–468.

Gregor, A. J. 1988. "Counterrevolutionaries." Pages 12–37 in *Human Rights in the People's Republic of China,* edited by Y. Wu, F. Michae, J. F. Cooper, T. Lee, M. S. Chang, and A. J. Gregor. Boulder, CO: Westview Press.

Gregory, D. 1996. "Beverly Harvard." *Essence,* March:56.

Griffin, Susan. 1971. "Rape: The All-American Crime." *Ramparts,* September:26–35.

Griswold, Eliza. 2001. "Faith of Her Fathers." *The New Republic,* February 26:13–15.

"Group Finds Health Care in Prisons Inconsistent." 2000. *New York Times,* February 5:B4.

Gullo, K. 2001. "Ashcroft Tells FBI It's a Credit to U.S., but Pep Talk Cites Its Recent Bungles." *San Diego Union-Tribune,* July 17:A4.

Gurr, T. R. 1989. "Political Terrorism: Historical Antecedents and Contemporary Trends." Pages 21–54 in *Violence in America: Protest, Rebellion, and Reform,* Vol. 2, edited by T. R. Gurr. Newbury Park, CA: Sage.

Haddad, Charles H. 2000. " 'Private Prisons Don't Work.'" *Business Week,* September 11:95–97.

Hagan, F. E. 1991. *Introduction to Criminology.* Chicago: Nelson-Hall.

Hagan, F. E. 1998. *Introduction to Criminology,* 4 ed. Chicago: Nelson-Hall.

Hagan, John. 1992. "The Poverty of a Classless Criminology—The American Society of Criminology 1991 Presidential Address." *Criminology,* 30(1):1–19.

Hagan, John, and Ronit Dinovitzer. 1999. "Collateral Consequences of Imprisonment for Children, Communities, and Prisoners." *Crime and Justice: A Review of Research,* 26:121–162.

Haines, Joe D., Jr. 2002. *Justice Judge Parker Style.* Available: http://littlerock.about.com/gi/dynamic/offsite.htm?site=

http://www.oklahombres.org/parker.htm (accessed April 10, 2002).

Half, C. 1997. "The Russian Mafia," *Harvard International Review*, 19(3):52–56.

Hall, J. C. 1996. "FBI Training on the New Federal Deadly Force Policy." *FBI Law Enforcement Bulletin*, 65(4):25–32.

Haller, M. H. 1976. "Historical Roots of Police Behavior: Chicago, 1890–1925." *Law and Society Review*, 10(Winter):303–324.

Hamilton, M. 1971. *The Policewoman—Her Service and Ideals*. New York: Arno Press and The New York Times. (Original work published 1924.)

Handelman, S. 1994. "The Russian Mafia." *Foreign Affairs*, 73:83–96.

Haney, Craig. 1997. "'Infamous Punishment': The Psychological Consequences of Isolation." Pages 428–437 in *Correctional Contexts: Contemporary and Classical Readings*, edited by James W. Marquart and Jonathan R. Sorensen. Los Angeles: Roxbury.

Harding, Richard W. 1998. "Private Prisons." Pages 626–655 in *The Handbook of Crime and Punishment*, edited by Michael Tonry. New York: Oxford University Press.

Harlow, Caroline Wolf. 1998. *Profile of Jail Inmates, 1996*. Washington, DC: Bureau of Justice Statistics, U.S. Department of Justice.

Harring, S. 1992. "The Development of the Police Institution in the United States." Pages 306–320 in *Policing and Crime Control, Part 3*, edited by E. H. Monkkonen. Westport, CT: Meckler.

Harring, S. L. 1983. *Policing a Class Society: The Experience of American Cities, 1865–1915*. New Brunswick, NJ: Rutgers University Press.

Harrington, P. E. 1999. "Equality Denied—The Status of Women in Policing: 1998." National Center for Women and Policing, A Division of the Feminist Majority Foundation.

Harrington, P. E. 2001. "Equality Denied—The Status of Women in Policing: 2000." National Center for Women and Policing, A Division of the Feminist Majority Foundation.

Harris, Anthony R., and James A. W. Shaw. 2000. "Looking for Patterns: Race, Class, and Crime." Pages 129–163 in *Criminology: A Contemporary Handbook*, edited by Joseph F. Sheley. Belmont, CA: Wadsworth.

Harris, D. 1999. "Driving While Black—Racial Profiling on Our Nation's Highways." *An American Civil Liberties Union Special Report*, June. Available: http://www.aclu.org/profiling/report/ndex.htm.

Harris, John C., and Paul Jesilow. 2000. "It's Not the Old Ball Game: Three Strikes and the Courtroom Workgroup." *Justice Quarterly*, 17:185–210.

Harris, M. G. 1997. "Cholas, Mexican-American Girls and Gangs." Pages 150–163 in *Gangs and Gang Behavior*, edited by G. L. Mays. Chicago: Nelson-Hall.

Harris, M. K., and R. P. Corbett, Jr. 1998. "Exploring the Implications of Four Sanctioning Orientations for Community Corrections." *Federal Probation*, 62(2):81–93.

Harrison, E. 1991. "Police Brutality in the U.S.: An Overview." Pages 16–21 in *Policing the Police*, edited by W. Dudley. San Diego, CA: Greenhaven Press.

Harrison, E. 1992. "Chicago Police Used Torture, Report Alleges." *Los Angeles Times*, February 2:A14.

Hart, Timothy C., and Brian A. Reaves. 1999. *Felony Defendants in Large Urban Counties, 1996*. Washington, DC: Bureau of Justice Statistics, U.S. Department of Justice.

"Hate and Bias Crimes." 1999. Available: http://www.ojp.usdoj.gov.ovc/ncvrw/1999.hate.htm.

"Hate Crime Legislation and the First Amendment." 2001. National Gay and Lesbian Task Force. Available: http://www.ngltf.org.statelocal/hcfirstamend.htm.

"Hate Group Count Tops 500; Number of Internet Sites Soars." 1999. *SPLC Report*, March:1.

Havemann, J. 1997. "A Nation of Violent Children." *The Washington Post Weekly Standard*, February 17:26.

Hawkins, J. David, Todd Herrenkohl, David P. Farrington, Devon Brewer, Richard F. Catalano, and Tracy W. Harachi. 1998. "A Review of Predictors of Youth Violence." Pages 106–146 in *Serious and Violent Juvenile Offenders: Risk Factors and Successful Intervention*, edited by Rolf Loeber and David P. Farrington. Thousand Oaks, CA: Sage.

Hawkins, Keith (ed.). 1993. *The Uses of Discretion*. New York: Oxford University Press.

"Hells Angels, Crime and Canada." 1998. *Economist*, March 28:33–34.

Hepburn, John. 1984. "The Erosion of Authority and the Perceived Legitimacy of Inmate Social Protest: A Study of Prison Guards." *Journal of Criminal Justice*, 12:579–590.

Herbert, B. 2002. "An Imaginary Homicide." *New York Times*, August 15:D10.

Herbert, Bob. 2000. "The Death Factory." *New York Times*, October 2:A27.

Herbert, S. 1997. *Policing Space: Territoriality and the Los Angeles Police Department*. Minneapolis: University of Minnesota Press.

Herbert, S. 1998. "Police Subculture Reconsidered." *Criminology*, 36(2):343–369.

Herbert, S. 2001. " 'Hard Chargers' or 'Station Queens'? Policing and the Masculinist State." *Gender, Place and Culture: A Journal of Feminist Geography*, 8(1):55–72.

Hernandez, R. 2001. "Study Details Sex Abuse of Kids." *San Diego Union-Tribune*, September 11:A5.

Herrington, N. L. 1997. "Female Cops—1992. Pages 385–390 in *Critical Issues in Policing*, edited by Roger C. Dunham and Geoffrey P. Alpert. Prospect Heights, IL: Waveland Press.

Heumann, M. 1981. *Plea Bargaining—The Experience of Prosecutors, Judges, and Defense Attorneys*. Chicago: The University of Chicago Press.

Hewitt, Bill, Bob Stewart, and Gabrielle Cosgriff. 2002. "Life or Death." *People Weekly*, March 4:83–87.

Hickey, E. W. 1991. *Serial Murderers and Their Victims*. Pacific Grove, CA: Brooks/Cole.

Hillenbrand, S. 1990. "Restitution and Victim Rights in the 1980s." Pages 188–204 in *Victims of Crime Problems, Policies, and Programs*, edited by A. J. Lurigio, W. G. Skogan, and R. C. Davis. Newbury Park, CA: Sage Publications.

Hindelang, Michael, Travis Hirschi, and Joseph G. Weis. 1981. *Measuring Delinquency*. Beverly Hills: Sage.

Hirschi, Travis. 1969. *Causes of Delinquency*. Berkeley: University of California Press.

Hirschi, Travis. 1995. "The Family." Pages 121–140 in *Crime*, edited by James Q. Wilson and Joan Petersilia. San Francisco: Institute for Contemporary Studies Press.

Hodgins, Sheilagh (ed.). 1993. *Mental Disorder and Crime*. Thousand Oaks, CA: Sage.

Hoffman, B. 1993. "Terrorism in the United States: Recent Trends and Future Prospects." Pages 220–225 in *Violence and Terrorism*, edited by B. Schechterman and M. Slann. Guilford, CT: Dushkin.

Hoffman, Jan. 1998. "Some Officers are Skirting *Miranda* Restraints to Get Confessions." *New York Times*, March 29:A1.

Holden, B. A., L. P. Cohen, and E. de Lisser. 1995. "Race Seems to Play an Increasing Role in Many Jury Verdicts." *The Wall Street Journal*, October 5:A1–A5.

Holmes, M. D., H. D. Daudistel, and W. A. Taggart. 1992. "Plea Bargaining Policy and State District Court Caseloads: An Interrupted Time Series Analysis." *Law & Society Review*, 26(1):139–159.

Holmes, R. M., and J. De Burger. 1988. *Serial Murder*. Newbury Park, CA: Sage.

Holmstrom, D. 1997. "Next Time in Mexico, Beware of Frisky Police." *Christian Science Monitor*, April 4:6.

Holscher, Louis M., and Rizwana Mahmood. 2000. "Borrowing from the Shariah: The Potential Uses of Procedural Islamic Law in the West." Pages 82–96 in *International Criminal Justice: Issues in a Global Perspective*, edited by Delbert Rounds. Boston: Allyn & Bacon.

Holten, N. G., and L. L. Lamar. 1991. *The Criminal Courts—Structures, Personnel, and Processes.* New York: McGraw-Hill.

Hopper, C. B., and J. Moore. 1997. "Women in Outlaw Motorcycle Gangs." Page 363–381 in *Gangs and Gang Behavior*, edited by G. L. Mays. Chicago: Nelson-Hall.

Horton, C. 1995. *Policing Policy in France.* London: Policy Studies Institute.

"How Effective Are '.08' Drunk-Driving Laws?" 1997. *Consumers Research Magazine*, 82(8):26–29.

Howell, James C., and J. David Hawkins. 1998. "Prevention of Youth Violence." *Crime and Justice: A Review of Research*, 24:263–315.

Hoyt, Charles A. 1981. *Witchcraft.* Carbondale: Southern Illinois Press.

Huff, C. 1997. "The Russian Mafia." *Harvard International Review*, 19(3):52–56.

Huff, C. R., A. Rattner, and E. Sagarin. 1997. "Convicted but Innocent: Wrongful Convictions and Public Policy." Pages 253–276 in *Order under Law—Readings in Criminal Justice*, edited by R. G. Culbertson and R. A. Weisheit. Prospect Heights, IL: Waveland Press Inc.

Huff, R. 1998a. "Criminal Behavior of Gang Members and At-Risk Youths." *National Institute of Justice—Research Preview*, March:1–4.

Huff, R. 1998b. "Comparing the Criminal Behavior of Youth Gangs and At-Risk Youths." *National Institute of Justice—Research in Brief*, October:2.

Huizinga, David, and Delbert S. Elliott. 1987. "Juvenile Offenders: Offender Incidence and Arrest Rates by Race." *Crime and Delinquency*, 33:206–223.

Human Rights Watch. 1998. "Report Charges Police Abuse in U.S. Goes Unchecked." Available: http://hrw.org/hrw/press98/july/polic707.htm.

Human Rights Watch. 2000. "Out of Sight: Super-Maximum Security Confinement in the United States." New York: Human Rights Watch.

Human Rights Watch. 2001a. "HIV/AIDS in Prisons." Available: http://www.hrw.org/hrw/advocacy/prisons/hiv-aids.htm. New York: Human Rights Watch.

Human Rights Watch. 2001b. "Prisons in the United States of America." Available: http://www.hrw.org/hrw/advocacy/prisons/u-s.htm. New York: Human Rights Watch.

Hunt, Geoffrey, Stephanie Riegel, Tomas Morales, and Dan Waldorf. 1993. "Changes in Prison Culture: Prison Gangs and the Case of the 'Pepsi Generation'." *Social Problems*, 40(3):398–409.

Hunt, J. 1999. "Police Accounts of Normal Force." Pages 306–324 in *The Police and Society*, edited by V. E. Kappeler. Prospect Heights, IL: Waveland Press.

Ianni, F. A. J., and E. Reuss-Ianni. 1972. *A Family Business: Kinship and Social Control in Organized Crime.* New York: New American Library.

Imber, C. 1997. *Ebu's-su'ud: The Islamic Legal Tradition.* Stanford, CA: Stanford University Press.

Impocco, J., and M. Guttman. 1993. "Firestorm!" *U.S. News & World Report*, November 8:12–17.

"Improving State and Local Criminal Justice Systems." 1998. Washington, DC: U.S. Department of Justice, Office of Justice Programs, U.S. Government Printing Office.

Inciardi, J. A. 1970. "The Adult Firestarter." *Criminology*, 8:145–155.

Inciardi, J. A. 1987. *Criminal Justice.* San Diego, CA: Harcourt, Brace, and Jovanovich.

Innocence Project. 2002. Available: http://www.innocenceproject.org.

"Innocence Project Honors 100th Freed Inmate." 2002. *Los Angeles Times*, January 19:B8.

"The Iron Fist and the Velvet Glove." 1999. Pages 80–92 in *The Police and Society*, edited by V. E. Kappler. Prospect Heights, IL: Waveland Press.

Irwin, John. 1980. *Prisons in Turmoil.* Boston: Little, Brown.

Irwin, John. 1998. "The Jail." Pages 227–236 in *Incarcerating Criminals: Prisons and Jails in Social and Organizational Context*, edited by Timothy J. Flanagan, James W. Marquart, and Kenneth G. Adams. New York: Oxford University Press.

Irwin, John, and Donald Cressey. 1962. "Thieves, Convicts, and the Inmate Culture." *Social Problems* 10:142–155.

Isikoff, Michael. 1989. "Drug Buy Set Up for Bush Speech." *The Washington Post*, September 22:A1.

Isikoff, M., and S. Taylor. 2001. "Justice in the Shadows." *Newsweek*, November 26:39.

Israel, J. H., and W. R. LaFave. 1988. *Criminal Procedure—Constitutional Limitations.* St. Paul, MN: West Group.

Israel, J. H., and W. R. LaFave. 2001. *Criminal Procedure—Constitutional Limitations.* St. Paul: West Publishing.

Ito, T. M. 1997. "Have Gun Will Shoot." *U.S. News & World Report*, September 15:7.

Jackson, Derrick Z. 2000. "Bush's Death Factory." *The Boston Globe*, October 25:A17.

Jacob, Herbert. 1978. *Justice in America: Courts, Lawyers, and the Judicial Process*, 3 ed. Boston: Little, Brown.

Jacobs, J. B. 1986. "Drinking and Crime." *Crime File Study Guide.* Washington, DC: National Institute of Justice.

Jacobson, Kristen C., and David C. Rowe. 2000. "Nature, Nurture, and the Development of Criminality." Pages 323–347 in *Criminology: A Contemporary Handbook*, edited by Joseph F. Sheley. Belmont, CA: Wadsworth.

Jameson, S. 1984. " 'Super-Cops of Japan'—The Glow Fades." *Los Angeles Times*, September 4.

Janny, S. 1995. "Group Psychology Explains Police Brutality." Pages 74–76 in *Police Brutality*, edited by W. Dudley. San Diego: Greenhaven Press.

Jary, D., and J. Jary. 1991. *Dictionary of Sociology.* New York: Harper Collins.

Jenkins, B. 1992. "Terrorism." Pages 427–453 in *Encyclopedia of Sociology*, edited by E. F. Borgatta. New York: Maxwell.

Jenne, Denise L., and Robert C. Kersting. 1996. "Aggression and Women Correctional Officers in the United States." *The Prison Journal*, 76:442–460.

Jensen, Eric L., and Jurg Gerber. 1996. "The Civil Forfeiture of Assets and the War on Drugs: Expanding Criminal Sanctions While Reducing Due Process Protections." *Crime and Delinquency*, 42:421–434.

Jensen, Eric L., and L. K. Metsger. 1994. "A Test of the Deterrent Effect of Legislative Waiver on Violent Juvenile Crime." *Crime and Delinquency*, 40:96–104.

Jerome, R. 1995. "Suspect Confessions." *New York Times Magazine*, August 13:28–31.

Johnson, David R., and Laurie K. Scheuble. 1991. "Gender Bias in the Disposition of Juvenile Court Referrals: The Effects of Time and Location." *Criminology*, 29(4):677–699.

Johnston, D., and D. Van Natta Jr. 2002. "Wary of Risk, Slow to Adapt, FBI Stumbles in Terror War." *New York Times*, June 2(sec. 1):1.

Johnson, Dirk. 2000. "Poor Legal Work Common for Innocents on Death Row." *New York Times*, February 5:A1.

Johnson, Robert. 1996. *Hard Time: Understanding and Reforming the Prison.* Belmont, CA: Wadsworth.

Johnson, Robert. 1998. *Death Work: A Study of the Modern Execution Process*, 2 ed. Belmont, CA: Wadsworth.

Jones, David A. 1986. *History of Criminology: A Philosophical Perspective.* New York: Greenwood Press.

Joseph, Janice. 1995. *Black Youths, Delinquency, and Juvenile Justice.* Westport, CT: Praeger.

Jost, K. 1999. "Plea Bargaining." *CQ Researcher*, 9(6):115–133.

Jurik, Nancy. 1985. "Individual and Organizational Determinants of Correctional Officer Attitudes toward Inmates." *Criminology*, 23:523–540.

"Jury." 1999–2000. Available: http://www.britannica.com.

"The Jury 1999–2000." 2000. *Encyclopedia Britannica*, www.britannica.com.

Kaczor, L. M., and Ryckman, R. M. 1991. "Observer Hypercompetitiveness and Victim Precipitation of Rape." *Journal of Social Psychology*, 131(1):131–134.

Kalven, H., and H. Zeisel. 1966. *The American Jury*. Boston: Little, Brown.

Kamisar, Y., W. R. LaFave, and J. R. Israel. 1999. *Basic Criminal Procedure—Cases Comments and Questions*. St. Paul, MN: West Group.

Kandel, Elizabeth, and Sarnoff A. Mednick. 1991. "Perinatal Complications Predict Violent Offending." *Criminology*, 29(3):519–529.

Kaplan, David E. 2000. "A Case Study in Policing for Profit." *U.S. News & World Report*, July 10:22–23.

Kappeler, V. E., R. D. Sluder, and G. P. Alpert. 1998. *Forces of Deviance—Understanding the Dark Side of Policing*. Prospect Heights, IL: Waveland Press.

Kappeler, Victor E., Mark Blumberg, and Gary W. Potter. 2000. *The Mythology of Crime and Justice*, 3 ed. Prospect Heights, IL: Waveland Press.

Karkorian, G., and R. Connell. 2002. "FBI Brass Accused of Apathy." *Los Angeles Times*, May 25:A20.

Karmen, A. 1980. "Auto Theft: Beyond Victim Blaming." *Victimology: An International Journal*, 5(2–4):161–174.

Karmen, A. 1990. *Crime Victims—An Introduction to Victimology*. Pacific Grove, CA: Brooks Cole.

Karmen, A. 1995. "Women Victims of Crime: Introduction." Pages 181–196 in *The Criminal Justice System and Women: Offenders, Victims, and Workers*, edited by B. R. Price and H. J. Sokoloff. New York: McGraw-Hill.

Katz, J. 1988. *Seductions of Crime*. New York: Basic Books.

Katz, Janet, and William J. Chambliss. 1995. "Biology and Crime." Pages 275–303 in *Criminology: A Contemporary Handbook*, edited by Joseph F. Sheley. Belmont, CA: Wadsworth.

Kauffman, Kelsey. 1988. *Prison Officers and Their World*. Cambridge, MA: Harvard University Press.

Kelly, D. 1990. "Victim Participation in the Criminal Justice System." Pages 172–187 in *Victims of Crime—Problems, Policies, and Programs*, edited by A. J. Lurigio, W. G. Skogan, and R. C. Davis. Newbury Park, CA: Sage.

Kelly, R. J. 1997. "Trapped in the Folds of Discourse: Theorizing about the Underworld." Pages 39–52 in *Understanding Crime in Global Perspective*, edited by P. Ryan and G. Rush. Thousand Oaks, CA: Sage.

Kelly, R. J., R. Schatzberg, and P. J. Ryan. 1997. "Primitive Capitalist Accumulation: Russia as a Racket." Pages 174–186 in *Understanding Crime in Global Perspective*, edited by P. Ryan and G. Rush. Thousand Oaks, CA: Sage.

Kempf, Kimberly L. 1993. "The Empirical Status of Hirschi's Control Theory." Pages 143–185 in *New Directions in Criminological Theory*, edited by Freda Adler and William S. Laufer. New Brunswick, NJ: Transaction.

Kennedy, R. 1997. *Race, Crime, and the Law*. New York: Pantheon Books.

Kennelly, M. F. 1994. "Pretrial Motions: Motions to Challenge the Indictment, Prosecutorial Misconduct, and Motions to Server." Pages 47–56 in *Federal Criminal Litigation*, edited by B. A. Reeves, G. C. Harris, and C. J. Loewenson, Jr. Chicago: American Bar Association.

Kershaw, A. 1998. *Jack London: A Life*. New York: St. Martin's.

Kessler, J. B. 1975. "The Social Psychology of Jury Deliberations." Pages 67–93 in *The Jury System in America*, edited by R. J. Simon. Beverly Hills, CA: Sage.

Kieffer, G., and E. Chemerinsky. 2000. "Police Commission Must Seize the Reigns." *Los Angeles Times*, March 16:B7.

Kilborn, Peter T. 2001. "Flood of Ex-Convicts Finds Job Market Tight." *New York Times*, March 15:A16.

Kim, Eun-Kyung. 2001. "Group Fights Back for Female Inmates." *Bangor Daily News*, March 7:B4.

Kindlon, Dan, and Michael Thompson. 1999. *Raising Cain: Protecting the Emotional Life of Boys*. New York: Ballantine Books.

King, Roy D. 1998. "Prisons." Pages 589–625 in *The Handbook of Crime and Punishment*, edited by Michael Tonry. New York: Oxford University Press.

"Kiss at Your Peril." 1998. *The Economist*, February 14:47.

Klaus, P. 1999. "Carjackings in the United States, 1992–1996." Washington, DC: Bureau of Justice Statistics, U.S. Department of Justice.

Klaus, P. A. 2000. *Crimes against Persons Age 65 or Older, 1992–97*. Washington, DC: U.S. Department of Justice, Office of Justice Programs.

Klaus, Patsy A. 1994. *The Costs of Crime to Victims*. Washington, DC: U.S. Department of Justice, Bureau of Justice Statistics.

Klein, Dorie. 1995. "The Etiology of Female Crime: A Review of the Literature." Pages 30–53 in *The Criminal Justice System and Women: Offenders, Victims, and Workers*, edited by Barbara Raffel Price, and Natlie J. Sokoloff. New York: McGraw-Hill.

Klockars, C. 1991. "The Rhetoric of Community Policing." Pages 427–445 in *The Police and Society*, edited by V. E. Kappeler. Prospect Heights, IL: Waveland.

Klockars, C. 1996. "A Theory of Excessive Force and Its Control." Pages 1–23 in *Police Violence*, edited by W. A. Geller and H. Toch. New Haven: Yale University Press.

Klockars, C. B. 1974. *The Professional Fence*. New York: Free Press.

Klockars, C. B. 1999. "The Dirty Harry Problem." Pages 388–394 in *The Police and Society*, edited by V. E. Kappeler. Prospect Heights, IL: Waveland.

Klofas, John M. 1998. "The Jail and the Community." Pages 244–258 in *Incarcerating Criminals: Prisons and Jails in Social and Organizational Context*, edited by Timothy J. Flanagan, James W. Marquart, and Kenneth G. Adams. New York: Oxford University Press.

Knickerbocker, B. 2001. "Hate Groups Try to Capitalize on September 11." *Christian Science Monitor*, November 21:2–3.

Kodluboy, D. W. 1996. "Basic Issues for Educators." National Alliance of Gang Investigators Associations. Available: http://www.nagia.org/asian_youth_gangs1.htm.

Kolata, G. 1996. "Experts Are at Odds on How Best to Tackle Teenagers' Drug Use." *New York Times*, September 18:B10.

Koppel, Herbert. 1987. *Lifetime Likelihood of Victimization*. Washington, DC: U.S. Department of Justice, Bureau of Justice Statistics.

Koss, M., and M. Harvey. 1991. *The Rape Victim: Clinical and Community Interventions*. Beverly Hills, CA: Sage.

Koss, M., C. Gidycz, and N. Wisniewski. 1987. "The Scope of Rape: Incidence and Prevalence of Sexual Aggression and Victimization in a National Sample of Higher Education Students." *Journal of Counseling and Clinical Psychology*, 55:162–170.

Kovaleski, Serge F. 2000. "D.C. Finds Dangers in Ailing Jail." *The Washington Post*, September 17:A1.

Kramer, John H., and Jeffery T. Ulmer. 1996. "Sentencing Disparity and Departures from Guidelines." *Justice Quarterly*, 13:81–106.

Kraska, P. B., and V. E. Kappeler. 1997. "Militarizing American Police: The Rise and Normalization of Paramilitary Units." *Social Problems*, 44(1):1–17.

Kraska, P. B., and V. E. Kappeler. 1988. "Police On-Duty Drug Use: A Theoretical and Descriptive Examination." *American Journal of Police*, 71:1–28.

Kravets, D. 2002. "Legal-Rights Limits Result in Concerns." *San Diego Union-Tribune*, September 13:A6.

Kravets, D. 2003. "California Supreme Court Says Rape Begins When Woman Says No." *Associated Press Newswires*, January 16.

Krivo, Lauren J., and Ruth D. Peterson. 1996. "Extremely Disadvantaged Neighborhoods and Urban Crime." *Social Forces*, 75:619–650.

Krohn, Marvin. 2000. "Sources of Criminality: Control and Deterrence Theories." Pages 373–399 in *Criminology: A Contemporary Handbook*, edited by Joseph F. Sheley. Belmont, CA: Wadsworth.

Kurtz, Howard. 1997. "The Crime Spree on Network News." *The Washington Post*, August 12:D1.

Kyl, J., and D. Feinstein. 1996. "At Issue: Victims' Rights." *American Bar Association Journal*, 82:82–83.

Lab, Steven F., and J. David Hirschel. 1988. "Climatological Conditions and Crime: The Forecast Is . . . ?" *Justice Quarterly*, 5:281–299.

Lab, Steven P. 2000. *Crime Prevention: Approaches, Practices and Evaluations*, 4 ed. Cincinnati: Anderson.

"L.A. Cop Convicted of 3 Rapes on Duty." 2003. *Los Angeles Times*, January 8:A7.

LaFranchi, H. 1994. "When Police Arrive, Mexicans Serve and Protect Themselves." *Christian Science Monitor*, November 2:9.

LaGrange, Randy L., and Helene Raskin White. 1985. "Age Differences in Delinquency: A Test of Theory." *Criminology*, 23:19–45.

LaGrange, Teresa C., and Robert A. Silverman. 1999. "Low Self-Control and Opportunity: Testing the General Theory of Crime as an Explanation for Gender Differences in Delinquency." *Criminology*, 37:41–72.

Lait, M., and S. Glover. 2000a. "Shooting Scenes Rigged Perez Says." *Los Angeles Times*, February 10:A1.

Lait, M., and S. Glover. 2000b. "LAPD Officer Corroborates Perez on Beating." *Los Angeles Times*, March 14:A1.

Lait, M., and S. Glover. 2000c. "LAPD Chief Calls for Mass Dismissal of Tainted Cases." *Los Angeles Times*, January 27:A1.

Landon, L. 2000. "School Policies Turn Troubled Youth into Young Offenders." *The Ottawa Citizen*, September 21:A10.

Landsman, Stephan. 1984. *The Adversary System: A Description and Defense*. Washington, DC: American Enterprise Institute for Public Policy Research.

Lane, C. 2002. "Supreme Court Turns Down Appeal by Killer Who Cited Bad Lawyering." *The Buffalo News*, May 29:A7.

Lane, R. 1967. *Policing the City: Boston 1822–1885*. Cambridge, MA: Harvard University Press.

Lane, R. 1992. "Urban Police and Crime Control in Nineteenth-Century America." Pages 6–48 in *Crime and Justice: An Annual Review of Research*, Vol. 15, edited by M. Tonry and N. Morris. Chicago: University of Chicago Press.

Langan, Patrick A., and Mark A. Cunniff. 1992. *Recidivism of Felons on Probation, 1986–89*. Washington, DC: U.S. Department of Justice.

Langbein, J. H. 1992. "On the Myth of Written Constitutions: The Disappearance of the Jury Trial." *Harvard Journal of Law and Public Policy*, (15)1:119–128.

"LAPD's Unlearned Lessons." 2000. *Los Angeles Times*, August 23:B4.

Larivee, John J., and Edward Davis. 2001. "Stacking the Deck against Released Prisoners." *The Boston Globe*, March 18:H2.

Laurent, B. 2001. "Eco-Vandals Put a Match to 'Progress.' " *Christian Science Monitor*, July 5:3.

Lauritsen J. L., and K. F. Davis-Quintet. 1995. "Repeat Victimization among Adolescents and Young Adults." *Journal of Criminology*, 11(2):143–166.

Lauritsen, J. L., R. L. Sampson, and J. H. Laub. 1991. "The Link between Offending and Victimization among Adolescents." *Criminology*, 29(2):265–292.

Le, B. P. 2002. "Asian Gangs: A Bibliography." *Asian Gang Index*. Available: http://www.communitypolicing.org/publications/iag/asian_gangs.

Lefkowitz, J. 1975. "Psychological Attributes of Policemen: A Review of Research and Opinions." *Journal of Social Issues*, 31(1):3–26.

Lehrer, Eli. 2001. "Hell behind Bars." *National Review*, February 5:24–25.

Leng, S., and H. Chiu. 1985. *Criminal Justice in Post-Mao China: Analysis and Documents*. Albany: State University of New York Press.

Leo, Richard A. 1996. "Miranda's Revenge: Police Interrogation as a Confidence Game." *Law & Society Review*, 30:259–288.

Leonard, Kimberley Kempf, Carl E. Pope, and William H. Feyerherm (eds.). 1995. *Minorities in Juvenile Justice*. Thousand Oaks, CA: Sage.

"Lessons from a Century of Drug Use Initiation Show World War II Was a Watershed." 1998. *The Brown University Digest of Addiction Theory and Application*, September:3–4.

Levin, David J., Patrick A. Langan, and Jodi M. Brown. 2000. *State Court Sentencing of Convicted Felons, 1996*. Washington, DC: Bureau of Justice Statistics, U.S. Department of Justice.

Levy, H. 1996. *And the Blood Cried Out*. New York: Basic Books.

Lewin, Tamar. 2000. "Racial Discrepancy Found in Trying of Youths." *New York Times*, February 3:A14.

Lewin, Tamar. 2001. "Little Sympathy or Remedy for Inmates Who Are Raped." *New York Times*, April 15:A1.

Lewis, A. D. E., and David J. Ibbetson. 1994. *The Roman Law Tradition*. New York: Cambridge University Press.

Lewontin, Richard C., Steven P. R. Rose, and Leon J. Kamin. 1984. *Not in Our Genes: Biology, Ideology, and Human Nature*. New York: Pantheon.

Lichtblau, E., and P. Meyer. 2002. "What U.S. Officials Claim to Have Known Pre 9/11." *New York Times*, April 30:A1.

Lilly, Robert J., and Mathieu Deflem. 1996. "Profit and Reality: An Analysis of the Corrections-Commercial Complex." *Crime and Delinquency*, 42:3–20.

Lindorff, D. 1999. "Police Culture." *Nation*, May 31:20.

Lindsay, Arthur G. 1998. "Abolish the Juvenile Court?" *Juvenile and Family Court Journal*, 49:51–58.

Lipton, Douglas, Robert Martinson, and Judith Wilks. 1975. *The Effectiveness of Correctional Treatment: A Survey of Correctional Treatment Studies*. New York: Praeger.

Lipton, Eric. 2001. "22 Years Later, Unsanitary Jail Conditions Still Exist, Judge Finds." *New York Times*, January 11:B3.

Liu, S., P. Z. Siegel, R. D. Brewer, A. H. Mokdad, D. A. Sleet, and M. Serdula. 1997. "Prevalance of Alcohol Impaired Driving: Results from a National Self-Reported Survey of Health Behaviors" *Journal of the American Medical Association*, 277(2):122–125.

"Loansharking Suspect Guilty on Two Counts." 1999. *The Providence Journal-Bulletin*, October 7:4B.

"Local Police Departments, 1997: Executive Summary." 1999. Washington, DC: U.S. Department of Justice, Office of Justice Programs.

Loeber, Rolf, and David P. Farrington (eds.). 1998. *Serious and Violent Juvenile Offenders: Risk Factors and Successful Interventions*. Thousand Oaks, CA: Sage.

Loeber, Rolf, and Magda Stouthamer-Loeber. 1986. "Family Factors as Correlates and Predictors of Juvenile Conduct Problems and Delinquency." Pages 29–149 in *Crime and Justice: An Annual Review of Research*, edited by Michael Tonry and Norval Morris. Chicago: University of Chicago Press.

Lomasky, L. E. 1991. "The Political Significance of Terrrorism." Pages 86–115 in *Violence, Terrorism, and Justice*, edited by R. G. Frey and C. W. Morris. Cambridge, Eng.: Cambridge University Press.

Lombardo, Lucien X. 1997. "Guards Imprisoned: Correctional Officers at Work." Pages 189–202 in *Correctional Contexts:*

Classical and Contemporary Readings, edited by James W. Marquart and Jonathan R. Sorensen. Los Angeles: Roxbury.

Lombroso, G. 1911. *Criminal Man According to the Classification of Cesare Lombroso.* New York: Putnam.

Long, Rob. 2001. "Free to Go Bad." *National Review,* December 31:22–23.

Longley, J., and B. Sheck. 2000. "Legal Genes." *People,* May 15 53(19):11–13.

Lubman, S. B., and G. C. Wajnowski. 1986. "Criminal Justice and the Foreigner." Pages 154–160 in *Law in the People's Republic of China,* edited by R. H. Folsom and J. H. Minan. Oceanside, NY: Professional Seminar Consultants.

Luckenbill, D., and D. P. Doyle. 1989. "Structural Position and Violence—Developing a Cultural Position." *Criminology,* 27:419–436.

Luckenbill, D. F. 1977. "Criminal Homicide as a Situated Transaction." *Social Problems,* 25:176–186.

Lundman, R. J. 1980. *Police and Policing—An Introduction.* New York: Holt, Rinehart & Winston.

Lurigio, A. J., and P. A. Resick. 1990. "Healing the Psychological Wounds of Criminal Victimization." Pages 50–68 in *Victims of Crime—Problems and Policies,* edited by A. J. Lurigio, W. G. Skogan, and R. C. Davis. Newbury Park, CA: Sage.

Lyall, Sarah. 2000. "A Rural Intruder's Slaying Unsettles England." *New York Times,* May 24:A1.

Lyman, M. D. 1987. *Narcotics and Crime Control.* Springfield, IL: Charles C. Thomas.

Lynch, D. R. 1999. "Perceived Judicial Hostility to Criminal Trials." *Criminal Justice and Behavior,* 26(2):217–233.

Lynch, James P. 1993. "A Cross-National Comparison of the Length of Custodial Sentences for Serious Crimes." *Justice Quarterly,* 10(4):639–660.

Lynch, James P., and William J. Sabol. 1997. *Crime Policy Report: Did Getting Tough on Crime Pay?* Washington, DC: The Urban Institute.

Lynch, Michael J., Raymond J. Michalowski, and W. Byron Groves. 2000. *The New Primer in Radical Criminology: Critical Perspectives on Crime, Power and Identity,* 3 ed. Monsey, NY: Willow Tree Press.

MacCharles, T. 2001. "Liberal Bill to Reform Young Offenders Act." *The Toronto Star,* February 6:A1.

Machan, Dyan. 2000. "Habilitation, Not Rehabilitation." Pages 133–134 in *Annual Editions: Criminal Justice, 2000/2001,* edited by Joseph L. Victor. New York: Dushkin/McGraw-Hill.

Maciak, B., and M. T. Moore. 1998. "Preventing Halloween Arson in an Urban Setting: A Model for Multisectoral Planning and Community Participation." *Health Education and Behavior,* 25(2):194–212.

MacKeen, Dawn. 1999. "Death Sentence?" Salon.com, May 20. Available: http://www.salon.com/health/feature/1999/05/20/condoms/index.html.

MacKenzie, Doris L. 1997. "Criminal Justice and Crime Prevention." Pages 9.1–9.61 in *Preventing Crime: What Works, What Doesn't, What's Promising,* edited by Lawrence W. Sherman, Don Gottfredson, Doris MacKenzie, J. Eck, P. Reuter, and S. Bushway. Washington, DC: National Institute of Justice, U.S. Department of Justice.

MacKenzie, Doris Layton, Robert Brame, David McDowall, and Claire Souryal. 1995. "Boot Camp Prisons and Recidivism in Eight States." *Criminology,* 33:327–357.

Maguire, Kathleen, and Ann L. Pastore (eds.). 2002. "Sourcebook of Criminal Justice Statistics 2000." Available: http://www.albany.edu/sourcebook.

Mahan, Sue. 1985. "An 'Orgy of Brutality' at Attica and the 'Killing Ground' at Santa Fe." Pages 73–78 in *Prison Violence in America,* edited by M. Braswell, S. Dillingham, and R. Montgomery. Cincinnati, OH: Anderson.

Mair, George. 1995. "Day Centres in England and Wales." Pages 131–138 in *Intermediate Sanctions in Overcrowded Times,* edited by Michael Tonry and Kate Hamilton. Boston: Northeastern University Press.

Males, Mike A. 1999. *Framing Youth: 10 Myths about the Next Generation.* Monroe, ME: Common Courage Press.

Mangold, T. 2002. "When Betrayal and Paranoia Are Part of the Job." *New York Times,* January 2:A15.

Mann, C. R. 1988. "Getting Even? Women Who Kill in Domestic Encounters." *Justice Quarterly,* 5:33–51.

Mann, Coramae Richey. 1993. *Unequal Justice: A Question of Color.* Bloomington: Indiana University Press.

Marano, Lou. 2001. "The Horror of Prison Rape." United Press International, February 20. Available: http://www.vny.com/cf/News/uipdetail.cfm?QID=161622.

Marciniak, Liz Marie. 2000. "The Addition of Day Reporting to Intensive Supervision Probation: A Comparison of Recidivism Rates." *Federal Probation,* 64:34–39.

Marcus, P., and C. H. Whitebread. 1996. *Gilbert Law Summaries: Criminal Procedures.* Chicago: Harcourt Brace Legal & Professional Publications.

Margolis, R. J. 1971. *Who Will Wear the Badge?* A Report of the United States Commission on Civil Rights. Washington, DC: U.S. Government Printing Office.

Marks, A. 1997. "More Police Are Willing to Break Code of Silence." *Christian Science Monitor,* August 20:1.

Marks, A. 1999a. "Black and White View of Police." *Christian Science Monitor,* June 9:1.

Marks, A. 1999b. "NYPD as Lab for Reducing Police Brutality." *Christian Science Monitor,* May 13:17–19.

Marks, A. 1999c. "Wall of Silence: Cracked but Not Crumbling." *Christian Science Monitor,* May, 27:1.

Marlantes, L. 2001. "Domestic Loners Top Suspect List in Anthrax Attacks." *Christian Science Monitor,* November 19:2–3.

Mars, G. 1983. *Cheats at Work—An Anthropology of Work Place Crime.* London: Unwin.

Martin, Randy, and Sherwood Zimmerman. 1990. "A Typology of the Causes of Prison Riots and an Analytical Extension to the 1986 West Virginia Riot." *Justice Quarterly,* 7:711–737.

Martin, S. E. 1980. *Breaking and Entering: Policewomen on Patrol.* Berkeley: University of California Press.

Martin, S. E. 1994. "Outsiders within the Station House: The Impact of Race and Gender on Black Women Police." *Social Problems,* 41(3):383–400.

Martin, S. E. 1997. "Women Officers on the Move: An Update on Women in Policing." Pages 363–384 in *Critical Issues in Policing: Contemporary Readings,* edited by R. G. Dunham and G. A. Alpert. Prospect Heights, IL: Waveland Press.

Martin, S. E., and N. C. Jurik. 1996. *Doing Justice, Doing Gender.* Thousand Oaks, CA: Sage.

Martinez, Pila. 1999. "Novel Attempt to Curb Prison Gang Violence." *Christian Science Monitor,* July 21:2.

Martinson, Robert. 1974. "What Works? Questions and Answers about Prison Reform." *Public Interest,* 35:22–54.

Maruschak, L. 1999. "DWI Offenders under Correctional Supervision." Washington, DC: Bureau of Justice Special Report. U.S. Department of Justice, Office of Justice Programs.

Maruschak, Laura M. 1999. *HIV in Prisons 1997.* Washington, DC: Bureau of Justice Statistics, U.S. Department of Justice.

Maruschak, Laura M. 2001. *HIV in Prisons and Jails, 1999.* Washington, DC: Bureau of Justice Statistics, U.S. Department of Justice.

Maruschak, Laura M., and Allen J. Beck. 2001. *Medical Problems of Inmates, 1997.* Washington, DC: Bureau of Justice Statistics, U.S. Department of Justice.

Marvell, Thomas B., and Carlisle E. Moody. 1994. "Prison Population Growth and Crime Reduction." *Journal of Quantitative Criminology,* June 2:10.

Marvell, Thomas B., and Carlisle E. Moody. 1996. "Specification Problems, Police Levels, and Crime Rates." *Criminology,* 34:609–646.

Marx, G. T. 1985. "Who Really Gets Stung? Some Issues Raised by Police Undercover Work." Pages 99–128 in *Moral Issues in Police Work*, edited by F. A. Elliston and M. Feldberg. Totowa, NJ: Roman and Allanheld.

Marx, K. 1971. *Economy, Class, and Social Revolution*. London: Michael Joseph Company.

Massey, A. 2000. "4 Dead, 2 Injured in Drunk Driving Accident at Colgate." *The Skidmore News*. Available: http://www.skidmore.edu/studentorgs/skidnews.

Masters, B. 2001. "Death Row to Freedom: A Journey Ends." *The Washington Post*, February 13:A1.

Mastrofski, S. 1993. "Information on the Beat." Pages 36–54 in *Police Work*, edited by R. Bennet. Beverly Hills, CA: Sage.

Mastroski, S. D., R. E. Worden, and J. P. Snipes. 1995. "Law Enforcement in a Time of Community Policing." *Criminology*, 33(4):539–563.

Matza, Michael. 1997. "Auditors to Eye Penn's Campus-Crime Data." *The Philadelphia Inquirer*, June 9:A1.

Mauer, Marc. 1999. *Race to Incarcerate*. New York: New Press.

May, John P. (ed.). 2000. *Building Violence: How America's Rush to Incarcerate Creates More Violence*. Thousand Oaks, CA: Sage.

McAlary, M. 1987. *Buddy Boys: When Good Cops Turn Bad*. New York: G. P. Putnam's Sons.

McBride, Duane, and Curtis VanderWaal. 1997. "Day Reporting Centers as an Alternative for Drug Using Offenders." *Journal of Drug Issues*, 27:379–407.

McCaghy, C. 1980. *Crime in American Society*. New York: Macmillan.

McCaghy, C., P. Giordano, and T. K. Henson. 1977. "Auto Theft: Offender and Offense Characteristics." *Criminology*, 15(3):367–386.

McCamant, J. F. 1984. "Grievance without Blood: Social Science's Antiseptic View of Rule; or The Neglect of Political Repression." Pages 11–42 in *The State as Terrorist: The Dynamics of Governmental Violence and Repression*, edited by M. Stohl and G. A. Lopez. Westport, CT: Greenwood.

McConville, M., and C. Mirsky. 1995. "Guilty Plea Courts: A Social Disciplinary Model of Criminal Justice." *Social Problems*, 42(2):216–234.

McCorkle, Richard C., Terance D. Miethe, and Kriss A. Drass. 1995. "The Roots of Prison Violence: A Test of Deprivation, Management, and 'Not-So-Total' Institution Models." *Crime and Delinquency*, 41:317–331.

McDonald, Douglas. 1992. "Punishing Labor: Unpaid Community Service as a Criminal Sentence." Pages 182–193 in *Smart Sentencing: The Emergence of Intermediate Sanctions*, edited by James M. Byrne, Arthur J. Lurigio, and Joan Petersilia. Newbury Park: Sage.

McDonald, Douglas C. 1999. "Medical Care in Prisons." *Crime and Justice: A Review of Research*, 26:427–478.

McDonald, W. F. 1977. "The Role of the Victim in America." Pages 37–52 in *Environmental Criminology*, edited by R. E. Barnett and J. Hagel III. Beverly Hills, CA: Sage.

McDonald, W. F. 1985. *Plea Bargaining: Critical Issues and Common Practices*. Washington, DC: U.S. Department of Justice, National Institute of Justice.

McDonald, W. F. 1992. "The Role of the Victim in America." Pages 87–98 in *Assessing the Criminal*, edited by R. E. Barnett and J. Hagel, III. Cambridge, MA: Ballinger.

McDonnell, P. J. 2001. "Visa Dates Give Notable Hijack Clues." *Los Angeles Times*, November 22:A1.

McDowall, David, and Colin Loftin. 1992. "Comparing the UCR and NCS over Time." *Criminology*, 30(1):125–132.

McFadden, R. D., and S. Saulny. 2002. "Reversal of Convictions in Rape Case Urged." *San Diego Union-Tribune*, December 6:A3.

McGoey, C. E. 1999. "Top 25 Stolen Cars." Available: http://www.crimedoctor.com/autotheft2.htm.

McGovern, G. S., and L. F. Guttridge. 1972. *The Great Coalfield War*. Boston: Houghton Mifflin.

McIvor, Gill. 1995. "CSOs Succeed in Scotland." Pages 77–84 in *Intermediate Sanctions in Overcrowded Times*, edited by Michael Tonry and Kate Hamilton. Northeastern University Press.

McLaughlin, A. 2001. "How Far Americans Would Go to Fight Terror." *Christian Science Monitor*, November 14:1.

McNaught, A. 2000. "Youth Crime Statistics and the Impact of the Young Offenders Act on Youth Crime." Legislative Research Services, Ontario Legislative Library, Legislative Assembly of Ontario. Available: http://www.ontla.con.ca/library/b27tx.h.

Meagher, M. S., and N. Yentes. 1986. "Choosing a Career in Policing: A Comparison of Male and Female Perceptions." *Journal of Police Science and Administration*, 14(4):320–327.

Meers, E. 1998. "Good Cop, Gay Cop." *Advocate*, March 3:26–35.

Megivern, James J. 1997. *The Death Penalty: An Historical and Theological Survey*. New York: Paulist Press.

Meier, Robert F., and Gilbert Geis. 1997. *Victimless Crime: Prostitution, Drugs, Homosexuality, and Abortion*. Los Angeles: Roxbury.

Mellili, K. J. 1992. "Prosecutorial Discretion in an Adversary System." *Brigham Young Law Review*, 3.

Mendelberg, Tali. 1997. "Executing Hortons: Racial Crime in the 1988 Presidential Campaign." *Public Opinion Quarterly*, 61:34–57.

Merton, R. 1947. *Social Theory and Social Structure*. New York: The Free Press.

Merton, Robert K. 1938. "Social Structure and Anomie." *American Sociological Review*, 3:672–682.

Messerschmidt, James W. 1997. *Crime as Structured Action: Gender, Race, Class, and Crime in the Making*. Thousand Oaks, CA: Sage.

Messner, Steven F., and Richard Rosenfeld. 2001. *Crime and the American Dream*, 3 ed. Belmont, CA: Wadsworth.

Meyer, J., and Weinstein, H. 2000. "Judge to Plead Guilty to Misconduct, Sources Say." *Los Angeles Times*, September 14:B1.

Michael, F. 1988. "Law—A Tool of Power." Pages 33–55 in *Human Rights in the People's Republic of China*, edited by Y. Wu, F. Michael, J. F. Cooper, T. Lee, M. S. Chang, and A. J. Gregor. Boulder, CO: Westview Press.

Miczek, Klaus A., Allan F. Mirsky, Gregory Carey, Joseph DeBold, and Adrian Raine. 1994. "An Overview of Biological Influences on Violent Behavior." Pages 1–20 in *Understanding and Preventing Violence: Biobehavioral Influences*, edited by Albert J. Reiss, Jr., Klaus A. Miczek, and Jeffrey A. Roth. Washington, DC: National Academy Press.

Miethe, T. D., and R. McCorkle. 1998. *Crime Profiles—The Anatomy of Dangerous Persons, Places, and Situations*. Los Angeles: Roxbury.

Miller, H. S., W. F. McDonald, and J. A. Cramer. 1978. *Plea Bargaining in the United States*. Washington, DC: National Institute of Law Enforcement and Criminal Justice, U.S. Department of Justice.

Miller, J. 1998. "Up It Up: Gender and the Accomplishment of Street Robbery." *Criminology*, 36:37–68.

Miller, Jerome G. 1996. *Search and Destroy: African American Males in the Criminal Justice System*. New York: Cambridge University Press.

Miller, Mark. 2000. "A War over Witnesses." *Newsweek*, June 26:55.

Miller, Ted, Marc Cohen, and Brian Wiersema. 1996. *Victim Costs and Consequences: A New Look*. Washington, DC: National Institute of Justice, U.S. Department of Justice.

Miller, W. 2000. "The Good, the Bad, & the Ugly." *History Today*, 50(8):29–35.

Milloy, Ross E. 2001. "Public Lives: For Seat-Belt Violator, a Jam, a Jail and Unmoved Justices." *New York Times*, April 28:A1.

Mills, Steve, Ken Armstrong, and Douglas Holt. 2000. "Flawed Trials Lead to Death Chamber." *Chicago Tribune*, June 11:A1.

Milner, B. 1999. "Speed Hot Issue in U.S. Policing." *The Globe and Mail*, March 24:A3.

Milton, P. 2001. "U.S. Won't Charge Police in Diallo Death." *The Buffalo News*, February 1:A7.

Ministry of Justice. 2001. Available: http://www.minjust.nl/ b_organ/wodc/publicaties/overige/pdf/11-icvs-h5.pdf. The Hague: Ministry of Justice, the Netherlands.

Mintz, J. 2002. "Tribunal Rules Aim to Shield Witnesses; Judges, Prosecutors May Be Anonymous." *The Washington Post*, March 22:A1.

"Miranda Survivor." 2000. *Washington Post Weekly*, July 3:25.

Mitcham, B. A. 1980. "Psychotherapy Techniques in Voir Dire Selection." *Association of Trial Lawyers of America*, 16(9):52–54.

Miyazawa, S. 1992. *Policing in Modern Japan—A Study in Making Crime*: Albany: State University of New York Press.

Monkkonen, E. H. 1992. "From Cop History to Social History: The Significance of the Police in American History." Pages 560–577 in *Policing and Crime Control, Part 2*, edited by E. H. Monkkonen. Westport, CT: Meckler.

Montgomery, D. 1987. *The Fall of the House of Labor.* Cambridge, MA: Cambridge University Press.

Moore, J. C., and C. P. Terret. 1999. "Highlights of the 1997 National Youth Gang Survey." *OJJDP Fact Sheet*, No. 97. Washington, DC: U.S. Department of Justice, Office of Justice Programs.

Moore, J. P., and C. P. Terrett. 1999. "Highlights of National Youth Gang Survey." *OJJP Fact Sheet*, March:1–4.

Moore, M. E. 1994. "Research Synthesis and Policy Implications." Pages 285–299 in *The Challenge of Community Policing*, edited by D. P. Rosenbaum. Thousand Oaks, CA: Sage.

Moore, Mark H. 1995. "Public Health and Criminal Justice Approaches to Prevention." Pages 237–262 in *Building a Safer Society: Strategic Approaches to Crime Prevention*, edited by Michael Tonry and David P. Farrington. Chicago: University of Chicago Press.

Moorehead, Caroline. 1999. *Dunant's Dream: War, Switzerland, and the History of the Red Cross.* St. Paul, MN: West Group.

Morales, E. 1989. *Cocaine—White Gold Rush in Peru.* Tucson: University of Arizona Press.

Moran, Nathan R. 2000. "The Netherlands: Policing Practices and Drug Policy." *Crime and Justice International*, 16(38):13–17.

Moran, Richard. 1981. *Knowing Right from Wrong: The Insanity Defense of Daniel McNaughton.* New York: Free Press.

Morash, Merry, Timothy S. Bynum, and Barbara A. Koons. 1998. *Women Offenders: Programming Needs and Promising Approaches.* Washington, DC: National Institute of Justice, U.S. Department of Justice.

Morash, Merry, Robin N. Haarr, and Lila Rucker. 1994. "A Comparison of Programming for Women and Men in U.S. Prisons in the 1980s." *Crime and Delinquency*, 40:197–221.

"More Than Sticky Fingers." 1988. *Psychology Today*, November:10.

Morgan, Kathryn. 1994. "Factors Associated with Probation Outcome." *Journal of Criminal Justice*, 22:341–353.

Morganthau, T. 1999. "Justice for Louima." *Newsweek*, June 8:42.

Morin, R., and C. Deane. 2002. "In Poll, Americans Back Security Agency." *The Washington Post*, June 11:A13.

Morris, Norval, and Michael Tonry. 1990. *Between Prison and Probation: Intermediate Punishments in a Rational Sentencing System.* New York: Oxford University Press.

Morrissey, M. C., R. C. Byrd, and E. A. Deitch. 1991. "The Incidence of Recurrent Penetrating Trauma in an Urban Trauma Center." *Journal of Trauma*, 31:1536–1538.

Moss, R. F. 1996. "TV Cop Shows Cop-Out on Race." *Commonwealth*, 123(19):12–13.

Mumola, Christopher J. 2000. *Incarcerated Parents and Their Children.* Washington, DC: Bureau of Justice Statistics, U.S. Department of Justice.

Munsterman, G. T., and J. T. Munsterman. 1986. "The Search for Jury Representativeness." *The Justice System Journal*, 11(1):59–78.

Myers, Martha A. 2000. "The Social World of America's Courts." Pages 447–471 in *Criminology: A Contemporary Handbook*, edited by Joseph F. Sheley. Belmont, CA: Wadsworth.

Nagin, Daniel S. 1998a. "Criminal Deterrence Research at the Outset of the Twenty-First Century." *Crime and Justice: A Review of Research*, 23:1–42.

Nagin, Daniel S. 1998b. "Deterrence and Incapacitation." Pages 345–368 in *The Handbook of Crime and Punishment*, edited by Michael Tonry. New York: Oxford University Press.

Naish, John. 2000. "Things That Go West in the Night." *The Times* (London), November 25:1.

Nardulli, Peter F., James Eisenstein, and Roy B. Flemming. 1988. *The Tenor of Justice: Criminal Courts and the Guilty Plea Process.* Urbana: University of Illinois Press.

Nasser, Haya El. 1995. "Crime-Weary Public Scoffs at 'Service' as Punishment." *USA Today*, July 6:6A.

Nathan, J. 1998. "Russia's Spiraling Nightmare." *USA Today Magazine*, March:19.

National Institute of Corrections. 1997. *Supermax Housing: A Survey of Current Practice.* Washington, DC: National Institute of Corrections, U.S. Department of Justice.

Neubauer, D. W. 1997. *Judicial Process—Law Courts and Politics in the United States.* Pacific Grove, CA: Brooks/Cole.

Neubauer, D. W. 1999. *America's Courts and the Criminal Justice System.* Belmont, CA: West/Wadsworth.

Newburn, Tim, and Elizabeth A. Stanko (eds.). 1994. *Just Boys Doing Business: Men, Masculinities and Crime.* London: Routledge.

Newman, Graeme. 1983. *Just and Painful: A Case for the Corporate Punishment of Criminals.* New York: Free Press.

Ng, W., and R. C. L. Lindsay. 1994. "Cross-Race Facial Recognition." *Journal of Cross-Cultural Psychology*, 25(4):217–232.

Nifong, C. 1997. "Dial 'M' to Stop Murders: Phone-Alert System Grows." *Christian Science Monitor*, September 24:1.

1999 Annual Report on Drug Use. 2000. Washington, DC: U.S. Department of Justice, Office of Justice Statistics.

Nolan, Martin F. 1995. "California Sees Prisons Filling as Colleges Decline." *The Boston Globe*, August 28:3.

Norway—Royal Ministry of Justice and the Police. 2001. Department of Justice and the Police, Department of Civil Affairs, Oslo, Norway.

O'Brien, Robert. 1985. *Crime and Victimization Data.* Beverly Hills: Sage.

O'Brien, Robert M. 2000. "Crime Facts: Victim and Offender Data." Pages 59–83 in *Criminology: A Contemporary Handbook*, edited by Joseph F. Sheley. Belmont: CA: Wadsworth.

O'Mara, J. J. 1972. "The Courts, Standard Jury Charges—Findings of Pilot Project." *Pennsylvania Bar Journal*, January:166–175.

One Nation: America Remembers September 11, 2001. 2001. Boston: Little, Brown.

Onishi, N. 1995. "Your Car, Sitting Duck." *New York Times*, March 19:CY10.

"On Your Bike." 1993. *The Economist*, October 10:28–29.

Orcutt, James D., and R. Faison. 1988. "Sex-Role Attitude Change and Reporting of Rape Victimization, 1973–1985." *Sociological Quarterly*, 29:589–604.

"Oregon City's Police Won't Aid FBI." 2001. *Los Angeles Times,* November 22:A34.

Orfield, M. W. 1987. "The Exclusionary Rule and Deterrence: An Empirical Study of Chicago Narcotics Officers." *University of Chicago Law Review,* 54(Summer):1016–1055.

Orr, D. A. 2000. "Weland v. State and the Battered Spouse Syndrome." *Florida Bar Journal,* 74(6):14–19.

Orwell, G. 1949. *Animal Farm.* New York: Harcourt, Brace and Jovanovich.

Osborne, D. R., D. Ellingworth, T. Hope, and A. Trickett. 1996. "Are Repeatedly Victimized Households Different?" *Journal of Quantitative Criminology,* 12(2):223–245.

Oster P. 1989. *The Mexicans: A Personal Portrait of a People.* New York: Harper & Row.

Ostrom, B. J., and R. A. Hanson. 2000. *Efficiency, Timeliness, and Quality: A New Perspective from Nine State Criminal Trials.* Washington, DC: U.S. Department of Justice, Office of Justice Programs, National Institute of Justice.

Ott, T. 1998. "Police Issue Fewer Tickets without 'Quotas.' " *Cleveland Plain Dealer,* October 17:1B.

Owen, Barbara. 1998. *"In the Mix": Struggle and Survival in a Women's Prison.* Albany: State University of New York Press.

Packer, Hérbert L. 1964. "Two Models of the Criminal Process." *University of Pennsylvania Law Review,* 113:1–68.

Padgett, T. 1998. "Laws of the Jungle." *Time,* January 12:58.

Palermo, G. B., M. A. White, L. A. Wasserman, and W. Hanrahan. 1996. "Plea Bargaining: Injustice for All?" *International Journal of Offender Therapy and Comparative Criminology,* 42(2):111–123.

"Panel Says Churches Are Still Targets." 1997. *New York Times,* June 9:A20.

Parent, Dale G., and Ronald P. Corbett, Jr. 1996. "Day Reporting Centers: An Evolving Intermediate Sanction." *Federal Probation,* 60:51–54.

"Parents Who Kill Their Children." 1995. *U.S. News & World Report,* May 5:14.

Parker, Karen F., and Patricia L. McCall. 1999. "Structural Conditions and Racial Homicide Patterns: A Look at the Multiple Disadvantages in Urban Areas." *Criminology,* 37:447–477.

Parker, Robert Nash, and Doreen Anderson-Facile. 2000. "Violent Crime Trends." Pages 191–213 in *Criminology: A Contemporary Handbook,* edited by Joseph F. Sheley. Belmont, CA: Wadsworth.

Parks, E. R. 1976. "From Constabulary to Police Society: Implications for Social Control." Pages 187–213 in *Whose Law What Order?* edited by W. J. Chambliss and M. Mankoffs. New York: Wiley.

Paternoster, Raymond. 1984. "Prosecutorial Discretion in Requesting the Death Penalty: A Case of Victim-Based Racial Discrimination." *Law & Society Review,* 18:437–478.

Peak, K. J. 1997. "African Americans and Policing." Pages 356–362 in *Critical Issues in Policing—Contemporary Readings,* edited by R. G. Dunham and G. P. Alpert. Prospect Heights, IL: Waveland Press.

Pease, K. 1992. "Preventing Burglary in a British Public Housing Estate." Pages 123–146 in *Situational Crime Prevention: Successful Case Studies,* edited by R. V. Clarke. New York: Harrow and Heston.

Pease, K. 1997. "Predicting the Future: The Role of Routine Activity and Rational Choice Theory." Pages 232–248 in *Rational Choice and Situational Crime Prevention: Theoretical Foundations,* edited by G. Newman, R. V. Clarke, and S. G. Shoham. Dartmouth, UK: Ashgate.

Pease, Ken. 1985. "Community Service Orders." Pages 51–94 in *Crime and Justice: An Annual Review of Research,* Volume 6, edited by Michael Tonry, and Norval Morris. Chicago: University of Chicago Press.

Pease, Kenneth (ed.). 1995. *Criminal Statistics: Their Use and Abuse.* Brookfield, VT: Dartmouth.

Pederson, D. 1997. "Go Get the Scumbags." *Newsweek,* October 20:32.

"People's Republic of China: The Death Penalty Log in 1998." 1998. Available: http://www.amnesty.org.ailib/aipub/1999/SUM/31705699.htm.

Pepinsky, Harold E., and Paul Jesilow. 1984. *Myths That Cause Crime.* Cabin John, MD: Seven Locks Press.

Perez, T. E. 2000. "External Governmental Mechanisms of Police Accountability: Three Investigative Structures." *Policing and Society,* 10(1):47–77.

Perez-Pena, Richard. 2000. "The Death Penalty: When There's No Room for Error." *New York Times,* February 13:WK3.

Perin, M. 1997. "Auto Theft: Costs Are High for Both Insurers and Victims." *Houston Business Journal.* Available: http:www.amcity/com.houston/stories/021797/focus1html.

Perkins, C. A. 1997. *Age Patterns of Victims of Serious Violent Crime.* Washington, DC: U.S. Department of Justice, Office of Justice Programs.

Petersilia, Joan. 1997. "Probation in the United States." *Crime and Justice: A Review of Research,* 22:149–200.

Petersilia, Joan. 1998. "Probation and Parole." Pages 563–588 in *The Handbook of Crime and Punishment,* edited by Michael Tonry. New York: Oxford University Press.

Petersilia, Joan. 1999. "Parole and Prisoner Reentry in the United States." *Crime and Justice: A Review of Research,* 26:479–529.

Petersilia, Joan. 2000a. "A Decade of Experimenting with Intermediate Sanctions: What Have We Learned." Pages 176–182 in *Annual Editions: Criminal Justice, 2000/2001,* edited by Joseph L. Victor. New York: Dushkin/McGraw-Hill.

Petersilia, Joan. 2000b. *When Prisoners Return to the Community: Political, Economic, and Social Consequences.* Washington, DC: National Institute of Justice, U.S. Department of Justice.

Petersilia, Joan, Peter Greenwood, and Martin Levin. 1978. *Criminal Careers of Habitual Felons.* Washington, DC: National Institute of Law Enforcement and Criminal Justice.

Petersilia, Joan, and Susan Turner. 1986. *Prison versus Probation in California: Implications for Crime and Offender Recidivism.* Santa Monica, CA: Rand Corporation.

Peterson, I. 1999. "Whitman Says Troopers Used Racial Profiling." *New York Times,* April 21:A1.

Petracca, M. J. 1996. "The Pedal-Pusher Patrol." *Women's Sport & Fitness,* 18(7):23.

Pfeifer, S. 2002. "Slain Teen Informant's Kin Settle for $1 Million." *Los Angeles Times,* August 27:B1.

"Philadelphia Police Recruitment." 1999. Available: http://www.lasalle.edu/philly/35-dist/recruit.htm.

Philliber, Susan. 1987. "Thy Brother's Keeper: A Review of the Literature on Correctional Officers." *Justice Quarterly,* 4:9–37.

Phillips, Amy K. 1997. "Thou Shall Not Kill Any Nice People: The Problem of Victim Impact Statements in Capital Sentencing." *American Criminal Law Review,* 35:93–118.

Platt, Anthony M. 1969. *The Child Savers: The Invention of Delinquency.* Chicago: University of Chicago Press.

Plungis, J. 2000. "Transportation Bill Conference Driven by National Drunken Driving Standard, Limitation of Truckers' Road Hours." *CQ Weekly,* August 5:1.

Podkopacz, Marcy Rasmussen. 1996. "The End of the Line: An Empirical Study of Judicial Waiver." *Journal of Criminal Law and Criminology,* 86:449–492.

"Police." 2000. Available: http://www.britannica.com.

"Police Claim Reverse Discrimination." 1996. *National Law Review,* 119(3):A8.

"Police Officer Recruitment." 2001. Available: http://www.ci.phoenix.az.us/POLICE/pdjob.html.

"Policing the Capital." 1998. *The Economist,* November 8:34.

"Policing the Cops." 1996. *The Economist,* May 11:26–27.

"Policing: The Sultans of Swat." 1999. *The Economist,* October 10:28.

Pollak, Otto. 1950. *The Criminality of Women.* Philadelphia: University of Pennsylvania Press.

Pollock, J. 1999. *Criminal Women.* Cincinnati, OH: Anderson.

Pollock, Joycelyn M. 1998. *Counseling Women in Prison.* Pacific Grove, CA: Brooks/Cole.

Pope, Carl, and Todd Clear. 1994. "Editors' Introduction." *Journal of Research in Crime and Delinquency,* 31:132–134.

Popenoe, David. 1996. *Life without Father: Compelling New Evidence That Fatherhood and Marriage Are Indispensable for the Good of Children and Society.* New York: Martin Kessler Books.

Pound, E. T., and B. Duffy. 2001. "The Ferrets and the Moles." *U.S. News & World Report,* September 10:30–32.

Pranis, K., and M. Umbreit. 1992. *Public Opinion Research Challenges Perception of Widespread Public Demand for Harsher Punishment.* Minneapolis: Citizens Council.

Pratt, Travis C., and Jeff Maahs. 1999. "Are Private Prisons More Cost-Effective Than Public Prisons? A Meta-Analysis of Evaluation Research Studies." *Crime and Delinquency,* 45:358–371.

Prendergast, Michael L., Jean Wellisch, and Gregory Falkin. 1997. "Assessment of and Services for Women Offenders in Community and Correctional Settings." Pages 318–326 in *Correctional Contexts: Contemporary and Classical Readings,* edited by James W. Marquart and Jonathan R. Sorensen. Los Angeles: Roxbury.

Prenzler, T. 1997. "Is There a Police Subculture?" *Australian Journal of Public Administration,* 56(4):47–56.

President's Task Force on Victims of Crime. 1982. Final Report. Washington, DC: U.S. Government Printing Office.

Prusher, I. R. 1997. "Worldwide Webs: Mafia's Reach Grows." *Christian Science Monitor,* October 8:2.

"Public Defenders." 1999. *The National Law Journal,* June 14:B15.

Public Health Reports. 1998. "Health Ranks Fifth on Local TV News." *Public Health Reports,* 113:296–297.

Purdy, Matthew. 2001. "Legal Powers Are Expanded in Bush Plan." *New York Times,* November 25:A1.

Quinn, J. F. 1983. "Outlaw Motorcycle Clubs: A Sociological Analysis." Master's thesis, University of Miami.

"Quote of the Day." 2002. *New York Times,* October 28:A1.

Rabinowtiz H. N. 1991. "The Conflict between Blacks and the Police in the Urban South, 1865–1900." Pages 237–256 in *The Colonies and the Early Republic,* edited by E. H. Monkkonen. New York: Meckler.

Radelat, A. 2002. "Ashcroft Likens WorldCom to Common Thieves." *Gannett News Service,* August 1:A1.

Rafter, Nicole Hahn. 1985. *Partial Justice: Women in State Prisons, 1800–1935.* Boston: Northeastern University Press.

Ralph, Paige H. 1997. "From Self-Preservation to Organized Crime: The Evolution of Inmate Gangs." Pages 182–186 in *Correctional Contexts: Contemporary and Classical Readings,* edited by James W. Marquart and Jonathan R. Sorensen. Los Angeles: Roxbury.

Ranalli, Ralph. 2000. "Debate Continues on Prison Alternative." *The Boston Globe,* May 7:B1.

"Rape and Sexual Assault." 1999. Available: http://www.ojp.usdoj.gov/ovc/ncvrw/1999/rape.htm.

Reaves, B. A. 1992. *Sheriff's Departments 1990.* Washington, DC: Department of Justice, Office of Justice Programs, Bureau of Justice Statistics.

Reaves, B. A. 1996. *Local Police Departments, 1993.* Washington, DC: U.S. Department of Justice, Office of Justice Statistics.

Reaves, B. A. 1998a. *Census of State and Local Law Enforcement Agencies, 1996.* Washington, DC: U.S. Department of Justice, Office of Justice Programs.

Reaves, B. A. 1998b. *Federal Law Enforcement Officers, 1996.* Washington, DC: U.S. Department of Justice, Office of Justice Programs.

Reaves, B. A., and A. L. Goldberg. 2000. *Local Police Departments, 1997.* Washington, DC: U.S. Department of Justice, Office of Justice Programs, Bureau of Justice Statistics.

Reaves, B. A., and J. Perez. 1994. *Pretrial Release of Felony Defendants, 1992.* Washington, DC: U.S. Department of Justice, Office of Justice Programs, U.S. Government Printing Office.

"Reforming Sao Paulo's Prison System: Tackle the Cause Not the Symptom." 2001. Available: http://amnesty.org.

Reichel, Philip L. 2001. *Corrections: Philosophies, Practices, and Procedures,* 2 ed. Boston: Allyn & Bacon.

Reid, A. 1998. "Metro Police Have Quotas, Are Writing More Tickets." *The Washington Post,* November 24:B6.

Reid, C. 2001. "Ramsey Case Cost Reaches $1.7M." *The Daily Camera,* December 18:A1.

Reiman, Jeffrey. 2001. *The Rich Get Richer and the Poor Get Prison: Ideology, Class, and Criminal Justice,* 6 ed. Boston: Allyn & Bacon.

Reiss, A. J. 1968. "Police Brutality—Answers to Key Questions." *Transaction,* 5(8):10–19.

Reitsma-Street, M. 1999. "Justice for Canadian Girls: A 1999's Update." *Canadian Journal of Criminology,* 41(3):335–363.

Reitz, Kevin R. 1998. "Sentencing." Pages 542–562 in *The Handbook of Crime and Punishment,* edited by Michael Tonry. New York: Oxford University Press.

Rennison, C. M. 1999. *Criminal Victimization 1998—Changes 1997–98 with Trends 1993–98.* Washington, DC: U.S. Department of Justice, Office of Justice Programs.

Rennison, C. M. 2001a. *Intimate Partner Violence and Age of Victim, 1993–1999.* Washington, DC: Bureau of Justice Statistics, U.S. Department of Justice.

Rennison, C. M. 2001b. *Criminal Victimization 2000: Changes 1999–2000 with Trends 1993–2000.* Washington, DC: Bureau of Justice Statistics, U.S. Department of Justice.

Rennison, Callie. 2002. *Criminal Victimization 2001: Changes 2000–01 with Trends 1993–2001.* Washington, DC: Bureau of Justice Statistics, U.S. Department of Justice.

Reno, Jamie, and Suzanne Smalley. 2001. "Using Students as Metal Detectors." *Newsweek,* March 19:28–30.

Renzetti, Claire M., and Lynne Goodstein (eds.). 2000. *Women, Crime, and Criminal Justice: Original Feminist Readings.* Los Angeles: Roxbury.

Report to the Nation on Crime and Justice. 1988. Washington, DC: U.S. Department of Justice, Bureau of Justice Statistics, U.S. Government Printing Office.

Reske, Henry J. 1995. "Prosecutor's Guilty Plea." *ABA Journal,* 91(8):32.

Reskin, B. F., and C. A. Visher. 1986. "The Impacts of Evidence and Extralegal Factors in Jurors' Decisions." *Law & Society Review,* 20(3):423–428.

Reynolds, H. 1986. *The Economics of Prostitution.* Springfield, IL: Charles C. Thomas.

Richardson, J. F. 1970. *The New York City Police: Colonial Times to 1901.* New York: Oxford University Press.

Richardson, J. F. 1974. "Corruption in the New York City Police Department." Pages 47–60 in *Police Corruption,* edited by L. W. Sherman. New York: Anchor Books.

Richardson, L. 1988. *The Dynamics of Sex and Gender: A Sociological Perspective.* 3d ed. New York: Harper & Row.

Richey, W., and K. Axtman. 2000. "Miranda Warning Survives." *Christian Science Monitor,* July 27:1.

Riding, A. 1989. *Distant Neighbors—A Portrait of the Mexicans.* New York: Vintage Books.

Rieber-Mohn, G. 1998. "The Dissolution of Core Values: Development of Crime and Society in Postwar Scandinavia with an Emphasis on Norwegian Circumstances." *Brigham Young University Law Review,* 4:1629–1643.

Riggs, D. S., and D. G. Kilpatrick. 1990. "Families and Friends—Indirect Victimization by Crime." Pages 120–138 in *Victims of Crime—Problems and Policies,* edited by A. J. Lurigio, W. G. Skogan, and R. C. Davis. Newbury Park, CA: Sage.

Riley, B. 1999. "2 Cops Lose in Appeal of Ticket Quota." *Newark Star-Ledger,* March 4:A1.

Riley, K. J., and B. Hoffman. 1995. *Domestic Terrorism: A National Assessment of State and Local Preparedness.* Santa Monica, CA: Rand.

Rimer, Sara. 2000. "Support for a Moratorium in Executions Gets Stronger." *New York Times,* October 31:A18.

Rimer, Sara. 2001. "Two Death-Row Inmates Exonerated in Louisiana." *New York Times,* January 6:A8.

Rimer, Sara, and Raymond Bonner. 2000. "Whether to Kill Those Who Killed as Youths." *New York Times,* August 22:A1.

Ritter, J. 2001. "From Big Cities to Rural Areas, the Costs Are Adding Up." *USA Today,* November 9:7A.

Roberg, R. R. 1994. "Can Today's Police Organizations Effectively Implement Community Policing?" Pages 249–257 in *The Challenge of Community Policing,* edited by D. P. Rosenbaum. Thousand Oaks, CA: Sage.

"Robert Philip Hanssen Espionage Case." 2001. Federal Bureau of Investigation. Available: www.fbi.gov/majcases/hanssen/hanssenmaj.html.

Roberts, Julian V. 1997. "The Role of Criminal Record in the Sentencing Process." *Crime and Justice: A Review of Research,* 22:303–362.

Robinson, Paul H. 2001. "Crime, Punishment, and Prevention." *The Public Interest,* Winter(142):61–71.

Roche, Timothy. 2002. "The Yates Odyssey." *Time,* January 28:42–50.

Rogers, P., and J. Campbell. 1999. "Lethal Force." *People,* April 19:54–59.

Rogers, Richard. 2000. *Conducting Insanity Evaluations.* New York: Guilford Press.

Rohrlich, T. 2001. "A Gap in Aviation Security." *Los Angeles Times,* November 5:A1.

Roncek, Dennis W., and Pamela A. Maier. 1991. "Bars, Blocks, and Crimes Revisited: Linking the Theory of Routine Activities to the Empiricism of 'Hot Spots'." *Criminology,* 29(4):725–753.

Rose, Dina R., and Todd R. Clear. 1998. "Incarceration, Social Capital, and Crime: Implications for Social Disorganization Theory." *Criminology,* 36:441–479.

Rosenberg, Irene Merker. 1993. "Leaving Bad Enough Alone: A Response to the Juvenile Court Abolitionists." *Wisconsin Law Review,* 1993:163–185.

Rosenfeld, Richard. 2000. "Patterns in Adult Homicide: 1980–1995." Pages 130–163 in *The Crime Drop in America,* edited by Alfred Blumstein and Joel Wallman. Cambridge: Cambridge University Press.

Rosenzweig, D. 2002. "No Charges in Tyisha Miller Case." *Los Angeles Times,* December 13:B1.

Rosoff, Stephen M., Henry N. Pontell, and Robert Tillman. 1998. *Profit without Honor: White Collar Crime and the Looting of America.* Upper Saddle River, NJ: Prentice-Hall.

Ross, H. L. 1984. "Social Control through Deterrence: Drinking and Driving Laws." Pages 21–35 in *Annual Review of Sociology,* edited by R. Turner and J. Short. Palo Alto, CA: Annual Reviews.

Rotella, S., and P. Gobbi. 2001. "8 Die, Thousands Held Hostage in Brazil Prison Riots." *Los Angeles Times,* February 19:A6.

Roth, A. 2002. "Experts Make Case for Defense Attorneys." *San Diego Union-Tribune,* September 22:A1.

Roth, Jeffrey A. 1994. *Psychoactive Substances and Violence.* Washington, DC: National Institute of Justice, U.S. Department of Justice.

Rothman, David J. 1995. "Perfecting the Prison: United States, 1789–1865." Pages 111–129 in *The Oxford History of the Prison: The Practice of Punishment in Western Society,* edited by Norval Morris and David J. Rothman. New York: Oxford University Press.

Rottman, D. B., C. R. Flango, M. T. Cantrell, R. Hansen, and N. LaFountain. 2000. *State Court Organization, 1998.* Washington, DC: U.S. Department of Justice, Office of the Justice Bureau, Bureau of Justice Statistics, U.S. Government Printing Office.

Rovella, D. E. 2000. "The Best Defense." *National Law Journal,* January, 22(3):A1-A2.

Rowe, P. 1999. "The Good Guys versus the Bad Guys versus the Mayor." *San Diego Union-Tribune,* August 3:E1.

Rubec, S. 2000. "Youth Doing More Time Than Adults: StatsCan." *The Toronto Star,* August 2:1.

Rubenstein, R. E. 1987. *Alchemists of Revolution: Terrorism in the Modern World.* New York: Basic Books.

Rubinstein, J. 1973. *City Police.* New York: Farrar, Strauss & Giroux.

Rudo, Z. H., and D. S. Powell. 1998. "The Effects of Violence in the Home on Children's Emotional, Behavioral, and Social Functioning: A Review of the Literature." *Journal of Emotional and Behavioral Disorders,* Summer:94–103.

"Rural Crime on the Rise." 2001. *Crime and Justice International,* April:11–12.

Russell, F. 1975. *A City in Terror.* New York: Viking Press.

Ryan, J. P., and J. J. Alfini. 1979. "Trial Judges' Participation in Plea Bargaining: An Empirical Perspective." *Law and Society Review,* 13(2):479–507.

Ryan, William. 1976. *Blaming the Victim,* revised ed. New York: Vintage Books.

Sack, K. 2001. "Focus on Terror Creates Burden for Police." *New York Times,* October 28:A1.

Safire, W. 2002. "Military Tribunals Modified." *New York Times,* March 21:A37.

Saks, M. J. 1996. "The Smaller the Jury, the Greater the Unpredictability." *Judicature,* 79(5):263–265.

Salama, M. M. 1982. "General Principles of Criminal Evidence in Islamic Societies." Pages 109–123 in *The Islamic Criminal Justice System,* edited by M. C. Bassiouni. London: Oceana.

Salkever, A. 1998. "Cities Compete for Cops to Fill Out Ranks." *Christian Science Monitor,* December 1:1.

Saltzburg, S. A., and D. J. Capra. 1992. *American Criminal Procedure—Cases and Commentaries.* St. Paul, MN: West Group.

Samaha, J. 1990. *Criminal Procedure.* St. Paul, MN: West Group.

Samborn, Randall. 1994. "Opinion Divided on Rape Shield; Fractious Appeals Ruling." *The National Law Journal,* January 24:13.

Sampson, Robert J. 1997. "Neighborhoods and Violent Crime: A Multilevel Study of Collective Efficacy." *Science,* 277(August 15):918–924.

Sampson, Robert J., and William Julius Wilson. 1995. "Toward a Theory of Race, Crime, and Urban Inequality." Pages 37–54 in *Crime and Inequality,* edited by John Hagan and Ruth D. Peterson. Stanford: Stanford University Press.

Sanad, Nagaty. 1991. *The Theory of Crime and Criminal Responsibility in Islamic Law: Shari'a.* Chicago: Office of International Criminal Justice, University of Illinois.

Sanborn, J. B. 1986. "A Historical Sketch of Plea Bargaining." *Justice Quarterly,* 3(2):111–138.

Sanders, W. B. 1983. *Criminology.* Reading, MA: Addison-Wesley.

Sands, A. 2001a. "Writer Jailed for 'His' Imagination." *The Ottawa Citizen,* January 8:D1.

Sands, A. 2001b. "U.S. Shooting a Vindication: OPP Officer." *The Ottawa Citizen,* March 8:A5.

Santobello v. New York. 2002. Available: http://www.caselaw.findlaw.

Sanz, C., and J. Hermes. 1995. "A Killer in Blue." *People,* October 10:131–134.

Sapp, A. 1994. "Sexual Misconduct by Police Officers." Pages 187–200 in *Police Deviance,* edited by T. Barker and D. L. Carter. Cincinnati: Anderson.

Sapsted, David. 2001. "DIY Police to Fight Rural Crime." *The Daily Telegraph,* May 24:1.

Sass, T. R., and J. L. Troyer. 1999. "Affirmative Action, Political Representation, Unions, and Female Police Employment." *Journal of Labor Research,* 20(4):571–577.

Schafer, S. 1968. *The Victim and His Criminal.* New York: Random House.

Scheer, R. 2001. "Liberty Dying, Liberal by Liberal." *Los Angeles Times,* November 20:B13.

Scheflin, A. W., and J. M. Van Dyke. 1995. "Merciful Juries—The Resilience of Jury Nullification." Pages 256–285 in *Courts and Justice—A Reader,* edited by G. Larry Mays and P. R. Gregware. Prospect Heights, IL: Waveland Press.

Scherer, R. 1999. "When Does the Police Mistake Become Murder?" *Christian Science Monitor,* March 5:1.

Scherer, R. 2002. "Police Mobilize to Support NYC Peers." *Christian Science Monitor,* January 11:1.

Schiraldi, V. 1999. "Making Sense of Juvenile Homicides in America." Available: http://www.findarticles.com.

Schlosser, Eric. 1998. "The Prison-Industrial Complex." *The Atlantic Monthly,* December:51–77.

Schmid, A. P., and A. J. Jongman. 1988. *Political Terrorism.* Amsterdam: North Holland Publishing.

Schmidt, J., and E. H. Steury. 1989. "Prosecutorial Discretion in Filing Charges in Domestic Violence Cases." *Criminology,* 27(3):487–510.

Schoeberger, K. 1989. "Legal Trap for Japanese." *Los Angeles Times,* April 28:A1.

Schreck, Christopher J. 1999. "Criminal Victimization and Low Self-Control: An Extension and Test of a General Theory of Crime." *Justice Quarterly,* 16:633–654.

Schweigert, F. J. 1999. "Moral Education in Victim Offender Conferencing." *Criminal Justice and Ethics,* 18(2):29–40.

Sciala, J. 1999. *Federal Pretrial Release and Detention, 1996.* Washington, DC: U.S. Department of Justice, Office of Justice Programs, U.S. Government Printing Office.

Scott, D. C. 1992. "Mexico City Police Strike over Corruption in Ranks." *Christian Science Monitor,* March 16:3.

Scruggs, K. 1994. "Among Police, New Chief Is Liked but Not Feared." *The Atlanta Journal and Constitution,* October 27:E1.

Sealey, G. 2002. "Confused Confessions." *abcNEWS.com,* September 25:1–4.

Sebastian, M. 2001. "Jury's Findings Still Secret." *The Daily Camera,* December 17:A1.

Sederberg, P. C. 1998. "Explaining Terrrorism." Pages 24–26 in *Violence and Terror,* edited by B. Schechterman and M. Slann. Guilford, CT: Greenwood.

Segrave, K. 1995. *Policewomen—A History.* Jefferson, NC: McFarland & Company.

Selcraig, Bruce. 2000. "Camp Fear." *Mother Jones,* November/December:64–71.

Sennott, Charles M. 1994. "Prison's Hidden Horror." *The Boston Globe,* May 1:1.

The Sentencing Project. 2001. *Drug Policy and the Criminal Justice System.* Washington, DC: The Sentencing Project.

The Sentencing Project. 2003. *Facts about Prisons and Prisoners.* Washington, DC: The Sentencing Project.

Serrano, R. A. 2001. "Detainee Caught in Backwash of Sept.11." *Los Angeles Times,* November 19:A1.

"Seven Years after Tiananmen, Repression Continues Unabated." 1996. Available: http://www.amnesty.org/news/1996/31705896.htm.

Sexton, J., and N. Brandt. 1986. *How Free Are We? What the Constitution Says We Can and Cannot Do.* New York: M. Evans.

Shafritz, J. M., E. F. Gibons, and G. E. J. Scott. 1991. *Almanac of Modern Terrorism.* New York: Facts on File.

Shannon, Lyle W. 1988. *Criminal Career Continuity: Its Social Context.* New York: Human Sciences Press.

Shapiro, B. 1997. "Victims and Vengeance." *Nation,* 264(5):11–16.

Sharkey, J. 1997. "Slamming the Breaks on Hot Pursuit." *New York Times,* December 14:D3.

Shaw, Malcolm N. 1997. *International Law,* 4 ed. Cambridge, Eng.: Cambridge University Press.

Shelden, Randall G. 2001. *Controlling the Dangerous Classes: A Critical Introduction to the History of Criminal Justice.* Boston: Allyn & Bacon.

Shelden, Randall G. 1982. *Criminal Justice in America: A Sociological Approach.* Boston: Little, Brown.

Sheley, Joseph F., and C. D. Ashkins. 1981. "Crime, Crime News, and Crime Views." *Public Opinion Quarterly,* 45:492–506.

Shenon, P. 2002. "Ex-FBI Agent Says Lax Security Made It Easy to Sell Secrets." *San Diego Union-Tribune,* April 5:A3.

"Sheriffs' Departments, 1997: Executive Summary." 1999. Washington, DC: U.S. Department of Justice, Office of Justice Programs.

Sherman, L. W. 1974a. "Narcotics and the Police in New York." Pages 125–145 in *Police Corruption,* edited by L. W. Sherman. New York: Anchor Books.

Sherman, L. W. 1974b. "Becoming Bent: Moral Careers of Police Officers." Pages 191–209 in *Police Corruption,* edited by L. W. Sherman. New York: Anchor Books.

Sherman, L. W. 1974c. "Introduction: Toward a Sociological Theory of Police Corruption." Pages 1–39 in *Police Corruption,* edited by L. W. Sherman. New York: Anchor Books.

Sherman, L. W., P. R. Gartin, and M. E. Buerger. 1989. "Hot Spots of Predatory Activities and the Criminology of Place." *Criminology,* 27(1):27–55.

Sherman, Lawrence W. 1990. "Police Crackdowns: Initial and Residual Deterrence." Pages 1–48 in *Crime and Justice: A Review of Research,* volume 12, edited by Michael Tonry and Norval Morris. Chicago: University of Chicago Press.

Sherman, Lawrence W., Denise C. Gottfredson, Doris L. MacKenzie, John Eck, Peter Reuter, and Shawn D. Bushaway. 1998. *Preventing Crime: What Works, What Doesn't, What's Promising.* Washington, DC: Office of Justice Programs, National Institute of Justice.

Shichor, David. 1995. *Punishment for Profit: Private Prisons/Public Concerns.* Thousand Oaks, CA: Sage.

Shichor, David, and Dale K. Sechrest (eds.). 1996. *Three Strikes and You're Out: Vengeance as Public Policy.* Thousand Oaks, CA: Sage.

Shinkai, Hiroyuki, and Ugljesa Zvekic. 1999. "Punishment." Pages 89–119 in *Global Report on Crime and Justice,* edited by Graeme Newman. New York: Oxford University Press.

Shover, N. 1973. "The Social Organization of Burglary." *Social Problems,* 20:499–514.

"Shrining Courtrooms." 1995. *Psychology Today,* March/April 28(2):20.

Siegel, L. J. 1998. *Criminology,* 6 ed. Belmont, CA: West/Wadsworth.

Simon, David R. 2002. *Elite Deviance,* 7 ed. Boston: Allyn & Bacon.

Simon, J. D. 2001. "Biological Terrorism: Preparing to Meet the Threat." *Journal of the American Medical Association,* 278(5):428–430.

Simon, R. J. 1975. *The Jury System in America.* Beverly Hills, CA: Sage.

Simon, R. J. 1992. "Jury Nullification, or Prejudice and Ignorance in the Marion Barry Trial?" *Journal of Criminal Law,* 20:261–266.

Simon, Rita James. 1975. *Women and Crime.* Lexington, MA: Lexington Books.

Simon, S. 2001. "Local Chiefs Want U.S. to Tell More on Safety Plans." *Los Angeles Times,* November 23:A1.

Simon, S. 2002. "Judges Push for Abused to Follow the Law." *Los Angeles Times,* January 22:A12.

Simpson, Sally S., Anthony R. Harris, and Brian A. Mattson. 1995. "Measuring Corporate Crime." Pages 115–140 in *Understanding Corporate Criminality,* edited by Michael B. Blankenship. New York: Garland Publishing.

Sims, D. W., B. A. Divins, F. N. Obeid, M. H. Horst, V. J. Sorenson, and J. J. Faith. 1989. "Urban Trauma: A Chronic Recurrent Disease." *Journal of Trauma,* 29:940–946.

Singer, Rena. 2001. "The Double-Edged Sword of Nigeria's Sharia." *Christian Science Monitor,* February 22:1.

Singer, Simon, and David McDowall. 1988. "Criminalizing Delinquency: The Deterrent Effects of the New York Juvenile Offender Law." *Law and Society Review,* 22:521–535.

Sink, L. 2001. "Terrorism Gives Hate Groups an Opportunity to Recruit." *Milwaukee Journal Sentinel,* November 19:B1.

Skolnick, Jerome H. 1968. "Coercion to Virtue: The Enforcement of Morals." *Southern California Law Review,* 41: 588–641.

Skolnick Jerome H. 1985. "Deception by Police." Pages 75–98 in *Moral Issues in Police Work,* edited by F. A. Elliston and M. Feldberg. Totowa, NJ: Rowman and Allanheld.

Skolnick, Jerome H. 1994. *Justice without Trial: Law Enforcement in a Democratic Society,* 3 ed. New York: Macmillan.

Skolnick, J., and J. Fyfe. 1993. *Above the Law: Police and the Use of Excessive Force.* New York: Free Press.

Slater, D. 1998. "Black Russians." *National Review,* 50(24):28–29.

Slevin, Peter. 2001. "Management Woes, Loss of Business Noted." *The Washington Post,* February 18:A03.

Small, D. I. 1999. *Going to Trial—A Step-by-Step Guide to Trial Practice and Procedure.* Chicago: American Bar Association.

Smith, B. L. 1994. *Terrorism in America: Pipe Bombs and Pipe Dreams.* Albany: State University of New York Press.

Smith, C. E. 1997. *Courts, Politics, and the Judicial Process.* Chicago: Nelson-Hall.

Smith, C. S. 2001a. "China's Efforts against Crime Make No Dent." *New York Times,* December 26:A1.

Smith, C. S. 2001b. "Wave of Executions Continues as China Battles Corruption." *San Diego Union-Tribune,* March 3:A19.

Smith, D., and J. Gray. 1985. *Police and People in London: PSI Report.* London: Aldershot Grower Company.

Smith, Douglas A. 1986. "The Neighborhood Context of Police Behavior." Pages 313–341 in *Communities and Crime,* edited by Albert J. Reiss, Jr., and Michael Tonry. Chicago: University of Chicago Press.

Smith, Douglas A., Christy A. Visher, and Laura A. Davidson. 1984. "Equity and Discretionary Justice: The Influence of Race on Police Arrest Decisions." *Journal of Criminal Law and Criminology,* 75:234–249.

Smith, M. 1993. "Region in Brief—Florida Seeks Aid on Tourist Attacks." *The Atlanta Journal and Constitution,* April 6:A3.

Smith, M. Dwayne. 2000. "Capital Punishment in America." Pages 621–643 in *Criminology: A Contemporary Handbook,* edited by Joseph F. Sheley. Belmont, CA: Wadsworth.

Smith, R. 2002. "The Economy: Fastow, Former Enron Officer, Indicted by U.S." *Wall Street Journal,* November 1:A2.

Smith, R. M. 2001. "With Justice for Some, Not All?" *Christian Science Monitor,* November 20:9.

Smith, S., and C. J. DeFrances. 1996. *Indigent Defense.* Washington, DC: U.S. Department of Justice, Office of Justice Programs, U.S. Government Printing Office.

Snell, Tracy L. 2001. *Capital Punishment 2000.* Washington, DC: Bureau of Justice Statistics, U.S. Department of Justice.

Snyder, H. H., M. Sickmund, and E. Poe-Yamagata. 1996. *Juvenile Offenders and Victims: 1996 Update on Violence.* Pittsburgh: National Center on Juvenile Justice.

Snyder, Howard. 2002. *Juvenile Arrests 2000.* Washington, DC: Office of Juvenile Justice and Delinquency Prevention.

Snyder, Howard, and Melissa Sickmund. 1999. *Juvenile Offenders and Victims: 1999 National Report.* Washington, DC: Office of Juvenile Justice and Delinquency Prevention.

Sommers, I., and D. R. Baskin. 1993. "The Situational Context of Violent Female Offending." *Journal of Research in Crime and Delinquency,* 30(2):136–162.

Sorensen, Jon, and Donald H. Wallace. 1999. "Prosecutorial Discretion in Seeking Death: An Analysis of Racial Disparity in the Pretrial Stages of Case Processing in a Midwestern County." *Justice Quarterly,* 16:559–578.

Sorenson, S. B., J. G. Manz, and R. Berk. 1998. "News Media Coverage and the Epidemiology of Homicide." *American Journal of Public Health,* 88:1510–1514.

Souryal, Sam S., Abdullah I. Alobied, and Dennis W. Potts. 1994. "The Penalty of Hand Amputation for Theft in Islamic Justice." *Journal of Criminal Justice,* 22:249–265.

Spaans, E. C. 1998. "Community Service in the Netherlands: Its Effects on Recidivism and Net-Widening." *International Criminal Justice Review,* 8:1–14.

Spaid, E. L. 1997. "Jurors and Judges Up the Penalties for Driving While Drunk." *Christian Science Monitor,* May 5:4.

Spelman, William. 2000. "The Limited Importance of Prison Expansion." Pages 97–129 in *The Crime Drop in America,* edited by Alfred Blumstein and Joel Wallman. Cambridge: Cambridge University Press.

Spencer, C. 2001. "New Police Chief Is among Few Women Commanders Nationwide." Associate Press State and Local Wire Service. Available: http://web.lexis-nexis.com/universe/docu.

Spencer, Cassie C. 1987. "Sexual Assault: The Second Victimization." Pages 54–73 in *Women, the Courts, and Equality,* edited by Laura L. Crites and Winifred L. Hepperle. Newbury Park, CA: Sage.

Spohn, C. 1990a. "Decision Making in Sexual Assault Cases: Do Black and Female Judges Make a Difference?" *Women and Criminal Justice,* 2:83–105.

Spohn, C. 1990b. "The Sentencing of Black and White Judges: Expected and Unexpected Similarities." *Law and Society Review,* 24:1197–1216.

"The Spy in the FBI." 2001. *National Public Radio.* Available: www.npr.org/programs/ . . . res/2001/dec/hanssen/011217.hanssen.html.

Stalkever, A. 1998. "Cities Compete for Cops to Fill Out Ranks." *Christian Science Monitor,* December 1:1.

Stark, Rodney. 1987. "Deviant Places: A Theory of the Ecology of Crime." *Criminology,* 25:893–911.

Starr, V. H., and M. McCormick. 1993. *Jury Selection—An Attorney's Guide to Jury Law and Methods.* Boston: Little, Brown.

Starr, V. Hale (ed.). 1994. *Jury Selection: Sample Voir Dire Questions.* Boston: Little, Brown.

State Court Organization, 1998. 1998. Washington, DC: Bureau of Justice Statistics, U.S. Department of Justice.

Statistics, Bureau of Justice. 2002. *Criminal Victimization in the United States, 1999: Statistical Tables.* Washington, DC: Bureau of Justice Statistics, U.S. Department of Justice. Available: http://www.ojp.usdoj.gov/bjs/pub/pdf/cvus9902.pdf.

Stead, J. 1983. *The Police of France.* New York: Macmillan.

Steffensmeier, Darrell. 1980. "Sex Differences in Patterns of Adult Crime, 1965–77: A Review and Assessment." *Social Forces,* 58:1080–1108.

Steffensmeier, Darrell, and Emilie Allan. 2000. "Looking for Patterns: Gender, Age, and Crime." Pages 85–127 in *Criminology: A Contemporary Handbook,* edited by Joseph F. Sheley. Belmont, CA: Wadsworth.

Steffensmeier, Darrell, and Miles D. Harer. 1999. "Making Sense of Recent U.S. Crime Trends, 1980 to 1996/1998: Age Composition Effects and Other Explanations." *Journal of Research in Crime and Delinquency* 36:235–274.

Steffensmeier, Darrell, and C. Hebert. 1999. "Women and Men Policymakers: Does the Judge's Gender Affect the Sentencing of Criminal Defendants?" *Social Forces,* 77(3):1163–1196.

Steffensmeier, Darrell, John Kramer, and Cathy Streifel. 1993. "Gender and Imprisonment Decisions." *Criminology,* 31(3):411–446.

Steffensmeier, Darrell, Jeffery Ulmer, and John Kramer. 1998. "The Interaction of Race, Gender, and Age in Criminal Sentencing: The Punishment Cost of Being Young, Black, and Male." *Criminology,* 36:763–797.

Steinberg, A. 1989. *The Transformation of Criminal Justice: Philadelphia, 1800–1880.* Chapel Hill: The University of North Carolina Press.

Steinhoff, P. G. 1993. "Pursuing the Japanese Police." *Law & Society Review,* 27(5):827–850.

Stephan, James J. 2001. *Census of Jails, 1999.* Washington, DC: Bureau of Justice Statistics, U.S. Department of Justice.

Stetz, M., and K. Thornton. 1999. "Cops to Collect Traffic-Stop Racial Data." *San Diego Union-Tribune,* February 5:A1.

Steury, E. H., and N. Frank. 1996. *Criminal Court Process.* Minneapolis, MN: West.

Stewart, J. Y. 2001. "Lest Hate Crime Be Forgotten." *Los Angeles Times,* January 25:A1.

Stitt, B. G., and R. H. Chaires. 1993. "Plea Bargaining: Ethical Issues and Emerging Perspectives." *Justice Professional,* 7(2):69–91.

Stodghill, R. 2002. "True Confession of the Central Park Rapist." *Time,* December 16:5.

Stolberg, Sheryl Gay. 2001. "Behind Bars, New Effort to Care for the Dying." *New York Times,* April 1:A1.

Stolzenberg, Lisa, and Stewart J. D'Alessio. 1994. "Sentencing and Unwarranted Disparity: An Empirical Assessment of the Long-Term Impact of Sentencing Guidelines in Minnesota." *Criminology,* 32(2):301–310.

Stop Prisoner Rape. 2001. Prisoner Rape: Fact Sheet. Fort Bragg, CA. Available: http://www.igc.org/spr/sections/about.html.

Storm, John P. 1997. "What United States Probation Officers Do." *Federal Probation,* 61:13–18.

Stout, K. D., and P. Brown. 1995. "Legal and Social Differences between Men and Women Who Kill Intimate Partners." *Affilia: Journal of Women and Social Work,* 10 (2):194–205.

Strauss, M. A., and R. Gelles. 1990. "How Violent Are American Families? Estimates from the National Family Violence Resurvey and Other Studies." Pages 256–263 in *Physical Violence in American Families: Risk Factors and Adaptations to Violence in 8,145 Families,* edited by M. A. Strauss and R. J. Gelles. New Brunswick, NJ: Transaction.

Strawn, D. U., and R. W. Buchanan. 1976. "Jury Confusion: A Threat to Justice." *Judicature,* 59(10):478–483.

Streib, Victor L. 2001. "The Juvenile Death Penalty Today: Death Sentences and Executions for Juvenile Crimes, January 1, 1973–December 31, 2000." Available: http://www.law.onu.edu/faculty/streib/juvdeath.htm.

Struckman-Johnson, Cindy, and David Struckman-Johnson. 2000. "Sexual Coercion Rates in Seven Midwestern Prison Facilities for Men." *The Prison Journal,* 80:379–390.

Struckman-Johnson, Cindy J., David L. Struckman-Johnson, L. Rucker, K. Bumby, and S. Donaldson. 1996. "Sexual Coercion Reported by Men and Women in Prison." *Journal of Sex Research,* 33:67–76.

"Study Criticizes Community Policing." 1991. *New York Times,* August 7:B2.

Stumpf, H. P. 1988. *American Judicial Politics.* San Diego: Harcourt, Brace and Jovanovich.

Sudetic, C. 1996. "Gay and Lesbian Officers Suing Police for Bias." *New York Times,* April 4:B7.

Sudnow, D. 1965. "Normal Crimes—Sociological Features of the Penal Code in a Public Defender Office." *Social Problems,* Winter:255–276.

"The Sultans of Swat." 1999. *The Economist,* October 2:28–29.

Surette, Ray. 1998. *Media, Crime, and Criminal Justice: Images and Realities,* 2 ed. Belmont, CA: Wadsworth.

Surrency, E. C. 1967. "The Courts in the American Colonies." *American Journal of Legal History,* 11:253–376.

Sutherland, E. 1947. *Principles of Criminology.* Chicago: J. B. Lippincott.

Sutherland, E. H., and D. R. Cressey. 1970. *Criminology.* Philadelphia: Lippincott.

Sutherland, Edwin H. 1939. *Principles of Criminology,* 3 ed. Philadelphia: Lippincott.

Sykes, G., and G. Matza. 1957. "Techniques of Neutralization: A Theory of Delinquency." *American Sociological Review,* 22:664–670.

Sykes, G. M., and D. Matza. 1970. "Techniques of Neutralization: A Theory of Delinquency." *American Sociological Review,* 22:664–670.

Sykes, Gresham M. 1958. *The Society of Captives: A Study of a Maximum Security Prison.* Princeton: Princeton University Press.

Symonds, M. 1975. "The Accidental Victim of Violent Crime." Pages 176–185 in *Violence and Victims,* edited by S. A. Pasternak. New York: Spectrum.

Tak, Peter J. P. 1995. "Sentencing and Punishment in the Netherlands." Pages 194–200 in *Sentencing Reform in Overcrowded Times: A Comparative Perspective,* edited by Michael Tonry and Kathleen Hatlestad. New York: Oxford University Press.

"Targeting Gangs and Violent Juveniles." 2001. Washington, DC: U.S. Department of Justice. Available: http://www.usdoj.gov/ag/anti-gang.htm.

Taxman, Faye S., and James Byrne. 1994. "Locating Absconders: Results from a Randomized Field Experiment." *Federal Probation,* 58:13–23.

Taylor, C. S. 1990. "Gang Imperialism." Pages 69–76 in *Gangs in America,* edited by C. R. Huff. Newbury Park, CA: Sage.

Tennessee v. Garner. 2001. Available: http://www.aclumontana.org/rights/garner/html.

Terry v. Ohio. 2001. Legal Information Institute. Available: http://suspct/law.cornell.edu.

"Testing and Selection Process." 1999. Available: http://www.sannet.gov/police/career/selection.shtm.

Tewksbury, Richard A. 1997. *Introduction to Corrections,* 3 ed. New York: McGraw-Hill.

Texas Lawyer. 2002. "Is It a Sign?" *Texas Lawyer,* 18(1) March 11:1.

"37 from Falun Gong Sentenced to Prison." 2001. *San Diego Union-Tribune,* March 3:A19.

Thomas, Cathy Booth, and Hilary Hylton. 2001. "A New Scarlet Letter." *Time,* June 11:82.

Thomas, Evan. 2001. "A Long, Strange Trip to the Taliban." *Newsweek,* December 17:30–36.

Thomas, G. C., III, 1996a. "Is Miranda a Real-World Failure? A Plea for More and Better Empirical Evidence." *UCLA Law Review,* 43(February):821–857.

Thomas, G. C. 1996b. "Plain Talk about the Miranda Debate: A 'Steady-State' Theory of Confessions." *UCLA Law Review,* 43(February):933–959.

Thomas, P. 1995. "Murder's Frightful New Face." *The Washington Post National Weekly Edition,* November:20–26.

Thomas, William I., and Dorothy Swaine Thomas. 1928. *The Child in America: Behavior Problems and Programs.* New York: Knopf.

Thornton, K. 1996. "Bad-Cop Investigation Soaring, and Maybe That's Good." *San Diego Union-Tribune,* June 17:A1.

Thornton, K. 1999. "Tragedy Stirs Debate over Police Pursuits." *San Diego Union-Tribune,* February 27:A1.

Thornton, K., and R. Huard. 1999. "Chief Gets the Word, Won't Stint Burglars." *San Diego Union-Tribune,* July 28:A1.

"Three Former Tyco Executives Charged with Looting $600 Million from Firm." *New York Daily News,* A1.

Thurman, Q. C., and A. Giacomazzi. 1993. "Research Note: Cops, Kids, and Community Policing—An Assessment of a

Community Policing Demonstration Project." *Crime and Delinquency,* 39(4):554–565.

Tillman, Robert, and Henry N. Pontell. 1992. "Is Justice 'Collar-Blind'?: Punishing Medicaid Provider Fraud." *Criminology,* 30(4):547–573.

Tipp, Stacey L. (ed.). 1991. *America's Prisons: Opposing Viewpoints,* 5 ed. San Diego, CA: Greenhaven Press.

Tittle, Charles R., and Robert F. Meier. 1990. "Specifying the SES/Delinquency Relationship." *Criminology,* 28:271–299.

Tjaden, Patricia, and Nancy Thoennes. 1998, April. "Stalking in America: Findings from the National Violence against Women Survey." Atlanta: National Institute of Justice Centers for Disease Control and Prevention Research Brief.

Tjaden, Patricia, and Nancy Thoennes. 2000. *Full Report of the Prevalence, Incidence, and Consequences of Violence against Women.* Washington, DC: National Institute of Justice and the Centers for Disease Control and Prevention.

Toch, H. 1996. "The Violence-Prone Police Officer." Pages 94–112 in *Police Violence,* edited by W. A. Geller and H. Toch. New Haven, CT: Yale University Press.

Toch, Hans. 1993. *Living in Prison: The Ecology of Survival.* Hyattsville, MD: American Psychological Association.

Tonry, Michael. 1994. *Malign Neglect: Race, Crime, and Punishment in America.* New York: Oxford University Press.

Tonry, Michael. 1996. *Sentencing Matters.* New York: Oxford University Press.

Tonry, Michael. 1998a. "Crime and Punishment in America." Pages 3–27 in *The Handbook of Crime and Punishment,* edited by Michael Tonry. New York: Oxford University Press.

Tonry, Michael. 1998b. "Intermediate Sanctions." Pages 683–711 in *The Handbook of Crime and Punishment,* edited by Michael Tonry. New York: Oxford University Press.

Tonry, Michael. 1998c. "Intermediate Sanctions in Sentencing Guidelines." *Crime and Justice: A Review of Research,* 23:199–253.

Tonry, Michael, and David P. Farrington (eds.). 1995. *Building a Safer Society: Strategic Approaches to Crime Prevention.* Chicago: University of Chicago Press.

"Too Poor to Be Defended." 1998. *The Economist,* April 11:36–37.

Torres, D. A. 1987. *Handbook of State Police, Highway Patrols, and Investigative Agencies.* New York: Greenwood Press.

Tracey, Paul E., Jr., Marvin E. Wolfgang, and Robert M. Figlio. 1990. *Delinquency Careers in Two Birth Cohorts.* New York: Plenum Press.

"Traffic Detainee Need Not Be Advised That Traffic Stop Is over Before Officer Requests Consent to Search; Court Adopts Rationale Urged in Amicus Curae Brief Filed by LELP Publisher." 1999. *Recent Court Decisions.* Available: http://www.xnet.com./~lelp/recent/ohio.htm.

Trasler, G. 1986. "Situational Crime Control and Rational Choice: A Critique." Pages 17–24 in *Situational Crime Prevention: From Theory to Practice,* edited by K. Heal and G. Laycock. London: Home Office Research and Planning Unit, Her Majesty's Stationery Office.

Travis, J. 1996. "NIJ Director Emphasizes Community Policing in Keynote Address." *Corrections Today,* 58(4):112–114.

"The Tricky Business" 2001. *The Economist,* October 20:31.

Truszkowska, Natalia. 2001. "Irreligious Police: Women's Rights in Saudi Arabia." *Harvard International Review,* 23(2):10–11.

Tuller, Roger H. 2001. *"Let No Guilty Man Escape": A Judicial Biography of "Hanging Judge" Isaac C. Parker.* Norman, OK: University of Oklahoma Press.

Tunnell, Kenneth D. 1996. "Let's Do It: Deciding to Commit a Crime." Pages 246–258 in *New Perspectives in Criminology,* edited by John E. Conklin. Boston: Allyn & Bacon.

Turner, Michael G., Judy L. Sundt, Brandon K. Applegate, and Francis T. Cullen. 1995. "Three Strikes and You're Out: A

National Assessment." *Federal Probation,* 59(September):16–35.

Tynan, T. 2002. "Medical Improvements Lower Homicide Rate." *The Washington Post,* August 12:A2.

Tyrangiel, Josh, Karen Tumulty, Sally Donnelly, Laura A. Locke, and Alex Perry. 2001. "The Taliban Next Door." *Time,* December 17:36–38.

Tyson, A. 1996. "Moves to Police: The Police Are Gaining Ground." *Christian Science Monitor,* November 13:4.

Ueno, H. 1994. "Police in Japan." Pages 231–284 in *Police Practices—An International Review,* edited by D. K. Das. Metuchen, NJ: Scarecrow Press.

Ulmer, J. T. 1994. "Trial Judges in a Rural Court Community." *Journal of Contemporary Ethnography,* 23(1):79–108.

Ulmer, Jeffery T., and John H. Kramer. 1996. "Court Communities under Sentencing Guidelines: Dilemmas of Formal Rationality and Sentencing Disparity." *Criminology,* 34:383–407.

Umbreit, M. 1994. *Victim Meets Offender: The Impact of Restorative Justice and Mediation.* Monsey, NY: Criminal Justice Press.

Umbreit, M. 1998. "Restorative Justice through Victim-Offender Mediation: A Multi-Site Assessment." *Western Criminology Review.* Available: http://wcr.sonoma.edu/v1n1/umbreit.html.

"Understanding the Federal Courts." 1999. Federal Court Home Page. Available: www.uscourts.gov/about/html.

Uniform Crime Reports, 1995—Crime in the United States. 1996. Washington, DC: U.S. Government Printing Office.

Urbonya, K. R. 1997. "The Fishing Gets Easier." *American Bar Association Journal,* 83(January):46–47.

"U.S. Asked to Intervene to Protect Falun Gong's Rights." 1999. Available: http://amnesty.org/hrw/press/1999/jul/china2207.htm.

"U.S. Called Capital of Gun Deaths." 1997. *Los Angeles Times,* February 7:A14.

U.S. Department of Justice. 1999. Available: http://www.fbi.gov/presserl/police.htm.

"U.S. Jury Finds Louise Guilty of Second Degree Murder." 1997. Available: http://news6.thdo.bbc.co.uk.

U.S. Sentencing Commission, 1996. *Sourcebook of Federal Sentencing Statistics.* Washington, DC: U.S. Sentencing Commission.

Useem, Bert. 1985. "Disorganization and the New Mexico Prison Riot of 1980." *American Sociological Review,* 50:667–688.

Useem, Bert, Camille Camp, and George Camp. 1996. *Resolution of Prison Riots: Strategies and Policies.* New York: Oxford University Press.

Useem, Bert, and Peter Kimball. 1989. *States of Siege: U.S. Prison Riots, 1971–1986.* New York: Oxford University Press.

Useem, Bert, and Michael Resig. 1999. "Collective Action in Prisons: Protests, Disturbances, and Riots." *Criminology,* 37:735–760.

van Dijk, Frans, and Jaap de Waard. 2000. *Legal Infrastructure of the Netherlands in International Perspective.* The Hague: Ministry of Justice, The Netherlands.

van Dijk, J., and C. H. D. Steinmetz. 1984. "The Burden of Crime in Dutch Society." Pages 29–43 in *Victimization and Fear of Crime,* edited by R. Block. Washington, DC: World Perspectives, U.S. Department of Justice, Bureau of Justice Statistics.

van Dijk, Jan, and Kristiina Kangaspunta. 2000. "Piecing Together the Cross-National Crime Puzzle." *National Institute of Justice Journal,* January:34–41.

Van Maanen, J. 1973. "Observations on the Making of Policemen." *Human Organization,* 32(4):407–418.

Van Maanen, J. 1999a. "The Asshole." Pages 346–367 in *The Police and Society,* edited by V. E. Kappeler. Prospect Heights, IL: Waveland Press.

Van Maanen, J. 1999b. "Kinsmen in Repose." Pages 220–237 in *The Police and Society,* edited by V. E. Kappeler. Prospect Heights, IL: Waveland Press.

Van Slambrouk, P. 1999. "Two Cities Tackle Racial Profiling." *Christian Science Monitor,* March 29:1.

Vanagunas, S., and J. F. Elliot. 1980. *Administration of Police Organizations.* Boston: Allyn & Bacon.

Vandiver, Margaret, and David Giacopassi. 1997. "One Million and Counting: Students' Estimates of the Annual Number of Homicides Occurring in the U.S." *Journal of Criminal Justice Education,* 8:135–143.

Vertuno, J. 2002. "Study: Faulty Appeals Representation Puts Innocent at Risk of Execution in Texas." December 3. Associated Press Newswires. Dow Jones Interactive.

"Victims of Crime Act Crime Victims Fund." 1999. Washington, DC: Office of the Victims of Crime, U.S. Department of Justice, Office of Justice Programs.

"Victims of Crime in 22 European Criminal Justice Systems." 2001. Available: http://www.victimology.nl/onlpub/brienenhogen/bh.html.norway.

Vidmar, N., S. Beale, M. Rose, and L. Donnelly. 1997. "Should We Rush to Reform the Criminal Jury?" *Judicature,* 80:286–290.

Vigil, J. D. 1988. *Barrio Gangs: Street Life and Identity in Southern California.* Austin: University of Texas Press.

Vigil, J. D., and J. M. Long. 1990. "Emic and Etic Perspectives on Gang Culture." Pages 149–157 in *Gangs in America,* edited by C. R. Huff. Newbury Park, CA: Sage.

Villmoare, E., and V. V. Neto. 1987. "Victim Appearance at Sentencing under California's Victims' Bill of Rights." *Research in Brief,* August:1–5.

Violanti, J. M. 1995. "The Mystery Within: Understanding Police Suicide." *FBI Law Enforcement Bulletin,* 64(2):123.

Violanti, J. M. 1996. *Police Suicide—Epidemic in Blue.* Springfield, IL: Charles C. Thomas.

Violence by Intimates. 1998. Washington, DC: U.S. Department of Justice, U.S. Government Printing Office.

Violent Relationships: Battering and Abuse among Adults. 2001. Wylie, TX: Information Plus.

Vise, D. 2001. *The Bureau and the Mole.* New York: Atlantic Monthly.

Vise, D. 2002. "From Russia with Love." *The Washington Post Sunday Magazine,* January 6:W18–W23.

Visher, Christy. 1986. "The Rand Inmate Survey: A Reanalysis." Pages 161–211 in *Criminal Careers and "Career Criminals,"* edited by Alfred Blumstein, Jacqueline Cohn, Jeffrey Roth, and Christy Visher. National Academy Press.

Visher, Christy A. 2000. "Career Offenders and Crime Control." Pages 601–619 in *Criminology: A Contemporary Handbook,* edited by Joseph F. Sheley. Belmont, CA: Wadsworth.

Vito, Gennaro F., Richard Tewksbury, and Deborah G. Wilson. 1998. *The Juvenile Justice System: Concepts and Issues.* Prospect Heights, IL: Waveland Press.

Vold, George, Thomas Bernard, and Jeffrey B. Snipes. 1998. *Theoretical Criminology,* 4 ed. New York: Oxford University Press.

Von Drehl, Dave. 1995. *Among the Lowest of the Dead: The Culture of Death Row.* New York: Times Books.

von Hentig, H. 1948/1967. *The Criminal and His Victim.* New York: Archon Books.

von Hirsch, Andrew. 1976. *Doing Justice: The Choice of Punishments.* New York: Hill and Wang.

von Hirsch, Andrew. 1985. *Past or Future Crimes: Deservedness and Dangerousness in the Sentencing of Criminals.* New Brunswick, NJ: Rutgers University Press.

von Hirsch, Andrew. 1998. "Penal Theories." Pages 659–682 in *The Handbook of Crime and Punishment,* edited by Michael Tonry. New York: Oxford University Press.

von Hirsch, Andrew, David Garland, and Alison Wakefield. 2000. *Ethical and Social Perspectives on Situational Crime Prevention.* Oxford: Hart.

Wade, R. C. 1972. "Violence in the Cities: A Historical Review." Pages 27–46 in *Cities in American History,* edited by K. T. Jackson and S. K. Schultz. New York: Knopf.

Walker, R. 2001. "Gangsta Girls in the Hood." Gangs. Available: http://www.gangsorus.com/gangs/ganggirls.html.

Walker, S. 1977. *A Critical History of Police Reform.* Lexington, MA: D.C. Heath.

Walker, S. 1984. " 'Broken Windows' and Fractured History: The Use and Misuse of History in Recent Police Patrol Analysis." *Justice Quarterly,* 1(1):75–89.

Walker, S. 1992. "Police Professionalism: Another Look at the Issues." Pages 858–869 in *Policing and Crime Control, Part 3,* edited by E. H. Monkkonen. Westport, CT: Meckler.

Walker, S. 1997. "Records of the Wickersham Commission on Law Observance and Enforcement." *Jurisprudence.* Available: http://www.lexisnexis.com/cispubs/guides/jurisprudence.

Walker, S. 1999. *The Police in America.* Boston: McGraw-Hill.

Walker, S., C. Spohn, and M. DeLone. 1996. *The Color of Justice: Race, Ethnicity, and Crime in America.* Belmont, CA: Wadsworth.

Walker, Samuel. 1998. *Popular Justice: A History of American Criminal Justice,* 2 ed. New York: Oxford University Press.

Walker, Samuel. 2001. *Sense and Nonsense about Crime and Drugs: A Policy Guide,* 5 ed. Belmont, CA: Wadsworth.

Walker, Samuel, Cassia Spohn, and Miriam DeLone. 2000. *The Color of Justice: Race, Ethnicity, and Crime in America,* 2 ed. Belmont, CA: Wadsworth.

Walker, T. G., and D. J. Barrow. 1985. "The Diversification of the Federal Bench: Policy and Process Ramifications." *Journal of Politics,* 47:596–617.

Wallace, Donald H. 1997. "Prisoners' Rights: Historical Views." Pages 248–257 in *Correctional Contexts: Contemporary and Classical Readings,* edited by James W. Marquart and Jonathan R. Sorensen. Los Angeles: Roxbury.

Wallace, Harvey, and Clifford Roberson. 2001. *Principles of Criminal Law,* 2 ed. Boston: Allyn & Bacon.

Wallace, J. M., and V. J. Yasmann. 1997. "Russia's Great Criminal Revolution: The Rule of the Security Services." Pages 187–200 in *Understanding Crime in Global Perspective,* edited by P. Ryan and G. Rush. Thousand Oaks, CA: Sage.

Walsh, E. 1995. "Inside the Blue Line, a Racial Gulf of Their Own." *The Washington Post National Weekly Edition,* December 18–24:8.

Walsh, M. S. 1994. "Voir Dire Follies—Humor in the Court." *Trial,* February:52–54.

Walters, Glenn D. 1992. "A Meta-Analysis of the Gene–Crime Relationship." *Criminology,* 30(4):595–613.

Ward, D. 2001. "Reassessing Terrorism." *Crime and Justice International,* 17(56):19–23.

Ward, David A., and Gene G. Kassebaum. 1965. *Women's Prison: Sex and Social Structure.* Chicago: Aldine.

Warner, Barbara D., and Glenn L. Pierce. 1993. "Reexamining Social Disorganization Theory Using Calls to the Police as a Measure of Crime." *Criminology,* 31(4):493–517.

Warr, Mark. 2000. "Public Perceptions of and Reactions to Crime." Pages 13–31 in *Criminology: A Contemporary Handbook,* edited by Joseph F. Sheley. Belmont, CA: Wadsworth.

Wasserman, Gail A., and Laurie S. Miller. 1998. "The Prevention of Serious and Violent Juvenile Offending." Pages 197–247 in *Serious and Violent Juvenile Offending: Risk Factors and Successful Interventions,* edited by Rolf Loeber and Davie P. Farrington. Thousand Oaks, CA: Sage.

Wasserman, Gail A., Laurie S. Miller, and Lynn Cothern. 2000. *Prevention of Serious and Violent Juvenile Offending.* Washington, DC: Office of Juvenile Justice and Delinquency Prevention, U.S. Department of Justice.

Watanabe T. 1992. "Victims of a Safe Society." *Los Angeles Times,* February 27:A1.

Watson, Alan. 1985. *The Evolution of Law.* Baltimore: Johns Hopkins University Press.

Watson, J. M. 1996. "Outlaw Motorcyclists: An Outgrowth of Lower Class Cultural Concerns." Pages 31–48 in *Deviant Behavior,* edited by D. H. Kelly. New York: St. Martin's Press.

Webb, G. 1999. "DWB." *Esquire,* April:118–128.

Webster, N. 1983. *Webster's New Twentieth Century Dictionary—Unabridged.* New York: Prentice-Hall.

Weinstein, H. 2002. "Georgia Fails Its Poor Defendants, Report Says." *Los Angeles Times,* December 13:A36.

Weisel, D. L., and J. E. Eck. 1994. "Toward a Practical Approach to Organizational Change—Community Policing Initiatives in Six Cities." Pages 53–72 in *The Challenge of Community Policing,* edited by D. P. Rosenbaum. Thousand Oaks, CA: Sage.

Weiss, C., and D. J. Friar. 1974. *Terror in the Prisons: Homosexual Rape and Why Society Condones It.* Indianapolis: Bobbs-Merrill.

Welch, Michael. 1999. *Punishment in America: Social Control and the Ironies of Imprisonment.* Thousand Oaks, CA: Sage.

"Welcome to the New World of Private Security." 1997. *The Economist,* April 21:21–24.

Wellford, Charles F., and Ruth A. Triplett. 1993. "The Future of Labeling Theory: Foundations and Promises." Pages 1–22 in *New Directions in Criminological Theory,* edited by Freda Adler and William S. Laufer. New Brunswick, NJ: Transaction.

Wells, L. Edward, and Joseph H. Rankin. 1991. "Families and Delinquency: A Meta-Analysis of the Impact of Broken Homes." *Social Problems,* 38(1):71–93.

Wells, R. 1990. "Considering Victim Impact—The Role of Probation." *Federal Probation,* 54(3):26–29.

"Wen Ho Lee Freed in Plea Bargain." 2000. The Acronym Institute. Available: http://www.acronym.org.uk/50Lee.htm.

"Wen Ho Released." 1999. *Unquiet Mind.* Available: http://www.unquietmind.com/wenholee.html.

Western, Bruce, and Becky Pettit. 2000. "Incarceration and Racial Inequality in Men's Employment." *Industrial and Labor Relations Review,* 54:3–16.

Weyant, J. M. 1986. *Applied Social Psychology.* New York: Oxford University Press.

White, J. R. 1991. *Terrorism: An Introduction.* Pacific Grove, CA: Brooks/Cole.

White, P. M. 1997. "Wonder Women." *Black Enterprise,* April: 114–117.

"White Officers Association." 1999. Available: http://home.sprynet.com/~schulze/history.htm.

White, Rob. 2000. "10 Arguments against Mandatory Sentencing." *Youth Studies Australia,* 19(2):22–24.

Wice, P. B. 1985. *Chaos in the Courthouse.* New York: Praeger Special Studies.

Wicker, Tom. 1975. *A Time to Die.* New York: Quadrangle Books.

Wiechman, Dennis J., Jerry D. Kendall, and Mohammad K. Azarian. 1999. "Islamic Law: Myths and Realities." Available: http://www.witness-pioneer.org/vil/Articles/shariah/ilw_myth_real.html.

Wilbanks, William. 1987. *The Myth of a Racist Criminal Justice System.* Monterey, CA: Brooks/Cole.

Wilgoren, Jodi. 2003. "Governor Assails System's Errors as He Empties Illinois Death Row." *New York Times,* January 12:A1.

Wilkens, J., and M. Sauer. 1999. "The Arrest." *San Diego Union-Tribune,* May 12:A1.

Wilkie, Curtis. 1995. "Miss. Flogging Debate Opens Old Wounds." *The Boston Globe,* February 21:1.

Wilkinson, P. 1986. "Terrorism versus Liberal Democracy: The Problem of Response." In *Contemporary Terrorism,* edited by W. Gutteridge. New York: Facts on File.

Williams, C. A. 2001. "So, This Is Heaven: Norway." *Los Angeles Times,* November 8:A1.

Williams, Frank P., III, Marilyn D. McShane, and H. Michael Dolny. 2000. "Predicting Parole Absconders." *The Prison Journal,* 80:24–38.

Williamson, L. 2001. "The 'New' YOA Is Even Worse," *The Toronto Star,* February, 11:C.

Wilson, Beth. 2000. "Mandatory Sentencing." *Legaldate* 12(March):8.

Wilson, James Q. 1968. *Varieties of Police Behavior.* Cambridge, MA: Harvard University Press.

Wilson, James Q. 1975. *Thinking about Crime.* New York: Basic Books.

Wilson, James Q. 1985. *Thinking about Crime,* 2 ed. New York: Vintage.

Wilson, James Q. 1994. "Prisons in a Free Society." *The Public Interest,* 117:37–40.

Wilson, James Q., and Allan Abrahamse. 1992. "Does Crime Pay?" *Justice Quarterly,* 9(3):359–377.

Wilson, James Q., and R. J. Herrnstein. 1985. *Crime and Human Nature.* New York: Simon & Schuster.

Wilson, T. W. 1986. "Gender Differences in the Inmate Code." *Canadian Journal of Criminology,* 28:397–405.

Wing-hung Lo, C. 1995. *China's Legal Awakening: Legal Theory and Criminal Justice in Deng's Era.* Hong Kong: Hong Kong University Press.

Winner, K. 1995. "Q & A—Ernesto Zedillo Ponce de Leon." *San Diego Union-Tribune,* July 23:G5.

Witherspoon v. Illinois, 1968. 2002. Find Law. Available: http://caselaw.lp.findlaw.com.

Witkin, G. 1995. "When the Bad Guys Are Cops." *Newsweek,* September 11:19–23.

Witkin, G. 1999. "The Ghosts of Waco." *U.S. News & World Report,* September 6:36.

Witkin, Gordon. 1998. "The Crime Bust." *U.S. News & World Report,* May 25:28–35.

Witt, Karen De. 1994. "Many in U.S. Back Singapore's Plan to Flog American Youth." *The New York Times,* April 5:A4.

Witt v. Wainright, 1985. 2002. Find Law. Available: http://caselaw.lp.findlaw.com.

Wolff, C. 1992. "Top Officer Sets Hiring of Blacks As Number One Goal." *New York Times,* October 18:1.

Wolfgang, M. 1958. *Patterns of Criminal Homicide.* Philadelphia: University of Pennsylvania Press.

Wolfgang, M. 1959. "Suicide by Means of Victim Precipitated Homicide." *Journal of Clinical and Experimental Psychopathology and Quantitative Review of Psychiatry and Neurology,* 20:335–349.

Wolfgang, Marvin E., Robert M. Figlio, Paul E. Tracy, and Simon I. Singer. 1985. *The National Survey of Crime Severity.* Washington, DC: U.S. Department of Justice.

"Women in Criminal Justice—A Twenty Year Update." 1998. Available: http://www.ojp.usdoj.gov/reports/98/Guides/wcjs98/welcome.html.

Wood, D. B. 1999. "Why the Police Are Hard to Police." *Christian Science Monitor,* September 27:1.

Wood, D. B. 2001. "9/11 Cuts Both Ways on Crime." *Christian Science Monitor,* November 20:1–2.

Wood, D. B. 2002. "Race Clouds a Police Chief's Future." *Christian Science Monitor,* March 11:1.

Wooden, W. 1985. "The Flames of Youth." *Psychology Today,* January:22–27.

Wooldredge, John D. 1994. "Inmate Crime and Victimization in a Southwestern Correctional Facility." *Journal of Criminal Justice,* 22:367–381.

Wooldredge, John D. 1998. "Inmate Lifestyles and Opportunities for Victimization." *Journal of Research in Crime and Delinquency,* 35:480–502.

Worden, A. P. 1995. "The Judge's Role in Plea Bargaining: An Analysis of Judges' Agreement with Prosecutors' Sentencing Recommendations." *Justice Quarterly,* 12(2):257–277.

Worden, R. E. 1996. "The Causes of Police Brutality: Theory and Evidence on Police Use of Force." Pages 23–51 in *Police Violence: Understanding and Controlling Police Abuse of Force,* edited by W. A. Geller and H. Toch. New Haven: Yale University Press.

World Almanac 2000. 1999. Mahwah, NJ: World Almanac Books, Primedia Reference Books.

Worsnop, R. L. 1995. "The History of Police Reform: An Overview." Pages 10–16 in *Policing the Police,* edited by P. A. Winters. San Diego: Greenhaven Press.

Wright, Richard T., and Scott Decker. 1994. *Burglars on the Job: Streetlife and Residential Break-ins.* Boston: Northeastern University Press.

Wright, Richard T., and Scott H. Decker. 1998. *Armed Robbers in Action: Stickups and Street Culture.* Boston: Northeastern University Press.

Wyoming v. Houghton. 2001. Legal Information Institute. Available: http://suspct.law.cornell.edu/suspct/html98–184.XS.html.

Yi, D. 1998. "Car-Chase Calculus." *Los Angeles Times,* July 12:B3.

"Youth and the Criminal Justice System." 1998. Office of the Legislative Assembly of Ontario, Toronto, Ontario, Canada. Available: http://www.johnhoward.ng.ca/pubed/yobar.htm.

Zamble, Edward. 1992. "Behavior and Adaptation in Long-Term Prison Inmates: Descriptive Longitudinal Results." *Criminal Justice and Behavior,* 19:409–425.

Zehr, H. 1990. *Changing Lenses.* Scottsdale, PA: Herald Press.

Zeilbauer, P. 1999. "Stellar Officer Is Mourned at Funeral after Suicide." *New York Times,* September 23:B5.

Zimbardo, Philip G. 1972. "Pathology of Imprisonment." *Society,* 9:4–8.

Zimmer, Lynn. 1986. *Women Guarding Men.* Chicago: University of Chicago Press.

Zimmer, Lynn. 1987. "How Women Reshape the Prison Guard Role." *Gender and Society* 1:415–431.

Zimring, Franklin E. 2000. *American Youth Violence.* New York: Oxford University Press.

Zimring, Franklin, and Gordon Hawkins. 1995. *Incapacitation: Penal Confinement and the Restraint of Crime.* New York: Oxford University Press.

Zoglin, Richard. 1996. "Now for the Bad News: A Teenage Timebomb." *Time,* January 15:52–53.

Zuniga, J. 1999. "Police 'Racial Profiling' Targeted—Minority Officers Urged to 'Step up to the Plate' to Fight Abuses." *Houston Chronicle,* July 29:33.

Name Index

Ford, C., 483
Ford, Marilyn Chandler, 333
Ford, Richard, 50, 51
Foss, Edward, 50, 51
Foster, Jodie, 115
Foucault, Michel, 380
Fox, James Alan, 69–70, 259–260
Frank, Antoinette, 244
Frank, N., 170, 273, 274, 282, 288, 299, 302, 323–324, 334
Frankel, Marvin E., 366
Franzen, R., 323
Frase, Richard S., 366
Frazier, Charles E., 360, 481
Freedman, Estelle B., 383–384
Freeh, Louis J., 243–244
Freud, Sigmund, 24, 40
Friar, D. J., 430
Fried, Michael, 322, 324
Friedman, Lawrence M., 4, 274, 275
Fritsch, Eric, 480
Fritsch, Jane, 115
Fry, Elizabeth, 384
Fry, Margaret, 154
Fuetsch, M., 174
Fuhrman, Mark, 256
Fyfe, James J., 125, 243, 254–255, 258, 260

Gaes, Gerald G., 352, 426–427
Gainsborough, Jenni, 6, 7, 406–409
Galloway, Joseph L., 429
Garcetti, Gil, 262
Gardner, Robert L., 228
Garland, David, 37–38
Garner, Edward, 123–124
Garofalo, M., 145
Gartin, P. R., 145
Garvey, Marcus, 186
Gates, Daryl, 257
Gault, Gerald, 476
Geerken, Michael, 32, 459
Geis, Gilbert, 13, 91, 154, 156
Geller, W. A., 256
Gelsthorpe, Loraine, 365
Gendreau, Paul, 470
Genovese, Kitty, 151
Gerber, Jurg, 37, 352, 467
Gerda, R. W., 185, 186
Gergen, K. J., 333
Gergen, M. J., 333
Gerstenzang, J., 171
Gesalman, Anne Belli, 106
Getlin, J., 252
Giacomazzi, A., 180
Giacopassi, David, 5
Giallombardo, Rose, 435
Gibbons, Don C., 387
Gibeaut, John, 99, 109, 337, 338
Gibons, E. F., 166, 167
Gideon, Clarence Earl, 273
Gidycz, C., 72
Gifford, Sidra Lea, 11, 12, 389, 390
Gifis, S. H., 64, 66, 121, 225, 282, 289, 295, 301, 302, 327

Gilbert, Martin, 167, 419
Gilliam, F. D., 5
Gilliard, Darrell K., 414–417
Ginger, James, 222
Ginsburg, Ruth Bader, 339
Giordano, Peggy C., 36, 44–45
Girshick, Lori B., 435
Giuliani, Rudy, 84–85
Glassner, Barry, 473
Glaze, Lauren E., 361, 414–417, 468
Gleick, E., 253, 260
Glick, H., 275
Glover, Scott, 118, 261–262
Glover, T. L., 190
Gobbi, P., 444
Gobert, J. J., 332, 333
Goffman, Erving, 419, 420
Goldberg, A. L., 202–203
Goldberg, Steven H., 329
Golden, A., 266, 267
Goldstein, Herman, 204
Goldstein, Joseph, 229
Gollner, P. M., 324–326
Goode, E., 85
Goodman, Ellen, 430
Goodstein, Lynne, 47, 421, 422
Gorman, T., 255
Gottfredson, Denise C., 49, 358, 408
Gottfredson, Michael, 45, 148
Gotti, John, 90
Gottschall, J., 284
Gould, James, 324
Gove, Walter, R., 32
Graham, Bob, 188
Graham, Gary, 400–401
Graham, Michael Ray, Jr., 400
Grasmick, Harold G., 99
Grassley, Charles, 310
Gray, J., 209
Green, Gary S., 91, 93
Greenberg, David F., 46, 55
Greenfeld, Lawrence A., 137, 384, 434, 438
Greenfield, N., 483
Greengard, S., 216
Greenhouse, Linda, 2, 114, 222, 274, 397
Greenwood, Peter W., 48, 357, 360, 408, 482
Greer, Kimberly R., 422, 433, 436
Gregor, A. J., 341
Gregory, D., 174
Griffin, Susan, 48
Griffith, C. T., 154
Griswold, Eliza, 19
Grotius, Hugo, 126
Groves, W. Byron, 47
Guggin, Claire, 470
Gullo, K., 188
Gurr, Ted R., 164–167
Guttman, M., 80
Guttridge, L. F., 167

Haarr, Robin N., 438
Haddad, Charles H., 392

Hagan, John, 7, 56, 93, 408, 409
Haines, Joe D., Jr., 349
Hall, J. C., 124
Haller, M. H., 178, 179
Hamilton, Alexander, 336
Hamilton, Mary, 193–194
Hammurabi, 107
Hampton, Ron, 206–207
Handelman, S., 94
Haney, Craig, 425
Hanrahan, W., 315
Hansen, Randall, 276–278
Hanson, Roger A., 278
Hanssen, Bonnie, 241–242
Hanssen, Robert, 241–243
Harachi, Tracy C., 471–472
Harding, Richard W., 390, 391
Hardyman, Patricia, 364
Harer, Miles D., 56
Harlow, Caroline Wolf, 414–418
Harring, Sidney L., 177–178
Harrington, P. E., 195
Harris, Anthony R., 32–33, 56–58, 68
Harris, D., 123, 230, 232
Harris, Donovan, 151
Harris, John C., 364
Harris, M. G., 101
Harrison, E., 257–259
Harrison, Paige M., 12, 362, 384, 385, 388, 389, 391, 413–414, 416–417, 434
Hart, Timothy C., 355, 362
Harvard, Beverly, 173–174
Harvey, M., 72
Havemann, J., 67–68
Hawkins, Gordon, 355, 357
Hawkins, J. David, 13–14, 471–472, 482
Hawkins, Keith, 350
Hawthorne, Nathaniel, 380
Hayes, Hennessey D., 459
Hayman, B. S., 124
Hebert, D., 283–284
Hemmens, Craig, 480
Henry, D. Alan, 364
Henry II, King of England, 294
Hepburn, John, 441
Herbert, Bob, 338, 401
Herbert, Steve, 209–210, 233–234
Hermes, J., 244
Herrenkohl, Todd, 471–472
Herrington, Nancy L., 196, 197
Herrnstein, R. J., 85
Heumann, Milton, 316, 320–321
Hewitt, Bill, 106
Hickey, E., 70
Hinckley, John, 115
Hindelang, Michael, 36
Hirschel, J. David, 59
Hirschi, Travis, 36, 44, 45
Hodgins, Sheilagh, 40
Hofer, Helmut, 19
Hoffman, B., 165–166
Hoffman, Jan, 124
Holden, B. A., 335
Holmes, M. D., 320

Holmes, R. M., 83
Holmstrom, D., 266, 267
Holscher, Louis M., 18–19
Holt, Douglas, 401
Holten, N. G., 276, 279, 285
Hoover, Herbert, 243
Hoover, J. Edgar, 186–187
Hope, T., 148
Hopper, C. B., 103
Horst, M. H., 148
Horton, C., 199
Horton, Willie, 6
Hotaling, G., 136
Houghton, Sandra, 123
Howard, John, 380
Howell, James C., 482
Hoyt, Charles A., 393
Huard, R., 223
Huff, C. Ronald, 336–340
Huff, R., 99, 100
Hughes, Michael, 32
Hugo, Victor, 378
Huizinga, David, 57
Hunt, Geoffrey, 428
Hunt, Jennifer, 254, 258
Hylton, Hilary, 453

Ianni, Francis A. J., 90
Ibbetson, David J., 107
Imber, C., 302
Impocco, J., 80
Inciardi, J. A., 79, 80
Irwin, John, 350, 387, 390, 391, 422, 423, 427
Isikoff, Michael, 6
Israel, J. H., 273, 293
Israel, J. R., 295
Iyengar, S., 5

Jackson, Derrick Z., 400
Jackson, Robert, 285
Jacob, H., 280–282, 285, 291
Jacob, Herbert, 371
Jacobs, J. B., 83
Jacobson, Kristen C., 39
Jameson, S., 237
Jary, D., 191
Jary, J., 191
Jenkins, Brian, 164
Jenne, Denise L., 443
Jensen, Eric L., 467, 481
Jensen, Vickie J., 57
Jerome, R., 226
Jesilow, Paul, 4, 364
John, King of England, 107–108
Johnson, David R., 480
Johnson, Dirk, 401
Johnson, Robert, 393, 424, 441–443
Johnston, D., 188
Jonassohn, K., 167
Jones, David A., 353
Jones, Joseph F., 387
Jongman, Albert J., 164
Jordan, Carol, 272
Jordan, W. E., 332, 333
Joseph, Janice, 480
Jost, K., 314, 320

Subject Index

Child pornography, 61–63
Child victimization, 136
Child welfare movement, 475
Chimel v. California, 119, 122
China, 167, 175
  criminal justice system in, 341–343
  political spying accusation and, 309–311
Chop shops, 79
Christian Bible Study, 81
Christopher Commission, 211, 246–247,
    251–252, 253, 256, 259, 260, 263
Chronic offenders, 59
Circumstantial evidence, 327
Citizen policing, in Great Britain, 50
Citizens' complaints, 29
Civil disobedience, 112
Civil law, 107–109
Civil Rights Act (1871), 439
Civil rights era, 190
Civil suits, 109
Civil War, 275
Civil wrongs, 109
Class. *See* Social class and crime
Classifications of law, 108–109
Climatology of crime, 58–59
Closing arguments, in jury trials, 329
Coalition for Federal Sentencing Reform,
    450, 451
Code of Hammurabi, 107
Code of Justinian, 107
Code of silence, 258–260, 265
Codification, 107
Collective efficacy, 41
Collective violence, in prisons, 427–429
College/university campus police, 189
Colombine High School (Colorado) mass
    murder, 67, 471
Colonial period
  courts in, 274–275
  criminal justice system in, 132
  death penalty in, 393
  juvenile crime in, 474–475
  law in, 108
  police in, 176
  probation in, 456
  punishment in, 380–382
Combat, judicial, 311
Commercialized vice, defined, 27
Commitment, in social control theory, 44
Common law, 107–108
Commonwealth attorneys. *See* Prosecutors
Community corrections, 454–470
  correctional supervision in, 454–455
  intermediate sanctions in, 455, 460–467
  parole in, 455–456, 467–470
  probation in, 455–460
Community policing, 202–205
  organizational dimension of, 204–205
  philosophical dimension of, 203
  strategic dimension of, 203–204
  tactical dimension of, 204
Community service, 461, 465–466
Community supervision, 3
Competence, in police subculture, 234
Complainants, 293
Complaints, 293
Concurrence, 110, 111
Conditional diversion, 286

Conference of Paris, 126
Confessions, false, 338–339
Conflict theory of crime, 46–47, 49, 177–178
Conformists, 42
Congregate model for prisons, 382
Consensual model of criminal justice, 18
Constables, 176
Contempt of cop, 258
Contract system, for indigent defendants,
    288, 289–292
  problems of, 291
  types of contracts, 290
Conviction, defined, 312
Cooper v. Pate, 439
Corporal punishment
  "eye for and eye" and, 353–354
  in historical perspective, 107, 379–382, 456
  juvenile crime and, 474–475
Correctional Association of New York, 449
Correctional officers, 441–443
  alienation and stress of, 442–443
  in Brazil, 444–445
  prisonization of, 442
  rape and sexual abuse of female prisoners,
    436–437
  women as, 443
Correctional supervision, defined, 454–455
Corrections. *See* Jails; Prisons and
    punishment
Corrections-commercial complex, 407
Corrections Corporation of America, 391, 392
Corruption, 245
Counsel, defined, 312
Counterfeiting, defined, 27
Counterintelligence, 188, 242
Counterterrorism, 168–169, 188
County attorneys. *See* Prosecutors
County of Riverside v. McLaughlin, 293
County of Sacramento v. Lewis, 222
Court of last resort (COLR), 275, 278, 279
Courts
  criminal. *See* Criminal courts
  juvenile, 476–477
Crackdowns, 31
CREEP (Committee to Reelect the
    President), 93
Creeping socialism, 158
Crime, 2–7
  age and, 55–56
  chronic offenders and, 59
  climatology of, 58–59
  criminal responsibility and legal defenses,
    111–115, 328–330
  defined, 109
  elements of, 110–111
  explaining, 37–48
  extent of, 3
  gender and, 24, 54–55
  geography of, 58–59
  get tough approach and, 6–7
  Islam and, 18–19
  media coverage of, 4–5
  occupational, 91–94
  organized, 89–91
  problem in understanding, 3–4
  public opinion on, 2–3
  race and, 56–58

  reducing, 48–49
  serious versus minor, 109–110
  social class and, 56
  statistics concerning, 25–37
Crime concealment arson, 80
Crime control model of criminal justice, 16
Crime displacement, 150–151
Crime Drop in America, The (Blumstein and
    Wallman), 408
Crime in the United States, 26
Crime myths, 5–6
Crime rates, 26–28, 406, 407–408
Crimes known to the police, 28–32
Crimes of violence, 61–75. *See also* Police
    violence; Victimization
  aggravated assault, 65, 73–74
  domestic violence, 74–75
  homicide, 64–71, 65
  in prisons, 427–433
  rape and sexual assault, 65, 72–73
  robbery, 65, 71
  serious and violent juvenile offenders
    (SVJ), 471–473, 482
Crime spillover, 151
Crime Victims Fund, 154–155
Criminal courts, 270–375
  defense attorneys in, 286–292
  federal, 279
  as formal organizations, 275–279
  history of, 274–275
  as informal organizations, 280–282
  judges in, 282–284
  plea bargaining and, 280–282, 285, 289,
    291, 294, 311–312
  pretrial procedures, 292–302
  prosecutors in, 280–282, 285–286, 294–295
  reforming, 340–341
  state courts, 276–278
  trial in, 116, 321–334
Criminal homicide, defined, 27
Criminal investigation, 223–226
Criminal justice system, 7–18
  in China, 341–343
  goals of, 12–13
  Islam and, 302–304
  models of criminal justice, 13–18
  public opinion on, 3
  sequence of events in, 8–10
  size and cost of, 10–12
  terrorism and, 169–171
Criminal law, 104–129
  classifications of law, 108–109
  criminal responsibility and legal defenses,
    111–115, 328–330
  defined, 106, 108–109
  elements of crime, 110–111
  history, 106–108
  procedural law and, 115–126
  serious crimes versus minor crimes,
    109–110
Criminal records, in wrongful convictions,
    340
Critical theory and crime, 45–48, 49
  conflict theory, 46–47, 49
  feminist perspective, 47–48, 49
  labeling theory, 45–46, 49
Cross-examination, 312, 328, 331
Cross-race effect, 337–338

Rockwell International Corporation, 91
Roman law, 107
Rotten apples explanation, of police corruption, 250
Rotten pockets explanation, of police corruption, 250
Routine activities theory of crime, 37–38
Ruffin v. Commonwealth, 438–439
Runaways, defined, 27
Rural crime
    geography of crime and, 58–59
    in Great Britain, 49–51
Russia
    organized crime in, 94–95
    political spying and, 241–243
Rwanda, 167

Sabotage arson, 80
Safety, in police subculture, 233
San Diego Police Department, 184, 213, 222–223, 244
San Francisco Police Department, 244
San Quentin (California), 385–386
Santa Fe, New Mexico state prison riot, 432–433
Scandinavia, prisons and punishment in, 402–403
Schooling, in social control theory, 44–45
Scott v. Illinois, 273–274
Seabury Committee, 245
Seat-belt violations, 1–2
Secondhand evidence, 294
Seductions of Crime (Katz), 71
Selective incapacitation, 356–357
Self-control theory, 45
Self-defense, 112–113, 330, 428
Self-incrimination, 117
Self-report surveys, 35–36
    defined, 35
    gender and, 54
    peer influence versus media and, 43–44
    race and, 57
    strengths and weaknesses of, 36
Senatorial courtesy, 282–283
Sentence, defined, 313
Sentencing and sanctions, 9–10, 346–375
    in Australia, 372–373
    determinants of, 368–371
    goals of, 350–360
    judicial discretion and, 350
    procedures for, 365–368
    reforms in, 363–365
    sentencing decisions, 283–284
    types of sentences, 360–365
    victims and, 158
Sentencing commissions, 366
Sentencing disparity, 369–371
Sentencing guidelines, 366–367
Sentencing hearings, 365–366
Sentencing Project, 409
September 11, 2001 terrorist attacks, 17, 112, 127, 131–132, 166, 168–171
Sequester, defined, 313
Serial killers, 68–71, 224
    characteristics of, 69–71
    types of, 69
Serious and violent juvenile offenders (SVJ), 471–473, 482

Serious crimes, 109–110
Serious felonies, in wedding cake model of criminal justice, 15
Seriousness of offense, as determinant of sentencing, 368–369
Sexism, 210
Sex offenses, defined, 27
Sexual abuse. *See* Rape and sexual assault
Sexual assault. *See* Rape and sexual assault
Sexual harassment, of female police officers, 196, 197, 244
Sexual misconduct of police, 244
Sexual shakedowns, 245, 250
Shadow jury, 326
Sheriff's departments, 183–185. *See also* Police
Shock probation, 461, 462–463
Shoplifting, 77–78, 273–274
Sick ins, 182
Simple assault, 27, 65
Sixth Amendment, 116, 117, 119–121, 151, 273–274, 291, 321
Skip tracers, 301
Smugglers, 88–89
Sniper killers, 69, 70, 224
Social class and crime, 56. *See also* Poverty
    crime victims, 138
    jail inmates, 417
    prison inmates, 413–414
    sentencing disparity and, 371
Social control theory, 44–45
Social ecology, 41
Socialization patterns, crime and, 47–48
Social marginality, 191–192
Society of Captives, The (Sykes), 420–421
Sociological theories of crime, 38, 41–49
Solitary confinement, 382, 424
Solitary model for prisons, 382
Sontobello v. New York, 312
Southern Poverty Law Center, 81
Special circumstances, 394
Special police forces, 189
Specific deterrence, 358, 359–360
Speedups, 182
Split-second syndrome, 255
Stalking, 82
State authority occupational crimes, 93
State criminal courts, 276–278
State police, 185–186
State's attorneys. *See* Prosecutors
State terrorism, 166–167
Statistics on crime, 25–37
    field research, 36–37
    National Crime Victimization Survey (NCVS), 33–35
    self-report surveys, 35–36
    Uniform Crime Reports (UCR), 26–33
Stocks, 380
Stolen property, defined, 27
Stoning, 393
Stop Prisoner Rape, 430
Strategic dimension, of community policing, 203–204
Street crime, 3, 4. *See also* Juvenile justice; Street gangs
    sentencing disparity and, 371
    victims of, 131, 139

Street gangs, 4, 98–102
    criminal behavior of, 100
    information on, 101–102
    names of, 99
    women in, 99–101
Street justice, 179
Stress
    of correctional officers, 442–443
    police and, 255
Strikes
    by police, 181–182
    police and control of, 177–178, 185–186
Strip searches, 437
Students for a Democratic Society (SDS), 166
Subculture
    defined, 233
    inmate, 421–422, 435–436
    police, 233–235, 253–260
    toddler beauty queen, 61–63
    of violence, 57–58
Subincarceration, 460. *See also* Intermediate sanctions
Subpoena, defined, 313
Substandard living conditions, in prisons, 423, 431–433, 444–445
Substantial capacity test, 116
Substantive law, 108, 109
Suicide, of police officers, 234–235
Supermax prisons, 424–425
Supplementary Homicide Reports (SHR), 32
Suspicion, defined, 27
Symbolic justice, 219–220
System model of criminal justice, 8, 13

Tactical dimension, of community policing, 204
Taliban, 23–24, 127
Target congruence, 147–148
Target-hardening, 169
Telemarketing fraud, 92
Telephones, 181
Ten Commandments, 107
Tennessee v. Garner, 119, 123–124
Terrorism, 164–171
    countering, 168–169, 188
    criminal justice and, 169–171
    defining, 164–165
    explaining, 167–168
    rape as act of, 73
    September 11, 2001, attacks, 17, 112, 127, 131–132, 166, 168–171
    types of, 165–167
Terry v. Ohio, 119, 122
Testimony, 313, 327
Testosterone, 39–40, 48
Texas Rangers, 185
Theft
    larceny–theft, 27, 77–78
    motor vehicle, 15, 27, 78–79, 145
    trends in, 15
Theft of a Nation (Cressey), 90
Theocracies, 18–19
Third degree, 243
Thompson v. Oklahoma, 396
"Three strikes" legislation, 364–365
Thrill-oriented killers, 69
Tiananmen Square massacre, 167, 342

Photo Credits